6TH EDITION

MANAGERIAL ECONOMICS

Analysis, Problems, Cases

LILA J. TRUETT

Professor of Economics
The University of Texas at San Antonio

DALE B. TRUETT

Professor of Economics
The University of Texas at San Antonio

SOUTH-WESTERN College Publishing

An International Thomson Publishing Company

Publisher/Team Director: Jack W. Calhoun
Acquisitions Editor: John Alessi
Developmental Editor: Eric Carlson
Production Editor: Sharon L. Smith
Production House: WordCrafters Editorial Services, Inc.
Internal Design: Lotus Wittkopf
Marketing Manager: Lisa L. Lysne

Library of Congress Cataloging-in-Publication Data

Truett, Lila J.
    Managerial economics : analysis, problems, cases / Lila J. Truett, Dale B. Truett.—6th ed.
        p.   cm.
    Includes bibliographical references and index.
    ISBN 0–538–86871–6
    1. Managerial economics.   I. Truett, Dale B.   II. Title.
HD30.22T78   1998
338.5′024′658—dc21   97–17187
                                                          CIP

    2   3   4   5   6   7   8   D1   3   2   1   0   9   8
Printed in the United States of America

International Thomson Publishing
South-Western College Publishing is an ITP Company.
The ITP trademark is used under license.

PREFACE

This book is designed primarily for use by business administration students who have done some introductory-level work in economics. As our title suggests, the objective of the book is to enhance students' understanding of the application of economic analysis to managerial decisions. We believe this goal can best be accomplished by providing a clear and brief statement of the principles of microeconomic decision making and supplementing this material with problems, examples, and cases that illustrate how such principles are applied.

Throughout the following chapters are numerical examples, applications, and minicases dispersed among discussions of decision criteria and rules. Chapters 2 through 15 end with questions and problems related to the materials covered. Answers to selected odd-numbered problems appear at the end of the book. In addition, we have provided Integrating Cases at the ends of the book's five major parts. Each case is somewhat longer than the typical end-of-chapter problem and integrates a number of concepts developed in the preceding chapters.

STUDY GUIDE, INSTRUCTOR'S MANUAL, SOFTWARE, AND TEST BANK

Student analytical skills in managerial economics can be enhanced by using the *Study Guide*, a learning tool that complements the problem-solving approach employed in the text. Virtually all of the *Study Guide* problems have been classroom tested, and step-by-step solutions are provided at the back of the guide. A unique feature of the guide is a prompting device called "Getting Started" that verbally walks the student through the steps that must be taken to solve a specific type of problem. The *Study Guide* is closely tied to the book by means of a cross-referencing system that indicates the specific end-of-chapter problem or problems that are similar to a given *Study Guide* problem. Finally, for most chapters, the *Study Guide* contains a set of Hand-In Problems that can be used as out-of-class or homework assignments.

Solutions for the Hand-In Problems are found in the *Instructor's Manual*. Many of the Hand-In Problems are set up in a way that allows the instructor to change the value of a key number to generate a variety of different answers. This allows instructors to vary the solutions from section to section of a given course or from one semester to another. The *Instructor's Manual* explains how to use this feature and provides some of the alternative values for the key numbers. The *Instructor's Manual* also contains step-by-step solutions to the end-of-chapter problems and all cases that appear in the book. We hope that instructors and students will use the problems and cases to the fullest possible extent: in our opinion, problem-solving experiences constitute the best way to develop an understanding of managerial economics.

The *Decision Assistant* is a software package that provides solution routines for various types of problems found in the text. These routines include maximization and minimization, linear programming, break-even analysis, and present value. In addition, the package contains both simple and multiple linear regression programs. Selected end-of-chapter problems in the book (those numbered D1, D2, etc.) are identified as candidates for solution with the *Decision Assistant*. Adopters of the book can obtain the *Decision Assistant* from South-Western College Publishing.

This edition of *Managerial Economics* is accompanied by an expanded and updated *Test Bank* prepared by Vincent DiMartino, who has many years' experience in business consulting and in teaching managerial economics. The *Test Bank* includes a substantial number of problems that are similar to those found in the text and the *Study Guide*, as well as multiple choice and true/false questions. Note that the Hand-In Problems in the *Study Guide* can also be used as testing materials by changing the key numbers as explained here and in the *Instructor's Manual*.

SIXTH EDITION FEATURES AND CHANGES

This edition of *Managerial Economics* retains the organizational change made in the fifth edition. That change placed the forecasting chapter (Chapter 4) immediately following the chapter on demand estimation. While clearly it is not obligatory to move directly to forecasting from the descriptive, theoretical, and statistical material on demand, some instructors may wish to do so, given the widespread availability of microcomputers. The Decision Assistant software described earlier contains a multiple regression program that supplements the demand estimation discussion in the text and can be used for a variety of purposes.

Two pedagogical devices introduced in a previous edition, Managerial Perspectives and Numerical Examples, have been revised and retained. The Managerial Perspectives are high-interest, current illustrations of how real-world firms have addressed or failed to address issues and decision problems discussed in the book. The Numerical Examples are set off from the running text and call attention to the steps that must be taken to solve specific types of problems (arc elasticity, cost minimization, profit maximization, present value, etc.) that students will encounter repeatedly in the end-of-chapter and/or *Study Guide* problems. We believe that students can greatly improve their abilities to handle these related kinds of problems if they take the time to work through the Numerical Examples.

As in previous editions, we have provided a Glossary at the end of the book. This one is somewhat expanded, partially as a result of our decision to style the text with running definitions in the body of each chapter. The aim of the running definitions, of course, is to make it easier for students to learn the economic jargon so necessary to understanding the analytical side of our discipline. There is also a Mathematical Appendix at the end of the text that will serve as an important learning tool for many students.

In the past eight to ten years, we have had the good fortune to be able to travel, study, and participate in economics conferences in a number of countries, ranging from Russia and China to England, Australia, Korea, and South Africa. These experiences, coupled with research and consulting related to a broad range of industries in the United States, Canada, and Mexico, have enhanced our understanding of business and public sector operations and decision making. We hope that what we have learned from these activities has helped to make this a better book, one that provides a unique, global perspective. That perspective is reinforced in the book's strategically placed International Capsules, designed to make students think about how operating in a global environment affects economic decision making.

Adopters familiar with previous editions of this book will find significant new material in Chapter 11. Specifically, the discussion of price discrimination has been expanded, and two new topics, two-part pricing and bundling, have been added. Discussions of these items have been handled in a way that should enhance students' understanding of pricing strategies that today's firms frequently employ.

In this edition, we have added a variety of new end-of-chapter problems, and the problem sets have been renumbered to make it easier for instructors to update course outlines and assignment sheets in the future. Problems that require calculus are now numbered C1, C2, etc., while those designed to be solved with the *Decision Assistant* software are numbered D1, D2, etc. Finally, the text has been thoroughly updated with many new references to current events and real-world examples.

COURSE DESIGN

Our own experience in teaching managerial economics leads us to caution both students and professors that this book contains more material than can normally be covered in a three-credit-hour, one-semester course. Where students can be expected to have no more than an average level of preparation in economic principles, it may not be possible to cover more than Chapters 1 and 2, 5 through 7, 9 through 12, 16, and 17. Students with more advanced backgrounds may progress swiftly enough to allow inclusion of Chapters 3 and 8 in the preceding list.

The book allows for some variation in emphasis. For example, to orient a course toward both private and public sector capital project analysis, Chapters 13, 14, and 15 could be substituted for the materials on demand estimation, forecasting, market structure, and complex pricing problems covered in Chapters 3, 4, and 11. For this kind of course, probably all of Part 5 should be covered.

For a two-course sequence, we suggest coverage of the basic materials (Chapters 1 through 3, 5 through 7, 9, 10, 12, 16, and 17) in the first course. The second course, which might well be launched as an elective if it is not possible to include it in the core requirements of a program, could include economic forecasting (Chapter 4), linear programming (Chapter 8), advanced topics in pricing (Chapter 11 and its appendix), project analysis (Chapter 13, its appendix, and Chapter 14), and public sector decision making (Chapter 15).

APPENDICES

As mentioned earlier, we have provided a Mathematical Appendix at the end of the book that can be used either for student review or to give the course a more quantitative slant. A statistical appendix following Chapter 3 and one on compounding and discounting following Chapter 13 serve similar purposes. The appendices to Chapters 2, 5, and 11 deal briefly with topics that are either too difficult or too time consuming, when fully developed, to be recommended as standard fare, unless the instructor has a special interest in them.

ACKNOWLEDGMENTS

For our backgrounds in microeconomics, we certainly owe debts of gratitude to James Jeffers and Gerald Nordquist of the University of Iowa, H. H. Liebhafsky and Wendell C. Gordon of the University of Texas at Austin, and the late Cliff Lloyd. We are grateful also to our colleagues, Robert E. Langley and Vincent DiMartino, for their diligent work on various editions of the *Test Bank* and certain other materials. The faculty, staff, and students of the Division of Economics and Finance at the University of Texas at San Antonio helped us immeasurably while the book was in preparation. Thanks are due as well to all of the instructors at other institutions who took the time to provide their comments on previous editions.

NOTE TO STUDENTS

In the short run (the present), playing your cards right gets you good grades. Over the long run (in the future), playing them right can get you success. We want to help you do both, and we wrote this book with that in mind.

Your immediate problem is going to be to cope with the course that goes with this book. Here's how.

1. Read your assignments *before* your instructor covers them in class. (If at first you do not understand the material, read through it again.)
2. Pay attention to the Numerical Examples that occasionally appear in the chapters. Work your way through them step by step with pencil and paper to make sure you understand them. It will help you to solve end-of-chapter, *Study Guide*, and exam problems.
3. Go down the list of questions at the end of each chapter. If there are some that you cannot answer, *review* the chapter and find the answer. Ask your instructor if you still are not sure.
4. Work *all* of the problems you are assigned, and do this *before* your instructor solves them for you.
5. When you think you understand a concept or method, make up a problem of your *own* (like the ones at the end of each chapter) and solve it.

We hope this book will help you develop useful skills for solving business or public economic problems or at least for evaluating the solutions or advice of others. These kinds of skills will likely be important to you long after your present course is over.

Much of what we discuss here is not too difficult if you put some thought into your study of it. One way to sharpen your economic IQ is to keep an eye on the news and on business periodicals such as *The Wall Street Journal* or *Business Week*. You will find, as we have, that the success or failure of many business undertakings hinges on how well management has understood many of the concepts we discuss in the chapters to follow. In fact, we cite some experiences of real businesses in almost every chapter, and as you work your way through the book, we expect that you will develop some definite opinions about which firms have played their cards wisely and which ones have not. All of this, we hope, will help you to play yours well in the future.

BRIEF CONTENTS

CONTENTS

PART 1

The Firm and Its Environment

1

INTRODUCTION, ENVIRONMENT, AND METHODOLOGY

MANAGERIAL ECONOMICS AND THE GLOBAL ECONOMY

The global economy has arrived! Actually, it has been with us in a substantial way for centuries, but the attention given it by both businesses and government policymakers has increased over the past decade or so. The globalization of economic activity has become increasingly important because technology has spread worldwide and because institutional arrangements (the rules that countries, individually and collectively fashion to regulate their economic and political lives) have increased both the interdependence of nations or trading groups and the efficiency with which we produce goods and services. Thus, in late 1993, Toyota Motor Company launched an advertising campaign in the United States trumpeting the fact that its Corolla automobile was assembled in Georgetown, Kentucky, with parts not only from Japan but also from 20 U.S. states. (It would not be surprising to find that the car contained numerous other non-Japanese and non-U.S. parts, since Toyota and some of its suppliers have been investing in the newly industrializing countries of Asia—Thailand, Malaysia, and even mainland China.) The Corolla is fast becoming a "world car," but the world car concept was not fashioned by the Japanese; it was the brainchild of Ford Motor Company. The car's name? Escort. As the World Bank (an international credit agency set up by the United States and Western Europe after World War II) has noted, the Escort is now and has for many years been made at various locations around the globe with parts from at least 10 European countries as well as from the United States, Canada, and Mexico.

The global economy presents managers with many more opportunities and many more choices than they have had in the past. These choices are not limited to the question of where to sell one's product. To be an efficient producer, a firm must now, more than ever, determine where to obtain both its inputs (labor, equipment, parts and materials, etc.) and its technology. This is not just a case of substituting cheap foreign labor for expensive domestic labor. It has to do with other considerations, such as the quality of labor for specific technical tasks and the type of technology best suited to the product line. While the United States, Japan, and Western Europe are technological giants, cutting-edge technologies have been developed and are available from such places as Mexico (directly reduced iron) and Russia (radial keratotomy, laser surgery equipment, rocket technology).[1]

Managerial economics focuses on the types of choices just described. Its central themes are:

1. Identifying problems and opportunities.
2. Analyzing alternatives from which choices can be made.
3. Making choices that are best (optimal) from the standpoint of the firm or organization.

Because managers are always confronted with situations involving choosing from among alternative policies or strategies (whether to go into a new product line, whether to employ a new technology, whether to consider production in a foreign market, and many other types of choices), the tools of managerial economics are important to them. It is certainly not true that all managers must also be managerial economists. However, managers who understand the way managerial economics applies basic economic analysis to the specific problems encountered by firms and other organizations are more likely to choose wisely than those who do not. This becomes increasingly the case as developments on the international scene broaden both our opportunities and our range of choices.

Globalization and the Firm

A fuller understanding of what the business firm faces in the new global environment follows from some perspective on how the world economy reached its present state. First, the United States has been a primary architect of this global transformation. Emerging as the noncommunist world's leading economic, political, and military power after the Second World War, the United States, with its wartime allies and even its former foes, Germany and Japan, fashioned policies that would greatly increase worldwide economic interdependence. Paramount among these was the **General Agreement on Tariffs and Trade (GATT)**, designed to reduce trade barriers among the major industrialized countries. During the Great Depression that preceded the war, most countries had tried to preserve their own citizens' jobs by imposing huge *import tariffs* (taxes) on foreign goods. The result was disastrous for world trade.

Signatories to GATT agree to the principles of *reciprocity* and *nondiscrimination*, as well as to work toward elimination of so-called nontariff barriers

The **General Agreement on Tariffs and Trade (GATT)** is the mechanism set up by the market economies after World War II to reduce barriers to international trade. It had over 100 member countries in 1993, and many former Eastern Bloc nations were hoping to join the group.

---

1 Michael A. Dornheim, "Rocket Technology Prevails Over Politics," *Aviation Week and Space Technology*, Vol. 147, No. 3 (August 14, 1995), pp. 51–52; and Dave Sarova, "The Hunt for Red Technology," *International Business*, Vol. 7, No. 4 (April 1994), pp. 60–64.

to trade (licenses or restrictions on the quantity of a specific good that can be imported, for example). Reciprocity means that if I reduce some of my tariffs, you agree to reduce some of yours in return. Nondiscrimination means if one country reduces a tariff or other barrier through reciprocal negotiations with another, third parties (other GATT members) will also get the reduction. GATT brings together representatives of its member countries (now about 100) to negotiate freer trade at meetings known as "rounds." The last two GATT rounds have taken place in Tokyo and in Uruguay. The GATT process has been extremely successful for manufactured goods. The average height of tariffs on manufactures among the GATT members was 40 percent in 1947, and it is less than 5 percent today. Unfortunately, GATT's success with agricultural products, which many countries both subsidize and protect with tariffs and other barriers, has not been as good.

In 1995 a new World Trade Organization (WTO) entered into force as a successor to GATT that would be a more formal entity and have broader mechanisms for both the enforcement of agreements and the settlement of disputes. The WTO proposal was one outcome of the *Uruguay Round* of GATT negotiations, which lasted many years and also resulted in some new agreements on agriculture and intellectual property (patents, copyrights).[2]

Importance of International Trade and Investment

GATT and the new WTO have provided the world's most productive countries with wide access to each other's markets. This fact has not been lost on business firms and public agencies who realize they can buy both finished products and inputs (parts, subassemblies, and even services) from suppliers in foreign countries. In addition, businesses can invest in one another's homelands, in manufacturing facilities and services as well as through the purchase of equity in other firms. U.S. corporations have accumulated huge amounts of investment in foreign operations (plants, equipment, plantations, licensing agreements, and other holdings) throughout the twentieth century. They have invested all over the globe. While for the most part these investments have flourished and contributed significantly to the profits of the investing firms, they have also been fraught with challenges from the societies that received them. Thus Latin Americans, sometimes even while in the act of gulping a Coke, often complain that the world is *"cocacolizado"* (Coca Cola-ized). Many feel that U.S. culture has been imposed on them, along with complex problems that U.S. technology has brought. In Central America, for example,

---

2 For more, see Salil S. Pitroda, "From Gatt to WTO: The Institutionalization of World Trade," *Harvard International Review*, Vol. 17, No. 2 (Spring 1995), pp. 46–47; and Jim Sanford, "World Trade Organization Opens Global Markets, Protects U.S. Rights," *Business America*, Vol. 116, No. 1 (January 1995), pp. 4–7.

a U.S. manufacturer produces glue that, according to a 1993 report by the news show, *Dateline NBC*, is sniffed and eaten by street children to stave off hunger by getting a "high."[3] This has led to severe criticism of the firm from several quarters. In today's global economy managers must learn how to cope with the myriad foreign environments they often face on a daily basis, whether at the home-country headquarters or far afield in a foreign land.

Another important development on the international scene has been *trading blocs*.[4] In part these exist because GATT and the WTO permit the formation of entities that free up trade among their member countries while erecting common external barriers against nonmembers. The world's leading trading bloc at the moment is the European Community (EC), an impressive market of over 350 million people that has been put together gradually over the past 30 years.[5] (The United States is only about 80 percent as large in terms of population.) The aggregate output of the EC is significantly larger than that of the United States. Moreover, the EC is a competitive producer of many manufactured goods and is home to many businesses with substantial foreign investments. At the end of 1992, the EC became for the most part a single, integrated market where goods could flow freely across national boundaries. (It is scheduled for a common currency in 1999.)[6] Several Eastern European countries have been extremely interested in joining the EC, especially those known as the Visegrad Three (Poland, Hungary, and the Czech Republic) that have made significant progress in economic and political reform.[7] While the EC members have had problems (especially in terms of agricultural policies, as the frequent protests and riots by French farmers will attest), the Community has been extremely successful in manufacturing, and much more growth is expected.

The reaction of U.S. firms to the EC has been to establish their own productive facilities within the trading bloc, thereby avoiding the trade barriers against goods produced outside the region. Because of this, the 1960s and 1970s became the decades of the *multinational corporation*, the firm that, while it may be headquartered in a given country, has subsidiaries or branch plants

---

3 The firm was H.B. Fuller Company, a very successful manufacturer of glues and household products. Fuller's management claims that the retailers in the region are responsible for the sales of glue to children. See "Sticking to Promises," *Dateline NBC* (Transcript produced by Burrell's Information Services), September 28, 1993, pp. 13–18.

4 We use the term "trading bloc" to indicate any group of countries that attempts to develop policies to foster freer trade among its members. For a fuller discussion of the types of arrangements that such groups may establish, see Franklin R. Root, *International Trade and Investment* (Cincinnati: South-Western, 1994), especially Chapter 10.

5 In 1996, members of the Community included Belgium, Denmark, France, Germany, Greece, Ireland, Italy, Luxembourg, the Netherlands, Portugal, Spain, the United Kingdom, and three countries who had just joined, Austria, Finland, and Sweden.

6 David Fairlamb, "Achtung! EMU is Coming," *Institutional Investor*, Vol. 30, No. 4 (April 1996), pp. 100–106.

7 "The Visegrad Three," Economist (March 1996), pp. 55–56.

in numerous other countries. The most attention-getting investments of U.S. multinationals probably have been those of Ford and General Motors in Europe. In Europe, one sees Ford's Mondeo and General Motors' Opel automobiles everywhere. But virtually every big-name corporation in the United States has some activity in Europe and elsewhere. You do not have to look far to find evidence of this phenomenon: the world is plastered with advertising for these firms. Take, for example, a typical issue of the London-based magazine, *EuroBusiness*. Alongside ads for Barclay's Bank of London and Swissair, you will find ads for Kodak, Digital Equipment, Citibank, and Coopers & Lybrand, to mention a few. Clearly, multinational corporations are here to stay, and many of them are neither American nor European. Asian multinationals (especially those based in Japan, Hong Kong, Korea, Taiwan, and Singapore) are also significant players in the global economy.

A recent development in trading blocs is the emergence of the North American Free Trade Agreement (NAFTA), designed to move the United States, Canada, and Mexico toward virtually complete removal of trade restrictions among them. NAFTA is a thorny issue, mainly because Mexico is a country with a much lower level of development than that of the United States or Canada. Workers in the United States and Canada are concerned about a flight of jobs to Mexico as freer trade occurs in the North American market. However, Mexico took the initiative by reducing many of its trade barriers against foreign goods, and U.S and Canadian trade barriers are already low (a bilateral, U.S.-Canada free trade pact has been in place since 1989). With the passage of NAFTA by the U.S. Congress in 1993, closer integration of markets in these three countries seems inevitable.[8]

Small Firms and the Global Environment

Not only in Mexico, but also as the Eastern bloc (former Soviet-aligned countries) and China open up, myriad new opportunities for international ventures will present themselves. An important point is that such opportunities will not be the exclusive territory of huge, multinational firms. In these less-developed areas, small firms can establish facilities with less investment and fewer competitors than they would have in, say, Western Europe. However, even highly competitive markets like those in Western Europe can provide many opportunities for smaller firms. For example, *Business Week* noted that a substantial number of U.S.-based firms with gross sales under $500 million do a great deal of their business on foreign turf (30 to 50 percent of sales). Two

---

8 For more on NAFTA, see Linda M. Aguilar, "NAFTA: A Review of the Issues," *Economic Perspectives* (Federal Reserve Bank of Chicago), Vol. XVII (January/February 1993), pp. 12–20, or G. C. Hufbauer and J. J. Schott, *North American Free Trade: Issues and Recommendations* (Washington, D.C., Institute for International Economics, 1992).

of these are Invacare of Elyria, Ohio, which manufactures home medical equipment in Europe; and Interlake Corporation, of Lisle, Illinois, which makes fluid-handling products at factories in Great Britain and Singapore. *Business Week* has dubbed such firms "mini-nationals." A CEO of one of them gave the formula for such international success: "Do what you know how to do. Do it right. And do it everywhere."[9]

The success formula for many small firms in the global business environment has been to develop a niche, to focus on specialized production where large firms cannot bury them with economies of scale (cost advantages of large-scale production). This means managers of small firms engaged in international business have to do their homework well, paying attention not only to what foreign markets want to buy, but also to the conditions of production and distribution in those markets. What is required is a great deal of research and a continuing commitment to learning, both about the external environment in which they are operating and the internal workings of the firm. Most of these companies try to stay very lean and efficient in terms of production and management. To accomplish this, managers have to understand what their alternatives are and make wise choices. As the global economy continues on its developing path, managers who are proficient decision makers are those most likely to succeed.

ECONOMICS AND THE MANAGEMENT OF ORGANIZATIONS

While the central themes in managerial economics—identifying problems and opportunities, analyzing alternatives, and making optimal choices—are vitally important to managers in firms with global operations, they are equally significant in the everyday affairs of firms and organizations that have little or no contact with international markets. It is interesting to note that a 1993 survey of the 1,000 largest corporations in the United States turned up the following: the college degree pursued by the chief executive officer (CEO) of a corporation in this group was most likely to have been either *engineering* or *economics*.[10] What these two disciplines have in common is in part their analytical toolkit. Both engineers and economists frequently analyze projects where the outcome can be determined with a great deal of precision using quantitative techniques. Even when they step outside their formal disciplines, they tend to analyze problems in terms of alternatives and expected outcomes. Thus, a CEO with this type of background seems always to be looking for the best alternative solution to a problem and, not surprisingly,

---

9 "Mini-nationals are Making Maximum Impact," *Business Week* (September 6, 1993), p. 67.
10 "Portrait of a CEO," *Business Week* (October 11, 1993), p. 64.

expecting fellow managers and co-workers to provide the substantive input required to find that solution.

Role of Managerial Economics in Problem Solving

We can expect that only a few students of managerial economics will become either managerial economists or CEOs, but whether one's major field is accounting, marketing, information systems, finance, or some other specialization, the analytical abilities that are sharpened by a familiarity with applied economics are extremely valuable. Take, for example, the issue of pricing. Suppose you are considering whether or not to reduce the price of a given product. The most fundamental question you can ask is "Will sales revenue *increase* or *decrease* as a result of this change in price?" Managerial economics can help to answer that question, and in a business someone who has those skills will be able to answer it, given the appropriate data. Whoever does answer it will probably refer to the *elasticity of demand* (discussed in Chapter 2), as relevant to the outcome. Others in the business, whether they fall above or below that person on the organization chart, must have some idea what this important technical relation is. For example, Herbert Kelleher, the CEO of Southwest Airlines and a lawyer by training, understood elasticity well and built a very strong firm on what he believed about it. (See "Building a Business on E_p," in Chapter 2.)

Managerial economics addresses problems not only in pricing, but also in areas such as production, input use, cost, profit, and investment decisions. Its analytic tools and techniques help people communicate their own thoughts and understand what others are saying.

The goal of both research and management activities is a set of decisions that are best for the firm or organization, given its environment and the resources it has to work with. These are called *optimizing decisions*. How managerial economics is related to the process of generating such decisions, as well as how it supplies tools to other areas in businesses and other entities is described graphically in Figure 1–1.

The figure should be read from the upper left, then clockwise and downward. Managerial economics is one of three basic analytical areas that supply decision techniques to people working in what are sometimes called *functional areas* in business: accounting, finance, marketing, and management. Quite simply, these areas are defined by the functions they perform. For example, accounting keeps the firm's records, marketing promotes the firm's product, and so on.

The two other basic analytical areas are mathematics/statistics and decision sciences. Although each basic analytical area has a different focus, all have certain tools and techniques in common: algebra, calculus, and linear algebra, for example. Managerial economics may be more concerned with how markets for products and inputs behave than is statistics or mathematics, yet

Figure 1–1   Relation of Managerial Economics to Decision Making in Firms and Other Organizations

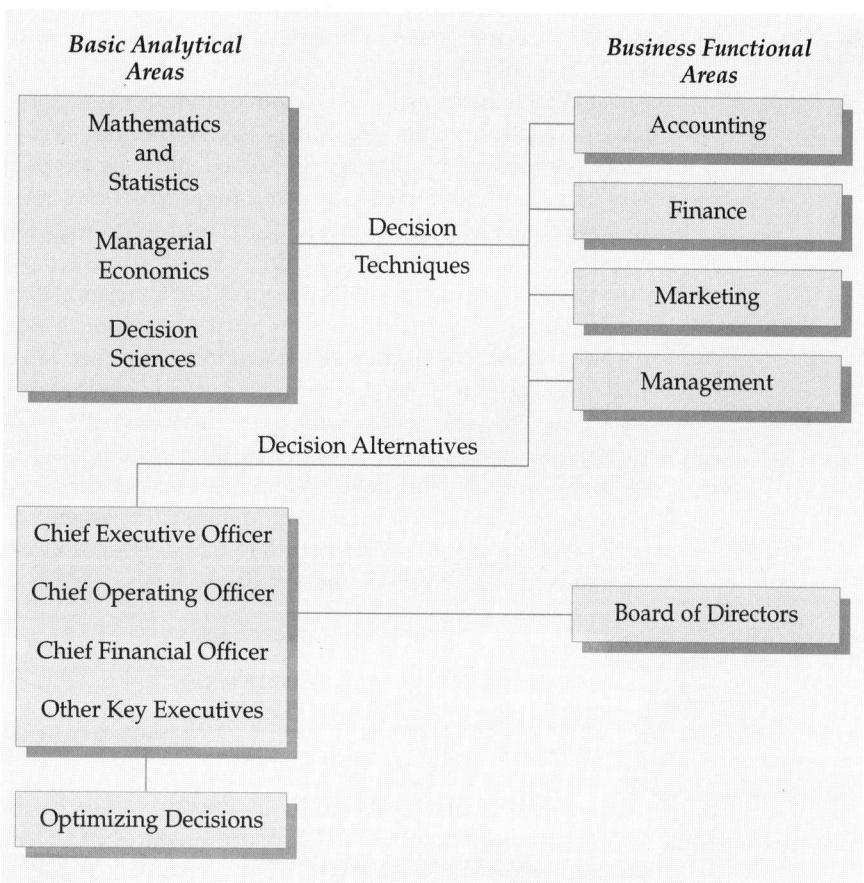

Read this figure from the basic analytical areas, then over to the right and down. Managerial economics is a key area in basic business analysis, along with mathematics, statistics, and decision sciences. All three provide quantitative techniques that are essential to decision makers in the firm or organization. People working in the business functional areas use the tools provided by the basic analytical areas to advise executives and board members who make key decisions. Information flows in both directions along the paths connecting the boxes in the figure.

managerial economists often draw on a widely used statistical technique, multiple regression analysis, to analyze a particular market. Together the basic analytical areas supply decision-making techniques to those who work in the functional areas of business and, ultimately, to the firm or organization's managers.

It is certainly reasonable to think of Figure 1–1 as a two-way street, since an organization's chief executives often either develop alternatives to be analyzed or identify problems to be solved and then ask people in the functional and basic analytical areas for input regarding both the development of further alternatives and the nature of the best or optimal decision. Thus, Figure 1–1 does not imply that everything depends on the basic analytical areas or on managerial economics, but simply that organizational decision making can be much enhanced by those who have good basic analytical tools. People employing those tools may be located in a variety of departments or divisions within the organization (the figure is *not* an organization chart). For example, someone in the marketing department may have the skills required to answer the chief financial officer's question about the impact of a price change on sales revenue. The employed techniques will be those studied in managerial economics. In summary, decision makers and researchers will communicate better if all have some background in managerial economics to help them understand the pricing issue more fully.

Macroeconomics, Microeconomics, and the Corporate Economist

Macroeconomics is the branch of economic analysis that deals with aggregate economic variables such as the economy's total output, central government spending and tax policy, and money supply and interest rates.

Microeconomics is the study of individual economic units such as consumers, business firms, or specific government agencies.

Economists generally divide their discipline into two branches, *macro*economics and *micro*economics. **Macroeconomics** focuses on the study of the economy as a whole and deals with issues such as the level of overall activity (gross domestic product or GDP), interest rates, federal budgets, international trade and currency issues, and federal taxes. **Microeconomics**, on the other hand, deals with the behavior of an individual economic unit, such as a consumer or a business firm. This book deals primarily with microeconomics, addressing how economic analysis can be used to make decisions within organizations. But the two branches are not mutually exclusive, and corporate economists are frequently asked to prepare research and suggest strategies relating to both macro- and microeconomic issues. This was underscored in 1992 by the results of a survey conducted by the economics organization of American Telephone and Telegraph Company (AT&T). Respondents were 32 large corporations with identifiable economics organizations, including such well-known firms as American Cyanamid, IBM, Phillips Petroleum, and Weyerhauser Company. Macro and industry-level forecasting were singled out as areas in which economists who work in these organizations spend a large percentage of their time. However, the same corporate economists were also called on to research specific products and markets, evaluate potential investments, provide environmental impact studies, and assist in litigations.[11]

Many firms and public-sector organizations are not large enough to support their own economics group and must rely on either consultants or in-house staff with some economics training to apply economic principles to decision problems. Most managers in these firms and organizations are interested in economic analysis only to the extent that it has something to say about questions that impact performance or profits. Thus they are even more likely to ask questions of a microeconomic nature than are certain of the managers of larger corporations or organizations.

The growing emphasis on the microeconomic side of economic analysis for businesses was noted almost 20 years ago, when *Business Week* stated that

> companies across the country are now demanding less of the old-style corporate economist who churned out sweeping economic forecasts, which often were swept into the wastebasket, and are turning instead to the new-style economist who can ply his skills in such fields as econometrics and industrial economics to help shape company policy. Indeed, an increasing number of them have joined the team of top-level executives who map business strategy.[12]

What *Business Week* was saying was that corporate economists are asked increasingly for input on issues specific to the performance of the firm. Their role has been redefined so that they spend less time providing general information and more time helping to analyze managerial decision problems. In fact, in a 1996 article, Walter E. Hoadley, a senior research fellow at the Hoover Institution, noted that a call is rising "... for a new breed of business economists who think and act like decision makers, broaden the multidisciplined dimensions of their work, and serve as scouts and shields for senior policy executives."[13] This is a further indication that the techniques provided by managerial economics have broad application to problem solving within

11 The results of the study are described in Dennis K. Hoover, "Business Economists: Not Just Forecasters," *Business Economics*, Vol. XXVII (July 1992), pp. 56–59.
12 "Executive Clout for Economists," *Business Week* (February 13, 1978), pp. 58, 60.
13 Walter E. Hoadley, "Who Needs Business Economists?—The Future of the Profession," *Business Economics*, Vol. 31, No. 1 (January 1996), p. 14. For more, see David Fettig, "Business Economists: Can't Live With 'em, Can't Live Without 'em," *Federal Reserve Bank of Minneapolis: The Region*, Vol. 8, No. 4 (December 1994), pp. 21–25.

firms and other organizations. Thus, even if one does not plan to become a managerial economist, being familiar with the techniques they employ can yield many benefits both in helping to solve problems and in communicating with other decision makers.

Managers and Their Objectives

The managers of a firm are responsible for making most of the economic decisions—the type of product produced, its price, the production technology utilized, and the financing of production—that will ultimately result in profits or losses for the firm. The firm's manager or managers may or may not be its owner or owners; therefore the goals of the managers may not be quite the same as those of the owners. There may be an incentive for the managers to act in ways that are not in the best interests of the shareholders. Economists call this type of problem a **principal-agent problem**. (Shareholders are principals and the managers are their agents.) In the early 1990s, there was a great deal of concern in the United States about the compensation of corporate chief executives, which to many observers seemed to have increased beyond all reason, especially in cases where companies were either losing money or not recording outstanding increases in profits. In 1992, it took an annual compensation of over $22 million to be among the top 10 U.S. CEOs, and the number-one package came to over $125 million. *Forbes* reported in 1996 that the highest paid CEO in the United States received a 1995 compensation package totaling $65.1 million, mostly in the form of stock.[14] While this may seem small in comparison with the top 1992 figure, quite a number of observers would still believe it to be excessive.

As a result of the furor over what many viewed as excessive rewards, a growing number of firms are revamping their executive compensation plans so that high-level managers will have incentives to maximize profits. Changes that have been undertaken include linking stock option awards to stock performance, requiring stock prices to rise a specified percentage before stock options can be exercised, improving disclosure of executive salaries to shareholders, and providing executive compensation committees with independent consultants. It is clearly in the interest of shareholders to structure executive compensation programs in ways that ensure that the firm maintains a satisfactory level of profits and, preferably, a high rate of profit

A **principal-agent problem** occurs when one party is entrusted with making a decision on behalf of another party in a setting where the goals of the two may differ.

---

14 Eric S. Hardy, "The People at the Top of Corporate America," Forbes (May 20, 1996), p. 192. See also John A. Byrne, "How High Can CEO Pay Go," *Business Week* (April 22, 1996) pp. 100–122.

growth. Thus more changes that tie managerial rewards to company performance are quite likely to take place.[15]

The recent debate over managerial compensation is related to various hypotheses about the nature of business firms. The most widely employed hypothesis in managerial economics is that firms will be operated in a way that leads to *profit maximization*.[16] While this seems to be a reasonable hypothesis, the principal-agent problem suggests that it is open to question. Economists and specialists in organizational management have derived other hypotheses about the behavior of firms and have done a great deal of research aimed at testing them. The following are some of the alternative hypotheses.

1. *Market share maximization.* A firm will behave in a way that maximizes market share (as measured by sales revenue, or perhaps proportion of quantity sold to total market).
2. *Growth maximization.* Increasing the size of the firm over time will take precedence over other objectives. Profit may be sacrificed to attain higher rates of growth in other variables.
3. *Maximization of managerial returns.* Managers will make choices that maximize their own interest, subject to generating sufficient profit to keep their jobs.

The results of empirical testing of these hypotheses, as well as tests of the profit maximization hypothesis, have been mixed.[17] At different points in time and under different states of the economy (expansion, recession), one or the other seems to have empirical support. However, economists have generally favored the profit maximization hypothesis for a variety of reasons. First and foremost, a firm that is not profitable is unlikely to survive in the long run. Second, while managerial rewards may be at some points in time and in some firms more closely correlated with sales or growth than with profit, as we have seen, shareholders and government regulators alike are interested in designing compensation packages that are tied to profit performance. Third, profit maximization requires careful study of factors such as

---

15 For more on the compensation issue, see Dyan Machan and Rana Dogar, "The Last Article You Will Ever Have to Read on Executive Pay? No Way," *Forbes* (May 20, 1996), pp. 176–183; "Executive Pay: The Party Ain't Over Yet," *Business Week* (April 26, 1993), pp. 56–62, and "The Pay Police: Lawmakers and the Media Have Declared War on CEO Compensation. How Angry Should You Be?" *Newsweek* (June 17, 1991), pp. 44–45.

16 This is often stated as maximization of the present value of the firm, defined as the present value of the future net cash flows into the firm. (See Chapter 13 for a discussion of present value.)

17 A very thorough survey of the literature on goals and objectives of the firm and its managers can be found in Donald A. Hay and Derek J. Morris, *Industrial Economics and Organization* (New York: Oxford University Press, 1991), especially Chapter 9. The relationship between market share and profitability is examined in N. Venkatraman and John E. Prescott, "The Market Share-Profitability Relationship: Testing Temporal Stability Across Business Cycles," *Journal of Management*, Vol. 16, No. 4 (1990), pp. 783–805.

demand and cost that will remain important even when the firm has another main objective or a set of more complex objectives. Finally, if one does not know what result a profit-maximizing strategy will yield, it is not possible to assess the cost to the firm of pursuing alternatives to it. For all of these reasons, this book will assume that the firm is a profit maximizer. This will give us an important benchmark from which we can assess any alternative behaviors that may present themselves. We will assume that in a business firm, the chief decision makers are interested enough in profit to want to know what strategy will maximize it. When we deal with a public-sector or not-for-profit organization, the usual assumption will be that the organization wishes to use its resources efficiently, thereby maximizing the net stream of benefits it produces.

In large, private-sector corporations, along with the CEO, some of the main decision makers of the firm usually include the president, the vice-president for sales, the vice-president for manufacturing, the vice-president for finance, the controller, and the board of directors. (The *controller* is the head accountant for the firm and is responsible for the collection of data regarding the firm's costs and revenues and for setting up its budgets, thereby performing a crucial role in the firm's decision-making process.) The aforementioned managers usually take joint responsibility for decision making. Thus their fortunes or careers may rise or fall depending on the skill with which they interpret economic problems and the data and advice they receive from staff economists or economic consultants, financial analysts, and market researchers. We shall see that the managers' responsibilities, although centered around achievement of the firm's profit goal, have been expanded to include both liability for criminal offenses and damages that result from the activities of the corporations that the managers oversee. In the important area of antitrust liability, managers must blend their knowledge of economic decision making with that of law, in order to avoid decision errors that could prove disastrous for themselves and their firms.

In this book it is not our objective to teach you to become a chief financial manager, a controller, the head of a marketing department, or even a full-fledged corporate economist. What we will attempt to do is to help you learn the economic principles that are relevant to decision making in all areas of firm management. An understanding of these principles will help the future firm manager know *which* questions to ask and thus *what data* are needed, as well as *what decision* to make once the data are obtained, in order to assist the firm in maximizing profits. If you do not eventually become a managerial economist, we hope that at least you will be able to communicate with economists and recognize when help from them can prove useful for problem solving.

The importance of utilizing economic principles in making managerial decisions is underscored by Small Business Administration statistics, which show that *50 percent* of all businesses fail within their *first two years* of operation and only *20 percent* survive for *five years*. We believe that the significance of these principles is further emphasized by the past bankruptcies or bankruptcy filings of such well-known companies as Federated Department Stores (Bloomingdale's, Rich's, Burdine's, and others), Continental Airlines, R. H. Macy, Foster Grant, and Orion Pictures,[18] as well as by some of the problems of other prominent firms, including Volkswagen, Woolworth's, Kmart, Sears Roebuck, and even McDonald's.[19]

As indicated previously, we shall usually assume that the goal of a firm is *profit maximization*, or making the greatest possible total profit over some specified time period. The corresponding goal of the public sector manager is assumed to be the *efficient use of resources*. Arguments can be made and are made with regard to the accuracy of these assumptions. Nevertheless, we think they are useful assumptions. That is because we believe that even when a firm or agency has more complex objectives, managers benefit by knowing the difference between an efficient, or profit-maximizing, strategy and one that sacrifices some efficiency or profit in order to achieve other goals.

OUR APPROACH TO PROBLEM SOLVING

Our emphasis here is on managerial problem solving, usually in a profit-maximizing context. In general, once managerial objectives are known, we take the following steps in arriving at a decision:

1. An *identification* of the problem or decision to be made.
2. A statement of *alternative solutions* to the problem.
3. A *determination of what data are relevant* to the decision, and an analysis of those data relative to the alternative solutions.

---

18 Murray Forseter, "The Big One Looms Over Retailing," *Chain Store Age*, Vol. 72, No. 1 (January 1996), p. 16; "Federated Stores Ends Chapter 11 Creditor Shield," *The Wall Street Journal*, February 6, 1992, p. A4; "This Time, Continental May Actually Fly," *Business Week* (May 10, 1993), pp. 70–71; "A 'Death Knell' at Macy's?" *Business Week* (January 27, 1992), pp. 28–29; "Foster Grant Runs for the Shade of Chapter 11," *Business Week* (September 3, 1990), p. 44; and "Orion Seeks Bankruptcy Court Protection," *The Wall Street Journal*, December 12, 1991, p. B6.
19 "Kmart Braces for 1996: Says Chapter 11 Not an Option," *Discount Store News*, Vol. 35, No. 1 (January 1, 1996), pp. 1, 52–53; "VW Figures Its Best Defense May be a Good Offense," *Business Week* (August 9, 1993), p. 29; "Woolworth to Shutter 10% of Its Stores," *The Wall Street Journal*, October 14, 1993, p. A3; "The Big Store May Be On a Big Roll," *Business Week* (August 30, 1993), pp. 82–85; "Can Ed Brennan Salvage the Sears He Designed?" *Business Week* (August 27, 1990), p. 34; and "McDonald's Isn't Looking Quite So Juicy Anymore," *Business Week* (August 6, 1990), p. 30.

4. The choice of *the best solution* consistent with our firm's or agency's objectives.

The time period under consideration will often be an important factor in our decision analysis. When decisions concern current operations and objectives are predetermined, alternatives may be very limited. In such cases step 2 may reduce to a simple statement of the conditions under which the objective will be met. For example, if management wishes to determine what rate of output per quarter will maximize profit from sales of a given product in a single market, there may be no alternative but to determine the output level that is consistent with this objective. However, if management wishes to decide which of a given set of investment projects will add the most to the value of the firm, a large number of alternatives may have to be analyzed. In general, the longer the time period in question, the greater the number of alternatives available to management.

The analyzing and choosing done in steps 3 and 4 rely heavily on standard and broadly accepted tools and criteria of economic analysis. As we progress through the definition of these tools and criteria and their application to specific economic problems of the firm, we will develop rules for decision making that will be applied time and time again. In general, these rules have their foundation in what is known as **marginal or incremental analysis**. Marginal analysis focuses on *changes* in economic variables and the results that occur directly from them. In a business the underlying principle of the marginal or incremental approach is that changes in economic variables controlled by the firm (output, price, resource use, investment) should be undertaken any time the result is to add more to the firm's revenues than to its costs—in other words, any time they add to profit. For public-sector management, we extend this concept to the effect of changes in public output on *social benefits* and *social costs*. These concepts take into account benefits and costs that accrue to or affect individuals or firms who are not directly involved in the transaction that yields them. An example of such an additional item would be benefits to the community as a whole of a program to provide vaccinations free of charge to low-income individuals. Another would be the costs of congestion borne by a neighborhood when a domed stadium is constructed there.

> **Marginal or incremental analysis** examines how changes in certain economic variables affect other economic variables; for example, how a change in the output of a firm affects both sales revenue and cost or how an increase in household income affects savings.

ORGANIZATION OF THIS BOOK

This book is organized in a way that we hope will help you quickly master some key economic concepts and recognize relevant data for decision making in business firms or other organizations. In fact, once Parts 1 and 2 are completed, virtually all of the tools and decision criteria necessary for the analysis of specific decision problems in the subsequent parts of the book will have been presented.

Analysis of Basic Concepts

Since a firm's total profit during any time period is equal to its *total revenue* (sales) less its total costs, an accurate economic analysis of the demand for the product of a firm and its *cost* is crucial to the achievement of the firm's goal of profit maximization. In fact, inadequate record keeping, which precluded careful analysis of these two factors, was one of the reasons for the mid-1970s demise of retailer W. T. Grant.[20] In 1990, another big merchandising firm, Ames Department Stores (Ames, G. C. Murphy, and Zayre stores) was in deep financial trouble, in part because of poor record keeping at several hundred stores it had acquired when it bought another company. Ames survived but had to settle for modest profits during the remainder of the 1990s.[21] Many other businesses have failed for similar reasons. By way of contrast, careful financial controls are a major factor in helping successful firms (such as DuPont, General Electric,[22] and USX[23]) to remain generally profitable and expand.

One of the first steps toward the development of a profit-maximizing strategy is to gain an understanding of the relationship between *demand* for a firm's output and the firm's revenue from sales. Chapter 2 is devoted entirely to a discussion of demand concepts, including (1) the relationship of price charged to quantity demanded, (2) the relationship of quantity demanded to total and incremental sales revenue, and (3) the effects on product demand of other variables, such as consumer income and prices of related goods. In Chapter 3, we turn to the empirical estimation of demand, relying primarily on modern statistical techniques that can be applied easily using a personal computer. Until recent years, small businesses rarely attempted statistical analysis of demand because most lacked computer facilities or the budget to hire consultants and mainframe time. Today, however, most businesses can do their own demand estimation.

---

20 See "Investigating the Collapse of W. T. Grant," *Business Week* (July 19, 1976), pp. 60–62.

21 "Ames Plans for Modest Gains in '96," *Discount Store News*, Vol. 35, No. 7 (April 1996), p. 3; and "They Took Their Shot at Being a Giant—and Missed," *Business Week* (May 7, 1990), p. 39.

22 Carol Kennedy, "The Company That Jack Welch Built," *Director*, Vol. 49, No. 2 (September 1995), pp. 42–48; "General Electric", *Industry Week*, Vol. 24, No. 19 (October 16, 1995), pp. 30–32; and "Cut Costs or Else," *Business Week* (March 22, 1993), pp. 28–29.

23 James P. Owen and David Elias, "Poised for Profits," *Chief Executive*, Vol. 102 (April 1995), p. 70; and "All That Lean Isn't Turning Into Green," *Business Week* (November 18, 1991), pp. 39–40.

Of course, large firms are performing more and more sophisticated demand analyses. For example, for over a decade firms in the airline industry have been using their computer systems to keep close tabs on air travel patterns and the effect of price changes on those patterns. As a result, they are able to adjust their fare structures quickly and precisely to adapt to changing markets.[24] Frito Lay, Kraft, Procter and Gamble, and RJR Nabisco are tracking consumer demand with software that analyzes data from supermarket scanners.[25] On the other hand, firms in the U.S. auto industry have had to make painful adjustments to the production of small cars and increased competition from foreign car manufacturers because they did not correctly anticipate consumer demand for lighter-weight, high quality cars.[26]

Historically, some firms have placed major emphasis on obtaining a greater market share as a means of expanding profit. Now, however, many firms are attaching increasing importance to *profit maximizing* and *flexible pricing* policies, as opposed to expanding sales volume. For example, Procter & Gamble, a major producer of detergents, diapers, cooking oils, and various foodstuffs, has recently placed new emphasis on the profit goal. They have revamped their pricing strategies to compete with low-price rivals and have set out on a serious drive to cut costs.[27] As strategy began to change several years ago, one company spokesman put it this way: "Before it had been share, share, share. We get the share, and the profits will follow." The company's revised approach is to focus more directly on profits.[28] To be a success at managing for profits requires a great deal of information, not only on markets and demand, but also on costs. This means that decision makers have had to increase their analytical skills as data collection and processing techniques have become more refined.

Chapter 4, the last chapter in Part 1, deals with *economic forecasting*, or predicting the future value of economic variables of interest to decision makers in the firm or agency. Forecasting is done at various levels of aggregation. For example, in a large firm it would not be unusual for the economics group to be asked to come up with a forecast of the country's GDP (gross domestic product) for the next quarter or year or to run various forecasts based on assumptions about changes in an important variable such as government tax policy or interest rates. However, the economists might also be asked to fore-

24 "Air Fares Rise, but Airlines Plan Sweeter Bonuses," *The Wall Street Journal*, September 13, 1993, p. A3, and "Airlines Use a Scalpel to Cut Fares in the Latest Round of Price Wars," *The Wall Street Journal*, November 26, 1985, p. 31.

25 "How Software is Making Food Sales a Piece of Cake," *Business Week* (July 2, 1990), p. 54.

26 "Detroit, Check Your Rearview Mirror," *Business Week* (June 6, 1994), pp. 26–27; "A New Era for Auto Quality," *Business Week* (October 22, 1990), pp. 85–96; and "Stumbling Auto Makers Face Tough '91," *The Wall Street Journal*, January 7, 1991, p. B1.

27 "Procter and Gamble Hits Back," *Business Week* (July 19, 1993), pp. 20–21.

28 "Can P&G Squeeze Profits Out of Orange Juice?" *Business Week* (January 23, 1989), p. 38.

cast demand for a single product that the firm sells. Our discussion will cover a variety of methods that are used to come up with such forecasts.

In Part 2 our emphasis shifts from demand and revenue analysis to the costs of the firm. Since profit maximization requires the greatest possible spread between total revenue and total cost, it is critical that managers understand how costs behave as output and sales of the firm change. Costs depend on the relationship between output and the inputs that are used to produce it.[29] For example, a manufacturing firm may purchase labor, machinery, raw materials, fuel, and managerial talent in order to make its product. In general, the firm's total cost will increase as output is increased, since more of these inputs will have to be bought to produce greater amounts of the product. Chapter 5 deals specifically with the way output varies as the amounts and kinds of inputs are changed. Our objective in Chapter 5 will be to determine for each possible output of the firm per given time period the combination of inputs that will minimize production cost. In Chapter 6 we show how the costs of the firm vary with its level of output, once the cost-minimization criteria of Chapter 5 are satisfied.

Finally, revenue and cost analyses are brought together in Chapter 7, where the criteria for profit maximization are fully developed. We will demonstrate in Chapter 7, for example, that maximization of profit does not necessarily mean that sales are maximized or that unit costs are minimized. In fact, we will show that for profit maximization, a firm must produce up to the point where the *incremental profit* (additional revenue less additional cost) received from the production of one more unit of output is zero.

In addition to profit-maximizing decision rules, Chapter 7 includes a comparison of profit maximization with break-even analysis, another well-known business approach to managerial decision making, and a reconsideration of profit maximization as a "real world" managerial goal. Again, once we reach this point in the book, most of the tools necessary for the analysis of the subsequent chapters will have been discussed and applied.

Environment of the Firm

A firm or other organization always operates in two environments, one internal and the other external. Its internal environment consists to a large extent of factors over which it has broad control. These include its technology,

---

29 Lee Iacocca, Chairman of Chrysler Corp., showed a keen awareness of cost when he chided his suppliers for developing a parking-brake cable that would hold up at 60 degrees below zero. Reportedly, Iacocca asked, "Why not 40 below? How many cars do we sell in Labrador? We've got to make sure we don't give our customers too much cost and not enough value." See "The Flashing Signal at Chrysler: Danger Dead Ahead," *Business Week* (June 18, 1990), p. 44.

its organizational structure, and its choice of products, materials, and other inputs. In the external environment, however, there are many factors and circumstances that the firm or agency cannot change. For example, if economic growth leads to higher wages for the type of labor a firm employs, it will most likely have to raise its workers' pay, since the alternative is to lose them to other firms. To situations like these it can only *react*, but its managers must take careful account of the factors outside the organization that affect its well-being in order to determine the optimal reaction.

Today more than ever the external environment has an international dimension. A development in international capital markets or a move made by a foreign government to improve the competitiveness of its producers may exert a direct impact on your firm or organization. In this book, we take into account such international dimensions by including special examples and observations in the chapters, by offering some international content in our Integrating Cases, and by discussing various international considerations in detail in our International Capsules. The latter are strategically placed after Chapters 6, 11, and 14 and are designed to both integrate topics from several chapters and extend the analysis to relevant international questions.

Parts 3, 4, and 5 deal specifically with some special factors in the environment in which managers must make economic decisions regarding the firm. The environment of the firm contains many factors that the firm must analyze and successfully cope with in order to maximize profits. These factors include (1) variables that determine consumer demand for its product, such as consumer income; (2) the presence, prices, and advertising of competing products; (3) population growth; and (4) consumer tastes and preferences, as discussed in Chapter 2.

However, of particular importance to the firm in determining its pricing strategy is the *type of product market* within which it operates. In Chapters 9 and 10 we define four basic product market structures, focusing primarily on the number of firms in a given market and the corresponding relationship of that number to the notion of competition. Profit maximization is first examined in Chapter 9 under conditions of theoretically perfect competition and its antithesis—pure monopoly. Still, most firms are faced with situations lying somewhere between these two extremes. Therefore, profit-maximizing price and output decisions in these more realistic and complex settings are discussed in Chapter 10.

Special pricing and production decisions—such as those associated with the internal transfer of a product from one division of a firm to another, jointly produced products, and price discrimination among different groups of buyers—are considered in Chapter 11.

Another environmental factor that affects the firm's costs is the current state of technology, which helps to determine the opportunities for economies of scale in production, as discussed in Chapter 5. However, the firm's costs are also affected by the fact that some of its inputs are fixed in the short run and by input market structures with which the firm must deal, as discussed in Chapter 12.

When a firm's management is contemplating new investments, the environmental elements in the decision-making process become more complex. For example, some of management's investment alternatives may involve lines of production with which management is not familiar. Also, the longer time horizon relevant to this type of decision brings forth the possibility that many more variables may change than would be expected in a short-run analysis of current operations. The analysis of *capital projects* (investment undertakings), which is the subject of Chapters 13 and 14, involves expansion of our decision-making goals to handle both the larger number of alternatives available in the long run and the fact that profits attributable to a decision will flow into the firm over some future time period. Moreover, we shall develop means for taking into account the *risk* associated with various future alternatives for the firm and for adjusting our analyses for differences in risk between alternatives.

The final part of this book, Part 5, deals with interrelationships between government, or the *public sector*, and the firm. We first show, in Chapter 15, how our decision analysis can be modified to deal with managerial problems in public agencies and to develop rules for the efficient use of public-sector resources. In Chapter 16 we consider government regulations as an element of the firm's environment and examine how profit maximization is affected by regulatory variables. These regulations affect both the pricing policies and the costs of the firm because the firm must meet numerous requirements regarding pricing, product safety, product quality, and plant safety.

Finally, in Chapter 17 we speculate about the future environment of the firm, focusing our attention on trends and impending changes that will likely affect the economic decisions of managers in years to come.

Other Tools for Decision Making

Besides the basic economic concepts and tools outlined in this chapter, other technical tools can greatly assist the manager in making decisions that will maximize firm profits. These tools include the calculus techniques of optimization (with or without a constraint), linear regression analysis, and linear programming.

A review of mathematical functions and graphs and an introduction to calculus are provided in the Mathematical Appendix at the end of the book. Optimization with calculus is covered in the appendix to Chapter 5 and in Chapter 7. Linear regression analysis, a statistical tool which assists the manager in estimating firm revenue and cost functions, is presented in Chapter 3 and its appendix. Chapter 8 discusses linear programming, a useful technique when a firm's relevant revenue and cost functions are linear but are subject to linear constraints that can be expressed in the form of inequalities.

Throughout the book are many numerical examples showing how to apply various analytical techniques. Be sure to work through these step by step as you read along; and remember, they can be used for review as well.

If mathematics is not your cup of tea, there is no reason to be discouraged. It is not necessary for you to master all of the quantitative tools we have mentioned before you can understand the basic economic principles involved in profit maximization or before you can find this book useful. Of course, various instructors will choose to place different emphases on the expertise you achieve in such methods. We believe, however, that a working knowledge of these tools will be very helpful to the business or public-sector manager in economic decision making.

APPENDIX 1

Demand, Supply, and Market Price: A Brief Review

The historian and philosopher Thomas Carlyle (1795–1881) once said that even a parrot could be taught to repeat "supply and demand" in response to any economic question. Thus, if we are to place ourselves at a level somewhere above the parrot, an understanding of the specifics of supply and demand analysis is warranted.

DEMAND AND THE DEMAND CURVE

In economic analysis, the term "demand" is used to refer to the various amounts of a good or service someone (a single consumer or a group of buyers) is both willing and able to buy at various possible prices. It is a functional relationship between a good's price and the quantity the buyer or buyers will take. When we are talking about the demand for a firm's product, we therefore mean the amounts of it that buyers will take at various possible prices. This kind of information is shown by either a *demand schedule* or a *demand curve* for the good. The amount that consumers will buy at any given price is usually called the "quantity demanded" of the good.

Let us assume for a moment that we are looking at the market demand for broccoli. Table 1A–1 shows the amounts of broccoli consumers will purchase per month at various possible prices per bunch. (Broccoli is sold in bunches with an average weight of about one pound.) The amount people are willing and able to buy at any given price appears in the quantity demanded column, labeled Q_b. In Figure 1A–1, the same data are presented as a demand curve. The demand curve, D_b, is just a plot of the price and quantity-demanded data from the table, with price shown on the vertical axis and quantity demanded on the horizontal axis.

Note that the demand curve slopes downward to the right (has a *negative* slope). For most goods, we expect this to be the case, since at lower prices people will tend to buy larger amounts per time period. This inverse relation between a good's own price and the quantity demanded of it is a reflection of the *law of demand*. The law of demand simply states that both individuals and groups of consumers will generally increase their purchases of a good when

Table 1A–1   Demand for Broccoli

Price of Broccoli per Bunch (P_b)	Quantity Demanded of Broccoli per Month (Q_b)
$1.20	100,000
1.10	125,000
1.00	150,000
.90	175,000
.80	200,000
.70	225,000
.60	250,000
.50	275,000

Figure 1A–1   Demand Curve for Broccoli

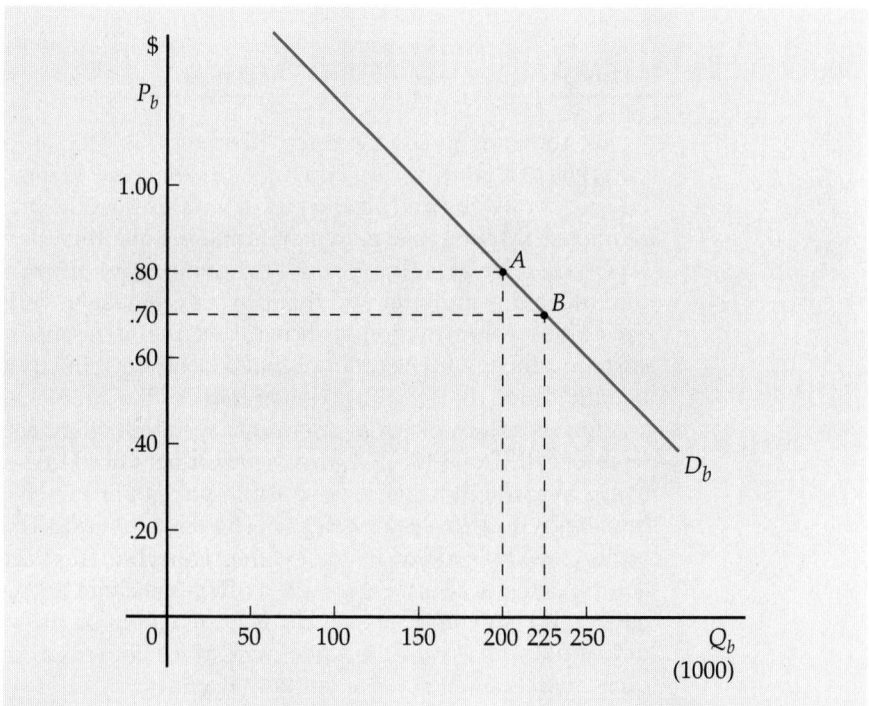

its price falls and decrease their purchases when its price rises. It holds for most goods but cannot be proven to hold for all goods in all circumstances. For example, we know that snob appeal sometimes causes people to buy *more* of a good when its price rises (designer clothes, luxury cars). However, these cases are relatively rare.

Since the law of demand holds in Figure 1A–1, we can see that a fall in the price of broccoli will lead to increased purchases of broccoli by consumers. If the price falls from $.80 per bunch to $.70 per bunch, consumers will increase their purchases from 200,000 bunches per month to 225,000 bunches. Such a change (from point *A* to *B* in Figure 1A–1), which takes place when the good's own price changes and there is a movement *along* a given demand curve, is called "change in quantity demanded."

Behind the demand curve is a broader concept, the *demand function*. The demand function explicitly recognizes that consumers' purchases of a given item depend on other things besides its price. For example, how much broccoli consumers will buy probably depends not only on the price of broccoli, but also on the prices of other green veggies such as brussels sprouts or green beans. It may also depend on consumer incomes, since cheaper vegetables might be bought instead if consumers were closely watching their budgets. We can represent all this as a demand function with the notational form $Q_b = f(P_b, P_v, I)$, where Q_b is the number of bunches of broccoli sold per month, P_b is the price of broccoli per bunch, P_v is the average price per unit of competing veggies, and I is a measure of consumers' monthly income. The variables other than P_b on the righthand side of the equation are called "determinants of demand."

In order to plot the demand curve as we did in Figure 1A–1, it is necessary that as we change the price of broccoli, other demand function variables such as the price of competing veggies and consumers' income remain constant. Why? Because the demand curve in the figure will *shift* if one of the other variables changes. Take income, for example. If income rises, some consumers who thought broccoli was too expensive for their dinner tables will decide to buy it. Thus at all possible prices there will be a greater demand for broccoli. In Table 1A–1 we would see a new column of data for quantity demanded, and in Figure 1A–1, the demand curve would shift to the right. Such a shift is illustrated in Figure 1A–2. This type of change is usually called a "change in demand." Thus *change in demand* is used to denote a shift in the demand curve, while *change in quantity demanded* refers to a movement along it. The latter would occur if the price of broccoli changed while income and the price of other green veggies remained constant. This was implicitly assumed earlier when we changed the price of broccoli from $.80 to $.70 per bunch and noted the movement from *A* to *B* along the demand curve in Figure 1A–1. When we hold other variables constant while we change only one key variable, the phrase "other things equal" is often invoked to indicate that only *one* of the variables is being altered.

Since an increase in income—other things equal—will shift the demand curve to the right, a decrease in income will shift it to the left. This will be the case for most goods. (Exceptions will be discussed in Chapter 2.) If we consider the effect on demand for broccoli of a change in the price of other green vegetables (*substitutes* for broccoli) it is easy to see that the change in the price of a substitute will also shift the demand curve. In our example, if the prices

Figure 1A–2   A Change in Demand for Broccoli

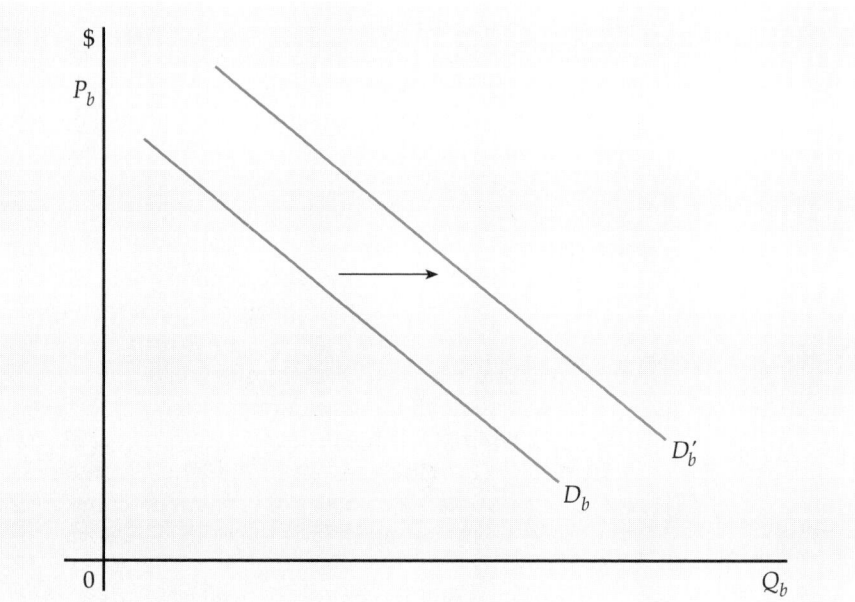

of other green vegetables fall while consumer incomes remain constant, we can expect the demand for broccoli to decrease (demand curve for broccoli to shift to the left). Why? Because some consumers will substitute the other, now relatively cheaper, vegetables for broccoli. A change in the price of a substitute good will always shift the demand curve in the same fashion: to the right for an increase in the substitute's price and to the left for a decrease in the substitute's price. If a related good is a complement (something used *with* the good in question, rather than instead of it), the shift relation reverses. More will be said about this in Chapter 2.

The basics of demand analysis can be summarized as follows:

1. *Demand* is a functional relationship between the price of a good and the quantity demanded of it per time period.
2. The demand curve for a good normally slopes downward to the right, reflecting the law of demand.
3. A demand function states the relation between the quantity of a good consumers will buy and the values of several independent variables, including its own price, prices of related goods, income, and other relevant determinants of demand.

4. When a good's own price changes but other demand function variables remain constant, there is a *change in quantity demanded* (movement along the demand curve).
5. If one of the determinants of demand changes, the demand curve will shift (there will be a *change in demand*). The direction of that shift will depend on whether there is a direct or an inverse relation between that independent variable and consumers' purchases of the good in question.

SUPPLY AND THE SUPPLY CURVE

In economic analysis, the term *supply*, like demand, refers to a functional relationship. It is the relation between the various possible prices of a good and the *quantity supplied* by sellers of it per time period. Supply can also be represented as a schedule or a curve. For example, we might say that at a price of $.60 per bunch sellers of broccoli will be willing and able to bring to market a quantity supplied of 100,000 bunches per month. That would describe *one point* on their supply curve of broccoli. If they will bring to market 300,000 bunches at a price of $1.00 per bunch, we have another point on their supply curve. Table 1A–2 is a supply schedule for broccoli, and Figure 1A–3 shows the broccoli supply curve. That curve has a positive slope (upward to the right), indicating that sellers will offer a larger quantity supplied at higher broccoli prices. We will often use upward-sloping supply curves in subsequent analyses, but occasionally we will consider circumstances where the supply curve does not slope upward. In the case of broccoli, it would be easy to justify an upward-sloping supply curve, since production costs would be likely to go up as broccoli production increased and less-suitable land was brought into cultivation of broccoli.

Table 1A–2   Supply of Broccoli

Price of Broccoli per Bunch (P_b)	Quantity Supplied of Broccoli per Month (Q_s)
$1.20	400,000
1.10	350,000
1.00	300,000
.90	250,000
.80	200,000
.70	150,000
.60	100,000
.50	50,000

Figure 1A–3   The Supply Curve of Broccoli

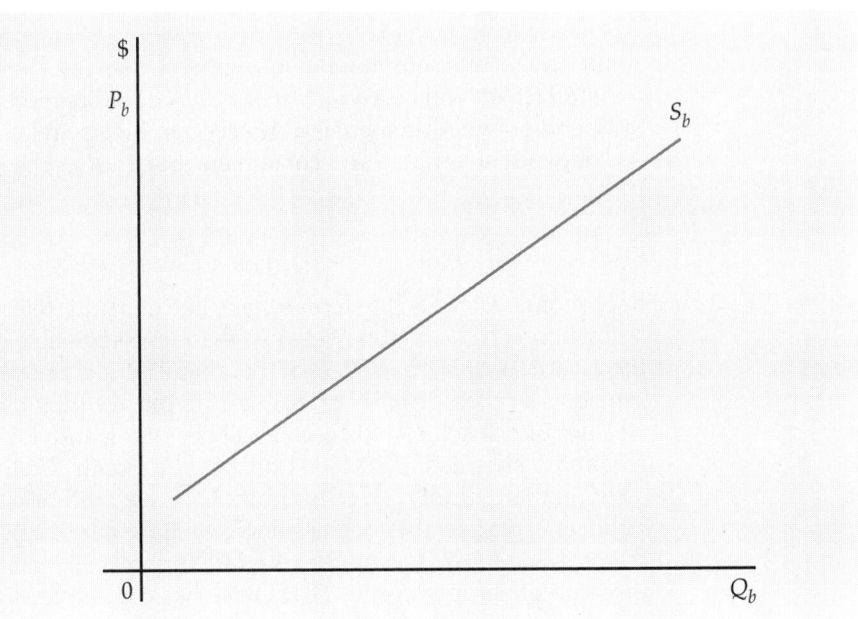

Just as we noted the existence of a demand function behind the demand curve, there is a supply function behind the supply curve. That function relates the amount of a good sellers are willing and able to offer for sale to both its own price and other relevant independent variables known as the "determinants of supply." For broccoli, the supply function might be of the form $Q_s = f(P_b, P_v, IN_p)$, where Q_s is the number of bunches of broccoli sellers will bring to market per month, P_b is the price of broccoli per bunch, P_v is the price of an alternative product (something the producers might wish to supply instead of broccoli), and IN_p is an index of input prices. If one of the determinants of supply changes, the supply curve will shift. For example, a fall in the price of fertilizer might lead suppliers to be willing to grow and bring to market more broccoli per month at every possible broccoli price. Thus the supply curve of broccoli would shift to the right. Clearly, rising input prices would do the reverse.

DETERMINATION OF MARKET PRICE

We are now ready to discuss the way supply and demand interact to determine market price. However, one caution is necessary. We will be assuming in what follows that the market in question (the broccoli market) is characterized by large numbers of sellers and buyers and that no individual firm or buyer in the market is powerful enough to affect the market price that is established. In other words, the going price that tends to hold for broccoli comes about as a result of the actions of the thousands of participants (buyers and sellers) in the market but not because any one of them is so large that he or she directly impacts the result. This is the condition known in economic theory as *perfect competition*. In a market characterized by perfect competition, the seller sees no need to lower the going price, since a large number of buyers are willing to pay that price. Similarly, the seller is aware that raising the price above the going level would result in zero sales, as the buyers know that a large number of sellers are willing and able to sell at the going price. For example, if broccoli is selling everywhere for $.80 a bunch, and seller Jilly Johnson decides she wants to charge $.85 per bunch, a higher price will not result, because buyers will simply purchase 80-cent broccoli from the other sellers.

The "going price" we have mentioned is an *equilibrium* value toward which the actions of the multitude of sellers and buyers in the market will cause price to move. This can be explained easily if we combine the demand and supply curve diagrams introduced in the earlier figures into one graph, as in Figure 1A–4. Now, the upward-sloping supply curve of sellers intersects

Figure 1A–4   Equilibrium in the Broccoli Market

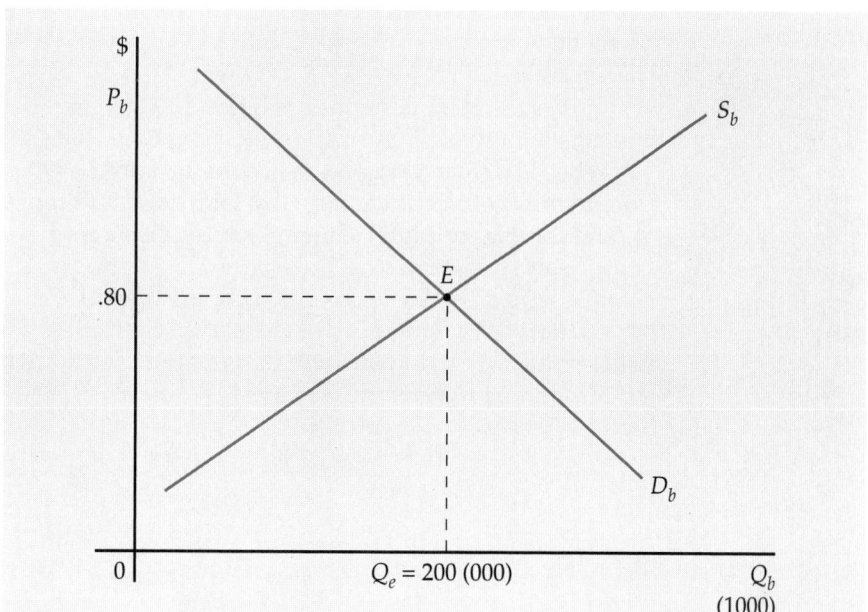

the demand curve of consumers at point E. Point E identifies the equilibrium values of both price and quantity demanded or supplied, since if price is either greater or less than P_e, market forces will cause price to return to that level. Note, of course, that P_e is the only price that will equate the quantity demanded by buyers with the quantity supplied by sellers. This quantity, the equilibrium quantity, is labeled Q_e and conforms to 200,000, if the supply and demand curves are plotted from Tables 1A–1 and 1A–2.

We can also solve algebraically for the equilibrium price and quantity in Figure 1A–4 as follows. The equation for the demand curve depicted in Figure 1A–1, corresponding to the data in Table 1A–1, is

$$Q_{d_b} = 400 - 250P_b,$$

Q_{d_b} is the quantity demanded of broccoli in thousands of bunches per month.

and

P_b is the price per bunch of broccoli in dollars.

Similarly, the equation for the supply curve depicted in Figure 1A–3, corresponding to the data in Table 1A–2, is

$$Q_{s_b} = -200 + 500P_b,$$

where

Q_{s_b} is the quantity supplied of broccoli in thousands of bunches,

and

P_b is the price per bunch of broccoli in dollars.

When the broccoli market is in equilibrium, $Q_{d_b} = Q_{s_b}$ at the going market price for broccoli. Thus we can solve for the equilibrium price by setting $Q_{d_b} = Q_{s_b}$ and solving for price. Therefore, at equilibrium,

$$Q_{d_b} = Q_{s_b}.$$

Substituting for Q_{d_b} and Q_{s_b} from the equations for the demand curve and the supply curve, respectively, we have

$$400 - 250P_b = -200 + 500P_b,$$

$$750P_b = 600,$$

and

$$P_b = \$.80.$$

We can find the equilibrium value for Q_b by substituting in $.80 for P_b in either the equation for the demand curve or the equation for the supply curve:

$$Q_{s_b} = -200 + 500P_b,$$

$$Q_{s_b} = -200 + 500(.80),$$

$$Q_{s_b} = -200 + 400 = 200 \text{ (in thousands)},$$

or

$$Q_{d_b} = 400 - 250P_b,$$

$$Q_{d_b} = 400 - 250(.80),$$

$$Q_{d_b} = 400 - 200 = 200 \text{ (in thousands)}.$$

As we found from Tables 1A–1 and 1A–2 and Figure 1A–4, the equilibrium price of broccoli is $.80 per bunch and the equilibrium quantity is 200,000 bunches.

The nature of the equilibrium at point E can be examined by asking what would happen if price were temporarily at some other value than P_e. In panel (a) of Figure 1A–5, suppose price is temporarily at P_H. This price is above the equilibrium price at E and results in a quantity supplied (Q_s) that exceeds

Figure 1A–5   Market Adjustment to Equilibrium

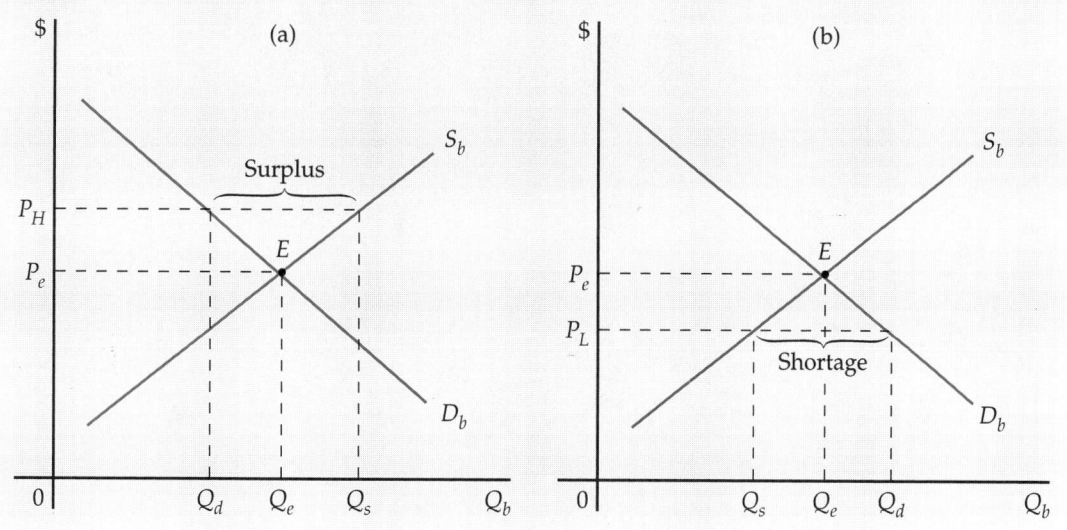

quantity demanded (Q_d). As the diagram shows, there will be a surplus of broccoli in the market because sellers will want to sell more at price P_H than buyers will be willing and able to buy. Sellers will build up inventories of the stuff, and they will have to reduce price in order to get rid of it. Note that this will be true for any price above P_e.

If, on the other hand, price is temporarily below P_e (as at price P_L in panel (b) of the figure), there will be a shortage of broccoli in the market, since quantity demanded (Q_d) will exceed quantity supplied (Q_s). Sellers will see their inventory levels drawn down and will be willing to increase quantity supplied only at higher prices. Consumers, as they become aware of the shortage, will be willing to pay higher prices. The result will be a tendency for price to rise until P_e is reached. Thus any price other than P_e is a disequilibrium price, which will bring on forces that will return the price to P_e and the quantity traded to an equilibrium volume of Q_e per month.

CARRYOVER TO ANALYSIS OF OTHER MARKETS

Perfect competition is an idealized market structure that is only approximated by markets in the real world. Nonetheless, many markets tend to adjust in ways *similar* to those described in the perfectly competitive case, so it is frequently useful to think of the frictionless, self-regulating market of perfect competition as the point of departure for examining markets where, perhaps, sellers are not so numerous and adjustments are not so smooth or automatic. Even in those situations, we will have to ask what we think sellers will do in terms of quantity supplied at various prices and what the demand of consumers for their product looks like. The notions about demand and supply that have been reviewed here will enter the picture time and time again, and we will have to consider whether and how to modify them on a case-by-case basis.

2

REVENUE OF THE FIRM

In his slapstick comedy, *Spaceballs*, Hollywood writer-producer-director-actor-comedian (did we leave anything out?) Mel Brooks, playing the great teacher "Yogurt," sets out to reveal the secret of The Force:[1] "Moichandising!" he declares to his young protégé in an accent betraying the urban East Coast, and goes on to reveal how high-powered marketing of toys, T-shirts, posters, and other products related to the movie will be a source of great wealth and power.

Certainly, marketing is important. Billions are spent on it each year, and broadcasters remind us annually how much it costs to buy an advertising minute during such spectacles as the Super Bowl. It seems that ads are showing up everywhere—not just on shopping carts and city buses but in church bulletins, on cash-register receipts, and now—whether by popular request or not—in some spots you cannot help but notice in washrooms at restaurants and other public establishments.[2]

What does the consumer want? Can you introduce new products that respond to consumer wants? Can businesses manipulate the wants of consumers? In the 1960s it was frequently argued that businesses could and did manipulate consumer wants.[3] An oft-cited example is the tailfins that appeared on certain automobiles just before the dawn of that decade—styling that served no purpose but was touted to consumers as the wave of the future. It was argued that such frills did not cater to any preexisting want, but that the desire for tailfins was created in the consumer's mind by the producer. The producer was characterized as not caring much about what the consumer wanted and being interested only in what resulted in the greatest profit for the firm.

In the 1990s, while the emphasis on the bottom line remains very much alive, some businesses are coming around to the view that the bottom line will not look good if consumers' wants are not carefully attended to. Gordon Bethune, chief executive officer of Continental Airlines, analyzed substantial losses in previous years at Continental this way:

---

1 In his own inimitable fashion, Brooks had renamed it "The Schwartz."
2 "Washroom Ads: 'Paid-for Graffiti,' " *Newsweek* (February 20, 1989), p. 42.
3 See John Kenneth Galbraith, "Time and the New Industrial State," *American Economic Review* (May 1988), pp. 373–382, as well as John Kenneth Galbraith and M. S. Randhawa, *The New Industrial State* (Boston: Houghton Mifflin, 1967), pp. 211–212.

> We had a crappy product, and we were trying to discount ourselves into profitability. Nobody wants to eat a crummy pizza, no matter if it's 99¢.[4]

Ford Motor Company Chairman Donald E. Petersen is reported to have said, "If we aren't customer-driven, our cars won't be either." Thus Ford and many other companies have solicited consumer input, not only regarding how satisfied customers are with the products and services they have chosen to buy, but also to determine what they want to see in the way of new products and product improvements. Ford, for example, now surveys about 2.5 million customers per year and has invited customers to "focus groups" that try to unravel design problems and anticipate consumer preferences.[5]

Despite the new attention businesses are paying to consumer wants, there is evidence that consumers are far from satisfied with what they are getting. A survey of American consumers done on behalf of *The Wall Street Journal* in 1989 found that only 5 percent believed business was "listening to them and striving to do its best." Consumers' attitudes were summed up by this quote from a 32-year-old professional in the computer industry:

> I live in the best country on the face of the earth, so I guess I'll put up with high prices, mediocre quality, and poor service.[6]

If consumers feel this way about American business, it presents business managers with both a challenge and an opportunity. Clearly, satisfied customers are beneficial to managers and their firms. Likewise, customer satisfaction is one of the ingredients that can make for a healthy bottom line. After going through years of restructuring through cost-cutting termed "re-engineering," "downsizing," "rightsizing," or sometimes "dumbsizing," the new buzz phrase for firm managers in the late 1990s appears to be *revenue management*. Robert Cross, called the "guru of revenue-management consultants" by *The Wall Street Journal*, states that revenue management is "knowledge-based pricing. Sometimes it's analyzing gigabytes of marketing data, and sometimes it's basic observation."[7]

Nevertheless, businesses cannot afford blind pursuit of revenue enhancement, either through better marketing or improved customer satisfaction strategies, to the exclusion of other considerations. In the final analysis, it is the difference between revenue and *cost* that determines a firm's profits; therefore the decisions that affect *both* of these factors are critical to business operations. It is no cause for amazement, then, that firms exert so much effort

---

4 "The Right Place, The Right Time," *Business Week* (May 27, 1996), p. 74.
5 "King Customer," *Business Week* (March 12, 1990), pp. 88–94.
6 Alix M. Friedman, "Most Consumers Shun Luxuries, Seek Few Frills But Better Service," *The Wall Street Journal*, September 19, 1989, p. B1.
7 "Finding New Ways to Meet Challenges From Debt to Diversity," *The Wall Street Journal*, January 5, 1996, p. B1; and "Many Firms See Gains of Cost-Cutting Over, Push to Lift Revenues," *The Wall Street Journal*, July 5, 1996, pp. A1, A2.

and expense trying to increase revenue while attempting to keep costs at as low a level as possible, *given a particular level of output*. Still, it is clear that without a market for its product, a firm will not be successful—no matter how low its costs. Accordingly, we emphasize the importance of managerial decisions relating to demand for a firm's product by discussing first how the firm manager should cope with both external and internal factors that affect dollar sales and, ultimately, the firm's success or failure. As we shall see early in this chapter, the term for total dollar sales is *total revenue* in the language of economists, and it will be our main focus for the present. Later, in Chapters 5 and 6, we will address the issue of cost, examining both the nature of the production process and its relation to the expenses the firm incurs in supplying output to its customers.

ADVERTISING, CONSUMER DEMAND, AND BUSINESS RESEARCH

The fact that U.S. corporations now spend $8 to $10 billion per year on network television advertising certainly suggests that they believe consumer demand for their products will be significantly affected as a result.[8] However, it should also be clear that advertising is not the only factor affecting the quantity that consumers demand of a particular product. In spite of advertising, consumers preferred "old" Coca Cola (now Classic Coke) to "new" Coke, and the RCA videodisc player was a flop. Other failed new products included the Fresh and Lite line of low-fat frozen Chinese entrées, the NeXT computer, and the Cadillac Allanté.[9]

Much to its dismay, top management in the U.S. automobile industry discovered in the 1980s that many consumers preferred Japanese cars to those produced by U.S. firms. In fact, General Motors is so concerned about what factors influence the demand for its automobiles that it invests money in a statistical analysis department, whose task, among other things, is to estimate the impact of various factors such as advertising, price, and personal income on the quantity of GM cars that potential consumers will purchase. Ford, too, has engaged in expensive research programs to determine both what consumers want to see in new cars and what they dislike about existing products.[10] By the early 1990s, the tables had turned in the automobile industry, and only partly because of the declining value of the dollar relative to the yen.

---

8 " 'Ad Space' Now Has a Whole New Meaning," *Business Week* (July 29, 1985), p. 52.
9 "Flops," *Business Week* (August 16, 1993), pp. 76–82.
10 "King Customer," *Business Week* (March 12, 1990), pp. 88–94. Research by General Motors on automobile demand has been going on for many years. An interesting older study of automobile demand done by one of their economists is H. F. Gallasch, Jr., "Elasticities of Demand for New Automobiles" (Societal Analysis Department, Research Laboratories, General Motors Corporation, Warren, Michigan, May 21, 1976).

The Honda Accord, the best-selling car in the United States from 1989 to 1991, was upstaged by a redesigned Ford Taurus in 1992. Even Toyota expected losses in 1993, and the Japanese were struggling to revive their market share in the United States. Honda introduced a new model in the fall of 1993, and the company's president remarked, "If this car fails, we won't survive."[11] Thus firm managers cannot be successful by simply assuming that advertising expenditures will solve all revenue problems; they must recognize that diverse factors affect product sales. In fact, a recent study suggests that advertising has little influence on consumer purchasing decisions. Only 25 percent of those surveyed stated that a television ad would convince them to try a new product or brand; the comparable figures for newspaper and magazine ads were 15 percent and 13 percent, respectively.[12]

To put matters in perspective, consider the fact that a consulting firm examining the success rates for 11,000 new products of 77 companies found that only about 56 percent of new products were still on the market five years after their introduction. Other studies estimate the long-term success rate of new products at approximately 65 percent, but even that figure is sobering when one considers that most new product ideas do not even get as far as test markets. One analyst stated that companies had only one successful product for every 13 new product ideas, and a Booz Allen & Hamilton Inc. study reported that "forty-six percent of all new-product development costs go to failures."[13] A marketing expert made this observation: "If companies can improve their effectiveness at launching new products, they could double their bottom line."[14] Clearly, successful development of new products is critical to the long-term survival of a company. According to the editor of the *Journal of Product Innovation Management*, "The companies that lead their industries in profitability and sales growth get 49 percent of their revenues from products developed in the past five years. The least successful get only 11 percent of sales from new products."[15]

Moreover, while consumers sometimes are entertained by whimsical and amusing ads, there is growing evidence that advertising that is offensive or out of place can create quite a backlash. *Time* magazine reported that consumers were putting up substantial resistance to advertising shorts run in movie theaters:

> Many are starting to rebel, and hoots and howls are common when commercials flash onto screens in New York City, where ticket prices run as high as $7.50.[16]

---

11 "A Car Is Born," *Business Week* (September 13, 1993), pp. 64–72. Also see "While Toyota Loses Its Hold . . . ," *Business Week* (April 26, 1993), pp. 28–29.
12 "Study Finds Ads Induce Few People to Buy," *The Wall Street Journal*, October 17, 1995, p. B10.
13 "Flops," pp. 76–77.
14 Ibid., p. 77.
15 Ibid., p. 82.
16 "Hoots and Howls at Ads," *Time* (September 18, 1989), p. 70.

Similarly, *Business Week* stated,

> ad executives say the hostility now is greater than ever before. "I have never seen such a volume and intensity of troubles with advertising," says . . . a retired chairman of Foote, Cone, and Belding Communications, Inc.[17]

In the face of all this, firms are becoming more and more interested in marketing in a much broader sense—the entire process of moving goods from the producer to the consumers. This far more inclusive view of marketing stresses the importance of determining consumer attitudes and wants and then analyzing the profitability aspect of proposed goods and services. Thus, businesses are finding that competition for consumers makes information regarding their tastes, preferences, and buying decisions critical to profitability. For example, Fingerhut has built a database that contains more than 500 bits of information on more than 50 million actual or potential customers. Using information technology to *micromarket*, Target adjusts its inventory to the particular tastes of customers in each location, so that stores within 15 minutes driving time of each other may contain different merchandise.[18]

As *Business Week* noted many years ago, firms have learned that decisions involving new products require

> conducting preliminary research, market identification, and product development; testing consumer reaction to both product and price; working out production capacities and costs; determining distribution; *and then deciding on advertising and promotion strategies.* [Emphasis added.][19]

Such market research is becoming particularly important as companies attempt to successfully enter international markets, where customer tastes may differ dramatically from those of domestic customers. For example, Frito-Lay found that the favorite flavor of potential Thai customers was shrimp, but that these potential customers also thought an American snack with that flavor would be inappropriate. As a result, Frito-Lay is cautiously sticking with their traditional flavors in the Thai market.[20]

A recent development in consumer market research is called "VALS"—the consumer Values and Lifestyles program of SRI International (formerly Stanford Research Institute). This methodology divides consumers into cate-

---

17 "Consumers Are Getting Mad, Mad, Mad, Mad at Mad Ave.," *Business Week* (April 30, 1990), p. 70.
18 "Data Is Power. Just Ask Fingerhut," *Business Week* (June 3, 1996), p. 69; "Target 'Micromarkets' Its Way to Success," *The Wall Street Journal*, May 31, 1995, pp. A1, A9; and "High-Tech Inventory System Coordinates Retailers' Clothes With Customers' Taste," *The Wall Street Journal*, June 12, 1996, pp. B1, B6.
19 "How GM Manages Its Billion Dollar R&D Program," *Business Week* (June 28, 1976), p. 54.
20 "Major U.S. Companies Expand Efforts to Sell to Consumers Abroad," *The Wall Street Journal*, June 13, 1996, pp. A1, A6.

gories based on their self-images, goals, and the products they use.[21] It looks at "who consumers are, how they live, what they buy—and more important, why they buy it."[22] This approach to consumer research is more comprehensive than the old one of looking only at demographic characteristics of consumers—age, education, income, and number of children, for example. Researchers are finding that consumers who used to have similar buying patterns now are parts of many different groups with diverse needs and interests. While the preceding steps are still important, a new wave in businesses' efforts to attract the consumer directs attention to service and customer satisfaction. Naturally, this strategy will require continuing emphasis on the wants and preferences of consumers as well as a great deal of research on how to attract—and keep—customers.

Understanding what economists are saying about these issues requires that you comprehend their special terminology and the precise definitions they attach to everyday expressions such as "changes in demand." Therefore we shall first define *demand* and other revenue terms. Later in this chapter, we provide some insights into what things influence the demand for a firm's product and how to deal with them, so that with proper management of these factors and their costs, the firm can achieve maximum profits. Most important, we hope that when you finish this chapter you will have gained a great respect for the power that consumers have in determining the success of an enterprise.

THE DEMAND FUNCTION

A **demand function** states how each of a number of relevant variables affects the amount of a good or service consumers will buy during some time period.

The **demand function** for a firm's product (or service) relates the quantities of a product that consumers would like to purchase during some specific period to the variables that influence a consumer's decision to buy or not to buy the good. Such variables often include the price of the product, the prices of other related goods, consumers' incomes, the season of the year, and dollars spent on advertising. For example, the quantity of a particular brand (Brand X) of microwave oven purchased by consumers during a year may be a function of the price of the oven, the price of a competing brand of oven, the number of women who work outside the home, consumer annual disposable income, and dollars spent yearly on advertising. We could represent this relationship in functional notation as

$$Q_X = f(P_X, P_Y, F, I, A),$$

---

21 Karen Malkowski, "Company Zestful in Targeting ZIP Code Areas," San Antonio *Express-News*, April 14, 1991, pp. 1-G, 2-G; and James Atlas, "Beyond Demographics," *The Atlantic* (October 1984), pp. 49–58.
22 "Wizards of Marketing," *Newsweek* (July 22, 1985), p. 42.

where

$$Q_X = \text{quantity demanded per year of Brand } X,$$
$$P_X = \text{the price of Brand } X,$$
$$P_Y = \text{the price of Brand } Y,$$
$$F = \text{the number of women who are employed,}$$
$$I = \text{the average annual per capita disposable income, and}$$
$$A = \text{the dollars spent per year on advertising.}$$

When the firm plans its operations, it would be useful for it to know the exact functional relationship between the quantity demanded of its product (Q_X) and the independent variables (P_X, P_Y, F, I, and A) that affect that quantity. We should note, however, that some of the independent variables in the demand function are completely beyond the control of the firm. The firm cannot significantly affect average household annual income or the number of women employed, even though its managers certainly should recognize how changes in these variables affect the quantity it can sell of its product. The firm may also not be able to affect the price of a competing good. Advertising and the price set for the firm's product, on the other hand, are variables controlled by management.

The price that the firm charges for its product is one of the variables that the firm can usually control. Therefore the firm often finds it particularly useful to give special attention to the relationship between quantity demanded over some specific time period and possible prices that the firm might charge during that period. The graphical representation of this relationship between price and quantity demanded is called the **demand curve**.

A **demand curve** is a curve or line showing the relation between the quantity demanded per time period of a good or service and various possible prices of that good or service.

For example, assume our hypothetical demand function for Brand X microwave ovens purchased per year had the following specific relationship:

$$Q_X = 26{,}500 - 100P_X + 25P_Y + .0001F + 2.6I + .02A$$

and that

$$P_X = \$400,$$
$$P_Y = \$500,$$
$$F = 40{,}000{,}000,$$
$$I = \$10{,}000,$$

and $A = \$50{,}000$. Solving for Q_X (the number of Brand X microwave ovens purchased per year), by letting the independent variables take on these values, we find that

$$Q_X = 26{,}500 - 40{,}000 + 12{,}500 + 4{,}000 + 26{,}000 + 1{,}000$$

$$= 30{,}000 \text{ ovens per year.}$$

If all of the independent variables remain at the values just stated, the firm will sell 30,000 microwave ovens per year.

If we hold all the variables except Q_X and P_X constant, we can graph the demand curve for Brand X ovens as shown in Figure 2–1. With all variables other than P_X and Q_X held constant, the demand function becomes

$$Q_X = 70{,}000 - 100P_X,$$

which is the equation for the straight line plotted in the figure. The equation for the demand curve is found by substituting in the given values for all of the variables except for Q_X and P_X in the preceding demand function.

Change in Demand

Change in demand refers to the shift in a demand curve that occurs when a demand function variable other that the own price of the item in question changes.

Change in quantity demanded refers to a movement along the demand curve for a given good or service in response to a change in its own price.

If one of the variables held constant when we drew the demand curve should change, the demand curve shifts. We call this event a **change in demand**. For example, if per capita income falls to $5,000 or rises to $15,000, the demand curve drawn in Figure 2–1 will shift, as shown in Figure 2–2. A change in demand, therefore, refers to a shift in the demand curve—as contrasted with a **change in quantity demanded**, which refers simply to a change in the amount of a good or service that consumers are willing to purchase over

Figure 2–1   Demand Curve for Brand X Microwave Ovens

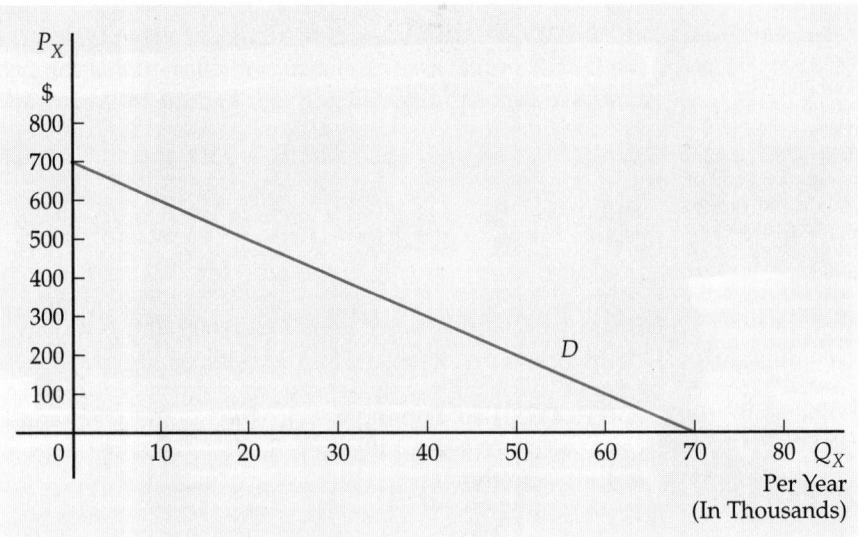

This graph depicts the demand curve, D, for Brand X microwave ovens. P_x represents the price of an oven, and Q_X is quantity demanded of ovens (in thousands) per year. At a price of $700 apiece, no ovens would be purchased. If the ovens were given away, 70,000 would be demanded per year.

Figure 2–2   Changes in Demand

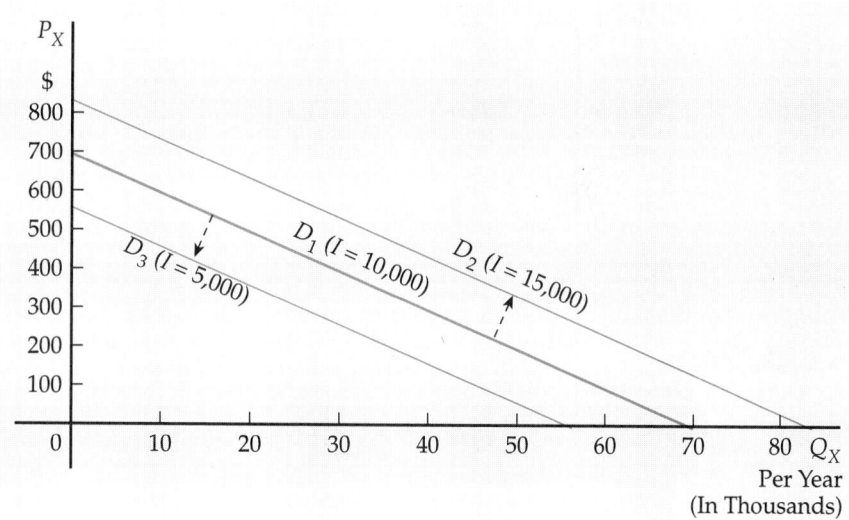

A change in income will cause the demand curve for Brand X microwave ovens to shift. If income increases from $10,000 to $15,000, demand will increase. If income decreases from $10,000 to $5,000, demand will decrease.

some time period *because of a change in the price* of the good. The behavior of consumers in the latter situation is represented by *a different point on the same demand curve*. A change in quantity demanded as P_X changes from $500 to $400 is illustrated in Figure 2–3.

Demand and Revenue

Total revenue is the total dollar sales of a firm during some particular time period. It is equal to the price of the product multiplied by the quantity sold.

The **total revenue** (total dollar sales) of a firm is directly related to the demand for the firm's product. In fact, if we know the demand curve equation for a firm's product and the price set by the firm, we can determine the firm's total revenue, which is just price times quantity demanded. To find total revenue, we would first substitute the value for the product's price in the demand curve equation and solve for quantity demanded. Total revenue is then found by multiplying price by quantity demanded (the number of units sold). Total revenue, therefore, is a function of price and quantity demanded, or $TR = g(P, Q)$. Since price can also be considered a function of the quantity demanded or sold, we can write price in terms of quantity and then write total revenue as a function only of quantity sold. Thus, for our microwave oven manufacturer,

$$Q_X = 70,000 - 100P_X,$$

Figure 2–3   Change in Quantity Demanded

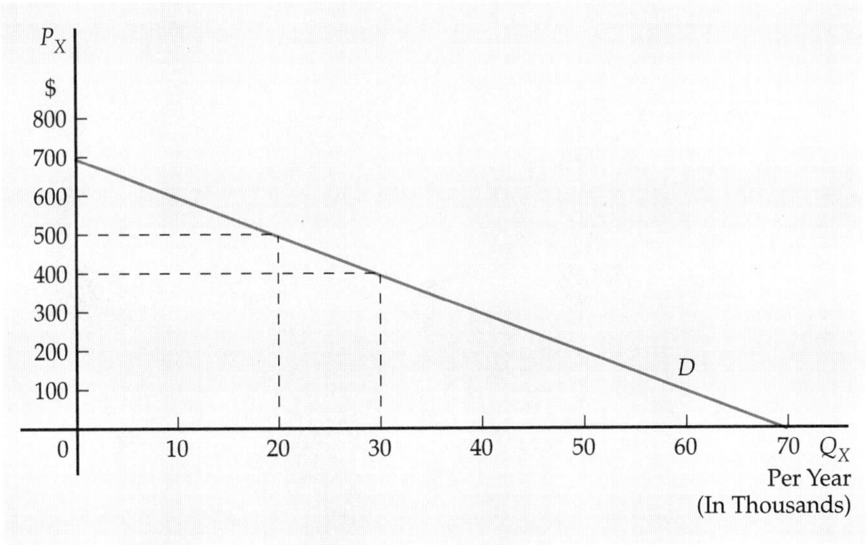

A change in the quantity demanded of microwave ovens occurs if there is a change in the price of the ovens. For example, if the price falls from $500 to $400, the quantity demanded will increase by 10,000 ovens per year.

and

$$-100P_X = -70{,}000 + Q_X.$$

Therefore

$$P_X = 700 - .01Q_X,$$

and

$$TR = P_X{\cdot}Q_X = (700 - .01Q_X)(Q_X) = 700Q_X - .01Q_X^2.$$

Average revenue is total revenue divided by quantity demanded. *When all units of the product are sold at the same price, average revenue is equal to the product's price.*

$$AR = \frac{TR}{Q} = \left(\frac{P \times Q}{Q}\right) = P,$$

Average revenue is the revenue received per unit of product sold. It is equal to total revenue divided by quantity sold and is equal to price if all units are sold at the same price.

where AR is average revenue, TR is total revenue, Q is quantity demanded, and P is price. We emphasize that the result that average revenue is equal to price requires all buyers to be charged the same price for the product, which we will assume is the case throughout most of this text. The special case of multiple prices for a single product will be discussed in Chapter 11. For the microwave oven demand curve, the AR formula is the same as the price equation we employed to get total revenue. In other words,

$$AR = P_x = 700 - .01Q_X.$$

Marginal revenue is the rate of change of total revenue
is the rate of change
of total revenue
from selling one
more unit of the
product.

Marginal revenue is the rate of change of total revenue with respect to quantity sold; it indicates how total revenue will change if there is a change in the quantity sold of the firm's product. An approximation of marginal revenue is the change in total revenue divided by the change in quantity sold, or

$$\text{Arc } MR = \frac{\Delta TR}{\Delta Q} = \frac{TR_2 - TR_1}{Q_2 - Q_1},$$

where TR_1 and Q_1 are the original total revenue and level of output, and TR_2 and Q_2 are the new total revenue and level of output, respectively. The *arc marginal revenue* value is only an approximation of marginal revenue because it measures the *average* rate of change of total revenue with respect to quantity sold over the range of output under consideration. This average rate of change will not be exactly equal to the rate of change of total revenue with respect to quantity at *some particular output level* if this rate of change is different for different levels of output. We call this approximation **arc marginal**

**Arc marginal
revenue** gives the
average rate of
change of total
revenue with
respect to quantity
sold over some
range of output.

revenue, since it measures the average rate of change of total revenue with respect to quantity sold over some range of output or over some arc.[23]

The relationships among the total revenue, average revenue, and marginal revenue functions for the manufacturer of Brand X microwave ovens are illustrated in Figure 2–4 and Table 2–1. Total revenue is depicted in the lower graph of the figure, while marginal revenue and average revenue are depicted in the upper graph. Geometrically, average revenue at some quantity is the slope of a line drawn from the origin to the point on the *TR* curve corresponding to that level of output. The average revenue in Figure 2–4 is always decreasing, as can be seen from a comparison of the slopes of line segments *OA* and *OB* in the lower graph. We should emphasize that since the *AR*

The three
fundamental
revenue concepts
are **total revenue,
average revenue,
and marginal
revenue,** where:

Total revenue =
$P \times Q$.

Average revenue =
$TR/Q = P$.

Marginal revenue =
$\frac{\Delta TR}{\Delta Q}$.

---

23 Technically, marginal revenue at a particular output level is the value of the derivative of the total revenue function with respect to quantity, dTR/dQ, at that point. Thus, for the manufacturer of Brand X microwave ovens discussed above,

$$TR = 700Q_X - .01Q_X^2, \text{ and }$$

$$MR = (dTR/dQ_X) = 700 - .02Q_X.$$

At an output level of 30,000 units, marginal revenue is $100. However, between $Q_X = 20,000$ and $Q_X = 30,000$, *arc* marginal revenue is $200, since $\Delta TR = \$2,000,000$ and $\Delta Q_X = 10,000$ (as shown in Table 2–1).

Figure 2–4   Geometrical Relationships Among Average Revenue, Marginal Revenue, and Total Revenue for Brand X Microwave Ovens

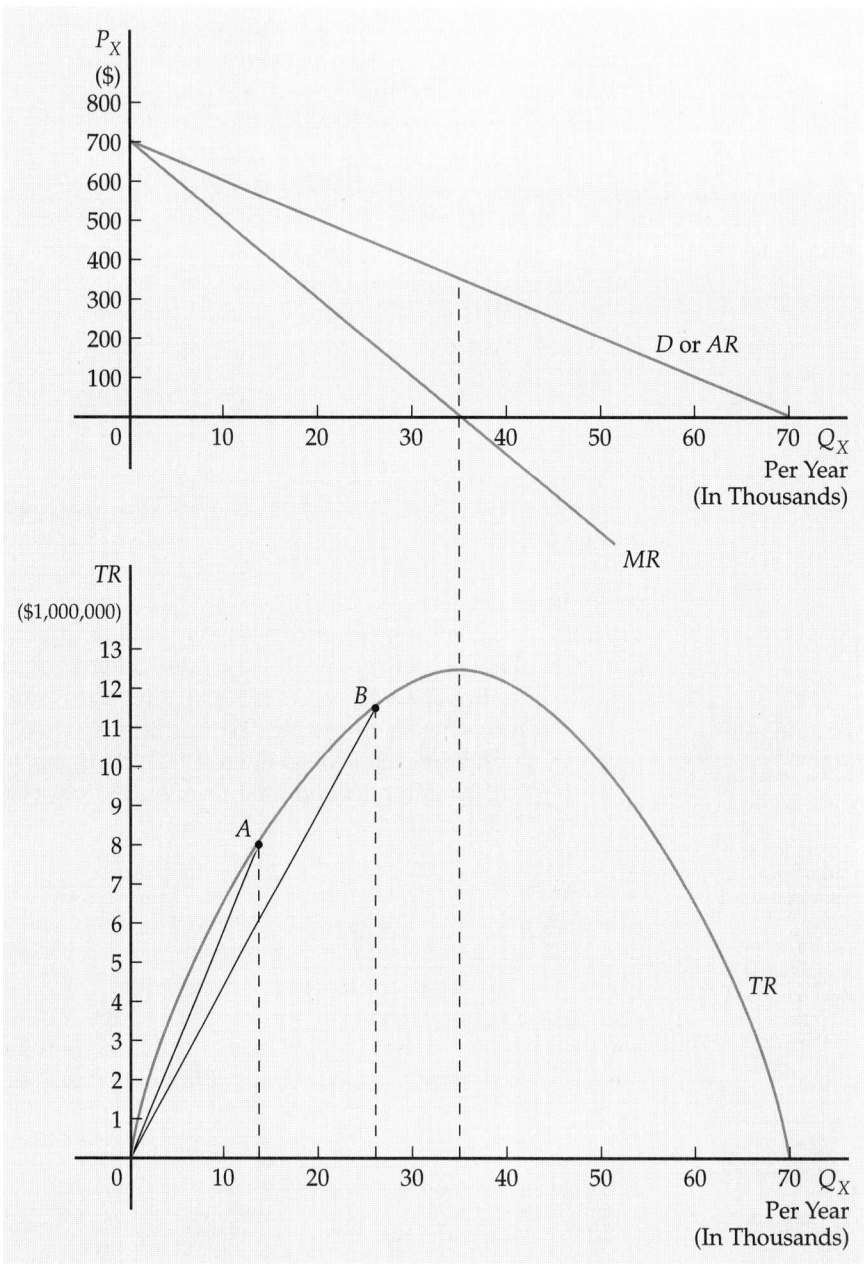

This graph depicts the geometrical relationships among average revenue (*AR*), marginal revenue (*MR*), and total revenue (*TR*) for Brand *X* microwave ovens. Marginal revenue is zero at a quantity of 35,000 ovens per month—the same point where total revenue is at a maximum. With a linear, downward-sloping demand curve, *MR* reaches zero at a quantity level (35,000 units) one half as large as that where average revenue is zero.

Table 2–1   Relationships Among Price, Total Revenue, and Arc
Marginal Revenue for Brand *X* Microwave Ovens

Price of X (Average Revenue)	Quantity of X Demanded	Total Revenue (P × Q)	Arc Marginal Revenue $\left(\dfrac{\Delta TR}{\Delta Q}\right)$
$700	0	0	
600	10,000	$ 6,000,000	$600
500	20,000	10,000,000	400
400	30,000	12,000,000	200
300	40,000	12,000,000	0
200	50,000	10,000,000	−200
100	60,000	6,000,000	−400

curve gives the relationship between price and quantity demanded for a firm, the *average revenue curve is also the firm's demand curve.*

Marginal revenue at some particular quantity is the slope of the *TR* curve at that quantity of output. In Figure 2–4, marginal revenue is also always decreasing and is equal to zero when total revenue reaches a maximum, at $Q_X = 35,000$.[24] Moreover, as long as the *AR* curve is linear, the *MR* curve will be linear with a slope twice as steep as the *AR* curve and will thus intersect the quantity axis at a level of output half as large as that at the point where the demand (*AR*) curve intersects the same axis.[25]

---

24 For TR to be at a maximum (or minimum) at a specific level of output, dTR/dQ must be equal to zero. Thus,

$$\frac{dTR}{dQ_X} = MR = 700 - .02Q_X = 0,$$

$$- .02Q_X = -700, \; or$$

$$Q_X = 35,000.$$

The second derivative

$$\frac{d^2TR}{dQ_X^2} = \frac{dMR}{dQ} = -.02,$$

which is less than zero so that the second-order condition for a maximum is satisfied.
25 If $TR = 700Q_X - .01Q_X^2$, then $AR = TR/Q_X = 700 - .01Q_x$ and, as stated above, $MR = 700 - .02Q_X$. The slope of the marginal revenue curve is −.02, which is twice as steep as the slope (−.01) of the average revenue curve. In more general terms, if

$$AR = a - bQ, \text{ then}$$

$$TR = aQ - bQ^2, \text{ and}$$

$$MR = a - 2bQ.$$

The slope of the marginal revenue curve is −2b, which is exactly twice the slope of the average revenue curve.

Figure 2–5   Horizontal Demand Curve ($P = MR$)

D is a horizontal demand curve. A firm can sell as many units of its product as it wishes to at the going market price. Price and marginal revenue are equal.

Both Figure 2–4 and Table 2–1 illustrate that *as long as price must decrease in order for the firm to increase the quantity demanded of its product, marginal revenue is less than price.* Marginal revenue is less than price because we are assuming that to sell a larger quantity, the firm must lower its price on *all* units sold. Hence, if the firm in Table 2–1 wishes to sell 30,000 units rather than 20,000, it must lower the price—from $500 to $400—on *all 30,000* of the units. Therefore the firm gives up the opportunity to sell the first 20,000 units at a price $100 higher.

We can show the effect of this price decrease on the revenue from the first 20,000 units sold as follows:

Gain in revenue from sale of an additional
    10,000 units = 10,000 × $400   = $4,000,000

Loss in revenue from sale of first 20,000 units
    at $400 rather than $500 = 20,000 × (–$100)   = –$2,000,000

Net increase in total revenue $2,000,000

$$\text{Marginal Revenue} = \frac{\Delta TR}{\Delta Q} = \frac{\$2,000,000}{10,000} = \$200$$

If the firm did not have to lower price to sell a larger quantity, the demand curve would be a horizontal line and price would equal marginal revenue, as shown in Figure 2–5.[26]

_____

26 If $TR = P \times Q$, then

NUMERICAL EXAMPLE:

The Demand for Draperies

Alicia Gartiz has estimated the following demand function for economical draperies sold by her firm, Pleats, Inc.:

$$Q_d = 1{,}200 - 20P_d + .1I + .08A,$$

where

Q_d = quantity demanded of pairs of drapes
P_d = price per pair of drapes
I = per capita income in the market area
A = her firm's advertising expenditure.

All data are on a monthly basis. The current values of the income and advertising variables are, respectively, $1,200 per month and $4,000 per month.

1. Assuming the above values for I and A remain constant, what is the equation of the demand curve for Pleats, Inc.'s drapes?
2. If Alicia wished to obtain the maximum monthly sales revenue, given the data above, what price would she charge and what would the revenue be?

Answer

1. Substituting the stated values into the demand function, we have $Q_d = 1{,}200 - 20P_d + .1(1{,}200) + .08(4{,}000)$, or $Q_d = 1{,}640 - 20P_d$.
2. The maximum total revenue will occur at the midpoint of the demand curve, where MR is zero and $Q_d = 820$. There, P_d will be $41. Total revenue will be $41(820) = $33,620. From the stated demand curve, $P_d = 82 - .05Q_d$, and, since MR will have the same intercept as AR on the vertical axis but be zero at the quantity corresponding to the midpoint of AR, $MR = 82 - .1Q_d$. This relationship holds because the MR curve's slope is twice as steep as that of the AR curve. Setting MR equal to zero locates maximum TR, or $82 - .1Q_d = 0$, so $Q_d = 820$. By substitution, $P_d = 82 - .05(820) = $41.

$$MR = \frac{dTR}{dQ} = P + Q\left(\frac{dP}{dQ}\right),$$

using the product rule for differentiation. If price does not change as quantity sold changes, $(dP/dQ) = 0$, and $MR = P$.

The relationships among demand and total and marginal revenue will be discussed later in this chapter. Moreover, in Chapter 7 we will see that marginal revenue plays a very important role in helping the firm locate its profit-maximizing level of output.

Firm Demand Versus Industry Demand

The demand function that we have been discussing relates the quantity purchased of a particular brand of microwave oven (Brand X) to other variables. Since there is more than one brand of microwave oven available, we could also talk about the factors that determine the total number of microwave ovens (all brands) purchased during a year. This relationship is the *industry demand function*—as contrasted with the demand function for Brand X microwave ovens, which is the demand function for a firm. Many of the same variables will appear in the industry demand function as in the demand function of the firm, although their coefficients will usually be different in size and sometimes in sign. For example, the price of Brand Y will affect the industry quantity demanded of microwave ovens (as well as the quantity demanded of Brand X and of Brand Y ovens). However, its coefficient will probably be *negative* in the industry demand function, indicating that an increase in P_Y will *decrease* the total quantity of microwave ovens demanded. In the demand function for Brand X ovens, the coefficient of P_Y had a *positive* sign, indicating that an increase in P_Y would increase the quantity demanded of Brand X ovens. In addition, in the preceding example, we would expect that the coefficients of (1) the number of women employed variable and (2) the average annual per capita income variable will be larger in the industry demand function than in the firm demand function, which indicates that a change in either one of these variables will have a greater effect on the *total quantity demanded* of microwave ovens than on the quantity demanded of Brand X. The size of the coefficient of the advertising dollars variable will depend on the extent that firm advertising serves to increase overall quantity demanded of microwave ovens—as opposed to merely increasing the quantity demanded of the microwave ovens of one firm at the expense of the sales of another firm.

Although most of the demand functions presented in this chapter are demand functions for the product of a *firm*, the concepts discussed can generally be applied to either industry or firm demand functions.

DETERMINANTS OF DEMAND

Any demand function variable that will cause a demand curve to shift is usually called a **determinant of demand**. In other words, for Brand X microwave

The **determinants of demand** for a given good or service are demand function variables other than its own price.

ovens, all of the variables on the right-hand side of the demand function equation except P_X are determinants of demand.

The determinants of demand are what cause consumers to change their view of how much they will buy of a given good or service at all possible prices that could be charged for it. Exactly what they are will depend on the good in question. For example, how many ice-cold drinks you want to buy at various possible prices is likely to depend on how hot the weather is. It would therefore be reasonable to include some measure of this (degrees Fahrenheit or Celsius) in the demand function for ice-cold drinks. But the weather is not likely to have a significant effect on your demand for ham sandwiches or pizza, and one would not likely include a weather variable in the demand functions for them.

If we tried to list all possible determinants of demand for goods and services, we would probably have a very long list. The following, however, are some of the most widely applicable:

1. Consumer incomes
2. Prices of related goods and services
3. Consumer tastes
4. Number of consumers in the market
5. Credit terms on loans
6. Advertising.

A **normal good** displays a positive relation between consumer purchases and income.

An **inferior good** displays a negative relation between consumer purchases and income.

We will consider each of these in turn, starting with two that are almost universally important, income and prices of related goods. Normally, as consumers' incomes increase, they tend to purchase more goods and services. If an individual consumer purchases more of a good when his or her income increases, that good is said to be a **normal good** with respect to income. If the reverse occurs, the good is an **inferior good**. It is often argued that hamburger is an inferior good for many people, since they will consume less hamburger and more of other meats (steaks, roast beef) if their incomes increase. In a demand function, a negative sign on the coefficient of the income variable indicates an inferior good, while the coefficient of the income term for a normal good will be positive. For a normal good, an increase in income will shift the demand curve to the right, while a decrease in income will shift it to the left. The reverse occurs for an inferior good.

A **substitute good** is a good that can be used in place of some other good.

The relation of the quantity purchased of a given good to the price of a related good depends, in a very basic sense, on whether the two are substitutes or complements. In the case of **substitute goods**, one can be used in place of the other and will, in fact, be substituted if one becomes relatively cheaper than the other. For example, frozen yogurt and ice cream are substitutes, and if the price of frozen yogurt drops while that of ice cream does not, some people will purchase yogurt instead of ice cream. In the demand function for ice cream, the coefficient of the price of the related good, frozen yogurt, will have a positive sign, indicating that a rise in the yogurt price would lead to greater quantity sold of ice cream, while a fall in the yogurt price would do the reverse. Likewise, one would expect a demand function for frozen yogurt to include the price of ice cream as an independent variable, with the coefficient taking a positive sign to indicate the substitute nature of the relation between the two goods. An increase in the price of a substitute, then, will shift the demand curve for a given good to the right, while a decrease in the price of a substitute will do the reverse.

For **complementary goods**, goods that are used together, the coefficient of the related good's price will be negative. For example, lettuce and salad dressing are complementary goods. If lettuce prices rise dramatically (as they have when freezing weather in California, Florida, and Texas has spoiled winter crops), people will buy less lettuce and less salad dressing. Thus the price of lettuce is a determinant of the demand for salad dressing. Lettuce price would appear in a demand function for salad dressing with a negative coefficient in front of it, since an increase in that price would lead to a reduction in purchases of salad dressing (demand curve for salad dressing shifts to the left).

Clearly, consumer tastes can serve as a determinant of demand also, but they are not always easy to measure. Sometimes a proxy variable for them can be used; for example, percent of consumers in a given age group or ethnic group. If a given good appeals to the particular preferences of teenagers, the percentage of teenagers in the market area might serve as a good proxy for taste in the demand function. The number of consumers in the market is also an important determinant of demand. Clearly, the demand curve for any good or service will shift to the right if more consumers enter the market for it. A good example would be the demand for housing in Florida, which has increased dramatically as older people from all parts of the United States have decided to retire there.

The remaining items on our determinants-of-demand list are credit terms and advertising. Credit terms (availability of loans as well as the interest rate on them) are especially important demand function variables for *durable goods*—goods that last a long time and for which purchases can be postponed for some length of time. Examples are houses, cars, and large home appliances like washers and dryers. The housing market reacts greatly to changes in availability of home mortgages and changes in mortgage interest rates. If interest rates increase or loans simply become difficult to qualify for, the demand for both new and used homes will fall. Likewise, people will postpone new car purchases if credit terms are unfavorable, and automobile manufacturers are well aware that sales can be stimulated by offering buyer incentives in the form of easy credit terms. Advertising, too, can shift the demand curve, and firms spend huge sums on it in attempts to do so. Normally, we expect increases in advertising expenditure by an individual firm to lead to a rightward shift of the demand curve for its product. However, in the face of competing advertising by rival firms, it is possible for this impact to be canceled out.

A NOTE ON DETERMINANTS OF SUPPLY

Determinants of supply are those variables other that a good's own price that change the quantity of the good sellers are willing and able to sell.

A supply function relates the amount that sellers will offer of a good to the independent variables that determine it. For example, a supply function for frozen yogurt might include as independent variables the price of frozen yogurt, the prices of the inputs used to make the yogurt, the prices of alternative products, and the number of suppliers in the market. The **determinants of supply** are those variables other than a good's own price that will increase or decrease the quantity of the good sellers are willing and able to sell. Besides the variables already mentioned, these might include government tax or subsidy policies, technology, and producer expectations about future market conditions.

If all of the determinants of supply remain constant, we can identify the supply curve of a given good as the curve or line showing the quantity of it that sellers will place on the market at various possible prices. The supply curve of a seller may slope upward to the right, indicating that the quantity supplied is a rising function of price. It probably does slope upward in many cases. (Figure 1A–3, in the appendix to Chapter 1, shows an example of an upward-sloping supply curve.) Later, when we examine market structures, more will be said about supply. However, the focus of the present chapter is demand, not supply, and it will be sufficient at this point to note that movements along a supply curve for a given good (changes in quantity supplied) take place when, other things being equal, the price of the good itself changes. The entire supply curve will shift, however, when one of the determinants of supply changes. (If you are unfamiliar with basic demand and supply analysis, read Appendix 1, which follows Chapter 1.)

ELASTICITY OF DEMAND

The managers of a firm must pay close attention to the responsiveness of the quantity demanded of its product to various factors, for only by understanding these relationships can they hope to make reliable predictions of sales. As we stated previously, the quantity demanded of a firm's product is determined both by factors outside the firm's control and by factors such as price and advertising, which are often within its control. The ability to predict revenue is crucial, for without an adequate level of sales relative to costs, the firm cannot be successful.

One measure of such responsiveness that is feasible if the demand function for the firm's product is known is merely to substitute different values for the independent variables in that function and then solve for the resulting quantity demanded and total revenue. However, it is also often useful for a firm to know the *relative responsiveness* of quantity demanded of its product to changes in the values of the variables that it knows affect that demand. Roughly speaking, the relative responsiveness of quantity demanded of

Brand X to a change in some variable Z is defined as the percentage change in Q_X divided by the percentage change in Z, or

$$E_Z = \frac{\text{percentage change in } Q_X}{\text{percentage change in } Z}$$

This responsiveness is called the *elasticity of demand* for Product X with respect to variable Z.

Arc versus Point Elasticity

Point elasticity of demand (for X) with respect to Z refers to the elasticity of demand *given* (or at) some specific value for Q_X and Z. Since the point elasticity of demand formula usually involves the use of partial derivatives, we will place our discussion of such elasticities in footnotes and concentrate on arc elasticity in the text. The *arc elasticity of demand* for product X with respect to variable Z refers to the average responsiveness of Q_X to a change in Z between two different values of Z, Z_1 and Z_2. The formula for arc elasticity of demand with respect to Z is given by[27]

$$E_Z = \frac{\Delta Q_X}{\dfrac{Q_{X_2} + Q_{X_1}}{2}} \div \frac{\Delta Z}{\dfrac{Z_2 + Z_1}{2}} \text{, or}$$

$$E_Z = \frac{\Delta Q_X}{\Delta Z} \cdot \frac{Z_2 + Z_1}{Q_{X_2} + Q_{X_1}}$$

Since with arc elasticity we are trying to measure the *average responsiveness* of Q_X to changes in Z *over some range of Z*, we use an average of the first and second values of both Q_X and Z.

For example, let us examine the elasticity of demand of Brand X microwave ovens with respect to P_X. The demand function given earlier in this chapter was

$$Q_X = 26{,}500 - 100P_X + 25P_Y + .0001F + 2.6I + .02A,$$

---

27 The general formula for point elasticity of demand for good X with respect to variable Z is

$$E_Z = \left(\frac{\partial Q_X}{\partial Z}\right)\left(\frac{Z}{Q_X}\right), \text{ or}$$

$$E_Z = \left(\frac{dQ_X}{dZ}\right)\left(\frac{Z}{Q_X}\right),$$

if Q_X is a function solely of Z.

and we said that if $P_X = \$400$, $P_Y = \$500$, $F = 40{,}000{,}000$, $I = \$10{,}000$, and $A = \$50{,}000$, then $Q_X = 30{,}000$.[28] By substituting $P_X = \$500$ in the preceding demand function, we find that at a price of $500 the quantity demanded falls to 20,000 microwave ovens per year. Thus, the arc price elasticity of demand between $P_X = \$400$ and $P_X = \$500$ is given by

$$E_P = \frac{\Delta Q_X}{\Delta P_X} \cdot \frac{P_{X_2} + P_{X_1}}{Q_{X_2} + Q_{X_1}} = \frac{Q_{X_2} - Q_{X_1}}{P_{X_2} - P_{X_1}} \cdot \frac{P_{X_2} + P_{X_1}}{Q_{X_2} + Q_{X_1}}$$

$$= \frac{-10{,}000}{100} \cdot \frac{900}{50{,}000} = -1.8.$$

The preceding equation assumes that $P_{X_2} = \$500$ and $P_{X_1} = \$400$, or that a price *increase* has occurred. However, a price decrease over this same range would also result in an elasticity coefficient of –1.8. This result holds because if price falls from $500 to $400, then the change in price will be –$100 and the change in quantity demanded will be +10,000. Therefore the only change in the elasticity calculation occurs in the signs of the numerator and denominator of $\Delta Q_X / \Delta P_X$.

We can illustrate why it is necessary to use both sets of prices and quantities in the arc elasticity formula with the following example. Suppose that we used only $P_{X_1} = \$400$ and $Q_{X_1} = 30{,}000$. Then

$$E_P = \frac{\Delta Q_X}{\Delta P_X} \cdot \frac{P_{X_1}}{Q_{X_1}} = \frac{-10{,}000}{100} \cdot \frac{400}{30{,}000} = -1.33.$$

On the other hand, if we were to use only P_{X_2} and Q_{X_2},

$$E_P = \frac{\Delta Q_X}{\Delta P_X} \cdot \frac{P_{X_2}}{Q_{X_2}} = \frac{-10{,}000}{100} \cdot \frac{500}{20{,}000} = -2.5.$$

Neither of these values (–1.33 or –2.5) adequately represents the price elasticity of demand over the entire price range from $500 to $400. Therefore, *the use of both prices and both quantities in the arc price elasticity formula appears to be one reasonable way of approximating the price elasticity of demand over this region*

---

28 At that point, the price elasticity of demand for Q_X is given by

$$E_P = \left(\frac{\partial Q_X}{\partial P_X} \right) \left(\frac{P_X}{Q_X} \right)$$

$$= -100 \left(\frac{400}{30{,}000} \right) = -1.33.$$

of the demand curve. As we found above, this approach gives us an intermediate value for E_p of –1.8.

We will examine the concept of price elasticity of demand further in the next section.

Price Elasticity of Demand

Price elasticity of demand measures the degree of responsiveness of quantity demanded to a change in the price of a good or service. It is the ratio of the percentage change in quantity demanded to the percentage change in price.

The **price elasticity of demand** measures the relative responsiveness of quantity demanded of a product to a change in its price. As indicated in the previous section, the arc price elasticity of demand is given by

$$E_P = \frac{\Delta Q_X}{\Delta P_X} \cdot \frac{P_{X_2} + P_{X_1}}{Q_{X_2} + Q_{X_1}}.$$

We also found that E_p for microwave ovens was equal to –1.8 between $P_X =$ $400 and $P_X =$ $500. This arc elasticity value means that over the interval between $P_X =$ $400 and $P_X =$ $500, a *1.0 percent increase* in P_X will result, on the average, in a *1.8 percent decrease* in quantity demanded.

As has been stated repeatedly, since the price of a firm's product is normally at least one of the variables in the demand function for its product over which the firm has some control, the price elasticity of demand is of far more than casual interest to the firm. Moreover, once the firm knows the price elasticity of demand for its product at some point (or over some price range), it also knows something about the behavior of its total revenue at that point (or over that price range). This fact is important because total revenue is one of the two factors (cost is the other) that determine a firm's total profit.

Since price and quantity usually move in opposite directions, the sign of E_p is usually negative, as we found previously. Therefore, we will classify E_p according to its *absolute value* (or absolute size, disregarding the negative sign). We denote the absolute value of something by two vertical lines, | |. We say, then, that if $|E_p|$ is less than one, the quantity demanded is *inelastic* with respect to price. If $|E_p|$ is greater than one, the quantity demanded is *elastic* with respect to price. If $|E_p|$ is equal to one, the quantity demanded is *unitary elastic* with respect to price. These classifications seem reasonable if we reflect that when $|E_p|$ is greater than 1, or elastic, it means that quantity demanded changes by a greater percentage than the percentage change in price. This occurrence means that quantity demanded is very responsive to a change in price; that is, it is *elastic*. On the other hand, if $|E_p|$ is less than one, it means that quantity demanded changes by a smaller percentage than the percentage change in price and therefore is relatively unresponsive or *inelastic*.

We use the same terminology in everyday life. If the waistband of a pair of slacks stretches (that is, if it is responsive to a pull), the waistband is said to be elastic. However, a cold iron rod is not very responsive if someone tries to stretch it. Thus the rod is said to be inelastic.

In the case where $|E_p|$ is greater than 1, we saw that quantity demanded would change by a large percentage relative to the percentage change in price. In other words, a change in price would result in a more-than-proportional change in quantity demanded. In this case we would expect that the firm might be inclined toward price decreases. However, *both cost and revenue* changes must be considered, as we will see in the next two sections of the chapter.

Note that quantity demanded usually falls when price is increased, regardless of whether demand is elastic or inelastic. Accordingly, quantity demanded rises when price is decreased—for either elastic or inelastic demand. It is the relative, or *proportional*, changes in quantity demanded and price that are important in determining the elasticity of demand.

Two extreme cases occur when $E_p = 0$ and $E_p = -\infty$. If $E_p = 0$, then the price elasticity of demand is completely inelastic and a change in price will not affect quantity demanded. The demand curve in this case is a vertical line, as in Figure 2–6, panel (a). If $E_p = -\infty$, then the price elasticity of demand is infinitely elastic, which means that if a firm raises price above the going market price, it will lose *all* of its sales. In this case the demand curve is a horizontal line (see Figure 2–6, panel (b)). These cases (where demand is either totally inelastic or infinitely elastic) are rarely found in the real world. For example, there is a price at which most people could not even afford necessities, such as medical treatment. Still, we do associate the horizontal demand curve with the perfectly competitive firm; and the demand for some products, such as table salt, over at least some price ranges is highly inelastic.

Of course, demand curves are not necessarily straight lines. For example, the demand curve shown in Figure 2–7 has the property that the elasticity of demand (in absolute value) is equal to 1.0 at all points on the curve. In this case quantity demanded will change by an exactly offsetting proportion as a result of a price change, and total revenue will be the same at all prices and quantities on the demand curve. For example, at point A in Figure 2–7, total revenue is equal to $\$10 \times 20 = \$200$. At point B, total revenue is equal to $\$5 \times 40 = \$200$, and at point C, total revenue is equal to $\$2.50 \times 80 = \$200$. Few, if any, demand curves in the real world are unitary elastic at *all* prices. However, a curve such as that shown in Figure 2–7 could represent the quantity of money demanded for transactions purposes (such as paying bills and buying goods) at various prices. Many economists have argued that this relationship is unitary elastic with respect to changes in the general level of prices. Other types of *nonlinear* (curved) demand curves would also be possible.

Determinants of Price Elasticity of Demand

The same factors that determine the size of changes in quantity demanded in response to a price change also affect the price elasticity of demand. For example, the *greater the number of substitute goods* that are available, the higher the price elasticity of demand. If the price of one of the products increases

Figure 2–6   Two Extreme Measures of Elasticity

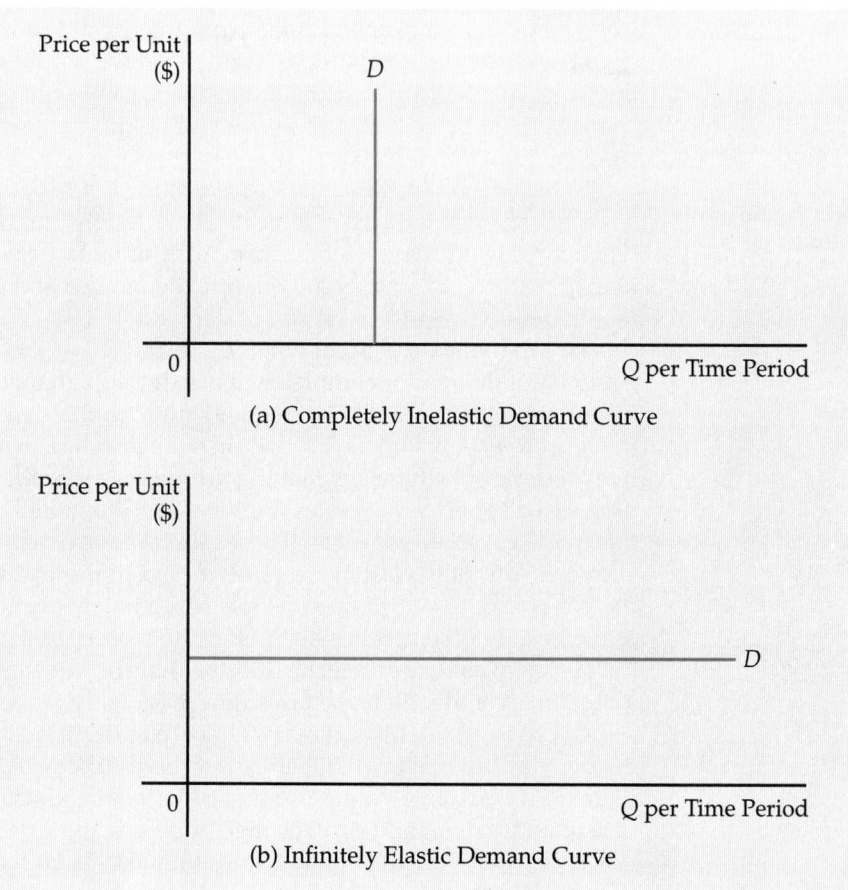

A completely inelastic demand curve is depicted in panel (a). The quantity demanded will not change in response to a change in price. Panel (b) shows an infinitely elastic demand curve. In this case, a firm can sell as many units of its product as it wishes to at the going market price, but it will sell zero units at a higher price.

while those of goods that are substitutes for it remain the same, we would expect consumers to switch some of their spending on the first product to purchases of the substitute goods. The greater the number of alternative goods available, the greater the opportunities for substituting spending on a product whose price has risen to purchases of a similar item whose price has remained the same.

Figure 2–7   A Unitary Elastic Demand Curve

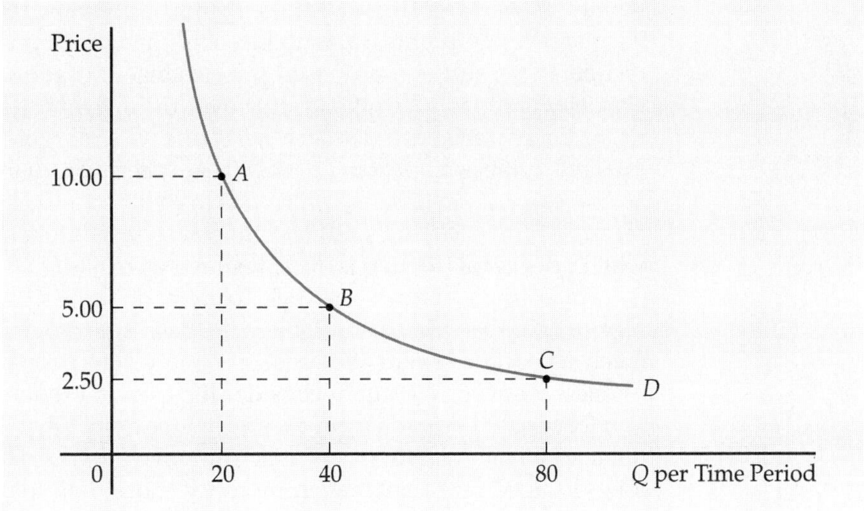

D is a unitary elastic ($|E_p| = 1$) demand curve. Unitary elastic demand curves have the property that total revenue ($P \times Q$) is the same for all prices.

Second, the price elasticity of demand will be higher the greater the *proportion* that spending on the item is of *consumers' total income*. Consumers usually do not spend a large fraction of their incomes on table salt or lead pencils. Consequently, even a substantial percentage increase in the price of table salt or the price of lead pencils is unlikely to have a major effect on their budgets if they continue purchasing the same amounts of these products as before. Third, the price elasticity of demand at a given point in time will depend on *consumer expectations* regarding future price changes. If a grocery store has soda pop on sale for a week, consumers will likely purchase more of it during that week if they believe that the price will return to its original level at the end of the week than if they believe that the price cut is a new "permanently" low price.

Finally, the price elasticity of demand will be greater the longer the time period allowed consumers to adjust their spending habits. During longer time periods consumers gain more information about the availability of alternative products, and additional substitute products are often developed. Purchases of smaller cars in response to gasoline price increases in the early 1970s are one example. In addition, consumers learned to develop new habits such as car pooling or using mass transit in response to an increase in gasoline prices.

Price Elasticity of Demand and Total Revenue

Finally, as we have already stated, the firm can know immediately whether its total revenue, or total sales dollars, will change in a positive or negative direction as a result of a proposed price change if it knows whether the price elasticity of demand for its product over the relevant range is inelastic, elastic, or unitary elastic. If demand is *inelastic* with respect to price, and price is lowered, total revenue will *decrease*. That is because quantity demanded will *not* increase *by a large enough proportion* to counteract the effect of a lower price received from each unit sold. The opposite effect occurs (for the same reason) when price is raised; that is, total revenue increases.

For example, the price elasticity of demand for basic household telephone service is probably inelastic. Unless the basic rate would increase drastically (such as a 100 percent increase), probably few people would have their phones removed. We might consider the frequent requests of Southwestern Bell for higher basic rates in Texas as evidence that Bell may believe that the demand for such service is inelastic. Moreover, in the last few years interstate long-distance rates have fallen by much more than local rates.[29] However, AT&T seems more interested in keeping rates on interstate long-distance phone calls relatively low, indicating that the company may believe the demand for such service to be significantly more elastic than the demand for basic local telephone service.

On the other hand, if demand is price *elastic* and price is lowered, total revenue will *increase*—an effect opposite to that obtained when demand is price inelastic. This result occurs because quantity demanded will increase by a sufficiently large percentage to more than make up for the lower price received on each unit sold. An example of this phenomenon might be the special price reductions offered periodically by restaurants. Another example might be the reduced prices of airline tickets when advance purchase requirements are met. Correspondingly, if demand is elastic and price is increased, total revenue will decrease. Finally, if demand is unitary elastic, a change in price will not affect total revenue, since price and quantity will change in equal proportions and therefore have exactly offsetting effects. These results are summarized in Table 2–2.

This information regarding price changes and total revenue can be very significant for the firm. For example, suppose that an ice-skating rink finds that quantity demanded by skaters is such that the rink is not being used close to its capacity level and that the (absolute value of the) price elasticity of demand is greater than 1. In such cases the rink should strongly consider lowering its price, since a large portion of its costs (such as interest on money

---

29 See, for example, "All Those Long-Distance Discounts Are Sweet, But . . . ," *Business Week* (September 19, 1994), p. 67. "Bell Tolls Again for Texas Users," *San Antonio Express-News*, April 2, 1985, p. 14-A; and "Repealed Phone Tax Still Collected," *San Antonio Express-News*, May 16, 1986, p. 1-B.

Table 2–2   Summary of Relationship Between Price Elasticity of Demand and Total Revenue

E_p	Classification	Effect of Price Change on Total Revenue
$|E_p| > 1$	Elastic	Increase in price lowers TR. Decrease in price raises TR.
$|E_p| < 1$	Inelastic	Increase in price raises TR. Decrease in price lowers TR.
$|E_p| = 1$	Unitary Elastic	Price change does not affect TR.

borrowed to finance the rink purchase and electricity to cool the ice) won't change very much. A similar situation could occur for a movie theater owner, which may help to explain the practice by theaters of offering matinee showings at bargain prices. A smart firm attempts to estimate the price elasticity of demand at different times of the day and for different movies. Movie theaters do, then, attempt to take advantage of such differences to some extent with special afternoon rates and different rates for different movies.

Even government policymakers have reason to be concerned about the price elasticity of demand. The U.S. government raised gasoline taxes by 4.3 cents a gallon (about 4.3 percent) in 1993, with the twin—but opposing—goals of increasing federal revenues (reducing the federal budget deficit) and reducing oil imports. An early estimate indicated that the demand for gasoline was inelastic—that the quantity demanded would fall by only 1.9 percent. As a result, the impact of the gasoline tax was likely to be greater on the federal budget than on the quantity of oil imports. Likewise, an increased tax on cigarettes was touted as a way to both raise funds for a federal health care plan and encourage people to stop smoking, which would lead to better health. Estimates of the price elasticity of demand for cigarettes ranged from −.4 in the short run to −.75 in the long run. Since these estimates were also in the inelastic range, they indicated that the effect of the higher taxes would likely be greater on government revenue than on quantity demanded.[30] In Sweden the government found out that its workers apparently became healthier when a new law was passed that cut back on sick-leave benefits. The new law specified that workers would receive only 75 percent, rather than 100 percent, of their pay for the first three days of illness. As a result, employee claims for sick-leave days fell by almost 20 percent.[31]

---

30 "Why There Won't Be Too Much Pain At The Pumps," *Business Week* (August 23, 1993), p. 14; "Taxes Curb Smoking," *The Wall Street Journal*, September 1, 1993, p. A1; and "Cigarette Smokers Will Quit—At a Price," *Business Week* (June 18, 1990), p. 20.
31 "Sick Pay Cuts Gives Swedes Healthier Lives," *San Antonio Express-News*, March 23, 1991, p. 4-A.

Price Elasticity of Demand, Average Revenue, and Marginal Revenue

Now that we know the relationships among E_p, price changes, and the effect on total revenue, we can discern the relationships among E_p, price changes, average revenue, and marginal revenue. Figure 2–4, showing the relationships among the latter three variables, is reproduced in Figure 2–8. In addition, the relationships among E_p, average revenue, and marginal revenue are indicated. Where $|E_p| > 1$, marginal revenue is *positive*, since a decrease in price increases total revenue. Where $|E_p| = 1$, marginal revenue is *zero*, since a decrease in price will not change total revenue. Finally, if $|E_p| < 1$, marginal revenue is *negative*, since a decrease in price will decrease total revenue.[32] As shown in Figure 2–8, with a linear demand curve, the price elasticity of demand will be equal to 1 in absolute value at the midpoint of the demand curve, the point where marginal revenue is equal to zero.

Nevertheless, a firm should not base its pricing decisions solely on the manner in which price affects total revenue; its costs must also be considered. When the price elasticity of demand is *inelastic*, the decision rule is straightforward: *raise price*. In this case total revenue will increase; and since quantity sold will decrease, total costs should at worst remain the same, resulting in an increase in total profit.

In the case of *elastic* demand, the situation is more complicated. A *decrease*

---

32 We can also derive another relationship among E_p, marginal revenue, and price. If

$$TR = P \cdot Q,$$

$$MR = \frac{dTR}{dQ} = P + Q\frac{dP}{dQ}, \text{ or}$$

$$MR = P + \left(1 + \frac{Q}{P} \cdot \frac{dP}{dQ}\right).$$

However, $\frac{Q}{P} \cdot \frac{dP}{dQ}$ is equal to $(1/E_p)$, so $MR = P(1 + 1/E_p)$.

As noted in a previous section of this chapter, if the demand curve is a horizontal line, price is equal to marginal revenue. We can now prove this statement with the use of the previously developed relationship. Since we know that $E_p = -\infty$ if the demand curve is horizontal, then in this case

$$MR = P(1 + 1/-\infty) = P(1 + 0) = P.$$

If $-\infty < E_p < 0,$

$$MR = P[1 + \text{some negative number}],$$

so $MR < P$, as already discussed in this chapter.

Finally, if $E_p = 0,$

$$MR = P(1 + 1/0) = \infty.$$

Figure 2–8   Relationships Among Total Revenue, Marginal Revenue, Average Revenue, and Price Elasticity of Demand

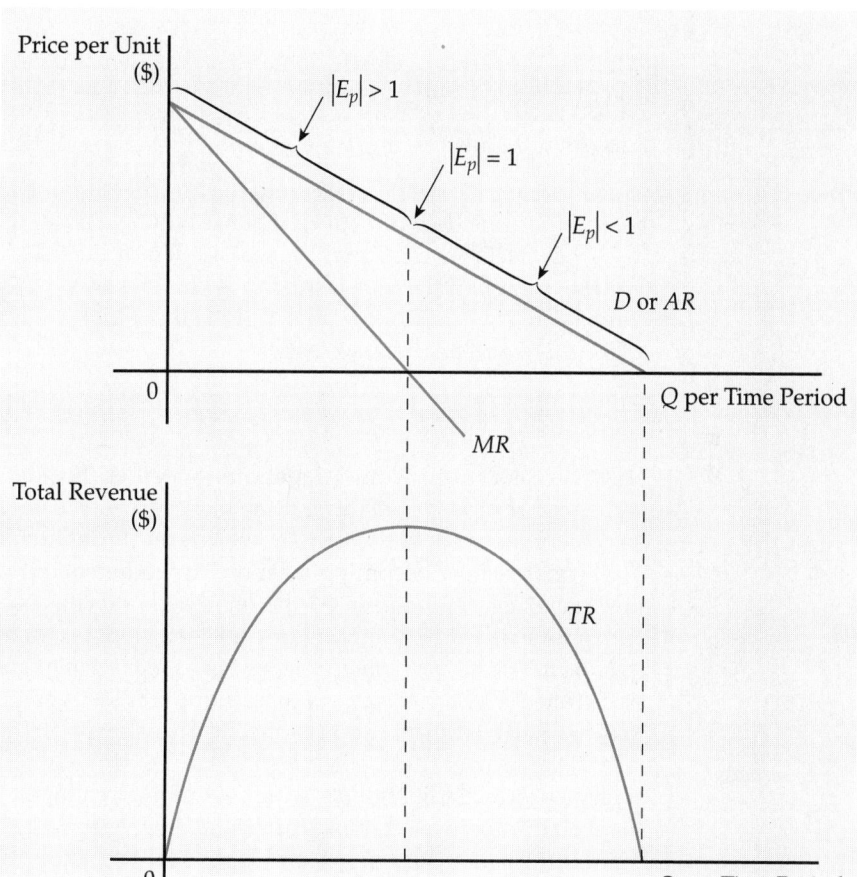

These graphs depict the relationships among total revenue (TR), marginal revenue (MR), average revenue (AR), and price elasticity of demand. When MR is positive, TR is rising and $|E_p|$ is greater than one. When $MR = 0$, TR is at a maximum and $|E_p| = 1$. When MR is negative, TR is falling and $|E_p|$ is less than one.

in price will *increase* total revenue, but the resulting increase in sales will likely increase total costs to some extent. *If the lower price causes output to increase sufficiently so that total revenue increases by a greater amount than total cost*, then the price cut will result in greater total profit. But, if a price cut results in a greater increase in total cost than in total revenue, total profit will fall. A similar analysis would hold for a price *increase*, except in this case the

NUMERICAL EXAMPLE:

Elasticity and the Straight-Line Demand Curve

Where is the range of elastic demand on the demand curve having the equation $Q_d = 8{,}000 - 50P$?

Answer

Demand is elastic from $Q_d = 0$ up to the midpoint quantity (where $MR = 0$) on the straight-line demand curve. Thus it will be elastic in the range $Q_d = 0$ up to $Q_d = 4{,}000$. From the equation, we can determine that $50P = 8{,}000 - Q_d$, and $P = 160 - .02Q_d$. Thus the elastic range can be stated in terms of price as that from $P = 160$ to $P = 80$. Of course, right at the midpoint, where $P = 80$ and $Q_d = 4{,}000$, there will be unitary elasticity.

effect on total profit would depend on whether the *decrease* in total revenue were greater or less than the *decrease* in total cost. We will reserve further discussion of the costs of the firm, however, until a later chapter.

Firms are now becoming far more concerned about pricing policies than they have been in the past. At the retail level this has become readily apparent as four major new pricing approaches have become popular. These are *yield management*, *price matching*, *everyday low pricing*, and *value pricing*. The first strategy, *yield management*, uses computer software to track sales volume and market conditions so that the firm can raise prices when demand increases and lower them when it slacks off, or quickly respond in other ways such as product adjustments when the market changes.[33] Airlines and large hotel chains have used this approach extensively. Basically, successful yield management depends on ascertaining how consumer demand differs over time as well as among consumers.

Price matching also involves a careful analysis of consumer behavior. Stores employing it have found that few consumers actually take advantage of the offer to match competitors' prices. *The Wall Street Journal* reports that, according to a pricing expert at UCLA,

> price-matching policies actually give merchants "a way to keep prices a little higher for loyal customers while giving a lower price" to new customers the store is trying to attract.[34]

---

33 See "Cost Cutting at Delta Raises the Stock Price But Lowers the Service," *The Wall Street Journal*, June 20, 1996, pp. A1, A8; "How Software Is Making Food Sales a Piece of Cake," *Business Week* (July 2, 1990), pp. 54–55; "No Cheap Hotel Room: Blame Yield Management," *The Wall Street Journal*, Nov. 4, 1988, p. 81; and "Computers Permit Airlines to Use Scalpel to Cut Fares," *The Wall Street Journal*, February 2, 1987, p. 25.

34 "Who Wins With Price-Matching Plans," *The Wall Street Journal*, March 16, 1989, p. B1.

As we will see in a later chapter, both yield management and price matching are special cases of market segmentation—basically, dividing up markets into segments with different elasticities of demand.

The third approach, *everyday low pricing*, has both a demand and a cost element. While firms such as Sears that have adopted the strategy expect it will enlarge their customer base, they also expected to reap cost savings from reductions in advertising and related expenditures.[35] *Business Week* and Sears' major rival provide the following observation:

> Everyday low pricing requires efficient operations to maintain profit margins. "If you can't be a low-cost player, forget it," says Bernard F. Brennan, chairman of Montgomery Ward & Co. Ward's, which has reduced operating costs by $100 million annually since 1985, began everyday low pricing in 1987.[36]

In recent years, U.S. discount retailers have even been invading the European market with everyday low prices.[37]

Most recently, firms, including General Motors and apparel stores, have been touting *value pricing*, or offering the "greatest value" for the price. Value pricing involves finding the optimal balance between product quality and price. Products that are too low in quality will not result in the greatest profit, even if they are offered at relatively cheap prices. Yet neither will products of the highest quality result in the greatest profit if they are offered at too high a price. Thus firms are under pressure to offer relatively high quality products at reasonable prices, a pressure that has resulted in the push for "total quality management," or TQM, in the business world.[38]

Income Elasticity of Demand

Income elasticity of demand is measured by the ratio of the percentage change in quantity taken of a product to the percentage change in income.

Income elasticity of demand measures the relative responsiveness of the quantity purchased of a product to changes in income. The arc formula for income elasticity of demand of Q_X is

---

35 In the case of Sears, it is not clear how well the everyday low pricing strategy has worked since the company still advertises frequently and includes some special sale prices.

36 "Little Prices are Looking Good to Big Retailers," *Business Week* (July 3, 1989), p. 44. Also see "What's This—Car Dealers With Souls," *Business Week* (April 6, 1992), pp. 66–67.

37 Kevin Helliker, "U.S. Discount Retailers Are Targeting Europe and Its Fat Margins," *The Wall Street Journal*, September 20, 1993, pp. A1, A4.

38 "Apparel Stores Seek to Cure Shoppers Addicted to Discounts," *The Wall Street Journal*, May 29, 1996, pp. A1, A10; "GM Expected to Expand 'No Haggle' Pricing Plan," *The Wall Street Journal*, April 24, 1996, pp. A3, A4; "GM to Stress Value Pricing for '94 Models," *The Wall Street Journal*, July 12, 1993, pp. A3, A9; "GM, Pitching Value, Scores Cavalier Upset," *The Wall Street Journal*, May 11, 1993, pp. B1, B2; and "Value Marketing," *Business Week* (November 11, 1991), pp. 132–140.

MANAGERIAL PERSPECTIVE:

Building a Business on E_p: The Saga of Southwest Airlines

Herb Kelleher, CEO of Southwest Airlines, tells the story more or less this way: Along about 1972, the founders of Southwest Airlines believed something that the industry leaders, as well as the CAB (Civil Aeronautics Board, which then was in charge of regulating U.S. air transportation), scoffed at. It had to do with how the low- and middle-income consumer felt about air travel. According to Kelleher, the CAB and the major airlines managers believed that air travel was largely reserved for people who had the ability to pay high fares—the rich and those flying on business budgets—while the average American would choose car travel over air travel for most needs. Ordinary people, they argued, viewed air travel as a luxury good and would not increase their purchases of it very much if prices were reduced any feasible amount from those then prevailing.

Mr. Kelleher and his associates believed the opposite—that lower fares would result in large increases in the quantity of air travel purchased by the general public: "We were certain that demand was much more elastic than any of them believed it to be." Because at that time the CAB regulated all interstate fares in the United States and did not permit price competition, Kelleher says the only way his group could test their proposition was to establish an *intra*state airline in a market area

$$E_I = \left(\frac{\frac{\Delta Q_X}{Q_{X_2} + Q_{X_1}}}{2} \right) \div \left(\frac{\frac{\Delta I}{I_2 + I_1}}{2} \right) = \frac{\Delta Q_X}{\Delta I} \cdot \frac{I_2 + I_1}{Q_{X_2} + Q_{X_1}}$$

$$= \frac{Q_{X_2} - Q_{X_1}}{I_2 - I_1} \cdot \frac{I_2 + I_1}{Q_{X_2} + Q_{X_1}} .$$

As stated earlier, in our microwave oven example, when $P_X = \$400$, $P_Y = \$500$, $F = 40,000,000$, $I = \$10,000$, and $A = \$50,000$, then Q_X is equal to 30,000. When all of the above independent variables except income (I) remain constant, and I increases to $12,000$, then Q_X increases to 35,200. Thus E_I between $I = \$10,000$ and $I = \$12,000$ is given by[39]

---

39 The point formula for income elasticity of demand is

large enough to make bargain air travel attractive to the consumer. That, he notes, had to be either California or Texas. They chose Texas. Southwest began by flying routes between the three large Texas cities, Dallas, Houston, and San Antonio. They offered "no frills" service. Refreshments never got fancier than peanuts and a drink, and there was only one class of seating, with no reserved seats. Ticket counters issued simple cash register receipts along with a reusable plastic boarding pass. In short, service was unpretentious, but the airline got the passengers to their destinations efficiently and *very* cheaply.

Consumer response to Southwest's low fares was tremendous. For a brief period, there was intense competition from Braniff on the intrastate routes, but Southwest persevered and kept to its game plan. It let consumers know that failure of Southwest would lead to the return of high fares in Texas, and they responded by being remarkably loyal to the firm. Southwest survived and has remained profitable. The price competition that was begun by Southwest and other upstarts in the industry led eventually to a new era in air transportation, with more discount fares, huge increases in traffic, and the eventual phaseout of the CAB. By 1990, however, mergers, bankruptcies, and buyouts had significantly reduced competition.

References: Based on a speech by Herbert D. Kelleher at The University of Texas at San Antonio, March 1990. For more on Southwest, see "Southwest Airlines: Flying High with 'Uncle Herb,'" *Business Week* (July 3, 1989), pp. 55–55, and "Southwest No. 1 in Quality Survey," *San Antonio Express-News,* April 12, 1994, p. 1-C.

$$E_I = \frac{5,200}{2,000} \cdot \frac{22,000}{65,200} = .88.$$

Since the above income elasticity of demand is greater than zero, we can say that Brand X microwave ovens are *normal goods*. In our previous discussion of the determinants of demand, normal goods are defined as products for which the quantity demanded increases as income increases (and vice versa). If $E_I > 1$, then the product is a normal good that is also a *superior good*.

$$E_I = \frac{\partial Q_X}{\partial I} \cdot \frac{I}{Q_X}.$$

In our microwave oven example, the point income elasticity of demand where $P_X = \$400$, $P_Y = \$500$, $F = 40{,}000{,}000$, $I = \$10{,}000$, $A = \$50{,}000$, and $Q_X = 30{,}000$ is given by

$$E_I = 2.6 \times \frac{10,000}{30,000} = .87.$$

Such a value for E_I means that the quantity demanded of superior goods increases more than proportionally to the percentage increase in income. Such goods are also often called *cyclical normal goods*, since the quantity purchased of them varies proportionally more than income does over the business cycle. If the income elasticity of demand is negative, it means that the quantity demanded of a good *decreases* as income *increases*. We call these products *inferior goods*.

Knowing the approximate income elasticity of demand for its product over the relevant region, a firm can estimate how a change in income will affect the quantity demanded of that good or service and can plan its production accordingly. This information is crucial to firms such as those in the automobile or appliance industries, where the demand for their products is very much affected by changes in the level of income. For example, consider the drastic production cutbacks in the automobile industry during 1991 and the early 1980s, when national income in *real terms* (that is, adjusted for price increases) was falling. The recessions also similarly affected the home-appliance and the furniture industries.[40]

The income elasticity of demand has also been a useful concept in describing one of the problems of firms in the agriculture industry in the United States during at least part of the twentieth century. The problem arises because the income elasticity of demand for agricultural products is less than 1—a fact that means the quantity demanded of agricultural products does not increase by as great a percentage as the percentage increase in income.

Cross Price Elasticity of Demand

Cross price elasticity of demand is measured by the ratio of the percentage change in quantity demanded of a product to the percentage change in price of a related product.

The **cross price elasticity of demand** for Product X with respect to the price of Product Y is a measure of the relative responsiveness of quantity demanded of Product X to changes in P_Y. The arc cross price elasticity of demand formula is

$$E_{XY} = \frac{\left(\dfrac{\Delta Q_X}{Q_{X_2} + Q_{X_1}} \right)}{\left(\dfrac{\Delta P_Y}{P_{Y_2} + P_{Y_1}} \right)} = \frac{\Delta Q_X}{\Delta P_Y} \cdot \frac{P_{Y_2} + P_{Y_1}}{Q_{X_2} + Q_{X_1}} = \frac{Q_{X_2} - Q_{X_1}}{P_{Y_2} - P_{Y_1}} \cdot \frac{P_{Y_2} + P_{Y_1}}{Q_{X_2} + Q_{X_1}}.$$

---

40 See, for example, "Tough Economic Times Are Knocking Stuffing Out of Many Furniture Stores," *The Wall Street Journal*, January 20, 1992, pp. B1, B2; "Big Three U.S. Car Output To Sink to a 33-Year Low," *The Wall Street Journal*, April 11, 1991, p. A2; and "Recession Hits Major-Appliance Makers, Causing Layoffs; Recovery Isn't in Sight," *The Wall Street Journal*, June 23, 1980, p. 12. The boom in single-family housing in 1986 also favorably affected the appliance industry. See "Consumers May Be Ready to Put on Their Shopping Shoes," *Business Week* (May 19, 1986), p. 34.

For our microwave oven demand function, when $P_X = \$400$, $P_Y = \$500$, $F = 40{,}000{,}000$, $I = \$10{,}000$, and $A = \$50{,}000$, then Q_X is equal to 30,000. If P_Y decreases to \$400, then Q_X decreases to 27,500 units. Therefore, between $P_Y = \$500$ and $P_Y = \$400$,[41]

$$E_{XY} = \frac{-2{,}500}{-100} \cdot \frac{900}{57{,}500} = .39.$$

If, as in the preceding situation, the cross price elasticity of demand is positive, we say that the two goods are *substitute goods*. A positive value for E_{XY} means that an increase in P_Y will result in an increase in Q_X (and vice versa), which indicates that an increase in P_Y causes some customers to purchase Brand X instead of Brand Y (and vice versa). If E_{XY} were negative, it would indicate that an increase in the price of Good Y would decrease the quantity purchased of Good X. In this case Good X and Good Y are said to be *complementary goods*. As stated previously in our discussion of the determinants of demand, complementary goods are, generally speaking, goods such that having more of one (at least to a point) increases the enjoyment a consumer obtains from the second. Examples of complementary goods are CDs and CD players, hamburger and hamburger buns, and gasoline and automobiles. If $E_{XY} = 0$, we say that the goods are *not related*.

Cross price elasticity information can be useful to the firm in several ways. If the firm produces two related goods or services, it is beneficial for it to be able to estimate how a change in the price of one will affect the quantity demanded of the other. For example, Procter & Gamble would like to know the effect of a price decrease for Crest toothpaste on the quantity demanded of the other brands of toothpaste that the company sells. A second situation in which cross price elasticity information is helpful occurs when another firm selling a related product has changed, or is expected to change, the price of that good or service. Thus Ford would like to know the impact of General Motors' rebates on the quantity sold of Ford vehicles. In the market for used cars, low prices on used rental cars sold by the automakers affected the quan-

---

41 The formula for point cross price elasticity of demand is

$$E_{XY} = \left(\frac{\partial Q_X}{\partial P_Y}\right)\left(\frac{P_Y}{Q_X}\right).$$

At the point where $P_X = \$400$, $P_Y = \$500$, $F = 40{,}000{,}000$, $I = \$10{,}000$, $A = \$50{,}000$, and $Q_X = 30{,}000$,

$$E_{XY} = 25\left(\frac{500}{30{,}000}\right) = .42.$$

tity demanded of other used cars.[42] Recently, cereal makers lowered the prices on many of their brands to allegedly counter a three-fold increase in the demand for bagels as a breakfast food.[43]

Finally, a third situation in which cross price elasticity information could be of critical importance is if the firm were defending itself in an antitrust case by demonstrating (1) that its product has a positive cross price elasticity relationship with other products, therefore (2) that there are recognized substitutes for the product, and (3) that it accordingly does *not* have a monopoly. This type of approach was quite helpful to du Pont in defending itself in a famous antitrust case.[44] Du Pont had nearly 75 percent of the market for cellophane wrapping materials. However, the company successfully argued that the relevant market was the entire market for flexible packaging materials, including waxed paper and aluminum foil; it supported its position by showing that there were positive cross price elasticities between cellophane and these products and that therefore the products were substitutes. When the total market for flexible packaging materials was considered, du Pont had a much smaller market share.

Other Elasticity of Demand Concepts

As we stated when the concept of elasticity (of demand) was introduced, we can use an elasticity coefficient to indicate the relative responsiveness of the quantity demanded of a product to a change in any variable that may affect it. In our microwave oven example, we could also talk of the advertising elasticity of demand and of the employment (of women) elasticity of demand. For some products, population growth and, hence, the population elasticity of demand might be significant. The wise firm will try to discover the values of those elasticities that it believes are important factors affecting its revenue.

Much of the information needed for demand studies can be obtained from Bureau of the Census data on population, income, and already existing businesses. Such reports can frequently be found in local libraries. Local planning authorities and trade associations are other important sources of information. In addition, consulting firms in the area of market research will be happy to supply and/or analyze data, for a fee. A more thorough discussion of demand estimation and forecasting techniques will appear in Chapters 3 and 4.

---

42 Neal Templin, "Sales of Used Rental Cars by Big Three Depress Other Second-Hand Auto Prices," The Wall Street Journal, January 6, 1992, pp. B1, B2.

43 "Cereal Makers Fight Bagels With Price Cuts," *The Wall Street Journal*, June 20, 1996, pp. B1, B8.

44 See *United States* v. *E. I. du Pont de Nemours and Co.*, 351 U.S. 377, 100 L. Ed. 1264, 76 S. Ct. 994 (1956).

MANAGERIAL PERSPECTIVE:
Some Dimensions of the Demand for Automobiles

Automobiles are a fixture of the American way of life, and it seems Americans are always interested in the attributes and prices of new cars. Economic studies of their demand for automobiles have produced some interesting results. First, there is a marked difference between demand for new cars in the aggregate and the demand for a given model of car. Second, consumers can always purchase a used car instead of a new one, so there is a substitute relationship not only between different makes of new cars but also between new and used.

The market demand for new automobiles has been estimated in a number of well-known studies. At different points in time and with different sets of data, these always seem to show the same result—that the price elasticity of demand for new cars is relatively low, usually around –1.1 to about –1.4. What this means is that when automobile manufacturers use rebates (a form of price cut) to help dealers entice customers to buy new cars, they realize very little, if any, increased revenue from those sales. However, the law of demand still works, so they do increase quantity sold and, therefore, reduce inventories. Since the automobile industry has long been dedicated to the "model year" concept of product development (introducing new models of most lines in the autumn each year), getting rid of excess inventory of this year's models is very important, especially if the release of next year's is not far off. Thus there is a pattern of rebating and offering other incentives at the end of each model year, even though it does not bring in big increases in revenue for the manufacturers.

While the elasticity of the aggregate demand for new cars is low, that for a specific model is much higher. This results from the fact that all cars are substitutes for one another, and some models of certain cars are very close substitutes for specific models of others. For example, a study published in 1983 found that the own-price elasticity for a Chevrolet Impala was –14.79 and that for a Ford Mustang was –8.42. The same study also found a cross-price elasticity of +19.30 for a Chevrolet Impala with respect to the price of a Pontiac Catalina, a close "cousin" of the Impala. Thus manufacturers (and dealers) can get buyers to switch purchases from one make of car to another by lowering price.

It has recently been noted that in the face of steep price increases by automobile manufacturers many consumers who did not view used cars as a close substitute for new ones have changed their minds. This change has probably been accelerated by the increasing availability of very-low-mileage used cars from corporate fleets and those marketed by car rental companies. Many cars offered by these sources are in nearly new condition and are sold with warranty terms that are quite comparable to those offered by new car sellers. Thus one variable that may have deterred many buyers from considering used cars close substitutes for new cars (risk of costly repair bills) has been largely eliminated.

References: F. Owen Irvine, Jr., "Demand Equations for Individual New Car Models Estimated Using Transaction Prices with Implications for Regulatory Issues," *Southern Economic Journal* 49 (January 1983), pp. 764–782; H. F. Gallasch, Jr., "Elasticities of Demand for New Automobiles" (Societal Analysis Department, Research Laboratories, General Motors Corporation, Warren, Michigan, May 21, 1976); "With Deals This Good, Why Settle for New?" *Business Week* (July 3, 1989), p. 81.

SUMMARY

Elasticity of Demand, Revenue, and the Firm

In this chapter we have emphasized one of the two most critical factors for the success of a firm: *the demand for its product*. We have defined the *demand function* as the mathematical relationship that indicates how the quantity demanded of a firm's product over some time period is affected by variables such as the price of the good (or service), prices of other goods, income of consumers, and advertising expenditures. The *demand curve* gives the relationship between the quantity demanded of a good and its price. The demand curve is obtained from the demand function by holding all variables (except price and quantity demanded) constant at some level. Those variables held constant when the demand curve is obtained are called *determinants of demand*. We noted that a change in a good's own price will cause a movement along its demand curve but that a change in one of the determinants of demand (income, prices of related goods, and tastes, for example), will shift the entire curve.

We also related the demand curve to the total revenue, average revenue, and marginal revenue functions. *Total revenue* relates total sales dollars received by the firm to quantity sold. Total revenue is equal to price times quantity purchased and can be derived from the equation for the demand curve. *Average revenue* is obtained by dividing total revenue by quantity sold and is equal to price. The average revenue curve, therefore, is the demand curve. *Marginal revenue* is the rate of change of total revenue with respect to quantity sold and is, consequently, the slope of the total revenue function. *Arc marginal revenue* is the average rate of change of *total revenue* with respect to some change in quantity sold, or

$$\text{Arc } MR = \frac{\Delta TR}{\Delta Q}.$$

We have emphasized that the profit-maximizing firm is concerned about the responsiveness of the quantity demanded of its product to changes in other variables—such as the price of the good or service, the prices of related goods, and the income of consumers. The measure of responsiveness that we have utilized here is *elasticity* of demand, which is given by

$$\frac{\text{percent change in quantity demanded}}{\text{percent change in a specific related variable}}.$$

In this chapter we discussed three types of elasticity of demand—price, income, and *cross price*. We classified price elasticity of demand according to whether it was *elastic*, *inelastic*, or *unitary elastic*; and in each case we related price changes to total revenue and marginal revenue. Given the income elasticity of demand, we classified a product as being either a *normal* (including superior) *good* or an *inferior good*. Using the cross price elasticity of demand between one product and another product, we can classify the two goods as *substitutes* or *complements*. We also demonstrated in each case various ways such information can be useful to the manager.

Before a firm commits much time and money to a given line of product or type of service, it should gather enough information to substantiate its belief that a sufficient market exists for the item it wants to sell. Once it has established that the market does exist for its product and therefore has gone into business, the wise firm will use its knowledge of the concepts we have discussed in this chapter to gather and analyze the information that will enable it to predict and increase its revenue. Thereby it will be well on its way toward maximizing profit.

In the next two chapters we will summarize some techniques of demand estimation and forecasting. Then, in the following chapters we consider production and the cost of production—the other major factor determining the degree of success or failure of an enterprise.

QUESTIONS

1. Define total revenue, marginal revenue, and average revenue. Why is knowledge of each of these elements important for the firm?

2. Define price elasticity of demand. How is E_p related to total revenue for a firm?
3. Explain what is meant by the *determinants of demand*.
4. Discuss two situations in which knowledge of the income elasticity of demand is helpful.
5. What factors do you think affect the price elasticity of demand?
6. Which demand curve do you think would generally be less price elastic—that for a firm's product or that for an industry's product? Why?
7. What is the relationship between goods that are substitutes? Between goods that are complements? How is the classification of goods in this manner related to cross price elasticity of demand?
8. What is the value of marginal revenue when total revenue is maximized?

PROBLEMS

1. The table that follows gives price and corresponding quantity demanded data for a firm.
   a. Complete the table by finding total revenue and arc marginal revenue.
   b. Plot the demand curve, the total revenue curve, and the arc marginal revenue curve. Note that the *arc marginal revenue between two levels of output should be plotted midway between the two levels*.
   c. Find the price elasticity of demand between $P = \$35$ and $P = \$30$ and between $P = \$15$ and $P = \$10$. In which price range is it more elastic?

P	Q	TR	ARC MR
$40	0		
35	5		_____
30	10		_____
25	15		_____
20	20		_____
15	25		_____
10	30		_____
5	35		_____
0	40		_____

2. Barker Cement Company is considering lowering the price on an 80-pound bag of cement from $3 to $2. Presently, Barker sells 10,000 bags of cement per week, and its market analysts believe the price elasticity of demand to be -2 over this price range.
   a. If Barker Cement Company lowers the price, will its total revenue increase, decrease, or remain unchanged? Why?
   b. What will be the new level of quantity demanded? Of total revenue?
3. a. Complete the following table by finding total revenue and price.

P	Q	TR	ARC MR
120	0	0	
			105
	10		
			75
	20		
			45
	30		
			15
	40		
			−15
	50		

   b. How would marginal revenue and price be related if price were constant? How are they related when price must decrease for quantity demanded to increase?
4. Jennie's Healthfoods now sells 2,000 lbs. of passion fruit per week at a price of $1.40 per lb. An economist has reported to management that the arc elasticity of demand for the fruit over the price range $1.40 to $1.20 per lb. is −2.0. Given that Jennie lowers her passion fruit price to $1.20 per lb., determine the following:
   a. How many lbs. of passion fruit will she sell per week?
   b. How much will her total revenue (TR) from passion fruit sales change?
5. Zeerok Shoe Company has hired a consultant to estimate the elasticity of demand for its most awesome basketball shoe. At present, Zeerok is charging $90 for a pair of the shoes. The consultant estimates that the arc price elasticity of demand for them is −1.40 for a price cut of $10.
   Currently, Zeerok is selling 20,000 pairs of the shoes per week at its 90-dollar price. If the consultant is correct and the company cuts its price from $90 to $80 per pair,
   a. What will be the new sales quantity per week of Zeerok's awesome shoe?
   b. Calculate the change in Zeerok's total revenue from sales of the shoe that follows from the change in part (a).
6. International Video Machines, Inc., is a manufacturer of a video-recording device. The firm is considering lowering the price of its product from $800 to $600. The company's market analysts have estimated the price

elasticity of demand to be –2 over this price range. Presently, this firm sells 1,000 video recorders per month.

a. What will be the new quantity sold if the price is lowered to $600?

b. What will be the new level of total revenue in part (a)?

c. What additional information does International Video Machines, Inc., need to know before it can determine whether or not a price decrease will increase the firm's profit?

d. Suppose that after International Video Machines lowers its price, its competitor, Videoview, lowers the price of its machine from $900 to $800. The cross price elasticity of demand between the quantity sold of International Video Machines' video recorders and the price of Videoview's machine is .5. What will be the effect of Videoview's price decrease on the quantity sold by International Video Machines? (Use the quantity you found in part (a) as Q_1. Round your answer to the nearest whole number.)

7. A manufacturer of stuffed animals, Texas Teddy Bear, Inc., is trying to determine the price of its stuffed animals (all sell at the same price) during the upcoming Christmas season. In the past the price of its stuffed animals has been $10, but the firm is getting worried because of the popularity of space toys. The firm has produced some new stuffed animals in an effort to increase its share in the toy market, but it is also considering a price decrease to $8. Texas Teddy Bear's market research department has estimated the price elasticity of demand for the firm's stuffed animals to be –1.5. The estimated quantity that would be sold this Christmas season (October–December) at a price of $10 is 40,000.

a. How many stuffed animals would be sold at a price of $8 if E_p were –1.5?

b. What would be the effect on the firm's total revenue if the price were lowered to $8?

8. Dirt Cheap Records, Inc., estimates its price elasticity of demand to be –4. Currently, DCRI sells 1,000 records per week at a price of $5 each. If DCRI lowers its price to $4,

a. What will happen to total revenue? How do you know?

b. What will be the new quantity sold?

9. Brand X auto manufacturer has just lowered the price of its new car by $2,000 (from $12,000 to $10,000), and Brand Y is concerned about the effect this action will have on the quantity demanded of its cars. At the old price, Brand Y sold 10,000 cars per month. If the cross elasticity of demand of Y's cars relative to X's prices is 1.5, what will be Y's new quantity sold?

10. Charles Sr., an East Coast fast-food chain, has been considering a price cut in its 1/4 lb. hamburger, the Astroburger. Currently, Astroburgers sell for $1.89, and Charles is selling 220,000 of the burgers per week. Charles's research department has suggested reducing the price of the

Astroburger to $1.65 and estimates that the arc elasticity of demand for the product is –1.80 over the range of the proposed price change.

a. If the research department is correct, what will be the weekly quantity sold of the Astroburgers after the price cut occurs?

b. What will be Charles's new total revenue from Astroburger sales?

Charles's major competitor, Mindy's, sells the Superburger, which is a close substitute for the Astroburger. Mindy's Superburger sells for $1.79, and, before Charles's price cut, 160,000 were sold per week. If the arc cross price elasticity of demand between the Superburger and the Astroburger is 2.20 over the range of the Charles price change:

c. Calculate the change in the quantity sold of Mindy's Superburger that occurs when Charles cuts the price of the Astroburger.

d. Calculate the dollar amount of change in Mindy's total revenue following the price cut by Charles.

11. The Hotel Madrileña, a small Spanish hotel, is considering lowering its room rates to increase occupancy during the low season. At the present time, the price of its rooms is $100 per night, and it rents an average of 25 rooms each night.

a. Find the new quantity of rooms rented per night if the Hotel Madrileña lowers its price to $80 and its price elasticity of demand is –1.5.

b. After the Hotel Madrileña lowers its price, a little pensión across the street lowers its room rate from $35 to $30 per night. Find the new quantity of rooms rented per night for the Hotel Madrileña after the pensión lowers its price if the cross price elasticity between the price of the pensión's rooms and the quantity demanded of the Madrileña's rooms is 1.0. (Hint: Use the number you found in part (a) as Q_1 in this problem.)

c. What will be the final effect of the price decreases in parts (a) and (b) on the Hotel Madrileña's total revenue?

The following problems require calculus:

C1. If $P = 120 - 1.5Q$ is the equation for the demand curve, find the corresponding total revenue function, marginal revenue function, and average revenue function.

C2. The statistics department of an appliance manufacturer has estimated that the demand function (number purchased annually) for their (Brand X) automatic washer is as follows:

$$Q_X = 197{,}000 - 100P_X + 50P_Y + .1I + .02A + 10{,}000P_L,$$

where

P_X = the price of the company's washer,
P_Y = the price of a major competitor's washer,
I = the average household income,
A = the annual dollars spent on advertising, and
P_L = cost of doing one load of wash in a self-service laundry.

a. If $P_Y = \$300$, $I = \$10,000$, $A = \$200,000$, and $P_L = \$.30$, find the price elasticity of demand between $P_X = \$350$ and $P_X = \$400$. (When $P_X = \$400$, with the values of the other variables as given above, then $Q_X = 180,000$.)

b. Is E_{P_X} elastic, inelastic, or unitary elastic? Why? If the price is cut, does total revenue increase, decrease, or not change?

c. Find the income elasticity of demand for Q_X, given $P_X = \$400$. The other variables are as given in part (a). Interpret your answer—i.e., what does it say, if anything, about the demand for Brand X washers?

C3. Alpha Company has estimated that the demand curve for its product is represented by the equation $Q = 2840 - 20P$, where Q is the quantity sold per week and P is the price per unit.

a. Based on the estimated demand curve, write the equations for Alpha's
   (i) Average revenue,
   (ii) Total revenue, and
   (iii) Marginal revenue.

b. What will be the maximum total revenue per week that Alpha can obtain from sales of its product? (Give the exact dollar amount and explain how you determine it.)

c. Calculate the point price elasticity of demand for Alpha's product when $Q = 1,600$. Is demand elastic or inelastic at this quantity? How do you know?

d. Calculate the *arc* price elasticity of demand for Alpha's product between $Q = 1,000$ and $Q = 1,100$. Interpret your result and relate it to what will happen to total revenue if Alpha is initially at $Q = 1,000$ and decides to cut price to increase its sales from 1,000 to 1,100 units.

C4. A mathematical demand function for new Cadillacs sold per year for a dealer is as follows:

$$Q_C = 200 - .01P_C + .005P_L - 10P_G + .01I + .003A,$$

where

P_C = the average price of Cadillacs,
P_L = the average price of Lincoln Continentals,
P_G = the price of gasoline,
I = per capita income, and
A = dollars spent annually on advertising.

a. Find the point price elasticity of demand if $P_C = \$25,000$, $P_L = \$20,000$, $P_G = \$1.00$, $I = \$15,000$, and $A = \$10,000$.

b. Is the price elasticity of demand elastic, unitary elastic, or inelastic? Why?

c. Find the arc cross elasticity of demand for Cadillacs and Continentals between $P_L = \$20,000$ and $P_L = \$22,000$. (All other figures except Q_C remain the same as in part (a).)

d. Are Cadillacs and Lincolns substitutes or complements? Why?

C5. Paradise Lake, Inc., is a developer of lakefront properties. Through statistical research, Paradise Lake has estimated the annual demand function for its lots to be as follows:

$$Q_L = 3,536 - .5P_L + .2P_C + .03I + .0001A,$$

where

Q_L = the number of Paradise Lake's lots purchased per year,
P_L = the price of a Paradise Lake lot,
P_C = the price of a competing land company's lots,
I = average annual household income, and
A = the annual amount spent by Paradise Lake on advertising.

a. Find the income elasticity of demand for Paradise Lake's lots where $P_L = \$10,000$, $P_C = \$8,000$, $I = \$12,000$, and $A = \$4,000$.
b. Are these lots a normal good or an inferior good? Why?
c. What does your answer in part (a) tell Paradise Lake about the demand for its lots?
d. Find the price elasticity of demand for Paradise Lake's properties at the same point as in part (a).
e. Is the price elasticity of demand for Paradise Lake's properties elastic, inelastic, or unitary elastic? How do you know?

C6. Smooth Sailing, Inc., has estimated the demand function for its sailboats (quantity purchased annually) as follows:

$$Q_S = 89,830 - 40P_S + 20P_X + 15P_Y + 2I + .001A + 10W,$$

where

P_S = the price of Smooth Sailing sailboats,
P_X = the price of Company X's sailboat,
P_Y = the price of Company Y's motorboat,
I = per capita income in dollars,
A = dollars spent on advertising, and
W = number of favorable days of weather in the southern region of the United States.

a. Suppose that $P_S = \$9,000$, $P_X = \$9,500$, $P_Y = \$10,000$, $I = \$15,000$, $A = \$170,000$, and $W = 160$. Find the price elasticity of demand at that point.
b. Is E_p elastic, inelastic, or unitary elastic in part (a)? Why?
c. What information does your answer in part (a) give Smooth Sailing that would be useful if the company were considering changing its price?
d. Find the cross price elasticity of demand for Smooth Sailing sailboats relative to Brand X sailboats between $P_X = \$9,500$ and $P_X = \$10,000$. Are the two boats substitutes or complements?

e. Find the income elasticity of demand for Smooth Sailing sailboats at the point given in part (a). Are the boats a normal good or an inferior good? Why?

C7. A firm's demand function for Product X has the following equation:

$$Q_X = 1420 - 20P_X - 10P_Y + .02I + .04A,$$

where

Q_X = the number of units of X sold per week,
P_X = the price charged per unit of X,
P_Y = the price charged for a related good, Y,
I = per capita income in the market area, and
A = the amount spent per week on advertising.

Suppose the firm spends $1,200 per week on advertising, that P_Y is $40, and that income in the market area is $8,000 per capita.

a. Write the equation of the demand curve for Product X.
b. Briefly explain how Product X is related to Product Y, given the equation for the demand function. (Is Y a substitute or a complement, and how can you tell?)
c. Given the stated values of the other independent variables in this problem, calculate the point price elasticity of demand for X at P_X = $50.
d. Given the stated values of P_Y, I, and A, at what price and quantity demanded will total revenue from sales of X be maximized? What will the maximum revenue be?

C8. Advanced Consumer Electronics manufactures digital video disc players, and its marketing department has estimated the following monthly demand function for the players:

$$Q_{ACE} = 180 - .6P_{ACE} - 3P_{VD} + .4P_C + .008I + .02A,$$

where

Q_{ACE} = the quantity of Advanced Consumer Electronics video disc players demanded per month,
P_{ACE} = the price of an Advanced Consumer Electronics video disc player,
P_{VD} = the price of a video disc,
P_C = the price of a competing video disc player,
I = annual average household income, and
A = monthly advertising expenditures.

a. Find the price elasticity of demand for ACE digital video disc players if P_{ACE} = $600, P_{VD} = $40, P_C = $500, I = $35,000, and A = $1,000.
b. Is the price elasticity of demand for these digital video disc players elastic, unitary elastic, or inelastic at the point specified in part (a)?

What does the value you found in part (a) tell you about the quantity demanded of ACE video disc players?

c. What is the cross price elasticity of demand between the quantity demanded of ACE video disc players and the price of the video discs? Are these two items substitutes or complements? What does the value of the cross price elasticity tell you about the demand for ACE video disc players?

d. What is the cross price elasticity of demand between the quantity demanded of ACE video disc players and the price of the competing brand of player at the point given in part (a)? Are the two brands of video disc players substitutes or complements?

e. Find the income elasticity of demand for ACE video disc players at the point specified in part (a). Are the players normal goods or inferior goods? Are they cyclically normal goods? Explain. What does this income elasticity of demand value tell you about the quantity demanded of ACE video disc players?

f. What is the equation for the demand curve for ACE video disc players given the values for P_{VD}, P_C, I, and A specified in part (a)?

g. What are the total revenue and marginal revenue functions that correspond to the demand function in part (f)?

This problem can be solved with Decision Assistant.

D1. Debra Ann Jones is the president of a successful merchandising operation, the DAJ Merchandising Corporation. In college, Debra received an electrical engineering degree with a minor in business administration. This combination provided her with excellent insight into the consumer electronics market. Debra had researched this market previously and determined that a very handsome profit could be made by concentrating on "hot, new consumer electronic items," such as electronic toys, telephones, and other novelties. Debra's research also revealed that quick reactions were the highest priority for success. That is, a firm had to spot a new product, buy the marketing or production rights, produce the product, and then sell it on a national scale before copies could be cheaply produced and sold. This marketing concept of striking quickly also enabled Debra to generate quick profits, and more attention was given to maximizing DAJ's revenue than to any other long-term consideration.

Debra has just been presented with one of those "hot items" she feels sure will add to the firm's success. The product is an electronic address book that can hold up to 50 names, addresses, and telephone numbers. As an additional unique feature it includes a voice synthesizer that "reads" any name, address, or telephone number stored in the device.

DAJ's marketing department has been hard at work to determine a demand function for the electronic address book. The best estimate of demand is determined by the following equation:

$$P = 500 - .25Q,$$

where P is the price to be charged and Q is the quantity demanded per month.

a. Use the Max/Min tool in the *Managerial Economics Decision Assistant* to see if you can assist Debra in determining the exact price DAJ should charge for the electronic address book if it wishes to maximize its total monthly revenue. Also determine the estimated total dollar sales per month assuming a total revenue maximizing price.

b. An alternative demand function has been proposed by several members of the marketing department. Determine the revenue maximizing price and quantity if the second demand function is given by the following equation:

$$P = 450 - .3Q,$$

where P is the price to be charged and Q is the quantity demanded per month.

SELECTED REFERENCES

Mansfield, Edwin. *Microeconomics: Theory and Applications*, 7th ed. New York: W.W. Norton, 1994, Chapters 3–5.

Landsberg, Steven E. *Price Theory and Applications*, 3d ed. Minneapolis/St. Paul: West, 1995, Chapters 1 and 4.

McGuigan, James R., and R. Charles Moyer. *Managerial Economics*, 5th ed. St. Paul, Minn.: West, 1989, Chapter 7.

Nicholson, Walter. *Microeconomic Theory: Basic Principles and Extensions*, 5th ed. Chicago: The Dryden Press, 1992, Chapters 3–7.

APPENDIX 2

Theory of Consumer Behavior

In Chapter 2 we looked at the relationship between price, quantity demanded, and total revenue. We also examined the concept of elasticity, and saw how it could be used to depict the effects of changes in variables such as income and the prices of related goods on the quantity demanded of a product.

It is also often useful to be aware of the notions about consumer behavior that lie in the background of the demand curve. In order to grasp the theory of consumer behavior put forth by economists, we must first recognize that the primary goal of consumers is assumed to be the maximization of their *utility* or *satisfaction*. In other words, consumers wish to achieve the greatest satisfaction possible within the bounds of their budget constraints.

CARDINAL UTILITY APPROACH

Early theories of consumer behavior implicitly assumed that personal utility or satisfaction could be measured in exact units of measurement, called *utils*, just as we measure length, temperature, and volume in inches, degrees, and liters. John and Sue Brown could say, for example, that they received 200 utils of satisfaction from an Anthony's super deluxe pizza and 50 utils of satisfaction from a bag of buttered microwave popcorn. With this type of measurement system, called a *cardinal* measurement system, we could say that John and Sue received four times as much satisfaction from a super deluxe pizza as from a bag of popcorn.

The *total utility* associated with a good or service is the total amount of satisfaction that the consumer obtains from the good or service. We can calculate marginal utility in the same way that we calculate other marginal values. *Arc marginal utility* is the addition to total utility provided by another unit of a good or service. For example, suppose your total utility is 1,500 utils. Someone gives you two bags of popcorn, and as a result, your total utility jumps to 1,600 utils. The marginal utility of a bag of popcorn in this case is equal to

$$\frac{\text{change in total utility}}{\text{change in bags of popcorn}} = \frac{100}{2} = 50 \text{ utils}.$$

In general, the *arc marginal utility of a good*, Good X, is given by

$$MU_X = \frac{\Delta TU_X}{\Delta X},$$

where MU is marginal utility and TU is total utility.

Economists have shown, and we can easily see, that given a cardinal utility function, consumers will maximize their satisfaction by dividing their budget among goods and services so that the marginal utility per additional dollar cost of another unit of each of these products is equal. For example, if you are dividing your monthly entertainment budget between pizza and compact discs, you will maximize your utility only if the

$$\frac{MU_{pizza}}{P_{pizza}} = \frac{MU_{CD}}{P_{CD}},$$

where

$$MU_{pizza} = \text{the marginal utility of a pizza,}$$
$$MU_{CD} = \text{the marginal utility of a compact disc,}$$
$$P_{pizza} = \text{the price of a pizza, and}$$
$$P_{CD} = \text{the price of a compact disc.}$$

Let us suppose that the price of a pizza is \$5.00, the price of a compact disc is \$10.00, the marginal utility of a pizza is 300 utils, and the marginal utility of a compact disc is 500 utils. In this case,

$$\frac{MU_{pizza}}{P_{pizza}} = \frac{300 \text{ utils}}{\$5.00} = 60 \text{ utils per additional dollar.}$$

while

$$\frac{MU_{CD}}{P_{CD}} = \frac{500 \text{ utils}}{\$10.00} = 50 \text{ utils per additional dollar.}$$

Here,

$$\frac{MU_{pizza}}{P_{pizza}} \text{ is greater than } \frac{MU_{CD}}{P_{CD}},$$

(60 is greater than 50).

Thus, to maximize your utility, you must reallocate your spending so that more pizza and fewer compact discs are purchased. For example, suppose you buy one less compact disc and two more pizzas. As a result, you will have a net gain of 100 utils for the same amount of money, as the following will show.

Buy one less compact disc:

$$\text{Change in utility} = -500 \text{ utils}$$

$$\text{Change in spending} = -\$10.00$$

Buy two more pizzas:

$$\text{Change in utility} = (2 \times 300) = 600 \text{ utils}$$

$$\text{Change in spending} = (2 \times \$5.00) = \$10.00$$

Net effect of budget reallocation:

$$\text{Net change in utility} = -500 \text{ utils} + 600 \text{ utils} = +100 \text{ utils}$$

$$\text{Net change in spending} = -\$10.00 + \$10.00 = \$0$$

Do these results mean that you should buy all pizzas and no compact discs? Certainly not! As you begin to purchase more pizzas and fewer CDs per month, you will probably find that the marginal utility of another pizza will fall, while that of another CD will rise. This phenomenon results from the *principle of diminishing marginal utility*, which states that as more and more units of a good or service are consumed, total utility may increase, but after some point the *marginal utility* of another unit will begin to fall.

Thus, as you begin to reallocate your monthly budget so that you are purchasing more pizzas and fewer compact discs, we would expect the marginal utility of another pizza to fall and that of another CD to rise. As a result, you would eventually reach a combination of pizzas and compact discs where your utility would be at a maximum, given your budget. This point might occur, for example, where the $MU_{pizza} = 275$ utils and the $MU_{CD} = 550$ utils, so that

$$\frac{MU_{pizza}}{P_{pizza}} = \frac{275}{\$5} = \frac{MU_{CD}}{P_{CD}} = \frac{550}{\$10} = 55 \text{ utils per } \$1.00.$$

At this point there is no way that you can reallocate your spending between these two goods and increase your total utility.

ORDINAL UTILITY THEORY

In recent years economists have placed increasing emphasis on the fact that the amount of utility a consumer receives from a particular combination of goods and services is a subjective phenomenon. Moreover, it may be quite difficult for the consumer to develop a utility function with cardinal measurements of utility even for himself or herself. Furthermore, twentieth-century economists have found that the important conclusions of their theory of consumer behavior could be derived from an *ordinal* utility function, which has the benefit of being much easier to construct.

An ordinal utility function does not require precise measurements of the actual utility received from a good or service; it requires only that consumers be able to state whether they prefer one combination of goods to another or are indifferent between them. A consumer who is *indifferent* between the two sets of goods likes them both equally well; they both yield the same amount of satisfaction. Two additional assumptions that economists make in the ordinal utility approach are (1) that consumers are consistent in their rankings and (2) that a consumer also prefers more to less of a good in the *relevant range* of choice. The first assumption means that if you prefer three hamburgers to four tacos but you prefer four tacos to two hot dogs, then you must also prefer three hamburgers to two hot dogs. The second assumption means that if someone offered you a choice between two hamburgers and three hamburgers for free, you would always choose three hamburgers.

Given these assumptions, we can construct an ordinal utility function for a consumer. All that is required is that the consumer tell us how he or she would rank combinations of goods and services in order of preference. We then can assign utility numbers to these combinations, following the rule that if one combination of goods and services is preferred to a second, then the first combination must have a higher utility number than the second. If a consumer is indifferent between two combinations of goods and services, they must have the *same* utility number assigned to them.

After the consumer's utility function has been constructed, we can draw indifference curves based on that data. An *indifference curve* shows various combinations of two goods and services that a consumer is indifferent among. Of course, each combination of goods and services on an indifference curve must have the same utility number assigned to it.

For example, Figure 2A–1 shows two indifference curves for combinations of compact discs and pizzas. The number of compact discs purchased per month is shown on the vertical axis and the number of pizzas on the horizontal axis. Each indifference curve represents a different level of utility. Points *A*, *B*, and *C* in the diagram indicate that this consumer is indifferent between ten compact discs and one pizza, six compact discs and three pizzas, and three compact discs and six pizzas.

We should pause here for a few moments to note some properties of indifference curves. First, indifference curves must have a *negative* slope—that is, they must slope downward to the right. This characteristic is the direct result of our assumption that a consumer always prefers more to less of a good. If some of one good is given up, more of the second good must be obtained for the consumer to remain at the same level of satisfaction and vice versa. Second, indifference curves cannot intersect. If they did intersect, that would mean that the combination of goods and services at the point of intersection gave a consumer two different levels of utility, which is impossible!

Figure 2A–1   Indifference Curves for Pizzas and Compact Discs

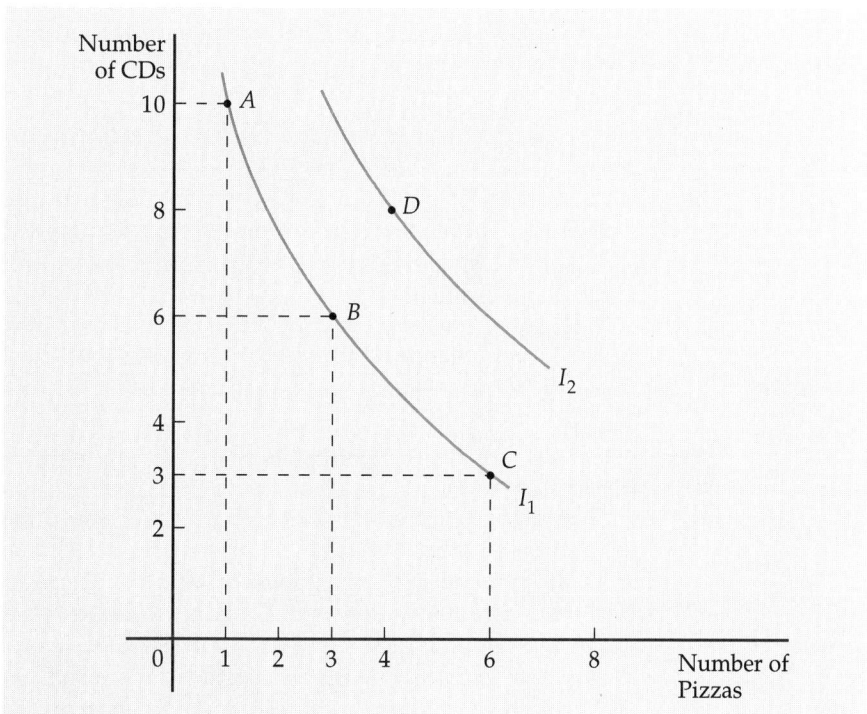

Third, higher (farther to the right) indifference curves must represent higher levels of utility. We can see why this relationship must hold by comparing points B on I_1 and D on I_2 in Figure 2A–1. Point D represents a combination of pizzas and compact discs that contains more of both goods than does B. Since a consumer prefers more to less of a good, I_2 must represent a higher level of satisfaction than does I_1.

MARGINAL RATE OF SUBSTITUTION

Points A, B, and C in Figure 2A–1 can be used to illustrate the marginal rate of substitution, a term that plays an important role in modern consumer theory. The *marginal rate of substitution* (*MRS*) indicates the rate at which a consumer is willing to substitute one good for another. In other words, it is the rate at which the consumer can substitute one good for another while remaining at the same level of satisfaction (on the same indifference curve). It is also equal to (–1) multiplied by the slope of the indifference curve at the relevant point. In general, we can write the marginal rate of substitution of Good

X for Good Y as $MRS = (-1)(\Delta Y/\Delta X)$, where Good Y is on the vertical axis and Good X is on the horizontal axis.

In Figure 2A–1, the marginal rate of substitution between points A and B is equal to

$$(-1) \ \frac{\text{change in number of compact discs}}{\text{change in number of pizzas}} = (-1) \ \frac{(-4)}{2} = 2.$$

In other words, between points A and B the consumer will maintain the same level of utility by giving up two CDs in exchange for another pizza. Between points B and C, the MRS is equal to

$$(-1) \ \frac{\text{change in number of compact discs}}{\text{change in number of pizzas}} = (-1) \ \frac{(-3)}{3} = 1.$$

Between points B and C the consumer is willing to trade only one compact disc for one pizza.

The change in the MRS between points A and B and points B and C illustrates the principle of diminishing marginal rate of substitution. A *diminishing marginal rate of substitution* of Good X for Good Y means that as consumers obtain more of Good X relative to Good Y, they are willing to give up less of Good Y to get one more unit of Good X. This principle is related to the notion of diminishing marginal utility, as we shall see shortly.

When we move from one point to another on an indifference curve, the amount of utility that we lose by giving up some of one good must be exactly offset by the utility we gain from getting more of the second good. Thus for two goods, X and Y, along an indifference curve,

(2A–1)
$$\left(\Delta Y \cdot \frac{\Delta TU}{\Delta Y} \right) + \left(\Delta X \cdot \frac{\Delta TU}{\Delta X} \right) = 0.$$

By subtracting $\Delta X(\Delta TU/\Delta X)$ from both sides of equation (2A–1), we obtain

(2A–2)
$$\Delta Y \cdot \frac{\Delta TU}{\Delta Y} = -\Delta X \cdot \frac{\Delta TU}{\Delta X}.$$

Dividing both sides of equation (2A–2) by $\Delta TU/\Delta Y$, we get

(2A–3)
$$\Delta Y = -\Delta X \cdot \frac{\left(\dfrac{\Delta TU}{\Delta X} \right)}{\left(\dfrac{\Delta TU}{\Delta Y} \right)}.$$

Finally, dividing both sides of equation (2A–3) by $-\Delta X$, we find

(2A–4)

$$-\frac{\Delta Y}{\Delta X} = \frac{\left(\dfrac{\Delta TU}{\Delta X}\right)}{\left(\dfrac{\Delta TU}{\Delta Y}\right)}.$$

The left-hand side of equation (2A–4) is equal to the *MRS* of Good *X* for Good *Y*. The right-hand side is equal to MU_X/MU_Y. Thus we have shown that

(2A–5)

$$MRS = -\frac{\Delta Y}{\Delta X} = \frac{MU_X}{MU_Y}.$$

If we think for a minute, equation (2A–5) makes a lot of sense. It states that the rate at which a consumer is just willing to trade Good *Y* for Good *X* is equal to the ratio of the marginal utility of Good *X* to that of Good *Y*. If the MU_X is 50 units and the MU_Y is 100, then the consumer would be willing to trade one unit of *Y* for two of *X*, or

$$MRS = \frac{1}{2} = \frac{MU_X}{MU_Y}.$$

Note that the consumer will give up less of the good with the higher marginal utility in exchange for the good with the lower marginal utility. In other words, the rate at which the consumer will trade Good *Y* for Good *X* *varies inversely* with the ratio of the marginal utility of *Y* to the marginal utility of *X*. Thus,

$$MRS = (-1)\frac{\Delta Y}{\Delta X} = \frac{MU_X}{MU_Y}, \; not \; \frac{MU_Y}{MU_X}.$$

CONSUMER EQUILIBRIUM

A consumer will maximize his or her satisfaction by allocating purchases in order to be on the highest indifference curve possible given the budget available. In Figure 2A–2 we see three indifference curves: I_1, I_2, and I_3. A consumer's budget line, denoted by $Y'X'$, is also drawn.

We can derive the equation for the consumer's budget line as follows. First assume that our consumer has B_0 dollars to spend on goods *X* and *Y*. Then the maximum amount that the consumer can spend on each good is given by

(2A–6)

$$P_Y \cdot Y + P_X \cdot X = B_0,$$

where

Figure 2A–2   Consumer Equilibrium

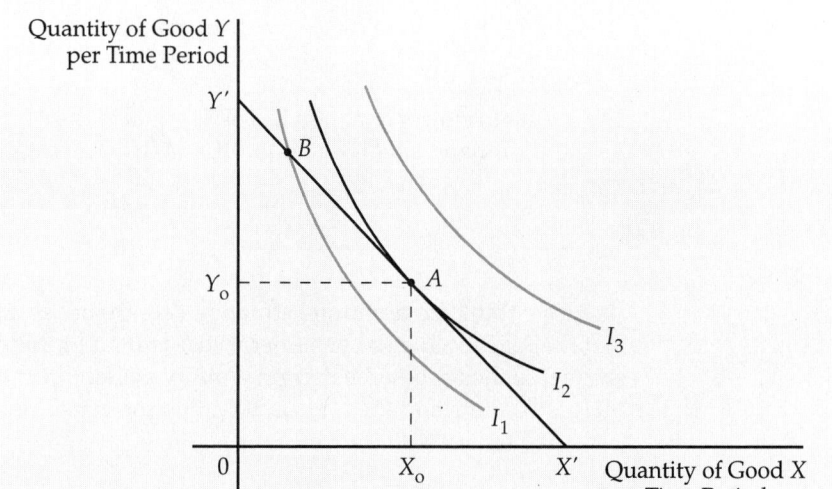

P_Y = the price of Good Y,
Y = the quantity purchased of Good Y,
P_X = the price of Good X, and
X = the quantity purchased of Good X.

Equation (2A–6) states that the price of Good Y multiplied by the quantity purchased of Good Y plus the price of Good X multiplied by the quantity purchased of Good X is equal to B_o.

To get equation (2A–6) in a form where it can be graphed easily, as in Figure 2A–2, we first subtract $P_X \cdot X$ from both sides of the equation, obtaining

(2A–7)
$$P_Y \cdot Y = B_o - P_X \cdot X.$$

Now, dividing both sides of this equation by P_Y, we get

(2A–8)
$$Y = \frac{B_o}{P_Y} - \frac{P_X}{P_Y} \cdot X.$$

Equation (2A–8) is in the familiar linear form of $Y = a + bX$. The Y-axis intercept, Y' in Figure 2A–2, is equal to B_o/P_Y. That is the number of units of Y that can be purchased if the consumer's entire budget is spent on Good Y. Similarly, the X-axis intercept, X' in Figure 2A–2, is given by B_o/P_X.

The slope of the consumer's budget line is equal to $-P_X/P_Y$. In other words, the rate at which a consumer can trade off spending on one good for spending on another is given by the ratio of their prices. More specifically, $\Delta Y/\Delta X$ along the budget line is equal to $-P_X/P_Y$.

As we can see from Figure 2A–2, the consumer will maximize his or her satisfaction at point A, on indifference curve I_2, by purchasing Y_0 units of Y and X_0 units of X. At this point, indifference curve I_2 is just tangent to the consumer's budget line.

Our consumer could, of course, manage to spend the entire budget by purchasing the quantities of Goods X and Y denoted by point B on indifference curve I_1. However, I_1 represents a lower level of utility than does I_2, so the consumer could do better than this point. On the other hand, no points on indifference curves higher than I_2 can be achieved with this budget. Consequently, this consumer will find that utility is maximized at point A, given the budget line.

Since the consumer's budget line must be tangent to the relevant indifference curve at the utility-maximizing point, the slope of the budget line and the slope of the indifference curve must be equal at that point. We just found the slope of the budget line to be $-P_X/P_Y$. The slope of the indifference curve is equal to $(-1) MRS = -MU_X/MU_Y$. Thus the consumer will maximize his or her satisfaction only if

(2A–9)
$$-\frac{P_X}{P_Y} = -\frac{MU_X}{MU_Y}.$$

We can easily show that equation (2A–9) is equivalent to the utility-maximizing rule developed with the cardinal utility approach. First, we multiply both sides of equation (2A–9) by $-MU_Y$ to find

(2A–10)
$$\frac{MU_Y}{P_Y} \cdot P_X = MU_X.$$

If we now divide both sides of equation (2A–10) by P_X we obtain our earlier utility-maximizing condition:

$$\frac{MU_Y}{P_Y} = \frac{MU_X}{P_X}.$$

DERIVING A DEMAND CURVE

We now need go only one short step further to derive a consumer's demand curve for a product. This process is illustrated in Figure 2A–3, which shows two budget lines for Jim Roberts, who is dividing his lunch-money budget be-

Figure 2A–3   Effect of a Price Change

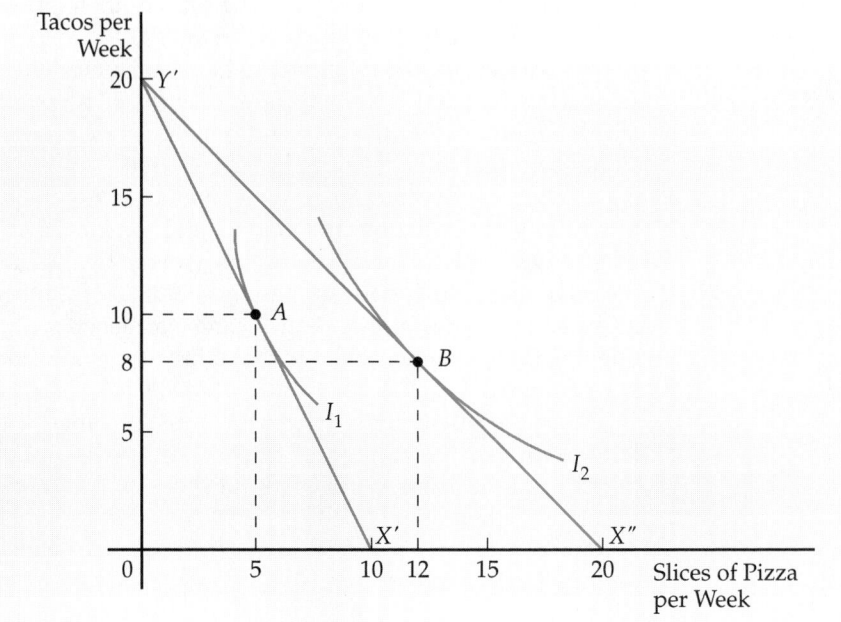

tween fajita tacos and slices of pizza. He can get either one *a la carte* at a shopping mall where he works. Initially, the price of a taco is $1, the price of a slice of thick, Sicilian pizza is $2, and Roberts has $20 a week to spend on lunches. (He drinks water for free.) This relationship is depicted by budget line $Y'X'$. With these prices and a budget of $20, Roberts will maximize his satisfaction at point A by purchasing ten tacos and five slices of pizza.

Suppose that the price of pizza falls to $1. The new budget will now be given by $Y'X''$. At the new price Roberts can now buy 20 rather than 10 slices of pizza if he spends all of his money on pizza. However, if he spends all of his budget on tacos, he can buy only the same number as before (20). With the new, lower price for pizza, Roberts will maximize his satisfaction by purchasing eight tacos and twelve slices of pizza, as shown in Figure 2A–3 at point B. As depicted in Figure 2A–4, we now have two points on Roberts's demand curve for pizza, given that the prices of other products and his budget in dollar terms remain the same. At a price of $2 Roberts will purchase five slices of pizza per week, whereas at a price of $1 he will purchase twelve slices of pizza per week.

We can separate the effect of the price change on the quantity purchased of pizzas into two parts: the (real) income effect and the substitution effect.

Figure 2A–4   Demand Curve for Pizzas

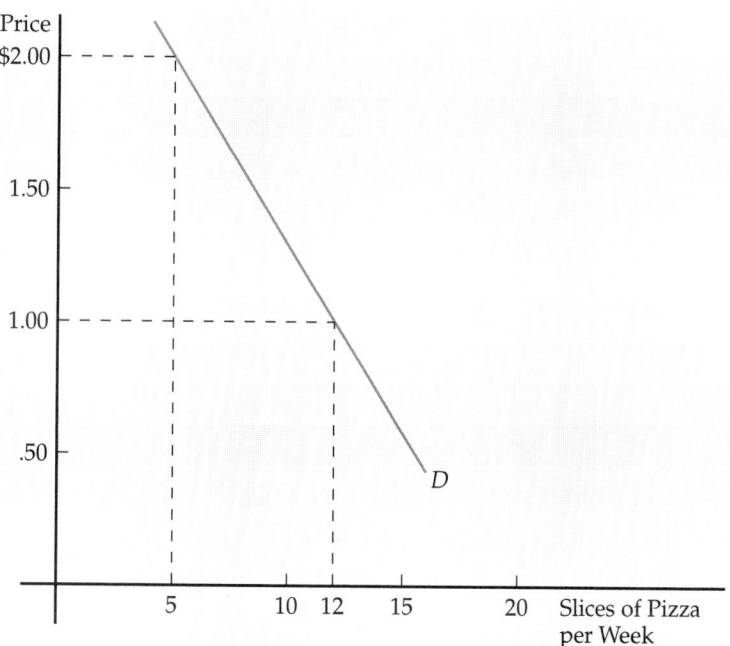

The *income effect* occurs because if the price of a good or service purchased by a consumer changes, it has an effect on the consumer's real budget or income—what that dollar budget can purchase. In Roberts's case, when the price of a slice of pizza falls, his real income rises (by $1 times the five slices of pizza he previously purchased). He can now buy ten slices of pizza for the same amount of money as he paid for five slices at a price of $2. The *substitution effect* occurs because the price of a slice of pizza is cheaper relative to the price of a taco than it was before.

Figure 2A–5 shows how the price effect can be separated graphically into the two parts. Lines $Y'X'$ and $Y'X''$ are the two budget lines from Figure 2A–3. Initially, Roberts purchases ten tacos and five slices of pizza per week, as shown at point A. After the decrease in the price of pizza, Roberts purchases eight tacos and twelve slices of pizza per week, at point B. Line RS is drawn parallel to the new budget line, $Y'X''$, but tangent to the original indifference curve, I_1. Consequently, line RS has the same price ratio (its slope) as the new budget line, but it allows the consumer to achieve only the same level of satisfaction as before the price decline. In this sense, budget line RS keeps the consumer's real income constant.

Figure 2A–5   Income and Substitution Effects

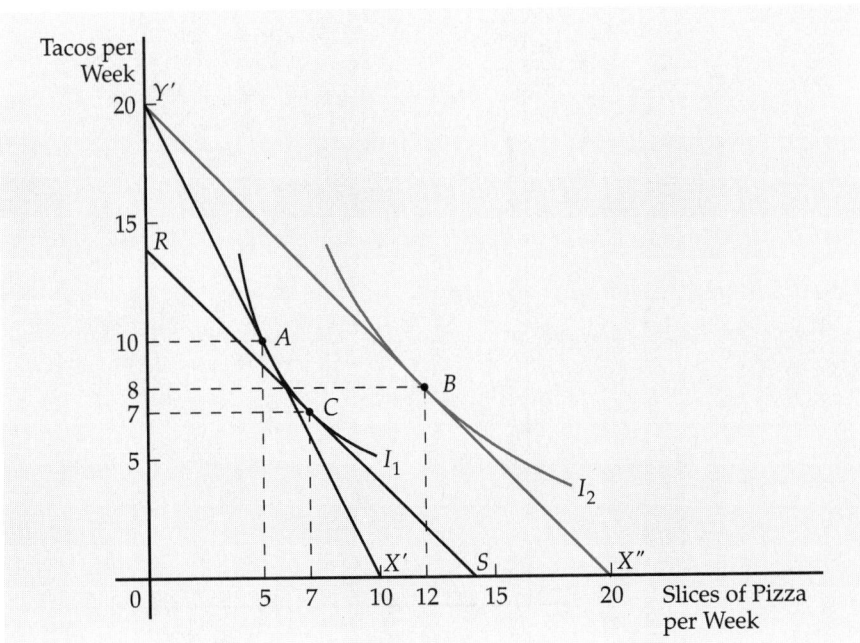

With budget line RS, Roberts will maximize his satisfaction by purchasing seven tacos and seven slices of pizza per week, at point C. The decrease by three units in the number of tacos purchased and the two-slice increase in the quantity of pizza purchased between points A and C show the substitution effect at work. The price ratio of the two goods has changed, but real income has remained constant.

The movement from point C to point B shows the income effect at work. The increase in real income Roberts experiences as a result of the fall in the price of pizza results in his purchasing five additional slices of pizza and one additional taco over what his position would be allowing for the substitution effect alone.

The substitution effect is always negative. That is, an increase in the price of a good or service relative to the prices of other products will always have a negative impact on our purchases of it. The opposite effect happens for a price decrease. The income effect may be either positive or negative, depending on whether a product is a normal or inferior good. In the preceding case, both tacos and pizza are normal goods.

3

TOPICS IN DEMAND ANALYSIS AND ESTIMATION

The primary objective of this chapter is to deal with the question of how the firm's managers can obtain information sufficient to put into operation the demand concepts we will repeatedly utilize in our discussions of revenue, profit maximization, and product markets. Obviously, *the more closely the firm can estimate demand conditions for its product, the more likely it is to determine correctly its profit-maximizing rate of output and price, or whether to produce a particular product at all.* The importance of accurate demand estimation is underscored by the results of a study that examined sales forecasts for 63 start-up computer software firms. The survey found that 43 percent of the companies' estimates of first-year sales were off by at least 30 percent; 77 percent of the companies' estimates were incorrect by at least 10 percent. On the average, the companies *overestimated* their first-year sales by 28 percent.

While the companies spent an average of $38,000 on demand estimation, the amount that they spent on these estimates had little relationship with the accuracy of the forecast. However, the accuracy of the forecasts did have a close relationship with how important firm owners *thought* it was to have accurate sales forecasts.[1] Ironically, an otherwise unnecessary business failure is likely to be the result of this lack of concern on the part of new firm owners.

Even well-established businesses have problems estimating the demand for their product or products. For example, RCA introduced its SelectaVision videodisc (CED) player in 1981. This machine had absorbed 15 years and $150 million in development costs. In 1984, RCA stopped production of the CED player after losses of $580 million. The company overestimated the demand for its players in the first few years after they were introduced because it did not foresee how rapidly the prices of videocassette recorders would fall during that period and the extent of consumer loyalty to the VCRs. Ironically, RCA finally abandoned the players just as their sales were rapidly increasing. Firm officials decided that sales would not grow sufficiently to make contin-

---

1 "Sales Projections: Facts or Wishful Thinking?" *The Wall Street Journal*, July 2, 1989, p. B3.

ued production of the players profitable.[2] That decision may have been RCA's second mistake, since the sales of videodiscs also fell dramatically when production of the players stopped. Over a longer time horizon, the combined production of players and discs may have become quite profitable.

Another example of incorrect market analysis is afforded by Ford Motor Company, which lost $250 million during the three years that it produced the Edsel. The Cadillac Allanté was abandoned by General Motors. In the 1980s, U.S. auto makers were still having trouble competing with cars made by foreign companies. However, by the early 1990s, the Japanese automakers were scrambling to regain market share in the United States.[3]

Even "Big Blue" (International Business Machines) is not immune to marketing blunders. Although IBM spent $40 million on the promotion alone of its home computer, PCjr, production of the PCjr was discontinued only slightly more than a year after it was introduced in late 1983. Sophisticated users were turned off by its limited capabilities, and casual consumers were unhappy with its relatively high price compared with the prices of other home computers.[4]

The extent to which demand is *actually analyzed* varies greatly from firm to firm. One reason for this is market structure. (Firms that are perfectly competitive are unlikely to view demand estimation as a very significant activity since they do not have a sufficient market share to significantly affect the market price of their product.) Another reason is lack of expertise or lack of the resources to obtain such expertise.

Thus demand estimation by firms runs the gamut from rough, rule-of-thumb decision making and "educated guesses" to the development of complicated econometric models relating a large number of variables to the quantity demanded of a given product. Nevertheless, more and more companies are investing substantial amounts of money as they move to "database marketing"—an approach to demand management that involves the use of computers to construct and analyze extensive data sets regarding customer characteristics.[5] We will begin with a discussion of market surveys and then consider statistical estimation of demand functions and techniques for the generation of market data.

2 See "Pioneer Electronics Videodisk Business Grows in Consumer Area That RCA Quit," *The Wall Street Journal*, January 9, 1985, p. 6; "CBS Will End Its Production of Videodisks," *The Wall Street Journal*, July 10, 1984, p. 8; "Slipped Disc," *Time* (April 16, 1984), p. 47; and "RCA's Rivals Still See Life in Videodiscs," *Business Week* (April 23, 1984), pp. 88–90.
3 See "A Car is Born," *Business Week* (September 13, 1993), pp. 64–72; "While Toyota Loses Its Hold . . . ," *Business Week* (April 26, 1993), pp. 28–29; "Will Japan Do to Europe What It Did to Detroit?" *Business Week* (May 7, 1990), pp. 52–53; "Motor City Madness," *Business Week* (March 6, 1989), pp. 22–23; "Ford Offers New Incentives to Spur Sales," *The Wall Street Journal*, March 30, 1989, p. B1; "Why Detroit Is Still Hooked on Sales Gimmicks," *Business Week* (May 19, 1986), p. 50; and "A Gallery of Goofs," *Time* (July 22, 1985), p. 51.
4 "Flops," *Business Week* (August 16, 1993), pp. 76–82; and "How IBM Made 'Junior' an Underachiever," *Business Week* (June 25, 1984), pp. 106–107.
5 "Database Management," *Business Week* (September 5, 1994), pp. 56–62.

MARKET SURVEYS

Many larger firms are able to allocate a substantial portion of resources and managerial effort to the task of demand analysis. More complicated demand functions involving variables other than price can be estimated from market data, and surveys or experiments can be undertaken to obtain a profile of consumer preferences. Generally, management can place a good deal more confidence in the results of a well-designed market experiment than in the results of a survey (that is, a questionnaire either filled out by respondents or administered by an interviewer), since the former provides information on how consumers actually react to certain changes, while the latter tells only how consumers *think* they will react *if* certain changes take place.

Surveys *can* be quite useful when questionnaires do not call for very fine discrimination by the respondents. For example, one might successfully survey consumer preferences regarding small cars versus large cars, since consumers may be able to differentiate easily between the two. However, it might be much more difficult for a consumer to determine whether a reduction in price of, say, 3 percent would be a sufficient incentive to buy a car this year instead of waiting until next year.

In addition to being limited in terms of what kind of information can be determined, large-scale market surveys can be quite expensive. Some years ago, for example, Clairol, Inc., undertook a consumer survey related to four of its hair-care products. The approach used combined advertising of the products with a mail questionnaire and a sweepstakes.[6] In other words, attention was drawn to the products in the *process* of administering the survey.

To conduct the survey, Clairol had to stand the expense of five full pages of color advertisements in each of four nationally circulated women's magazines, as well as $22,000 in sweepstakes prizes for respondents and all promotional and research expenses. (However, we should note that the purposes of the survey were probably dual: to advertise four of Clairol's products *and* to sample consumer preferences.)

Only three questions were asked about each product, and all of the questions related to product differentiation rather than to price. *Example:* Why do you think Nice 'n Easy sells the most?

1. It leaves hair looking natural.
2. It leaves hair looking healthy.
3. It's easy to use; you just shampoo it in.

To the extent that customers participated in the survey, Clairol saved the cost of a stamp per response by having its respondents supply their own postage stamps on the mail-back questionnaires. However, management also

---

6 See *Family Circle* (February 1977), pp. 1–4.

obviously believed that the sweepstakes prizes were necessary to get a large number of responses.

It is clear that small businesses cannot undertake such ambitious campaigns as Clairol did to measure subjective perceptions of product traits. Nor is it necessary, as historical market data or data from smaller-scale market surveys or experiments can be utilized. Using some form of statistical analysis, small businesses, as well as Clairol's researchers, could examine the data that they obtained. We discuss one type of statistical technique, *linear regression analysis*, in the following section.

DEMAND ESTIMATION WITH REGRESSION ANALYSIS

Regression analysis is a statistical technique used to "fit" an equation to empirical data in order to estimate the relationship between a dependent variable and one or more independent variables. In demand estimation, when regression analysis is employed, the dependent variable is the quantity of some product purchased or sold per unit of time; and the independent variables usually include such items as price of the product, prices of related goods (substitutes or complements), consumer income, advertising expenditure, and credit terms. The regression equation is usually linear or log-linear (a form in which the natural logarithm of the dependent variable is usually a linear function of the logs of the independent variables).[7] If there is more than one independent variable, the equation-fitting technique is called *multiple regression*.

Figure 3–1 provides a simple vehicle for explaining what regression analysis does. Suppose the quantity of frozen bagels sold is envisioned to be affected solely by the price of the bagels. In order to estimate monthly demand, we obtain data from a group of supermarkets (of about the same size and located in similar neighborhoods) over a period of time short enough so that any other factors that might affect bagel purchases will remain constant.

The points labeled Y_1, Y_2, etc., in panel (a) of Figure 3–1 represent the price-quantity observations we obtained from the data on supermarket sales of bagels (each Y_i is a price-quantity sold combination that existed at some point in time in *one* of the supermarkets). Thus panel (a) of Figure 3–1 constitutes a scatter diagram of the relationship of the quantity of bagels sold to price per package of bagels. We can see that the set of points forms a kind of band that slopes downward to the right.

Using a linear regression model, a statistician can estimate a straight-line demand function, given a set of data points such as those in Figure 3–1, in a way that will ensure a statistical "best fit" to the scatter diagram. In panel (b)

---

7 We discuss natural logarithms in the appendix to this chapter.

Figure 3–1   Price and Quantity-Sold Observations and Corresponding Regression Line

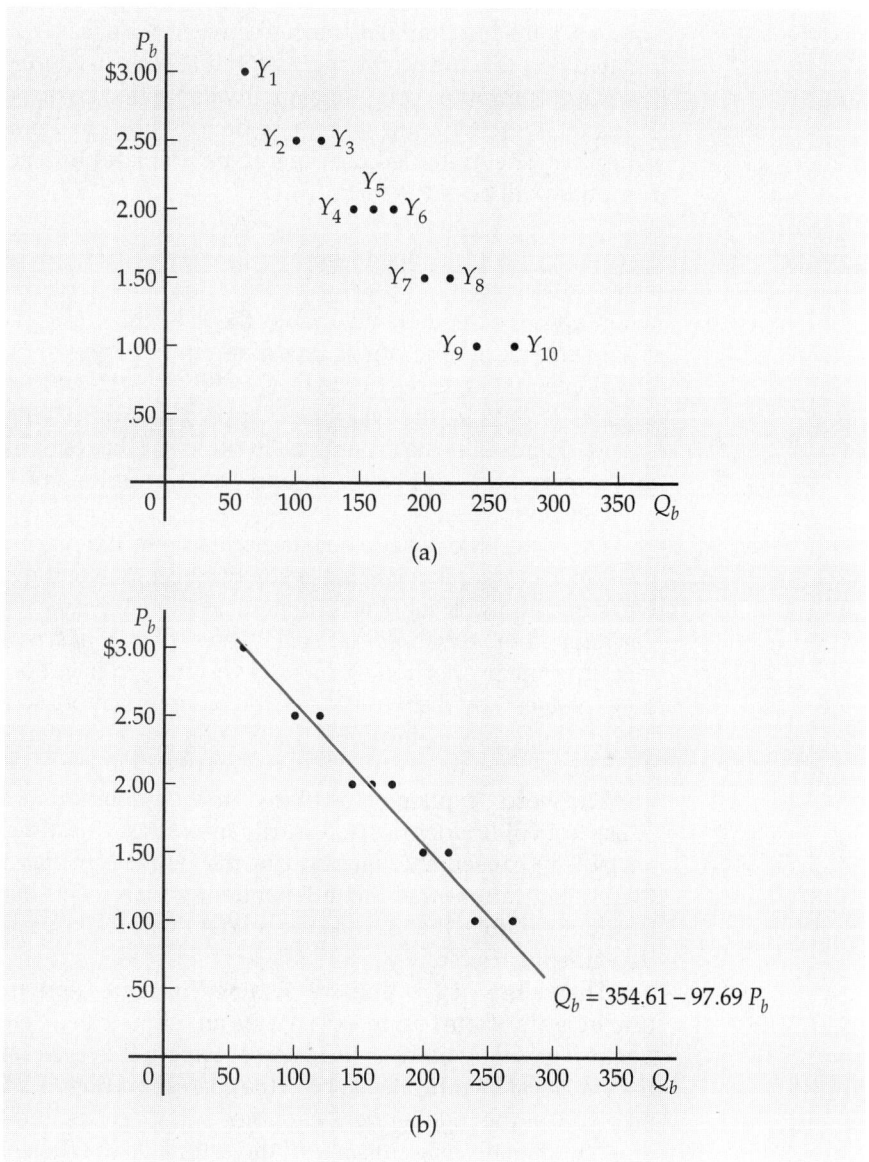

(a)

(b)

$$Q_b = 354.61 - 97.69\,P_b$$

In panel (a), data are plotted showing different prices charged for bagels and corresponding quantities sold by a firm. In panel (b), a regression equation, $Q_b = 354.61 - 97.69P_b$, has been estimated. This equation represents the best linear approximation of the relationship of quantity sold of bagels to bagel prices.

of Figure 3–1, the line drawn through the scatter diagram is a *regression line* representing the best linear approximation of the relationship of quantity sold of bagels to bagel prices. It is a best fit in the sense that the sum of the squares of the horizontal distances between the observed data points and estimated points lying on the regression line have been minimized.[8]

Many computer programs are available that perform the task of calculating the regression line when raw data on observed points are fed into the computer. The multiple linear regression demand function estimated by the computer will be of the form

$$Q_d = \alpha + \beta_1 X_1 + \beta_2 X_2 + \ldots + \beta_n X_n + \varepsilon,$$

where Q_d is the dependent variable, the X_i are the independent variables, and ε is an error term. For our scatter diagram in panel (b) of Figure 3–1, the regression equation turns out to be $Q_b = 354.61 - 97.69 P_b$, which, given the current set of data, is the best linear approximation of the demand curve for bagels. (Here, Q_b is the number of 16-ounce packages of bagels sold per week in a supermarket of given size and characteristics, and P_b is the price of a package in dollars.)

The closer the observed data points lie to the regression line, the more confidence we can have in the predictive accuracy of the regression model. A measure of how closely the estimated relationship reflects or accounts for the variation in the observed data is R^2, the *coefficient of determination*. Briefly, R^2 measures the proportion of the total variation in the dependent variable that is "explained" by the variation of the independent variable(s). For our bagel model, the R^2 of 0.97 indicates that 97 percent of the variation in bagel quantity sold is "explained" by the variation of bagel prices.

The word "explained" is placed inside quotation marks because a large (close to 1.00) R^2 does not necessarily mean that variation in the independent variable(s) caused the variation in the dependent variable. Large R^2s are merely indications that the independent variables are *correlated* with the dependent variable; that is, the independent variables "vary together" with the dependent variable.

The values of R^2s that are obtained in regression analysis vary widely (theoretically, from 0.00 to 1.00). When an estimate of a demand function using linear regression analysis has been obtained, it is then important to analyze the statistical significance of both the corresponding R^2 and the estimated coefficients of the independent variables and, perhaps, the constant term.

The statistical significance of the estimated coefficients as well as the estimated constant term are tested by calculating a t statistic. The t statistic to

---

8 The *horizontal* distances are minimized because we are placing the *dependent* variable, Q_b, on the horizontal axis, as is customarily done for demand functions in economics.

test whether an estimated coefficient, b, is statistically significantly different from some hypothesized value for the true coefficient, β, is calculated with the following formula:

$$t = \frac{b - \beta}{\hat{\sigma}_b}.$$

The statistical significance of the calculated value for t is then checked by using a table showing the probabilities associated with different values of t. These topics are discussed more carefully in the appendix to this chapter.

One needs a course in advanced statistics to understand thoroughly the regression model and to learn how to interpret the obtained results. Nevertheless, the manager of a firm is often able to hire the expertise necessary to perform a statistical demand analysis and to establish a degree of confidence in its predictions. The cost of such a study can be quite small if the manager has kept accurate records of the relevant data. Furthermore, without too much effort, the manager can learn enough about statistics to be able to communicate with such experts and to utilize effectively the results of their analyses in making pricing and output decisions. We turn now to some actual cases of demand estimation utilizing regression analysis.

Examples of Regression Studies

It is difficult to obtain regression studies of demand that have been prepared by private firms, because firms generally avoid making public any information that might prove useful to competitors. Moreover, it is only on rare occasions that small firms will engage the expertise necessary to execute a soundly constructed regression analysis of demand. Because of such limitations, available studies tend to deal with product demand at fairly high levels of aggregation. Nevertheless, we shall discuss three such studies in the following pages.

Chow: The Demand for Automobiles

The demand for automobiles in the United States has been examined numerous times. A classic regression analysis is that done by Gregory Chow and published in 1960.[9] Chow's estimated automobile demand function is

$$X_t = -0.7247 - 0.048802P_t + 0.025487I_{e_t},$$

---

9 See G. C. Chow, "Statistical Demand Function for Automobiles and Their Use for Forecasting," *The Demand for Durable Goods*, edited by A. C. Harberger (Chicago: University of Chicago Press, 1960), p. 158.

where

X_t = The per-capita stock of automobiles at the end of time period
    t given in hundredths of a unit,

P_t = an automobile price index, and

I_{e_t} = expected per-capita income.

The R^2 for Chow's equation is 0.895.

Since the coefficient of P_t is negative while that of I_{e_t} is positive, the equation indicates that an increase in automobile prices will reduce X_t, whereas an increase in expected income will increase X_t—which is as we would expect. As we learned in Chapter 2, it is possible from Chow's equation to calculate price and income elasticities of demand for *car ownership* when P_t and I_{e_t} are specified.[10] For the year 1960, Chow computed these elasticities to be about −0.6 and + 1.5, respectively. Thus Chow's study supports the hypothesis that auto sales are much more likely to respond to increases in expected consumer income than to price reductions. Subsequent studies, some a good deal more complicated than Chow's, tend to support his results.[11] The generally low price elasticities may explain auto makers' past reluctance to reduce list prices, even though they have been known to offer sizable rebates when caught with large inventories in periods of declining expected real consumer incomes. (The rebates and other incentives offered consumers during the 1980s and early 1990s are a case in point.)[12]

In a more recent study involving the automobile industry, Carlson and Umble estimated the following demand function:

$$D_t^i = \beta_0 + \beta_1 Y_t^D + \beta_2 P_t^i + \beta_3 G_t + \beta_4 Z_t^E + \beta_5 Z_t + \varepsilon_t,$$

10 For example, if P_t = 120.0, and I_{e_t} is $600, then

$$X_t = -0.7247 - 0.048802(120.0) + 0.025487(600) = 8.71126.$$

Thus

$$E_p = (\partial X_t / \partial P_t) \times (P_t / X_t) = -0.048802\,(120.0/8.71126) = -0.672261,$$

or approximately −0.67.

Also,

$$E_I = (\partial X_t / \partial I_{e_t}) \times (I_{e_t} / X_t) = 0.025487\,(600/8.71126) = 1.755452,$$

or approximately +1.76. Chow estimates that the price and income elasticities of demand for *new cars* are −1.2 and +3.0, respectively.

11 For example, see H. F. Gallasch, Jr., "Elasticities of Demand for New Automobiles," Societal Analysis Department, Research Laboratories, General Motors Corporation, Warren, Michigan (May 21, 1976). However, Gallasch obtained estimates of price elasticity of demand between −1.6 and −1.3 and of income elasticity of demand of +1.0.

12 See Joseph B. White, "Stumbling Auto Makers Face Tough '91," *The Wall Street Journal*, January 7, 1991, p. B1; "Motor City Madness," *Business Week* (March 6, 1989), pp. 22–23; and "Detroit's Sad New Year," *Newsweek* (February 15, 1982), p. 68.

where

D^i = the demand for car of size i;

Y^D = real (adjusted for inflation or deflation in the economy) disposable income, seasonally adjusted and adjusted for population size;

P^i = the average car price (adjusted for general inflation or deflation in the economy) for size i;

G = gasoline price (not adjusted for general price changes);

Z^E = a dummy variable to indicate periods of gasoline shortages;

Z = a dummy variable to indicate United Auto Worker strikes; and

ε = an error term.[13]

Carlson and Umble found that of the independent variables, disposable income appeared to have the greatest impact on the demand for automobiles. The coefficient of the automobile price variable was also statistically significantly different from zero, with the expected negative sign. The coefficient of the gasoline price variable was statistically significant and positive in the estimated demand equations for subcompact and compact cars, significant and negative in the equation for standard full-size cars, and not significantly different from zero in the equation for luxury cars. The coefficient of the variable for gasoline shortages was statistically significant and positive in the estimated equation for subcompact cars, not significantly different from zero in the equation for compact cars, and significant and negative in the equations for the other models.

Harp and Miller: The Demand for a New Convenience Food

Regression analysis can also be applied to the estimation of demand for a new product. The easiest way to approach this problem is to examine data for goods that are close substitutes for the new product in question. Since only about 10 percent of new products introduced survive one year, it is important for firms to have an estimate of the potential demand for a new product.[14] In research done under the auspices of the U.S. Department of Agriculture, H. H. Harp and M. Miller provide a regression equation that is an estimate of the demand function for a new convenience food.[15] The Harp and Miller equa-

13 See Rodney L. Carlson and M. Michael Umble, "Statistical Demand Functions for Automobiles and Their Use in Forecasting in an Energy Crisis," *Journal of Business* Vol. LIII (April 1980), pp. 193–204.

14 See H. H. Harp and M. Miller, "Convenience Foods: The Relationship Between Sales Volume and Factors Influencing Demand," *Agricultural Economic Report No. 81*, Economic Research Service, U.S. Department of Agriculture, revised October 1965.

15 Ibid.

tion is in log form and relates annual sales in 100 million serving units of product to nine independent variables. The equation is

$$\log Y = -0.6 - 0.60 \, (\log X_1)^2 - 0.85 \log X_2$$
$$+ \, 0.28 \, (\log X_3)^2 + 0.31 \log X_4$$
$$+ \, 0.65 \log X_5 - 0.16 \, (\log X_5)^2$$
$$+ \, 0.44 \log X_6 + 0.23 \log X_7$$
$$- \, 0.58X_8 + 0.33X_9,$$

where the variables are defined in the following manner:

Y = sales in units of 100 million servings,
X_1 = cents per serving of convenience foods,
X_2 = percentage market share of convenience foods that are close substitutes for the new one,
X_3 = cents per serving of fresh or home-prepared foods,
X_4 = cents per serving of highest volume near-substitute convenience food,
X_5 = importance of convenience food group in question in the consumer purchase pattern,
X_6 = index of availability in supermarkets,
X_7 = sales of highest volume competing good, and
X_8, X_9 = dummy variables to adjust for unusually high or low predicted sales.

In the Harp and Miller equation, the *coefficients* of the independent variables (such as X_2, X_4, X_6, and X_7), which are expressed in log form and are not squared, give estimates of their respective elasticities of demand. In other words, when the dependent variable and the independent variables are in log form, a *constant* elasticity of demand is estimated for each of the independent variables.[16] Since variables X_3 and X_4 refer to the cost of substitutes for the new convenience food, the positive values of the estimated coefficients of the terms involving those variables support our expectations that they would

---

16 For example, suppose we have a hypothesized demand function,

$$Q_d = \alpha X_1^{\beta_1} X_2^{\beta_2},$$

which in natural log form is

$$\log Q_d = \log \alpha + \beta_1 \log X_1 + \beta_2 \log X_2.$$

The estimated β_i values give us estimates of the elasticity of demand with respect to X_1 and X_2, respectively.

have positive cross price elasticities of demand. Variables X_1 and X_2, respectively, relate to the cost of the new convenience food and the market share of competing foods. As we would expect, we find that the estimated coefficients of the terms involving those variables are negative, indicating negative elasticities of demand with respect to X_1 and X_2.

Regression analysis is a powerful tool on which a large proportion of market research studies are based. If sufficient data can be obtained without unreasonable expense, a firm's management might be wise to undertake demand estimation using the regression approach whenever it is uncertain about the demand and revenue situation it faces. However, the regression model and its results must be carefully examined to ensure that the functional relationship specified is one that constitutes a reasonable depiction of the actual demand situation.

Since, as was stated earlier, variables that are related statistically do not necessarily have a cause-effect relationship to one another, management must always be careful in its use of statistically estimated demand functions. Moreover, important variables may have been excluded. In the Harp and Miller study, for example, an R^2 of 0.87 was obtained for the regression equation stated previously. However, the authors cautioned that their model is limited by the exclusion of three variables—product quality, brand promotion (advertising), and product life cycle.

Wilson: The Demand for Electricity

An example of an estimated demand function that has an unclear interpretation is the following:

$$Q = 21{,}737 - 1{,}178P + 144G - 1.370Y + 47.9R + 0.069C,$$

To see why this is so, recall that the elasticity of demand with respect to variable Z is given by

$$E_z = \frac{\partial Q_d}{\partial Z} \cdot \frac{Z}{Q_d}.$$

If we examine the elasticity of demand with respect to X_1, we find

$$\frac{\partial Q_d}{\partial X_1} = \alpha \beta_1 X_1^{\beta_1 - 1} X_2^{\beta_2}, \text{ and}$$

$$E_{X_1} = \alpha \beta_1 X_1^{\beta_1 - 1} X_2^{\beta_2} \cdot \frac{X_1}{Q_d}$$

$$= \alpha \beta_1 X_1^{\beta_1 - 1} X_2^{\beta_2} \cdot \frac{X_1}{\alpha X_1^{\beta_1} X_2^{\beta_2}}$$

$$= \beta_1, \text{ since } X_1^{\beta_1 - 1} \text{ times } X_1 = X_1^{\beta_1}.$$

where

Q = quantity of electricity demanded by households,
P = Federal Power Commission's computed typical bill for 500 kilowatt-hours in the corresponding (to the household) city,
G = price of natural gas in cents per therm,
Y = median annual family income,
R = average number of rooms per housing unit, and
C = number of degree days.[17]

As we would expect, the coefficient of the price variable is negative, which indicates negative price elasticity of demand. The coefficient of the gas price variable is positive, which indicates both a positive cross price elasticity of demand and that gas and electricity are substitutes, which is also as we would expect.

However, the sign of the income variable coefficient is *negative*, which indicates a negative income elasticity of demand and implies that as incomes rise, people use *less* electricity. While it seems realistic to hypothesize that the income elasticity of demand is quite small (at least at high income levels), it is difficult to think of a reason why it should be negative. The problem may be the way in which the study was set up—it covered a cross section of 77 cities during one time period. It is possible that the negative income elasticity coefficient resulted because many of the higher income households were in areas where a large percentage of homes were heated by natural gas rather than by electricity.

Also, the coefficient of the house size variable was not significantly different from zero at the 10 percent level of statistical significance (those of the other variables were significant). The R^2 was only .52. Thus the researcher in this case perhaps should have tried to change the estimated demand function to see if a regression relationship could be obtained without the problems mentioned previously. For example, a variable could be added that would indicate whether or not most homes in a particular area were heated with gas or electricity. Such matters are discussed in greater detail in the appendix to this chapter.

MARKET EXPERIMENTS

Where there is uncertainty about product demand and the data required to perform a regression analysis are not available, it may be possible or desirable to conduct a market experiment that will generate such data. In a market ex-

---

17 John W. Wilson, "Residential Demand for Electricity," *Quarterly Review of Economics and Business* Vol. 11 (Spring 1971), pp. 7–22.

periment, those variables that are anticipated to be determinants of the quantity sold of a product are changed by the seller. For example, if management believes the quantity of its product that can be sold is primarily a function of price and advertising, it can adjust (change) these two variables over a certain period of time or across different markets and study the relationship of these variables to quantity sold.

Market experiments, although useful, are inherently risky and expensive. For example, an experiment in which price is increased could lead to both a temporary reduction in revenues and a permanent loss of customers to rival firms. If the experiment includes increases in advertising, additional costs will be incurred. Another problem is that there are almost always some relevant variables that the experimenters cannot control (income, tastes, and prices of related goods). Finally, because of their expense, the size and duration of market experiments are usually limited; therefore such experiments may not generate a sufficiently large number of observations to allow much confidence in their results.

An example of the pitfalls of market experiments is provided by the introduction of "no-frills" fares in the airline industry during 1975.[18] At the request of National Airlines, the Civil Aeronautics Board (CAB) permitted experimentation with discount fares (reductions of up to 35 percent) on selected routes for a period of about 10 weeks. National's competitors on the routes, Eastern Airlines and Delta Airlines, also were allowed to try out the lower fares, although they were opposed to the experiment.

When the experiment was over, National claimed to have exhaustively studied the effects of the fares on passenger traffic (quantity sold) and revenues, and its experts concluded that both the number of passengers and the sales revenues on the routes increased substantially because of the lower fares. While National claimed the thrift fares increased its revenue by $4 million over the trial period, Eastern and Delta claimed that their revenues fell (Eastern by over $500,000). Moreover, National engaged in a vigorous advertising campaign emphasizing the thrift fares. Thus the increases in traffic it experienced may well have been at the expense of the other two airlines, even though National claimed that 56 percent of the passengers it carried at thrift fares were new passengers who would not otherwise have flown.[19] However, National did decide to end the no-frills fares—at least with the 35 percent discount—in the spring of 1976.[20]

With CAB approval, the airlines continued experimenting with their fare structures in the late 1970s and early 1980s. On December 31, 1984, the CAB

18 "National Says 'No Frills' Air Fare Helps, but Eastern Counters that Loss Resulted," *The Wall Street Journal*, July 8, 1975, p. 7.
19 Ibid.
20 Todd E. Fandell, "National To End 'No-Frills' Fare: TWA Will File for 2% Domestic Increase," *The Wall Street Journal*, March 22, 1976, p. 2.

completely lost its power to control routes and fares as provided for in the Airline Deregulation Act of 1978.[21]

Since that time there has been a great deal of competition among the airlines with respect to fares as well as other promotional items, including frequent-flyer bonuses and discounts on hotels and car rentals. New airlines entered the industry, but a significant number of companies have declared bankruptcy. Some of the remaining airlines are having trouble making a profit.[22] However, in recent years the airline industry has become more consolidated as airlines have either gone out of business or merged with other airlines, and ticket prices have started to increase again. Although fare sales still occur, the prices on which the percent discounts are offered are higher, so that the sale prices are not as low as in earlier years.[23] Moreover, with the help of computers, airlines are able to track travel patterns more closely now than in the past. As a result, companies receive quicker feedback on their pricing experiments and are better able to design their fare structures to fit the market.[24] Still, it is interesting how history repeats itself: in the fall of 1996, Delta began a discount service targeting the Florida market.[25]

---

21 See "The CAB Flies into the Sunset Today," *The Wall Street Journal*, December 31, 1984, p. 8; and "CAB Flies into the Sunset, 'Closed Forever,' " *San Antonio Express News*, January 1, 1985, p. 1-C.

22 See, for example, "Fast Growth Lands Low-Cost Airline in Trouble," *The Wall Street Journal*, September 10, 1996, pp. B1, B4; "Piloted by Bethune, Continental Air Lifts Its Workers' Morale," *The Wall Street Journal*, May 15, 1996, pp. A1, A8; "Up, Up, and Away—Again," *Business Week* (April 22, 1996), p. 40; "USAir's European Squeeze Play," *Business Week* (September 2, 1996), pp. 62–63; "Conditions Are Ideal For Starting an Airline And Many Are Doing It," *The Wall Street Journal*, April 1, 1996, pp. A1, A5; "Takeoff Is Bumpy for Start-Up Airlines as They Try to Grab a Piece of the Sky," *The Wall Street Journal*, July 1, 1993, pp. B1, B11; "Behind the Rise and Fall of Air Florida," *Business Week* (July 23, 1984), pp. 122–125; and "Earning Wings the Hard Way," *Time* (February 3, 1986), p. 56. Pan Am and Eastern have ceased operations, although it appears that Pan Am may be resurrected in some form. See "Pan Am to Fly on Low-Cost Strategy," *San Antonio Express-News*, January 31, 1996, p. 1E; "Pan Am Ceases Operations, Race Opens to Get Its Valuable Latin American Routes," *The Wall Street Journal*, December 5, 1991, p. A6; "Eastern: The Wings of Greed," *Business Week* (November 11, 1991), pp. 34–36.

23 See "Southwest Air Offers $25 One-Way Fare on Nonstop Flights, and Majors Follow," *The Wall Street Journal*, July 15, 1996, pp. A3, A4; "Air Fares Rise Under Restored Tax," *San Antonio Express-News*, September 8, 1996, p. 4K; "American Air Says Its Growth Will Trail That of Industry Because of Higher Costs," *The Wall Street Journal*, September 11, 1996, p. B6; "America West Announces Lower Fares to 11 Cities," *San Antonio Express-News*, September 5, 1996, pp. 1E, 3E; "One Sure Result of Airline Deregulation: Controversy About Its Impact on Fares," *The Wall Street Journal*, April 19, 1990, pp. B1, B4; and "Skies Are Deregulated, But Just Try Starting a Sizable New Airline," *The Wall Street Journal*, July 19, 1989, pp. A1, A8.

24 "Air Ticket-Pricing Gets Overhaul," *San Antonio Express-News*, April 8, 1991, p. 1-C; "Computers Permit Airlines to Use Scalpel to Cut Fares," *The Wall Street Journal*, February 2, 1987, p. 25; "Airlines Use a Scalpel to Cut Fares in the Latest Round of Price Wars," *The Wall Street Journal*, November 26, 1985, p. 31; and "Finding the Best Air-Travel Deal Gets Harder as Restrictions Grow," *The Wall Street Journal*, March 31, 1986, p. 21.

25 See "Delta Express or 'Delta Distress,' " *Business Week* (August 26, 1996), p. 31; and "Up, Up, and A Ways to Go," *Business Week* (September 16, 1996), p. 88.

MANAGERIAL PERSPECTIVE:

Peter Rabbit, Fatal Attraction, and Market Experiments

Recently, Waldenbooks, the largest bookseller in the United States, began a market experiment with certain books. Waldenbooks negotiated an agreement that in exchange for not returning certain unsold books to the publisher, it could initially purchase these books at cheaper-than-usual prices. To be included were some children's books such as *Peter Rabbit* and *The Wind In The Willows*, some former bestsellers such as *Eat to Succeed*, and some art books.

Waldenbooks planned to keep track of the time each of these books spent on the shelf in its stores. If a book was not sold within 60 days, its price would be lowered. If it remained unsold for 90 days, the price would be lowered again. After 120 days, the price might be lowered for a third time, depending on the original price of the book. The in-store location of a book would change as each price reduction was made; presumably it would be displayed more prominently as a sale or bargain book. Dara Tyson, senior manager for public relations and promotions at Waldenbooks, described the program as "very revolutionary. It represents value and spontaneous buying."

Although Waldenbooks recognized that the new policy might reduce profit margins on these books, it anticipated that volume—and, correspondingly, inventory—turnover would increase sufficiently so that there would be a net positive effect on total profit. Some competing bookstore owners predicted that the new plan would not work and offered such comments as "I don't think the public can be fooled," and "If they don't want to buy a book, they won't, regardless of the price."

The authors have not seen a report on the results of this particular experiment; however, they have noted the presence of "bargain" books at a number of bookstores in recent years.

Waldenbooks was not the only company engaged in market experiments. Movie studios such as Paramount were conducting market experiments with home videos. While Paramount was pricing videotapes of some hit movies, such as *Fatal Attraction*, at $89.95, it listed others—*Top Gun*, for example—at $26.95. Disney took a similar approach when it set the list prices of *Lady and the Tramp* and *Good Morning Vietnam* at $29.95. While Paramount sold 500,000 copies of *Fatal Attraction* the first three months after its release, Disney sold 2 million copies of *Good Morning Vietnam* in the *first month* after its release. Disney figured that it had to sell 1.6 million copies of the movie at the lower price for it to make a greater profit than at a price of $89.95. (However, the expected sales volume at a price of $89.95 was not specified.) By September 1988, customers had purchased 3 million copies of *Top Gun* and 3.2 million of *Lady and the Tramp. E.T.* was expected to be a sure winner at $24.95.

Still, deciding which movies will have a sufficiently high price elasticity of demand for the cheaper prices to be profitable is not always easy. According to Robert Klingsmith, president of Paramount's video division, "It should be highly repeatable family fare that has comedy, music or action-adventure. Heavy drama like *Fatal Attraction* isn't the kind of program you put on TV every Saturday night for family viewing."

References: "Waldenbooks to Cut Some Book Prices in Stages in Test of New Selling Tactic," *The Wall Street Journal*, March 29, 1988, p. 32; "Sales Can Soar, If the Price Is Right," *The Wall Street Journal*, September 23, 1988, p. 19. Also see "Movie Studios Produce Uneven Picture With Efforts to Win More Video Buyers," *The Wall Street Journal*, June 6, 1990, pp. B1, B4.

SUMMARY

Techniques of Demand Estimation

This chapter has examined several techniques of demand analysis and demand estimation. At the beginning of the chapter, we discussed *market surveys*, devices through which firms question customers about their preferences or their probable reaction to certain changes, such as changes in the price of a good. Although a market survey is certainly one method of obtaining information about consumer tastes and spending, we pointed out that consumer surveys do not guarantee sufficiently detailed or reliable data to present a firm with a precise estimate of its demand function.

Linear regression analysis, one of the main statistical techniques that a firm can use to estimate its demand function, was also examined. We discussed the interpretation of the estimates of the coefficients of the independent variables in the demand function as well as that of the coefficient of determination, R^2. We pointed out that even though a given firm's management may not have the expertise to carry out a statistical demand estimation procedure, it is possible to hire someone to perform such an analysis; we noted that without a great deal of study, one can gain enough knowledge of statistics to interpret and utilize the results of such an investigation.

Finally, we pointed out that if the firm does not have sufficient data available for statistical demand analysis, it may wish to conduct market experiments by changing price and/or the amount of advertising and recording the corresponding quantity sold. However, we also cautioned that market experiments may be costly, especially in terms of lost sales.

We have emphasized both in this chapter and in Chapter 2 the importance of a firm's knowing the demand function for its product. Without such insight on the part of the firm, profit maximization would be the result of sheer luck. However, the firm must decide *how much* data it will obtain and in what ways that data will be gathered, taking into consideration both the cost and the accuracy of the information. The firm should always be aware of the value of keeping records of prices charged, advertising expenditures, and corresponding quantities sold; these statistics comprise one source of information regarding its demand.

In Chapter 4 we examine different types of forecasting techniques that business firms and government policymakers can use to predict future values of economic variables. As you might expect, some of these employ the statistical tool of regression analysis, which was discussed in this chapter and is explained in greater detail in appendix 3.

Then, in Chapters 5 and 6, we turn our attention to production and cost. As we will see later, two elements are essential if a business firm is to maximize its profit: an accurate analysis of the demand for the product and efficient production of that good or service.

QUESTIONS

1. What is a market survey? What are some of the problems associated with the use of market surveys to estimate the demand for a firm's product?
2. What information is obtained through the use of linear regression analysis?
3. Discuss market experiments: what they are, how they may be used, and any drawbacks that they might have.
4. Explain how a hotel in Miami Beach might estimate the demand for its rooms. Be specific, including a description of what variables you would consider and why, as well as any other relevant information as to how you would conduct the experiment.
5. Using linear regression analysis, Estate Lighting Company estimated its demand function for a particular chandelier with the following results:

$$Q_E = 995 - 2.51P_E + 1.78P_C + 0.05I,$$

where

Q_E = quantity sold per year of the Estate Lighting chandeliers,
P_E = price of the Estate Lighting chandelier,
P_C = price of a competing firm's chandelier, and
I = average annual household income.

    a. How can Estate Lighting use this information to find its price, income, and cross price elasticities of demand?

    b. What would an R^2 of 0.84 indicate?

    c. Can you think of a potentially important variable that Estate Lighting has ignored in its demand analysis?

6. In the Wilson article cited in this chapter (page 103), a log (base 10) form of the demand function for electricity was also estimated with the following results:

$$\log_{10} Q = 10.25 - 1.33 \log_{10} P + 0.31 \log_{10} G - 0.46 \log_{10} Y +$$

$$0.49 \log_{10} R - 0.04 \log_{10} C, \ (R^2 = 0.566),$$

where

    Q = quantity demanded (kilowatts) of electricity,
    P = cost of the Federal Power Commission's typical bill for 500 kilowatt-hours per month,
    G = average price of natural gas (cents per therm),
    Y = median annual family income,
    R = average size of housing units, and
    C = degree days.

    a. What does each of the estimated coefficients represent in the preceding demand function? Interpret the economic significance of each of them.

    b. What does a value of $R^2 = 0.566$ mean?

SELECTED REFERENCES

Brennan, Michael J., and Thomas M. Carroll. *Preface to Quantitative Economics & Econometrics*, 4th ed. Cincinnati: South-Western, 1987.

Greene, William H. *Econometric Analysis*, 3d ed. New York: Macmillan, 1997.

Griffiths, William E., R. Carter Hill, and George G. Judge. *Learning and Practicing Econometrics*. New York: John Wiley & Sons, 1993.

Johnston, J. *Econometric Methods*, 3d ed. New York: McGraw-Hill, 1984.

Maddala, G. S. *Introduction to Econometrics*, 2d ed. New York: Macmillan, 1992.

Mirer, Thad W. *Economic Statistics and Econometrics*. New York: Macmillan, 1983.

Verleger, Philip K., Jr. "Models of the Demand for Air Transportation," *The Bell Journal of Economics and Management Science*, Vol. III (Autumn 1972), pp. 437–457.

APPENDIX 3

Linear Regression Analysis

In this appendix we will try to aid the interested student in achieving a better understanding of how a linear regression model is constructed and how it can be interpreted.

THE LINEAR REGRESSION MODEL AND UNDERLYING ASSUMPTIONS

If a researcher uses linear regression analysis, the assumption is made that two variables, Y and X, are related in the following manner:

(3–1)
$$Y_i = \alpha + \beta X_i + \varepsilon_i$$

which states that Y is a linear function of X plus an error term.[1] Researchers usually include an error term in a regression model because they believe that while *on the average*, $Y = \alpha + \beta X$, there may also be other variables representing less important factors affecting Y that are left out of the regression model. Also, there may be measurement errors present. Another way to state what we have just said is that it is assumed that

(3–2)
$$\mu_{YX} = \alpha + \beta X,$$

where μ_{YX} is the *mean or average* value of Y given a particular value for X, α is the Y-axis intercept, and β is the slope of the function.

For example, suppose a supermarket has sold milk at a price of $.80 per half gallon for only four weeks and that during week 1, week 2, week 3, and week 4, it sold 100, 80, 90, and 110 cartons of milk, respectively. The average value of Y or Q_d, given X, or $P = \$.80$, is

$$\frac{100 + 80 + 90 + 110}{4} = \frac{380}{4} = 95.$$

---

[1] We first discuss the case of one independent variable and one dependent variable. The case of more than one independent variable (multiple linear regression) is conceptually quite similar and will be explained briefly at the end of this appendix.

Thus the mean, μ_{YX}, of Y *given* X is found by adding up all of the Y values corresponding to that particular X value and dividing by the number of observations. Thus

$$\mu_{YX} = \frac{\sum_{i=1}^{n} Y_i | X}{n}$$

where n is the number of observations of Y associated with that particular value of X.

In order to compute some of the statistics and to interpret the statistical significance of the results obtained in most linear regression analyses done in the area of economics, the following additional assumptions must usually be made:

1. The error term, ε_i, is a random variable with a normal (bell-shaped curve) distribution.
2. The mean or expected value of ε is zero. We write this as $E(\varepsilon) = 0$. This assumption means that while some values of ε may be positive, some negative, and others zero, the *average* value of ε is zero.
3. The *variance* of the ε_i terms *given each X value* is assumed to be the same and equal to σ_{YX}^2. We find the variance, σ_{YX}^2, by finding

$$\sum_{i=1}^{n} \frac{(Y_i - \mu_{YX})^2}{n}$$

Thus we sum the squared differences or deviations of each Y value from its mean, μ_{YX}, given a particular X. For our milk example,

$$\sigma_{YX}^2 = \frac{(100 - 95)^2 + (80 - 95)^2 + (90 - 95)^2 + (110 - 95)^2}{4}$$

$$= \frac{25 + 225 + 25 + 225}{4} = \frac{500}{4} = 125.$$

The *standard deviation* is given by

$$\sqrt{\sigma_{YX}^2} = \sqrt{125},$$

which is approximately equal to 11.18 in the milk carton example. We also assume that $E(\varepsilon_i \varepsilon_j) = 0$, *where i does not equal j*, which means that ε_i and ε_j are not related.

4. In economic research we usually assume that X is a random variable with a normal distribution. (In a controlled experiment, the X values could be fixed.)

Estimators of the Slope and Intercept Terms

If we could observe all of the combinations of X and Y that have occurred in the past or would occur in the future for all possible values of X, our task of finding α and β or "fitting" the relationship hypothesized in equation (3–1) would be made much easier. All of these observations of X and Y are called the *population*. Unfortunately, in economics we usually cannot observe the entire population because obtaining all of the data is either impossible or too expensive. Thus we must make do with a *sample* (which we assume is randomly drawn) from the population data. This situation is one in which we must rely a great deal on the laws of statistics.

In the real world, therefore, our task is to find an estimate of α and β in equation (3–1) from a sample of data. Thus we want to find

(3–3)
$$\hat{Y} = a + bX,$$

where a and b are estimates of α and β, respectively, and $\hat{Y}$ is the computed value of Y given a particular value of X and our estimated relationship. Then

$$Y_i = a + bX_i + e_i,$$

where e_i is the error term for our estimated relationship and is an estimate of ε_i, the population error term. Thus

$$Y_i - \hat{Y}_i = e_i.$$

We would like our estimates of α and β to have at least two characteristics. First, if we took repeated samples and estimated α and β for each sample, we would like the mean or expected value of a to be equal to α and the mean or expected value of b to be equal to β. In other words we want $E(a) = \alpha$ and $E(b) = \beta$. In this case we say a and b are *unbiased estimators*. Second, we would like the values of a and b, which are found from each sample, to vary as little as possible among the samples. Thus we want σ_a^2 and σ_b^2 to be minimized.

Furthermore, we want our regression equation to be such that the sum of the squared error terms, $\sum_{i=1}^{n} e_i^2$ (*where n is the number of sample observations*), is minimized. We want to minimize the sum of the *squared* error terms because if our assumptions are correct, the sum of the error terms themselves should equal zero. It turns out that if we use a mathematical method to find a and b that minimizes $\sum_{i=1}^{n} e_i^2$, these estimators of α and β will also have the other two desirable properties (unbiasedness and minimum variance) mentioned previously. These estimators are

(3–4)
$$a = \bar{Y} - b\bar{X}$$

and

(3–5)
$$b = \frac{\sum_{i=1}^{n} (X_i - \overline{X})\,(Y_i - \overline{Y})}{\sum_{i=1}^{n} (X_i - \overline{X})^2}\,,$$

where $\overline{Y}$ is the average or mean value of Y for the *whole sample* and $\overline{X}$ is the average or mean value of X for the sample.[2]

---

2 We can derive a and b in the following manner. Recall that

$$e_i = Y_i - \hat{Y}_i = Y_i - a - bX_i.$$

Then

(3–6)
$$\sum_{i=1}^{n} e_i^2 = \sum_{i=1}^{n} (Y_i - a - bX_i)^2.$$

We wish to find values of a and b such that $\sum e_i^2$ is minimized. To minimize $\sum e_i^2$, we take the first (partial) derivatives of equation (3–6) with respect to a and b and set them equal to zero to satisfy the first order conditions:

(3–7)
$$\frac{\partial \sum e_i^2}{\partial a} = -2 \sum_{i=1}^{n} (Y_i - a - bX_i) = 0$$

and

(3–8)
$$\frac{\partial \sum e_i^2}{\partial b} = -2 \sum_{i=1}^{n} X_i(Y_i - a - bX_i) = 0.$$

Simplifying equations (3–7) and (3–8), we obtain the *normal equations*

(3–9)
$$\sum_{i=1}^{n} Y_i = na + b\sum_{i=1}^{n} X_i$$

and

(3–10)
$$\sum_{i=1}^{n} X_iY_i = a\sum_{i=1}^{n} X_i + b\sum_{i=1}^{n} X_i^2.$$

When equations (3–9) and (3–10) are solved simultaneously, we obtain

$$a = \overline{Y} - b\overline{X}$$

and

$$b = \frac{\sum_{i=1}^{n} (X_i - \overline{X})\,(Y_i - \overline{Y})}{\sum_{i=1}^{n} (X_i - \overline{X})^2}.$$

The term $\bar{Y}$ is somewhat different from μ_{YX} discussed earlier, which is the *population mean of Y given a specific X value*. It is also different from μ_Y, which is the *population mean of all the Y values*. We usually cannot observe the population means, so we must therefore "make do" with the sample means. We call the estimators *a and b for* α and β, respectively, which can be found from equations (3–4) and (3–5), given previously—the *least squares estimators* because they minimized $\sum e_i^2$. We can also say that *a* and *b* are the *best linear unbiased estimators (BLUE)* because they have the additional two desired properties of minimum variance and unbiasedness. If the sample we take has *n* observations (values of *X* and *Y*), we can easily use an electronic calculator to compute *a* and *b*:

(3–4′)
$$a = \frac{\sum Y}{n} - b \frac{\sum X}{n},$$

and

(3–5′)
$$b = \frac{n \sum XY - \sum X \sum Y}{n \sum X^2 - \left(\sum X\right)^2},$$

where the sums are taken over the n sample observations.

Table 3A–1 gives an example of a sample of milk prices and quantity sold data collected by our supermarket. Notice that there are *six* observations, so $n = 6$. Given the information in Table 3A–1, we find

$$b = \frac{n \sum XY - \sum X \sum Y}{n \sum X^2 - \left(\sum X\right)^2}$$

$$= \frac{6(480) - 700(4.30)}{6(3.19) - (4.30)^2}$$

$$= \frac{2880 - 3010}{19.14 - 18.49}$$

$$= \frac{-130}{.65}$$

$$= -200,$$

and

$$a = \frac{\sum Y}{n} - b \frac{\sum X}{n}$$

$$= 116.67 - (-200)(.72)$$

$$= 260.67.$$

Table 3A–1   Data for Milk Demand Problem

Quantity Demanded Y	Price of Milk X	XY	X²
160	$.50	80	.25
140	.60	84	.36
120	.70	84	.49
110	.80	88	.64
90	.80	72	.64
80	.90	72	.81
$\Sigma Y = 700$	$\Sigma X = \$4.30$	$\Sigma XY = 480$	$\Sigma X^2 = 3.19$

$$\frac{\Sigma Y}{n} = 116.67 \qquad \frac{\Sigma X}{n} = .72 \qquad (\Sigma X)^2 = 18.49$$

Thus our estimated demand function is $\hat{Y} = 260.67 - 200X$. In order to check casually to see how closely our estimate of the demand function reflects the actual sample points, we compute $\hat{Y}$ at $X = \$.70$ and find $\hat{Y} = 120.67$. In this case the error, e_i, which is equal to $Y - \hat{Y} = 120 - 120.67 = -0.67$. Similarly, at $X = \$.90$, we find $\hat{Y} = 80.67$ and $e_i = 80 - 80.67 = -0.67$. The sample points and the estimated demand function are shown in Figure 3A–1.

Interpretation of the Regression Statistics

Our casual observation indicated that our estimated regression equation "fairly closely" approximated the actual Y_i values in the sample. However, we usually wish to determine, using standard statistical measures, how closely an estimated function fits the sample data and what inferences we can draw from the estimate, which is based on the *sample*, regarding the *population* (quantities that would be demanded at *all possible prices*). Thus we will discuss statistics that give us an indication of the statistical significance of the coefficient estimates and of the coefficient of determination, R^2. Finally, we will discuss a statistic that will allow us to find a confidence interval for Y, given X.

Statistical Significance of Estimates of α and β

First, let us examine the statistical significance of an estimate, b, of a coefficient, β, of the independent variable, X. Frequently in regression analysis, one of the prime concerns of the statistician is to determine whether or not the *actual* coefficient is different from zero (and sometimes whether it is positive or negative). This information is very important because it indicates the rela-

Figure 3A–1   Sample Points and $\hat{Y} = a + bX$

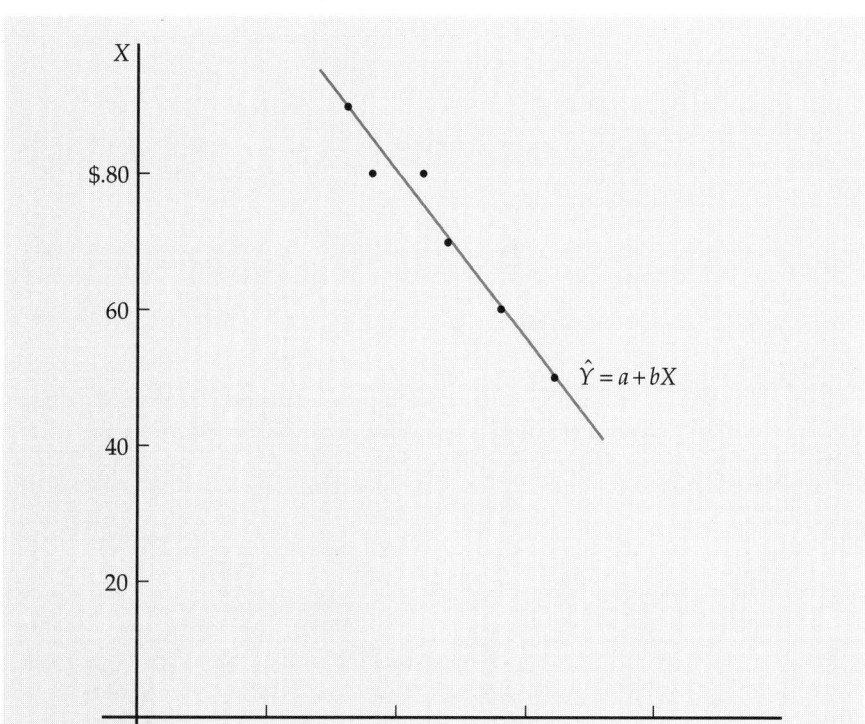

The sample points indicating the quantity demanded of milk and corresponding prices and the estimated demand function are shown here.

tionship between the independent variable and the dependent variable, which is the relationship of primary interest to the researcher in that type of situation. It turns out that we can use a statistical test to tell us whether or not we can reject the hypothesis (called the *null hypothesis*) that the coefficient in question is equal to zero (or some other number), *given a particular level of probability or chance that we are rejecting the hypothesis when it is true.*

To set up this test, we must calculate a *t statistic*. The *t* statistic has a distribution similar to the normal (bell-shaped) distribution when the sample size is large, and either the *t* distribution or the normal distribution could be used to analyze the statistical significance of the coefficients in this case. However, when the sample size is small, perhaps less than 40 observations, the *t* statistic should be used.

The *t* statistic that we need to calculate is given by

$$t = \frac{b - \beta}{\hat{\sigma}_b},$$

(3–11)

where b is the estimate of β and $\hat{\sigma}_b$ is the estimate of the standard deviation (square root of the variance) of b. We already know for our example that $b = 200$. The formula for $\hat{\sigma}_b$ is

$$\hat{\sigma}_b = \sqrt{\hat{\sigma}_b^2} = \sqrt{\frac{\hat{\sigma}_{YX}^2}{\sum (X - \overline{X})^2}}$$

The term $\hat{\sigma}_{YX}^2$ is called the estimated standard deviation of the regression or the estimated standard error of the estimate. We can find $\hat{\sigma}_{YX}^2$ from the following relationship:

$$\hat{\sigma}_{YX}^2 = \frac{1}{n - 2} \ \Sigma (Y - \hat{Y})^2$$

(3–12)

Since $Y - \hat{Y}$ represents the "error," or difference between the *actual* value of Y and our *estimate* of Y or $\hat{Y}$, it is easy to see how $\hat{\sigma}_{YX}^2$ got its name. The YX subscript indicates that we estimated the functional relationship between Y and X, or $Y = f(X)$. The term $n - 2$ represents *degrees of freedom* which, briefly, indicate the number of elements or values that can vary freely in computing t. We get six degrees of freedom from the sample observations ($n = 6$) for computing $Y - \hat{Y}$, but we lose two degrees of freedom because a and b—which we use to find $\hat{Y}$—are already determined by the regression equation. Thus for our example the degrees of freedom equal 4.

In Table 3A–2 we give the original sample values of X and Y and the computed values for $(X - \overline{X})$, $(X - \overline{X})^2$, $\hat{Y}$, $(Y - \hat{Y})$, and $(Y - \hat{Y})^2$. Thus we can find

$$\hat{\sigma}_{YX}^2 = \frac{1}{n - 2} \ \Sigma (Y - \hat{Y})^2$$

$$= \frac{1}{4} \ (202.694) = 50.674 \,.$$

Now we can find

$$\hat{\sigma}_b = \sqrt{\frac{\hat{\sigma}_{YX}^2}{\Sigma (X - \overline{X})^2}} = \sqrt{\frac{50.674}{.106}}$$

$$= \sqrt{478.057} = 21.86 \,.$$

Table 3A–2   Calculations for $\hat{\sigma}_{YX}^2$

Quantity Demanded Y	Price of Milk X	$X - \bar{X}$*	$(X - \bar{X})^2$	$\hat{Y}$	$Y - \hat{Y}$	$(Y - \hat{Y})^2$
160	$.50	−.22	.048	160.67	−.67	.449
140	.60	−.12	.014	140.67	−.67	.449
120	.70	−.02	.000	120.67	−.67	.449
110	.80	.08	.006	100.67	9.33	87.049
90	.80	.08	.006	100.67	−10.67	113.849
80	.90	.18	.032	80.67	−.67	.449

$$\Sigma(X - \bar{X})^2 = .106 \qquad \Sigma(Y - \hat{Y})^2 = 202.694$$

$$\hat{\sigma}_{YX}^2 = \frac{\Sigma(Y - \hat{Y})^2}{n - 2} = 50.674$$

* Recall from Table 3A–1 that $\bar{X} = \dfrac{\Sigma X}{n} = .72$.

The calculated value for t now becomes

(3–13)

$$t = \frac{b - \beta}{\hat{\sigma}_b} = \frac{-200 - \beta}{\hat{\sigma}_b}$$

$$= \frac{-200 - \beta}{21.86}$$

If we wish to test the hypothesis that $\beta = 0$, we substitute $\beta = 0$ into equation (3–13) and obtain

$$t = \frac{-200}{21.86} = -9.15.$$

To interpret this value for t, we must look at a table for the t distribution. A partial t table is given in Table 3A–3. Each value of t given in the table indicates the probability for ϕ degrees of freedom that t would be greater than the value given, assuming the hypothesis used to calculate t is true. A corresponding interpretation holds for t being less than (minus one) times the value given in the table. Thus from Table 3A–3 we see that for $n = 4$ degrees of freedom, the $P(t > 2.132) = .05$ or 5 percent. Also, the $P(t < -2.132) = .05$ or 5 percent, where P stands for the probability or chance of some event occurring. The statement $P(t > 2.132) = .05$ means that in only 5 out of 100 times (on the average) would we calculate a t value greater than 2.132 *if the null hypothesis were true*. A similar interpretation holds for the figures in the 1 percent column.

Table 3A–3   The t Distribution

ϕ Degrees of Freedom	γ 5 Percent	γ 1 Percent
1	6.314	31.821
2	2.920	6.965
3	2.353	4.541
4	2.132	3.747
5	2.015	3.365
6	1.943	3.143
7	1.895	2.998
8	1.860	2.896
9	1.833	2.821
10	1.812	2.764

Source: R. A. Fisher, *Statistical Methods for Research Workers*, 14th ed. (New York: Hafner Press, 1972), abridged from Table IV.

The kind of probability statements just given are called *one-tailed tests* because they indicate the probability of t being *greater than* some number, or the probability of t being *less than* some number if we consider $P(t < -2.132)$. If we wish to find the probability that t lies outside the interval given by plus or minus the t value given in the table, we must multiply the stated probability percentage by two (there is a .05 + .05 probability that t will be in either one or the other "tail"). Thus

$$P(t > 2.132 \text{ or } t < -2.132) = .10$$

for four degrees of freedom. We call this probability statement a *two-tailed test*. We could also state that the

$$P(-2.132 < t < 2.132) = .90,$$

since the probability of t being *outside* an interval plus the probability of t being inside the interval must equal 1.00.[3]

Now let us examine the t statistic that we computed for b, based on the null hypothesis that $\beta = 0$. In this case our computed value for $t = -9.15$. We see from Table 3A–3 that for four degrees of freedom,

---

3 The probability of a *certain* event occurring is 1.00; the probability of an *impossible* event occurring is 0; and the sum of the probabilities of individual events occurring, one and only one of which must and can occur (but is not predetermined to occur), must be 1.00.

$$P(t < -3.747) = .01, \text{ and}$$

since our computed value for t is *smaller* than -3.747, we can say that the chances are less than 1 in 100 that we would obtain a t value of -9.15 if the null hypothesis were true. Therefore, we can reasonably reject the null hypothesis and accept the hypothesis that β is less than zero. Another way of stating our conclusion is to say that b is significantly less than zero at the 1 percent level of significance.

We can also compute a t statistic for a, the estimate of the Y-axis intercept. The computed value of t for a is given by

(3–14)
$$t = \frac{a - \alpha}{\hat{\sigma}_a},$$

where

(3–15)
$$\hat{\sigma}_a = \sqrt{\hat{\sigma}_a^2} = \sqrt{\frac{\hat{\sigma}_{YX}^2 \, \sum X^2}{n \sum (X - \overline{X})^2}}$$

From Tables 3A–1 and 3A–2, we can find

$$\hat{\sigma}_a = \sqrt{\frac{50.674\,(3.19)}{6\,(.106)}}$$

$$= \sqrt{254.167}$$

$$= 15.94.$$

If our null hypothesis is $\alpha = 0$ and our alternative hypothesis is $\alpha > 0$, then

$$t = \frac{260.67 - 0}{15.94}$$

$$= 16.35.$$

From Table 3A–3 it is obvious that we can reject the null hypothesis that $\alpha = 0$ and can accept the alternative hypothesis that $\alpha > 0$; we can say that a is significantly greater than zero at the 1 percent level of significance.

The Coefficient of Determination: R^2

Another measure of the statistical significance of the regression line that we have found from the sample points is the coefficient of determination, or R^2. To understand what R^2 represents, note first that we may separate the deviation of the actual Y values from the *sample mean* into two parts in the following manner:

(3–16)
$$Y - \bar{Y} = (Y - \hat{Y}) + (\hat{Y} - \bar{Y}).$$

(Total
Deviation)
(Unexplained
Deviation)
(Explained
Deviation)

The term $(\hat{Y} - \bar{Y})$ represents the portion of the deviation of the Y values that is "explained" by the regression equation that was obtained from the sample points. You should recall that $Y - \hat{Y} = e_i$. It is also true, given our assumptions at the beginning of this appendix, that

(3–17)
$$\sum \left(Y - \bar{Y} \right)^2 = \sum \left(Y - \hat{Y} \right)^2 + \sum \left(\hat{Y} - \bar{Y} \right)^2.$$

$\sum (Y - \bar{Y})^2$ is called the *total* sum of squares, $\sum (Y - \hat{Y})^2 = \sum e_i^2$ is the *unexplained* sum of squares, and $\sum (\hat{Y} - \bar{Y})^2$ is the *explained* sum of squares. If we divide equation (3–17) by $\sum (Y - \bar{Y})^2$, we obtain

(3–18)
$$1 = \frac{\sum(Y - \hat{Y})^2}{\sum(Y - \bar{Y})^2} + \frac{\sum(\hat{Y} - \bar{Y})^2}{\sum(Y - \bar{Y})^2}.$$

R^2 is defined as

(3–19)
$$R^2 = \frac{\sum(\hat{Y} - \bar{Y})^2}{\sum(Y - \bar{Y})^2},$$

or the ratio of the explained sum of squares to the total sum of squares. When the *unexplained* deviation equals zero, $Y = \hat{Y}$ and

$$R^2 = \frac{\sum(\hat{Y} - \bar{Y})^2}{\sum(Y - \bar{Y})^2} = \frac{\sum(Y - \bar{Y})^2}{\sum(Y - \bar{Y})^2} = 1.$$

When the *explained* deviation equals zero, $\hat{Y} = \bar{Y}$ and

$$R^2 = \frac{\sum(\hat{Y} - \bar{Y})^2}{\sum(Y - \bar{Y})^2} = 0.$$

Consequently, the *maximum* value that R^2 can be is 1, and the minimum value that R^2 can be is zero.

In Table 3A–4 we have computed the values for the total sum of squares, the unexplained sum of squares, and the explained sum of squares for our example. Thus we can find

$$R^2 = \frac{\sum(\hat{Y} - \bar{Y})^2}{\sum(Y - \bar{Y})^2} = \frac{4,336}{4,533.334} = 0.956.$$

Table 3A–4   Analysis of Variance

Y	$Y - \bar{Y}$*	$(Y - \bar{Y})^2$	$\hat{Y}$	$Y - \hat{Y}$	$(Y - \hat{Y})^2$	$\hat{Y} - \bar{Y}$*	$(\hat{Y} - \bar{Y})^2$
160	43.33	1,877.489	160.67	−.67	.449	44	1,936
140	23.33	544.289	140.67	−.67	.449	24	576
120	3.33	11.089	120.67	−.67	.449	4	16
110	−6.67	44.489	100.67	9.33	87.049	−16	256
90	−26.67	711.289	100.67	−10.67	113.849	−16	256
80	−36.67	1,344.689	80.67	−.67	.449	−36	1,296
		$\Sigma(Y - \bar{Y})^2 = 4,533.334$			$\Sigma(Y - \hat{Y})^2 = 202.694$	$\Sigma(\hat{Y} - \bar{Y})^2 = 4,336$	

* Recall from Table 3A–1 that $\bar{Y} = \dfrac{\Sigma Y}{n} = 116.67$.

Therefore, the regression line we estimated from sample points can account for almost 96 percent of the variation in the observed values of Y.[4] In the case where X and Y can both vary (as we have assumed here is true), the correlation coefficient, R, which is the square root of R^2, also can be interpreted as a measure of the degree of *covariability* of X and Y (of the extent to which X and Y vary together).[5]

---

4 An R^2 value adjusted for degrees of freedom is often computed as

$$R'^2 = 1 - \frac{\dfrac{\Sigma(Y - \hat{Y})^2}{n - 2}}{\dfrac{\Sigma(Y - \bar{Y})^2}{n - 1}}$$

$$= 1 - \frac{\Sigma(Y - \hat{Y})^2}{\Sigma(Y - \bar{Y})^2} \times \frac{n - 1}{n - 2},$$

where $n - 2$ is the degrees of freedom of $\hat{\sigma}^2_{YX}\left[= \dfrac{\Sigma(Y - \hat{Y})^2}{n - 2}\right]$ and $n - 1$ is the degrees of freedom of $\hat{\sigma}^2_Y = \dfrac{\Sigma(Y - \bar{Y})^2}{n - 1}$. This latter term loses one degree of freedom because $\bar{Y}$ is fixed.

For our example,

$$R'^2 = 1 - \frac{202.694}{4,533.334} \times \frac{5}{4}$$

$$= 1 - 0.054$$

$$= 0.946.$$

In our case R'^2 is quite close to R^2; and, in general, they will be very close when the degrees of freedom are large.

5 This matter is discussed extensively in Taro Yamane, *Statistics: An Introductory Analysis*, 3d ed. (New York: Harper and Row, 1973), Chapter 15.

Confidence Interval for Y

Suppose we wish to make a prediction regarding an individual Y value—such as a prediction about the quantity demanded of milk when the price of milk = $1.00. Usually, we would like to have some objective measure of the confidence we can place in our prediction, and one such measure is a *confidence interval* constructed for Y.

A confidence interval for a predicted Y, given a value for X, can be constructed in the following manner. We first find the value of a t statistic for Y where

(3–20)

$$t = \frac{Y - \hat{Y}}{\hat{\sigma}_{YX} \sqrt{1 + \dfrac{1}{n} + \dfrac{(X - \overline{X})^2}{\Sigma(X - \overline{X})^2}}}$$

with $n - 2$ degrees of freedom. We also know that

$$P(-t_{.05} < t < t_{.05}) = .90,$$

which means that

(3–21)

$$P\left[-t_{.05} < \frac{Y - \hat{Y}}{\hat{\sigma}_{YX} \sqrt{1 + \dfrac{1}{n} = \dfrac{(X - \overline{X})^2}{\Sigma(X - \overline{X})^2}}} < t_{.05}\right] = .90.$$

Multiplying both sides of the inequality by $\hat{\sigma}_{YX}$ times

$$\sqrt{1 + \dfrac{1}{n} + \dfrac{(X - \overline{X})^2}{\Sigma(X - \overline{X})^2}}$$

we obtain

$$P\left[-t_{.05}\,\hat{\sigma}_{YX} \sqrt{1 + \dfrac{1}{n} + \dfrac{(X - \overline{X})^2}{\Sigma(X - \overline{X})^2}} < Y - \hat{Y}\right.$$

$$\left. < t_{.05}\,\hat{\sigma}_{YX} \sqrt{1 + \dfrac{1}{n} + \dfrac{(X - \overline{X})^2}{\Sigma(X - \overline{X})^2}}\right] = .90,$$

or

$$P\left[\hat{Y} - t_{.05}\,\hat{\sigma}_{YX}\,\sqrt{1 + \frac{1}{n} + \frac{(X - \overline{X})^2}{\Sigma(X - \overline{X})^2}} < Y\right.$$

$$\left. < \hat{Y} + t_{.05}\,\hat{\sigma}_{YX}\,\sqrt{1 + \frac{1}{n} + \frac{(X - \overline{X})^2}{\Sigma(X - \overline{X})^2}}\,\right] = .90.$$

If we wish to find the 90 percent confidence interval for quantity demanded (or Y) at a price of \$1.00 (or $X = \$1.00$) for our preceding example, we first compute

$$\hat{Y} = 260.67 - 200(1.00) = 60.67.$$

From Table 3A–3 we find $t_{.05}$ for four degrees of freedom = 2.132. We know $\hat{\sigma}_{YX} = \sqrt{50.674} = 7.119$. Finally, we compute

$$\sqrt{1 + \frac{1}{n} + \frac{(X - \overline{X})^2}{\Sigma(X - \overline{X})^2}}$$

$$= \sqrt{1 + \frac{1}{4} + \frac{(1.00 - .72)^2}{.106}}$$

$$= \sqrt{1.25 + \frac{.078}{.106}}$$

$$= \sqrt{1.986} = 1.409.$$

Consequently, the 90 percent confidence interval for Y, given $X = \$1.00$, is given by

(3–22)

$$P[60.67 - 2.132(7.119)(1.409) < Y < 60.67 + 2.132(7.119)(1.409)]$$
$$= P(60.67 - 21.38 < Y < 60.67 + 21.38) = .90,$$

or

$$P(39.29 < Y < 82.05) = .90.$$

We can interpret our confidence interval (3–22) as follows: if we were to select 100 samples and construct 100 corresponding confidence intervals for $X = \$1.00$, we should expect that 90 out of 100 of those confidence intervals will contain the actual value of Y corresponding to $X = \$1.00$.

Notice that the term

$$\sqrt{1 + \frac{1}{n} + \frac{(X - \overline{X})^2}{\Sigma(X - \overline{X})^2}}$$

gets larger as the given X value $\left[\text{in the numerator of } \dfrac{(X - \overline{X})^2}{\Sigma(X - \overline{X})^2}\right]$ gets far-

ther and farther away from the sample mean, $\overline{X}$. Consequently, the farther the given X for which we wish to predict Y is from $\overline{X}$, the wider the confidence interval for Y for a given probability level, and our prediction of Y is less reliable. This last statement is particularly relevant if the given X value is outside the range of the sample observations.

Multiple Linear Regression

Our discussion until now has focused on simple linear regression, analyses that involve one dependent variable and one independent variable. In many cases in economics, however, the value of a dependent variable is determined by more than one independent variable. Chapter 2 noted that the quantity demanded of a product is typically affected not only by its own price but also by the prices of related goods and the incomes of consumers. Other variables such as advertising expenditures, credit terms, and the climate may also be important factors affecting the quantity demanded of certain products. Wilson's estimated demand function for electricity, for example, included the price of electricity, the price of natural gas, median annual family income, the average number of rooms per housing unit, and the number of degree days as independent variables. We can examine the relationship between a dependent variable and a *group* of independent variables through the use of *multiple* regression analysis.

Let us assume, for example, that we have a regression model where Y is related to X_1, X_2, and X_3 in the following manner:

$$Y_i = \alpha + \beta_1 X_{1i} + \beta_2 X_{2i} + \beta_3 X_{3i} + \varepsilon_i$$

In multiple regression analysis, we make the same basic assumptions regarding the error terms, ε_i, that were made earlier in the chapter in the case of simple linear regression analysis. In addition, we assume that no one of the X variables is determined by any linear combination of the other two. If this latter assumption does not hold, then the independent variables are not really free to vary independently of one another, and we have the problem of *multicollinearity*, discussed in the next section. The value of R^2 in the case of multiple regression that is analogous to R^2 in the case of simple regression is called the *coefficient of multiple determination*, and its positive square root, R, is called the *multiple correlation coefficient*. Tests of the significance of the estimates of α and the coefficients of the X variables can be done using the t statistic in the same manner as in the case of simple linear regression. The degrees of freedom will be equal to $n - k - 1$, where n is the number of observations and k is the number of independent variables.

For example, suppose we wish to investigate the nature of a demand function for a video game, "Fantastic Frieda." Table 3A–5 gives data on the quantity demanded per year of the games, Q_F, the price of the games, P_F, the price of competing games, P_C, median annual family income, Y, and monthly advertising expenditures, A. In this case, our regression model is given by

$$Q_{F_i} = \alpha + \beta_1 P_{F_i} + \beta_2 P_{C_i} + \beta_3 Y_i + \beta_4 A_i + \varepsilon_i.$$

A wide variety of computer software packages, including one in the *Decision Assistant*, are available that will make the calculations necessary for the estimates of α, the coefficients of P_F, P_C, Y, and A, the coefficient of multiple determination (R^2), and the values of the t statistic for α and each estimated coefficient. Using any of the standard multiple regression computer packages and the data in Table 3A–5, you should be able to obtain the following estimated demand function for "Fantastic Frieda" video games:

$$Q_{F_i} = 10{,}749.360 - 2{,}979.179 P_{F_i} + 2{,}785.712 P_{C_i} + 1.337 Y_i + 0.467 A_i.$$

$$(9{,}986.243)\quad(1{,}344.300)\quad(1{,}397.794)\quad(0.825)\quad(1.488)$$

The standard error of each coefficient is given in parentheses under the respective coefficient. The R^2 is equal to .96, and R'^2 (the adjusted coefficient of multiple determination) = .94. The t values can be calculated for each estimated coefficient by dividing it by its respective standard error. Thus, the t values for α, β_1, β_2, β_3, and β_4, respectively, are 1.076, –2.216, 1.993, 1.621, and

Table 3A–5   Demand for Video Games Data

Year	Q_F	P_F ($)	P_C ($)	Y^a ($)	A
1983	50000	18	20	24580	7500
1984	60000	16	20	26433	10500
1985	55000	16	18	27735	10500
1986	61000	17	20	29458	11500
1987	63000	17	21	30970	12000
1988	65000	18	22	32191	12400
1989	75000	16	21	34213	13000
1990	70000	20	24	35353	12500
1991	75000	20	24	35939	14000

[a] **Source:** *Statistical Abstract of the United States*, Washington, D.C.: U.S. Government Printing Office, 1992, p. 449; and *Economic Report of the President*, Washington, D.C.: U.S. Government Printing Office, 1993, p. 380.

0.314. The degrees of freedom are equal to $n - k - 1 = 9 - 4 - 1 = 4$. Therefore, the estimated value of β_1 is significantly less than zero at the 5 percent level of significance, and the estimated values of β_2 and β_3 are significantly greater than zero at the 10 percent level of significance. However, the estimated values of α and β_4 are not significantly greater than zero at the 10 percent level of significance.

Possible Problems in Linear Regression

Several problems may occur in linear regression analysis. If there is more than one independent variable, two of these variables may be so closely related that estimation of the relationship between these variables and Y is made very difficult. This is the problem of *multicollinearity*.

Another problem may occur when the ε_i terms are not statistically independent. In this case $E(\varepsilon_i \varepsilon_j) \neq 0$, for $i \neq j$, σ_b will usually be *underestimated* and, as a result, the statistical significance of b overestimated. This problem is called *autocorrelation*.[6] Although the least squares estimators of the coefficients will still be unbiased, they will not satisfy the minimum variance property. In other words, the least squares estimators are no longer the *best* linear unbiased estimators.

A third problem may occur if the variance of ε_i is not the same for each value of X. In this situation we have the problem of *heteroscedasticity*. Again, least squares estimates of the coefficients will be unbiased, but they will no longer be the estimates that have the minimum variance. Also, the estimated

---

6 One common statistic that can be used to test for the presence of autocorrelation is the Durbin-Watson statistic, computed as follows:

$$d = \frac{\sum_{t=2}^{n} (e_t - e_{t-1})^2}{\sum_{t=1}^{n} e_t^2}$$

where the subscript t refers to time period. Durbin and Watson computed values for d_L and d_U such that:

if $d < d_L$,	reject the hypothesis that there is no autocorrelation and accept the alternative hypothesis of *positive* autocorrelation;
if $d > 4 - d_L$,	reject the hypothesis of no autocorrelation and accept the alternative hypothesis of *negative* autocorrelation;
if $d_U < d < 4 - d_U$,	do not reject the hypothesis of no autocorrelation;

otherwise, the test is inconclusive.

See J. Durbin and G. S. Watson, "Testing for Serial Correlation in Least-Squares Regression," *Biometrika*, Vol. 37 (1950), pp. 409–428, and Vol. 38 (1951), pp. 159–178.

standard errors calculated for the least squares estimators will in general no longer be correct, so that confidence intervals and hypothesis tests may give misleading results.

Finally, the fourth problem that we will mention is that of *identification*. The identification problem occurs because the data points that we observe, and therefore use in our statistical analyses, are various *equilibrium* values for price and quantity. Thus, to observe more than one data point (one value for P and Q), either the demand curve or the supply curve (or both) must shift. If *only* the supply curve shifts, the price and quantity equilibrium points will trace out the demand curve. However, if the demand curve shifts or if *both* the demand curve and the supply curve shift, the equilibrium price and quantity pairs will not be on a single demand curve. Figure 3A–2 illustrates the results we could get if the demand curve were shifting or if both the demand and the supply curves were shifting while the sample observations were gathered. Thus, if we attempt to estimate a demand function for a good with its price as the only independent variable, we must assume that all variables other than price that affect quantity demanded are held constant, so that the demand function is stable over that period.

We will leave a discussion of possible solutions to these problems to more advanced statistics texts.[7] At this point, we merely wish to warn our readers that such problems might occur.

LOGARITHMIC TRANSFORMATIONS

In this last section, we will discuss logarithms. Since *linear* regression analysis can be used only for the direct estimate of linear relationships between two (or more) variables, logarithmic transformations are often a useful means of changing a nonlinear function, which we cannot directly estimate, into an equivalent linear relationship, which we can.

Before we discuss this procedure, we will first briefly explain what a logarithm is. The *logarithm* of a number is the power to which *another* number, called the base, must be raised in order for the whole term to be equal to the original number in question. Thus, since $3^2 = 9$, we can say that $\log_3 9 = 2$, where 3 represents the base. We can also say that $\log_2 16 = 4$, since $2^4 = 16$. In this case, 2 is the base. In general we can say that $\log_a N = x$, which means that $a^x = N$. Two bases that are commonly used are the base 10 and the base e. Logs taken to the base 10 are called *common* logarithms and are often used in computations. Logs taken to the base e are called *natural* logarithms, where e is approximately equal to 2.718. The base e is often used in studies involving

---

7 See J. Johnston, *Econometric Methods*, 3d ed. (New York: McGraw-Hill, 1984), Chapters 6–12, for a more detailed discussion of these problems and possible solutions. Also see Yamane (note 5), Chapter 23.

Figure 3A–2   Effect of a Shifting Demand Curve

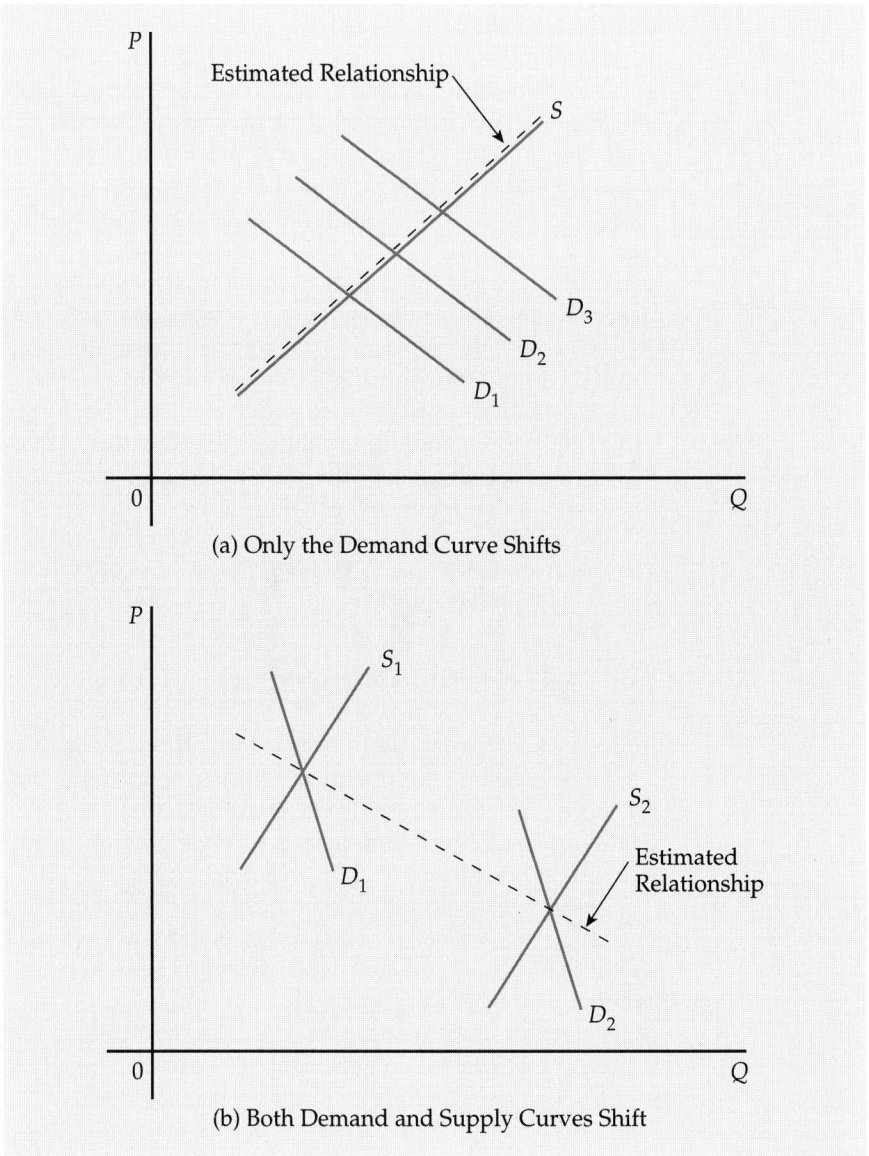

(a) Only the Demand Curve Shifts

(b) Both Demand and Supply Curves Shift

If the demand curve shifts over the period for which the demand function is being estimated, identification of the relationship becomes a problem. If only the demand curve shifts, as in panel (a), the supply curve may be estimated. If both the demand and the supply curves shift, as in panel (b), identification of which relationship (if any) is being estimated becomes more difficult.

growth or decay over time, since an amount A_0 growing constantly at rate r for t time periods is equal to A_t, where

$$A_t = A_0 e^{rt}.$$

The following rules hold for logarithms to *any base*, although we shall state them in terms of logs to base e.

1. Log of a Product

$$\log_e (XY) = \log_e X + \log_e Y.$$

   The log of the product of two numbers is equal to the sum of the logs of each number.
2. Log of a Quotient

$$\log_e (X/Y) = \log_e X - \log_e Y.$$

   The log of the quotient of two numbers is equal to the log of the denominator of the original fraction subtracted from the log of the numerator.
3. Log of a Number Raised to an Exponent

$$\log_e (X)^n = n \log_e X.$$

   The log of a number raised to an exponent is the exponent multiplied by the log of the number.
4. $\log_e e = 1$, since $e^1 = e$.

As previously indicated, logarithms, especially natural logarithms, are frequently used to transform nonlinear relationships into equivalent linear relationships, which can then be estimated using linear regression analysis. For example, suppose we wish to estimate α, β_1, and β_2 in the following hypothetical demand function:

$$Q_d = \alpha P^{\beta_1} Y^{\beta_2} e^{\varepsilon}$$

where

> Q_d is quantity demanded per time period of a product,
> P is price per unit of this product,
> Y is income, and
> ε is an error term.

We can transform this expression into a linear function by taking the logs of both sides of the equation as follows:

$$\log Q_d = \log \alpha + \beta_1 \log P + \beta_2 \log Y + \varepsilon.$$

As we stated and proved earlier in Chapter 3, β_1 and β_2 represent the price and income elasticities of demand, respectively. Thus this type of demand function has constant elasticities of demand.

SUMMARY

The Linear Regression Model

In this section we will summarize our assumptions regarding the linear regression model and the statistics that we have discussed.

A. Assumptions
1. The two variables Y and X are related in the following manner:

$$Y_i = \alpha + \beta X_i + \varepsilon_i,$$

where ε_i is the population error term.
2. The error term ε_i is a random variable with a normal distribution.
3. The mean or expected value of ε is zero.
4. The variance of ε *for each* X value is the same. Also, $E(\varepsilon_i\varepsilon_j) = 0$, where i *does not equal* j, which means that ε_i and ε_j are not related.
5. X and Y can both vary.

B. The Regression Model
From a sample of values for X and Y, we wish to estimate a and b such that

$$\hat{Y} = a + bX,$$

where the expected value of a equals α $[E(a) = \alpha]$, and $E(b) = \beta$. The best linear unbiased estimators of a and b are given by

$$a = \bar{Y} - b\bar{X}$$

and

$$b = \frac{\Sigma(X - \bar{X})\ (Y - \bar{Y})}{\Sigma(X - \bar{X})^2} = \frac{n\Sigma XY - \Sigma X\ \Sigma Y}{n\Sigma X^2 - (\Sigma X)^2},$$

where $\bar{Y}$ is the mean value of Y $(= \Sigma Y_i/n)$ for the sample, $\bar{X}$ is the mean value of $X (= \Sigma X_i/n)$ for the sample, and n is the number of observations in the sample. Each sum is to be taken over the sample observations.

C. Tests of Statistical Significance
1. Test for b.

$$\text{Compute } t = \frac{b - \beta}{\hat{\sigma}_b}$$

$$\text{where } \hat{\sigma}_b = \sqrt{\frac{\hat{\sigma}_{YX}^2}{\Sigma(X - \overline{X})^2}}$$

$$\text{and } \hat{\sigma}_{YX}^2 = \frac{\Sigma(Y - \hat{Y})^2}{n - 2}.$$

The degrees of freedom are given by n - 2. We can use a table for the t distribution to decide whether or not to reject a null hypothesis regarding β.

2. Test for a.

$$\text{Compute } t = \frac{a - \alpha}{\hat{\sigma}_a},$$

$$\text{where } \hat{\sigma}_a = \sqrt{\frac{\hat{\sigma}_{YX}^2 (\Sigma X^2)}{n \Sigma(X - \overline{X})^2}},$$

and then use a t table to test a null hypothesis regarding α.

3. The Coefficient of Determination: R^2.

$$R^2 = \frac{\text{explained sum of squared deviations}}{\text{total sum of squared deviations}}$$

$$= \frac{\Sigma(\hat{Y} - \overline{Y})^2}{\Sigma(Y - \overline{Y})^2}.$$

Briefly, R^2 gives a measure of how much of the variation in Y can be accounted for by the variation in X, according to the estimate of the relationship between the two variables. A large R^2, however, does not mean that a change in X *caused* a change in Y but merely that the two variables vary together.

4. Confidence Interval for Y Given X.

The 90 percent confidence interval for Y given X can be found by computing

$$P\left[\hat{Y} - t_{.05} \hat{\sigma}_{YX} \sqrt{1 + \frac{1}{n} + \frac{(X - \overline{X})^2}{\Sigma(X - \overline{X})^2}} < Y \right.$$

$$\left. < \hat{Y} + t_{.05} \hat{\sigma}_{YX} \sqrt{1 + \frac{1}{n} + \frac{(X - \overline{X})^2}{\Sigma(X - \overline{X})^2}} \right] = .90,$$

for n - 2 degrees of freedom.

PROBLEMS

1. Given the following sample points for sales of milk and corresponding prices for the supermarket mentioned in the appendix:

Quantity Demanded (Y)	Price of Milk (X)
240	$.20
230	.30
200	.40
160	.50
150	.50
140	.60
120	.70
110	.80
90	.80
80	.90

a. Find the least squares estimators a and b of α and β, where

$$Y_i = \alpha + \beta X_i + \varepsilon_i, \text{ and } \hat{Y} = a + bX.$$

b. Compute the R^2 for the regression line that you found above.
c. Test the hypotheses that $\alpha = 0$ and that $\beta = 0$.
d. Compute the 90 percent confidence interval for Y, given $X = \$.50$.
e. Would you expect the estimates of α and β to be more reliable for a small sample or a large sample? Why?

These problems can be solved with Decision Assistant.

2. Eastern Electric produces a 25-inch thin-walled television. The company wants to get a better grasp on the sensitivity of the quantity demanded of its product to the various factors that affect it.

   You have been hired as a consultant to estimate the following demand function:

$$Q_E = \beta_0 + \beta_1 P_E + \beta_2 P_G + \beta_3 I,$$

where

Q_E = the average monthly quantity demanded of Eastern Electric's televisions during a given calendar year.
P_E = the price of Eastern Electric's television,
P_G = the price of a television set made by a competing company, Generally Excellent, and
I = average annual household income.

a. Find the estimated values for β_0, β_1, β_2, and β_3.
b. Which of the estimated values that you found in part (a) are signifi-

Quantity of Televisions	Price of Eastern Electric Televisions	Price of Generally Excellent Televisions	Average Annual Household Income
250	$900	$1400	30000
400	800	1500	30000
330	800	1200	30000
360	800	1200	32000
445	700	1200	32000
380	700	1000	31000
440	675	1000	32000
400	675	900	32000
450	630	900	32000
500	630	950	38000
440	630	800	38000
500	595	800	38000
470	595	750	38000
520	595	750	42000
480	595	700	42000
440	625	700	42000
410	625	700	39000
460	625	750	39000

cantly different from zero (one-tailed tests) at the 5-percent level of significance? Why?

c. What is the value of R^2?

3. Connie Jefferson is the primary flower retailer in her home town of San Flores. Connie has watched the sales volume of her favorite flower, the yellow rose, change over the past 10 weeks. The changes are due to an experiment that Connie is conducting. She has been told she could sell more roses by reducing the price, and Connie tends to agree. In her experiment, Connie has set out to determine the relationship between the price charged for yellow roses and the quantity demanded. Over the last 10 weeks, Connie has carefully tracked the selling price of her roses and the quantity sold. Her data are as follows:

Week	Price (in dollars)	Quantity Sold
1	30	50
2	8	270
3	10	240
4	27	90
5	25	110
6	21	130
7	12	200
8	15	190
9	19	160
10	20	150

a. Use the Linear Regression tool in the *Managerial Economics Decision Assistant* to assist Connie in the following:
   (i)   Determining the relationship between price and quantity demanded using regression analysis. (Determine the demand function.)
   (ii) Graphing the relationship between price and quantity demanded.
   (iii) Determining R^2. What does this answer mean? How reliable is your estimate of the demand function?

b. (Requires prior completion of Chapter 2 in the textbook.) Using the demand function you helped Connie determine in part (a), assist her in the following:
   (i)   Determining the total, average, and marginal revenue functions for the demand function of yellow roses.
   (ii) Obtaining graphic representation of those three functions.
   (iii) Determining the revenue-maximizing quantity and price. What total revenue will be generated given this price?

SELECTED REFERENCES

Brightman, Harvey, and Howard Schneider. *Statistics for Business Problem Solving.* Cincinnati: South-Western, 1992.

Griffiths, William E., R. Carter Hill, and George G. Judge. *Learning and Practicing Econometrics,* New York: John Wiley & Sons, 1993.

Johnston, J. *Econometric Methods,* 3d ed. New York: McGraw-Hill, 1984.

Maddala, G. S. *Introduction to Econometrics,* 2d ed. New York: Macmillan, 1992.

Mansfield, Edwin. *Statistics for Business and Economics.* New York: W.W Norton, 1980.

Yamane, Taro. *Statistics: An Introductory Analysis,* 3d ed. New York: Harper & Row, 1973.

4

ECONOMIC FORECASTING

In Chapters 2 and 3, the importance of accurate revenue data to a profit-maximizing firm was stressed; in Chapter 6, the corresponding importance of accurate cost data will be highlighted. In Chapter 3 and its appendix, various procedures for estimating a firm's demand function were examined; and in Chapter 5, several techniques for estimating a firm's cost function will be described.

In this chapter we turn specifically to the issue of forecasting. **Forecasting** refers to the process of analyzing available information regarding economic variables and relationships and then predicting the future values of certain variables of interest to the firm or economic policymakers. As we will see later, economic forecasting has been one of the fastest growing industries in the United States.

Forecasting is the process of analyzing available data on economic variables and relationships and predicting future values of certain economic variables.

TYPES OF ECONOMIC FORECASTS

Forecasts are made regarding a great variety of economic variables. For example, on an *aggregate* (national economy or macroeconomic) level, forecasts are made regarding future levels of the gross national product or gross domestic product, investment spending, consumption spending, government expenditures, and net exports.

Gross national product (GNP) is the final market value of goods and services produced with factors of production owned by the residents of a country during some time period. In the United States, the time period under consideration is usually one year. The gross national product is measured by the *final* market value of newly produced goods and services in order to avoid double counting. For example, a ton of iron ore may pass through several stages and forms (such as sheet metal) before it finally becomes part of an automobile. Nevertheless, the value of all of the work that takes place on the iron ore and steel will eventually be reflected in the price of the automobile when it is sold to a consumer.

Gross national product for a country is the market value of all final goods and services produced with factors of production owned by residents of the country during some particular time period, usually one year.

It is important also to note that GNP refers to the value of goods and services *produced* during the time period in question. For example, if you sold your old car to a friend, the price of your car to your friend would not be included in GNP, since the car was not newly produced. (However, the *profits* of used-car dealers are included because the dealers do perform a productive service.)

In 1991, the U.S. Department of Commerce began emphasizing gross *domestic* product rather than gross *national* product. Many other countries have traditionally emphasized GDP as a measure of the economic activity occurring within the country, and the change in emphasis by the Commerce Department reflects the integration of the United States into the global economy. The difference between the gross national product and the gross domestic product is that gross national product measures the market value of final output produced annually by all labor and other assets supplied by U.S. residents, *regardless of where the labor and property are located*, whereas **gross domestic product** (GDP) measures the market value of final output produced annually *within the United States, regardless of the ownership of the productive factors*. Although GDP is believed to be a more accurate index of economic activity within a nation, GNP more accurately reflects the income of a nation's citizens and permanent residents. Since many other countries report GDP statistics, reporting GDP as part of U.S. national income and product accounts makes U.S. data more easily compared with data of other nations.[1]

Investment spending refers to the purchases of new plants, equipment, and inventories by businesses. It also includes purchases of new residential housing by individuals. Inventory investment varies to a greater degree than the other two types of investment spending when the level of GNP changes.

Consumption spending refers to expenditures by individuals and nonprofit organizations on newly produced goods and services (except for housing). Consumption spending is frequently broken down into three categories: nondurable goods, durable goods, and services. *Nondurable goods* are consumption goods with an expected useful life of less than three years.[2] Accordingly, *durable goods* have an expected useful life of at least three years. By contrast, *services* cannot be stored but must be consumed at the point of production. Consumer expenditures on durable goods are most affected by changes in GNP.

Government expenditures are expenditures for goods and services by state and local governments and the federal government. These expenditures include such items as national defense goods and wages for firefighters and teachers. Government expenditures do not include such things as welfare payments. These are considered to be transfers of income, not payment for goods and services.

Finally, **net exports** is the term denoting the value of newly produced U.S. goods and services purchased by foreigners (exports) less the value of newly produced foreign goods purchased by the United States (imports). Net

Gross domestic product is the market value of all final output produced within the geographical area of a country during a given time period (generally one year).

Investment spending includes all purchases of capital goods, including buildings, equipment, and inventories by private businesses and nonprofit institutions. It also includes all expenditures for residential housing.

Consumption spending is the market value of purchases of newly produced goods and services by individuals and nonprofit organizations and the value of goods and services received by them as income in kind. It includes the value of owner-occupied houses but does not include the purchase of dwellings, which are considered to be capital goods.

---

1 Currently, the difference between GNP and GDP for the United States is not large. In 1994, GDP was reported to be greater than GNP by .1 percent. See *Economic Report of the President*, Washington, D.C.: U.S. Government Printing Office, 1996, p. 304.

2 See U.S. Department of Commerce, Bureau of the Census, *Historical Statistics of the United States, Colonial Times to 1970*, Bicentennial Edition, Part 1, p. 218.

Government expenditures are expenditures for newly produced goods and services, including government investment expenditures, by all levels of government.

Net exports are equal to the purchases of new goods and services produced in the home country by foreigners (*exports*), less the purchases of new foreign-produced goods and services by the residents of the home country (*imports*).

exports make an allowance for the excess of goods produced in the United States but purchased by foreigners over the value of goods produced abroad but purchased by U.S. citizens.

In addition to the aggregate levels of gross national product, investment spending, consumption spending, government expenditures, and net exports, forecasts are made regarding the regional (such as southwestern United States or northern Florida) or local (such as Kansas City, Missouri) values of these variables. Forecasts are also made for individual components of each type of production and spending—for example, federal government spending on defense equipment, business expenditures on new plants, and consumer expenditures on durable goods. Forecasts are also made at the industry, the firm, and the individual product levels—for example, the annual sales of the automobile industry, of General Motors Corporation, and of Chevrolet Caprices, respectively.

Forecasts can be short run or long run. In many cases a business needs to forecast its quarterly, monthly, or even weekly sales. A bakery will try to predict accurately its *daily* sales. However, when a firm makes decisions regarding long-term investment projects, it is important for the firm to obtain accurate forecasts of sales and costs perhaps five, ten, or even twenty years in the future. In practice, some inputs are *not* variable in the short run. Consequently, a firm manager finds making decisions about investment in plant and equipment to be a hopeless task without forecasts. The recent difficulties of some firms in the automobile, airline, and steel industries are just a few examples of the need for accurate forecasting.

TWO MAJOR KINDS OF DATA

Time series data are observations of a particular variable over a number of time periods.

Cross-section data are observations of a variable at a specific point in time.

The two general types of data that are used by forecasters are time series data and cross-section data. **Time series data** are observations regarding a specific variable over a number of time periods. For example, data giving the sales of Ford Motor Company over the last 10 years would be time series data. **Cross-section data** are observations regarding a particular variable at a single point in time. For example, the sales of each of the U.S. automobile manufacturers in 1998 would be cross-sectional data.

FACTORS AFFECTING ECONOMIC VARIABLES

The types of factors that affect the values of economic variables are often classified into four general categories: trend, seasonal, cyclical, and other.

Trend factors are related to movements in economic variables over time.

Trend Factors

Trend factors are those that reflect movements in economic variables over time. One example of a trend factor that would affect the demand for automobiles is the average annual rate of growth of real GNP over several years. (*Real GNP* is the value of gross national product adjusted for inflation so that it better reflects changes in the production of goods and services that have occurred over the period in question.) Another relevant trend factor would be the population growth rate. A third trend factor would be a change in consumer tastes that occurs progressively over time.

Seasonal Factors

Seasonal factors are connected with a specific season of the year.

Seasonal factors are those related to a specific season of the year (spring, summer, fall, or winter) that affect the economic variable or variables in question. For example, more bathing suits are generally sold during the spring than during the fall. More construction activity is usually carried on during the summer than during the winter. More snowmobiles and sleds are sold during the winter than during the summer.

Cyclical Factors

Cyclical factors are related to fluctuations in the general level of economic activity.

Cyclical factors are those related to fluctuations in the general level of economic activity. Economists often use the term *business cycle* to refer to these fluctuations.

A business cycle consists of four parts—a peak, a contraction, a trough, and an expansion, as shown in Figure 4–1. At the peak, economic activity has reached its greatest positive deviation from the long-term trend index of business activity. During a contractionary period, real GNP is falling and unemployment is rising. At the trough, economic activity has reached its greatest (in absolute value) negative deviation from the trend. During an expansionary period, aggregate real GNP is rising and unemployment is falling.

Other Factors

This category includes all other factors that affect the values of an economic variable. Changes in consumer tastes or preferences not specifically related to the passage of time would be one example of an "other" factor. The level of advertising by a firm's competitors could also be an "other" factor.

It is frequently rather difficult in practice to separate the effects of trend, seasonal, cyclical, and other factors. Linear regression analysis, discussed in the appendix to Chapter 3, is one means of breaking down the effects of various factors. Other techniques for dealing with this problem involve less sophisticated and less formal procedures.

Some of the general types of forecasting techniques will be discussed in the next section.

Figure 4–1   A Business Cycle

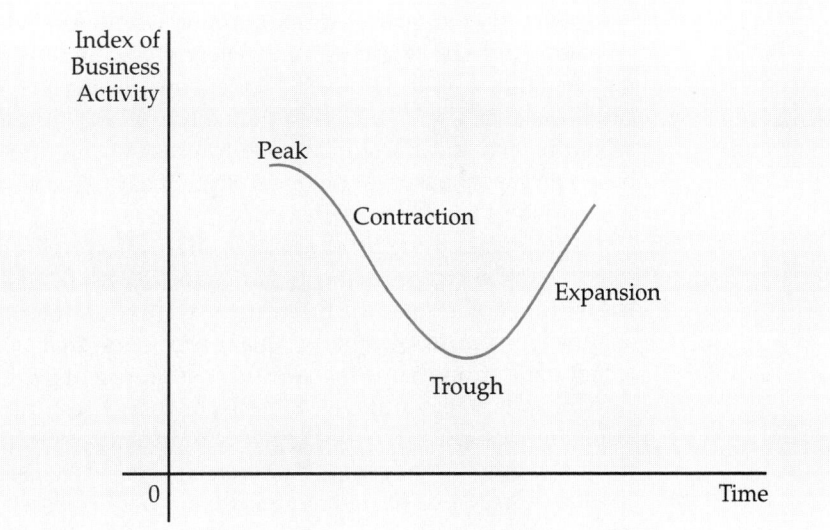

A business cycle consists of four parts—a peak, a contraction, a trough, and an expansion. At the peak, economic activity has reached its greatest positive deviation from the long-term trend index of business activity. At the trough, economic activity has reached its greatest (in absolute value) negative deviation from the trend.

FORECASTING METHODS

Six different types of forecasting techniques are discussed in this chapter: trend analysis, ARIMA models, barometric forecasting, surveys, econometric models, and input-output analysis. Each procedure has its advantages and its disadvantages; thus, in a given situation, a firm may find it worthwhile to use more than one of the procedures.

Trend Analysis

Trend analysis is a forecasting technique that relies primarily on historical data to predict the future.

Trend analysis relies primarily on historical data to predict the future. The more naive models emphasize the manipulation of historical data in order to discern a long-run trend (rate of change over time) and treat as less important the understanding of the underlying causal relationships.

Probably the simplest form of forecasting using trend analysis is the projection into the future of the current value of an economic variable. For example, we might forecast that $Y_{t+1} = Y_t$, where Y_{t+1} is the dollar value of a firm's sales during the coming year and Y_t is the dollar value of sales for the year just completed.

A slightly more sophisticated model would predict that next year's dollar sales would be a function of this year's sales and the change in dollar sales between this year and last year. For example, a marketing department might predict that $Y_{t+1} = Y_t + \gamma(Y_t - Y_{t-1})$, where $(Y_t - Y_{t-1})$ is the increase in dollar sales this year over last year. The forecasters might estimate a value for γ based on casual observation or through linear regression analysis (discussed in Chapter 3) using time series data.

A forecaster using trend analysis might also predict the dollar value of future sales by sketching a line that appears to "best fit" the historical data, plotted with Y (dollar sales) on the vertical axis and time (t) on the horizontal axis, as shown in Figure 4–2. Finally, linear regression analysis could be used to determine the straight line that would best represent the historical data. In this case the forecaster would use those techniques to estimate α and β in an equation of the form $Y_{t+1} = \alpha + \beta t$, where t represents the number of time periods that have passed since some base period.

Far more sophisticated models than those discussed here may be used in trend analysis, and they may be quite useful in making long-run forecasts. However, regardless of their sophistication, models that consider *only* trend factors will probably not be as useful, at least for short-run forecasts, as will

Figure 4–2   Forecasting by Sketching a "Best Fit" Line

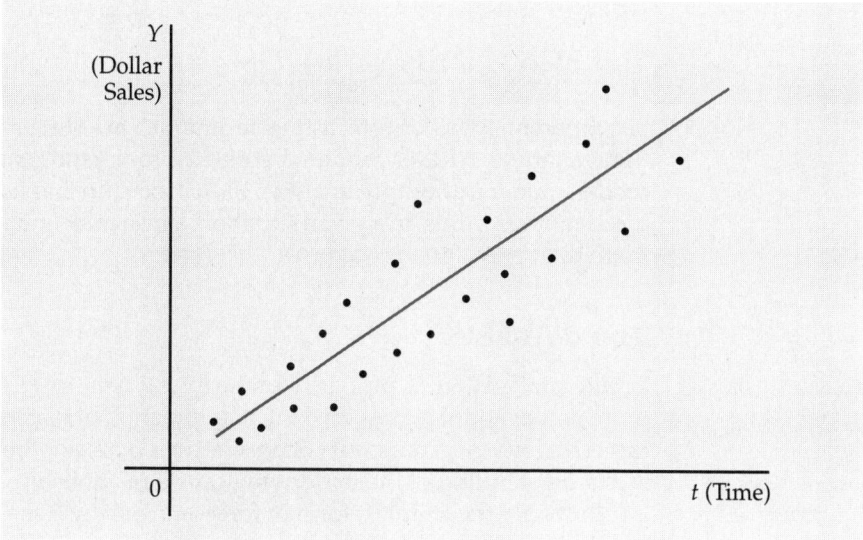

Using this method, a forecaster predicts the dollar value of future sales by sketching a line that appears to "best fit" the historical data.

models that attempt to incorporate causal relationships that include adjustments for seasonal, cyclical, and other factors. Seasonal factors will be quite important when forecasting the monthly sales of items such as bathing suits, boats, snowblowers, snow and water skis, air conditioners, and coats, for example. Cyclical factors will be important in forecasting the sales of products such as automobiles, new houses, and automatic dishwashers, since the level of consumer income is an important determinant of consumer spending on such items.

ARIMA Models[3]

Autoregressive integrated moving average (ARIMA) models are a general class of models used often in forecasting time series. These models are based on the hypothesis that adequate forecasts of future values of a time series can be obtained from past values of the series. In general, ARIMA models are linear functions of the sample data, and the sample data must generally constitute a stationary series.[4] The assumption of stationarity is important because the ARIMA models by their nature, based solely on past observations of the series to be forecasted, assert that there is some regularity to the process that is generating the series. Such a situation will not occur, for example, if the value of a series is constantly growing over time. In addition, these models are most useful for nonseasonal data or data from which the seasonality aspect has been removed.[5] ARIMA models are frequently utilized by forecasters because they yield adequate representation of the time series under investigation with relatively few parameters. This attempt to find efficiently parameterized

---

3 This section may be omitted without loss of continuity. It will be helpful to students to be familiar with the appendix to Chapter 3 on linear regression analysis before they read this section.

4 A *stationary* time series is one that has both a constant mean and a constant variance over time. We state these conditions more formally as follows.
A time series, X_t, is weakly stationary if the following three conditions are satisfied:

1. The mean, μ, is constant at all points in time:

$$E(X_t) = \mu \text{ for all } t.$$

2. The variance, σ_X^2, of the series is the same over time:

$$\text{Var}(X_t) = E[X_t - \mu)^2] = \sigma_t^2 = \sigma_x^2 \text{ for all } t.$$

3. The covariance between any two values of the series depends only on the number of time periods between them, not on their absolute location in time:

$$\text{Cov}(X_t, X_{t-k}) = E[(X_t - \mu)(X_{t-k} - \mu)] = \gamma_k$$

for all t, where γ_k is the covariance between any two values separated by k time periods.

5 More advanced ARIMA models can be constructed to deal with seasonal data. See Paul Newbold and Theodore Bos, *Introductory Business & Economic Forecasting*, 2d ed., (Cincinnati: South-Western, 1994), pp. 319–356.

models is known as the *principle of parsimony*. Some of the special subclasses of the general ARIMA models are discussed next.

Autoregressive Models

Autoregressive models are based on the assumption that future values of a series are a function of the past values of the series. For example, a first-order autoregressive model is of the form

$$X_t = A + \phi_1 X_{t-1} + \varepsilon_t,$$

where A is a constant, ϕ is the autoregressive parameter, and ε_t is an error term. The assumptions regarding ε are similar to those involving the error term in linear regression analysis discussed in the appendix to Chapter 3: it is assumed that (1) ε is a random variable with zero mean and constant variance over all time periods, and (2) the ε_t are not autocorrelated, so there is no correlation between ε_t and the error in any other time period.[6] A more general form of the autoregressive model of order p, denoted by $AR(p)$, is given by

$$X_t = A + \phi_1 X_{t-1} + \phi_2 X_{t-2} + \ldots + \phi_p X_{t-p} + \varepsilon_t.$$

Some statistical programs estimate this model in a slightly different form where the constant term, A, is omitted and the mean, μ, of the series is subtracted from each value of X:

$$\dot{X}_t = \phi \dot{X}_{t-1} + \phi_2 \dot{X}_{t-2} + \ldots + \phi_p \dot{X}_{t-p} + \varepsilon_t,$$

where $\dot{X}_t = X_t - \mu$.

Moving Average Models

Moving average models express a time series as a function of past and present values of the ε terms, where the ε_t series exhibits all of the properties discussed above and is said to be generated by a white noise process. A first-order moving average model is of the form

$$X_t - \mu = \dot{X}_t = \varepsilon_t + \Theta_1 \varepsilon_{t-1},$$

where Θ is a fixed parameter and ε_t is white noise. A more general moving average model of order q, denoted by $MA(q)$, has the following form:

$$X_t - \mu = \dot{X}_t = \varepsilon_t + \Theta_1 \varepsilon_{t-1} + \Theta_2 \varepsilon_{t-2} + \ldots + \Theta_q \varepsilon_{t-q},$$

where $\Theta_1, \Theta_2, \ldots \Theta_q$ are moving average parameters.

---

6 A series formed by $X_t = \varepsilon_t$, where ε_t has a zero mean, constant variance, and the correlation $(\varepsilon_t, \varepsilon_s) = 0$, where $t \neq s$, is often said to be generated by a *white noise* process.

Autoregressive Moving Average Models

Autoregressive moving average (ARMA) models are a combination of autoregressive and moving average models. An autoregressive moving average model of order (p,q), denoted by ARMA(p,q) is of the form

$$\dot{X}_t = \phi_1 \dot{X}_{t-1} + \dots + \phi_p \dot{X}_{t-p} + \varepsilon_t + \Theta_1 \varepsilon_{t-1} + \dots + \Theta_q \varepsilon_{t-q},$$

where $\dot{X}_t = X_t - \mu$ and ε_t is white noise. For example, a first-order autoregressive moving average ARMA(1,1) model is

$$\dot{X}_t = \phi_1 \dot{X}_{t-1} + \varepsilon_t + \Theta_1 \varepsilon_{t-1}.$$

Pure autoregressive models and pure moving average models are special subclasses of the more general ARMA models. The advantage of this more general model is that it can at times provide an acceptable representation of the behavior of a series using fewer parameters than would be necessary using only a pure autoregressive model or a pure moving average model.

Integrated Moving Average Models

We stated earlier that the models discussed previously could be used when a series is stationary. However, many times business and economic data cannot be represented by a stationary series. Such would be the case, for example, when the series grows over time. Series of GNP data, consumption, and investment spending for the United States over time would be nonstationary series. A nonstationary series can frequently be transformed into a stationary series by taking the *first differences* of the series. The first differences of the series X_t are given by $X_t - X_{t-1}$. An autoregressive moving average model is then fitted to the series of first differences. In some cases *second differencing*, or differencing of the first differences, may be necessary to achieve stationarity. A process for which differencing is necessary to achieve stationarity is called an *integrated process*, and autoregressive moving average models applied to such data are called *autoregressive integrated moving average (ARIMA)* models. General autoregressive integrated moving average models are denoted by ARIMA (p,d,q), where p is the order of the autoregressive process, d is the degree of differencing, and q is the number of moving average terms in the model. Two simple models that are special cases of ARIMA models are the random walk model and a simple exponential smoothing model.

The *random walk* model is of the form

$$X_t - X_{t-1} = \varepsilon_t.$$

It is denoted by ARIMA (0,1,0). It states that the change in the series from one period to the next is generated by a random process. Some investigators have found such a model to provide an adequate description of the behavior of prices in speculative markets, such as the stock market and foreign currency markets.

A simple *exponential smoothing* model is of the form

$$X_t - X_{t-1} = \varepsilon_t - (1-\alpha)\varepsilon_{t-1},$$

where α is a smoothing parameter. Such a process is an ARIMA (0,1,1) model, which means that the first differences of the series follow a first-order moving average process.

Simple exponential smoothing models like the preceding one are relatively easy to estimate and are frequently used when forecasts of a large number of time series are required on a regular basis. For example, such models can be utilized by a firm with a number of mature product lines when the firm wishes to estimate the monthly sales of each one.

An alternative specification of an exponential smoothing model that can be used for forecasting nonseasonal time series with a constant mean is

$$X_t = \alpha X_{t-1} + \alpha(1-\alpha)X_{t-2} + \alpha(1-\alpha)^2 X_{t-3} + \ldots + \varepsilon_t,$$

where α is the smoothing constant. This is in the form of an autoregressive equation with $\phi_j = \alpha(1-\alpha)^{j-1}$, $j = 1, 2, 3 \ldots$. However, for small values of α, a large number of the autoregressive terms may be needed to obtain adequate forecasts. In this case, the preceding model can be easily transformed into the ARIMA(0,1,1) exponential smoothing model discussed earlier.

Such exponential smoothing models use a weighted average of past values of a series to forecast a future value. It would be possible to use a simple arithmetic average of the past values of the series to forecast the future. Such a procedure results in each past value of the series being given equal weight in the forecasted value, although in many cases it may seem appropriate to give greater weight to values in the more recent past. The other extreme would be to consider only the value in the most recent past to forecast the future. Exponential smoothing models are a compromise between these two positions in that they consider data over a number of periods but the weights attached to each value decrease as the values fall further in the past.

Box and Jenkins have developed a procedure for estimating ARIMA models. Basically, this methodology involves an iterative procedure with three steps. The first task is to select a specific model from the general class of ARIMA models. This means that the autoregressive order p, the degree of differencing parameter d, and the moving average order q must be specified. These decisions are made based on statistics calculated from the sample data. The second step is to estimate the parameters of the chosen model, and the third step is to check the estimated model to see if it adequately represents the series. A number of computer programs written for personal as well as mainframe computers are available for the Box-Jenkins procedure.[7]

---

7 See G. E. P. Box and G. M. Jenkins, *Time-Series Analysis, Forecasting and Control* (San Francisco: Holden-Day, 1970).

Barometric Forecasting

Barometric
forecasting uses
current values of
certain variables,
called indicators,
to predict future
values of other
economic variables.

Barometric forecasting involves the use of current values of certain economic variables called *indicators* to predict the future values of other economic variables.

The philosophy behind barometric forecasting is that if researchers can find a set of economic variables whose fluctuations in value consistently *precede* similar fluctuations in other economic variables, then the first set of variables—called *leading indicators*—can be used to predict future values of the second set of variables. Much of the current barometric forecasting, at least on a macroeconomic level, is based on work done at the National Bureau of Economic Research by Arthur Burns, Geoffrey Moore, Julius Shiskin, and Wesley C. Mitchell.[8]

As we have stated, variables whose current changes give an indication of future changes in other variables are called leading indicators. Variables whose changes roughly coincide with changes in other economic variables are called *coincident indicators*. Finally, variables whose changes typically follow changes in other economic variables are called *lagging indicators*.[9]

The Conference Board publishes a monthly report on the indicator variables entitled *Business Cycle Indicators*.[10] These indicators are subdivided according to the aspect of the economy being described and their timing at business cycle peaks and troughs. The seven general classification headings are employment and unemployment; production and income; consumption, trade, orders, and deliveries; fixed capital investment; inventories and inventory investment; prices, costs, and profits; and money and credit.

In the past, the Department of Commerce published (and it appears that the Conference Board will continue to publish) a shorter list of 22 indicator variables, shown in Table 4–1. These variables were selected on the basis of six characteristics—economic significance, statistical adequacy, consistency of timing at business peaks and troughs, conformity to business expansions and contractions, smoothness, and prompt availability. Of the 22 superior indicators, 11 are leading indicators, 4 are coincident indicators, and 7 are lagging indicators.

Each group of indicators (leading, coincident, or lagging) is then used to

8 See, for example, A. F. Burns and W. C. Mitchell, *Measuring Business Cycles* (New York: National Bureau of Economic Research, 1946); W. C. Mitchell and A. F. Burns, *Statistical Indicators of Cyclical Revivals*, Occasional Paper 69 (New York: National Bureau of Economic Research, 1938); and G. H. Moore and J. Shiskin, *Indicators of Business Expansions and Contractions* (New York: National Bureau of Economic Research, 1967).
9 The values of coincident and lagging indicators may be used to confirm short-run trends in the economy previously indicated by the leading indicators.
10 Prior to 1966, the Department of Commerce published data on more than 100 leading, coincident, lagging, and unclassified indicators in the *Survey of Current Business*, also a monthly publication.

Table 4–1   Short List of Economic Indicators

Indicator	Median Lead (–) or Lag (+) in Months
Leading indicators (11 series)	
Building permits, private housing units	–9.5
Common stock prices, index	–5.5
Initial claims, unemployment insurance	–5.5
Change in sensitive materials prices	–5.5
Vendor performance, slower deliveries	–6.0
Average workweek, manufacturing	–4.5
Plant and equipment contracts and orders (1987) dollars)	–3.5
New orders, manufacturing, consumer goods and materials (1987 dollars)	–4.5
Money supply (M2) (1987 dollars)	–10.0
Consumer expectations index	–4.0
Change in manufacturers' unfilled orders, durable goods (1987 dollars)	–7.0
Coincident indicators (4 series)	
Industrial Production Index	0.0
Employees, nonagricultural payrolls	0.0
Personal income less transfer payments, 1987 dollars	0.0
Sales, manufacturing and trade, 1987 dollars	–1.5
Lagging indicators (7 series)	
Change in labor cost per unit of output, manufacturing	+10.0
Ratio, consumer installment credit to personal income	+6.0
Average prime rate charged by banks	+5.5
Average duration of unemployment	+3.5
Ratio, inventories to sales, manufacturing and trade, 1987 dollars	+10.0
Commercial and industrial loans outstanding, 1987 dollars	+4.5
Change in CPI for services	N.A.*

*Not available

Source: U.S. Department of Commerce, Bureau of Economic Analysis, *Handbook of Cyclical Indicators* (1984), pp. 172–173; and U.S. Bureau of the Census, *Statistical Abstract of the United States: 1995* (115th ed.), Washington, D.C.: U.S. Government Printing Office, p. 539.

calculate a *composite*, or overall, indicator for the group.[11] Since they give diversified economic coverage based on a superior set of indicators, the composite indexes tend to give more reliable signals than do the individual indicators. The relationship of the values of these variables to the growth rate of gross domestic product from 1980 to 1994 is illustrated in Table 4–2.

11 See George R. Green and Barry A. Beckman, "Business Cycle Indicators: Upcoming Revision

Ideally, to be good predictors, changes in leading indicators would consistently precede changes in the values of other variables that the researchers are trying to predict. Moreover, these changes should not only always precede changes in the other variables, but also consistently precede them by a certain length of time, such as one month or six months.

Unfortunately, the leading indicator variables are not always that reliable. As a result, the notion of a diffusion index has been developed. A *diffusion index* indicates what percentages of values of the leading indicators are rising (with half of the unchanged components considered rising). Thus, if the values of all of the leading indicators are rising, the diffusion index is equal to 100. If all of the values are falling, the diffusion index is equal to zero. Moore found that the diffusion index is usually above 50 percent during business cycle expansions and below 50 percent during business cycle contractions.[12]

Barometric techniques are frequently used to forecast turning points in the level of general economic activity in a country. They may also be useful in forecasting the *direction of change* in the values of other economic variables. However, these forecasting methods are not as useful in predicting the *magnitude* (size) of such changes.

Surveys

The use of surveys by firms in estimating the demand for their products was discussed in Chapter 3. However, surveys are also used to predict future levels of general economic activity.

Surveys can be quite useful in indicating the plans of businesses to purchase new plants and equipment. Such investment spending can have a relatively large impact on the economy-wide demand for goods and services.

Several agencies regularly conduct surveys of business investment in plant and equipment. For example, McGraw-Hill conducts a survey of such plans twice a year and publishes the results in *Business Week* in November and April. The McGraw-Hill survey covers all large corporations and a great number of medium-sized firms. A joint quarterly survey is conducted by the Department of Commerce and the Securities and Exchange Commission and published in the third month of each quarter in the *Survey of Current Business*. The National Industrial Conference Board surveys capital expenditures commitments made by the boards of directors of 1,000 manufacturing firms. The results of these surveys are also published in the *Survey of Current Business*.

---

of the Composite Indexes," *Survey of Current Business*, Vol. 73, No. 10 (October 1993), pp. 44–51; and Geoffrey H. Moore (ed.) for the National Bureau of Economic Research, *Business Cycle Indicators, Volume 1: Contributions to the Analysis of Current Business Conditions* (Princeton, N.J.: Princeton University Press, 1961), Chapter 3, especially p. 72.

12 Ibid.

Table 4–2 Index of Cyclical Indicators and Rate of Growth of Real GDP

	1980	1985	1986	1987	1988	1989	1990	1991	1992	1993	1994	1995
Rate of Growth of Real GDP	−0.3	3.7	3.0	2.9	3.8	3.4	1.3	−1.0	2.7	2.2	3.5	2.0
LEADING INDICATORS												
Composite index, 1987 = 100	88.6	95.3	97.7	100.0	100.1	99.7	98.5	97.2	98.2	98.8	101.8	101.3
Indexes:												
Building permits.[1] 1967 = 100	96.7	138.1	141.2	122.9	115.8	107.7	89.6	75.4	87.6	96.3	86.4	84.2
Common stock prices.[2] 1941–43 = 10	118.8	186.8	236.4	286.8	265.8	322.8	334.6	376.2	415.7	451.4	460.3	541.6
Consumer Expectations, U. of Michigan,[6] 1966: 1 = 100	56.8	86.5	85.8	81.3	85.2	85.3	70.2	70.3	70.3	72.8	83.8	83.2
Percent:												
Change in sensitive materials prices[3,4]	4.3	−8.2	3.4	12.3	5.0	0.6	−3.0	−7.3	3.2	−3.1	2.2	2.9
Vendor companies reporting slower deliveries	41	48	51	57	58	48	48	47	50	52	60	53
Initial claims, unemployment insurance (1,000)	480	383	370	314	305	327	383	444	411	365	337	355
Avg. workweek, manufacturing[5] (hours)	39.7	40.5	40.7	41.0	41.1	41.0	40.8	40.7	41.0	41.4	42.0	41.6
Plant and equip. contracts and orders (1987 dols.) (bil. dol.)	358	350	341	373	422	437	420	381	401	447	535	623
New orders, manufacturing, consumer goods and materials (1987 dols.) (bil. dol.)	1,016	1,114	1,167	1,226	1,264	1,250	1,227	1,186	1,231	1,305	1,431	1,455
Money supply (M2) (1987 dols.) (bil. dol.)	2,163	2,631	2,795	2,874	2,908	2,885	2,883	2,855	2,829	2,784	2,688	2,670
Change in manufacturers' unfilled orders, durable goods (1987 dols.) (bil. dols.)[4]	−1.1	0.3	0.1	1.7	1.5	1.8	1.1	−1.2	−3.1	−2.9	−0.7	N.A.

COINCIDENT INDICATORS

Composite index, 1987 = 100	85.6	95.0	97.2	100.0	103.5	105.8	106.7	105.3	106.7	109.4	114.2	117.7
Industrial production index, 1987 = 100	84.1	94.4	95.3	100.0	104.4	106.0	106.0	104.3	107.6	112.0	118.1	122.0
Employees, nonagric. payrolls (mil.)	90.4	97.4	99.3	102.0	105.2	107.9	109.4	108.3	108.6	110.5	114.0	116.6
Personal income less transfer payments (1987 dols.) (bil. dol.)	2,722	3,110	3,200	3,260	3,357	3,436	3,469	3,416	3,477	3,523	4,562	4,722
Sales, mfg. and trade (1987 dols.) (bil. dol.)	4,522	5,109	5,307	5,505	5,736	5,825	5,837	5,755	5,929	6,262	6,688	6,963

LAGGING INDICATORS

Composite index, 1987 = 100	99.0	98.9	100.2	100.0	102.1	104.6	104.7	102.1	97.3	96.3	97.4	101.7
Percent:												
Change in labor cost per unit of output, manufacturing[4]	10.1	1.8	-0.2	-2.5	4.6	2.6	3.0	2.8	0.1	-0.2	-2.3	-0.5
Ratio, consumer installment credit to personal income	13.2	14.3	15.3	15.5	15.7	16.0	15.7	15.0	14.2	14.1	14.7	15.9
Average prime rate charged by banks	15.3	9.9	8.3	8.2	9.3	10.9	10.0	8.5	6.2	6.0	7.1	8.8
Change in CPI for services[4,8]	15.2	5.0	4.8	4.2	4.7	5.0	5.9	4.5	3.8	3.8	3.1	3.5
Average duration of unemployment, weeks	11.9	15.6	15.0	14.5	13.5	11.9	12.1	13.8	17.9	18.1	18.8	16.6
Ratio inventories to sales, mfg. and trade (1987 dols.)	1.6	1.6	1.6	1.5	1.5	1.6	1.6	1.6	1.6	1.5	1.5	1.5
Commercial and industrial loans outstanding (1987 dols.) (bil. dol.)[7]	231	338	359	364	375	400	413	398	373	371	384	513

— Represents zero. [1]New private housing units authorized. [2]Standard and Poor's 500 stocks. [3]Producer prices of selected crude and intermediate materials and spot market prices of selected raw industrial materials. [4]Smoothed by an autoregressive-moving-average filter developed by Statistics Canada. [5]Production workers. [6]Copyrighted by the University of Michigan's Survey Research Center. [7]Includes commercial paper issued by nonfinancial companies. [8]Consumer price index. N.A. Not available.

Source: U.S. Bureau of Economic Analysis, *Survey of Current Business* (October 1995); *Economic Report of the President, 1996*; and U.S. Department of Commerce, *Statistical Abstract of the United States, 1996*.

MANAGERIAL PERSPECTIVE
The Economic Indicators: Astronomy, Astrology, or Gambling?

In the spring of 1990, Alan Greenspan, chairman of the Federal Reserve Board, told Congress that there was only a 20 percent chance of a recession in 1990, compared with a 30 percent chance predicted a year earlier. He went on to say, moreover, that the National Bureau of Economic Research's monthly Experimental Recession Index indicated that the risk of an economic slowdown was even lower—only a 10 percent chance. Of course, that prediction was made before Iraq invaded Kuwait in August of that year and oil prices skyrocketed.

While we cannot expect Mr. Greenspan to have been able to predict the actions of Iraqi President Saddam Hussein, the predictions of the Federal Reserve Board and other economic soothsayers have not always been accurate in the past, even in the absence of unanticipated international crises. Among other things, the Federal Reserve's predictions are based on an analysis of the Conference Board's (formerly the Department of Commerce's) leading economic indicators. Unfortunately, these indicators have had only a 64 percent accuracy record for predicting recessions over the last 40 years. The NBER forecasters give less weight to manufacturing performance than does the Conference Board. The NBER also excludes stock prices from the data used in preparing its forecasts.

Some economic forecasting skeptics assert that Greenspan's predictions would be as nearly accurate (or no more inaccurate) if he used the "Hemline Index" or the "Super Bowl Index." During the 1940s, 1950s, and 1960s, it appeared that there was a relationship between the length of women's dresses and the economy: when hemlines rose, the economy tended to grow; when hemlines fell, the economy declined. The Japanese equivalent to the hemline index is the bikini index. Some fund managers argue than an increase in bikini sales at Tokyo department stores is an indicator of confidence in the economy.

Another interesting predictor variable is the winner of the Super Bowl, which so far has a 89.7 percent accuracy rate. In 26 of the 29 years since Super Bowl I, a National Football Conference team winning the Super Bowl was followed by rising stock prices and a booming economy. On the other hand, an American Conference team winner was followed by falling stock prices. Although an NFC team won the 1990 and 1991 Super Bowls, the economy grew only slightly in real (inflation-adjusted) terms in 1990, and real GDP decreased in 1991. However, the relationship between an NFC team win and a growing economy did hold from 1992-1995. (The Japanese equivalent of this index is the performance of the Tokyo Giants baseball team—a winning season for the Giants bodes well for the economy.)

Some economists contend that the reason forecasts based on the leading indicator series sometimes do not pan out is that some of the variables that make up this series are no longer as relevant as they should be. For example, Professor Paul Samuelson has stated that the indicators do not properly consider inflation. Others argued that there was a problem with how the Commerce Department constructed its series on contracts and orders for plant and equipment because it did not reflect orders placed with foreign firms. In addition, it has been suggested that the service sector is not adequately represented by the indicator series. Other recommended additions to the series include a Dow Jones price index for 20 corporate bonds, a measure of the number of operating businesses, the rate of worker layoffs, and the rate at which workers quit their jobs. Recognizing the difficulties facing economic forecasters, David Hale, chief economist for Kemper Financial Services, stated: "I have more in common with seismologists than with meteorologists."

References: "The Real Truth About the Economy," *Business Week* (November 7, 1994), pp. 110–118; "If the Poky Truck Driver Wears a Bikini, Good Times Are Here," *The Wall Street Journal*, June 20, 1994, p. B1; "Laying Odds on a Recession: How the Game Is Played," *Newsweek* (February 12, 1990), p. 43; "A Mess of Misleading Indicators," *Time* (June 13, 1988), p. 49; and "Shaky Statistics Pose Peril for Forecasters," *The Wall Street Journal*, May 9, 1988, p. 1.

Consumer spending has an important effect on the aggregate level of income (GNP) through its impact on aggregate demand. Both the Bureau of the Census and the Survey Research Center at the University of Michigan conduct surveys regarding consumer intentions to purchase specific products. The information gathered by the Census Bureau is published quarterly in "Consumer Buying Indicators," *Current Population Reports* (Series P-65). The Survey Research Center surveys consumer attitudes and buying plans, and an index of general attitudes is calculated. The results of these surveys are reported annually in the *Survey of Consumer Finances*, published by the Survey Research Center. The Conference Board also publishes a Consumer Confidence Index, based on five survey questions that relate to consumers' current perceptions of local business conditions and job availability and their expectations for the next six months.[13]

Surveys regarding business expectations of future sales and business

---

13 See "Forecasting Consumer Spending: Should Economists Pay Attention to Consumer Confidence Surveys?" Federal Reserve Bank of Kansas City *Economic Review* (May/June, 1991), pp. 57–71; and Dawn M. Spinozza, "Two Indexes Track Consumer Confidence," Federal Reserve Bank of Richmond *Cross Sections* (Summer 1991), pp. 8–9.

plans for inventories are also conducted by the Department of Commerce and the Securities and Exchange Commission. These results are published quarterly in the *Survey of Current Business*.

Econometric Models

Econometric models are a fourth way of forecasting in the field of economics. These models range from simple linear demand functions for the product of a firm to very large models containing hundreds of equations, designed to describe many of the economic relationships in an entire nation, including its global environment. Both models describing firm- or industry-level relationships and models describing relationships involving economic aggregate variables (covering large sectors of or an entire national economy) can be quite useful to firm managers.

For example, we have already explained how important it is for a firm to know the nature of the demand function for its product. Given estimates of consumer incomes, competitors' prices, advertising expenditures, and the price it plans to charge, a firm can make a prediction about the future sales of its product. However, the larger econometric models can be quite valuable to a firm in developing forecasts of general business conditions in the economy and, consequently, what consumer incomes and competitors' prices will be in the future. This information, in turn, is necessary in making forecasts regarding the sales of the individual firm. The procedure for estimating the demand function for an individual firm was discussed at length in the appendix to Chapter 3. In this chapter, therefore, we will concentrate on explaining the nature of larger econometric models.

One of the first mathematical models describing the workings of an entire economy was developed in 1939 by the Nobel prize-winning Dutch economist, Jan Tinbergen. However, this model was not sufficiently well specified to be very useful for forecasting. Since that time, however, many advances have been made in the areas of mathematical economics, statistics, and the development of computers and computer programs. Three of the largest current econometric models are those of Wharton Econometric Forecasting Associates (headed by Nobel prizewinner Lawrence Klein); Data Resources, Incorporated; and Chase Econometrics.

All econometric models have two types of equations—behavioral equations and identities. *Behavioral equations* describe how the values of one or more economic variables are related to the behavior of economic units and, therefore, the value of another economic variable. *Identities* are equations that must be true by definition—for example, $(4/2) \equiv 2$. The sign $\equiv$ means "identically equal to."

The workings of a macroeconomic econometric model can be illustrated by the following simple one. Suppose that aggregate consumption spending, C, is a function of aggregate income or GNP last period, Y_{t-1}, plus the change in income during this time period, ΔY_t. We can write one version of this relationship as follows:

$$C_t = \alpha + \beta_1 Y_{t-1} + \beta_2 \Delta Y_t + \varepsilon_t.$$

The subscript t refers to values for the current period, and $t{-}1$ refers to values for the last period. As discussed earlier in this chapter and in the appendix to Chapter 3, the term ε_t is a term reflecting random errors, with an expected value of zero. Furthermore, let us hypothesize that aggregate investment spending (new plant and equipment, residential housing, and inventories) will be a value determined by factors outside our model. Thus $I_t = I_t^*$.

Finally, if there were no government expenditures or foreign trade, as we will assume is true in our simple model, the aggregate level of income in an economy must, by definition, be equal to the sum of consumption and investment spending. Therefore

$$Y_t \equiv C_t + I_t.$$

In other words, everything that is produced in an economy during period t must be demanded by some economic unit—consumers or businesses. (However, businesses might find that some of their investment spending has gone for inventories in excess of desired levels.)

Our simple model, therefore, consists of the following three relationships:

(4–1) $$C_t = \alpha + \beta_1 Y_{t-1} + \beta_2 (Y_t - Y_{t-1}) + \varepsilon_t,$$

(4–2) $$I_t = I_t^*,$$

and

(4–3) $$Y_t \equiv C_t + I_t.$$

Equations (4–1) and (4–2) are behavioral relationships because they indicate something about the behavior of consumption and investment spending, respectively. Equation (4–3) is an identity. The variables C_t and Y_t are called *endogenous* variables because their values will be determined within the framework of our model.

Investment, I_t^*, is an *exogenous* variable because its value is determined by factors outside this model. In this case Y_{t-1} is a *predetermined* variable—its value has already been determined by the time we are ready to try to predict C_t and Y_t. The remaining terms—α, β_1, and β_2—are called *parameters*. Although their values may change from time to time, they represent numerical constants that describe the behavior of economic units (consumers, in this case). They are not thought to vary as much as the values of the endogenous variables.

If we substitute equations (4–1) and (4–2) into (4–3) for C_t and I_t, respectively, we can obtain the following equation for Y_t, which involves only predetermined or exogenous variables and parameters, except for Y_t itself:

$$Y_t = \alpha + \beta_1 Y_{t-1} + \beta_2(Y_t - Y_{t-1}) + I_t^* + \varepsilon_t.$$

Subtracting $\beta_2 Y_t$ from both sides, we obtain

$$Y_t - \beta_2 Y_t = \alpha + \beta_1 Y_{t-1} - \beta_2 Y_{t-1} + I_t^* + \varepsilon_t.$$

Factoring out $(1 - \beta_2)$ on the left-hand side, we get

$$Y_t(1 - \beta_2) = \alpha + \beta_1 Y_{t-1} - \beta_2 Y_{t-1} + I_t^* + \varepsilon_t.$$

Finally, dividing by $1 - \beta_2$, we obtain

$$Y_t = \frac{\alpha}{1-\beta_2} + \left(\frac{\beta_1}{1-\beta_2}\right) Y_{t-1} - \left(\frac{\beta_2}{1-\beta_2}\right) Y_{t-1} + \left(\frac{1}{1-\beta_2}\right) I_t^* + \left(\frac{1}{1-\beta_2}\right) \varepsilon_t,$$

or

(4–4)
$$Y_t = \frac{\alpha}{1-\beta_2} + \left(\frac{\beta_1 - \beta_2}{1-\beta_2}\right) Y_{t-1} + \left(\frac{1}{1-\beta_2}\right) I_t^* + \left(\frac{1}{1-\beta_2}\right) \varepsilon_t.$$

Now, substituting for Y_t from equation (4–4) into equation (4–1), we find

$$C_t = \alpha + \beta_1 Y_{t-1}$$

$$+ \beta_2 \left[\left(\frac{\alpha}{1-\beta_2}\right) + \left(\frac{\beta_1 - \beta_2}{1-\beta_2}\right) Y_{t-1} + \left(\frac{1}{1-\beta_2}\right) I_t^* + \left(\frac{1}{1-\beta_2}\right) \varepsilon_t - Y_{t-1}\right] + \varepsilon_t,$$

or

$$C_t = \alpha + \beta_1 Y_{t-1}$$

$$+ \beta_2 \left[\left(\frac{\alpha}{1-\beta_2}\right) + \left(\frac{\beta_1 - \beta_2}{1-\beta_2} - 1\right) Y_{t-1} + \left(\frac{1}{1-\beta_2}\right) I_t^* + \left(\frac{1}{1-\beta_2}\right) \varepsilon_t\right] + \varepsilon_t,$$

Simplifying, we get

$$C_t = \alpha + \left(\frac{\alpha\beta_2}{1-\beta_2}\right) + \left[\frac{\beta_2(\beta_1 - \beta_2)}{(1-\beta_2)} - \beta_2 + \beta_1\right] Y_{t-1}$$

$$+ \left(\frac{\beta_2}{1-\beta_2}\right) I_t^* + \left(\frac{\beta_2}{1-\beta_2}\right) \varepsilon_t + \varepsilon_t,$$

$$C_t = \left(\frac{\alpha - \alpha\beta_2 + \alpha\beta_2}{1 - \beta_2} \right) + \left[\frac{\beta_2\beta_1 - \beta_2^2 - \beta_2 + \beta_2^2 + \beta_1 - \beta_2\beta_1}{1 - \beta_2} \right] Y_{t-1}$$

$$+ \left[\frac{\beta_2}{1 - \beta_2} \right] I_t^* + \left[\frac{\beta_2 + 1 - \beta_2}{1 - \beta_2} \right] \varepsilon_t ,$$

and

(4–5)
$$C_t = \left(\frac{\alpha}{1 - \beta_2} \right) + \left(\frac{\beta_1 - \beta_2}{1 - \beta_2} \right) Y_{t-1} + \left(\frac{\beta_2}{1 - \beta_2} \right) I_t^* + \left(\frac{1}{1 - \beta_2} \right) \varepsilon_t .$$

Equations (4–4) and (4–5) are said to be in *reduced form* because they express the relationships for Y_t and C_t, respectively, in terms of only exogenous and predetermined variables and the parameters.

Using historical data and regression analysis techniques, an econometrician could now statistically estimate the values for $[\alpha/(1 - \beta_2)]$, $[(\beta_1 - \beta_2)/(1 - \beta_2)]$, and $[1/(1 - \beta_2)]$ in equation (4–4). The same procedure could also be used to estimate the constant term and the coefficients of Y_{t-1} and I_t^* in equation (4–5). Once these relationships are statistically estimated, the current value of Y_t and the expected value of I_{t+1}^* could be used to forecast Y_{t+1} and C_{t+1}.[14]

In recent years, econometric models have been developed for use on personal computers. At least one of these programs, the FAIRMODEL, has performed quite favorably compared with the larger models. The personal computer versions of the models are much cheaper to use than the big models, and economists anticipate that these smaller models will be quite helpful to businesspeople in forecasting the future path of economic activity.[15]

Input-Output Analysis

Input-output analysis is concerned with the connection between the demand for final output and the productive efforts required of individual industries and their interrelationships. For example, an increase in the quantity demanded of automobiles by consumers will require an increase in the quantity of steel, aluminum, tires, and glass produced. It will also require an increase in the quantity produced of brake drums, engines, transmissions, and drive

---

14 Other methods of statistically estimating relationships involving simultaneous equations may be desirable. See J. Johnston, *Econometric Methods*, 3d ed. (New York: McGraw-Hill, 1984), Chapter 11.

15 "How Personal Computers Are Changing the Forecaster's Job," *Business Week* (October 1, 1984), pp. 123–124.

shafts. Some of these items will be totally or partially produced by industries other than the automobile industry, while some will be produced by the automakers themselves. As may be obvious already, these relationships can get quite complicated. Input-output tables are one method of organizing and depicting them.

If we classify the gross national product by type of spending, it can be divided into four categories: investment spending, consumption spending, government expenditures, and net exports (all defined previously). GNP can also be divided into the types of income that were created when the gross national product was produced. These categories of income include wages, rent, profit, interest, a capital consumption allowance (basically depreciation), and certain indirect business taxes and net surpluses of government businesses.

The division of the gross national product into expenditure categories and into income categories in an input-output framework is shown in Table 4–3. The top line of the table shows the expenditure categories, and the first column of the table shows the income categories. Note that rent, interest, profit, and the capital consumption allowance are combined into one type of income. It should also be pointed out that income taxes are *not* included in the government sector. They are included in the other two sectors as a part of wages and "profit-type" incomes. Indirect business taxes are taxes (such as sales taxes) that are not directly related to the level of a firm's profits.

Table 4–3 shows only the final demand for the products produced and the categories of income that their production creates. In this case both the items in the top *row* of the table and the items in the first *column* of the table sum to GNP. Table 4–4 is an expanded version of Table 4–3 that includes the interindustry relationships among the producers. Now, the top row of the table indicates both the final markets for agricultural products plus the *purchases of agricultural products by other industries*. This type of input-output table showing the flow of goods and services and incomes among the various sectors of an economy is called an *input-output flow table*.

Table 4–5 shows a portion of an actual input-output flow table for the U.S. economy for 1967. It was prepared by the Bureau of Economic Analysis (BEA) of the Department of Commerce. The BEA periodically constructs such tables, some far more detailed than that shown here. The value of the total output produced in the United States can be computed by summing the column totals for the four final markets. For example, $490,660 + 120,477 + 5,132 + 179,119 = $795,388 million, the value of GNP in producers' prices for 1967. The value of GNP can also be found by reading the value in the *total* output column corresponding to the *value-added row*. Each *row* of Table 4–5 shows the *distribution* of an industry's *output*. Each *column* shows the *inputs* used in producing each industry's output.

A *direct requirements table* is a form of input-output table that is quite useful for economic forecasters. A direct requirements table indicates the fraction of each dollar of an industry's *output* that is made up of inputs from each other industry. The direct requirements table is constructed by dividing each

Table 4–3 The Gross National Product in Input-Output Format

	Producers	*Persons*	*Investors*	*Foreigners*	*Government*	
Producers		Personal consumption expenditures	Gross private domestic investment	Net exports of goods and services	Government purchases of goods and services	Gross national product
Employees	Employee compensation					
Owners of business and capital	Profit-type income and capital consumption allowances					
Government	Indirect business taxes and current surplus of government enterprises, etc.					
	Gross national product					

Source: U.S. Department of Commerce, Bureau of the Census, *Historical Statistics of the United States: Colonial Times to 1970* (Washington: U.S. Government Printing Office, 1975), p. 268.

Table 4–4 Input-Output Flow

	Producers								Final Markets			
	Agriculture	Mining	Construction	Manufacturing	Trade	Transportation	Services	Other	Persons	Investors	Foreigners	Government
Producers Agriculture									Personal consumption expenditures	Gross private domestic investment	Net exports of goods and services	Government purchases of goods and services
Mining												
Construction												
Manufacturing												
Trade												
Transportation												
Services												
Other												
Value added Employees	Employee compensation								Gross national product			
Owners of businesses and capital	Profit-type income and capital consumption allowances											
Government	Indirect business taxes and current surplus of government enterprises, etc.											

Source: U.S. Department of Commerce, Bureau of the Census, *Historical Statistics of the United States: Colonial Times to 1970* (Washington: U.S. Government Printing Office, 1975), p. 269.

input item in a column in the input-output flow table by the corresponding column value for total inputs in that table.

Table 4–6 is a direct requirements table corresponding to Table 4–5. It indicates that 18,542/63,097 (or 29.4 cents) of each dollar of final output produced by the agricultural industry consists of intermediate products produced by the agricultural industry itself. Table 4–6 also shows that 2,451/63,097 (or 3.9 cents) of each dollar of final output of the agricultural industry is made up of products from the chemical industry. Similar computations can be made between the products of all of the other industries.

A third input-output table that is very important for economic forecasting is the *total requirements table*. A total requirements table indicates the value of the total inputs (direct and indirect) required per dollar of an industry's product produced for final demand. The total requirements table must take into account all of the interrelationships among the inputs and products of the various industries.

The total requirements table can be constructed from the direct requirements table (Table 4–6) in the following manner. By looking at the column for the metal-mining industry, we can see that each dollar of final mining products produced requires an input of 9.5 cents of metal-mining industry products. Thus the metal-mining industry must produce $1.095 of output for each dollar of final output produced. Hence the production of $100 of final output for the mining industry requires the production of $109.50 worth of metal-mining products. This production, in turn, will require $109.50 × .00497 = $.54 worth of products from other mining industries, $109.50 × .01359 = $1.49 worth of products from the construction industry, $109.50 × .00062 = $.07 worth of products from the textile industry, and so on. Each of these industries will need products from other industries to produce the required increases in their products, and the circle continues.

The calculations necessary to construct a total requirements table for the U.S. economy would be quite laborious if done by hand. However, such calculations can be done quickly by a computer. A total requirements table has been calculated by the Bureau of Economic Analysis for a more detailed level of industry classification than that shown in Table 4–6.

Sometimes an *output distribution table* is also constructed. This table is obtained by dividing each item of a row of the input-output flow table by the value of the total output for that row. For example, the first entry in the output distribution table would show that 18,542/63,097 = .294 or 29.4 percent of the output of the agriculture industry is used by the agriculture industry itself. The first entry in each of the next three columns would have zero values. The first entry of the construction column would show that 263/63,097 = .0042 or .42 percent of the output of the agriculture industry is distributed to the *construction* industry.

Input-output analysis can be quite useful to forecasters in tracing the interindustry effects of a change in the final demand for some product or group of products. It can be used by government policymakers, industry associa-

Table 4–5   Value of Input-Output Transactions Among Industries in the U.S. Economy: 1967 (in millions of dollars at producers' prices)

Industry No.	Producing industry	Intermediate Markets								
		Agriculture, forestry, and fisheries	Metal mining	Petroleum and natural gas mining	Other mining	Construction	Food, feed, and tobacco products	Textile products and apparel	Wood products and furniture	Paper, printing, and publishing
	1967									
1	Agriculture, forestry, and fisheries	18,542	–	–	–	263	28,505	1,603	1,125	–
2	Metal mining	–	320	–	9	–	–	–	–	–
3	Petroleum and natural gas mining	–	–	374	1	–	–	–	–	–
4	Other mining	138	17	(Z)	535	930	53	20	8	154
5	Construction	603	46	476	50	30	264	91	94	224
6	Food, feed, and tobacco products	3,762	–	–	–	–	16,493	47	6	135
7	Textile products and apparel	201	2	5	31	279	145	18,954	511	352
8	Wood products and furniture	123	14	(Z)	23	5,528	124	28	4,683	1,212
9	Paper, printing, and publishing	161	1	2	26	295	3,225	402	216	11,213
10	Chemicals and chemical products	2,451	78	173	125	1,477	874	3,298	379	1,477
11	Petroleum and coal products	1,113	10	33	112	2,024	220	51	118	172
12	Rubber, plastics, and leather	216	23	34	64	749	739	324	404	434
13	Stone, clay, and glass products	33	4	83	131	7,128	1,002	99	198	34
14	Primary and fabricated metals	192	101	230	201	15,192	2,438	81	1,203	614
15	Machinery, except electrical	322	118	276	222	1,842	250	169	137	200
16	Electrical equipment and supplies	55	3	171	17	2,509	6	19	35	27
17	Transport equipment and ordnance	38	8	–	1	5	4	4	45	6
18	Other manufacturing	12	2	16	3	535	84	448	97	341
19	Transportation and trade	4,144	214	321	203	10,839	5,970	1,960	1,374	2,293
20	Electric, gas, and sanitary services	304	89	172	187	74	645	331	180	514
21	Other services	5,235	318	2,886	606	7,824	5,730	1,795	991	3,794
22	Government enterprises	9	3	6	5	66	94	76	20	301
23	Scrap and secondhand goods	–	14	86	21	14	1	39	–	239
DI	Directly allocated imports	36	–	–	–	101	1,318	62	2	3
TrI	Transferred imports	1,025	858	1,076	203	–	1,355	825	791	1,387
I	Intermediate inputs, total	38,716	2,244	6,420	2,776	57,705	69,539	30,727	12,616	25,127
VA	Value added	24,382	1,117	8,611	3,762	45,575	27,852	15,638	8,584	19,402
T	Total inputs	63,097	3,362	15,031	6,538	103,280	97,391	46,365	21,200	44,529
Tr	Transfers	1,189	1,024	1,298	365	–	2,922	1,358	1,443	2,003

Sources: "The Input-Output Structure of the U.S. Economy: 1967," *Survey of Current Business*, Vol. 54 (February, 1974), pp. 24–56; and U.S. Department of Commerce, Bureau of the Census, *Historical Statistics of the United States: Colonial Times to 1970* (Washington: U.S. Government Printing Office, 1975), pp. 272–273.

tions, or firm managers to spot potential bottlenecks in the supply of certain inputs. It also can be used by firm managers as one tool in forecasting the demand for their products. Less aggregated versions of Tables 4–5 and 4–6 would be more useful at the firm level.

However, some assumptions implicit in the construction of input-output tables should be kept in mind. First of all, *these tables are valid only as long as*

| | Intermediate markets—Con. | | | | | | Final markets | | | | | | |
Other manu-facturing	Trans-porta-tion and trade	Electric, gas, and sanitary services	Other services	Govern-ment enter-prises	Scrap and second-hand goods	Personal con-sump-tion expendi-tures	Gross private domestic invest-ment	Net exports	Govern-ment pur-chases	Total output	Trans-fers	Industry No.
												1967
21	196	–	3,014	392	–	6,152	1,162	3,301	–1,314	63,097	4,006	1
3	1	1	14	–	–	–	38	158	60	3,362	25	2
–	25	2,521	165	–	–	–	257	82	–	15,031	1,138	3
9	16	896	89	145	–	128	145	538	47	6,538	366	4
62	1,833	1,137	9,191	1,771	–	–	54,338	15	31,231	103,280	–	5
31	1,067	2	3,797	121	10	66,244	1,089	2,507	1,131	97,391	4,397	6
358	433	17	434	25	72	20,227	640	583	645	46,365	605	7
199	252	1	54	–	–	4,293	2,017	413	528	21,200	467	8
2,694	2,103	44	11,395	75	129	5,694	564	924	1,442	44,529	12,410	9
693	679	58	2,628	165	–	7,867	607	2,863	2,656	44,999	1,609	10
43	3,374	275	1,644	141	12	10,194	541	765	1,370	26,975	2,509	11
618	1,042	23	1,434	43	14	5,928	187	385	589	19,069	913	12
136	340	1	456	7	–	562	166	322	111	14,808	562	13
1,883	1,134	78	2,163	25	588	1,232	2,636	2,253	983	87,906	3,834	14
262	746	39	2,020	33	108	812	22,108	5,249	2,648	53,593	3,242	15
809	554	74	1,723	24	96	8,566	7,312	1,989	7,964	46,759	3,537	16
179	1,022	3	1,545	18	168	17,271	16,828	4,300	20,221	82,831	3,258	17
1,422	959	31	3,492	29	35	6,047	2,919	1,222	2,181	22,288	2,032	18
998	11,447	765	14,285	1,440	58	120,763	8,108	6,506	6,091	216,165	10,201	19
101	2,757	6,888	3,242	1,268	–	13,935	–	74	1,942	37,321	188	20
1,601	30,671	1,002	51,351	1,392	11	178,786	3,142	1,599	12,459	335,588	132	21
35	3,931	5,610	3,660	23	–	2,148	–	106	819	17,337	9,768	22
–	16	–	40	(Z)	–	1,286	–3,042	580	554	1,991	–	23
182	942	–	290	341	–	9,870	558	–18,221	3,967	–	–	DI
870	1,363	145	376	–	689	–	–	–20,807	–	–	20,807	TrI
13,210	66,904	19,609	118,502	7,480	1,991	–2,047	122,320	2,908	–861	–	–	I
9,078	149,261	17,712	217,087	9,857	–	4,701	–1,843	4,517	81,654	795,388	–	VA
22,288	216,165	37,321	335,588	17,337	1,991	490,660	120,477	5,132	179,119	–	–	T
4,283	8,466	5,947	28,062	–	1,991	–	–	–	–	–	–	Tr

the relative prices of the various inputs and products remain the same. Constant prices were assumed when the tables were constructed. Second, *it is assumed that the same production relationships hold over all output levels.* For example, it is assumed that $1 worth of metal-mining products always requires 2.3 cents worth of chemical products (see Table 4–6). Finally, the usefulness of the input-output tables to forecasters will depend on the accuracy of the predicted changes in the final demand for the various products. An inaccurate forecast of the final demand for these goods and services will certainly reduce the usefulness of input-output tables.

Table 4–6   Direct Requirements per Dollar of Gross Output: 1967 (in dollars, producers' prices)

Industry No.	Producing industry	Agriculture, forestry, and fisheries	Metal mining	Petroleum and natural gas mining	Other mining	Construction	Food, feed, and tobacco products
	1967						
1	Agriculture, forestry, and fisheries	.29386	–	–	–	.00254	.29268
2	Metal mining	–	.09527	–	.00136	–	–
3	Petroleum and natural gas mining	–	–	.02487	.00017	–	–
4	Other mining	.00219	.00497	.00002	.08189	.00901	.00055
5	Construction	.00956	.01359	.03168	.00760	.00029	.00271
6	Food, feed, and tobacco products	.05962	–	–	–	–	.16935
7	Textile products and apparel	.00319	.00062	.00032	.00477	.00270	.00148
8	Wood products and furniture	.00194	.00428	(Z)	.00352	.05353	.00127
9	Paper, printing, and publishing	.00255	.00033	.00011	.00396	.00286	.03311
10	Chemicals and chemical products	.03885	.02317	.01149	.01918	.01430	.00898
11	Petroleum and coal products	.01764	.00289	.00220	.01708	.01960	.00226
12	Rubber, plastics, and leather	.00343	.00687	.00227	.00982	.00725	.00759
13	Stone, clay, and glass products	.00052	.00110	.00552	.01999	.06902	.01028
14	Primary and fabricated metals	.00304	.03019	.01534	.03077	.14709	.02503
15	Machinery, except electrical	.00510	.03507	.01839	.03394	.01784	.00257
16	Electrical equipment and supplies	.00088	.00104	.01136	.00255	.02429	.00007
17	Transport equipment and ordnance	.00060	.00235	–	.00011	.00005	.00004
18	Other manufacturing	.00018	.00074	.00105	.00054	.00518	.00087
19	Transportation and trade	.06568	.06371	.02134	.03105	.10495	.06130
20	Electric, gas, and sanitary services	.00482	.02659	.01145	.02854	.00071	.00662
21	Other services	.08297	.09468	.19198	.09275	.07576	.05883
22	Government enterprises	.00014	.00080	.00042	.00076	.00064	.00097
23	Scrap and secondhand goods	–	.00422	.00573	.00315	.00014	.00001
DI	Directly allocated imports	.00058	–	–	–	.00098	.01353
TrI	Transferred imports	.01624	.25512	.07159	.03108	–	.01391
VA	Value added	.38641	.33237	.57287	.57542	.44128	.28598
T	Total inputs	1.00000	1.00000	1.00000	1.00000	1.00000	1.00000

Source: U.S. Department of Commerce, Bureau of the Census, *Historical Statistics of the United States: Colonial Times to 1970* (Washington: U.S. Government Printing Office, 1975), pp. 278–279.

ACCURACY OF FORECASTS

As we have indicated, forecasts may be either long run or short run in nature. Businesses use short-run forecasts, for example, to plan short-run production schedules and inventory holdings. Long-term forecasts are essential for decisions regarding investment in plant and equipment. Many of the best-known macroeconomic forecasts are short run (that is, they cover not more than two years in the future), and we will discuss their reliability next.

Stone, clay, and glass products	Primary and fabricated metals	Machinery except electrical	Electrical equipment and supplies	Transport equipment and ordnance	Other manu-facturing	Transpor-tation and trade	Electric, gas, and sanitary services	Other services	Govern-ment enter-prises	Scrap and second-hand goods	In-dustry No.
											1967
–	–	–	–	–	.00094	.00091	–	.00898	.02262	–	1
.00149	.02971	–	.00017	–	.00012	(Z)	.00003	.00004	–	–	2
–	–	–	–	–	–	.00012	.06756	.00049	–	–	3
.06365	.00878	.00024	.00020	.00027	.00041	.00008	.02400	.00027	.00836	–	4
.00881	.00543	.00308	.00304	.00260	.00276	.00848	.03047	.02739	.10216	–	5
.00041	.00012	.00014	–	–	.00141	.00494	.00005	.01131	.00696	.00502	6
.00571	.00120	.00113	.00144	.01061	.01607	.00200	.00045	.00129	.00147	.03631	7
.00597	.00424	.00256	.00789	.00691	.00895	.00116	.00003	.00016	–	–	8
.03329	.00729	.00495	.01159	.00276	.12089	.00973	.00118	.03395	.00435	.06493	9
.02606	.01441	.00283	.01429	.00725	.03110	.00314	.00156	.00783	.00949	–	10
.00750	.00299	.00394	.00213	.00245	.00195	.01561	.00737	.00490	.00812	.00583	11
.01467	.00463	.01061	.01629	.01465	.02771	.00482	.00061	.00427	.00248	.00718	12
.10276	.00411	.00718	.01489	.00684	.00609	.00157	.00002	.00136	.00042	–	13
.02187	.29260	.16884	.11176	.14788	.08449	.00525	.00210	.00645	.00145	.29533	14
.01619	.03243	.12591	.02720	.05127	.01175	.00345	.00105	.00602	.00189	.05409	15
.00329	.01006	.06476	.16299	.03270	.03628	.00256	.00198	.00514	.00140	.04801	16
.00101	.00794	.01835	.01608	.22469	.00804	.00473	.00008	.00460	.00106	.08422	17
.00500	.00362	.00597	.01117	.00992	.06381	.00444	.00083	.01041	.00168	.01778	18
.07871	.05823	.04325	.03943	.03583	.04480	.05295	.02049	.04257	.08305	.02938	19
.03334	.01787	.00582	.00664	.00485	.00452	.01276	.18456	.00966	.07313	–	20
.06800	.04600	.06558	.07156	.05232	.07183	.14189	.02684	.15302	.08028	.00567	21
.00154	.00077	.00107	.00131	.00115	.00158	.01819	.15031	.01091	.00134	–	22
.00068	.02003	.00112	.00005	.00257	–	.00007	–	.00012	.00001	–	23
.00005	.00072	.00055	.00185	.00096	.00818	.00436	–	.00087	.01970	–	DI
.01829	.04403	.02545	.02527	.01189	.03903	.00631	.00389	.00112	–	.34626	TrI
.48171	.38281	.43670	.45275	.36964	.40729	.69050	.47458	.64688	.56858	–	VA
1.00000	1.00000	1.00000	1.00000	1.00000	1.00000	1.00000	1.00000	1.00000	1.00000	1.00000	T

Short-Run Forecasts

The American Statistical Association and the National Bureau of Economic Research have collected the short-run forecasting records of over 50 separate forecasting operations since 1968. These organizations then put together a median (middle value) forecast based on the figures.[16] Several studies have now been made of these forecasts.

---

16 The American Statistical Association and the National Bureau of Economic Research (NBER) publish the median (middle value) forecasts in the *American Statistician and Explorations in Economic Research*, published by the NBER.

According to an investigation by Su and Su, the root-mean-square errors in terms of 1958 dollars of the median forecasts for the period from late 1968 to mid-1973 were $3.0 billion and $6.1 billion for quarterly and annual nominal (current dollar) predictions of GNP and $3.4 billion and $7.0 billion for forecasts of real GNP.[17] There is also evidence to indicate that the forecasting errors were larger during the first half of the 1970s than during the earlier (but partly overlapping) period.[18] The errors usually amounted to approximately one-fourth of the *change* for nominal quarterly forecasts but only about one-eighth of the change for nominal annual forecasts. The corresponding figures for forecasts of real GNP are one-half and one-third, respectively.[19] Annual forecasts tend to be more nearly accurate than quarterly forecasts because the impact of short-run events (such as strikes, production bottlenecks, and inventory adjustments) is less significant over an entire year.

Approximately 60 percent of the forecasts whose predictions are compiled by the American Statistical Association and the National Bureau of Economic Research used a judgmental approach, basing forecasts on the forecaster's judgment and exogenous variables. About 20 percent used primarily econometric models, whereas 10 percent used a leading indicators approach. According to one source, the differences between the forecasting errors resulting from the use of judgmental methods and those resulting from the use of econometric models have been relatively small—with the judgmental forecasts tending to be more nearly accurate. However, the accuracy of the econometric models was improved when their use was combined with a judgmental approach with respect to such things as the future values of exogenous variables. The record of those forecasters using the indicators approach reflected greater errors than did the other two approaches with respect to nominal GNP and greater errors than did the judgmental approach with respect to real GNP.[20]

---

17 See Vincent Su and Josephine Su, "An Evaluation of ASA/NBER Business Outlook Survey Forecasts," *Explorations in Economic Research* 2 (Fall 1975), pp. 588–618, especially p. 600. The root-mean-square error is equal to

$$\left[\frac{\sum_{t=1}^{n}(GNP_t - G\hat{N}P_t)^2}{n} \right]^{1/2},$$

where GNP_t is the actual value of GNP, $G\hat{N}P_t$ is the predicted value of GNP, and n is the number of time periods.
18 See Stephen K. McNees, "How Accurate are Economic Forecasts?" *New England Economic Review* (November/December 1974), pp. 2–19; and Stephen K. McNees, "An Evaluation of Economic Forecasts," *New England Economic Review* (November/December 1975), pp. 3–39.
19 William Ascher, *Forecasting: An Appraisal for Policy-Makers and Planners* (Baltimore: Johns Hopkins University Press, 1978), p. 74.
20 Ibid., pp. 75–76, 81.

In another study, Professor Geoffrey Moore found that since the 1950s business executives have generally outperformed economists in forecasting inflation rates for the coming year. There was hardly any relationship between the previous year's inflation rate and the businesspeople's predictions; however, economists' forecasts were highly correlated to past inflation rates.[21] Thus, these results further reinforce the conclusion that the performance of forecasters using econometric techniques could be improved if they would also use a judgmental approach in analyzing the results from the models.

Stephen McNees, of the Boston Federal Reserve Bank, compared the record of seven forecasters using econometric models with a naive prediction that the future growth rate of GNP would be equal to the latest observed growth rate. These forecasts were also compared to those from a simple forecasting rule espoused by economist Milton Friedman that GNP in one quarter would be proportional to the average level of the money supply two quarters *earlier*. McNees summarizes his findings this way:

> Clearly, the naive same-change rule is far inferior to the monetarist [Friedman's] forecasting procedure. All of the economic [econometric model] forecasters, on the other hand, were more successful than the monetarist rule. The margin of superiority varies widely: the Fair model's forecasting errors were, on average, about 10 percent smaller than the monetarist technique while the most successful GNP forecasters' errors are only a little more than half as large as the monetarist formula.[22]

In another recent study, McNees compared the accuracy of the official forecasts generated by the Council of Economic Advisors (CEA), the Congressional Budget Office (CBO), and the Federal Open Market Committee (FOMC) Humphrey-Hawkins forecasts with a number of private-sector forecasts. His results were consistent with the hypothesis that the one-year-ahead forecasts of the CEA, the CBO, and the private sector are about equally accurate and more accurate than simple rules of thumb. However, his findings were also consistent with the hypothesis that the multiyear real GNP forecasts of prominent private forecasters and the CBO were more accurate than those of the CEA. The FOMC's July forecasts for the coming year had somewhat greater accuracy than a standard private-sector forecast.[23]

In another study, Howrey compared annual forecasts of real GNP growth, the rate of inflation, the civilian unemployment rate, and the Treasury Bill rate generated by the Research Seminar in Quantitative Economics (RSQE), based on the Michigan Quarterly Econometric Model, with those of

---

21 See "Executives Make the Best Inflation Forecasters," *Business Week* (June 9, 1986), p. 24.
22 Stephen K. McNees, "How Accurate Are Economic Forecasts?" *New England Economic Review* (November/December 1974), p. 19. The FAIRMODEL is relatively judgment free.
23 See Stephen K. McNees, "An Assessment of the 'Official' Economic Forecasts," *New England Economic Review* (July/August 1995), pp. 13–23.

a four-variable vector autoregressive (VAR) model. His findings were that the RSQE forecasts of the rate of inflation, the unemployment rate, and the interest rate were more nearly accurate than those of the VAR forecasts. However, the VAR forecasts of the annual rate of growth of real GNP were slightly better than those of the RSQE.[24]

Long-Run Forecasts

Five well-known organizations that make long-term economic forecasts include the National Planning Association, the Joint Economic Committee of the U.S. Congress, McGraw Hill, the Committee for Economic Development, and the Organization for Economic Cooperation and Development. Short-term factors, such as temporarily high interest rates or a temporary change in government spending, have a less significant effect on long-run forecasts than on short-run forecasts. Still, since many of these forecasts rely on estimates of the long-run productive capacity of the economy and give less consideration to demand factors, they tend to be overly optimistic with regard to their projections of GNP growth.[25]

The Current Prognosis

Economic forecasters continue to have problems with the accuracy of their forecasts. Many forecasters did not predict the recession that began in the summer of 1990. In May 1990, only 19 percent of the forecasters surveyed by the *Blue Chip Economic Indicators* predicted a recession to begin in that year.[26] Moreover, once it began, the recession lasted longer than was expected. A 1980 *Business Week* article argued:

> Not only have the economists missed the intensity and timing of each of the seven postwar recessions, but their forecasts seem to be getting worse, even as their acceptance by policymakers and businessmen rises.[27]

The difficulties of the forecasters, especially those using econometric models, can be explained at least partly by changes in the structure of the economy

---

24 E. Philip Howrey, "An Analysis of RSQE Forecasts: 1971–1972," *Atlantic Economic Journal*, Vol. 23, No. 3 (September 1995), pp. 203–219. Forecasters in the United Kingdom and the other countries in the Group of 7 (Canada, France, Germany, Italy, and Japan) besides the United States also have difficulty with the accuracy of their forecasts. See "Dismal Science: Dismal Record," *Barclays Economic Review* (November 1992), pp. 19–34; and David Poulizac, Martin Weale, and Garry Young, "The Performance of National Institute Economic Forecasts," *National Institute Economic Review*, No. 156 (May 1, 1996), pp. 55–62.

25 William Ascher, *Forecasting: An Appraisal for Policy-Makers and Planners* (Baltimore: Johns Hopkins University Press, 1978), p. 92.

26 Mark W. Watson, "Using Econometric Models to Predict Recessions," Federal Reserve Bank of Chicago *Economic Perspectives*, Vol. XV, No. 6 (November/December 1991), p. 22.

27 "1980: The Year the Forecasters Really Blew It," *Business Week* (July 14, 1980), p. 88.

since the 1960s. For example, during the 1970s and early 1980s, inflation was a far more important factor than it had been in the 1950s and 1960s. Supply shortages of some basic materials developed, and the structure of the international oil market changed. Furthermore, the impact of international product and money markets on the domestic economy has expanded, and there have been some significant shifts in consumer behavior. The fact that the Gulf War and its preceding hostilities were not predicted probably had a significant impact on consumer confidence and, as a result, on household purchasing decisions. Finally, economic forecasters have not always correctly anticipated the monetary and fiscal policies that were implemented over the last two decades.

When structural factors in the economy change, the parameters in large econometric models estimated using historical data may no longer be valid. Robert Solow, an economist at the Massachusetts Institute of Technology, summarized the problem this way:

> One advantage the physicist has over the economist is that the velocity of light has not changed over the past thousands of years, while what was in the 1950s and 1960s a good wage and price equation is no longer so.[28]

Another problem forecasters face is inadequate data. Government spending on data gathering in real terms has increased little since the 1970s, although the economy is much larger and more complex. A recent *Fortune* article quoted Harvard University economist Zvi Griliches:

> Our data are weakest in precisely those areas where economic change has been most dynamic, such as technological innovation, the service sector, and trade.[29]

It is argued that measurement errors regarding inflation cause the greatest distortions because these affect wage and productivity data as well as growth of GDP. Also, U.S. data regarding exports of products and services probably significantly underestimate their true values.[30]

Nevertheless, econometrics has been one of the fastest-growing industries in the United States. Its annual revenues were estimated to be over $100 million in the early 1980s; and its customers included most major corporations as well as large governmental departments.[31] McNees concludes:

> When revisions often change actual outcomes by several tenths of a percentage point even well after the fact, it would be naive to expect forecast errors of essentially zero. From this perspective, it is comforting to see that

---

28 "Theory Deserts the Forecasters," *Business Week* (June 29, 1974), p. 53.
29 Louis S. Richman, "Why the Economic Data Mislead Us," *Fortune* (March 8, 1993), p. 108.
30 Ibid., pp. 108–113; "The Real Truth About the Economy," *Business Week* (November 7, 1994), pp. 110–118; and "Silver Lining in a Flawed CPI," *Business Week* (October 9, 1995), p. 30.
31 "Where the Big Econometric Models Go Wrong," *Business Week* (March 30, 1981), p. 70.

multiple-percentage-point errors are rare. Far more often than not, macro-economic forecasts have anticipated the level of the inflation and unemployment rates a year or more into the future within 1 percentage point. Simple rules of thumb have been far less reliable.[32]

More and more corporations are beginning to use *consensus forecasting*, a technique that involves making a composite forecast based on the predictions of many other forecasters. Chrysler Corporation maintains that this technique has worked successfully with regard to forecasts of GNP and inflation, though not so well for interest rates.[33] Another study of the *Blue Chip Economic Indicators* consensus forecast computed from those of 50 leading economists found that the consensus forecasts performed best with respect to October forecasts of the growth of real GNP for the next year. The forecasts of inflation for the next year were not quite as accurate as those for real GNP. However, forecasts of quarterly growth rates had average errors more than twice those of the other predictions.[34] Finally, a recent study examined the track record of individual participants in the semiannual survey of economic predictions reported by *The Wall Street Journal*. It suggested that combining the forecasts of a few individuals with superior records in the past would result in a forecast with greater accuracy than combining the forecasts of all participants into one consensus forecast.[35]

John Mahaffie has argued that forecasts are the best guess among many plausible alternatives, and those who wish to make forecasting a predictive science will probably be disappointed. He states that even with improvements in predictive tools, forecasting is likely to remain an art. He lists eight common errors of forecasters: failure to examine assumptions, going beyond one's expertise, being too conservative in considering possibilities for the future, neglecting real world constraints, excessive optimism, reliance on mechanical extrapolation, making forecasts before all factors are considered, and being overly specific. Mahaffie believes that it is important for forecasters to blend quantitative statistical data and qualitative information in making their predictions. Moreover, forecasts will be most helpful if the purpose of a forecast is clearly stated, several possible future outcomes are presented and analyzed, the assumptions used in making the forecast are stated, and social and technological forces are accounted for.[36]

32 Stephen K. McNees, "An Assessment of the 'Official' Economic Forecasts," *New England Economic Review* (July/August 1995), p. 22.
33 John Koten, "They Say No Two Economists Ever Agree, So Chrysler Tries Averaging Their Opinions," *The Wall Street Journal*, November 3, 1981, p. 29.
34 See Jim Eggert, "Consensus Forecasting—A Ten-Year Report Card," *Challenge* (July-August 1987), pp. 59–62.
35 See Dong W. Cho, "Forecast Accuracy: Are Some Business Economists Consistently Better Than Others?" *Business Economics*, Vol. 31, No. 4 (October 1996), pp. 45–49.
36 John B. Mahaffie, "Why Forecasts Fail," *American Demographics*, March 1995, pp. 34–40.

In any event it seems apparent that despite the problems associated with economic forecasting, corporate managers still believe that an attempt must be made to predict the economic future. After all, it is on the basis of such projections that many managers must bet the life—or at least the good health—of their firms.

SUMMARY

Economic Forecasting and the Firm

Economic forecasts can be made regarding a great variety of economic variables. On an aggregate level, for example, forecasts are made regarding future levels of the gross national product, investment spending, consumption spending, government expenditures, and net exports. On a microeconomic level, forecasts are made regarding such variables as sales of a firm and its competitors and the level of input prices. Forecasts may be either long run or short run in nature.

Forecasters use two major types of data in studying the nature of economic relationships—time series data and cross-section data. *Time series data* are observations of a specific variable over a number of time periods. *Cross-section data* are observations of a particular variable at a single point in time.

The types of factors that affect the values of economic variables are often classified into four general categories: trend, seasonal, cyclical, and other. *Trend factors* are those that reflect long-term movements in economic variables. *Seasonal factors* are related to a specific season of the year. *Cyclical factors* are related to fluctuations in the general level of economic activity. Other factors include such things as changes in consumer tastes not specifically related to the passage of time.

We discussed six forecasting methods—trend analysis, ARIMA models, barometric techniques, surveys, econometric models, and input-output analysis. *Trend analysis* relies primarily on historical data to predict the future. These techniques range from rather simple projections of past data to more sophisticated methods.

Autoregressive integrated moving average (ARIMA) models are a general class of models used in forecasting time series based on the hypothesis that adequate forecasts of future values of a time series can be obtained based solely on past information of the series. In general, ARIMA models are linear functions of the sample data, and the sample data must generally constitute a nonseasonal, stationary series. Autoregressive models and moving average models are subsets of the more general ARIMA model class. The random walk model and an exponential smoothing model are two relatively simple ARIMA models that are sometimes used in economic forecasting.

Barometric forecasting involves the use of current values of certain economic variables called *indicators* to predict the future value of other economic variables. The indicator variables are divided into three categories: leading, coincident, and lagging. *Leading indicators* are variables whose current changes give an indication of future changes in other economic variables. *Coincident indicators* are variables whose changes roughly coincide with changes in other economic variables. *Lagging indicators* are variables whose changes typically follow changes in other economic variables.

The use of *surveys* by firms in estimating the demand for their products was discussed in Chapter 3. Surveys are also conducted by various governmental agencies and private firms regarding business investment and consumer spending plans and expected sales and inventory changes.

Econometric models are a fifth method of economic forecasting. These models range from simple, linear demand functions for the product of a firm to very large models containing hundreds of equations, designed to describe many of the economic relationships in an entire nation and its global environment. Econometric models have two types of equations—behavioral equations and identities. *Behavioral equations* describe how the changes in certain economic variables are related to changes in another economic variable. *Identities* give relationships that are true by definition.

Input-output analysis is concerned with the connection between the demand for final output and the productive efforts required of individual industries and their interrelationships. An input-output table showing the flow of goods and services and incomes among the various sectors of an economy is called an *input-output flow table*. A *total requirements table* indicates the value of the total inputs (direct and indirect) required per dollar of an industry's product produced for final demand. Such tables are prepared periodically for the United States by the Bureau of Economic Analysis of the Department of Commerce.

Unfortunately, none of the forecasting methods discussed in this chapter yields completely accurate forecasts. Nevertheless, economic forecasting, particularly econometrics, has been one of the fastest-growing industries in the United States. Its customers include major corporations as well as large governmental departments.

QUESTIONS

1. What is the difference between time series data and cross-section data?
2. Explain how barometric forecasting is done. What are indicator variables?
3. What is trend analysis? How does it work?
4. What is an econometric model? Can you construct a simple one?
5. What are input-output tables? How are they utilized in forecasting? Give an example using only two products.

6. List and explain four general categories of factors that may affect the quantity demanded of a product. Give an example.
7. Explain how forecasts involving aggregate economic (macroeconomic) variables can be useful to a businessperson. Give some examples.
8. What are two sources of survey information regarding planned business investment and planned consumer spending?
9. Discuss the accuracy of economic forecasts in recent years. What factors have led to problems in making forecasts? How might forecasters improve their accuracy?

SELECTED REFERENCES

Burns, Arthur F. *The Business Cycle in a Changing World*. New York: National Bureau of Economic Research, 1969. Distributed by Columbia University Press, New York.

Granger, C. W. J. *Forecasting In Business and Economics*, 2d ed. Boston: Academic Press, 1989.

Henry, William R., and W. Warren Haynes. *Managerial Economics: Analysis and Cases*, 4th ed. Dallas: Business Publications, Inc., 1978, Chapters 4 and 5.

Johnston, J. *Econometric Methods*, 3d ed. New York: McGraw-Hill, 1984.

Lansing, John B., and James N. Morgan. *Economic Survey Methods*. Ann Arbor: Institute for Social Research, The University of Michigan, 1971.

McGuigan, James R., R. Charles Moyer, and Frederick H. deB. Harris. *Managerial Economics*, 7th ed. St. Paul: West, 1996, Chapter 6.

Newbold, Paul, and Theodore Bos. *Introductory Business & Economic Forecasting*, 2d ed. Cincinnati: South-Western, 1994, especially Chapter 7.

Simon, Julian L. "Great and Almost-Great Magnitudes in Economics," *Journal of Economic Perspectives* IV (Winter 1990), pp. 149–156.

INTEGRATING CASE 1A

Are There Two Markets for Microwave Ovens?[1]

Master Cook, Inc. (MCI), which manufactures microwave ovens, is trying to determine its optimal pricing strategy. In the past MCI has been manufacturing a deluxe model of oven for people in the upper-middle-income bracket. The demand function of people (in this category) for the deluxe model is given by

$$Q_H = 60,000 - 50P_H + 25P_C + 10F_H + .14I_H + .0001A_H,$$

where

Q_H = annual sales (number of units) of the deluxe model,
P_H = price of the deluxe model,
P_C = price of a competing-brand oven,
F_H = number of women (in 1,000s) employed whose families are members of this income bracket,
I_H = average annual income of families in this bracket, and
A_H = annual dollar expenditures on advertising for the high-priced model.

Currently, $P_H = \$600$, $P_C = \$500$, $F_H = 5$, $I_H = \$40,000$, $A_H = \$500,000$, and $Q_H = 48,200$.

For several years after the deluxe model was introduced, demand grew rapidly. Now, however, MCI believes that the market for this model is fairly well saturated and that prospects for future growth in sales are limited. (Note the small size of the coefficients of I_H and A_H.)

Consequently, MCI is trying to determine if its profits would be greater if it added a second model—less elaborate, but cheaper—to its product line. Some researchers in the marketing department have argued that there exists a large potential market among middle- and lower-middle-income consumers if MCI were to develop a substantially cheaper model that performed

---

1 For an article on microwave oven sales, see "Raves for Microwaves," *San Antonio Express-News*, October 6, 1993, p. 4B.

the basic function of fast cooking. In fact, the researchers were so convinced such a market existed that they mailed a questionnaire to 10,000 families living in the suburbs of several large U.S. cities. They selected residents of housing developments populated primarily by people in the target income bracket.

From the 5,000 questionnaires that were returned and from U.S. government statistics indicating the number of families in the target income range, the market researchers estimate that the demand function for the cheaper microwave oven is

$$Q_L = 34{,}800 - 100P_L + .05F_L + .7I_L,$$

where

Q_L = annual sales (number of units) of the lower priced model,
P_L = price of lower priced model,
F_L = number of women (in 1,000s) in the labor force whose
          families are members of these income brackets, and
I_L = average annual income of families in the target income range.

Currently, F_L = 40,000 and I_L = $16,000.

QUESTIONS

1. If management is prepared to design a microwave oven specifically for the moderate-income market, how can it use the estimated demand curve for the lower priced product to assess the relationship of its pricing decision to quantity sold and to the behavior of sales revenue? Suppose the managers were particularly interested in the following possible sales prices:

   P_L = $480, $450, $425, $400, $375, $350, $325, $300, $275, $250,
        $225, $200, and $175.

   What would be the estimated quantity sold at each price, and how would total revenue and arc marginal revenue vary from price to price?
2. Over what price range is the estimated demand for the low-priced oven *elastic*? Is it *inelastic* at any price or prices? If so, which?
3. What is the income elasticity of demand for this product between I_L = $16,000 and I_L = $18,000? (Assume P_L = $400 and F_L = 40,000.) What do you think the prospects are for future sales growth as income rises? Why?

4. What is the effect of employed women on the quantity demanded of this product? Be sure that your answer is complete and precise.

5. What other variables (not in the estimated demand function for the cheaper model given above) might affect the demand for this product? How might the firm obtain information on their effects on demand after the new model is introduced?

6. Suppose that the additional cost incurred by MCI as a result of producing more of the cheaper models is $95 per oven over its feasible range of output. Can you determine from the table you constructed in Question 1 the optimal quantity of this oven for MCI to produce? Why? (We shall discuss this issue carefully in Chapters 5, 6, and 7.)

INTEGRATING CASE 1B

Omega Distributing Company I

Omega Distributing Company specializes in supplying laundry and cleaning products to chain grocery stores. One of the products it sells is a fabric softener marketed under the brand name Blast. Although the product has generated substantial net revenues for Omega, management is unsure of its pricing and advertising strategies and has undertaken, with the cooperation of some retail stores, to conduct a statistical analysis of demand for the product in its market area.

Omega's analysts believe that the principal determinants of consumer purchases of Blast are (1) the price charged for Blast, (2) the price of Cloud (a competing brand of softener sold by a rival firm), and (3) advertising expenditures on Blast. The following data were collected from a group of representative stores.

$Q =$ Weekly Quantity of Blast Sold (hundreds)	$P_b =$ Price of Blast (dollars)	$P_c =$ Price of Cloud (dollars)	$A =$ Advertising dollars (ten thousands)
1027	1.45	1.42	3.97
1204	1.29	1.45	4.54
974	1.47	1.39	3.77
1111	1.33	1.43	3.29
1042	1.44	1.40	3.49
1304	1.32	1.47	4.27
1054	1.33	1.38	4.11
997	1.35	1.37	3.50
1223	1.31	1.43	3.97
1247	1.30	1.44	3.88
1049	1.46	1.43	3.99
1250	1.27	1.47	4.54
972	1.47	1.38	3.75
1184	1.32	1.46	3.31
1054	1.43	1.41	3.49

In the table, the price of Cloud is the retail price charged consumers, while the price of Blast is the price Omega charges its customers. However, since the retailers use markup pricing, the price charged by Omega does determine what consumers pay for Blast.

Omega's analysts hypothesized that a linear demand function of the following form would describe the relation between quantity sold and the set of independent variables shown in the table:

$$Q = B_0 + B_1(P_b) + B_2(P_c) + B_3(A)$$

Using multiple regression analysis and the data in the table, they estimated the values of the coefficients B_0 through B_3 to be the following:

$$B_0 = -820$$

$$B_1 = -689$$

$$B_2 = 1,972$$

$$B_3 = \quad 18 \quad \text{(all rounded to the nearest whole number)}$$

QUESTIONS

1. Assume that Omega's analysts found no statistical reason to reject the regression results or any of the estimates of the coefficients of the demand function. Management asks what the demand function indicates about how the sales volume of Blast is related to its price, the price of Cloud, and advertising expenditures on Blast. Duncan Haynes, a member of the team that carried out the study states that a number of important conclusions can be drawn by setting each of the variables in the table equal to its mean value and determining the quantity sold that the demand model estimates. He says that the signs of the estimated coefficients and the elasticity of the sales quantity with respect to each of the independent variables will indicate that Omega should consider some alterations in its current pricing and advertising strategies.

   Using the mean values of the independent variables in the table with the estimated regression equation, determine what strategy changes Duncan would be likely to suggest.

   This exercise should be carried out only by students who have access to a computer and a multiple regression program and have the statistical background to interpret the results.

2. Using the data obtained by Omega and the form of regression equation given above, estimate a linear regression equation for Omega's sales volume of Blast. Check to see whether your results agree with the linear function estimated by Omega's analysts. Interpret the results of the equation with regard to (a) overall goodness of fit and (b) significance of the estimated coefficients of the independent variables.

PART 2

Production, Cost, and Profit Maximization

5

THEORY OF PRODUCTION

The basic function of a firm is that of readying and presenting a commodity or service for sale—presumably *at a profit*. When the firm's activities center around a tangible product rather than a service, the firm may merely obtain the item from another enterprise and sell it to a third party, or it may also undertake the partial or complete (from raw materials) manufacture of that item. We will use the term "production" in a broad sense so that it refers to all of the procedures that a firm may go through to present its good or service for sale.

Not long ago, the popular press was bemoaning the advent of the "hollow corporation" in the United States.[1] In the sense used here, a *hollow corporation* is one that has shifted its manufacturing base overseas or buys many parts and intermediate products abroad while maintaining its management base in the United States. In the mid-1980s, it seemed clear that American manufacturing companies were going to have to achieve more efficient production methods in order to be internationally competitive and bolster manufacturing activity and employment in their home country. Fortunately, it appears that many U.S. businesses have responded to that challenge.[2]

One of the latest developments in corporate structure is the *virtual corporation*. The virtual corporation consists of a partnership of firms, wherein each one contributes some specific competency at which it excels in a cooperative effort to produce a good or service. These virtual corporations may consist of companies at many different locations—even different countries—linked by informational networks. These organizations may be temporary, depending on the nature of the market that is being met.[3] A very interesting virtual corporation in the baking business is majority owned by former football star

---

1 Robert Heller, "The Dangers of Deconstruction," *Management Today* (February 1993), pp. 14–17; Edward W. Davis, "Global Outsourcing: Have U.S. Managers Thrown Out the Baby With the Bath Water?" *Business Horizons* (July/August 1992), pp. 58–65; and "The Hollow Corporation," *Business Week* (March 3, 1986), pp. 57–85.

2 For an example, see "More and More, Made in the U.S.A.," *Nation's Business* (February 1996), p. 42.

3 Sidney Hill, "The 'Virtual' Corporation," *Manufacturing Systems*, Vol. 14, No. 3 (January/February 1996), pp. 32–40; and "The Virtual Corporation," *Business Week* (February 8, 1993), pp. 98–103.

Franco Harris.[4] Harris's company subcontracts the major responsibilities of manufacturing, selling, and shipping to other firms. Its in-house activities consist of managing, contracting, quality control, and product development. In fact, Franco Harris retained a master baker to develop improved product formulations for the subcontract baking companies.

When making product decisions, a firm's management must consider both what is to be produced and *how* to produce it. Companies that are successful over long periods of time usually have performed outstandingly well in both of these areas. General Motors is a firm that in the past achieved long-run success attributable at least in part to careful product design and efficient organization of production. However, in the early 1990s the automaker's attempts to more fully automate its plants with robots ran into difficulties. GM's Japanese competitors, with less automation, high productivity, and their just-in-time inventory system, were able to achieve lower costs both in their U.S. and in their Japanese plants. In fact, much of the automation in GM's Cadillac plant in Hamtramck, Michigan, caused so many problems that it was removed.[5] Product quality also became a problem at GM, and the company's share of the U.S. new-car market declined from 46 percent to only 35 percent.[6]

In the eight-year period from 1982 to 1990, GM sunk over $3.5 billion into a new division, Saturn, to produce the Saturn automobile with production technology and organizational approaches that were, in many instances, completely new to the company. The subsidiary is said to have a "dream plant," located in Spring Hill, Tennessee. New production methods include "lost foam casting," which improves the precision of cast metal parts and reduces machining costs by as much as 30 percent. Innovative assembly lines allow for the manufacturing of both automatic and manual transmissions in any sequence, and materials and subparts flow smoothly from one part of the plant to another. Even loading docks have been placed at critical distances from the points where materials are used.[7] The Saturn experience generally has been viewed as a success, and, certainly, GM has learned a lot from it that can and has been carried over to its other operations.[8]

Industrial giants such as GM are not the only organizations that have

---

4 Tim R. Davis and Bruce R. Darling, "How Virtual Corporations Manage the Performance of Contractors: The Super Bakery Case," *Organizational Dynamics*, Vol. 24, No. 1 (Summer 1995), pp. 70–75.

5 "Some Manufacturers Drop Efforts to Adopt Japanese Techniques," *The Wall Street Journal*, May 7, 1993, pp. A1, A12; and "Auto Makers Discover 'Factory of the Future' Is Headache Just Now," *The Wall Street Journal*, May 13, 1986, pp. 1, 12.

6 "What Went Wrong?" *Time* (November 9, 1992), pp. 42–50; and "Crisis at GM," *Business Week* (November 9, 1992), pp. 84–87.

7 "At Saturn, What Workers Want Is . . . Fewer Defects," *Business Week* (December 2, 1991), pp. 117–118; and "Here Comes GM's Saturn," *Business Week* (April 9, 1990), pp. 56–62.

8 Earl Hitchner, "In the Rings of Saturn," *National Productivity Review*, Vol. 13, No. 2 (Spring 1994), pp. 297–303.

been revamping production processes. Small steel mills such as North Star Steel in Minneapolis have been able to produce some types of steel more efficiently than have the large ones. Their efficiency is partly the result of modern equipment, including the electric arc furnace and the continuous caster, and a successful effort to keep overhead low and improve intraplant communication.[9]

America's business schools also have been responding to the challenge in manufacturing. Donald P. Jacobs, Dean of Northwestern University's Kellogg School said in 1989,

> we take the threat to our manufacturing competitiveness very seriously. For the first time in our history we have . . . a triple "M," a masters of management in manufacturing. . . . But what shocked us is that we don't even have a brochure out explaining the program and we've already had 800 requests for information.[10]

More recently, the interest in technology management courses and degree programs has continued to expand, not only in the United States but also in Great Britain, where a consortium of schools has set up a "Universities in Technology" initiative.[11]

Today's business publications are full of stories about trends toward "smart factories," "work teams," "concurrent engineering," "flexible manufacturing," and the "quest for quality" in U.S. industry.[12] Computer-integrated manufacturing (CIM) and computer-aided design (CAD) are two tools that have helped firms to be more efficient and respond quickly to market changes. However, as the examples just cited have shown us, no mechanical or electronic device will substitute for careful, efficient, on-the-ball management. Making the right choices at the right time, simplifying and reorganizing production for greater efficiency, and producing products that are qualitatively equal to or better than imported alternatives depend on people

---

9 See Jim Thompson, "The Future for Minimills," *Iron Age New Steel* (February 1996), p. 80; "Minimill Inroads in Sheet Market Rouse Big Steel," *The Wall Street Journal*, March 9, 1992, pp. B1, B2; "Is Your Company Too Big?" *Business Week* (March 27, 1989), pp. 84–94; and "Small Is Beautiful Now in Manufacturing," *Business Week* (October 22, 1984), pp. 152–156. National Steel, one of the healthiest of the major U.S. steel companies, in the mid-1980s sold a half interest to a Japanese steel company, Nippon Kokan (NKK). The Japanese firm quickly found 300 practices that needed to be changed to cut costs at National. See "National Steel's New Game Plan Is Made in Japan," *Business Week* (June 3, 1985), p. 78.

10 "Shifting the Focus at B-Schools," *New York Times*, December 31, 1989, p. 4F.

11 George A. Schillinger and Anthony J. Wiener, "Responding to Global Competition: The Technology Management Program," *Review of Business*, Vol. 14, No. 3 (Spring 1993), pp. 5–9; and "Universities in Technology Initiative," *Personnel Management*, Vol. 25, No. 8 (August 1993), p. 49.

12 See Brian McWilliams, "Re-engineering the Small Factory," *Inc.* (January 1, 1996) pp. 44–47; Gary S. Vasilash, "Lean—and Beyond," *Automotive Production*, Vol. 108, No. 1 (January 1996), pp. 60–63; "Small, Flexible Plants May Play Crucial Role in U.S. Manufacturing," *The Wall Street Journal*, January 13, 1993, pp. A1, A2; and "Quality," *Business Week* (November 30, 1992).

skills, not just automation or robotics. In fact, General Motors is said to have benefited more from the management techniques it learned from Toyota in its California joint venture (Geo) than from what it found out about Japanese robotics or factory automation.[13]

However, some firms are finding that Japanese techniques must be adapted carefully to fit U.S. culture if they are to be profitable for production in the United States.[14] For example, Whirlpool found that quality circle discussions tended to waste time on minor issues, such as the color of paint in the bathrooms. As an alternative, Whirlpool instituted gain-sharing plans through which workers shared in the savings resulting from quality improvements. In some plants, GE has replaced quality circles with Work-Out, where workers and managers meet periodically and workers are encouraged to offer radically new ideas. In contrast to quality circles and similar to Whirlpool's gain-sharing plans, Work-Out offers individual rewards for profitable ideas.[15]

In Chapter 2, we discussed the necessity of producing a product for which a sufficient market could be obtained, and in Chapters 3 and 4 we considered ways to estimate and forecast the size of that market. In the next two chapters, we will discuss how a firm's manager can use economic principles to ensure that its product is produced at the lowest possible cost, *given a certain desired level of output.*

In the **long run** all inputs are variable, whereas in the **short run** some input or inputs are fixed.

As we discuss production, it will be helpful to distinguish between two general categories of time periods—the long run and the short run. The **long run** is distinguished from the short run by being a period of time long enough for all inputs, or factors of production, to be variable as far as an individual firm is concerned. The **short run**, on the other hand, is a period so brief that the amount of *at least* one input is fixed. Certainly the length of time necessary for all inputs to be variable may differ according to the nature of the industry and the structure of the firm. For example, the long run for General Motors would likely be a greater length of time than that for a firm specializing in temporary office help. In a practical sense, economists think of the long run as a planning period involving decisions regarding investment in new plant and equipment, while the short run involves operations from existing plant and equipment.

---

13 "The Five Hottest Manufacturers in Silicon Valley: NUMMI, Focusing on the Individual," *Production*, 107, No. 5 (May 1995), pp. 64–65; Susan A. Mohrman, Edward E. Lawler III, and Gerald E. Ledford, Jr., "Do Employee Involvement and TQM Programs Work?," *Journal for Quality and Participation*, Vol. 19, No. 1 (January/February 1996), pp. 6–10; and "Downsizing Detroit: The Big Three's Strategy for Survival," *Business Week* (April 14, 1986), p. 87.

14 Taunco Kekale and Jouni Kekale, "A Mismatch of Cultures: A Pitfall of Implementing a TQM Approach," *International Journal of Quality and Reliability Management*, Vol. 12, No. 9 (1995) pp. 210–220. For a discussion of difficulties encountered in transferring Japanese techniques to Australia, see Patrick Dawson, "Troubles with TQM: Pirelli Cables Australia, Ltd." *Managing Service Quality*, Vol. 5, No. 6 (1995), pp. 18–20.

15 Amal Kumar Naj, "Some Manufacturers Drop Efforts to Adopt Japanese Techniques," *The Wall Street Journal*, May 7, 1993, pp. A1, A12.

THE PRODUCTION FUNCTION AND THE LONG RUN

The economic analysis of production can be undertaken by either first considering the long run and then the short run, or vice versa. Here we have chosen to begin with the long run for the following reason: *The condition for obtaining the cost-minimizing combination of inputs for a given level of output in the long run also applies in the short run to all variable inputs.* Thus the long-run case provides a rule with general applicability to the question of choosing the proper combination of what may be very numerous available combinations of variable inputs. After developing our picture of the long run, it will be easy to turn to the short run, which has the added restriction that some inputs are fixed in amount.

The **production function** is a statement of how inputs can be combined to get various quantities of output of some given product.

We will begin our discussion of the long run by concentrating on the nature of the production function itself. Briefly, a **production function** is a mathematical statement of the way that the quantity of output of a particular product depends on the use of specific inputs, or resources. In the long run, it is possible to vary the amount of each input that is included in the function and therefore to use virtually any combination of the inputs to obtain output. For each possible combination of inputs, the production function indicates the *maximum quantity of output that can be produced*. For example, one production function might be $Q = L^2 + 2KL$, where Q equals quantity of output, K is quantity of capital, and L is quantity of labor. Another production function might be $Q = 10K^{1/2}L^{1/2}$. Table 5–1 gives some approximate quantities of output for the latter production function corresponding to different amounts of capital and labor. We say that the production function indicates *maximum* quantities that can be produced with each combination of inputs because we assume *all* inputs are being utilized efficiently; that is, none are idle or wasted. In other words, no workers are playing cards when they are supposed to be tightening bolts on an assembly line.

Marginal Product of an Input

The **marginal product** of a variable input is the rate of change of total product with respect to the input, all other inputs kept fixed.

A fuller understanding of the meaning of a production function can be gained by examining what happens to output if the amount of just one input is changed. If we select some combination of inputs from Table 5–1 and assume a firm is operating with it, there will be specific changes in output that occur from changing one or the other of the two inputs. For example, if the firm is using three units of K with two of L, output will be 24.49. If K is increased by one unit, output will expand to 28.28. The change in output that occurs, 28.28 minus 24.49 or 3.79 is called the **marginal product** of input K. It tells us the impact on output (Q) of a one-unit change in K and can also be written

$$MP_K = \frac{\Delta Q}{\Delta K}.$$

Similarly, the marginal product of a unit of L is $\Delta Q/\Delta L$, and if the firm is currently using 3 units of K with 2 units of L, the marginal product of *a third unit*

Table 5–1   Values of Q, K, and L for the Production Function
$Q = 10K^{1/2}L^{1/2}$

K	Output Quantity (Q)				
5	22.36	31.62	38.73	44.72	50.00
4	20.00	28.28	34.64	40.00	44.72
3	17.32	24.49	30.00	34.64	38.73
2	14.14	20.00	24.49	28.28	31.62
1	10.00	14.14	17.32	20.00	22.36
	1	2	3	4	5 L

of L will be 30 minus 24.49 or 5.51. You should examine Table 5–1 enough to see that at other combinations of K and L, the marginal products of the two inputs are not the same as they are at $K = 3$ and $L = 2$. The reason for this is that while inputs may be partial substitutes for one another, they also generally complement one another in some way, so that the marginal product of one of them will be greater the more of another it has to work with. Thus, in the table, when $L = 2$ but $K = 4$ rather than 3, the marginal product of L will be 34.64 minus 28.28 or 6.36—higher than it is when K is only 3. That is because when $K = 4$ instead of 3, labor has more capital to work with; therefore an additional unit of labor can add more to total output.

Marginal product is usually written as MP with a subscript for the name of the input. Thus MP_K indicates the marginal product of K and MP_L the marginal product of L. In this book we will also adopt the convention that calculation of marginal product from tabular data (also called discrete data) will be called *arc marginal product*. This is the same convention we used in Chapter 2 when arc marginal revenue was defined. There we were interested in how much total revenue changed per unit of output as output (Q) changed by one or more units. Here we focus on how much *output* changes per unit of *input*, as some input such as capital or labor changes by one or more units. Thus, if a firm employs four more workers and its daily output rises by 20, we will say that the arc marginal product of a worker is 5 units of output per day (assuming no other inputs are changed). When combined with knowledge of *how much the firm must pay* to obtain an additional unit of a given input, the marginal product of an input provides extremely useful information on choosing the best input combination, as will be shown a bit later in this chapter.

Isoquants and the Production Function

In general, we can represent the production function for a firm as

$$Q = f(a,b,c, \ldots ,z),$$

where a, b, c, . . . ,z are amounts of various inputs and Q is the level of output for a firm. Although a firm usually has more than two types of inputs and a more general case can be handled mathematically without too much difficulty, we will restrict our discussion to a situation in which there are only two inputs. Thus we will use a production function of the form

$$Q = f(a,b),$$

where a and b are factors of production (inputs) and Q is quantity of output. We are limiting our discussion to the two-input case because it can be illustrated easily and because all of the economic principles that we derive from this case apply to a more general case as well. The production function relationship $Q = f(a,b)$ can be graphed as a surface in three-dimensional space so that the surface generally reaches higher altitudes as the quantities used of inputs a and b increase (see Figure 5–1). Such a function indicates that a greater level of output can be achieved with greater amounts of the inputs—an assumption that seems realistic.

As we will see later, the economic way of looking at the most efficient (that is, the cheapest) combination of two inputs that will produce a particu-

Figure 5–1   The Production Function

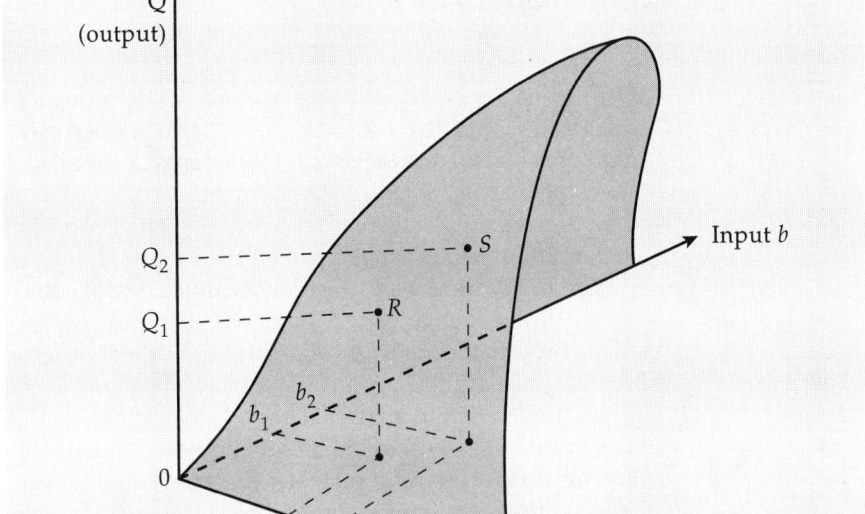

Figure 5–1 depicts a production function—the relationship between the quantity produced (Q) and the quantities utilized of two inputs, a and b. For example, at R with a_1 of input a and b_1 of input b, Q_1 units of output can be produced. A similar explanation holds for a_2, b_2, and Q_2 at point S.

lar level of output is most easily understood if we first visualize the production surface in Figure 5–1 as consisting of a series of isoelevation contours (lines of equal height above the *ab* plane), each of which corresponds to a particular level of output (see Figure 5–2).

> An **isoquant** is a contour line that shows the various combinations of two inputs that will produce a given level of output.

Now imagine that these contours have been projected down into the *a*, *b* (input) plane (see Figure 5–3). These contours, which are called **isoquants** (meaning, literally, *equal quantity*), give the various combinations of inputs *a* and *b* that would enable a firm to produce a particular level of output. Thus each isoquant corresponds to a specific level of output and shows different ways, all technologically efficient, of producing that quantity of output. As we proceed northeastward from the origin, the output level corresponding to each successive isoquant increases because, as we stated earlier, a higher level of output usually requires greater amounts of the two inputs.

Slope of an Isoquant (Marginal Rate of Substitution)

The slope of an isoquant is significant because it indicates the rate at which factors *a* and *b* can be substituted for each other while a constant level of pro-

Figure 5–2   Iso-Quantity Contours on the Production Surface

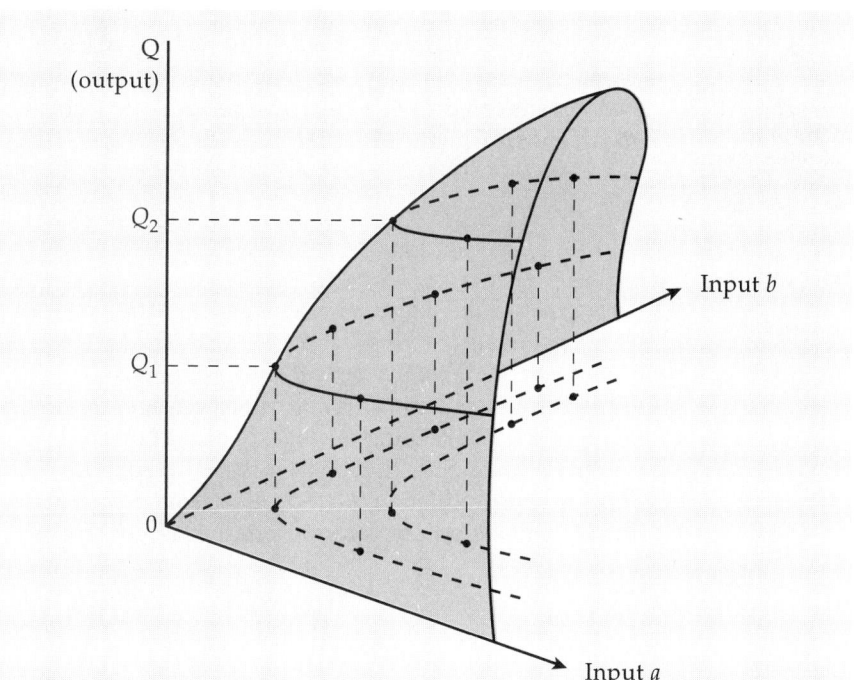

The iso-quantity contours depict various combinations of inputs *a* and *b* that can be used to produce levels of output equal to Q_1 and Q_2, respectively.

Figure 5–3   Isoquant Curves

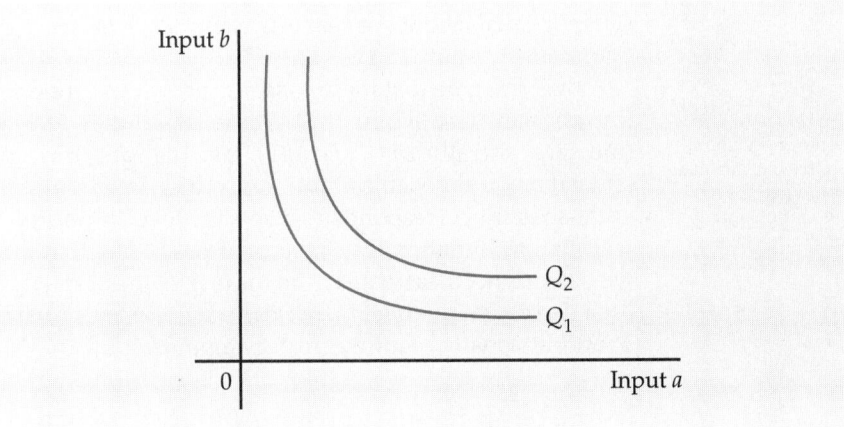

The iso-quantity contours depicted in Figure 5–2 are projected onto the input (a,b) plane in Figure 5–3. Here, they are called isoquants.

duction is maintained. Specifically, the slope of an isoquant in Figure 5–3, or $\Delta b / \Delta a$, can be obtained by finding the amount of input b that can be given up if one more unit of input a is added while the level of output is held constant. Economists call the negative of this term$(-\Delta b / \Delta a)$ the **marginal rate of (technical) substitution (MRS)** of input a for input b:

The **marginal rate of (technical) substitution (MRS)** is the negative of the slope of an isoquant and shows how much of one input can be substituted for another, output constant.

$$MRS = -\left(\frac{\Delta b}{\Delta a}\right)_{Q \text{ constant}} = (-1) \times \text{ isoquant slope.}$$

In Figure 5–4 the marginal rate of substitution between points C and D is 3, whereas between points E and F it is 2/3. The MRS has decreased because inputs a and b are *not* perfect substitutes for each other. Therefore, as more of input a is added, less of input b can be given up in exchange for another unit of input a while keeping the level of output unchanged.

In Figure 5–5 we find an isoquant corresponding to an output level of 20 units for the production function illustrated in Table 5–1. That table indicated that 20 units of output could be produced in the ways shown here:

Level of Output (Q)	Amount of Capital (K)	Amount of Labor (L)
20	4	1
20	2	2
20	1	4

Figure 5–4   Diminishing Marginal Rate of Substitution

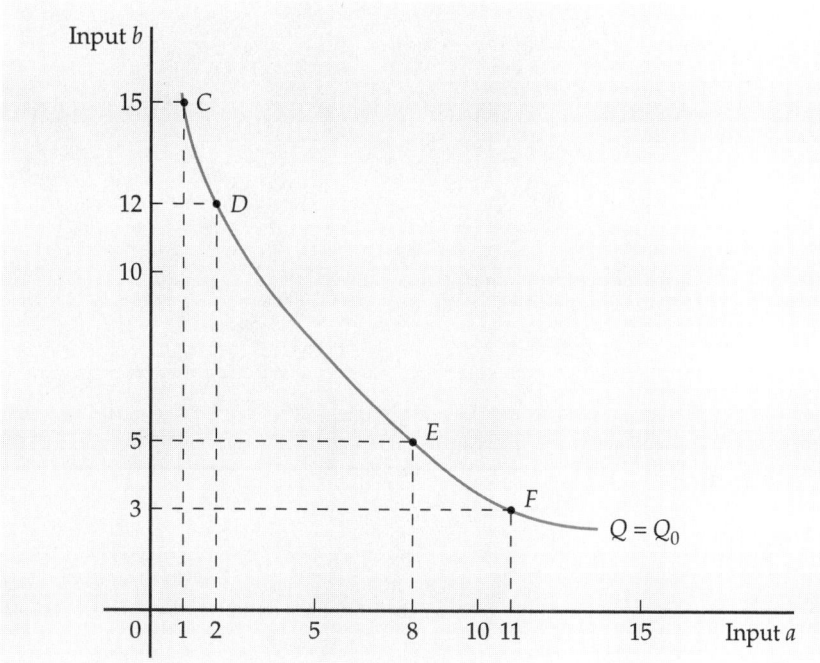

In Figure 5–4 the marginal rate of substitution of input *a* for input *b* decreases as the amount of input *a* used relative to input *b* increases. Between points C and D, MRS = −(Δb/Δa) = −(−3/1) = 3. Between points E and F, MRS = −(−2/3) = 2/3.

The two inputs involved are capital, measured on the vertical axis, and labor, measured on the horizontal axis. The marginal rate of substitution of labor for capital between points *A* and *B* is equal to −(ΔK/ΔL) = −(−2/1) = 2. Between points *B* and *C*, the marginal rate of substitution is equal to −(ΔK/ΔL) = −(−1/2) = 1/2. In this case also, the marginal rate of substitution is decreasing, and the inputs (capital and labor) are imperfect substitutes.

Relation of *MRS* to Marginal Product of Inputs

The marginal rate of substitution −(Δb/Δa) is equal to the ratio of the *arc* marginal product of input *a* to the *arc* marginal product of input *b*. As we explained earlier in the chapter, the arc marginal product of an input is the average change in output resulting from a one-unit increase in that input, holding the other input(s) constant. Thus $MP_a = \Delta Q/\Delta a$ and $MP_b = \Delta Q/\Delta b$. Along an isoquant, the *increase* in output resulting from the addition of input

Figure 5–5   An Isoquant for 20 Units of Output

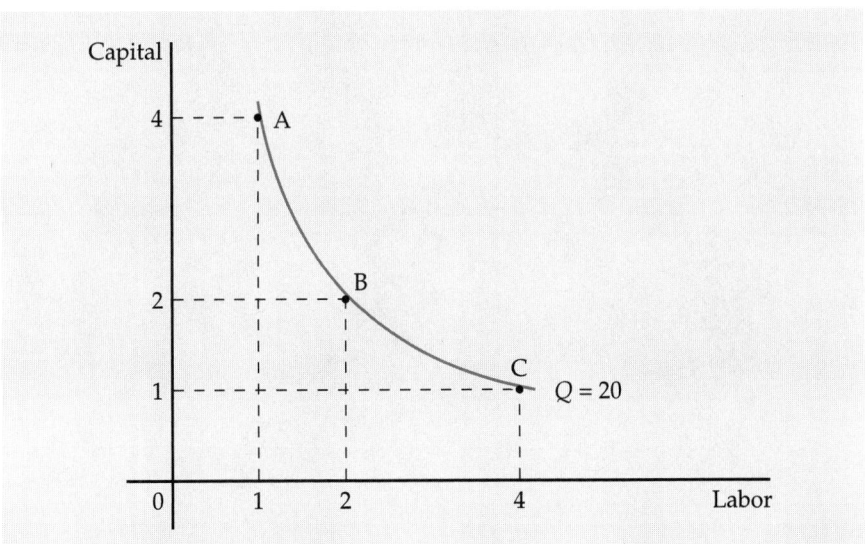

Figure 5–5 depicts an isoquant for 20 units of output. That level of output can be produced using 4 units of capital and 1 of labor, 2 units of capital and 2 of labor, or 1 unit of capital and 4 of labor.

a must be exactly offset by the *decrease* in quantity from a reduction in input b, or $\Delta Q = 0 = MP_a(\Delta a) + MP_b(\Delta b)$. Thus $MP_a(\Delta a) = -MP_b(\Delta b)$, and dividing both sides by $\Delta a(MP_b)$, we obtain the following equation:[16]

$$\frac{MP_a}{MP_b} = -\frac{\Delta b}{\Delta a}, Q \text{ constant.}$$

If we think about it, it must be the case that the rate at which one input can be substituted for another, while maintaining the same level of output, is inversely related to their relative productivities. For example, if 1 unit of capital will add 20 units of output per hour and 1 unit of labor will add 10 units

---

16 Precisely, in calculus terms, the slope of an isoquant is db/da, with quantity constant. We can find the slope of the isoquant by first finding the total differential of the production function. If $Q = f(a,b)$, then the total differential is

$$dQ = \left(\frac{\partial Q}{\partial a}\right)da + \left(\frac{\partial Q}{\partial b}\right)db.$$

Along an isoquant, $dQ = 0$, since quantity of output does not change and so $(\partial Q/\partial a)da + (\partial Q/\partial b)db = 0$. Solving for db/da, we find $db/da = -(\partial Q/\partial a)/(\partial Q/\partial b)$, the slope of the isoquant. Finally, $\partial Q/\partial a$ is the marginal product of input a, and $\partial Q/\partial b$ is the marginal product of input b; so $db/da = -MP_a/MP_b$.

of output per hour, then we can substitute 2 units of *labor* for *1* unit of *capital*. This relationship holds, since in this case one unit of labor is only *half* as productive as one unit of capital [$MP_L = 10 = (1/2)MP_K$]. Thus

$$MRS = -\left(\frac{\Delta K}{\Delta L}\right)_{Q\text{ constant}} = -\left(\frac{-1}{2}\right) = \frac{1}{2} = \frac{10}{20} = \frac{MP_L}{MP_K}.$$

Substitutability of Inputs

Three general types of shapes that an isoquant might have are shown in Figure 5–6. In Figure 5–6, panel (a), the isoquants are right angles, indicating that inputs *a* and *b* must be used in fixed proportions and therefore are *not substitutable*. An example of this type of situation would be yeast and flour for a specific type of bread. Tires and a battery for an automobile would be another example. In any such case of nonsubstitutable inputs, the *MRS* will be zero along the horizontal portion of the isoquant, since when an additional unit of *a* is used, there is no amount of *b* that can be given up if output is to remain constant. (The *MRS* is undefined along the vertical portion of the isoquant, since no amount of input *a* can be given up in exchange for a greater amount of input *b*.)

The other extreme case—where inputs *a* and *b* are *perfect substitutes*—is shown in Figure 5–6, panel (b). In this case, input *a* can be substituted for input *b* at a fixed rate, as indicated by the straight-line isoquants (which have a constant slope and *MRS*). In the area of baking, honey and brown sugar are often nearly perfect substitutes. Natural gas and fuel oil are close substitutes in energy production.

The most common situation is depicted in Figure 5–6, panel (c) (and was discussed previously). In this situation the inputs are *imperfect substitutes*, and the rate at which input *b* can be given up in return for one more unit of input *a* while maintaining the same level of output (the *MRS*) diminishes as the amount of input *a* being used increases (observe points C, D, E, and F in Figure 5–4). In farming, combines and labor for harvesting grain provide an example of a diminishing *MRS*; and, in general, capital and labor are imperfect substitutes.

The choice of which input combination to use is easy in the cases of inputs that are not substitutable and inputs that are perfect substitutes. In the first situation, there is no decision to be made. An automobile requires one engine, one transmission, and four wheels; no other combination of these inputs will do.

In the case of perfectly substitutable inputs, it is easy to calculate which, if either, of the two inputs is cheaper relative to its productive ability. For example, suppose 10,000 cubic feet of natural gas can produce the same amount of energy as one barrel of oil. Furthermore, suppose that 1,000 cubic feet of natural gas costs $3.30 and that one barrel of oil costs $36.00. In this case (all other factors being equal) a firm would use natural gas to produce its energy,

Figure 5–6   Substitutability of Inputs

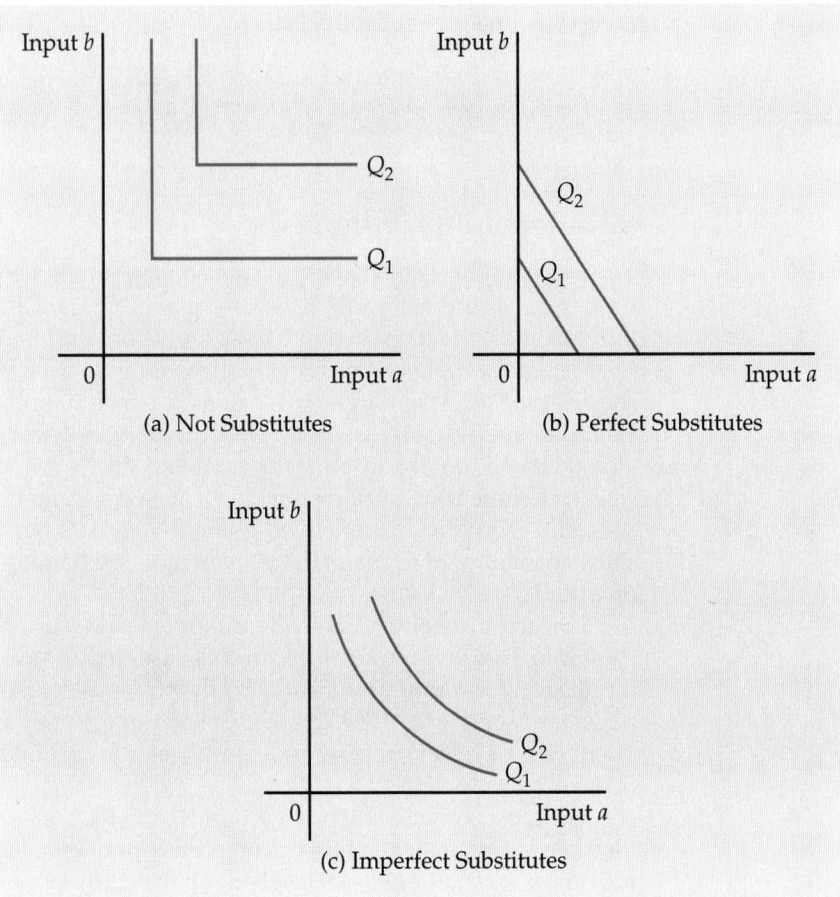

(a) Not Substitutes

(b) Perfect Substitutes

(c) Imperfect Substitutes

Panel (a) depicts the case of two inputs that are not substitutable. In this case one particular combination of inputs is required to produce a specific level of output. Output cannot increase without increased quantities of both inputs. Panel (b) depicts the case of two inputs that are perfect substitutes. They can be substituted for each other at a constant rate while the firm maintains the same level of output. Panel (c) depicts the case of inputs that are imperfect substitutes. They can be substituted for each other at changing rates, while the firm maintains the same level of output.

since $10 \times \$3.30 = \$33.00$ (the cost of 10,000 cubic feet of natural gas) and $\$33.00$ is less than $\$36.00$ (the cost of one barrel of oil).

Since the decision-making process is relatively simple in cases where inputs are not substitutable or are perfect substitutes, we will concentrate most of our attention on the case of inputs that are *imperfect substitutes*. Determining the cheapest combination of inputs that will enable a firm to produce a given level of output is somewhat more complicated in the last case, as we will see shortly.

Least Cost Combination of Inputs

An **isocost line** shows the various combinations of two inputs that can be bought for a given dollar cost.

Once we have established the *technical* (physical) trade-off possibilities between inputs a and b in production, in order to make an *economic* (profit-maximizing) decision on their employment we still need to consider the rate at which they can be exchanged in the firm's budget. To aid our thinking in this regard, economists have developed the concept of the **isocost** (equal cost) **line**, which shows all combinations of inputs a and b that can be employed for a given dollar cost. Therefore the equation for an isocost line is of the form

$$C_0 = P_a(a) + P_b(b),$$

where C_0 is the firm's total cost of inputs for some specific time period, P_a and P_b are the prices of input a and input b, respectively, and a and b represent the physical quantities of the two inputs. Verbally, the isocost equation states that when the firm's total cost is C_0, the price of input a times the *amount* of input a purchased (used) plus the price of input b times the *amount* of input b purchased (used) must equal C_0.

In Figure 5–7 we have drawn isocost lines for $C_1 = \$50$, $C_2 = \$80$, and $C_3 = \$100$, where $P_a = \$5$ and $P_b = \$10$. Note that these three isocost lines are *parallel*. They must be parallel because the slope of each line is equal to $-P_a/P_b$, or $-5/10 = -1/2$.[17] Note that the slope of an isocost line must be equal to $-P_a/P_b$, since that represents the rate at which input a can be substituted for input b while maintaining the same level of cost. In the preceding example, if $P_a = \$5$ and $P_b = \$10$, then we can substitute 2 units of a for every 1 unit of b while maintaining the same cost level. Thus

$$\left(\frac{\Delta b}{\Delta a}\right)_{\text{cost constant}} = -\frac{P_a}{P_b} = -\frac{\$5}{\$10} = -\frac{1}{2}.$$

The b axis intercept for each isocost line is equal to C_i/P_b, since dividing the total amount of expenditure by the price of an input will give the maximum amount of the input that can be purchased if no other input is purchased. Thus for C_1, the b axis intercept is $C_1/P_b = \$50/\$10 = 5$. For C_2 it is $C_2/P_b = \$80/\$10 = 8$. Similarly, the a axis intercept is $C_1/P_a = 10$ in the case of isocost line C_1, and it is $C_2/P_a = 16$ for isocost line C_2.

To obtain the combination of inputs a and b that will enable a firm to produce the *greatest output* for a *given cost* (or what is the same thing, to produce a *given* output at the lowest possible cost), the firm owner must employ the two inputs in such a manner that the isocost line corresponding to the given

---

17 If the equation for an isocost line is $P_a(a) + P_b(b) = C_0$, then the slope of the isocost curve (when b is on the vertical axis) can be found by solving for b and observing the resulting coefficient of a. Thus $P_b(b) = -P_a(a) + C_0$, and $b = -(P_a/P_b)a + C_0/P_b$. Therefore, as long as P_a/P_b remains constant, the slopes of the isocost curves will remain the same.

Figure 5–7   Isocost Curves

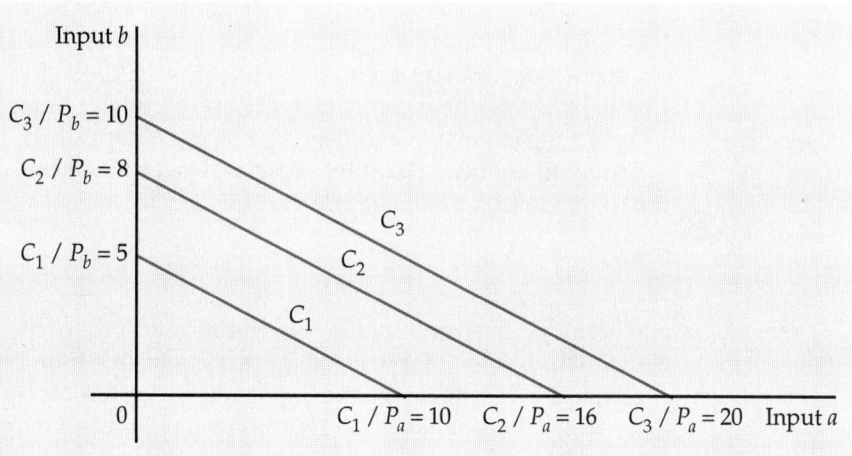

Figure 5–7 shows three icocost lines for inputs a and b. C_1, C_2, and C_3 represent cost levels of $50, $80, and $100, respectively. The price of input a, P_a, is assumed to be $5; and the price of input b, P_b, is assumed to be $10. If the firm wishes to maintain a cost level of C_1 = $50, it can use $50/$5 = 10 units of input a or $50/$10 = 5 units of input b. It can also use the other combinations of inputs a and b depicted by C_1.

A **least cost combination of inputs** requires that the marginal product per additional dollar spent on each input be equal. This condition will hold at the point of tangency between an isocost line and an isoquant.

level of expenditure (cost) touches the highest isoquant possible. Such a point will occur where the isocost line is just *tangent* to an isoquant, and the point of tangency will identify the input combination that is most economical (see Figure 5–8). This result requires that the slopes of the isoquant curve and the isocost line be equal at that point, or $-P_a/P_b = (\Delta b/\Delta a)$ when output is held constant.[18] We call this combination of inputs the **least cost combination of inputs**. (We should note here that this formula for the least cost combination of inputs is valid only if the firm can assume that P_a and P_b are constant. We will discuss this matter further in Chapter 12.)

In Figure 5–8, if P_a = $5 and P_b = $10, then –5/10 (or –1/2) must be equal to $\Delta b/\Delta a$ at point X, where 6 units of input a and 2 units of input b are employed at a total cost outlay of $50 to produce 100 units of output. The same quantity of output could be produced using other combinations of a and b; for example, a = 10 units and b = 1 unit (point Y) or a = 3 units and b = 4 units (point Z), but they would cost more ($60 and $55, respectively). Moreover, there is no way to produce a quantity greater than 100 units with a cost limitation of $50. Thus at point X the firm is producing 100 units of output in the

---

18 A least cost combination of inputs requires that $-P_a/P_b = (db/da)$ when Q is held constant, using calculus terms.

Figure 5–8   A Least Cost Combination of Inputs

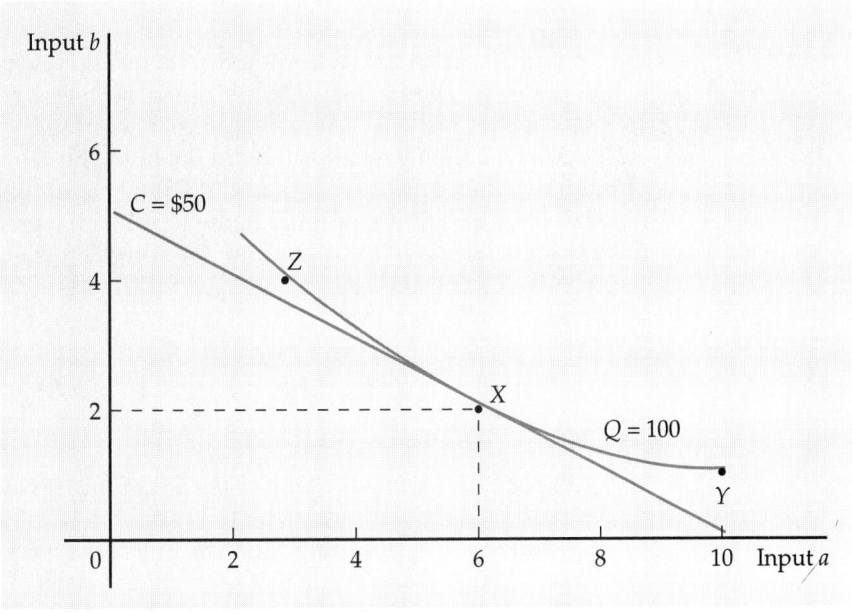

A least cost combination of inputs will be found where an isocost line (C = $50) is tangent to an isoquant curve (Q = 100). In this case the cheapest way to produce 100 units of output is with 6 units of input a and 2 units of input b. This combination of inputs will also yield the greatest output (100 units) for a cost of $50.

cheapest manner possible or, alternatively, producing the greatest level of output possible for $50 cost.

Since $-\Delta b/\Delta a$ (the MRS) along the isoquant is equal to MP_a/MP_b, it must also be true that for the firm to be using the least cost combination of inputs for a given output,

$$-\frac{P_a}{P_b} = -\frac{MP_a}{MP_b}.$$

Rearranging terms and dividing by minus one, we can see that this condition also requires that[19]

---

19 Given $-(P_a/P_b) = -(MP_a/MP_b)$, we can multiply both sides of the equation by $(-MP_b)$ and obtain $MP_b \cdot (P_a/P_b) = MP_a$. Dividing both sides of the equation by P_a, we obtain $MP_b/P_b = MP_a/P_a$.

$$\frac{MP_a}{P_a} = \frac{MP_b}{P_b}.$$

This equation states that for the firm to be employing a *least cost* combination of inputs *a* and *b*, the *additional output obtainable from spending another dollar on input* a *must equal the additional output obtainable from spending another dollar on input* b. If this relationship did not hold, the firm would be better off purchasing either less of the input with a lower additional output per additional dollar expenditure or more of the input with a greater additional output per additional dollar expenditure, or both. For example, if the firm has two inputs—capital and labor—and if $MP_L = 5$, $P_L = \$5$, $MP_K = 40$, and $P_K = \$25$ (all in per-hour terms), then

$$\frac{MP_L}{P_L} = \frac{5 \text{ units}}{\$5} < \frac{MP_K}{P_K} = \frac{40 \text{ units}}{\$25},$$

or 1 unit per $1 is less than 1.6 units per $1. In this situation the firm would be better off using less labor and more capital.

For example, suppose that the firm used 5 fewer units of labor and 1 more unit of capital. Assuming that each of the 5 units of labor removed had the same marginal product, the results that follow would be obtained.

From using 5 fewer units of labor:

Change in cost = $-5 \times \$5 = -\$25$ per hour

Change in output = -5×5 units $= -25$ units per hour

From using 1 more unit of capital:

Change in cost = $1 \times \$25 = \$25$ per hour

Change in output = 1×40 units $= 40$ units per hour

Net change in cost = $0

Net change in output = $+ 15$ units per hour

Thus, by substituting 1 unit of capital for 5 units of labor, the firm would obtain an additional 15 units of output per hour without incurring any additional cost.

However, the firm would probably not find it in its best interest to fire all its workers and utilize *only* capital. Why not? The reason is that as more and more capital is substituted for labor, the marginal product of capital will most likely fall and the marginal product of labor will rise. This phenomenon occurs because the inputs are not perfect substitutes, and, as stated previously, in this case the marginal rate of substitution will vary as more of one input is used relative to another input.

This point is easy to understand if we visualize a plumbing contractor who has the job of digging a trench for a water line. The use of some capital equipment, such as trenching machines and jackhammers, may be less costly than using all labor. Nevertheless, at the extreme it is hard to imagine trenching machines and jackhammers running themselves in a very productive fashion—some amount of labor will be required for a least cost combination of inputs.

Example of a Production Problem

Now let us consider a more realistic situation that a manager might face. Alert Concrete Company is considering modernization of its concrete-batching plant. Presently, it takes two workers to operate the plant at a rate of 30 yards of concrete batched per hour. If a third worker is employed in batching, output will increase to 40 yards per hour.

The result that can be obtained by modernizing the plant and retaining only two workers is an output rate of 45 yards per hour. The wage rate of the workers is $6.40 per hour, and management estimates that the additional costs associated with the modernization of the plant (depreciation, fuel, opportunity cost of funds, etc.) will be $14,400 per year, based on 265 working days of 8 hours each. Should the company hire an additional worker or should it modernize the plant?

To answer this question, the firm must get all of the figures on the same *per-unit basis*, such as per hour or per year. All of the figures given in the preceding two paragraphs are on a *per-hour* basis except for the cost of modernizing the plant. Therefore we will transform the latter figure. If plant modernization will result in costs of $14,400 per year, based on 265 working days of 8 hours each, the *per-hour* cost of plant modernization is $14,400 divided by 2,120, or $6.80. (The figure 2,120 is 265 times 8, the total number of hours the plant is in operation per year.)

Now, to determine whether Alert Concrete should hire another worker or modernize its plant, we must compare marginal product per hour relative to cost per hour for a third worker versus modernizing the plant. For a third worker, $MP_L/P_L = 10/\$6.40 = 1.6$ units per additional dollar spent. For modernizing the plant, $MP_K/P_K = 15/\$6.80 = 2.2$ units per additional dollar spent. Thus the firm would get the most additional output per additional dollar spent by modernizing the plant.

We should point out, however, that the firm might want to go beyond our simple least cost rule and consider over what period of time it would desire to produce a higher level of output and how much higher that output should be. That is because modernizing the plant would give the firm less flexibility in regard to level of cost relative to level of output than would hiring another worker. Additionally, the firm would need to consider how wage rates might rise in the future relative to unit costs for modernizing the plant.

NUMERICAL EXAMPLE:

The Least Cost Input Combination

Letterperfect, Inc. is now providing word processing services to its customers using ABM X86 computers. It leases the computers from ABM for $100 per month each and can lease more for this same amount. Letterperfect's business has increased, and it is planning to lease an additional computer. The ABM representative has told management that if it leases a new PSY86 computer, word processing output on that machine should be about 54 standard pages per day—a high figure for their type of business. The new computer leases for $140 per month.

   If Letterperfect's past experience indicates that an additional ABM X86 model yields 40 standard pages per day, should management lease the new computer or just another unit of the X86 model? Explain, relating your answer to the least cost input rule. (Assume 20 work days per month.)

Answer.
Relate pages per additional machine (marginal product) to the respective machine's price. On a monthly basis, this would be 800 pages for the ABM X86 and 1080 pages for the PSY86. So

$$\frac{MP_{ABM}}{P_{ABM}} = \frac{800}{100}; \quad \frac{MP_{PS}}{P_{PS}} = \frac{1080}{140}$$

$$8 > 7.71$$

Since the *MP* of $1 worth of the ABM X86 model exceeds the *MP* of $1 worth of the PSY86 model, there is no reason to lease the newer model computer. The old model, while less productive per unit, provides more bang for the buck!

Economic Region of Production

Finally, we should emphasize that there are certain combinations of inputs that the firm should not use in the long run *no matter how cheap they are* (unless the firm is being paid to use them). These input combinations are represented by the portion of an isoquant curve that has a positive slope. A positively sloped isoquant means that merely to maintain the *same level* of production, the firm must use more of *both* inputs if it increases its use of one of the inputs. What is happening in this situation is that the marginal product of one input is negative; using more of that input would actually cause output to *fall* unless more of the other input were also employed.

This situation is illustrated in Figure 5–9. Point C on I_0 marks the spot where $MP_b = 0$. Beyond that point (greater amounts of b) on I_0, the MP_b is negative. We can see that beyond point C, if we use more of input b, we must also use more of input a to maintain the same level of output. At point D, the MP_a is 0, and if a greater quantity of input a is used, its marginal product becomes negative. At point E on I_1, the MP_b is zero; and at point F, the MP_a is zero. Lines such as $0X$ and $0Y$, which connect the points on the isoquants where the marginal product of each respective input becomes zero (MP_b for $0X$, MP_a for $0Y$), are called **ridge lines**.[20] They bound the **economic region of production**, since the marginal product of one input is negative outside the ridge lines.

Expansion Path of the Firm

Given fixed input prices and our assumption about the slope of the isoquants (diminishing marginal rate of substitution), and if we assume the isoquant is a *smooth* curve, there will be one least cost combination of inputs for each level of output. The line connecting all such points is called the **expansion path** of the firm (see Figure 5–10). As we will see later, the point that the firm finally chooses when it maximizes profit will depend on revenue considerations as well as on cost.

Returns to Scale

Returns to scale is a term that refers to how output changes when *all* inputs are increased by the same multiple (for example, doubled or tripled). If output increases by a greater multiple than that by which the inputs are increased, then *increasing* returns to scale are present. If output increases by the same multiple, *constant* returns to scale are present. Finally, if output increases by a smaller multiple, *decreasing* returns to scale are present.

For example, suppose a firm's production function is given by $Q = 2K^2 + LK + L^2$, where K is the quantity of capital and L is the quantity of labor. If the firm uses 5 units of labor and 5 units of capital, output equals 100. If labor and capital are both doubled to 10 units each, $Q = 400$, which is more than double the original quantity. In this case the firm has increasing returns to scale. On the other hand, if the firm's production function is $Q = 10K^{1/2}L^{1/2}$, and $L = 2$ and $K = 2$, then $Q = 20$. If capital and labor are doubled (to 4 units each), $Q = 40$, which is exactly double the original level of output. In this case the firm has constant returns to scale. Finally, if the firm's production function is $Q = 100 + 5K + 10L$, and $L = 5$ and $K = 5$, then $Q = 175$. If labor and capital are doubled to 10, $Q = 250$, which is less than double the original output level. In this case the firm faces decreasing returns to scale.

Ridge lines: The lines connecting the points where the marginal product of an input is equal to zero (one line for each input) in the isoquant map and forming the boundary for the economic region of production.

The **economic region of production** is the range in an isoquant diagram where both inputs have a positive marginal product. It lies inside the ridge lines.

The **expansion path** is the path of least cost input combinations in the isoquant diagram that occurs as the firm expands its long-run output at *given* input prices.

Returns to scale measures the effect on output of increasing all of the inputs in a production function by the same proportion (e.g., doubling all inputs).

---

20 Ridge line $0X$ connects points where the isoquants are vertical ($MP_a/MP_b = MP_a/0 = \infty$), and ridge line $0Y$ connects points where the isoquants have a zero slope ($MP_a/MP_b = 0/MP_b = 0$).

Figure 5–9   The Economic Region of Production

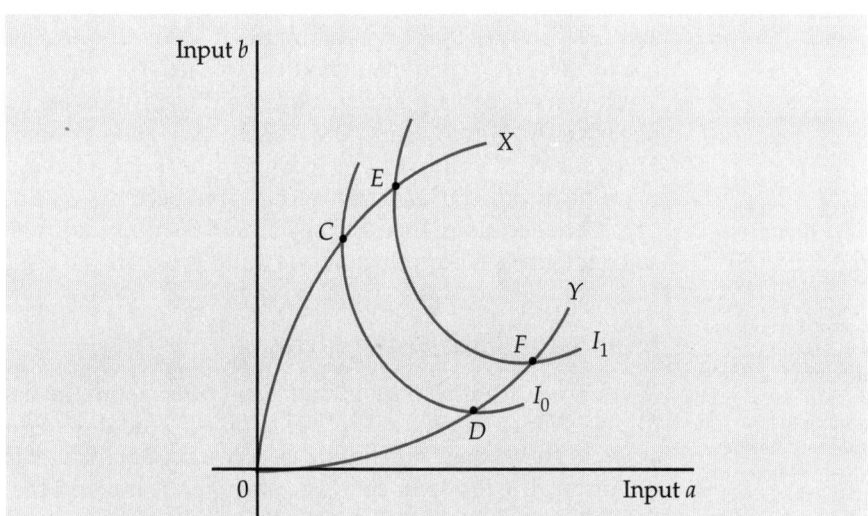

Ridge line $0X$ connects the points where the MP_b is zero. Ridge line $0Y$ connects the points where the MP_a is zero. A profit-maximizing firm will try never to produce using input combinations outside the ridge lines.

Figure 5–10   The Expansion Path

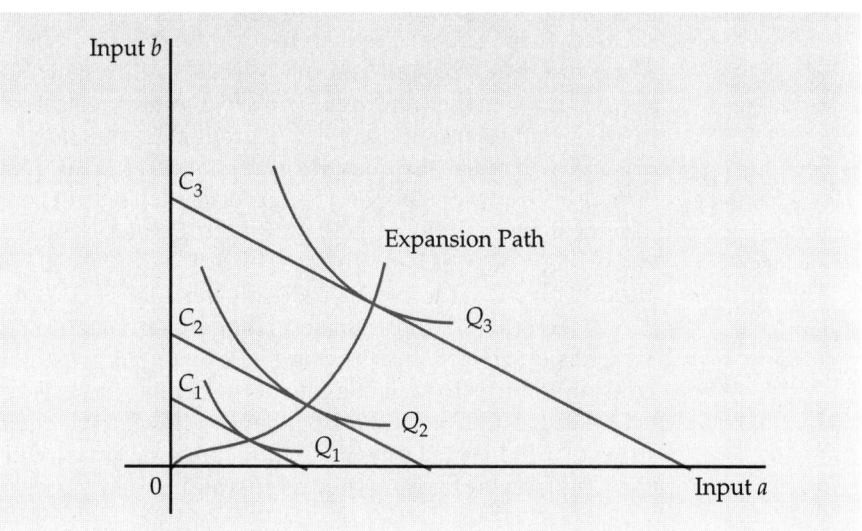

The expansion path connects least cost combinations of inputs for different levels of output. It is assumed that the input price ratio is constant.

As we will see in Chapter 6, with fixed input prices, if a firm has increasing returns to scale, its cost per unit of output will decline as output increases. On the other hand, if a firm has decreasing returns to scale, its cost per unit of output will increase as output increases. Finally, if a firm has constant returns to scale, its cost per unit of output will remain constant.

The nature of its returns to scale is very important to a firm, not only because of the way returns to scale affect its own costs, but also because of the way in which such returns affect the firm's ability to compete with other firms of various sizes in the same industry. It is likely that three firms among those most aware of this principle are General Motors, Ford, and Chrysler, since it has long been argued that increasing returns to scale is an important phenomenon in the automobile industry.[21] However, the nature of returns to scale in this industry may be changing as production shifts to smaller cars and is assisted by computer-integrated manufacturing and computer-aided design.[22]

Relation of Long-Run Least Cost Condition to the Short Run

The short run was defined earlier as a period of time when one or more inputs in a multi-input production function is fixed in amount. It is usually viewed as corresponding to a situation wherein the firm has determined its plant size or production capacity and is able to vary only the use of other inputs (labor, materials, fuel, equipment that would not require a major investment, etc.). In the short run, substitution of the latter type of variable inputs may be possible. Thus if a firm had 5 short-run fixed inputs and 20 short-run variable inputs, the MP_i/P_i condition would still apply to any of the variable inputs that were substitutable for one another. For example, a firm that produces kitchen cabinets might have to decide the optimal combination of electric staple drivers and air-driven staple drivers to use in applying trim to its wood cabinets. The prices of these two types of tools will probably not be equal, and neither will their marginal products. The optimal combination of the two to employ will be the one that comes closest to yielding the same marginal product per dollar spent on each type of tool. Again, the point we are making is that the condition for a least cost combination of variable inputs in the short run is the same as that for *all* inputs in the long run. This is why we chose to discuss the long run first in our examination of production.

---

21 See *Administered Prices: Automobiles*. Report of the Subcommittee On Antitrust and Monopoly of the Committee of the Judiciary, United States Senate, Eighty-Fifth Congress, Second Session, November 1, 1958, especially pp. 13–16.

22 See "Two Sides of a Giant: GM Can Learn a Few Lessons from its Dynamic European Offshoot," *Time* (February 19, 1990), pp. 68–70; "Is Your Company Too Big?" *Business Week* (March 27, 1989), pp. 84–94; John Koten, "Ford Decides Bigness Isn't a Better Idea," *The Wall Street Journal*, September 16, 1981, p. 25; and "Small Is Beautiful Now in Manufacturing," *Business Week* (October 22, 1984), pp. 152–156.

MANAGERIAL PERSPECTIVE

Changing Production Functions in U.S. Manufacturing

Good news! In a world of global competition, many American firms have come around to the view that the best defense is a good offense. Recent examples of firms that have taken the offensive in manufacturing include one small firm in the steel industry and one very large firm that makes automobiles. Nucor Corporation, of Darlington, South Carolina, has become a leading innovator in the steel industry. In late 1989, the firm began to ship steel from its revolutionary thin-slab plant, creating quite a stir among steel producers. Nucor had revised the production function for making flat-rolled steel sheets in a way that changed the face of its industry. The process, which creates a much thinner piece of steel for the rolling mill than any previous technology, has reduced the number of worker hours required per ton of sheet steel by 75 percent.

Nucor's latest development may be even more striking than its success in thin slabs. It is coming on line with a process to make liquid iron from iron carbide. Steel made from this process requires no input of coke and little or no scrap metal, something quite revolutionary in the industry. USX Corporation (formerly United States Steel), a giant among producers, is so impressed that it has formed a joint venture with Nucor to build a pilot project mill to test the new technology.

In the automobile industry, production functions have also changed. Ford Motor Company has spent more than a billion dollars on a new breed of engine plant. Located in Romeo, Michigan, the plant focuses on a modular engine design which reduces parts by 25 percent. Flexible manufacturing techniques at the new plant allow for the production of more than a dozen different sizes of engines on the same production line. In addition, the engines have many interchangeable parts, and alternators, smog pumps, and other self-contained units are bolted directly onto the engine block rather than requiring complicated brackets. Reportedly, the new approach has reduced the retooling costs for new V-8 engines from a typical $500 million figure to about $60 million. After construction of the Romeo plant, Ford also decided to produce modular engines at Cleveland and at Windsor, Ontario.

References: Stephen Baker, "The Odd Couple of Steel," *Business Week* (November 7, 1994), pp. 106, 108; "Big Steel is Facing David vs. Goliath Test," *The Wall Street Journal*, October 17, 1989, p. A16; Gary S. Vasilash, "Making Modular Engines at Ford Windsor," *Automotive Production*, Vol. 108, No. 3 (March 1996), pp. 34–35; and "A Dozen Motor Factories—Under One Roof," *Business Week*, November 20, 1989, pp. 90, 94.

Note that making a decision like the one facing our cabinet manufacturer, while it involves some outlay for tools or equipment, is not the same as determining what size plant to build. In other words, a given cabinetmaker in the short run definitely might have some flexibility regarding the purchase or lease of certain types of equipment, but this decision is very different from one about establishing a completely new manufacturing facility or substantially expanding an old one. The latter are long-run decisions. However, there is more to say about the firm's production in the short run, as the next section will show.

TOTAL PRODUCT CURVES AND THE SHORT RUN

Although all inputs are variable in the long run for a firm, they usually are *not* all variable in the short run. In this section we will return to the two-input production function $Q = f(a,b)$ and assume that input b is a fixed input.

Because we are treating input b as being fixed, we will make use of a function that relates total output to levels of input a only. Accordingly, we will define the **total product function** of input a (TP_a) as the function that indicates the maximum level of output possible with various amounts of input a and a fixed amount, b_0, of input b, so that $TP_a = f(a, b_0)$. We can also define the **average product** of input a as the total product of a divided by the quantity of a in use, or

The **total product function** of a variable input indicates the maximum output that can be obtained from different amounts of the input, while all other inputs are kept fixed.

$$AP_a = \frac{TP_a}{a}.$$

The **average product** of a variable input is equal to total product divided by the number of units of the input in use.

Finally, the marginal product of input a gives the rate of change of total output with respect to changes in input a. As has already been indicated, arc marginal product of input a is defined as the average addition to output or total product obtained by adding one more unit of input a, or

$$MP_a = \frac{\Delta TP_a}{\Delta a}.$$

Arc marginal product is an approximation to marginal product over some range of output and is equal to the change in total product divided by the change in the variable input.

As arc marginal revenue was an approximation to marginal revenue, so is **arc marginal product** of input a an *approximation* to the marginal product of input a. That is because arc marginal product of input a measures the average rate of change of total output with respect to input a over *some* range of values for input a, rather than measuring the rate of change at a *single value* for input a.[23] The *short-run product functions* of the firm are

---

23 Technically, the marginal product of input a is given by $dTP_a/da = \partial Q/\partial a$, where input b is held constant at some level, b_0.

Total product = total output per time period related to different
amounts of a variable input;

Average product = output per unit of variable input; and

Marginal product = rate of change of output as variable input increases.

As we have already seen, managers of the profit-oriented firm are deeply interested in how its output will vary with respect to the quantity used of an input. The reason, of course, is that such information is essential for determining the profit-maximizing level of output.

Law of Diminishing Returns

Figure 5–11 demonstrates the relationships among total product, average product, and marginal product. At point A, marginal product (which is the slope of the total product curve) reaches a maximum, and beyond that point, diminishing returns to input a set in. The portion of the marginal product curve after point A illustrates the economic **law of diminishing returns** (or diminishing marginal productivity). This law asserts that if equal increments of one variable input are added while keeping the amounts of all other inputs fixed, total product may increase; but *after some point, the additions to total product* (the marginal product) *will decrease.* This law merely recognizes the fact that inputs are usually not perfect substitutes. For example, in farming, the first unit of labor, when combined with some machinery and a field of wheat, might increase total product significantly. After some point, however, the next unit of labor will surely increase the total bushels of wheat produced by a smaller amount than did the previous unit of labor employed.

Examples of the law of diminishing returns are shown in Tables 5–2 and 5–3, which are derived from Table 5–1. In Table 5–2, diminishing returns to factor L set in after the first unit of L is added (input K is fixed at 1 unit). Diminishing returns to K also set in after the first unit of K is added in Table 5–3.

The average product for a particular amount of input a (AP_a) is given by the slope of a line segment extending from the origin to the point on the

The **law of diminishing returns** states that in the short run the marginal product of a variable input will eventually fall as output is increased.

Table 5–2   Total, Average, and Marginal Product of Input L, Given $K = 1$

L	TP_L	AP_L	$Arc\ MP_L$
0	0	—	
1	10.00	10.00	10.00
2	14.14	7.07	4.14
3	17.32	5.77	3.18
4	20.00	5.00	2.68
5	22.36	4.47	2.36

Figure 5–11   Total Product, Average Product, and Marginal
Product Curves

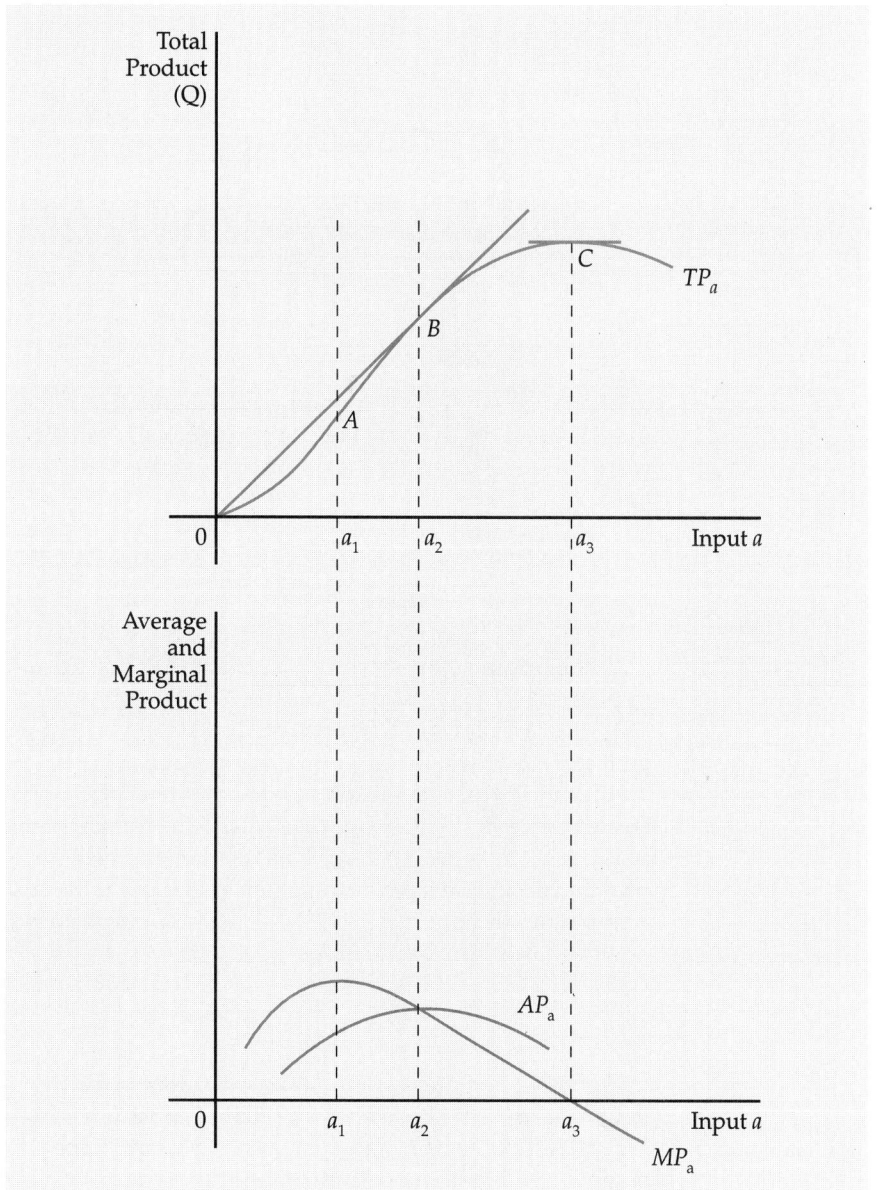

Figure 5–11 depicts the relationships among the total product (TP_a), average product (AP_a), and marginal product (MP_a) of input a. The TP_a is at a maximum when $MP_a = 0$. Also, $MP_a = AP_a$ when AP_a is at a maximum.

Table 5–3   Total, Average, and Marginal Product of Input K, Given $L = 4$

K	TP_K	AP_K	$Arc\ MP_K$
0	0	—	
			20.00
1	20.00	20.00	
			8.28
2	28.28	14.14	
			6.36
3	34.64	11.55	
			5.36
4	40.00	10.00	
			4.72
5	44.72	8.94	

total product curve corresponding to that quantity of the input. We know that the AP_a must be given by the slope of the line segment from the origin to the corresponding point on the TP_a curve, because the slope of that segment is equal to

$$\frac{\text{change in vertical distance}}{\text{change in horizontal distance}} = \frac{TP_a}{a},$$

with the origin as the starting point. The AP_a reaches a maximum at point B in Figure 5–11, where line segment OB is tangent to TP_a. At this point, $MP_a = AP_a$, since MP_a for some amount of input a is given by the slope of the line tangent to TP_a at the corresponding output level.

Total product attains its maximum at point C, where the total product curve reaches its peak. Since the slope of the total product curve is zero at this point, MP_a must also be zero. This relationship becomes obvious if we recognize that if TP_a is at a maximum, then at that point the addition of another unit of input a will not change the level of total output produced. By definition, however, this fact means that MP_a is zero.

Average-Marginal Relationship

Because of the **average-marginal relationship**, an average curve cannot rise unless the related marginal curve is above it; the average cannot fall unless the marginal is below it.

In Figure 5–11, there is an important quantitative relationship between the average and marginal product curves for the variable input a. Note that when MP_a falls, it passes through the maximum point of the AP_a curve. When an average curve has a maximum point, the corresponding marginal curve will pass through that point. This is because of a mathematical property known as the **average-marginal relationship**. The reason the AP_a is rising to the left of its maximum is that the amount added to total product by the next unit of input is greater than the average product of previous units. This *causes* the average to rise. To the right of the maximum of AP_a, an additional unit of

NUMERICAL EXAMPLE:

Relation of Average and Marginal Product to Total Product

Complete the table below, assuming that the firm is in the short run and the L is the only variable input.

Units of L	TP_L	AP_L	Arc MP_L
0	0	—	
2		80	
4	340		
			70
6			

Answer.
  a. The first missing TP_L is 160, which is $AP_L(L)$, or 80(2). The second missing TP_L is 480, which is obtained by multiplying the given MP_L of 70 times the change in L of 2, and adding on to the previous TP_L of 340, or $70(2) + 340 = 480$. This follows from the definition $MP_L = \Delta TP_L/\Delta L$. So, $MP_L(\Delta L) = \Delta TP_L$.
  b. The missing AP_L values are $340/4 = 85$ and $480/6 = 80$, since $AP_L = TP_L/L$.
  c. Since $MP_L = \Delta TP_L/\Delta L$, the missing MP_L values are $160/2 = 80$ for the change from $L = 0$ to $L = 2$ and $180/2 = 90$ for the change from $L = 2$ to $L = 4$.

input a adds less to total product than the average amount added by previous units, thereby lowering the average. In short, anytime a marginal curve is *above* its corresponding average curve, the average curve will be *rising*; anytime the marginal is *below* the average, the average will be *falling*. You can verify this numerically by looking at Table 5–4, where data on TP_a, AP_a, and MP_a are shown.

In Table 5–4, when the second and third units of input a are added to the production process, the average product of a rises, since the marginal product of the additional unit is greater than the previous average in both instances ($200 > 100$, and $300 > 150$). However, beyond $a = 3$, average product declines. This is because the marginal product of each additional unit is lower than the average of all the previous units ($140 < 200$, $100 < 185$, and $60 < 168$).

The average-marginal relationship holds even if the average curve does not have an extreme value (maximum or minimum). For example, if you re-

Table 5–4   Total, Average, and Marginal Product of a for a Case Where AP_a Has a Maximum

Units of a (a)	TP_a (Q)	AP_a (Q/a)	MP_a ($\Delta Q/\Delta a$)
1	100	100	
			200
2	300	150	
			300
3	600	200	
			140
4	740	185	
			100
5	840	168	
			60
6	900	150	

view Tables 5–2 and 5–3, you will see that the average product of the variable input always falls in those tables. This is because the marginal product (shown in the right-most column) is always less than the average. If you go back to Chapter 2, you can verify that this relationship also holds for marginal revenue and average revenue.

In fact, the average-marginal relationship is not restricted to economics. You may note that if you have a "B" overall grade average (3.0 on a 4-point system) but only manage to turn in a "C" performance for this term, your average will fall. On the other hand, if this turns out to be an "A" term for you, your average will rise. The average-marginal relationship will turn up again in the next chapter, which is on cost.

Production in the Short Run Versus the Long Run

We can contrast a short-run situation of one fixed input and one variable input with the long-run situation (all inputs are variable) by utilizing the isoquant map in Figure 5–12. Points A, B, C, and D represent *least cost* combinations of inputs a and b required to produce the levels of output represented by I_1, I_2, I_3, and I_4, respectively. Assume the firm has been operating at point C (with b_0 units of b and a_0 units of a) and that b is fixed in the short run. In the short run, therefore, the firm must operate along the line b_0b_0, and its costs for producing any output level different from that of I_3 will be greater than would be necessary with the optimal combination of inputs.

As we discussed earlier in this chapter, point E on I_1 illustrates a point at which the combination of a and b is especially undesirable—where the marginal product of one input (b) is negative. This result is clear if we observe that I_1 has a positive slope at E—which indicates that if more of input b is used in production, more of input a must also be used to maintain the *same* level of

Figure 5–12   Effect of a Fixed Input on Cost of Production

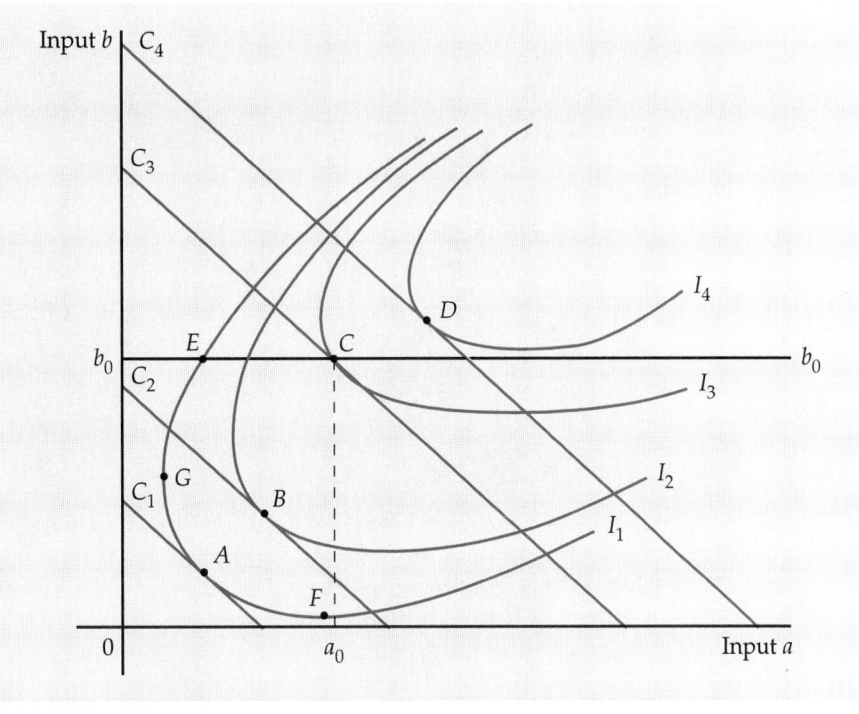

The input combination of a_0, b_0 is the least cost combination of inputs for the output level represented by I_3. However, if input b is fixed at b_0 in the short run, the costs of the firm will be higher at any other level of output than they would be with a least cost combination of inputs.

output. Similarly, the marginal product of input a is negative beyond point F on I_1. The profit-maximizing firm would not plan to be in a position where the marginal product of an input is negative unless the firm were paid for using the input.

In Figure 5–12, if input b was fixed as far as expenditure was concerned but *not fixed in its utilization*, and if the firm desired to produce the quantity represented by I_1, the *short-run* best combination of inputs would be achieved by utilizing input b only to the point where its marginal product became zero. That is because decreases or increases in the *use* of this input will have no effect on expenditures for it in the short run. This position is represented by point G. One example of such a reduction in utilization of an input that is relatively fixed in expenditure is the closing off of dining areas in a restaurant during less busy periods when they are not needed for seating. A smaller number of servers are able to give good service to a given number of people if the people are seated in an area that is not so large. Another example is the

MANAGERIAL PERSPECTIVE
Getting "People Power" Into the Manufacturing Process

"You have a friend in the business," trumpets one ad from Gateway 2000, a Sioux City manufacturer of IBM-compatible personal computers. In fact, Gateway 2000 computers are very nice, and what you are now reading was originally written on one. Throughout the 1990s, Gateway was a leader in its field, selling thousands of computers per week. Gateway attributes at least a part of its success to the way it assembles components from many suppliers into a top-quality, competitively priced PC. Each PC is assembled by a single person who is responsible for his or her own quality control and rewarded according to how satisfied customers are with the product. Thus, production workers are not doing just the monotonous, routine installation of a single part on a fast-moving assembly line.

Replacing assembly-line manufacturing with processes that yield more employee involvement with the product is not new, but it is certainly receiving more attention recently as companies place increased emphasis on both quality and efficiency. Volvo pioneered the break with the assembly line in the auto industry, and in 1987, its chairman, Roger Holtback, dedicated a new plant in Uddevala, Sweden, by assembling a Volvo 740t *all by himself.* Holtback reportedly said, "It started nicely, but it wouldn't have been delivered to a customer." Volvo does not anticipate having individual workers assemble an entire car; at Uddevala it uses teams of from seven to ten workers. The reason for Volvo's approach has to do with the Swedish work force, which is highly educated and independent-thinking. Management at Volvo be-

shutting down of one assembly line in a factory or the shutting down of one plant of a firm with multiple plants.[24]

Optimal Use of Variable Inputs in the Short Run

We will leave a thorough discussion of the optimal use of variable inputs for a later chapter. Here we will merely state that such optimal use requires that a variable input be employed up to the point where the additional revenue

---

24 General Motors has begun working with its suppliers to use plants and workers that it has idled. In some cases, GM may even pay part of the workers' wages, since after GM employees are laid off for 36 weeks, they receive full pay from a GM-funded Jobs Bank, whether they work or not. See "Smart Step for a Wobbly Giant," *Business Week* (December 7, 1992), p. 38.

lieves that monotonous, assembly-line work produces high absenteeism and poor quality from a work force that is looking for a challenge in what they do.

The teamwork approach to manufacturing has been breaking out in the United States as well. Xerox has formed employee teams to encourage cooperation on the shop floor and spur innovation and problem solving. *Business Week* reports that in 1989, numerous U.S. corporations were using the work-team approach, including Boeing, Caterpillar, Digital Equipment, General Electric, and General Motors. Procter and Gamble is reported to have started using work teams as early as 1962. The name of the game in the team strategy is similar to that at Gateway— pride in accomplishment, greater worker satisfaction, higher quality, and increased productivity.

Approaches that increase employee involvement are not without critics. From the management side there are warnings that it is not for everybody and that, while it may instill craftsmanship, it is not as efficient as assembly-line production. From the labor side come complaints that management uses the teamwork concept to erode the collective bargaining system and to introduce changes that yield more for the company than for its production workers. But the teamwork and employee involvement approaches appear to be here to stay, and in many industries, production in the twenty-first century is unlikely to be accomplished the same way it was during much of the twentieth.

References: *Computer Shopper* (September 1996); *PC Magazine* (May 15, 1990), pp. 129–132; "Volvo's Radical New Plant: The Death of the Assembly Line?" *Business Week* (August 28, 1989), pp. 92–93; "The Payoff From Teamwork," *Business Week* (July 10, 1989), pp. 56–62; and "Making It Better," *Time* (November 13, 1989), pp. 78–81.

brought into the firm by the last (or next) unit of that input is just equal to its marginal cost, or the cost of that additional unit. We call this additional revenue the **marginal revenue product of an input**; it is equal to the marginal (physical) product of the input times the additional net marginal revenue (marginal revenue net of raw materials or components cost) that the firm can obtain from output produced. If we state this principle for input a, the firm would employ input a until

Marginal revenue product of an input is the rate of change of total revenue with respect to change in the variable input.

$$MRP_a \equiv (MP_a \cdot NMR) = MC_{a'}$$

where MRP_a is the marginal revenue product of input a, MP_a is the marginal (physical) product of input a, NMR is the net marginal revenue obtained from each additional unit of output, and MC_a is the marginal cost of input a. While the condition that $MRP_a = MC_a$ is relevant to the optimal use of input a, it is really a profit-maximizing condition rather than just a production decision rule. Thus further discussion of it will be deferred to Chapter 12, where the relationship between employment of inputs and profit is examined.

SUMMARY

Production and the Firm's Profit

We have repeatedly emphasized that only two main factors are of concern to the profit-maximizing firm: *revenue* and *cost*. In this chapter we have shown that if its profit is to be at the maximum level, the firm must be using a combination of inputs that will minimize cost *at the optimal level of output*. Production at the lowest possible cost *for a given level of output* requires that the additional output that would be obtained per additional dollar spent for another unit of one input is equal to that obtained per additional dollar spent for every other input. We called this a *least cost combination of inputs.*

While deriving the condition for achieving the least cost combination of inputs, we developed the concepts of the production function, isoquant and isocost curves, and the marginal rate of substitution of one input for another. The *production function* indicates the maximum quantities of output a firm can produce using various combinations of inputs. An *isoquant* curve shows different combinations of two inputs that can be used to produce a specific level of *output*, whereas an *isocost* curve indicates different combinations of two inputs that can be utilized for a given dollar cost. The *marginal rate of substitution* is the negative of the slope of an isoquant curve, and it indicates the rate at which one input may be substituted for another while the same level of output is maintained. The least cost combination of inputs for a particular level of output is located where an isocost curve is tangent to the isoquant curve corresponding to that level of output. At this point, the marginal rate of substitution equals the ratio of the input prices, or

$$\frac{MP_a}{MP_b} = \frac{P_a}{P_b}.$$

The set of all least cost input combinations makes up the *expansion path* of the firm.

It is also important for a firm to be aware of the *returns to scale* of its operations so that the firm can estimate how its unit costs will be affected as it expands or contracts its scale of operations. If the firm has *increasing returns* to scale, an increase in its scale of operations will more than proportionally increase its output and thereby lower unit costs. If the firm has *constant returns* to scale, an increase in its scale of operations will increase output by the same proportion, and unit costs will remain constant. Finally, with *decreasing returns* to scale, an increase in the scale of the operations of a firm will increase its output by a smaller proportion, so that unit costs will increase.

We also pointed out that in the short run, some inputs a firm employs are fixed (at least in regard to cost outlay), so the firm may not be able to achieve the least cost combination of inputs at its optimal level of output at all times. This latter possibility emphasizes the importance to the firm of predicting accurately what its profit-maximizing level of output will be in the future. Fulfillment of the desire of the profit-oriented firm to produce at least cost (*given* the level of output) requires that it be able to at least estimate parts of its production function and future input prices.

In the short run, the profit-oriented firm should be aware of how its output varies with respect to changes in the amount of its variable input or inputs. In this connection we introduced the following terms: total product, average product, and marginal product. The *total product* of a variable input indicates the maximum output that can be obtained from different amounts of one variable input, keeping all other inputs fixed. The *average product* of a variable input is obtained by dividing total output by the number of units of the input in use. The *marginal product* of an input is the rate of change of total product with respect to changes in the amount of the input. The *law of diminishing returns* states that the marginal product of an input will decrease after some point.

To maximize profit in the short run, the firm should employ a variable input (say, input *a*) up to the point where the additional revenue that another unit of input will bring in is just equal to its cost, or where the marginal revenue product of input *a* equals its marginal cost ($MRP_a = MC_a$). Even though the *cost* associated with the fixed inputs of a firm may be fixed in the short run, their *utilization* may not be fixed. In this case the firm should avoid using so much of a fixed input that its marginal product becomes negative.

In the next chapter, we relate level of cost directly to level of output for a firm. We will also discuss several cost concepts that the profit-maximizing firm must understand and be able to utilize.

QUESTIONS

1. What is a production function? How does it differ from a total product function?
2. What condition(s) must be satisfied for a firm to achieve a least cost combination of its inputs? Why can't the firm always attain a least cost combination of inputs in the short run?
3. Does the obtaining of a least cost combination of inputs assure a firm that it is maximizing profit? Why or why not?
4. Compare the concepts of diminishing marginal productivity and decreasing returns to scale.

5. Define isoquant and isocost curves. Why would information given by these two curves be useful to the firm?
6. What are ridge lines? What is their significance to a firm?
7. Explain the meaning of the expansion path for a firm. What might cause it to change?

PROBLEMS

1. Yolanda Von Sweeny owns an art factory in Palermo, Italy. She is thinking of expanding her exports of large-size paintings of picturesque Italian cityscapes. She has had little difficulty recruiting new artists to Palermo to work a 40-hour week in the factory. The weekly wage is now up to 672,000 lira, which translates to $480 in U.S. currency, and she thinks she can hire as many artists as she needs for that rate. An additional artist normally adds 96 paintings per week to the output of the factory. However, Yolanda has been approached by a Hong Kong dealer who is selling remarkable computerized robots that can closely duplicate the work of some of her current artists. A robot can paint 210 pictures per week and has a daily operating and financing cost of $168 (U.S. currency) per operating day. Regardless of whether she uses the robots or additional artists, Yolanda plans to operate the factory only 5 days per week.
   a. Employ the least cost input rule to determine whether Yolanda should consider buying the robots. (It will be easier if you use dollars rather than lira.)
   b. Given the current daily cost of robots, what artist wage would make Yolanda indifferent between employing the robots and hiring more artists?
   c. What other considerations might influence Yolanda's decision?
2. Suppose a firm has the total product curve shown on page 217, assuming that input L is its only variable input and that Q = output per time period. (Note: Plot MP_L values at the midpoint of each ΔL that you use to determine them.)
   a. In the quadrant below the given diagram, sketch the curves of marginal product and average product of input L. (Provide an appropriate scale on the vertical axis.)
   b. What is the maximum value of AP_L?
   c. Can you employ geometry to determine the value of MP_L when it is at a maximum? (Hint: Draw a tangent to TP_L at its inflection point and evaluate its slope.)
3. Diamond Brewery is reevaluating its optimal combination of inputs as a result of recent union-negotiated wage rate increases. At the present time,

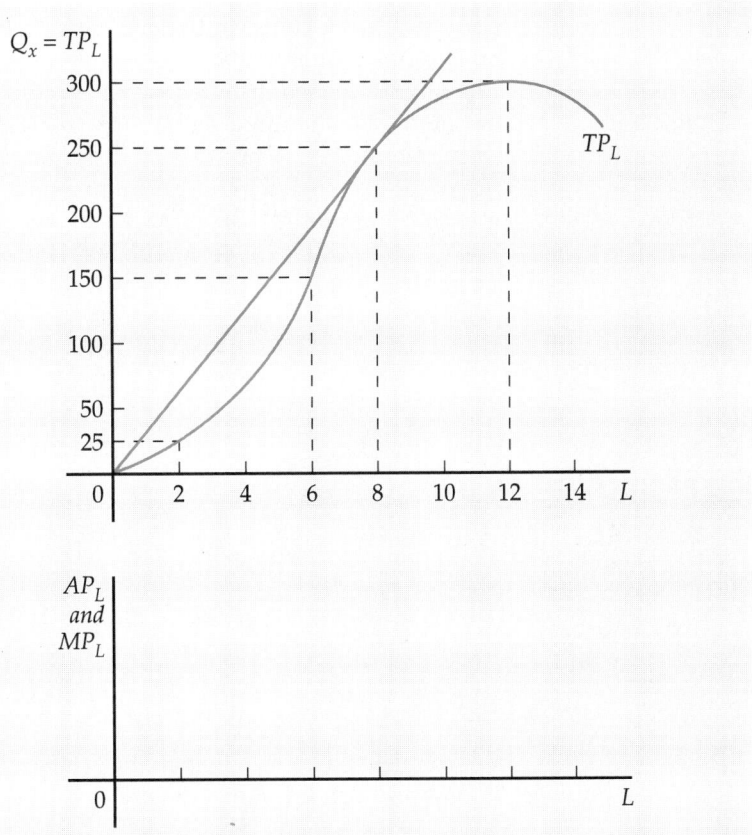

the MP of labor on the production line is 5 cases of beer per hour and the wage rate is $6. The MP of capital is 10 cases of beer per hour, and the price of a unit of capital's services for one hour is $10. Is the combination of inputs at Diamond optimal? Why or why not?

4. State whether each of the following production functions exhibits increasing, constant, or decreasing returns to scale.
   a. $Q = 100{,}000 + 500L + 100K$
   b. $Q = .01K^3 + 4K^2L + L^2K + .0001L^3$
   c. $Q = 50K^{1/2}L^{1/2}$
   d. $Q = .001M + 50{,}000$
   e. $Q = 15K + .5KL + 30L$
   f. $Q = AK^{1-\alpha}L^{2\alpha}, \alpha > 0$

5. Shiny Apple Company can use either labor or a combination of labor and machines to pick apples. Labor can be obtained very cheaply—the going rate is $7 per hour, while the cost (depreciation, gasoline, maintenance, etc.) of using a machine for one hour is $30. The firm is currently using only labor to pick apples, reasoning that labor is cheaper in dollars per

day than the machine. In the present situation, the marginal product of an additional unit of labor is 4 bushels of apples per hour, while the additional product contributed by an apple-picking machine is 40 bushels per hour. You are hired by the firm managers as a consultant to advise them on whether or not to purchase such a machine. What recommendation do you make? What additional data might you also want to take into consideration?

6. Use the following table to complete this problem.

MP_L	L	Q	AP_L
	0	0	—
	5	20	
8.0			
	10		
	15	90	
	20	110	
	25		5.0
2.0			
	30		
	35	140	

a. Complete the table, given that L is labor units, Q is units of output per day, and that L is the only variable input.

b. Suppose the firm is producing between 90 and 110 units of output per day and that the price of a unit of input L is $40. If at that level of production the marginal product of its only fixed input, capital, is 24 units of output per day, should it consider adding to its capital equipment if the price of a unit of capital is $120? Explain.

7. The following table gives the quantities of output that can be produced with different amounts of capital and labor utilized by a firm.

Units of K	Units of Output						
6	122	174	213	244	274	300	
5	112	158	194	224	250	274	
4	100	142	173	200	224	244	
3	87	122	150	173	194	213	
2	71	100	122	142	158	174	
1	50	71	87	100	112	122	
0	1	2	3	4	5	6	Units of L

a. What are the returns to scale for this firm over the range of capital and labor shown in the table? Why?

    b. Compute the marginal product and average product of capital for $L = 3$ units as K varies from 1 unit to 6 units.

    c. Compute the marginal product and average product of labor for $K = 1$ unit as L varies from 1 unit to 6 units.

    d. Suppose the firm is producing 87 units of output using 1 unit of capital and 3 units of labor. The cost of a unit of labor is $10, and the cost of a unit of capital is $20. Is the firm using a *least cost* combination of inputs? Why or why not?

8. A small local plumbing contractor is trying to decide whether to rent a backhoe or to hire more labor for an especially large plumbing job. The contractor estimates that 600 tons of dirt and rocks must be dug and moved. It is believed that a backhoe could move 10 tons of dirt per hour and would cost $30 per hour to rent (including the operator). On the average a worker can move 1 ton of dirt per hour, and the wage rate is $4.50 per hour.

    a. Should the contractor rent a backhoe or hire enough workers to do the job? Why?

    b. Suppose the backhoe could be rented on a full eight-hour-day basis only (a full day would be charged for any partial days). Would this change your answer in part (a)? Why or why not?

9. A total product curve for input a is drawn in the following diagram:

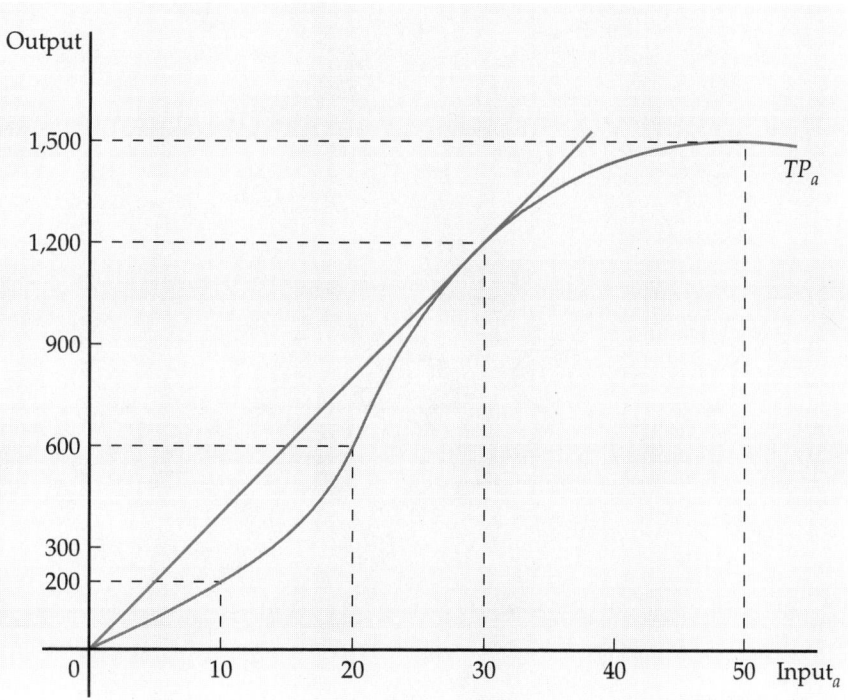

      a. Find the average product of input a at amounts of a equal to 10, 20, 30, and 50 units.

      b. Find the marginal product of a between 0 and 10 units, 10 and 20 units, 20 and 30 units, and 30 and 50 units.

      c. Sketch the average and marginal product curves for a, and label the axes appropriately.

      d. Where is AP_a at its maximum? Where is MP_a at its maximum?

      e. At what point do diminishing returns to input a set in?

10. Use the isoquant diagram that follows to fill in the blank spaces in statements a through e.

      a. At point _____ the total product of input a will reach its maximum when input b is fixed at b_1.

      b. Point _____ and point _____ represent least cost combinations of inputs, given the isocost curves drawn in the diagram.

      c. With expenditures limited to the level represented by isocost curve NN', a firm would produce at point _____ in the short run where $b = b_1$. In the long run, with the same budget, it would produce the level of output represented by isoquant _____.

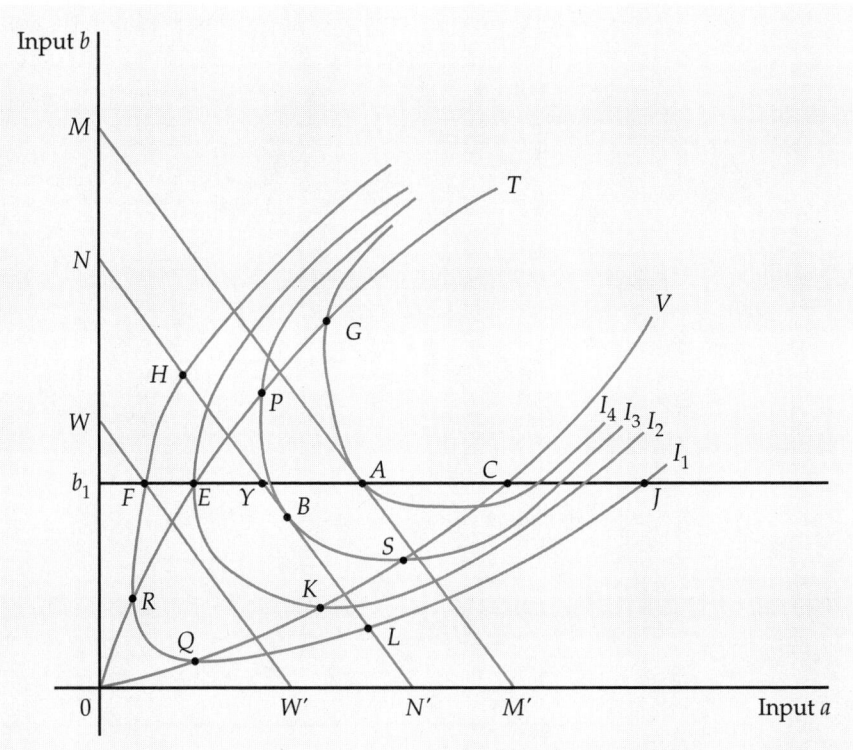

     d. On I_1, the marginal product of b equals zero at point _____; at point _____ on the same isoquant, the marginal product of a equals zero.

     e. In the short run, with plant size b_1 (and fixed in utilization at b_1), output level I_1 could be produced at point _____ or at point _____. However, the cost-minimizing firm with plant size b_1 (but not fixed in utilization) would choose to produce I_1 at point _____ .

11. An automobile manufacturer is considering buying a robot to paint automobiles. One robot can paint 40 cars an hour and costs $12,000 a year (based on 240 working days of eight hours each). A person can paint 60 cars an hour and costs $11.50 per hour. Should the firm purchase the robot or hire a person if it wishes to maximize profit? Why?

12. The following table gives corresponding values for amounts of labor and capital used by a firm and the corresponding maximum quantities of output that can be produced.

Units of K	Units of Output						
7	70	140	210	280	350	420	490
6	60	120	180	240	300	360	420
5	50	100	150	200	250	300	350
4	40	80	120	160	200	240	280
3	30	60	90	120	150	180	210
2	20	40	60	80	100	120	140
1	10	20	30	40	50	60	70
0	1	2	3	4	5	6	7 Units of L

     a. Complete the following table when capital is fixed at 4 units.

Units of L	TP_L	AP_L	Arc MP_L
1			
2			
3			
4			
5			
6			

b. If the cost of a unit of capital's services (P_K) is $30 and the cost of a unit of labor's services is $10, is $K = 4$ and $L = 3$ a least cost combination of inputs? Why or why not?

c. Given the information in part (b) and in the table, what is the cheapest way this firm can produce 120 units of output?

d. Does the production function depicted in the table have constant, increasing, or decreasing returns to scale? Why?

e. What happens to the marginal product of labor as the amount of capital used by the firm increases? Why?

13. Suppose a firm operates in a *perfectly competitive market* (for definition, see Appendix 1 following Chapter 1) where it can sell any amount of its product for $8 per unit. This means that its marginal revenue will be $8. Now let's suppose that it has two variable inputs, labor and materials. The materials cost per unit of output is $3, and the firm must pay $12 per unit of labor that it hires, or $MC_L = 12$. If L is the number of units of labor hired and the firm's marginal product of labor in the short run is $MP_L = 20 - 0.2L$, answer the following:

a. How much labor would be employed if the firm operated its plant at capacity (maximum output)?

b. Given the $12 price of labor, how many units of labor should the firm hire in order to maximize profit (minimize loss)?

The following problems require calculus.

C1. A production function for a firm has the following relationship between the level of output (Q) and the levels of capital (K) and labor (L).

$$Q = 4KL + 3L^2 - (1/3)L^3$$

a. Find the isoquant equation for $Q = 100$.

b. Derive the expression, or function, that gives the slope of the isoquant (in terms of quantities of K and L).

c. Derive the marginal product of labor function from the preceding production function if K is fixed at 5 units.

d. If K is fixed at 5 units, where do diminishing returns to labor set in?

C2. A given firm has the following simple short-run total product function:

$$Q = 400L - 0.5L^2,$$

where

$$Q = \text{output per month, and}$$
$$L = \text{units of labor.}$$

a. What is the equation for the firm's average product?

b. What is the equation for its marginal product?

c. At what level of labor use is marginal product zero?

d. What is the firm's maximum output per month?

C3. Suppose a firm has the following production function:

$$Q = 12KL + KL^2 - (1/12)KL^3$$

If the firm is operating in the short run and capital (K) is fixed at $K = 4$, determine the following:
a. The maximum output that the firm can produce when $K = 4$;
b. The level of use of input L where AP_L is at a maximum;
c. The output level where diminishing marginal returns to input L occurs.

C4. Toadhall Company has the following total product function with input Z as its only short-run variable input:

$$Q = 160Z + 18Z^2 - (1/3)Z^3$$

a. At what Z value will the MP_Z for this firm equal zero?
b. What will be the maximum short-run output the firm can produce?
c. What is the numerical value of the marginal product of Z (MP_Z) when MP_Z is at its maximum?
d. At what Z value will the average product of Z be maximized?

C5. Suppose Zeta Company has the following total product function, where Q is output per time period and L is the number of units of labor hired.

$$Q = 44L + 10L^2 - \frac{1}{3}L^3.$$

(Show all calculations.)
a. What will be the maximum short-run output the firm can produce?
b. At what L value will the MP_L for this firm be at its maximum?
c. At what level of output will the firm reach the point of diminishing marginal returns to L?
d. What will be the numerical value of AP_L when it is at its maximum?

C6. Excellence Company has the following total product function with labor (L) as its only short-run variable input:

$$Q = 84L + 11L^2 - \frac{2}{3}L^3$$

a. At what L value will the MP_L for this firm equal zero?
b. What will be the maximum short-run output the firm can produce?
c. What L value corresponds to the maximum point of AP_L?
d. What will be the numerical value of MP_L when it is maximum?

C7. Where L is the only variable input, suppose that on a daily basis the short-run total product curve for a firm is $TP_L = Q = 50L - 0.1L^2$. The firm must pay a fixed price of $130 a unit (one worker day) for labor, so that $MC_L = 130$. It sells in a perfectly competitive market (see definition in Appendix 1 that follows Chapter 1) and can sell all of the product it wants to for $20 per unit. It uses only labor and materials to produce output, and the materials cost per output unit is $7. Determine:

a. The maximum short-run output the firm can produce; and

b. The output that is consistent with optimal use of the variable input L.

SELECTED REFERENCES

Bilas, Richard A. *Microeconomic Theory*, 2d ed. New York: McGraw-Hill, 1971, Chapter 6.

Hyman, David N. *Modern Microeconomics*, 3d ed. Homewood, IL: Richard D. Irwin, 1993, Chapter 7.

Lyons, Ivory L., and Manuel Zymelman. *Economic Analysis of the Firm*. New York: Pitman, 1966, Chapter 15.

McGuigan, James R., R. Charles Moyer, and Frederick H. deB. Harris. *Managerial Economics*, 7th ed. St. Paul: West, 1996, Chapter 7.

Miller, Roger LeRoy, and Raymond P. H. Fishe. *Microeconomics: Price Theory in Practice*. New York: HarperCollins, 1995, Chapter 8.

Pashigian, B. Peter. *Price Theory and Applications*. New York: McGraw-Hill, 1995, Chapter 5.

Pindyck, Robert S., and Daniel L. Rubinfeld. *Microeconomics*, 2d ed. New York: Macmillan, 1992, Chapter 6.

Wibe, Sören. "Engineering Production Functions: A Survey," *Economica* 51 (November 1984), pp. 401–411.

APPENDIX 5

Mathematics of Determining the Least Cost Combination of Inputs

We can mathematically solve for the least cost combination of inputs to produce a given level of output or (what is essentially the same sort of problem) to find the combination of inputs that will maximize output subject to the condition that only a particular level of cost be incurred by the firm. Mathematical methods often have the advantage of being simpler and more precise than graphical techniques.

The simplest mathematical technique *if* the cost and production functions are mathematically simple is that of substitution. For example, assume that our production function is

(5–1)
$$Q = L^2 + 5LK + 4K^2,$$

that the price of a unit of labor services and a unit of capital services is $5 and $10, respectively, and that our cost limitation is equal to $1,000 per time period. Our goal, then, is to find the quantities of K and L that will maximize output (Q) subject to the condition that

(5–2)
$$5L + 10K = 1,000.$$

If we solve equation (5–2) for L in terms of K and substitute in equation (5–1), we obtain

(5–3)
$$L = 200 - 2K,$$
$$Q = (200 - 2K)^2 + 5(200 - 2K)K + 4K^2,$$
$$Q = 40,000 - 800K + 4K^2 + 1,000K - 10K^2 + 4K^2,$$

and

(5–4)
$$Q = 40,000 + 200K - 2K^2.$$

Using the first-order condition for an extremum, we find dQ/dK and set it equal to 0, as shown in equation (5-5)

(5–5)
$$dQ/dK = 200 - 4K = 0.$$

Solving equation (5–5) for K, we find $K = 50$, and substituting in equation (5–3), we find $L = 100$. The second-order condition for a maximum is also satisfied.

If the functions are such that the substitution method is difficult, the Lagrangian multiplier method is useful. The Lagrangian multiplier method essentially involves adding the constraint (in a form in which it will equal zero when it is satisfied) to the original function to be maximized or minimized. Then, through creation of a new independent variable (the Lagrangian multiplier), the satisfaction of the constraint becomes a first-order condition for a new function.

Using our production function in equation (5–1), we obtain a new, augmented function to be maximized:

(5–6)
$$Z = L^2 + 5LK + 4K^2 + \lambda(1{,}000 - 5L - 10K).$$

Here, the Greek λ is the Lagrangian multiplier. In this form, λ is readily interpretable as the marginal effect on the production function (on output) of relaxing the cost constraint.

Now, applying the optimizing conditions for a function of more than one independent variable, we find the following first-order conditions:

(5–7)
$$\frac{\partial Z}{\partial L} = 2L + 5K - 5\lambda = 0,$$

(5–8)
$$\frac{\partial Z}{\partial K} = 5L + 8K - 10\lambda = 0,$$

and

(5–9)
$$\frac{\partial Z}{\partial \lambda} = -5L - 10K + 1{,}000 = 0.$$

Note that we are treating λ the same way as any regular independent variable. Solving equations (5–7) through (5–9) simultaneously, we find $L = 100$, $K = 50$, and $\lambda = 90$.

PROBLEMS

1. A firm's production function is given by $Q = L^2 + 10LK + K^2$, and its cost function is given by $TC = 5L + 20K$. What is the maximum quantity the

firm can produce for a cost of $1,150? What quantities of capital and labor should it utilize?

2. Miller Company uses two inputs, X and Y, in its production function. The production function is:

$$Q = 40X^{.5}Y^{.5},$$

where inputs and output are in units per week.

The market price of input X is $100 per unit and that of input Y is $20 per unit. Miller has a budget constraint of $16,000 per week. Find its best input combination and the maximum weekly output it can produce.

6

COST OF PRODUCTION

Cost, as we have repeatedly emphasized, is one of the two major factors with which profit-maximizing firms *must* deal wisely. Successful managers are certainly aware that it is the *level of cost relative to revenue* that determines the firm's overall profitability. In the 1980s and 1990s, the motto across all sectors of manufacturing in the United States seemed to be "Cut Costs Or Else!" as companies struggled to remain profitable or to become profitable once again. Big manufacturers such as General Motors and General Electric pressured their suppliers to cut costs or lose their business, and GM was trying to transfer more of its in-house parts-making operations to sources outside the company. In 1996, it was estimated that GM's costs per car were $598 higher than Chrysler and $443 higher than Ford because General Motors produced a larger proportion of its parts rather than purchasing them outside the company. Small companies, especially those supplying component parts to larger companies, also felt the pinch. Sears, Roebuck & Co. was under pressure to cut costs so that it could compete with Wal-Mart and Kmart. Frito-Lay, Marriott, U.S. Steel, and Macy's were other well-known firms engaged in efforts to cut costs substantially.[1] To cut costs, some hospitals have changed "housekeepers" into "service partners" whose job descriptions include wielding mops, feeding patients, and even performing CPR.[2] The Chicago Hyatt Regency found that it could save $220,000 a year by eliminating the nightly ritual of turning down the beds.[3]

One of the most memorable things about the airline industry in the 1980s was the number of companies in trouble. This list included Continental, Eastern, Pan American World Airways, TWA, and Braniff, to name a few.[4] By the

---

1 "GM's Per-Car Costs Higher Than Rivals Due to Reliance on Own Parts-Making," *The Wall Street Journal*, June 25, 1996, p. A2; "Hardball Is Still GM's Game," *Business Week* (August 8, 1994), p. 26; Cut Costs Or Else," *Business Week* (March 22, 1993), pp. 28–29; "The Big Squeeze on Small Businesses," *Business Week* (July 19, 1993), pp. 66–67; "All That Lean Isn't Turning Into Green," *Business Week* (November 18, 1991), pp. 39–40; "Companies vs. Costs," *Newsweek* (March 17, 1980), p. 76; and " 'What If' Help for Management," *Business Week* (January 21, 1980), pp. 73–74.
2 "Daily Grind," *The Wall Street Journal*, June 25, 1996, p. A1.
3 "Why Hyatt Is Toning Down the Glitz," *Business Week* (February 27, 1995), p. 92.
4 See "All Lorenzo Needs Now Is a Few Billion More in Assets," *Business Week* (April 23, 1990), p. 33; "Ailing Pan Am Still Relying on Asset Sales," *The Wall Street Journal*, March 12, 1990, p. A4; "Pan Am Seeks Chapter 11 Shield, Gets UAL-Backed Cash Infusion," *The Wall Street Jour-*

early 1990s, Pan Am and Eastern were out of business, and Braniff no longer existed in its previous form.[5] However, Southwest Airlines, maintaining a low cost and efficient operation, did quite well while its competitors were having difficulties. One source estimated that its average costs were approximately 20 percent less than those of its rivals, and by its twenty-second year Southwest had won the Department of Transportation's "triple crown"—best on-time performance, fewest lost bags, and fewest overall complaints in a given month—eleven times. In the summer of 1996, Southwest celebrated its twenty-fifth anniversary by offering $25 one-way fares on nonstop flights or $50 fares for destinations with published direct or connecting service. Given its low operating costs relative to the rest of the airline industry, Southwest can reportedly increase profit by offering these low fares with restricted availability.[6]

Before the airlines were deregulated in the United States, some companies, protected by high fares and limited competition, were not as careful about costs as they might have been. However, Northwest Airlines strove to control costs and increase productivity to obtain even greater profit. When deregulation did occur, Northwest was considered to be the most efficient of the major airlines.[7] As a result, the firm was in far better shape to cope with the fierce competition that gripped the airline industry in the 1980s. In the latter part of the 1980s American Airlines was in a strong position as a result of developing the airline industry's best computer reservation and yield-management systems. Union concessions also helped to lower American's costs below those of United and Delta.[8] Nevertheless, by the early 1990s, all of the major U.S. airlines were plagued with losses while they watched Southwest consistently make an operating profit. As a result, the major carriers searched for ways to cut costs without compromising customer satisfaction.[9]

---

nal, January 9, 1991, p. A3; "Braniff Files For Protection From Creditors," *The Wall Street Journal,* September 29, 1989, pp. A3, A14; "Can a 'Labor of Love' End TWA's Tailspin?" *Business Week* (April 19, 1993), pp. 80–82; and "Behind the Rise and Fall of Air Florida," *Business Week* (July 23, 1984), pp. 122–125.

5 See "Pan Am Ceases Operations, Race Opens to Get Its Valuable Latin American Routes," *The Wall Street Journal,* December 5, 1991, p. A6; "Eastern: The Wings of Greed," *Business Week* (November 11, 1991), pp. 34–36; and "Braniff Hopes to Shrink Itself Into a Charter," *The Wall Street Journal,* November 8, 1989, p. A8.

6 See "Southwest Air Offers $25 One-Way Fares On Nonstop Flights, and Majors Follow," *The Wall Street Journal,* July 15, 1996, pp. A3, A4; "Southwest Flies Circles Around United's Shuttle," *The Wall Street Journal,* February 20, 1996, pp. B1, B8; "Prince of Midair," *Time* (January 25, 1993), p. 55; and "Southwest Airlines Is A Rare Air Carrier: It Still Makes Money," *The Wall Street Journal,* October 26, 1992, pp. A1, A7.

7 "At Northwest Airlines, Emphasis on Keeping Costs Low Pays Off," *The Wall Street Journal,* October 31, 1983, pp. 1, 12. Also see "U.S. Seeks Delay in Northwest Air, Republic Merger," *The Wall Street Journal,* February 19, 1986, p. 6.

8 "American Aims For the Sky," *Business Week* (February 20, 1989), pp. 54–58.

9 James S. Hirsch, "With Fewer Attendants Aboard Jets, Mood of Passengers Turns Turbulent," *The Wall Street Journal,* July 23, 1993, pp. B1, B3.

The entertainment industry affords us another example of how important efficient operation is to a firm's success. Paramount Pictures has been known for careful cost management. It is also the producer of such successful films as *Raiders of the Lost Ark*. However, behind the scenes of this and other popular films some tough decisions were made.

For example, when George Lucas and Steven Spielberg first brought *Raiders* to Paramount, it was estimated that the *opening scene alone* would cost $25 million. However, Michael Eisner, then president of Paramount, insisted that the entire movie be produced for $20 million, and the final cost was actually less than that. According to Eisner, "You've got to . . . pretend you're playing with your own money."[10] Because Paramount kept its costs per film relatively low, it was able to produce a greater number of films each year than many other studios. As a result, its chances of producing a hit were also greater.[11]

Moreover, low-budget filmmakers have become a significant force in the movie industry. They typically produce movies for much less than half the average cost of a major-studio film ($15.8 million), yet they have achieved some spectacular successes.[12] More recently, other large filmmakers have begun to exert much greater effort to control costs.[13] When the musical *Rent* opened on Broadway, its weekly costs were estimated at $250,000 compared with *Beauty and the Beast's* $400,000. As a result, *Rent* was expected to begin making a profit within six months. It took *Beauty and the Beast* at least a year to reach that point.[14]

The frantic drive of the auto industry to control costs and become profitable in the early 1990s is another example of an industry in trouble. *Business Week* reported that in 1992 Volkswagen's costs were so high that it *could not have made a profit even operating at 100 percent of capacity*.[15] In late 1993, Ford introduced a new version of the Mustang after spending only about 75 percent as much time and 70 percent of the money typically required to introduce new models of comparable products. It was a car that almost never came to be. In 1989, Mustang's sales slumped to half their 1987 level, and Mustang was Ford's most trouble-plagued model. Anticipating the costs required to

---

10 "Hollywood's Penny Pinchers," *Newsweek* (April 9, 1984), p. 83.

11 "Thrift Becomes Paramount in Hollywood As Big-Budget Films and Economy Falter," *The Wall Street Journal*, January 17, 1991, pp. B1, B5; and "A Slasher Is Loose on Paramount's Lot," *Business Week* (January 28, 1991), pp. 52–53.

12 See "A Down-Home Movie Mogul," *Newsweek* (January 12, 1987), p. 41; "Lights! Camera! Cut the Budget!" *Time* (March 30, 1987), p. 57; and "Studio Commandos," *Newsweek* (May 12, 1986), pp. 58–59.

13 Richard Behar, "Small Wonders," *Time* (February 11, 1991), pp. 63–64.

14 "Putting on a Musical for a Song," *Business Week* (May 6, 1996), p. 44.

15 "VW Figures Its Best Defense May Be a Good Offense," *Business Week* (August 9, 1993), p. 29. Also see "GM Tightens the Screws," *Business Week* (June 22, 1992,), pp. 30–31, and "GM Slices and GM Slashes, But the Flab Survives," *Business Week* (December 23, 1991), p. 27.

accommodate the Mustang to passive restraints (required after September 1, 1993), Ford was ready to abandon it. However, a group of people at Ford convinced senior management to let them form "Team Mustang" with the goal of developing a new Mustang that would inspire consumer demand at a reasonable cost. By the fall of 1993 the new version was completed under budget, and its estimated average variable cost was less than the targeted figure.[16]

Remanufacturing is a cost-saving approach that is becoming more and more popular—and *profitable*—for many things, including automobiles, robots, airplane engines, and telephones. Remanufacturing involves using both old and new parts to make a piece of equipment "as good as new" again. Using this approach, the remanufacturers can sell their products for far less than the corresponding new items and still make a substantial profit. For example, a remanufactured bus with a new body can be sold for about $110,000 compared with a price of $170,000 for a new one. That difference represents a 35 percent savings.[17]

It is clear that careful cost management can be critical to a firm's survival. In addition to the preceding examples, many other industries, including computer manufacturing, have vividly illustrated this fact. According to *Business Week*:

> Companies across the country are focusing on one of the basics of business: making a better product faster and cheaper. They are recognizing that the best-conceived strategic plans or marketing analyses are useless if products are too costly to produce or too shoddy to sell. And they are putting in corporate wide programs aimed at spotting every quick and lucrative fix available to increase manufacturing productivity at the lowest possible cost.[18]

If a firm can reduce its unit costs over those of comparable firms in its industry, it has a head start in making a profit—either by selling its product at the same price as its rivals and reaping the benefits of a greater price-cost differential or by being able to lower price and successfully capture a larger market share.

Nevertheless, cost cutting must be done carefully or it can reduce the profitability of a company. Some of the downsizing and restructuring that occurred in the 1990s as companies attempted to become more competitive has been dubbed "dumbsizing" for its negative impact on consumer satisfaction and firm profits. For example, Delta Airlines embarked on an aggressive cost-cutting mission in the mid-1990s. However, the airline also fell to last place among the 10 largest airlines in on-time performance, and con-

---

16 Joseph B. While and Oscar Suris, "How a 'Skunk Works' Kept Mustang Alive—On a Tight Budget," *The Wall Street Journal*, September 21, 1993, pp. A1, A12.
17 "A Growing Love Affair with the Scrap Heap," *Business Week* (April 29, 1985), pp. 69–72.
18 "Business Refocuses on the Factory Floor," *Business Week* (February 2, 1981), p. 91.

sumer satisfaction fell. As management consultant Eileen Shapiro stated, "What you want to be is *low-cost relative to the benefits* you offer customers" (emphasis added).[19]

TYPES OF COSTS

There are many different types of costs that a firm may consider relevant under various circumstances. Such costs include historical costs, opportunity costs, fixed costs, variable costs, incremental costs, private costs, and social costs. **Historical costs** or **explicit costs** are costs of the firm for which *explicit payment* has been made sometime in the past or for which the firm is committed in the future. These are the costs that a financial accountant attempts to record as data and are gathered for the firm's income statement.[20] Examples of explicit costs include wages and salaries, rent, materials costs, depreciation (related to the amount paid for a machine), and interest payments. The obvious advantage of restricting cost figures to those based on historical costs is that of objectivity—records of transactions should exist from which the figures can be verified.

However, most economists consider the concept of explicit or historical costs to be too narrow when estimating the total costs of the firm, and they would include *implicit opportunity costs* that the firm incurs as well as explicit costs in the firm's cost figures. **Implicit costs** are those that do not involve actual payment by a firm to factors of production but nevertheless represent costs to the firm in the sense that in order to use certain inputs in the production process, the firm has had to abandon opportunities to use them elsewhere.

For example, let us suppose that John and Ruth Brown (1) have opened a delicatessen in a building that they own in a shopping mall; (2) have invested $20,000 of their own financial capital in it; and (3) consider its management to be John's full-time job. A monthly income statement such as might be prepared by an economist is shown in Table 6-1. Notice that both explicit and implicit costs are included.

Historical costs or **explicit costs** are those costs of production that involve a specific payment by the firm to some person, group, or organization outside the firm.

Implicit costs are the costs of using firm-owned resources. They are opportunity costs that cannot be accounted for by payments to outsiders. These costs represent opportunities that a firm gives up by using a resource in one way rather than another.

19 "Call It Dumbsizing: Why Some Companies Regret Cost-Cutting," *The Wall Street Journal*, May 14, 1996, p. A6. Also see "Some Companies Cut Costs Too Far, Suffer 'Corporate Anorexia,'" *The Wall Street Journal*, July 5, 1995, pp. A1, A5. Cost Cutting at Delta did raise the stock price, however. See "Cost Cutting at Delta Raises the Stock Price But Lowers the Service," *The Wall Street Journal*, June 20, 1996, pp. A1, A8; and "A Slimmer Delta Still Loves to Fly But Does It Show?" *The Wall Street Journal*, January 26, 1996.

20 The Securities Exchange Commission in the past required that some firms adjust their cost figures to reflect the current value of assets used in the production process. See Fredrich Andrews, "Replacing Cost Accounting Plan Adopted by SEC," *The Wall Street Journal*, March 25, 1976, p. 6. The Financial Accounting Standards Board in late 1986 issued a new statement that relieved these companies of this requirement. They still are encouraged to provide this information on a voluntary basis. See *Management Accounting* (January 1987), p. 9, and FASB No. 82.

Table 6–1   John and Ruth's Deli
Statement of Economic Profit
for Month Ended July 31, 1997

Total Revenue (sales)		$120,000
Less Cost of Goods Sold		84,000
Gross Profit		$ 36,000
Less Operating Expenses		30,000
Operating (accounting) Net Income		$ 6,000
Less		
Implicit Rental Income	$2,000	
Implicit Salary Income	2,600	
Implicit Interest Income	160	4,760
Economic Profit		$ 1,240

The first part of the income statement is straightforward, resulting in an income figure consistent with that found by using currently accepted accounting principles. From that amount, however, we have subtracted amounts for the firm owners' implicit opportunity costs—estimated rental income that the firm's owners could have earned on the building by leasing it to another business, the monthly salary that John could expect to make if he worked for someone else, and an expected return on the $20,000 capital if invested elsewhere (with equal risk). Note the presence of the words *expected* or *estimated* in the list of opportunity costs. Such words reflect the fact that the firm must estimate what revenue its resources would bring in if they were employed according to the *next best* opportunity. This nonobjectivity of the implicit cost figures bothers some accountants and is the main reason that such figures are not generally acceptable in financial statements for use by stockholders or investors. Still, if implicit costs are positive, actual economic costs for a firm will be larger than accounting costs, and therefore economic profit generally will be smaller than accounting profit. Thus the inclusion of implicit costs is important for managerial decision making by a firm's owner(s) because it helps the owner(s) to better understand the economic implications of the demands that the firm is placing on *all* resources.

We will now briefly consider the other cost items listed at the beginning of the chapter. **Fixed costs** are those costs that are fixed in the short run and therefore do not vary with the level of output produced by the firm during that time period. **Variable costs** are those costs that do vary with the level of production of the firm. Note that *in the long run, all costs of the firm are variable*. It is possible to distinguish a third category, **semivariable costs**, which are fixed over some ranges of output and variable over others. Two examples might be a firm's water bill and the wages paid to supervisors. For simplicity

Fixed costs are costs that do not vary with the level of output in the short run.

Variable costs are costs that increase or decrease as a firm's output increases or decreases.

Semivariable costs are costs that are fixed over some ranges of output and variable over others.

MANAGERIAL PERSPECTIVE
The Cost of Being Your Own Boss

Many people dream of owning their own business—being their own boss, gathering the respect of the community as a successful business person, and, certainly, making a lot of money. In a recent article, however, *Business Week* may have brought some of these dreamers back to reality with a discussion of "sweat equity." Sweat equity is the value that people build in a business (or home) by investing their time and, usually, plenty of hard work and brainpower as well.

A three-year-study by the National Federation of Independent Business found that 53 percent of the owners of firms that had been in business for 18 months spent 60 or more hours a week in that endeavor. For some, the time commitment was even more substantial: 11 percent of those who started their own company and 14 percent of those who bought companies reported spending 80 or more hours a week in managerial duties. However, recent studies indicated that less than 20 percent of executives in big corporations spent that much time on the job. Moreover, almost 20 percent of new business owners claimed to be working additional part-time or full-time jobs as well.

When one considers the preceding data regarding the expenditure of managerial blood, sweat, and tears along with the fact that only 20 percent of all businesses survive for five years, it is clear that owning your own business is not an easy road to riches. While we certainly do not wish to discourage any budding entrepreneurs, they cannot make an economic decision regarding a new enterprise without counting the considerable cost in their own time and energy.

References: "Like 60-Hour Weeks? Try Your Own Business," *Business Week* (August 10, 1987), p. 75; Geoffrey Leavenworth, "Small Business: Still a Gamble," *Texas Business & Texas Parade* (June 1978), p. 65.

Incremental cost is the additional cost that a firm will incur if it undertakes one more activity, or if it takes one course of action rather than another.

The **private costs** of a firm include all of the costs of resource use, both explicit and implicit, the firm must bear to produce its output.

The **social costs** of a firm are the private costs of the resources that the firm uses plus any additional costs imposed on society by the firm's operation.

we will assume that all short-run costs fall into one of two categories—fixed or variable—and that *all* cost items are variable in the long run.

Incremental costs associated with some decisions by the firm are the additional costs that a firm would incur if it took one course of action rather than another. In many instances the profit-maximizing firm owner makes decisions based on a comparison of incremental revenue and incremental costs. We will discuss this topic further in Chapter 7.

Finally, the **private costs** of a firm are the sum of the explicit and implicit costs that it incurs, as we have already discussed. The **social costs** of a firm are those that society in general bears because of the firm's activities. Social costs would include the private costs of a firm, since presumably all of the firm's resources could be used elsewhere in producing goods of value to (at least some members of) society. However, social costs would also include costs paid for by society but not by the firm, even though such costs were a result of production by the firm. Examples might include air, water, and noise pollution. A firm could, in addition, generate *negative* social costs (social benefits) such as the beauty of a well-kept golf course and the resultant increase in the values of surrounding properties. Most people would be pleased that an exclusive country club had decided to locate near their property—even if they wanted only to sell that property for a profit. Social costs are important considerations in economic decision making (and law making) by society in general. However, since the part of social cost that is not included in private cost is not usually considered by the *profit-maximizing* firm in its decision-making process, it will generally be ignored in our discussion of the firm. We will now turn to a more detailed discussion of the firm's private costs.

COSTS IN THE LONG RUN

Long-run total cost is the minimum economic cost of producing each possible level of output when the time period is sufficiently long to change all inputs of the firm's production function.

Once we know the production function and the prices and quantities of its inputs, we can then easily discover how total costs vary with the level of output. As in Chapter 5, we will continue to use $Q = f(a,b)$ for a firm's production function, where Q is the quantity of output and a and b are inputs. In Figure 6–1, panel (a), we have shown a series of optimal input combinations (at points A, B, C, D, and E) corresponding to different levels of production derived using the rules for least cost production discussed in Chapter 5. In Figure 6–1, panel (b), we have graphed corresponding output levels and **long-run total cost** (*LTC*). Note that we are still assuming that both inputs, a and b, are variable so that *LTC* in Figure 6–1, panel (b), is applicable only when the firm can achieve the lowest cost input combination for its desired level of output. In other words, the firm must be operating on its expansion path [line $0X$ in Figure 6–1, panel (a)]. Thus *LTC* in Figure 6–1, panel (b), must be the long-run total cost curve of the firm. As stated in Chapter 5, the least cost combination of inputs for each level of output requires that

$$\frac{MP_a}{P_a} = \frac{MP_b}{P_b} = \ldots = \frac{MP_n}{P_n},$$

Long-run average cost is equal to long-run total cost divided by the level of output. It measures cost per unit of output when all inputs are variable.

for all inputs of the firm, where MP_i is the marginal product of input i and P_i is the price of input i (and assumed to be constant).

Long-run average cost (LAC), or per-unit cost, at some output level Q can be found by dividing *long-run total cost* (*LTC*) by *output* (*Q*):

$$LAC = \frac{LTC}{Q}.$$

Figure 6–1   Variation of Total Cost

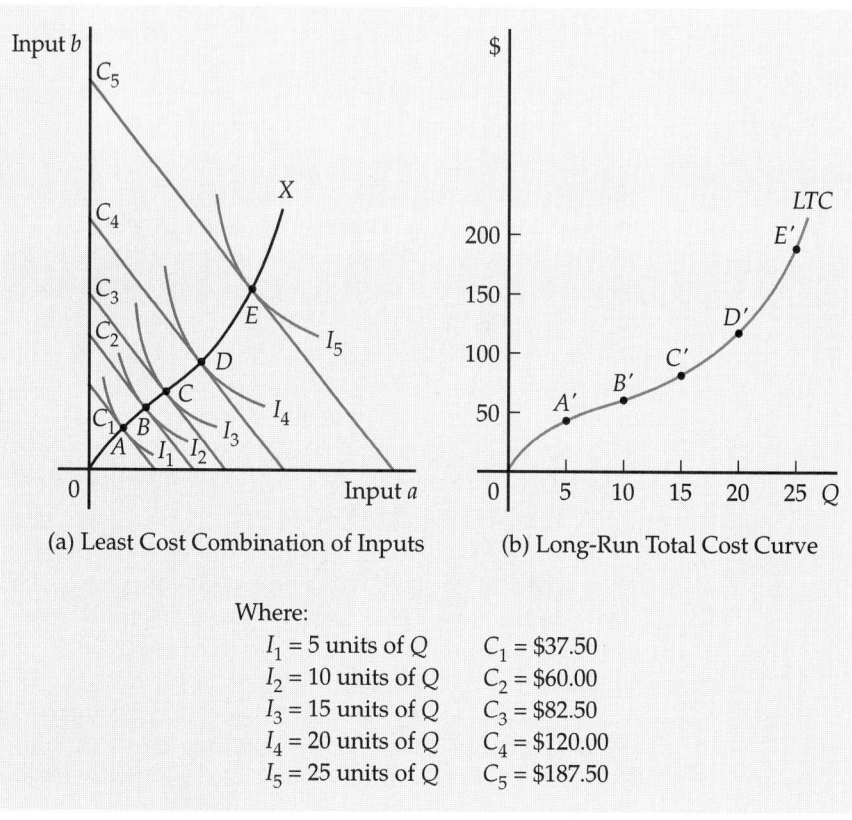

(a) Least Cost Combination of Inputs   (b) Long-Run Total Cost Curve

Where:

I_1 = 5 units of Q	C_1 = \$37.50
I_2 = 10 units of Q	C_2 = \$60.00
I_3 = 15 units of Q	C_3 = \$82.50
I_4 = 20 units of Q	C_4 = \$120.00
I_5 = 25 units of Q	C_5 = \$187.50

Least cost combinations of inputs for levels of output corresponding to I_1, I_2, I_3, I_4, and I_5 are given by points A, B, C, D, and E, respectively, in panel (a). These points then determine corresponding points (A', B', C', D', and E', respectively) on the long-run total cost curve (LTC), in panel (b).

Since *long-run average cost* gives the cost per unit of output in the long run when all costs are variable, it follows that *LAC* for a particular output level is calculated by dividing *LTC* at that level of output by the number of units of output. We would find the average value of anything else in the same manner: divide the total value by the number of cases involved. For example, the average weight of the students in your classroom would be obtained by adding up the weight of each student in the room and dividing by the number of students.

Geometrically, *LAC* for a particular level of output is equal to the *slope* of the line segment drawn from the origin to *LTC* at that same level of output. The slope of this line must be equal to *LAC* because its slope is equal to the change in the vertical distance divided by the change in the horizontal distance between any two points on the line. Between the origin and any other point on the long-run total cost curve, the vertical change is equal to the value

Figure 6–2   Deriving Average Cost from the Total Cost Curve

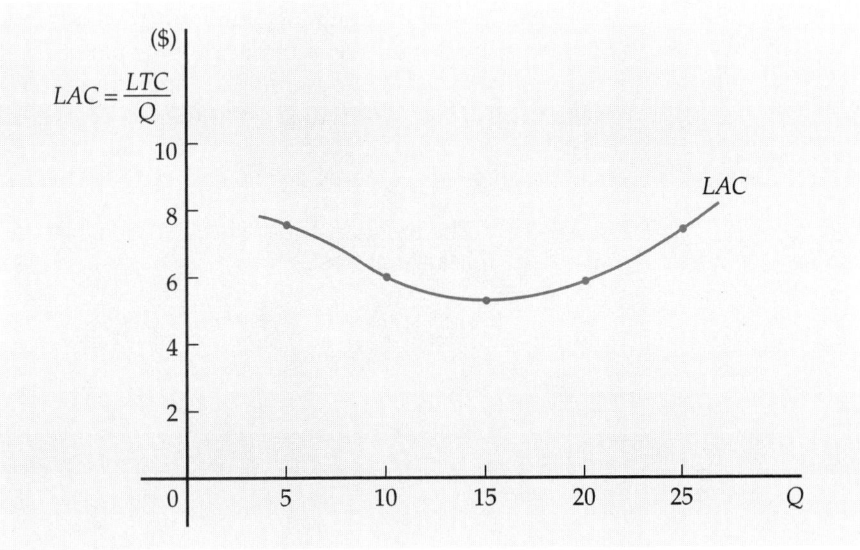

The long-run average cost curve can be derived from the long-run total cost curve by dividing each *LTC* figure by the corresponding quantity of output.

of *LTC* at that point, and the horizontal change is equal to the value of Q at that point. Thus the slope of the line is equal to LTC/Q, which is the definition of long-run average cost. The long-run average cost curve corresponding to *LTC* in Figure 6–1, panel (b), is drawn in Figure 6–2.

Long-run marginal cost is the rate of change of long-run total cost as the level of output changes.

Long-run marginal cost, or the rate of change of long-run total cost with respect to output, at a particular quantity of output is given by the slope of the total cost curve at that output level.[21] In discrete terms, *arc marginal cost* is an approximation to marginal cost and is the *average rate of change* of total cost with respect to the quantity of output *between two levels of output*. Thus *marginal cost answers the question, "How much will production of one more unit of output cost the firm?"* Arc long-run marginal cost (*LMC*) can be found by dividing the change in total cost by the change in the quantity of output, or

$$\text{Arc } LMC = \frac{\Delta LTC}{\Delta Q}.$$

---

21 For example, at Q_1 this slope is equal to the slope of a line tangent to *LTC* at LTC_1; and, mathematically,

$$LMC_1 = \frac{dLTC}{dQ} \text{ at } Q_1.$$

The long-run total cost curve (*LTC*) drawn in Figure 6–1, panel (b), has first decreasing, then increasing, marginal cost.

The relationships among long-run total, average, and marginal costs for the long-run total cost curve in Figure 6–1, panel (b), are further demonstrated in Figure 6–3. We observe that long-run marginal cost (*LMC*) is decreasing until $Q_1 = 10$, at which point the *LTC* curve has its smallest slope.

Figure 6–3   The Relationships Among Total Cost, Average Cost, and Marginal Cost

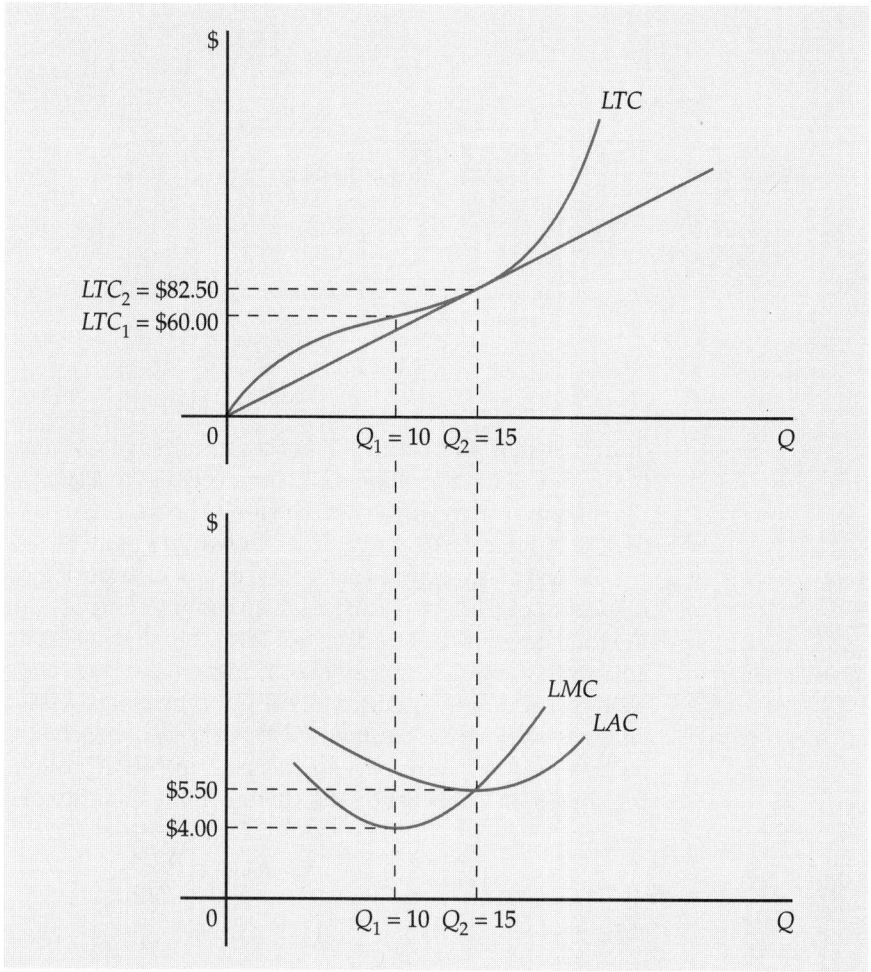

Figure 6–3 depicts the relationships among long-run total cost (*LTC*), average cost (*LAC*), and marginal cost (*LMC*). *LMC* reaches its minimum where the slope of *LTC* reaches its smallest value. *LMC* is equal to *LAC* when *LAC* is at a minimum.

Minimum long-run average cost (*LAC*) is reached at $Q_2 = 15$, where a line drawn from the origin to point LTC_2 is just tangent to *LTC*, since this is the least steeply sloped line that can be drawn from the origin to a point on the long-run total cost curve. At Q_2 also, marginal cost equals average cost = $5.50, since long-run marginal cost is by definition the slope of a line tangent to *LTC* at the point under consideration. We also know that marginal cost must be equal to average cost when average cost is at a minimum because of the marginal-average relationship. When marginal cost is greater than average cost, average cost must be rising; and when marginal cost is less than average cost, average cost must be falling. Only when marginal cost is equal to average cost does average cost not change, and this happens only when average cost is at a minimum.

The numerical relationships among long-run total cost, long-run average cost, long-run marginal cost, and arc long-run marginal cost are also summarized in Table 6–2. Note that both the data in this table and the per-unit curves in the lower panel of Figure 6–3 are consistent with the average-marginal relationship. Thus the *LMC* curve passes through the minimum of the *LAC* curve.

It should be emphasized, however, that the cost curves discussed previously give the firm information on costs when the *lowest possible* cost for a particular level of output can be achieved, *given current input prices*. These cost curves assume that the firm can vary all inputs and thus achieve a least cost combination of inputs for every possible level of output. It follows that they are relevant *only* for long-range planning by the firm regarding level of production, size of plant, and other similar decisions. In the next section we will discuss the short-run cost situation of the firm.

Table 6–2   Summary of Numerical Values for *LTC*, *LAC*, *LMC*, and Arc *LMC**

Q	LTC	LAC	LMC	Arc LMC
0	$ —	Undefined	$10.00	
5	37.50	7.50	5.50	$ 7.50
10	60.00	6.00	4.00	4.50
15	82.50	5.50	5.50	4.50
20	120.00	6.00	10.00	7.50
25	187.50	7.50	17.50	13.50

* These relationships are easily derived mathematically. The total cost function drawn in Figure 6–1, panel b, is given by $LTC = 10Q - .6Q^2 + .02Q^3$. The long-run average cost function is given by $LAC = LTC/Q = 10 - .6Q + .02Q^2$. The long-run marginal cost function is obtained by taking the derivative of *LTC* with respect to Q, $LMC = dLTC/dQ = 10 - 1.2Q + .06Q^2$. *LMC* reaches its minimum when $dLMC/dQ = -1.2 + .12Q = 0$, or $Q = 10$. At this point, $LMC = 10 - 1.2(10) + .06(100) = \$4.00$. *LAC* reaches its minimum where $dLAC/dQ = -.6 + .04Q = 0$, or where $Q = 15$. At this point, $LAC = 10 - .6(15) + .02(15)^2 = \$5.50$.

NUMERICAL EXAMPLE

Given the following diagram:

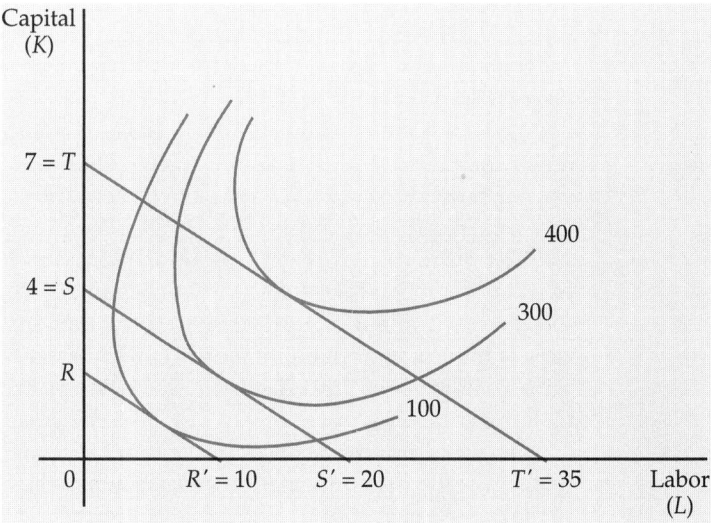

If the price of a unit of labor, P_L = $50, complete the following.

a. At an output of 400, TC = _____.
b. The price of a unit of capital, P_K = _____.
c. The maximum number of units of capital that could be purchased with a budget represented by line RR' is _____.
d. From the three outputs shown, the lowest average cost obtainable is _____.

Answer:

a. TC = $1,750, which is the value of the budget on line TT', or the same as $L(P_L)$ = 35($50).
b. P_K = $250. Anywhere along TT', for example, $1,750 is spent. This includes point T, where K = 7. Thus P_K = $1,750/7 = $250.
c. At point, R, K = 2. Anywhere along RR', TC = $500 = $L(P_L)$ at R' = 10($50). Since P_K = $250, only two units of K can be bought with the budget represented by RR'.
d. Minimum AC for these outputs occurs when Q = 300 and AC = $1,000/300 = $3.33. The other two ACs are $500/100 = $5.00 and $1,750/400 = $4.38, respectively, for the 100 and 400 output levels.

COSTS IN THE SHORT RUN

In the short run, *at least one* input is fixed, so a firm may not be able to achieve the best combination of inputs for its desired level of output. In Figure 6–4, panel (a), input b is fixed at b_0. Thus, in the short run, the least cost combination of inputs can only be achieved for the level of output associated with I_3, since this is the only point on b_0 that is also on the expansion path for the firm, given current input prices. If the firm should desire to produce any other level of output in the short run, it must do so at a greater cost than it could achieve with an optimal combination of inputs. In Figure 6–4, panel (b), the *STC* curve associated with input b fixed at b_0 is higher than the long-run total cost curve (*LTC*) at all output levels except for Q_3. Moreover, in general, short-run costs will be greater than long-run costs except for those output levels for which the fixed inputs are at their optimal levels. In Figure 6–4, panel (a), if input b were fixed at b_1 units, short-run total cost would be greater than the lowest possible cost for every output level except Q_2 [see Figure 6–4, panel (b)].

Because of the presence of both fixed and variable costs in the short run, we can identify seven different types of short-run cost curves: total fixed cost, total variable cost, total cost, average fixed cost, average variable cost, average total cost, and marginal cost. Although these short-run cost terms represent seven different cost concepts, the facts that (1) their names tell us what they are and (2) the relationships among the total, average, and marginal cost functions in the short run are in many ways similar to the relationships among total, average, and marginal cost in the long run make it relatively easy to remember them. The relationships among the short-run cost curves are illustrated in Figure 6–5. **Total fixed cost** (*TFC*) is a horizontal straight line at an amount equal to $P_b \cdot b$ if input b is fixed. **Short-run total variable cost** (*TVC*) is given by $P_a \cdot a$, where a is the variable input. **Short-run total cost** (*STC*) is the summation (vertical) of *TFC* and *TVC*, or

$$STC = TFC + TVC.$$

Directing our attention to unit costs, we observe that **average fixed cost** (*AFC*), or fixed cost per unit of output, is found by dividing a given dollar amount of fixed cost by larger and larger levels of output:

$$AFC = \frac{TFC}{Q}.$$

Thus, *AFC* approaches, but does not reach, zero (the quantity axis) and is the shape of a rectangular hyperbola.[22] **Short-run average variable cost** (*AVC*),

---

Total fixed cost is the private economic cost of the firm's fixed inputs in the short run. The *TFC* curve is a horizontal line since these costs do not vary with the level of output in the short run.

Short-run total variable cost is the sum of all private economic costs of the firm that vary with its level of output in the short run.

Short-run total cost includes all of the private economic costs of the firm in the short run. Short-run total cost is equal to total fixed cost plus short-run total variable cost.

Average fixed cost is fixed cost per unit of output in the short run. Average fixed cost is equal to total fixed cost divided by the level of output.

Short-run average variable cost is the variable cost per unit of output produced in the short run. It is equal to short-run total variable cost divided by the level of output.

---

22 A rectangular hyperbola is given by the functional form $XY = a$ where a is a constant.

Figure 6–4   Short-Run Costs and Production

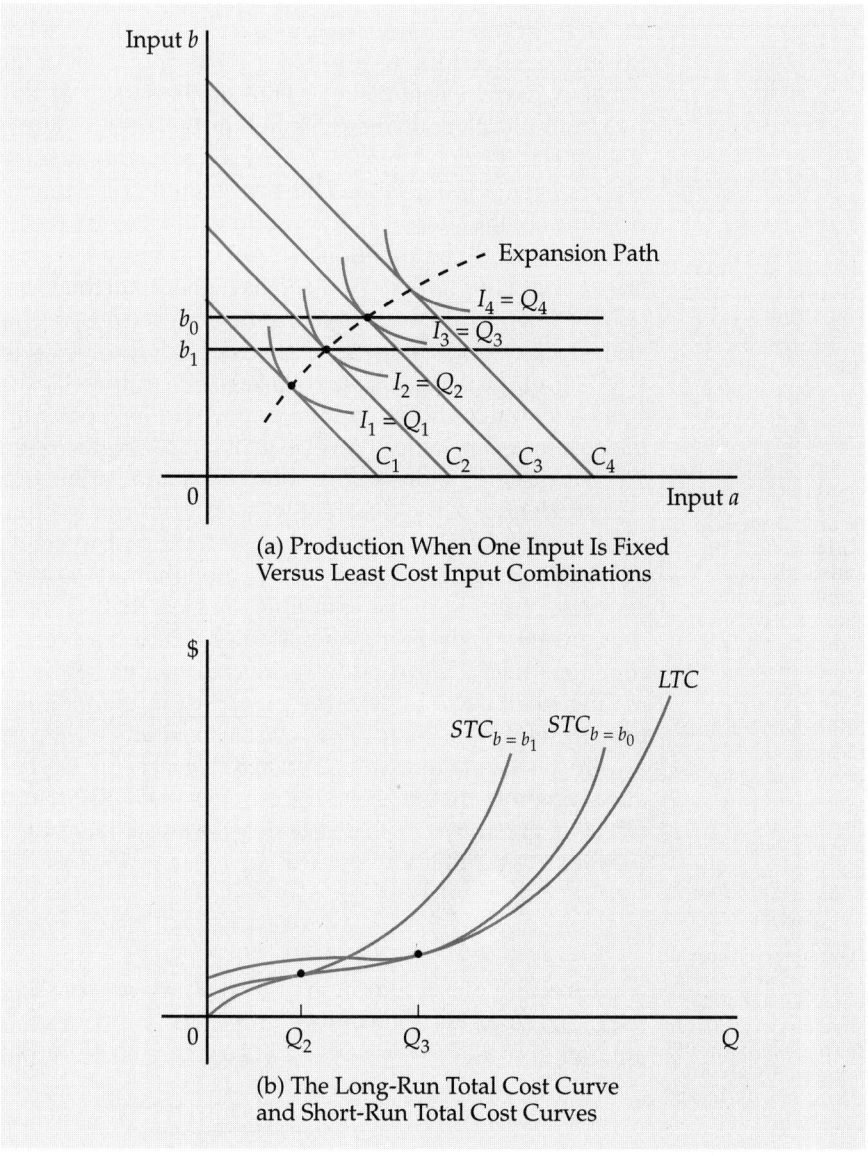

(a) Production When One Input Is Fixed
Versus Least Cost Input Combinations

(b) The Long-Run Total Cost Curve
and Short-Run Total Cost Curves

The expansion path of the firm determines the long-run total cost curve (LTC). However, in the short run, the firm may not be able to achieve a least cost combination of inputs. For example, if input b is fixed at b_0 in the short run, the total cost curve appropriate for various levels of output will be $STC_{b=b_0}$. It will represent a least cost combination of inputs at Q_3 only. At other levels of output, $STC_{b=b_0}$ is greater than LTC. A similar explanation holds if input b is fixed at b_1.

variable cost per unit of output, is found by dividing short-run total variable cost by the corresponding level of output:

$$AVC = \frac{TVC}{Q}.$$

Short-run average total cost is the cost per unit of output in the short run. It is equal to short-run total cost divided by the level of output. It is also equal to average fixed cost plus short-run average variable cost for each level of output.

Short-run average total cost (SAC), average total cost per unit of output, can be found by dividing short-run total cost by the level of output or by adding AFC and AVC:

$$SAC = AFC + AVC = \frac{STC}{Q}.$$

As indicated in our discussion of long-run costs, per-unit (average) costs for a particular level of output can be obtained geometrically by finding the slope of a line segment extending from the origin to the point on the total cost curve corresponding to that quantity of production. The same procedure can also be used to find AFC and AVC from the TFC and TVC curves, respectively. Thus in Figure 6–5 short-run average cost at Q_3 is the slope of line segment OA.

Short-run marginal cost is the rate of change of *either* short-run total cost or short-run total variable cost as the level of output changes in the short run.

Short-run marginal cost is defined in the same manner as marginal cost is defined in the long run: the rate of change of short-run total cost with respect to the level of output. *Arc short-run marginal cost* (SMC) between two levels of output can be found by dividing either the change in short-run *total cost* or the change in short-run *total variable cost* by the change in quantity:

$$\text{Arc } SMC = \frac{\Delta TVC}{\Delta Q} = \frac{\Delta STC}{\Delta Q}.$$

Since fixed cost does not change in the short run, the changes in STC and TVC must be equal. Therefore arc short-run marginal cost measures the average rate of change in either total variable cost or total cost with respect to changes in the level of output in the short run.[23] Table 6–3 gives a numerical illustration of all of the short-run cost functions.

---

23 Instantaneous short-run marginal cost (or short-run marginal cost *at some level of output*) is obtained by finding $dTVC/dQ$ or $dSTC/dQ$ and is the slope of both the short-run total cost and the short-run total variable cost curves:

$$SMC = \frac{dTVC}{dQ} = \frac{dSTC}{dQ}.$$

For example, if

$$STC = 1{,}000 + 80Q - 6Q^2 + .2Q^3,$$

Figure 6–5   Graphical Relationships Among the Short-Run Cost Curves

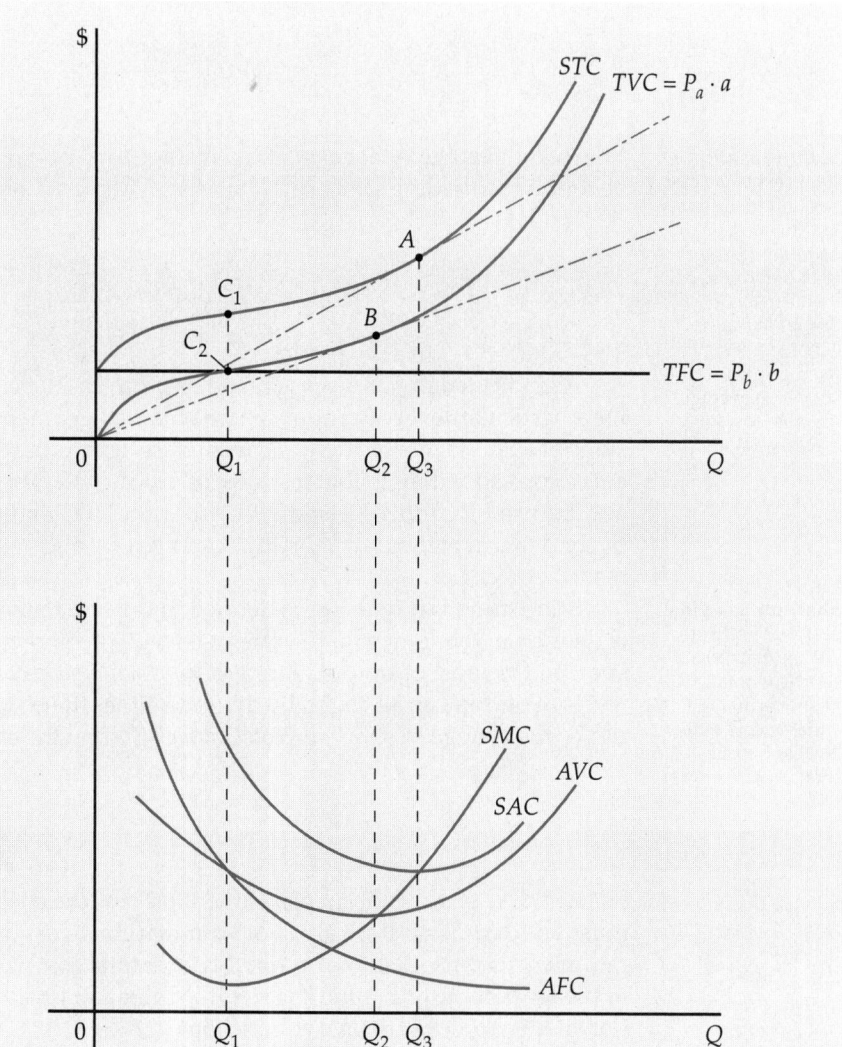

In Figure 6–5 it is assumed that input b is fixed and that input a is variable. Total fixed cost (TFC) is equal to the price of input b (P_b) multiplied by the quantity of input b. Total variable cost (TVC) is equal to $P_a \cdot a$. Short-run total cost (STC) is equal to $TVC + TFC$. Average fixed cost (AFC) is equal to TFC/Q. Average variable cost (AVC) = TVC/Q. Short-run average cost (SAC) is equal to $STC/Q = AVC + AFC$. Short-run marginal cost (SMC) is equal to the slope of the STC curve. SMC is equal to AVC and SAC at their respective minimum points.

Table 6–3 A Numerical Example of the Relationships Among Short-Run Cost Curves

Q	TFC	TVC	STC	AFC	AVC	SAC	SMC	Arc SMC
0	$1,000	$ —	$1,000	$ —	$ —	$ —	$ 80	
								$ 55.00
5	1,000	275	1,275	200.00	55.00	255.00	35	
								25.00
10	1.000	400	1,400	100.00	40.00	140.00	20	
								25.00
15	1,000	525	1,525	66.67	35.00	101.67	35	
								55.00
20	1,000	800	1,800	50.00	40.00	90.00	80	
								115.00
25	1,000	1,375	2,375	40.00	55.00	95.00	155	
								205.00
30	1,000	2,400	3,400	33.33	80.00	113.33	260	

Finally, we observe in Figure 6–5 that SMC reaches its minimum where STC and TVC reach their respective flattest points—that is, where their slopes are least (at C_1 and C_2). Also, AVC reaches its minimum where the slope of a line segment from the origin to a point on the TVC curve is at its minimum (at point B in Figure 6–5). At this point, AVC = SMC, since both are equal to the slope of 0B, which is tangent to TVC at quantity Q_2. For the same reasons, SAC reaches its minimum at Q_3, and SMC = SAC at that point. Again, we know that marginal cost must be equal to average variable cost and to short-run average total cost at their respective minimum points because of the average-marginal relationship. When marginal cost is greater than average variable cost, AVC must be rising, and when marginal cost is less than average variable cost, AVC must be falling. Only when marginal cost is equal to AVC does AVC not change, and this is true only at its minimum point. The same relationship must also hold for short-run average total cost and marginal cost. Notice that SAC reaches its minimum later (at a larger quantity) than AVC because of the presence of fixed costs. As explained earlier, the SMC *passes through the respective minima of AVC and SAC*, in keeping with the average-marginal relationship.

It should be readily apparent that costs need not always vary with output according to the relationships hypothesized in Figure 6–5. In fact it is often assumed in managerial accounting, at least in the relevant range of production in the short run, that average variable cost (and therefore marginal

---

then

$$TVC = 80Q - 6Q^2 + .2Q^3$$

and

$$SMC = \frac{dSTC}{dQ} = \frac{dTVC}{dQ} = 80 - 12Q + .6Q^2.$$

Table 6–3 gives a numerical illustration of all of the short-run cost functions.

Figure 6–6   Short-Run Cost Curves with Constant Average Variable Cost

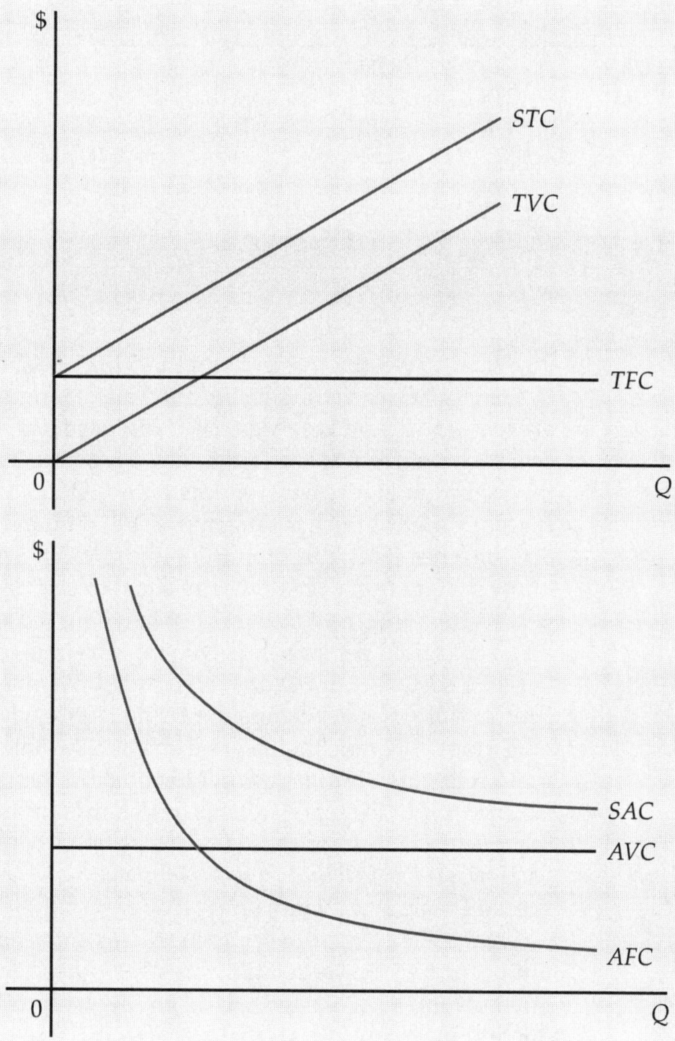

If average variable cost (*AVC*) is constant, *STC* and *TVC* are straight lines. *AVC* = *SMC* in this case.

cost) is constant. Appropriate cost curves, given the assumption of constant unit variable costs, are shown in Figure 6–6. This assumption greatly simplifies analysis of the costs and, consequently, of the corresponding profit-maximizing position of the firm. Moreover, for many firms in the short run and over relatively small ranges of production, such an assumption is probably a fair approximation of reality.

RELATIONSHIP OF SHORT-RUN COST CURVES TO SHORT-RUN PRODUCT CURVES

The total product, average product, and marginal product curves discussed in Chapter 5 are closely related to total variable cost, average variable cost, and marginal cost in the short run. We can demonstrate the reason this statement is true in the following manner. First, assume we have a general production function of the type used in Chapter 5.

$$Q = f(a,b),$$

where a and b are inputs, Q is output, and input b is *fixed* in the short run at 4 units. We will assume that the corresponding total product of a, average product of a, and marginal product of a are as given in Table 6–4.

Turning to the cost curves, we recall from Figure 6–5 that short-run total cost is composed of total fixed cost plus total variable cost, or

$$STC = TVC + TFC.$$

Also, total fixed cost is equal to $P_b \cdot b$, and total variable cost is equal to $P_a \cdot a$, where P_a and P_b are the prices of inputs a and b, respectively, and a and b are the quantities of the inputs. We have stated that b is fixed at 4 units and that P is equal to \$50. Thus, since both P_b and b are fixed, total fixed cost is a horizontal line at $P_b \cdot b = \$50 \times 4 = \$200$, as shown in Figure 6–7.

Total variable cost $(= P_a \cdot a)$ is derived from the TP_a curve by multiplying each amount of input a by P_a and plotting the obtained TVC value against its respective level of output or Q value (Q on the horizontal axis), as shown in Figure 6–8. (In Figure 6–8 we have assumed that P_a is \$36.) For example, at $Q = 50$ units, a is equal to 5 units, and TVC is equal to $\$36 \times 5 = \$180$. At $Q = 54$ units, a is equal to 6 units, and TVC is equal to $\$36 \times 6 = \$216$.

Important relationships exist among the AP_a curve and the MP_a curve

Table 6–4   Relationships Between Productivity of Variable Input and Short-Run Cost Curves*

Input a (Units)	Input b (Units)	Output (Q) (Units)	AP_a	Arc MP_a	Arc SMC	AVC	AFC	SAC	TVC	TFC	STC
0	4	0	—			—	—	—	0	\$200	\$200.00
				5	\$7.20						
2	4	10	5			\$7.20	\$20.00	\$27.20	\$ 72.00	200	272.00
				15	2.40						
4	4	40	10			3.60	5.00	8.60	144.00	200	344.00
				10	3.60						
5	4	50	10			3.60	4.00	7.60	180.00	200	380.00
				4	9.00						
6	4	54	9			4.00	3.70	7.70	216.00	200	416.00
				2	18.00						
7	4	56	8			4.50	3.57	8.07	252.00	200	452.00

* P_a is \$36, and P_b is \$50.

Figure 6–7   Short-Run Total Cost, Total Variable Cost, and Total
Fixed Cost

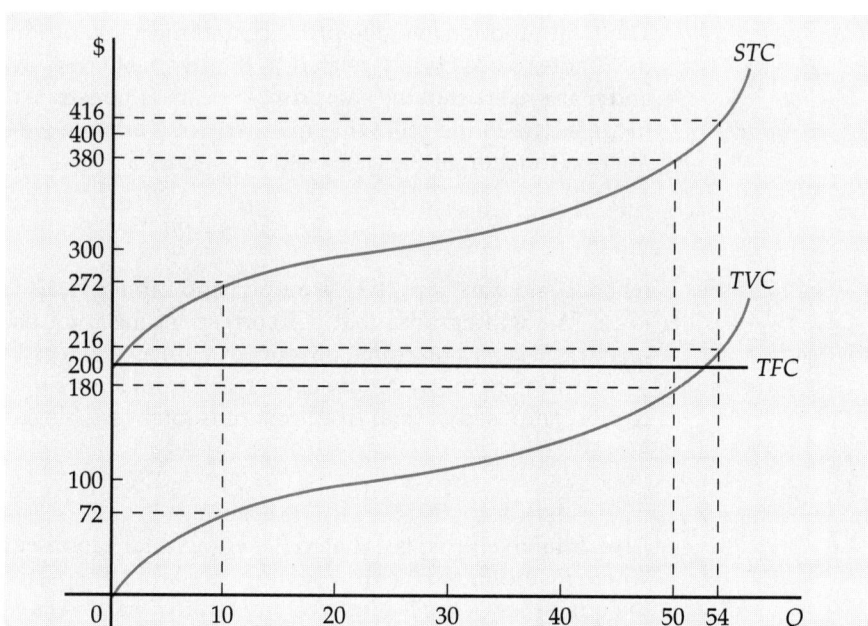

Since input b is fixed at 4 units and $P_b = \$50$, $TFC = P_b \cdot b = \$200$. $STC = TVC + TFC$.

and the average variable cost, short-run average total cost, and short-run
marginal cost curves. We know that

$$SAC = \frac{STC}{Q} = \frac{TFC}{Q} + \frac{TVC}{Q} = AFC + AVC.$$

If

$$TFC = P_b \cdot b \text{ and } TVC = P_a \cdot a,$$

then

$$AFC = \frac{P_b \cdot b}{Q} \text{ and } AVC = \frac{P_a \cdot a}{Q},$$

and

$$SAC = \frac{P_b \cdot b}{Q} + \frac{P_a \cdot a}{Q}.$$

Figure 6–8   Relationship Between Total Product of Input *a* and Total
Variable Cost

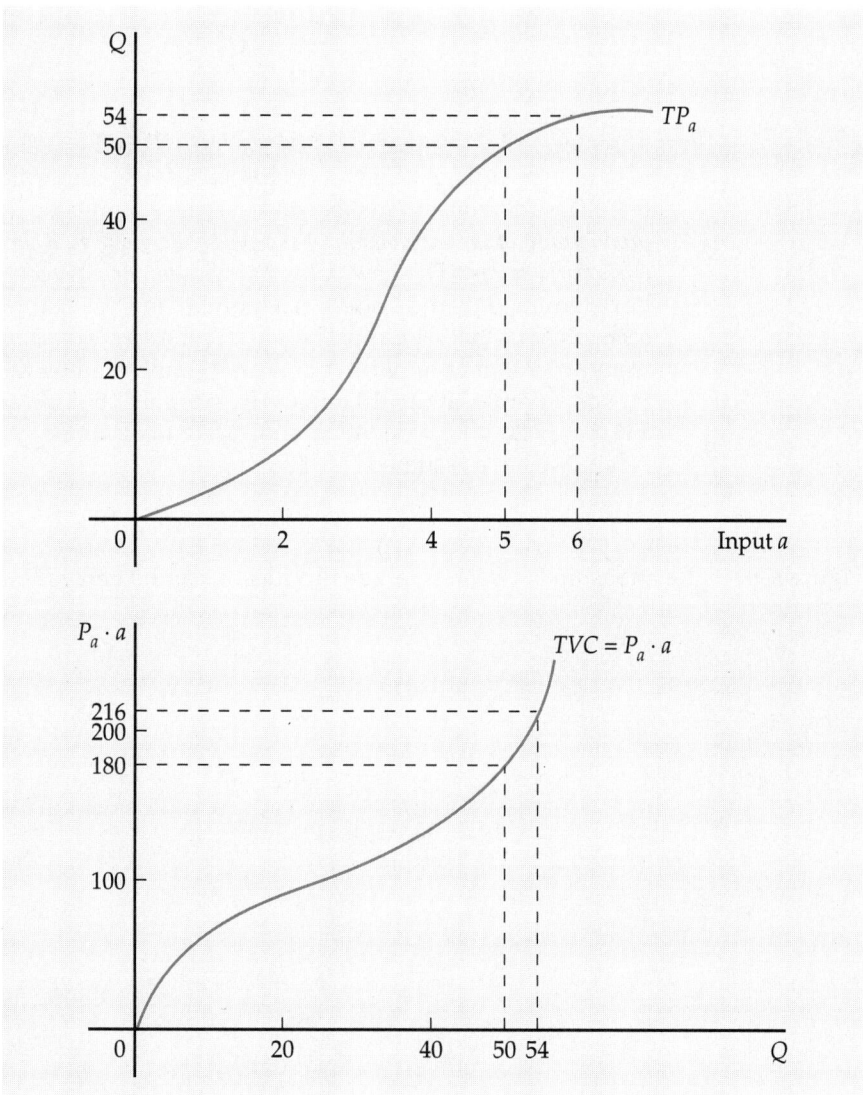

The productivity of a variable input and short-run costs vary inversely. If input *a* is the only variable input, $TVC = P_a \cdot a$. Note that the more steeply sloped the TP_a curve, the less steeply sloped the TVC curve (or the greater the MP_a, the smaller the SMC).

Since $AVC = (P_a \cdot a)/Q$, we can write

$$AVC = \left(\frac{a}{Q}\right) \cdot P_a = \frac{1}{\left(\dfrac{Q}{a}\right)} \cdot P_a = \frac{1}{AP_a} \cdot P_a = \frac{P_a}{AP_a}.$$

Therefore, AVC is equal to P_a/AP_a where AP_a is the average product of input a. In other words, AVC is the reciprocal of AP_a, multiplied by P_a (see Figure 6–9). This relationship makes sense, because it must be true that *if the average productivity of the variable input increases, there will be a corresponding fall in average variable cost.* The new value of average variable cost, however, will also be determined by the price of the input. In fact, if we think about it, it would seem obvious that AVC must be equal to the *average amount of the variable input required per unit of output, $a/Q = 1/AP_a$,* multiplied by the price of the input, P_a. For example, at $Q = 10$ units, AP_a is equal to 5 units and $AVC = P_a/AP_a = \$36/5 = \$7.20$. At $Q = 50$, AP_a is equal to 10 units and $P_a/AP_a = \$36/10 = \$3.60$. Again, we have assumed $P_a = \$36$.

Figure 6–9   Relationship Between Average Product of a and Average Variable Cost

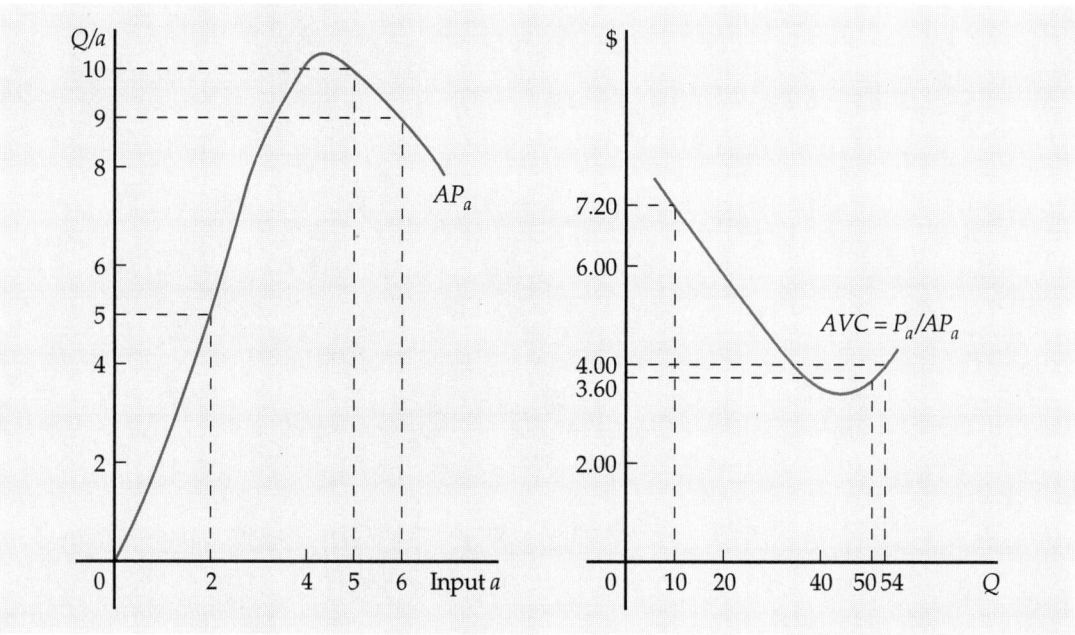

The greater the average product of the variable input (input a), the smaller AVC. For example, when the amount of input a is 2 units, $AP_a = 5$ units. $AVC = P_a/AP_a = \$36/5 = \$7.20$. When 5 units of input a are utilized, then $AP_a = 10$ units and $AVC = \$3.60$.

As shown in Figure 6–5, the average fixed cost curve is a rectangular hyperbola, since $P_b \cdot b$ is constant. Some points on the AFC curve for $TFC = \$200$ are shown in Figure 6–10. The SAC curve is shown in Figure 6–10 as the vertical summation of AFC and AVC.

Finally, we will consider the relationship between the marginal product of input a and short-run marginal cost. In Chapter 5 we said that

$$\text{arc } MP_a = \frac{\Delta Q}{\Delta a} = \frac{\Delta TP_a}{\Delta a},$$

and in this chapter we have said that

Figure 6–10   Short-Run Average Cost, Average Variable Cost, and
Average Fixed Cost

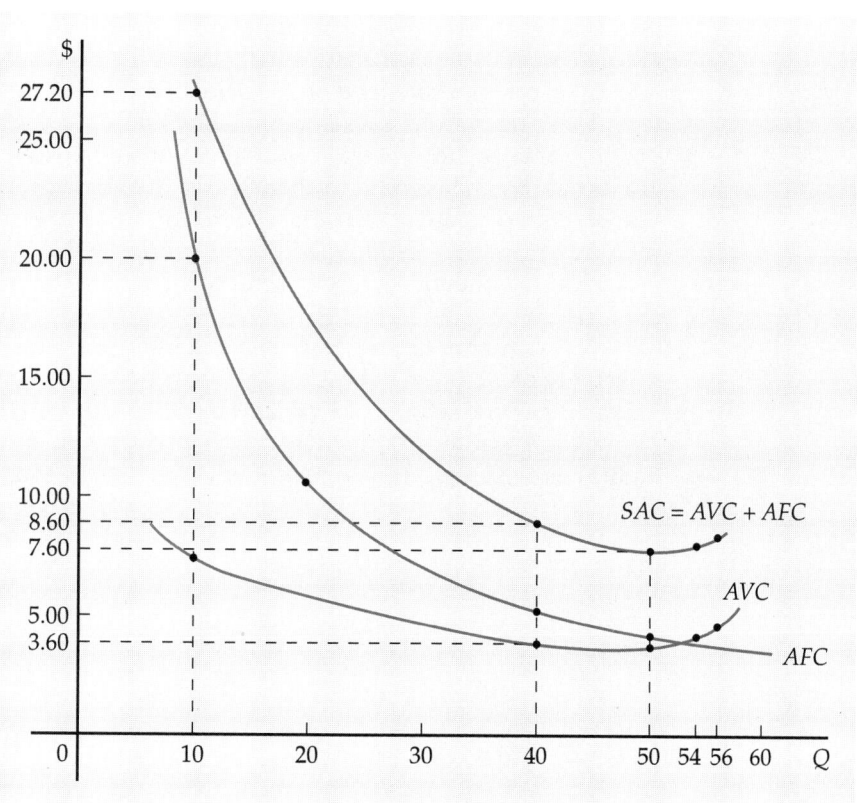

Short-run average cost (SAC) is equal to $AVC + AFC$. For example, at 10 units of output, $AVC = \$7.20$, $AFC = \$20.00$, and $SAC = \$7.20 + \$20.00 = \$27.20$.

$$\text{arc } SMC = \frac{\Delta STC}{\Delta Q} = \frac{\Delta TVC}{\Delta Q}.$$

We know that $TVC = P_a \cdot a$ (as long as P_a remains constant). Then

$$\text{arc } SMC = \left(\frac{\Delta a}{\Delta Q}\right) P_a = \left[\frac{1}{\left(\dfrac{\Delta Q}{\Delta a}\right)}\right] \cdot P_a$$

$$= \left(\frac{1}{\text{arc } MP_a}\right) \cdot P_{a'}$$

where MP_a is the marginal product of input a. Thus SMC is the reciprocal of the marginal product of a multiplied by P_a, or P_a/MP_a, as shown in Figure 6–11.[24] Again, it makes sense that if the *marginal product* of a variable input *rises*, there will be a corresponding *fall* in *short-run marginal cost*, and if the *marginal product* of a variable input *falls*, *short-run marginal cost* must *rise*. Moreover, how much a change in the marginal product of an input changes marginal cost must depend on the price of the input.

These relationships seem reasonable if one thinks about them for a moment. Suppose the average worker on a soda pop assembly line turns out 4 cases of soda an hour and the hourly cost of one worker is $6.00. The *average variable cost* per case of soda must be $P_a/AP_a = \$6.00/4$ cases $= \$1.50$ per case. If the *marginal product* of an additional worker is 3 cases per hour, then the *marginal cost* of another case of soda will be $P_a/MP_a = \$6.00/3$ cases $= \$2.00$ per case.[25]

By examining Figures 6–7, 6–9, and 6–11, we can observe that the productivity of an input and costs vary inversely. Other things being equal, the greater the productivity of a variable input, the lower the short-run costs of a firm. The lower the productivity of an input, the higher the short-run costs of a firm. For example, in Figure 6–9, when the AP_a is equal to 5 units, average

---

24 In calculus terms,

$$MP_a = \frac{\partial Q}{\partial a} \text{ and } SMC = \left(\frac{\partial a}{\partial Q}\right) \cdot P_{a'}$$

so

$$SMC = \left(\frac{1}{MP_a}\right) \cdot P_a.$$

25 We are temporarily ignoring the cost of additional containers and other materials. In reality the per-case amounts of these items would be added onto the AVC and SMC figures. We discuss the matter of component costs more thoroughly in Chapter 12.

Figure 6–11   Relationship Between Marginal Product of a and Short-Run
Marginal Cost

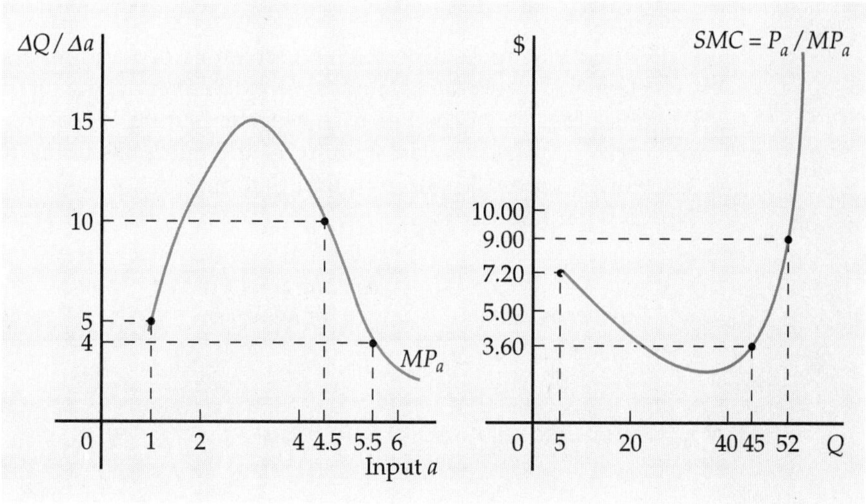

The greater the marginal product of a variable input, the lower the short-run marginal cost
(SMC). For example, the marginal product of the first unit of input a is 5 units. The marginal cost
of those first 5 units of output is equal to $P_a/MP_a = \$36/5 = \$7.20$. The marginal product of the
fifth unit of a is 10 units. SMC at this point (between 40 and 50 units of output) = \$3.60.

variable cost is equal to \$7.20. When AP is doubled to 10 units, AVC is cut in
half. In Figure 6–11, when the MP_a is 5 units, SMC is equal to \$7.20. When MP_a
decreases to 4 units, SMC rises to \$9.00. Certainly these relationships mesh
with what our common sense would lead us to conclude.

Figure 6–12 shows the relationship between the short-run marginal cost
curve and the AVC and SAC curves. Note that the rising SMC curve passes
through the minimum point of the AVC curve as well as the minimum point
of the SAC. This is in keeping with the *average-marginal relationship,* which was
discussed in the preceding chapter and mentioned again earlier in this chapter. The reason the AVC is falling to the left of its minimum is that the amount
added to total cost by the next unit of output is less than the average variable
cost of previous units. In the case of a single variable input, we can say this
occurs because the marginal product of additional units of that input exceeds
its average product, causing AP to rise. Rising AP yields falling AVC. Once
the MP of the input falls below its AP, AP will fall; therefore AVC will rise.
This happens to the right of minimum AVC, where an additional unit of output adds more to total cost than the average variable cost of previous units.
If input a is the only variable input, it will follow that the output level where

NUMERICAL EXAMPLE:

Relation of Short-Run Product to Cost

The following data pertain to Dynamo Corporation, a small firm that employs college students to do fast-food delivery using bicycles. Each employee must furnish his or her own bicycle. Naturally, there is no allowance for fuel. Complete the last column of the table, assuming that each additional worker is paid $6 per hour and that marginal product is measured in deliveries per hour.

Number of Workers	Arc Marginal Product of a Worker	Marginal Cost
0		
1	5	
2	8	
3	6	
4	4	
5	2	

Answer:

The easiest way to obtain marginal cost from these data is to use the relation $SMC = P_a/MP_a$, where a is the variable input. Thus, for the first worker, we have $SMC = (\$6/5) = \$1.20$, and for the second, $SMC = (\$6/8) = \$0.75$. For the third, fourth, and fifth workers, the respective SMCs are $1.00, $1.50, and $3.00. If you use $SMC = \Delta TVC/\Delta Q$, you will obtain the same results.

$SMC = AVC$ is the *same* output where $MP_a = AP_a$, or that *minimum AVC* corresponds to *maximum AP_a*.

RELATION OF SHORT-RUN TO LONG-RUN AVERAGE COSTS

Once again we emphasize that for any given output, short-run total cost (and therefore short-run average cost) is unlikely to be as low as the level achievable when all inputs are variable. Typically, *only one* of all possible output levels attainable in a short-run setting will be characterized by cost data equal to long-run least possible cost for that level of output. Accordingly, short-run total cost will exceed long-run total cost for all other possible short-run outputs. (An exception, discussed on p. 258, is the case in which all inputs are not divisible.)

Figure 6–12   Relation of *SMC* to *AVC* and *SAC*.

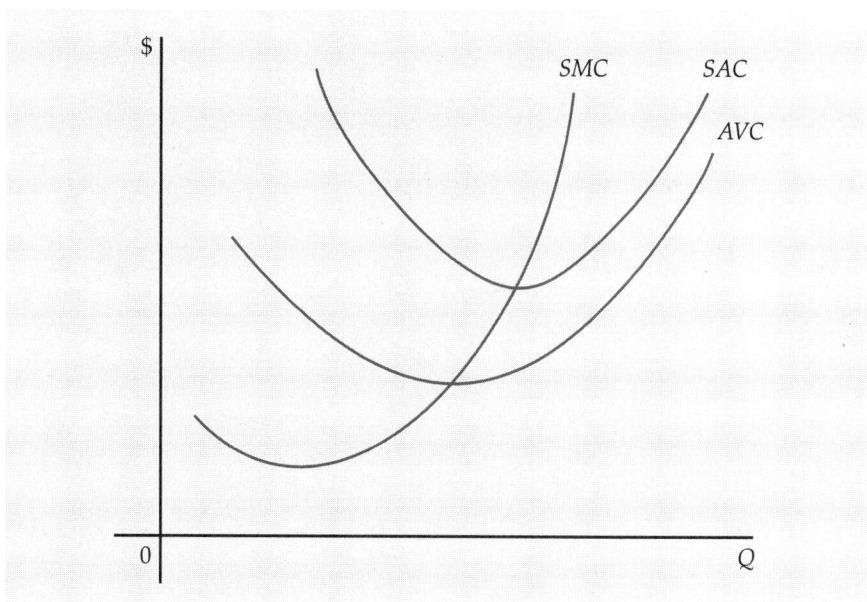

A marginal curve will always pass through the extreme value of the corresponding average curve. Thus, as it rises, *SMC* passes through the minimum of *AVC and* through the minimum of *SAC*.

Economies of scale are technological and organizational advantages that accrue to the firm as it increases output in the long run. Economies of scale reduce long-run average costs.

Diseconomies of scale are technological and organizational disadvantages that the firm encounters as it increases output in the long run. Diseconomies of scale increase long-run average costs.

In Figure 6–4 we indicated the relationship between short-run total cost curves and the long-run total cost curve. In Figure 6–13 the relationship between short-run average cost curves and the long-run average cost curve is demonstrated. Notice that the long-run average cost curve is an *envelope* curve for the short-run average cost curves. In other words, it is made up of points that indicate the lowest unit costs obtainable for each level of output. We further observe that such points are not necessarily the minimum points of the short-run average cost curves. In fact, for outputs smaller than that corresponding to the minimum point of the long-run average cost curve, the short-run average cost curves are tangent to the long-run curve to the *left* of their respective minimum points. This occurs because of the existence of **economies of scale**, which means that smaller unit costs can be obtained by producing with a larger size plant than by producing at the minimum short-run average cost corresponding to a smaller plant size. (See point *A* in Figure 6–13.) The opposite result occurs if **diseconomies of scale** are present, so that it is cheaper to produce beyond the point of minimum short-run average cost corresponding to a smaller plant than by producing at the minimum short-

Figure 6–13   Relationship Between Short-Run Average Cost Curves and the Long-Run Average Cost Curve.

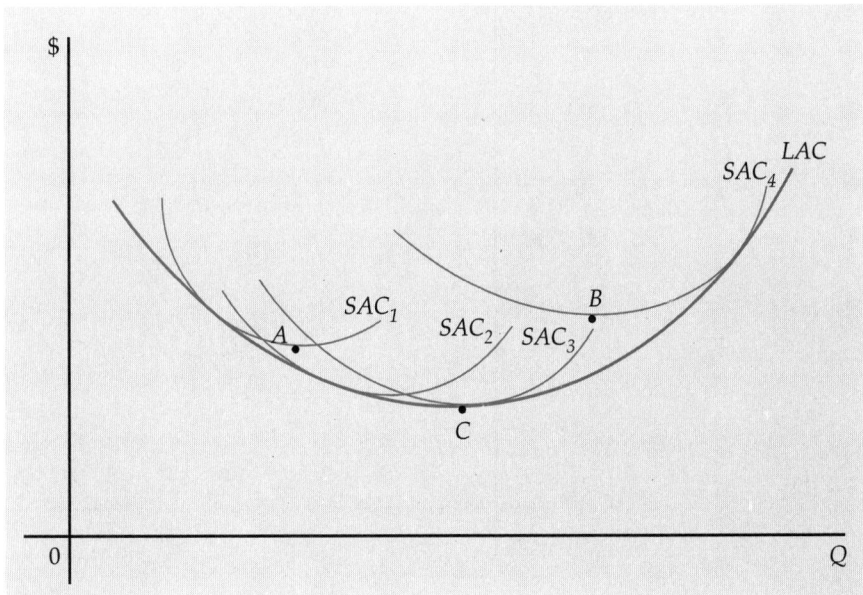

Each point on the long-run average cost curve (*LAC*) represents a least cost combination of inputs and a point on one short-run average cost curve.

run average cost point corresponding to a larger plant. (See point *B* in Figure 6–13.) Only at the minimum point of the long-run average cost curve, where constant returns to scale are obtained, can the firm produce a given level of output most cheaply by producing at the minimum point of a short-run average cost curve. (See point *C* in Figure 6–13.) The regions of economies of scale, diseconomies of scale, and constant returns to scale are summarized in Figure 6–14. These economies and diseconomies of scale occur because of the nature of the firm's production function and are *not* caused by changes in external data such as input prices. Thus they are sometimes called *internal* economies and diseconomies.

The cost elasticity reflects the presence of either economies or diseconomies of scale. **Cost elasticity**, E_C, is defined as the percentage change in long-run total cost from a 1 percent change in output:

Cost elasticity is the percentage change in long-run total cost from a 1 percent change in output.

$$E_c = \frac{\text{percentage change in } LTC}{\text{percentage change in } Q}.$$

Figure 6–14   Long-Run Average Cost and Returns to Scale

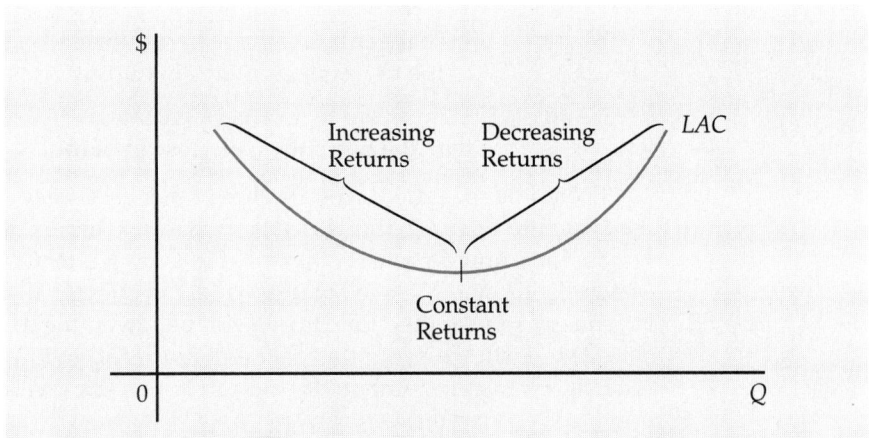

When the firm experiences increasing returns to scale, *LAC* declines. When the firm has constant returns to scale, *LAC* is constant. When the firm has decreasing returns to scale, *LAC* is increasing.

It measures the relative responsiveness of long-run total cost to changes in the level of output. The formula for *arc cost elasticity* is given by[26]

$$E_c = \frac{\Delta LTC}{\Delta Q} \cdot \frac{Q_2 + Q_1}{LTC_2 + LTC_1}.$$

If the cost elasticity is less than 1, then a given percentage increase in output will result in a smaller percentage increase in long-run total cost, and economies of scale will be present. On the other hand, if the cost elasticity is greater than 1, then *LTC* will increase by a greater percentage than the percentage change in output, and diseconomies of scale will occur. If *LTC* and output change by exactly the same percentage, then constant returns to scale will be present. These relationships are summarized as follows:

---

26 The formula for point cost elasticity is

$$E_c = \frac{\partial LTC}{\partial Q} \cdot \frac{Q}{LTC}.$$

$E_C < 1$ *LTC* increases by a smaller percentage   economies of
       than the percentage increase in output.   scale

$E_C = 1$ *LTC* changes by the same percentage   constant returns
       as the percentage change in output.   to scale

$E_C > 1$ *LTC* increases by a larger percentage   diseconomies of
       than the percentage increase in output.   of scale

Economies of scale, or the absence of them, can play an important role in the structure of firms, industries, and markets. For example, Kraft General Foods, Inc., found that its sales people from Kraft, General Foods, Oscar Mayer Foods, and Maxwell House would frequently all appear at a particular grocery store at the same time, all of them wanting to talk to the manager simultaneously. To avoid this pandemonium and to lower costs as well, the four divisions were combined into Kraft Foods, Inc., with a single sales force organized around marketing teams, and each team was assigned to one chain of stores. In the steel industry, economies of scale were thought to be very important. However, in recent years, technological changes have made it possible for smaller minimills to achieve the same or even lower unit costs than the large steel mills. A similar phenomenon is occurring in computer chip factories, where "minifabs"—smaller, more automated, and more flexible versions of wafer fabrication plants—are becoming competitive with respect to costs or even more efficient than the traditional, larger plants.[27] Other things remaining equal, when technology enables small firms to achieve the same or lower per-unit costs as large firms, the probability of greater competition in that industry and market is increased.

We should point out that drawing the *LAC* curve as a smooth, U-shaped curve implies that all inputs are perfectly divisible. In reality, all inputs are not necessarily infinitely divisible. For example, only a limited number of sizes of blast furnaces are readily available. When inputs are indivisible, the firm's long-run average cost curve merely consists of those points on the short-run average cost curves corresponding to the sizes of plant that are available that represent the lowest unit cost possible for each level of output. This situation produces a scalloped long-run average cost curve, such as that shown in Figure 6–15.

THE LEARNING EFFECT

Some authorities in the area of production and cost have observed that average costs of production for a given level of output decline as a firm's *cumulative* output of a product (total output produced to date) increases. In this

27 "Will So Many Ingredients Work Together?" *Business Week* (March 27, 1995), pp. 188, 191; and "Huh? Chipmakers Copying Steelmakers?" *Business Week* (August 15, 1994), pp. 97–98.

Figure 6–15   Long-Run Average Cost Curve when Four Plant Sizes
Are Available

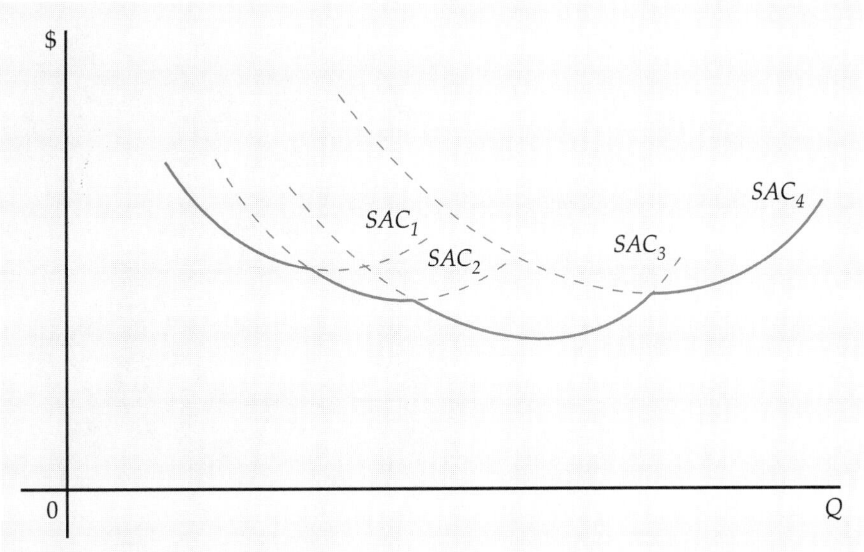

If only four plant sizes are available, the *LAC* curve will be determined by finding the plant size
with the lowest per-unit costs for each level of output, SAC_1, SAC_2, SAC_3, and SAC_4 are short-run
average cost curves corresponding to the four plant sizes. The long-run average cost curve is the
heavy black line.

situation, the firm's production of additional units of output causes its long-
run average cost curve to shift downward. This phenomenon is attributed to
a *learning effect* of increased production on the part of both management and
labor. Costs are reduced as both management and labor become more familiar with the production processes required to manufacture the item and, as a
result, become more efficient in its production.

ECONOMIES OF SCOPE

Economies of scope
occur when the
average cost of
undertaking two or
more activities
together is less than
the sum of the costs
of each activity
separately.

Economies of scope occur when it is cheaper for a firm to undertake two or
more activities together than the sum of the costs that the firm would incur
to pursue each activity separately. For example, the average cost of selling an
insurance policy per dollar of premium received may be lower for a firm that
sells life insurance together with home and automobile insurance than for a
firm that sells only life insurance *or* home insurance *or* automobile insurance.
The lower cost per premium dollar could be achieved because one customer
could be sold all three types of premiums during the same visit.

MANAGERIAL PERSPECTIVE
Lean, Mean, and Green

It hardly seemed worth bothering. The blades on the saws in Georgia Pacific sawmills could be made half as thick as they were before, thanks to a new, stronger metal alloy used to make the blades. Yet that smaller blade will result in 800 additional railcars of Georgia Pacific products each year rather than sawdust on the mill floor.

And Georgia Pacific is not alone in its effort to reduce waste. Companies all over the United States are finding that they must become more efficient if they are to survive in the international market environment in which they find themselves. Rockwell International found that by investing in an $80,000 laser to etch contract numbers on communications systems sold to the Pentagon, the company could save not only $4,000 annually in direct labor cost, but—much more important—$200,000 per year in inventory holding costs. Through automation of its refineries, weeding out unprofitable service stations, and modernizing high-volume stations, Exxon has been able to increase the volume sold through the stations by one-third. The paper industry and the steel industry have also been heavily involved in an effort to become more competitive by closing plants, restructuring, and layoffs. As a result, productivity in manufacturing grew at an annual rate of almost 4 percent between 1981 and 1987, a great improvement over the 1.3 percent rate of growth that prevailed between 1973 and 1981.

Of course, cost-cutting that is not carefully planned and thought through can be harmful to a firm's health. General Motors' problems with its new automated, state-of-the-art plants have been well publicized. Certainly, firms must be careful not to reduce plant capacity to such an extent that they lose market share when the demand for their products increases. Nor can they afford to ignore product development and quality control and improvement. One company recently supplied Ford Motor Company with 1.6 million oil pump parts without a single defect. According to its president, the company found that quality control that once was believed to be impossible is now necessary for survival. Xerox found that quality improvements could save as much as $2 billion on sales of $10 billion, certainly a significant figure. David Kearns, chief executive officer of Xerox, stated, "Over the years, you grow up thinking that the greater quality you give a customer, the higher the price. We now know that's not true. Quality drives costs down." The cost saving comes because doing it right the first time is often cheaper than repairing manufacturing defects and working to regain loyalty from dissatisfied customers.

Companies are finding that being "green" is profitable as well. Measures to improve the environmental impact of their products help companies to avoid obvious costs like fines and lawsuits. However, environmentally responsible policies can result in lower production and marketing costs as well. In 1989, Exxon endured an avalanche of bad publicity, not to mention more than $3 *billion* in environmental charges, as a result of the Valdez oil spill. ARCO Chemical found that it could reduce its energy costs by 35 percent by using a new, more efficient plant. Union Carbide recycled or sold 82 million pounds of waste in the first six months of 1989, generating $3.5 million in revenue and saving $8.5 million of disposal costs. By getting workers on the shop floor to buy into the notion of reducing hazardous wastes, General Electric was able to trim waste oil at an aircraft engines plant by 20 percent.

Clearly, careful cost management has become imperative for successful companies as they enter the twenty-first century, and environmentally sound policies with respect to resource use and disposal are a part of this mandate as well.

References: "America's Leanest and Meanest," *Business Week* (October 5, 1987), pp. 78–80; "The Productivity Paradox," *Business Week* (June 6, 1988), p. 104; "U.S. Parts Makers Just Won't Say 'Uncle,' " *Business Week* (August 10, 1987), p. 76; "Culture Shock at Xerox," *Business Week*," (June 22, 1987), p. 110; and "The Greening of Corporate America," *Business Week* (April 23, 1990), p. 100.

CHOOSING THE OPTIMAL PLANT SIZE: AN EXAMPLE

To get an idea of the type of analysis a firm must go through in trying to determine its optimal plant size, consider once more the case of John and Ruth Brown and their delicatessen, discussed at the beginning of this chapter. In Table 6–5 the income statement presented in Table 6–1 is reproduced with some additional information. Suppose that the deli, by selling 20,000 meals per month, is operating near its capacity level and that the Browns are contemplating expanding their restaurant.

In fact, assume that John and Ruth are considering two possibilities for expansion. The first possibility would involve building an addition onto the original deli, so that the back wall would extend further into the mall parking area. This plan would increase the deli's capacity by 50 percent to 30,000 meals per month and would involve an initial outlay of $60,000 for construction and equipment. John and Ruth have $20,000 additional money of their own that they could invest, and they know where they can borrow the remaining $40,000 at 9 percent interest. *If* the expanded restaurant were to operate at capacity, its income statement (with additional information) would be like that presented in Table 6–6.

Table 6–5   John and Ruth's Deli
Statement of Economic Profit
for Month Ended July 31, 1997

Total Revenue (20,000 meals @ average price of $6.00)		$120,000
Less		
Cost of Goods Sold (food and beverages—20,000 meals @ $4.20)		84,000
Gross Profit		$ 36,000
Less		
Operating Expenses		
Fixed	$20,000	
Variable (20,000 meals @ $0.50)	10,000	30,000
Operating (accounting) Net Income		$ 6,000
Less		
Implicit Rental Income	$ 2,000	
Implicit Salary Income	2,600	
Implicit Interest Income	160	4,760
Economic Profit		$ 1,240

Table 6–6   John and Ruth's Deli
Statement of Economic Profit
for Month Ended _____
(At Capacity Under Expansion Plan 1)

Total Revenue (30,000 meals @ average price of $6.00)		$180,000
Less		
Cost of Goods Sold (food and beverages—30,000 meals @ $4.20)		126,000
Gross Profit		$ 54,000
Less		
Operating Expenses		
Fixed	$29,000	
Variable (30,000 meals @ $0.46)	13,800	42,800
Operating Net Income		$ 11,200
Less		
Explicit Interest Expense		300
Accounting Net Income		$ 10,900
Less		
Implicit Rental Income (existing building)	$ 2,000	
Implicit Salary Income	2,600	
Implicit Interest Income	320	4,920
Economic Profit		$ 5,980

The second expansion possibility involves buying the small vacant building adjoining the deli in the mall. This additional area would double the deli's capacity to 40,000 meals per month, and the Browns could get a good deal on the building, so that the initial outlay necessary for the building, remodeling, and equipment would be only $100,000. Again, the Browns could put up $20,000 of their own money and borrow the remaining $80,000 at 9 percent interest. If the restaurant were to follow this expansion plan *and were to operate at capacity*, John and Ruth expect that their monthly economic profit statement would be similar to that presented in Table 6–7. Note that if the Browns expand the restaurant to double the capacity, they *do* expect to be able to take advantage of some external and internal economies, such as greater volume buying of both food and other operating supplies and more efficient use of equipment.

If John and Ruth think they have a high probability of being able to sell 40,000 meals per month, then obviously they should decide in favor of the larger expansion plan. However, suppose that they expect to be able to sell only 29,000 meals per month for the next few years. Then, assuming they cannot take advantage of volume food buying at that level of business under either plan, they expect monthly results under each expansion plan to be similar to those computed in Tables 6–8 and 6–9. In this case, without addi-

Table 6–7	John and Ruth's Deli Statement of Economic Profit for Month Ended _____ (At Capacity Under Expansion Plan 2)		
Total Revenue (40,000 meals @ average price of $6.00)			$240,000
Less			
Cost of Goods Sold (food and beverages—40,000 meals @ $4.10)			164,000
Gross Profit			$ 76,000
Less			
Operating Expenses			
Fixed		$35,500	
Variable (40,000 meals @ $0.40)		16,000	51,500
Operating Net Income			$ 24,500
Less			
Explicit Interest Expense			600
Accounting Net Income			$ 23,900
Less			
Implicit Rental Income (existing building)		$ 2,000	
Implicit Salary Income		2,600	
Implicit Interest Income		320	4,920
Economic Profit			$ 18,980

Table 6–8   John and Ruth's Deli
                    Statement of Economic Profit
                    for Month Ended _____
            (At 29,000 Meals Under Expansion Plan 1)

Total Revenue (29,000 meals @ average price of $6.00)		$174,000
Less		
Cost of Goods Sold (food and beverages—29,000 meals @ $4.20)		121,800
Gross Profit		$ 52,200
Less Operating Expenses		
Fixed	$29,000	
Variable (29,000 meals @ $0.46)	13,340	42,340
Operating Net Income		$ 9,860
Less Explicit Interest Expense		300
Accounting Net Income		$ 9,560
Less		
Implicit Rental Income (existing building)	$ 2,000	
Implicit Salary Income	2,600	
Implicit Interest Income	320	4,920
Economic Profit		$ 4,640

Table 6–9   John and Ruth's Deli
                    Statement of Economic Profit
                    for Month Ended _____
            (At 29,000 Meals Under Expansion Plan 2)

Total Revenue (29,000 meals @ average price of $6.00)		$174,000
Less		
Cost of Goods Sold (food and beverages—29,000 meals @ $4.20)		121,800
Gross Profit		$ 52,200
Less Operating Expenses		
Fixed	$35,500	
Variable (29,000 meals @ $0.40)	11,600	47,100
Operating Net Income		$ 5,100
Less Explicit Interest Expense		600
Accounting Net Income		$ 4,500
Less		
Implicit Rental Income (existing building)	$ 2,000	
Implicit Salary Income	2,600	
Implicit Interest Income	320	4,920
Economic Profit		$ (420)

tional factors to consider, it appears that John and Ruth should select the smaller expansion plan.

Nevertheless, the Browns may well wish to consider some additional factors before they make their final decision. For example, they would perhaps wish to consider a longer time horizon than three or four years, especially if they expect sales to continue expanding. As they expand the time period under consideration, the second plan may look more and more desirable. The Browns would also want to consider the risks associated with each expansion plan in the event that their projected levels of sales are incorrect. They should also consider the possibilities for expanding their restaurant *after* they have already used the first expansion plan. We will discuss further the techniques John and Ruth should use in this type of analysis in Chapters 13 and 14. They would also be wise to consider the results after changing their price structure and probably should do some investigation of the demand function of their deli's product. Demand analysis, demand estimation, and forecasting were discussed at length in Chapters 2, 3, and 4. Profit analysis is explained in Chapter 7, and alternative pricing strategies are considered in much greater depth in Chapter 11.

ESTIMATION OF COST

One of the tasks with which a profit-maximizing firm manager must contend is that of estimating what the costs of the firm will or should be for different levels of output. For example, strong financial controls and cost estimation have contributed significantly to the profitability of the General Electric Company; the lack of such controls has hurt Westinghouse.[28] In Detroit, Ford and General Motors make cost calculations to fractions of a cent.[29]

There are two general methods of estimating costs: one is through utilization of historical cost data, and the second is through utilization of estimates by engineers. Managers who choose the historical cost method try to estimate future costs from data about actual costs incurred by the firm in the past. These historical cost figures must be adjusted to include opportunity costs and to take into consideration any changes in input prices or technology that will affect a firm's costs. An attempt should be made to separate short-run cost data from long-run cost data. Such an analysis will necessitate a study of those cost-output combinations that were obtained with a least cost combination of inputs and those that were not. Moreover, an attempt must be made to match historical costs with the appropriate level of output. Some costs, such as certain maintenance and repair expenses, may not always be in-

---

28 "The Opposites: GE Grows While Westinghousᵢe Shrinks," *Business Week* (January 31, 1977), pp. 60–66.
29 "Detroit's New Appetite for Electronic Controls," *Business Week* (August 29, 1977), p. 66.

curred by the firm at the same time that the responsible level of output was produced. Finally, historical cost figures must also be adjusted for inflation if they are to be useful in estimating future costs.

Once the historical cost figures have been adjusted, firm managers can use various methods to estimate a firm's cost function or functions. We will briefly discuss three of them here—the high-low method, the visual-fit method, and the regression method. To use the high-low method, one merely draws a straight line connecting the highest and lowest cost figures on a scatter diagram showing the adjusted historical cost data, as demonstrated in Figure 6–16. Employing the visual-fit method, one draws a line through points on a scatter diagram that appears to be most representative of (or "best fits") the underlying cost data. This method is illustrated in Figure 6–17. The third method, regression analysis, requires the use of more sophisticated statistical techniques to estimate the cost function and the correlation of cost with the level of output. This method, although more precise, is also more difficult to use. It was discussed in Chapter 3 and its appendix in connection with demand estimation.

There are several different forms of the long-run total cost function that

Figure 6–16   High-Low Method of Cost Estimation

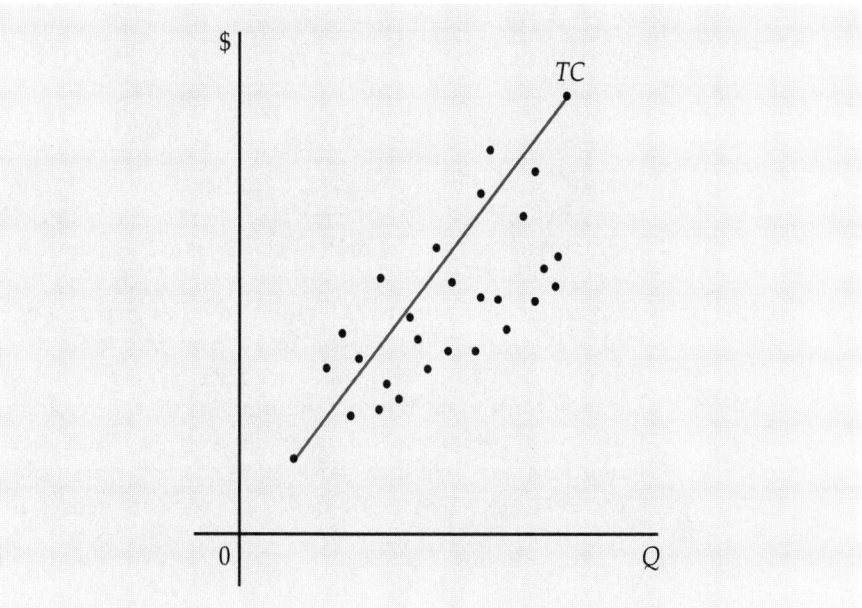

The high-low method of cost estimation involves drawing a total cost curve by connecting the lowest level of cost with the highest level of cost.

Figure 6–17   Visual-Fit Method of Cost Estimation

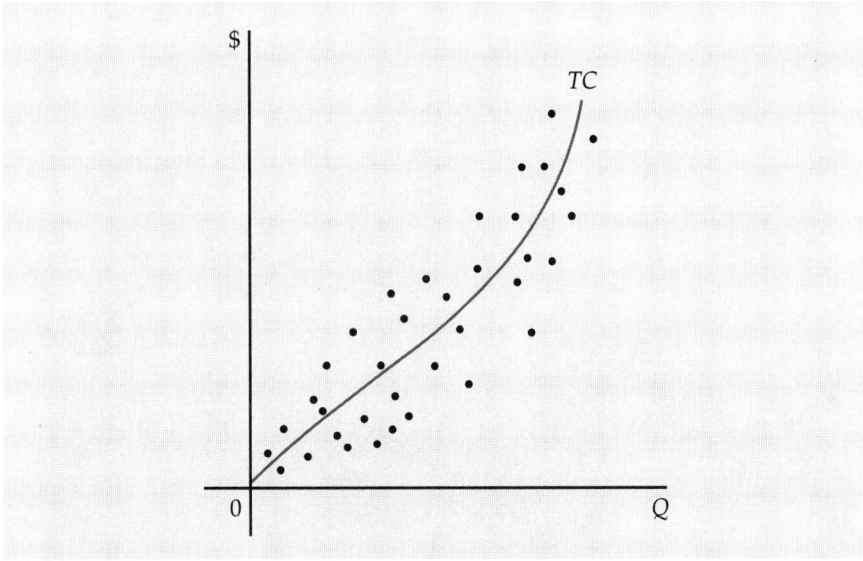

The visual fit method of cost estimation involves sketching that total cost curve which appears to "best fit" the historical cost data.

a firm might estimate through regression analysis. The simplest one is a linear cost function of the form

$$LTC = \alpha Q + \sum_{i=1}^{n} \beta_i X_i + \varepsilon,$$

where

LTC = long-run total cost,
Q = quantity of output, and
X_i = other factors that affect long-run total cost, such as input prices.

In this case, if input prices did not change, marginal cost would be constant and equal to α.[30]

---

30 In this case,

$$LMC = \frac{\partial LTC}{\partial Q} = \alpha.$$

Nonlinear forms of the long-run total cost function are also estimated. One type is a function that is quadratic with respect to the quantity of output:

$$LTC = \alpha_1 Q + \alpha_2 Q^2 + \sum_{i=1}^{n} \beta_i X_i + \varepsilon,$$

where LTC, Q, and X_i are defined as before. In this case marginal cost would be a straight line given by the equation $\alpha_1 + 2\alpha_2 Q$.[31] A second type of nonlinear function that can yield the typical marginal cost curve frequently found in economics textbooks is a cubic cost function:

$$LTC = \alpha_1 Q + \alpha_2 Q^2 + \alpha_3 Q^3 + \sum_{i=1}^{n} \beta_i X_i + \varepsilon,$$

where LTC, Q, and X_i are defined as before. In this case marginal cost is equal to $\alpha_1 + 2\alpha_2 Q + 3\alpha_3 Q^2$.[32] With appropriate values for α_1, α_2, and α_3, marginal cost will first decrease, reach a minimum, and then increase.

A third type of nonlinear cost function that is estimated is a *multiplicative cost function*. The following is one example of this type of function:

$$LTC = Q^\alpha X_i^\beta \varepsilon,$$

where the variables are still defined as before. In this form, α would be equal to the cost elasticity with respect to output, E_C. The β_i terms would represent the elasticity of LTC relative to each respective X_i variable. In this case, marginal cost depends on the values of the X variables.[33] As we discussed in Chapter 3 and its appendix, multiplicative functions can be transformed into linear equations by taking the logarithms of the variables:

$$\log LTC = \alpha \log Q + \sum_{i=1}^{n} \beta_i \log X_i + \log \varepsilon.$$

---

31 Again, marginal cost is given by

$$LMC = \frac{\partial LTC}{\partial Q} = \alpha_1 + 2\alpha_2 Q.$$

32 As before, marginal cost is found as

$$LMC = \frac{\partial LTC}{\partial Q} = \alpha_1 + 2\alpha_2 Q + 3\alpha_3 Q^2.$$

33 Marginal cost is now equal to

$$LMC = \frac{\partial LTC}{\partial Q} = \alpha Q^{\alpha-1} X_i^\beta \varepsilon.$$

MANAGERIAL PERSPECTIVE

Estimating Product Cost the Modern Way

Computers invaded industry decades ago, and they are now a common fixture on production lines as well as in corporate offices. What everyone has learned is that these wondrous information processors are only as good as the software designed to run them. Often the capabilities of computers are underutilized because no one has developed appropriate applications programs. Computer-aided design (CAD) and computer-aided manufacturing (CAM) are examples of fields in which there has been an outpouring of software development.

Now comes the Parts Cost Estimating (PCE) program. This new breed of software utilizes a base of existing knowledge in specific types of manufacturing to generate cost estimates for yet-to-be-built products. Thus, once the CAD folks have come up with a design, the PCE people can check out its likely production cost. The brainchild of Geoffrey Boothroyd, a professor at the University of Rhode Island, the first PCE program was for machining parts made of metal. However, modifications of the program can handle parts made by injection molding, bending of sheet metal, forging, and other methods. The PCE program calculates how long certain operations will take, how much material they use, and finally their cost.

Reference: "Software That Tells You How Much That New Widget Will Cost," *Business Week* (April 4, 1988), p. 63.

In recent years other types of cost functions involving flexible functional forms have been developed.[34]

Engineering cost estimates are another technique of cost estimation. This method of cost estimation utilizes engineering and other manufacturing experts in the firm to develop the cost function. Engineering cost estimates have an advantage in that the cost figures obtained in this manner should already be based on current technology and current prices. Also, there should not be the problem of separating long-run and short-run cost figures nor the problem of matching costs incurred with the relevant levels of production. However, engineering cost estimates are still only that—*estimates*. The better the engineers understand the nature of a firm's production relationships and the

---

[34] One example of this type of cost function and a discussion of its features can be found in Lila J. Truett, Dale B. Truett, and Bobby Apostolakis, "The Translog Cost Function and Import Demand: The Case of Mexico," *Southern Economic Journal*, Vol. 60, No. 3 (January 1994).

more closely they can estimate future prices, the more nearly accurate their cost estimates will be. Even these figures, however, must still be adjusted to reflect implicit or opportunity costs.

Thus it is evident that the estimation of a firm's costs is rarely a simple task. Still, the difficulty of estimating a firm's costs does not diminish the importance of that information to the firm managers. Managers face the job of finding a proper (profit-maximizing) balance between more precise information regarding the firm's costs and the corresponding cost of obtaining it and less reliable, but cheaper, information.

SUMMARY

Costs and the Firm

We have repeatedly emphasized the crucial role that costs play in determining the profitability of the firm. The profit-oriented firm manager must consider both opportunity costs and explicit costs in order to use time, money, and physical resources economically. Obviously, a firm does not always have totally accurate information about its costs; but it is very important that it have reliable *estimates* of its fixed costs, of how its costs vary with respect to output over the relevant range of production, and of whether or not its costs would be lower (and if so, how much) with a different size plant.

We have discussed three general types of cost classifications in this chapter: (1) *explicit*, or *historical*, costs and *implicit*, or *opportunity*, costs; (2) *fixed* and *variable* costs; and (3) *private* and *social* costs. Explicit costs are costs for which the firm has made direct payment or will make direct payment in the future and are the basis for most accounting cost figures. Opportunity costs are costs that the firm incurs by utilizing its resources in one activity when such resources could also be used in another manner, even though no explicit payment is being made by the firm for their use. Examples of such resources are the owner-manager's time and money. A consideration by the manager of both the explicit and implicit costs of a firm is necessary to ensure that *all* of the firm's resources are being used to maximize profits. Thus *economic costs* include both explicit and implicit costs. Fixed costs are costs that do not vary with the level of a firm's output in the short run, whereas variable costs do vary with the level of output. By classifying costs in this manner, a firm manager can separate opportunities and decisions relevant to the short run from opportunities and decisions that are relevant to long-run planning. Private costs are costs that a firm incurs, whereas social costs are those borne by society as a whole. A classification of costs as to which are private and which social is most useful for decisions involving social policy.

Next, we discussed the long-run costs of a firm, all of which are assumed to be variable and are derived by finding a series of least cost combinations of inputs. The long-run costs were discussed in terms of *total cost*, *average cost*, and *marginal cost*. Long-run total cost is all of the costs that a firm incurs, given that the firm is producing with the optimal input mix. Average cost is the average cost per unit of output, or LTC/Q. Marginal cost is the rate of change of total cost with respect to the level of output.

Because of the existence of fixed costs in the short run, short-run costs must be discussed in terms of *total cost, total fixed cost, total variable cost, average total cost, average fixed cost, average variable cost,* and *marginal cost.* The definition of each of these terms is similar to that for corresponding long-run terms (total, average, or marginal). Of course, *total fixed cost* and *average fixed cost* have no long-run counterparts, since all costs are variable in the long run. We also demonstrated the close relationships between short-run product curves and cost curves.

Moreover, we discussed the relationships among short-run average cost, long-run average cost, and returns to scale. We also gave a simple example of some of the analysis that a profit-maximizing firm manager should undertake when determining the optimal plant size for the firm.

Finally, we ended this chapter with a brief discussion of cost estimation techniques. The two general types of methods used are the historical cost method and the engineering cost method, and data used in both methods usually require some adjustments. Obtaining information about a firm's costs can be an expensive project for a manager, who must determine when (and how much of) that expense is in the best interests of the firm.

As those who operate successful businesses understand, in order to be profitable, a firm must produce a good or service that people desire, market it well, and price it correctly, *in addition to* keeping its unit costs low relative to those of other firms in the same industry.[35] In the next chapter we will discuss how the profit-maximizing firm determines its optimal level of output (and price), given its cost and revenue data.

QUESTIONS

1. Define and compare historical costs, accounting costs, opportunity costs, economic costs, private costs, and social costs.
2. Why is it important that a firm owner consider opportunity costs when making economic decisions regarding the firm? Give some examples of opportunity costs.
3. What is a least cost combination of inputs? How do such input combinations relate to the long-run total cost curve for a firm?
4. What is the difference between the long run and the short run for a firm? How do the firm's costs differ in the two time periods?

---

35 See, for example, "Kodak Chief Is Trying For the Fourth Time, To Trim Firm's Costs," *The Wall Street Journal,* September 19, 1989, pp. A1, A8.

5. How are the short-run average cost curves and the long-run average cost curve related?
6. Why can arc short-run marginal cost be found by finding either $(\Delta STC / \Delta Q)$ or $(\Delta TVC / \Delta Q)$?
7. How do returns to scale affect the shape of the long-run average cost curve?

PROBLEMS

1. a. Complete the following table, which gives short-run cost data for a firm.

Q	STC	TFC	TVC	SAC	AFC	AVC	Arc SMC
0	10,800		0	—	—	—	
1,000			1,000				
2,000			1,600				
3,000			2,400				
4,000			3,600				
5,000			5,000				
6,000			7,200				

b. Sketch the cost curves, given the data that you have computed in the preceding table.
2. a. In the following table, complete the cost data for a firm.
b. Sketch the cost curves, given the data in part (a).

Q	STC	TFC	TVC	SAC	AFC	AVC	Arc SMC
0			0	—	—	—	
							20
1					120		
							16
2							
							12
3							
							16
4							
							21
5							
							29
6							

3. Given that $Q = f(a,b)$, as shown in the following diagram, and that $P_a = \$1$ and $P_b = \$2$, answer the questions in parts (a) through (e).

a. If $b_3 = 450$ units of input b, what is the total cost of producing 300 units of output?

b. What is the long-run *average* cost of producing 300 units of output? Is this consistent with point H' in the lower diagram?

c. Assuming the curve in the lower diagram *is* long-run average cost, how many units of a is a_1 equal to in the upper diagram?

d. What is the dollar amount of TC_2?

e. If $a_4 = 1,400$ units and $Q_4 = 400$ units, find average cost at point J in the upper diagram.

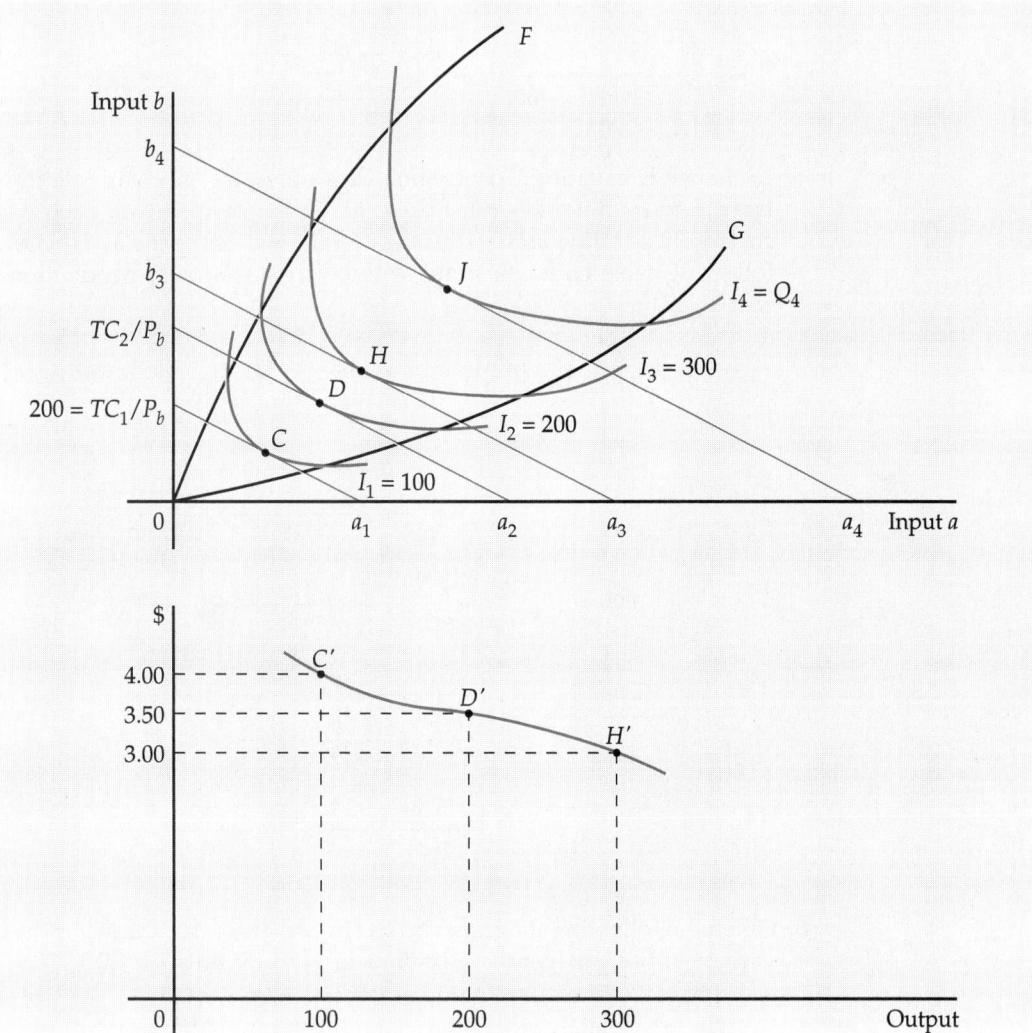

4. Complete the following table, given that the price of input a is constant and that a is the only variable input. (Hint: The price of input a and total fixed cost can be determined from the information given in the table.)

Input a (Units)	Q (Output in Units)	Arc MP_a	Arc SMC	AVC	SAC
0	0			Unde-fined	Unde-fined
			$10.00		
1	5			$10.00	$30.00
2	20				
3	40				
4	55				
5	65				

5. Exclusive Excavating Corporation digs holes. Its only variable input is labor, and each worker must bring his or her own shovel. Each worker costs $100 per day, and Exclusive's total fixed cost per day is $300. The following table contains some of the company's daily production and cost data.
   a. Complete the table.
   b. Where is SMC at a minimum? Where is MP_L at a maximum?

SMC	MP_L	Q	L	TVC	SAC
		0	0	0	—
		40	2		12.50
		100	4		
4.00					
		150	6		
		190	8		
5.88					
		224	10		
		254	12		5.91
		274	14		
		284	16		

6. Given the following diagram and the information that input a is the only variable input, answer the questions in parts (a) through (d).
   a. What is the maximum value of AP_a?
   b. At approximately what quantity of input a will MP_a be at a maximum?
   c. If P_a is $96, what is the minimum AVC?

      d. If P_a is \$96 and TFC is \$4,800, find STC and SAC at an output level of 60 units.

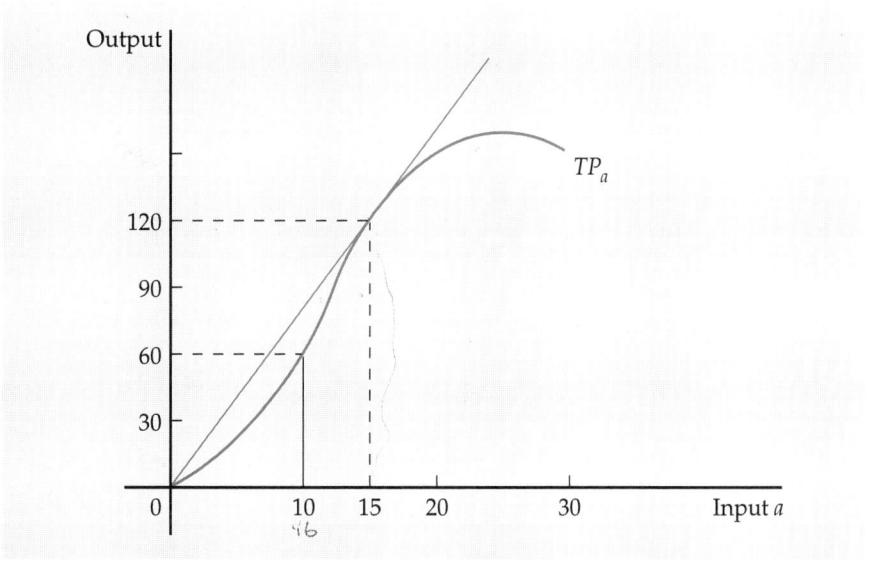

7. Complete the following table, assuming that the firm is in the short run, that input a is the only variable input, and that $P_{a'}$, the price of input a, is fixed.

Input a (Units)	Output (Units)	AP_a	Arc MP_a	Arc SMC	AVC	AFC	STC
0	0	—			\$ —	\$ —	
			5.0	\$ 40.00			
2	10				40.00		
				22.22			
4		7			28.57		
			10.0				
6	48					14.00	
				50.00			
8	56	7			28.57		
10		6					
			1.5	133.33			
12	63				38.10		

* Take note in your calculation of marginal product that Δa is 2 units of a between output values.

8. Complete the following table, assuming that L is the only variable input and that its price, P_L, is fixed.

SMC (Marginal Cost)	MP_L (Marginal Product)	L (Input)	TP_L = Q_X (Output)	TVC (Total Variable Cost)	STC (Total Cost)
		5	100	200	600
		10	200		
		15	450		
		20	550		
4.00	10				
		25	600	1,000	
		30	625		
10.00	4				
		35	645		
		40	660		2,000

a. Now calculate the following:
   (i) Average fixed cost at an output of $Q = 200$.
   (ii) Average product of L at an output of $Q = 600$.
b. Suppose total fixed cost is increased by 25 percent. Which of the numbers in the table would change? Why?

9. The following data represent the quantities of Product X that can be obtained from various combinations of two inputs, Y and Z.

Units of Input Y	Output of Product X						
6	122	205	277	345	408	468	
5	112	190	256	317	374	429	
4	100	168	228	283	334	383	
3	86	145	197	245	289	331	
2	70	119	160	200	236	270	
1	50	84	114	142	167	191	
0	1	2	3	4	5	6	Units of Input Z

a. How will the long-run average cost curve for the production of X behave? Explain how you know from the given data.
b. Suppose the price of a unit of Y is $14 and that of a unit of Z is $12. Do one unit of Y and two units of Z constitute a least cost combination of inputs for an output of 84 units of Product X? Explain why or why not.
c. Suppose input Z is fixed at $Z = 4$. Complete the following table, assuming the same production function and input prices. (Assume also that no output can be obtained if $Y = 0$.)

SMC	MP_Y	Output of X	Input of Y	AP_Y	AVC	STC
		0	0	—	—	

10. In the following table, assume that L is the only variable input and that P_L, the price of a unit of labor, is fixed.
    a. Given that L is labor units and Q is units of output per time period, complete the table.

MP_L	L	Q	STC	AFC	AVC	TVC	MC
	0	0	120	—	—	0	
	2	20		6		160	
	4	60					
	6	90				480	
	8	110					
	10	125					

   b. Explain what a 25 percent increase in total fixed cost would do to the concepts listed in the table.
11. Suppose a firm has two inputs, a and b, and that b is fixed in the short run. Its short-run total product is described by the following table.

a	Q = Output
0	0
2	50
4	120
6	180
8	230
10	270
12	300

a. Fill in the table below, assuming that the price of a unit of input *a* is $40.

SMC	MP_a	Output (Q)	Input of a	AP_a	AVC	STC
			0			
						744

b. What will be the value of average fixed cost when output is at a level of $Q = 180$? How do you know?

c. Suppose the price of a unit of *b* is fixed, and that the amount employed of *b* is constant at $b = 12$. How much is the firm paying per unit of *b*? (What is *b*'s price?) Explain how you know.

12. Suppose a firm determines that its average variable cost can be represented by the equation $AVC = 10 + 4Q$, where Q is its daily output. Suppose also that its total fixed cost is $TFC = 100$. Do the following:

a. Plot the firm's AVC curve for the range $Q = 1$ to $Q = 15$ units of output per day.

b. Plot its AFC over the same range of output.

c. Add the two curves to develop the short-run average cost SAC curve. Does SAC appear to have a minimum point? If so, at what output? If not, explain why not.

The following problems require calculus.

C1. A firm has the following short-run total cost function:

$$STC = \$1{,}000 + 240Q - 4Q^2 + (1/3)Q^3.$$

a. Write equations for the firm's SMC, AVC, and SAC.

b. Determine the output level at which SMC will be minimized.

c. Determine the output level at which AVC will be minimized.

C2. Suppose a firm has the following total cost function:

$$STC = 300 + 40Q - 8Q^2 + (2/3)Q^3$$

$$300 \qquad 40 - 8Q + 2/3Q^2$$

a. Write equations for

(i) Average fixed cost

(ii) Average variable cost

b. What will be the value of short-run average cost when $Q = 60$?

c. Write the marginal cost equation for this firm.

d. What will marginal cost be when $Q = 20$?

e. For this firm, what will be the dollar value of AVC at its minimum?

C3. Juno Corporation has the short-run total cost function

$$STC = TFC + TVC = 800 + 60Q - 4.5Q^2 + 0.15Q^3,$$

where Q is output. Answer the following:

a. What is the dollar value of average fixed cost at an output of 20 units?

b. At what level of output will marginal cost be at its minimum?

c. What will be the value of average variable cost when it is at its minimum?

C4. A firm has the following long-run total cost function:

$$LTC = 180Q - 3Q^2 + .02Q^3$$

a. Write expressions for long-run marginal cost and long-run average cost.

b. Does the LAC curve have a minimum? If so, at what quantity? If not, explain why.

c. What does your answer to part (b) suggest about returns to scale in this firm's production function?

C5. IMOVISION, a maker of liquid crystal display screens for scientific plotting calculators, is considering production of a new model screen in a foreign location. It plans to make 400 of the screens per day whether it produces them at its home plant or at the foreign location. Estimated daily U.S. dollar costs, including all fixed costs are as follows:

$$\text{Home plant: } STC = 5,000 + 10Q + .02Q^2$$

$$\text{Foreign plant: } STC_F = 6,400 + 9Q + .01Q^2$$

a. In which plant will the firm attain the lowest *minimum* average cost for the projected 400-unit-per-day output?

b. In which plant will the firm attain the lowest *minimum* average cost per screen?

c. Suppose that $1,800 of the daily fixed cost in the home plant consists of allocated fixed costs that would exist whether or not production of the screen in question occurs there, but that all of the fixed costs in the foreign plant are directly associated with the production of the new screens. What advice would you give to management regarding the choice between home and foreign production?

C6. Consider the following short-run total cost function.

$$STC = 400 + 6Q + .01Q^2$$

     a. Briefly describe what this total cost function will look like when plotted as a diagram.

     b. Will short-run marginal cost have a minimum point? Explain.

     c. What kind of line or curve would represent the average variable cost curve related to this *STC*?

     d. Will *SAC* have a minimum point? If so, explain, and give the minimum value of *SAC*.

C7. Suppose the total cost function is $550 + 9Q - .15Q^2 + .005Q^3$.

     a. Find the marginal cost, average variable cost, average cost, and the average fixed cost functions.

     b. Sketch the functions that you derived in part (a).

     c. At what level of output does the *SMC* reach its minimum? *AVC*? *AFC*?

     d. Find *SMC* and *AVC* when *AVC* is at its minimum.

SELECTED REFERENCES

Bailey, Elizabeth E., and Ann F. Friedlander. "Market Structure and Multiproduct Industries," *Journal of Economic Literature,* 20, no. 3 (September 1982), pp. 1024–1048.

Cookenboo, Leslie, Jr. "Production Functions and Cost Functions: A Case Study," *Crude Oil Pipe Lines and Competition in the Oil Industry.* Cambridge, Mass.: Harvard University Press, 1955.

Leftwich, Richard H., and Ross D. Eckert. *The Price System and Resource Allocation,* 9th ed. Hinsdale, Ill.: The Dryden Press, 1985, Chapter 10.

Mansfield, Edwin. *Microeconomics: Theory and Applications,* 7th ed. New York: W. W. Norton, 1994, Chapter 8.

McGuigan, James R., R. Charles Moyer, and Frederick H. deB. Harris. *Managerial Economics,* 7th ed. St. Paul, Minn.: West, 1996, Chapter 8.

Moore, Frederick T. "Economies of Scale: Some Statistical Evidence," *Quarterly Journal of Economics* 78, no. 2 (May 1959), pp. 232–236.

Moroney, John R. "Cobb-Douglas Production Functions and Returns to Scale in U.S. Manufacturing Industry," *Western Economic Journal* 6, no. 1 (December 1967), pp. 39–51.

Nicholson, Walter. *Microeconomic Theory: Basic Principles and Extensions,* 5th ed. Chicago: The Dryden Press, 1992, Chapter 12.

Willig, Robert D. "Multiproduct Technology and Market Structure," *The American Economic Review Papers and Proceedings,* 69, no. 2 (May 1979), pp. 346–351.

INTERNATIONAL CAPSULE I

Some International Dimensions of Demand, Production, and Cost

As a business firm develops its strategy regarding product lines, organization of production, and efficiency in the use of its resources, its managers frequently perceive that there are opportunities to sell in markets other than those of its home country. In addition, foreign sales of a product are often followed by a managerial decision to produce that product at a foreign location or, in some cases, to *purchase* certain component parts from foreign suppliers. Although these options are available to firms of all sizes, those that have been most successful in pursuing them are large multinational corporations, many of which are headquartered in the United States. Some examples are General Motors, Ford, and Chrysler; large drug manufacturers such as Eli Lilly; and chemical companies such as Celanese.

THE BASIS FOR INTERNATIONAL TRADE

In order to understand why firms enter international markets, we must first look at the economic rationale underlying foreign trade. Economic theory argues that international trade occurs because of country-to-country differences in relative prices. More precisely, it is argued that a country will export goods that are relatively cheap in its home market and import those that are relatively expensive. A simple example will help to illustrate this point.

Suppose we consider two countries, the United States and Germany, both of which produce two goods: white table wine and Cheddar cheese. Assume at first that there is no trade between the two countries. Each will be willing to give up some of one of the two goods only if it gets a suitable amount of the other in return. Thus we are examining a basis for two-way trade, where each country both exports to and imports from the other.

Of course, in this example and in international trade generally, each country's internal prices will be stated in its own currency. This will not deter us from identifying goods that are relatively cheap or relatively expensive, since the relative value of any good can be measured in terms of how much of some other good must be given up in order to obtain it. Let us suppose that in Germany a bottle of white table wine sells for 20 marks, while a pound of Cheddar cheese sells for 10 marks. In other words, a bottle of wine is worth two pounds of cheese. Now suppose that in the United States either one bottle of wine or one pound of cheese can be bought for $3.00. Thus a bottle of wine is worth only one pound of cheese to U.S. consumers. In relative terms, then, wine is expensive in Germany, while cheese is expensive in the United States.

Table I–1 summarizes the price information. How can we determine whether two-way trade will occur? The answer is that we must know the *exchange rate* between marks and dollars in order to analyze this situation. For example, suppose that in the market for currencies, a dollar can be obtained for 4 marks. The exchange rate is thus 4 marks per dollar, or $0.25 per mark (the mark is 1/4th of a dollar).

As Table I–2 shows, the German internal prices of wine and cheese (20 marks and 10 marks, respectively) translate into $5.00 per bottle for wine and $2.50 per pound for cheese. On the other hand, the U.S. internal prices ($3.00 for either good) translate into 12 marks for either wine or cheese. German

consumers will find U.S. wine attractive at 12 marks per bottle, since equivalent German wine costs 20 marks. Likewise, U.S. consumers will be attracted by the price of German cheese—$2.50 per pound—since equivalent U.S. cheese costs them $3.00 per pound. Thus we do have a basis for two-way trade at the exchange rate of 4 marks per dollar. Germany will export cheese, and the U.S. will export wine.

The importance of the exchange rate cannot be overstressed. If, in the example just cited, the exchange rate had been 3 marks per U.S. dollar, the dollar price of German cheese would be 10/3 or $3.33 per pound, while German wine would be priced at 20/3 or $6.67 per bottle. Thus U.S. consumers would not wish to buy either product from Germany, since both would be cheaper produced in the United States ($3.00 per unit). However, German consumers would find both U.S. products attractive. There would be a basis for one-way trade, but not for two-way trade.[1]

Why Relative Prices Differ

Until the last 20 years or so, the most widely accepted explanation for international differences in relative prices was variation in production costs from country to country. Thus, in our example, it would be argued that production costs for cheese were lower in Germany than in the United States, while for wine the reverse was true. The supposed reason for the lower production costs was said to be relative abundance or scarcity of resources. The relative production cost expla-

Table I–1   Local Currency Prices of Wine and Cheese in Germany and the United States

	Price of:	
	Wine in Local Currency	Cheese in Local Currency
Germany	20 marks	10 marks
United States	$3.00	$3.00

Table I–2   Translation of Internal Prices to Foreign Currency

	Money Price of Product in:			
	Marks		Dollars	
Country	Wine	Cheese	Wine	Cheese
Germany	20	10	5.00	2.50
United States	12	12	3.00	3.00

1 One-way trade is not feasible for very long. In this example, the desire of Germany to buy both wine and cheese from the United States would flood the currency markets with marks and cause the price of the mark to fall until some German goods became attractive to American buyers.

nation (called the Heckscher-Ohlin theorem after the two Swedish economists who developed it) was widely accepted, since it seemed to do a good job of explaining why countries with an abundance of unskilled labor (Latin American countries, India, and some Asian countries) tended to export products that required relatively large doses of labor to produce. Of course, it also seemed to explain why industrialized countries such as the United States, Japan, and Germany tended to export goods that required relatively large amounts of capital goods to produce. However, the production cost approach did not seem to explain why most of world trade occurs *among* the industrialized countries, all of which are relatively capital abundant. One answer was put forth by Staffan Linder, who argued that different relative prices might well depend as much on demand as on cost of production.

Linder looked at modern trade patterns and observed that the lion's share of world trade is carried out by the industrialized countries (United States, Japan, Western Europe) trading among themselves. These countries both import and export large amounts of manufactured goods, and all of them have an abundance of capital equipment, skilled labor, and advanced technology. Since all of them can supply manufactured goods at relatively low costs of production, why do they trade so much with one another? Linder reasoned that the explanation could be found in overlapping patterns of demand. The industrialized countries in general have large internal markets and relatively affluent consumers. Thus products that can be sold in one of them can probably be sold in all of them. If a company introduces a battery-powered electric face scrubber in the United States, it probably will find a market for that product in Germany and France. However, it is unlikely to find much of a market for it in Peru. Many other U.S. products might be suc-

cessfully marketed in a country like Peru, but the *range* of products Peruvians will buy is much smaller than the range of products that can be sold in Western Europe.

Different intensities of demand certainly can account for different relative prices, even if production costs are the same in the United States as in Europe. For example, if Germans become absolutely wild about designer sweatsocks, the relative price of these garments may become much higher in Germany than it is in the United States, opening up an opportunity for U.S. manufacturers to sell them in Germany.

PAYMENT FOR EXPORTS

What we have said about the importance of exchange rates in determining trade leads to a further question: If a firm exports merchandise to a foreign buyer, what can the seller do to make sure that payment for the merchandise is received?

Three types of risk are involved—*default risk*, *inconvertibility risk*, and *foreign exchange risk*. Default risk is basically the same kind of risk that sellers face in domestic trade. Thus a seller firm must evaluate the ability of the buyer to make payment. If goods are received by the buyer before payment is made, even if the seller and buyer are both in the same country, the seller is assuming some risk regarding the creditworthiness of the buyer. However, default risk is more of a problem in international trade because legal actions against debtors may be more costly and less likely to succeed when debtors are located in a foreign country.

Inconvertibility risk is the risk that the government of a given country will impose controls that make its currency impossible to exchange for some other currency. There are several ways an exporter can avoid default and inconvertibility risk. One option, of course, is to demand payment in your own currency in advance. However, this generally occurs in international trade only when the buyer has extremely poor credit or the buyer's currency is very weak. Somewhat more common is the confirmed, irrevocable letter of credit. This is a document issued by the buyer's bank. When it is *confirmed* by a bank in the seller's home country, that bank agrees to allow the exporter (seller) to draw the funds from the bank when proof is presented that the merchandise has been shipped. Aside from payment in advance, the confirmed, irrevocable letter of credit is the least risky payment instrument for exporters. But because this method is burdensome to importers, they tend to seek sellers who will accept simpler terms of payment. As a result, most exports are paid for by *commercial drafts* drawn by the exporter on the importer, with commercial banks in both countries serving as intermediaries. However, this method depends on the importer alone for payment and is therefore more risky than cash in advance or a letter of credit. Commercial drafts are also subject to inconvertibility risk.

Foreign exchange risk is the risk that the exchange rate between the currency of the seller and that of the buyer will change before payment for merchandise occurs. For example, suppose the exchange rate between British pounds and U.S. dollars is £1 = $1.50. If you export a piece of equipment to England and the buyer agrees to pay you £10,000 for it, that will translate into a payment of $15,000. However, if by the time payment is made the pound depreciates to £1 = $1.35, you will receive only $13,500. There are two methods for dealing with foreign exchange risk. The easiest, of course, is to make a contract that calls for payment in your own currency. Note, however, if you are an exporter, that what this does is transfer the foreign exchange risk to the importer in the other country. No mat-

ter how the contract is drawn, one party will face a foreign exchange risk. Since exporters and importers seldom wish to become speculators in foreign exchange, when they face foreign exchange risk they normally use a method called *hedging* to offset it.

Hedging is the process of buying or selling an asset (such as foreign currency) for the purpose of offsetting the risk of a change in its value. For example, if you are a U.S. exporter who wants to receive a payment equal to $15,000 for a piece of equipment sold to someone in England who agrees to pay in pounds 60 days in the future, you can hedge against the possibility that the number of dollars in a pound may fall by selling to someone a contract to deliver pounds on that date. There is a futures market in foreign exchange known as the *forward market*. What you will have to do is to calculate the number of pounds equal to $15,000 at the forward rate. Let's assume that today's exchange rate (known as the *spot rate*) is £1 = $1.50, but that the 60-day forward rate is £1 = $1.40. Thus the number of pounds you will need to obtain $15,000 by selling them forward is $15,000/1.4 = £10,714. You will quote this pound price to the English buyer instead of the £10,000 that would be equivalent to $15,000 at the spot rate. As soon as the contract for purchase of the equipment is signed, you will sell in the forward market a forward exchange contract to deliver £10,714 in 60 days. You will immediately receive £10,714(1.4) = $15,000 from whoever purchases the forward contract. In effect, the export has been paid for in dollars. In 60 days, when the pound payment is made by the English buyer of the equipment, the pounds are simply delivered to the buyer of the forward contract. Naturally, there are some transactions costs associated with hedging, but they are generally regarded as small relative to the benefit produced by virtually eliminating foreign exchange risk.

THE PROBLEM OF TRADE BARRIERS

Today's world is full of pitfalls to international trade that make it imperative for a company entering a foreign market to proceed with caution. One commonly encountered problem is trade barriers. These take two forms: tariffs and nontariff barriers. Import tariffs are taxes levied on imported goods. They are frequently used to protect home industries from foreign competition. Sellers of an imported good simply view the import tariff as an additional cost of production, and they are willing to supply the imported good only at a price that will cover the costs of production *including* the tariff.[2] Thus the tariff raises the price of the imported good and may actually make it impossible for the imported good to compete with equivalent locally produced goods. In many developing countries, local manufacturing is protected by very high import tariff rates—perhaps 100 percent or more of the invoice price of the imported article. In effect, these tariffs totally prohibit the importation of many kinds of goods (automobiles and television sets, for example).

Nontariff barriers may actually prohibit imports in a more decisive fashion than do import tariffs. Two examples of these devices are the *import quota* and the *import license*. An import quota is a limitation on the physical amount of a particular good that will be allowed to enter the country. For example, if Pulistonia decides to establish an annual import quota of 200 motorcycles, then no more than 200 motorcycles will be allowed to enter the country each year. This has a more certain

effect than a tariff, since a tariff pushes price up but does not specifically limit quantity. Presumably, anyone wishing to pay the tariff can still import the good. Quotas are usually accompanied by a licensing system, since the government must keep track of the quantity of imports and determine who gets to do the importing. Thus Pulistonia would require a license to import motorcycles and devise some means for dividing the quota among the licensees (auctioning off the licenses, for example, or giving them only to in-laws of government officials).

Licensing often occurs even when there is no quota. In other words, under a system that appears to rely mainly on import tariffs for protection, a license may also be required to import a particular item and thereby enjoy the privilege of *paying* the tariff. Mexico has employed such a system in the past; the government simply refused to give out licenses whenever it wished to prohibit the importation of some particular good. During the 1960s, Mexico had an elaborate system of tariffs on automobiles; the rates were meaningless, however, since almost no one could get a license to import a car anyway.

These are not the only kinds of trade barriers firms encounter when they attempt to enter a foreign market. Frequent restrictions are placed on size and labeling. (Example: "Do not send product in quart bottles, we allow only liters," or "Do not label product on the side, only on the bottom.") A firm may also find that government agencies are allowed to purchase its product only if locally produced output is nonexistent, regardless of price differentials between the two. In fact, something like the latter restriction is used by many state governments in the United States ("Buy American" laws). The moral is that no firm should seriously consider entering a foreign market without first determining the nature and extent of trade barriers found in that market. This may require considerable re-

---

2 Economic theory shows that the price paid by consumers in the importing country will rise by less than the amount of the tariff if foreign supply is not infinitely elastic.

search at significant expense, but it is *absolutely necessary*. If insurmountable trade barriers are present, a firm may have to choose between giving up a specific foreign market or entering it by investing in production facilities located there.

Analyzing Foreign Demand

Whether a firm is considering export or foreign production, an important step in its decision process will be the assessment of potential foreign demand for its product. For a product that has been successful in the home market, the firm might simply choose to look for foreign markets where consumer preferences are likely to be similar to those in its own country. If its product is not unique, there are likely to be other firms already selling in the chosen foreign market. Statistical data on production, consumption, and imports in that market may make it possible for the firm to estimate a market demand function for the product or at least estimate the rate of growth of demand. (Statistical procedures for demand estimation were discussed in Chapter 3.)

Rapid growth of demand is one indicator that a foreign market is ripe for entry. However, even if data on a firm's product are not available, an assessment of potential demand can be made from other information on the characteristics of the foreign market. For example, for many countries, data on population, per capita income, and income distribution are easily obtained. As Staffan Linder suggested, for certain manufactured goods it would be important to identify sizable markets where the middle class is large and per capita income is relatively high. Although this set of circumstances seems to describe the industrialized countries only, it also applies to the urban middle-class consumers found in many of today's developing

countries (Brazil and Mexico, for example). Moreover, a firm might find that a smaller country constitutes a feasible export market simply because there is no local production of its product.

Data Sources

To make an evaluation of foreign demand requires knowledge of basic sources of secondary data (data not directly gathered by the firm). The U.S. Department of Commerce produces many publications that contain data on foreign markets, including not only data on U.S. exports by commodity and country (Report FT 927), but also an international marketing information series. The latter provides (1) global market surveys covering 15 or more countries for certain target industries or products; (2) foreign country market surveys covering leading industrial sectors in a single country; (3) "Overseas Business Reports" including background data and economic conditions for both industrialized and developing countries; and (4) a variety of other valuable information on foreign economic trends and new developments in world trade. There is also a great deal of basic data available from international agencies such as the United Nations, the Organization of American States, and the Organization for Economic Cooperation and Development (for industrialized countries).

The governments of most industrialized countries and many of the developing countries provide data on their own production, consumption, and foreign trade. In fact, these are the basic sources of much of the statistical data published by the international agencies. Statistics vary widely in terms of both availability and accuracy. For some countries, there is a great deal of lag in data publication, so that the latest available information may pertain to the economy of five years ago rather than that of the present. Other countries do not even gather economic and demographic data on a regular basis. For example, it was reported in 1984 that Oman had never taken a census and that the People's Republic of China did not take a census between 1953 and 1982.[3]

Where secondary data are not available, a firm may have to either collect its own information or rely on expert opinion regarding a foreign market opportunity. It may be relatively easy to have survey research done on a potential market in an industrialized country, although pitfalls related to cultural and language differences must be avoided. (Do not ask about the size of a car "trunk" in a country where the luggage compartment is called a "boot.") In a developing country the obstacles to market research may be substantial, since many consumers will not have telephones or even access to reliable mail service. The best sources of information in such cases may be local experts such as consultants, industry colleagues, or economic officers assigned to embassies or consulates.

Product Adaptation

Analysis of the need for product adaptation often goes hand in hand with analysis of foreign demand. Product adaptation means changing the product to fit the characteristics of the foreign market environment. It may involve production costs. For example, electrical appliances presently manufactured for 110-volt current in the home market may have to be redesigned for 220-volt current in the foreign market. Sometimes product adaptation has more to do with how the product is *presented* to potential buyers in the foreign market than with its physical characteristics. A case in point is the Chevrolet Nova, a car that was produced and sold by General Motors in a number of countries. The name of the car presented a problem in the Spanish-speaking world, since *no va* in Spanish means "it won't run." There are other cases in which cultural norms make product adaptation imperative. For example, one U.S. candy manufacturer reportedly planned to introduce a chocolate candy with peanuts into the Japanese market. Fortunately, the firm found out in time that an old Japanese belief held that eating peanuts with chocolate would cause nosebleeds.[4] In a case like this, it would probably be advisable to develop a new product aimed at local tastes and preferences rather than attempt to change the perception of the existing product.

It is clear that the product adaptation question has at least three dimensions: (1) change in the physical attributes of the product; (2) change in buyer perception of the product; and (3) development of an entirely new product for foreign consumers. While the second item has mainly to do with marketing, the economics of production is of substantial importance for the other two. Production can take place, in whole or in part, either at home or in a foreign location.

Producing in a Foreign Country

Having examined various dimensions of identifying a foreign market for a product, the time has come to consider what it means to produce a product in a foreign location. There are numerous advantages to such a

3 For more on sources of secondary data, see Edward W. Cundiff and Marye Tharp Hilger, *Marketing in the International Environment* (Englewood Cliffs, N.J.: Prentice-Hall, Inc., 1984), especially pp. 199–203.

4 Philip R. Cateora, *International Marketing* (Homewood, Ill.: Irwin, 1983), p. 270.

strategy, but it is an arena into which a firm should enter only after a good deal of careful study.

The decision to produce abroad is usually made either for reasons of cost or for political reasons. When a firm produces in its home market and exports to a foreign market, its production costs are determined by resource prices in its home country. To sell abroad, it must also pay transportation costs and any other costs incurred in getting the good to the foreign market. In the foreign location, the firm may find that certain resources are lower priced than at home. This could be reason enough to consider producing all or part of the good in the foreign country rather than at home. However, political factors may also determine the location of production.

Many developing countries provide incentives for firms to invest in production facilities. These range from tax breaks and loan guarantees for foreign investors to provision of plant space in government-sponsored industrial parks. Often such incentives are coupled with barriers against importation of finished products, so that the only access to the country's market is through local production or assembly of the final product. To some extent, firms in industrialized countries are pushed into establishment of foreign production facilities when they realize that their only hope for gaining a foothold in a potentially large foreign market is through such investments.

The Product Cycle

Where costs rather than government policies determine foreign investment, the development of foreign production facilities often follows the pattern described by the *product cycle* theory of international trade. This theory, popularized by Raymond Vernon of Harvard

University, argues that new product development takes place in advanced, industrialized nations. The firm that develops such a product is likely to be its first producer, and the product is aimed first at consumers in the home market. Once the product is successful, the firm may look to foreign markets for increased sales. It may also try to reduce costs by seeking foreign sources of certain parts, even though final production still occurs at home. Finally, it may decide to set up a foreign subsidiary to manufacture the good. If foreign production proves cheaper than home country production, the firm may choose to shut down its home country facilities. The result is that the home country then becomes an *importer* of the very product that it first exported.

The product cycle theory seems to provide a reasonable approximation of how U.S.-based multinational corporations have expanded into overseas production, especially in Europe and parts of Asia. Here, costs rather than government policies attracted the firms' investment. In situations like these, deciding whether or not to set up foreign plants is based rather straightforwardly on the kinds of cost analyses firms are familiar with from their operations at home. If long-run production costs are minimized by producing in the foreign location, and if investing there does not appear to be overly risky, then foreign production may well be the strategy to choose.

Analysis of Foreign Costs

In comparing foreign costs with those at home, it is important to be aware of political or environmental differences that may make the total cost of inputs higher than their nominal price. For example, seemingly lower labor costs often make foreign production appear to be attractive, but firms have learned that low wage rates may be offset by both lagging worker productivity and government requirements for such benefits as social security, medical services, paid holidays, and severance pay. In terms of the production analysis presented in Chapter 5, this means that the marginal product of labor is lower in the foreign location than at home and that the price of foreign labor is actually much higher than its wage rate implies. Further, the cost of foreign labor may escalate rapidly if a politically powerful union can make unwarranted demands on foreign-owned firms.

Other dimensions of foreign cost analysis include the availability of raw materials and intermediate goods, added costs related to communications and transportation, the costs of training and work-force development, and the cost implications of such government policies as restrictions on employment of non-native personnel. Costs for the firm can be substantially increased if it must purchase inputs from local suppliers who are either inefficient or corrupt. Tariffs against imported inputs may have been put in place to forward the interests of such producers at the expense of both consumers and foreign investors. The costs of transporting inputs within the foreign country may not be comparable with those at home, and communications may not measure up to those in the home country (in some countries telephone service is unreliable). Nationalistic fervor often leads to the passage of labor laws that discriminate against the employment of foreign technicians and managers and cause firms to employ less-experienced or less-qualified local personnel.

The foregoing are just a few of the issues a firm must investigate before taking as bold a step as investing in foreign production facilities. Thus analysis of foreign production costs requires perhaps even more scrutiny than analysis of foreign demand.

QUESTIONS AND PROBLEMS

1. How are relative prices related to the basis for international trade?
2. Given the following table, answer parts (a)–(c).

Units of Labor Required to Produce One:

	Tablecloth	Barrel of Wine
Greece	10	5
Belgium	4	4

a. Explain why the data *do* provide a basis for two-way trade between Greece and Belgium. (Assume labor costs reflect relative prices in each country.)

b. Which good will be exported by Greece? Why?

c. Assume that the numbers in the table represent domestic prices (in drachmas for Greece and francs for Belgium) instead of labor costs. If one drachma = one franc is the exchange rate, will two-way trade occur? (If *yes*, explain why. If *no*, tell what would have to take place in order for two-way trade to occur.)

SELECTED REFERENCES

Caves, Richard E., Jeffrey A. Frankel, and Ronald W. Jones. *World Trade and Payments*. New York: HarperCollins, 1993.

Cundiff, Edward W., and Marye Tharp Hilger. *Marketing in the International Environment*. Englewood Cliffs, N.J.: Prentice-Hall, 1984.

Keegan, Warren J. "Multinational Product Planning: Strategic Alternatives," *Journal of Marketing* 33 (January 1969), pp. 58–62.

Linder, Staffan B. *An Essay on Trade and Transformation*. New York: Wiley, 1961.

Vernon, Raymond. "International Investment and International Trade in the Product Cycle," *Quarterly Journal of Economics* 80, no. 2 (May 1966), pp. 190–207.

7

PROFIT ANALYSIS OF THE FIRM

Profit maximization: Making the greatest economic profit possible.

Throughout this book we are assuming that the primary concern of the firm is its level of *profit*. Some firms may have other subsidiary goals, such as a large volume of sales or a good company image. We assume, however, that any such concerns are *definitely secondary* in nature to the concern for generating profits, and we recognize that often the attention paid to such secondary goals merely reflects the impact company officials believe such variables may have on future company profits. Thus, assuming that the overriding goal of the firm is **profit maximization**—obtaining the greatest economic profit possible—we will direct our attention to decision rules for determining the corresponding optimal price and level of output for the individual firm.

Although profit maximization is the primary goal of a firm, we do not mean to suggest that the firm maximize profit with no regard for legal or ethical considerations. The firm that wishes to remain a successful and responsible part of our society in the long run must consider the ethical ramifications of its actions. Henry Ford II once remarked:

> There is no such thing as planning for a minimal return less than the best you can imagine—not if you want to survive in a competitive market. It's like asking a professional football team to win by only one point—a sure fire formula for losing. There's only one way to compete successfully—all out. If believing this makes you a greedy capitalist lusting after bloated profits, then I plead guilty. The worst sin I can commit as a businessman is to fail to seek maximum long-term profitability *by all decent and lawful means* [emphasis added]. To do so is to subvert economic reason.

Maximizing profit is an obligation that corporate managers have to the company's shareholders, but it is also an obligation to society. If the firm is not maximizing profits, scarce resources are typically being wasted. Yet, as Mr. Ford intimated, both the business enterprise and society are benefited in the long run only when the goal of maximum profit is achieved by "decent and lawful means."

To understand the importance of the profit-maximizing guidelines presented in this chapter, we must first recognize the fact that things can go sour—even for a firm that has apparently established itself. A classic example is W. T. Grant Company (Grant's). Grant's was the seventeenth-largest retailer in the United States with sales of $1.6 billion and $38 million in profits in 1972, and it seemed poised to do in the 1970s what Wal-Mart accomplished

MANAGERIAL PERSPECTIVE

On Profit Maximization and Business Ethics

There is no doubt that the profit strategies of certain businesses have raised ethical questions. For example, 1996 saw a rash of charges leveled at U.S. firms that subcontracted to domestic producers who ran sweatshops or to foreign sweatshop operators who employed child labor. Such well-known names as Nike, Wal-Mart, and Kathie Lee Gifford were involved in the controversies that flared when the situation was publicized. Naturally, these discoveries raised questions regarding ethics and profit-maximizing behavior.

In 1994, two business ethics scholars, Patrick Primeaux and John Stieber, produced an interesting article that addressed the connection between profit maximization and the laws, ethics, and mores of society. Primeaux, a Marist Father and theology professor at St. Johns University (New York), and Stieber, a professor of finance and economics at Southern Methodist University (Dallas) argued that profit-maximizing managerial decisions are inherently quite consistent with ethical behavior. Primeaux and Stieber began their analysis with the proposition that in business, as in football and baseball, there are rules of the game. Those rules are related to the role of the manager in the social system as a whole, where business managers serve the function of allocating scarce resources.

Primeaux and Stieber explained that managers are driven to be efficient in the use of resources, because, if they are not, their businesses will not be profitable, or, at least, will not be as profitable as they *could be*. Thus, there is an ethical dimension to profit maximization, since failure to produce the "right" amount of output (failure to operate where $MR = MC$) misallocates resources, resulting in the supply of either too little or too much of the firm's product. When resources are misallocated, society as a whole pays the bill, so that consumers, shareholders, managers, and employees will eventually be worse off. The authors stated:

> From a behavioral perspective, profit maximization is defined as *the act of producing the right kind and the right amount of goods and services the consumer wants at the lowest possible cost (within the legal and ethical mores of the community).*

They added that the phrase, "within the legal and ethical mores of the community," was placed in parentheses because the community standards are already contained within the costs of the firm.

The idea that the legal and ethical mores of society are contained within the costs of the firm deserves some explanation. What Primeaux and Stieber had in mind was the concept of opportunity cost. They argued that managers ". . . are aware (and if not, should be aware) that opportunity costs can be significant for any decision." Legal and ethical considerations are a part of such opportunity costs. Thus, businesses face the prospects of losing customers or being saddled with litigation expenses, payments for damages, and fines if their managers make decisions that violate community standards. A real-world example that Primeaux and Stieber offered was the case of General Motors having chosen to install Chevrolet engines in Oldsmobiles produced in 1977. To GM, they stated, this appeared to be a decision that would reduce costs and improve efficiency. However, if it considered adverse reactions at all, GM clearly miscalculated the cost of public indignation, bad publicity, customer compensation, and legal expenses that, when all was said and done, proved to be some of the opportunity costs of its decision. (GM offered a cash settlement to the affected car buyers and, of course, had to bear substantial legal expenses and suffer a monumental loss of customer good will.)

A more startling case not discussed by Primeaux and Stieber was that of the Ford Pinto gas tank shield. In that instance, Ford managers actually were aware that deletion of a shield from the gas tank area of the subcompact Pinto would lead to horrible injuries and numerous deaths from fiery explosions that would occur when the car was struck from behind. However, they calculated that the costs to the firm in litigation and damages expenses would be outweighed by the savings in the production costs of the cars. It would be easy to argue that this was a calculation so terrible that it should never have been made. But other cases are less clear cut. For example, should all cars have *side impact* air bags and anti-lock brakes? Or, should automakers have installed passenger-side air bags when they apparently did have some knowledge that the bags could injure or kill children placed, with or without infant safety seats, in the front passenger area?

While managers who are behaving properly when they make profit-maximizing decisions certainly should *try* to take into account the ethics-related opportunity costs of those decisions, it is likely that in many cases imperfect information will lead to miscalculations. In addition, there will always be some managers who see opportunities to profit from decisions that wrongfully harm some members of society but are not likely to affect the firm's bottom line because of the inability of the parties who are negatively affected to obtain redress. However, none of this is reason to condemn profit-maximizing behavior in general. As Primeaux and Stieber stressed, when properly carried out, profit maximization demands that the ethics and mores of the community become integral to the decision-making process.*

Sources: "Pangs of Conscience: Sweatshops Haunt U.S. Consumers," *Business Week* (July 29, 1996), pp. 46–47; Marilyn M. Helms and Betty A. Hutchins, "Poor Quality Products: Is Their Production Unethical?" *Management Decision*, Vol. 30, No. 5 (1992) pp. 35–46; and Patrick Primeaux and John Stieber, "Profit Maximization: The Ethical Mandate," *Journal of Business Ethics*, Vol. 13, No. 4 (April 1994), pp. 287–294.

* Primeaux and Stieber do not carefully consider the impact of market structure or possible divergences between private and social costs and benefits in their analysis. More will be said about these issues in Chapter 15.

much later. However, Grant's filed for bankruptcy in October 1975. Was it the result of calamitous factors external to the firm? *Apparently not.* Significantly, there are indications that during Grant's rapid expansion years from 1969 to 1973, the company exercised little control over accounts receivable, cost of goods sold, and inventories. Moreover, the company apparently did not keep accurate records of how individual items were selling and at what prices and costs.[1]

More recently, Allied Stores Corporation and Federated Department Stores, Incorporated, filed for protection under Chapter 11 of the Bankruptcy Code; at the time, it was the largest bankruptcy filing of retail stores in history. These companies include such venerated retailers as Abraham & Straus, Bloomingdale's, Rich's, Burdines, Lazarus, Jordan Marsh, and Bon Marché. Other well-known retailers that have recently filed for Chapter 11 bankruptcy-law protection include R. H. Macy, P. A. Bergner (owner of Carson Pirie Scott), McCrory, and Best Products.[2] Lack of effective cost management and marketing seems also to have played a significant role in the recent

---

1 See William Weitzel and Ellen Jonnson, "Reversing the Downward Spiral: Lessons from W. T. Grant and Sears Roebuck," *Academy of Management Executive*, Vol. 5, No. 3 (August 1991), pp. 7–22; and "Investigating the Collapse of W. T. Grant," *Business Week* (July 19, 1976), pp. 60–62.

2 "American Retailing: Bounced Out of Bankruptcy?" *Economist* (January 8, 1994), pp. 61–62; "The Bankruptcy Game," *Time* (May 18, 1992), pp. 60–61; "Macy's Is Counting On a Number-Cruncher," *Business Week* (June 22, 1992), pp. 72–73; Jeffrey A. Trachtenberg, "McCrory Files for Protection of Chapter 11," *The Wall Street Journal*, February 27, 1992, pp. A2, A5; "The Wrong Way to Hit the Big Time," *Business Week* (September 9, 1991), p. 44; Peter Pae, "Best Products Co.'s Filing Adds to Creditors' Bad-Debt Burdens," *The Wall Street Journal*, January 7, 1991, p. A4; "It'll Be A Hard Sell," *Business Week* (January 29, 1990), pp. 30–31; and "Bankruptcy Petition Brings Fresh Risks for Allied, Federated," *The Wall Street Journal*, January 16, 1990, pp. A1, A6. Federated emerged from bankruptcy in 1992. See "Short Chapter, Happy Ending," *Business Week* (February 10, 1992), pp. 126–127.

problems of General Motors, John Deere, Sears, Kmart, and even the venerated Lloyds of London, to cite further examples.[3]

If a firm knows little about both the demand for its product or products and its costs, it has, as a result, slight opportunity for effective management and probably little chance for survival, not to mention success. An article in *The Wall Street Journal* put it bluntly:

> Accountants see it all the time—management by ignorance. An owner doesn't realize his business is in trouble until it is too late. "Many businesses go under," says Aubrey D. Boutwell, a CPA in Pascagoula, Miss., "and owners don't even know what their problems are. All they know is they end up with no money and can't pay their bills."[4]

Effective use of the profit-maximizing decision rules that we will discuss requires that a firm be able to estimate its revenue and cost over the relevant ranges of production. Later in the chapter we will examine break-even analysis, a modification of the more traditional economics of profit maximization.

PROFIT MAXIMIZATION

The decision rule for profit maximization can be explained by using either total or marginal curves, and we will do both in this chapter. In the simplest terms, total profit is equal to total revenue minus total cost. In Chapter 2, total revenue was defined as the total sales of a firm, equal to the price multiplied by the quantity sold of each product. Chapter 6 explained that the total cost of a firm includes both explicit and implicit, or opportunity, costs. Thus we can define **total profit** as the "pure" or "economic" profit remaining after all explicit and implicit costs—including a normal or average return for the funds invested in this business—have been subtracted from total revenue.

Total profit or **economic profit** for a firm is equal to total revenue minus total cost, where total cost includes all opportunity costs associated with the firm's activities.

In Figure 7–1 we have drawn a total revenue curve, a total cost curve, and a total profit curve. Since we are assuming that the goal of the firm is to maximize profit, we wish to establish a decision rule that will enable the firm to find that output level and price which will make total profit (that is, total sales

---

3 See "As Kmart Teeters, An Industry Holds Its Breath," *Chain Store Age*, Vol. 72, No. 1 (January 1996), pp. 70–80; "Lloyds' Runoff Not an Option, *Business Insurance*, Vol. 30, No. 5 (January 29, 1996) pp. 17, 19; "Who Profits From Sears' Demise," *Catalog Age*, Vol. 10, No. 3 (March 1993), p. 5; "Crisis At GM," *Business Week* (November 9, 1992), pp. 84–86; "Coup at the Top," *Time* (November 9, 1992), pp. 42–50; "Two Sides of a Giant," *Time* (February 19, 1990), pp. 68–70; "Will the Big Markdown Get the Big Store Moving Again?" *Business Week* (March 13, 1989), pp. 110, 114; "Now Sears Has Everyday Low Profits, Too," *Business Week* (August 21, 1989), p. 28; "As John Deere Sowed, So Shall It Reap," *Business Week* (June 6, 1988), pp. 84–86.

4 "Watch the Numbers to Learn if the Business Is Doing Well," *The Wall Street Journal*, August 26, 1985, p. 17.

Figure 7–1   Total Revenue, Total Cost, and Total Profit

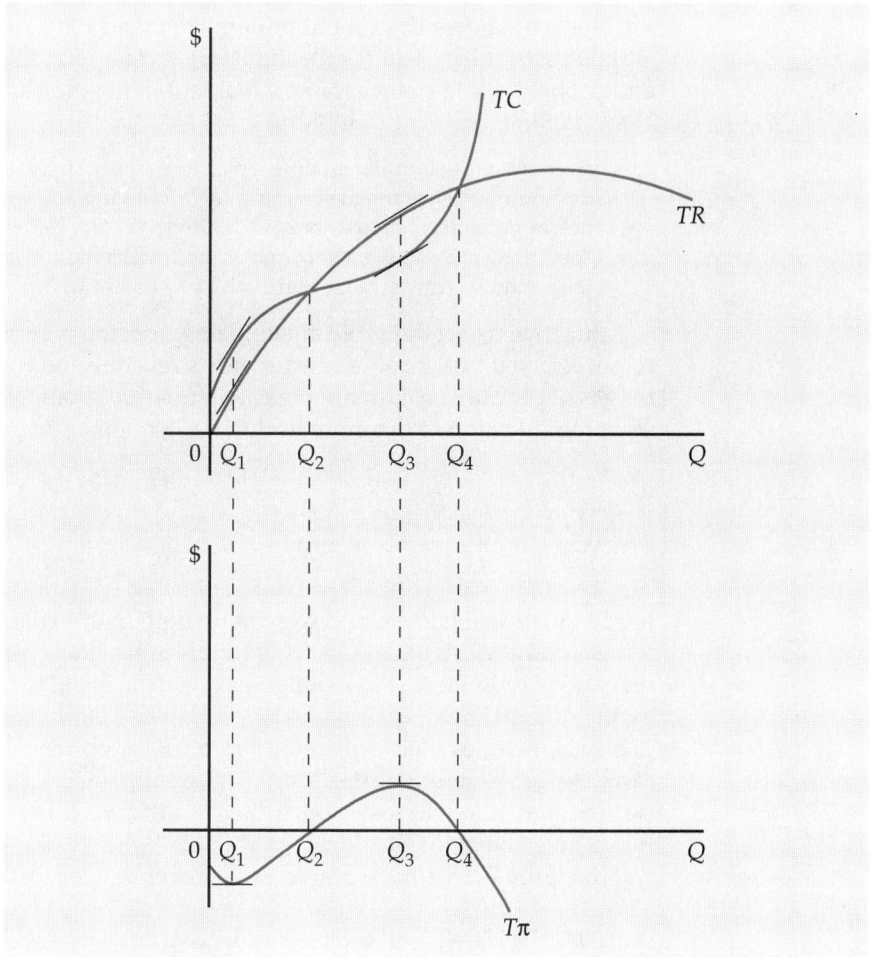

Total profit ($T\pi$) will be maximized at the level of output where total revenue (TR) minus total cost (TC) is at its greatest positive level. At this point, the slope of the TR curve (marginal revenue) will equal the slope of the TC curve (marginal cost).

revenue less total cost) the greatest amount possible. In Figure 7–1 the profit-maximizing output is Q_3.

Notice that at Q_3, the slopes of the total revenue and total cost curves are equal, and the slope of the total profit curve is zero. In Chapter 2 we pointed out that the slope of the total revenue curve at a particular output level is marginal revenue at that level of output; and, correspondingly, we stated in Chapter 6 that the slope of the total cost curve is marginal cost. In the same

Marginal profit is the rate of change of total profit with respect to changes in the level of output.

manner, the slope of the total profit curve is **marginal profit**, or the rate of change in the total profit of the firm with respect to output.[5] Marginal profit can be approximated by the change in total profit divided by the change in quantity produced between two levels of output:

$$M\pi = \frac{\Delta T\pi}{\Delta Q} = \frac{T\pi_2 - T\pi_1}{Q_2 - Q_1}.$$

This latter value we call *arc marginal profit*, as it gives the average rate of change of total profit with respect to output *between two levels of output*. Marginal profit can also be found by subtracting marginal cost from marginal revenue:

$$M\pi = MR - MC.$$

Thus, for profit maximization, the profit to be gained by producing another unit of output must be zero, or $M\pi = 0$. Moreover, $M\pi = 0$ implies $MR - MC = 0$, so that $MR = MC$. In other words, at the profit-maximizing level of output, the additional revenue to be gained from another unit of output must be equal to the additional cost the firm incurs by producing it.

Therefore, at Q_3 in Figure 7–1, marginal revenue equals marginal cost, marginal profit is zero, and total profit is at a maximum. In Figure 7–2 we have sketched the marginal revenue, marginal cost, and marginal profit curves corresponding to the total revenue, total cost, and total profit curves in Figure 7–1.

To emphasize what we have shown so far, we reiterate that it is not a coincidence that marginal revenue and marginal cost are equal where profit is maximized. The fact that marginal profit ($M\pi$) is zero at the profit-maximizing level of output means that $MR - MC = 0$. By adding MC to both sides of this equation, we see that it must be true that $MR = MC$ at the profit-maximizing level of output. Again, recall that marginal revenue is the additional revenue the firm receives from selling another unit of output. Marginal cost is the cost of producing another unit of output. As long as the additional revenue from producing another unit is greater than the cost of the unit (that is, if marginal profit is positive), the firm will find it profitable to expand its output.

For example, if the marginal revenue from producing another television set is $200, and the set's marginal cost is $100, the firm will add $100 to profit

---

5 Mathematically speaking, instantaneous or point marginal profit is the derivative of the total profit function with respect to quantity:

$$M\pi = \frac{dT\pi}{dQ}.$$

Figure 7–2   Marginal Revenue, Marginal Cost, and Marginal Profit

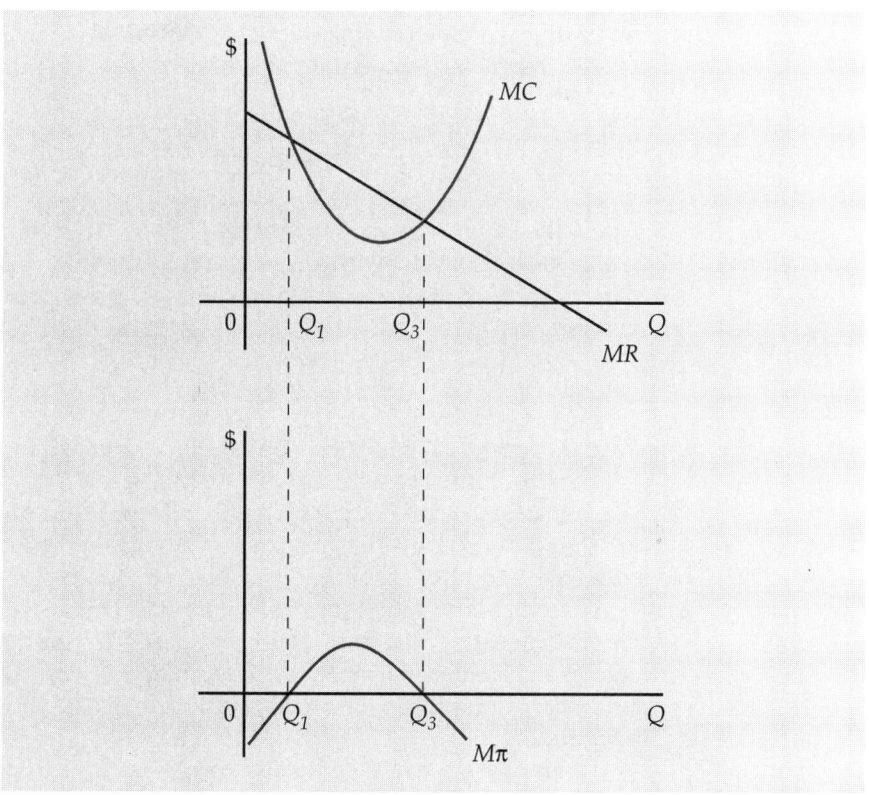

Total profit is maximized at Q_3, where marginal profit ($M\pi$) is equal to zero, and MC is greater than MR at higher levels of output. At Q_1, $M\pi$ is equal to zero, but MC is less than MR at higher levels of output. In this case the firm will increase profit by expanding output.

by producing the TV. Even if the marginal revenue of a television set were $175 and the set's marginal cost were $174, the firm would still add $1 to profit by producing the TV. On the other hand, if the marginal revenue from producing another TV is $160 and the TV's marginal cost is $180, the firm's profit will decrease by $20 if it produces another TV. Only when the additional revenue from producing another unit of output is equal to its cost will profit be maximized.

However, we need to add a condition to our decision rule that the profit-maximizing level of output occurs where $M\pi = 0$. If marginal profit is zero at a particular level of output (such as Q_3 in Figure 7–2), that fact *may* be an indication to the firm that at larger output levels, *marginal profit* will be *negative* and total profit will consequently decline. However, we can also observe that $MR = MC$ and $M\pi = 0$ at Q_1 in Figure 7–2. At this point, total profit reaches a relative *minimum* and will increase if the level of output is increased. Thus the decision rule that the firm should follow to maximize total profit is the following one:

> Produce at the level of output where $MR = MC$ ($M\pi = 0$) and MR *is below* MC at higher output levels.[6]

The firm can find its corresponding profit-maximizing price by substituting in that level of output for quantity demanded in its demand function or by dividing the corresponding total revenue by that quantity.

In Figure 7–3 we demonstrate both the relationships among *average* revenue, *average* cost, and *average* profit and the relationships among *marginal* revenue, *marginal* cost, and *marginal* profit. *Marginal profit* is maximized at Q_1, where the difference between MR and MC is the greatest positive amount.

Average profit is the profit per unit sold. It is equal to total profit divided by quantity of output. It is also equal to price minus average cost.

Average profit is maximized at Q_2, where the difference between AR (price) and AC is the greatest positive amount. However, *total profit* for the firm is maximized at a level of output (Q_3) that is *greater than* either Q_1 or Q_2. In other words, total profit is usually maximized *not* where average or unit profit is maximized, but rather at a higher level of output. We can find total profit at Q_3 by multiplying $A\pi_3$ by Q_3. Total profit is also equal to ($P_3 - AC_3$) multiplied by Q_3, since P_3 (or AR_3) minus AC_3 must equal $A\pi_3$. Total profit is, therefore, identical in value to the area of rectangle P_3STAC_3; and, given the curves drawn in Figure 7–3, this area will be greatest at Q_3. Remember:

> The greatest profit per unit is *not* the goal of the firm; rather, the firm's goal is the greatest *total* profit.

An understanding of these relationships will be quite helpful in Part 3 of this text.

In Table 7–1 we can see once again how our $MR = MC$ decision rule can be utilized by the firm to maximize profit. Between 5 and 10 units of output,

---

6 The condition that MR be below MC at higher levels of output is merely a statement in economic terms of the mathematical second-order condition for a maximum, given in the Mathematical Appendix to this book. The first-order condition for maximum total profit is that the first derivative of the total profit function be equal to zero. Since

$$T\pi = TR - TC,$$

then the first-order condition is that

$$M\pi = \frac{dT\pi}{dQ} = \frac{dTR}{dQ} - \frac{dTC}{dQ} = MR - MC = 0,$$

or

$$MR = MC.$$

The second-order condition is that

$$\frac{d^2T\pi}{dQ^2} = \frac{dMR}{dQ} - \frac{dMC}{dQ} < 0,$$

which requires that marginal revenue be less than marginal cost at higher levels of output.

Figure 7–3   Relationships Among Marginal Revenue, Marginal Cost, and Marginal Profit and Average Revenue, Average Cost, and Average Profit

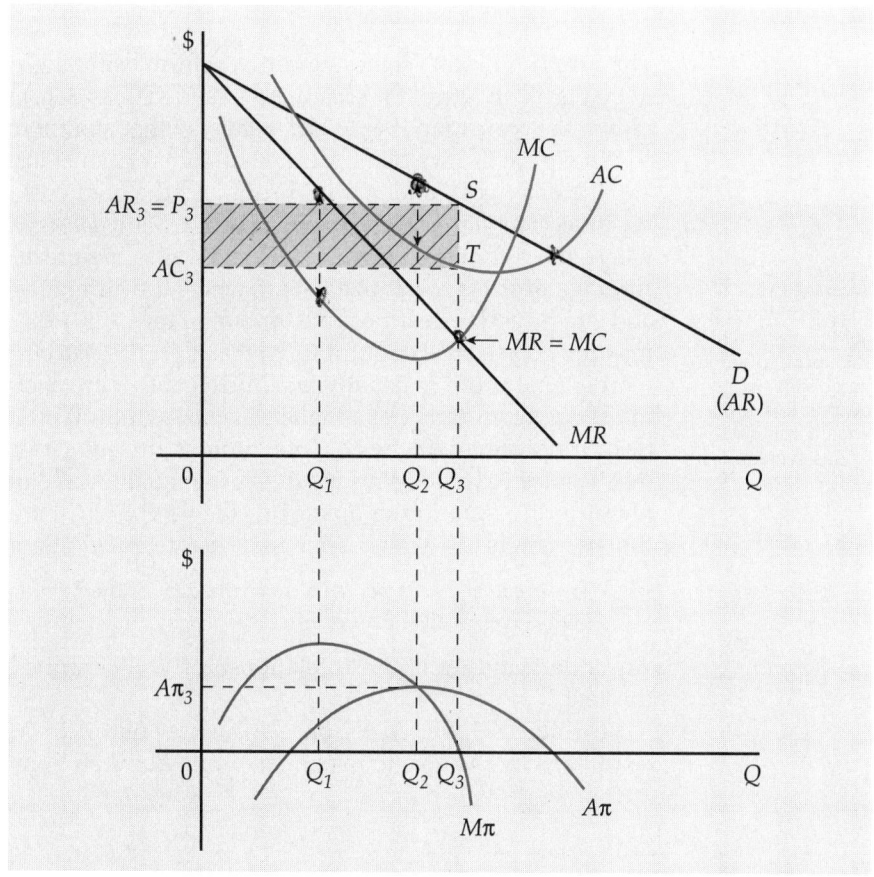

marginal profit is zero. However, marginal cost is falling below marginal revenue, so marginal profit is positive at higher levels of output. Profit is maximized between 30 and 35 units of output, where marginal revenue and marginal cost are again equal and marginal profit is zero. Beyond 35 units of output, marginal revenue falls below marginal cost, and marginal profit becomes negative. Thus, to summarize what we have been saying, the firm should expand its output up to the point where the production of additional units would *add more to the firm's costs than to its revenues.*[7]

---

7 Using calculus, a firm manager can find the precise level of output that would maximize total

Table 7–1   Revenue, Cost, and Profit Maximization

Q	P	TR	TC	Tπ	Arc MR	Arc MC	Arc Mπ
0	200	0	200	−200			
5	190	950	1,200	−250	190	200	−10
10	180	1,800	2,050	−250	170	170	0
15	160	2,400	2,450	−50	120	80	40
20	140	2,800	2,700	100	80	50	30
25	120	3,000	2,850	150	40	30	10
30	105	3,150	2,950	200	30	20	10
35	93	3,255	3,055	200	21	21	0
40	80	3,200	3,180	20	−11	25	−36

profit if the firm's total revenue and total cost functions are known. For example, suppose the firm's total revenue function is

$$TR = 100Q - 2Q^2,$$

and the total cost function is

$$TC = 30 + 120Q - 5Q^2 + (1/12)Q^3.$$

The total profit function would then be given by total revenue minus total cost or

$$T\pi = -(1/12)Q^3 + 3Q^2 - 20Q - 30.$$

To find the level of output that would maximize total profit, we find the marginal profit function, set it equal to zero, and solve for the quantity of output. Therefore

$$M\pi = \frac{dT\pi}{dQ} = -(1/4)Q^2 + 6Q - 20 = 0.$$

To solve this equation, we first multiply both sides by −4 and then factor:

$$Q^2 - 24Q + 80 = 0$$

and

$$(Q - 20)(Q - 4) = 0.$$

Thus, at $Q = 20$ and at $Q = 4$, marginal profit is zero.

Nevertheless, we must still check the second-order condition for a maximum to see if profit is maximized at either $Q = 4$ or $Q = 20$. The second derivative of $T\pi$ is

$$\frac{dM\pi}{dQ},$$

and

$$\frac{d^2 T\pi}{dQ^2} = \frac{dM\pi}{dQ} = -.5Q + 6.$$

At $Q = 4$ the second derivative is positive, so $T\pi$ is minimized at that level of output. At $Q = 20$ the second derivative is negative, so profit is maximized at that level of output.

NUMERICAL EXAMPLE:

Algebra of Profit Maximization

A firm has the following total and marginal cost functions, where Q is output per week:

$$STC = 500 + 20Q + .05Q^2$$

$$SMC = 20 + .1Q$$

What will be its profit-maximizing output, assuming it faces a fixed market price of \$40 for its product? How much will the maximum profit be?

Answer.

To find the profit-maximizing quantity, set marginal profit or $(MR - MC)$ equal to zero.

$$40 - 20 - .1Q = 0$$

Thus

$$20 = .1Q,$$

and

$$Q = 200.$$

Profit equals

$$TR - STC = \$40(200) - 500 - 20(200) - .05(40,000)$$

$$= 8,000 - 500 - 4,000 - 2,000$$

$$= \$1,500$$

We can tell that a profit *maximum* occurs at $Q = 200$ since at higher levels of output MR is less than MC.

SHUT-DOWN POINT

There is *one more qualification* to our profit maximization decision rule. The firm maximizes profits by producing where $MR = MC$ (with marginal revenue thereafter *below* marginal cost) *as long as price is greater than or equal to average variable cost*. If price is less than average variable cost, the firm should not produce at all—even in the short run.

For example, suppose a restaurant has fixed costs of $4,000 per month, an average price of $4.00, and an average variable cost of $4.50 for each meal served. If the restaurant operates for a month selling 10,000 meals, its total sales revenue will be $40,000 and its total variable cost will be $45,000. In this case the firm's revenues will not cover $5,000 of its variable costs or any of the $4,000 fixed costs, so the firm will be losing $9,000 per month (see Table 7–2). If the firm did not produce at all, the most it could lose would be the $4,000 per month fixed cost. Therefore the firm will minimize its loss by temporarily shutting down. Firms frequently make this choice during recessionary periods, when demand falls but is expected to increase in the future. Of course, a firm would go out of business permanently if it were not able to increase revenue or reduce costs enough so that it could eventually make a normal return or a profit.

On the other hand, if the average price of a meal were $4.60, the average variable cost were $4.40, and the firm were to sell 9,000 meals, then the firm's total revenue would be $41,400, its total variable cost would be $39,600, and its total loss would be $2,200 (see Table 7–3). This last example illustrates the

Table 7–2   Total Loss for a Restaurant When Price Is Less Than Average Variable Cost

Total Sales (10,000 meals @ $4.00 each)	$40,000
Less:	
Total Variable Cost	
(10,000 meals @ $4.50 each)	45,000
	($ 5,000)
Less:	
Total Fixed Cost	4,000
Net Income (loss)	($ 9,000)

Table 7–3   Total Loss for a Restaurant When Price Is Greater Than Average Variable Cost But Less Than Average Total Cost

Total Sales (9,000 meals @ $4.60 each)	$41,400
Less:	
Total Variable Cost	
(9,000 meals @ $4.40 each)	39,600
	$ 1,800
Less:	
Total Fixed Cost	4,000
Net Income (loss)	($ 2,200)

The **profit-maximizing rule** (or **loss-minimizing rule**) is to produce up to the point where marginal revenue is equal to marginal cost and at higher output levels marginal revenue is less than marginal cost, as long as price is greater than or equal to average variable cost in the short run or long-run average cost in the long run.

principle that in the short run, it is in the firm's best interests to continue to operate as long as it can cover its variable costs and make something toward covering its fixed costs.

In the long run, of course, the firm presumably would require that *all* of its economic costs be covered if it is to stay in business. An exception to this principle would be owner-managed enterprises where an opportunity-cost loss of the owner's time and/or money is accepted in return for the pleasure of owning the business and "being your own boss." However, this type of owner violates our profit maximization assumption; therefore we will disregard this possibility throughout the remainder of the book. The **profit-maximizing rule** (or **loss-minimizing rule**) is that a firm produce up to the point where marginal profit is zero, as long as price is at least as great as av-

NUMERICAL EXAMPLE:
Profit Maximization, Tabular Data

Complete the following table and find the profit-maximizing output, assuming total fixed cost is $400.

Arc MR	Q	P	TR	TVC	Arc MC
95	0	100	0	0	60
	10	95	950	600	
	20	90	1,800	1,000	60
75	30	85	2,550		
65	40	80	3,200		70
	50	75	3,750	3,150	

Answer.

The missing MR values are 85 and 55, each obtained by calculating $\Delta TR/\Delta Q$. The missing MC values are 40 and 85, each obtained by calculating $\Delta TVC/\Delta Q$. Finally, the missing TVC values are 1,600 and 2,300, each obtained by multiplying the relevant MC by ΔQ and adding on the ΔTVC to the preceding TVC value.

Profit is maximized where, for an increase in Q, $MC > MR$. This occurs at $Q = 30$, since increasing Q to 40 would result in $MC = 70$, but $MR = 65$. Profit is $TR - TC = 2,550 - 1,600 - 400 = 550$.

MANAGERIAL PERSPECTIVE

The Fall and Resurrection of "The Steel"

It was March, 1986. Walter Williams had just been given the job of chief executive officer of Bethlehem Steel, an honor that less courageous men would have refused. The company, called "The Steel" by its employees, had enjoyed four straight years of losses, was anticipating a fifth, and had only a few month's worth of cash available. Its stock price had fallen to its lowest value ever.

Bethlehem was not prepared for the 1982 decrease in steel demand, the worst in 40 years, coupled with an influx of high-quality and low-cost Japanese steel. To make matters worse, Bethlehem was inefficient and the quality of its steel was poor. Campbell's Soup, Caterpillar, and Firestone were among the customers that almost abandoned Bethlehem.

Williams's predecessor had cut 39,000 jobs, closed some steel mills, and spent several billion dollars rehabilitating others, and implemented stronger accounting controls. Williams sold 16 operations unrelated to the mills (for example, a plastics company), got wage concessions from the workers, and worked to improve the quality of the steel and the productivity of the mills. In fact, Bethlehem was able to reduce by 50 percent the number of worker hours required to make a ton of steel; some mills' productivity exceeds that of their Japanese counterparts. These efforts were rewarded when Bethlehem had record profits in 1988, with the highest profit per ton of the U.S. mills. (Bethlehem was also helped when the demand for steel increased that year.)

In mid-1989, however, "The Steel" had not yet completely conquered its problems. Substantial expenditures were still needed to further modernize the mills and to meet a huge unfunded pension liability. Rising wage rates were making further productivity increases imperative. Bethlehem's labor costs were 18 percent greater than mills in Japan and five times those in South Korea, and the Japanese mills were working hard to increase productivity. Nonetheless, Bethlehem continued to get its house in order, concentrating on cost cutting and technological improvements that would improve its profitability. During the 1990s, its fortunes improved substantially as steel prices rose and it took steps to increase its efficiency at its Burns Harbor, Indiana, plant, a unit that produces high-valued sheet steel for the automobile industry.*

---

*John Schriefer, "Steelmakers Finish 1994 Strong," *Iron Age New Steel*, Vol. 11, No. 3 (March 1995), pp. 42–43; "New Efficiencies at Bethlehem's Burns Harbor Mill," *Iron Age New Steel*, Vol. 10, No. 3 (March 1994), p. 9; and "Forging the New Bethlehem," *Business Week* (June 5, 1989), pp. 108–110.

erage variable cost in the short run or as great as long-run average cost in the long run. This point will be where marginal revenue is equal to marginal cost.

BREAK-EVEN ANALYSIS

Break-even analysis is in some respects a simplification of profit-maximization analysis. In a typical break-even problem, a constant price, a constant average variable cost, and a specific level of fixed costs are assumed; and the resulting level of output (or sales) necessary for the firm to cover its total costs (to break even) is then calculated. Alternatively, the firm may wish to determine the level of output required to cover its total costs and achieve a target level of income. With these assumptions we can derive the formula for break-even output quite easily.

To break even, a firm's revenue must equal its costs, or

(7–1)
$$TR = TC = TVC + TFC.$$

We can write total revenue as price times quantity ($P \times Q$) and total variable cost as average variable cost times quantity ($AVC \times Q$), so that equation (7–1) becomes

(7–2)
$$P(Q) = AVC(Q) + TFC.$$

If we subtract $AVC \times Q$ from both sides of equation (7–2), we obtain

(7–3)
$$P(Q) - (AVC)(Q) = (P - AVC)(Q) = TFC.$$

Dividing both sides of equation (7–3) by $(P - AVC)$, we get the formula for break-even point quantity, which is

(7–4)
$$Q_{BEP} = \frac{TFC}{P - AVC}.$$

The term $(P - AVC)$ is called the *unit contribution margin*, since it indicates the contribution that each unit sold will make toward covering fixed cost and, eventually, generating profit.

To see how break-even analysis is used, assume that the Magic S (for "magic sandwich") is a fast-food restaurant that specializes in submarine sandwiches. The Magic S has fixed costs per month of $40,000. Most of the revenue for this firm is derived from its featured meal: a hot submarine sandwich, small drink, and french fries for $4.00. The average variable cost of the meal is approximately constant at $2.40 over the relevant range of production.

To find out how many of the specials the Magic S must sell per month to break even, we substitute these figures into equation (7–4) and obtain

$$Q_{BEP} = \frac{\$40,000}{\$4.00 - \$2.40} = 25,000 \text{ specials.}$$

Moreover, we could find out how many specials the Magic S would have to sell to make a target income of, say, $24,000 per month by substituting fixed costs plus $24,000 in place of only fixed costs and obtain

$$Q = \frac{\$64,000}{\$1.60} = 40,000 \text{ specials.}$$

The assumptions of a constant price and constant unit variable cost enable us to graph the total revenue and total variable cost curves for the Magic S as straight lines, and we obtain a graphical solution for the break-even quantity for the Magic S, as shown in Figure 7–4. The break-even point is, of course, where the total revenue curve cuts and rises above the total cost curve. We can translate break-even quantity to break-even dollar sales merely by multiplying break-even point quantity by price. For the Magic S, break-even point dollar sales are 25,000 × $4.00 = $100,000.

Moreover, if we multiply both sides of our break-even point quantity formula [equation (7–4)] by price, we can derive the break-even dollar sales formula, which is

$$P(Q_{BEP}) = \frac{P(TFC)}{P - (AVC)} = \frac{TFC}{[1 - (AVC/P)]} = \frac{TFC}{\text{contribution margin ratio}}.$$

Note that $[1 - (AVC/P)]$ is called the *contribution margin ratio*, since this term is the ratio of the unit contribution margin to price. The contribution margin ratio indicates the fraction of the price of each unit sold that contributes to covering fixed cost and, eventually, generating a profit. Break-even dollar sales could thus be found graphically by using dollar sales, rather than units sold, along the horizontal axis.

Firms often use break-even analysis to determine expected profits under several different, but presumably feasible, alternatives being considered—with various prices, for instance, or different unit variable costs, different fixed costs, or some combination of those possibilities. For example, suppose an electric motor manufacturing company has current plant capacity of 1 million motors per year. Unit variable costs associated with this plant are $10, and fixed costs are $1 million. The current capacity number of motors can be sold for $20 each. The firm is considering expanding and modernizing its plant facilities so that the current capacity will be doubled. Under this pro-

Figure 7–4   Break-Even Quantity for the Magic S

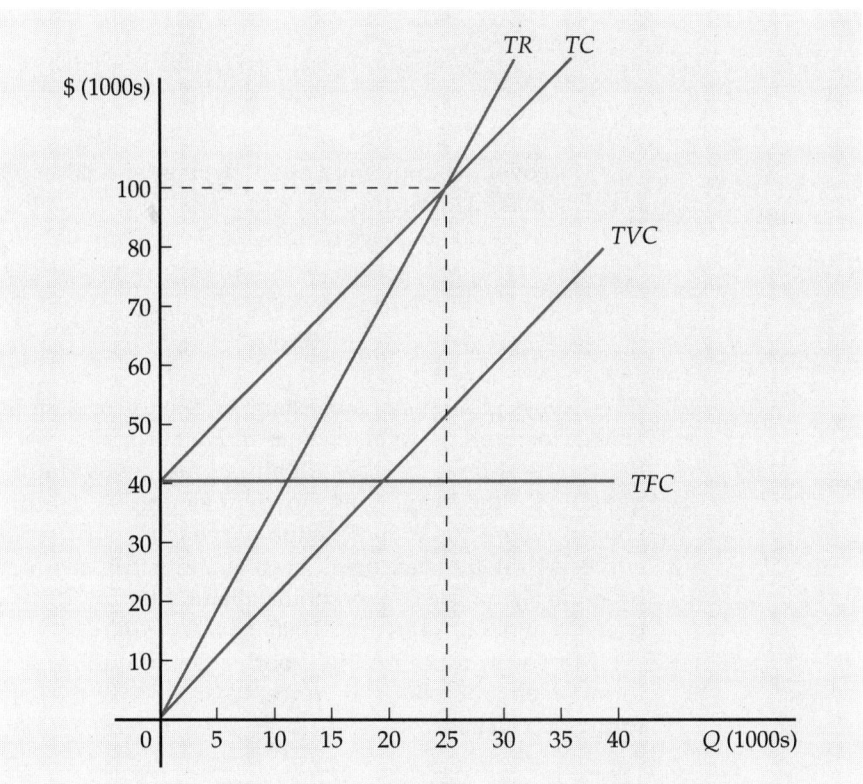

Total cost (*TC*) is equal to *TVC* + *TFC*. The break-even level of output occurs where total revenue (*TR*) = *TC*, at an output level of 25,000 specials per month.

posal, unit variable costs would be expected to decrease to $5, and fixed costs would be expected to increase to $2 million. The firm estimates that it could sell 1.5 million motors at a price of $15.

Two things in which the motor company would be vitally interested are the quantities required to break even for both the present plant and the proposed plant and the expected profits from each plant. Break-even points for the two plants are found as follows:

$$\text{Present plant}: \ Q_{BEP} = \frac{1,000,000}{10} = 100,000 \text{ motors};$$

$$\text{Proposed plant}: \ Q_{BEP} = \frac{2,000,000}{10} = 200,000 \text{ motors}.$$

The expected profits from each plant would be the following:

Present Plant
Quantity Sold:	1,000,000	
Price: $20		
Total Revenue:		$20,000,000
Less:		
Total Variable Costs:		10,000,000
		$10,000,000
Less Fixed Costs		1,000,000
Net Income Before Taxes		9,000,000

Proposed Plant
Expected Quantity Sold:	1,500,000	
Price: $15		
Total Revenue:		$22,500,000
Less:		
Total Variable Costs:		7,500,000
		$15,000,000
Less Fixed Costs		2,000,000
Expected Net Income Before Taxes		$13,000,000

Thus our data indicate that the expected profits would be greater with the larger plant. Nevertheless, before it makes a final decision on so significant a matter, the firm might want to consider expected profits with an intermediate-sized plant. It might also want to consider expected profits from using different prices with each sized plant. Further, the risk associated with each plant should be taken into account (see Chapter 14).

A person considering starting a new enterprise could also find break-even analysis a useful tool in obtaining a rough estimate as to whether or not the business could reasonably be expected to be successful under any of several proposed plans.[8] For example, suppose that our Magic S sandwich place has not yet been built and that the prospective owners believe that they cannot expect to sell 25,000 submarine specials per month. The prospective owners could, among other things, consider the feasibility of lowering fixed costs by building a smaller establishment or of increasing demand by offering a greater variety of sandwiches. They could also consider increasing quantity demanded by lowering price.

---

8 For example, see "Tigers, A Volcano, Dolphins, and Steve Wynn," *Business Week* (November 20, 1989), pp. 70–71; and "Vacancy Signs Are Lit, But More New Hotels Are on the Way," *Business Week* (March 17, 1986), pp. 78–79.

PROFIT MAXIMIZATION VERSUS BREAK-EVEN ANALYSIS

Break-even analysis in its most sophisticated usage is a simplified approximation to profit maximization. In traditional profit maximization analysis, the firm presumably knows its revenue and cost functions and chooses to produce at the level of output and charge the price that will maximize profits (where marginal revenue equals marginal cost). Price and average variable cost are *not* required to be constant.

On the other hand, when it uses break-even analysis, a firm *usually assumes* a constant price and a constant average variable cost in the relevant range of production and recognizes explicitly or implicitly a capacity limitation. The firm then solves for the quantity of sales necessary to break even or to achieve some target level of income.[9]

The firm may use break-even-type analysis to reach a fairly close approximation to profit maximization by considering expected profits under a variety of alternatives. Such alternatives would include various prices, different-sized plants, and different levels of advertising expenditures. However, if the firm has enough information regarding the preceding variables to approximate the results achieved using profit maximization analysis, it would most likely be easier for the firm to construct total revenue and total cost functions corresponding to its best information and to produce where marginal revenue equals marginal cost (and marginal revenue is falling below marginal cost).

Break-even analysis offers some advantage over traditional profit maximization analysis when the information available to the firm regarding its future costs and revenues is seriously limited, and a rough approximation to profit maximization is the best that the firm owner may reasonably expect to accomplish. If more detailed information is available, then profit maximization is more efficient.

INCREMENTAL PROFIT ANALYSIS

Incremental profit is equal to incremental revenue less incremental cost resulting from a specific change in the activity of a firm.

Incremental profit analysis is simply a variation of traditional profit maximization and represents a quite useful way of thinking about a current or prospective sales order, change in equipment, or other activity of the firm. All that is required for incremental profit analysis is that the firm ask itself whether the sales order, equipment change, or other activity contributes (or will contribute) more to total revenue than to total cost—that is, whether its

---

9 It is possible to use nonlinear total revenue and cost functions (price and average variable cost are not constant) in break-even analysis. However, this approach is not used frequently.

contribution to the total profit of the firm will be *positive*. When the firm considers whether or not the incremental profit is positive, it should ignore all revenue that will be obtained and all costs that will be incurred by the firm regardless of the decision it makes on the matter under consideration. In other words, it merely considers the **incremental revenue** and *incremental cost* pertaining to the activity being considered.

Incremental revenue is the additional revenue that a firm will receive by undertaking a particular project.

When examining the incremental costs associated with a particular undertaking, a firm usually must distinguish between direct and indirect costs. *Direct costs* associated with a particular product or activity are costs that can be obviously and physically identified with that product or activity. *Indirect costs*, while they may be associated with a product or activity, generally must be allocated on some basis, since the precise amount required for (or associated with) each line of endeavor is less clear. For example, the cost of materials or intermediate products that physically make up a final product is a direct cost. The cost of the labor required to process and/or assemble these materials is also a direct cost. On the other hand, the cost of warehouse storage space that is shared by several products is an indirect cost. Direct costs associated with an activity will be incremental costs, while indirect costs frequently will not.

The use of incremental profit analysis can be illustrated with the example of a retail firm that sells three brands of appliances—Brand *X*, Brand *Y*, and Brand *Z*. Table 7–4 shows total revenue, total direct costs, and total indirect costs attributed to each product line. In this case, indirect costs are assigned to each product line according to the proportion that total revenue from each line's sale is of the total revenue of the firm.

After a quick glance at Table 7–4, it appears that Brand *Z* is subtracting from the total profits of the firm by the amount of the net loss attributed to it ($5,000). However, a more in-depth analysis is required before that conclusion is justified. This analysis should include answers to such questions as how much, if any, will indirect costs be lowered if the firm no longer carries Brand *Z*? Is there another, more profitable, brand of merchandise that the firm could carry rather than Brand *Z*? For example, if the indirect costs will be unchanged if the firm no longer carries Brand *Z* (or a third product line) and if the firm has no more profitable brands that it can sell in place of Brand *Z*, then total profits of the firm would actually be *reduced* by $15,000 if the firm

Table 7–4   Revenue and Costs for an Appliance Store

	Brand X	*Brand Y*	*Brand Z*
Total Revenue	$150,000	$100,000	$50,000
Total Direct Costs	60,000	50,000	35,000
Total Indirect Costs	60,000	40,000	20,000
Net Income (loss)	$ 30,000	$ 10,000	$(5,000)

NUMERICAL EXAMPLE:

Incremental Profit Analysis

Ventana Corporation makes high-speed video cards for personal computers. The cards are sold to numerous small computer assemblers and wholesale parts vendors who buy 50 to 100 cards at a time. Currently, the cards are priced at $150 each, and sales are 4,000 cards per month. Ventana has been approached by a mid-sized personal computer manufacturer located in Mexico to supply 1,500 cards per month for a two-year period. The price this buyer is willing to pay is 476 Mexican "new" pesos per card. The "new" peso has been relatively stable at 3.4 pesos per U.S. dollar. Because it has some old, high-interest debt it wishes to pay off, Ventana's management does not wish to expand capacity beyond the current 4,000 cards per month. Savings that would accrue to Ventana by taking the proposed deal are related to packaging, distribution, and advertising costs. Specifically, it is estimated that the company's advertising budget could be reduced by $15,000 per year if the deal is accepted. In addition, packaging and distribution costs would fall by $2.50 per unit on the cards sold to the computer manufacturer. Ventana could also lay off two sales representatives who now receive $24,000 per year plus 10 percent commission on the cards they sell.

Using incremental profit analysis, determine the following:

1. The incremental changes in total revenue and total cost that would occur if Ventana were to accept the deal.
2. The price of cards that would be acceptable to Ventana, assuming management would commit only 1,500 units of output to a single buyer for an incremental profit of at least $270,000 per year, which is $22,500 per month.

Also identify specific factors related to the international nature of the transaction that Ventana's management would have to take into consideration in making its decision.

Solution:

1. In U.S. dollars, the Mexican firm is offering only $476/3.4 = \$140$ for the cards. Therefore, total monthly revenue will change by $\Delta P \times 1,500 = -10(1,500) = -\$15,000$. Total monthly cost will change in a number of ways. First, monthly advertising cost will change by $-\$15,000/12 = -\$1,250$. There will be a change in monthly packaging and distribution cost of $-\$2.50(1,500)$, and the reduction in sales force will result in a cost change of $-\$48,000/12$ in salaries and $-.10(1,500)(\$150)$ in commissions. Thus

$$\Delta TC = -1,250 - 2.5(1,500) - 4,000 - .1(1,500)(150) = -\$31,500$$

and

$$\Delta\pi = \Delta TR - \Delta TC = -15,000 - (-31,500) = \underline{\underline{\$16,500}}.$$

The incremental profit is positive and equals $16,500 per month.

2. The difference between the required incremental profit of $22,500 per month and the estimated amount of $16,500 per month tells how much monthly TR would have to increase. Since $TR/Q = P$, it follows that $\Delta TR/Q = \Delta P$. Thus

$$\Delta P = (22,500 - 16,500)/Q = 6,000/1,500 = \$4.00.$$

Therefore the price would have to be

$$\$140 + \$4.00 = \$144.00.$$

Given that the price was quoted by the buyer in Mexican pesos, Ventana would need to assess its foreign exchange risk. If the peso depreciates, 476 pesos will no longer equal $140 (nor will the required price of $144 be 144(3.4) = 489.6 pesos. It would be advisable for Ventana to insist on payment in dollars and require a letter of credit from a U.S. bank (generally, an irrevocable document backed by the issuing bank) for each shipment. Also, the overall solvency of the foreign buyer will be important, since any contract with it will have international legal ramifications and may be difficult to enforce.

were to drop Brand Z! Let's see why this is so. If the $20,000 of indirect costs assigned to Brand Z would be incurred even if the firm did not carry a third brand of appliance, then the sale of Brand Z *does contribute* $15,000 toward covering those costs.

Nevertheless, the firm should be careful to consider its alternatives in both the long run and the short run. In the long run, it may be possible for the firm to eliminate the $20,000 of indirect costs if the firm does not sell a third brand of appliance. It may also be possible to become a dealer in a more profitable third brand. Moreover, dropping Brand Z may increase the revenue from sales of Brand X and Brand Y. Thus the firm must consider how its decision about Brand Z will affect both long-run and short-run revenue and cost. Still, all of these deliberations are merely utilizing a version of the profit maximization rule, which states that the firm should continue to produce as long as marginal revenue is greater than marginal cost and should not produce when marginal revenue is less than marginal cost.

MANAGERIAL PERSPECTIVE

Earnings versus Cash Flow

"Earnings, Schmernings—Look At The Cash" reads the headline in a *Business Week* article.* The point of the article was that a single-minded emphasis on a firm's net income is shortsighted. The cash flow of a firm is its net cash receipts over the period in question. The cash flow of a firm will be affected by the net income of a firm, but the two figures are typically not equal to one another.

Accounting net income reflects total sales less total accounting costs. However, the cash flow to the firm may be something entirely different for the period. For one thing, most firms allow some customers to purchase their goods on credit. As a result, the total dollar sales of the firm for a particular period, say a month, and the cash collected by the firm from those sales may be quite different. The credit sales may merely be reflected by an increase in accounts receivable. On the other hand, the firm may have some cash receipts from collections of accounts receivable from sales in prior months. The firm, in turn, may purchase some inputs on credit; thus, the variable input costs for the period may not always be immediately reflected in cash outflows. Alternatively, the firm may have to pay the entire purchase price for a new machine at the time it is acquired, and a cash outflow equal to the entire amount spent for the machine will be incurred immediately. The entire amount paid for the machine will not be reflected as a cost in the firm's income statement for the period, however; it will be written off as depreciation over a period of time that reflects the expected life of the machine. Thus, in those later periods, depreciation will be a cost item that does not represent a cash outflow. On the other hand, debt payments (not including interest payments) represent outflows of cash that are not costs, although they may very well be related to costs incurred in the past.

Three categories of net cash flows can be distinguished for the firm. The broadest classification is operating cash flow (OCF)—the net cash flow from the ordinary operations of the firm, but before repayments of debt and interest payments are made. The second concept of cash flow is the one that is commonly referred to when the term "cash flow" is used. It includes net income adjusted for such things as changes in accounts receivable and accounts payable, plus accounting charges to net income, such as depreciation, depletion, or amortization expenses, that

---

* "Earnings, Schmernings—Look at the Cash," *Business Week* (July 24, 1989), pp. 56, 57. See also "What Do Shareholders Want?" *Accountancy*, Vol. 115, No. 221 (May 1995), p. 44.

do not require the current use of cash. The third category of cash flow is perhaps most important for the firm's viability: the *free* cash flow, or what remains after essential capital expenditures have been made and dividends have been paid. A firm with free cash flow can decide to pay additional dividends, pay off debt, or buy back shares, among other things. Because a firm with free cash flow can develop a cushion of cash assets as a reserve against a temporary decline in sales, it is less vulnerable to the movements of the business cycle. Firms that have no free cash flow may not be able to make principal and interest payments on their debt during periods of temporary declines in sales; thus they may find their very existence in jeopardy.

Net income may not always reflect accurately the growth in assets of a firm. For example, amortization is a write-down of intangible assets such as goodwill. (Goodwill is the difference between what a company paid for an asset and its book value.) Accounting rules require that goodwill be written off over a period of years, whether or not the asset's market value is declining. Furthermore, tangible assets that are being depreciated may actually be increasing in value.

The *Business Week* article concludes with this comment:

> The case for cash flow doesn't mean that profits are passé. For most investors, net income will remain the handiest snapshot of a company. Even so, following the cash as it flows through a company . . . "gives you insight into the quality of earnings." Indeed, if profits are soaring, but the cash flow isn't, a company's good fortunes may prove to be short-lived.

Continental Airlines made explicit use of incremental profit analysis in adjusting certain parts of its fare structure in 1982.[10] There is also evidence that restaurants use incremental profit analysis when determining their price structure.[11]

SUMMARY

Profit Maximization and the Real World

We have assumed that the goal of the firm is to maximize its profits. Accordingly, in this chapter we have developed a decision criterion that, when fol-

---

10 "Most Big Airlines Cut Intercontinental Fares," *San Antonio Express*, February 10, 1982, p. 1B.
11 See "With Liquor Sales Slipping, Restaurants Try Fancier Desserts and Higher Prices," *The Wall Street Journal*, June 14, 1985, p. 23.

lowed, will ensure profit maximization. That criterion is to *produce up to the point where marginal revenue equals marginal cost, subject to the conditions that marginal revenue is less than marginal cost at higher levels of output and that price is at least as great as average variable cost.* If price is less than average variable cost, the firm should at least temporarily shut down.

In reality a firm manager does not always have precise information regarding the firm's costs and revenue and obtaining such information may be costly. In this situation a firm manager often uses break-even analysis to determine what level of output is necessary for the firm to break even or to achieve a target level of income. When using this type of analysis, the firm manager assumes that price and average variable cost are constant, a simplification that is *not* necessary with traditional profit maximization techniques. In these circumstances the formula for break-even output is

$$Q_{BEP} = \frac{TFC}{P - AVC}.$$

The manager may use break-even analysis to determine approximately the profit-maximizing price and level of output by considering expected profits under a variety of alternatives (such as various prices, different plant sizes, and different levels of advertising expenditures).

However, break-even analysis offers some advantages over traditional profit maximization analysis only when the information available to the firm manager regarding the firm's costs and revenues is quite limited and a rough approximation to profit maximization is the best that can be expected. Still, the firm manager may find that the firm falls far short of profit maximization unless some reliable estimates of its revenue and costs relative to the level of output can be obtained. The wise firm manager, therefore, must attempt to gain such information about its costs and the demand for its product up to the point where the expected cost of obtaining additional information is greater than the expected benefits of such information. Some techniques of demand estimation were discussed in Chapter 3. Cost estimation techniques were briefly summarized in Chapter 6.

Finally, we discussed *incremental profit analysis*—a variation of traditional profit maximization analysis that is useful to the firm manager when he or she is analyzing such problems as accepting an additional sales order, trading in a piece of equipment, adding or dropping a product line, or similar alternatives. We stated that the profit-oriented manager should undertake an activity as long as its *incremental revenue less incremental cost* (its *marginal profit*) is greater than zero.

In the next chapter, we will discuss linear programming—a profit maximization technique the firm can use when its revenue and cost functions and any other constraining functions are linear.

QUESTIONS

1. What do we mean when we say that the goal of a firm is profit maximization?
2. Is the assumption of profit maximization a realistic goal? Why or why not?
3. Compare break-even analysis and (the more traditional) profit maximization. How are they alike? How are they different?
4. What is incremental profit analysis? Give several examples of situations in which it would be useful.

PROBLEMS

1. Complete the following cost and revenue table and indicate the profit-maximizing output and price.

Q	Arc MR	TR	P	Arc MC	AFC	AVC	SAC	TC
0			21		—	—	—	
	20			25				
1					28			
	18			15				
2								
	16			11				
3								
	14			5				
4								
	12			4				
5								
	8			6				
6								
	6			11				
7								
	4			19				
8								

2. Penny Car Rental has fixed costs per month of $300,000 and variable costs per car rented per day of $6. If Penny charges $30 per day to rent a car, how many car-rental days (the number of cars rented times the number of days each is rented) must Penny have each month to break even? To make $60,000 before taxes?

3. Complete the following cost and revenue data and find the profit-maximizing price and output.

Q	P	TR	Arc MR	Arc MC	TFC	AVC	Arc Mπ
0	$5.00	0				—	
			$4.90	$3.00			$1.90
10		49					
				1.00			
20		96			60		
				1.00			
30		135					
				.50			
40		160					
				1.00			
50		175					
				1.50			
60		180					
				2.00			
70		175					
				3.00			
80		144					
				4.50			
90		90					
				7.00			
100		10					

4. A firm making sofas has the following income data for one week:

Sales (50 sofas at $1,000)		$50,000
Less cost of goods sold:		
Variable manufacturing costs	$20,000	
Fixed manufacturing costs	5,000	25,000
Gross margin		$25,000
Less selling and administrative expenses:		
Variable	$10,000	
Fixed	5,000	15,000
Net income		$10,000

a. Find the firm's break-even quantity.
b. Find the firm's new break-even output if it builds a new plant that will raise fixed manufacturing costs to $10,000 but decreases variable manufacturing cost to $300 per unit. Assume average variable selling expenses, fixed selling expenses, and selling price remain the same.

5. In the following table, complete the cost and revenue data for a particular model of side-by-side refrigerator-freezer sold in a department store. What is the profit-maximizing price and output?

P	Q	TR	Arc MR	Arc MC	AFC	TVC	TC	Arc Mπ
900	0				—			
				500				
875	10							
				400				
850	20							
				350				
800	30							
				300				
750	40				150			
				250				
675	50							
				200				
600	60							
				180				
500	70							
				200				
400	80							
				300				
200	90							

6. For the month of October, the Crossroads Diner had the income situation shown in the table.

Crossroads Diner
Income Statement
for Month Ended October, 1997

Gross sales (10,000 meals @ average price of $6.00)		$60,000
Less cost of goods sold:		
Cooks	$ 9,000	
Servers, etc.	9,500	
Food	21,000	
Utilities (prorated—food service)	900	
Depreciation (prorated—kitchen, dining area, and equipment)	4,500	44,900
Gross margin		$15,100
Less administrative and selling expenses:		
Monthly advertising expense	$ 6,900	
Transportation expense	1,500	
Office salaries and supplies	3,000	
Utilities (prorated—office)	600	
Depreciation (prorated—office)	600	12,600
Operating income		$ 2,500
Less interest expense		6,000
Net income (loss)		($3,500)

a. Compute the number of meals that the diner would have to sell monthly to break even. You may assume in this part that average variable costs and average revenue per meal are constant. *Do state whether and why you classify each cost item (or some portion thereof) as variable or fixed.*

b. What implicit costs do you think would have been incurred by the owners of the Crossroads Diner but are not presented in the (accounting) income statement?

c. As the economic consultant for the Crossroads' owners, what suggestions can you make to help them improve their income from the diner? *Tell why* you think each of your suggestions will be helpful.

7. The next table gives monthly sales and cost data for a bicycle manufacturer.

a. Complete the table.

b. What is the profit-maximizing price and level of output for the firm? Why?

Price	Quantity	Total Revenue	Marginal Revenue	Marginal Cost	TVC	AFC	Marginal Profit
$200	0				$0	—	
190	1,000				150,000		
	2,000	360,000			290,000	6.00	
170	3,000				420,000		
160	4,000				540,000		
150	5,000			100			
140	6,000			80			
130	7,000			75			
120	8,000			80			
	9,000		30	100			
	10,000		10		1,095,000		
90	11,000				1,235,000		

8. The following annual income statement is for Alamo Chemical Company, which produces slug and snail bait. Of the $300,000 advertising expense, $250,000 is variable, and all but $100,000 of the travel expense is variable. Alamo considers $50,000 of the office salaries to be variable.

a. Find the break-even quantity for Alamo Chemical.

b. Alamo is considering installing some new machinery that would raise its fixed manufacturing costs to $1,000,000. This machinery would

Sales (1,000,000 two-pound bags @ $5)		$5,000,000
Less cost of goods sold:		
Direct labor	$700,000	
Direct materials	350,000	
Variable overhead	150,000	
Fixed overhead	600,000	1,800,000
Gross margin		$3,200,000
Less administrative and selling expenses:		
Sales commissions (@ $.50 per bag)	$500,000	
Travel expenses	600,000	
Advertising expense	300,000	
Office supplies	10,000	
Office salaries	90,000	1,500,000
Net operating income		$1,700,000
Less interest expense		500,000
Net income before taxes		$1,200,000

(handwritten annotations: check marks by Direct labor, Direct materials, Variable overhead; "F" by Fixed overhead; "E" by Sales commissions; "500 –V , 100 – F"; "–E" by Travel expenses; "– F" by Advertising expense; "VE" by Office supplies; "V" by Office salaries; "50 – VC" and "40 – F" near Less interest expense)

lower the direct labor cost to $.15 per bag and double the firm's capacity to 2,000,000 bags. (Presently, the firm is operating at capacity.) Interest expense would also increase to $1,000,000. *The firm believes it can sell to the new capacity level if it lowers price to $4.50 per bag.* Other average variable costs and fixed costs would not change.

Do you recommend that Alamo install the new machinery? Why or why not? What will be its expected new level of net income before taxes if the machinery is installed and the price lowered to $4.50?

9. Mueller Brewery manufactures a full-flavored, dark German beer. Shown in this problem is Mueller's income statement for a month earlier this year.

Sales (100,000 cases @ $7 per case)		$700,000
Less cost of goods sold:		
Direct materials (nonreturn bottles)	$195,000	
Direct labor	210,000	
Fixed manufacturing expenses	50,000	455,000
Gross margin		$245,000
Less administrative and selling expenses:		
• Delivery expenses	$ 30,000	
• Sales commissions	50,000	
• Advertising expenses	10,000	
• Travel expenses	5,000	
Fixed administrative and selling expenses	10,000	105,000
Net income before taxes		$140,000

    a. Find the number of cases of beer Mueller's must sell per month to break even.

    b. Mueller expects to sell, on the average, 100,000 cases per month for the rest of the year. Its capacity is 120,000 cases per month. Because of a strike by brewery workers in a foreign country that usually does not import Mueller's beer, a major hotel chain in that country has made an all-or-nothing offer to import 40,000 cases per month for the next three months at a price of $5.75 per case. Mueller's can supply from inventory only 30,000 of the total additional cases required for the three-month period because it did not anticipate receiving such an order. There will be no delivery expense, sales commissions, travel expense, or advertising expense connected with this order. Should Mueller agree to supply the hotel chain with the beer? *Why or why not?*

10. Kokkakola Company is a firm located in Athens, Greece, that produces a popular soft drink normally sold in single-serving cans. Because of government price controls, it knows that the wholesale price it can charge for the drink is 80 drachmas per can. Its market studies show there is nothing to be gained by charging less. If Kokkakola's total cost function per month in drachmas is

$$TC = 8{,}000{,}000 + 20Q + .0001Q^2,$$

and its marginal cost therefore is

$$MC = 20 + .0002Q,$$

determine

    a. how many cans of the drink it should sell, and

    b. how much its total monthly profit will be.

11. A firm estimates the following demand information for daily sales of its product, where Q is the quantity sold and P is the price:

$$Q = 136 - 0.4P$$
$$P = 340 - 2.5Q$$
$$MR = 340 - 5Q$$

    a. If its marginal cost is described by the function

$$MC = 40 - 10Q + Q^2,$$

    what will be its profit-maximizing output and price?

    b. Suppose the total cost function from which the above marginal cost was derived is

$$TC = 3{,}000 + 40Q - 5Q^2 + (1/3)Q^3,$$

    and determine how much profit the firm will have per day.

12. Squiggly Wiggly Corporation sells fishing worms in the wholesale market. The company has monthly fixed costs of $1,960, and it sells worms for $5.00 per gallon.
    a. If its AVC is constant at $2.20 per gallon of worms, how many gallons will it have to sell in order to break even?
    b. Suppose Squiggly Wiggly desires to have an economic profit of $12,000. If the preceding costs are the total economic costs of the firm, what monthly quantity of worm sales will yield the desired profit? (Round to nearest gallon.)

13. Omygosh Corporation has estimated the following average and marginal revenue equations for its product:

$$AR = 370 - Q$$

$$MR = 370 - 2Q.$$

The company's cost analysts say that total cost can be approximated by the equation $STC = 10{,}500 + 10Q + Q^2$ and that, therefore, its short-run marginal cost is $SMC = 10 + 2Q$. Determine the firm's profit-maximizing output, the price it should charge, and the amount of its total profit.

The following problems require calculus.

C1. A firm has the following total revenue and total cost functions:

$$TR = 21Q - Q^2$$

$$TC = (1/3)Q^3 - Q^2 + 9Q + 6$$

    a. At what level of output does the firm maximize *total revenue*?
    b. At what level of output does the firm maximize *total profit*?
    c. How much is the firm's total profit at its maximum?

C2. Find the maximum profit for a firm if its total revenue function is $TR = 50Q - Q^2$ and its total cost function is $TC = 100 - 4Q + 2Q^2$.

C3. Suppose a firm s estimated demand curve has the equation

$$Q = 220 - P,$$

and its total cost function is

$$TC = 1{,}000 + 80Q - 3Q^2 + (1/3)Q^3.$$

    a. Write an equation for the firm's total revenue function.
    b. Determine the *output* level and *price* that will maximize profit (or minimize short-run loss) for the firm.
    c. Calculate the firm's economic profit or loss at the optimum point.

C4. Suppose a firm has the following short-run total cost function:

$$STC = 4{,}850 + 40Q - 1.5Q^2 + 0.04Q^3,$$

where Q is output, and the constant in the equation represents total fixed cost. Answer the following:

a. What is the dollar value of average fixed cost at an output of 25 units?

b. At what level of output will marginal cost be at a minimum?

c. At what level of output will AVC be at a minimum?

d. If the firm has a fixed product price of $190 per unit, at what level of output will it choose to operate, and what will be its economic profit or loss?

C5. Traumco sells a specialized medical monitoring device. It estimates the monthly quantity demanded to be represented by the equation

$$Q = 350 - .25P, \text{ where } P \text{ is price.}$$

Its monthly cost function is

$$STC = 20{,}000 + 200Q - 9Q^2 + (1/3)Q^3.$$

Determine the profit-maximizing quantity sold and price for the monitor. How much will the maximum monthly profit be?

C6. Suppose that for a given time period a firm faces the following demand curve:

$$Q = 75 - .5P.$$

If its total cost function for the same period is

$$STC = 500 + 30Q - 3Q^2 + (1/3)Q^3,$$

a. Write the MR equation for the firm.

b. Find:

i) The sales quantity that will maximize its profit.

ii) The price it should charge if profit is maximized.

iii) The dollar value of its total profit at the maximum.

C7. Maurice's makes and sells dog collars studded with genuine semi-precious stones. Based on data collected over a 36-week period, Maurice has estimated that in his area the demand function for such collars is given by the equation

$$Q_c = 50 - 2P_c + 0.1F + 0.002I - 0.01K,$$

where Q_c = number of collars sold per week

P_c = price per collar

F = number of resident french poodles in area = 2,000

I = average annual income of dog owners in area
= $90,000

K = number of resident cats in area = 15,000.

Maurice estimates that his variable cost for the collars is

$$TVC = 20Q_c + 1.5Q_c^2$$

How many collars should Maurice plan to sell per week? What price should he charge, and what will be the total profit contribution from the sales of the collars?

Problems C8 and C9 require both partial differentiation and constrained maximization. They should be attempted only if you have covered the material in the appendix that follows Chapter 5.

C8. Lone Star Instruments, Inc., makes two deluxe printing models of calculators—a scientific model and a business and financial model. The demand function for the scientific model is

$$Q_S = 20,000 - 100P_S,$$

where

Q_S = annual quantity demanded of the scientific model,

and

P_S = price of the scientific model.

The demand function for the business and financial model is

$$Q_B = 50,000 - 400P_B,$$

where

Q_B = annual quantity demanded of the business and
financial model,

and

P_B = price of the business and financial model.

The total cost function for LSI is given by

$$STC = \$100,000 + 25Q,$$

where

$$Q = Q_S + Q_B.$$

LSI also has a capacity limitation of 17,500 calculators per year.
a. Find the profit-maximizing quantity and price for each model of calculator.
b. Solve for the Lagrangian multiplier. What does its value tell you?
C9. Stanislaw's Ping-Pong Emporium sells two types of memberships. One is the individual membership (*I*), which allows unlimited use of facilities

for one person. The second type of membership is the corporate membership (C), which allows the member and his/her family to use the facilities with some restrictions. Stan believes he has 500 units of membership capacity and that an individual membership will use up one unit of capacity, while a corporate membership will use up 1.5 units of capacity, because of the added load from family members.

Stan's monthly total profit function is as follows:

$$\pi = 52C - .06C^2 + 70I - .1I^2 + .01CI - 8{,}000$$

where C is the number of corporate memberships sold and I is the number of individual memberships sold,

a. Subject to the capacity constraint, what combination of the two types of memberships will maximize Stan's profit? (Solve by Lagrangian method.)
b. How much will Stan's maximum monthly profit be?
c. Would Stan be wise to consider expanding his capacity? Explain, relating your answer to the Lagrangian multiplier, lambda.

These problems can be solved with Decision Assistant.

D1. Bill Roberts operates Southwest Distributing Company, a distribution firm that buys large quantities (freight cars or large trucks) of fresh fruits, repackages them, and then sells the repackaged merchandise to local grocery stores. Bill has been considering expanding the firm to include a selection of standard vegetables such as carrots, lettuce, tomatoes, and potatoes.

Carrots: Bill has determined the total revenue function for carrots is given by the equation

$$TR = \$100Q - \$0.5Q^2,$$

where Q represents the quantity of bushels of carrots sold. The total cost function for carrots is given by the equation

$$TC = \$1{,}500 - \$10Q + \$.05Q^2,$$

where Q represents the quantity of bushels of carrots purchased.

Lettuce: Bill has determined the total revenue function for lettuce is given by the equation

$$TR = \$200Q - \$0.5Q^2,$$

where Q represents the quantity of crates of lettuce sold. The total cost function for lettuce is given by the equation

$$TC = \$1{,}500 - \$20Q + \$.05Q^2,$$

where Q represents the quantity of crates of lettuce purchased.

Tomatoes: Bill has determined the total revenue function for tomatoes is given by the equation

$$TR = \$350Q - \$0.5Q^2,$$

where Q represents the quantity of flats of tomatoes sold. The total cost function for tomatoes is given by the equation

$$TC = \$1{,}500 - \$35Q + \$.05Q^2,$$

where Q represents the quantity of flats of tomatoes purchased.

Potatoes: Bill has determined the total revenue function for potatoes is given by the equation

$$TR = \$450Q - \$0.5Q^2,$$

where Q represents the quantity of sacks of potatoes sold. The total cost function for potatoes is given by the equation

$$TC = \$1{,}500 - \$45Q + \$.05Q^2,$$

where Q represents the quantity of sacks of potatoes purchased.

Use the Max/Min tool in the *Managerial Economics Decision Assistant* to determine profit-maximizing quantity and price for each of the products (carrots, lettuce, tomatoes, and potatoes).

D2. Jeff Anderson has approached this day with great reservations. His company, Marble Extraction Services, Inc., is at a crossroads in its life. The company has had a successful past mining marble and selling it to various companies who in turn process it into slabs, tile, etc. However, the open pit mine used in the past is virtually depleted, and it is no longer economically feasible to continue with the mining operations.

Jeff has researched the possibilities of moving the operations and has been fortunate to locate a suitable area that has been tested and found to contain an excellent grade of marble. A long-term lease has been signed on the property, and now all that remains is to determine the type of mining operation to be used at the new site. Great advances in automation have occurred in the mining industry since the original mining operation commenced, and Jeff is now faced with a decision that will affect the company's fortunes for the next 25 years.

The director of mining operations, Mike Wilson, has studied various options concerning the new facilities. From his study he has determined there are three possibilities which will be consistent with the site itself and with the grade of marble being mined.

Plant A is highly automated with some of the latest electronic and robotic equipment in the industry. The average variable cost for extracting a ton of marble is estimated to be $500 per ton. Fixed cost, mostly due to the price and quantity of equipment, is estimated to be $3 million per year.

Plant B is slightly less automated and therefore relies on more labor in the mining process. Fixed costs are estimated to be $2 million per year. Average variable costs will be approximately $750 per ton.

Plant C relies on the more traditional, labor-intensive methods of marble mining and has the lowest fixed costs of $1 million per year. Estimated average variable costs are $1,000 per ton.

The director of marketing, Anne Stephens, has studied the marketplace for the type of marble to be mined and determined the average price for marble of similar quality is $2,000 per ton.

a. As an economist for the company, you have been asked to provide an analysis of each plant. The Break-Even Analysis tool in the *Managerial Economics Decision Assistant* can be used to evaluate the profitability of each plant type. What is the break-even quantity for each type of plant?

b. In addition to other information you consider important, Jeff specifically wants the answers to the following questions.

   i) At each of the following production levels, what level of profit would be generated by each plant?

   > 5,000 tons per month
   > 4,000 tons per month
   > 3,000 tons per month
   > 2,000 tons per month
   > 1,000 tons per month

   ii) Assuming that Anne Stephens is predicting the higher volume of 5,000 tons per month, which plant should be used? Under what conditions would your answer change? Be specific and give reasons for your logic.

SELECTED REFERENCES

"Airline Takes the Marginal Route," *Business Week* (April 20, 1963), pp. 111–114.

Cyert, R. M., and C. L. Hedrick. "Theory of the Firm: Past, Present, and Future: An Interpretation," *Journal of Economic Literature* X, no. 2 (June 1972), pp. 389–412.

Dean, Joel. "Measuring Profits for Executive Decisions," *Accounting Review* (April 1951).

Denzau, Arthur. *Microeconomic Analysis: Markets and Dynamics*. Homewood, IL: Richard D. Irwin, 1992, Chapters. 17 and 26.

Eaton, B. Curtis, and Diane F. Eaton. *Microeconomics*. Englewood Cliffs, NJ: Prentice-Hall, 1995, Chapters. 9 and 10.

Enke, Stephen. "On Maximizing Profits: A Distinction Between Chamberlin and Robinson," *American Economic Review* XLI (September 1951), pp. 566–578.

Landsburg, Stephen E. *Price Theory and Applications*, 3d ed. St. Paul: West, 1995, Chapter 5.

Nicholson, Walter. *Microeconomic Theory: Basic Principles and Extensions*, 5th ed. Chicago: The Dryden Press, 1992, Chapters 13 and 14.

Williamson, O. F. "The Modern Corporation: Origins, Evolution, Attributes," *Journal of Economic Literature* XIX (December 1981), pp. 1537–1538.

8

LINEAR PROGRAMMING AND THE FIRM

Linear programming is a mathematical tool for solving maximization and minimization problems characterized by linear functions and constraints that can be stated as inequalities.

In the preceding chapters, we have discussed optimizing decisions made by the firm regarding demand, production, cost, and profit-maximizing output and price, using techniques that depended on the mathematics of calculus. In this chapter we will discuss some of those decisions, using the tools of a different branch of mathematics—that of **linear programming**. Linear programming is a mathematical decision-making tool for optimization problems with a linear objective function and linear constraints that are in the form of inequalities.

RELATIONSHIP BETWEEN LINEAR PROGRAMMING AND CALCULUS TECHNIQUES

As one should expect since we are including a discussion of decision making using both tools in this book, calculus and linear programming *each* have areas of applicability where the other cannot be used. For example, linear programming can be used only when the relevant functions or relationships involved are linear.[1] This restriction means the cost, revenue, and total profit functions must all be graphed as straight lines as long as only one independent variable is involved. If there is more than one independent variable, no variable (X_i) must be raised to a power other than 1 or multiplied by any other variable. Thus all functions must be of the form

$$Y = a_0 + a_1X_1 + a_2X_2 + \ldots + a_nX_n,$$

where the a_i are constants. Linear programming techniques require constant returns to scale, constant marginal productivity of a variable input (if we are using short-run cost functions), constant input prices, and constant output prices.

Obviously, such requirements are not necessary for the application of calculus techniques, since many of the functions that we used in the production

---

1 There is a branch of mathematical programming—nonlinear programming—for which the linearity assumption is not required. However, that topic is too advanced for this book.

and cost chapters were *not* linear; and, indeed, over wide variations in levels of output, these relationships are probably nonlinear for most firms. However, as we indicated in our discussion of break-even analysis, over small variations in levels of production the assumption of linearity may be realistic.

On the other hand, linear programming can be utilized in situations where certain constraints or limitations faced by the firm can be expressed in terms of *inequalities*, whereas the traditional calculus techniques can be used only when these constraints can be expressed as *strict* equalities. Thus, for example, it is easy to see the usefulness of linear programming in a situation in which a firm has certain capacity limitations such that it may utilize either none of a particular input or various amounts of it up to some maximum amount available. A firm may wish to maximize short-run profit, subject to some minimum requirement on dollar sales. A manufacturing firm may wish to minimize the cost of producing a good, subject to certain minimum safety and/or quality requirements. Later in this chapter we discuss a marketing problem that involves linear programming, and there are also many uses for linear programming in the area of finance. For example, a firm may wish to maximize the expected return on its investment portfolio, subject to certain minimum constraints on the amounts held of certain types of assets.

The use of linear programming (and calculus) by a firm implies, however, that fractional solution values for the decision variables at the optimal point are acceptable and that, if necessary, the decision maker can round to the profit-maximizing whole number. In cases where such an assumption is unwarranted, a more complex procedure—integer programming—may be necessary. This technique is beyond the scope of this book, but further reading may be done in sources listed at the end of this chapter.

THE PRIMAL PROGRAM

Each linear programming problem has two programs: the *primal program* and the *dual program*. The *primal program* explicitly states the objective of the firm and its constraints and is, therefore, easier to understand. For this reason we will begin this chapter with an example of a primal maximization program, leaving a discussion of the dual program for later.

Profit Maximization with Input Constraints

As we have already stated, frequently a firm wishes to maximize profit but is constrained because there are maximum amounts available of certain inputs. For example, suppose a winery produces two products—white wine and champagne. In the short run, the firm has three capacity limitations: fermenting capacity, bottling capacity, and champagne purifying capacity. For those who are not familiar with the production processes involved in making champagne, we should explain that champagne requires a double fermentation. This double process is done so that the partially fermented grape juice, along with some grape pulp, is sealed in bottles and allowed to undergo further fermentation to acquire the bubbles and effervescence characteristic of champagne. The champagne mixture is then partially frozen so that the bubbles will not escape when the bottles are unsealed and the sediment is removed. By this means, the champagne is purified and then rebottled.

The maximum amount of initial fermenting capacity becoming available in casks is 600 units each week, the maximum amount of bottling capacity available per week is 500 units, and the maximum amount of champagne purifying capacity available each week is 150 units. Production of one bottle of champagne requires three units of fermenting capacity, two units of bottling capacity, and one unit of champagne purifying capacity. Production of one bottle of white wine requires only one unit of fermenting capacity and one unit of bottling capacity. These relationships are summarized in Table 8–1.

The Graphical Solution

In Figure 8–1 we have graphed three straight lines indicating the *maximum* amounts of white wine and/or champagne the firm can produce, *given* the three input constraints. These three straight-line relationships were derived in the following manner from the information presented in Table 8–1. First, consider the constraint on fermentation. If we were to express the information relevant to that constraint presented in the table as a mathematical relationship, we could state that three times the number of bottles of champagne produced plus one times the number of bottles of white wine produced must be less than or equal to 600 units, which is the maximum available amount of inputs required for fermentation. In mathematical notation

$$3Q_c + Q_w \leq 600,$$

where Q_c is the number of bottles of champagne and Q_w is the number of bottles of white wine. Thus, this mathematical relationship summarizes the fer-

Table 8–1   Input Requirements for Producing White Wine and Champagne

Input	Units of Input Required per Bottle		Maximum Number of Units of Input Available
	Champagne	*White Wine*	
Fermentation	3	1	600
Bottling	2	1	500
Champagne Purifying	1	0	150

Figure 8–1   Maximum Quantities of White Wine and Champagne that Can Be Produced, Given Fermenting, Bottling, and Champagne Purifying Constraints

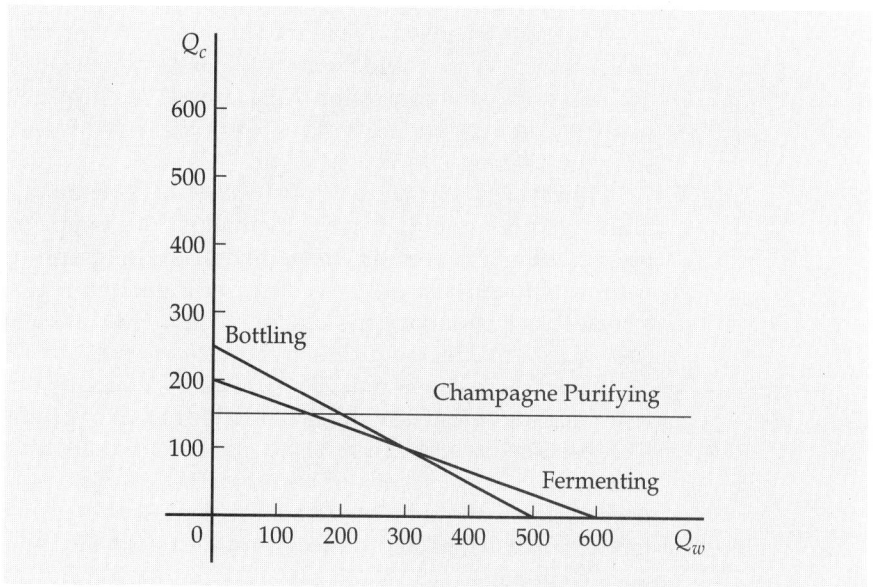

The bottling constraint indicates the maximum quantities of champagne and wine that can be produced with current bottling capacity. The champagne purifying and fermenting constraints have similar interpretations.

mentation constraint because it combines the information that (1) it takes three units of fixed fermentation input to produce one bottle of champagne, (2) it takes one unit of fixed fermentation input to produce one bottle of white wine, and (3) a maximum of 600 units is available. In a similar manner we can derive mathematical expressions for the other two constraints, which are presented in Table 8–2.

If we remove the inequality sign from each of these constraints, thus making them strict equalities, we obtain the relationships that indicate the *maxi-*

Table 8–2   Mathematical Expressions of the Fermenting, Bottling, and Champagne Purifying Constraints

Fermenting	$3Q_c + Q_w \leq 600$
Bottling	$2Q_c + Q_w \leq 500$
Champagne Purifying	$Q_c \leq 150$

mum quantity of champagne and/or wine that could be produced under each constraint if all available units of the input were utilized. These equations are presented in Table 8–3 and are the equations for the straight-line functions graphed in Figure 8–1.

Note that when we consider only one constraint, the firm may be able to produce any one of a wide variety of combinations of wine and champagne and still satisfy the constraint. For example, the firm could produce 200 bottles of champagne and no wine or 600 bottles of wine and no champagne and still meet the fermenting constraint.

However, the firm must satisfy *all* of the constraints and, consequently, is able to produce only those combinations of champagne and wine that are in (including the boundary) the region of the graph in Figure 8–1 that is within all three constraints. We have indicated this region in Figure 8–2 with a heavy black boundary and diagonal lines. The combinations of champagne and wine in this region make up the *feasible region* of production.

Given these constraints, the firm can produce any combination of wine and champagne that is within the feasible region of production. However, we have assumed that the firm wishes to produce that combination of products that will *maximize its profit* (or minimize its loss). To achieve this goal, the firm needs to know the *profit contribution* (price less average variable cost) per unit for each product that it produces. Assume that the profit contribution per bottle of champagne is $2.50, whereas the profit contribution per bottle of white wine is $1.00. With this information the firm can use *isoprofit curves* to graphically find its optimal quantities of wine and champagne. Similar to other economics curves with an *iso-* prefix, an **isoprofit curve** indicates the various combinations of two products that will yield *equal profit* for the firm. (Recall from Chapter 5, for example, that an *isocost curve* indicates the combinations of two inputs that are of *equal cost*.)

In Figure 8–3 we have graphed three isoprofit curves and the feasible region from Figure 8–2. We were able to obtain the equation for each isoprofit line by substituting different values for total profit contribution (πC) in the following function:

$$\pi C = \$2.50 Q_c + \$1.00 Q_w.$$

An **isoprofit curve** indicates the different combinations of two products that will result in equal profit for the firm.

Table 8–3   Equations Expressing Maximum Quantities of Wine and Champagne that Can Be Produced Under Each Constraint

Fermenting	$3Q_c + Q_w = 600$
Bottling	$2Q_c + Q_w = 500$
Champagne Purifying	$Q_c \quad\quad = 150$

Figure 8–2   Feasible Region of Production of Wine and Champagne

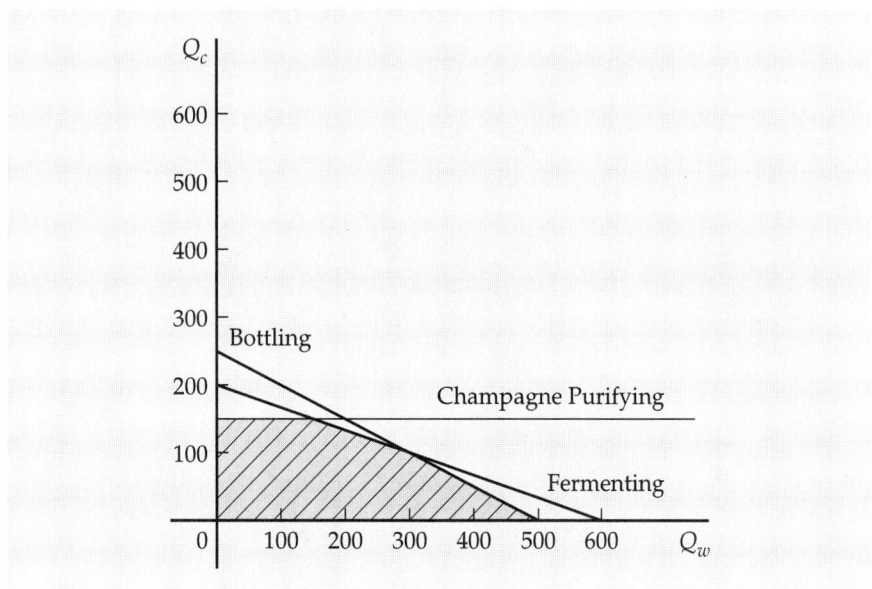

The feasible region of production, indicated by the diagonal lines, represents the quantities of wine and champagne that the firm can produce with its current capacity.

This function states that the total profit contribution of the firm must be equal to $2.50 times the number of bottles of champagne produced plus $1.00 times the number of bottles of wine produced. By substituting $375 for πC, we can find the equation that indicates the different combinations of wine and champagne that will result in a $375 level of profit contribution. To derive the equations for the other isoprofit curves, we do the same thing for $\pi C = \$550$ and $\pi C = \$650$. (The amounts $375, $550, and $650 were picked because they involved combinations of champagne and wine that were near the boundary of the feasible region.)

If the firm is to maximize profit, it must be on the highest isoprofit curve possible, given its constraints. In Figure 8–3 we observe that the isoprofit line for $\pi C = \$550$ just touches an outside corner (point A) of the feasible region; therefore a profit contribution level of $550 is the greatest amount that the firm can achieve, given its capacity constraints. Point A also indicates the profit-maximizing combination of champagne and wine that the firm should produce in this situation—100 bottles of champagne and 300 bottles of wine. Note that while point A is the optimal point, the firm still has some excess champagne purifying capacity.

Figure 8–3   Isoprofit Lines and the Feasible Region of Production

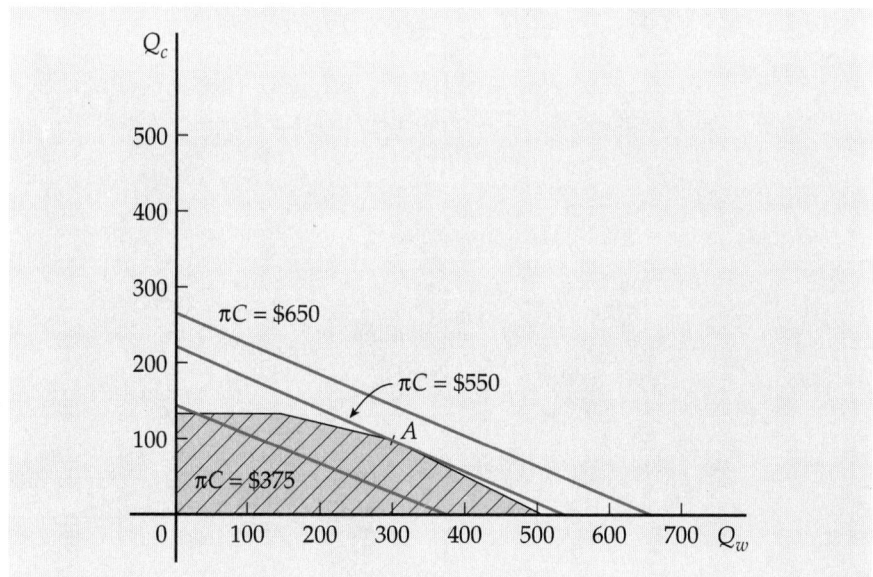

The equation for each isoprofit curve is obtained by substituting each respective level of profit contribution in the equation.

$$\pi C = \$2.50 Q_c + \$1.00 Q_w,$$

where πC is the total profit contribution, Q_c is the number of bottles of champagne, and Q_w is the number of bottles of wine. The isoprofit curve for $\pi C = \$550$ just touches an outside corner (point A) of the feasible region, and it indicates the profit-maximizing quantities of champagne and wine.

The Algebraic Solution Method

The graphical method of finding the profit-maximizing combination of products is quite useful for illustration. However, algebraic methods are more precise and more practical when the number of decision variables is greater than two, because graphing is difficult when there are more than two variables. There are a variety of algebraic methods in use, and often these operations would be performed by a computer. Consequently, in this book we will discuss only one of the simplest algebraic procedures.

As indicated in the preceding paragraph, the objective function (or goal) of the firm is to maximize

$$\pi C = \$2.50 Q_c + \$1.00 Q_w,$$

subject to the following constraints (see Table 8–2):

Fermenting	$3Q_c + Q_w \leq 600,$
Bottling	$2Q_c + Q_w \leq 500,$ and
Champagne purifying	$Q_c \quad\quad \leq 150.$

To solve this problem algebraically, we create three new variables called *slack* variables. Each of these slack variables represents excess capacity in some area, and since there cannot be *negative* excess capacity, the value of each of these variables must be greater than or equal to zero. The values of Q_c and Q_w must likewise be greater than or equal to zero.

Since each slack variable represents excess capacity in some area, we place one slack variable in each of the preceding constraints, which changes it to an equality:

(8–1)
$$3Q_c + Q_w + S_F = 600,$$

(8–2)
$$2Q_c + Q_w + S_B = 500,$$

and

(8–3)
$$Q_c \quad\quad + S_P = 150.$$

In this case, S_F represents excess fermenting capacity, S_B represents excess bottling capacity, and S_P represents excess champagne purifying capacity. The addition of these slack variables transforms these constraints into equalities because the amount of a particular kind of input used in producing champagne and wine, plus the excess capacity left over, must equal the total available amount of the input.

Before proceeding any further, we should note that in this case corners of the boundary (also called *extreme points*) of the feasible region occur (1) where two constraints intersect, (2) where a constraint intersects either the horizontal or vertical axis, or (3) at the origin. Therefore, at any extreme point, at least *two* of the five variables (Q_c, Q_w, S_F, S_B, and S_P in the constraint equations) must be zero. It is also true in the general case with m constraints and n decision variables that the number of *zero-valued* variables must be great enough so that the number of *nonzero-valued* variables is no greater than the number of constraints. Usually, if there are m constraints, there will be m variables that are nonzero.

To draw each constraint line, we assumed that all available capacity of the corresponding input was being utilized. This means that along a capacity constraint line, the value of the corresponding slack variable is zero. Thus, in Figure 8–4, at point A, Q_c and Q_w are zero; at point B, Q_w and S_P are zero; at point C, S_P and S_F are zero; at point D, S_F and S_B are zero; and at point E, S_B and Q_c are zero.

Observe that not all points where two of these variables are zero are *necessarily* part of the feasible region. For example, at point F, S_P and S_B equal

Figure 8–4   Constraints and the Boundary of the Feasible Region

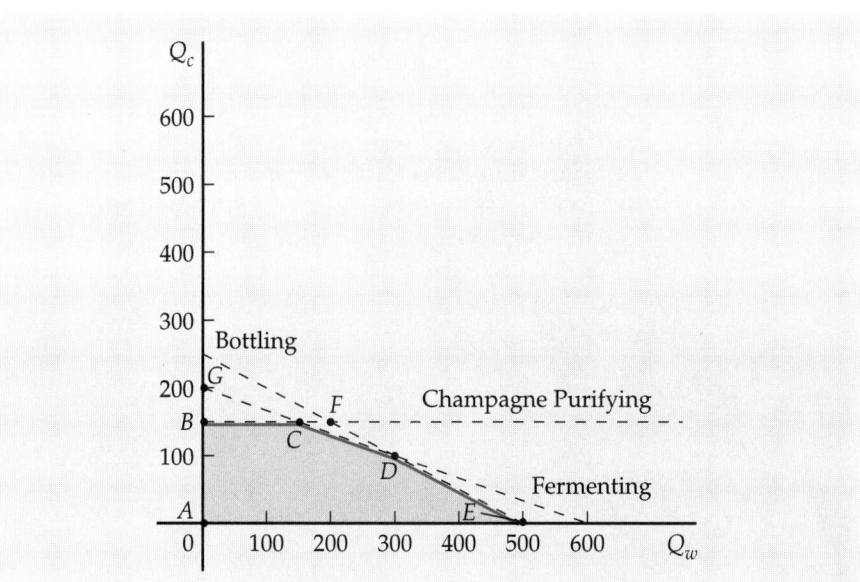

Points A, B, C, D, and E mark the corners of the boundary of the feasible region of production. Points G and F lie outside the feasible region.

zero, but point F is not part of the feasible region because it is outside the fermenting constraint. At point G, Q_w and S_F are zero, but point G is also outside the feasible region.

Furthermore, *at least one* of the extreme (boundary corner) points of the feasible region will mark a profit-maximizing combination of champagne and wine to be produced. (If a constraint happens to coincide with an iso-profit curve, then two extreme points, both on the constraint, and all points in between, will be equally profitable.) Therefore, by solving the constraint equations for Q_c and Q_w at each extreme point of the feasible region and determining the corresponding πC from the objective function, we can discover the optimal combination of champagne and wine.

As long as the profit contribution per unit of output is positive, we can ignore the origin, since at that point, $Q_c = 0$, $Q_w = 0$, and $\pi C = 0$. At point B, S_P and Q_w are zero, and substituting those values into equations (8–1) through (8–3), we obtain the following equations:

$$3Q_c + S_F = 600,$$

$$2Q_c + S_B = 500,$$

and

$$Q_c = 150.$$

Substituting $Q_c = 150$ in the first and second equations, we obtain $S_F = 150$ and $S_B = 200$. From the objective function, we find that $\pi C = \$2.50(150) + \$1.00(0) = \$375$. The values of the slack variables tell us that there are 150 excess units of fermenting capacity and 200 excess units of bottling capacity.

At point C, S_P and S_F are zero, and substituting these values in equations (8–1) through (8–3), we obtain

$$3Q_c + Q_w = 600,$$

$$2Q_c + Q_w + S_B = 500,$$

and

$$Q_c = 150.$$

Substituting $Q_c = 150$ in the first equation, we find $Q_w = 150$. Substituting $Q_c = 150$ and $Q_w = 150$ in the second equation, we find $S_B = 50$. From the objective function, we find $\pi C = \$2.50(150) + \$1.00(150) = \$525$.

At point D, S_F and S_B are zero, and substituting those values into equations (8–1) through (8–3), we obtain

$$3Q_c + Q_w = 600,$$

$$2Q_c + Q_w = 500,$$

and

$$Q_c + S_P = 150.$$

Subtracting the second equation from the first, we obtain $Q_c = 100$. Substituting $Q_c = 100$ in either of those equations, we find $Q_w = 300$. Substituting $Q_c = 100$ in the last equation, we get $S_P = 50$. From the objective function, we find $\pi C = \$2.50(100) + \$1.00(300) = \$550$.

At point E, Q_c and S_B equal zero, and in a manner similar to that used for the other points, we obtain $Q_w = 500$, $S_F = 100$, $S_P = 150$, and $\pi C = \$500$.

The information that we have obtained by examining each of the boundary corners of the feasible region is summarized as follows:

Point A	Point B
$Q_c = 0$, $Q_w = 0$	$Q_w = 0$, $S_P = 0$
$S_F = 600$, $S_B = 500$, $S_P = 150$	$Q_c = 150$, $S_F = 150$, $S_B = 200$
$\pi C = 0$	$\pi C = \$375$

Point C

$S_F = 0$, $S_P = 0$
$Q_c = 150$, $Q_w = 150$, $S_B = 50$
$\pi C = \$525$

Point D

$S_F = 0$, $S_B = 0$
$Q_c = 100$, $Q_w = 300$, $S_P = 50$
$\pi C = \$550$

Point E

$Q_c = 0$, $S_B = 0$
$Q_w = 500$, $S_F = 100$, $S_P = 150$
$\pi C = \$500$

As we have already found graphically, the optimal combination of champagne and wine is given by point D, where $Q_c = 100$, $Q_w = 300$, and $\pi C = \$550$—the highest profit contribution level obtainable by this firm.

How did we know that points A, B, C, D, and E made up the boundary corners of the feasible region, as opposed to points like F and G? Before we solved for the values of the nonzero slack variables, the only way we could tell was from the graph. *After* we solved for the values of the nonzero slack variables, we could tell because the values of those variables were positive. At points such as F and G, the value of at least one slack variable will be negative, meaning that at least one constraint is being violated. For example, at point G, $S_P = -50$, meaning that the purifying constraint has been violated. However, it is often helpful to use a graph together with the algebraic method of finding the profit-maximizing point in order to locate more easily the corners of the feasible region boundary (as long as the number of decision variables is not too large).

We now turn to an example of the primal program in a cost minimization problem.

Example of a Linear Programming Cost Minimization Problem

Linear programming is quite useful for certain types of cost minimization decision problems, as well as for profit maximization problems, so long as the linearity requirement is met. For example, suppose that a manufacturer of high quality (and relatively high priced) speakers for stereo component systems is trying to decide on the optimal combination of advertisements in two magazines. The cost per ad in the first magazine is $500, while the cost per ad in the second magazine is $400. The firm has certain minimum quantities of different types of people whom it wants to reach through these advertisements. Specifically, it wants to reach at least 600,000 people under 50 years of age, at least 180,000 people with annual incomes of $40,000 and over, and at least 260,000 people who already own stereo systems.

The firm believes that no person subscribes to both magazines, as the characteristics of people who read the first magazine differ significantly from the characteristics of those who read the second magazine. Accordingly, the firm believes that each ad placed in the first magazine will reach 20,000 *new* readers who are under 50 years of age, 15,000 new readers who have annual incomes of at least $40,000, and 10,000 new readers who already have stereo systems. The corresponding figures for the second magazine are believed to be 30,000 new readers under 50 years of age, 5,000 with incomes of $40,000 and over, and 10,000 who already own stereo systems.

The objective of the stereo speaker manufacturer is to minimize the total cost of the advertisements while fulfilling the minimum goals for reaching each type of audience. Thus our linear programming problem becomes this:

$$\text{Minimize } TC = \$500Q_1 + \$400Q_2,$$

where Q_1 is the number of advertisements placed in the first magazine and Q_2 is the number of advertisements placed in the second magazine, subject to the following constraints:

Age	$20{,}000Q_1 + 30{,}000Q_2 \geq 600{,}000,$
Income	$15{,}000Q_1 + \ 5{,}000Q_2 \geq 180{,}000,$ and
Stereo ownership	$10{,}000Q_1 + 10{,}000Q_2 \geq 260{,}000,$
where	

$$Q_1 \text{ and } Q_2 \text{ are } \geq 0.$$

The first constraint states that 20,000 times the number of ads placed in the first magazine (which will equal the number of people under 50 years old reached by that magazine) plus 30,000 times the number of ads placed in the second magazine (which should equal the number of people under 50 years old reached by the second magazine) must be greater than or equal to 600,000, the *minimum* number of people under 50 years of age that the speaker manufacturer wishes to reach. The second and third constraints have similar interpretations. Note that the constraint inequalities in this minimization problem are in the form of greater-than-or-equal-to constraints, whereas in the maximization problem they were less-than-or-equal-to constraints. This difference occurs because in the first case the constraints are placing a limit on making something *larger*, while in the second case they are placing a limit on making something *smaller*. The constraints and the feasible region for the stereo speaker manufacturer are graphed in Figure 8–5, and the respective extreme points are designated by points *A, B, C,* and *D*.

Using the algebraic method developed in the previous section, we use slack variables to transform the constraints into strict equalities as follows:

(8–4)
$$20{,}000Q_1 + 30{,}000Q_2 - S_A = 600{,}000,$$

(8–5)
$$15{,}000Q_1 + \ 5{,}000Q_2 - S_I = 180{,}000,$$

Figure 8–5   Constraints and the Feasible Region for Advertisements in
Two Magazines

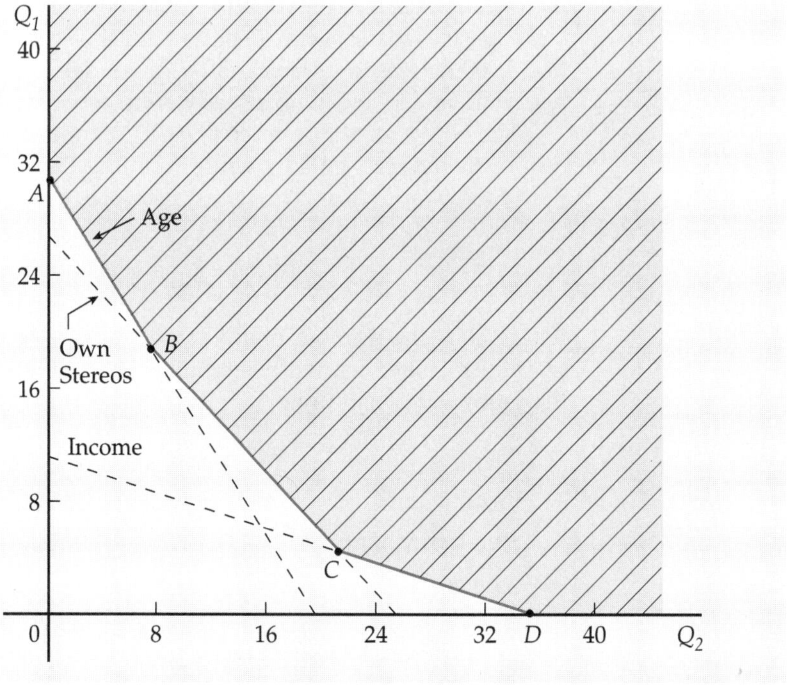

In this case the feasible region, denoted by the diagonal lines, is above *ABCD*.

and

(8–6)

$$10{,}000Q_1 + 10{,}000Q_2 - S_O = 260{,}000.$$

Here, the slack variables represent the *additional* people reached by advertisements in a particular classification above the minimum number required. As before, the values of all variables must be greater than or equal to zero.

We now examine each boundary corner point. At point A, S_A and Q_2 are equal to zero. Substituting these values into the constraint equations (8–4) through (8–6), we obtain:

$$20{,}000Q_1 \qquad = 600{,}000,$$

$$15{,}000Q_1 - S_I = 180{,}000,$$

and

$$10,000Q_1 - S_O = 260,000.$$

From the first constraint, we find $Q_1 = 30$, and substituting for Q_1 in the second and third constraints, we find $S_I = 270,000$ and $S_O = 40,000$. From the objective function, we obtain $TC = \$500(30) + \$400(0) = \$15,000$.

At point B, S_A and S_O are zero, and substituting these values into the constraint equations, we obtain the following:

$$20,000Q_1 + 30,000Q_2 \quad\quad = 600,000,$$

$$15,000Q_1 + \;\;5,000Q_2 - S_I = 180,000,$$

and

$$10,000Q_1 + 10,000Q_2 \quad\quad = 260,000.$$

By subtracting twice the third equation from the first equation, we obtain $10,000Q_2 = 80,000$ or $Q_2 = 8$. Substituting for Q_1 in the third equation, we find $Q_1 = 18$. Substituting for Q_1 and Q_2 in the second equation, we find $S_I = 130,000$. From the objective function, we can obtain $TC = \$500(18) + \$400(8) = \$12,200$.

In a similar fashion, we can find the values for Q_1, Q_2, S_A, S_I, S_O, and TC at points C and D. Our results are summarized as follows:

Point A

$Q_1 = 30, Q_2 = 0, S_A = 0$
$S_I = 270,000, S_O = 40,000$
$TC = \$15,000$

Point B

$Q_1 = 18, Q_2 = 8, S_A = 0$
$S_I = 130,000, S_O = 0$
$TC = \$12,000$

Point C

$Q_1 = 5, Q_2 = 21,$
$S_A = 130,000$
$S_I = 0, S_O = 0$
$TC = \$10,900$

Point D

$Q_1 = 0, Q_2 = 36,$
$S_A = 480,000$
$S_I = 0, S_O = 100,000$
$TC = \$14,400$

Thus the firm will minimize its advertising cost, given these constraints at point C, where $Q_1 = 5$, $Q_2 = 21$, and $TC = \$10,900$. Therefore the firm should advertise 5 times in the first magazine and 21 times in the second magazine. In Figure 8–6 we have graphed the boundary of the feasible region and the isocost curve for $TC = \$10,900$, and we have indicated the optimal values of Q_1 and Q_2.

Figure 8–6   The Least Cost Combination of Advertisements in Two
Magazines

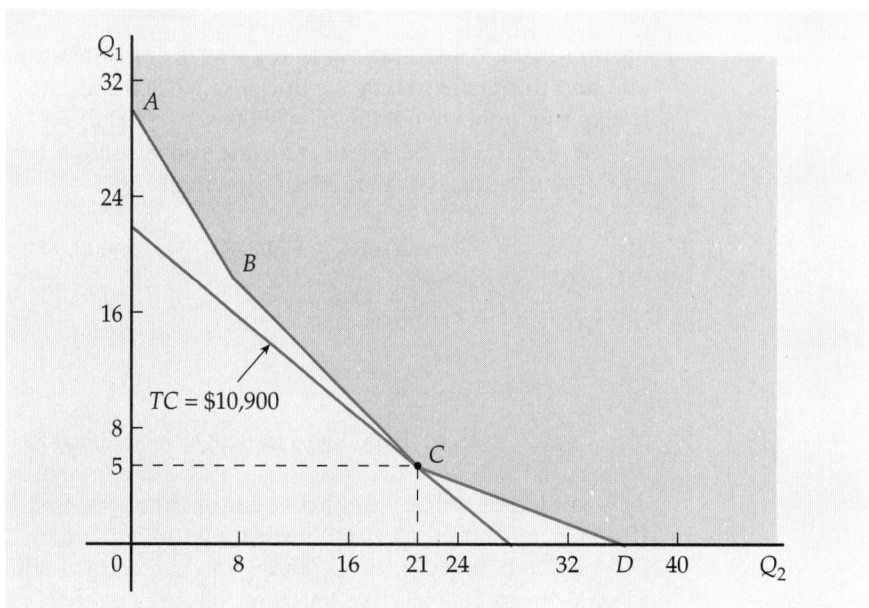

The firm will minimize advertising cost at point C, with 5 advertisements in the first magazine
and 21 in the second magazine.

Summary of Primal Program Solution Procedure

The steps that should be followed to obtain the optimal solution to a primal
program using a combination of graphical and algebraic methods are summarized as follows:

1. Set up the objective function and the constraints in mathematical notation.
2. Graph the constraints by considering them to be strict equalities and determine the extreme points of the boundary of the feasible region, recall-
   ing that the values of all slack variables and the quantities produced of
   the products must be greater than or equal to zero. Moreover, these corner points must include *the* optimal point or at least *one of a set* of equally
   optimal points. If the constraints cannot be graphed easily, go to the third
   step, using the algebraic technique described earlier to examine each
   point where the number of nonzero variables is at least no greater than
   the number of constraints.
3. Using the algebraic technique described earlier, examine each of the extreme points in turn, solving for the quantities of each of the products and
   the slack variables at each point and the resulting level of profit contri-

bution or cost in order to determine at which point profit will be maximized or cost will be minimized. (It will often be helpful to graph an isoprofit/isocost curve that falls near the outermost/innermost boundary of the feasible region as an aid in eliminating some extreme points from consideration without having to solve the constraint relationships for each point algebraically.)

In the next section, we examine the nature of the dual programs in the two examples of the optimization problems presented previously.

THE DUAL PROGRAM

Every linear programming problem that involves maximizing or minimizing an objective function has a corresponding linear programming problem called the *dual* program. As we have indicated, the original programming problem that directly states the objective of the firm is called the *primal* program. For every primal *maximization* problem, there can be constructed a corresponding dual *minimization* problem; conversely, for every primal minimization problem, there can be constructed a corresponding dual maximization problem. Both the primal and the dual programs will give the same values for the *decision variables* in the *primal* objective function at their respective optimal points. Also, the optimal value for the primal objective function will equal the optimal value for the dual objective function.

The dual program is useful for two reasons. First, it may be easier to find the optimal values of the decision variables in the primal program by solving the dual program. Second, the dual program gives an imputed value of the opportunity cost to the firm of the decision variables in the primal objective function and of the constraints.

Dual Minimization Problem

Consider the primal maximization problem that we discussed earlier in this chapter. The primal objective function that the firm wished to maximize was

$$\pi C = \$2.50Q_c + \$1.00Q_w,$$

where Q_C and Q_W were the quantities of champagne and wine, respectively, to be produced by the firm, and $2.50 and $1.00 were their respective profit contributions per unit. This objective function was to be maximized subject to the following constraints (see Table 8–2):

Fermenting	$3Q_c + Q_w \leq 600,$
Bottling	$2Q_c + Q_w \leq 500,$ and
Champagne purifying	$Q_c \qquad \leq 150,$

where Q_c and Q_w are ≥ 0.

The corresponding dual program is concerned with finding the *minimum* values that can be assigned to the three inputs represented by the capacity constraints and still account for *all* of the unit profit contribution of each product. These minimum values of the fixed inputs represent their marginal value or opportunity cost to the firm in terms of the profit contribution that results from their use by the firm.

Thus the dual objective function that the firm wishes to minimize in this case is

$$TOC = 600V_F + 500V_B + 150V_P,$$

where TOC is the total opportunity cost to the firm of the three resources, V_F is the marginal opportunity cost of the fixed resources used in fermentation, V_B is the marginal opportunity cost of the fixed bottling resources, and V_P is the marginal opportunity cost of the fixed champagne purifying resources. The coefficients 600, 500, and 150 represent the total available amounts of fixed resources used in fermenting, bottling, and champagne purifying, respectively.

As should be expected, the constraints set limits on the values to be assigned to the three resources, and these limits are stated in terms of the unit profit contribution of each product. Accordingly, the constraints are

(8–7)
$$3V_F + 2V_B + V_P \geq \$2.50,$$

and

(8–8)
$$V_F + V_B \geq \$1.00.$$

These two constraints state that the sum of the marginal value or opportunity cost of each input times the amount of that input used to produce a unit of a particular product must be greater than or equal to the unit profit contribution for that product. Thus the first constraint applies to champagne and indicates that three units of the fixed fermenting resource, two units of the fixed bottling resource, and one unit of the champagne purifying resource are needed to produce one bottle of champagne with unit profit contribution of $2.50. A similar interpretation can be made of the second constraint, which applies to wine.

Since it is difficult to graph in three-dimensional space (V_F, V_B, and V_P necessitate three dimensions), we shall solve the dual program algebraically. First, as with the primal, the inequalities must be transformed into equalities by adding new variables:

$$3V_F + 2V_B + V_P - L_c = \$2.50,$$

and

$$V_F + V_B - L_w = \$1.00,$$

where L_c and L_w are greater than or equal to zero. In this case L_c represents the *net* opportunity cost to the firm of producing champagne, and L_w represents the *net* opportunity cost of producing wine.[2] If, for example, L_c were positive, it would indicate to the firm that the opportunity cost of the resources used in producing a bottle of champagne was greater than its unit profit contribution. In this case the profit-maximizing firm would not produce *any* champagne and the optimal Q_C would be zero. A similar interpretation holds for L_w.

Unfortunately, if we do not already know the optimal Q_c and Q_w (and since we cannot easily eliminate any *un*feasible solutions by graphing), we have ten possible solution points to consider.[3] Recall that at any boundary corner of the feasible region there will be *at least* a sufficient number of zero-valued variables in the constraint equations so that the number of remaining variables is equal to (or possibly less than) the number of constraints. We have listed the results for all ten possibilities as follows:

Point 1

$V_F = 0, L_c = 0, L_w = 0$
$V_B = \$1.00, V_P = \$.50$
$TOC = 600(0) + 500(\$1.00) + 150(\$.50)$
$\quad = \$575$

Point 2

$V_B = 0, L_c = 0, L_w = 0$
$V_F = \$1.00, V_P = -\$.50$
Not a feasible solution, $V_P < 0$

Point 3

$V_P = 0, L_c = 0, L_w = 0$
$V_F = \$.50, V_B = \$.50$
$TOC = 600(\$.50) + 500(\$.50) + 150(0)$
$\quad = \$550$

Point 4

$V_F = 0, V_B = 0, L_c = 0$
$V_P = \$2.50, L_w = -\$1.00$
Also not a feasible solution, as $L_W < 0$

Point 5

$V_F = 0, V_B = 0, L_w = 0$
Impossible—violates the second constraint

Point 6

$V_F = 0, V_P = 0, L_c = 0$
$V_B = \$1.25, L_w = \$.25$
$TOC = 600(0) + 500(\$1.25) + 150(0)$
$\quad = \$625$

---

2 The *net* opportunity cost is the cost incurred by the firm from producing a particular product because the opportunity cost of the fixed resources used up is greater than the profit contribution of the product.
3 The number of possible solution points is obtained by finding the number of possible combinations of five things taken three at a time, since there are five variables (three of which must be zero at any solution point). The formula for the number of possible combinations of five things taken three at a time is

$$C_3^5 = \frac{5!}{3!\,2!} = \frac{5 \cdot 4 \cdot 3 \cdot 2 \cdot 1}{3 \cdot 2 \cdot 1 \cdot 2 \cdot 1} = 10.$$

Point 7

$V_F = 0$, $V_P = 0$, $L_w = 0$

$V_B = \$1.00$, $L_c = -\$.50$

Not a feasible solution, $L_C < 0$

Point 8

$V_B = 0$, $V_P = 0$, $L_c = 0$

$V_F = \$.83$, $L_w = -\$.17$

Not a feasible solution, $L_w < 0$

Point 9

$V_B = 0$, $V_P = 0$, $L_w = 0$

$V_F = \$1.00$, $L_c = \$.50$

$TOC = 600(\$1.00) + 500(0) + 150(0)$

$= \$600$

Point 10

$V_F = 0$, $V_B = 0$, $V_P = 0$

$L_C = -\$2.50$, $L_w = -\$1.00$

Not a feasible solution, as L_C

and L_w are negative

By examining the solution values at the ten points, we find that the opportunity cost for the firm is minimized at point 3, where $V_F = \$.50$, $V_B = \$.50$, $V_P = 0$, $L_c = 0$, $L_w = 0$, and $TOC = \$550$. Moreover, as we interpret the meaning of these values and relate them to the primal solution, it will become obvious that, given the primal solution, we could have immediately picked point 3 as the optimal solution to the dual program.

First, L_c and L_w being equal to zero means that for both champagne and wine the sum of the opportunity cost valuations placed on the resources necessary to produce one unit of each product is just equal to the respective unit profit contributions of both wine and champagne, and both products will therefore be produced. That V_P is zero indicates that the opportunity cost of using the fixed champagne purifying resources is zero, which means that at the optimal point there is excess or slack champagne purifying capacity. Thus, since we knew from the primal that at the optimal point Q_c and Q_w were positive, we then knew that at the optimal point for the dual program L_c and L_w must be zero. We also knew from the primal program solution that there was excess champagne purifying capacity, so that V_P must be equal to zero.

The value of V_F indicates the marginal effect the fixed fermenting input has on the level of profits for the firm. Thus, another unit of the fixed fermenting resource would add \$.50 to the total profit of the firm. A similar interpretation of V_B holds for the fixed bottling resource. If the market price of a unit of these resources is below \$.50, the firm may wish to make plans to increase its fermenting and/or bottling capacity in the future. It may also wish to reduce its champagne purifying capacity. Note also that the minimum value of TOC (equal to \$550) is equal to the maximum πC, which is as it should be, since it states that the opportunity cost valuation of the fixed resources is equal to their contribution to the firm's profit at the optimal point.

In the next section, we construct and solve the dual program for the primal cost minimization problem discussed earlier in the chapter.

Dual Maximization Problem

In this section we will discuss the dual to the cost minimization problem presented earlier. The original objective was to minimize

$$TC = \$500Q_1 + \$400Q_2,$$

where TC was total advertising cost, Q_1 was the number of advertisements in Magazine 1, and Q_2 was the number of advertisements in Magazine 2. The firm wished to minimize TC subject to the following constraints:

Age	$20{,}000Q_1 + 30{,}000Q_2 \geq 600{,}000,$
Income	$15{,}000Q_1 + 5{,}000Q_2 \geq 180{,}000,$ and
Stereo ownership	$10{,}000Q_1 + 10{,}000Q_2 \geq 260{,}000.$

These three constraints state that the firm wishes the advertisements to reach at least 600,000 people under 50 years of age, at least 180,000 people with incomes of \$40,000 or greater, and at least 260,000 people who already own stereo systems.

For the dual program, the objective now becomes to maximize

$$Z = 600{,}000V_A + 180{,}000V_I + 260{,}000V_O$$

subject to the constraints that

$$20{,}000V_A + 15{,}000V_I + 10{,}000V_O \leq \$500 \text{ (Magazine 1)},$$

and

$$30{,}000V_A + 5{,}000V_I + 10{,}000V_O \leq \$400 \text{ (Magazine 2)}.$$

In this case Z represents an imputed value or cost to the firm of the three age, income, and ownership constraints in the primal program, which is obtained by finding an imputed value that is really the *marginal cost* to the firm of changing each individual constraint. The first constraint for the dual program states that the marginal cost to the firm of the age constraint times 20,000 (the number of people under age 50 that an advertisement in Magazine 1 reaches) plus the marginal cost to the firm of the income constraint times 15,000 (the number of people with annual incomes of at least \$40,000 that one advertisement in Magazine 1 reaches) plus the marginal cost to the firm of the stereo ownership constraint times 10,000 (the number of people who own stereo systems who are reached by an advertisement in Magazine 1) must be less than or equal to \$500 (the cost of placing one advertisement in Magazine 1). A similar interpretation holds for the second constraint. Basically, the constraints state that the imputed value or marginal cost of each of the primal constraints times the number of people in each category reached by an advertisement in a particular magazine must be less than or equal to the cost of such an ad.

If we transform the constraints into equalities, we obtain

$$20{,}000V_A + 15{,}000V_I + 10{,}000V_O + L_1 = 500,$$

and

$$30{,}000V_A + 5{,}000V_I + 10{,}000V_O + L_2 = 400.$$

The two variables L_1 and L_2 represent the net opportunity cost or *relative inefficiency* of using Magazine 1 and Magazine 2, respectively, as advertising media. If neither magazine is relatively inefficient, L_1 and L_2 will both be zero and the firm will advertise in both magazines.

At the optimal primal solution, we found TC = \$10,900, Q_1 = 5, Q_2 = 21, S_A = 130,000, S_I = 0, and S_O = 0. Since Q_1 and Q_2 are positive, we know that L_1 and L_2 must be zero at the optimal primal solution; that is, both magazines are relatively efficient advertising media. As before, since S_A is positive, there is an excess over the minimum required number of people under age 50 being reached at the optimal point; therefore, the marginal cost of increasing the age constraint, V_A, must be zero at that point. Following a similar line of reasoning, we can also conclude that at the optimal point, V_O and V_I must be positive. Thus we can conclude that the optimal point for the dual program will be found where L_1, L_2, and V_A equal 0.

Substituting these values into the dual constraint equations, we get

$$15{,}000V_I + 10{,}000V_O = \$500,$$

and

$$5{,}000V_I + 10{,}000V_O = \$400.$$

Subtracting the second equation from the first, we obtain $10{,}000V_I$ = \$100, or V_I = \$.01. Substituting V_I = \$.01 in the second equation, we find that V_O = \$.035. We can now find that optimal Z = 600,000(0) + 180,000(\$.01) + 260,000(\$.035) = \$10,900, the minimum value we found for TC in the primal program.

To utilize the values obtained for V_I and V_O, the firm must have a reliable estimate of the actual value or marginal benefit to the firm (in terms of increased profit contribution) obtained by increasing the income and stereo ownership constraints, respectively. For example, if the marginal benefit from increasing the income constraint is greater than \$.01, the firm should consider increasing this constraint. On the other hand, if the marginal benefit is less than \$.01, the firm should consider reducing the minimum number of people it reaches who have annual incomes of at least \$40,000. A similar analysis would apply for the stereo ownership constraint.

Summary of How to Construct the Dual Program

In this section we summarize the steps for setting up the dual program from the primal.

1. The dual objective function will be obtained by assigning a valuation variable to each of the primal constraints and summing the values of these variables multiplied by the numbers that represent the maximum or minimum values of their respective primal constraints. If the primal objective function is to be maximized, the dual objective function should be minimized, and vice versa.
2. The dual constraint inequalities are obtained by finding the sum of each *valuation variable* in the dual objective function multiplied by the *coefficient* of the corresponding *primal objective function* variable in the corresponding primal constraint. There will be one dual program constraint for each primal decision (objective function) variable. Also, the direction of the dual program constraint inequalities will be the reverse of those in the primal program constraints.

We present two general examples of the relationships between the primal and the dual linear programs, as follows:

■ Example 1

Primal

Maximize $\pi = \pi_1 X_1 + \pi_2 X_2$

Subject to $a_1 X_1 + b_1 X_2 \le Y_1$,

$\quad\quad a_2 X_1 + b_2 X_2 \le Y_2$,

$\quad\quad a_3 X_1 + b_3 X_2 \le Y_3$,

$\quad\quad$ and $X_1, X_2 \ge 0$.

Dual

Minimize $TC = Y_1 V_1 + Y_2 V_2 + Y_3 V_3$

Subject to $a_1 V_1 + a_2 V_2 + a_3 V_3 \ge \pi_1$,

$\quad\quad b_1 V_1 + b_2 V_2 + b_3 V_3 \ge \pi_2$,

$\quad\quad$ and $V_1, V_2, V_3 \ge 0$.

■ Example 2

Primal

Minimize $TOC = C_1 X_1 + C_2 X_2$

Subject to $a_1 X_1 + b_2 X_2 \ge Y_1$,

$\quad\quad a_2 X_1 + b_2 X_2 \ge Y_2$,

$\quad\quad a_3 X_1 + b_3 X_2 \ge Y_3$,

$\quad\quad$ and $X_1, X_2 \ge 0$.

Dual

Maximize $Z = Y_1 V_1 + Y_2 V_2 + Y_3 V_3$

Subject to $a_1 V_1 + a_2 V_2 + a_3 V_3 \le C_1$,

$\quad\quad b_1 V_1 + b_2 V_2 + b_3 V_3 \le C_2$,

$\quad\quad$ and $V_1, V_2, V_3 \ge 0$.

ACTIVITY ANALYSIS: ONE PRODUCT

In this final section of the chapter, we discuss another kind of decision problem for which linear programming is useful. This is a situation where, given fixed amounts of certain inputs, a firm wishes to determine the optimal combination of processes that it should use to produce the greatest quantity possible of a single product. A type of activity analysis is needed in this case, where each of the processes may be considered to be an activity.

For example, suppose a firm can produce a product using any one of three different processes. Using process A, the firm needs three units of capital and one unit of labor to produce one unit of the final product. Using the second process, process B, the firm needs two units of capital and two units of labor to produce one unit of output. If the firm uses process C, it requires one unit of capital and four units of labor to produce one unit of the product. In Figure 8–7 we have drawn three rays, each of which represents a different process. Points A_1, A_2, A_3, and A_4 represent the inputs needed to produce one, two, three, and four units of output, respectively, using process A. A similar interpretation holds for B_1, B_2, B_3, and B_4 and for C_1, C_2, C_3, and C_4. We have also drawn *isoquants* for levels of *output* equal to one, two, three, and four units, where the segment of an isoquant between two production process rays implies that a *combination* of the two processes is being used to produce that particular level of output.

Figure 8–7   Three Production Process Rays and Isoquant Curves for Four Levels of Output

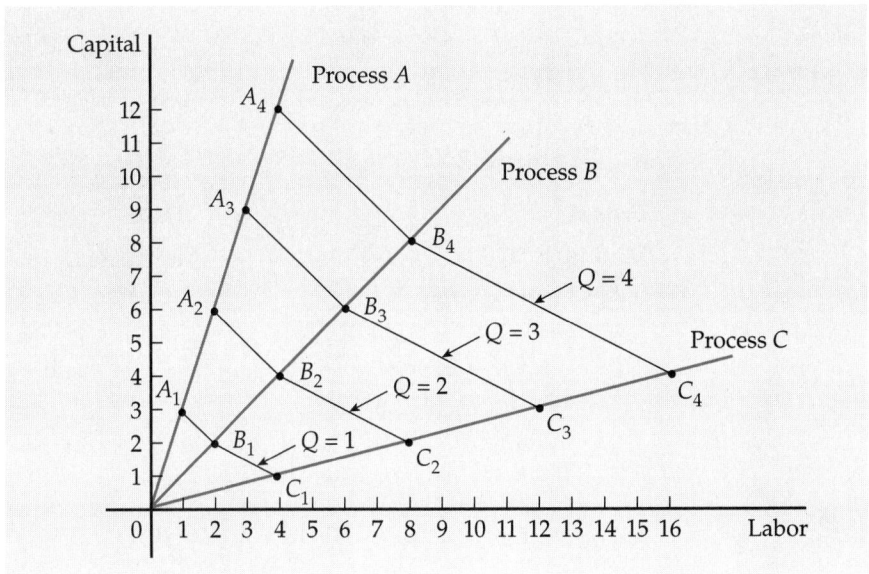

Using process A, the firm needs three units of capital and one unit of labor to produce one unit of the final product. Using process B, the firm needs two units of capital and two units of labor to produce one unit of the final product. Using process C, it needs one unit of capital and four units of labor for each unit of output.

Figure 8–8   The Least Cost Process for Producing Three Units of Output

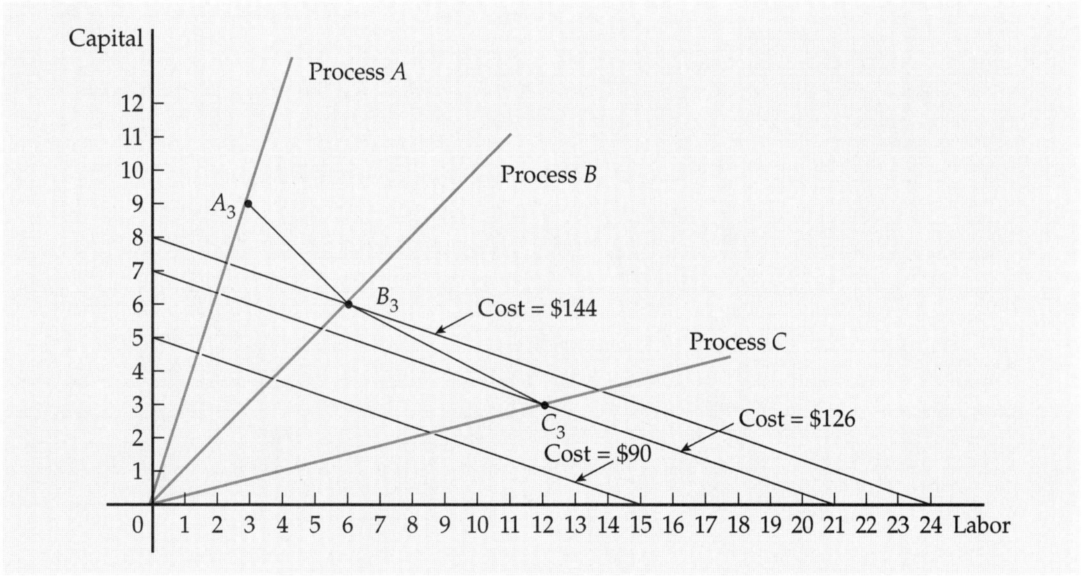

Three isocost lines, for $90, $126, and $144, respectively, are shown here. $A_3B_3C_3$ is the isoquant for three units of output. The least cost combination of inputs for three units of output is at C_3 with a cost of $126.

If the firm wishes to find the production process that would minimize the cost of producing a particular level of output, say three units, it can use an isocost and isoquant analysis similar to that presented in Chapter 5. As before, the firm would wish to be on the lowest isocost line possible and still achieve the desired level of production.[4]

In Figure 8–8 we have drawn three isocost lines for cost levels of $90, $126, and $144, respectively, assuming the price of a unit of capital is $18 and the price of a unit of labor is $6. We have also drawn the isoquant curve for $Q = 3$. In this case we see that the least cost process for producing three units of output is process C, where the quantity used of capital is three units, the quantity used of labor is twelve units, and total cost is $126.

However, suppose the goal of the firm is to produce the maximum level of output possible, given that it has available only four units of capital and ten units of the skilled labor necessary to manufacture this product. In Figure 8–9

---

4 At the optimal point, however, the marginal rate of substitution of labor for capital would not necessarily equal (minus-one times) the ratio of the price of labor to the price of capital. In Figure 8–8 the slope of the isocost line is not equal to the slope of the isoquant at the optimal input combination.

Figure 8–9   Optimal Production Processes, Given Input Constraints

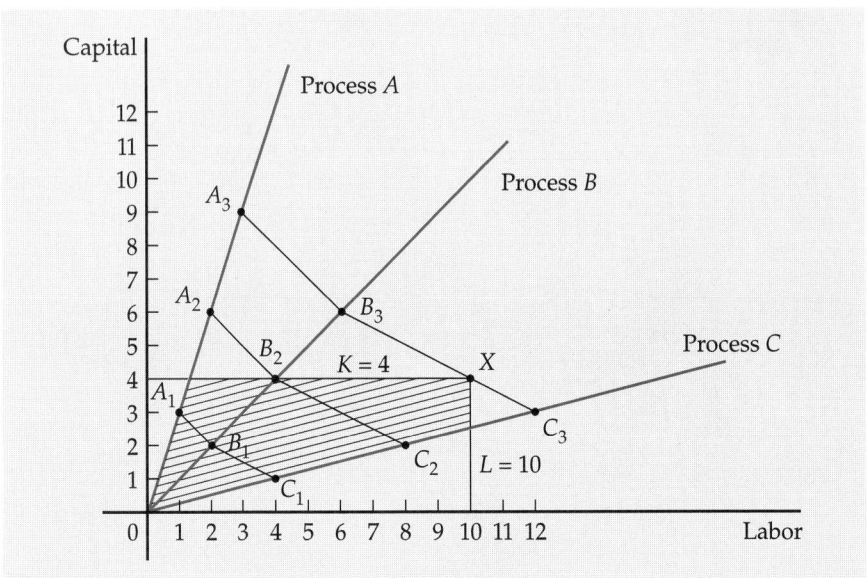

The production process rays are the same as in Figures 8–7 and 8–8. In this case, however, only four units of capital and ten units of labor are available. The feasible region is now indicated by the diagonal lines.

we have drawn the three production process rays; the isoquant curves for the production of one, two, and three units of output; and the input constraints. We have also shaded in the feasible region of production.

It is obvious from Figure 8–9 that, given these input constraints, the greatest level of output that this firm can produce is three units, using the combination of process B and process C represented by point X. We can find the number of units to be produced by each process by drawing a line parallel to the process C ray beginning at point X and continuing toward the origin until it touches the process B ray, which it does at B_1 in Figure 8–10. The fact that this line intersects the process B ray at B_1 indicates that one unit of output should be produced using process B and that the remainder, two units in this case, should be produced using process C.

We could also easily solve for the optimal quantity to be produced by each production process using an algebraic method. We can express the objective of the firm as to maximize

$$Q_A + Q_B + Q_C,$$

where

Figure 8–10   Finding the Optimal Production Process Combination

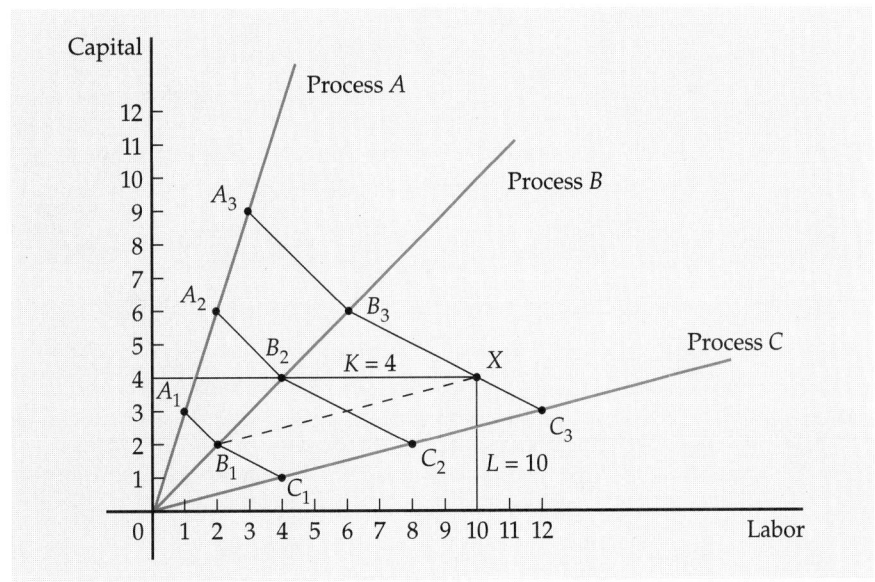

The maximum amount of output that can be produced with four units of capital and ten units of labor is three using a combination of processes B and C (point X). Line segment B_1X indicates that one unit should be produced using process B and two units using process C.

Q_A is the quantity of output produced by process A,
Q_B is the quantity produced by process B, and
Q_C is the quantity produced by process C.

The input constraints will be

Capital $3Q_A + 2Q_B + (1)Q_C \leq 4$, and

Labor $(1)Q_A + 2Q_B + 4Q_C \leq 10$.

The first constraint indicates that the number of units of capital it takes to produce one unit of output using process A times Q_A *plus* the units of capital necessary to produce one unit of output using process B times Q_B *plus* the units of capital necessary to produce one unit of output using process C times Q_C must be less than or equal to four units—the total amount of capital available. A similar interpretation can be given to the labor constraint.

If we add a slack variable for capital in the first equation and a slack variable for labor in the second equation, we get

$$3Q_A + 2Q_B + Q_C + S_K = 4,$$

and

$$Q_A + 2Q_B + 4Q_C + S_L = 10.$$

We know from Figure 8–9 that at the optimal point S_K, S_L, and Q_A equal zero. Substituting these values into the preceding equations, we obtain

$$2Q_B + Q_C = 4,$$

and

$$2Q_B + 4Q_C = 10,$$

and subtracting the second equation from the first, $-3Q_C = -6$ or $Q_C = 2$. We then can find $Q_B = 1$, which gives us the same solution as we found graphically. A combination of graphical and algebraic methods, where feasible, may offer the easiest and most precise solution.

SUMMARY

Linear Programming as an Optimizing Tool

In this chapter we have discussed linear programming, a mathematical decision-making tool particularly useful when a firm faces an optimizing problem that can be specified in terms of a linear objective function and linear constraints in the form of inequalities. The primal program directly specifies the objective of the firm in terms of the decision variables, whereas the dual program gives information regarding various opportunity costs connected with the problem. However, as we demonstrated, it is possible to find the optimal values of the decision variables using either the primal or the dual program.

In this chapter we have demonstrated only the simplest algebraic and graphical methods of solving linear programs in order to give some examples of how this tool can be used by business without being too complex. In many real-world situations with more variables than those in our examples, decision makers are likely to utilize more sophisticated algebraic techniques, such as the simplex method, as well as the computer. Moreover, linear programming is only one of a class of mathematical tools called mathematical programming. These other techniques, including nonlinear programming and dynamic programming, are beyond the scope of this book, but the interested reader can learn more about them from the sources in the list of references at the end of this chapter.

QUESTIONS

1. Compare the techniques of linear programming and calculus. For what types of decision problems is calculus more useful? For what types of decision problems is linear programming more useful?
2. Give some examples of specific business decisions where linear programming could be useful.
3. Why is maximizing the *total profit contribution* of the firm's inputs equivalent to maximizing its total profit in the short run?
4. What type of information does one get by solving the dual program that one does not obtain by solving the primal program? Give an example.
5. Why may the dual problem be easier to solve than the primal problem? How can the optimal values of the primal problem be found from those of the dual? Give an example.

PROBLEMS

1. Polynesian Pineapple, Inc., is a company that imports raw pineapples. It markets two products, canned pineapple slices and raw pineapples. Polynesian has capacity limitations in three areas: warehouse space, canning facilities, and crating facilities. A raw pineapple requires .6 of a unit of warehouse space before it is shipped, .2 of a unit of crating facilities, and no canning facilities. One can of pineapple slices requires .3 of a unit of warehouse space, .2 of a unit of crating facilities, and .1 of a unit of canning facilities.

   The total available monthly amount of warehouse space is 1,200,000 units; of crating facilities, 600,000 units; and of canning facilities, 250,000 units. The profit contribution is $.20 per raw pineapple and $.25 per can of slices.
   a. Find the monthly profit-maximizing quantities of raw and canned pineapple, respectively, for Polynesian Pineapple.
   b. What is the total monthly profit contribution from pineapples in part (a)?
2. Holiday on Wheels (HOW) manufactures two types of recreational vehicles. One is a trailer that is towed behind a car or pickup, and the other is a motorized vehicle that moves under its own power. HOW is trying to determine the optimal combination of trailers and motor homes to produce per day, given that three of the inputs (power train assembly, paint and trim line, and body assembly) needed to produce these products are

available in limited amounts. Manufacture of one motor home requires 2.0 hours of power train assembly capacity, 2.5 hours of paint and trim capacity, and 3.0 hours of body assembly capacity, whereas the production of one trailer requires only 2.0 hours of paint and trim capacity and 2.0 hours of body assembly capacity.

HOW has available on a daily basis 300 hours of power train assembly capacity, 500 hours of paint and trim capacity, and 540 hours of body assembly capacity. The profit contribution of a motor home is $4,000, while that of a trailer is $3,000.

a. Using both algebraic and graphical solution methods, find the profit-maximizing combination of motor homes and travel trailers that HOW should produce daily.

b. What is HOW's daily contribution to profit at the optimal point?

3. Set up the dual program for Holiday on Wheels using the data in Problem 2.

a. What useful information would Holiday on Wheels obtain by solving the dual program? Explain.

b. What is the optimal solution to this dual program?

c. State the economic significance of the values of each of the dual variables at the optimal point.

4. Hill Country Concrete, Inc. (HCC) does asphalt and concrete paving. HCC is now trying to make a short-run decision on the optimal mix of asphalt and concrete paving, given capacity constraints involving road grader, roller, and power trowel time. The maximum number of hours of road grader time available per month is 640; of roller time, 1,500; of power trowel time, 150. It takes 2 hours of road grader time and 5 hours of roller time for each 1,000 square feet of asphalt paving; and each 1,000 square feet of concrete paving requires 2 hours of road grader time, 3 hours of roller time, and .5 hour of power trowel time. The profit contribution for 1,000 square feet of asphalt paving is $200; for 1,000 square feet of concrete paving it is $300.

a. How many square feet of concrete paving and of asphalt paving should HCC do per month to maximize profit? Why? Use both graphical and algebraic solution methods.

b. What is the total monthly profit contribution from paving for Hill Country Concrete?

5. Set up the dual program for Hill Country Concrete using the data in Problem 4.

a. What economic interpretation can be given to each of the dual decision variables, the objective function, and the constraints?

b. At the optimal point, what is the opportunity cost associated with using the road grader? The roller? The power trowel?

c. At the optimal point, what is the net opportunity cost to HCC of doing asphalt paving? Of doing concrete paving? Why?

6. A firm that manufactures and retails a variety of women's clothes from the moderately priced department store lines to the more expensive bou-

tique styles is expanding its market and, accordingly, is trying to determine how many stores of each type it will lease. The firm wishes to lease its department store space in large shopping areas, such as larger malls. On the other hand, the boutique stores that the firm wishes to lease are in small, elite shopping centers in very high income areas of cities. The choice department stores lease for $10,000 per month, and boutique stores in good locations lease for $2,000 per month.

Given its product mix, the firm wishes to be in locations such that *at least* 10,500 customers under 45 years of age and at least 1,150 customers with annual household incomes over $50,000 will, on the average, visit its stores daily. Moreover, the firm believes that 420 people under 45 years of age and 5 people with incomes over $50,000 will visit each of the department stores daily, while an average of 20 people under 45 years of age and 10 people with annual incomes over $50,000 will visit each of its boutique stores daily.

a. Given the above information, how many of each type of store should the firm lease if it wishes to minimize leasing costs?

b. What is the total cost to the firm of leasing these stores at its optimal point?

c. What is the marginal cost to the firm of increasing the age constraint? The income constraint?

d. Given your answers in part (c), do you think the firm should consider changing the income or age constraints and/or other alternatives to leasing stores? Why or why not?

7. A firm can manufacture its product using any one or a combination of three processes. Production of 1 unit of output per month using process *A* requires 10 units of capital and 2 units of labor, whereas production of 1 unit of output using process *B* requires 5 units of capital and 5 units of labor, and production of 1 unit of output using process *C* requires 3 units of capital and 10 units of labor. Since this product is classified top secret by the government and all inputs must receive a security clearance, there are fixed amounts of capital and of labor available to the firm in the short run. In fact, at this point in time, the firm has available on a monthly basis 24 units of labor and 40 units of capital.

a. Find the maximum quantity of output that this firm can produce per month under these constraints.

b. How much of this output is produced using each of the three available processes?

8. A commercial feedlot operation, Best-Fed Beef, Inc. (BFB) is trying to determine the least cost combination of two types of feed that will meet the nutritional requirements of its cattle. The first kind of feed is a grain mixture, and each ton of grain contains, on the average, 200 pounds of protein, 1,000 pounds of carbohydrates, and 300 pounds of roughage plus 500 pounds of miscellaneous minerals, vitamins, fats, and water. The second feed is a type of silage, and an average ton of silage contains 40 pounds of protein, 400 pounds of carbohydrates, and 600 pounds of

roughage, as well as a substantial amount of water and some minerals, fats, and vitamins.

BFB believes that its cattle need a minimum of 1,200 pounds of protein, 8,000 pounds of carbohydrates, and 3,600 pounds of roughage daily. The grain mixture costs $80 per ton, and the silage costs $30 per ton.

a. Find the least cost combination of grain and silage that will meet the daily nutritional requirements of BFB's cattle.

b. What is the total cost of the optimal combination of feeds found in part (a)?

c. Set up the dual program, find its optimal solution, and explain the economic significance of the values you found for the dual decision variables.

d. How would the information that you found in part (c) be useful to BFB? Why?

9. Malibu Motor Company is trying to decide the optimal number of two automobile models to maintain in inventory. Model 1 is a mid-sized car, and Model 2 is a luxury sports car. The company has a showroom and lot space constraint, a financing constraint, and a constraint on the number of Model 2 cars that the manufacturer will allow it to keep in inventory. One car of Model 1 type takes up 600 square feet of showroom or lot space, and one car of Model 2 type takes up 450 square feet of space. The firm would need $3,200 financing for each car of Model 1 and $6,400 for each car of Model 2. Moreover, Malibu can keep a maximum number of 40 Model 2 cars on hand in inventory. The maximum total amount of showroom and lot space available is 60,000 square feet, while the maximum total amount of financing available is $400,000. The profit contribution is $1,000 per Model 1 car and $3,000 per Model 2 car.

a. Using *both* algebraic and graphical solution methods, find the optimal combination of Model 1 and Model 2 cars for Malibu Motors.

b. What is the total profit contribution at the point you found in part (a)? What are the values of all slack variables?

c. What is the marginal value to the firm of one more square foot of showroom or lot space? Of one more dollar of financing?

10. Intergalactic Products, Inc. (IPI) manufactures two different products, surgical gloves and toy balloons. It has capacity limitations on three inputs in the production process: latex heating, injection molding, and sterile packaging. Specifically, it has 780 units of latex heating capacity, 630 units of injection molding capacity, and 180 units of sterile packaging capacity available per day. Both surgical gloves and balloons are sold to distributors in boxes of 500. For IPI, profit contribution per box of gloves is $100, while that per box of balloons is $40. Production of one box of surgical gloves requires 2.4 units of latex heating, 2.8 units of injection molding, and one unit of sterile packaging. Production of one box of balloons requires 4 units of latex heating, 2 units of injection molding, and no sterile packaging.

a. Using both algebraic and graphical solution methods, find the optimal combination of surgical gloves and toy balloons that IPI must produce to maximize its total profit. What are the values of the slack variables at this point?

b. What is the total profit contribution for IPI at the point you found in part (a)?

c. How much would the per-unit profit contribution of surgical gloves have to decrease to change the optimal combination of surgical gloves and toy balloons?

This problem can be solved with Decision Assistant.

D1. Abe Jackson learned the cabinetmaking business from his father, as his father did before him. Because pride is built into every cabinet Abe and his crew make, quantity demanded always seems to exceed quantity supplied. In addition, the business expands slowly because Abe himself carefully selects each worker. Abe often says he would rather lose a sale than produce a cabinet that his grandfather could not be proud of. The summer of this year has proved to be no exception with regard to demand.

Abe's son, Robert, who has been away at college, is working in the shop as he has in summers past. However, this year Robert brings more to his summer job than just his skills in cabinetmaking. Having just completed a college course in linear programming, Robert knows he can assist his father even more this year. In previous years, production scheduling and determination of the product mix has been completed by Abe, who relied on his past experiences and intuition. This year Abe has decided to produce equal quantities (5 per day) of each type of cabinet. Robert thinks he can do better, although it will be no easy task to convince his father there might be a "better way."

Before setting out to convince his father, Robert gathers the following data about the shop's operation:

• Two basic styles of cabinets are being produced: standard and designer. Standard cabinets are cut, sanded, stained, and varnished in the shop. Designer cabinets are produced the same as standard cabinets with the addition of an extra step of applying antiquing. The standard cabinet has a profit contribution of $12 while the designer cabinet contributes $9 in profit.

• All cutting and sanding is done in the preparation department. It takes 1 hour to cut either type of cabinet. A total of 10 hours per day could be devoted to the cutting and sanding of cabinets.

• Staining and finishing is done in the finishing department where a total of 32 hours per day are available for these activities. It takes 4 hours to stain and finish each standard cabinet and 2 hours to stain and finish each designer cabinet. (Designer cabinets actually take less time to stain because they will be antiqued.)

• Between the staining and finishing steps in the finishing department, each designer cabinet goes to the antiquing department where skilled craftspeople apply a special antiquing. A total of 21 hours per day are available in the antiquing department. It requires 3 hours for each designer cabinet to go through this step.

Armed with this data, Robert feels confident he can improve on the shop's performance. Do you agree? Use the linear programming (graphical method) tool in the *Managerial Economics Decision Assistant* to help you answer the following questions:

a. How many cabinets of each type will Robert recommend be produced?

b. How much profit will the shop make under Abe's plan (calculate manually) and under Robert's plan?

c. Under Robert's proposed solution, how many "extra" hours (if any) will be available in each of the three departments: preparation, finishing, and antiquing?

Use the linear programming (simplex method) tool in the *Managerial Economics Decision Assistant* to assist you with working the dual program to answer the following questions (you will need to restate your constraints and objective function):

d. If the business were to expand, which department(s) would need to be expanded?

e. How much should Abe be willing to pay to expand each department?

SELECTED REFERENCES

Chiang, Alpha C. *Fundamental Methods of Mathematical Economics*, 3d ed. New York: McGraw-Hill, 1984, Chapters 19–21.

Childress, Robert L. *Mathematics for Managerial Decisions*, 2d ed. Englewood Cliffs, N.J.: Prentice-Hall, 1989, Chapters 5–8.

Dorfman, Robert. "Mathematical, or Linear, Programming," *American Economic Review*, XLIII (December 1953), pp. 797–825.

Garvin, W. W., H. W. Crandall, J. B. John, and R. A. Spellman. "Applications of Linear Programming in the Oil Industry," *Management Science* III (July 1957), pp. 407–430.

Kamien, Morton I., and Nancy L. Schwartz. *Dynamic Optimization: The Calculus of Variations and Optimal Control in Economics and Management*. New York: North Holland, 1981.

Silberberg, Eugene. *The Structure of Economic Analysis*, 2d ed. New York: McGraw-Hill, 1990, Chapter 14.

Takayama, Akira. *Mathematical Economics*, 2d ed. Hinsdale, Ill.: Dryden Press, 1985, Chapter 1.

INTEGRATING CASE 2A

Frontier Concrete Products Company[1]

Frontier Concrete Products Company is planning to open a new concrete plant in another city. The owner-manager of the company is currently trying to determine the optimal size plant to build, given the estimated cost and revenue data presented in Table 1.

The data in Table 1 show that Frontier Concrete Company has determined that there are at least 4 different combinations of plant size and labor that would enable the firm to produce a given level of output. Since the company believes that its optimal level of output will be between 30 and 60 cubic yards of concrete per hour, it is considering only 12 different plant sizes.

Table 1   Various Combinations of Capital and Labor Needed to Produce 30, 45, and 60 Cubic Yards of Concrete per Hour

Q = 30 Cubic Yards per Hour

Plant 1	Plant 2	Plant 3	Plant 4
K = 4	K = 3	K = 2	K = 1
L = 1	L = 2	L = 5	L = 10

Q = 45 Cubic Yards per Hour

Plant 5	Plant 6	Plant 7	Plant 8
K = 6	K = 4.5	K = 3	K = 1.5
L = 1.5	L = 3	L = 7.5	L = 15

Q = 60 Cubic Yards per Hour

Plant 9	Plant 10	Plant 11	Plant 12
K = 8	K = 6	K = 4	K = 2
L = 2	L = 4	L = 10	L = 20

---

1 This case is based on production and cost information from an antitrust case in the ready-mix concrete industry.

In Table 1 the company has prepared the input figures in terms of standardized units of capital and standardized units of labor. A unit of capital is estimated to increase the expenses (depreciation, repairs and maintenance, interest expense, and utilities) of the firm by $18,000 per year, based on a year consisting of 260 eight-hour working days. The estimated cost to the firm for one unit of labor is $7.00 per hour. Other costs—for raw materials and delivery, which were not included in Table 1—are estimated to be as follows (*per cubic yard* of concrete produced):

Aggregate (rock)	$3.34
Cement	$7.50
Delivery costs	$4.00

The company has also estimated the demand for its product, and these figures are presented in Table 2.

Table 2   Estimated Demand for Frontier Concrete Produced by the New Plant

Cubic Yards per Hour	Price per Cubic Yard
20	$24.00
30	22.34
40	21.26
50	20.40
60	19.66
70	19.00
80	18.38

QUESTIONS

1. How do Frontier's total manufacturing costs (exclusive of raw materials and delivery costs) vary for each of the four capital-labor combinations given, as output is increased from 30, to 45, to 60 cubic yards per hour? Does it appear that this production function has increasing, decreasing, or constant returns to scale?
2. What are the total costs, including raw materials and delivery costs, for each of the capital-labor combinations in Question 1?
3. Which capital-labor combination is a least cost combination of inputs for each of the three levels of output?

4. Frontier's owner has plotted a curve showing how the minimum total delivered cost for each output varies when all inputs—including capital, labor, raw materials, and delivery costs—are variable. What should this curve be called? Given the preceding data, what does it look like?

5. What are the long-run average cost figures and the long-run marginal cost figures that correspond to the curve drawn in Question 4?

6. What are the firm's total revenue schedules and marginal revenue schedules, given the information presented in Table 2?

7. Suppose that Frontier had decided to build Plant 10. Suppose also that of the $108,000 annual capital expenses connected with the plant, $96,000 were fixed costs and the remainder were variable. If all labor costs are assumed to be variable and a yard of concrete includes the average variable raw material and delivery costs stated previously, what is the break-even point for this plant, assuming the price of concrete is $20 per cubic yard?

8. Based on the values computed in Question 7, what is the profit-maximizing level of output per hour for Frontier Concrete's new plant?

9. Based on the values computed in Questions 5 and 6, what is the profit-maximizing level of output per hour for Frontier Concrete if all inputs are variable? (Assume $LAC = \$16,17$ for any level of output per hour.)

10. If the cost figures presented here are *accounting costs*, what *types* of adjustments do you think would be needed to transform them into *economic cost* figures?

INTEGRATING CASE 2B

Shanghai Magnificent Harmony Foundry I

X. C. Fei is in charge of export sales analysis for a large firm in the People's Republic of China, Shanghai Magnificent Harmony Foundry (SMHF). Most of the foundry's cast-iron output has been destined for the domestic market, principally the locomotive, rail-car, and machinery industries. It has been suggested to Fei that he investigate the overseas market for manhole covers, a product that is simple to manufacture and for which there seems to be endless demand. The target market he has chosen is the United States. Fei's research assistant has found that India is currently the main source of cast-iron manhole covers that are imported into the United States and that many small Indian foundries make the product. Further, competition is always forthcoming from other less-developed countries, since the United States has a favorable trade policy for such producers.

It is evident to Fei that SMHF will have to meet the world market price for the covers. In addition, he believes that the amount of output he wishes to sell can be marketed in the United States without cutting price below the world level. Currently, the covers are selling for $0.48 per pound, landed at U.S. West Coast ports. The tariff on such castings is $.02 per lb., but less-developed-country producers can qualify for trade preferences that will reduce the tariff to zero. India and certain other producers have successfully qualified for the reduction.

A further consideration that has troubled Fei is the price of iron ore, which China imports. He expects that while some of his foreign competitors that do not import iron ore will not experience a change in production costs in the near future, his company may have to pay higher ore prices, which could increase the raw materials cost of cast manhole covers by as much as 20 percent.

The central management committee of SMHF has told Fei that 6,500 short tons per year (one short ton = 2,000 lbs.) of casting capacity can be utilized for the manhole cover exports but that this type of production will have to carry allocated fixed overhead in the amount of 1,500,000 Renminbi Yuan (RY) annually. The plant must sell all dollar proceeds from its exports to the Chinese government at an official fixed rate of 4.8 RY to the U.S. dollar. The government is not expected to change this rate for at least three years.

The committee has requested that Fei prepare a report on the manhole cover exports and has directed that he specifically analyze three cases. First, the best-case scenario, which conforms to (a) obtaining U.S. trade preferences and paying no tariff and (b) not being faced with the 20 percent materials cost increase; second, a case in which the trade preferences are *not* granted, but materials costs remain at their current level; and third, the worst-case scenario, in which the firm does not obtain the trade preferences and also faces a 20 percent increase in raw materials cost.

Fei has been instructed to render the analysis in U.S. dollars, since materials, freight, and the final product are normally priced in dollars in the international market. For the best-case scenario, he has estimated the following unit costs per pound:

Direct materials	$0.10
Fuel	0.11
Direct labor	0.08
Variable selling expenses	0.03

Fei knows that the average U.S. manhole cover weighs 160 pounds and will use this figure to determine how many he can export. Currently, he believes he will be able to sell all of the covers he can make to U.S. buyers, and he foresees no new investment in plant and equipment to produce the output. He has checked into ocean freight rates and figures the transport cost per pound of finished product will be 10 U.S. cents.

QUESTIONS

1. Complete the best-case scenario for Fei's report.
2. Explain how the results would change if materials costs were to remain constant but SMHF could not obtain the U.S. trade preference to eliminate the $.02 per lb. tariff. (Assume SMHF "absorbs" the tariff in its selling price to keep the landed U.S. price at the $0.48 level.)
3. Complete the worst-case scenario, assuming that the tariff must be paid *and* that materials costs rise by 20 percent.

PART 3

Markets and the Behavior of the Firm

9

PERFECT COMPETITION AND MONOPOLY: THE LIMITING CASES

To determine its revenue and therefore its profit-maximizing level of output and product price, the individual business firm must develop some notion of the demand for its product. Certain basic demand propositions were reviewed in Chapter 2 and reintroduced in Chapter 7 in connection with our discussion of the conditions for profit maximization. The present chapter deals exclusively with two theoretical market models that represent the opposite ends of a very broad spectrum of possible market situations in which a given firm might find itself.

The first limiting case is *perfect competition*, a market structure where the firm takes market price as given and therefore needs only to determine what cost/output combination maximizes its net revenue or profit. Our second limiting case is *monopoly*, where there is only one seller of a particular product and the *market* demand curve of consumers is the *firm's* demand curve. Most firms in the real world have to deal with market conditions that lie between the two extremes of perfect competition and monopoly, but we will leave these other market structures until Chapter 10. In this chapter we will concentrate on gaining some insights into how firms in the two extreme situations should act to maximize profits, so that it will be easier to understand how firms that are between the two extremes behave.

PERFECT COMPETITION AND ITS SETTING

We have noted that the perfectly competitive firm is a *price taker* in the sense that it views market price as a given on which it can have no effect. We must now take a closer look, from the viewpoint of the firm, at the market situation that produces such an outcome. Normally, **perfect competition** is described as a product market structure characterized by the following set of conditions:

Under **perfect competition**, there are many small firms, and the individual firm takes the market price as a given.

1. There is a very *large number of buyers and sellers* in the market.
2. The *product* of each seller is identical to that of every other seller (*homogeneous product*).
3. There are *no artificial interferences* with the activities of the buyers and sellers (for example, government price controls).

370

4. All buyers and sellers have *perfect knowledge* of market conditions and of any changes in market conditions that occur.
5. Over the long run (the period of time in which it is possible to build or get rid of a plant), there is *freedom of entry* into or *exit* from the industry.

These conditions have some very important implications as far as the operation of the perfectly competitive model is concerned. For example, the existence of a very large number of buyers and sellers in the market (condition 1) and the situation that products of all firms are identical (condition 2) are the basis for the proposition that the individual firm takes market price as given. If a firm knows (condition 4) that there are many other sellers of a product identical to its own and that there is nothing it or anyone else can do to interfere with the activities of such sellers (condition 3), it will conclude that if it raises price, it will lose all its customers to the other firms, since there is no reason to assume that other firms will also raise price. (There are too many firms to be able to get together and effectively agree on restricting quantity supplied and raising price, as many national farm organizations have discovered.) On the other hand, because there are many buyers in the market willing to pay the going price, the firm has no reason to *lower* price either. In a very important sense, the assumption of perfect competition makes the individual firm insignificant with respect to the total market for its product, and that is why it must take price as given.

Our assumptions also ensure one other result: that firms will enter or leave the perfectly competitive industry over the long run depending on the level of profit in that industry. If there are no artificial barriers to entry and there is perfect knowledge of market conditions, there will be incentives for new firms to be established when the industry is more profitable than other industries. When profit is less than in other industries, some firms will leave the industry. We identify the level of profit necessary to keep the number of firms in the industry constant as "normal profit." If there is **free entry** in *any market structure*, greater than normal profit will lead to entry, and less than normal profit will cause firms to leave. The result, of course, is that industries characterized by freedom of entry will tend toward only normal profit over the long run, which we can think of as a rate of return on investment similar to that attainable in closely related industries. Finally, as stated in Chapter 7, we will consider normal profit to be a *cost of production*, since over the long run, there would be no output produced if the firm's owners did not receive at least a normal return on investment. Thus all of our cost curves for the firm will include normal profit as an opportunity cost.

What we have said thus far allows us to easily paint a verbal picture of the perfectly competitive model. It is a market structure where individual firms, each of which is insignificant with respect to the total market, go about maximizing profit based on a fixed market price and tend over the long run to attain only normal profit. We can, however, supply a good deal more detail regarding how all of this comes about, and we will do so in the sections that follow.

In a market that is characterized by **free entry**, profit serves the function of drawing new firms into the industry when greater than normal and causing them to leave when less than normal.

Market Demand Versus Firm Demand

The demand curve for the homogeneous product of a perfectly competitive *industry* (i.e., all of the firms that produce the same product) is determined by the preferences of consumers. At any given point in time, if this demand curve is "normal" in the economic sense, it will be characterized by an inverse relationship between the going market price for the product and the quantity consumers are willing to purchase per unit of time (that is, price must be lowered to entice consumers to buy a larger quantity). The demand curve in Figure 9–1, D_i, conforms to such a case. The supply curve of the industry, S_i, shows the amounts that producers are willing to place on the market at various prices. In the short run, we expect such a curve to exhibit a direct relationship between price and the quantity supplied, since production cost per unit (particularly marginal cost, as we saw in Chapter 6) rises as the firms in the industry near their physical capacity per month. An equilibrium price, P_e, is established where the amount of output that producers are willing to put on the market per month is exactly equal to that which consumers are willing to buy.

It is obvious in Figure 9–1 that price P_e is the only price at which the quantity that producers are willing to place on the market is equal to that which consumers are willing to buy. Further, we can explain a tendency for this price to be established and to hold as the "going price" by considering what

Figure 9–1   Industry Demand and Supply

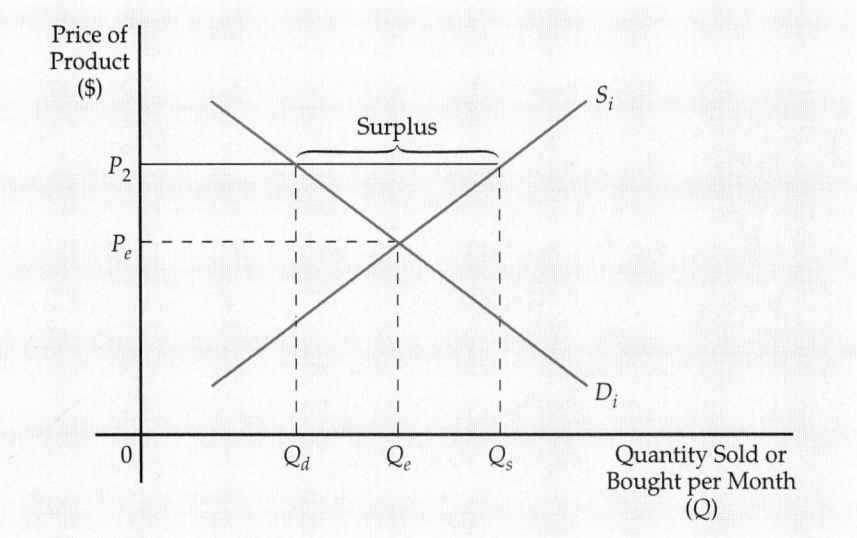

Equilibrium in this market occurs at P_e, Q_e. Any price higher than P_e will result in a surplus and lead to price reductions. Prices below P_e will result in shortages and price increases.

would happen if some other price were temporarily in effect. At P_2, for example, producers would want to put Q_s per month on the market, while consumers would be willing to buy only Q_d. There would be a surplus of $Q_s - Q_d$ units of output in the market, producers' inventories would pile up, and producers would cut price in order to sell more product. This would be the case for any price above P_e. It can easily be verified that for prices *lower* than P_e, the quantity consumers would want to buy in the market would exceed the quantity producers would wish to supply. Consequently, buying activity would reduce producers' inventories and lead to rising prices as consumers bid for the insufficient quantity of output coming into the market. (Use Figure 9–1 to illustrate this situation by drawing a horizontal line over to the S_i and D_i curves for some price lower than P_e. Identify for yourself the shortage in quantity supplied that exists for the lower price.)

An **equilibrium price** is one that equates quantity demanded in the market with quantity supplied so that there is no surplus or shortage of the product being traded.

It is clear that the **equilibrium price**, P_e, is the only price that can exist for any length of time when market conditions are such as those given by demand curve D_i and supply curve S_i.

It is important to note that D_i, the demand curve of the perfectly competitive industry in Figure 9–1, is *not* the demand curve facing an individual firm in that industry. Remember, we established early in this chapter that the individual competitive firm takes the market price, P_e, as given and believes it cannot by itself have any effect on this price. Figure 9–2 illustrates the relationship of the market demand curve to that of the individual firm. In panel (b) we see

Figure 9–2   Relation of Perfectly Competitive Firm's Demand Curve to the Industry

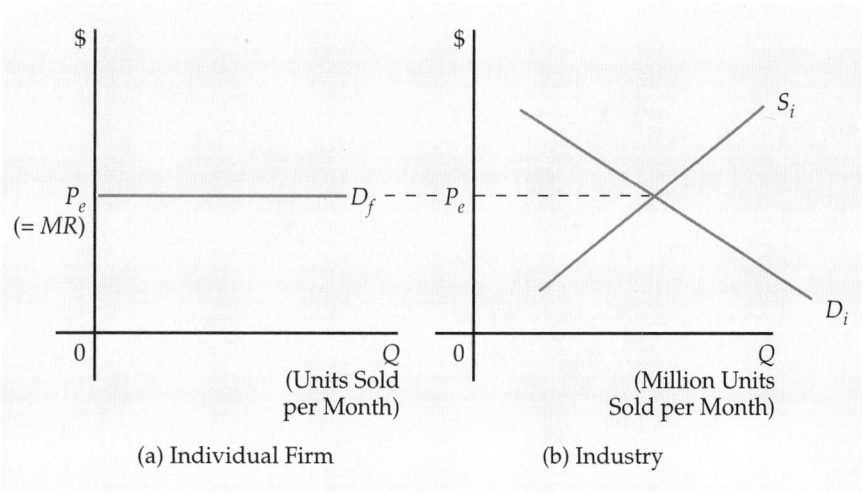

(a) Individual Firm   (b) Industry

The perfectly competitive firm views its demand curve as horizontal at the market price of its product.

the same market situation that was depicted in Figure 9–1. Panel (a), however, shows the demand curve for the product as it is perceived by the individual perfectly competitive firm. Since the firm takes the market price as given, the horizontal line P_eD_f in panel (a) is its demand curve. Note that the Q axis of panel (a) measures the firm's output in *units* of output per month, whereas the Q axis of panel (b) measures market quantities sold and bought in *millions* of units per month. The point is that movements along P_eD_f in panel (a) are so insignificant that they do not materially affect the equilibrium price and quantity of panel (b). This is a realistic notion as long as the output of the firm is very small with respect to the total market for the product.

From the standpoint of profit maximization, the situation depicted in panel (a) has some further implications for the perfectly competitive firm. First of all, as we know from Chapter 2, the horizontal line P_eD_f is both the marginal and the average revenue curve for the firm, since revenue per unit never changes as output is increased.[1] Finally, since MR is the rate of change of TR, the TR curve must be a straight line emanating from the origin, as in break-even analysis.

Profit Maximization Under Perfect Competition

If a perfectly competitive firm has short-run cost curves similar to those depicted in Chapter 6 and is incurring greater than normal profit, we can easily illustrate its profit-maximizing output using either marginal and average cost and revenue curves or total cost and total revenue curves. In Figure 9–3, panel (a), we see the firm's total cost and total revenue curves along with a net rev-

---

1 More formally, we know

$$TR = P \cdot Q,$$

and

$$MR = \frac{dTR}{dQ} = P + Q\frac{dP}{dQ}.$$

Where P is constant,

$$\frac{dP}{dQ} = 0,$$

and

$$MR = P.$$

Also,

$$AR = \frac{TR}{Q} = \frac{P(Q)}{Q} = P,$$

the same constant.

Figure 9–3   Perfectly Competitive Firm with Profit Greater than Normal

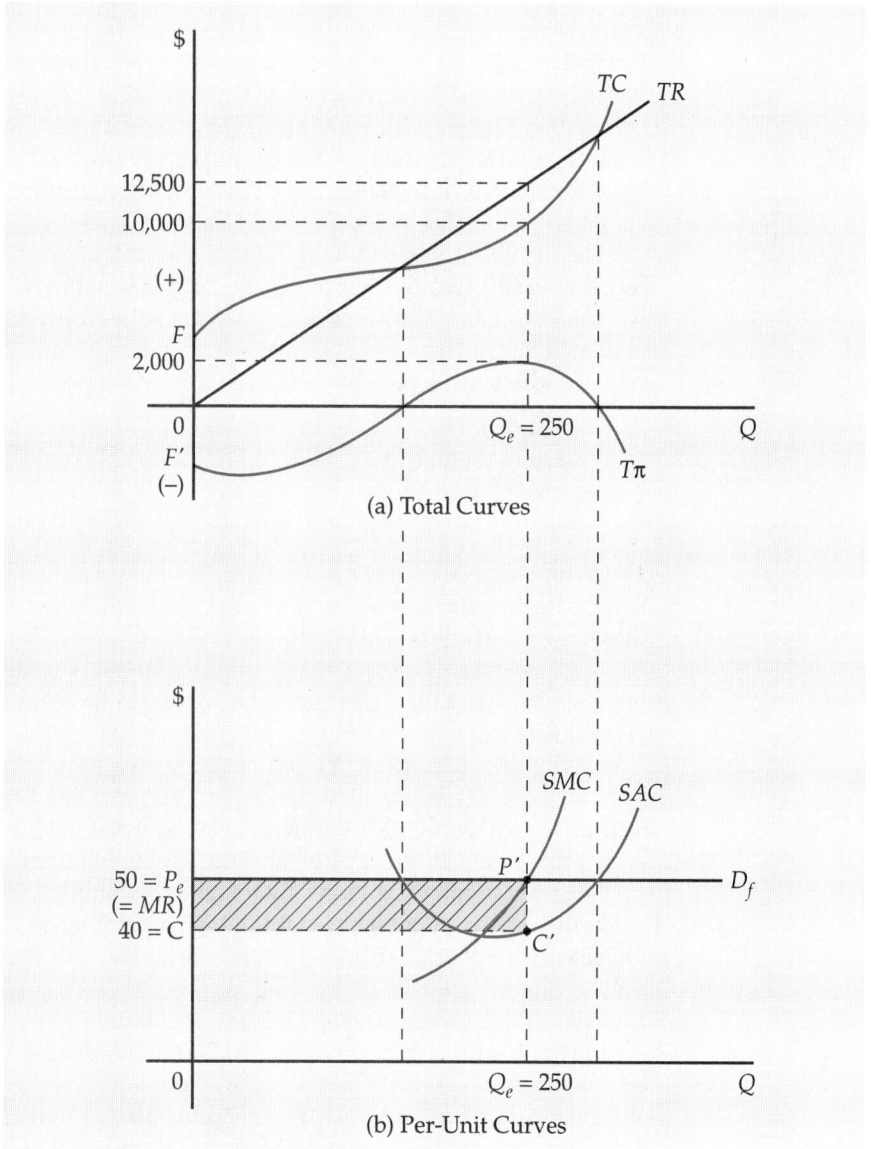

The firm maximizes profit where $SMC = MR$, which corresponds to the peak of the $T\pi$ curve in panel (a). In panel (b) profit is equal to the area of the shaded rectangle, or $(P - SAC)$ multiplied by Q_e.

enue or profit curve, $T\pi = TR - TC$. The firm maximizes profit at Q_e, where the $T\pi$ curve has its peak and where the slope of the TR curve, MR, equals that of the TC curve, SMC, as we learned in Chapter 7. In panel (b) the Q axis is identical to that of panel(a), but the $\$$ axis measures per-unit cost and revenue rather than total cost and total revenue. At Q_e in panel (b), $SMC = MR$ and economic profit per unit is $(P_e - C)$. Total profit may be calculated by taking the per-unit profit $(P_e - C)$ times the number of units sold ($0Q_e$ or CC') and is, therefore, equal to the area of rectangle $CP_eP'C'$. No output greater or less than Q_e will yield a profit as large as the one that exists at Q_e when the market price is P_e.

The firm in Figure 9–3 has profit greater than normal at Q_e, since $T\pi > 0$. This is a feasible result for a perfectly competitive firm in the *short run*, since the number of firms in the industry remains constant and the entry of new producers cannot drive price downward. However, market conditions could easily produce three other possible results for the perfectly competitive firm:

1. normal profit,
2. operating loss, or
3. temporary shutdown.

Panels (a) and (b) of Figure 9–4 provide total and average or per-unit curves for a firm with only normal profit in the short run. Panels (c) and (d) do the same for a firm operating at a loss. Note that in each diagram, the condition $SMC = MR$ holds at the equilibrium output, Q_e. *In panels (a) and (b), $T\pi = 0$, $C = P_e$, and there is only normal profit. In panels (c) and (d), $T\pi < 0$, $C > P_e$, and* there is a loss equal to $0L$ in the upper diagram or to the area $CP_eP'C'$ in the lower diagram.

An important point in this latter case is that the operating loss at output Q_e, $0L$ in panel (c), is less than fixed cost, $0F$. Since fixed cost is $0F$ even when output is zero, the firm should shut down only when $0L$ exceeds $0F$ (or $0F'$), as we learned in Chapter 7. You should be able to verify that the firm in Figure 9–5 will minimize its losses by temporarily shutting down.

In the short run, the firm that is a loss minimizer as well as a profit maximizer will not produce when price is below AVC but will produce at $SMC = MR = P_e$ when price is above AVC. It follows from this profit-maximizing principle that the *short-run supply curve* of a perfectly competitive firm is that portion of its marginal cost curve (SMC) that lies above AVC. Note in Figure 9–6 that as price (and MR) moves upward from P_1 to P_2 to P_3 in response to shifting market demand, the firm's equilibrium output increases from Q_1 to Q_2 to Q_3. Because the firm's SMC (above minimum AVC) gives the relationship between price and the quantity supplied by the firm, the short-run industry supply curve, S_i in panel (b), which is the sum of the firms' short-run supply curves, is also the sum of the SMCs of all firms in the industry. In other words, for each price, we sum the quantities of output supplied by the various firms (sometimes called a "horizontal" sum). It follows that S_i or ΣS_f will shift outward in the long run if firms enter the industry and inward if firms leave the industry.

Figure 9–4   Normal Profit and Operating Loss Under Perfect Competition

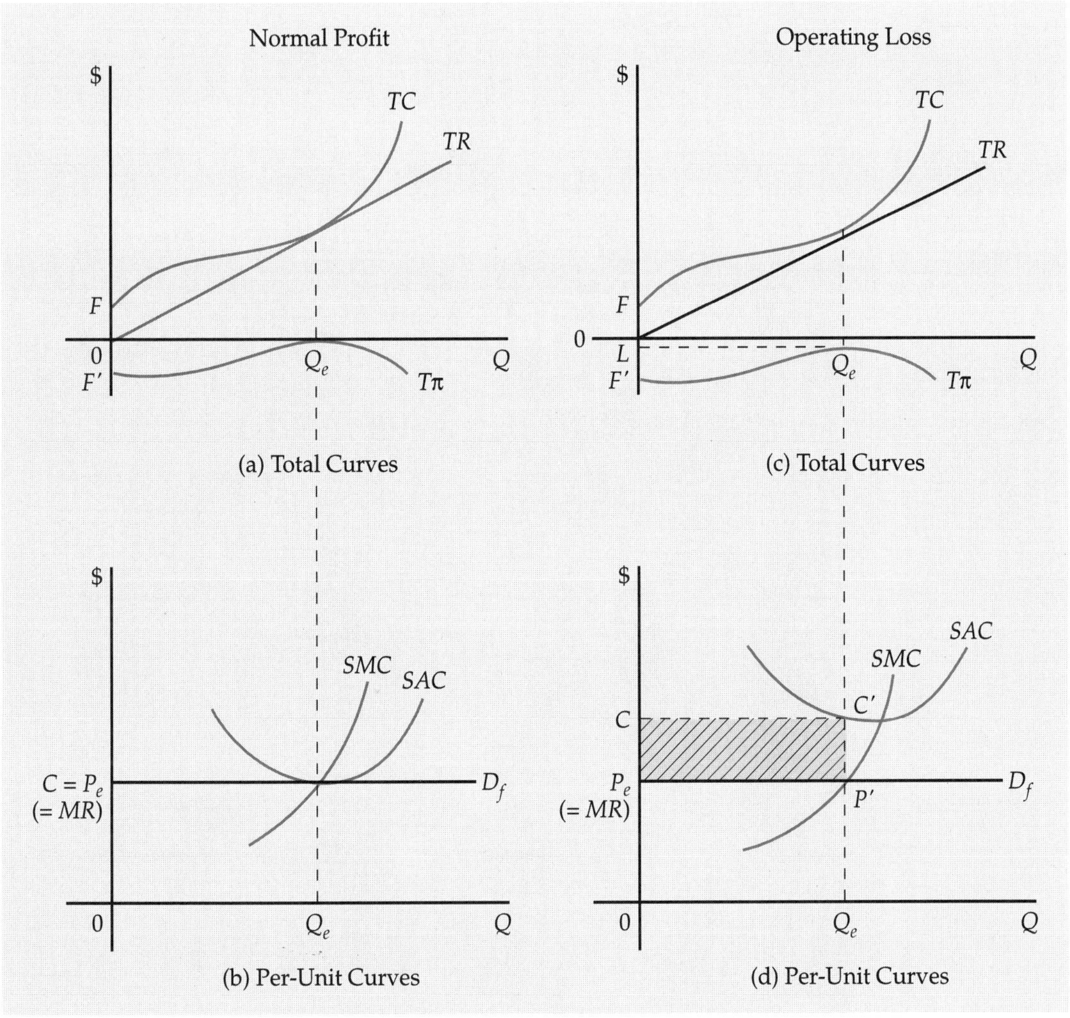

In panels (a) and (b), $T\pi = 0$, since $TC = TR$ and $P = SAC$ at Q_e. In panels (c) and (d), the firm has a loss at Q_e but should operate, since the loss is less than total fixed cost.

The Long Run Under Perfect Competition

In the long run, the firm will maximize profit by equating long-run marginal cost to the going market price and its constant marginal revenue ($LMC = P_e = MR$). As we indicated in Chapter 7, this involves adjusting plant size to that plant that has a short-run average cost just equal to long-run average cost

Figure 9–5   Shutdown Conditions Under Perfect Competition

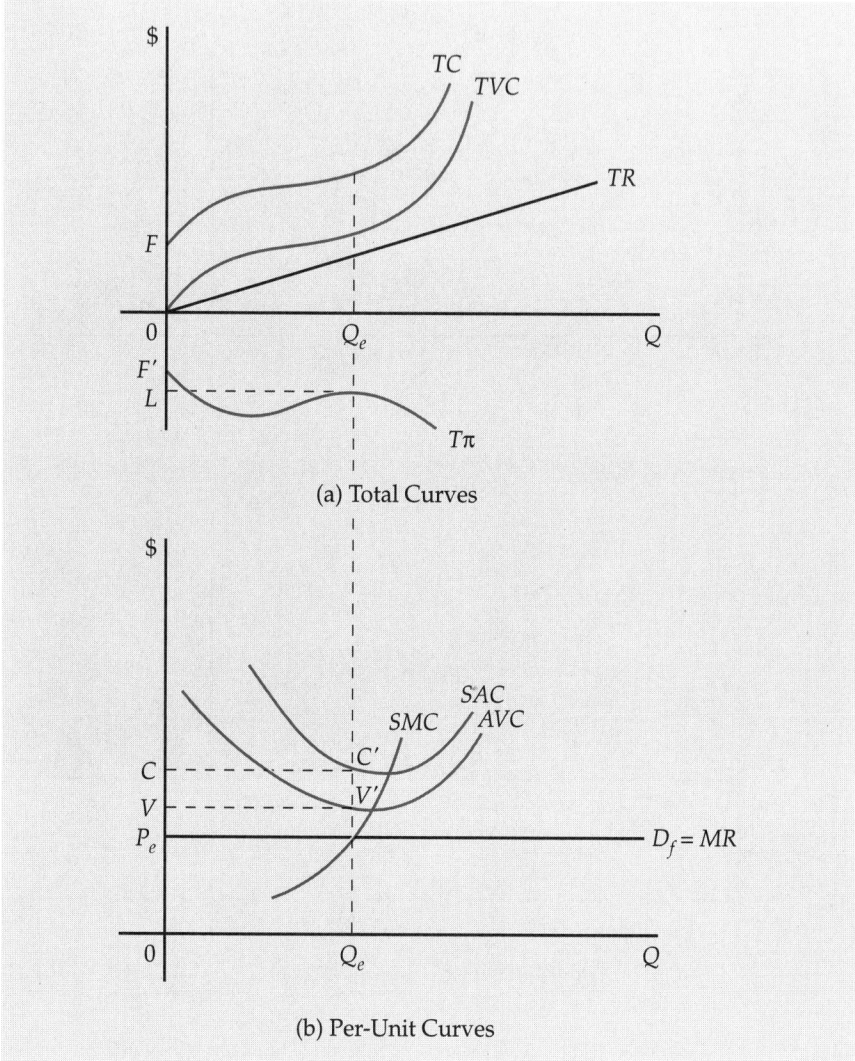

(a) Total Curves

(b) Per-Unit Curves

The firm in these diagrams should temporarily shut down, since its operating loss at Q_e would exceed total fixed cost.

at the long-run, profit-maximizing output ($LAC = SAC$). This occurs where the SAC curve is tangent to LAC and also where $SMC = LMC = P_e = MR$. Under perfect competition in the long run, there will be only normal profit for the typical firm in the industry. If profit is greater than normal, new firms will enter the industry, thereby increasing industry supply and reducing

Figure 9–6   Short-Run Supply Under Perfect Competition

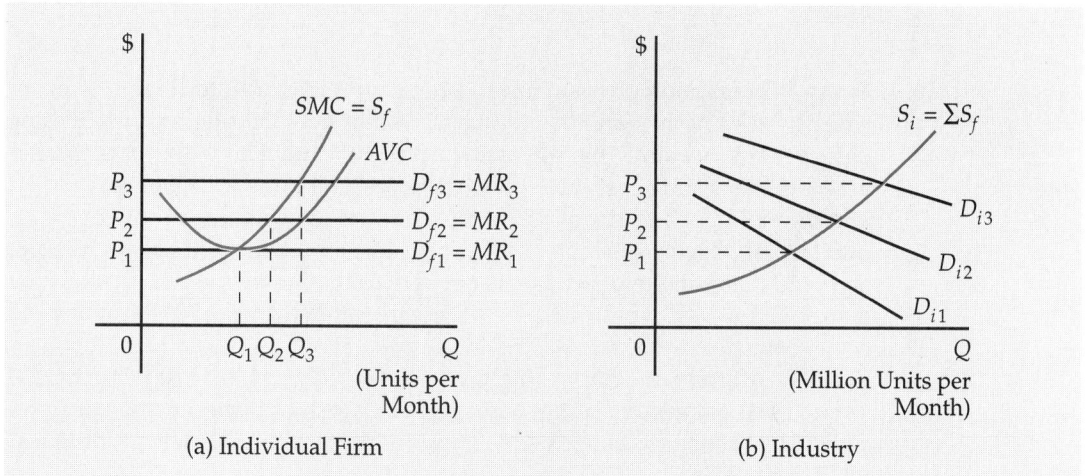

(a) Individual Firm   (b) Industry

The perfectly competitive firm's short-run supply curve is its *SMC* curve for the range where *SMC* is above *AVC*. The industry supply curve is the horizontal sum of all the firms' *SMC* curves over the same range.

market price. Entry will continue to take place as long as profit is greater than normal.

In terms of the short- and long-run average cost curves of the individual firm, the long-run equilibrium position is shown in Figure 9–7, panel (a). The industry adjustment to the equilibrium price, P_e, is shown in panel (b). If the short-run industry supply curve is initially at S_i and price is P', the typical firm will have greater than normal profit. [In panel (a), P' would intersect *SMC* well above the minimum point on the *SAC* curve.] The entry of new firms attracted by the greater than normal profit shifts the industry supply curve rightward to S'_i where it intersects the market demand curve at a price consistent with attainment of only normal profit by the typical firm. This price must be P_e in Figure 9–7, since minimum long-run average cost is equal to P_e. At any price higher than P_e, the typical firm would still have greater than normal profit, and entry would continue. If S_i were to shift out further than S'_i, price would fall below P_e. In this instance some firms would leave the industry, and S_i would shift leftward until P_e was established.

As long as there are no changes in input prices or technology, the industry long-run equilibrium price will be P_e. This is the long-run equilibrium price because Q_f is the only level of output at which $P (= MR) = LMC$, so the firm's profit maximization rule is met, and $P = LAC$, so there are no economic profits. Of course, if industry expansion is accompanied by rising input prices, P_e will rise over time. Falling long-run input prices or improvements in technology, on the other hand, could lead to decreases in P_e as the indus-

NUMERICAL EXAMPLE:

Perfect Competition and Sunk Costs in Farming

Pansy Witherspoon grows natural cabbage (no chemical fertilizers or pesticides used). She has an 800-acre farm. While her planting and cultivating costs per acre are sunk (have been incurred and cannot be reduced) at $10 per acre, her harvesting costs are still variable. Pansy's land is of uneven quality, and the yield per acre drops as she incorporates less and less productive land into her cabbage production. She has 150 acres that will yield 20 bushels per acre, 150 that will yield 18 bushels per acre, 200 that will yield 16 bushels per acre, 150 that will yield 14 bushels per acre, and another 150 that will yield only 10 bushels per acre.

Pansy figures the harvesting costs for the cabbage are $30 per acre. Assuming she planted the entire acreage, how much of it should she harvest if when the cabbage is mature the going market price that she can obtain is $2.75 per bushel?

Answer.

Pansy should harvest all but that grown on the lowest-yielding land (the 150 acres that yield only 10 bushels per acre). We have a sunk cost problem here, because the planting and cultivating costs are already expended by harvest time. Thus, the relevant marginal cost for decision making is the marginal cost per bushel for harvesting. For each class of land, this is the acre cost divided by the yield per acre, the figure that appears in the right-hand column below:

Acres	Yield	$30/yield = MC per Bu. to Harvest
150	20	1.50
150	18	1.67
200	16	1.88
150	14	2.14
150	10	3.00

Since Pansy's marginal revenue is $2.75 (assume perfect competition), the lowest-yielding land will not be worth harvesting, and the plants should just be left to decay and then ploughed under when ploughing time comes. Pansy will have a profit contribution of $10,750 on the 650 acres she harvests, assuming all variable costs are accounted for in the harvesting costs stated earlier. (At this point, the planting and cultivating costs are sunk costs and must be treated like fixed costs as Pansy makes her decision with regard to how many acres to harvest.)

Figure 9–7   The Long Run Under Perfect Competition

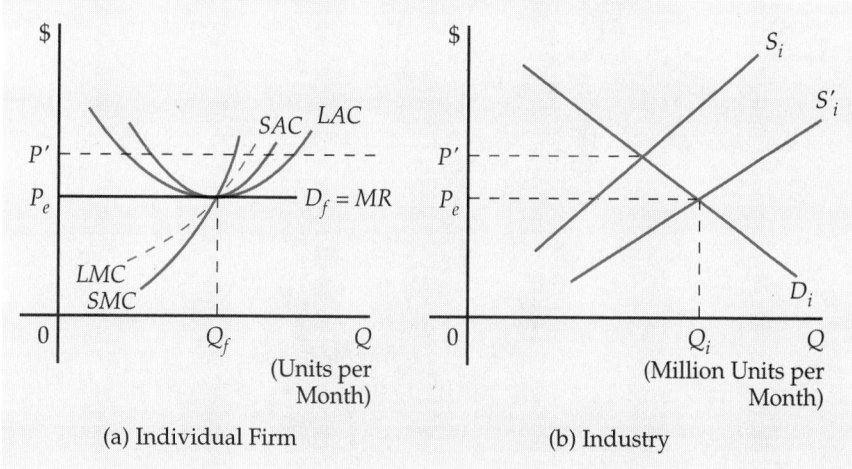

(a) Individual Firm   (b) Industry

In the long run under perfect competition, profit will tend toward normal (zero economic profit), since firms will enter whenever profit exceeds normal and leave whenever profits are below normal.

try expands. Whatever the result in terms of long-run price, firms will tend toward operation at the bottom of the *LAC* curve, with price equal to average cost, and they will tend to settle on the size of plant that has its minimum *SAC* tangent to the lowest point on *LAC*.

Overview of Perfect Competition

We can now summarize the perfectly competitive model and relate it to behavior of firms in the real world. First, the model assumes that the firm has no market power—in the sense that it can obtain no price higher than the going price for its output and that price cutting is made unnecessary by its ability to sell all it wishes at the going price. In the short run, the firm takes the fixed market price as its marginal revenue curve and maximizes its profit at the output where $SMC = MR = P$. It may operate with normal profit, greater than normal profit, or less than normal profit, but it will temporarily shut down only if market price is less than average variable cost.

In the long run, firms in the perfectly competitive industry will tend to have only normal profit, since entry will occur when profit is greater than normal, whereas less than normal profit will cause some firms to leave. The typical firm will adjust its plant size over the long run to a size that is consistent with minimum long-run average cost, since higher-cost plants will not be able to achieve normal profit. Productive efficiency in terms of the least pos-

MANAGERIAL PERSPECTIVE

The Cocoa Industry and the Competitive Model

It is frequently argued that the model of perfect competition would apply reasonably well to agriculture if there were no government intervention such as price support and acreage restriction programs. It is also argued that certain world commodity markets would conform closely to perfect competition, if there were no international commodity agreements to help stabilize them.

Alas, poor cocoa. After many years of operating with price support from the London-based ICCO, an international organization set up to buy surplus production of cocoa and resell it during periods of shortage, the industry in the 1990s was in a shambles. The price of cocoa had plummeted from a 1977 high of about $5,500 per ton to less than $850 per ton, and, for producers, there seemed to be no relief in sight. At the bottom of the trouble was the shortage of 1977, which not only brought on the $5,000-plus price level and huge industry profits but also prompted many new growers in tropical countries to plant vast tracts of seedling trees. As the trees matured, the cocoa supply curve shifted to the right, and prices fell markedly.

It would be easy to get the idea that cocoa production takes place on a few huge plantations owned by the descendants of foreign adventurers who went to the tropics a century or more ago to exploit the land. However, while there are no doubt some very wealthy third- or fourth-generation planters, there are also many, many smaller growers. In its poverty-stricken Northeast, Brazil alone counts more than 20,000 small cocoa growers, and small planters are also found in West Africa, Malaysia, and Indonesia.

As noted earlier, the profits reaped by growers in the late 1970s led to entry. As the new cocoa plants matured, prices began their downward trend. There were simply too many new producers bringing too much output to market, and efforts by both the ICCO and the governments of producer nations only had limited impacts on market supply.

In the early 1990s the ICCO toiled to come up with a new Cocoa Agreement that would regulate supply. A five-year pact was signed in 1994, but many observers believed that it was not likely to have much impact, especially because Indonesia, one of the world's largest producers, would not join the ICCO.

References: "Hot Chocolate," *Economist* (June 11, 1994), p. 62; "Stockpiles and Shortages," *Futures* (December 1993), pp. 52, 54; and "Bitter Times for Cocoa Growers," *Business Week* (April 4, 1988), p. 83. For another example of the effects of entry, see "Dentists Step Up Services and Marketing As Competition Increases in Crowded Field," *The Wall Street Journal*, November 20, 1987, p. 29.

sible cost per unit of output is thus assured in the perfectly competitive industry, and this result is one reason why perfect competition is frequently used as a norm or standard against which to assess other types of market structures and their consequences.

Many firms, particularly small firms, face some of the conditions of the perfectly competitive model in their everyday operations. However, it is rare that all of the perfectly competitive assumptions prevail. After all, the U.S. economy and industrial economies in general are characterized by the corporate form of business organization, where certain lines of production are dominated by a few very large enterprises. In many of these industries, entry of new firms is extremely difficult, similar products are differentiated from one another by superficial changes and heavy advertising, and the activities of one firm have very substantial effects on others.

It is significant, though, that small firms often cannot block entry into their markets or differentiate their products sufficiently to have much effect on their competitors. In a large city, Hank's Garage may try to develop a reputation for fair prices and good service, but Hank is unlikely to be able to charge prices that are much different from other garages, and he can do little or nothing to keep Rosa Alonso from opening a new garage in his market area. If Hank is an efficient operator, however, he will be able to run his business at a normal level of profit. Many other small businesses are in much the same position. In such a setting they may have greater than normal profit for some short period of time, but this is the exception and not the rule. The small businessperson who "makes a killing" is generally one who was in the right place at the right time and thus was able to cash in on *temporarily* greater than normal profits.

MONOPOLY AND ITS SETTING

Monopoly, in its purest form, is the case of a single seller. The market demand for its product is the only constraint on the firm's pricing policies. Barriers to entry prevent new firms from coming into the industry.

Monopoly is the name applied to the extreme case in which there is only one seller of a given product. In a sense it lies at the opposite end of the product market spectrum from perfect competition, and we will see later that the monopoly model provides the basic analytical framework for virtually all less than perfectly competitive product market structures.

The monopoly structure's key requirement of a single seller with a product not duplicated by other firms leads directly to two results:

1. The market demand curve is the firm's demand curve.
2. Entry is blocked over the long run.

Of course, if the firm is a monopolist, it can hardly be unaware that it is the only seller in the market for its product; therefore it must know that to the extent that it can estimate market demand, it has estimated the demand curve it faces. To remain a monopolist, the firm must be in a setting where entry is effectively blocked. This is possible if the firm controls the sole source of a mineral, for example, or if it has a patent or license that prohibits others from producing its product or selling a similar product within a given geographical area.

We expect the monopolist to have a downward-sloping demand curve that will be elastic over some range. In spite of the fact that a firm is the sole seller, it will be able to raise the price sufficiently to cause a proportionately large reduction in the number of buyers who will want to or be able to purchase its product. Since the monopolistic firm knows it faces such a demand curve, it is aware that the quantity of output it can sell will depend on the price it sets.

Profit Maximization Under Monopoly

If the monopoly firm's demand curve is linear, we can expect its profit-maximizing short-run equilibrium to look like Figure 9–8 whenever it is fortunate enough to have greater than normal profit. Note that where $SMC = MR$ and the $T\pi$ curve is at its peak, *both* the *market price* and the *quantity produced* are determined. If one compares Figure 9–8 to Figure 9–3, it is apparent that the differences between the graphical analyses of monopoly and perfect competition stem from their respective assumptions concerning the demand curve of the firm. TR in Figure 9–3 is a straight line from the origin because D_f is a horizontal line, meaning price is constant and equal to marginal revenue. In Figure 9–8, TR is a curve with a maximum because the demand curve, D, is a downward-sloping line. In addition, MR lies below D or AR in the lower panel of Figure 9–8 because price must be lowered on *all* units sold to sell larger levels of output, as was explained in Chapter 2.

The profit-maximizing monopoly must determine its equilibrium (profit-maximizing) output where $MR = MC$ or where $M\pi = 0$, subject to the usual condition that $M\pi$ is negative for greater output levels. Thereafter, the firm must set its price at the demand curve point that corresponds with its equilibrium output. The firm depicted in Figure 9–8 would first find Q_e, the profit-maximizing output. The corresponding profit-maximizing price, P_e, would then be determined. Suppose, for purposes of illustration, that $Q_e = 200$. *If the firm's demand curve is given by the equation $Q = 800 – 2P$*, it would follow that at Q_e, $200 = 800 – 2P$. Solving for P, we find:

$$2P = 800 – 200 = 600,$$

and

$$P = 300 = P_e.$$

Thus, to maximize profit, the monopoly would set its price at $300 per unit, where consumers would buy exactly 200 units of output per time period.

Although the monopolist of Figure 9–8 has greater than normal profit, it

Figure 9–8   Monopoly in the Short Run with Profit Greater than Normal

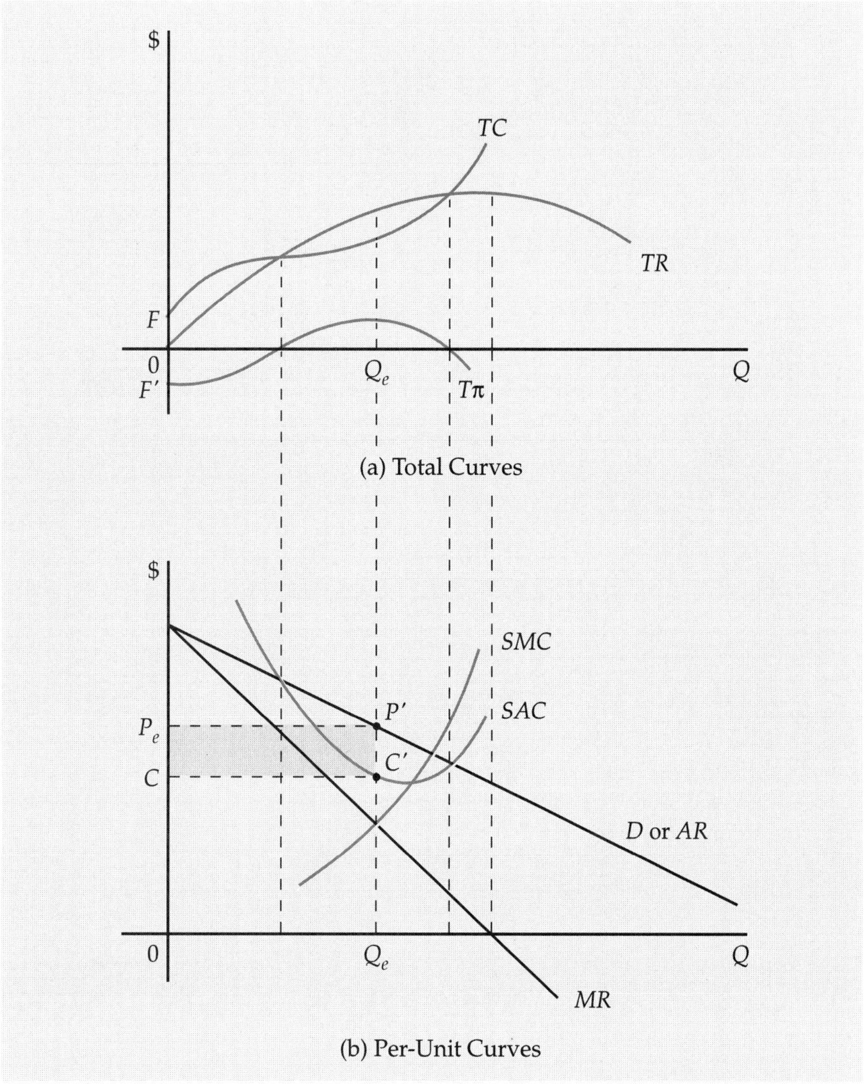

(a) Total Curves

(b) Per-Unit Curves

In panel (a), profit is maximized at Q_e, where the $T\pi$ curve has its peak. In panel (b), $SMC = MR$ at Q_e and profit equals $(P_e - C)$ multiplied by Q_e.

should be understood that in the short run, the monopoly firm (just like the firm under perfect competition) can also have only normal profit, *or* operate at a loss, *or* temporarily choose to cease production, depending on the relationship of demand to the firm's short-run cost structure. In Figure 9–9, panels (a) and (b) show the monopolistic firm operating with only normal profit,

Figure 9–9   Monopoly in the Short Run: Normal Profit and Operating Loss Cases

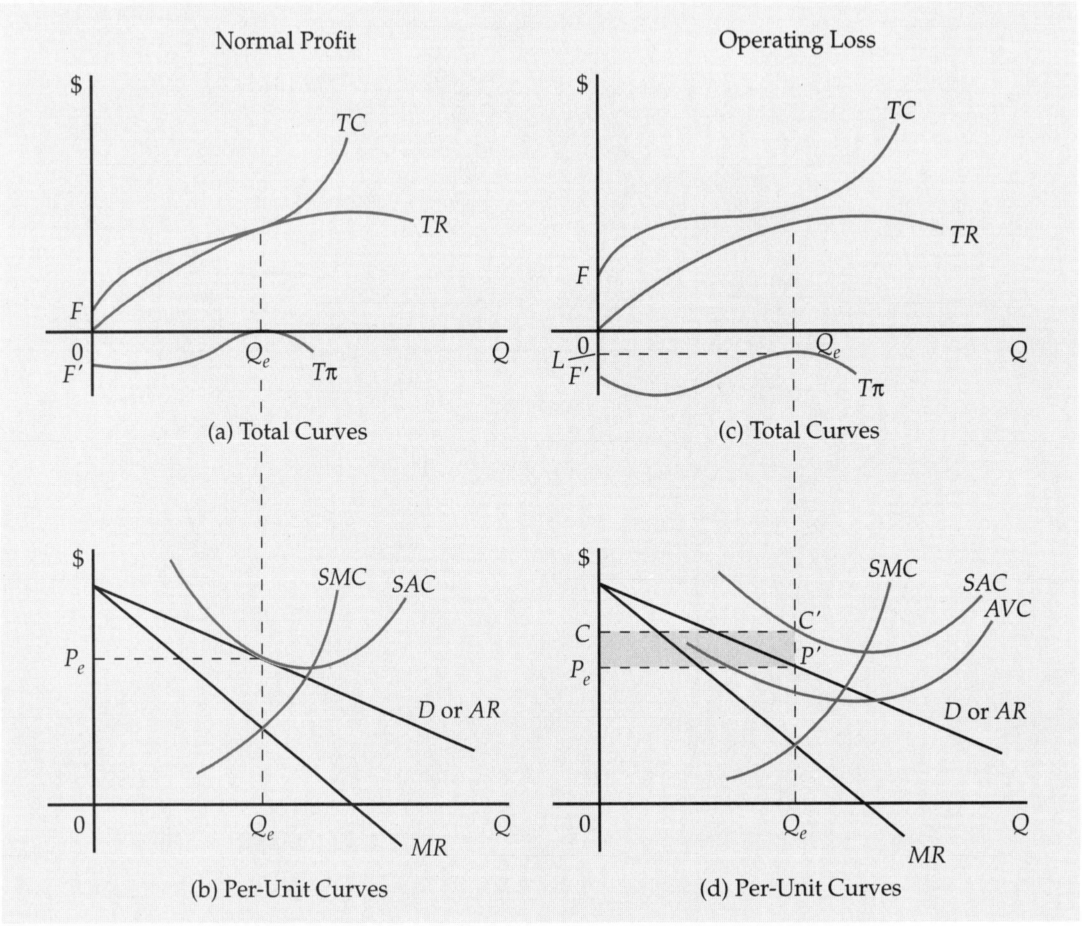

The monopoly in panels (a) and (b) has $T\pi = 0$, since at Q_e, $TC = TR$ and $P = SAC$. In panels (c) and (d), the firm has a loss, since at Q_e, $TR < TC$ and $P < SAC$. However, it should operate, since its operating loss is less than total fixed cost.

while panels (c) and (d) illustrate short-run operation with negative profit. Operation at Q_e in the latter case is rational, since in the upper panel, $0L$ is less than $0F$ (or $0F'$), and in the lower panel, P_e exceeds AVC. If price does not exceed average variable cost at the $SMC = MR$ level of output, the monopolist should temporarily shut down and lose only the fixed costs.

The Long Run Under Monopoly

In the long run, the monopoly firm continues to determine both its profit-maximizing rate of output and its selling price where (long-run) marginal cost is equal to marginal revenue. As in pure competition, if a monopolistic firm has predicted its optimal long-run output correctly, it can produce that output with the optimal combination of inputs; therefore, its long-run cost curves are appropriate for determining its profit-maximizing output. As in the short run, the firm may or may not have greater than normal profit. However, in the event that profit *is* greater than normal, entry will not occur, since other firms are not free to come into the industry. It follows that greater than normal profit can exist indefinitely. Figure 9–10 depicts such a case. Note that Figure 9–10 differs from panel (b) of Figure 9–8 only by the inclusion of the firm's long-run average and marginal cost curves.

If Q_e is a long-run profit-maximizing output, then it must be true that both *SMC* for the appropriate-sized plant and *LMC* are equal to *MR*. The long-run equilibrium of Figure 9–10 differs from that of the perfectly competitive firm in Figure 9–7 not only by the existence of a greater than normal profit, but also by the operation of the firm at a level of output where *LAC* is falling, which means that even the least cost plant for producing Q_e produces it at an average cost higher than the long-run optimum plant under perfect competition. (The appropriate plant under perfect competition is the one

Figure 9–10   Monopoly in the Long Run with Greater than Normal Profit

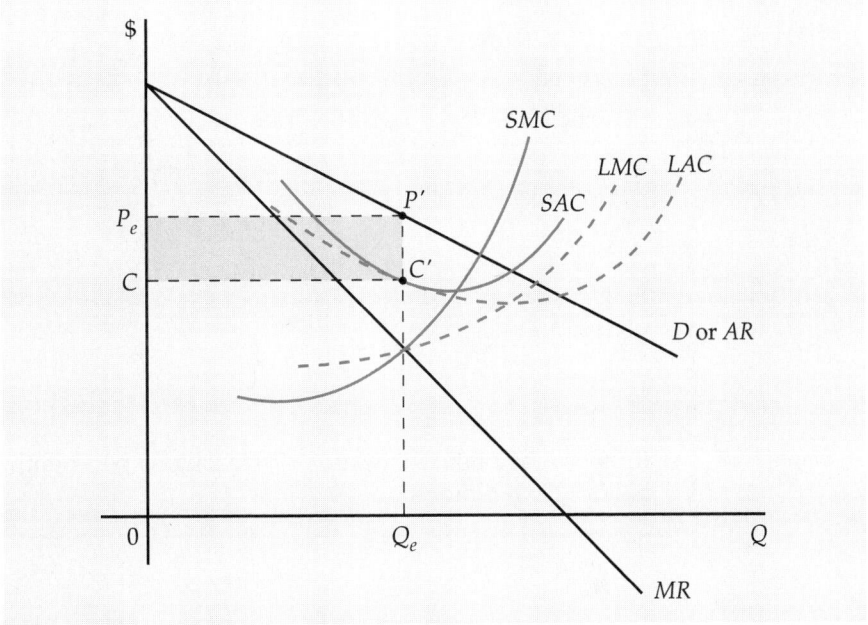

Since there is no entry in the long run under monopoly, the firm can have greater than normal profit indefinitely. In this case profit is equal to $(P_e - C)$ multiplied by Q_e.

NUMERICAL EXAMPLE:

The Pricing of Water in a New Housing Development

Artie Fender, a developer in Saugus, California, has opened a new housing tract just outside of town where he also owns the water system. Artie figures that, based on average home size, the demand for water in the development is expressed in the following equation:

$$Q_w = 80,000 - 2000P_w,$$

where Q_w is the number of thousands of gallons of water consumed per month and P_w is the price per 1,000 gallons. If Artie's marginal cost of producing the water is constant at $5 per 1,000 gallons, what price should he charge for the water? If the average home consumes 10,000 gallons per month, what will be the household's water bill? (Assume Artie's company faces no regulation.)

Answer.

Since Artie is a pure monopolist, he should just set his marginal cost equal to the marginal revenue from the preceding demand curve. Transposing the demand equation yields

$$P_w = 40 - .0005Q_w$$
$$MR_w = 40 - .001Q_w.$$

Setting $MR = MC$,

$$40 - .001Q_w = 5$$
$$.001Q_w = 35$$
$$Q_w = \underline{35,000}.$$

Substituting,

$$P_w = 40 - .0005(35,000) = \underline{\$22.50}.$$

If the average household uses 10,000 gallons per month, it will pay a water bill of $225 per month.

whose *SAC* is tangent to *LAC* at its minimum point and is both larger and has a lower per-unit cost associated with it than that in monopoly.) In fact, under monopoly we can draw no special conclusion regarding plant size in the long run when profit is greater than normal, since the long-run equilibrium output for a monopoly in this case may be to the left, right, or at the output level where minimum *LAC* can be achieved.

When profit is only normal, however, the monopolist must be producing a level of output where the *LAC* is falling, since normal profit requires that the two appropriate average cost curves (*SAC* and *LAC*) be tangent to the downward-sloping demand curve (*P* must equal *SAC* and *LAC*). Figure 9–11 illustrates the case of a monopolist with only normal profit in the long run.

Since, as we have shown, monopoly firms can indefinitely sustain greater than normal long-run profit, the government has undertaken the regulation of monopoly in many cases. There are two basic tools utilized by public agencies in the regulation of monopolies: taxes and price regulation. When taxes are used, the monopolist's costs are increased and profit is reduced. If the tax is a variable cost, output will also be reduced. When price regulation is used, the regulatory authority must determine whether the firm can cover costs with the price that is set. If it cannot, subsidization will be required to keep the firm from going out of business. We will investigate these topics further in Chapter 16.

Figure 9–11   Monopoly in the Long Run with only Normal Profit

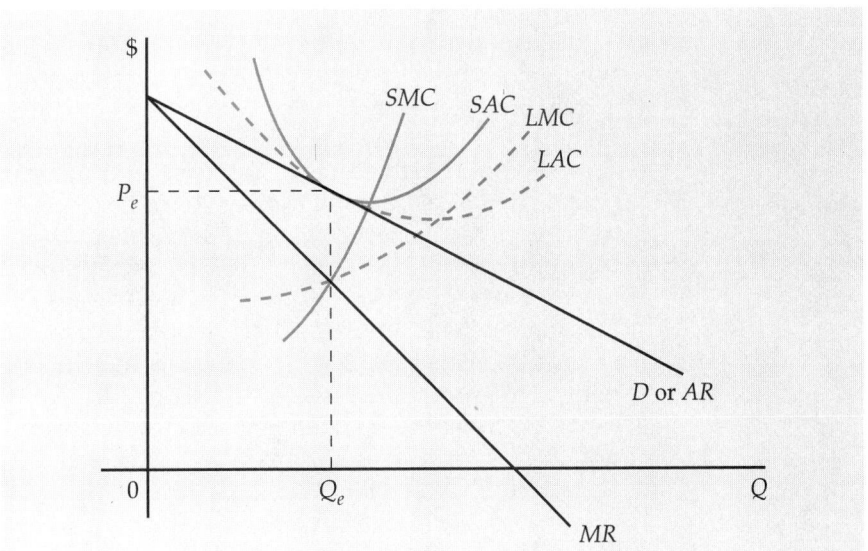

Normal profit is a possibility under monopoly. However, as this diagram shows, the monopoly firm with $P = SAC$ and $T\pi = 0$ will operate in a plant that lies on the falling portion of *LAC*.

MANAGERIAL PERSPECTIVE

A New World for Your Local Cable TV Monopoly

In the Orwellian year of 1984, Big Brother decided to deregulate the cable TV industry. At the time, Congress thought such an action would stimulate the growth of the industry and encourage both entry and competition. Well, the industry certainly grew, and some of the firms in it became extremely profitable. Following passage of the 1984 Act, cable prices in some New York areas rose by as much as 74 percent over a span of only 4 years. Similar rate increases occurred in many other parts of the country.

While the 1990s can be characterized by substantial entry into the cable programming industry at the *national level*, where a number of large firms were slugging it out for market share, consumers typically dealt with only one company at the *local level*. Some of these companies were quite small when compared with the national cable networks such as ESPN, CNN, TBS, or USA. However, the 1984 decision of Congress covered these companies too, thereby approving of deregulated monopoly at the local level. There was often no entry possible at that level, because a single firm held a franchise let by local government. Thus the firms were free to set a profit-maximizing price that moved upward as cable demand increased with no corresponding increase in supply. Many local cable operators enjoyed greater than normal returns with a perfect barrier to entry, the franchise.

Consumers complained loudly about the rate increases deregulation brought, and in 1994 the Federal Communications Commission passed a regulation that rolled back prices on nonpremium programming. Needless to say, the cable industry grumbled and argued that growth would be stifled. However, a new era dawned for cable TV with passage of the Telecommunications Act of 1996. The Act was passed because Congress believed the growth of digital, satellite, cellular, and fiber-optic cable technologies, as well as that of the Internet, were paving the way for increased competition in the delivery of cable television, telephone, and related services to consumers. The Act allows competition between cable TV companies and telephone companies in both communications and broadcasting. It also frees local cable providers from price regulation when they face competition from other nonsatellite carriers, and it provides for the end of rate regulation of large cable TV systems within three years of its passage. While the increase in competition the Act fosters certainly has the potential eventually to bring better and cheaper service to consumers, it is interesting to note that the ink was hardly dry on the new law when one major cable company (TCI, which serves Denver and Northern California) announced rate increases of from 15 to 20 percent.

References: Shira McCarthy, "Cable TV Industry Finds Freedom From Rate Regulation Chains," *Telephony*, Vol. 230, No. 16 (April 15, 1996), p. 8; "Hold the Phones! A Telcom Bill After All," *Fortune* (January 15, 1996), p. 14; Jim McConville, "TCI Boosts Rates 15%–20%," *Broadcasting and Cable*, Vol. 126, No. 11 (March 11, 1996), pp. 12–16; Charles F. Mason, "FCC Vote Reduces Cable TV Rates," *Telephony*, Vol. 226, No. 9 (February 28, 1994), pp. 16–18; "Tune In, Turn On, Sort Out," *Time* (May 29, 1989), p. 68; and "Untangling the Debate Over Cable TV," *The Wall Street Journal*, March 19, 1990, pp. B1, B6.

Overview of Monopoly

Briefly, we can summarize the monopoly case as that of a firm that is the sole seller of some product and maximizes profit in both the short and long run by equating marginal cost to marginal revenue, having derived marginal revenue from the market demand curve for the product. In determining its equilibrium output, the firm also determines the price of its product, since both price and marginal revenue depend on the amount sold. This can easily be seen from the firm's downward-sloping demand and marginal revenue curves. The monopoly firm may have greater than normal profit, normal profit, or losses in the short run, depending on the relation between its costs and the market demand. If it remains in business over the long run, it can be expected to have at least normal profit.

We should note that the analysis of any firm that perceives or estimates a downward-sloping demand curve is graphically identical to that of monopoly, except that the firm's demand (or *AR*) curve is not the market demand curve for the product when there is more than one seller in the market. In the chapters that follow, therefore, we will see a good deal more of the downward-sloping demand and marginal revenue curves. However, in contrast to monopoly, the market situations to be examined next generally assume that a number of firms are engaged in the production and sale of identical, or at least similar, products.

SUMMARY

Competition, Monopoly, and Analysis of the Firm

In this chapter we provided a brief review of the two limiting cases in the microeconomic analysis of the firm: perfect competition and monopoly. The discussion was in large part theoretical, since we believe that few real-world firms exactly fit the assumptions of either case. However, the point was made that there are many real-world firms that face situations characterized by such attributes of perfect competition as a market with many buyers and sellers, similar costs from firm to firm, and relatively free entry in the long run. In addition, it was argued that a large number of firms in modern industrial economies depart from the perfectly competitive situation and, in fact, must be viewed in an entirely different light. For such firms the pure monopoly case holds some analytical keys that will be useful in the chapters that follow.

Our review of perfect competition extended the profit analysis of Chapter 7 to the setting of a firm too small to have any effect on its own price and situated in an industry characterized by long-run freedom of entry. In the short run, the firm acted as a price taker, and management's task was simply to determine the rate of output that would maximize profit or minimize loss. It was seen that the firm could do any of the following in the short run: operate with a greater than normal profit; operate with only normal profit; operate with a loss less than total fixed costs; or temporarily shut down, losing only fixed costs. In the long run, however, it was argued that the firm would have only normal profit because of freedom of entry into the industry. Thus any occurrence of temporarily greater than normal profits would be followed by entry of new firms and an increase in industry supply, which would depress the market price and eliminate the abnormal profits of older firms. Below normal profits would occur only temporarily, since they would provide an incentive to leave the industry in search of higher returns. In this chapter the long-run equilibrium of the perfectly competitive market was shown to result not only in normal levels of profit but also in economic efficiency, since all firms tended toward operation at the minimum point of the long-run average cost curve.

The discussion of monopoly noted that although the monopoly firm determines not only its profit-maximizing output, but also the appropriate price to charge for its product, it is still somewhat at the mercy of its demand curve. By this we mean that the monopoly firm's demand curve, which is the market demand curve for the product, might not provide the firm with any opportunities for greater than normal profit. In fact (as we showed previously) in regard to profit, the monopoly firm in the short run has all the same possible outcomes as the perfectly competitive firm, including normal profit, operating loss, and temporary shutdown. In the long run, however, the monopoly firm may reap greater than normal profit indefinitely, since entry into the industry is effectively blocked. The lack of entry that characterizes monopoly market situations may also lead to inefficiency in production, since there is no assurance that the monopoly firm's profit-maximizing output will occur in an optimum-sized plant. Because of the profit and efficiency problems, monopolies are usually subject to rather strict regulation by government. The nature of such regulation is discussed in Chapter 16.

Many firms that are not monopolies operate under market conditions that approximate monopoly much more closely than they do perfect competition. The giant industrial enterprises of the United States and Europe are cases in point. The issue of government regulation of such firms is controversial and centers around the question of antitrust law. This subject will also be taken up in Chapter 16. Meanwhile, the next few chapters will further extend our analysis of managerial decision making to market situations notably more complex than the two limiting cases that we have reviewed here.

QUESTIONS

1. Under what conditions can we expect to find a perfectly competitive firm with greater than normal profit?
2. What is the profit expectation for a perfectly competitive firm in the long run? Why?
3. How is the short-run supply curve of a perfectly competitive *industry* derived? Is there anything that would ensure that such a curve would slope upward and to the right?
4. What control does the individual perfectly competitive firm have over the price it charges for its product? Explain.
5. The agricultural sector of the U.S. economy is often said to approximate a perfectly competitive market situation. Do you think this characterization is appropriate? What would you predict about the chances for success of farmers' strikes and protest marches (tractor parades), as well as of farm organizations bent on securing higher prices, given what you know about the perfectly competitive model?
6. What kind of market demand situation can we expect a monopolistic firm to face? Why?
7. Must monopoly firms always have greater than normal profits in the short run? Why or why not?
8. Under what conditions would a monopoly firm have only normal profit in the long run? (Assume no regulation.)
9. Why can an unregulated monopoly firm have greater than normal profit indefinitely over the long run?
10. If an unregulated monopoly firm has only normal profit in the long run, will it be operating at the minimum point of its long-run average cost curve? Why or why not?

PROBLEMS

1. Diagram the following situations using both total and per-unit (average, marginal) cost and revenue curves.

a. A perfectly competitive firm producing output but minimizing its short-run loss.
b. A monopoly producing its long-run profit-maximizing output with only normal profit.
c. A perfectly competitive firm in the short run with greater than normal profit.
d. A monopoly operating but minimizing loss in the short run.

2. Suppose a firm has the following short-run cost data:

SMC	MP_b	Output of X	Input of b	AP_b	AVC	STC
		0	0	—	—	
		100	2		0.40	240
		250	4			
		350	6			
		425	8			
		475	10			
		500	12			

a. Complete the table.
b. Find its best short-run output if it has no choice but to sell its product at the prevailing market price of $0.78.

3. Determine whether the following perfectly competitive firm should produce output in the short run or temporarily shut down. Given

$$P = MR = \$60$$

$$TC = 4{,}000 + 204Q - 3Q^2 + 0.02Q^3$$

$$SMC = 204 - 6Q + 0.06Q^2$$

where

$$Q \text{ is units produced per month.}$$

If the firm does not operate, it will lose its $4,000 of fixed costs. What profit or loss will it have if it operates where $SMC = MR$?

4. Suppose a firm is operating under highly competitive market conditions and the going price for its product is $P_x = \$260$. If the firm's short-run total cost function is

$$TC = 1{,}000 + 80Q_x - 6Q_x^2 + 0.2Q_x^3,$$

and therefore marginal cost is

$$MC = 80 - 12Q_x + 0.6Q_x^2,$$

what is the firm's profit-maximizing output? (Show work.) How much profit will the firm have? (Assume all data pertain to monthly operations.)
5. Examine the following diagrams.

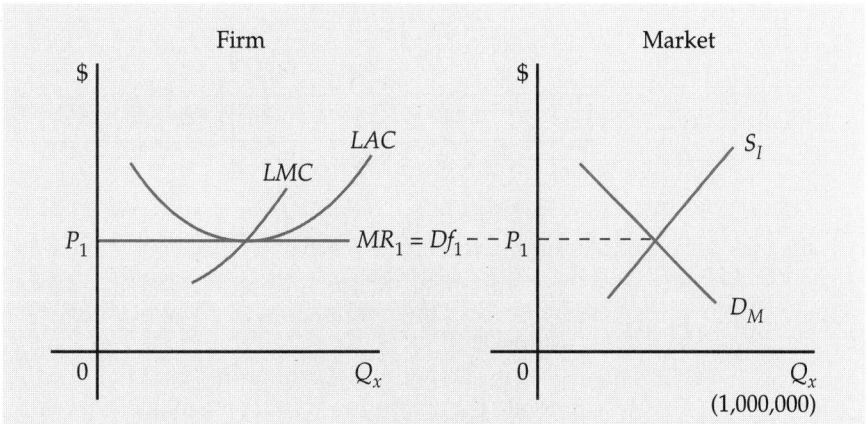

The industry is perfectly competitive. *Explain* and *illustrate* what would happen if market demand increased. That is, what adjustments would occur in the *long run*? (Assume the cost curves do not shift in any way.)

6. The following data pertain to a monopoly firm's demand and costs per quarter.

Q (quantity sold)	P (unit price)	TVC (total variable cost)
0	$20	0
5,000	18	$100,000
10,000	16	120,000
15,000	14	180,000
20,000	12	250,000
25,000	10	330,000
30,000	8	420,000
35,000	6	520,000
40,000	4	640,000

If total fixed costs are $10,000 per quarter, what will be the firm's maximum profit output? How much will profit be at this output level?
7. Complete the following table, assuming that the firm is in the short run and L is the only variable input.

TC	AFC	AVC	AP_L	Input of L	$TP_L =$ Output	MP_L	SMC
—	—	—		0	0		
						10	
960.00	90.00	6		1	10		
						18	3.33
		4.29		2	28		
		3.75		3	48		
		4.29	14.0	4			
						4	
	15.00			5	60		
						3	20.00
	14.29	5.71	10.5	6			

Assuming the firm operates in a perfectly competitive market and faces a market price of $12 per unit for its product, answer the following:
a. At which of the outputs in the table will it have the greatest profit (lowest loss)?
b. How much will the above profit (loss) be?

8. Complete the revenue and cost data in the following table, assuming that the firm, Calabasa Consolidated Cable, is a monopoly that has been allowed to set its own price for home TV cable service in the very small town of Calabasa, Wisconsin. (Q refers to number of subscribers, and the revenue and cost data are per month.)

MR	P	Q	TR	STC	AVC	TVC	MC
	110		1100			600	
	100	20		1500	35.00		
		30	2700	1700		900	20
	80	40		2000			30
	70		3500		32.00		
		60	3600				50
	50	70		3500		2700	

a. What output and price will Calabasa Cable choose? Explain why, relating your answer to the general condition for a profit maximum.
b. How much total profit will Calabasa have at the maximum?
c. In the table, $300 per month of the cable company's total fixed cost is a franchise fee paid to the city. If no other data change, but the city raises the franchise fee to $500 per month, what will be the effect on the company's output, price, and total profit? *Explain.*

9. Gina Redonda has the only ready-mix concrete company in Hot Pepper, New Mexico. She believes that concrete batching and delivery costs can be viewed as relatively constant at $18 per cubic yard of concrete sold. If she estimates the monthly demand in her market area to be given by the demand curve $Q = 1200 - 10P$ so that $MR = 120 - .2Q$:
   a. How many yards of concrete should she sell per month?
   b. What price should she charge per yard, and how much will her total profit contribution from concrete sales be?

The following problems require calculus.

C1. Suppose the typical firm in a perfectly competitive industry has the following long-run total cost function:

$$LTC = 240Q_x - 6Q_x^2 + 0.08_x^3.$$

If this function remains stable, what will be the long-run going price for Product X?

C2. Assume a perfectly competitive firm has the following total cost function for the short run:

$$STC = 700 + 90Q - 4.5Q^2 + (1/3)Q^3.$$

   a. Determine its profit-maximizing or loss-minimizing output for the short run, given that the market price of its product is $180 per unit.
   b. What will be the firm's short-run profit or loss?

C3. A monopoly firm has the following demand curve:

$$Q = 2,000 - 25P,$$

where Q is its monthly output. Assuming its monthly short-run total cost is described by the function

$$STC = 500 + 8Q + .035Q^2,$$

answer the following questions.
   a. What will be its profit-maximizing price and output?
   b. How much profit will it have at the preceding output?

C4. The following is a demand curve that has been estimated for a monopoly firm:

$$Q_x = 4,000 - 20P_x,$$

where Q_x is the quantity of Product X sold per month, and P_x is the price charged by the firm.

   If its marginal cost is constant at $20 per unit, at what price and quantity will it maximize profit?

C5. a. Solve Problem C4 for a monopoly firm with the same demand curve but the following short-run total cost function:

$$TC = 8{,}750 + 176Q_x - 2.93Q_x^2 + 0.02Q_x^3.$$

  b. Indicate the dollar amount of profit for the firm at the preceding output per month.

C6. Suppose a monopoly firm has the following demand and short-run total cost curves:

$$Q = 100 - P;$$

$$STC = 250 + 180Q - 13Q^2 + (1/3)Q^3.$$

  a. At what output and price will the firm maximize total *revenue*?
  b. At what output and price will the firm maximize total *profit*?
  c. Compare the maximum profit obtainable with the profit that the firm would have if it chose a revenue-maximizing strategy. (Show calculations.)

C7. Suppose a perfectly competitive firm has the following total cost function for the short run:

$$STC = 5{,}000 + 150Q - 12Q^2 + (1/3)Q^3.$$

  a. Determine its profit-maximizing or loss-minimizing output for the short run, given that the market price of its product is $330 per unit.
  b. What will be the firm's short-run profit or loss?
  c. Now disregard the preceding cost function, and suppose its *long-run* total cost is:

$$LTC = 660Q - 9Q^2 + 0.05Q^3.$$

  i. Write an equation for long-run average cost.
  ii. Indicate the firm's long-run price, quantity sold, and profit, assuming the industry is in long-run equilibrium.

C8. Stanley Straing has a soft drink concession monopoly at the Fort Tippecanoe, Indiana, County Fair. He believes his total cost for supplying the drinks will be

$$STC = 800 + 0.2Q + 0.0001Q^2.$$

If the County Fair Board tells him he must charge $0.80, and demand for the drinks during the fair is given by the demand curve $Q = 5{,}000 - 2{,}500P$, determine the following:

  a. The number of drinks sold and Stanley's total profit at the fixed price of $0.80 per drink.
  b. Whether the amount Stanley wants to sell is consistent with the amount consumers want to buy at the $0.80 price.
  c. Stanley's profit-maximizing output, price, and profit if he were allowed to set his own price instead of having to charge $0.80.

This problem can be solved with Decision Assistant.

D1. The Herridge family has been actively involved in growing oranges in the family orchard for four generations. Over that period many factors have contributed to periods of profit and loss. Next year is shaping up to be "one of those years." A mild winter in Texas and Florida translated to bumper crops and lower prices for the Herridge's oranges.

Jack Herridge is trying to predict next year's profit potential and is reviewing a recent trade-publication article that predicts a price of $10 per bushel for the variety of oranges Jack's family grows.

Although the price of oranges has fluctuated widely over the years, the cost of producing oranges has been fairly constant as given by the following total cost function:

$$TC = 5,000 + 4Q + .001Q^2,$$

where Q is the quantity in bushels of oranges grown and sold on the Herridge orchard.

Jack is now ready to project the profit (or loss) for the family business. (*Hint: TR* is $P(Q)$ or $TR = 10Q$.)

Use the Max/Min tool in the *Managerial Economics Decision Assistant* to complete the following:

a. Determine the quantity of oranges Jack's orchard should grow and send to market.

b. Suppose the price of oranges rises to $12 per bushel. What will be the new quantity of oranges grown and sent to market?

c. Suppose the price of oranges falls to $9 per bushel. What will be the new quantity of oranges grown and sent to market?

SELECTED REFERENCES

Amacher, Ryan C., and Holly H. Ulbrich. *Economic Principles and Policies.* Cincinnati: South Western College Publishing, 1995, Chapters 23 and 24.

Maurice, S. Charles, and Owen R. Phillips. *Economic Analysis*, 6th ed. Homewood, Ill.: Irwin, 1992, Chapters 12–14.

McConnell, Campbell R., and Stanley L. Brue. *Economics*, 13th ed. New York: McGraw-Hill, 1996, Chapters 23 and 24.

Miller, Roger LeRoy, and Raymond P. H. Fishe. *Microeconomics: Price Theory in Practice.* New York: HarperCollins, 1995, Chapters 10 and 11.

Nicholson, Walter. *Microeconomic Theory: Basic Principles and Extensions*, 5th ed. Fort Worth: The Dryden Press, 1992, Chapters 15–19.

Truett, Dale B., and Lila J. Truett. *Economics.* St. Louis: Times Mirror/Mosby College Publishing, 1987, Chapters 21 and 22.

10

MONOPOLISTIC COMPETITION, OLIGOPOLY, AND RIVALROUS MARKET STRUCTURES

In the preceding chapter, our examinations of perfectly competitive and monopolistic firms demonstrated that such firms had two important points in common: (1) neither type of firm was motivated to differentiate its product from that of other sellers through advertising or other means and (2) neither type of firm needed to be concerned about the effects of rival firms' activities on its own operations or reactions by such firms to its decisions. However, most real-world firms are vitally concerned with one or both of the foregoing considerations. They know that what they do affects firms that are their rivals in the marketplace, and they are aware that they can capture a certain share of the market by convincing buyers that their product or service is superior to that of other sellers. (Thus Wendy's, Inc., goes to a lot of trouble trying to convince the world that its hamburgers are better than those of McDonald's; and likewise, the amount and kind of advertising done by McDonald's is often a function of the activities of its rivals.) What businesses attempt to do when they whittle away a certain portion of the market for themselves is to create a sort of mini-monopoly position for their individual firm. This is why monopoly analysis, rather than the perfectly competitive model, provides a suitable point of departure for examination of market structures where sellers are few enough in number that they are likely to be aware of the problem of rivalry among themselves.

Oligopoly is a market structure characterized by few sellers and interfirm rivalry.

Economists have settled on the term **oligopoly** to describe product market situations that are characterized by relatively few sellers (few enough so that nothing that approaches perfect competition will exist). More recently, the terms *rivalrous competition* and *rivalrous market structures* have been used to describe a broad range of oligopolistic situations that lie somewhere between the extremes of monopoly and perfect competition. These market structures range from cases in which the number of sellers is very few and the product is homogeneous to cases in which there are relatively large numbers of sellers with products that vary markedly. In fact, efforts to differentiate the firm's product from similar goods produced by rival firms is an

MANAGERIAL PERSPECTIVE

Oligopoly Advertising and The Pickup Truck Wars

One characteristic frequently found in oligopolistic markets is product differentiation so fierce that it takes the form of negative advertising that literally runs down the product of a rival firm. A classic oligopoly advertising battle raged between General Motors (GM) and Ford in the pickup truck market from 1988 to 1990. GM's Chevrolet division marketing gurus whipped up a slate of macho ads that pitted the full-size Chevy pickup against similar Fords and, supposedly, proved the latter to be puny by comparison. In one ad, the 4-wheel-drive version of the Ford was left bogged down in a "Ditch of Doom," while a Chevy cruised on by. In another a Ford was shown to lose a tug of war with a Chevy and plunge into a "Crater of Fire."

Ford's marketing experts said there was "no value" in such negative advertising but soon retaliated with similar comparison ads. The negative advertising war ended after a survey by Ford indicated consumer displeasure with the ads. Ford decided to emphasize its own product quality rather than attack or counterattack Chevrolet. This strategy seemed to succeed for a number of years, and, in 1996, Ford unveiled a redesigned full-size pickup (F-150 for 1997) that analysts believed would enhance its already impressive position in the light truck market.

References: "How Ford's New F-150 Lapped the Competition," *Business Week* (July 29, 1996), pp. 74–76; "Ford Calls a Truce in Battle With GM With New Ad Campaign for Its Trucks," *The Wall Street Journal*, April 12, 1990, p. B4; and "Chevy Turns to Negative Ads in an Effort to Topple Ford as Pickup-Truck Leader," *The Wall Street Journal*, December 12, 1988, p. B1.

Product differentiation refers to a wide variety of activities, such as design changes and advertising, that rival firms employ to attract consumers to their products.

important strategy tool in many rivalrous markets. Such **product differentiation** may take the form of actual physical changes in the product or may be limited to advertising that makes people *think* the product is somehow superior to that produced by rivals. Oligopoly analysis is difficult because it tries to deal with some of the most complex interfirm relationships encountered in the real world, and many of these structures are characterized by *uncertainty*. In some cases, therefore, we are able to predict an outcome with respect to price and quantity sold only if certain rather heroic assumptions are allowed to hold. In others the best we can do is describe a range in which the solution will be found.

MONOPOLISTIC COMPETITION:
A CASE OF MANY FIRMS

Monopolistic competition is the name applied to a market structure with numerous firms that sell slightly differentiated products.

One market structure that is less than perfectly competitive and, as a result, draws on the tools of monopoly analysis is the case called **monopolistic competition**. The theory of monopolistic competition, developed by Harvard economist E. H. Chamberlin in the 1930s, occupies an in-between area in the analysis of market structures because it is not really an explanation of oligopoly or rivalrous competition but does allow for the element of product differentiation. Consequently, individual firms do have some control over price. We can describe monopolistic competition as a situation characterized by a relatively large number of sellers of somewhat differentiated products where each seller firm is not particularly concerned about the relationship between its individual actions and those of other firms in the industry. Each firm attempts to retain or increase its market share by differentiating its product from the output of other firms, either by making the product physically different, by advertising, or by combining both methods.

The individual firm thus perceives the relevant portion of its demand curve to be highly elastic (similar to the demand curve under perfect competition), but *not* perfectly so. In this setting very small price changes cause large changes in quantity demanded; and once the firm locates its profit-maximizing output and price, it tends not to tamper further with price adjustments but rather to focus its attention on product differentiation as a market weapon. It could, through this choice, increase its sales and profit at or near the existing price by enticing customers away from other firms.

Short-Run and Long-Run Equilibria Under Monopolistic Competition

Although firms do not explicitly recognize the interdependence of their prices under monopolistic competition, prices of the differentiated versions of the product do tend to move together. This occurs because the market has many buyers and sellers and will tend toward an equilibrium in a manner similar to that described for perfect competition.

Analysis of profit maximization by the individual monopolistically competitive firm requires that we not only consider the highly elastic demand curve (perceived or estimated by the firm on the assumption that it can adjust its price independently of other firms), but also a curve that shows what will happen if all firms' prices change together. This latter curve is called the firm's **market share curve**. In Figure 10–1, d is the demand curve perceived by the firm, and M, which looks like a less-elastic demand curve, is the individual firm's market share curve.

The **market share curve** describes the amounts the firm can actually sell at various prices as all firms in the industry adjust price together.

Points on M show the quantities of output the firm can sell at various prices if (1) all firms' prices change together and (2) the firm neither increases

Figure 10–1   Demand Curve, Market Share Curve, and Marginal Revenue Curve of the Firm Under Monopolistic Competition

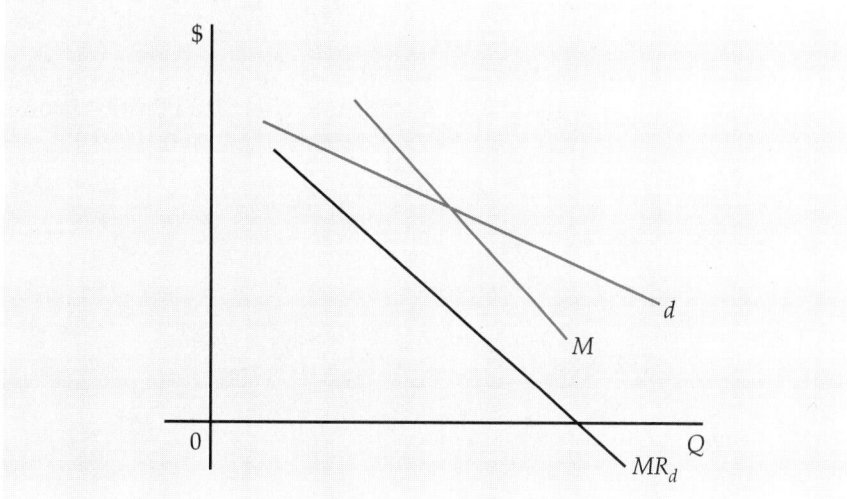

The monopolistically competitive firm ignores its rivals and estimates demand curve d and the marginal revenue curve, MR_d. The market share curve, M, shows how price and this firm's quantity demanded will be related when all firms' prices tend to move together.

nor decreases its share of the total market. The marginal revenue curve, MR_d, is based on the d curve, since that curve reflects the firm's view of demand.

Because of the tendency for firms' prices to reach a level consistent with a market-wide equilibrium, the individual firm in equilibrium will always be at the intersection of its d curve with its M curve. In other words, it will be selling the quantity consistent with its current price and market share and it will believe that it can do just that. If its belief is not consistent with its market share, it will adjust its price or differentiate its product (or both) until it reaches an intersection of d with M that is consistent with the profit-maximizing condition, $SMC = MR_d$.

The adjustment process could involve *both* revision of its estimate of d and the actual shifting of M as product differentiation alters its market share. With all firms in the industry practicing product differentiation, it is likely that they will just counteract one another's efforts. In this instance, M would hold still, and the path to profit maximization would entail shifting only the d curve.

Suppose a monopolistically competitive industry is in a period of falling costs and reductions in price by all firms. As adjustment takes place, an individual firm may find itself in a position such as that shown in panel (a) of Figure 10–2. At price P_a, the firm expected to maximize profit by selling Q_a but finds it can only sell Q_b. Why?

Because its market share, shown by the M curve, is not sufficient to sell Q_a at price P_a. The firm must therefore adjust its estimate of d. It may also adjust its price in order to find the profit maximum. Once it has done this, its solution will look like that in panel (b) of Figure 10–2, where its new estimated

Figure 10–2   Adjustment to Short-Run Profit-Maximizing Output Under Monopolistic Competition

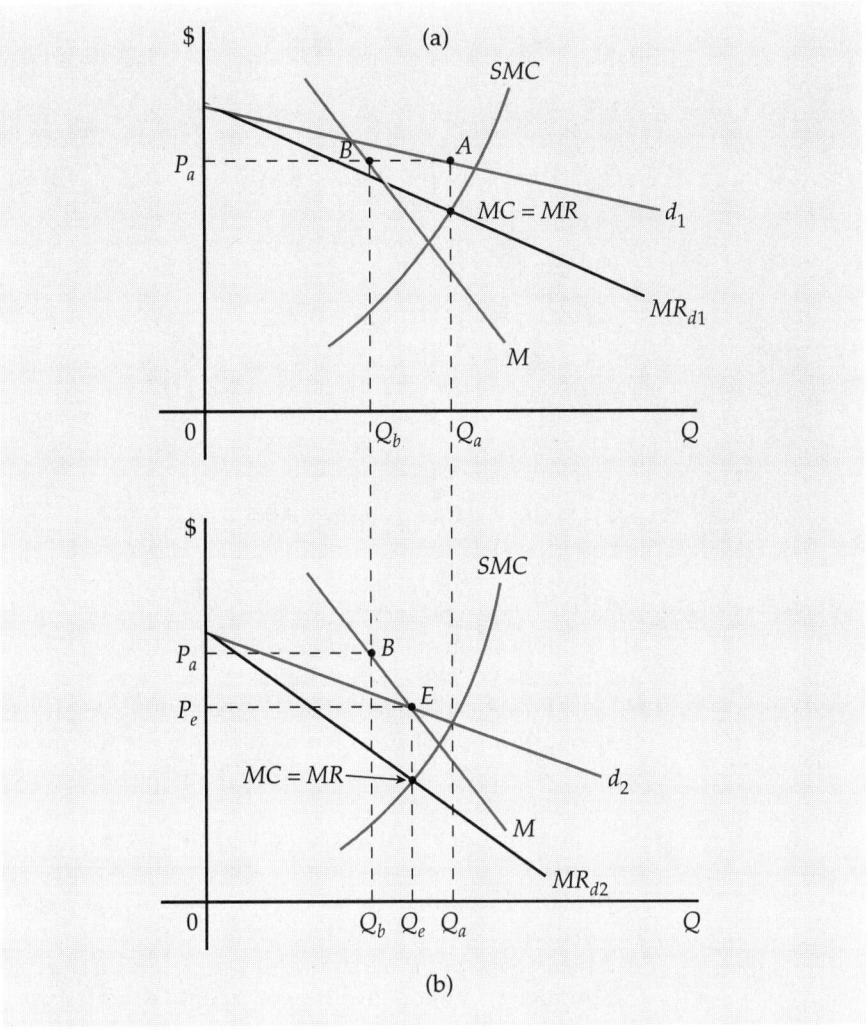

The firm is not in equilibrium in panel (a), since it cannot sell its estimated quantity, Q_a, but only amount Q_b, which is consistent with its market share. In panel (b) equilibrium and profit maximization occur at Q_e and P_e, a combination of output and price that lies on both d_2 and the firm's market share curve, M.

demand curve, d_2, and M intersect at the output consistent with $MR_{d2} = SMC$. In this example, the equilibrium price, P_e, is lower than the original one, P_a, and the quantity, Q_e, is higher than Q_b but lower than the previously anticipated quantity, Q_a. We have posited no change in market share, so the M curve in panel (b) is the same as the original one in panel (a).

The question arises as to whether, when all is said and done, the firm will regard segment BE of the M curve as its demand curve. This will not be the case, since the firm continues to believe that other firms will ignore its price changes and that demand will be very elastic, as shown by d_2. Since it believes it has attained a profit maximum relative to d_2 at Q_b, product differentiation (increase in market share) is viewed as the only route to higher profits. Successful product differentiation will move both d and M to the right.

In the long run under monopolistic competition, there is freedom of entry, and therefore firms will tend to have only normal profit. However, the long-run profit-maximizing position of the monopolistically competitive firm differs from that of the perfectly competitive firm because the firm's demand curve, d, has some downward slope. The negative slope of d ensures that the normal-profit, long-run position of the firm will occur at a level of output where the LAC is falling and, therefore, that the firm will utilize a somewhat smaller plant than it would have under perfect competition. In Figure 10–3, the tangency of d to LAC at Q_e shows that the firm believes it can obtain only

Figure 10–3   Long-Run Equilibrium Under Monopolistic Competition

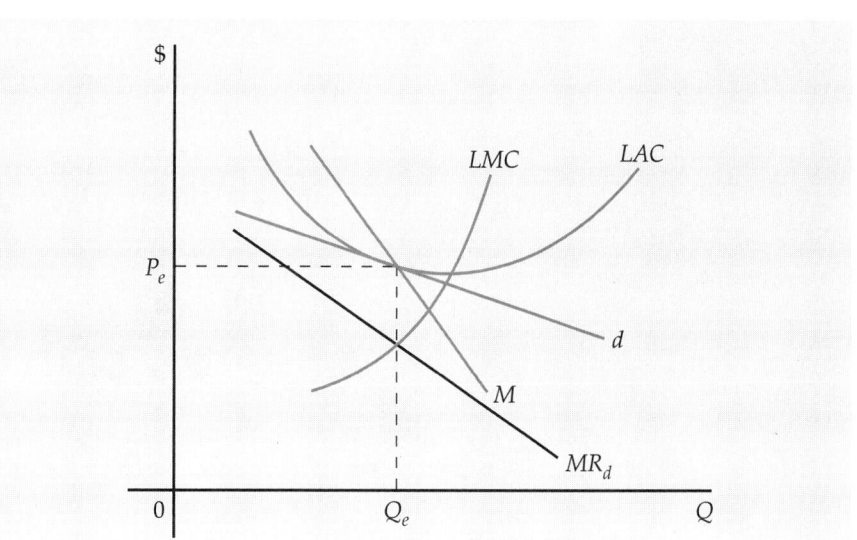

With free entry the long-run result under monopolistic competition is that $T\pi = 0$ and $P_e = LAC$ at Q_e. However, the firm does not produce at minimum LAC.

NUMERICAL EXAMPLE:

Monopolistic Competition

Bonnie's Brake Shop is an independent auto repair facility that specializes in quick-service brake jobs. It is one of many similar firms operating in a large metropolitan area. Bonnie currently averages 80 brake jobs per month on American cars at her standard price of $190. Bonnie is about to embark on a new advertising campaign that she believes will increase her market share to the point where she will be able to sell 110 of the brake jobs per month at the same price.

    a. If Bonnie's market share curve can be described by the equation $Q_m = 185 - 0.5P$ after the advertising campaign is in place, will she be able to sell 110 brake jobs per month? (Q is monthly output and P is price.)

    b. Suppose Bonnie's marginal cost at her new output is $100. If, after determining the result of her advertising campaign, she reestimates her demand curve to be $Q = 280 - P$, will she be maximizing profit? (Assume AVC is covered.)

Answer.

a. Bonnie will only be able to sell 90 brake jobs, since her market share at $P = 190 is

$$Q_m = 185 - 0.5(190) = 185 - 95 = \underline{90}.$$

b. Bonnie will be maximizing profit if $MC = 100, since for her estimated demand curve, $Q = 280 - P$,

$$P = 280 - Q, \text{ and } MR = 280 - 2Q,$$

therefore

$$MR = 280 - 180 = $100.$$

Thus

$$MR = MC.$$

normal profit, while the intersection of d and M at this same point indicates that Q_e, P_e is consistent with the market share of the firm.

Monopolistic Competition and the World of Business

When we look at the real world for examples of the monopolistically competitive market structure, a number of industries stand out as reasonable candidates. Certainly, most of the elements of monopolistic competition are found in independent retail trade in large metropolitan areas. In any given metropolitan market area, businesses such as boutiques, hairstyling salons, bars, and men's furnishings stores abound. Each has a slightly differentiated product in terms of location, brand names handled, atmosphere, or a combination of these characteristics. To the extent that one is more profitable than another, product differentiation will often be the key. However, extraordinary profits are unlikely to persist for any given firm unless it can block entry in the sense of keeping other firms from securing as good a location, array of merchandise, or atmosphere. Other markets that exhibit most of the characteristics of monopolistic competition are the "no name" clone personal computer market and the mail order market for cameras and video equipment. Sellers in these markets slightly differentiate their products, and entry or exit is relatively easy. Prices tend to be clustered very closely together.

Obviously, the manager of a firm in this kind of industry will be more successful over the long run to the extent that the firm's operations are adjusted in terms of product differentiation in a way that will provide the firm with at least temporary periods of greater than normal profit. If location or some other factor allows the firm to operate with greater than normal profit on a regular basis, then one would have to conclude that the firm is not monopolistically competitive but rather has succeeded in redefining its own market structure as something closer to differentiated oligopoly (oligopoly with differentiated product) or monopoly.

DUOPOLY: AN OLIGOPOLY WITH TWO FIRMS

As we noted earlier in this chapter, many conceivable oligopolistic situations can be analyzed using tools developed in the monopoly case. Even nineteenth-century economists recognized this relationship, and some tried to extend monopoly by asking what would happen if there were just *two* sellers of a specific product—a case known as *duopoly*. It is important to consider duopoly for two reasons. First, the models show that outcomes in oligopolistic situations will depend on what a given firm believes others will do. Second, study reveals that even in the apparently simple case of only two firms, a wide variety of results can occur.

Cournot's Model

A Frenchman, Augustin Cournot, examined the case of a costless monopolist whose market was entered by a second firm. He argued that if a monopolist selling spring water that was produced at zero cost encountered a rival with a spring yielding the same water at no cost, the two would end up supplying a combined quantity equal to two-thirds of the quantity that would be taken by consumers at a price of zero. Cournot's case is illustrated in Figure 10–4.

Figure 10–4   Cournot's Case of the Costless Duopoly

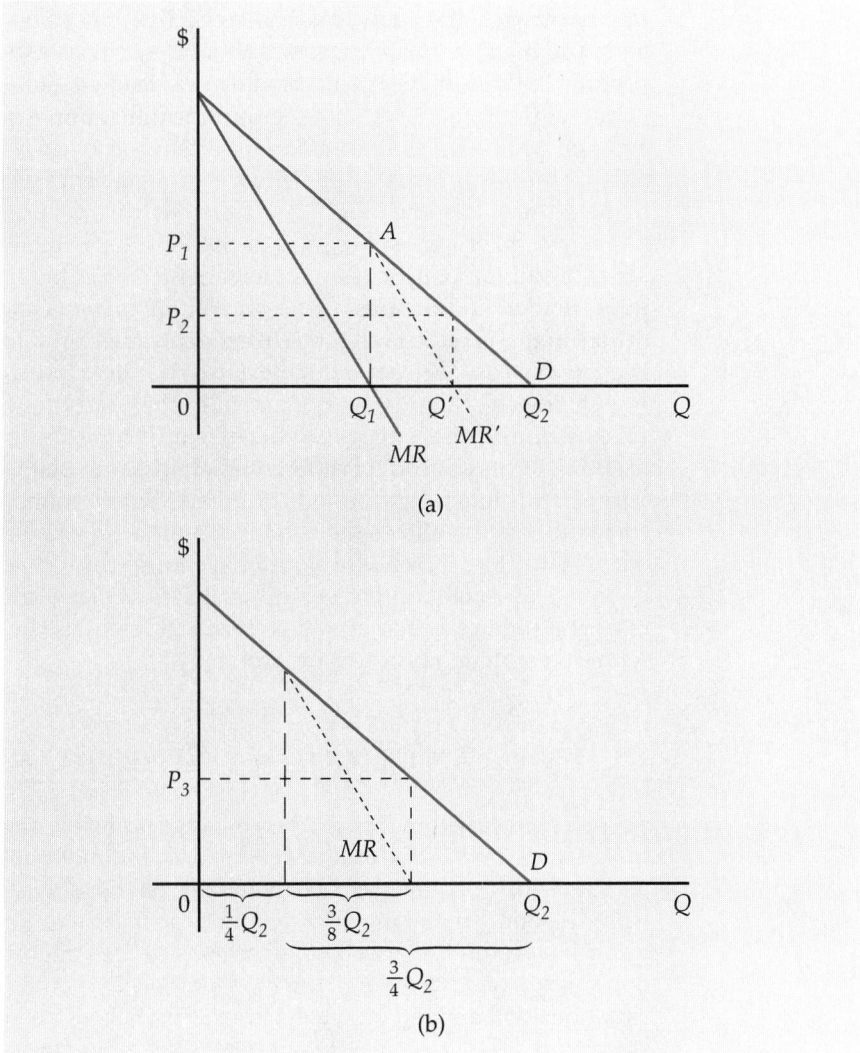

In panel (a) the second firm, believing the first will remain at Q_1, views its demand curve as segment *AD*. The second firm will, therefore, maximize profit at Q'. In panel (b) the first firm assumes the second will continue supplying $\frac{1}{4}Q_2$ and maximizes profit by selling $\frac{3}{8}Q_2$.

Cournot assumed that each of the two firms would profit maximize based on the belief that the other would keep its *output* constant. In panel (a) of Figure 10–4, we see Firm 1, the costless monopolist, facing market demand curve *D*. Q_2 is the amount of spring water consumers would take if it were given away free ($P = 0$). The monopoly firm maximizes profit by selling $Q_1 = \frac{1}{2}Q_2$ and charging P_1. With $MC = 0$, total profit is maximized where total revenue is maximized, or where $MR = 0$. With a straight-line demand curve, $MR = 0$ at Q_1, which is exactly one-half the output level where $P = 0$, or Q_2.

When the rival firm appears on the scene, it assumes that the first seller will keep output at Q_1 and then profit maximizes on the remaining market Q_1Q_2. Its demand curve is segment AD of the market demand curve, considering Q_1 as the origin, and from this relationship it derives MR'. It will profit maximize by selling quantity Q_1Q' or $\frac{1}{2}Q_1Q_2$, which is $\frac{1}{4}Q_2$. The two firms together are now supplying $\frac{1}{2} + \frac{1}{4} = \frac{3}{4}$ of the zero-price output. However, if Firm 1 tries to maintain price P_1, it will likely lose some of its customers to Firm 2. If Firm 1 assumes Firm 2 will keep its output constant at $\frac{1}{4}Q_2$, it will readjust to maximize profit based on the remaining $\frac{3}{4}$ of the market. In Figure 10–4, panel (b), we see Firm 1 profit maximizing at $\frac{3}{8}Q_2$ by allowing $\frac{1}{4}Q_2$ for Firm 2 and setting price P_3 based on $\frac{1}{2}$ of the remaining $\frac{3}{4}Q_2$ (in other words $\frac{1}{2} \times \frac{3}{4}Q_2 = \frac{3}{8}Q_2$). Now, the $\frac{3}{8}Q_2$ of Firm 1 plus $\frac{1}{4}$ or $\frac{2}{8}Q_2$ allowed Firm 2 places the total quantity on the market at $\frac{5}{8}Q_2$. However, Firm 2 will now react. It will assume that Firm 1 keeps output constant at $\frac{3}{8}Q_2$ and will maximize profit on the remaining $\frac{5}{8}Q_2$. This means that Firm 2 will increase its output to $\frac{5}{16}Q_2$. In Table 10–1 we summarize our results.

Note that if Firm 1 has an output of $\frac{1}{3}Q_2$ and Firm 2 maximizes profit on the remaining $\frac{2}{3}Q_2$, Firm 2 will sell $\frac{1}{2}$ of $\frac{2}{3}Q_2 = \frac{1}{3}Q_2$, which leaves $\frac{2}{3}Q_2$ not taken by Firm 2. Firm 1 now will maximize profit by producing $\frac{1}{2}(\frac{2}{3})Q_2$, leaving $\frac{2}{3}Q_2$ for Firm 2. The situation is stable. Each firm finds the other settling on $\frac{1}{3}Q_2$, and together they cover $\frac{2}{3}$ of the zero-price output.

Cournot showed that for costless producers with a straight-line market demand curve, the general production solution is:

$$\frac{n}{n+1}(Q_2),$$

where n is the number of firms in the market and Q_2 is the zero-price output. The larger the number of firms, the closer $n/(n + 1)$ approaches 1 and the

Table 10–1   Behavior of Firms Under Cournot Assumptions

	Round 1	Round 2	Round 3	Final Round
Firm 1	$\frac{1}{2}Q_2$	$\frac{3}{8}Q_2$	$\frac{11}{32}Q_2 \ldots\ldots$	$\frac{1}{3}Q_2$
Firm 2	$\frac{1}{4}Q_2$	$\frac{5}{16}Q_2$	$\frac{21}{64}Q_2 \ldots\ldots$	$\frac{1}{3}Q_2$
Total Market	$\frac{3}{4}Q_2$	$\frac{11}{16}Q_2$	$\frac{43}{64}Q_2 \ldots\ldots$	$\frac{2}{3}Q_2$
or,	$(0.750Q_2)$	$(0.688Q_2)$	$(0.672Q_2) \ldots$	$(0.667Q_2)$

closer we get to the perfectly competitive solution, which with zero-cost would be $P = 0$ and $Q = Q_2$.

It would be hard to justify Cournot's assumption that each firm makes decisions based on the other's keeping its output constant, for there is no particular reason for either firm to believe this. Surely after one complete round of decisions is made, each firm must know the other will indeed adjust its quantity. Furthermore, if there are only two firms, we can ask why they don't get together and set the price and total market quantity back at Q_1, P_1, which, with the given market demand curve, will maximize their joint total revenue and therefore their joint total profit.

Bertrand's and Edgeworth's Theories

Cournot was criticized even in his own time for the constant quantity assumption. Joseph Bertrand, a French mathematician and economist who wrote later in the nineteenth century, argued that each of the duopolists would assume that the other's *price* would not change, paying no attention to the rival's quantity. In Bertrand's analysis the price simply falls to zero as each duopolist tries to steal the other's customers by cutting price again and again.

At the close of the nineteenth century, British economist F. Y. Edgeworth argued still another solution to the costless duopoly problem. Edgeworth stated that if the duopolists each had limited productive capacity with respect to the quantity consumers would demand at zero price, a lower limit would be established below which price would not fall. However, Edgeworth showed that this price would not be stable, for once it is reached, one firm will assume that the other will stay at the price where it reaches its capacity limit and perceive that under these circumstances (1) the rival firm can sell no more because it is at capacity, and (2) an increase in price will increase profit. Accordingly, one of the firms will now raise price to the level that will give it maximum profit on the remaining market. The other will follow suit but will raise price only to a level slightly *below* the one established by the first. The reaction of the first firm will be to cut price, and, with successive rounds of cutting, the price will fall back to the lower limit. This restores the opportunity for one of the two to gain by raising price, and the price moves back up. This goes on *ad infinitum*, as long as each assumes the other will not follow a price change.

Chamberlin and Duopoly Theory

Of course, the Cournot, Bertrand, and Edgeworth analyses are all based on assumptions of extreme naivete on the part of the two firms. E. H. Chamberlin, who developed the monopolistic competition analysis we surveyed earlier in this chapter, stated in 1933, "When a move by one seller evidently forces the other to make a countermove, he is very stupidly refusing to look further than his nose if he proceeds on the assumption that it will not."[1] Chamberlin argued that the duopolists would recognize their interdependence and settle on a price that conformed to the monopoly price, splitting the profits between them. An agreement was not required, he stated, because the firms would realize quickly that any other strategy would be disastrous over the long run.

Chamberlin's approach to the problem of duopoly and certain of the notions he developed in his study of monopolistic competition represent a clear improvement over the older assumptions of naive behavior on the part of the individual firm or its managers. The key to Chamberlin's approach is what he called the recognition of *mutual interdependence* among oligopolistic firms. By this he meant that a firm in an oligopolistic situation will realize that its decisions affect other firms and that decisions made by other firms affect it. Some ideas about what constitutes rational behavior, from a profit-maximizing standpoint, are bound to emerge from this kind of setting.[2]

The most obvious solution to the management problem of competing or rivalrous oligopolists is to get together (collude) to formulate a strategy that is at least satisfactory to all the parties. The problem with this approach is that in the United States and many other countries, such action would be viewed as a conspiracy in restraint of trade and therefore a violation of antitrust laws. Another possible solution is to merge the firms into a single unit, but such mergers are also prohibited when not clearly in the public interest. What, then, are we left with when oligopolistic firms recognize their mutual interdependence? The answer, of course, is what Chamberlin suggested. The firms' managers will have to analyze their environment carefully and try to adjust their operations in a manner that signals to other firms in their group the desire to be profitable without being destructively rivalrous. After all, a price war, even in an industry with a fairly large number of firms, might leave many firms in a position similar to that of Bertrand's poor duopolists—out of business! Moreover, in a setting where one firm is much larger and perhaps more efficient than its rivals, any attempt to crowd out the smaller firms is likely to meet with antitrust action. (The role of government in preventing business behavior that is not in the public interest or that is unfair to rival firms will be discussed in Chapter 16.) We turn now to several oligopoly situations in which some standard tools of analysis can be applied to determine the appropriate strategy for managers of an individual firm.

---

1 E. H. Chamberlin, *The Theory of Monopolistic Competition* (Cambridge, Mass.: Harvard University Press, 1933), p. 46. Chamberlin's book includes an exhaustive bibliography in which the original references for the Cournot, Bertrand, and Edgeworth theories can be found.

2 For an interesting case of duopoly that apparently did not lead to joint profit maximization, see Ray Rees, "Collusive Equilibrium in the Great Salt Duopoly," *The Economic Journal* 103, No. 419 (July 1993), pp. 833–848.

THE QUESTION OF ENTRY

Duopoly analysis, in addition to raising the issues of rival reaction, strategy, and collusion, calls attention to the significance of entry. Usually, as we have seen, industry total profit is lower after entry occurs than monopoly profit was before entry. Even if joint profits are maximized (as Chamberlin argued), the original monopoly firm would logically have to give up some profit to its rival. Thus, in duopoly or other forms of oligopoly, existing firms will benefit in the long run if entry by new firms is somehow restricted. The matter of how entry is deterred or what conditions, known as **barriers to entry**, may keep new firms from coming into an industry is a matter of considerable debate in economics. However, if there are effective barriers to entry, oligopolistic firms, like monopolies, can have greater than normal profits in the long run.

Barriers to entry are conditions that make it difficult for new firms to enter an industry or market where existing firms have long-run interests.

Barriers to Entry

A brief survey of the economics literature on barriers to entry turns up several prominent candidates. One is *entry-limit pricing*. Entry-limit pricing is the practice of setting a price lower than the one that maximizes profit in order to discourage potential rivals from entering the market. Of course, it is a viable strategy only if existing firms' long-run costs are lower than those possible for new firms. This situation might occur in a mineral industry, for example, where existing firms had bought up the best ore deposits and new firms could enter only by working inferior deposits at higher than existing industry average costs.

Excess capacity and *economies of scale* are also often cited as barriers to entry. Excess capacity in existing firms can serve as a signal to potential entrants that the former will cut price and expand output in the face of any new firm's attempt to gain a share of the market. Further, if there are economies of scale, to be able to price competitively a new entrant may have to come into the market with substantial sales volume, something that will also depress price and perhaps make entry unattractive.

Capital requirements are another frequently identified barrier to entry. The argument here is that new firms will have to raise tremendous amounts of investment funds to install the plant and equipment needed to enter an industry where existing firms have had many years to build up their facilities. The automobile industry may be a good case in point. It takes a huge investment to establish a new firm in automobile manufacturing, so much that it is difficult to do so without support from a government. The Western economies witnessed two attempts to establish new automobile companies during the 1970s and 1980s. These were Bricklin (Canada) and DeLorean (Northern Ireland). Both had substantial government backing, but neither succeeded. (In Asia, however, Korean producers have managed to enter the industry and even to export to the United States.)

Another way firms can deter entry is through *product differentiation*. If existing companies have managed to establish a preference on the part of consumers for their products, it may be very difficult for new firms to attract customers. Existing preferences, in fact, may have various dimensions, ranging from brand identification based on advertising to consumer experiences with products that provide verification of product quality. Indeed, a long-term study of several hundred U.S. firms found that quality of products and services was very important as a determinant of profitability.[3] Moreover, if existing firms spend large amounts on advertising and promotion, new ones will have to do the same, something that further raises the capital requirements for entry.

Other barriers to entry have been identified (research and development expenditures, government policies, sales networks, economies of scope).[4] In any given industry, more than one barrier may be relevant, and some may be stronger in one industry than in another. Over the long run, barriers certainly are important to managers, who may either employ them to enhance the firm's position or be wary of them when entering new markets or lines of product. In the global marketplace, entry barriers may be even more important: consumer preferences are partly defined by culture, foreign governments may impede entry through regulatory means, and large multinational corporations may present newcomers with tremendous obstacles in terms of economies of scale and scope, capital requirements, and product differentiation.

Contestable Markets

During the 1980s, William J. Baumol and others advanced a new theory of oligopolistic markets that focused on entry.[5] Specifically, they defined what are called **contestable markets** as markets with few sellers but characterized by free entry. The theory, which predicts that oligopolies in such markets will price at perfectly competitive levels and have only normal long-run profits, rests on three assumptions:

Contestable markets are oligopolistic markets characterized by free and costless entry and exit and by a lack of rival reaction on the part of existing firms.

1. Entry is free and costless.
2. New firms can enter with no price reaction (or other reaction) from existing firms.
3. Exit is also free and costless.

---

3 R. Buzzell and B. Gale, *The PIMS Principles Linking Strategy to Performance* (New York: Free Press, 1987).

4 For a more thorough discussion of barriers to entry, see Dennis W. Carlton and Jeffrey M. Perloff, *Modern Industrial Organization* (Glenview, IL: Scott, Foresman/Little, Brown, 1990), especially pp. 172–176.

5 W. J. Baumol, J. C. Panzar, and R. D. Willig, *Contestable Markets and the Theory of Industry Structure* (New York: Harcourt, Brace, Jovanovich, 1982).

MANAGERIAL PERSPECTIVE

Soda Pop Wars and Duopoly Theory

While Coca Cola Company and Pepsico are not the only players in the soft drink market, they are certainly the dominant ones for cola beverages. There is, of course, a tremendous amount of image-oriented marketing hype pumped out by both companies. However, the two firms battle it out on the price front as well. It is easy to observe this at the local grocery store, where one or the other of the two brands is on sale very often.

Coke versus Pepsi has the basic elements of a duopoly case, since neither firm is worried to any great extent about what some third party will do. The pricing pattern of these two soda-pop giants appears to have elements of both the Bertrand and the Edgeworth approaches to duopoly. Certainly, there is price cutting as Bertrand described. However, as in Edgeworth's analysis, a point is reached after which prices begin to rise. Edgeworth attributed the eventual increase in prices to one firm's having run out of production capacity, thereby making it "safe" for the second one to raise price. In the cola market, analysts do not believe the price oscillations can be traced to such a cause. Rather, they argue that Coke and Pepsi both have focused on enlarging market share as a major corporate goal and have adopted strategies aimed at getting buyers to switch from one brand of drink to the other.

The switching strategy suggests corporate managers believe that, over the long run, greater market share will be synonymous with a higher value of the firm and, therefore, higher stock prices. However, long and frequent price wars may cost both firms more than either can hope to gain in market share. Industry research shows that about half of all soft-drink consumers are habitual brand switchers and are not likely to stay with a given brand when its price rises relative to that of a substitute. As one executive of a smaller beverage producer put it: "It is a battle between two very powerful companies that borders on a battle for bragging rights. . . . It's ego."

References: "Pepsi Revamp Lacks Sparkle," *Marketing Week* (July 12, 1996), pp. 26–27; "The Cola Kings Are Feeling a Bit Jumpy," *Business Week* (July 13, 1992) p. 112; "The Soda War Fizzes Up," *Newsweek* (March 19, 1990) p. 38; and "Coke and Pepsi Step Up Bitter Price War," *The Wall Street Journal*, October 10, 1988, p. B1.

The contestable markets theory was immediately criticized, primarily on the grounds that entry and exit generally are far from costless in an oligopolistic setting and that existing firms will most likely respond to entry (or even a threat of entry) with some price cuts or other types of rivalrous reaction. Some economists have suggested that contestable markets exist only in the minds of the proponents of the theory, while others have stated that the assumption of no reaction from existing firms " . . . stretches credulity to the limit."[6]

Probably the most important aspect of the contestable markets theory is that it points out that because of differences in strength or effectiveness of entry barriers, some oligopolistic markets are easier than others to enter. However, in virtually all such markets we can expect that there will be entry and exit costs and that existing firms will in some way react to incursions by new firms. From the standpoint of managerial decision making, then, the important conclusion is that these types of costs and potential rival reactions must be taken into account carefully when planning to enter an existing market.

By their very nature, the issues of entry barriers and contestable markets deal with the long run. However, there are many short-run situations in oligopoly analysis that can be analyzed using the tools we have developed in the contexts of perfect competition, monopoly, and monopolistic competition. We turn now to the kinked oligopoly demand curve, which is a direct descendant of Chamberlin's monopolistic competition model.

THE KINKED OLIGOPOLY DEMAND CURVE: PRICE RIGIDITY WITHOUT COLLUSION

The two demand curves used by Chamberlin in his analysis of monopolistic competition have also been applied to the case of price rigidity in *noncollusive oligopolies* (oligopoly situations where firms do not make any agreement among themselves regarding price, market share, or other conditions).[7] By *price rigidity* we mean the tendency for all firms in an industry to charge approximately the same price for a specific product over long periods of time. Such a phenomenon can be an indication that prices are being administered by collusive agreements in the industry, but it can also mean simply that each firm, acting independently, has determined that it cannot gain by departing from the prevailing price.

In Figure 10–5 we redraw Chamberlin's d and M curves (as in monopolistic competition), but we now use them to describe the situation faced by an

6 Donald A. Hay and Derek J. Morris, *Industrial Economics and Organization*, 2d ed. (New York: Oxford University Press, 1991), p. 579.
7 The kinked demand curve was first used by Paul Sweezy in a 1939 article, "Demand Under Conditions of Oligopoly," *Journal of Political Economy* (August 1939), pp. 568–573.

Figure 10–5   The Kinked Oligopoly Demand Curve

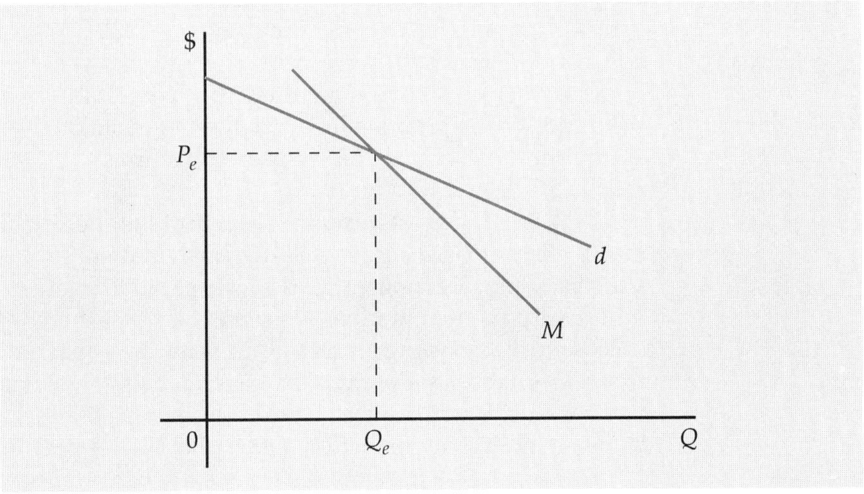

With a kinked demand curve, the firm believes that the *d* curve will apply for prices higher than P_e but that the *M* curve will apply for prices lower than P_e.

oligopolistic firm where mutual interdependence is recognized but firms do not collude. Unlike the monopolistically competitive firm, which always believed that some *d* curve was its actual demand curve, the oligopolistic firm is aware of the existence of both *d* and *M*. It knows that *d* shows what will happen if it changes price but no one else follows suit and that *M* shows what will happen if all firms change price together. However, the firm believes that if it raises price, no one else will (quantity will react along *d*) and customers will be lost to other firms. If it lowers price, everyone will follow suit (there will be a price war, and quantity will react along *M*) and few new customers will be acquired. In either case profit is likely to fall, since *d* is highly elastic and *M* is relatively inelastic. The firm thus takes the view that the demand curve consists of *d* to the left of Q_e, and *M* to the right of Q_e. It has a kink in it at Q_e, P_e; and price will, under most circumstances, remain at this kink. The reason for the inflexibility of price is that management will usually determine that no other attainable price-quantity combination will yield more profit than the one that exists at Q_e, P_e.

A **kinked demand curve** consists of an elastic range for price increases and a less elastic (perhaps inelastic) range for price decreases. In oligopoly, a firm facing a kinked demand curve will seldom wish to change price.

The preceding point is examined further in Figure 10–6, where the marginal revenue curve relevant to the **kinked demand curve** is introduced. Note that at Q_e there is a gap in the *MR* curve. To the left of Q_e, the *MR* curve is derived from the elastic portion of the demand curve (a segment of *d*). As the firm's output moves through Q_e, *MR* falls from a relatively high level to a relatively low level and is now derived from the inelastic portion of the demand curve. Finally, SMC_1 represents the lowest short-run marginal cost curve that

Figure 10–6   Kinked Demand Curve Related to Marginal Revenue and Various Marginal Cost Curves

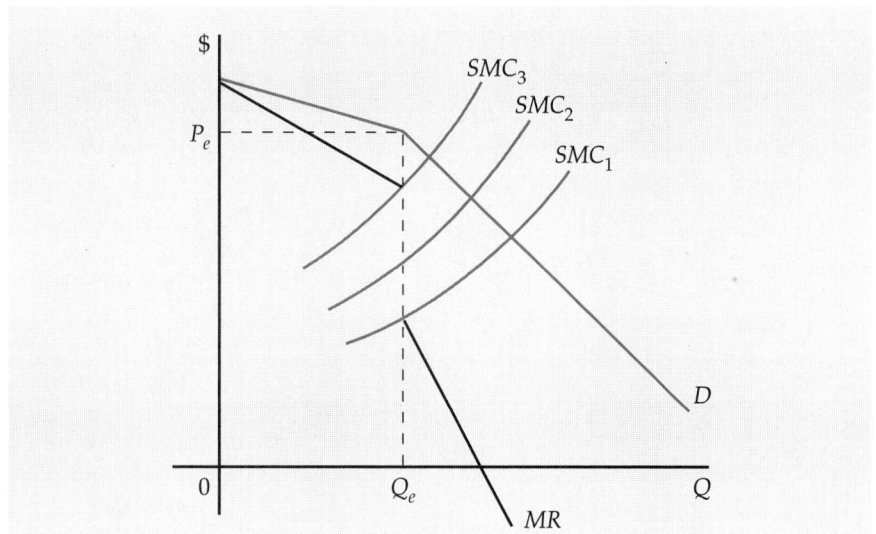

Since the kinked demand curve results in a gap in the *MR* curve, various marginal cost curves yield an equilibrium at Q_e and P_e.

would result in profit maximization at Q_e. We know profit will be maximized at this quantity, since to the left of Q_e, $MR > SMC_1$ and to the right of Q_e, $MR < SMC_1$. However, notice that this relationship also holds for SMC_2 and SMC_3. Thus the firm could have a wide range of marginal cost curves, and management still would have to conclude that Q_e and P_e would be the profit-maximizing output and price, respectively. We should note also that shifts in demand and related changes in the quantity sold might not change the profit-maximizing price, since the kink still might occur at price P_e. (Imagine the demand curve in Figure 10–6 shifting outward so that the kink is at a greater Q_e but is at the same P_e—a quite conceivable result.) Returning again to the question of managerial strategy, we note that all of the preceding simply suggests that where the firm expects rivals to match a price cut but ignore a price increase, it is unlikely that profit can be increased by altering price.

Nevertheless, in an inflationary environment such as was characteristic of western economies some years ago, an oligopolistic firm operating under conditions described by the kinked demand curve could easily find itself temporarily in a position where a price increase would make sense whether or not other firms followed suit. In Figure 10–7, the demand curve that management has estimated is dCM. The firm initially has marginal cost curve MC_1 and maximizes profit at Q_1,P_1. If rising input prices push marginal cost

Figure 10–7   Adjustment of Product Price and Quantity Under Kinked Demand Curve Oligopoly After an Increase in Production Cost

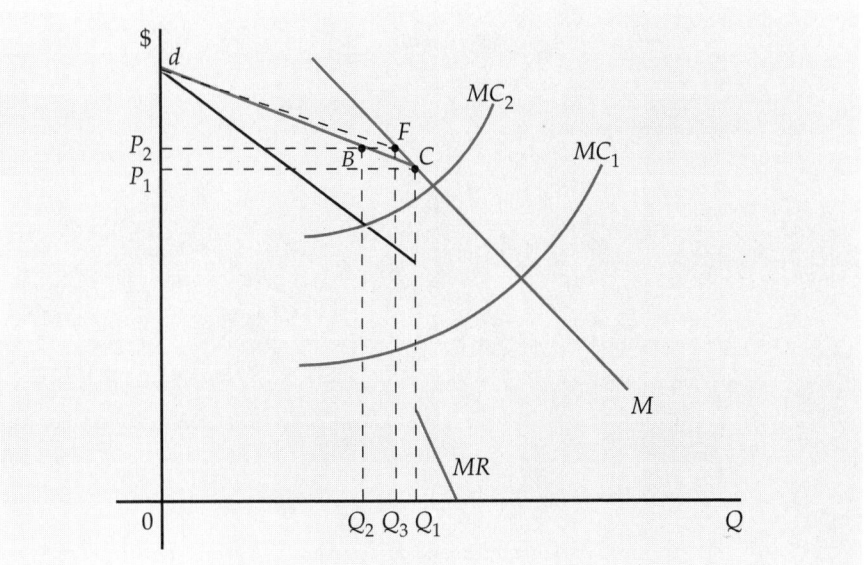

With inflation, this firm's *SMC* curve (MC_2) intersects the upper segment of *MR*. Thus, it should raise price to P_2. If all firms' costs rise, a new kink will develop at point *F*.

upward to MC_2, the firm should not wait to see whether other firms raise price, since over the short run it will profit maximize at Q_2,P_2 (which corresponds to point *B* on the elastic portion of *dCM*). If other firms follow suit (inflation would ensure this result), the first firm will adjust to point *F* on *M*, thereby increasing its quantity sold at price P_2 to Q_3. Ultimately, management would adjust its view of the market so that the kinked demand curve would be *dFM* and the firm would again be profit maximizing at the kink.

The Kinked Demand Curve Applied

When managers of a firm believe they face a market situation characterized by a kinked demand curve, it will be necessary for them to determine whether or not they can maximize profit at about the same price charged by their rivals. Furthermore, they may wish to look into the prospects for increasing market share (moving the *M* curve to the right) through product differentiation.

It is unlikely that a given firm will be able to maximize profit by pricing to the right of the kink in the demand curve, since this would require either extremely low or even negative marginal cost (an impossibility). However, when the industry is characterized by high rates of profit, some high-cost firms might well price to the left of the kink in their demand curves.

Suppose a firm selling electronic minicalculators of the type commonly sold in drugstores is operating in a market where management believes that price cutting will lead to retaliation by other firms but that other firms are unlikely to follow a price increase. (Industry profits are high at the going price.) The firm is currently pricing its machine at $10, but its marketing consultants have just come up with a new estimate of demand. Specifically, they state that if all firms change price equally, the monthly demand curve will be $Q_M = 1,500 - 50P$. However, if the firm can change its price independently of rival reactions, the monthly demand curve will be $Q_d = 3,000 - 200P$. The firm's total cost function is $TC = 1,500 + 3Q + .0025Q^2$.

In Figure 10–8 we see the marketing consultant's plot of the two demand

Figure 10–8   Kinked Demand Curve Analysis for a Firm Selling Electronic Minicalculators

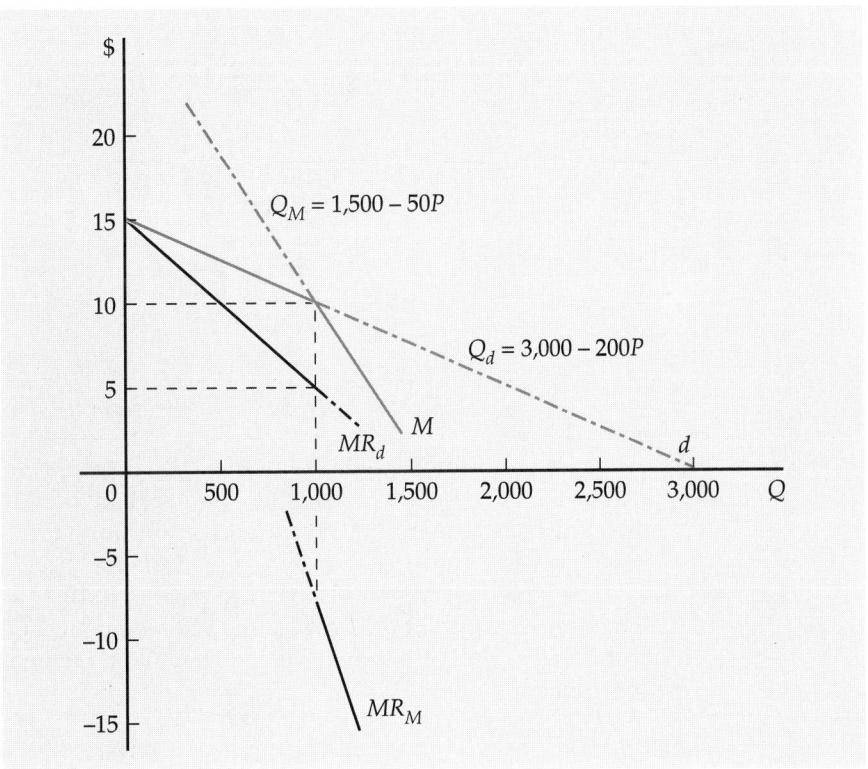

For this firm the gap in *MR* occurs at $Q = 1,000$, where $MR_d = \$5$. As long as *SMC* is less than $5 at this output, the firm should charge $10 per unit for its calculators.

curves for the firm's calculators. By solving for the intersection of the two curves ($Q = Q_d = Q_M$ and $P = P_d = P_M$), we obtain the maximum quantity the firm can sell without encountering a precipitous drop in MR. (MR will not always be negative for outputs greater than that at the intersection of d and M.) This occurs at $Q = 1,000$, $P = \$10$, or where

$$3,000 - 200P = 1,500 - 50P,$$

$$1,500 = 150P,$$

and

$$P = \$10.$$

Using the d demand function ($Q_d = 3,000 - 200P$), we can solve for P and obtain $P = 15 - .005Q_d$. In this case

$$TR_d = P \cdot Q_d = 15Q_d - .005Q_d^2,$$

and

$$MR_d = \frac{dTR_d}{dQ_d} = 15 - .01Q_d.$$

Using the market share demand function ($Q_M = 1,500 - 50P$), we obtain $P = 30 - .02Q_M$. For this demand function,

$$TR_M = P \cdot Q_M = 30Q_M - .02Q_M^2$$

and

$$MR_M = 30 - .04Q_M.$$

If we substitute 750 for Q_M in the MR_M function, we can see that MR_M will be negative for any level of Q_M greater than 750. However, MR_M is not the firm's *actual* marginal revenue function until *after* the kink in the demand curve.

The kink in the demand curve occurs at $P = \$10$, $Q = 1,000$, and $MR_d = 5$. However, the firm should only charge $10 per unit if at $Q = 1,000$ its marginal cost is $5 per unit or lower. Given management's estimate of the firm's total cost function,

$$TC = 1,500 + 3Q + .0025Q^2,$$

and

$$SMC = \frac{dTC}{dQ} = 3 + .005Q.$$

At $Q = 1{,}000$, $SMC = \$8$ and $TC = \$7{,}000$. Since $TR = 1{,}000(\$10)$, the firm would have an economic profit of $(\$10{,}000 - \$7{,}000) = \$3{,}000$ if it were to continue charging a price of $10.

If the firm's managers are astute, however, they will notice that at $Q = 1{,}000$, $MR < SMC$, since $MR_d = \$5$ and $SMC = \$8$. In Figure 10–9 we show the marketing consultant's demand curves along with management's marginal cost curve. Obviously, $MR_d = SMC$ at an output *lower* than 1,000 units per month. Specifically, where $MR_d = SMC$,

$$15 - .01Q = 3 + .005Q,$$

$$12 = .015Q,$$

and

$$Q = 800.$$

Along demand curve d, $P = \$11$ when $Q_d = 800$. If the firm charges $11 and sells 800 units, TR will be $8,800, TC will be $5,500, and economic profit will

Figure 10–9   Profit-Maximizing Output and Price for the Minicalculator Firm

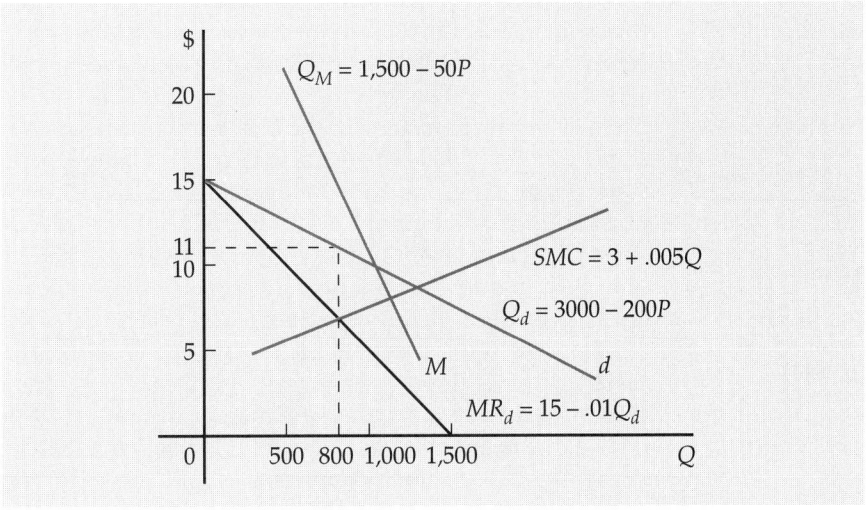

Since the firm's SMC curve intersects MR_d at $Q = 800$, a price of $11 per calculator should be charged, even though the kink in the demand curve occurs at $P = \$10$.

be ($8,800 – $5,500) = $3,300 per month. Since this profit is greater than the $3,000 per month economic profit at P = $10, the price should be adjusted to $11 per unit, even though management does not expect rival firms to follow a price increase.

TACIT COLLUSION AND PRICE LEADERSHIP

It should not be assumed from the analysis of the kinked demand curve that oligopolistic firms always determine their market strategies in the absence of interfirm negotiation or unwritten agreements. At the local level of operation, the existence of trade associations (the local homebuilders' association, for example) provides ample opportunity for exchange of information and tacit live-and-let-live agreements, even for relatively small and numerous firms.

In manufacturing industries characterized by large firms that are few in number, the incentive to avoid independent behavior detrimental to the group will be quite strong. However, in the United States, virtually any kind of specific communication agreement that has an effect (even a remote effect) on interstate commerce is subject to prosecution under the antitrust laws. Thus local firms that engage in price fixing in a given city but do not sell across state lines may still face federal prosecution if they have out-of-state competitors or buy inputs supplied from out of state. In short, it is only under rare circumstances that collusive business practices are immune from the antitrust laws, although some illegal practices do escape detection.

In many instances consumers are the only ones damaged by unfair business practices, and generally they are able to mount organized local campaigns against oligopolistic lawbreakers only when harm has been widespread and the identity of wrongdoers is obvious. Given the difficulty of prosecution of firms that utilize tacitly collusive business practices, it is not surprising that rather specific pricing patterns have developed in many oligopolistic industries. One of the best known patterns is that of **price leadership**. Usually, when the firm that is the leader changes its price, other members of the group shortly follow suit. In the United States such leadership has prevailed in the steel, automobile, rubber, and petroleum industries, although in any given industry the identity of the leader may have changed from time to time. Two market situations in which there is a clear reason for the price leader's identity are the *efficient firm case* and the *dominant firm case*.

Figure 10–10 depicts price leadership by an efficient firm where the market structure is duopoly. Here, Firm *A* is the efficient firm because of its lower marginal and average costs. The market demand curve is *D*, and if the two firms agree to split the market equally, each firm faces demand curve *D'*. (*D'* shows one-half as much quantity as does *D* for each price.) Price will be P_a, and quantity Q_a will be sold by each firm. Note that this is the price-quantity combination that maximizes profit for Firm *A* but that Firm *B*'s managers would rather sell a smaller quantity (Q_b) at a higher price. However, Firm *B*

Price leadership occurs when specific firms in an oligopolistic group (perhaps even one firm) set a price that subsequently determines what other members of the group will charge.

Figure 10–10   Price Leadership by an Efficient Firm

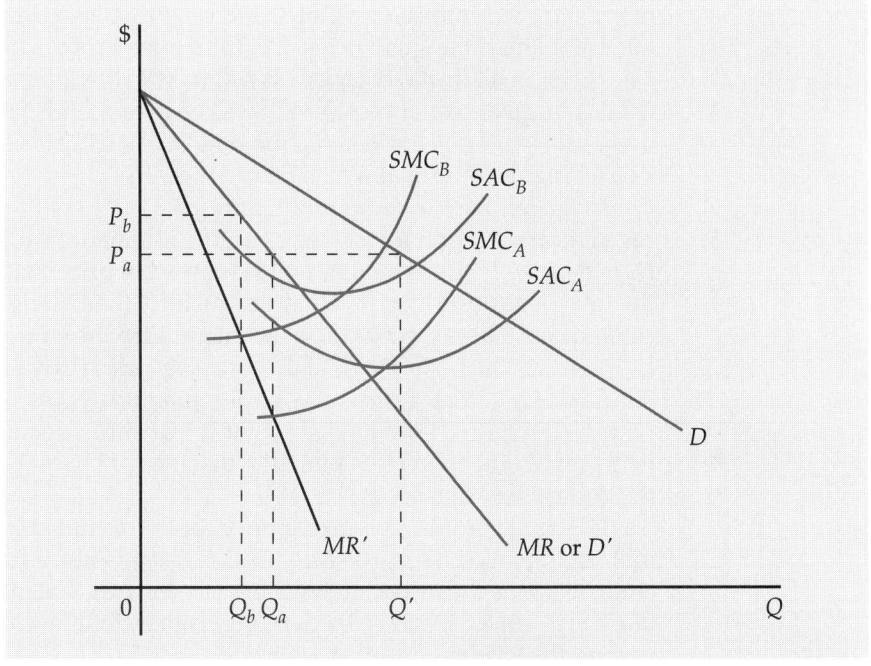

Since Firm A has the lowest MC curve, it will establish price P_a and Firm B will be forced to follow.

will have to be content with price P_a, since if it charged P_b, it would at least temporarily lose customers to Firm A. If Firm B persisted in charging P_b, it would get customers only to the extent that they were unaware of Firm A's price or that Firm A's output was depleted. At the latter point, something would have to give, but that something might be that Firm A would expand or duplicate its plant, thereby putting Firm B out of business. The conclusion can be generalized to an oligopoly of many more firms: Inefficient firms will have to follow the pricing decisions of efficient firms in order to survive, even if such action means lower than desired rates of profit for the followers. Of course, if following the price leader still produces normal or greater than normal profits for the less efficient firm and if other alternatives are risky, then followership may indeed be management's best strategy.

The dominant firm case of price leadership is usually described as one in which a single large firm is the price leader and smaller firms in the industry simply take its price as the going price, maximizing profit on this assumption. The problem for the dominant firm's management is to determine how much of the market small firms will absorb at each possible price and, based on this information, to choose the specific price that will maximize the profit of the dominant firm. In Figure 10–11 the dominant firm's estimate of market demand and the supply curve of the small firms is shown in the right-hand quadrant. Since the small firms take the leader's price as given, for them $P_e = MR_s$. Each small firm will equate its MC to MR_s; therefore the sum of the small firms' marginal cost curves, ΣMC_s, will be their supply curve, S_s. If the dominant firm were to set price at P_h, the small firms would absorb the entire market, selling the output at which S_s intersects D_M.

In the left-hand quadrant of Figure 10–11, we see the demand, marginal revenue, and marginal cost curves of the dominant firm. The demand curve D_L is derived by determining for each possible price the difference between the total quantity demanded and the quantity that would be supplied by the small firms. Since the small firms would absorb the entire market at price P_h, D_L intersects the vertical axis at this price. At price P_e we see in the right-hand quadrant that small firms will supply quantity Q'_s, the quantity consistent with $MR_s = \Sigma MC_s$, leaving $Q'_M - Q'_s$ of the quantity demanded for the dominant firm. Point A on D_L is plotted a distance of $Q'_M - Q'_s = 0Q'_L$ to the left of the vertical axis at price P_e.

If P_e is the profit-maximizing price for the dominant firm, it must be true that at Q'_L, P_e we find $MC_L = MR_L$. This is true in Figure 10–11, so we can conclude that P_e is the price that will be set by the firm's management. The dominant firm would locate P_e by deriving its marginal revenue curve, MR_L, and finding the level of output at which $MR_L = MC_L$.

Of course, the dominant firm may be sufficiently powerful in terms of its

Figure 10–11   Price Leadership by a Dominant Firm

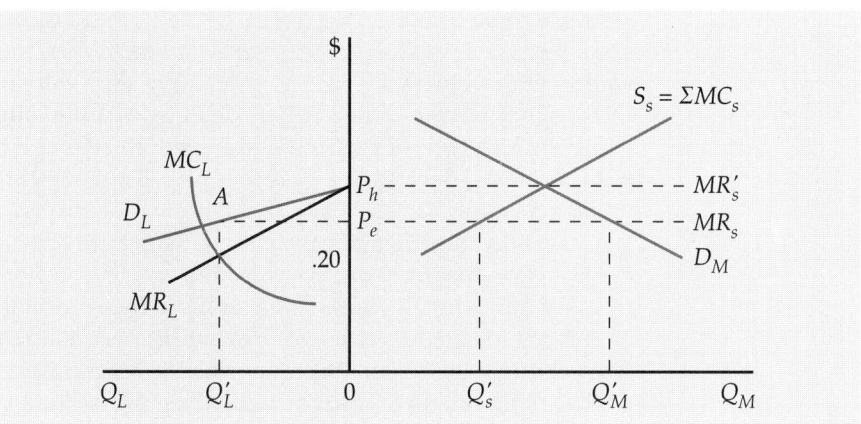

The dominant firm's demand curve, D_L is obtained by subtracting the quantity supplied by the small firms from the market quantity demanded at each possible price. The dominant firm then sets price P_e at quantity Q'_L which corresponds to the intersection of MC_L with MR_L.

ability (1) to sustain losses for a period of time, (2) to drive the smaller rival firms from the market, and (3) to establish a monopoly price based on the market demand curve, D_M. In the United States, the management of such a dominant firm would probably not take this step because of the provision against *predatory price cutting* (cutting price to an unreasonably low level in order to eliminate competition) in the antitrust laws.

U.S. Steel: The Dominant Firm Case Applied

In September 1985, it was reported that domestic steelmaking firms, "following U.S. Steel Corp.'s pricing action," would raise selling prices of sheet steel products some 3 to 4 percent.[8] At the time, this move amounted to an increase of approximately $18 per ton on cold-rolled sheet steel, the type used in the manufacture of automobile bodies. For many years, United States Steel Corporation (hereafter USS, although today its name is U.S. Steel Group, a unit of USX Corporation) was the dominant firm in its industry.[9] Over the past 20 years, the development of minimills that use scrap as their primary input has led to an increase in the number of small firms selling certain products alongside this giant firm. The new minimills are very efficient, lean on management, and in most cases nonunion. Thus, while the pricing policies of USS are still important in the steel market, the firm does not play the dominant role that it did 10 or 15 years ago.[10]

Things were quite different back when USS was more clearly the dominant firm. A particularly interesting case of price leadership in cold-rolled sheet steel took place in 1976. In April of that year, William Verity, chairman of Armco Steel Corporation, stated at his company's shareholders' meeting that there was a "desperate need for adequate price relief [increases] for the flat-rolled carbon steels, which continue to bear a disproportionate burden in the fight against inflation."[11] However, *The Wall Street Journal* reported that when questioned further, Armco's officers said they would not *initiate* such a price increase.

In mid-August 1976, USS announced that it would increase the base prices of its flat-rolled products an average of 4.5 percent. The price of one of the major items in this category, Class I cold-rolled sheet, would be raised from $296 a ton to $309 a ton.[12]

---

8 "Big Steelmakers Raising Prices to Fight Slump," *The Wall Street Journal*, September 26, 1985, p. 5.

9 The name of the parent firm was changed to USX Corporation in 1986.

10 In fact, in 1994 USS entered a joint venture with Nucor Corporation, a leading minimill producer, to perfect a new process for making steel from iron carbide. See "The Odd Couple of Steel," *Business Week* (November 7, 1994), p.106.

11 "Bethlehem Steel Joins Price Rises on Certain Items," *The Wall Street Journal*, April 26, 1976, p. 8.

12 "U.S. Steel Pricing Likely to Prompt Industry Boosts," *The Wall Street Journal*, August 16, 1976, p. 6.

The Wall Street Journal reported that some of the other firms in the industry were not happy with USS's decision to raise prices by only $13 a ton on cold-rolled sheet. However, it is quite possible that a larger price change would not have been in USS's interest. We can use the dominant firm model to investigate the *type* of situation USS faced, even though we do not have the firm's actual data.

Suppose that USS estimates the supply curve of the smaller firms in the industry over the relevant range to be

$$Q_s = 0.9P + 150,$$

where Q_s is the quantity of cold-rolled sheet that small firms will put on the market (measured in thousands of tons of product per month), P is the market price, and industry demand for the product is (in thousand tons per month)

$$Q_M = 1{,}403 - 2.6P.$$

Figure 10–12 illustrates these two curves in the $200–$400 per ton price range. USS would know that at a price of $358 per ton, $Q_s = Q_M$ and the smaller firms would produce enough cold-rolled sheet to supply the entire market.

By subtracting the supply curve of the small firms from the market demand curve, the demand curve for USS (Q_L) can be obtained. Thus

$$Q_L = 1{,}403 - 2.6P - (0.9P + 150)$$

$$= 1{,}253 - 3.5\text{P}.$$

From the preceding, it follows that

$$P_L = 358 - 0.2857Q_L,$$

$$TR_L = 358Q_L - 0.2857Q_L^2,$$

and

$$MR_L = 358 - 0.5714Q_L,$$

where TR_L and MR_L are USS's total and marginal revenue, respectively.

Suppose now that over the relevant range of production for the problem in question, USS estimates its marginal cost for cold-rolled sheet to be constant at $260. At the existing price of $296 per ton, the preceding demand curve shows that $Q_L = 1{,}253 - 3.5(296) = 217$. Accordingly, $MR_L = 358 - (0.5714)(217) = 234. Since marginal revenue is less than marginal cost ($234

Figure 10–12   Demand Curve for Cold-Rolled Sheet and Solution to U.S. Steel Price Leadership Problem

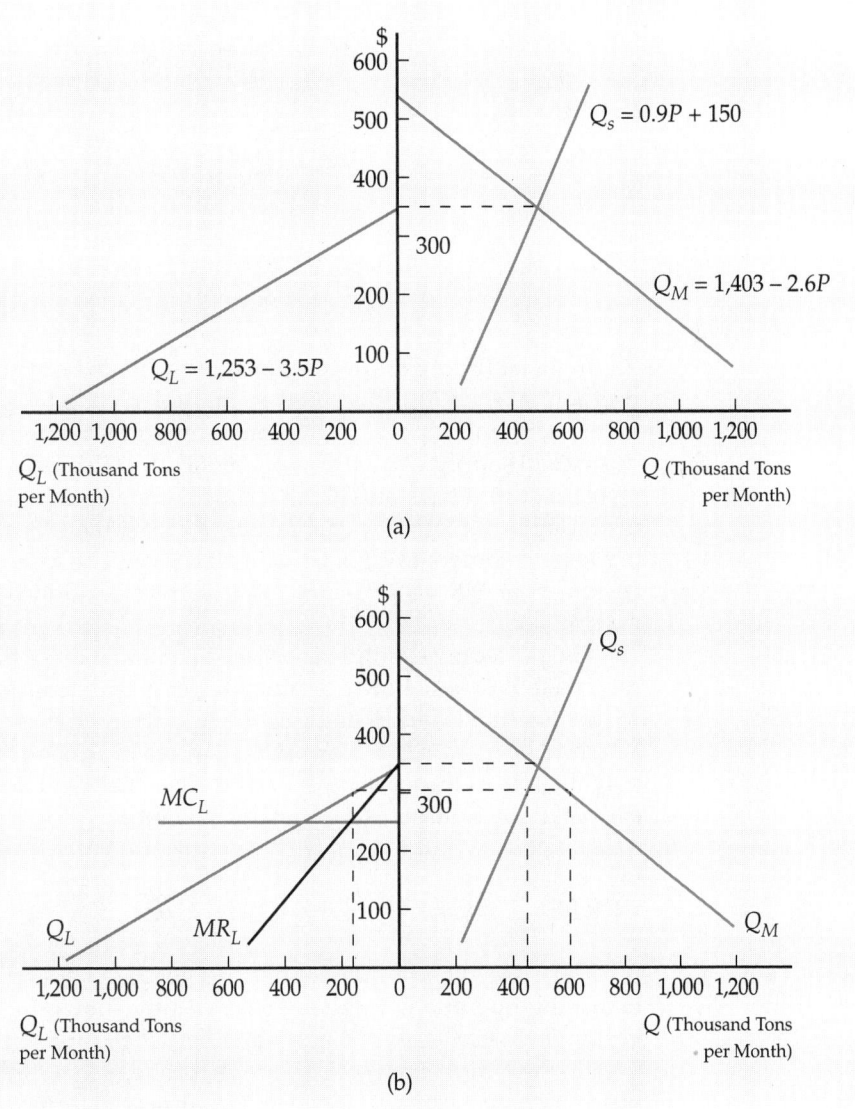

In panel (a), Q_L is equal to $(Q_M - Q_s)$. In panel (b), the leader's price is established at $309, since this price corresponds with the output where $MR_L = MC_L$. The small firms accept the $309 price.

< \$260), a price increase and reduction in quantity sold are warranted. USS should adjust its output to the point where $MR_L = \$260 = MC_L$ and charge the corresponding price. We can easily see that the above condition is met where

$$MR_L = 358 - 0.5714Q_L = 260,$$

or where

$$Q_L = 171.5 \text{ thousand tons per month}$$

and

$$P_L = 358 - (0.2857)(171.5) = \$309 \text{ per ton.}$$

In panel (b) of Figure 10–12, we illustrate the outcome of USS's pricing decision. At the \$309 price, total quantity demanded will be 599,600 tons per month. USS will supply 171,500 tons per month, and the other firms in the industry will supply 428,100 tons per month. If USS's capacity is such that it can increase output substantially at a constant marginal cost of \$260, then other firms cannot successfully charge a price higher than \$309, since they will simply lose customers to USS. Of course, USS will be quite happy to take their customers at $MR = \$309$, since this is a great deal more than the firm's \$260 marginal cost.

The preceding example has used a combination of actual and hypothetical data to illustrate how a dominant firm might determine a market price it wishes to establish for a single product. Currently, the steel industry is characterized by a more complex pricing system in which other firms sometimes play the role of leader. However, it is clear that rival firms still keep a close eye on USS, because it is such a large producer.[13]

PERFECT COLLUSION—THE CARTEL

A **cartel** is a group of firms that have joined together to make agreements on pricing and market strategy.

A **cartel** exists when a number of firms get together and agree on a policy of managing operations in a way that will maximize the joint profits of the group. *Perfect collusion* is simply another label applied to this market situation. In the United States, firms are prohibited from forming cartels for purposes of domestic trade. However, U.S. firms can form cartels for purposes of foreign trade, and a number of such organizations have been important in U.S. industry.

---

13 "U.S. Steel to Raise Certain Prices 6% as Demand Slides," *The Wall Street Journal*, November 29, 1991, p. A4.

In terms of the conditions for profit maximization, there is absolutely no difference between the optimal managerial strategy of a cartel and that of a monopolistic or oligopolistic firm that has several different plants. Still, the cartel's management does face the additional problem of *distribution* of profits among its members once the profit-maximizing price has been established, and there is no particular rule that must be followed in that distribution. Moreover, the main difference between the cartel and an oligopolistic firm with several plants is that the latter must estimate a demand curve that is something other than the market demand curve. Thus it should be clear that there are a number of good reasons to examine carefully the case of the multiple-firm cartel.

To maximize profit, managers of a cartel must allocate *production* to the individual member firms based on the "rule of marginal cost." Simply stated, this rule dictates that marginal or incremental output should always be allocated to the firm that has the lowest marginal cost. Thus, if the cartel consists of two firms, Firm A and Firm B, and management is adjusting output in a situation where $MC_B < MC_A$, then additional output should be allocated to Firm B. Presumably, as Firm B's output is increased, its marginal cost will increase. When marginal cost reaches a level equal to that in Firm A, additional output may be allocated to Firm A. In fact, at any time that $MC_A \neq MC_B$, the cartel can gain by switching output from the firm with higher marginal cost to the one with lower marginal cost. Thus, where profit is maximized, it must be true that $MC_A = MC_B = MR$.

This condition can be generalized to a cartel consisting of any number of firms. For example, a graphical solution for a cartel consisting of three firms is shown in Figure 10–13. Management determines the cartel's total output and price at Q_T, P_e, in the quadrant to the extreme right. This quantity-price

Figure 10–13   Allocation of Production by a Centralized Cartel

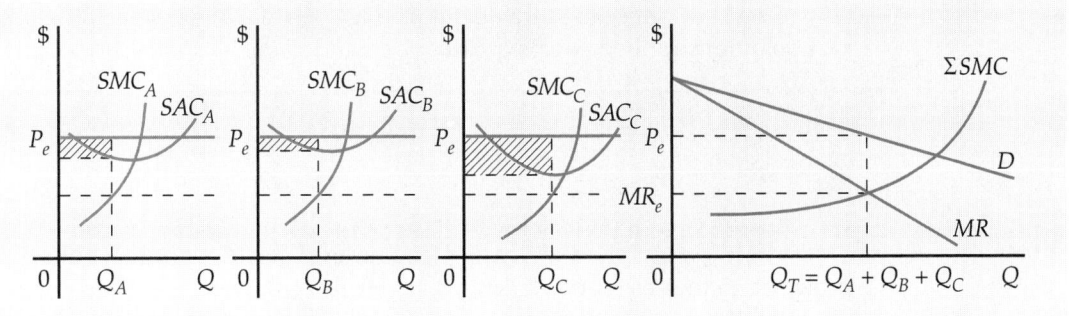

The marginal cost curves of Firms A, B, and C are summed horizontally to obtain the ΣSMC curve. The cartel's price is established in keeping with $\Sigma SMC = MR$, and output is allocated to each firm at the quantity where its $SMC = MR_e$.

NUMERICAL EXAMPLE:

Cartel Output Allocation

Producers in three countries, Irun, Sheran, and Uwaq have formed a cartel to sell highly prized desert oasis water in the world market. Suppose world demand for the water is consistent with the equation $P = 8.30 - .0005Q_T$, where Q_T is total cartel sales, and that the producers have managed to maximize profit at a price of \$5.65 per gallon. Suppose also that the countries have the following marginal production costs:

Irun: $MC_i = .25 + .00125Q_i$.

Sheran: $MC_s = .60 + .002Q_s$.

Uwaq: $MC_u = .15 + .0015Q_u$.

How much production should cartel managers allocate to each country?

Answer.

If the cartel has succeeded in maximizing profit at the \$5.65 price with the given demand curve, then all three of the above marginal cost functions will be equal to MR at that price ($MC_i = MC_s = MC_u = MR$). The marginal revenue function for the given demand curve will have the same dollar axis intercept as the demand curve and twice the negative slope, so it is $MR = 8.30 - .001Q_T$. To determine Q_T, substitute the price of \$5.65 into the demand curve to obtain $.0005Q_T = 2.65$ and $Q_T = 5,300$. Substituting $Q_T = 5,300$ into the MR function yields $MR = 8.30 - 5.30$, so that $MR = 3$. Setting each of the three MCs equal to 3 will yield the following:

$$Q_i = 2.75/.00125 = 2,200.$$

$$Q_s = 2.40/.002 \quad = 1,200.$$

$$Q_u = 2.85/.0015 \ = 1,900.$$

Of course, the sum of the three quantities (2,200 + 1,200 + 1,900) is 5,300, so that quantity supplied equals quantity demanded.

combination corresponds to the intersection of ΣSMC (the horizontal sum of SMC_A, SMC_B, and SMC_C) with MR. MR_e, the level of MR consistent with P_e, is projected to the cost curve diagrams for Firms A, B, and C, and each firm is allocated the output at which its $SMC = MR_e$. The cartel's total profit is the sum of the areas of the profit rectangles for the three firms, or $(P_e - SAC_A)Q_A + (P_B - SAC_B)Q_B + (P_C - SAC_C)Q_C$.

The cartel agreement might prescribe that each firm keep the amount of profit it produces, or it might provide for some other division of the total. For example, some of the profits of high-cost firms might be redistributed to the lower-cost firm (Firm *C* in Figure 10–13) as an incentive for the lower-cost firm to cooperate with the cartel. Otherwise it might try to break away and increase its market share by lowering price.

Usually the managers of a cartel place high priority on strategies that will keep the cartel from breaking up, since under rivalrous competition both group and individual firm profits are likely to be smaller in the long run. Nonetheless, bickering among cartel members over output and pricing decisions certainly can occur. The oil cartel, OPEC, represents such a case, where failure to agree on economic strategy led in 1990 to the Iraqi invasion of Kuwait and subsequent disasters.

The possibility of cartel breakup explains why managers might depart from the optimal solution of Figure 10–13 to some lower profit (for the short run) strategy that has a higher probability of keeping the organization intact. For example, where the cartel's markets are geographically widespread, the managers might decide only to divide markets, allowing prices to settle around a level so that price differentials are so small that it is not profitable for intermediaries to attempt to buy from one cartel member and sell in another member's territory. This approach might allow a higher-cost producer to charge a somewhat higher price, particularly if that producer's territory is somewhat removed from those of other producers. Thus, while the perfect collusion approach to cartel management provides a point of departure for cartel strategy, it is easy to see that the decisions made by cartel management experts in any given case may differ significantly from the theoretically optimal solution.

PRODUCTION WITH MULTIPLE PLANTS

If a firm has multiple plants, the condition for optimal allocation of output is the same as for a cartel—that is, the marginal cost of production should be the same in each plant or total cost can be reduced by shifting output from one plant to another. Of course, many large corporations have multiple production facilities and are faced with decisions regarding how much output to place in any one facility. Sometimes these facilities are located in a single country, but in today's global economy, multinational corporations frequently have to decide how to allocate production among plants located in several countries.

The appropriate allocation method can be illustrated with a simple example. Suppose Benwag Corporation has plants for relining brake shoes in the United States, Canada, and Mexico. All output sold in the U.S. market is shipped to a distribution center in Kansas, and shipping costs from the three plants to the center do not differ significantly. Canadian and Mexican domestic sales are small compared with sales in the United States. If the plants have the marginal costs given in the table that follows, what is the optimal allocation of a total output of 14,000 units per week?

United States		Canada		Mexico	
Quantity	Marginal Cost	Quantity	Marginal Cost	Quantity	Marginal Cost
0		0		0	
	6.40		6.40		6.00
1,000		1,000		1,000	
	6.20		6.50		6.14
2,000		2,000		2,000	
	6.24		6.69		6.29
3,000		3,000		3,000	
	6.30		6.89		6.46
4,000		4,000		4,000	
	6.50		7.10		6.70
5,000		5,000		5,000	
	6.71		7.32		7.00
6,000		6,000		6,000	
	7.00		7.55		7.40
7,000		7,000		7,000	
	7.35		7.79		7.90
8,000		8,000		8,000	

Recall that the condition for optimal allocation, as in the cartel model, is that the marginal cost should be the same in all plants. With the given tabular data, each increment of 1,000 units of output should be allocated to the plant that can produce it at the lowest marginal cost. Thus the first 1,000 units would be allocated to the Mexican plant, where marginal cost is $6.00. In fact, 3,000 units can be allocated to the Mexican plant before any are allocated to the U.S. or Canadian plants, since their initial marginal costs are both $6.40. Production of 4,000 units would be accomplished at least cost by producing the incremental 1,000 in either the U.S. or the Canadian plant, since their marginal costs of $6.40 are below the Mexican marginal cost of $6.46 for the next increment. The optimal allocation for the required 14,000 units is highlighted in the table: 6,000 units for the U.S. plant, 3,000 for the Canadian plant, and 5,000 for the Mexican plant. The marginal costs of the last units produced in each plant are approximately the same, or about $6.70. It would not be rational to increase the output of one of the plants and decrease that of another, since for each plant, an increase beyond its current allocation would yield marginal cost greater than $6.71, the marginal cost of the last 1,000 units that were allocated to the plant in the United States.

SUMMARY

Oligopoly Analysis and Business Behavior

In this chapter we have taken an important step from the rather simplistic analyses of the perfectly competitive and monopolistic market structures to the more complex world of monopolistic competition and oligopoly. The importance of this chapter lies in the fact that the situations we have discussed encompass many additional elements with which a majority of U.S. firms must deal in the development of their managerial strategy. These elements (product differentiation, rival reactions, price leadership, and collusion) may be significant in the decision process any time a seller's market is not characterized by perfect competition or monopoly.

We have stated that a firm in an industry structure characterized by monopolistic competition maximizes profit at a level of output where its perceived demand curve intersects its market share demand curve and $MR_d = SMC$. In the long run, a monopolistically competitive firm can expect to make only a *normal* profit because of entry of other firms.

In the case of an oligopolistic market structure, however, there are substantial barriers to entry, and long-run economic profits are possible. Early in this chapter we discussed the duopoly theories of Cournot, Bertrand, and Edgeworth in which a firm makes naive assumptions regarding the behavior of the other firm, in spite of contradictory experiences. (Cournot indicated that each firm believes the other firm will not change its level of output, whereas Bertrand and Edgeworth assumed that each firm believes the other firm will hold price constant.)

Later in the chapter we discussed more realistic theories of oligopolistic firm behavior, each based to some extent on Chamberlin's assumption that such firms recognize their *mutual interdependence*. These theories included the kinked demand curve, price leadership, and cartel hypotheses. We have shown that what actually happens in an oligopolistic market structure is influenced to a large extent by its legal environment and by the extent to which the firms in an industry cooperate with one another.

We have only scratched the surface of the number of conceivable oligopoly situations, but we hope to have demonstrated that it is possible to apply the tools developed in earlier chapters to management's decision problems in a wide variety of oligopolistic settings. (An additional analytical device, game theory, is discussed in the appendix to this chapter.) In Chapter 11, we will continue to apply now-familiar approaches to realistic situations, analyzing a number of specific pricing problems that firms in monopolistically competitive or oligopolistic markets are likely to face.

QUESTIONS

1. What is the significance of product differentiation in a market characterized by monopolistic competition?
2. How is the kinked oligopoly demand curve related to the demand curve faced by a monopolistically competitive firm? How does the oligopolistic firm's perception of the inelastic portion of its demand curve differ from the perception of the monopolistically competitive firm regarding its demand?
3. Give some examples of product markets in your community that can be identified as monopolistically competitive. Why do you believe they fit the case?
4. Why do the nineteenth-century oligopoly models generate different conclusions about duopoly? Can you see any relationship between Chamberlin's critique of the duopoly models and the cases of price leadership discussed in this chapter?
5. Under what conditions would an oligopolistic firm facing a kinked demand curve charge a price different from the one that occurs at the kink?
6. Although General Motors is not always the price leader in the U.S. automobile industry, do you think it can be characterized as the dominant firm? Why or why not?
7. Can you state simply the rule by which a cartel should allocate output among its members to maximize profit? Why might a cartel choose to do otherwise?
8. Why can we expect that monopolistically competitive firms will tend to have only normal profits in the long run, whereas oligopolistic firms may well have greater than normal profits?
9. Gasoline stations have often been used to describe kinked demand curve oligopoly. Why do they appear to fit the case?
10. Briefly explain how a large and dominant firm's demand curve may be related to the market demand curve for its product under the assumption that smaller firms will follow its price leadership.

PROBLEMS

1. The firm in the diagram is in the short run in a monopolistically competitive market.
   a. Derive the firm's marginal revenue curve.

b. Indicate its short-run profit-maximizing output, supplying an appropriate *SMC* curve in the diagram.

c. Add a short-run average cost curve such that the firm has greater than normal profit.

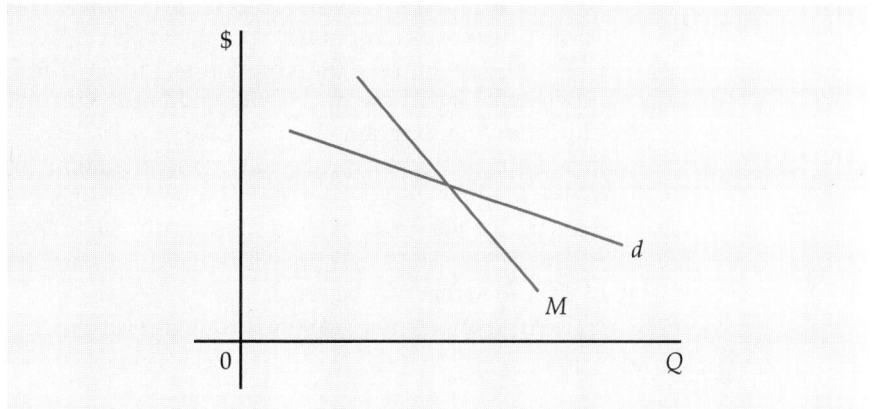

2. The monopolistically competitive firm in the following diagram is not in a long-run profit-maximizing position. Why not? What changes would have to occur for it to get to such a position? (*Hint:* Compare this diagram with Figure 10–3 in this chapter.)

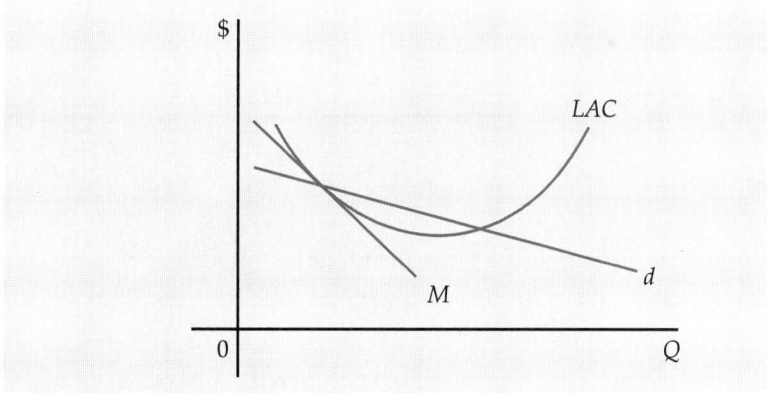

3. Suppose your favorite charity is participating in a fund-raising carnival that will run for three nights. You have been put in charge of managing the kissing booth. All labor at the carnival is voluntary, including that of the kissers, so you believe that you have a costless monopoly. Given your estimate of the nightly demand for kisses,

$$Q_k = 5{,}000 - 25{,}000P_k,$$

a. What price will yield the most revenue for your charity?
b. If another charity opens a kissing booth adjacent to yours but demand remains as above (assume the product is undifferentiated), what price will prevail and how much revenue will each booth generate under the Cournot assumption?
c. Could you improve the situation in part (b) through collusion? If not, why not? If so, how, and what would be the result in terms of revenue?

4. The following diagram shows a case of price leadership by a dominant firm. SMC_L is the marginal cost curve of the dominant firm, S_s is the sum of the marginal cost curves of the "follower" firms, and D_M is the market demand for the product. Find graphically the following information:
a. The demand and marginal revenue curves of the price leader.
b. The price that will be set.
c. The quantity sold by (i) the leader and (ii) the follower firms.

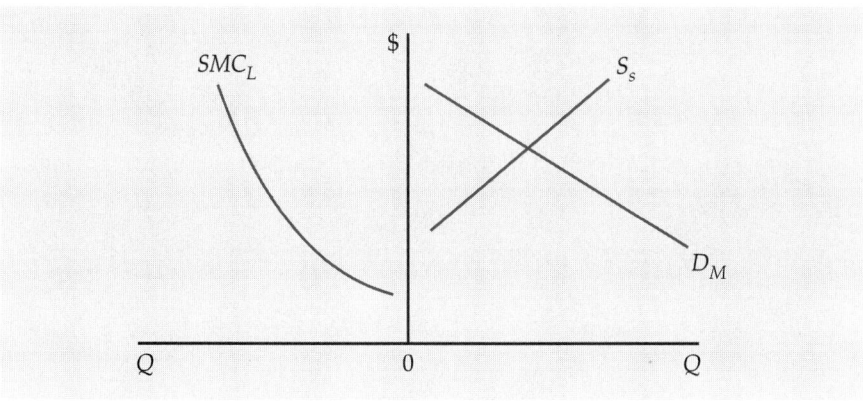

5. Suppose a large firm that is a price leader in an industry characterized also by many small, competing firms estimates the market demand for its product to be

$$Q_M = 81{,}000 - 200P,$$

and that it expects small firms in the industry to supply output according to the following function:

$$Q_s = 1{,}000 + 50P.$$

The large firm's marginal cost function is

$$MC_L = 100 + .014Q_L.$$

   a. What price will the large firm set?
   b. How much will the large firm sell?
   c. What quantity will the small firms sell?

6. The two firms in the following diagram decide to form a cartel. Find graphically the following information:
   a. The market price of their output.
   b. The quantity each firm will sell.
   c. The total profits of the cartel.

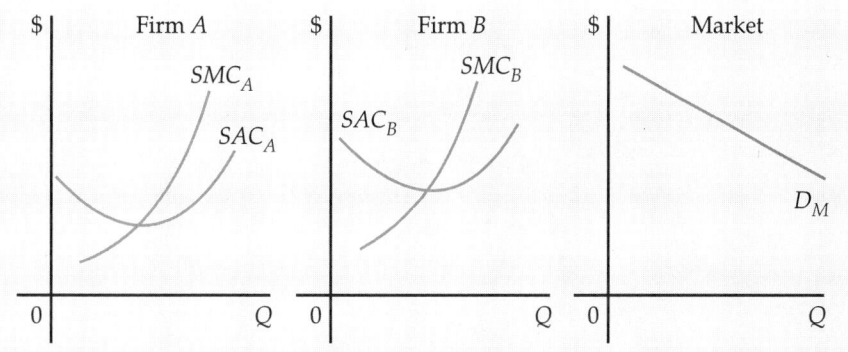

7. A cartel is maximizing profit at a price of $37.50 per barrel for its product. The demand curve for the members' product is given by the equation $Q = 200,000 - 4,000P$, so that $MR = 50 - .0005Q$. Suppose there are three firms in the cartel with the following respective marginal cost functions:

$$MC_1 = 2 + .001Q_1,$$

$$MC_2 = 1.9 + .0012Q_2,$$

and

$$MC_3 = 9.5 + .002Q_3.$$

How much output should be allocated to each cartel member? (Assume that Q_i is yearly output in barrels and that MC_i is marginal cost per barrel.)

8. Suppose an oligopolistic firm has the following cost and revenue data.
   a. Fill in the blank spaces in the table.
   b. What output should the firm produce? Why?
   c. What price should the firm charge, and what will be its economic profit?

MR	Q	P	TR	TVC	AVC	AFC	SMC
	0	120	0	0	—	—	
———	10		1150	600		60	———
———	20		2200		40		———
———	30	105	3150	900			———
———	40	100		1120			———
———	50	95			30		———
———	60		5400		40		———
———	70		5950		50	8.57	———
———	80		6400	4800		7.50	———
———	90	75		7200		6.67	———

9. The following diagram is for an oligopolistic firm that faces a kinked demand curve. Complete it by constructing the firm's marginal revenue curve and adding a marginal cost curve that is consistent with maximizing profit at the price and quantity that occur at the kink.

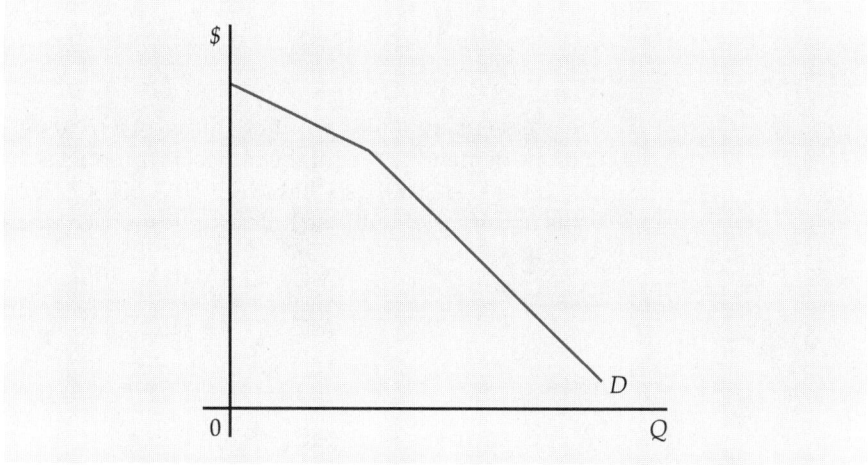

The following problems require calculus.

C1. Gnoma Pest Control Company specializes in pest control services for single-family homes. Entry is easy in the local market, and a large number of local firms offer similar services. The typical contract provides wholehouse service, including one interior spraying per month and a yearly foundation spray. The cost to the company can be regarded as a constant amount per unit at

$$AVC = \$5 \text{ per month per home.}$$

Advertising and image are important to pest control firms in the local market, since this method is about the only way they can differentiate what is otherwise a fairly homogeneous output. Gnoma's management advertised heavily to get the firm established but has recently cut the firm's advertising by one-half. Management now estimates the firm's demand curve for household service to be

$$Q = 25{,}000 - 2{,}000P,$$

where Q is the quantity of homes under service contract and P is the *monthly* service charge.

a. Based on management's estimate of demand, at what price and quantity sold should Gnoma be able to maximize profit?

b. If monthly fixed costs are $12,000, what will monthly profit be?

    After the reduction in advertising, Gnoma's sales fell to 5,250 homes under monthly contract. A market analyst states that this drop occurred because Gnoma's market share fell when advertising expenditures were cut. The analyst further states that under conditions of the current advertising level, Gnoma should estimate its demand curve as

$$Q' = 22{,}000 - 2{,}000P.$$

The analyst states that Gnoma can either maximize profit subject to the preceding demand curve (Q') or spend an additional $5,000 per month on advertising and move back to the originally estimated demand curve, recovering its market share.

c. If Gnoma's management maximizes profit subject to

$$Q' = 22{,}000 - 2{,}000P,$$

what is the firm's optimal output and price?

d. Is the preceding profit greater or less than the profit that would be obtained by spending the $5,000 per month on advertising and returning to

$$Q = 25{,}000 - 2{,}000P?$$

e. What should Gnoma do?

C2. A firm's research department has estimated that if other firms in the industry are indifferent to changes in the price of its product, its demand curve will be

$$Q = 700 - 50P.$$

However, if other firms always charge the same price it does, the firm's demand curve will be

$$Q' = 200 - 10P$$

a. If the firm's marginal cost equals $8.00, what output and price will maximize profit? (Assume that the other firms will not follow a price rise above $12.50 but that they will follow a price cut below $12.50.)

b. If the firm's marginal cost equals $11.50, what output and price will maximize profit?

C3. The following is a demand curve that has been estimated for an oligopolistic firm:

$$AR = P_x = 160 - (1/2)Q_x,$$

where Q_x is the quantity of Product X sold per month, and P_x is its price per unit. If the firm's total cost function is

$$TC_x = 500 + 40Q_x - 1.5Q_x^2 + (1/3)Q_x^3,$$

a. Determine the quantity produced (sold) that will maximize profit.

b. Indicate the dollar amount of profit for the firm at the preceding output per month.

C4. Phunny Phaucet Corporation of America (PPCA) operates in a noncollusive oligopolistic market where firms tend to base their strategies on fear of their rivals. PPCA believes that at its current price its demand curve will be $Q = 400 - 4P$ if it raises price, since it expects that other firms will not follow a price increase. For price cuts, however, it believes its demand curve is $Q = 250 - 2P$, since other firms are expected to follow a reduction in price.

a. With the above assumptions, what are PPCA's current price and quantity sold?

b. Suppose PPCA's total cost function is

$$STC = 50 + 20Q + 0.1Q^2.$$

Is PPCA maximizing its profit at the quantity and price you found in part (a)? Explain why or why not.

c. Now suppose that PPCA has made an error in the estimate of its total cost function so that the actual total cost is

$$STC = 60 + 30Q + 0.25Q^2.$$

With this revised total cost function, what is the firm's best output and price?

C5. Aqualor Corporation is a very large producer of swimming pool electronic control valves. Aqualor typically charges a standard price for a valve that fits many different brands of swimming pool equipment. Aqualor's management realizes that smaller firms in its industry will always charge exactly the price that Aqualor sets and currently estimates the market demand curve for the valves to be

$$Q_M = 7{,}520 - 75P.$$

Aqualor's total cost function can be represented by the equation $TC = 85{,}000 + 8Q + .001Q^2$. In addition, it has estimated that the smaller firms' supply curve can be represented by the equation $Q_s = 120 + 25P$.

a. What price will Aqualor charge for its valves, and how many will it sell?

b. How many valves will the smaller firms supply?

c. What will be the total profit or loss of Aqualor Corporation?

C6. Starcom Communications of America (SCA) operates in a noncollusive oligopolistic market where firms tend to base their strategies on good old-fashioned fear. SCA believes that at its current price its demand curve will be $Q = 3{,}000 - 20P$ if it raises price, since it expects that other firms will not follow a price increase. For price cuts, however, it believes its demand curve is $Q = 1{,}800 - 10P$, as other firms are expected to follow a reduction in price.

a. With the above assumptions, what are SCA's current price and quantity sold?

b. Suppose SCA's total cost function is

$$STC = 20{,}000 + 3Q + .05Q^2.$$

Is SCA maximizing its profit at the quantity and price you found in part (a)? Explain why or why not.

c. Now suppose that SCA has made an error in its estimate of the total cost function so that the actual total cost is

$$STC = 20{,}000 + 7Q + .08Q^2.$$

With this revised total cost function, what is the firm's profit-maximizing price, output, and total profit?

C7. Lullabye Corporation produces inexpensive baby crib mattresses that it sells to furniture manufacturers. For its segment of market demand, it currently estimates the demand curve it faces to be $Q = 3{,}800 - 100P$, where Q refers to monthly output. Lullabye has two plants, one located in No Hope, Arkansas, and another in Dime Box, Texas. The marginal cost in the Arkansas plant is $MC_A = 10 + .02Q_A$. In the Texas plant it is $MC_T = 8 + .03Q_T$. (In both, Q_i is monthly output.) Management believes it will maximize profit at a price of $29 per mattress. Assuming the price is correct, how much output should be allocated to each plant?

C8. Ajax Roofing Company is located in a small metropolitan area where it is one of six companies that specialize in reshingling. Management knows that basic reshingling jobs are selling in its market area for $82 per square (100 sq. ft.). From data on its past price increases, none of which were followed by the other firms, Ajax has estimated that its demand can be represented by the equation $Q = 1,260 - 10P$, where Q is the number of squares of replacement roofing installed per month. Its monthly total cost is $STC = \$10,000 + 34Q$, where Q is, again, the number of squares installed. Past experience shows that it is useless for Ajax to lower price below the prevailing one, since this results in a price war and almost no gain in quantity sold. (Demand at the firm level proves to be inelastic.) Is $82 the profit-maximizing price for Ajax? Explain.

These problems can be solved with Decision Assistant.

D1. CAM Automotive, Inc., is in a highly interactive market for its remote-controlled toy vehicle, the Cyclone. CAM knows if it raises the price of the Cyclone, no other manufacturers will follow, and CAM will receive a relatively larger loss of sales in proportion to the price increase. Conversely, if CAM lowers the Cyclone's price, the interacting competitors will do the same.

Sarah Burg, vice president of marketing at CAM, is reviewing sales projections for next year's Cyclone. Her marketing research department has estimated if CAM raises the price of the Cyclone, the appropriate demand function is given by the following equation:

$$Q_1 = 85 - P_1,$$

where Q is the quantity (in thousands) of Cyclones demanded per month and P is the price. Likewise, the marketing department has estimated if CAM lowers the Cyclone's price, the demand function is given by the following equation:

$$Q_2 = 32.5 - .25P_2,$$

where Q is the quantity (in thousands) of Cyclones demanded per month and P is the price.

After meeting with the production department, Sarah has determined that the following equation describes the Cyclone's total cost function:

$$TC = 375 + 25Q + .6Q^2,$$

where Q is the quantity (in thousands) of Cyclones produced per month.

Use the Oligopoly-Kinked tool in the *Managerial Economics Decision Assistant* to complete the following:

a. Given the preceding information, determine the selling price and the quantity of Cyclones that CAM should produce per month.

b. Sarah knew the estimate of the Cyclone's total cost function from the production department would be critical in determining the proper quantity of Cyclones to produce. Accordingly, she has asked for two additional total cost functions to be provided: one based on slightly less optimistic cost data (resulting in a demand function with higher total manufacturing costs) and one based on an optimistic prediction that CAM would be able to successfully negotiate lower prices with four of its major suppliers. The total cost functions are, respectively,

$$TC_2 = 375 + 40Q + .6Q^2,$$

and

$$TC_3 = 375 + 2.9Q + .1Q^2,$$

where Q is the quantity (in thousands) of Cyclones produced per month.

Determine the selling prices and quantities of Cyclones CAM should produce and sell each month under each of these two equations.

D2. Better Built Motors, Inc., manufactures large electric motors. The company is the largest, most efficient manufacturer in its industry and has been very successful. There are ten smaller firms that follow Better Built Motors' pricing.

A new model year is approaching and Florence Langford, marketing manager for Better Built Motors, Inc., is reviewing pricing practices. Better Built Motors has always allowed the smaller competing firms to sell all they wish at the price it established. This year, Florence projects the total market demand for large electric motors to be

$$Q_M = 40,000 - 20P,$$

where Q_M is the market quantity demanded and P is the price in dollars. Better Built Motors' expected marginal cost function for large motors is

$$MC_{BBM} = 200 + .02Q_{BBM}.$$

Florence has further estimated that the supply function of the ten smaller firms is

$$Q_s = 10,000 + 5P.$$

Use the Oligopoly-Price Leadership tool in the *Managerial Economics Decision Assistant* to assist Florence in determining the following:
a. Her firm's profit-maximizing output and price, assuming that Better Built Motors will again act as the dominant firm in the industry.
b. The output for the combined smaller firms.

SELECTED REFERENCES

Adams, Walter, and James Brock. *The Structure of American Industry*, 9th ed. Englewood Cliffs, N.J.: Prentice Hall, 1995.

Besanko, David, David Dranove, and Mark Shanley. *Economics of Strategy*. New York: Wiley, 1996.

Borenstein, Severin. "The Dominant-Firm Advantage in Multiproduct Industries: Evidence From the U.S. Airlines," *Quarterly Journal of Economics* 106, no. 4 (November 1991), pp. 1237–1266.

Chamberlin, Edward H. *The Theory of Monopolistic Competition*. Cambridge, Mass.: Harvard University Press, 1933.

Eaton, B. Curtis, and Diane F. Eaton. *Microeconomics*. Englewood Cliffs, N.J.: Prentice Hall, 1995, Chapters 11 and 12.

Lipsey, Richard G., Peter O. Steiner, Douglas D. Purvis, and Paul N. Courant. *Economics*. New York: Harper & Row, 1990, Chapter 14.

Prager, Jonas. *Applied Microeconomics*. Homewood, Ill.: Irwin, 1993, Chapters 13 and 14.

Shepherd, William G. " 'Contestability' vs. Competition," *American Economic Review* 74, no. 4 (September 1984), pp. 572–587.

Truett, Dale B., and Lila J. Truett. *Economics*. St. Louis: Times Mirror/Mosby College Publishing, 1987, Chapter 23.

Venkatraman, N., and John E. Prescott. "The Market Share-Profitability Relationship: Testing Temporal Stability Across Business Cycles," *Journal of Management* 16, no. 4 (1990), pp. 783–805.

APPENDIX 10

Game Theory in Oligopoly Analysis

Emphasized in Chapter 10 as an important characteristic of certain oligopoly situations is the recognition by managers that their individual firms' success or failure may well depend on a strategy decision made by a rival firm. In some of the market situations we surveyed, rather restrictive assumptions were made regarding the behavior of a firm's rivals. From a strictly theoretical point of view, the horizon for describing alternative decision strategies based on various modes of rival reaction was much expanded by pioneering work in *game theory* during the period since 1944.[1] However, interest in the subject outside the academic world has waned since the 1960s, largely because the new technique and applications failed to provide concrete solutions to many oligopoly problems using real-world data. Nonetheless, some degree of familiarity with the approach broadens one's perspective of the problems faced by oligopolistic firms.

In theoretical jargon a "game" is a situation involving a payoff for a specified number of players, each of whom knows that the strategies chosen by other players will affect each individual player's success. A strategy consists of a well-defined course of action a player will take, given each possible contingency of the game. The game can be as simple as tic-tac-toe or as complicated as chess, military strategy, or a firm's marketing decisions. Many conceivable games are indeterminate; that is, their outcomes cannot be predicted. A very simple form of game can be used to show the potential usefulness of the approach in the decision analysis of the business firm. This form is the two-person, zero-sum game.

A two-person game, as its name implies, has only two players. If the game is zero-sum, this means that the sum of the gains and losses equals zero, or that one player's gains are the other's losses. It has been shown in theory that a two-person, zero-sum game will have a determinate solution as long as a specific rule, known as the *minimax principle*, holds and mixed strategies

---

1 The pioneer effort in this field was John von Neumann and Oskar Morgenstern, *Theory of Games and Economic Behavior*, 3d ed. (Princeton, N.J.: Princeton University Press, 1953).

are permitted.[2] The minimax principle is simply an assumption that each player believes the opposition will counter a given strategy with one that will leave the first player with the worst possible result. One assumes, then, that for each strategy one chooses, the other side will choose a strategy that maximizes its share of the payoff. Therefore one chooses a strategy that minimizes the opponent's maximum gain. This can be stated alternatively as a strategy that maximizes one's own minimum gain (*maximin*).

A suitable example can be drawn from a situation in which two rival firms are contemplating advertising or product differentiation strategies that will have predictable effects on the share of the total market obtained by each. It is a zero-sum game, since if Firm A gets 30 percent of the market, that would be 30 percent not obtained by Firm B. There is only 100 percent to be had, and one firm's gains are the other's losses. Hypothetical data for such a market share game are presented in Table 10A–1, which shows the outcomes in terms of Firm A's percentage of total sales in the market where it has three possible marketing strategies (A_1, A_2, and A_3), each of which may be countered by one of three different strategies of Firm B (B_1, B_2, and B_3).

In the setting of Table 10A–1, Firm A will adopt a maximin strategy—that is, one that maximizes the firm's minimum gain. It does so by examining the possible outcomes for each one of its own strategy options and determining the worst possible result. For example, strategy A_1 will yield Firm A 90 percent of the market if Firm B counters with strategy B_1, 65 percent of the market if firm B counters with strategy B_2, and 40 percent of the market if Firm B counters with strategy B_3. Since strategy combination A_1,B_3 yields the worst result for Firm A, its managers will expect this to be the outcome from their own choice of A_1. This follows from their assumption that Firm B will always counter with whatever is worst for Firm A. We place an asterisk (*) in the upper right-hand box in Table 10A–1 to indicate Firm A's expected result when strategy A_1, is chosen.

When strategies A_2 and A_3 are examined, we find that the worst possible result under A_2 is A_2,B_3, which leaves Firm A with 60 percent of the market, while under A_3 the worst result for Firm A is A_3,B_1, which yields it only 20 percent of the market. We have placed asterisks in boxes A_2,B_3 and A_3,B_1 to indicate that these outcomes are expected by Firm A's managers under strategy options A_2 and A_3, respectively. Since strategy A_2 yields the maximum of the three minimum gains, Firm A's managers will choose this strategy.

Under the conditions of Table 10A–1, Firm B will choose a *minimax* strategy; that is, it will choose the Firm B strategy that minimizes Firm A's maximum gain. For example, Firm B's managers believe that if they choose

---

2 Mixed strategies allow for the assignment of statistical probabilities to the payoffs accompanying each alternative strategy. Because the introduction of such strategies complicates the analysis, we will not concern ourselves with them here. The zero-sum game example to follow will produce a solution without our having to consider mixed strategies.

Table 10A–1   Payoff Matrix for a Two-Firm, Zero-Sum Game (Outcomes in Terms of Firm A's Percentage Share of Market)

A's Strategy	B's Strategy		
	B_1	B_2	B_3
A_1	90#	65	*40
A_2	75	70#	*60#
A_3	*20	30	50

strategy B_1, Firm A will counter with A_1, to maximize its share of the market. We have placed a crosshatch (#) in the upper left-hand corner of Table 10A–1 to indicate the outcome expected by Firm B. Similarly, if Firm B chooses strategy B_2, its managers will expect Firm A to counter with A_2; and for strategy B_3, Firm A is expected to counter with A_2 once again. We have placed crosshatches in boxes B_2,A_2 and B_3,A_2 to indicate Firm B's expected outcomes under strategy options B_2 and B_3, respectively. Firm B's managers will choose strategy B_3, since this is the strategy that yields the least maximum gain for their rival, Firm A.

Note that in Table 10A–1, only the box A_2, B_3 contains both an asterisk and a crosshatch. This is so because it represents the solution to the game, as we have shown by the preceding logic. In theoretical jargon the game we have examined is "strictly determined"; that is, the strategy chosen by Firm A produced the expected countermove from Firm B, and vice versa. However, if the game had not been strictly determined or the firms had not been assumed to play by the complementary maximin-minimax strategies, things could have become much more complicated—perhaps even to the point that no solution could be found.

More advanced forms of game theory and decision theory generally introduce even greater information requirements than were required for the preceding game. For example, the probability of occurrence of each outcome must be known by the players. The introduction of probability into the analysis is very appealing intellectually, since it broadens the range of solvable game situations. For example, two-person, zero-sum games that are not strictly determined can be solved when the various outcomes are weighted by their *known* probabilities. However, as one economic theorist noted some years ago, in the more difficult and interesting games," . . . the probability that the probabilities are known is negligible."[3]

_____

3 C. E. Ferguson, *Microeconomic Theory*, 3d ed. (Homewood, Ill.: Irwin, 1972), p. 348.

11

SELECTED TOPICS IN PRICING AND PROFIT STRATEGY

In preceding chapters our analysis of the firm and its markets has included only situations in which the firm produces and sells a single product in one market and charges a uniform price on all units sold. We have always assumed that the objective of the firm's managers is to maximize net or economic profit in both the short run and the long run. The main objective of the present chapter is to expand our analysis to take into account situations in which the firm produces more than one product, uses special pricing approaches to enhance both revenue and profit from sales of a single product, sells a single product in more than one market, or considers the level of profit to be only a secondary goal. First, however, we will look at the practice of marking up merchandise by specific proportions (percentages) to show how this simple approach to pricing is related to the economics of profit maximization.

MARKUP PRICING

In **markup pricing** a percentage of cost or price is added to cost of goods sold to obtain market price.

Markup pricing is a pricing technique whereby a certain percentage of cost of goods sold or of price is added to the cost of goods sold in order to obtain the market price. In many industries or lines of merchandise, the experienced manager will be familiar with rules of thumb concerning the typical markup on goods sold. However, the term *markup* is understood by different people to mean different things. What some would call a 50 percent markup others would define as a 100 percent markup. For example, suppose an item costs $50 to produce and is sold for $100. In some industries this would be known as a 50 percent markup, whereas in others it would be considered a markup of 100 percent. The difference, of course, is that in the first instance the margin is a *markup on price* (the proportion of the *selling price* that represents an amount added to the cost of goods sold), whereas in the second case the markup is a *markup on cost* (the proportion of *cost of goods sold* that is added on to that figure to arrive at the selling price). In the material that follows, we will use the *markup-on-cost* approach. To avoid confusion, we recommend that when analyzing any particular industry, one begins by determining the conventional use of the term "markup" in that industry.[1]

Markup pricing has long been a traditional way of doing business for large U.S. manufacturing companies. Firms tried to set price at a level that would allow them to achieve a certain long-run target rate of return at a particular volume of production. Price cutting in periods of short-term declines in demand was not looked on with much favor. (However, especially with the availability of computer technology, which allows a firm to do market research and to maintain sophisticated cost controls more easily, target pricing is currently not being used as rigidly as it has been in the past.)[2]

When a manager decides on a given markup for a product, the manager anticipates some specific result over the planning period in terms of quantity sold and sales revenue. To the extent that such a decision maximizes profit, the manager will have correctly estimated the elasticity of demand for the product. Alternatively, a correct estimation of the elasticity of demand for the product will allow management to determine the appropriate markup.

We can demonstrate this point by examining the general relationship between marginal revenue and price elasticity of demand. We know from Chapter 2 that

$$MR = P\left(1 + \frac{1}{E_p}\right),$$

and from Chapter 7 that

$$MR = MC$$

where profit is maximized.[3] If incremental costs of production are relatively constant and average variable selling and administrative costs are immaterial, MC is approximately equal to AVC. (If the firm is a manufacturing firm, fixed manufacturing overhead per unit must also be immaterial.) Thus, at the profit-maximizing output and price,

$$P\left(1 + \frac{1}{E_p}\right) = MC = AVC,$$

---

1 In the garment industry, for example, the term *keystoning* is used to mean pricing an item at twice its wholesale cost. However, in the trade, this practice is also called a "markup of 50 percent."

2 Bill Pearson, "Get Your Markup Where You Can," *Stores*, Vol. 67, No. 7 (July 1994), pp. 65–66; and "Flexible Pricing," *Business Week* (December 12, 1977), pp. 78–88.

3 See Chapter 2, footnote 32. Also, Chapter 7, section on profit maximization.

and

$$P = \frac{AVC}{1+\dfrac{1}{E_p}}.$$

We can simplify the right-hand side of this equation by first writing the denominator as one fraction and then inverting and multiplying as follows:

$$P = \frac{AVC}{1+\dfrac{1}{E_p}} = \frac{AVC}{\dfrac{E_p+1}{E_p}} = AVC\left(\frac{E_p}{E_p+1}\right).$$

By addition and subtraction of 1 in the numerator, we can break this last term into two terms in the following manner:

$$P = AVC\left(\frac{E_p}{E_p+1}\right) = AVC\left(\frac{E_p+1-1}{E_p+1}\right)$$

$$= AVC + AVC\left(\frac{-1}{E_p+1}\right)$$

$$= AVC + mAVC,$$

where m is the proportion of markup on *cost*. Of course,

$$m = \frac{-1}{E_p+1},$$

so the estimation of a profit-maximizing output and price is tantamount to estimating the elasticity of demand, E_p. Note that as long as E_p (which is nearly always negative) has an absolute value larger than 1, m will be *positive*. (As we showed in Chapter 2, $|E_p|$ will be greater than 1 whenever MR is positive.) Moreover, if one knows P^*, Q^*, and E_p at point Q^*, a linear equation approximating the demand curve around that point can be found.[4]

---

4 For example, if $P^* = 2$, $Q^* = 10$, and $E_p = (dQ/dP) \cdot P^*/Q^* = -2.0$, then $-2.0 = (2/10) \cdot dQ/dP$, or $dQ/dP = -10$. Since dQ/dP is the slope (b) of the linear demand curve, $Q_d = a + bP$, we know that $Q_d = a - 10P$ is the equation for a linear demand curve, given the above information. We can find the intercept term a by substituting $Q^* = 10$ and $P^* = 2$ in that equation, so $10 = a - 10(2)$, or $a = 30$. Thus, $Q_d = 30 - 10P$ is a linear approximation of the demand function at the point $Q^* = 10$, $P^* = 2$.

Naturally, in a small business, management might not recognize the technical side of what is taking place when it determines the appropriate markup. However, the foregoing analysis certainly makes it clear that the manager who correctly chooses the profit-maximizing markup, given the unit variable costs, either has a good feel for demand conditions in the market or has made a lucky guess.

DECISIONS INVOLVING MULTIPLE PRODUCTS

Given both the large number of technologically related products sharing today's consumer markets and the trends toward merger and acquisition in the modern business world, multiproduct firms presently outnumber single-product firms in the United States and other industrialized countries. A major task of management in a multiproduct enterprise is to analyze carefully the profitability of the various final and intermediate products that compete internally for a share of the firm's resources. For example, in the mid-1980s one of America's corporate giants, General Electric Company, was reshuffling its product mix in an effort to improve its future profitability. Specifically, it had left the small-appliance field and sold off its subsidiaries that produced minerals and oil, choosing to enter markets in microcircuits, computer graphics, and radio and television broadcasting; in addition it had moved to increase its market share in major home appliances. By 1993, GE manufactured and sold a wide variety of products from jet engines to medical systems to commercial lending operations all over the world, including Europe, Japan, Mexico, India, and China. In India alone, it has factories making medical-imaging equipment, kitchen appliances, plastics, and lamps.[5]

The Gillette Company provides another good example of a firm that faces many decisions involving multiple products. Gillette's U.S. production includes razors, blades, and many other consumer items; its European subsidiary, Braun, makes more than 400 products, most of which are in the electrical appliance line. Prior to 1977, Braun's output consisted of more than 600 products; but in order to improve its profit picture, Gillette's management dictated that about one-third of the products be eliminated.[6]

Like Braun, many of today's multiproduct firms are subsidiaries or divisions of very large companies. Moreover, the affiliation between such productive units often occurs in a setting where one of the entities responsible to

---

5 William H. Miller, "General Electric," *Industry Week*, Vol. 24, No. 19 (October 16, 1995), pp. 30–32; "GE's Brave New World," *Business Week* (November 8, 1993), pp. 64–70; and "Can Jack Welch Reinvent GE?," *Business Week* (June 30, 1986), pp. 62–67.
6 "The Gillette Advantage," *Industry Week*, Vol. 24, No. 1 (January 3, 1994), p. 28; and "Gillette after the Diversification that Failed," *Business Week* (February 28, 1977), pp. 58–62.

a firm's top management must either *supply inputs to* an affiliate or *obtain inputs from* an affiliate. Thus the multiple product question has two major dimensions: (1) the determination of the optimal output combination for jointly produced products, and (2) the establishment of an appropriate price (known as the *transfer price*) for a product sold by one division of a firm to another division of the (same) firm. We will consider the joint product question first.

The Joint Product Problem

A multiproduct firm that has separate production facilities for each product will maximize its short-run profit by producing each product at the level of output where $MC = MR$, subject, of course, to the condition that MC is higher than MR at greater levels of output. Over the long run, the firm should move resources out of less profitable product lines and into more profitable ones. However, if the products are produced in the same plant and they are joint products or co-products in the sense that one cannot be produced without getting some of the other (in this case one of the products might be called a by-product), the firm will face a very special kind of problem in determining the profit-maximizing price and output combination for each product. When joint products are produced in fixed proportions, the analysis is relatively simple, but it becomes more complex when proportions can be varied.

In the former case (that is, joint products produced in fixed proportions), each increment of output, Q, consists of a certain amount of each jointly produced product. For example, if there are two products, A and B, one unit of Q might consist of one unit of Product A and one unit of Product B. Marginal revenue would in this case consist of $MR_A + MR_B = MR_J$. Marginal cost would be the increase in total cost as Q increases, and profit would be maximized where $MR_J = MC$, *provided that neither MR_A nor MR_B is negative.* The necessity for this latter qualification can be made clear by considering Figure 11–1.

In Figure 11–1 the demand and marginal revenue curves for Products A and B are shown, and the two MR curves are vertically summed (add $MR_A + MR_B$ at each level of output) between the origin and Q^* to obtain MR_J. The firm should never sell more than Q^* of Product B, since for larger outputs, MR_B is negative. The relevant marginal revenue curve for the firm is MR_J between the origin and Q^* and MR_A to the right of Q^*. If the firm's marginal cost curve were SMC, management's profit-maximizing strategy would be to sell Q_e of each product. On the other hand, it should be clear that if the firm's marginal cost curve is SMC', Q'_e of Product A should be sold, but only Q^* of Product B should be put on the market. An amount of Product B equal to $Q'_e - Q^*$ should be withheld from the market, even though the firm has to produce it. If storage costs are not too great and demand is expected to increase, the excess output may be stored until market conditions for Product B are such that it is rational to sell more. Alternatively, if Product B is a perishable product or if its cost of storage is high, it may be rational for the firm to destroy the excess output.

Figure 11–1   Profit-Maximizing Output Rates for Two Joint Products
Produced in Fixed Proportions

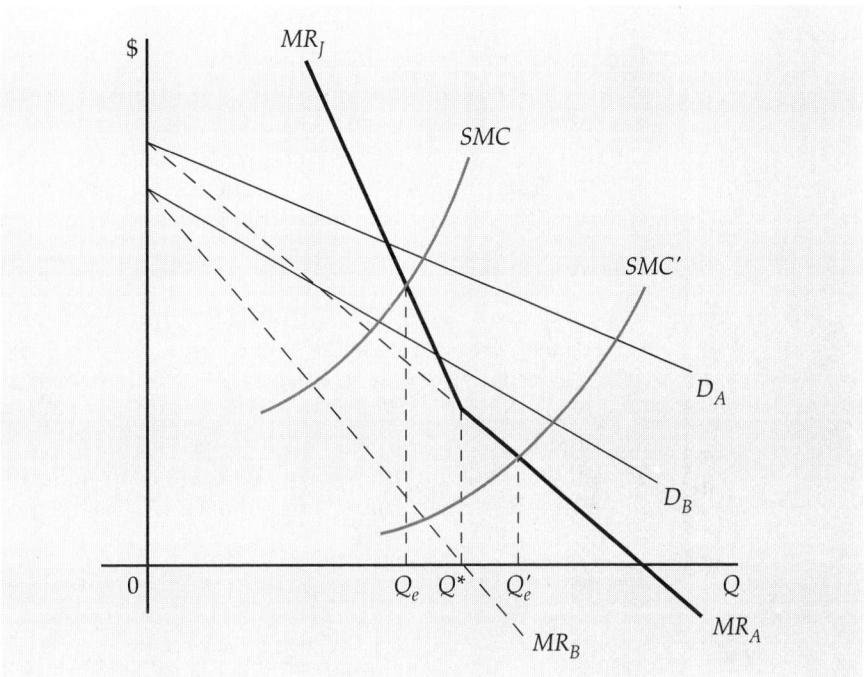

The relevant MR curve is MR_J for quantities less than Q^* and is MR_A for quantities greater than Q^*. If the marginal cost curve is SMC, Q_e of both products should be sold. However, if the marginal cost curve is SMC', an amount equal to $(Q_e' - Q^*)$ of Product B should be withheld from sale.

One would not have to search very far in the real world to find cases that conform to the situation just described. In Canada producers of natural gas obtain sulphur as a co-product in the process of scrubbing poisonous gases from the fuel. During the early 1970s, sulphur markets became so weak relative to world supply that the Canadian producers' stockpiles reached 10 million tons, enough to supply all U.S. industry for an entire year. The Canadian firms could not sell their natural gas without obtaining the sulphur, and there was no way to destroy the excess output. Hence the sulphur just piled up on the ground and became an environmental problem in western Canada.[7] Processors of foodstuffs face similar problems with joint products, although disposal of excess output is usually possible. For example, pineapple packers

---

NUMERICAL EXAMPLE:

Joint Products in Fixed Proportions

Pacific Porchposts produces fine ornamental wood columns in standard eight-foot lengths. For every column it produces, it obtains one pound of wood chips that can be sold as a by-product. The demand for columns is estimated to be $Q_n = 1,400 - 20P_n$, while that for wood chips is $Q_w = 800 - 1,000P_w$. If its marginal cost of production for the two joint products is constant at $18, will it be able to sell all of the wood chips profitably?

Answer:

The company will not be able to sell all of the wood chips. This can be determined easily by noting that for wood chips, $P_w = 0.8 - .001Q_w$ and $MR_w = 0.8 - .002Q_w$. The latter equals zero when $Q = 400$. However, if $Q = 400$, since $P_n = 70 - .05Q_n$ and $MR_n = 70 - .1Q_n$, $MR_n = 70 - 40 = \$30$. Since this is greater than MC of $18, the firm will wish to produce beyond the output where $MR_w = 0$. Thus it will obtain more wood chips than it can sell profitably. (If you carry this example further, you will find that $Q = 520$ is the profit-maximizing production level.)

in many instances obtain more juice than they can feasibly market, and orange juice producers are bound to wind up with a lot more rind than is likely to be marketable as a spice.

In cases where it is possible to vary the proportions in which joint products are produced, management must determine the output combination that maximizes profit. The easiest approach to this problem is to determine the various possible outputs *for each level of total cost* and identify the output that yields maximum total revenue (at least one for every level of cost). The set of profit-maximizing cost-output combinations can be determined, and the highest of these will define the firm's optimal strategy. We can employ a set of *product transformation curves* (production possibilities curves) to describe the cost-output combinations.

In Figure 11–2, panel (a), the contour A_1B_1 is a product transformation curve representing the possible output combinations the firm can produce with a given total cost. It is concave toward the origin because resources cannot be perfectly transferred from the production of Product A to the production of Product B. If the market prices of Products A and B are given (for example, if there is perfect competition), isorevenue lines such as TR_1 and TR_2 will show the various combinations of Products A and B that will yield a specific total revenue. With a total cost of $50, the firm could attain a total revenue of $55 by producing at R or S or at a point inside the product transformation curve on segment RS. However, if it produces at D, where the

Figure 11–2   Product Transformation Curves and Profit-Maximizing
Output Combinations for Joint Products Produced in
Variable Proportions

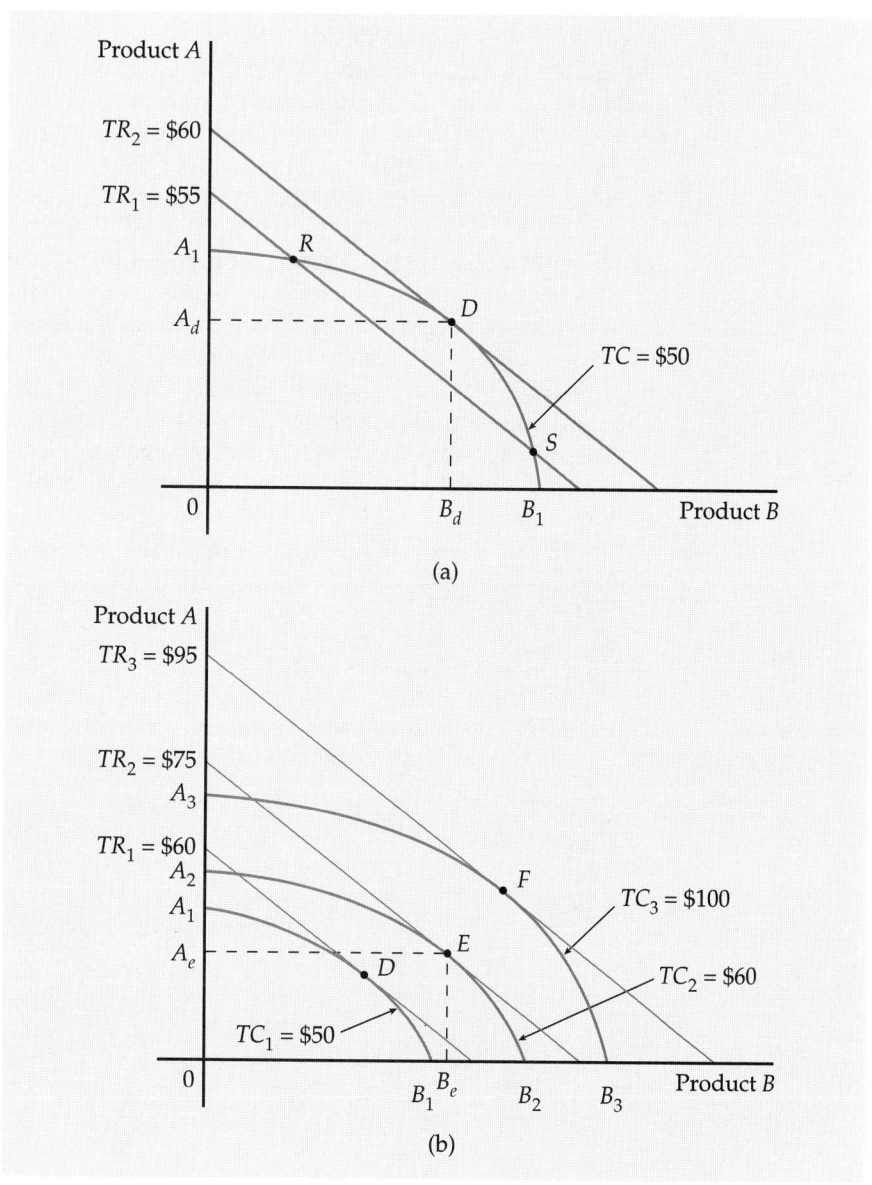

(a)

(b)

In panel (a) profit is maximized at point D, where combination A_d, B_d of the two products is produced and sold. In panel (b) the firm chooses to operate with two shifts at point E, since this strategy provides the highest profit.

transformation curve is tangent to TR_2, the firm will attain a total revenue of $60 and thus maximize profit for the $50 level of total cost.

In panel (b) of Figure 11–2, we depict transformation curves for the $50, $60, and $100 levels of total cost. The situation is similar to one in which management would have to decide whether to operate a plant on one, two, or three shifts, given that both costs and the possible output combinations increase as we move from (transformation) curve A_1B_1 to curve A_2B_2 to curve A_3B_3. Assuming that the market prices of Products A and B remain given, the profit-maximizing output combinations for the three transformation curves are D, E, and F, respectively. Management would choose combination E as the best of these three, since here $\pi = TR_2 - TC_2 = \$15$, which is the greatest profit attainable. At point D profit is only $10, and at point F it is –$5.

The foregoing analysis seems to require that the firm's managers obtain a great deal of information in order to ascertain the exact nature of the transformation and isorevenue curves. However, in any given case, management might be able to perform a perfectly satisfactory analysis by identifying only a few feasible output combinations at each cost level, rather than trying to describe completely the product transformation curve. (Indeed, smooth transformation curves such as those of Figure 11–2 may not even exist for the firm.)

In Figure 11–3 we show a transformation "curve" for a firm in which management believes it is technologically feasible to produce Product A ex-

Figure 11–3   Product Transformation Curve When Only One Joint Output Combination Exists

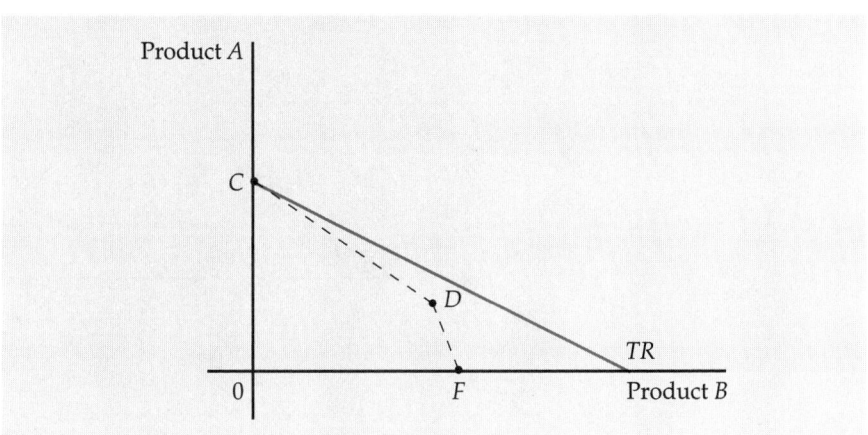

With transformation curve CDF and isorevenue curve TR, the firm would produce Product A only. It would produce both products when the isorevenue curve is less steep than DF but steeper than CD.

MANAGERIAL PERSPECTIVE

Cows and Farmers Mad at Good Ol' Jack Daniel

It seems the famous Jack Daniel Distillery in Lynchburg, Tennessee, produces not only sippin' whiskey, but also an interesting by-product called "thick slop," which is used as a fortifier for cattle feed. Around Lynchburg, a feedlot industry burgeoned for decades. The cows reportedly just loved the slop-laced feed; one farmer said they would ". . . stick their snoots in all the way up beyond their eyes."

Jack Daniel at first gave the slop away to farmers who would pick it up in tank trucks. Eventually, it began to charge for the stuff, first $2 a thousand gallons, later $4. When the cattle industry grew so much that manure was polluting local streams, Daniel announced it would continue to sell slop only to farmers who invested in pollution control. However, in 1984 Jack Daniel decided to switch to the "dry house" method of handling slop, which allowed the firm to recover from it grain that could be sold for $10 per ton. The remaining thin slop did not have many nutrients, and farmers argued they could not afford to buy grain to replace what Jack Daniel had removed. Eventually, they sued Jack Daniel's parent company, Brown-Forman Distillers, arguing that Jack Daniel was requiring them to invest in pollution control at the same time it was planning to do away with thick slop. Meanwhile, the cattle industry in the area has declined significantly.

Reference: "Tennessee Cattlemen Are Suin' Jack Daniel Instead of Sippin It," *The Wall Street Journal*, February 12, 1986, pp. 1, 19.

---

clusively, Product *B* exclusively, or a combination consisting of 25 percent *A* and 75 percent *B*. In this case the transformation curve consists only of the points *C*, *D*, and *F*, and the combinations represented along the dashed lines connecting these points cannot be produced. If Product *B* is relatively low priced (as expressed by isorevenue line *TR*), the firm will produce only Product *A*, operating at point *C*. If the slope of the isorevenue line is identical to that of line segment *CD*, the firm will attain its maximum total revenue at either *C* or *D*. As the isorevenue line becomes steeper than *CD*, *D* will become the revenue-maximizing output combination. When its slope is equal to that of segment *DF*, both *D* and *F* will yield the same total revenue; if steeper than *DF*, the firm's best output will occur at *F*. Thus, in the setting of Figure 11–3, it will be relatively easy for managers to compile a complete description of the alternatives and their profit outcomes, making an output decision based on the maximum profit attainable.

Table 11–1   Revenue, Cost, and Profit Outcomes with Two Products and Three Shifts

Output Combinations

No. of Shifts	100% *Product A*	25% Prod. A 75% Prod. B	100% *Product B*
1	$TR = 50$ $TC = \underline{45}$ $\pi = 5$	$TR = 45$ $TC = \underline{45}$ $\pi = 0$	$TR = 30$ $TC = \underline{45}$ $\pi = -15$
2	$TR = 80$ $TC = \underline{65}$ $\pi = 15$	$TR = 70$ $TC = \underline{65}$ $\pi = 5$	$TR = 65$ $TC = \underline{65}$ $\pi = 0$
3	$TR = 95$ $TC = \underline{85}$ $\pi = 10$	$TR = 92$ $TC = \underline{85}$ $\pi = 7$	$TR = 80$ $TC = \underline{85}$ $\pi = -5$

Finally, if we return to the problem of choosing whether to employ one, two, or three shifts with the kind of product transformation limitations illustrated in Figure 11–3, a complete description of the alternatives and their outcomes might be given by a table such as Table 11–1. Here, it would take an analysis of nine possible outcomes to make a decision on the best strategy in production and sale of the joint products. Under current market conditions, management would determine that profit will be maximized when two shifts are used to produce only Product *A*.

The Transfer Product Problem

Many large firms are vertically integrated, which means that at least one division of the firm produces a good that is an *input* for the product of another division. When a vertically integrated firm's top management sets out to maximize profit, it must ensure that the divisions of the firm that supply inputs produce such goods in a quantity that is consistent with profit maximization for the entire firm. The appropriate quantity, as we will see, may be less than, equal to, or greater than the needs of the division of the firm to which the inputs are transferred, depending on the state of the external market for the transferred input. To maximize firm profit, the price of the transfer product will be determined internally by the firm's management if there is no external market for the transfer product, and by the market if there is a perfectly competitive external market for the transfer product. In the event that the external market is not perfectly competitive, different internal and external prices will exist for the transfer product.

To simplify our discussion, we will use throughout as an example the case of a firm having just two divisions—a final product division and a transfer product division. Further, we will consider only cases in which one unit of the transfer product is required per unit of final product output.

Where there is no external market for the transfer product, the final product division can be viewed as either a distribution division for the transfer product or a division that combines the transfer product with other inputs to produce a different final good. The marginal cost of the entire firm, MC_e (marginal cost of the enterprise), will be the sum of MC_F (the marginal cost of the final product division excluding the transfer price finally assigned to the transferred product) and MC_T (the marginal cost of the transfer product division), which is shown as follows:

$$MC_e = MC_F + MC_T.$$

The firm generates external revenue solely from the sale of the final good. If D_F is a downward-sloping demand curve for the final good and MR_F is the marginal revenue curve derived from it, the firm will maximize profit where

$$MC_e = MR_F.$$

This is shown in Figure 11–4, panel (a), at E—where Q_e is the profit-maximizing output of both the final product and the transfer product. Since $MC_e = MC_F + MC_T$, we can restate the profit-maximizing condition as follows:

$$MR_F = MC_F + MC_T.$$

Subtracting MC_F from both sides of the equation, we get

$$NMR_F = MR_F - MC_F = MC_T.$$

Net marginal revenue is marginal revenue from the sale of a firm's final product *minus* a specific portion of marginal production cost. In the case of transfer pricing, the portion of marginal production cost that is deducted from MR to obtain final product net marginal revenue (NMR_F) is the marginal cost of the final division, not including the cost of the transfer product.

Now, for the firm as a whole, the left-hand term above is the **net marginal revenue** (NMR_F) obtained from selling the final product after deduction of all incremental costs except that of the transfer product. The net marginal cost (NMC_F) of the *final product* is MC_T (the difference between the marginal cost of the entire enterprise, MC_e, and MC_F, the marginal cost of the final division):

$$MC_T = MC_e - MC_F = NMC_F.$$

We can restate the profit-maximizing condition as

$$NMR_F = MR_T = MC_T = NMC_F$$

In panel (b) of Figure 11–4, the preceding condition is met at E'. E' must occur directly below E, since NMC_F is MC_e reduced by MC_F and NMR_F is MR_F reduced by the same amount.

Figure 11–4   Optimal Production of Final and Transfer Product with No
External Market for the Transfer Product

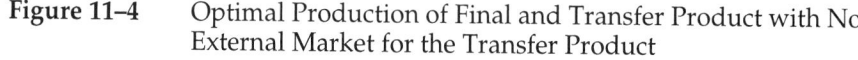

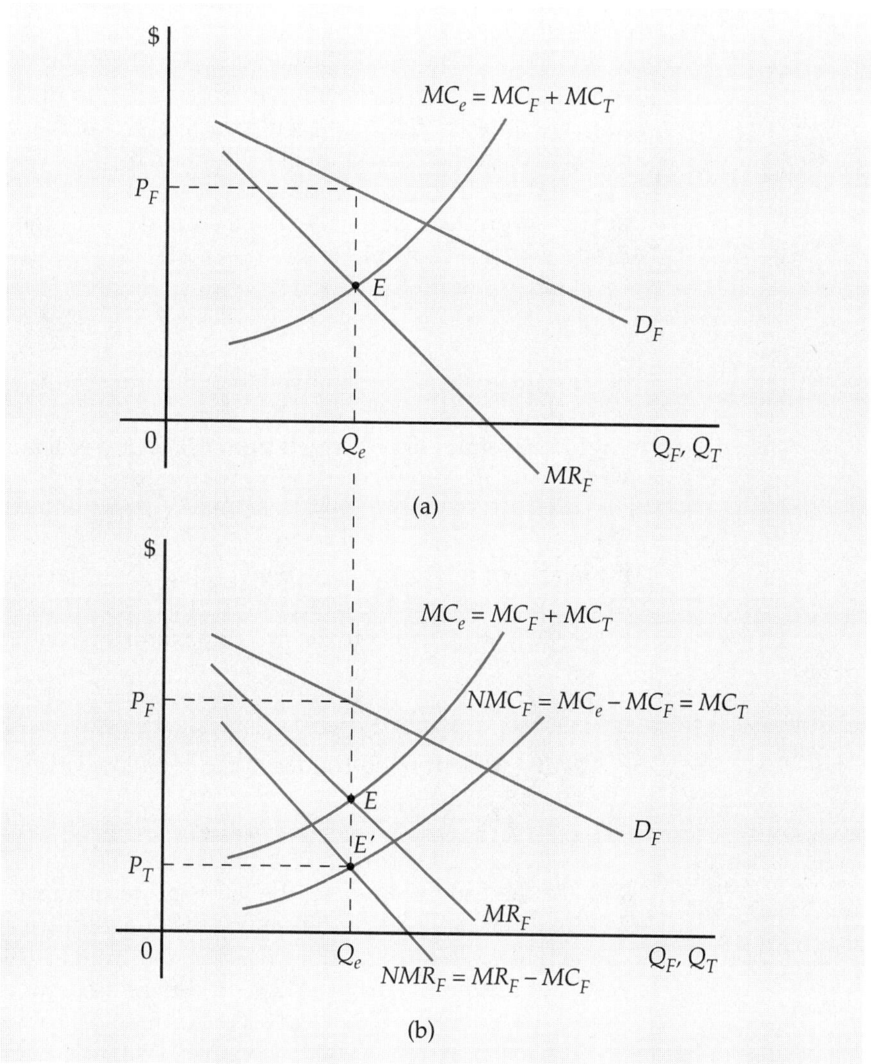

In panel (a) the firm maximizes profit at Q_e, where $MC_e = MR_F$. Panel (b) shows that with no external market for the transfer product, profit maximization is consistent with the condition $NMR_F = MC_T$.

Given the preceding profit-maximizing conditions, management must develop a strategy that will ensure the following two results:

1. The transfer product division will supply Q_e of the transfer product.
2. The final product division will demand Q_e of the transfer product.

These results can be accomplished by either of two strategies. First, management might decide to let the final product division fix the price of the transfer product, giving precise information on the marginal cost curve of the division producing the transferred product and instructing the division to set the transfer price of the transfer product equal to the marginal cost of the transfer product at the optimal level of output. The final product division would then know that the price it sets will constitute the MR curve of the transfer product division, since like a perfectly competitive firm facing a fixed price, the latter will regard its situation as one in which $P = MR$. The transfer product division will profit maximize where $P_T = MR_T = MC_T$, and the final product division will have set the transfer price equal to MC_T at Q_e, the output that maximizes the firm's profit. In terms of Figure 11–4, the price would be P_T, determined by the intersection of NMC_F with NMR_F. Note that $NMC_F = MC_T$, since after accounting for all variable costs of the final product division, the remaining marginal costs will consist of those attributable to the transfer product division.

The second strategy that management might follow to ensure that Q_e of the transfer product is produced and that P_T is established as the transfer price would involve letting the transfer product division set P_T based on the final product division's *demand curve* for Product T. Since NMR_F in Figure 11–4, panel (b), shows the amount of Product T that the final product division would purchase when it equates a given P_T to NMR_F, it is the final product division's demand curve for Product T. With this information available, the transfer product division would be instructed to expand output up to the point at which the price that the final product division is willing to pay is exactly equal to MC_T. Again, this will occur at E' in Figure 11–4, panel (b).

Where there is a perfectly competitive external market for the transfer product, the final product division should not pay the transfer product division a price in excess of that at which the transfer product can be obtained from outside suppliers. Likewise, the transfer product division should not sell to the final product division at a price that is *less* than it can obtain in the external market. All of this leads to the conclusion that the appropriate transfer price will be the prevailing, perfectly competitive, external market price. This being the case, there is no assurance that the transfer product division will produce an amount of Product T equal to that demanded by the final product division when profits are maximized for the firm.

Figure 11–5 presents two situations in which there is a perfectly competitive external market for the transfer product and the output of the transfer product division is not equal to the quantity demanded by the final product division when firm profits are maximized. In panel (a) the demand curve facing the transfer product division is $AR_T = MR_T$ since the price of the product, P_T, is determined in the perfectly competitive market. At the final product equilibrium quantity, P_T is also equal to NMR_F. NMR_F is obtained by subtracting MC_F from MR_F.

The final product division maximizes profit at Q_F, P_F, since this is consistent with the intersection of NMR_F with AR_T at E. In this case P_T, given by AR_T,

Figure 11–5   Optimal Production of Final Product and Transfer Product

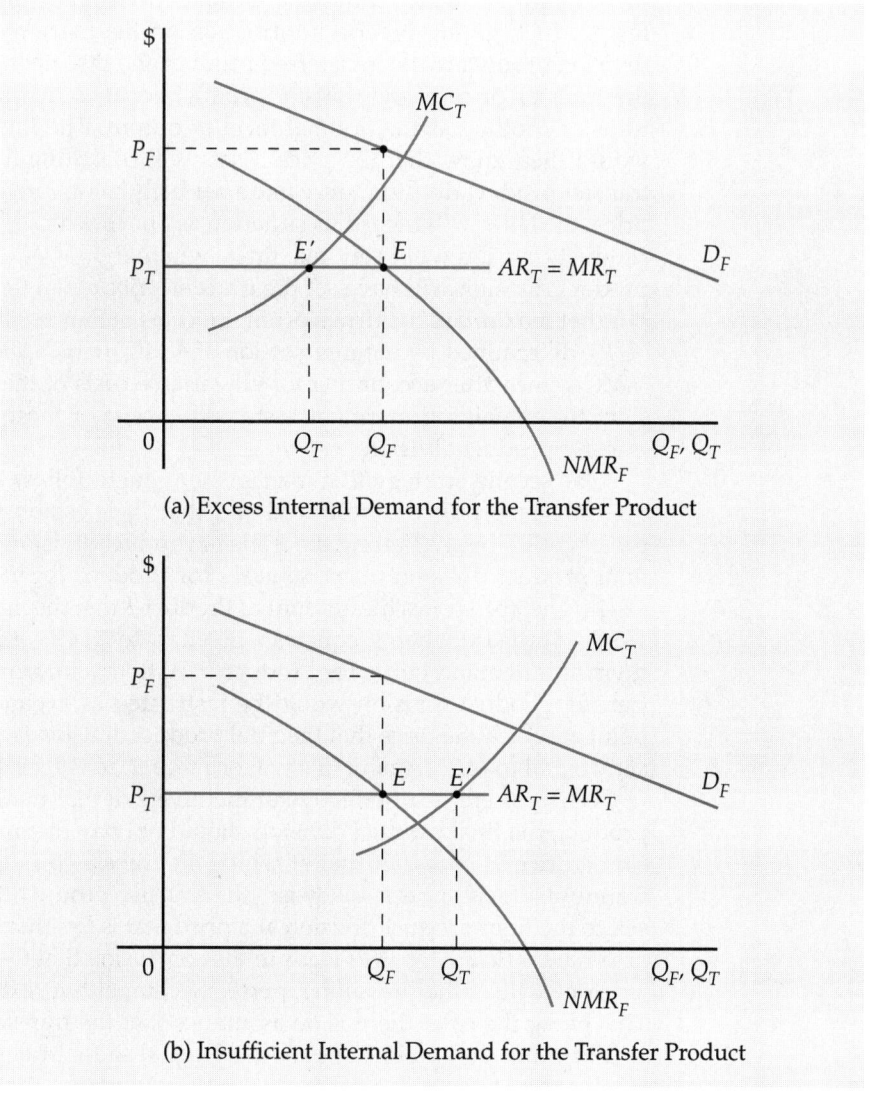

(a) Excess Internal Demand for the Transfer Product

(b) Insufficient Internal Demand for the Transfer Product

In panel (a) the final product division produces Q_F and obtains $(Q_F - Q_T)$ of the transfer product from outside suppliers. In panel (b) the transfer product division sells $(Q_T - Q_F)$ to outside purchasers.

represents the appropriate marginal cost of the transfer product to the final division. MC_T no longer gives the appropriate marginal cost of the transfer product to the final division because where $MC_T < P_T$, the firm incurs an opportunity cost if it sells the transfer product to the final product division at a price less than P_T. That is because the transfer product could be sold in the external market for P_T. On the other hand, if $MC_T > P_T$, it would not be economically sound to produce the transfer product and sell it to the final product division at a price greater than P_T, since that division could always purchase the transfer product externally at a price of P_T.

The profit-maximizing condition for the transfer product division is met at E', where $MR_T = P_T = MC_T$. Thus only Q_T is produced by the transfer product division, and the final product division must purchase $Q_F - Q_T$ of the transfer product in the external market. Since the transfer product division cannot produce units of output beyond Q_T at a marginal cost as low as the external price, P_T, the final product division should not force the transfer product division to supply the additional amount needed to maximize firm profit.

Figure 11–5, panel (b), illustrates a situation in which firm profits are maximized when the transfer product division produces *more* output than is needed by the final product division when the latter is maximizing profit from the sale of the final good. In this instance the quantity $Q_T - Q_F$ of the transfer product should be sold in the external market for P_T per unit—the prevailing market price. Such activity clearly adds to the total profit of the firm, since $MC_T < MR_T = P_T$ between Q_F and Q_T.

It is obvious that the transfer pricing problem is one that must be confronted by many firms and that it has numerous dimensions. The foregoing discussion only scratches the surface of the issue. For example, the analysis becomes more complex when the transfer product can be sold in a less than perfectly competitive external market and the external price is not a given. (See Appendix 11A.)

Transfer pricing is an especially important issue in international business. If a transfer product is sold across international boundaries by a multinational corporation, management must take into account the tax consequences of accruing divisional profits in one location rather than another. In this setting, transfer prices may be manipulated to move profits out of divisions located in countries with high taxes or restrictions on capital flows and accumulate them in divisions located in lower tax areas with freer movement of capital. Some very large multinational corporations have established divisional "profit centers" to which profits from certain designated geographical areas are transferred.[8] Needless to say, such practices may have noticeable effects on the economies of countries in which the multinational corporations operate, and many nations have taken steps to curb the use of transfer pricing as a mechanism for changing the locus of profits.

---

8 For a good discussion of transfer pricing in multinational business, see David K. Eiteman and Arthur I. Stonehill, *Multinational Business Finance*, 5th ed. (Reading, Mass.: Addison-Wesley, 1989) pp. 555–561.

NUMERICAL EXAMPLE:

Transfer Pricing

Camgo Company makes inexpensive, fixed-focus 35mm cameras. Its subsidiary, Focrude, Inc., makes the lenses for the cameras. The market for such lenses is highly competitive, and they can be either bought or sold at the equilibrium market price of $2. Camgo estimates the demand for its cameras to be $Q_c = 12{,}000 - 400P_c$, so that $MR_c = 30 - .005Q_c$. The marginal cost of manufacturing the cameras, *not* including the lenses, is constant and equal to $5. The marginal cost of the Focrude division for making the lenses is given by the equation $MC_f = .30 + .0004Q_f$. Each camera requires one lens. Will Focrude be able to both supply Camgo's required number of lenses and sell profitably in the outside market?

Answer.

To find out how many cameras Camgo should sell to maximize profit, set net marginal revenue from camera sales equal to the price of the transfer product:

$$\text{Definition: } NMR_c = MR_c - MC_c = 30 - 0.005Q_c - 5$$
$$= 25 - 0.005Q_c$$

Because of the external competitive market, $NMC_c = 2$. Thus

$$25 - .005Q_c = 2; \text{ and } Q_c = 4{,}600.$$

The Focrude division will maximize profit where its marginal cost equals the marginal revenue of $2 from sales both inside and external to the firm. So

$$.30 + .0004(Q_f) = 2,$$
$$.0004(Q_f) = 1.70;$$

and

$$Q_f = 4{,}250.$$

Focrude will be unable to supply Camgo with enough lenses to meet its requirements, and Camgo will buy 350 of them on the external market.

PRICE DISCRIMINATION

Price discrimination is the practice of charging different prices for the same product, either by offering buyers lower prices on marginal or incremental quantities purchased or by dividing groups of buyers into separate markets. The latter is also known as **market segmentation**.

Price discrimination involves either (1) charging different prices for additional units of a good purchased by a consumer or (2) separating groups of consumers into **market segments** and charging different prices to each segment. In economic jargon, the former type of discrimination may be either second or first degree, while the latter is called third degree. All three types of price discrimination are used by firms to increase profit.

Second- and First-Degree Discrimination

An easy way to approach price discrimination is to consider a costless monopolist as we did in the Cournot analysis of Chapter 10 and assume that we are looking at the demand curve of just one consumer. In the Cournot analysis, the monopolist simply maximized total revenue (therefore profit, since total cost was assumed to be zero) by setting price at the level where $MR = 0$. In Figure 11–6, with a demand curve $Q_x = 10 - P_x$, this would occur at P_M and

Figure 11–6   Second-Degree Price Discrimination by a Costless Monopolist

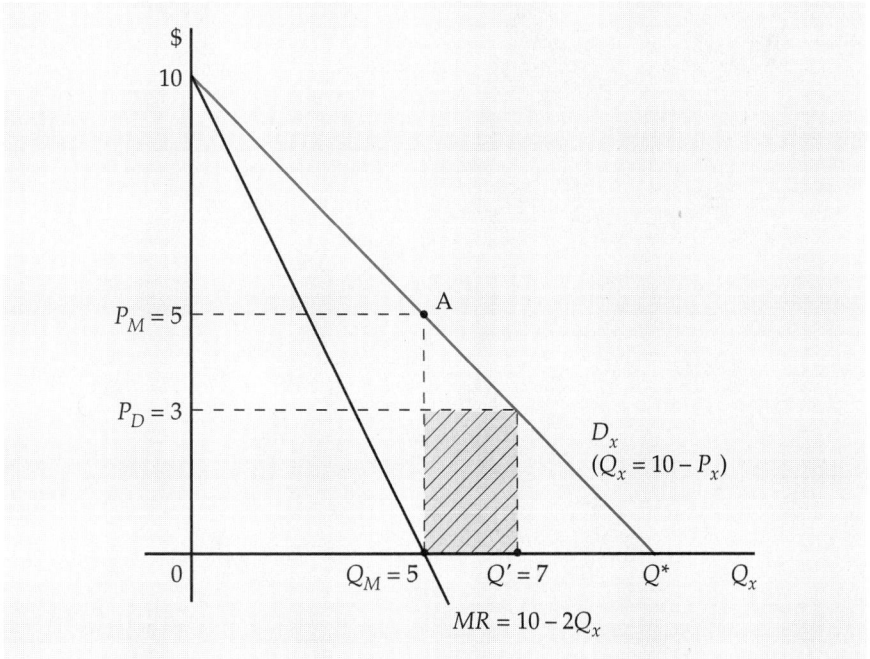

With no discrimination, profit is maximized where $MR = 0$ at $Q = 5$. Employing second-degree discrimination, a discount of $2 is offered on purchases in excess of 5 units. The consumer buys two additional units for $3 each, and profit increases by $6.

0.5Q^*, or Q_M, would be sold. Could the monopolist increase the total revenue by charging the consumer *more than one price*? The answer is yes. The seller could charge the consumer P_M for the first Q_M units sold and then offer a discount of $(P_M - P_D)$ on as many additional units as the consumer will buy. Our consumer would then choose to buy $(Q' - Q_M) = 2$ additional units at price P_D, which is $3. This increases the monopolist's TR to the original amount (area $0P_MAQ_M$) *plus* the shaded rectangle. That rectangle adds $3(2) = $6 to the seller's total revenue. The original TR was $5(5) = $25, but with the discount for additional units, it rises to $25 + 6 = $31. This is a case of **second-degree price discrimination**, also known as *block pricing*. In our example, the seller employed only two price blocks. However, the more price blocks the seller establishes, the greater will be the TR, and the limit on TR will be the entire area under the demand curve. That is what is obtained if the seller charges a different price for each unit sold, a situation conforming to **first-degree price discrimination**.

Figure 11–7, with the same demand curve as Figure 11–6, illustrates first-degree price discrimination for sales of four units, where the first unit is sold

Second-degree price discrimination is the practice of charging successively lower prices for block-type increases in quantity purchased.

First-degree price discrimination is a theoretical concept that refers to charging a different amount, specifically the maximum amount a consumer is willing and able to pay, for each unit purchased.

Figure 11–7   First-Degree Price Discrimination and Consumer's Surplus for Purchases of Four Units of X

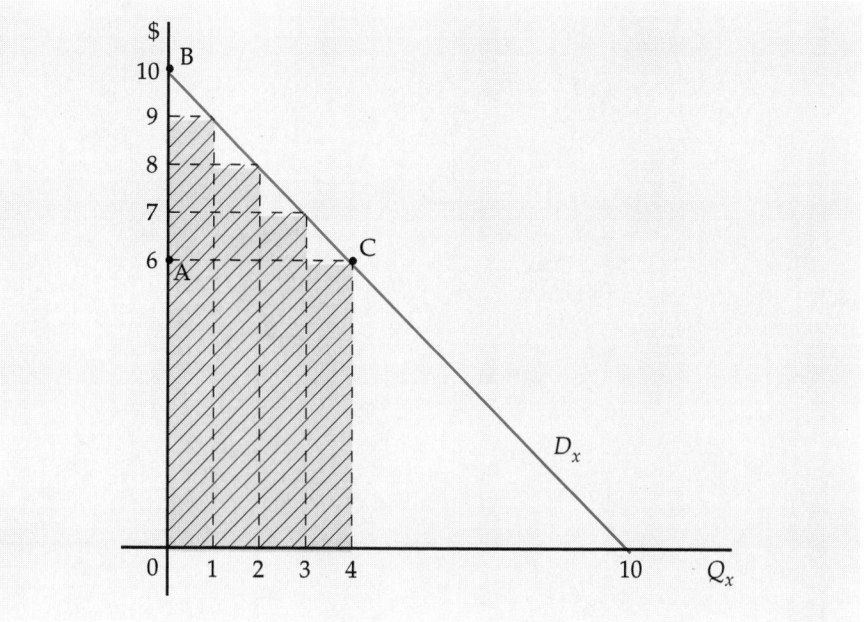

By charging $9 for the first unit, $8 for the second unit, $7 for the third unit, and $6 for the fourth, the seller obtains total revenue equal to the shaded area. By dividing the product into smaller units and increasing the number of prices charged, the unshaded triangles can also be added to total revenue.

for $9, the second unit for $8, the third unit for $7, and the fourth unit for $6. In this case, *TR* will be the entire area under the demand curve, except for the small unshaded triangles at the top, if $1 less is charged for each additional unit of output to $Q = 10$. If the firm charged a different price for each 1/2 unit (or each 1/4, or 1/8, or 1/16 unit), the triangles would be much smaller and the *TR* much closer to the entire area under the demand curve. That complete area is the maximum *TR* the costless monopolist could obtain if first-degree discrimination were employed.

Consumer's Surplus

Consumer's surplus is the difference between the maximum value a consumer places on a given quantity of a good he or she purchases and the money amount that is actually paid to obtain that quantity.

In economic theory, the difference between the maximum value that a consumer places on a given quantity of a good and the amount that he or she actually pays for that quantity is called the **consumer's surplus**. In Figure 11–7, the consumer values the first unit of *X* at $9, the second unit at $8, the third unit at $7, and the fourth unit at $6. If the consumer in this figure were to buy four units of *X* at $6 each, he or she would spend $24 for units of *X* valued at $9 + 8 + 7 + 6 = $30 and obtain a consumer's surplus of $6. (Note that this is equivalent to the portion of the shaded area lying within the triangle ABC.) Where does this extra $6 go? The answer is that it is simply additional purchasing power that the consumer can spend on other things. Part and parcel of the consumer's decision to buy four units of *X* at a price of $6 each was the consumer's understanding that the purchase yielded a surplus over the maximum he or she was willing to pay, and that the surplus could be spent on other goods and services. As a limit, this surplus approaches the area of triangle *ABC*, which, by geometry is $1/2(10 − 6)(4) = 8, but this would require that *X* be divisible into infinitely small units.[9]

What have we found out? Basically it is that both second- and first- degree price discrimination increase the seller's total revenue and profit by capturing all or part of the consumer's surplus. First-degree price discrimination is rare, although some observers have suggested that at a market demand level something close to it occurs when automobile salespersons try to get the highest possible price from each consumer who comes in to buy a car. One individual may pay $20,000, another $19,700, and another $19,500 for identically equipped vehicles. Second-degree price discrimination is frequently found in water and electricity rates, where a high rate is charged for an initial amount of usage and lower rate blocks apply to additional consumption.[10]

---

9 Technically, the consumer's surplus as given here would accurately measure the benefit from consumption of *X* only if demand for *X* were independent of income (no income effect when there is a change in P_x). However, it has been argued that this measure is useful when the proportion of income spent on *X* is small. See Robert D. Willig, "Consumer's Surplus Without Apology," *American Economic Review*, Vol. 66, No. 4 (September 1976), pp. 589–597.

10 Recent efforts to promote conservation of water and energy have made such rate schedules less common, since penalty rates have been applied to high-volume users.

The concept of consumer's surplus will again become important when we examine access fees, also called two-part pricing, later in this chapter. Now, however, we will turn to our remaining type of price discrimination, third degree, also known as market segmentation.

Third-Degree Price Discrimination (Market Segmentation)

Third-degree price discrimination is the practice of dividing groups of consumers into separate markets and charging a different price in each market.

In **third-degree price discrimination**, buyers are separated into distinct markets or market segments. For example, consumers of water might be segmented into a residential market and an industrial market, or airline passengers might be segmented into an advance purchase market and an unrestricted purchase market. Two economic conditions must hold for third-degree price discrimination to yield enhanced revenues and profit: (1) the market segments must be kept apart, and (2) the buyers must have different elasticities of demand for the product. The first condition ensures that buyers who purchase at a low price cannot resell to those in a higher-priced market segment, and the second is required because identical elasticities lead to a profit-maximizing solution with identical, rather than different, prices.

Third-degree price discrimination is legal in some settings but illegal in others. Briefly, in the United States, price discrimination is prohibited in interstate commerce when its effect is to lessen competition substantially or when it tends to create a monopoly. It is permitted when it can be justified on the basis of differences in grade, quality, or quantity sold; differences in transportation costs; or the lowering of price in good faith to meet competition. The prohibition against price discrimination applies only to products that will be resold; it does not apply to sales to the final consumer.[11]

Firms in many different lines of business take advantage of opportunities to increase profits by selling what is essentially the same product to different groups of consumers at different prices. Persons attending conventions get lower hotel room rates than are regularly charged. Theaters charge afternoon moviegoers a lower price than is paid by those who see the same films at night. So-called commercial rates abound in everything from electric power to rental cars. Many of the discriminations in price that occur daily in the United States have not been tested in the courts, but such testing would undoubtedly prove a large proportion of them to be justifiable. The individual firm must seek competent legal guidance in the question of pricing for multiple markets, but it must also be prepared to recognize opportunities to increase profit through acceptable forms of market segmentation.

The mechanics of increasing profit through the separation of markets are easily understood. We will use convention rates at hotels to illustrate the

---

11 Lawrence S. Clark and Peter D. Kinder, *Law and Business: The Regulatory Environment*, 3d ed. (New York: McGraw-Hill, 1991), pp. 912–915.

steps taken by management in the multiple price-setting decision. First, management must determine whether it is actually better off to establish a convention rate and a regular rate, rather than charge the same rate to all occupants of rooms of a given quality. This latter question will depend on the *elasticity* of demand for rooms in the general market as opposed to that in the convention market. (Our definition of the "general market" is that in which rooms are rented singly or in small quantities, and the "convention market" is that in which rooms are blocked in large quantity and subsequently rented to members of a special group.) We will see that if the elasticity of demand in the general market is lower than that in the convention market, management should establish a general market room rate that is higher than the rate it charges in the convention market.

Let us say that we are looking at the multiple rate question from the standpoint of a big-city hotel that can expect to do a considerable amount of convention trade at all times during the year. Management wishes to maximize daily profit from combined general market trade and convention market trade. The hotel has 1,600 rooms of equal quality that it expects to rent in the $60 to $90 per day category. Based on studies of the general and convention markets for hotel rooms in the city in which it is located and management's experience in other large cities, the demand curves for rooms in the two markets have been estimated to conform to the following equations:

$$General\ market \quad R_g = 1{,}400 - 10P_g,$$

where R_g is the number of rooms rented per day and P_g is the room rate for the general market.

$$Convention\ market \quad R_c = 2{,}400 - 20P_c,$$

where R_c is the number of rooms rented per day and P_c is the room rate for the convention market. These two demand curves are plotted, along with their respective marginal revenue curves, in panels (a) and (b) of Figure 11–8. The curves are drawn with solid lines only in the $60 to $90 range, where management expects to establish prices.

Now, suppose that management has estimated the total cost function for the hotel to be

$$TC = 18{,}200 + 30R_g + 30R_c,$$

where R_g and R_c are, respectively, the number of general rate and convention rate rooms rented per day and daily fixed cost is $18,200. It should be clear from the preceding formula that the marginal cost of a room, whether rented to an occupant in the convention market or the regular market, is $30. Short-run average cost, however, will fall as the daily fixed cost is divided by an increasing quantity of rooms rented.

Figure 11–8   Hotel Pricing Analysis with and Without Discrimination Between Convention and General Markets

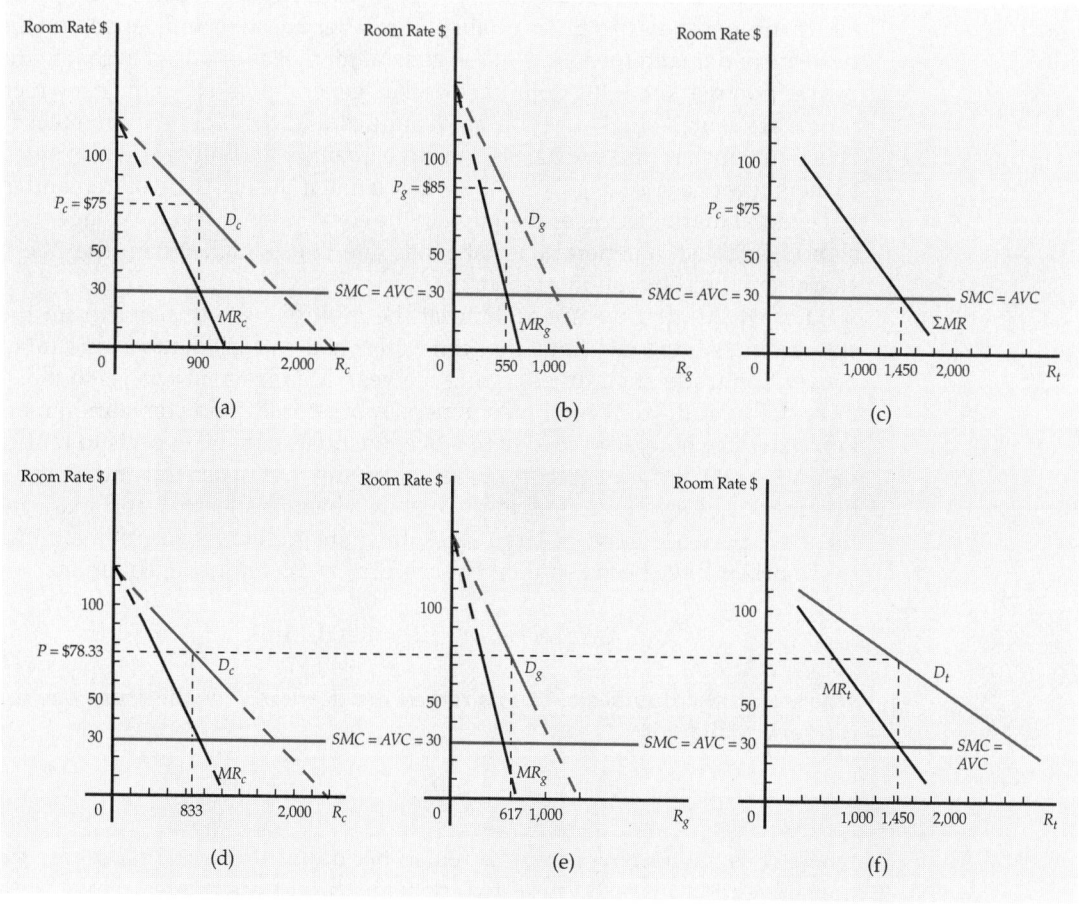

Panels (a), (b), and (c) show the hotel practicing price discrimination and charging a $75 convention rate but an $85 general rate. In panels (d), (e), and (f), there is no discrimination and both groups of consumers are charged $78.33.

The average variable cost and marginal cost curves appear in panel (c) of Figure 11–8. The ΣMR curve in panel (c) is derived by summing the quantities that correspond to each MR level in panels (a) and (b). For example, at the $30 level of MR, MR_c corresponds to 900 rooms rented in the convention market, and MR_g corresponds to 550 rooms rented in the general market. Thus we show the sum of these, 1,450 rooms, as the total quantity that can be rented (along ΣMR) when $MR = \$30$.

The profit-maximizing condition when selling in two markets is that marginal cost is equal to marginal revenue in both markets, or (in terms of our hotel)

$$MR_g = MR_c = SMC.$$

To understand why this must be so, consider any situation where $MR_g \neq MR_c$. For example, if $MR_g > MR_c$, the hotel can increase total revenue simply by renting one less room in the convention market and one more in the general market. As in other profit-maximizing problems, output should be increased as long as marginal cost is less than MR_g and MR_c, or up to the point where $SMC = \Sigma MR$ in panel (c) of Figure 11–8. This locates the optimum output, which for the hotel is 1,450 rooms rented per day. We satisfy the condition $MR_g = MR_c = SMC$ in panels (a) and (b) by projecting $\Sigma MR = SMC = \$30$ back to each MR curve. The price and quantity relevant to each market can then be determined as those corresponding to the intersection of $\Sigma MR = SMC = \$30$ with the individual market MR curves. For the general market, the profit-maximizing quantity is 550 rooms per day and the rate per room is \$85. For the convention market, the optimum quantity is 900 rooms per day and the rate per room is \$75. Mathematically, this information is expressed as follows:

(11–1)
$$P_g = 140 - .1R_g,$$

$$TR_g = 140R_g - .1R_g^2,$$

$$MR_g = 140 - .2R_g;$$

(11–2)
$$P_c = 120 - .05R_c,$$

$$TR_c = 120R_c - .05R_c^2,$$

$$MR_c = 120 - .1R_c.$$

Since SMC is constant at \$30, when profit is maximized,

(11–3)
$$30 = MR_g = MR_c,$$

(11–4)
$$30 = 140 - .2R_g,$$

$$R_g = 550;$$

(11–5)
$$30 = 120 - .1R_c,$$

$$R_c = 900.$$

From equations (11–1) and (11–2), we can then obtain $P_g = \$85$ and $P_c = \$75$. Profit is calculated as follows:

$$\pi = TR - TC$$

$$= R_g(P_g) + R_c(P_c) - 18{,}200 - 30R_g - 30R_c$$

$$= 550(85) + 900(75) - 18{,}200 - 30(550) - 30(900)$$

$$= \$52{,}550 \text{ per day.}$$

It can be shown that no single price could produce as much profit for the hotel as the two previous prices, given the two demand curves in panels (a) and (b) of Figure 11–8. The mathematics of this situation are somewhat complicated; however, we present a simple graphical explanation in panels (d), (e), and (f) of Figure 11–8. Panels (d) and (e) contain the same demand and MR curves represented in panels (a) and (b). In panel (f), instead of summing the MR quantities from each market, we sum the quantities demanded at each price to obtain an aggregate demand curve, D_t. This curve expresses the total amount sold at various prices subject to the condition that $P_g = P_c$. The curve MR_t in panel (f) is the marginal revenue curve relevant to D_t. Where $SMC = \$30$ intersects MR_t, we establish the optimum quantity, 1,450 rooms, and the price, \$78.33. Note, however, that when this price is applied to the demand curves in panels (d) and (e), quantities are obtained that do not correspond to the intersection of $SMC = 30$ with MR_g and MR_c. In fact, we can see that at a price of \$78.33, $MR_g < SMC$ and $MR_c > SMC$. In terms of profit, the hotel is worse off, since

$$\pi = 1{,}450(78.33) - 18{,}200 - 30(1{,}450)$$

$$= \$51{,}879 \text{ per day.}$$

Clearly, if the law permits discrimination between the two markets, the hotel's management should establish a higher rate for general market customers than for convention market customers.

Earlier we noted that when markets are segmented, the market with the lowest (in absolute value) elasticity of demand would have the highest price when profit is maximized. This can be established from the general relationship between marginal revenue and elasticity of demand, which was introduced in Chapter 2 and is expressed as follows:

$$MR = P\left(1 + \frac{1}{E_p}\right) = P\left(1 - \frac{1}{|E_p|}\right), \text{ since } E_p < 0.$$

Recall that in the two-market case, $MR_g = MR_c$ when profit is maximized. Therefore it must also follow that

$$P_g\left(1 - \frac{1}{|E_g|}\right) = P_c\left(1 - \frac{1}{|E_c|}\right).$$

MANAGERIAL PERSPECTIVE
Computers and Price Discrimination

Price discrimination is becoming increasingly common in two large U.S. service industries, hotels and airlines. Travelers who use the airlines regularly are quite aware of the term "limited seat availability" that almost always appears in the fine-print footnote to air carriers' ads that trumpet special discount fares. This qualification allows the companies to switch seats from the discount market to the full-fare market when demand on a given route heats up. The discount fares are based on a specific demand estimate for each class of travel (discount, full coach, first class, etc.). With computer booking now pervasive in the industry, it is easy to track changes in demand and reduce the availability of discount seats if higher marginal revenue can be obtained from sales of nondiscounted seats. The hotels have learned from the airlines, and now the big chains that have computerized booking also reduce the availability of advertised discount rooms when demand in the nondiscount market increases. Some state attorneys general have eyed the practice warily, fearing that consumers will be unfairly treated if insufficient numbers of the advertised rooms are not made available.

References: Nikhil Hutheesing, "Keeping the Seats Warm," *Forbes*, Vol. 15, No. 1 (January 1, 1996), pp. 62–63; Allison Lucas, "Making Sure the Price is Right," *Sales and Marketing Management*, Vol. 148, No. 5 (May 1996), pp. 92–93; "No Cheap Room? Blame Yield Management," *The Wall Street Journal*, January 4, 1988, p. 8; and "Computers Permit Airlines to Use Scalpel to Cut Fares," *The Wall Street Journal*, February 2, 1987, p. 25.

From the preceding equation we can see that when $P_g > P_c$ it must be true that $|E_g| < |E_c|$, or, in the case of our hotel, the elasticity of demand for rooms is higher in the convention market than in the general market.

Of course, there are numerous cases in which management may be faced with a multiple-market pricing decision. We can expect the possibility of profit maximization through price discrimination or market segmentation to exist any time that distinct groups of consumers purchase a product in different quantities, at different times of the year, or of slightly different attributes (first class vs. tourist transportation, for example). In many cases such discrimination in pricing will be justifiable. Thus the competent manager must be able to recognize such possibilities if the firm is to be guided to maximum profit. This is especially important when the firm deals in international trade, because there may be significant differences between domestic and foreign elasticities of demand.

TWO-PART PRICING (ACCESS FEES)

Two-part pricing is a strategy that divides the amount a consumer pays for a good or service into an access fee and a price per unit.

While market segmentation allows firms to enhance profits by charging different prices to distinct groups of consumers, there are other strategies employing more than one price that do not involve discrimination but can also significantly add to profits. One such strategy is to separate the price to the consumer into two parts, an access fee and a price per unit consumed. Such **two-part pricing** is used by many firms.[12] Examples are telephone or cellular services that impose a fixed monthly fee to have a phone plus an additional charge per time unit of phone use; golf courses that charge a membership fee plus a green fee per unit of use; and amusement parks that charge an entry fee plus an additional fee for using each ride or attraction.

To understand how two-part pricing works, we will first consider the case of a market consisting of just a single consumer, and we will suppose that the marginal cost of output is constant. Let us say that the consumer's demand curve is given by the equation $P = 4 - 0.1Q$ and that $MC = AVC = \$1$. Suppose the firm charged no access fee and wanted to maximize profit contribution on sales to this one consumer. What price would it charge, and how much would its profit contribution be? Consider Figure 11–9. Here it is easy to see that profit contribution would be maximized where $SMC = MR$, so that $4 - 0.2Q = 1$. Thus, $3 = 0.2Q$ and $Q = 15$. Price would be \$2.50, and total profit contribution would be $(P - AVC)Q = \$1.5(15) = \$22.50$.

Now let's suppose the firm decides to charge an access fee to the consumer, so that in order to buy *any* units of the product a membership or entry fee must be paid. How much could the firm charge this consumer as an entry fee, assuming it charges the \$2.50 price in Figure 11–9? The answer can be easily obtained from the figure if one notes that triangle ABC represents the consumer's surplus on the 15 units bought at $P = \$2.50$.[13] (Keep in mind that the demand curve tells us what the consumer values each unit of the good at, so that all units between $Q = 0$ and $Q = 15$ are worth more to the consumer than the \$2.50 price that was paid for them.) What is the value of the area of triangle ABC? By geometry it is one-half the height of the triangle multiplied by its base—that is, $(1/2)(\$4 - \$2.5)(15) = \$11.25$. Where P^* is the price axis intercept of the demand curve, P is the current price, and Q is the quantity purchased, we can say the consumer's surplus $= (1/2)(P^* - P)(Q)$. Thus, the 15 units of product bought by the consumer for $\$2.5(15) = \$37.50$ have a value to this consumer of $\$37.50 + \$11.25 = \$48.75$. This means that the firm could charge an access fee of \$11.25, and the consumer would still buy the 15 units

---

12 In economic jargon, the term "two-part tariff" is frequently used to refer to this type of pricing. When so used, "tariff" just means "price" and has nothing to do with international trade, where it usually refers to a tax on imports or exports.

13 Consistent with the previous discussion of consumer surplus, we continue to assume that the income effect of a change in the price of this good is negligible.

Figure 11–9   Maximization of Profit Contribution Employing
Two-Part Pricing

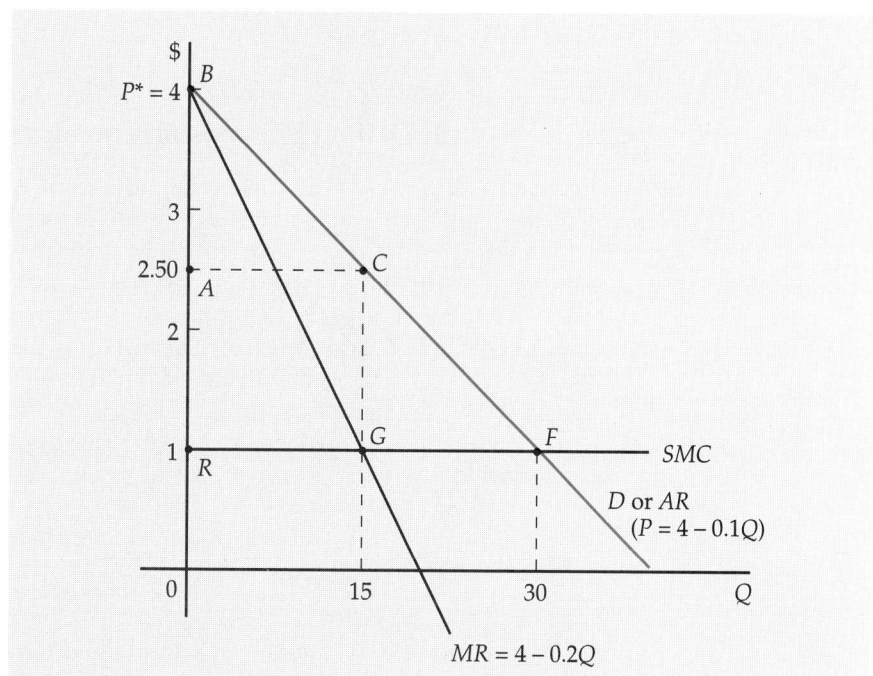

With unit pricing only, the firm would charge $2.50 and have a total profit contribution of $22.50. However, with the same unit price it could also charge an access fee equal to the area of triangle *ABC*. The maximum total profit contribution equals the area of triangle *RBF* and is obtained by charging a $1 price per unit with an access fee of $45.

of output for $2.50 per unit since he or she values them at $48.75. The firm's profit contribution, therefore, rises by the amount of the access fee and will total the original $22.50 *plus* the access fee of $11.25, or $33.75. This is an increase in profit contribution of 50 percent, so it is easy to see why the firm might be interested in a two-part pricing strategy.

Now we must ask whether $33.75 is the most the firm can get in profit contribution from using the two-part pricing approach. The answer is no. In fact, in this case the firm's profit will be maximized by setting $P = SMC$ and charging an access fee equal to the area of triangle *RBF* in Figure 11–9. The consumer will then purchase 30 units of output at a price of $1 per unit. Profit contribution increases because the additional variable cost of output is covered by the unit price, while the new access fee captures both the earlier profit contribution (area *RACG*) and the previous access fee (area *ABC*), and adds to them the area of triangle *GCF*. Since price and *AVC* are equal, total profit contribution now consists only of the access fee (area of triangle RBF) which is $(1/2)(\$3)(30) = \$45$. This is the maximum profit contribution obtainable.[14] The firm will therefore find it rational to charge an access fee of $45 and a price of $1 per unit.

Access Fees with Different Types of Consumers

While the preceding analysis is fairly straightforward, two-part pricing becomes more complex if consumers have different demand curves for the product. To illustrate, let us now suppose that instead of dealing with a single consumer, the firm has to consider two types of consumers with different demand curves. Again, it plans to employ two-part pricing, but one of the two types of consumers exhibits greater demand for the product than does the other. We will retain the demand curve from the previous example for the low-demand type of consumer and introduce another for the high-demand type. Additionally, the firm will *not* engage in price discrimination. The two demand curves follow.

$$P_L = 4 - 0.1Q_L \qquad \text{(low demand)}$$

$$P_H = 5 - 0.1Q_H \qquad \text{(high demand)}$$

In these expressions, the P terms are prices and the Q terms are the quantities demanded. (While our two demand curves are not greatly different, they will suffice to illustrate the case. Moreover, if the high-demand type of consumer differs too greatly from the low-demand type, the solution will be not to sell any to the latter.)

A special problem now arises because at every possible price per unit the consumer's surplus of the high-demand type of consumer exceeds that of the low-demand type. (In our preceding equation for the area of the consumer's surplus triangle, P^* will equal 5, rather than 4, for the high-demand consumer.) This will limit the access fee the firm can charge to the amount of the consumer surplus of the low-demand type of consumer. The reason for this is that charging an amount greater than that will lead the low-demand consumer to reject purchasing *any* of the product. If F_L is the consumer surplus of the low-demand type of consumer, the firm, by charging that amount as an access fee, can collect $2F_L$ from the two types of consumers. Assuming selling to both types of consumer is more profitable than just selling to the high-demand type, we can set up a profit contribution function (where AVC stands for average variable cost) as follows:

---

14 It can be shown graphically that $\Delta TR < \Delta TC$ if price is dropped to a level less than SMC. You may wish to work this out for yourself.

$$T\pi_c = 2F_L + (P - AVC)(Q_L + Q_H).$$

This simply says that the total profit contribution will consist of the two access fees plus the unit profit contribution multiplied by the sum of the quantities sold in the two markets. In the preceding expression, again using the geometrical formula for the area of a right triangle, $2F_L = 2(1/2)(P^* - P)Q_L$, where P^* is the dollar axis intercept of the demand curve of the low-demand type of consumer (in this case, 4), P is the price charged per unit, and Q_L is the quantity sold in the low-demand market. Note that since both types of consumer will be charged the same unit price, $P = P_L = P_H$, so that for our given demand curves,

$$4 - 0.1Q_L = 5 - 0.1Q_H$$

$$0.1Q_H = 0.1Q_L + 1, \text{ and}$$

$$Q_H = Q_L + 10.$$

This allows us to write the total profit contribution function as

$$T\pi_c = 2(1/2)(4 - 4 + 0.1Q_L)(Q_L) + (3 - 0.1Q_L)(2Q_L + 10)$$

$$= -0.1Q_L^2 + 5Q_L + 30.$$

For prices ranging from \$3.50 to \$0.50, Table 11–2 shows the results in

Table 11–2   Profit Contribution Data for Example of Two-Part Pricing with Low- and High-Demand Types of Consumers

P	Q_L	Q_H	F_L	F_H	$2F_L$	$T\pi_c$	$M\pi_c$
3.50	5	15	1.25	11.25	2.50	52.50	
							1.75
3.00	10	20	5.00	20.00	10.00	70.00	
							1.25
2.50	15	25	11.25	31.25	22.50	82.50	
							0.75
2.00	20	30	20.00	45.00	40.00	90.00	
							0.25
1.50	25	35	31.25	61.25	62.50	92.50	
							−0.25
1.00	30	40	45.00	80.00	90.00	90.00	
							−0.75
0.50	35	45	61.25	101.25	122.50	82.50	

Note: $F_L = (1/2)(P^* - P)(Q_L)$ and is the consumer's surplus of the low-demand type of consumer, where $P^* = 4$ is the price intercept of the relevant demand curve. F_H is the consumer's surplus of the high-demand type of consumer and can be calculated by the same formula where $P^* = 5$ is the appropriate demand curve intercept.

terms of both total and marginal profit contribution ($M\pi_c$) along with the quantities sold, the access fee ($2F_L$), and the respective consumer surpluses (F_L and F_H) for the two types of consumer. (Remember that if F_H is charged as the access fee, the low-demand type of consumer will not buy the product. Thus, charging F_H would yield a $T\pi_c$ equal to $F_H + (P - AVC)Q_H$ which is, at every price, *less* than the $T\pi_c$ shown in the table. You can check this for yourself.) As the table shows, the maximum profit contribution occurs when $P = \$1.50$. There, the firm will charge an access fee of \$31.25 and sell 25 units in the low-demand market plus 35 units in the high-demand market. Thus,

$$T\pi_c = 2F_L + (P - AVC)(Q_L + Q_H)$$

$$= 2(31.25) + (1.5 - 1)(60)$$

$$= 62.50 + 30 = \underline{\$92.50}.$$

Note also that the firm's marginal profit contribution is positive for quantity sold less than 60 but negative for quantity sold greater than 60.[15] As a practical matter, when consumers are diverse and, therefore, have different consumer surpluses, the firm may have to do a substantial amount of experimentation to determine what combination of access fee and unit price constitutes the best two-part pricing approach. Indeed, some firms, including theme park operators such as the Disney Corporation, have decided that it is optimal to use only an access fee and not charge a price per unit for partaking of the attractions. (In these businesses, however, the pricing of food, refreshments, and souvenirs is, of course, another matter.)[16]

BUNDLING

Bundling is a strategy that offers a package deal to consumers on the purchase of two or more products.

Bundling is a pricing strategy that takes a number of forms, but its principal characteristic is that it offers the buyer a package consisting of two or more goods that is more attractive than the alternative of buying the goods separately. Like many of the other strategies we have examined, it can enhance both revenue and profit. Bundling is used by tour companies, when they offer deals that can include airfare, hotel, rental car, and even meals at one package price; by cable television companies that offer combinations of channels at package prices cheaper than the separate prices for the same channels; by computer retailers who offer package deals including a computer, soft-

---

15 The calculus solution is straightforward and agrees with the table. To obtain marginal profit contribution, take the first derivative of the total profit contribution function. This yields $M\pi_c = -0.2Q_L + 5$. Setting $M\pi_c = 0$, one obtains $Q_L = 5/0.2 = \underline{25}$, and since $Q_H = Q_L + 10$, $Q_H = \underline{35}$.

16 One of the best-known articles on two-part pricing did, in fact, deal with Disneyland. See Walter Oi, "A Disneyland Dilemma: Two-Part Tariffs for a Mickey Mouse Monopoly," *Quarterly Journal of Economics* 85 (1971): pp. 77–96.

ware, and a number of peripherals; and even by fast-food restaurants that offer "meal deals" at prices lower than those charged for the same items bought separately.

How the firm gains from bundling is most easily demonstrated with a numerical example. Like certain other strategies, bundling is based on differing demand patterns of consumers. What is required for bundling to be attractive to the firm is a situation in which two consumers (or consumer groups) have an inverse relation between the amounts they are willing to pay for two different goods. To illustrate, let us imagine a wholesale travel company in New Orleans that advertises in selected newspaper travel pages and deals directly with consumers using a toll-free telephone number. Its research has indicated that there are basically two types of consumers in the target market. The *Type A* consumer is only mildly interested in jazz and creole cuisine but likes to take day trips to nearby attractions such as gardens, plantations, and beaches. The *Type B* consumer comes to New Orleans mainly for the jazz music and food but has only slight interest in the attractions of the surrounding area.

The maximum amounts that the two types of consumer would be willing to pay per day for a room and a rental car are shown in Table 11–3. The *Type A* consumer will pay up to $85 for a room and up to $40 for a rental car. The *Type B* consumer will pay up to $120 for a room but only values a rental car at $20 per day, since he or she is not terribly interested in traveling to the surrounding attractions. We can see that if more than $85 is charged for a room, the *Type A* consumer will not be interested in getting a room through this company. Likewise, if more than $20 is charged for a car, the *Type B* consumer will not be interested in booking a car through the company. If the company wishes to attract both consumers to rent a car and a room, the maximum separate prices it can charge for them is $85 for the room and $20 for the car. Then, both consumers will buy both items, and a total revenue of 2($85 + $20) = $210 will be obtained.

Now let's consider bundling the room and the car in a package deal. With the data in Table 11–3, we can see that the *Type A* consumer is willing to pay $125 per day for the combination of a room and a car, whereas the *Type B* consumer is willing to pay $140. Clearly, then, both will buy the bundle if the firm charges $125. This yields total revenue of 2($125) = $250, which is a

Table 11–3   Maximum Amounts That Two Types
of Consumers Would Pay Per Day
for a Room or a Rental Car

Consumer	*Room*	*Rental Car*
Type A	$ 85	$40
Type B	$120	$20

NUMERICAL EXAMPLE
Bundling

Whatsupwit U. has decided to allow beer consumption at its football games. You have been fortunate enough to secure the franchise for that operation, which is also authorized to sell hot dogs. Because you are a business school graduate, you have done some survey research that indicates the following are the maximum amounts spectators of two different persuasions would be willing to pay for those two items.

	One Hot Dog	One Beer
Male	$3.00	$2.50
Female	$4.00	$1.00

Your research indicates that attendance at the games will be about equally divided between males and females.

Questions

1. If the two items are priced separately, what combination of prices will yield the maximum total revenue?
2. What price would be charged if the two items are bundled, and how much would this strategy affect total revenue?

Solution

If the two items are priced separately, the firm will do best to charge $3.00 for a hot dog and $1.00 for a beer. This yields a total revenue of $8.00 from one male and one female. If hot dogs are priced above $3.00, the male will not buy any, and the female forgoes beer if it is priced above $1.00. At the maximum prices of $4.00 for a hot dog and $2.50 for a beer, only $6.50 would be obtained from one male and one female, since the male forgoes hot dogs and the female forgoes beer.

With bundling, the firm will charge $5.00 for the two items. Both males and females will buy the package, yielding $10 in revenue from one male and one female. This is a $2 gain from the unbundled result.

far better result for the firm than the $210 it would obtain if the two items were sold separately at prices that would attract both types of buyers.

In the foregoing example, bundling provided a gain because the preferences of the two consumers were inversely related. That is, the *Type A* consumer was willing to pay *less* for a room but *more* for a car than was the *Type B* consumer. If the data are altered to destroy this relation, for example, by reducing the amount the *Type B* consumer will pay for a room to $84, there will be no gain from bundling. You should try this, or any other combination where one consumer is willing to pay more for both items than is the other, to prove to yourself that the inverse relation is required.

Finally, we should note that the example we have given is one known as *pure bundling*. This means that we considered only offering the two items separately or as a package and did not take into account the possibility of offering them both separately and at a special price for the bundle. The latter would constitute *mixed bundling*. Mixed bundling, which includes offering separate items at the same time as, perhaps, a variety of different bundles, is an appropriate strategy where there are groups of consumers with imperfectly correlated inverse preferences and where there are differential marginal costs associated with the various products or packages. In fact, many of the bundling approaches that firms use today fall into the mixed category.

ALTERNATIVES TO PROFIT MAXIMIZATION

All of the situations discussed thus far in this chapter—and indeed, throughout this book—have focused on the managerial goal of profit maximization. Although it seems reasonable to accept profit maximization as at least the long-run goal of a firm's managers, there are good reasons to question this assumption. One of the well-recognized characteristics of business in the United States today is *separation of ownership and control*.

Since modern corporations are owned by shareholders but controlled by managers who may or may not have the shareholders' interest as their prime concern, there is a possibility that profit maximization, even when desired by shareholders, will not be the objective of the firms' managers. In other words, as we noted in Chapter 1, there is an *agency problem*, since the managers are acting as agents for the shareholders. For example, a corporate manager whose goal is personal success, measured in terms of either income or prestige, might perceive that personal rewards are more closely tied to the *size of the firm* than to profitability. In this setting, the manager might wish to expand sales beyond the point of profit maximization in order to capture a larger share of the market or to give the illusion of rapid growth. The firm might then be led to operate where *sales* are maximized, subject to the constraint that profit is sufficient to keep shareholders satisfied.[17]

---

17 See Seth Mendelson, "Market Share Vs. Bottom Line," *Supermarket Business*, Vol. 5, No. 2 (February 1996), p. 59; Daryl N. Winn and John D. Shoenhair, "Compensation-Based (Dis)Incentives for Revenue-Maximizing Behavior: A Test of the Revised 'Baumol Hypothesis,' " *Review of Economics and Statistics*, Vol. 70, No. 1 (February 1988), pp. 154–158; "GE's Wizards Turning from the Bottom Line to Share of the Market," *The Wall Street Journal*, July 12, 1982, pp. 1, 14; and "Position Wanted: Corporate Strategists Giving New Emphasis to Market Share, Rank," *The Wall Street Journal*, February 3, 1978, pp. 1, 23.

The preceding situation is described in Figure 11–10, where instead of operating at Q_e, the firm operates at Q^*. At output level Q^*, sales revenue is maximized but profit is less than at Q_e. Presumably, shareholders will not complain because profit at Q^* is still greater than normal. Of course, for certain firms, appreciation of stock prices may be more closely correlated with growth than with profits during one time period or another. In such a setting both shareholders and management might be more interested in sales increases than in maximum profit.

Although profit maximization and the conditions necessary to attain it are bound to be of importance to every manager, it is clear that the question of objectives of the firm includes a number of other considerations. Survival is not the least of these, and in a world characterized by oligopoly, risk aversion on the part of management could easily take precedence over profit maximization. In fact, in the game-theory model we presented in the appendix to Chapter 10, the firm was seen to choose a strategy that would maximize its *minimum* market share (the least market share it could obtain given rival reactions to its various possible strategies). Finally, we must note that most profit-maximizing rules based on market demand tend to be utilized where

Figure 11–10   Maximization of Sales Revenue Compared with Profit Maximization

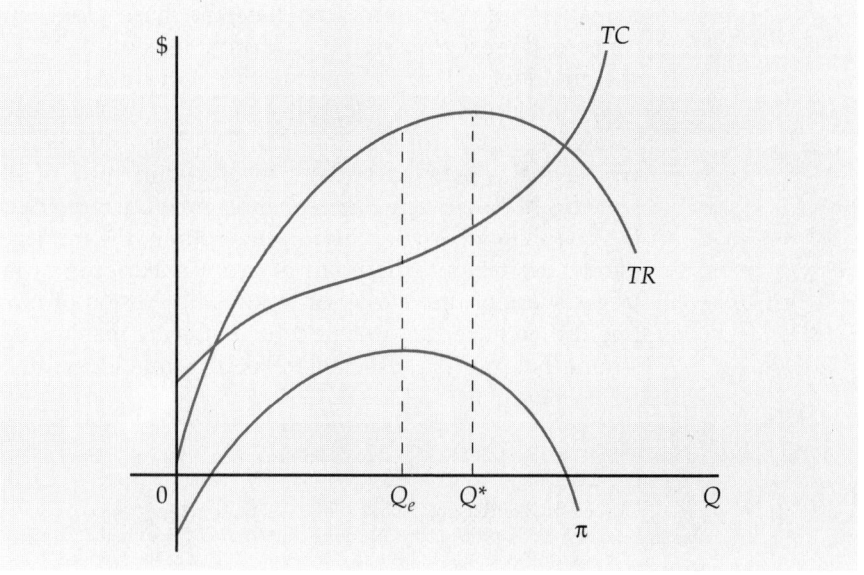

If the firm chooses to maximize sales revenue, it will operate at Q^*, even though maximum profit would be obtained at Q_e, a lower output.

rather short-run views of the market are estimated. As the time horizon pertinent to a management decision becomes longer, the difficulty in estimating demand increases, since more variables are likely to become relevant. Further, the possibility exists that short-run profit maximization may not be consistent with long-run profit maximization. A firm might choose in the short run to have lower profit and higher sales because over the long run or in subsequent periods, the consequences of early market penetration may have a very positive effect on profit. In other words, capturing additional markets today at rather low rates of profit may mean greatly increased profits in the future. To some extent the capital budgeting approach to long-run planning of the firm takes into account the effects of strategies that produce differential profit outcomes over time. This approach, which is an extension of the profit-maximizing analyses we have been using all along, will be discussed in Chapter 13.

SUMMARY

Multiple Products, Segmented Markets, and the Firm

In this chapter we have discussed pricing and output decisions of the firm in more complex situations than those assumed to exist in previous chapters. At the beginning of the chapter we examined markup pricing and found that it is not inconsistent with the conditions for profit maximization. More complex pricing problems were then discussed, beginning with the profit-maximizing behavior of firms that produce multiple products. The first case considered was that where two products can or must be produced jointly. If the two products *must* be produced in fixed proportions, the firm will maximize profit if it produces where the joint marginal revenue of the two products is equal to their joint marginal cost. (If the marginal revenue of one of the products becomes negative before this point is reached, some of the output of this product should be either destroyed or stored.) We also demonstrated that the situation is much more complex if the products can be produced in variable proportions.

Next we directed our attention to the case in which one division of a firm produces a product, called the *transfer product*, that is also used as an intermediate product in making the product of another division of the firm, the *final product* division. We discussed how the firm would determine the profit-maximizing quantities of the final division product and the transfer product and the appropriate price that should be charged the final product division for the transfer product. We saw that the determination of the optimal transfer price and quantities of both products differed, depending on whether or not the transfer product could be sold in an external market.

We then considered price discrimination, which occurs in various forms. We focused attention on *third-degree* price discrimination, where a firm that sells the same product in two separate markets can legally charge a different price in each market. As we saw, for price discrimination to be economically sound, customers in the two markets must have different elasticities of demand, and the firm must be able to prevent customers in the higher-priced market from buying the product in the lower-priced market.

Following the discussion of price discrimination, we developed models of both *two-part pricing*, where unit prices are supplemented by access fees, and *bundling*, where revenue and profit are enhanced by offering package deals on multiple products. Finally, we discussed alternative goals to profit maximization, such as sales maximization. Here, we noted the possibility that firm *managers* are more likely to have goals other than profit maximization if they are not also the firm's owners.

In the next chapter we return to the simpler case of the firm producing one product for one market and discuss how the firm can determine the short-run, profit-maximizing quantity of a variable input to be employed, assuming that all other inputs are fixed.

QUESTIONS

1. Under what set of circumstances would a firm that produces two joint products in fixed proportions be forced to withhold a portion of one product from the market?
2. How can a product transformation curve be employed to illustrate profit maximization with joint products produced in variable proportions? How is revenue represented in such a setting?
3. What is a transfer product? Under what circumstances might such a product be sold externally, as well as transferred?
4. State in two different ways the necessary condition for optimal production of a transfer product in the case of no external market for the transfer product.
5. What is meant by the term *consumer's surplus*? How is this concept related to both first- and second-degree price discrimination?
6. What is meant by *market segmentation* or *price discrimination*? Where a firm is selling in two separate markets, what is the condition that must be fulfilled in order to maximize the firm's profit?
7. Under what circumstances would it be useless (although not illegal) to charge different prices in two separate markets?
8. What is meant by the term *two-part pricing*? Give an example of a market where two-part pricing is frequently found.
9. What is *bundling*? Given two different types of consumers, what kind of preferences must exist for bundling to increase revenue?

10. Why might a firm's management choose to operate at a rate of output greater than the rate that maximizes profit? How can such behavior be reconciled with the profit maximization norm?
11. Why is transfer pricing an important issue in international business?
12. Under what circumstances is price discrimination legal in the United States?
13. Name some industries in your community in which firms legally and overtly practice price discrimination.
14. What is meant by markup pricing? Has it been used by firms as a long-run or a short-run pricing strategy? Explain.

PROBLEMS

1. Given the following product transformation curve, indicate the amount of X and Y that will maximize profit for the firm if the selling price per unit of X is 1/2 the price per unit of Y.

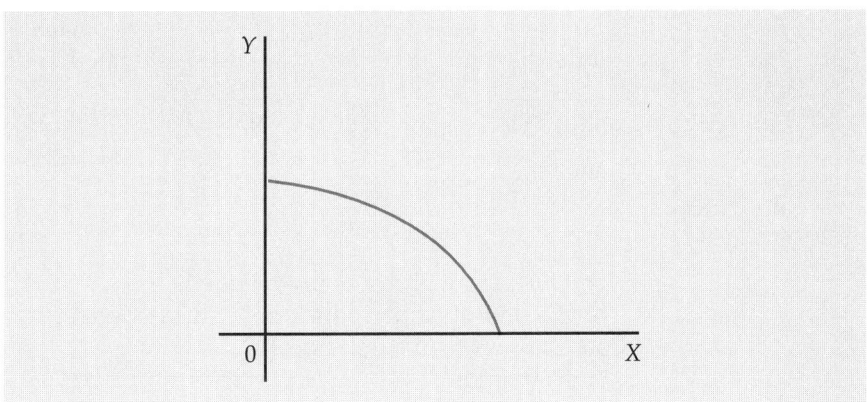

2. Sketch a product transformation curve for a firm that produces two joint products (X and Y) but has only the following input-output production possibilities:
   a. 100 percent X
   b. 75 percent X and 25 percent Y
   c. 50 percent X and 50 percent Y
   d. 25 percent X and 75 percent Y
   e. 100 percent Y
   Note: Assume that resources cannot be perfectly transferred from the production of X to the production of Y.

3. Suppose Randy Corporation is selling its product both in the United States and overseas and faces the two demand curves illustrated here. If the company's marginal cost is constant at $7.50 per unit of output, determine from the graphs what price it will charge in each market. (The United States has a large tariff on the product.)

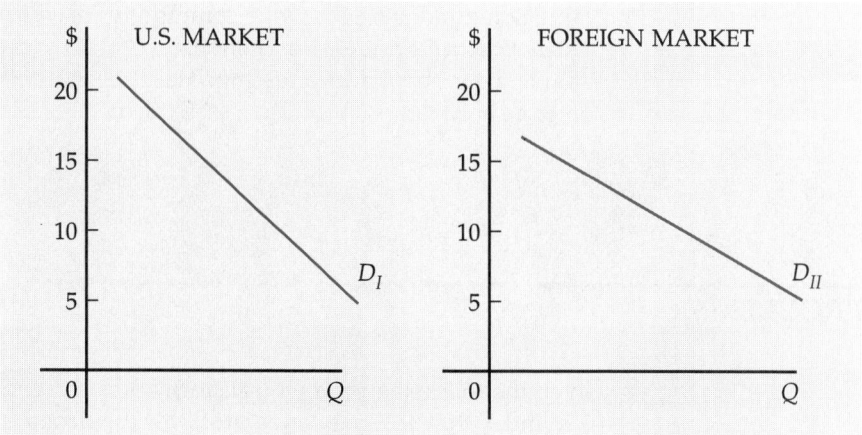

4. Suppose a company produces two products, A and B, and the production process is such that one unit of A is always obtained with one unit of B. If the demand curves for A and B are estimated to be

$$Q_A = 100 - P_A, \text{ (so that } MR_A = 100 - 2Q_A)$$

and

$$Q_B = 120 - 0.8P_B, \text{ (so that } MR_B = 150 - 2.5Q_B),$$

and the marginal cost of production is $MC = 4 + 1.5Q_J$, where Q_J consists of one unit of each product, how much of each product should the firm sell in order to maximize profit?

5. A company that produces plastic products by using injection molding machines has the following production and revenue alternatives for three products (A, B, and C) that are feasible to produce with the existing plant and equipment:

Product Combinations

No. of Shifts	100% A	50% A 50% B	100% B	75% A 25% B
1	TR = 200	TR = 225	TR = 275	TR = 200
2	TR = 380	TR = 410	TR = 500	TR = 400
3	TR = 490	TR = 575	TR = 575	TR = 600

TR is in thousands of dollars per month. *Total* cost for the first shift is $125,000 per month—of which $80,000 is labor, $40,000 is other variable costs, and $5,000 is fixed cost. As the number of shifts is increased, fixed cost remains at $5,000 per month while variable costs other than labor remain the same *per shift*. For the second shift, labor must be paid 1.25 times the amount paid in the first shift; for the third shift, labor must be paid 1.50 times what it receives in the first shift.

a. Determine total cost for the two-shift and three-shift alternatives.

b. Indicate the product combination and shift level that maximizes profit.

6. The Maxton Company produces a number of household appliances, including an electric coffee pot. The final product division of the company manufactures the metal pot and all plastic parts and then assembles, packages, and distributes the product. The electrical components unit of the coffee pot (consisting of a heating element, a thermocouple, and related wiring items) are produced by a separate electrical parts division of the firm.

The electrical parts division could sell the coffee pot components unit in the open market to a number of assemblers at a standard price of $2.80. There is vigorous competition in the electrical components industry, and it is unlikely that any but the going price can be obtained. Management has determined that the demand curve for quantity sold per month of the final product is

$$Q_f = 3{,}000 - 125P_f, \text{ (so that } MR_f = 24 - .016Q_f),$$

while the marginal cost of the final product, *excluding* the cost of the electrical components unit, is

$$MC_f = .004Q_f.$$

In addition, management has determined that the marginal cost of the transfer product division is

$$MC_t = .008Q_t,$$

where Q_t is the quantity of the transfer product produced.

a. At what final product price and rate of output will the firm maximize profit?

b. How much of the transfer product should be produced?

c. Should the final product division obtain *all* of its electrical components units for the coffee pot from its own components division? Why or why not?

d. Construct a diagram corresponding to the above situation. Show the equilibrium output for each division.

7. The management of Castle's Fried Chicken is planning a pricing policy based on market segmentation. M. J. Pyronic, the firm's sales manager, argues that the eat-in customer can be differentiated from the carry-out customer because the latter will generally purchase a large quantity of chicken to serve a group of people at home. Pyronic estimates that carry-out demand is more elastic than eat-in demand and states that carry-out buckets should be priced at a lower rate per serving of chicken (one wing, one drumstick, and one thigh) than the price per serving for eat-in customers.

Pyronic's estimate of carry-out demand is

$$Q_c = 10{,}000 - 2{,}000P_c, \text{ (so that } MR_c = 5 - .001Q_c),$$

where Q_c is the number of carry-out orders sold per week and P_c is the price per carry-out serving. She estimates the eat-in demand per week to be

$$Q_j = 6{,}000 - 1{,}000P_j, \text{ (so that } MR_j = 6 - .002Q_j),$$

where P_j is the price per eat-in serving. Marginal cost per serving is constant at $1.20.

   a. Should the price per serving for the carry-out market be lower than that for the eat-in market?
   b. How many servings per week should be sold in each market to maximize profit?
   c. What price or prices should be charged?
   d. Diagram the case showing the profit-maximizing rates of output and the average revenue.

8. Salmagam Corporation purchases video camcorder batteries from a manufacturer in Hong Kong and distributes them to retail stores throughout the United States. Salmagam's management has estimated that within the range of feasible prices for the batteries, the elasticity of demand of the retail stores for them is –3.5. If Salmagam can obtain any quantity of the batteries from the manufacturer for a fixed price of $18, answer the following:

   a. What will be its profit-maximizing markup percentage?
   b. What price should it charge for the batteries?

9. Smales Labs is a mail-order color film processing company. They have recently installed equipment that will allow them to expand their services to include supplying computer photodisks of customers' 35mm and Advanced Photo System prints. Smales has identified two major types of customer, those who favor prints (*Type P*) and those who favor photodisks (*Type D*). The maximum amounts each type of customer would pay per roll of film (24 or 25 exposures) for prints and a photodisk appear in the following table.

Type of Customer	Prints	Photodisk
Type P	$7.50	$4.00
Type D	$5.50	$8.00

Smales is considering offering its processing only as a bundle consisting of both prints and photodisk. Given the preceding data, what price would you advise the company to charge for the bundle? Explain how this yields more revenue than unbundled pricing that would attract each type of customer to buy *both* prints and disk.

10. Water Hyperwonderland, a theme park that features dolphin shows, estimates that the typical customer who likes the shows enough to want a season discount card has an annual demand curve represented by the equation $Q = 18 - P$, where P is the price charged per admission and Q is the number of times per year the person will visit the park. The park's marginal cost per visit for any type of client is $2. Based on the foregoing demand curve, to maximize profit contribution from discount-card customers, what should be (a) the price of a season discount card and (b) the per-visit ticket price for a discount card holder?

The following problems require calculus:

C1. Schmooker Chemical Company produces bubble bath powder using a process that yields a joint product of one unit of deadly Z41 pesticide for each unit of bubble bath produced. Schmooker's demand curve for bubble bath is $Q_b = 3,800 - P_b$. Its demand curve for Z41 has the equation $Q_z = 6,000 - 5P_z$. Schmooker's total cost function for the two joint products is $TC = 500 + 20Q + .095Q^2$. Answer the following:
   a. How much of each product should Schmooker sell?
   b. What price should it charge for each product?
   c. Should it withhold any of either product from the market? If so, which one (and how much) should it keep off the market?

C2. Taipei Electronics makes compact disc players under license from CRA Corporation. One of Taipei's subsidiaries, Lenscan Corporation, makes the optical stylus for the players. The total dollar cost of production of the stylus by Lenscan is

$$TC_s = 12,000 + 2Q_s + .0001Q_s^2.$$

Taipei's marginal cost (in dollars) for the final production of the disc players (not including the cost of the stylus) is $MC_d = 10 + .003Q_d$. The demand curve for the disc player is

$$Q_d = 70,000 - 400P_d, \text{ where } P_d \text{ is in dollars.}$$

If the optical stylus can be bought or sold in the open market at a fixed price of $5 per unit, determine the following:

a. The number of disc players Taipei should sell.
b. The price that should be charged for the players.
c. The number of optical styli the Lenscan subsidiary should produce.
d. The price that Lenscan should charge for the stylus.

C3. Down Under Products is an Australian firm that produces wine for sale to manufacturers of wine coolers. Due to spoilage in the production process, it also sells a co-product, wine vinegar. The ratio of vinegar to wine it produces is constant and equal to one case of vinegar for each case of wine produced. Down Under's current estimate of wine demand is represented by the following equation:

$$Q_w = 12{,}000 - 100P_w,$$

where Q_w is the number of cases of wine sold per month and P_w is the price obtained per case of wine.

Respectively, the demand curve for wine vinegar and the firm's total cost function are the following:

$$Q_v = 6{,}000 - 200P_v,$$

where Q_v is the number of cases of vinegar sold per month, and P_v is the price per case; and

$$TC = \$100{,}000 + 4.16Q + 0.006Q^2,$$

where $100,000 is monthly fixed cost, and Q represents the number of case equivalents of the two products it produces.

Down Under's present strategy is to maximize profit from the sales of the two products, given that there is no disposal cost for any excess product. Find the profit-maximizing quantities sold of the two products, their prices, the amount of excess product not sold, if any, and Down Under's total profit from sales of the two joint products.

C4. Gongalong Company makes grandfather's clocks. One of its subsidiaries, Boing, Inc., makes the mainsprings for the clocks. The market for such springs (which have many other novel uses) is highly competitive, and the going market price for them is $28.00 per unit. Gongalong estimates the demand for its clocks to be $Q_c = 14{,}000 - 20P_c$. The marginal cost of manufacturing the clocks, *not* including the mainsprings, is given by the function $MC_c = 23 + .12Q_c$. The marginal cost of the Boing division for making the mainsprings is $MC_s = 4 + .005Q_s$. There is one mainspring in each clock. Answer the following:

a. How many clocks should Gongalong produce, and what price should it charge per clock?
b. How many mainsprings should Boing, Inc., produce, and what price should it charge Gongalong per spring?
c. Will Gongalong have to buy any mainsprings from suppliers other than Boing? If not, why not? If so, how many?

C5. Peixe Louco is a Portuguese company that processes codfish. It also produces a co-product, codfish oil. Its production ratio of oil to fish is constant and equal to one gallon of oil for each case of fish produced. Peixe Louco's current estimate of fish demand is represented by the following equation:

$$Q_f = 10{,}000 - 100P_f,$$

where Q_f is the number of cases of fish sold per month, and P_f is the price obtained per case of fish.

Respectively, the demand curve for fish oil and the firm's total cost function are the following:

$$Q_o = 7{,}000 - 200P_o,$$

where Q_o is the number of gallons of oil sold per month and P_o is the price per gallon; and

$$TC = \$100{,}000 + 4.06Q + 0.003Q^2,$$

where \$100,000 is monthly fixed cost, and Q represents the number of case and gallon equivalents of the two products it produces.

Peixe Louco's present strategy is to maximize profit from the sales of the two products, given that there is no disposal cost for any excess product. Find the profit-maximizing *quantities sold* of the two products, their *prices*, the amount of *excess product* not sold, if any, and the company's *total profit* from sales of the two joint products.

C6. Aunt Jane's Fitness Center is planning to utilize price discrimination to set its family and corporate rates. For a family membership, its estimated demand curve is

$$Q_f = 984 - 20P_f.$$

For the corporate market, its estimated demand curve is

$$Q_c = 2{,}070 - 50P_c.$$

In both equations, Q represents quantity of members and P represents the monthly membership fee. The center's weekly total cost is

$$TC = 12{,}000 + 10Q,$$

where Q is total number of members ($Q_f + Q_c$).
   a. With price discrimination, how many memberships will be sold in each market?
   b. What price will Aunt Jane's charge in each market?
   c. What will be the center's monthly profit?

Problem C7 requires both partial differentiation and constrained maximization. It should be attempted only if you have covered the material in the appendix that follows Chapter 5.

C7. The Chilidome Regency Hotel is planning to use price discrimination between convention and general room rates. For a standard double room, its estimated demand curve for the general market is

$$Q_g = 4{,}344 - 20P_g.$$

For the convention market, its estimated demand curve is

$$Q_c = 5{,}800 - 50P_c.$$

In both equations, Q represents weekly quantity of rooms and P represents price per night. The hotel's weekly total cost is

$$TC = 112{,}000 + 40Q + .01Q^2,$$

where Q is weekly total number of rooms rented ($Q_g + Q_c$).
a. With price discrimination, how many rooms will be rented in each market?
b. What price will the hotel charge in each market?
c. What will be the hotel's weekly profit?
d. Compare the results from both (b) and (c), in terms of both price and profit, with what the firm could obtain if it did not practice price discrimination.

C8. The small city of Olpeson, Kansas, has a municipal golf course. For years, the golf course has been available at no charge to users. However, due to declining population and increasing costs of maintenance, the city council has decided to institute both a membership fee and a greens fee (fee charged per round played) for golf patrons. Research shows there are two kinds of patrons, city residents and persons who live in the surrounding rural area. The council believes it is not politically feasible to charge the rural users different fees than those paid by the city residents. Its research staff estimates that the typical city resident golfer's demand can be represented by the equation $Q_c = 20 - 0.4P_c$. For the typical rural golfer, the estimated demand curve is $Q_r = 18 - 0.4Q_r$. (In either equation, the P_i represents the greens fee and the Q_i represents the annual number of times it is paid.) If research estimates that the average variable cost (maintenance, fee administration, etc.) to the course of an individual's round of golf is $3.00, what combination of membership fee and greens fee will maximize the return to the city? How many rounds of golf per year will the typical city resident golfer play, and how many will the typical rural golfer play?

This problem can be solved with Decision Assistant.

D1. For many years, VHG Press, Inc., has published travel guides for all regions of the United States. These travel guides have been received with great enthusiasm by travelers because of the accuracy of the material they contain, the inclusion of many unique out-of-the-way sites not listed in other guides, and the many outstanding discount coupons that are bound into each edition.

The president of VHG Press, Victor Garrett, has been watching the recent trends of increasing visits to the United States by English-speaking Europeans. Victor knows this trend presents a unique opportunity to VHG Press—the possible marketing of the company's existing guides through various large European outlets. The opportunity is unique in two ways: no additional fixed costs would be incurred, as the current English edition could be used, and VHG Press could possibly charge a different price in its European market.

The marketing department has provided the following information:

$$\text{Domestic Demand} \quad Q_d = 30 - P_d,$$

where Q_d is the quantity demanded (in thousands) in the domestic market and P_d is the domestic price, and

$$\text{International Demand} \quad Q_i = 22 - P_i,$$

where Q_i is the quantity demanded (in thousands) in the international market, and P_i is the international price.

The production department has provided the total cost function for the production of travel guides as being

$$TC = 2Q_t + .1Q_t^2,$$

where TC is total costs and Q_t is the total quantity printed (in both markets).

Use the Price Discrimination tool in the *Managerial Economics Decision Assistant* to assist Victor in preparing a report on the feasibility of this new venture. The report should include the following information:

a. The price currently charged and the quantity being sold in the domestic market.

b. The proposed price in the international market along with the estimated quantity to be sold in the international market.

c. The profit-maximizing price and quantity in the domestic market with the proposal.

SELECTED REFERENCES

Adams, Walter (ed.). *The Structure of American Industry*, 6th ed. New York: Macmillan, 1982.

Carlton, Dennis W., and Jeffrey M. Perloff. *Modern Industrial Organization*, 2d ed. New York: HarperCollins, 1994, especially Chapters 11 and 12.

Lanzillotti, Robert F. "Pricing Objectives in Large Companies," *American Economic Review* (December 1958), pp. 921–940.

Miller, Roger LeRoy, and Raymond P. H. Fishe. *Microeconomics: Price Theory in Practice*. New York: HarperCollins, 1995, especially Chapter 12.

Plott, Charles R. "Industrial Organization Theory and Experimental Economics," *Journal of Economic Literature* (December 1982), pp. 1485–1527.

Scherer, F. M. *Industrial Market Structure and Economic Performance*, 3d ed. Boston: Houghton Mifflin, 1990.

APPENDIX 11A

Transfer Pricing with a Less-Than-Perfectly Competitive Market for the Intermediate Product

In this appendix we analyze the transfer pricing problem facing managers of a two-division, two-product firm when the transferred product can be sold externally in a market that is less than perfectly competitive. The relationship of the transfer product division to the final product division remains unchanged from the examples covered in this chapter; that is, the transfer product division knows it must price its output at marginal cost when selling to the final product division. Presumably, with an oligopolistic external market for the transfer product, T, the final product division cannot be supplied its T inputs from rival firms at a price as low as the level of the marginal cost of Product T when profit for the firm is maximized. However, if the T division has the opportunity to sell its product in such an external market, management will need to determine the combination of final and transfer product outputs that maximizes profit, as well as the profit-maximizing prices of each of the products.

In this situation, the firm's profit will be maximized when MC_T, the marginal cost of product T, is equal to the net marginal revenue of the entire enterprise, NMR_e. In the chapter, NMR_F was identified as $MR_F - MC_F$, the marginal revenue remaining after all marginal costs except that of Product T are subtracted from the marginal revenue resulting from the sale of the final product. However, with an external market for T that is less than perfectly competitive, the T division finds itself selling in what is essentially a two-market setting (internal and external) or a situation similar to the case of two-market price discrimination (also discussed within Chapter 11). From management's point of view, then, the NMR_e will consist not only of $MR_F - MC_F$, but also of MR_T—the marginal revenue obtainable from sales of T in the external market.

The firm as a whole will be able to increase profit by switching output of T from the internal market to the external market whenever $MR_T > (MR_F - MC_F)$. Note, however, that this can be accomplished only by also varying the amount produced and sold of the final product, as well as the price of the final product. Such a result follows because the amount of T supplied to the final product division cannot be reduced without also reducing the output of the final product itself.

Figure 11A–1 provides a graphical solution to the profit-maximizing problem that exists when management knows it can sell some amount of T in an oligopolistic external market. As in previous examples in Chapter 11, we depict a situation in which there is a fixed amount of T used in the manufacture of one unit of the final product. Thus the Q axis of panel (a) will measure both production of the final product, F, and utilization of T by the final product division. In panel (a) the curve $MR_F - MC_F$ is derived from D_F in the usual manner. The external market for Product T is illustrated in panel (b), where MR_T is derived from the external demand curve D_T. Finally, in panel (c) the two curves $MR_F - MC_F$ and MR_T are summed horizontally (quantities added for each level of MR) to obtain NMR_e—the net marginal revenue of the enterprise.

Profit maximization occurs in Figure 11A–1 where $NMR_e = MC_T$. By projecting the profit-maximizing level of MC_T (that is, MC_T^*) leftward to panels (b) and (a), we find the quantities of T sold to the final product division (Q_e) and the external market for the transfer product Q'_{T_x} such that $MC_T^* = MR_T = MR_F - MC_F$. The equality of $MR_F - MC_F$ with MR_T ensures that the firm cannot gain by switching output from the internal market to the external market, or vice versa. Since the transfer product division is instructed to set a transfer price equal to MC_T, $P_{T_i} = MC_T^*$ will be the price charged the final product division for its inputs of T. However, in the external market, a price of P_{T_x} will be charged [panel (b)]. Back in panel (a), the final product division can be seen to produce Q_e of final product F and charge a price of P_F.

Figure 11A–1   Transfer Pricing With a Less-Than-Perfectly Competitive Market for Transferred Product

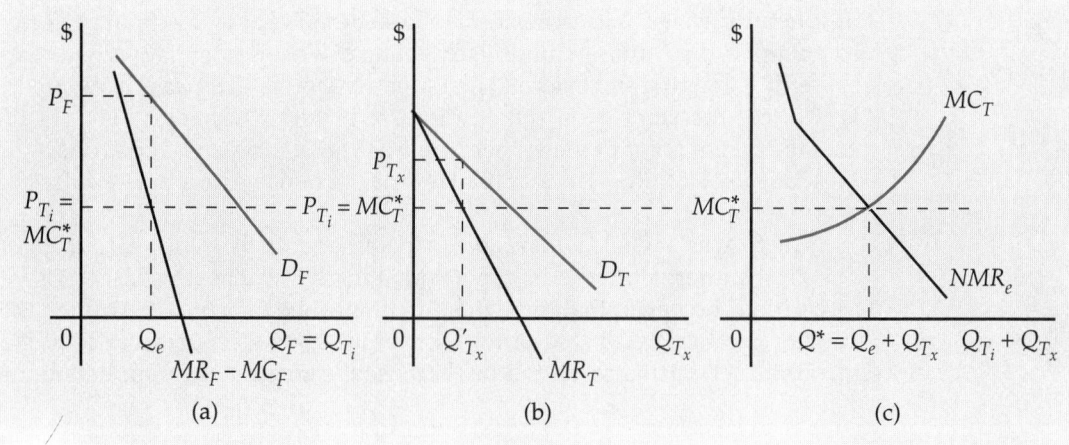

The situation depicted in Figure 11A–1 is illustrative of the kind of analysis that must be done in order for managers to maximize profit where a transfer pricing decision must be made and the external market for the transfer product is not perfectly competitive. It should be clear from the preceding that sales of the transfer product to purchasers outside the firm may contribute importantly to the firm's total revenue and profit. Another way to examine this issue is to ask what would happen if the external demand for the transfer product were to increase (D_T and MR_T shift to the right). In terms of Figure 11A–1, we can verify that NMR_e would also shift toward the right, thereby intersecting MC_T at a level higher than MC_T^*. This would undoubtedly lead to increased sales in the external market for the T product, but what would happen to Q_F? If final product demand has not changed, then Q_e must fall and P_F must rise when the profit-maximizing level of MC_T rises above MC_T^*. Thus the firm would actually be best off to reduce sales of its final product and increase the final product's price in order to be able to market more of Product T externally.

The lesson to be learned from the preceding analysis is that a change in one of the markets faced by a multiple-product, multiple-market firm can have pervasive effects on several aspects of the firm's operations. However, these effects may be predictable to some degree if the firm has sufficient information on demand and costs. Another example that could be illustrated by making some changes in Figure 11A–1 is a situation in which demand for the final product has increased [D_F shifts rightward in panel (a)] but D_T has not. The reader should be able to verify that in this setting, less of T should be sold externally and P_{T_x} should be increased.

APPENDIX 11B

Mathematics of Price Discrimination[1]

The model of two-market price discrimination discussed in Chapter 10 was developed only for the case of constant marginal cost, since the mathematics of the situation is somewhat complex if marginal cost is variable. To illustrate why, we will return to the example of hotel pricing used in the chapter and use the same demand data found there with a total cost function characterized by increasing marginal cost. The demand curves given for the hotel example were the following

General market: $P_g = 140 - 0.1R_g$.

Convention market: $P_c = 120 - 0.05R_c$.

P_g and P_c are the prices charged in the two markets, respectively, while the R terms denote the quantity of rooms demanded in each market per day.

Whereas the original example was developed with a constant marginal cost of \$30 per additional room rented, we will now suppose that the hotel has the following total and marginal cost functions:

$$TC = 18{,}200 + 4R + 0.02R^2$$

$$MC = 4 + 0.04R.$$

In these two expressions, R is the number of rooms rented in *both* markets. From the example in the chapter, it might appear that profit could be maximized by just setting the above MC equal to the marginal revenue equation for each market. However, this will not yield the correct answer, since the renting of an additional room in *one* of the two markets changes the marginal cost of the next room rented in *either* market.

---

1 This material utilizes both partial differentiation and the Lagrangian multiplier approach to constrained maximization. It is highly recommended for students who have sufficient mathematical preparation to have been introduced to these techniques in the appendix to Chapter 5.

SOLUTION PROCEDURE IF DISCRIMINATION IS PERMITTED

The usual approach to solving the price discrimination problem when marginal cost is variable is to set up a profit function where both revenue and cost depend on two independent variables, the quantities sold in each market. From the demand equations, it follows that the total revenue function for sales in both markets is

$$TR = 140R_g - 0.1R_g^2 + 120R_c - 0.05R_c^2.$$

The profit function results when the total cost function stated earlier is subtracted from this total revenue equation. However, we restate the "R" term in the cost function as $(R_g + R_c)$.

$$\pi = 140R_g - 0.1R_g^2 + 120R_c - 0.05R_c^2 - 18,200 - 4R_g - 4R_c$$
$$- 0.02R_g^2 - 0.04R_cR_g - 0.02R_c^2;$$

or, collecting terms,

$$\pi = 136R_g - 0.12R_g^2 + 116R_c - 0.07R_c^2 - 0.04R_gR_c - 18,200.$$

To solve for the profit-maximizing quantities of R_g and R_c, we now take the two partial derivatives of the profit function and set each equal to zero. This will satisfy the necessary conditions for a maximum.[2].

$$\frac{\partial \pi}{\partial R_g} = 136 - 0.24R_g - 0.04R_c = 0$$

$$\frac{\partial \pi}{\partial R_c} = 116 - 0.04R_g - 0.14R_c = 0$$

These two partials can be solved easily by multiplying the second equation by -6 and adding it to the first, an operation that yields

$$-560 + 0.80R_c = 0,$$

$$R_c = 700,$$

---

2 We will deal only with first-order conditions here. Second-order conditions are discussed in the mathematical appendix at the end of the book.

and substituting 700 for R_c in either partial,

$$R_g = 450.$$

Thus the hotel should rent 1,150 rooms, 700 in the convention market and 450 in the general market. From the demand equations for each market, it follows that the prices will be

$$P_g = 140 - 0.1(450) = \$95,$$
$$P_c = 120 - 0.05(700) = \$85.$$

The total daily profit of the hotel with price discrimination will be

$$95(450) + 85(700) - 18,200 - 4(1,150) - 0.02(1,150)^2 = \$53,000.$$

No other combination of prices and quantities sold in the two markets will yield a higher profit.

SOLUTION PROCEDURE IF DISCRIMINATION IS NOT PERMITTED

Using calculus, it is possible also to show that profit with price discrimination is greater than it would be if the firm were to charge a uniform price in both markets. In effect, this is a constrained maximization problem where the constraint is that the price in one of the two markets must be equal to that in the other. For the preceding case, this would mean that $P_g = P_c$, or

$$140 - 0.1R_g = 120 - 0.05R_c,$$

which can be rewritten as

$$20 - 0.1R_g + 0.05R_c = 0.$$

To solve for the quantities that will maximize profit subject to this constraint, we form the Lagrangian function as follows.

$$L\pi = 136R_g - 0.12R_g^2 + 116R_c - 0.07R_c^2 - 0.04R_gR_c - 18,200$$
$$+ \lambda(20 - 0.1R_g + 0.05R_c).$$

To solve for the profit-maximizing quantities of R_g and R_c, we now take three partial derivatives of the Lagrangian function and set each equal to zero. This will satisfy the necessary conditions for a maximum.

$$\frac{\partial L\pi}{\partial R_g} = 136 - 0.24R_g - 0.04R_c - 0.1\lambda = 0.$$

$$\frac{\partial L\pi}{\partial R_c} = 116 - 0.04R_g - 0.14R_c + 0.05\lambda = 0.$$

$$\frac{\partial L\pi}{\partial \lambda} = 20 - 0.1R_g + 0.05R_c = 0.$$

The Lagrangian multiplier, λ, can be eliminated from the first two expressions by multiplying the second equation by 2 and adding it to the first one. This yields the following:

$$368 - 0.32R_g - 0.32R_c = 0.$$

Finally, R_g, can be eliminated by multiplying the partial derivative with respect to λ by -3.2 and adding it to the preceding expression. This results in

$$304 = 0.48R_c, \text{ and } R_c = 633.33.$$

Substituting the preceding value of R_c into the constraint equation, we find that $R_g = 516.67$. Thus, to the nearest room, the profit-maximizing quantities are 633 rooms in the convention market and 517 rooms in the general market.

If this answer is correct, we should expect to find that the room rate charged is the same for both markets. To demonstrate this, we return to the unrounded values of R_g and R_c. From the demand curve equations initially given,

$$P_g = 140 - 0.1(516.67) = \$88.33,$$

and

$$P_c = 120 - 0.05(633.33) = \$88.33.$$

Thus the room rate should be set at \$88.33. Note that this price is between the two prices that were charged with discrimination and that quantity has increased in the general market but decreased in the convention market. However, the total quantity of rooms rented is still 1,150 per day. Quantity will always be the same as under discrimination, since what happens when discrimination takes place is that rooms with low marginal revenue (general market) are switched for rooms with higher marginal revenue (convention market) until both of the marginal revenues are equal to marginal cost.

As we stated earlier, profit will be less with a uniform price than it was with discrimination. Recall that with discrimination profit was calculated to be \$53,000. Without discrimination it is

$$\$88.33(1,150) - 18,200 - 4(1,150) - 0.02(1,150)^2$$
$$= 101,579.50 - 49,250 = \$52,329.50.$$

Thus the hotel makes $670.50 per day more with price discrimination than without. Note that total cost is the same in either case, but that price discrimination increases total revenue. This will always be the case.

PROBLEM

Trenchwich Corporation manufactures power trenching machines in the United States. It also sells them in the international market. The company spends a lot of money on lobbying and has been successful in obtaining a high tariff on competing foreign output. The annual domestic demand for its product is given by

$$Q_{US} = 30,000 - 2P_{US}.$$

Annual foreign demand for the same machine is given by the equation

$$Q_f = 50,000 - 4P_f.$$

Trenchwich's total cost function is

$$TC = 200,000 + 2,000Q + .5Q^2.$$

a. Assuming the firm practices price discrimination, what will be its price per unit in each of the two markets, and how many machines will it sell in each market?
b. Calculate the firm's total profit under the preceding conditions.
c. Find the firm's profit-maximizing price, sales quantity in each market, and total profit under the assumption that it does not discriminate in pricing.

INTERNATIONAL CAPSULE II

Markets and Pricing Strategy in International Trade

As Chapters 9 through 11 have shown, an important problem facing the firm is the *structure* of the market or markets in which it sells its product. By this we mean the nature of both consumer demand and competition from other firms. Although we cannot cover all of the possible market structures encountered in international trade in this brief capsule, a number of the situations discussed here are frequently faced by firms that deal outside their own national boundaries, and an introductory review of them will provide some food for thought regarding both the opportunities and difficulties associated with pricing strategies in world markets. We will begin with a strategy that is frequently employed by firms, that of market segmentation.

MARKET SEGMENTATION IN INTERNATIONAL TRADE

Chapter 11 showed that firms often have opportunities to employ price discrimination or market segmentation to increase their sales revenues from markets that are physically separated and characterized by different elasticities of demand. Of course, this concept carries over to the international market, as does another important maxim, the rule that it pays to sell incremental output as long as

the price of that output exceeds its average variable cost.

Low-Priced Foreign Sales

Any firm that sells both at home and in a foreign market must make some determination regarding whether to charge different prices in the two outlets. How can it make the choice?

Our discussions of the determinants of demand (Chapter 2) and the impact of various market structures (Chapters 9 and 10) lead to the conclusion that the price elasticity of demand for any product is likely to be greater the larger the number of substitute goods available. Thus, if a firm sells in a largely unfettered world market where there are many substitute products, it may well maximize profit by selling at a *lower* price in the international market than at home. For many products, the world market is vastly larger and more competitive than any one country's internal market. Therefore the foreign elasticity of demand may be the greater of the two. As the hotel pricing example in Chapter 11 showed, in the case of two-market price discrimination, profit maximization dictates that the market with the higher elasticity of demand be the one that will be charged the lower price.

There are other reasons a firm may choose to sell outside its national boundaries at a price below that charged domestic consumers. First, as noted earlier, in incremental analysis it is argued that incremental sales add to profit as long as price exceeds average variable cost. A firm that has already covered all of its fixed costs from profit contribution on home country sales would be rational to sell outside the country at *any* price that is above its average variable cost. When foreign sales are viewed strictly as an incremental decision, the firm may choose to sell in the foreign market at prices that are so far below the home price that they *appear* to be unprofitable. However, such sales likely are actually adding to profit, as Figure II–1 shows. Here it is assumed that the world market is perfectly competitive with a prevailing price of P_w, that marginal cost is rising in straight-line fashion, that $P_w > AVC$ at E_f, and that the home market is insulated from foreign sellers (perhaps by a nontariff barrier). In panel (a), the firm maximizes profit on home country sales at the output where $MC = MR_h$ and charges price P_h to domestic consumers. However, in panel (b) it sells an additional amount, $0Q_w$, to foreign purchasers at the world market price. The addition to its profit from the foreign sales is triangle P_wZE_f, which measures the difference between MR and MC on the $0Q_w$ units sold. (Note that this is a price discrimination problem that differs from those discussed in Chapter 11 in that the firm itself sets only one of the two prices, and the firm has not obtained the maximum possible profit, since $MR_w > MR_h$ at Q_h. Thus the firm would be better off to switch output from home to foreign sales until it reaches a combination where $MR_h = MR_w$).

Thus far we have seen that both price discrimination and incremental analysis support

Figure II–1   One Rationale for a Low Foreign Price

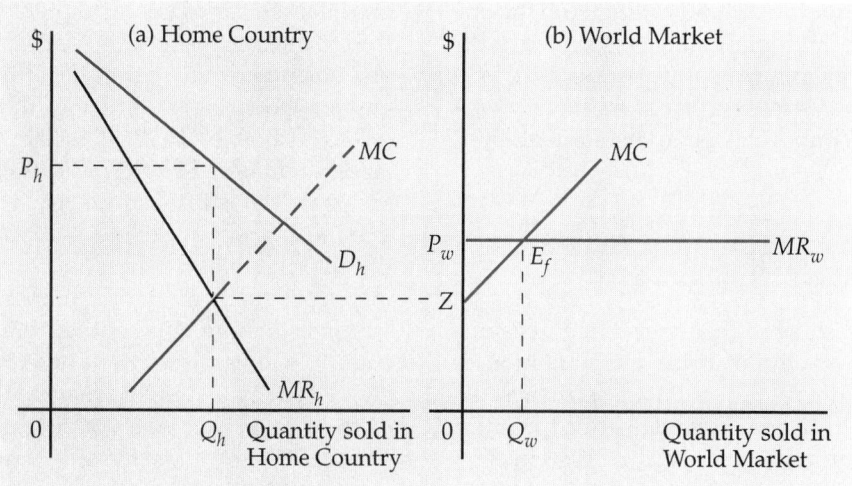

This firm maximizes profit in the home market and then sells an additional amount, $0Q_w$, in the world market until $MC = MR_w$. While this strategy adds to profit, the firm is not maximizing profit since $MR_w > MR_h$. To maximize profit, it must sell less at home and more in the world market.

the possibility that a firm might charge a lower price internationally than at home for the same product. There is another reason, also related to the discussion of Chapter 11, that could account for selling at a low price to foreign purchasers. Suppose a firm produces two joint products. If there is limited domestic demand for one of them, foreign sales might provide an outlet that is cheaper than paying for disposal of unwanted product at home. In fact, if a firm bases its production quantity of two joint products strictly on the domestic demand for them, and one product is produced in excess quantity, it will be rational to sell an amount in the foreign market equal to the excess *plus* any amount of domestic sales for which domestic marginal revenue is below foreign marginal revenue. Here again, there may be a strong incentive to sell outside the home market at a very low price.

High-Priced Foreign Sales

While we have emphasized foreign market prices that are below home market prices, we should realize that firms also have opportunities to maximize profit by charging *higher* prices in the foreign market than at home. After all, price discrimination just says that the higher price should be charged where demand is least elastic; it does not say home demand is always less elastic than foreign. What kinds of situations might conform to a lower foreign demand elasticity than at home? Again, our earlier observation about market size gives a hint. If the foreign market is small in comparison with the home market, it may pay to charge a higher price on foreign sales. This may be the case for luxury goods that are in common use in the market of a highly developed country such as the United States but would be purchased by only a small proportion of consumers in many less-developed countries. Keeping in mind that demand is a "willing and able" concept, we

note that in some countries many consumers are willing but *not* many are able to buy certain types of goods. Within the markets of those countries, goods exported from the industrialized countries may command very high prices, and the demand of the small consuming group for such goods will likely be less elastic than that found in the industrialized countries. In addition, less-developed countries are characterized by both limited and uncertain domestic production of many types of manufactured goods, and these characteristics on the supply side of such markets can also lead to higher prices than those found elsewhere.

THE PROBLEM OF DUMPING

The term "dumping" has a very specific meaning in international trade. It refers to the practice of selling in a foreign market at a price that is lower than the home market price.[1] Since we have seen that there are a good number of reasons for a firm to charge foreigners a low price, it should be no surprise that dumping often occurs. In some cases, the main result of dumping is just that some consumers get a bargain price on foreign goods. However, there are laws regulating dumping that can cause serious difficulties for a firm, particularly if its managers are unaware of how a foreign government may react. If consumers in the country where goods are dumped get them at bargain prices, what is the issue? The problem is that

1 Some of the laws that regulate dumping state that it occurs when the foreign price is below the home cost of production. These laws usually are difficult to administer, since precise data on home cost are not easily obtained and definitions of cost vary. Note that if the definition of cost is average variable cost, a firm that is dumping is doing so for negative incremental profit.

producers in the same country may view dumping as a form of unfair competition. After all, to remain in business they must generate sufficient revenues to cover both variable and fixed costs. The firm that is dumping in a foreign market probably has already covered its fixed costs from home sales and, as we have already noted, can sell profitably to foreigners at any price above average variable cost.

To keep foreign firms from damaging domestic firms through dumping, national governments have enacted antidumping laws that may deal rather harshly with foreign firms. The United States has one of the most actively used antidumping laws in the world—the Antidumping Act of 1921. Under this act, as modified by later legislation, the U.S. Treasury Department is required to initiate an investigation whenever a U.S. firm or group of firms files a complaint alleging that it is being "injured" by competition from foreign goods dumped in the U.S. market. If Treasury investigators do find dumping, the next step is hearings before the United States International Trade Commission (ITC), which must make a determination regarding the question of injury. In the event the ITC does find injury, antidumping duties may be assessed against the U.S. firms that *purchased* the dumped merchandise, and the foreign exporters' shipments may be subject to surveillance for several years. Although antidumping duties may be substantial, in many cases the litigation costs of defending an antidumping charge far exceed the penalties.[2]

A U.S. firm that exports its goods to a foreign country may find that it faces a similar situation to that faced by foreign firms that dump in the United States. Dumping in the foreign market could not only disrupt its export activities but also lead to substantial foreign legal expenses.[3]

WEBB-POMERENE AND EXPORT TRADING COMPANIES

In 1918, largely as a response to German cartels that were set up before World War I, the U.S. Congress passed the Webb-Pomerene Act, which allows U.S. firms to form export trade associations to market their products abroad. In effect, it permits for export trade purposes a number of practices—such as price fixing and division of markets—that in domestic trade are in violation of the antitrust laws (see Chapter 16). What this means for U.S. firms is that they need not compete with each other in the international market and have the alternative of taking a cartel approach to pricing and division of markets in foreign trade.

Historically, the U.S. export trade associations have been important in certain natural-resource-based industries such as minerals and forest products. The associations have

---

2 New provisions against dumping are also included in the recently completed Uruguay Round of negotiations of the General Agreement on Tariffs and Trade accord. See "Trade Pact Is Set by 117 Nations, Slashing Tariffs, Subsidies Globally," *The Wall Street Journal*, December 16, 1993, pp. A3, A13; and other articles on pages A12–A13 of that issue.

3 We should note also that in the United States the antidumping law has sometimes served as a nontariff trade barrier. By this we mean that U.S. firms that are *not* in danger of significant injury from imports file antidumping complaints simply to discourage foreign competition of any kind. Part of the job of the International Trade Commission is to fend off groundless complaints so that the U.S. market will not be unduly restricted. Antitrust authorities from the Federal Trade Commission frequently attend the ITC hearings and give testimony when they believe a U.S. industry is using the antidumping law as a market weapon to restrict competition.

had a checkered past, since they have at times engaged in anticompetitive practices that may have had an adverse impact on the domestic market in the United States as well as on foreign markets. For example, in the 1930s the Sulphur Export Corporation suppressed a newly discovered Norwegian process for sulphur production by purchasing a patent to ensure that no one outside Norway would ever be able to employ it without their consent.[4] Further, throughout the Great Depression, U.S. domestic prices of sulphur were quite stable and differed from the export price by only $2 per ton. In the 1960s the Phosphate Export Corporation sold phosphate rock to Korea for an export price substantially above the U.S. domestic price. It was later discovered that the phosphate was purchased with U.S. aid money and that the U.S. government (and its taxpayers) had been charged the foreign price.

Despite the less than satisfactory results of the Webb-Pomerene Act, there has been much interest in the establishment and promotion of new U.S. export trading companies. The reason for this development is the great success of Japanese export trading companies in world markets. These companies have specialized in representing broadly based consortia of corporations, in league with banking interests, to market a very large number of different products. In 1982, the U.S. Congress passed the Export Trading Companies Act (PL 97-290), which amended the Webb-Pomerene Act and provided for active government promotion of export trading companies. The new law allowed a variety of financial institutions to invest in export trading companies and authorized the Export-Import Bank (a government institution)

to provide loan guarantees to trading companies. With regard to the antitrust laws, it clarified the position of U.S. firms that formed trading companies and set up a certification procedure for establishing limited antitrust immunity.

Although there has not been a rush to take advantage of the new law, the apparatus is now in place to allow U.S. firms to harmonize their international pricing through the trading company approach. This could have far-reaching consequences in the future.

THE EFFECTS OF TRADE RESTRICTIONS ON PRICES

As indicated in our first international capsule, tariffs and other trade restrictions may be important considerations affecting a firm's prospects for selling abroad. Clearly, if the tariff wall surrounding a given foreign market is so high as to be totally prohibitive, export sales to that market will not be possible. However, we should ask what happens when a new tariff that is not prohibitive is levied on an export product of a firm. In general, economic theory shows that the foreign market price will rise by *less* than the amount of the tariff if the foreign supply elasticity is not infinite. In other words, if the country imposing the tariff is large enough that its purchases will impact the world market price, its domestic price will rise by less than the amount of the tariff. This happens because there is a drop in the quantity of foreign goods purchased after imposition of the tariff, which means sellers will move down their supply curves and thereby absorb some of the tariff in a lower supply price.

We can illustrate this for a two-country case as follows. Suppose the exporting industry is in the United States and the amount its producers are willing to supply abroad is represented by the export supply curve SX_{us} in

4 U.S. Federal Trade Commission, *Report of the Federal Trade Commission on the Sulphur Industry and International Cartels* (Washington, D.C., 1947), p. 56.

Figure II–2. S is the supply curve of producers in the foreign country, and SS is the horizontal sum of the two supply curves. SS is the curve that will define equilibrium in the country's internal market when both imported and internally produced output are available. Imposition of a per-unit import tariff equal to t will shift SX_{us} to SX'_{us} and SS to SS' and move the importing country's equilibrium point from E to E', raising its internal price from P to P'. However, note that the amount of the price increase will be less than t, since t is the vertical distance between the old SX_{us} supply curve and the new one, SX'_{us}, and is larger than $(P' - P)$. Thus the price U.S. producers receive for their exports will fall (to level P_s). Any U.S. firm that is exporting this

product can expect to sell less *and* realize a lower price after the tariff is imposed.

Of course, import tariffs are not the only type of trade restriction that may affect prices or sales volume in foreign markets. Import quotas and other types of quantitative restrictions will have similar effects. This is true because any reduction in quantity of exports sold will be accompanied by a fall in price if the supply curve of those exports is upward sloping. While the type of analysis we have been employing here does not give an exporting firm a way to predict *when* trade restrictions will be imposed, it does help to show what the effects of such restrictions will be when and if they are imposed. Given that trade restrictions are a fact of life in many for-

Figure II–2   Price Effect of a Per-Unit Import Tariff

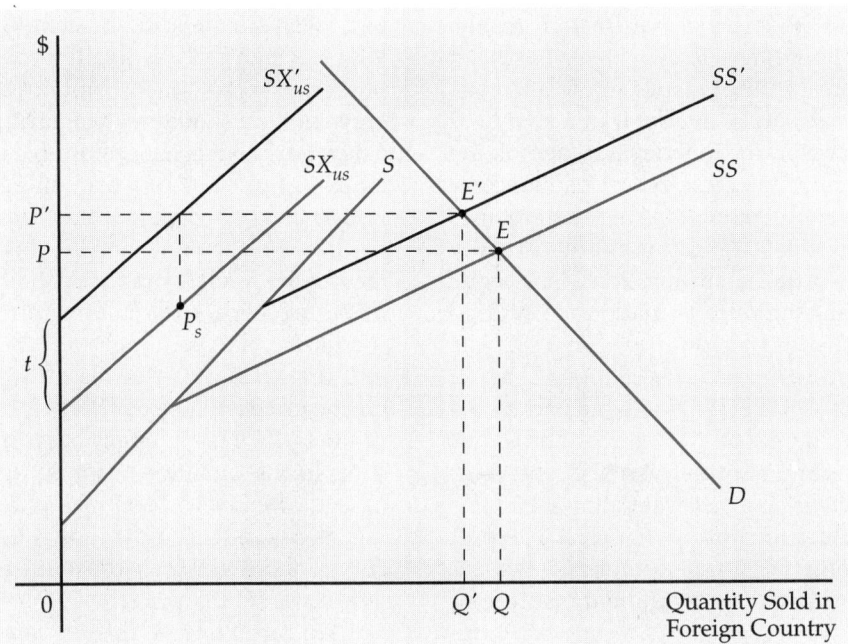

Imposition of a per-unit tariff equal to t (the vertical distance between SX_{us} and SX'_{us}) causes price to rise to P' in the foreign country, while quantity sold falls. The price increase $(P' - P)$ is less than the amount of the tariff. The price received by producers after the tariff is shown by P_s.

eign markets (particularly in less-developed countries, where they are used to promote industrialization), it is useful to have some idea of how to analyze their impact on a firm's exports and the prices it receives for them.

INTERNATIONAL TRANSFER PRICING

Our final topic in this brief survey is transfer pricing, a subject that is significantly more complicated in the international marketplace than in a single country. As Chapter 11 showed, the optimal transfer price within divisions of a firm that do not trade across international boundaries is argued to be a price equal to the marginal cost of the transfer product. While a situation *could* exist in international trade where a transfer product is exchanged between two units of the same firm at a price equal to its marginal cost, a number of factors make this unlikely.

When products are transferred internationally, they move from one country with one set of laws, regulations, and financial institutions to another country with different laws, regulations, and financial institutions. Thus the transfer prices may be employed as a device to obtain a wide variety of results, given the objectives of the firm. For example, suppose a firm has a subsidiary in a developing country where the government places restrictions on remitting profits to foreign investors. This would mean that the subsidiary is limited in the amount of profit it can send to the parent company. To keep profits from piling up in the subsidiary, the parent may decide to charge very high prices for goods transferred to the subsidiary, thereby switching profits from the latter to the parent.[5]

The firm may use transfer pricing for a variety of other purposes. For example, it may choose to use a low transfer price when shipping goods to a subsidiary located in a country with high duties on those goods. Another strategy relates to income tax minimization and calls for arranging transfer prices to shift profits to units of the firm located in low-tax countries. Finally, transfer pricing may be used to "dress up" financial statements by reporting high profits for units located in countries where borrowing and other financing are likely to take place.

QUESTIONS AND PROBLEMS

1. Explain how each of the following strategies discussed in earlier chapters is related to pricing problems firms frequently encounter in international trade.
    a. Incremental profit analysis
    b. Price discrimination
    c. Pricing of joint products
2. Discuss the problem of dumping in international trade. Under what circumstances might a firm be likely to have legal problems if it dumped in a foreign market?

3. What is an export trading company? How is it related to recent U.S. interest in more permissive laws regulating business?
4. Suppose a firm sells in only two markets, its home market and one foreign market.

---

5 It is not surprising that many countries have enacted laws regulating transfer pricing in an attempt to thwart such activity.

Its total cost function is $TC = 200,000 + 120Q$. Suppose its home demand curve has the equation $Q_h = 10,000 - 20P_h$ and the foreign market demand curve has the equation $Q_f = 7,500 - 12.5P_f$.

a. Will the prices in the two markets be the same, assuming no trade barriers in the foreign market? Explain, and calculate the price(s) the firm will charge as well as its profit from sales in the two markets.

b. If the importing country imposes an import tariff of $10 per unit, what price will be charged in that country after the tariff? Calculate the firm's profit after the tariff.

5. How does transfer pricing in international business differ from that in firms that do not operate across national boundaries?

SELECTED REFERENCES

Cateora, Phillip R. *International Marketing*, 6th ed. Homewood, Ill.: Irwin, 1987, especially Chapter 16.

"EEC Acts on Japanese Dumping," *Business Europe* (January 25, 1985), p. 31.

Exporter's Encyclopedia. Dunn & Bradstreet, Inc., New York (annual).

Grennes, Thomas. *International Economics*. Englewood Cliffs, N.J.: Prentice-Hall, 1984, especially Chapters 6 and 7.

Kistler, Robert. "Export Pricing in Today's Market," *Business America* (July 9, 1984), p. 21.

Robock, Stefan H., and Kenneth Simmonds. *International Business and Multinational Enterprises*, 3d ed. Homewood, Ill.: Irwin, 1983.

12

FACTOR MARKETS AND PROFIT-MAXIMIZING EMPLOYMENT OF VARIABLE INPUTS

In the first edition of this book, we stated that two major newsworthy events affecting productive inputs were wage rate *increases* negotiated by the United Auto Workers (UAW) and OPEC hikes in the price of oil. In later years news headlines proclaimed wage rate *concessions* made by the UAW and *decreases* in the price of oil.[1]

In our earlier editions, we predicted that the wage rate increases by the UAW would tend to encourage the automobile manufacturers to become more capital intensive—and that prediction was accurate. High wage rates and competition from foreign automobile manufacturers provided the incentives for U.S. automakers to begin significantly increasing their use of robots.[2] The increasing use of robots and the recession of the early 1980s (with its corresponding effects on the demand for automobiles and the employment of auto workers) prompted the UAW to make virtually unheard-of wage concessions.[3] The earlier increase in the price of oil resulted in higher energy

---

1 See "A Barrel of Troubles for the Oil Market," *Business Week* (August 9, 1993), p. 31; "Labor Draws an Empty Gun," *Time* (March 26, 1990), pp. 56–59; The GM Settlement Is a Milestone for Both Sides," *Business Week* (October 8, 1984), pp. 160–162; "2001: A Union Odyssey," *Newsweek* (August 5, 1985), pp. 40–42; "Oil-Price Drop Spurs Many Firms to Switch from Using Gas, Coal," *The Wall Street Journal*, April 7, 1986, pp. 1, 10; "Slowing the Decline in the Auto Work Force," *Business Week* (October 25, 1976), pp. 114–118; "How OPEC's High Prices Strangle World Growth," *Business Week* (December 20, 1976), pp. 44–50; and "Detroit's New Balance of Power," *Business Week* (March 1, 1982), p. 90.

2 "High Tech to the Rescue," *Business Week* (June 16, 1986), pp. 100–108; and "Detroit Area Is Becoming Home to Robotics," *The Wall Street Journal*, April 10, 1985, p. 6.

3 However, the price of oil has been rising again, and the most recent contract negotiated between the UAW and the automakers does provide for wage rate increases, while allowing for more flexibility on the part of General Motors to reduce its work force because of jobs lost to productivity gains, market-share declines, and the sale of uncompetitive plants. See "UAW Delegates Endorse Pact With GM," *The Wall Street Journal*, November 7, 1996, pp. A2, A10. Although robots have been used and are still being introduced in a number of manufacturing plants in a variety of industries, their use has not always been as profitable as managers anticipated. See "Some Manufacturers Drop Efforts to Adopt Japanese Techniques," *The Wall Street Journal*, May 7, 1993, pp. A1, A2; "Limping Along in Robot Land," *Time* (July 13, 1987), pp. 46–47; "Factory of the Future Becomes a Vision of the Past," *The Wall Street Journal*, September 1, 1988, p. 1; and "GM Bets an Arm and a Leg On a People-Free Plant," *Business Week* (September 12, 1988), pp. 72–73.

prices, which tended to reduce the usage of capital equipment because the cost of operating such machinery increased. However, the primary impact of the price increases seemed to be the encouragement of industry to develop more fuel-efficient equipment. As a result of increased fuel efficiency (and also a recession), oil suppliers in the 1980s found themselves saddled with huge surpluses; thus crude oil prices began to fall. As we will discover later in this chapter, the net result of all these events on the capital intensity of firms will depend on the marginal productivity of labor relative to its marginal cost, as compared with the marginal productivity of capital relative to its marginal cost with the new prices.[4]

Some of the most critical decisions a firm manager must make concern the employment of factors of production by the firm; such factors account for a large portion of the firm's *costs*. The firm with a goal of profit maximization wishes to produce at its optimal level of output and to do so at the lowest possible cost, given the market structures within which it operates. To accomplish this goal, the firm manager must make economic judgments with regard to how much of each input to use and, often, corresponding decisions with regard to the prices paid for inputs or for their services. We will begin this chapter with a discussion of how the profit-maximizing quantity of a variable input is determined, and then relate this analysis to the determination of the demand curve for an input and the equilibrium price and quantity of the input.

As we stated in Chapter 5, the least cost combination of inputs *a* and *b* associated with a given level of output requires that

$$\frac{MP_a}{P_a} = \frac{MP_b}{P_b}$$

as long as the firm cannot affect P_a and P_b. However, we also stated that in the short run the firm may not be able to achieve the least cost combination of inputs for its optimal level of output because the amounts of some of its inputs may be fixed. The relevant question in such a situation becomes this: *How can the firm maximize profits in the short run by utilizing the inputs that are variable?*

PROFIT-MAXIMIZING EMPLOYMENT OF ONE VARIABLE INPUT

Consider the plight of a local soda-pop bottler. It has $1 million worth of capital equipment and another $1 million invested in the building and land. The

---

4 The least cost condition for inputs capital, K, and labor, L, requires that $(MP_K/P_K) = (MP_L/P_L)$. As we will see later, this rule applies only if the firm considers P_K and P_L to be "given." The net result of higher oil prices on total employment depends on the net effects of all of these changes on the marginal productivity of each input as well as its price.

equipment, building, and land are relatively fixed in the short run. The only decisions the firm's management needs to make regarding them are in the nature of long-range planning decisions. What management must determine now is how much labor (of various types) should be employed and what level of output should be produced to maximize profits, *given* the plant and equipment.

Directly related to the managerial decisions involving the bottler's labor force and level of output will be decisions regarding raw materials and intermediate goods, such as concentrated soda mix, aluminum for cans, and empty bottles. Certainly, in the real world, the amounts of raw materials and intermediate products could vary widely per unit of output produced (and sold), as workers are more or less careless (and drink more or less of the product) while on the job. However, we will assume for the sake of simplicity that such inputs are used in fixed proportions to the level of output produced. We will also assume that when the firm decides on the level of its labor force and, correspondingly, its level of output, it will have automatically decided on the required amounts of the raw materials and intermediate-good inputs. How does the bottler determine the optimal labor force and level of production in the short run? To some extent the minimum number of workers necessary to operate the plant will influence its decision. However, the plant could operate and function well with many different quantities of labor above the minimum required. So how is the profit-maximizing quantity determined?

To employ one variable factor of production (labor, in this case) in a manner so that profits will be maximized, the firm should follow the same type of marginal rule as it does with respect to output: *Continue using additional units of the input until the last unit just pays for itself.* (That is, continue employment of additional units of a factor of production until the additional revenue resulting from employment of one more unit of the input is just equal to the amount the input adds to the costs of the firm.) If we (the authors) have done our job well, such a decision rule should seem obvious at this point. We emphasize again that the situation we are considering is one in which the firm has the problem of trying to decide how much of one particular variable input to use, *given* certain fixed inputs and a fixed quantity of raw materials and intermediate goods required for each unit of output.

To phrase our rule—*continue to employ an input until the last unit just pays for itself*—in the language of economists, we state that the firm should continue to employ an input until its marginal revenue product is equal to the input's marginal cost. Thus the manager of the bottling company should employ labor until the marginal revenue product of the last person hired is just equal to that person's marginal cost—both with respect to some specific time period, of course, such as per hour, day, or week.

We have already defined marginal revenue product of an input in Chapter 5, but we will do so in greater depth here to ensure that its meaning is understood. The *arc* **marginal revenue product of input *a*** (MRP_a) is defined as

MANAGERIAL PERSPECTIVE
Profit and Chocolate-Loving Cows

Farmer McGregor is feeding Hershey bars to dairy cows and increasing profits. As a result, the cows are happy and so is McGregor.

Feeding chocolate bars to cows may seem hardly a profitable way to run a dairy business, but it is apparently more profitable than giving them only things that would seem to be more nutritious—like hay and corn, for example. As most human chocoholics who are concerned about their weight know, a chocolate bar has a plentiful supply of carbohydrates and fat, which translates into calories. In humans, eating chocolate bars may merely result in unwanted pounds. Dairy cows do not gain weight from the bars, but the butterfat content of their milk rises, which means that the price the farmer can receive for the milk increases. More specifically, the basic butterfat standard for whole milk is 3.5 percent. For every .1 percent of butterfat above the 3.5 standard, a farmer received an increase in price of 1.28 cents per gallon.

The situation is almost too good to be true—very rare in the business world, where typically every move to increase productivity has its price. In the case of the chocoholic cows, feeding chocolate both lowers costs and raises revenue. The farmers in Maryland, New Jersey, and Pennsylvania obtained damaged chocolate bars from Hershey Foods Corporation in Hershey, Pennsylvania, at $60 a ton, while the price of corn was $85 a ton. Even better, the energy content of a candy bar is about twice that of an ear of corn.

The chocoholic cows on these farms get an average of four to eight pounds of chocolate a day mixed in with their hay and grain. One farmer, Stephen Mason, calculated that adding chocolate to his cows' diet raised the fat content of their milk to 3.9 percent. That translated to a higher price of 5.12 cents per gallon.

There are not many situations in business where a firm can so painlessly reduce cost while simultaneously increasing output and revenue. In fact, as more farmers discover the profit possibilities in feeding chocolate to dairy cows, the price of damaged chocolate bars may increase to the point where the tradeoff between chocolate and corn becomes closer to what economists would expect to see given the least cost combination of inputs condition. In the meantime, profit-maximizing employment of inputs for dairy farmers means that they should continue to feed chocolate bars to their cows up to the point where the marginal revenue received from another chocolate bar is just equal to its marginal cost. Apparently this strategy makes for both happy farmers and *very* happy cows.

Reference: "Now the Question Is: How Do You Get Rid of a Cow's Pimples?" *The Wall Street Journal*, June 1, 1988, p. 25.

The **marginal revenue product of input** *a* is equal to the net marginal revenue of input *a* multiplied by the marginal product of input *a*: $MRP_a = NMR_a \times MP_a$.

The **marginal product of input** *a* is the additional output that the firm can produce by adding one more unit of input *a*: $MP_a = (\Delta Q / \Delta a)$.

Net marginal revenue is marginal revenue from the sale of a firm's final product *minus* a specific portion of marginal production cost. In determining the optimal amount of a variable input, net marginal revenue is defined as marginal revenue minus marginal cost of components.

the arc net marginal revenue the firm can obtain by selling an additional unit of output produced by input *a* multiplied by the number of additional units of output produced per additional unit of input *a*. (As we stated in Chapter 5, input *a*'s **marginal product**, MP_a, equals $\Delta Q / \Delta a$.) The *arc* **net marginal revenue** (*NMR*) the firm can get from selling one more unit of output produced by input *a* is the addition to total revenue that the sale of one more unit of output will bring in—or arc marginal revenue of the output ($\Delta TR / \Delta Q$)—less the cost of raw materials and the intermediate goods required for each additional unit of output.[5]

$$NMR \equiv MR - MC_M,$$

where MC_M is the marginal cost of raw materials and intermediate goods per unit of output. Obviously, we cannot consider *all* of the additional revenue going to the bottler as a result of the sale of another case of soda produced by the last person hired as being solely the result of that person's efforts, as the firm still had to contribute additional raw materials for the soda and the packaging materials. Thus, if the sale of an additional case of soda would bring in additional revenue of \$2 and the additional mix and other materials needed cost \$.50 per case, the arc net marginal revenue, *NMR*, would be equal to \$1.50 per case of soda.

However, we need a little more information to find the arc marginal revenue *product* of input *a*. The net marginal revenue of input *a* and its marginal revenue product are usually *not* equal because an additional unit of input *a* frequently does not produce *exactly* one additional unit of output during the time frame of reference the firm is using. For example, suppose the last worker hired enabled the firm to produce four more cases of soda per hour. The arc marginal revenue product, or the additional revenue per hour that *the worker* would bring in for the firm, would be the net marginal revenue of \$1.50 per case *multiplied by* the four cases per hour added to production, or \$6.00. Thus, in this case,

$$MRP_L \equiv MP_L \times NMR = 4 \times \$1.50 \equiv \$6.00.$$

At last we are in a position to restate our profit-maximizing rule for employing input *a*: Employ input *a* until its arc marginal revenue product equals its marginal cost, or until

---

5 In calculus terms, the marginal revenue product of input *a* equals net marginal revenue times the marginal product of *a*, or

$$MRP_a \equiv NMR \cdot MP_a \equiv \left(\frac{dTR}{dQ} - \frac{d \text{ materials cost}}{dQ} \right) \cdot \frac{\partial Q}{\partial a}.$$

$$MRP_a \; (\equiv NMR \times MP_a) = MC_a.$$

MC_a is the change in a firm's total costs as a result of using another unit of input a:[6]

$$MC_a \equiv \frac{\Delta TC}{\Delta a}.$$

The marginal cost of an input is the increase in the firm's total cost from employing one more unit of the input: $MC_a = (\Delta TC/\Delta a)$. If the price of an input is constant, the marginal cost of the input is equal to its price.

If the price of input a is *constant*, the **marginal cost of an input** is equal to its price. In our soda-pop bottling company worker example, if the marginal

---

6 We can mathematically derive this decision rule in the following way. If $TR = P \cdot Q$, where $P = f(Q)$, the production function is given by $Q = Q(a,b)$, and the total cost is given by $TC = (P_a \cdot a) + (P_b \cdot b)$, then the total profit function is

$$T\pi = [P \cdot Q(a,b)] - (P_a \cdot a) - (P_b \cdot b).$$

A firm manager who wishes to find the quantities of inputs a and b that will maximize profits must find the first partial derivatives of $T\pi$ with respect to inputs a and b and set them equal to zero, so that

(12–1)
$$\frac{\partial T\pi}{\partial a} = P \cdot \frac{\partial Q}{\partial a} + Q \frac{dP}{dQ} \frac{\partial Q}{\partial a} - P_a - \frac{dP_a}{da} \cdot a$$

$$= \left(P + Q\frac{dP}{dQ}\right)\frac{\partial Q}{\partial a} - \left(P_a + \frac{dP_a}{da} \cdot a\right) = 0,$$

and

(12–2)
$$\frac{\partial T\pi}{\partial b} = P \cdot \frac{\partial Q}{\partial b} + Q \frac{dP}{dQ} \frac{\partial Q}{\partial b} - P_b - \frac{dP_b}{db} \cdot b$$

$$= \left(P + Q\frac{dP}{dQ}\right)\frac{\partial Q}{\partial b} - \left(P_b + \frac{dP_b}{db} \cdot b\right) = 0.$$

The term $[P + Q(dP/dQ)]$ is the marginal revenue to the firm from selling the output. It follows that $[P + Q(dP/dQ)](\partial Q/\partial a)$ and $[P + Q(dP/dQ)](\partial Q/\partial b)$ are the marginal revenue products of inputs a and b, respectively, if there are *no* marginal materials costs. If there *are* marginal materials costs ($= MC_M$), these must be subtracted from $[P + Q(dP/dQ)]$ to get *net* marginal revenue, so

$$NMR = P + Q(dP/dQ) - MC_M,$$

$$MRP_a = [P + Q(dP/dQ) - MC_M]\left(\frac{\partial Q}{\partial a}\right),$$

and

$$MRP_b = [P + Q(dP/dQ) - MC_M]\left(\frac{\partial Q}{\partial b}\right).$$

Notice that as long as dP/dQ is negative and/or MC_M is positive, NMR is less than P.

The terms $[P_a + (dP_a/da) \cdot a]$ in equation (12–1) and $[P_b + (dP_b/db) \cdot b]$ in equation (12–2) measure the marginal costs of inputs a and b, respectively. Thus equations (12–1) and (12–2) state that for profit maximization of inputs a and b, revenue product of the *last* person hired was $6.00 per hour and the additional worker *cost* the firm $6.00 per hour, the bottler would maximize profit by holding its employment of labor at that level. If the worker cost the firm $7.00 per hour, that person should be let go (a gentle phrase for "fired"). If the worker cost the firm only $5.00, the firm manager should consider hiring another worker, as the additional worker might bring in additional profit after all additional costs were subtracted from additional revenue. (In this case, the last person hired would have added $1 per hour to the total profit of the firm.)

(12–3)
$$MRP_a - MC_a = 0$$

and

(12–4)
$$MRP_b - MC_b = 0.$$

We could rewrite equations (12–3) and (12–4) as

(12–5)
$$MRP_a = MC_a$$

and

(12–6)
$$MRP_b = MC_b.$$

If both inputs are variable, *both* equations (12–5) and (12–6) must be satisfied.

We can find a more general condition for obtaining the least cost combination of inputs than developed in Chapter 5 by dividing equation (12–5) by equation (12–6) and rearranging terms:

(12–7)
$$\frac{MRP_a}{MRP_b} = \frac{MC_a}{MC_b},$$

and

(12–8)
$$\frac{MRP_a}{MC_a} = \frac{MRP_b}{MC_b}.$$

Dividing both sides of this equation by NMR, which is equal to $[P + Q(dP/dQ) - MC_M]$, we obtain the more general form of the least cost combination of inputs rule:

(12–9)
$$\frac{MP_a}{MC_a} = \frac{MP_b}{MC_b}.$$

If the firm cannot significantly affect P_a or P_b by using more or less of input a or input b, dP_a/da and $dP_b/db = 0$, $MC_a = P_a$, $MC_b = P_b$, and equation (12–9) becomes

(12–10)
$$\frac{MP_a}{P_a} = \frac{MP_b}{P_b},$$

our previous rule for the least cost combination of inputs. In this case equations (12–5) and (12–6) become

(12–11)
$$MRP_a = P_a$$

and

(12–12)
$$MRP_b = P_b.$$

NUMERICAL EXAMPLE:

Profit-Maximizing Input Use

Complete the following table and find the profit-maximizing level of use of input L. Assume that L is the only variable input, that its price (P_L) is $110 per unit, that there are no components costs, and that total fixed cost (TFC) is $350.

Arc MP_L	L	Q	P	TR	Arc MR	Arc MRP_L
	0	0	22	0		
10					20	200
	2		20	400		
					14	
	4	60	16	960		
15					7	
	6	90	13	1,170		
					2	
	8	110	11	1,210		
6					0.8	4.80
	10		10	1,220		

Answer.

The missing MP_L values are 20 and 10, each obtained by calculating $\Delta Q / \Delta L$. The missing Q values are 20 and 122, each obtained by multiplying the relevant MP by ΔL and adding on the ΔQ to the preceding Q value. The missing MRP_L values are 280, 105, and 20, each calculated as $MR(MP_L)$.

Profit is maximized where $P_L \leq MRP_L$ but for an increase in L, $P_L > MRP_L$. This occurs at $L = \underline{4}$, since increasing L to 6 would result in $P_L = 110$, but $MRP_L = 105$. Profit is $TR - TC = 960 - L(P_L) - TFC = \$960 - 440 - 350 = \underline{\$170}$.

Unfortunately, the process of finding the optimal amount of an input is usually a bit more complicated in the real world than we have made it appear up to this point. One reason is that the marginal product of an input usually does not stay constant as more units of the input are added (remember the law of diminishing returns). A second reason is that marginal revenue may also change—usually in a downward direction, since many firms have to lower price to sell larger quantities of output.

Moreover, once we acknowledge the fact that the marginal product of an input may first increase and then decrease, we must recognize the possibility that the MRP of an input may also first rise and then fall. In this case we must

The **profit-maximizing rule for employing a variable input**, say input *a*, is to employ that input until its marginal revenue product is equal to the marginal cost of the input; that is, to where $MRP_a = MC_a$, and at higher levels of output $MRP_a < MC_a$.

add another condition to our **profit-maximizing rule for employing a variable input:** Employ the input up to the point where its *MRP* is equal to its marginal cost, *as long as the marginal cost of the input would be at least equal to or above the MRP of the input for a greater quantity of the input.* Thus, if the last soda-pop bottler hired had an *MRP* of $6.00 and a marginal cost of $6.00, but the *next* person to be hired would have an *MRP* of $7.00 and a marginal cost also of $6.00, then the firm should continue to hire workers until there are no further opportunities to hire a worker whose *MRP* is above marginal cost. This is another way of saying employ the input until the last unit just pays for itself, but additional units of the input will cost more than the additional revenue they would bring to the firm.

For example, in Table 12–1 we give revenue and labor productivity data for the manufacturer of a black-and-white portable television. Arc marginal revenue is obtained by finding $\Delta TR/\Delta Q$, and *NMR* is obtained by subtracting the $20 components cost from *MR* at each level of output. The marginal product of labor is obtained by finding $\Delta Q/\Delta L$. The MRP_L is then found by multiplying *NMR* by MP_L. If the wage rate is fixed at $9.00, then the price of labor also equals the MC_L. In this case, the firm maximizes profits (assuming labor is the only variable input besides the components) where *output* is between 48 and 53 television sets per hour and the firm's *labor force* is between 50 and 60 people. Between 48 and 53 units of output, the $MRP_L = \$9.00$ and $MC_L = \$9.00$. Between 53 and 55 units of output, the $MRP_L = \$.80$ and $MC_L = \$9.00$. Thus 70 workers would clearly be too many to employ in order to maximize profits, since workers 61 through 70 would each bring in an average of $.80 net revenue per hour but would each cost $9.00 per hour.

Finally, if more inputs than one are variable, changes in the quantity utilized of one will affect the productivity of the others *if* the inputs are *related*, thereby changing their optimal levels. The resulting changes in those inputs will in turn affect the optimal level of the first input. In this kind of situation, we define related inputs as being either substitutes or complements. Two inputs are *substitutes* if utilizing more of one *decreases* the marginal product of the other. Two inputs are *complements* if utilizing more of one *increases* the marginal product of the other. Two inputs could be substitutes or complements, depending on the situation. For example, the use of a paint sprayer by a painter would probably reduce the marginal product of a paint roller. However, the use of a computer by a research institution might well increase the marginal product of an employee engaged in research. In the first example, the paint sprayer and the paint roller are substitutes. The paint sprayer might also be a substitute for an additional painter with a brush. In the second example, the computer and the employee are complements. We will leave further consideration of related inputs to a more advanced text. It is sufficient at this point to be aware of the possibility (and probability) of relatedness among inputs and to take that possibility into account when determining the optimal levels of variable factors of production for the firm.

Table 12–1 Revenue, Labor Productivity, and Cost Data for a Manufacturer of Black-and-White Televisions

Quantity Produced per Hour	Price (P)	Total Revenue (TR = P·Q)	Arc Marginal Revenue $\left(MR = \dfrac{\Delta TR}{\Delta Q}\right)$	Components Cost (per Unit)	Arc Net Marginal Revenue of Labor (NMR$_L$ = MR − Marginal Components Cost)	Quantity of Labor (L)	Arc Marginal Product of Labor $\left(MP_L = \dfrac{\Delta Q}{\Delta L}\right)$	Arc Marginal Revenue Product of Labor (MRP$_L$ = NMR·MP$_L$)	Hourly Wage Rate	Arc Marginal Cost of Labor $\left(MC_L = \dfrac{\Delta TC}{\Delta L}\right)$
0	$240	$ 0	$230	$20	210	0	.5	$105.00	$9.00	$9.00
5	230	1,150	200	20	180	10	1.0	180.00	9.00	9.00
15	210	3,150	150	20	130	20	1.5	195.00	9.00	9.00
30	180	5,400	100	20	80	30	1.0	80.00	9.00	9.00
40	160	6,400	64	20	44	40	.8	35.20	9.00	9.00
48	144	6,912	38	20	18	50	.5	9.00	9.00	9.00
53	134	7,102	24	20	4	60	.2	.80	9.00	9.00
55	130	7,150		20		70			9.00	9.00

DETERMINATION OF EQUILIBRIUM PRICES FOR INPUTS: PERFECT COMPETITION IN THE INPUT MARKET

In the opening section of this chapter we concentrated on developing a profit-maximizing decision rule for a business firm to use in employing inputs. There, we assumed that the firm knew what the price—and consequently the marginal cost—of another unit of the input would be. Now we turn to the question of what factors determine the market price of an input. As you might expect from the discussion of the profit-maximizing price and output in the product markets, the *structure* of an input market is an important factor affecting the determination of its price. We consider first the case of perfect competition in the input market.

As in the output market, if *perfect competition* exists in the market for an input, there are many buyers and sellers of that input, and an individual firm considers the price of the *input* to be "given." Since the amount demanded of an input by an individual firm is too small relative to the total market demand and supply of the input to influence its price significantly, the marginal cost of a unit of the input is constant and equal to its price. When we considered the case of a firm *selling its output* in a perfectly competitive market, we said (1) that the firm considered the price it received for its *output* to be given, (2) that the *demand curve* for its product was a horizontal line, and (3) that *output price was equal to marginal revenue*. On the other hand, when a firm is *buying an input* in a perfectly competitive market, it accepts (1) that the input price is given, (2) that the *supply curve* of the input *to the firm* is horizontal, and (3) that the *input price equals the input's marginal cost* (as was the case in the example in Table 12–1).

In this situation, therefore, the firm's profit-maximizing condition for utilizing input *a* is to employ input *a* up to the point where the *marginal revenue product of a is equal to its price*, which (as we have just said) is equal to its marginal cost:[7]

$$MRP_a = P_a = MC_a.$$

We need to add one more qualification to this decision rule: the firm should employ input *a* up to the point where $MRP_a = P_a$ as long as MRP_a *is decreasing*. Thus, the firm's *demand curve* for input *a* is given by the portion of the marginal revenue product curve for input *a* where MRP_a is decreasing. This part

---

[7] If the firm also *sells* its *output* in a perfectly competitive market, marginal revenue equals price and NMR = price minus marginal materials cost. In this case economists also call MRP_a the *value of the marginal product of a*, or VMP_a.

of the MRP_a curve is the demand curve for input a because it indicates the quantity of input a the profit-maximizing firm will employ at each price.[8]

In Figure 12–1 we have shown the firm's demand curve for input a, the supply curve for input a, and the profit-maximizing quantity of a (Q_a^*) for the firm to employ. In the case of the television manufacturer discussed in the previous section, Q_L is approximately equal to 55 and $P_L = \$9.00$ (see Figure 12–2). We say that Q_L is approximately equal to 55 because we are using arc values for MRP_L, which gives an *average* value for a particular interval (such as $L = 50$ to $L = 60$). We must plot such figures at the midpoint of the interval.

We now understand the process by which a firm manager determines how much of an input the firm should employ to maximize its profit, *given the price of the input*. However, how is the price of the input determined? The answer is that in perfectly competitive input markets, the input price is determined by the total market demand for and supply of the input. A rough approximation to the *market demand* for the input is obtained by summing the quantity of the input that each firm that utilizes the input will demand at each

---

8 However, the output price must also be sufficiently high to cover AVC, or the firm will at least temporarily shut down. With *more than one variable input*, a change in the amount used of one input, say input a, may affect the MRP(s) of the other variable input(s), which will change the profit-maximizing quantity(ies) of the other input(s). A change in the quantity(ies) utilized of that input (those inputs) will cause the MRP_a to shift because the MP_a will change. Whether the MRP_a shifts rightward or leftward will depend on whether input a is being increased or decreased in the first step. For example, if the inputs are substitutes, then the use of more of input a will decrease the marginal product of the other variable input(s) and the quantity used of it (them) will decrease. This decrease, in turn, will cause the MP_a to *increase*, shifting the MRP_a curve to the right. If the inputs are complements, then an increase in the use of input a will increase the marginal product of the other input(s) and the quantity used of it (them) will increase. This increase will also cause the MP_a to *increase*, again shifting the MP_a curve to the right. The demand curve will consist of points where $MRP_a = P_a$, but each point will be on a different MRP curve, as shown:

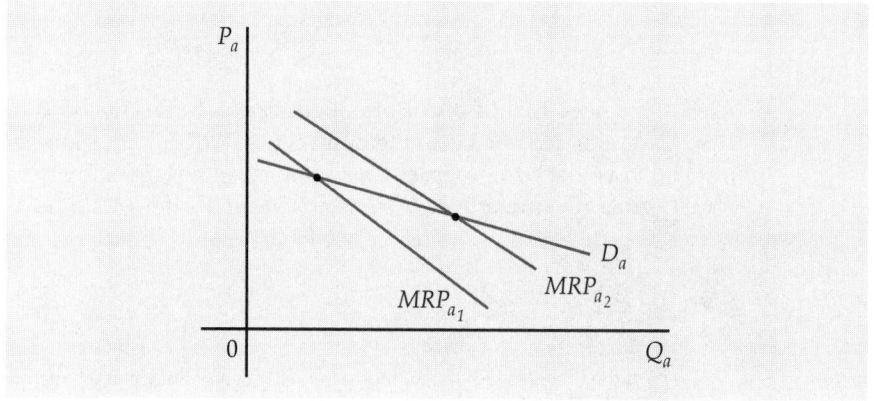

Figure 12–1   Optimal Employment of an Input in a Perfectly
Competitive Input Market

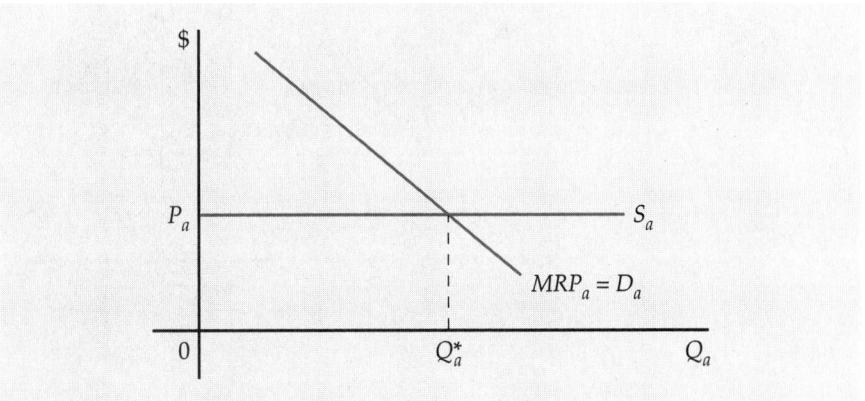

The marginal revenue product curve for input a, MRP_a, is the firm's demand curve for input a.
The supply curve of the input to the firm is a horizontal line, S_a, at the market-determined price
of P_a. The firm will maximize profit by employing Q_a^* units of input a at price P_a.

Figure 12–2   Demand and Supply Curves of Labor for a Television
Manufacturer

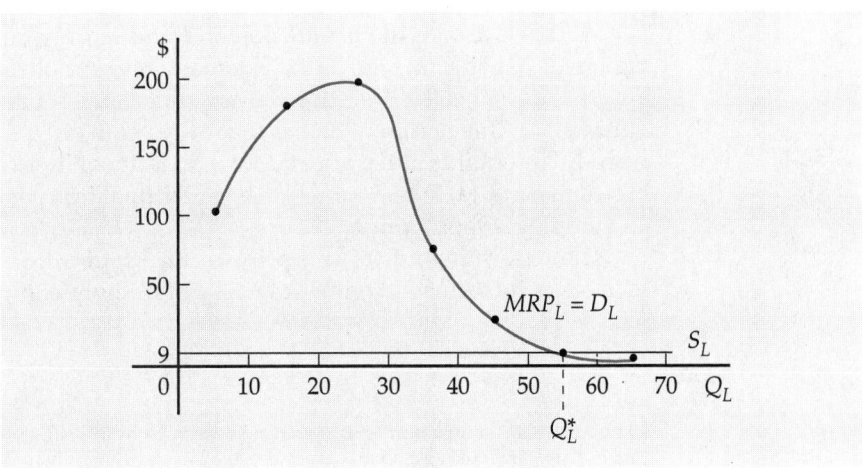

In this case the supply curve of workers to a television manufacturer is a horizontal line at $9
per hour. The firm will employ workers up to the point where the $MRP_L = \$9$, at $Q_L^* = 55$, ap-
proximately.

Figure 12–3   Demand and Supply Curves for Input *a*

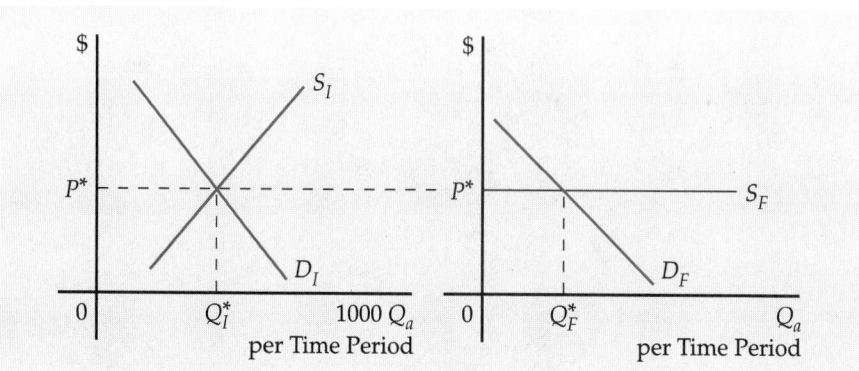

In panel *(a)* the industry supply and demand curves for input *a* determine the input's price, P^*, and the total quantity sold of input *a*, Q_I^*. In panel *(b)* an individual firm accepts the price of input *a*, P^*, as given (S_F is horizontal). The firm employs Q_F^* units of input *a* at a price of P^*, where D_F intersects S_F.

price.[9] Thus we obtain the *market demand* curve for an *input* in a perfectly competitive input market much as we determined the market *supply* curve in a perfectly competitive *output* market. The market supply curve of the *input* merely reflects the quantity of the input that will be supplied at each price. We will assume, as is generally realistic, that the market supply curve for an input is upward sloping, which means that more of the input will be supplied at higher prices.

We have drawn the *market* demand and supply curves for input *a* in Figure 12–3, panel (a), and a *firm's* demand and supply curves for input *a* in Figure 12–3, panel (b). Note that the horizontal axis of panel (a) is in *thousands* of units per time period, whereas that of panel (b) is in single units per time period. The equilibrium price and total quantity of input *a* utilized are determined in panel (a) to be P^* and Q_I^*. The individual firm considers P^* to be fixed and employs Q_F^* of input *a*.

The determination of the price of an input when the market for its services is imperfectly competitive is a little more complicated, as we will now see.

---

9 This horizontal summation of firm demand curves for inputs is only an approximation to the market demand curve for an input because as all firms in an industry expand, the market price and marginal revenue for a firm's product may fall more than is indicated by an individual firm's demand and marginal revenue curve. For example, the horizontal demand curve of a perfectly competitive firm is drawn under the assumption that only the individual firm is changing its level of output and therefore that price will not be affected. The market demand curve for an input must take into account the effects on the price and marginal revenue of the firm's product caused by factors external to the firm.

MANAGERIAL PERSPECTIVE

The Age of Agrimation

Robots in the factory are now an everyday fact of life, but the use of robots in agriculture has been much less prevalent. If researchers at a number of universities and countries around the world are successful, however, the age of agrimation is not far away.

Through automation, the direct labor cost of most items manufactured by mass-production methods has been reduced to 5 to 15 percent of their selling price. However, direct labor costs may be as much as 30 percent of the selling price of agricultural products, and proponents of agrimation contend that robots could reduce costs significantly in the production of agricultural goods. Take fruit, for example. These researchers state that a worker hired to harvest fruit could pick approximately 1,000 pieces of fruit per hour during six- to eight-hour working days. However, one-armed robots have already been developed that can pick fruit almost as quickly as a person, and two-armed robots are under consideration. In one laboratory test, a one-armed robot picked 15 oranges per minute, while an experienced human picker did 20 oranges per minute. France is developing an apple picker that technicians believe will be able to pick 30 apples a minute, more than double that of a skilled apple picker. Moreover, these machines would be willing to put in 24-hour days, so that fruit could be picked at the optimal time. The new robots also handle the fruit far more gently than the old mechanical pickers, which shook the trees or blasted them with air to force the fruit to fall to the ground, often bruising it in the process. The researchers figure that even if the robots cost as much as $100,000, they will pay for themselves in three seasons.

Even European milkmaids may soon feel competition from their steel-collared counterparts. Vicon, a Netherlands-based company is spending $3 million to develop a "cowbot," that will feed dairy cows, hook them up to the milking machines, and later clean the equipment. Such a helper could save dairy farmers more than four hours each day. Vicon estimates that if the robot costs less than $100,000 the machine would pay for itself in four years.

Clearly, if these new robots are successfully developed, farmers will have to consider the productivity and cost of human labor compared with that of robots. In turn, farm workers may be forced to consider ways to increase their productivity, working for lower wages, or new careers.

References: "Robots Head for the Farm," *Business Week* (September 8, 1986), pp. 66–67; and "Moo! Those Hands Are Cold!" *Business Week* (September 8, 1986), p. 67.

DETERMINATION OF EQUILIBRIUM PRICES FOR INPUTS: MONOPSONY IN THE INPUT MARKET

A **monopsony** is a market with one buyer.

An **oligopsony** is a market with a few buyers, or a few dominant buyers.

A market characterized by **monopsonistic competition** has many buyers of a differentiated product.

Monopsony is the label we attach to a market structure that is characterized by one *buyer* of some particular product or service. In this case we will use the term *monopsony* to refer to the situation where there is one firm that demands the services of an input. You will recall that we used the term *monopoly* to describe the situation where there is only one firm that *supplies* a product, *oligopoly* where there are a few suppliers of a product, and *monopolistic competition* where there are many suppliers of a differentiated product. In a similar fashion we also use the terms **oligopsony** to describe the market structure where there are a few *buyers* of a product and **monopsonistic competition** where there are many buyers of a differentiated product. We will discuss only the case of monopsony in the input market in this book, but the profit-maximizing decision rule discussed here applies to oligopsony and monopsonistic competition as well. In this section we will further assume that the *suppliers* of the input are perfectly competitive in the sense that they do not organize and attempt to affect the price received for the services of the input.

In a monopsonistic input market, the firm *buying* the input knows that the price of the input will be determined by the quantity of the input that it purchases. In this case, changes in the quantity of an input demanded by the firm will appreciably affect the input's price because we have assumed that the market supply curve of the input is upward sloping, meaning that a greater quantity of the input will be supplied only at a higher price. Since there is only one buyer of that input, changes in the quantity demanded of the input by that buyer will noticeably affect the input's price.

In this situation, the profit-maximizing firm that is utilizing the input will still follow the decision rule stated earlier in this chapter: *Employ the input until its marginal revenue product is equal to its marginal cost.* Unlike the case of perfect competition in the input market, however, for the monopsonistic firm the price of an input is (theoretically, at least) *not* equal to its marginal cost. The marginal cost of another unit of an input is greater than its price because it is assumed that the monopsonistic firm has to pay a higher price to get an additional unit of the input per time period. Moreover, it is also assumed that if a firm pays a higher price for one more unit of the input, it must pay the same price for *all units* of the input.

Consider the following situation, which the only garage in a small town might face if it wishes to hire another mechanic. The garage has three mechanics currently working for it at $10.00 an hour and can hire a fourth mechanic for $12.00 an hour. If it hires the fourth mechanic for $12.00 an hour, the firm will find that the first three mechanics will be unhappy unless their wage rates are also raised to $12.00 per hour. In fact, their dissatisfaction may cause their productivity to decline unless their salaries are raised. In this case the marginal cost of the fourth mechanic is $18.00 per hour, which is $12.00 for the fourth mechanic's wage plus $2.00 per hour for each of the other three mechanics. The supply and marginal cost schedules of mechanics to the garage are given in Table 12–2, and the corresponding curves are drawn in Figure 12–4.

The profit-maximizing garage should now follow the decision rule stated at the beginning of this chapter: Employ an input up to the point where its

Table 12–2   Supply and Marginal Cost Schedules of Mechanics to a Garage

Number of Mechanics	Hourly Wage Rate	Marginal Cost of Labor (MCL)
0	$ 4.00	
		$ 6.00
1	6.00	
		10.00
2	8.00	
		14.00
3	10.00	
		18.00
4	12.00	
		22.00
5	14.00	

Figure 12–4   Supply and Marginal Cost of Mechanics to a Garage

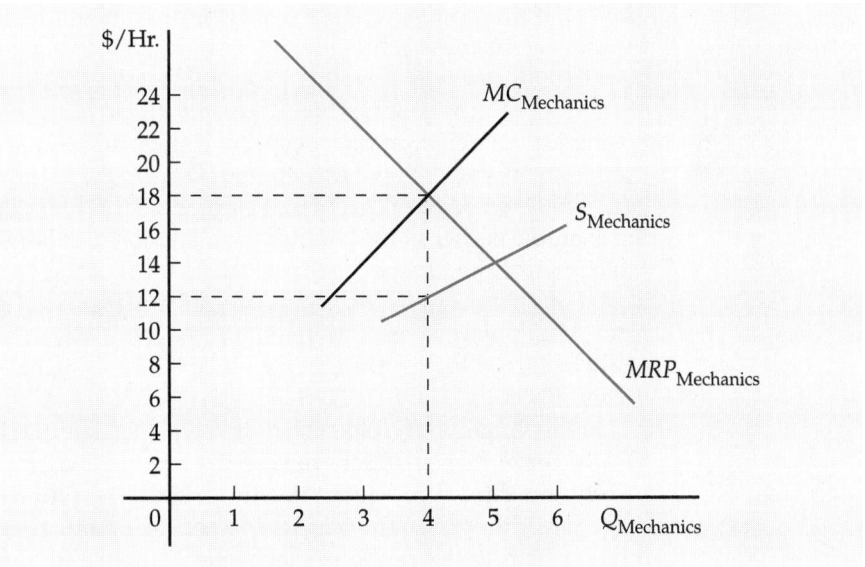

Here, the supply curve of mechanics to a garage is upward sloping, which means that the marginal cost of another mechanic to the firm, given by $MC_{Mechanics}$, also increases as the number of mechanics employed increases. In this case the firm will employ mechanics up to the point where the $MRP_{Mechanics} = MC_{Mechanics}$, at 4 mechanics and an hourly wage of $12.00.

marginal revenue product is equal to its marginal cost. Therefore the *profit-maximizing rule for employment of a variable input in a monopsonistic input market* is to employ that input until its marginal revenue product is equal to its marginal cost. In this case, the price of the input will be less than its marginal cost.

In Figure 12–4, the *MRP* of mechanics is just equal to the marginal cost of mechanics when the garage hires four mechanics. Note that whereas the marginal cost of the fourth mechanic is $18.00 per hour, all of the mechanics are actually being paid only $12.00 per hour. Since the garage is the only buyer of this input, the number of mechanics it employs to maximize profits will determine both the total number of mechanics employed in this town and their wage rate. Thus $12.00 per hour is the market wage rate, at least in this limited market for mechanics.

In the next section, we will discuss a third extreme case involving an input market—the situation of bilateral monopoly in which there is only one buyer and *one seller* of an input.

DETERMINATION OF EQUILIBRIUM PRICES FOR INPUTS: BILATERAL MONOPOLY IN THE INPUT MARKET

Bilateral monopoly in the input market means that there is one buyer and one seller of the input.

Bilateral monopoly in the input market means that there is only *one buyer* and *one seller* of an input. Admittedly, we are talking about an extreme case, but bilateral monopoly may more nearly approximate the market structure between "big business" and "big labor" in industries such as automobiles and steel than does any of the other cases we have described.

Since both the seller of the input and the buyer of the input are the sole businesses involved on their respective sides of the market, the *seller* of the input may wish to behave as a monopolist and the *buyer* may wish to behave as a monopsonist. Suppose all of the potential mechanics in the small town in the example earlier in the chapter form a union and bargain as a group with the owner of the garage. In Figure 12–5 we have redrawn Figure 12–4 and added one more curve, which indicates the marginal revenue to the *supplier* from selling another unit of the *input* under the assumption that the buyer could be forced to pay a wage rate equal to the marginal revenue product of the input.

In this situation the old supply curve of mechanics is now not really their supply curve *if* their union behaves as a profit-maximizing monopolist. It merely indicates what quantities they would be willing to supply at each wage rate *if* they thought they had to accept whatever wage rate the garage offered them *or* not work as mechanics. If their old supply curve in some sense measures their marginal cost of supplying labor, the mechanics will maximize their group profit by selling their services up to the point where the marginal cost *to themselves* of their services is equal to the marginal revenue brought in by those services. At point *A* the marginal revenue brought in by the mechanics' services is just equal to the marginal cost to the mechanics of

Figure 12–5   A Case of Bilateral Monopoly

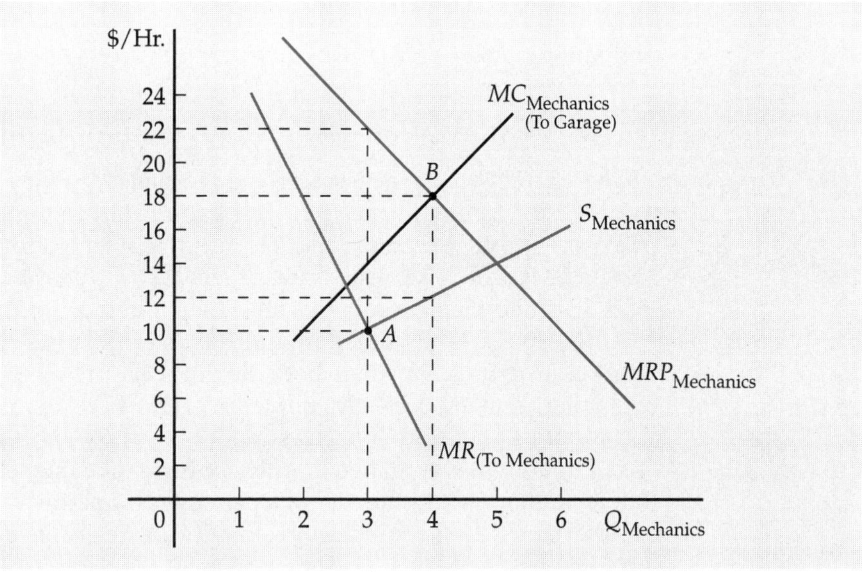

This figure describes a case of bilateral monopoly. Both the mechanics selling their services and the firm buying their services have some monopoly power. As in Figure 12–4, the marginal cost of mechanics increases as the quantity of mechanics employed increases, and $MC_{Mechanics}$ is above $S_{Mechanics}$. The marginal revenue to mechanics from selling their services is given by $MR_{(To\ Mechanics)}$. The firm will wish to employ 4 mechanics at a wage rate of $12 per hour, where $MRP_{Mechanics} = MC_{Mechanics}$. Mechanics will wish to offer their services up to the point where $MR_{Mechanics} = S_{Mechanics}$, at an hourly wage of $22 for 3 workers. The final result will depend on the relative bargaining strength of the firm and of the mechanics.

supplying their services, and the mechanics' union would like to have three people employed at a wage rate of $22.00.

However, it would be quite a feat for the mechanics' union to get three people hired at a wage rate of $22.00, because when a seller gets a buyer to pay the *maximum* price the buyer would be willing to pay for that particular quantity of the product (or input) in question, the buyer usually assumes any monopsony power previously held has been lost in bargaining for a lower price. Such a case should not occur here. The garage should perceive that it has some monopsonistic power, and it would like (as we indicated in Figure 12–4) to employ four workers at a wage rate of $12.00. That is because at point *B* the marginal revenue product of mechanics is equal to their marginal cost to the firm, at least if we consider $S_{Mechanics}$ to be the supply curve of mechanics. In this situation where bilateral monopoly exists, presumably the mechanics and the garage owner will bargain, and the wage rate agreed upon will be somewhere between $12.00 and $22.00. The level at which the wage rate is finally established will depend on the relative persuasiveness of the mechanics' union and the garage owner.[10]

SUMMARY

Profit Maximization and Employment of Inputs

In this chapter we have discussed the decision rule that a firm must follow in order to determine the *quantity* of a variable input that it should utilize to maximize profit: Employ a variable input, input a, up to the point where the $MRP_a = MC_a$. If P_a is constant for all levels of input a employed by the firm, $MC_a = P_a$, and the firm should utilize the input until $MRP_a = P_a$.

We have also discussed input *price* determination under three types of market structures: (1) where both the firms buying the input and the suppliers of the input are perfectly competitive, (2) where there is only one buyer of the input (monopsony) but the suppliers view the market as perfectly competitive, and (3) where there is only *one* buyer and *one* seller of the input (bilateral monopoly). In the case of a perfectly competitive market for an input, the market price and equilibrium quantity are determined by market demand and supply. In the case of a monopsonistic input market, the market price and equilibrium quantity are determined by the quantity of the input utilized by the one buyer of the input. This firm employs an input (for example, input a) until $MRP_a = MC_a$. Finally, in the case of bilateral monopoly, the market price and equilibrium quantity of an input are determined through a bargaining process.

It is fairly easy to find an approximation to a perfectly competitive (buyer and seller) type of market structure for an input—the market for unskilled, nonunion labor in a large metropolitan area is one example. It is somewhat more difficult to find an example of a monopsonistic firm that is faced with quite the situation we described earlier; that is, facing a perfectly competitive market on the supply side for an input. Recall that such a firm was forced to pay a higher price for *all* units of that input that it employed in order to obtain additional units of the variable input. Consider the case of the finance de-

---

10 An alternative theory regarding this situation is based on a joint profit maximization model, which yields a determinate level of employment of the input and a corresponding determinate level of final product output and price. See A. L. Bowley, "Bilateral Monopoly," *The Economic Journal* (December 1928), pp. 651–659; Roger D. Blair, David L. Kaserman, and Richard E. Romano, "A Pedagogical Treatment of Bilateral Monopoly," *Southern Economic Journal* 55, no. 4, pp. 831–841; and Dale B. Truett and Lila J. Truett, "Joint Profit Maximization, Negotiation, and the Determinacy of Price in Bilateral Monopoly," *The Journal of Economic Education*, 24, no. 3, pp. 260–270. The limiting cases of the input price described in the Blair, Kaserman, and Romano model depend, however, on the assumption that the dominant firm can force the other firm to purchase (or sell) a quantity of the input that is not consistent with the usual marginal profit requirements for profit maximization. However, an equilibrium input price would exist at the joint profit-maximizing quantity where the *MRP* of the input is equal to the marginal cost of supplying it.

partment in a university where the university is the only institution of higher education in a given area. The university will probably find that to get an *additional* finance professor, it may have to pay that *professor* more than the salary paid to comparable professors already working for the institution. However, to the extent that the university has monopsony power in the area in regard to the employment of finance professors, it may not have to *increase* the salaries of the professors it is currently employing but has hired previously. We have observed such a phenomenon first-hand numerous times in academic departments. Only when faculty members who were hired earlier are *willing* and *able* to accept jobs elsewhere in lieu of a raise at their present university must the university also raise the pay of the current employees to correspond to that of the new employee in order to keep the department intact. To have any clout with the university, the current employees must have alternative job opportunities elsewhere that they have convinced the university they are willing to accept—a situation that means that the firm really was not a monopsonist after all. (However, the market for these professors is still imperfectly competitive.) It is illegal to price discriminate purely on the basis of race or sex, but it is not illegal to price discriminate solely on the basis of when someone was hired. To the extent that a firm can do such discriminating with regard to wages paid employees, the marginal cost of another employee will still be that employee's *wage rate*, even though that wage rate is greater than the wage rate of employees hired previously.

Finally, concerning bilateral monopoly, we suggest that in the case of big labor and big business—for example, the UAW and the automakers—our wage-determination model may be somewhat inappropriate to the extent that the labor union involved does not behave as a profit-maximizing monopolist. The union must be concerned about the level of employment of its members, *as well as* their wage rate(s); thus the assumption that the goal of a union is profit maximization may be neither meaningful nor realistic. The bilateral monopoly model might be realistic in a situation where the U. S. government was purchasing some classified military equipment from a firm that had the sole patent for the product. Even in this situation, however, we would have to assume that the Department of Defense behaved as a profit-maximizing monopsonist.

Still, none of the foregoing comments alters our basic decision rule for a firm interested in employing the profit-maximizing quantity of a variable input: *Employ the input until its marginal revenue product equals its marginal cost.*

QUESTIONS

1. What is meant by profit-maximizing employment of one variable input?
2. What is the general decision rule for determining the profit-maximizing employment of one variable input?

3. Compare the general decision rule for determining the profit-maximizing employment of one variable input when its price is fixed and when its price is variable.
4. How are the market price and equilibrium quantity of a variable input determined when the input is sold in a perfectly competitive market?
5. How are the market price and equilibrium quantity of a variable input determined when the input is sold in a monopsonistic market?
6. How would your answer to Question 5 change if the input were sold in a market characterized by bilateral monopoly?
7. Compare the decision rule for the least cost combination of inputs and that for profit-maximizing employment of one variable input. What does each tell the firm? How are they different? Under what circumstances should each be used?

PROBLEMS

1. The following table shows worker, quantity of output, and output price information for a sweatshirt manufacturer. The cost of materials used in each sweatshirt is $.50.
   a. Complete the table below.

Workers per Hour	Quantity (Total Product) per Hour	Price of Output	Total Revenue	Arc Marginal Revenue	Arc Net Marginal Revenue of Labor	Arc Marginal Revenue Product of Labor	Arc Marginal Revenue Product of Labor
0	0	$2					
1	10	2					
2	25	2					
3	45	2					
4	60	2					
5	70	2					
6	77	2					
7	81	2					
8	84	2					
9	85	2					

b. How many sweatshirts should the company produce to maximize profits if the wage rate is $4.50 per hour? Why?

2. Shown in the following table is the relationship between the number of workers per hour and the total product per hour for a tire company. The relationship between output produced per hour and the price at which it can be sold is also given. Assume that the cost of materials in tires is $6.50.

Number of Workers	Quantity (Total Product) per Hour	Price of Output	Total Revenue	Arc Marginal Revenue	Arc Net Marginal Revenue of Labor	Arc Marginal Product of Labor	Arc Marginal Revenue Product of Labor
0	0	$50.00					
10	200	40.00					
20	300	35.00					
30	350	32.50					
40	380	31.00					
50	400	30.00					
60	410	29.50					

a. Complete the table.
b. If the wage rate is $5 per hour, how many workers should this firm hire to maximize profits? Why?

3. Suppose the workers in Problem 2 organize, form a union, and succeed in bargaining the wage rate up to $9.50 per hour. How many workers should the tire company employ now? Does your answer to this question indicate a reason why a labor union would not necessarily want to bargain for the highest wage rate it might achieve? Why or why not?

4. Wizard, Inc., produces electronic business calculators. Revenue and labor productivity data are given in the following table. The components cost for one calculator is $20. The wage rate is constant and equal to $7.00 per hour.
a. Complete the table.
b. How many workers should Wizard employ? Why?
c. How much output per hour should Wizard produce and what price should it charge?
d. What is the marginal cost of a calculator at this point? (You should be able to determine this figure using relationships discussed in Chapter 6.)

Price of Output	Number of Calculators per Hour	Quantity of Labor	Total Revenue	Arc Marginal Revenue	Arc Net Marginal Revenue of Labor	Arc Marginal Revenue Product of Labor	Arc Marginal Revenue Product of Labor
$100.00	0	0					
						1.0	
95.00	10	10					
						2.0	
85.00		20					
						1.5	
77.50		30					
						1.0	
72.50		40					
						.5	
70.00		50					
						.2	
69.00	62	60					

5. The bar in a small town is faced with the situation depicted in the table on page 535 in regard to revenue per night from the sale of drinks, the number of bartenders working per evening, and the wage rate paid the bartenders. The average cost of ingredients in one drink is $.50. The average price of one drink varies with the number of customers because more people patronize the bar as more "specials" are offered on various drinks.

    a. How many bartenders should this bar employ and what should be the average price of drinks in order to maximize profit? Why?

    b. What is the equilibrium wage rate?

6. Vinox Company makes portable copying machines. Demand and labor productivity data per month are given in the table. The components cost per machine is $200. The average monthly cost of labor is $1,800.

Quantity of Labor	Quantity of Copiers	Price	Total Revenue	Arc Marginal Revenue	Arc NMR	Arc MP_L	Arc MRP_L
0	0	$1,000					
10	100	900					
15	200	800					
25	300	700					
45	400	600					
70	500	500					

    a. Complete the table.

Table for Problem 5

Number of Drinks Sold per Hour	Number of Bartenders	Average Price of One Drink	Total Revenue per Hour	Arc Marginal Revenue	Arc Net Marginal Revenue	Arc Marginal Product of Bartenders	Arc Marginal Revenue Product	Hourly Wage Rate	Arc MC of Bartenders
0	0	$5.00						—	
20	1	4.00						$4.00	
50	2	3.40						5.00	
70	3	3.00						6.00	
85	4	2.70						7.00	
95	5	2.50						7.75	
100	6	2.40						8.50	

b. What is the profit-maximizing number of copiers to be produced monthly, price, and number of workers for Vinox? Why?

c. If Vinox tried to produce and sell 100 more copiers than it does at the profit maximum you identified, what will be the arc marginal cost per copier over this range? Explain how the profit-maximizing number of copiers that you found in part (b) is consistent with the $MR = MC$ condition for copiers.

7. Rio Grande Fitness Machines, Inc., makes muscle toner exercise machines. Daily production and revenue data and corresponding labor requirements for the machines are given in the following table. The daily cost of one worker is $80. The cost of components for each exercise machine is $30.

a. Complete the following table.

Quantity of Labor (L)	Quantity of Machines (Q)	Price of a Machine (P)	Total Revenue (TR)	Marginal Revenue (MR)	Net Marginal Revenue (NMR)	Marginal Product of Labor (MP_L)	Marginal Revenue Product of Labor (MRP_L)
0	0	$200					
10	20	190					
15	40	180					
19	60	170					
24	80	160					
29	100	150					
35	120	140					
43	140	130					
53	160	120					
68	180	110					
88	200	100					

b. What is the profit-maximizing number of exercise machines for Rio Grande to produce, the corresponding price of an exercise machine, and the quantity of labor to employ? Why?

c. What is the marginal cost of producing another exercise machine at the point found in your answer to part(b)? Show your work!

The following problems require calculus.

C1. Suppose the total product (per hour) of labor for a restaurant is given by $TP_L = 38L - 2L^2$.

a. Find the MP_L function.

b. How many workers should the restaurant employ if the wage rate is $4, the average price of a meal is $6, and the average cost per meal of the food ingredients is $2? Why?

C2. In Problem C3 of Chapter 5, a firm was said to have the following short-run total product curve:

$$TP_L = Q = 48L + 4L^2 - (1/3)L^3,$$

where labor, L, is the only variable input and TP_L is the total output produced per day. Suppose the firm faces a fixed price of $2 per unit for its output.

a. If the firm must pay a market-determined wage rate of $78 per day for each unit of labor hired, how much labor should it employ?

b. If the firm's daily fixed costs total $250, what will be its total profit per day?

C3. A firm uses a single variable input, L, in its production process. Its total product function for daily output in the short run is given by the equation

$$Q = 200L - L^2,$$

where L is the number of workers employed per day. The firm sells its output in a perfectly competitive market for $2 per unit.

a. Make a sketch of the firm's labor demand curve.

b. Suppose labor is bought in a perfectly competitive market and that the going wage is $40 per day. Determine the amount of labor the firm will employ. (Show calculation.)

c. Now suppose the market wage rises to $52. Determine how much labor the firm will employ.

SELECTED REFERENCES

Bilas, Richard A. *Microeconomic Theory*, 2d ed. New York: McGraw-Hill, 1971, Chapter 11.

Lyons, Ivory L., and Manuel Zymelman. *Economic Analysis of the Firm: Theory and Practice*. New York: Pitman, 1966, Chapters 15 and 16.

Mansfield, Edwin. *Microeconomics: Theory and Applications*, 8th ed. New York: Norton, 1994, Chapters 13 and 14.

McCloskey, Donald N. *The Applied Theory of Price*, 2d ed. New York: Macmillan, 1985, Chapters 22–26.

INTEGRATING CASE 3A

German-American Metals Corporation

German-American Metals Corporation (GAMC) is an affiliate of a Stuttgart firm that uses a patented process to recover lead and other nonferrous metals from very fine-sized mixed metallic scrap. The process used by GAMC is based on thermal separation of metals in a smelter. The smelting plant consists of a drying system, a lead-smelting separator, separating equipment for other nonferrous metals, and an exhaust purification system with related utility devices. GAMC uses natural-gas-fired burners to generate heat for the smelter, and it currently has a long-term contract guaranteeing it natural gas at $4 per 1,000 cubic feet for the next two years.

GAMC's overall production is dependent on the lead segment of its operations, since its source material contains predominantly lead scrap. The company has two primary outlets for the lead it recovers. First, there is the general market for lead ingots, an oligopolistic market in which GAMC must follow the price leadership of a large, established domestic firm. Its second outlet is sales to one of its own U.S. subsidiaries, Southern Electrical Devices, Inc., a producer of lead battery plates for large industrial batteries.

A forecast prepared by GAMC's planning department indicates that the lead component of its scrap purchases next year will cost $0.15 per pound. On the surface this appears to management to be a favorable development, since lead ingot is expected to sell for $520 per short ton (2,000 lbs.). GAMC has been studying its recovery plant data to come up with reasonably accurate cost projections in the light of high but stable energy prices. The firm's engineers have indicated that, given the quality of scrap available, 20,000 cubic feet of gas must be burned to recover a short ton of lead. Fixed overhead and fixed labor costs comprise most of the remaining costs of lead recovery. However, because of pollution control expenses, marginal cost is expected to rise by $.02 per ton of lead recovered up to GAMC's capacity of 8,500 tons per year.

GAMC's subsidiary, Southern Electrical Devices (SED), may choose to purchase lead ingot either from GAMC or from other outside suppliers.

This case is based on research conducted in Germany in 1982. We wish to thank the officers and management of Texas Shredder Parts, Inc., as well as their German counterparts, for their help in making it possible for us to carry out our investigation.

Not including the expected price of lead ingot for next year, SED's total cost function for the production of battery plates has been estimated to be the following:

$$TC_B = 4,000,000 + 80Q_B + 0.1Q_B^2,$$

where total cost (TC_B) is in dollars, and Q_B is the number of tons of battery plates produced. The SED plant makes efficient use of all the lead it purchases, so that one ton of ingot yields one ton of battery plates. SED's management is not certain whether to plan to purchase lead from outside suppliers next year or to restrict its production of battery plates to those it can make from GAMC's total lead output. Its marketing department has estimated a statistical demand function for the battery plates such that

$$Q_B = 131,720.0 - 80.0P_B + 255.5P_n + 0.5I,$$

where Q_B is the number of tons of battery plates produced, P_B is the sales price per ton of plates, P_n is an index number of regional industrial production, and I is regional per-capital income. SED has contracted with an economic forecasting firm that regularly supplies it with forecasts of a large set of economic variables relating to output, prices, and income levels. For next year the forecasters have estimated that the average value of the regional production index will be 210 and that regional per-capita income will average $13,250.

QUESTIONS

Given the foregoing data, answer the following questions.
1. What strategy will maximize the joint profits of GAMC and its SED subsidiary?
2. For the two products (lead and battery plates), what will be the prices and outputs consistent with a profit-maximizing strategy during the coming year?
3. For next year, should SED plan to restrict its output to what can be produced from the ingot output of GAMC? Why or why not?

INTEGRATING CASE 3B

Bonco, Incorporated: A Firm in Transition

Bonco, Inc., produces a patented surgical device known as the incis-a-matic. The device has been sold successfully in the U.S. market, but it has been produced in two of the company's outdated Ohio plants, one in Columbus and one in Cincinnati.

Barry Cosgrove, a young economist hired to assist management in making decisions regarding the future of incis-a-matic production and marketing strategies, has been developing cost and revenue data relevant to next year's operations.

His boss, Mary Thompson, has argued that for next year, the company should plan to duplicate this year's annual output of 2,400 units and raise price from $10,000 to $12,000 per unit. Thompson's reasoning is that the company plans to build a new plant that will begin operating year after next and has arranged to dispose of its two old plants. She believes they should simply "mark time" as far as output is concerned (in the old facilities) but raise price to cover some anticipated overall inflation in the economy.

Cosgrove's data for the two plants are as follows:

Columbus Plant		Cincinnati Plant	
Output per Month	Arc MC	Output per Month	Arc MC
0		0	
	$ 4,000		$ 3,000
100		100	
	7,000		5,000
200		200	
	9,000		7,200
300		300	
	11,000		9,200
400		400	
	13,000		11,000
500		500	

From the company's chief accountant, Cosgrove has learned that total fixed costs per month will be $700,000 in the Columbus plant and $600,000 in the Cincinnati plant. He has discovered that no one in the company has ever attempted to estimate a demand curve for the incis-a-matic and that Thompson has always based her pricing and output recommendations on her general impressions about the state of the economy. In order to estimate the demand for the incis-a-matic, Cosgrove performed a survey of hospital administrators and department chiefs. The result was the following demand schedule:

Price per Unit	Quantity Sold per Month
$16,000	0
14,000	100
12,000	200
10,000	300
8,000	400
6,000	500
4,000	600

QUESTIONS

Given Cosgrove's demand data, answer the following questions.

1. What should Cosgrove recommend regarding next year's total output and price per unit of the incis-a-matic?
2. How should next year's total output be allocated between the two plants? Why?
3. What will be next year's profit from sales of the incis-a-matic if Cosgrove's data are accurate and his recommendations are followed?
4. How does the Cosgrove recommendation compare with Thompson's strategy in terms of profit?

Beginning year after next, Bonco will be operating in its new plant, where a constant marginal cost of $5,000 per unit can be achieved over the 200- to 1,200-unit-per-month output range. Cosgrove has been asked to study the prospects for both U.S. and foreign sales of the incis-a-matic once the new plant is operational. For two years from now, based on analysis of surgical data for foreign hospitals and projections of U.S. demand, Cosgrove has estimated the following demand curves:

$$AR_f = 20{,}000 - 15Q_f$$

$$AR_{us} = 21{,}000 - 20Q_{us},$$

where

AR_f = average revenue from foreign sales,
Q_f = quantity sold per month in the foreign market,
AR_{us} = average revenue from sales in the U.S. market, and
Q_{us} = quantity sold per month in the U.S. market.

In addition, preliminary data on the new plant indicate that in the first year of operation, total fixed costs will be $800,000 per month.

Given the data on costs and on U.S. and foreign demand, answer the following questions for the first year of operations in the new plant:

5. What price should be charged in the U.S. market?
6. What price should be charged in the foreign market?
7. What will be the amount sold in each market if the preceding prices are charged?
8. What will be the maximum profit obtainable from incis-a-matic sales for the year?

INTEGRATING CASE 3C

A Hare-Raising Decision

On January 24, 1983, the AP news wire reported that Rex Rabbit, Inc., a firm in West Lafayette, Indiana, was launching a fast-food business specializing in rabbit dinners. Rex Rabbit's 42 ranches in the area raised rabbits for the fur trade. The restaurant venture was initiated to develop a market for by-product rabbit meat. The following case was suggested by the Rex Rabbit undertaking, but all of the data are hypothetical and not intended to be an exact representation of any firm—hopping or dead.[1]

Wonder Bunny, Inc., raises rabbits and sells their pelts to manufacturers of fur hats and accessories. For the past 10 years, it has also sold a by-product, unprocessed rabbit meat, to packinghouses that use it as an ingredient in canned pet foods. Chico Saltar, a production manager for Wonder, has noted recent disposal problems with the rabbit meat because packinghouse demand for the product has tapered off. As a result, Wonder has had to pay a waste disposal firm to haul away and destroy the excess meat. Currently, disposal costs are running $0.30 per unit on all unsold meat (production of one rabbit pelt yields one unit of meat). For the foreseeable future, Chico does not expect a recovery in packinghouse demand for the meat.

His current estimate of this demand is represented by the following equation:

$$Q_m = 12,000 - 5,000P_m,$$

where Q_m is the number of units of meat sold per quarter and P_m is the price obtained per unit of meat. Respectively, he has estimated the demand function for pelts and the firm's total cost of production to be

$$Q_f = 3,600 - 4,000P_f + 1,000P_s + 1.8I,$$

where Q_f is the number of rabbit pelts sold per quarter, P_f is the price per rabbit pelt, P_s is the price of squirrel pelts, and I is household income; and

$$TC = \$38,000 + 1.8Q + 0.0001Q^2,$$

---

1 "Firm Hopping into Fast-Food Bunny Trade," *San Antonio Express*, January 24, 1983, p. 3-D.

where $38,000 is quarterly fixed cost and Q represents the number of rabbits processed or production of one pelt *and* one unit of the by-product meat. Wonder's present strategy is to maximize profit from the sales of the two products, given the disposal cost per unit applicable to any amount of excess meat.

Mariel Hutch, a financial consultant for Wonder, has come to the company with a proposal that it stop selling rabbit meat to packinghouses and process the meat for sale to a new market, fast-food restaurants specializing in rabbit dinners. She has estimated that Wonder's demand curve for sales in this market is given by the equation

$$Q_r = 18,500 - 5,000P_r,$$

where Q_r is the number of units of meat sold per quarter and P_r is the price charged for a unit of meat. (The unit of meat remains the amount obtained with the production of one pelt.) While this demand clearly exceeds Chico's current estimate of demand in the packinghouse market, the changeover would require an increase in fixed costs of $14,000 per quarter as well as additional marginal costs of $0.28 per rabbit to process the meat to specifications of the new market. The cost increases will be applicable to all production of pelts and meat because of once-over changes that will have to be made in the processing line. In other words, the new costs cannot be allocated to meat production alone. Moreover, it would not be feasible for Wonder to sell in both the restaurant market and the packinghouse market, since the decision to interrupt sales to the latter would likely cause a permanent loss of customers there. In the event that all of the meat cannot be sold in the restaurant market, it will still be possible to use the previously described waste disposal alternative.

Wonder must make a decision regarding the two by-product market possibilities within the next few weeks. As far as the pelt market is concerned, the company believes that the demand function variables other than the rabbit pelt price will remain constant. The current price of squirrel pelts is $3.20, and household income is $18,000. Given this additional information, what should Wonder do?

Hint: It is rational for Wonder to accept negative marginal revenue from meat sales as long as the negative MR per unit is less than the disposal cost per unit.

INTEGRATING CASE 3D

Omega Distributing Company II

(Note: This case is a continuation of the analysis done in Integrating Case 1B, Omega Distributing Company I, which is found at the end of Part I. A review of that case would be helpful for understanding this one.)

Duncan Haynes, a member of the team that developed a demand function for Omega Distributing Company's Blast fabric softener, has been assigned the task of determining whether the price of the product should be changed. (Duncan had earlier suggested changing price, since the results of a regression analysis of demand indicated that the company had been pricing the product in the inelastic range of its demand curve.) The demand function for Blast from the earlier analysis is

$$Q = -820 - 689P_b + 1{,}972P_c + 18A.$$

Q is denominated in hundreds in the equation and refers to the number of hundreds of units of Blast sold per week.

Duncan has decided that the pricing decision can best be analyzed by assuming that the price of the competing brand of softener, Cloud (P_c in the preceding equation) remains at its average recent value, $1.42 per unit, and that his own company cuts its advertising expenditure on Blast (A in the equation, denominated in ten thousands) to $20,000 per week ($A = 2.0$). This leaves only P_b, the price per unit of Blast, as an unknown in the preceding equation.

Duncan knows that Omega pays the manufacturer of Blast $0.875 and that Omega's unit variable cost for the product is equal to 112 percent of the amount it pays the manufacturer. Given that the price of Blast and that of Cloud in the estimated demand function are denominated in dollars, what sales price per unit should Duncan recommend? What impact on profit would these changes in price and advertising have as compared to the profit Blast would generate with the average price and advertising levels determined in Integrating Case 1B (P_b = $1.37, P_c = $1.42, and A = 3.86)? Should Omega be cautious about instituting the price increase that Duncan's demand curve calls for? Why or why not?

PART 4

Analysis of Project Decisions

13

FUNDAMENTALS OF PROJECT EVALUATION

In many of the preceding chapters, our primary concern was the way a firm's managers identify a profit-maximizing rate of output and its corresponding price under various types of market situations. Over the short run, as we defined it, a significant proportion of the firms' inputs were envisioned as fixed (plant and equipment, for example), and the issue of investment in new capacity did not arise. Generally, when we considered the long run, the firm remained in a given industry or product line even though it might change the size of its plant. Moreover, product differentiation or an adjustment in the share of output of joint products did not constitute a change in the type of activity undertaken by the firm.

In the present chapter, we change our emphasis to the question of management's analysis of investment opportunities, which include wholly new undertakings of the firm. Such ventures range all the way from the expansion of capacity in a given line of activity to entry into a new and different industry. It is a characteristic of today's industrial society that firms typically have many investment opportunities before them; and as the firms grow, their managers must be prepared to determine not only how and when to expand existing operations but also whether to steer the firm toward new types of activities in which profitable investments can be made. The large U.S. and European business conglomerates are an obvious case in point. Many of these giant corporations, such as Eastman Kodak, Gulf + Western Industries, and Textron, are characterized by divisions that produce totally unrelated types of output. The managers of these large firms must constantly review the expansion alternatives before them; and in a given firm, viable alternatives may range from developmental expenditures in space technology to the introduction of a new pastry snack into the consumer market.

A recent example of a firm faced with vexing investment alternatives is General Electric Corporation, which had to make a decision on what path to take in developing an engine for the new Boeing 777 jumbo jet. GE's competitors, Pratt & Whitney and British Rolls-Royce PLC, each spent about $750 million to modify existing engine designs. General Electric, however, decided to spend $1.5 *billion* to develop a totally new engine, a decision that was particularly difficult because both the commercial aviation industry and the defense industry's demand for new plane engines were depressed at the time. The new engines were introduced in 1995. However, by early 1996 a price war had developed among the three engine makers, and it was estimated that the engines were selling for only about half of their full cost, including allocated development costs. Moreover, the GE engine still lacked certification for flights over water because of some problems with parts burning up. It was estimated that the program would not break even for at least 10 years, twice as long as GE had originally anticipated. In fact, a GE manager stated, "It's a 30-year business."[1] All three companies have been battling fiercely for orders in Asia, as airlines in that region have been among those placing the largest orders for 777s. The competition has been so keen that British Prime Minister John Major was involved in an effort to assist Rolls in Tokyo.[2]

Even the venerable Walt Disney Productions is not exempt from the need to evaluate investment projects carefully: Mickey Mouse alone does not ensure financial success. For example, the company invested $4 billion to build Euro Disneyland, near Paris. The park opened in April 1992, and Disney soon found that its earlier estimates of attendance—as well as the amount of money that each visitor would spend once inside the park—were far too optimistic. The park lost $905 million in its second fiscal year, and Euro Disney stated that it needed to restructure its finances. In 1995, Euro Disney finally had its first profitable year [a profit of 114 million French francs (including 112 million francs from a buyback of convertible bonds), compared with a loss of 1.8 *billion* francs the previous fiscal year].[3]

Smaller firms also must face important decisions regarding new product development. For example, the Ball Corporation—an old-line manufacturer of glass bottles, mason jars for home canning, and metal containers—has in recent years added copper-zinc penny blanks, small satellites, and aircraft instruments to its product mix. Although it was reported in 1982 that Ball's traditional products still contributed 80 percent of the firm's profits, growth in the canning and packaging industry was slow. Thus a 24 percent increase in Ball's 1981 profits was attributed to "an upturn in its small industrial products operation." Richard M. Ringoen, Ball's president and chief executive officer at the time, was pursuing a strategy of expansion in high-technology aerospace products, which he believed would attain greater earnings growth in the future.[4]

---

1 "Defying the Law of Gravity," *Business Week* (April 8, 1996); and "Clash of the Flying Titans," *Business Week* (November 22, 1993), pp. 64–67.

2 Ibid., p. 67.

3 "Euro Disney Posts First Annual Profit, Stock Slides 14%," *The Wall Street Journal*, November 16, 1995, p. A17; "Mickey's Trip to Trouble," *Newsweek* (February 14, 1994), pp. 34–39; "A Goofy Kind of Year," *Business Week* (October 18, 1993), p. 57; "Photo Finish," *Business Week* (November 22, 1993), p. 52; and "The Mouse Isn't Roaring," *Business Week* (August 24, 1992), p. 38.

4 "Ball: Reaching Beyond Mason Jars to Satellites and High Technology," *Business Week* (August 16, 1982), pp. 76–77.

A major factor on the recent business scene has been the emergence of what are virtually stateless corporations. These firms represent a further evolution of multinational businesses that once were based primarily in one country, such as the United States, with subsidiary operations in other parts of the world. Frequently, these foreign appendages produced goods designed and developed in the home country. As *Business Week* put it, "The chain of command and nationality of the company were clear."[5] Today, however, the national identities of these corporations are becoming much less clear. *Business Week* continued:

> With the U.S. no longer dominating the world economy or holding a monopoly on innovation, new technologies, capital, and talents flow in many different directions. The most sophisticated manufacturing companies are making breakthroughs in foreign labs, seeking to place shares with foreign investors and putting foreigners on the fast track to the top. A wave of mergers, acquisitions, and strategic alliances has further clouded the question of national control.[6]

As a result of the new world market environment, managerial decision making, particularly with regard to new investment, has become far more complex than it was in the past. A company can no longer afford to ignore the impact of the international business community on the firm's operations, including its proposed capital projects.

CAPITAL BUDGETING AND PROJECT ANALYSIS

Capital budgeting is the analysis of alternative investment opportunities by a firm.

The analysis of alternative investment opportunities is the focus of a subject area known as **capital budgeting**, which encompasses both economics and finance. We can view capital budgeting as the process by which a firm's managers determine how to allocate investment expenditures among alternative projects. The projects that are the subject of analysis usually include only those that will yield dollar returns to the firm for periods longer than one year. *Capital project analysis* is a major part of the capital budgeting process, since it provides managers with the raw materials in terms of data that are necessary to carry out capital budgeting decisions. Accordingly, we will first consider the analysis of a single undertaking (investment project) and later turn to the question of deciding which of a number of alternative investment projects should be accepted.

---

5 "The Stateless Corporation," *Business Week* (May, 14, 1990), p. 98.
6 Ibid.

COSTS IN NEW UNDERTAKINGS

From our earlier analysis of the firm, we know that any operation of a given size (plant) normally has both fixed and variable costs of production. Thus, to analyze a specific capital project, it is necessary to determine such costs and compare them with the revenues the project will generate. However, a *new* undertaking has one-time costs associated with obtaining and organizing the resources necessary to bring it into existence, and project analysis must also take these costs into account. For convenience we will call this latter set of costs the *price* or *initial cost outlay* of the project. A capital project's price includes initial outlays for land, buildings, and equipment, as well as developmental costs both for the undertaking itself and for the product it is intended to produce. Another item that should be included in a project's price is the cost to the firm of any increase in working capital requirements attributable to the project. Finally, if the project involves replacement of existing capital goods, the after-tax salvage value of the old equipment should be deducted from the project's price.

Capital budgeting puts managers into an accept-or-reject framework with respect to the individual capital project. The following general rule for acceptance of a single project is simple:

> A project should be accepted as long as the *present value* of the expected *net receipts* it generates *equals or exceeds its price* (the net outlay required).

In other words, worthy investments are those that yield returns at least equal to their costs, where the costs include a normal or target rate of return on invested capital. *Returns* from the project are defined as the present value of net receipts, or a discounted stream of *net cash flows*. Such a concept will be familiar to students who have had a course in finance, but others should give it particular attention. The following section provides a summary of how to calculate the discounted stream of net receipts. More detailed information on the use of discounting and compounding methodologies appears in the appendix to this chapter.

STREAM OF RECEIPTS OR RETURNS

In general, capital projects have a finite life, even though it is not always clear to the project analyst how long a given venture might be expected to yield net operating returns to the firm. Even if the life of a particular project were viewed as indefinitely long or infinite, it would be possible to calculate just what one would be willing to pay today in order to obtain an infinite stream of annual receipts of a given amount per year. In approaching this problem, we would quickly find out that we would not be willing to pay very much for an amount that is not to be received until many, many years in the future. To understand this point, ask yourself what you would be willing to pay for a piece of paper that guarantees you will receive $50 thirty years from today. Not much! The exact answer, assuming no inflation, would depend on the interest rate.[7]

To examine the effect of interest rate considerations on management's evaluation of net receipts from a capital project, let us suppose a firm's project analysts are reasonably certain that a given project will generate net receipts for the firm for the next ten years. Specifically, let us suppose that in terms of today's prices (this means that inflation is adjusted out of all calculations), $100,000 will be generated each year. We will assume that the first annual receipts of the project are received at the end of one year's time from completion of the project and will treat the project's net outlay as a current value (paid immediately, at time-period zero). Thus the first $100,000 is received at the end of year one, the second $100,000 at the end of year two, and so forth.

The value at the time of project completion of $100,000 of receipts that will be earned at the end of, say, year three is not $100,000, but rather something less. In particular it is the amount of money that would *accumulate* to $100,000 at the end of year three if it were invested today at some specific rate of interest per year. This is so because the firm at project completion and initiation of production is in the same position as the person who is promised a given sum of money at some future time. The current value, or **present value**, of that promised amount is something less than the future amount itself. If the interest rate is 6 percent, the present value of $100,000 received at the end of year three is $83,961.93. Alternatively, if we receive $83,961.93 *now* and put it into an account paying 6 percent interest per year, at the end of this year we will have ($83,961.93)(1.06) = $88,999.64. If we do not remove any of the funds from the account, at the end of year two we will have ($88,999.64)(1.06) = $94,339.62; and at the end of year three we will have ($94,339.62)(1.06) = $100,000.00. Thus we can say that if the interest rate is 6 percent, $83,961.93 in our hands today is *equivalent* to $100,000 received at the end of year three. Similarly, both of the foregoing are equivalent to $94,339.62 received at the end of year two. The process by which we have determined the amount or **future value** that the $83,961.93 will accumulate to is called **compounding**. In the foregoing example, 6 percent interest was compounded at the end of each year. This means that at the end of each year, the interest for that period is

The **present value** of a future payment or series of payments represents the amount received today that would be equivalent in value to the future payment or payments.

The **future value** of a sum of money held today is the amount that would be accumulated at some future date if we invested that sum of money now at a particular rate of interest.

Compounding is the process of computing the value of a current sum of money at some future date.

---

7 We use the term "interest rate" very loosely at this point. In general, when we employ the term, we are referring to the rate of return expected from alternative uses of funds. If we are certain that the funds paid out for the guarantee of receiving $50 thirty years from now can be placed in a risk-free account paying 6 percent interest compounded annually, we could ascertain that $8.71 placed in such an account would reach a value of $50 in 30 years. Therefore we would not want to pay more than $8.71 for the paper guaranteeing $50 at the end of 30 years.

Discounting is the process of computing the present value of sums of money to be received in the future.

The **discount rate** is the rate of interest used to compute present values.

added to the amount that was in the account at the beginning of the year. Therefore the 6 percent interest is paid on a larger amount the next year.

The proposition that discounted future amounts are equal to a certain present amount is known as the *concept of equivalency*. The process by which we determine the present value of an amount to be received at some time in the future is called **discounting**, and the interest rate we use in the determination of the present value is called the **discount rate**.

Clearly, the farther out in time a future amount is received, the lower its present value. Returning to the previous project with a $100,000 annual net receipts figure, for year ten the present value of $100,000 is only $55,839.47 if a discount rate of 6 percent is applied. Such a present value is found by the formula

(13–1)

$$PV = \frac{FV_n}{(1+r)^n}$$

where

$$PV = \text{present value,}$$
$$FV_n = \text{future value at the end of year } n,$$
$$r = \text{applicable discount rate, and}$$
$$n = \text{number of periods (years) until the amount is received.}$$

In the preceding case, n would be 10 and r would be 0.06. We can derive the present value formula by further examining the concept of equivalency previously discussed. We have already seen that when $r = 0.06$, $100,000 received at the end of year three is equal to a present value of $83,961.93. Note that the $100,000 received at the end of year three is equal to an initial amount of $83,961.93 increased by 6 percent at the end of year one to $88,999.64, compounded at 6 percent again at the end of year two to $94,339.62, and compounded at 6 percent at the end of year three to $100,000.00. So we have the following:

Amount at the end of

year one: 　　　　　　　($83,961.93)(1.06) = $88,999.64

year two: 　　　　　　($83,961.93)(1.06)(1.06) = $94,339.62

　　　　　　　　　　　　　　　　　= ($83,961.93)(1.06)^2

year three:　　($83,961.93)(1.06)(1.06)(1.06) = $100,000.00

　　　　　　　　　　　　　　　　　= ($83,961.93)(1.06)^3

or for each year,

(13–2)

$$FV_n = PV(1.06)^n,$$

where FV is received at the end of n periods in the future. If we divide both sides of the preceding expression by $(1.06)^n$, we get

(13–3)
$$PV = \frac{FV_n}{(1+.06)^n}.$$

Since 0.06 is the discount rate, r, we have

(13–4)
$$PV = \frac{FV_n}{(1+r)^n},$$

which is identical to equation (13–1).

We can also state equation (13–4) as

(13–5)
$$PV = FV_n(PVF\ r, n),$$

where $(PVF\ r, n) = 1/(1+r)^n$ is the *present value factor*. Tables have been developed for the value of the PVF (also known as the present value of $1) for given rates of interest and numbers of periods in the future. In Appendix B at the end of the text, Table B–3 gives the values of the PVF. To find the present value of $100,000 received at the end of the third year for the preceding project, we simply multiply $100,000 times the present value factor from the table, which for $n = 3$ and $r = 0.06$ is 0.8396. (Read down the 6 percent column of Table B–3 to $n = 3$.) Thus

$$\$100,000(PVF\ 6\%, 3) = \$100,000(0.8396) = \$83,960,$$

which corresponds closely to the $83,961.93 in the previous example. The slight difference in the result is due to the rounding of the PVF, which is more precisely given by 0.83962.

To evaluate our example of $100,000 per year stream of annual net receipts for 10 years, we construct Table 13–1, using the 6 percent present value factors from Appendix B, Table B–3. Each of the 10 annual $100,000 amounts is multiplied by its respective 6 percent present value factor, and the present values in the fourth column are then summed to obtain the present value of the entire 10-year stream of receipts. From Table 13–1, we can see that the present value of the 10-year flow of $100,000 in net receipts per year is $736,020—the sum of the *discounted* future values where the applicable discount rate is 6 percent.

However, this result can be obtained more easily by multiplying $100,000 times the present value factor for an annuity (PVF_a) of 10 years discounted at 6 percent. Defined briefly, an *annuity* is a constant amount payable at the end of each year for a specified number of years. In the case of our current example, if we let $A = \$100,000$, then PV_a (the present value of the 10-year stream of $100,000 per year) is

Table 13–1   Present Value of $100,000 per Year Stream of Net Receipts Discounted at 6 Percent per Year

Period (n)	FV = Future Value (At End of Period)	PV Factor (PVF 6%, n)	Present Value (FV × PVF)
1	$100,000	0.9434	$ 94,340
2	100,000	0.8900	89,000
3	100,000	0.8396	83,960
4	100,000	0.7921	79,210
5	100,000	0.7473	74,730
6	100,000	0.7050	70,500
7	100,000	0.6651	66,510
8	100,000	0.6274	62,740
9	100,000	0.5919	59,190
10	100,000	0.5584	55,840
		PV of 10-year stream	$736,020

(13–6)
$$PV_a = \frac{A}{(1+r)^1} + \frac{A}{(1+r)^2} + \dots + \frac{A}{(1+r)^n},$$

where $n = 10$. Factoring out the A, we obtain

(13–7)
$$PV_a = A\left[\frac{1}{(1+r)^1} + \frac{1}{(1+r)^2} + \dots + \frac{1}{(1+r)^n}\right].$$

The present value factor for the annuity is the term in brackets in the preceding equation, or

(13–8)
$$PVF_a = \left[\frac{1}{(1+r)^1} + \frac{1}{(1+r)^2} + \dots + \frac{1}{(1+r)^n}\right],$$

so that we can state $PV_a = A(PVF_a\, r, n)$. A table of present value of annuity factors also appears in Appendix B. For a discount rate of 6 percent and 10 periods (PVF_a 6%, 10), the present value factor is 7.3601. Thus, in the case of our example, we have

$$PV_a = \$100,000(PVF_a\, 6\%, 10) = \$100,000(7.3601) = \$736,010.$$

In round numbers, then, we have determined that the present value of the net receipts stream anticipated from our example project is $736,000. This assumes, of course, that management has determined that 6 percent per year is an appropriate rate of discount to apply.

According to the general rule stated in the preceding section, the project

MANAGERIAL PERSPECTIVE
The Saturn: A Product Made in Heaven?

"All-new aluminum engine, fail-safe sophisticated marketing research and highly automated assembly technique . . . a revolutionary change from a company and industry that heretofore have stressed slow, evolutionary change." These words could have been used to describe General Motors' Saturn, a new small car introduced in the fall of 1990, but here *The Wall Street Journal* was quoting them from J. Patrick Wright's 1979 book, *On a Clear Day You Can See General Motors*. And where did Wright pick them up? From General Motors' claims for the Vega, a car introduced in 1970. An indication of the Vega's success, or lack thereof, can be gleaned from a comment by Mr. Richard LeFauve, the boss at General Motors' Saturn subsidiary, who admits: "We've had many letters from people saying, 'Don't let this be another Vega.'"

Work on the Saturn began in 1983, and General Motors spent $4.5 billion to bring the car to market. The Saturn was envisioned as a top-quality small car that would be more technologically advanced than competing Japanese cars. The Spring Hill, Tennessee, plant that manufactures the new cars cost $1.9 billion with an initial capacity of 240,000 cars a year. However, Thomas G. Manoff, Saturn's vice-president of finance, calculated that plant capacity would have to double if Saturn were to become profitable.

General Motors began the Saturn project by attempting to design a plant that would be so automated that very little human labor would be required. Later, however, the company had to modify that plan because comparable equipment in other General Motors facilities was not performing as well as had been hoped.

In contrast, Honda began developing a U.S. plant in 1982 in Marysville, Ohio, at a cost of about $2 billion. Initially, the degree of automation at the plant was relatively low, but Honda gradually added sophisticated equipment as workers became more adept at using it. The company also added capacity as demand for the car expanded. Although the plant began by building an existing model of the Accord, by 1985 it had introduced a new Accord model. For approximately the same cost as General Motors' Saturn project, Honda got two assembly plants with a total annual capacity of 510,000 cars as well as a factory capable of building nearly all of the engines, transmissions, and related parts needed by its auto assembly plants plus a motorcycle plant.

The Saturn was approximately the size of a Toyota Corolla, which had a base price of $9,000 to $13,000. The Saturn's projected price range was $10,000 to $13,000. GM hoped that the Saturn would get 80 percent of its sales from customers who previously purchased competing cars made by other companies: the Honda Civic, for example, and Mazda MX6 Coupe, as well as the Toyota Corolla.

As a result of a limited capital budget and capital rationing decisions, the allocation of funds to develop the Saturn caused a delay in the development of a new line of four-door, mid-sized cars to compete with Ford Motor Company's Taurus and Sable. That delay allegedly contributed to a decline in GM's U.S. market share from 44 percent in 1983 to 35.7 percent in 1990. Moreover, even Saturn's management believed in 1990 that it would be at least five years before the company would know if Saturn was a profitable project for General Motors.

By Fall 1996, Saturn had been making an operating profit for three years, but GM had still not recovered its original investment in the car. Nevertheless, the company announced it was planning to build a new, mid-size version of the Saturn, and analysts estimated the project would cost another $1 billion. In addition, the company planned to spend another billion dollars to develop a new world engine to be used first in the new Saturn. However, the new model was to be built in GM's Wilmington, Delaware, assembly plant rather than at the Spring Hill plant. (The Wilmington plant had previously been scheduled to close.) Clearly, the Saturn project remains a work-in-progress whose overall profitability still remains to be determined.

References: "GM's Saturn Division Plans to Build a Midsize Car to Keep Customers Loyal," *The Wall Street Journal*, August 6, 1996, p. B5; "GM Confirms Plan for Midsize Saturn, Available by 1999," *The Wall Street Journal*, August 7, 1996, p. C18; "GM's Plan for Saturn, To Beat Small Imports, Trails Original Goals," *The Wall Street Journal*, July 9, 1990, pp. A1, A12.

> The **net present value** (*NPV*) of an investment is the present value of its net cash inflows minus the present value of its cost outlays. An investment project is acceptable if its *NPV* is greater than or equal to zero.

> The **net cash flow** of a project is equal to any increase in revenues brought about by the project less any increase in operating expenses and depreciation, multiplied by $(1 - T)$, where T is the firm's marginal income tax rate. The incremental depreciation associated with the project is then added to the above sum.

should be accepted as long as its price (the net outlay) is not more than $736,000. Another way of stating this requirement is to say that the **net present value** (*NPV*) of the project must be *nonnegative* (zero or greater). The net present value of a project is the difference between the discounted stream of expected **net cash flows** from the project and the project's price, or

(13–9)

$$NPV = \sum_{i=1}^{n} \frac{(TR_i - TC_i)(1 - T) + D_i}{(1 + r)^i} - C_P,$$

where TR is total revenue, TC is total operating cost (short run and including depreciation for the project), T is the firm's marginal income tax rate, D is depreciation, and C_P is the price or net outlay for the project. Equation (13–9) indicates that we should determine the *net* receipts for each time period (i) and discount such receipts at the rate r for all time periods for one through n; then we should sum them (the Greek letter Σ, sigma, indicates that we should sum all items with an i subscript from $i = 1$ to $i = n$) and subtract the price of the project to obtain the *NPV*.

If the *NPV* in equation (13–9) turns out to be zero, the project will yield a return identical to the return that would be received if an amount equal to C_P were put into an account paying ($r \times 100$) percent interest compounded annually. Where *NPV* is greater than zero, the project yield will exceed the discount rate, r.

In fact, it is possible to determine the net annual percentage yield of a project (its **internal rate of return** or ***IRR***) when its price and annual dollar receipts are known by setting *NPV* equal to C_P and solving for r in equation (13–9). Thus we find r such that

The **internal rate of return (*IRR*)** of a project is the discount rate that will result in a net present value of zero for the project.

$$\sum_{i=1}^{n} \frac{(TR_i - TC_i)(1 - T) + D_i}{(1 + r)^i} = C_P.$$

The r value can be found by trial and error or by interpolation. There is no simple formula for finding it, and not all financial calculators have this capability. However, there are computer programs available for determination of the internal rate of return.[8] Later in this chapter an example of trial-and-error determination of a project's internal rate of return will be introduced.

A SIMPLE CAPITAL PROJECT ANALYSIS

Any investor, whether a large corporation or an individual, must go through an analysis similar to that outlined previously in order to make an appropriate accept-or-reject decision on a capital project. For the large enterprise contemplating a major undertaking, the process of enumerating project costs and returns may be very tedious and expensive. For an individual or a small business, however, the procedure may be relatively simple.

Let us consider as an example the case of a small firm, Clickwash, Inc., that operates a chain of coin laundries in a given area. The firm's managers are quite experienced in the construction and operation of such facilities but are now considering opening a coin-operated car wash in a location that appears to be desirable. A car wash franchising company owns the site and has offered Clickwash an attractive ground lease in exchange for a franchise fee of 30 percent of sales revenue.

---

8 As long as the project cash flows follow the pattern of negative cash flows in the first few periods and positive cash flows thereafter, there will usually be only one positive-valued solution for the *IRR* (the others are negative or imaginary). However, if there is a mixture of positive and negative cash flows during future periods, it is possible to have more than one positive-valued solution for the *IRR*. In such cases one reverts back to the *NPV* method to determine the acceptability of the project in question.

According to our prior discussion of project analysis, Clickwash's management will have to determine the following:

1. The price or net outlay of the project.
2. Anticipated annual sales revenues from the project.
3. Annual operating costs of the project.
4. A salvage value at the end of the project's life.

Based on its experience with coin laundries, management has determined that five years is an appropriate project life, since the machinery receives rather rough use and leases on suitable locations can seldom be negotiated for a term greater than five years. The car wash will have seven bays made of structural steel and aluminum siding. The bays and washing equipment can be dismantled and sold or moved at termination of the project; however, driveway pavement, the concrete slab on which the bays rest, and plumbing placed in the slab will all be abandoned when the project is over. The initial cost of the bays and washing equipment is $159,000. They can be sold at the end of the project for $66,500. The paving, slab, nonsalvageable plumbing, and plant installation cost an additional $20,000. The management of Clickwash thus knows that the price or net outlay of the project will be $C_p = \$179,000$.

The next step for management is to calculate the annual net receipts from the project and determine the present value of the five-year receipts stream. Suppose they have the following information:

1. The car wash will operate an average of 360 days a year.
2. An average of 36 car washes per day will occur at each of the seven bays.
3. The average receipts for a single wash are $0.875. This result is based on an assumption that the average wash will yield $1.25 in revenues (some people will spend four quarters per wash and others six) but that 30 percent of that amount belongs to the franchising company ($0.375).
4. Variable costs per wash are as follows:

Utilities and water	$0.08
Soap and supplies	0.04
Maintenance of machinery	0.02

5. Fixed costs per month are as follows:

Rent	$750.00
Utilities (fixed portion)	90.00
Site maintenance	80.00
Labor	190.00
Administrative expense	100.00

6. Depreciation is $22,500 per year.
7. The company is in the 34 percent income tax bracket.

From 1, 2, and 3, it can be determined that annual receipts from sales will be

$$7 \text{ bays} \times 36 \text{ washes} \times 360 \text{ days} \times \$0.875 = \$79{,}380.$$

Based on the preceding cost information, management can determine the annual cost of the car wash project as in Table 13–2. Our format in Table 13–2 is a hybrid of the economic and accounting costs discussed in Chapter 6. At this point we do not take into account the opportunity cost to the firm of using its own funds for the project. However, the discount rate applied to the future net receipts and the criterion that the present value of such receipts be greater than the price of the project do account for the opportunity cost of investing the funds in another way.

Table 13–2   Annual Operating Cost of Car Wash Project

Variable Costs:		
Utilities and Water (0.08 × 90,720 washes per year)	$7,258	
Maintenance of Machines (0.02 × 90,720 washes per year)	1,814	
Soap and Supplies (0.04 × 90,720 washes per year)	3,629	
		$12,701
Fixed Costs:		
Utilities (fixed portion, $90 per month)	$1,080	
Rent ($750 per month)	9,000	
Site Maintenance ($80 per month)	960	
Labor ($190 per month)	2,280	
Administrative Expense ($100 per month)	$1,200	
		14,520
Depreciation		22,500
Total Annual Operating Cost of Project		$49,721

Table 13–3 is a worksheet for the project itself. Here, the anticipated receipts from sales are reduced by the annual cost of operations from Table 13–2 and by federal income taxes, which are 34 percent of net income before taxes. In order to obtain the annual net inflow of cash from the project, the firm's managers must add back the yearly depreciation figure, since depreciation is charged against current receipts but not paid to anyone else outside the firm.[9] As Table 13–3 shows, after this adjustment the annual net inflow from the project is $42,075. Then management applies a discount rate of 10 percent to analyze the project. (The question of choosing the appropriate discount rate will be discussed later in this chapter.)

---

9 Depreciation expense is an accounting concept employed to reflect the using up of certain fixed assets (that is, having them wear out or become obsolete) in the production process of the firm. On the firm's income statement, depreciation is an expense, but no cash is paid out. Because of this the firm's *net flow of cash benefits* will exceed net income. Therefore we must add the depreciation back to the net income to account for its contribution to the benefits stream.

Table 13–3   Worksheet for Car Wash Project *NPV* Analysis

Annual Receipts from Sales		$ 79,380
Less:		
Annual Cost of Operations	$49,721	
Net Income Before Taxes		29,659
Less:		
Income Tax	10,084	
Net Income		19,575
Plus:		
Depreciation	22,500	
Annual Net Inflow from Project		$ 42,075
PV of Five-Year Net Inflow[1]		$159,498
Salvage Value of Equipment		
$66,500		
PV of Salvage Value[2]	41,290	
GPV of Project		200,788
Price of Project (C_P)		(179,000)
NPV of Project		$ 21,788

[1]This amount is $42,075(PVF_a$ 10%, 5) = $42,075(3.7908). See the discussion of PVF_a earlier in the chapter, and consult Table B–4 in Appendix B.

[2]This amount is $66,500(PVF$ 10%, 5) = $66,500(0.6209). See Table B–3 for *PVF*.

The present value of a cash inflow of $42,075 for five years when discounted at 10 percent is $159,498, a figure substantially lower than C_P, the price of the car wash project ($179,000). However, we must recall that management estimates the equipment to have a salvage value of $66,500 at the end of the five-year project life, and the present value of that salvage amount (discounted at 10 percent) is $41,290.[10] This gives a gross present value (*GPV*) figure for the project of $159,498 + $41,290 = $200,788. Since C_P is only $179,000, the project is acceptable. Alternatively, it is shown in Table 13–3 that the net present value of the project is $21,788. Since the net present value is greater than zero, the project meets the general rule for acceptability.

PROJECT YIELD OR RATE OF RETURN

Management will also be interested to know the return that is generated by the project in terms of a percentage yield or rate of return on the $179,000 of

---

10 In this example, the salvage value is exactly equal to the book value of the equipment at the end of five years. If these two values were not equal, the income tax due (saved) on the gain (loss) as a result of the sale of the equipment would have to be considered.

invested capital. Logically, the project has a return of more than 10 percent per year, since its *NPV* is greater than zero. If the *NPV* were zero, the net inflows from the project discounted at 10 percent per year would exactly equal $179,000. In financial analysis the *internal rate of return* (*IRR*) of a project is its yield. As explained earlier in the chapter, the *IRR* can be defined as the discount rate that will just equate the present value of the stream of net receipts with the price of the project. To estimate the *IRR* in the context of our car wash project, we would want to find a discount rate such that the five-year stream of $42,075 in net receipts per year plus the present value of the salvage amount (*PV* of $66,500) is just equal, in present value terms, to C_P, or

$$\$42,075(PVF_a\ IRR\%, 5) + \$66,500(PVF\ IRR\%, 5) = \$179,000.$$

Mathematically, solving for the *IRR* is a difficult process. However, it is quite easy to estimate a project's *IRR* using an ordinary financial calculator or a set of present value tables and employing a trial-and-error method. In the preceding case, we know that the *IRR* is greater than 10 percent. We can calculate the present value of the stream of annual receipts plus the salvage amount at discount rates of 12 and 14 percent and see which most closely approximates $179,000. The following are the *PVs* of the five-year stream of $42,075 per year plus the salvage value for the preceding rates of discount.

Discount Rate (IRR)	PV of $42,075/yr. + $66,500 (n = 5)
12%	$189,404
14%	$178,987

The *PV* for 12 percent is too high, indicating that the *IRR* exceeds 12 percent. In fact, the *IRR* must be about 14 percent. For 14 percent, if we calculate the *PV* of an annual net inflow of $42,075 for five years plus the *PV* of the $66,500 salvage value, we get $178,987, which is very close to the project price. Thus we can conclude that Clickwash's management will enjoy a yield of approximately 14 percent on its investment in the car wash project. Since this yield is greater than the 10 percent discount rate, the project should be undertaken. This analysis provides a new and slightly different statement of the accept-reject rule: An individual project is acceptable if its *IRR* equals or exceeds the discount rate.[11]

---

11 Some exceptions to this rule exist, particularly when there are multiple positive-valued solutions for the *IRR*. For more information on this topic see J. Fred Weston and Thomas E. Copeland, *Managerial Finance*, 9th ed., (Chicago: The Dryden Press, 1992), Chapter 9.

PROJECT RANKING IN CAPITAL
BUDGETING ANALYSIS

We have shown how to determine whether a single given project is acceptable from an investment standpoint. However, we have not yet developed any rules for ranking alternative projects in terms of their relative acceptability. In the context of our hypothetical firm, Clickwash, this issue would emerge if management had to decide not only whether a car wash would be an acceptable investment but also whether such an investment would be *better* than several other alternatives that have the same initial price and project life.

For example, Clickwash might be faced with whether it should build the car wash, take over an existing pizzeria, build a donut shop, add another laundromat to its chain, or build an automobile muffler shop—each of which would entail an outlay (project price) of $179,000 and have a planned project life of five years. Under these circumstances there is little difficulty choosing the most desirable project. In this case, the appropriate procedure for choosing among the projects is simply to go through the *NPV* analysis for each of the five projects and select the one with the highest *NPV*. Further, if the firm had enough funds to undertake four of the five projects, management could decide which one to reject by determining which had the lowest *NPV*.

If the projects were of different size (price) but the same planned life, the *NPV* approach to ranking them could be applied, but management would have to take into account the possibility that various *combinations* of projects might generate different aggregate *NPV*s. Thus management would end up ranking various feasible *packages* of projects, rather than each project individually. Returning to the example of Clickwash, suppose that the five projects previously stated are analyzed and the following results are obtained:

Project	Price	NPV
Car wash	$179,000	$21,788
Pizzeria	100,000	15,200
Donut shop	70,000	10,150
Coin laundry	80,000	10,800
Muffler shop	181,000	18,100

All of the projects meet the general rule for acceptability, since each has an *NPV* greater than zero. Suppose that the firm has only $360,000 to allocate for new investments. Management will then have to devise a plan for *capital rationing*; that is, deciding which of the numerous projects to undertake, given the limited capital budget of $360,000. Management's objective should be to select the combination of projects that provides the greatest aggregate *NPV* for an outlay of $360,000 or less.

Our first step is to rank-order the projects by price, as in Table 13–4. This

Table 13–4   Clickwash, Inc., Project Array in Rank Order by Price

Project	Price	NPV
1. Muffler Shop	$181,000	$18,100
2. Car Wash	179,000	21,788
3. Pizzeria	100,000	15,200
4. Coin Laundry	80,000	10,800
5. Donut Shop	70,000	10,150

provides a way to determine both the minimum and maximum number of projects that can be accepted. From Table 13–4 we can see that the minimum number of projects is two (Projects 1 and 2, which exhaust the $360,000). Further, all combinations of two projects require $360,000 or less and thus could be undertaken. However, it is easy to see that no other two-project combination will yield as much as the combination 1,2. We illustrate this with a complete enumeration of the possible two-project combinations in Table 13–5. Since none of the two-project combinations has an *NPV* greater than combination 1,2 or greater than $39,888, we can drop all two-project combinations other than 1,2 from consideration.

Mathematics would indicate that there are also 10 possible three-project combinations from the list of Table 13–4, since

$$C_b^a = \frac{a!}{b!\,(a-b)!}$$

Table 13–5   Clickwash, Inc., Analysis of Possible Two-Project Investment Combinations

Project Combination	Price	NPV
1,2	$360,000	$39,888
1,3	281,000	33,300
1,4	261,000	28,900
1,5	251,000	28,250
2,3	279,000	36,988
2,4	259,000	32,588
2,5	249,000	31,938
3,4	180,000	26,000
3,5	170,000	25,350
4,5	150,000	20,950

is the formula for the number of combinations of a things taken b at a time. In Table 13–6 we enumerate all three-project combinations, showing their respective aggregate *NPV*s and prices. Note that only six three-project combinations fall within the capital budget constraint of $360,000. Of these, combination 2,3,4 has the greatest aggregate *NPV*—$47,788. This particular combination of projects has a total *NPV* that exceeds that of the best two-project combination—combination 1,2 (aggregate *NPV* of only $39,888). The conclusion is that combination 2,3,4 (the car wash, the pizzeria, and the coin laundry) should be undertaken.

In the preceding analysis, the alternative projects all had the same planned project life (five years). Obviously, firms can be faced with making accept-reject decisions on capital undertakings of unequal project life. There are a number of ways to handle the problem of unequal project life in capital budgeting analysis. One way is to set up "replacement chains," which would extend the capital budgeting analysis to the number of years divisible by the respective project lives. For example, if we are comparing two projects—one that has a life of two years and one that has a life of three years—we could use six years as our period for comparison, assuming that we would repeat the first project three times over the period and the second project twice over the period. This would be a reasonable approach to use in a case such as the evaluation of two machines, one of which is more durable than the other. Employing such an approach, management could decide whether to use a less durable machine that would be replaced every two years or a more durable one that would be replaced every three years.

We should also note that where alternative projects have rather long lives (30 to 40 years or more), it might be reasonable to compare them using some arbitrary point (say, 30 years), that is set as the "life" of each alternative. This is so because as the flow of project returns is extended into the more distant

Table 13–6   Clickwash, Inc., Analysis of Possible Three-Project Capital Budgeting Combinations

Project Combination	Price	NPV
1,2,3	$460,000	$55,088
1,2,4	440,000	50,688
1,2,5	430,000	50,038
1,3,4	361,000	44,100
1,3,5	351,000	43,450
1,4,5	331,000	39,050
2,3,4	359,000	47,788
2,3,5	349,000	47,138
2,4,5	329,000	42,738
3,4,5	250,000	36,150

future, not only does the present value of far-off receipts fall, but also the uncertainty of their occurrence increases.[12]

COST OF CAPITAL AND THE DISCOUNT RATE

The **marginal cost of capital (MCC)** is the discount rate which represents the marginal cost of investment funds to the firm. It is calculated as a weighted average of the after-tax cost of funds from each source.

As our example of Clickwash, Inc., has shown, the discount rate is an extremely important item in conducting a capital project analysis. Thus far we have not discussed how a firm goes about determining the discount rate used to calculate the present value of project cash flows. In its most basic form, this rate represents the cost to the firm of obtaining new funds to invest. It is called the **marginal cost of capital**.

Generally, firms have two principal sources of investment funds—debt and equity. In other words they can obtain new financing either by borrowing or by using owner-supplied funds (the latter can be internally generated or raised by issuing new stock). Since interest paid on borrowed funds is tax deductible, it is the after-tax cost of debt that is relevant to estimating the effect of debt on the firm's overall marginal cost of capital. Its marginal cost of capital at any point in time will then be the weighted average of its cost of debt and cost of equity.

To illustrate, let's assume that the interest rate on new bonds issued by the firm is 12 percent and that the firm's owners expect a return of 14 percent on funds that they invest. Further, assume that the best capital structure for the firm is 60 percent debt and 40 percent equity.[13] If the corporate income tax rate (T) is 34 percent, the firm's marginal cost of debt will be the interest rate on borrowed funds (*bond rate*) multiplied by the quantity $(1 - T)$, or $0.12(1 - 0.34) = 0.0792$. Its marginal cost of capital will be this rate multiplied by the proportion of debt in its capital structure *plus* the expected rate of return on equity (14 percent) multiplied by the proportion of owner-supplied funds in the capital structure. For the preceding numbers, the marginal cost of capital (k) is calculated as follows:

$$k = 0.0792(0.6) + 0.14(0.4) = 0.0475 + 0.056 = 0.1035.$$

Ordinarily, as a firm expands the amount of its new investment at any point in time, the marginal cost of capital will rise. This occurs because the firm must turn to more and more expensive means of financing as the total

---

12 Another technique that is used to evaluate projects with unequal lives is that of the equivalent annual annuity approach, which essentially assumes that the replacement chains extend to infinity for each project. For more information on comparing projects with unequal lives see Eugene F. Brigham and Louis C. Gapenski, *Financial Management*, 8th ed. (Chicago: The Dryden Press, 1997), pp. 448–451.

13 By *best* or *optimal capital structure* we mean the combination of debt and equity that will minimize the weighted average cost of capital for the firm, all other factors remaining the same. For a more thorough discussion of this issue see Brigham and Gapenski, *Financial Management*, op. cit., Chapters 8 and 12.

amount of investment funds to be raised is increased. Thus a curve relating the marginal cost of capital to the size of the capital budget will look something like the *MCC* curve in Figure 13–1. Similarly, one can construct a curve that relates the internal rates of return of available investment alternatives to the amount of investment undertaken. This is done by rank-ordering capital projects in decreasing order of internal rate of return. The *IRR* curve of Figure 13–1 reflects the decrease of the internal rate of return as less and less profitable projects are undertaken.

If we recall the rule that states that a project is acceptable as long as its internal rate of return exceeds the firm's discount rate, we can find both the equilibrium size of the capital budget and the firm's *MCC* in Figure 13–1. This occurs where the rising *MCC* curve intersects the falling *IRR* curve. Beyond Q^*, the return on additional projects is less than the firm's marginal cost of capital, so these projects will not be undertaken. Thus k^* is the firm's marginal cost of capital for the given *MCC* and *IRR* curves.

Of course, firms generally have to choose among investment alternatives that not only are risky but also vary in riskiness. Therefore it is necessary to modify capital project analyses to take explicit account of the problem of risk. In Chapter 14, several approaches to handling the problem of decision making under risk will be discussed.

Figure 13–1   Determination of the Firm's Capital Budget and Marginal Cost of Capital

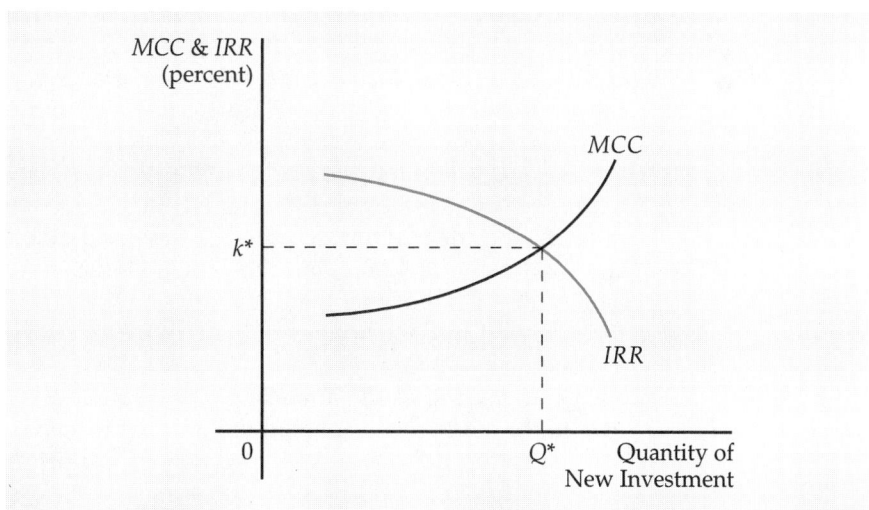

As the quantity of new investment undertaken increases, the firm's marginal cost of capital rises. However, the internal rate of return falls because less and less attractive new investments are undertaken. At k^*, where $MCC = IRR$, the optimal size capital budget and the firm's *MCC* are determined.

MANAGERIAL PERSPECTIVE

The Leverage Roller Coaster

In the world of corporate finance, the 1980s were known as the decade of the leveraged buyout (LBO)—the purchase of a company typically by management primarily through the use of borrowed money. By the end of 1989, $1.3 trillion had been spent on mergers and acquisitions and leveraged buyouts; between 1982 and 1988, nonfinancial companies doubled their debt from $.9 to $1.8 trillion. The biggest deals of the decade included Philip Morris's purchase of Kraft for $12.6 billion and Kohlberg Kravis Roberts's leveraged buyout of RJR Nabisco for $24.7 billion.

Borrowed money became a popular means of financing corporate takeovers because *if* a company is highly profitable, the after-tax cost of debt is typically cheaper than the cost of equity financing. For example, if a corporation is in the 34 percent income tax bracket and borrows money at a 12 percent annual rate of interest, the after-tax cost of debt is $(1 − .34) \times 12\% = 7.92\%$. The return that stockholders will require to keep their money invested in the firm will depend on the level of interest rates in the economy and the risk associated with a particular company's stock, together with the riskiness of the stock market as a whole. The rate of return on a long-term U.S. government bond, considered virtually risk-free in terms of default risk, has been around 9 percent on an annual basis. The added-on amount, called the market risk premium, associated with general market riskiness, has historically ranged from 4 percent to 7 percent per year. If an individual company's stock is perceived to be riskier than the market as a whole, an additional risk premium will be required as well. Thus, since it is not tax deductible, the cost of equity capital can easily exceed 15 percent on an annual basis.

Although debt may be a relatively inexpensive source of funds for a firm, it may increase the risk of bankruptcy. If a company's stock does not yield the rate of return required by the stockholders, the price of the stock will very likely fall, but this situation does not force a firm into bankruptcy. On the other hand, if a company cannot meet the required payments for its debt, holders of the firm's debt can force it to resort to a declaration of bankruptcy.

One measure of the amount of corporate leverage is the ratio of debt to the market value of equity. This ratio reached its highest value, 106 percent, in 1974, as a result of generally low prices for stocks. As a result of rapidly increasing stock prices in the 1980s, this ratio fell to 75 percent in spite of the increased amount of corporate borrowing. Moreover, this ratio is about twice as large for similar foreign companies.

Nevertheless, the increases in leverage for some U.S. companies do appear to be impacting the bankruptcy statistics: in 1984, 54 large companies defaulted on $11 billion of debt, whereas in 1987, 87 companies defaulted on $21.4 billion of debt. Some noteworthy LBOs that eventually led to Chapter 11 bankruptcy protection filings included that of Revco, Hillsborough Holdings (involving an LBO of Jim Walter Corporation), and Dart Drug Stores.

On the other hand, an increase in the percentage of a firm's financing from debt may have positive effects in addition to its lower component cost. Obligations for the repayment of debt and interest payments place pressure on firm management to control cost and carefully plan corporate strategy; the margin for error diminishes as leverage increases. A company may become more innovative and more profitable as a result. In fact, some LBOs, including Allegheny Ludlum, Metromedia, and Wilson Sporting Goods were quite profitable.

Thus, while a high amount of corporate leverage may result in a lower cost of capital and substantially higher earnings per share for stockholders, it frequently also means "betting the company." A successful future for a highly leveraged company requires astute management at the very minimum.

References: "All That Leverage Comes Home to Roost," *Business Week* (September 10, 1990), pp. 76–77; "The Best and Worst Deals of the '80s," *Business Week* (January 15, 1990), pp. 52–62; "Learning to Live With Leverage," *Business Week* (November 7, 1988), pp. 138–143; and "What Does Equity Financing Really Cost?" *Business Week* (November 7, 1988), pp. 146, 148. The risk premium attached to the stock of an individual company will increase as the percent of the value of the company financed by debt increases, all other factors remaining the same.

SUMMARY

Project Analysis and Capital Budgeting

In this chapter we have examined the application of interest and discount rate methodologies to managerial decisions concerning capital projects or new investments. We defined *capital budgeting* as the process by which a firm's managers determine how to allocate investment expenditures among alternative projects. The evaluation of individual investment undertakings, or *capital project analysis*, was shown to be a major part of the capital budgeting process.

The concept of *equivalency* was introduced to show that a present amount of money is equal in value to a discounted future amount. The present value of an amount received n years in the future, we saw, can be found by the formula

$$PV = \frac{FV_n}{(1+r)^n},$$

where r is the applicable discount rate (a target yield or rate of return on similar alternative investments). Tables of *present value factors* were introduced to simplify the mathematics of the discounting process.

Application of the preceding concepts led us to the conclusion that the present value of an anticipated stream of net receipts generated by a capital project is something less than the additive amount of such receipts. In particular the present value is the discounted value of the stream. We argued that a given capital project is *acceptable* when adjustments are made for depreciation and salvage value as long as such a *discounted stream of net cash flows is at least equal to the price of the project*. The *net present value* (*NPV*) of the project (*PV* of net receipts minus project price) would thus be equal to or greater than zero. This criterion was related to an alternative statement: namely, that the yield on the project's price, or its *internal rate of return* (*IRR*), should be at least equal to the marginal cost of capital for the firm. A simple capital project analysis involving a coin-operated car wash (Clickwash, Inc.) was introduced as an example of the steps management must go through to make an accept-or-reject decision on a new undertaking.

Later in the chapter we discussed the *capital rationing* aspect of the capital budgeting process. Here we examined the special problem of allocating a limited amount of investment dollars to various feasible combinations of capital projects. The net present value approach was extended to this setting, and a methodology for identifying the combination of projects producing the greatest aggregate *NPV* was developed. The simple methodology we employed is usable for projects with different prices and equal planned project lives but must be modified somewhat if projects with unequal lives are being analyzed.

Finally, we introduced the notion of the firm's *marginal cost of capital* and its marginal cost of capital curve. The equilibrium quantity of investment and marginal cost of capital was defined by the intersection of the firm's *MCC* curve with its *IRR* curve.

This chapter did not deal with the problem of differences in the risk associated with dissimilar capital projects. For example, in the case of our hypothetical firm, Clickwash, we treated the flows of returns from investments in endeavors (muffler shop, pizzeria, donut shop) unfamiliar to the firm as being either risk free or equal in risk to undertakings (an additional laundromat) that are thoroughly covered by management's prior experience. It is unlikely that such a view would be taken by managers in real-world capital budgeting situations. Generally, managers will attempt to take into account differences in the risks associated with alternative capital projects. In Chapter 14, we will examine some methodologies that allow for comparison of projects with unequal risk.

QUESTIONS

1. From an economist's point of view, would you characterize capital budgeting decisions as long- or short-run decisions? Why?
2. Which of the following would you include as part of the price of a capital project undertaken to expand a company's production of minicomputers? (For each item you *exclude*, give a brief explanation of why it should not be considered a part of the project price.)
   a. Production labor for minicomputers
   b. Product development costs
   c. Interest on construction loan for new building to house project
   d. Components for assembly of minicomputers
   e. Architectural fees for new building
   f. Present value of expanded working capital requirements
   g. Cost of fuel to heat new building
   h. New machine tools for manufacture of minicomputer parts
3. What is the definition of the net present value (*NPV*) of a capital project? What *NPV* rule should be followed in classifying capital projects as acceptable or unacceptable?
4. How would you define the internal rate of return of a capital project?
5. A certain capital project has anticipated net cash receipts of $180,000 per year for 10 years and a salvage value of $20,000. What is the maximum price a firm should pay for this project if the appropriate discount rate is 12 percent?
6. If a capital project has estimated net receipts of $8,000 per year and a life of 15 years with no salvage value, what would be its *NPV* if its price were $54,487 and the applicable discount rate were 9 percent?
7. What is the *IRR* (internal rate of return) of the preceding project?
8. Briefly explain how a firm's managers can use the *NPV* approach to allocate a limited capital budget among a number of acceptable capital projects, each having the same life and price.
9. Suppose a firm has a given-size capital budget. Explain how the best combination of a number of acceptable capital projects with *different* prices but the *same* lives can be determined using the *NPV* approach.

PROBLEMS

1. A project has an anticipated stream of annual net receipts of $23,500. Its life is 12 years. No salvage value is expected at the end of the 12 years.

Compute the net present value of the project if its price is $130,000 and the applicable discount rate is each of the following:

a. 6 percent

b. 9 percent

c. 12 percent

2. Gretna Corporation is about to sell some used equipment to Allied Leasing. Allied has offered the following two payment schemes:

a. $100,000 now and $250,000 at the end of five years.

b. $100,000 now, $50,000 at the end of two years, and $215,000 at the end of eight years.

If the appropriate discount rate for either transaction is 6 percent, which would be the better of the two alternatives for Gretna? Why? Show your work.

3. In the preceding problem, what would you advise Gretna's management to ask for if it desired to settle the transaction this year for a single cash payment?

4. Jayne Corporation has decided to undertake a capital project that has a life of eight years and estimated annual net inflows of $27,460. At a discount rate of 6 percent, what is the present value of the eight-year receipts stream?

5. Hamstrung, Inc., is contemplating an investment in a new food processing plant. Management's best estimate of the project's price is $620,000. The plant will have an indefinite life, but management expects to divest it at the end of 12 years at an estimated after-tax salvage value of $273,000. Annual net inflows from operations are expected to be $60,000. Is the project acceptable at a discount rate of 9 percent? Why or why not? What would happen if a discount rate of 6 percent were applied to the project?

6. Pickadilly Peppers is trying to decide whether to invest in a new cannery, to set up a wholesaling operation that would eliminate intermediaries currently selling its product, or to computerize several older plants. All three alternatives are viewed as having the same project life of 15 years. However, different project prices are applicable to each, and each has a different expected stream of annual net inflows. The firm's managers believe that a discount rate of 6 percent is appropriate for evaluating the alternatives. Data are as follows:

Project	Price	Annual Net Inflows
(a) New Cannery	$190,000	$20,000
(b) Wholesale Operation	168,000	18,000
(c) Plant Computerization	159,000	17,000

After examining the project prices, management finds it has a sufficient capital budget to undertake two of the projects. Assuming that the cash flows from the projects are independent of one another (i.e., that undertaking one of the projects will have no effect on the returns from another), which two projects should be undertaken?

7. All of the following projects have an initial cost (project price) of $87,500. Which are acceptable at a discount rate of 9 percent?

   a. Purchase of a vintage car that can be sold for $120,000 at the end of five years.

   b. Investment in a restaurant partnership that will return you a net inflow of $5,000 per year for 10 years and will provide a buyout of your share for $100,000 at the end of 10 years.

   c. Purchase of a piece of machinery that will generate net inflows of $18,000 per year for eight years and have an after-tax salvage value of $7,000 at the end of the period.

8. The following is a list of four projects that Capital Corp. must choose from for the coming year:

Project	Project Price	Annual Net Inflows	Internal Rate of Return
A	$700,000	$118,861	11%
B	670,000	109,039	10%
C	184,000	32,549	12%
D	273,000	48,305	12%

John Smart, a junior vice-president of the company, has argued that Projects A, C, and D should be accepted, since they all have higher internal rates of return than Project B and their prices sum to less than the capital budgeting constraint of $1,700,000. Jane Cranston, a consultant to the company, politely suggests that Smart is not so smart and that Projects A, B, and D should be undertaken. If the appropriate rate of discount for all four projects is 9 percent and each has a life of 10 years, who is right— Smart or Cranston? (Assume no salvage values.)

9. The managers of Zeron Corporation have determined that their firm's optimal capital structure is 40 percent debt financing and 60 percent equity. The current interest rate is 14 percent for borrowers like Zeron, and the company's shareholders expect a return on equity of 16 percent. The company's corporate income tax rate is 40 percent, and interest is a deductible expense.

   a. What is Zeron's marginal cost of capital?

   b. If Zeron is considering an investment project with a life of 10 years, an annual net flow of benefits of $470,000, a project cost of $2,500,000, and no salvage value, what advice would you give to management?

10. Lagrange Chicken Farm is considering the installation of new automated chicken feeders. The feeders are more efficient and will reduce wastage of chicken feed. The new feeders will cost $160,000 and will have an expected life of five years with a salvage value of $10,000. They are expected to result in a cost savings of $30,000 a year. The old feeders were

purchased five years ago at a cost of $65,000 and have been depreciated on a straight-line basis with an expected life of 10 years and a salvage value of $5,000. Their current market value is $40,000. The firm's marginal cost of capital is 12 percent, and its marginal tax rate is 40 percent. The firm will also be able to get an investment tax credit equal to 5 percent of the cost of the new feeders. (Do not adjust the cost basis of the feeders to reflect the tax credit when calculating depreciation.)

a. What is the initial cash outlay required for the new machine?

b. What are the annual after-tax cash flows from the new feeders in years one through four?

c. Should the company purchase the new feeders? Why or why not?

d. Suppose that the cost saving on the new feeders will be $30,000 the first year but will increase by 10 percent a year each year for the next four years. What is the *NPV* of the new feeders now?

11. Transcendental Research Laboratories is considering replacing their old supercomputer with a new terraflops computer. TRL believes that the new computer would enable the company to increase the sales revenues from research projects by $8,500,000 per year with a corresponding increase in operating costs (not including depreciation) of $500,000 per year. The new computer will cost $42,500,000 and will have an expected life of 10 years. It will be depreciated using straight-line depreciation with an assumed salvage value of $2,500,000. The old supercomputer was purchased five years ago for $22,500,000 and depreciated on a straight-line basis with an expected life of 15 years and no salvage value. The current market value of the old computer is $10,000,000 (before any tax consequences of the sale are considered). The marginal cost of capital is 12 percent, and the marginal income tax rate is 40 percent.

a. Calculate the net outlay that would be required for TRL to purchase the new computer. This net outlay figure should consider the sale proceeds from the old machine and all initial tax consequences of the sale of the old computer and the purchase of the new one.

b. Calculate the net present value of replacing the old computer with the new one. Do you recommend that TRL purchase the new computer? Why or why not?

This problem can be solved with Decision Assistant.

D1. SA Service Bureau, Inc., is a small data processing service bureau that has experienced rapid but sound growth over the past 10 years. SA Service Bureau has just signed a new major customer with such a large volume of payroll transactions that SA would be required to expand its data processing facilities. The new contract is expected to produce incremental billings (revenues) of $50,000 per year for the next five years.

Bill Lane, chief financial officer for SA, has asked the purchasing department and the data processing department to work together to determine several different approaches to meeting the new processing requirements. Helen Trask, a financial analyst working for Bill Lane, has been provided with all the information generated by the purchasing and data processing departments. The data follow:

Expansion Plan 1: This plan represents a "modular" approach to the problem of the expansion. A new minicomputer, completely compatible with the existing hardware and software, would be purchased and dedicated to processing the new client's data. Data for this plan are

Initial cash outlay:	$135,000
Estimated annual costs:	$15,000
Estimated project life:	5 years

Expansion Plan 2: This plan utilizes the existing minicomputer and upgrades it (more memory, storage capacity, etc.) to perform the increased workload. Additional personnel will also be hired to run a second shift. Data associated with this plan are

Initial cash outlay:	$75,000
Estimated annual costs:	$25,000
Estimated project life:	5 years

Use the Net Present Value, Future Value, *IRR* tool in the *Managerial Economics Decision Assistant* to complete the following.

a. Assume you are helping Helen Trask and prepare an analysis of the two projects from an economic and financial point of view (calculate the net present value and the internal rate of return). SA Service Bureau uses a 10 percent discount rate. (Do not consider data processing strategy, as this will be discussed and decided on by Mr. Lane.)

b. Using a 12 percent discount rate, recalculate the net present value for the two projects.

c. Using an 8 percent discount rate, recalculate the net present value for the two projects.

SELECTED REFERENCES

Adams, Walter, and James W. Brock. *Dangerous Pursuits: Mergers and Acquisitions in the Age of Wall Street*. New York: Random House, 1989.

"Capital Budgeting," *Financial Management* 18, no. 1 (Spring 1989), pp. 10–17.

"Divisional Hurdle Rates and the Cost of Capital," *Financial Management* 18, no. 1 (Spring 1989), pp. 18–25.

Engler, George N. *Business Financial Management*. Dallas: Business Publications, Inc., 1975, Chapters 5 and 6.

Flannery, Mark J., Joel F. Houston, and Subramanyam Venkataraman. "Financing Multiple Investment Projects," *Financial Management* 22, no. 2 (Summer 1993), pp. 161–172.

Gitman, Lawrence J. *Principles of Managerial Finance*, 7th ed. New York: Harper & Row, 1994, Chapters 8, 9, and 10.

Grant, Eugene L., and W. Grant Ireson. *Principles of Engineering Economy*, 4th ed. New York: The Ronald Press, 1964, Chapters 3–9.

Mao, James C. T. *Corporate Financial Decisions*. Palo Alto, Cal.: Pavan, 1976, Chapters 7 and 8.

Moyer, R. Charles, James R. McGuigan, and William J. Kretlow. *Contemporary Financial Management*, 6th ed. St. Paul: West, 1995, Chapters 9, 10, 11, and 12.

Neveu, Raymond R. *Fundamentals of Managerial Finance*, 3d ed. Cincinnati: South-Western, 1989, Chapters 9, 10, and 14.

Pohlman, Randolph A., Emmanuel S. Santiago, and F. Lynn Markel. "Cash Flow Estimation Practices of Large Firms." *Financial Management* 17, no. 2 (Summer 1988), pp. 71–79.

Rao, Ramesh K. S. *Fundamentals of Financial Management*. New York: Macmillan, 1989, Chapters 10 and 11.

Ross, Marc. "Capital Budgeting Practices of Twelve Large Manufacturers," *Financial Management* 15, no. 4 (Winter 1986), pp. 15–22.

Roubi, Raafat R., Richard T. Barth, and Alex Faseruk. "Capital Budgeting Use in Canada: Sophistication and Risk Attributes," *Journal of Applied Business Research* 7, no. 4 (Fall 1991), pp. 83–89.

Statman, Meir, and David Caldwell. "Applying Behavioral Finance to Capital Budgeting: Project Terminations," *Financial Management* 16, no. 4 (Winter 1987), pp. 7–15.

Taylor, George A. *Managerial and Engineering Economy*. New York: D. Van Nostrand, 1980, Chapters 7–9.

Weston, J. Fred, Scott Besley, and Eugene F. Brigham. *Essentials of Managerial Finance*, 11th ed. Chicago: The Dryden Press, 1996, Chapters 13, 15, and 16.

APPENDIX 13

Compounding and Discounting

COMPOUND INTEREST

The process of determining the amount to which a given sum will accumulate over a specified number of time periods at a stated rate of interest per period is known as *compounding*. An example of a compound interest problem would be the determination of the amount to which a $1,000 savings deposit will accumulate in 10 years if 6 percent interest is added to the account at the end of each year. We can analyze this problem as follows:

		Account Balance	Interest Earned = .06 × Previous Account Balance
Initial Deposit:		$1,000.00	
Amount at End of Year:	1	1,060.00	$ 60.00
	2	1,123.60	63.60
	3	1,191.02	67.42
	4	1,262.48	71.46
	5	1,338.23	75.75
	6	1,418.52	80.29
	7	1,503.63	85.11
	8	1,593.85	90.22
	9	1,689.48	95.63
	10	1,790.85	101.37

If the account is left untouched and each year's interest is compounded on the previous year's ending balance (including interest), the 10-year result will be $1,790.85. Each entry in the "Interest Earned" column is .06 times the previous year-end balance; for example, year 5 will yield $75.75 = .06 × $1,262.48, the ending balance for year 4.

It is easy to derive a formula for the amount that the $1,000 will accumulate to at the end of year 10. Denote FV (future value) as the account balance at the end of a given period. For the end of year 1, we have

$$FV_1 = PV(1.06),$$

where PV is the initial deposit (a present value). At the end of year 2, FV will be increased by 6 percent so that

$$FV_2 = FV_1(1.06) = [PV(1.06)](1.06) = PV(1.06)^2.$$

At the end of year 3, we will have

$$FV_3 = FV_2(1.06) = [PV(1.06)^2](1.06) = PV(1.06)^3.$$

For each period that we compound the interest, the exponent of the above expression will rise one digit. Thus for 10 years we have

$$FV_{10} = PV(1.06)^{10},$$

or

$$FV_{10} = \$1,000(1.06)^{10} = \$1,000(1.7909) = \$1,790.90,$$

a rounded-off version of the answer we obtained in the preceding calculations.

Compound interest tables are commonly used to determine future values, as stated previously. Such tables contain the values of the term $(1 + r)^n$ where r is the rate of interest and n is the number of periods the interest is compounded. In the preceding example, $(1 + r)^n = (1 + .06)^{10} = 1.7909$. The number 1.7909 is called a compound interest factor, CIF, and it is the amount to which one dollar will accumulate in 10 years with interest annually compounded at 6 percent. To find the future value of $1,000 compounded at 6 percent for 10 years, we simply multiply the CIF for a 6 percent interest rate and 10-year term (CIF 6%, 10) times the present amount ($PV = \$1,000$):

$$FV_{10} = PV(CIF\ 6\%,\ 10)$$

$$= \$1,000(1.7909) = \$1,790.90.$$

Table B–1 in the Interest Factor Tables at the end of the book provides compound interest factors. To use the table, simply look up the CIF for the number of periods that interest will be compounded and multiply the factor times the principal or present value. The result will be the future amount. Thus, if we wished to determine the future value of $25,000 compounded at 9 percent annually for 18 years, we would find

$$FV_{18} = \$25,000(CIF\ 9\%,\ 18)$$

$$= \$25,000(4.7171) = \$117,927.50.$$

PRESENT VALUE AND DISCOUNTING

The present value of some amount to be received at a specific future date is equal to the present amount that would accumulate to the future amount by the date in question at some appropriate rate of interest. The rate of interest applied to such calculations is called the *discount rate*, since the present value will be smaller than the future value by a specific percentage per year.

Discounting, then, is the reverse of compounding. To understand this, ask how much you would be willing to give for $1,790.90 received 10 years from now if you expect you can easily make 6 percent interest per year on any present amount you have on hand. From our above discussion of compounding, it is clear that $1,000 will accumulate to the sum of $1,790.90 in 10 years if 6 percent interest is compounded annually. Thus the discounted value of $1,790.90 received 10 years from now is $1,000.00, and 6 percent is the discount rate.

Alternatively, from our formula for compounding, we know

$$FV_{10} = PV(1 + r)^{10}.$$

Therefore,

$$PV = \frac{FV_{10}}{(1 + r)^{10}} = FV_{10}\left[\frac{1}{(1 + r)^{10}}\right].$$

The term in brackets is the *present value factor*, PVF. For the preceding problem, we can write

$$PV = FV_{10}(PVF\ 6\%,\ 10),$$

where, for the term in brackets, $r = .06$ and $n = 10$. This factor appears in Table B–3 in the Interest Factor Tables and its value is 0.5584. Thus, for a future value of $1,790.90, we have

$$PV = \$1,790.90(0.5584) = \$1,000.04 \approx \$1,000.$$

The slight error is due to the rounding of the present value factor, which is more accurately 0.558394.

The notion of present value is extremely important in managerial economics and finance, since project decisions generally involve evaluations of benefits or receipts that are generated at some future date or over some period of years in the future. For further discussion of this point, see the relevant sections within this chapter.

ANNUITIES

An annuity is a fixed sum received at the end of each period for some specified number of periods in the future. The *compound* or *future* value of an annuity is the amount to which such period-end payments would accumulate if each payment were left in an account at a specified rate of interest compounded annually. For example, if you are to receive an annuity of $1,000 for 10 years and you leave all of the payments in an account with 6 percent interest compounded annually, at the end of the tenth year you will have $13,180.80. The compound value is determined as follows, where A is the amount of each period-end payment and n is the number of periods:

Year 1	Year 2	Year 3	Year 10
$FV_a = A$	$A + A(1 + r)$	$A + [A + A(1 + r)](1 + r)$	$A[(1 + r)^0 + (1 + r)^1$
or	or	or	$+ \ldots + (1 + r)^9]$
$FV_a =$	$A[(1 + r)^0$	$A[(1 + r)^0 + (1 + r)^1$	
$A(1 + r)^0$	$+ (1 + r)^1]$	$+ (1 + r)^2]$	

Therefore the general formula is

$$FV_{a_n} = A[(1 + r)^0 + (1 + r)^1 + \ldots + (1 + r)^{n-1}].$$

Again, tables have been developed for the term in brackets, which is the compound value factor for an annuity, CVF_a. For 6 percent and 10 years, CVF_a 6%, 10 equals 13.181 (see Appendix B, Table B–2). For our $1,000 annuity, we can write

$$FV_{a_{10}} = \$1,000(CVF_a\ 6\%,\ 10)$$

$$= \$1,000(13.181) = \$13,181.$$

The *present value of an annuity* is the amount that, if received today, would accumulate to the same amount as an annuity received for a specified number of periods with interest compounded at the end of each period. With a 6 percent interest rate, the present value of the $1,000 per-year annuity discussed previously is $7,360.27, which is its future compound value, $13,181, discounted at the given rate of interest. From our formula for the compound value of an annuity, we derive the formula for the present value of an annuity, PV_a, in the following way.

We know that the present value of the annuity is the same as the PV of $13,181 received 10 years from now, or

$$PV_a = \frac{FV_a}{(1 + r)^n} = \frac{A[(1 + r)^0 + (1 + r)^1 + \ldots + (1 + r)^{n-1}]}{(1 + r)^n}$$

$$= A\left[\frac{(1 + r)^0}{(1 + r)^{10}} + \frac{(1 + r)^1}{(1 + r)^{10}} + \ldots + \frac{(1 + r)^9}{(1 + r)^{10}}\right]$$

$$= A\left[\frac{1}{(1 + r)^{10}} + \frac{1}{(1 + r)^9} + \ldots + \frac{1}{(1 + r)}\right].$$

The term in brackets in the last expression is the present value factor for an annuity, and its general formula is

$$PVF_a(r\%, n) = \left[\frac{1}{(1+r)^n} + \frac{1}{(1+r)^{n-1}} + \dots + \frac{1}{(1+r)} \right].$$

Table B–4 in the Interest Factor Tables contains such factors for up to 60 payment periods. For the present problem, we have PVF_a (6%, 10) = 7.3601. Therefore PV_a = \$1,000 (PVF_a 6%, 10) = \$7,360.10, which is the same (except for rounding) as the present value of \$13,181 received 10 years in the future where the discount rate is 6 percent.

In capital project analysis, the present value of an annuity approach can be used to determine the present value of project benefits or inflows when a certain fixed dollar return per period is expected to be generated by the project for a specified number of periods in the future. For a direct application of this method, review the case of Clickwash, Inc., in Chapter 13.

PROBLEMS

1. To what amount will \$20,000 left untouched in an account accumulate at the end of 13 years if 9 percent interest is added to the account at the end of each year?
2. What is the present value of a single payment of \$187,000 received eight years in the future if the discount rate is 12 percent?
3. Suppose your company puts \$2,000 per year into an annuity for you at the end of each year and you are guaranteed to receive 6 percent per annum interest on all funds left in your annuity account. How much will your account balance be at the end of six years if you are not permitted to make any withdrawals?
4. A retiring executive of Pygmalion Enterprises has offered to sell her 20-year annuity back to the company for cash. She or her survivors were to receive \$18,000 per year at year-end over the 20-year period. If the company normally applies a 6 percent discount rate to such transactions, how much will it be willing to pay for the annuity?
5. Barclay Concrete Company owes its supplier, Ace Cement, \$172,000 for trade credit extended to Barclay's account for cement purchases. Barclay has had cash flow problems and cannot pay off the account with current revenues. Ace's management has offered to convert the account to a long-term debt, extending a 10-year balloon note at 9 percent compound interest per year. If the principal and interest are not due until the end of

the 10 years, how much will Barclay have to pay Ace when the note comes due?

6. A given investment project is expected to yield $10,000 in net receipts per year for each of 10 years following its undertaking. If the discount rate is 12 percent, what is the present value of the net receipts stream?

7. You are offered a risk-free investment that you can sell at the end of three years for $14,000. You know that you can easily and safely earn 6 percent interest on your funds. What is the maximum amount you would be willing to pay for the investment?

14

RISK IN PROJECT ANALYSIS

Chapter 13 introduced some tools for the analysis of capital projects or alternative investment possibilities. Throughout that chapter we assumed that the decision maker was certain about the outcome of each project that was evaluated. Combinations of projects were also compared without considering the possibility that the success of an individual undertaking might depend on whether the undertaking was combined with a related project.

Our task in the present chapter is to analyze the problem of risk in capital projects or investments in general and to describe a workable approach to decision making under risk. We begin with discussions of the nature of risk and the application of both economic theory and statistical methods to the evaluation of risky situations. A practical example from real estate development is used to introduce the notion that risk can be viewed as the variance of a probability distribution of uncertain outcomes. The chapter moves from a two-project, single-payoff analysis toward situations that are more complex in terms of cash flows over time and interrelationships between projects. Finally, we discuss a practical approach to decision making under risk.

CERTAINTY VERSUS RISK

A situation is certain when there is absolutely no doubt as to its outcome. Most people would regard the purchase of a certificate of deposit (CD) at a bank as an investment characterized by certainty. It is clear to the decision maker who has made the purchase that a given return will be received if the CD is held to maturity. A situation is characterized as *risky* when there is some doubt regarding the occurrence of its expected outcome. Thus a person who invests in a restaurant may expect to receive a given return from the investment if the restaurant is successful in attracting enough customers and if costs of operation do not change. Clearly, this type of investment is something different from the purchase of a CD. It is a risky alternative, since the decision maker is faced with some doubt about the outcome of the decision.

Fundamentally, the analysis of risk has to do with the comparison of alternatives having outcomes that are certain with alternatives having outcomes about which there is doubt. Differences in the degree of riskiness of various alternatives can be analyzed using statistical methods. The statistical approach will be outlined after we discuss what economic theory has to say about risk and human behavior.

RISK IN ECONOMIC ANALYSIS

A **risk-averse** investor is one that given a choice between two investments with the same expected return will always prefer the less risky one.

To analyze risk from an economic point of view, we must first make a behavioral assumption about the decision maker who is confronted with alternatives of unequal risk. In project analysis the assumption usually made is that the decision maker is **risk averse**. Simply stated, this means that the decision maker will prefer a situation that promises a guaranteed or certain return of a given amount of money to a situation in which the receipt of the same amount of money is less certain. From our preceding example, a risk averter would choose to invest, say, $5,000 in a certificate of deposit rather than in a restaurant if both investments were expected to yield a net return of $2,000 at the end of five years. That is because the return from the CD is certain and the return from the restaurant is not. Whenever the amount invested, the term of the investment (the time elapsed to maturity or final receipt of returns), and the expected amount of return are identical, the risk averter will choose the certain investment over the risky investment.

A **risk seeker** is an investor that given a choice between two investments with the same expected return will prefer the riskier one.

A **risk-neutral** investor is indifferent between two investments with the same expected return, regardless of their risk.

Economic theory also recognizes the possibility that a decision maker may be a risk seeker or have a neutral attitude toward risk. If the decision maker in the previous example were a **risk seeker**, the restaurant investment would be chosen, even though the money return expected from it was the same as that for the CD. A **risk-neutral** decision maker would be indifferent between the two alternatives. It has been argued that very wealthy decision makers (individuals *or* firms) will be risk neutral when confronted with investment alternatives involving amounts of money that are small in comparison with their wealth. This would follow from the notion that the differences in the outcomes that are attributable to riskiness are virtually inconsequential to the wealthy decision maker. In the discussion that follows, we focus mainly on the risk-averse decision maker, since risk seeking is viewed as a relatively uncommon attitude in project analysis and since risk analysis is unnecessary if the decision maker is risk neutral.

RISK-RETURN INDIFFERENCE CURVES

A risk-return indifference curve shows combinations of risk and return that are equally attractive to a given investor. Figure 14–1 illustrates two risk-return indifference curves. We assume that risk is measurable and that it increases along the vertical axis. (The question of how risk can be measured is taken up in a later section.) For the moment we will use the numbers 1, 2, 3, and 4 to indicate increasing levels of risk. The horizontal axis of the diagram shows money returns expected by the investor. A single risk-return indifference curve traces out combinations of risk and expected money return that will make the investor equally happy. Consider curve I_5 in Figure 14–1, for example. It indicates that the investor would be indifferent between combination A (which consists of zero risk and a return of $1,000) and combination B

Figure 14–1   The Risk-Return Indifference Curve Concept

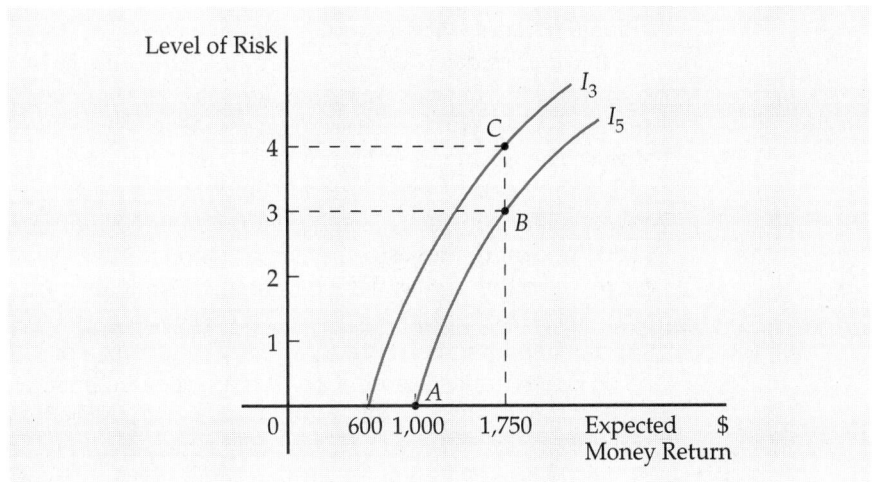

Risk-return indifference curve I_3 is less desirable to the investor than I_5, since each combination of risk and return on I_3 is equal to a certain return of only $600, which is much less than the certain return of $1,000 associated with I_5 combinations.

(which consists of a risky return of $1,750). The risk-return indifference curve slopes upward to the right because the risk-averse investor will be indifferent toward higher risk only if he or she expects a greater return to be associated with it. The curvature of the indifference curve reflects one further assumption—that as risk increases, progressively larger increments in expected return will be required to offset given increments in risk (in order to keep the investor equally happy).

In Figure 14–1, combinations of risk and return that lie on risk-return indifference curve I_3 are less satisfying to the investor than those that lie on I_5. Why? Clearly, it is because the combinations of risk and return on I_3 all involve either higher risk for any given return or a lower return for any given level of risk. For example, point C, which corresponds to a return of $1,750, is less satisfying to the investor than is point B. This is because the return associated with C is the same as with B, but B is on a lower level of risk.

In general, for a risk-return indifference curve diagram such as Figure 14–1, we view the quadrant as being filled with indifference curves such as I_5 and I_3, all of which are nonintersecting. Return decreases and risk increases as we move toward the northwest area of the quadrant, so that less desirable indifference curves lie to the northwest of any given point (risk-return combination), while more desirable indifference curves lie to the southeast. The risk-return indifference curve is a concept similar to the equal-output isoquants employed in production analysis (Chapter 5). However, risk-return indifference curves are concave toward the X or "return" axis, since at the margin the decision maker's willingness to accept additional risk for an additional dollar's worth of return diminishes.

If we consider a whole family of risk-return indifference curves for a given investment decision maker, we can conclude that for any amount of expected money return, the risk averter will be less happy the greater the level of risk. This is shown in Figure 14–2. Note that the investor regards point A on I_5 as a risk-return combination equivalent to a certain return of $1,000. If, however, we consider a combination involving more risk than level 4 for a $1,300 return, the investor is seen to be on a lower risk-return indifference curve (the *certain return*, which is viewed as equally desirable to the risky return, *falls*). Thus points B, C, and D represent successively less desirable risk-return combinations for an expected money return of $1,300.

If we retain the assumption of risk aversion, then, we can conclude that the economic nature of risk is that its presence *lessens the desirability* of a given undertaking or investment project. Further, the more risky a given undertaking, the less desirable it will be in comparison to other alternatives having the same expected money outcome. At this point, however, we cannot go further until we have a way to measure risk or to differentiate among risky undertakings those that are more risky and those that are less so. It is to this matter that we now turn.

Figure 14–2   A Family of Risk-Return Indifference Curves

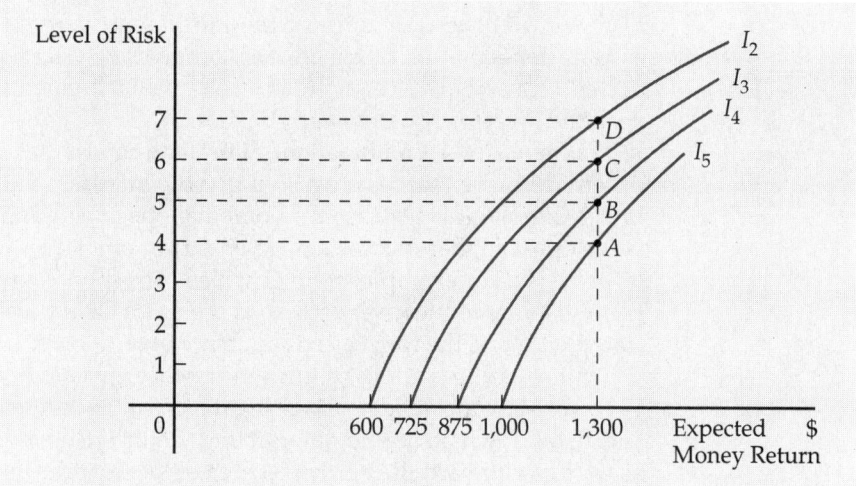

Assuming the investor is risk averse, higher risk levels associated with a given expected return yield less and less satisfaction. Thus, for an expected return of $1,300, the investor's satisfaction decreases progressively from point A through points B, C, and D.

PROBABILITY AND UNCERTAINTY

To measure risk in a meaningful way, we must apply the tools of statistics known as *probability analysis*. In probability analysis the term *event* is used to designate an outcome. The probability of a particular event is a numerical value measuring the uncertainty that the event will occur. More specifically it is the proportion of times under identical circumstances that the event can be expected to occur, or

$$P(E) = \frac{\text{number of times event occurs}}{\text{number of times situation is repeated}}.$$

If an event is certain to occur, its probability is one. If it can never occur, its probability is zero. An event's probability can be viewed as the *odds* that the event will occur or the percentage of times it will take place when a given set of circumstances is repeated many times. Running an experiment where a situation is repeated many times is a way to determine empirically the probability of a specific event. However, it is also possible to determine an event's probability deductively if enough information is available. For this, we need a few more definitions.

Each event in a listing of all the possible outcomes of a given situation is called an *elementary event*. For example, in picking a card from a deck of 52 cards, each card is an elementary event. A *composite event* consists of a number of elementary events, and an *event set* consists of all the elementary events that satisfy a particular outcome. Thus we can restate our formula for the probability of an event as

$$P(E) = \frac{\text{number of elementary events in event set}}{\text{number of equally likely elementary events}}.$$

From the preceding, we can see that the probability of picking a two of spades from a deck of 52 cards is 1/52, but the probability of picking a deuce is 4/52, since the event set includes the four elementary events: two of spades, two of hearts, two of diamonds, and two of clubs. For a deck of 52 cards, the sum of the probabilities of all the cards (elementary events) is one (there are 52 elementary events, each having a probability of 1/52). In general, any time a listing of all possible events includes every conceivable outcome—one of which *must* occur—the sum of the probabilities of all the elementary events will be one.

There are many situations in which probabilities can be ascertained empirically or through experimentation. The card-picking examples are cases in point. For the composite event "pick a deuce," a deck of cards can be shuffled and a card picked. This can be repeated a very large number of times, and the more the experiment is run, the closer the ratio of deuces picked to the total number of cards picked will approach 4/52. It is also true that in many cases probabilities can be ascertained logically. Again, card picking suffices as an example. Since we know there are 52 possible elementary events, four of which constitute the event set "pick a deuce," the odds (or probability) of picking a deuce equal 4/52.

When the probability of events in an uncertain situation cannot be ascertained either empirically or logically, we enter the realm of *subjective probability*. A subjective probability is simply a probability value *assigned* to an event by an investigator. It is a judgmental estimate rather than strictly an empirical one. Subjective probability is used in the analysis of investment projects, since decision makers frequently must rely on expert opinion (their own personal judgment, perhaps) regarding the likelihood of any particular event. For example, the decision maker may be able to estimate how successful in terms of dollar return a project will be, *given* various rates of growth in personal income for a particular region or state; but there may be a great deal of uncertainty about the occurrence of each possible rate of growth in income. An approach that employs the subjective probabilities of the possible rates of growth in income may be used to determine both a weighted average outcome for the project and a measure of its riskiness. In the following section, we provide an example of the probability approach to project analysis under risk.

APPLICATION OF PROBABILITY ANALYSIS TO RISK

Statistical analysis of risk becomes quite complicated when the time horizon for a payoff or return from an investment is long or when alternatives consisting of multiple-project combinations are being considered. However, we can gain considerable insight into the application of probability to risk situations from a simple example involving a choice between two investments—each of which has a single cash payoff that is received one year in the future. To illustrate, we choose an example from real estate investment.

Suppose the Texland Corporation has obtained similar tracts of land in Houston and Dallas at identical cost and is considering subdivision and marketing alternatives for next year. Management has information indicating that the cost of subdividing and marketing the land will be the same in each city and that under even the most pessimistic assumptions, either project will yield a positive net present value. However, the firm's financial condition and resource base are such that it cannot develop both tracts in the coming year.

From past experience Texland's managers are confident that the returns from either project will depend on the rate of growth of personal income in Texas during the year. Their estimates of the cash inflow generated by each alternative appear in Table 14–1. Texland's managers do not believe that the rate of income growth in the state will fall below 6 percent or exceed 14 percent, but they are uncertain about the probabilities of occurrence of various

Table 14–1   Cash Flow Estimates for Two Land Development Projects

Percentage Rate of Growth in State Personal Income	Estimated Cash Inflow	
	Dallas Project ($1,000)	Houston Project ($1,000)
6	$ 600	$770
8	700	790
10	800	800
12	900	810
14	1,000	830

growth rates within this range. As the table shows, the potentially higher payoffs associated with the Dallas project are attractive, but it is clear from the payoff estimates that the Dallas alternative will yield less than the Houston alternative if the rate of growth of personal income is relatively low.

To help analyze the growth rate problem, Texland has employed an economist from Austin Commerce College who has provided the following subjective probabilities for the growth rates in Table 14–1.

Rate of Growth in State Personal Income	Probability of Occurrence
6%	0.15
8%	0.20
10%	0.30
12%	0.20
14%	0.15

The **expected value** of an investment is found by multiplying each possible outcome by the probability that it will occur, then summing these values.

Texland's management then used the preceding probabilities to construct the payoff tables shown in Table 14–2. For each project an **expected value** is calculated. The expected value is a weighted average of the possible outcomes, and it is obtained by multiplying each outcome by the probability associated with it and then summing the individual outcome values (sum of the fourth column of each payoff table). In effect, each payoff is associated with an event (rate of growth in personal income) that has a subjective probability. Weighting the payoffs by their respective associated probabilities and summing the weighted values, one obtains the expected value of the project. It is this kind of weighted average that appears on the "return" axis of the indifference curve diagrams in Figures 14–1 and 14–2.

As Table 14–2 shows, Texland found that the expected values of the two alternatives were exactly the same. We will see, however, that this does not mean there is no basis for choosing one project over the other. To complete

Table 14–2   Payoff Tables for Land Development Projects

(a) Dallas Project

Percentage Rate of Growth in State Personal Income (Event)	Subjective Probability (P_i)	Cash Flow Payoff (X_i) ($1,000)	X_iP_i ($1,000)
6	0.15	$ 600	$ 90
8	0.20	700	140
10	0.30	800	240
12	0.20	900	180
14	0.15	1,000	150
		$\bar{X}$ = Expected Value = ΣX_iP_i =	$800

(b) Houston Project

Percentage Rate of Growth in State Personal Income (Event)	Subjective Probability (P_i)	Cash Flow Payoff (X_i) ($1,000)	X_iP_i ($1,000)
6	0.15	$ 770	$115.5
8	0.20	790	158.0
10	0.30	800	240.0
12	0.20	810	162.0
14	0.15	830	124.5
		$\bar{X}$ = Expected Value = ΣX_iP_i =	$800.0

the analysis, we must consider the risk of each alternative; and, in fact, the information of Table 14–2 does provide a means for quantifying risk and differentiating between the two projects.

An acceptable way to measure risk is to examine the *probability distribution* of the possible outcomes of a given situation. A probability distribution may be represented by a rod graph relating the probability of each growth rate (event) to its outcome in terms of cash inflow. For the data of Table 14–2, probability distributions are constructed in Figure 14–3. In each panel of Figure 14–3, the payoffs associated with each possible growth rate appear on the horizontal axis, and the probability value associated with each payoff appears on the vertical axis.

The probability distributions of Figure 14–3 are called *discrete* probability distributions because they do not include information on the probabilities associated with payoffs that might occur at growth rates in between those of Table 14–2. (For example, we do not have any information on the probability of a growth rate between 8 and 10 percent.) A *continuous* probability distribution would be represented by a line rather than a bar graph and would contain information on the probability values associated with a wide range of

Figure 14–3   Rod Graphs of Probability Distributions of Returns from
Two Land Development Alternatives

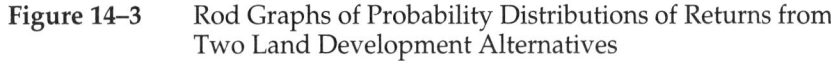

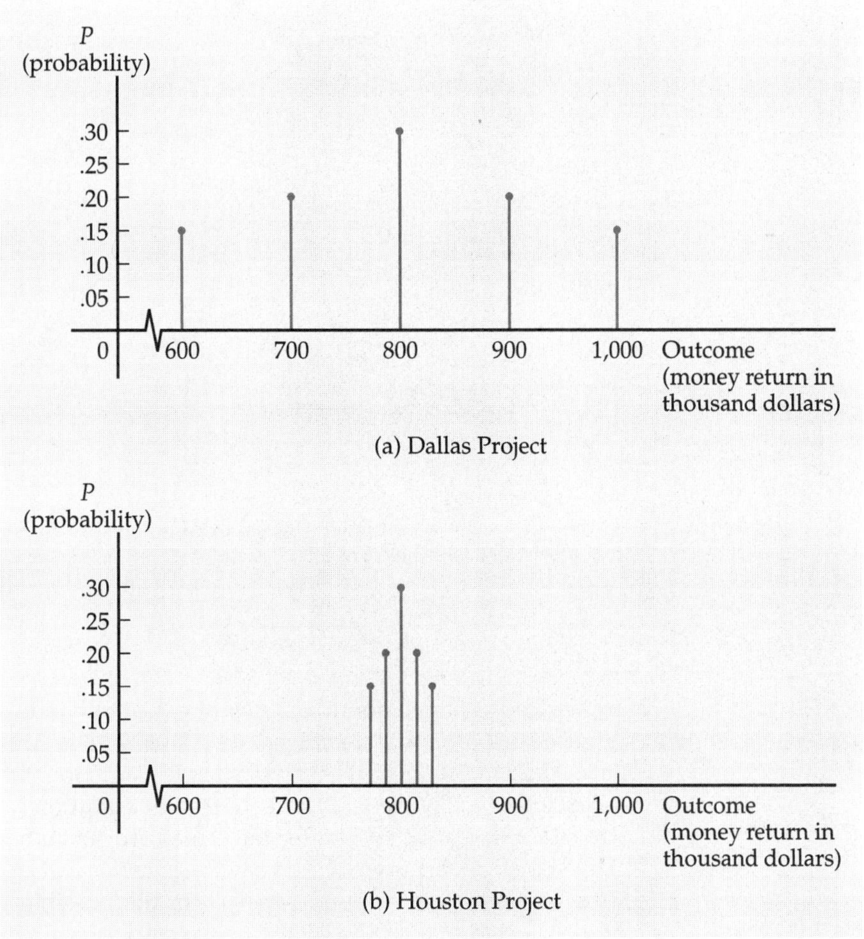

P
(probability)

.30
.25
.20
.15
.10
.05

0   600   700   800   900   1,000   Outcome
(money return in
thousand dollars)

(a) Dallas Project

P
(probability)

.30
.25
.20
.15
.10
.05

0   600   700   800   900   1,000   Outcome
(money return in
thousand dollars)

(b) Houston Project

The rod graphs above show that the Dallas project is riskier than the Houston project, since the expected money outcomes associated with the Dallas project display greater dispersion.

possible payoffs. It might look like Figure 14–4. If we added up all of the probability values associated with the outcomes in Figure 14–4 (i.e., in calculus terms, if we "integrated the area under the probability distribution"), we would get a value of one for their *cumulative* probability. In other words, we would say that it is certain that one of the outcomes will occur. Similarly, we could ascertain the probability of obtaining a result between *a* and *b* by integrating the area under the curve between these two values. A particularly useful continuous probability distribution is the *normal* distribution, which is

Figure 14–4   A Continuous Probability Distribution

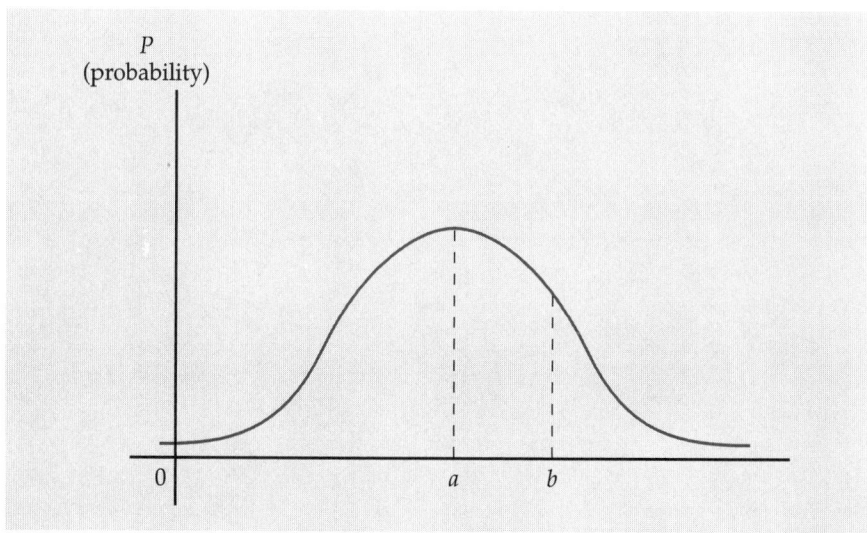

A continuous probability distribution that is normal will plot as a bell-shaped curve. The cumulative probability of obtaining a result between *a* and *b* above is equal to the area under the curve between *a* and *b*.

The **variance** of the possible returns of a project is found by subtracting the expected value of the project from each possible outcome, squaring each of these values, multiplying each squared deviation by the probability of each respective outcome, and summing the resulting products. The variance, a measure of the dispersion of possible project outcomes, is one indicator of risk.

symmetrically shaped about its *mean* or expected value (the value at point *a* in Figure 14–4). We will use such a distribution here to help interpret the results of the risk analysis of Texland's Dallas and Houston projects.

Returning to Figure 14–3, note that the distribution of outcomes along the horizontal axis is much wider for the Dallas project than for the Houston project. In statistical terms we would say that the *range* of the Dallas outcomes is greater or that there is more *dispersion* of the possible outcomes about the mean (expected) value, $800,000. The **variance** of a given set of data is a statistic that measures the dispersion about the mean of the set of probable outcomes or payoffs. It is calculated by squaring the difference between each probable outcome and the weighted average (mean or expected value) of the outcomes, multiplying each such squared value by its associated probability, and summing these multiplied values. In other words we have

$$\text{variance} = \sigma^2 = \sum_{i=1}^{n} \left(X_i - \overline{X} \right)^2 P_i ,$$

where σ^2, a standard notation for variance, is read "sigma squared"; the X_i are the outcomes; $\overline{X}$ is the expected value; and the P_i are the respective probabilities associated with the outcomes.

In project analysis the variance of the distribution of probable returns (payoffs or cash inflows) is often employed as a measure of risk. Generally, the higher the variance of the distribution, the greater the risk. In Table 14–3, variance calculations are shown for the Dallas and Houston tract development projects of Texland Corporation. The variance is frequently an extremely large number, since it expresses dispersion in terms of original units (dollars, in this case) squared. For the Dallas project, we obtain a variance of $16,000,000,000, whereas the variance for Houston is only $310,000,000.

It is sometimes quite useful to calculate the square root of the variance,

$$\sqrt{\sigma^2} = \sigma = \sqrt{\sum_{i=1}^{n}\left(X_i - \overline{X}\right)^2 P_i},$$

The **standard deviation**, another measure of risk, is the square root of the variance.

which is called the **standard deviation** of the probable outcomes (payoffs). The standard deviation is also used as a measure of risk. For the Dallas project, $\sigma = \$126{,}490$; whereas for the Houston project, it is $17,610.

Whether the variance or the standard deviation is used as a measure of

Table 14–3   Variance Calculations for Two Land Development Projects

(a) Dallas Project

Percentage Rate of Growth in State Personal Income	P_i	$(X_i - \overline{X})$ ($1,000)	$(X_i - \overline{X})^2$ ($1,000)	$(X_i - \overline{X})^2 P_i$ ($1,000)
6	0.15	$–200	$40,000,000	$ 6,000,000
8	0.20	–100	10,000,000	2,000,000
10	0.30	0	0	0
12	0.20	100	10,000,000	2,000,000
14	0.15	200	40,000,000	6,000,000

Variance = σ^2 = $16,000,000
Standard Deviation = σ = $126,490

(b) Houston Project

Percentage Rate of Growth in State Personal Income	P_i	$(X_i - \overline{X})$ ($1,000)	$(X_i - \overline{X})^2$ ($1,000)	$(X_i - \overline{X})^2 P_i$ ($1,000)
6	0.15	$– 30	$ 900,000	$ 135,000
8	0.20	– 10	100,000	20,000
10	0.30	0	0	0
12	0.20	10	100,000	20,000
14	0.15	30	900,000	135,000

Variance = σ^2 = $ 310,000
Standard Deviation = σ = $17,610

MANAGERIAL PERSPECTIVE

A Gamble on Tigers, Dolphins, and a Volcano

What do tigers, dolphins, a volcano, and beds have in common? They are all part of the Mirage casino and hotel in Las Vegas. The hotel, opened several years ago, is the brainchild of Stephen Wynn and had an initial estimated cost of from $620 million to over $700 million. Its features include a five-story volcano that erupts with gray smoke every five minutes, a lobby displaying white tigers behind a glass wall and several sharks in a 20,000-gallon aquarium, dolphins in a tank near the pool, and a $37 million golf course containing 10,000 transplanted pine trees. Moreover, the annual hotel operating costs included such things as $11.5 million for magicians.

At the time it opened, the Mirage was the largest hotel in Las Vegas, with 3,056 rooms. Industry analysts estimated then that the Mirage would have to generate $1 million per day to break even; Wynn himself put the daily break-even revenue at $800,000. Of all the casino-hotels in Las Vegas, only Caesar's Palace did that kind of volume.

Mr. Wynn owns 31 percent of the equity in Golden Nugget, Incorporated. Once construction began on the Mirage, Golden Nugget's debt increased to over $900 million, so that equity was only 12 percent of the firm's capital. In 1988, Golden Nugget lost $7.6 million, and in the first nine months of 1989 it lost $11.4 million. Its revenues decreased 21 percent in 1991, when the Mirage was in operation.

Nevertheless, in its first two years of operation, the Mirage turned out to be a profitable gamble, and Wynn undertook the building of another $430 million hotel, Treasure Island, that opened in late 1993. Treasure Island has a large water-filled canal where mock pirate ships simulate gun battles and stuntmen leap into the air as their ships are apparently destroyed. Still, Wynn estimated that the room rates would have to be $50 or less to attract the volume of customers necessary to make it profitable. The price of rooms at the Mirage was nearly double that figure.

Moreover, the competition in the hotel industry is heating up in Las Vegas. During Fall 1993, Circus Circus Enterprises opened a new $390 million luxury casino-hotel, the Luxor, shaped like a pyramid. MGM Grand also opened a new billion-dollar 5,000-room casino-hotel that includes a 33-acre theme park. Some industry analysts were predicting a substantial excess-capacity problem for the industry in the future, and five older casino-hotels had recently gone bankrupt. While the MGM Grand reportedly lost $1.1 million in the first half of 1995, a strategy of cost reduction, better targeted marketing, and a remodeled casino resulted in an operating profit of $97.8 million in the first half of 1996. Not content with the situation, the company is spending another $250 million to upgrade the hotel as well as participating in building a $460 million casino nearby called New York, New York. In the meantime, Circus Circus made plans to expand the Luxor, whose profits had suffered as the MGM Grand and the Mirage's Treasure Island hotels opened. The company also paid $153 million for a 120-acre plot of land next to the Luxor on which it plans to build as many as four more casinos.

In April 1996, Grand Casinos opened the Las Vegas Stratosphere Tower, Hotel, and Casino, a $550 million complex containing the highest free-standing observation tower in America. However, by November of that year, Stratosphere Corp. was seeking to restructure its debts and even considering a bankruptcy filing. In June, the Monte Carlo Resort and Casino, a $344 million joint venture of Mirage Resorts and Circus Circus, had increased the competition in Las Vegas by adding another 3,000 hotel rooms. An even bigger project, a $1.3 billion resort called the Bellagio, is scheduled to open in 1998.

Still, MGM Grand's chief executive argued that since only 15 percent of Americans had ever been to Las Vegas, there was a lot of potential to expand the market. Whether this forecast is accurate remains to be determined.

References: "Roller-Coaster Ride of Stratosphere Corp. Is a Tale of Las Vegas," *The Wall Street Journal*, October 29, 1996, pp. A1, A6; "MGM's Grand Ambition," *Business Week* (September 23, 1996), pp. 87, 90; "Newest Mega-Resort Set for Vegas Debut," the *San Antonio Express-News*, June 15, 1996, p. 1E; "At Circus Circus, It's Build, Build, Build," *Business Week* (September 25, 1995), pp. 84–85; "Will Too Many Players Spoil the Game?" *Business Week* (October 18, 1993), pp. 80–82; "Wynn's World: White Tigers, Blackjack, and a Midas Touch," *Business Week* (March 30, 1992), pp. 74–75; and "Tigers, A Volcano, Dolphins, and Steve Wynn," *Business Week* (November 20, 1989), pp. 70-71.

risk, it is clear from the preceding calculations that the Dallas project is riskier than the Houston project, since both statistics are higher for Dallas than for Houston. Using the standard deviation as a risk measure, we can carry the analysis one step further if we are willing to assume that the distribution of probable returns in each case is normal or forms a symmetrical, bell-shaped curve (such as that in Figure 14–4) around the expected value. This assumption may be acceptable if the outcomes constitute values of a continuous random variable, which means a variable that is measured on a continuous scale (dollars, heights, weights, etc.), and the outcomes have values determined by chance only after the experiment (project) is over.

Statistics tells us that for a normal distribution, approximately 68 percent of the distribution (its *area*) lies within plus or minus *one* standard deviation about the mean, and that approximately 95 percent of the distribution lies within *two* standard deviations of the mean. In the case of the Dallas project, this would mean that we expect only a 5 percent probability that we would get a cash inflow outside the range

$$\$800,000 \pm 2(\$126,490),$$

or that there is a 95 percent probability of a cash inflow between \$547,020 and \$1,052,980. However, with the Houston project, our 95 percent probability is between \$764,780 and \$835,220. If Texland's managers are risk averters, they will choose the Houston project.

Now we can return to the concept of risk-return indifference curves to complete our analysis of the Texland decision. Figure 14–5 is very similar to Figure 14–1. As we noted in our earlier discussion, the assumption of a risk-averse decision maker assures a preference structure in which less desirable combinations of risk and expected money return lie on indifference curves that are, in general, successively further toward the northwest area of the indifference curve map. Alternatively, indifference curves representing less and less desirable combinations of risk and return will have successively lower and lower intercepts on the expected-money-return axis (the intercept being the risk-free equivalent dollar value of the risky returns that lie on a given indifference curve).

As Figure 14–5 shows, the risk-return combination for the Dallas project must correspond to a lower risk-free return and lie on a less desirable indif-

Figure 14–5   Risk-Return Combinations for Two Land Development Projects

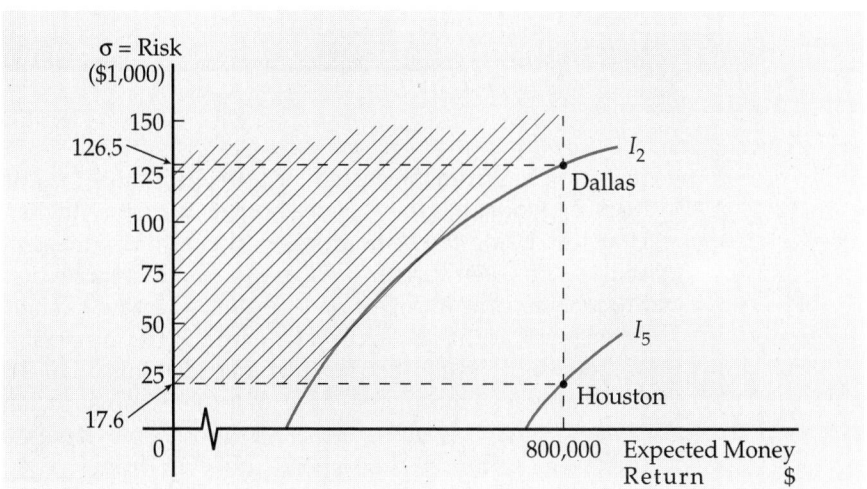

Risk-return indifference curves for the Dallas and Houston land development projects show that the Dallas project is less desirable, since both projects have an expected return of \$800,000 and the standard deviation of the return is much higher for Dallas.

ference curve than the Houston combination, since both have the same expected value and the Dallas combination has higher risk (a larger σ). Again,
we must conclude that if Texland's managers are risk averters, they will
choose the Houston project.

One final observation can be made about Figure 14–5 as it applies to decisions involving more than two projects. Even if we do not know the shape
of I_5, the Houston project will be preferred over all other projects that have
any of the following: (1) a lower expected money return but an identical σ; (2)
a higher σ but an identical expected money return; or (3) a lower expected
money return *and* a higher σ. Thus graphically we can say that the Houston
project is preferred not only to the Dallas project but also to any project that
falls in the shaded area of the indifference curve diagram. In more advanced
analysis of decision making under risk, this notion (which is called *dominance*) provides a means of defining an efficient set of risk-return alternatives.

An **efficient portfolio** is a project or a combination of projects or investments that have the lowest risk for a given rate of return. In other words, there
is no other investment that has the same expected return but lower risk. A
risk-averse investor would prefer such a portfolio to any other portfolio with
the same expected return and higher risk. The **efficient set** is the set of all efficient portfolios.

Thus many portfolios (and projects) can be systematically rejected because they lie outside the efficient set. In Figure 14–6 we provide an example.
Here, points *A*, *D*, and *E* dominate points *B*, *C*, and *F*, respectively. Therefore
points *B*, *C*, and *F* lie outside the efficient set. However, among points *A*, *D*,

> An **efficient portfolio** is a project or a combination of investments that will involve the least risk for a given rate of return.
>
> The **efficient set** is the set of all efficient portfolios.

Figure 14–6   The Concept of Dominance in Risk Analysis

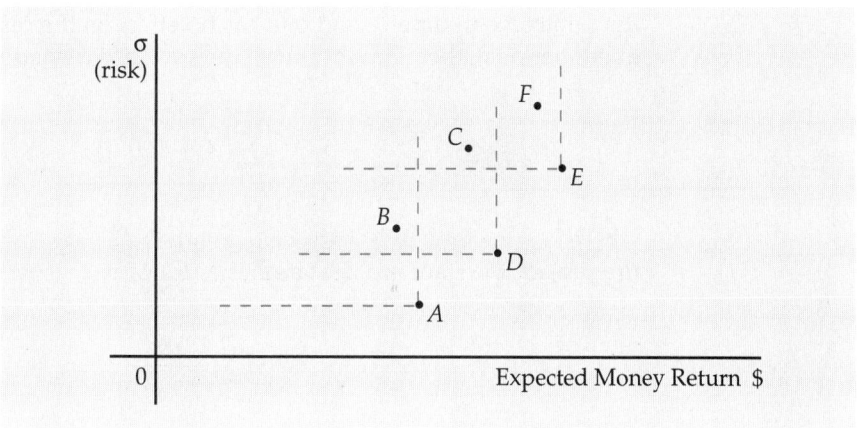

A risk-return combination will dominate other combinations of either equal risk and lower return *or* greater risk and the same return. Thus, combination *A* dominates *B*, combination *D* dominates *B* and *C*, and combination *E* dominates *C* and *F*. Among combinations *A*, *D*, and *E*, none
dominates.

and E, none clearly dominates either of the others. The optimal portfolio (or project) among those in the efficient set is determined for each investor by his or her preferences regarding risk and expected return.

EVALUATING RISKY STREAMS OF RECEIPTS

Unlike the preceding Texland example, many project analyses deal with more than one expected return per project. Where an individual project has a number of periodic returns, such as a flow of annual receipts over a number of years, there will be a probability distribution of payoffs for each year. In such cases the standard deviation of the entire stream of discounted receipts must be calculated in order to measure the project's risk.

The procedure for determining the expected present value of a stream of risky returns is summarized in the following formula:

$$E(PV) = \sum_{t=1}^{n} \frac{\overline{X}_t}{(1+r)^t},$$

where

$$\overline{X}_t = \text{expected value of net receipts in period } t,$$
$$r = \text{the appropriate discount rate, and}$$
$$t = \text{the time period.}$$

The formula simply says to sum up the discounted expected values of the future net cash inflows.

If the future cash flows are independent of one another (that is, if the cash flow outcome in time period one has no effect on the cash inflows in subsequent periods), then for *each period*, the standard deviation is:

$$\sigma_t = \sqrt{\sum_{i=1}^{m} \left(X_{it} - \overline{X}_t\right)^2 P_i},$$

where P_i is the probability associated with the ith net cash inflow. For the entire project, the standard deviation is as follows:

$$\sigma = \sqrt{\sum_{t=1}^{n} \frac{\sigma_t^2}{(1+r)^{2t}}}.$$

Although derivation of the preceding three formulas is beyond the scope of this text, some of the selected references at the end of this chapter provide more detail for the interested student.

If cash flows are *interdependent* (in other words, if the net cash flow in one time period has some relationship to that in another time period), the calculation of expected value and variance for the stream of receipts becomes more complicated. In such a case (and many projects will necessarily fit this case), the *covariances* of the probable returns must also be taken into account. Defined briefly, the covariance of one probable return with respect to another is a measure that reflects the degree to which the first return is correlated with the second. To the extent that two returns are positively correlated, when a high value occurs for the first, a high value will also occur for the second. In general, other things equal, the greater the degree of correlation between a project's cash flows, the greater the standard deviation of the expected present value of the project. Thus it is important to recognize the existence of interdependence between individual period cash flows in the stream of receipts.

PROBABILITY APPROACH TO MULTIPLE PROJECT ALTERNATIVES

The analysis of our previous chapter culminated with a discussion of methodologies for selecting the optimal combination of projects under conditions of certainty. As we have indicated, the probability approach to risky investment alternatives can be extended to encompass the evaluation of alternative combinations (*portfolios*) of projects. For each portfolio, such a procedure involves an analysis of the degree of interdependence of cash flows over time. Thus the analyst of alternative portfolios would have to calculate the expected present value or expected return of each portfolio, taking into account not only the interdependence of cash flows in each single project but also the interdependence of cash flows *between* projects in each alternative combination of projects. Once the expected present value of each portfolio is determined and its variance or standard deviation is calculated, the dominance approach described earlier can be applied to define the efficient set of portfolios. Again, the optimal portfolio will be determined by the investor's preferences regarding risk and expected return.

The portfolio approach to multiple-project alternatives is usually modified when it is applied to capital budgeting situations for a variety of reasons. First, the approach was developed for application to the question of analyzing portfolios of securities, primarily common stock.[1] It is possible to divide

---

1 One interesting result obtained from portfolio theory supports the old adage about not putting all of one's eggs in the same basket. In particular it can be shown that adding new projects to a portfolio can reduce its overall risk (standard deviation) as long as the projects are not perfectly positively correlated. In the literature of finance, such risk reduction through diversification of investments is known as the *portfolio effect*.

a common stock portfolio into almost any combination of available stocks. However, the share of a total capital budget allocated to a given physical capital undertaking often is not divisible. Such projects must be either accepted or rejected in total, and the possibility of undertaking, say, one-half of one project and one-fourth of two others just does not exist. In addition the covariances and correlation coefficients that are needed to analyze interdependent projects are much more difficult to obtain for capital projects than for common stocks. Finally, there is the problem of identifying the risk-return preferences of a firm. For any given firm, management may consist of a group of decision makers, each group member having his or her own preference set (set of risk-return indifference curves); furthermore, the preferences of managers, either singly or in the aggregate, may not reflect the wishes of the owners (shareholders) of the firm.

ACCEPTABLE SHORTCUTS TO RISK ANALYSIS

Although the portfolio approach outlined in the preceding section is generally viewed as a theoretically correct approach to risk evaluation and project selection problems, some shorter methodologies that directly adjust present values for perceived differences in project riskiness are widely used. These methodologies are (1) the risk-adjusted discount rate approach and (2) the certainty equivalent approach.

Risk-Adjusted Discount Rate

The risk-adjusted discount rate approach simply alters the standard present value formula by substituting a higher discount rate, k, for the risk-free rate, r, that was employed in Chapter 13. Thus we would have

$$k = r + \rho,$$

where ρ (the Greek letter *rho*) is called the *risk premium*. The present value formula would then be

$$PV \mid k = \sum_{t=1}^{n} \frac{\overline{X}_t}{(1 + k)^t}.$$

Since k is larger than r, the effect of the risk-adjusted discount rate is to lower the value of PV for a risky future return. The higher the risk premium, the more risky the project and the lower the risk-adjusted PV for each future cash inflow.

For two projects of equal size (cost), equal lives, and approximately equal subjective risk, the selection procedure is simply to choose the one with the higher risk-adjusted net present value. If the risks of the two projects differ, then it is appropriate to apply a higher discount rate to the project judged to be riskier. The selection of the discount rate may be a subjective matter, a point that will be discussed further in the following section.

If we were to apply the preceding methodology to the Texland example, management would evaluate the Dallas project using a higher discount rate than the one applied to the Houston project. Suppose that instead of one-year lives, the land development alternatives were expected to have four-year net cash inflows of $200,000 per year and that each alternative had a price of $550,000. If management chose to apply a 12 percent discount rate to the Dallas project and a 9 percent rate to the Houston project, the result would be as follows:

Dallas Project

$NPV \mid k_D = \$200,000\ (PVF_a\ 12\%,\ 4) - \$550,000 = \$57,460$

and

Houston Project

$NPV \mid k_H = \$200,000\ (PVF_a\ 9\%,\ 4) - \$550,000 = \$97,940.$

Clearly, the Houston project would be the best choice.

Certainty Equivalent Approach

Remaining for the moment with the question of evaluating two mutually exclusive projects with uncertain cash flows, we turn now to the certainty equivalent approach. This approach relates closely to the risk-return indifference curve trade-off we discussed in connection with the portfolio approach. It adjusts the present value of an uncertain return through the numerator of the present value formula as follows:

$$PV \mid \alpha_t = \sum_{t=1}^{n} \frac{\alpha_t \overline{X}_t}{(1+r)^t},$$

where α_t is a "certainty equivalent adjustment factor" and r is the risk-free discount rate. For all but completely certain returns, $0 < \alpha_t < 1$. Thus $\alpha_t = 1$ would indicate that the tth return (X_t) was certain, whereas $\alpha_t = 0$ would indicate that the probability of the tth return was zero. Thus very risky projects will have low α_ts whereas less risky ones will have α_ts closer to one.

The certainty equivalent adjustment factor, in theory, is derived from the decision maker's risk-return preferences, as indicated in a set of risk-return indifference curves. In Figure 14–7 we illustrate two risk-return indifference curves and the expected money returns and risk levels (α_i) of two projects,

Figure 14–7   Relation of Risk-Return Indifference Curves to Certainty
                        Equivalent Adjustment Factor

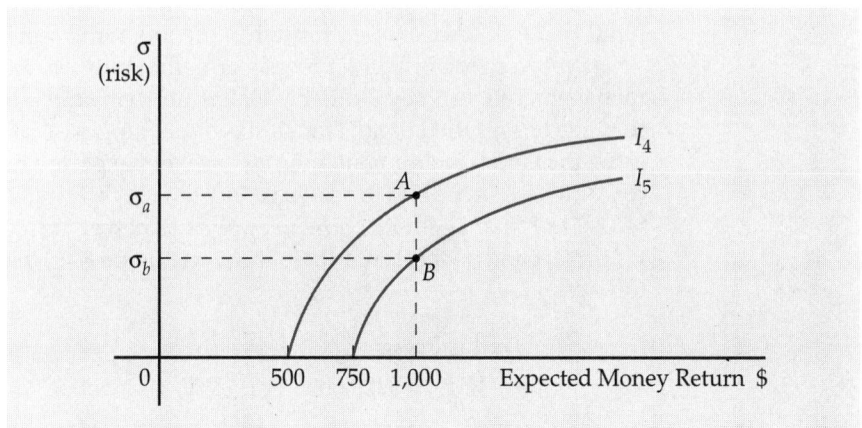

The certainty equivalent adjustment factor is equal to the ratio of the certain return (indifference
curve intercept on the return axis) to a given equivalent risky return. Thus, the certainty equivalent adjustment factor for risk-return combination A is 0.5, while that for combination B is 0.75.

A and B. The risk-return indifference curves show that the certain return
equivalent to the expected money value of Project A is \$500, while that equiv-
alent to Project B is \$750. For either project the certainty equivalent adjust-
ment factor is

$$\alpha_t = \frac{\text{certain return}}{\text{equivalent risky return}}.$$

Thus we have for Project A

$$\alpha_A = \frac{500}{1,000} = 0.5,$$

and for Project B

$$\alpha_B = \frac{750}{1,000} = 0.75.$$

In the analysis of any given project, the certainty equivalent adjustment
factor can be different for each future return. Thus, if a project is believed to
become less risky as time passes, higher αs can be applied to the cash flows

for more distant periods. Returning again to our land development alternatives, Texland may be virtually certain it can sell all of either tract at its desired prices by the end of four years, but management may believe that the cash flows early in the projects' lives are less certain. For example, management might choose to apply the following α_ts to the two projects:

Year	α_t Dallas	α_t Houston
1	0.78	0.85
2	0.84	0.85
3	0.90	0.90
4	0.90	0.95

Given a risk-free discount rate of 8 percent, our earlier projected annual inflows of $200,000, and project prices of $550,000, we have for the Dallas project

$$NPV \mid \alpha_t = \frac{0.78(\$200,000)}{(1.08)^1} + \frac{0.84(200,000)}{(1.08)^2} + \frac{0.90(\$200,000)}{(1.08)^3}$$

$$+ \frac{0.90(\$200,000)}{(1.08)^4} - \$550,000$$

$$= \$13,672.81,$$

and for the Houston project

$$NPV \mid \alpha_t = \frac{0.85(\$200,000)}{(1.08)^1} + \frac{0.85(200,000)}{(1.08)^2} + \frac{0.90(\$200,000)}{(1.08)^3}$$

$$+ \frac{0.95(\$200,000)}{(1.08)^4} - \$550,000$$

$$= \$35,700.68.$$

Again the Houston project would be judged the better alternative on the basis of its adjusted NPV. The difference in the two NPVs reflects both the generally lower α_ts of the Dallas project and the higher certainty equivalents of the Houston inflows *early* in the life of the project.

It is argued that the certainty equivalent approach is superior to the risk-adjusted discount rate approach when project returns do not become increasingly risky over time. Still, the risk-adjusted discount rate approach is more frequently used because (1) it is easier to calculate NPV and (2) the two approaches, it can be shown, will yield the same result whenever

$$\alpha_t = \frac{(1+r)^t}{(1+k)^t} = \frac{PVF\ k,\ t}{PVF\ r,\ t}.$$

That is, the two approaches yield identical results whenever the certainty equivalent adjustment factor for each future period equals the ratio of the present value factor (including a risk premium) to the risk-free present value factor. It follows that if far-off returns are viewed as increasingly less certain, the risk-adjusted discount rate approach will frequently be chosen.

RISK ADJUSTMENT IN PRACTICE

With the exception of the risk-adjusted discount rate, most of the approaches to the problem of risk that were described in the previous sections are the result of systematic examination of risk problems by financial and economic experts during the period since 1960. Corporations—and to some extent, public sector agencies—have applied these tools selectively, but many of them are not in common use by practical decision makers. This is particularly true of the probability approach, since the probabilities can be ascertained only roughly and the entire procedure becomes quite cumbersome when future cash flows are interdependent.[2]

While much of the literature on project analysis published in economics and finance journals is highly theoretical, academicians do occasionally conduct survey research on how risk analysis is employed by corporate financial planners. Three well-known surveys were conducted during the 1970s. James C. T. Mao[3] interviewed executives of several medium- and large-sized corporations and concluded from their responses that (1) the executives tended to characterize risk as not meeting a target rate of return, especially in the case of small investments, and (2) there was a tendency to emphasize downside risk, so that in the case of large projects the danger of insolvency was carefully considered.

Mao found that the executives frequently employed the risk-adjusted discount rate approach when evaluating capital projects. However, this rate

---

2 We note at this point that an extension of the probability approach in decision theory, the decision tree methodology, has become popular with some analysts although it relies on probabilities that are unlikely to be known. (See the game theory discussion in the appendix to Chapter 10.) Decision trees are usually covered in quantitative management courses, so we omit the discussion of them here. For a managerial economics text that makes primary use of the decision tree approach, see Julian Simon's *Applied Managerial Economics*, listed in the selected references at the end of this chapter. The probability approach also is at the foundation of the *capital asset pricing model* (CAPM), a method of calculating risk-adjusted discount rates that is sometimes used by large firms.

3 James C. T. Mao, "Survey of Capital Budgeting: Theory and Practice," *Journal of Finance* XXV (May 1970), pp. 349–360.

seemed to be quite high in relation to the return realized on common stock or a rate that would reflect a typical company's cost of capital (roughly, the rate at which new funds can be obtained). He attributed the tendency to choose high rates of discount to a desire to offset overly optimistic projections of returns or cover for items of project cost that might be overlooked (federal regulations requiring special facilities for handicapped workers, for example).

In 1977 and 1978, the results of surveys conducted by several other academic researchers were published.[4] These surveys indicated that corporate decision makers still relied heavily on risk-adjusted discount rates and that subjective methods were used to estimate the rates. One of the studies reported that 56 percent of the sample firms attempted to assess risk subjectively, while another 4 percent did not assess risk at all. However, this study also found that of the 40 percent that did attempt formal analysis of risk, the probability distribution approach was the most widely employed method. Another study published in 1986 revealed that certain large firms did not ordinarily perform a thorough financial analysis of small-sized capital projects, but instead penalized them by subjecting them to excessively high rates of discount.[5]

It is evident from the available surveys that most financial executives do attempt to make some adjustment for risk in the analysis of capital projects. It seems likely that the outpouring of theoretical literature on risk analysis, the increased exposure of business students to that literature, and the availability of computer programs to simulate the possible outcomes of risky investment projects will lead to more widespread application of formal risk assessment techniques by firms of all sizes. However, one must keep in mind that any sophisticated technique is only as good as the information it is used to analyze.

Given the realities of investment project evaluation, one might ask whether there is a feasible shortcut approach to the identification of an optimal combination of projects when a limited capital budget is available. For example, without too much difficulty could we expand the *NPV* approach of Chapter 13 to encompass risky investments? The answer is yes, and the methodology would be simply to evaluate each project using a risk-adjusted discount rate and thereafter select from the possible combinations the one that yields the highest aggregate adjusted *NPV*. The main caution to observe in this procedure relates to what we have learned about the interdependence of cash flows. The project combination yielding the highest *NPV* might well

---

4 Lawrence D. Schall, Gary L. Sundem, and William R. Geijsbeek, Jr., "Survey and Analysis of Capital Budgeting Methods," *Journal of Finance* XXIII (March 1978), pp. 281–287; and Lawrence J. Gitman and John R. Forrester, Jr., "A Survey of Capital Budgeting Techniques Used by Major U.S. Firms," *Financial Management* 6 (Fall 1977), pp. 66–71.
5 Marc Ross, "Capital Budgeting Practices of Twelve Large Manufacturers," *Financial Management*, 15, No. 4 (Winter 1986), pp. 15–22.

MANAGERIAL PERSPECTIVE
Risk, Capital Budgeting, and Kevlar

In the early 1960s a group of chemists at Du Pont's experimental lab in Wilmington, Delaware, began work on developing a material made of carbon molecules that would be extraordinarily strong. Initially known as Fiber B, the cloth-like material that was eventually developed was named Kevlar. The development process took place over a 25-year period and entailed $700 million in capital costs together with an additional $200 million in operating losses. By 1987, its annual sales had finally reached $300 million, and Du Pont estimated that these revenues would grow by 10 percent a year over the next five years.

Unfortunately, the early sales projections for Kevlar were too optimistic. By 1980, more than half of the Kevlar produced by Du Pont was being used in automobile tires, and some people expected that eventually Kevlar would be the only material used in tires. As a result Du Pont invested in its first commercial Kevlar plant, capable of making 45 million pounds each year. Soon after Du Pont began construction on the $500 million plant, the tire manufacturers chose steel instead of Kevlar for tires, arguing that Kevlar was too expensive and that customers were more attracted to steel-belted tires. At that point, the new plant appeared to be an investment with little chance of becoming profitable.

Kevlar was used in race cars and trucks, where its added durability made it worth its higher price. In addition, Du Pont asked the U.S. Army to consider Kevlar as a replacement for nylon in flak jackets, because nylon did not protect soldiers from shrapnel. Kevlar then went through seven years of testing by the Army and further development to meet the Army's specifications. The Army was finally satisfied when 100 goats were covered with half-inch-thick blankets of Kevlar and shot with .38-caliber pistol bullets and sustained only minor bruises from the experience. Bulletproof vests made of Kevlar also were demanded by other law enforcement entities. Still, the specialty tire market and the bulletproof-vest market were not sufficiently large to make Du Pont's investment profitable.

As a result, Du Pont began to look for people who would be willing to devote their careers to finding new markets for Kevlar. The company decided to change its marketing strategy so that rather than trying to think of new uses for Kevlar on its own, it would try to discover customer needs that might be appropriate for the material, and then to further develop Kevlar so that it would meet those needs. As a result, Kevlar has become one of the materials specified by aerospace engineers in their plans, a substitute for asbestos, and an insulator of fiber optic cable. Kevlar is now also used to make gloves, and Du Pont is considering using it to reinforce the heels and toes of socks to keep them from wearing out. The late Sam Walton, founder of Wal-Mart Stores, Incorporated, suggested that Kevlar booties be designed to protect the feet of hunting dogs.

Not all of the Kevlar products developed by Du Pont initially performed as anticipated. Cables designed for off-shore drilling platforms for Exxon snapped when they were tightened. Kevlar sails also initially tore in the wind. However, both products have been redesigned, and it appears that these problems have been corrected.

By 1987, Du Pont reported that Kevlar had generated operating profits for the last two years. Although the intrinsic value of Kevlar was no longer doubted, some industry analysts questioned whether the investment would eventually turn out to be profitable, particularly since Du Pont's basic patents on the material would begin expiring in 1990 and other competing fibers were becoming available.

The saga of the development of Kevlar illustrates that even a large company such as Du Pont cannot develop a new product without risk. Clearly, a careful analysis of potential markets, corresponding revenues, and costs in such a situation combined with an estimate of the risk involved is extremely important.

Reference: "Du Pont's Difficulties in Selling Kevlar Show Hurdles of Innovation," *The Wall Street Journal* (September 29, 1987), pp. 1, 20.

be carefully reviewed alongside those having *NPVs* that are not greatly different, since a subjective evaluation of the correlation between the projects in each combination might lead to some revision of *NPVs* based on the effect of such correlation on the standard deviation or risk of the project combinations.

EXTERNALITIES AND THEIR NATURE

The cautious attitude of executives toward new capital projects and their tendency to apply what might seem to be excessive risk-adjusted discount rates to project inflows may in many cases be a sign of prudence rather than of paranoia. A hint about the problems underlying such behavior is found in the preceding assertion that certain elements of cost, such as federal requirements concerning facilities for the handicapped, may have been overlooked by project analysts. There is a tendency in project evaluation to analyze first and foremost the estimated revenue and operating cost components of the flow of annual benefits and to compare the discounted net amount of those two figures with project price. However, the operating cost item directs attention to nuts-and-bolts aspects of annual cost that are very much *internal* to the firm. In other words the emphasis is on those cost items over which the firm has direct control through management's ability to plan and organize the process of production.

For any given project, there are likely to be elements of cost markedly affected by changes in data that are *externally* determined—that is, over which management has no control. Changes in input prices are perhaps the most obvious of such external factors. A firm may be faced with rising input prices because it is in an industrial sector where many rapidly expanding firms are bidding against one another for relatively scarce resources. Thus costs may rise for an individual firm even though no changes have occurred in its production function. Such externalities, which economists have called *pecuniary externalities*, are occasionally overlooked by project evaluators. More likely to be overlooked are certain other types of externalities, particularly those associated with what have come to be known as *public goods*.

A public good is a good that is jointly consumed by many people and, once it is made available, the marginal cost of increased consumption is zero. A highway bridge provides a good example. Once the bridge has been built, it can handle any amount of traffic up to the capacity per unit of time of the roadway. If it is being used at one-half its capacity, and an additional user wishes to cross it, the additional user will be able to do so at zero addition to the cost of the bridge. Theoretically, no price should be charged for using the bridge, since marginal cost equals zero; therefore the perfectly competitive $P = MC$ market solution is price equals zero. The users of public goods who benefit from but do not pay for them through market transactions enjoy what are known as *third-party benefits*.

The cost of operation of an investment undertaking in the private sector is seldom affected by such public goods as a bridge, although we could certainly imagine circumstances where it might be. (In an underdeveloped country or region, the roads, the bridges, and the electric power plants often are externalities on which successful private capital projects ultimately depend.) However, over the past few decades we have come to the realization that clean air, clean water, the preservation of wildlife, and a relatively quiet environment are public goods that have often been neglected in our economic calculus. This neglect has provided the business sector an array of public-good externalities, such as free water, zero-cost dumping of pollutants, and the prerogative to increase noise and temperature levels at will.

The recent awakening of both the general public and governmental authorities to the fact that much private sector output is produced in a setting where external costs are imposed on third parties has caused business decision makers to be wary about regulatory changes and penalties that might well *internalize* such costs.

AN EXAMPLE OF INTERNALIZATION

On January 6, 1978, *The Wall Street Journal* reported that Foothills Pipe Lines, Ltd., a Canadian corporation organized for the purpose of constructing and operating a 2,000-mile stretch of the Alaska Highway Natural Gas Pipeline, had been informed by the Canadian government that it would have to bear all operating costs of a new government agency established to monitor the pipeline.[6] In addition, Foothills was told that it would be assessed penalties of up to $10,000 per day if it failed to comply with any order of the agency.

According to the *Journal*, Foothills had not planned on paying the costs of the monitoring agency, and such costs apparently were not included in its original estimate of project price or annual cost. Obviously, the Canadian government's move caused the costs of pipeline monitoring (which were at first presumed to be external to the firm) to be *internalized* by the firm. For the firm to continue to have a feasible project, it would be necessary to ensure that the future revenue stream would be sufficient to yield the desired return on investment, given the required alterations in project price and annual cost of operations. If provisions were not made to increase the annual cash inflows to Foothills, the entire project could become unattractive. In terms of standard capital project analysis, where

$$NPV = \sum_{i=1}^{n} \frac{X_i}{(1+k)^i} - C_P,$$

the initial costs of the monitoring agency would increase C_P, while its annual costs after the pipeline is completed would reduce the X_i. Further, if k is a risk-adjusted discount rate, uncertainty regarding *changes* in the regulatory picture might warrant reevaluating the project with a higher k.

Fortunately for Foothills Pipe Lines, the Canadian government made an adjustment in the tariffs charged for gas transported through the line, thereby allowing for an adequate return on investment while transferring most of the burden of financing the monitoring agency to natural gas consumers in the United States.[7]

The preceding example calls attention to the fact that externalities do have to be anticipated by project evaluators, particularly because of their effects on project price and annual costs. Government has many ways in which

---

6 "Foothills Must Pay for Agency to Monitor Pipeline Construction," *The Wall Street Journal*, January 6, 1978, p. 2.
7 Since the increase in tariff would probably cause a reduction in quantity sold, some of the burden would still be borne by Foothills.

it can cause third-party costs attributable to a firm to become internal. Among these are legislation of standards and penalties, user charges, taxes, and assignment of property rights. However, many private capital projects also create external *benefits* as well as costs, and project evaluators must be aware of the prospects for internalization of such flows.

One of the best recent examples of an attempt to internalize the potential third-party benefits of a capital project is Walt Disney World in Florida.[8] When Walt Disney Productions constructed the original Disneyland in California, only enough land was purchased by the Disney interests to provide for the amusement park and a few related activities. The result was that the project supplied tremendous external benefits to owners and users of surrounding property in the development boom that the area experienced after Disneyland opened. In planning the Florida Disney World project, the corporation ensured its own capture (internalization) of many of the potential external benefits that it would create by purchasing 6,000 acres of land, thereby assuring control over nearby related activities. There were still some spillover benefits to third parties who owned land or set up businesses on the perimeter of the Disney World tract, but the distance of these sites from the park itself much reduced external benefits and enhanced the long-run profitability of the Disney project. The moral is clear: Successful investors take into account opportunities to internalize project-related external benefits. If at first they do not, they will indeed *learn* to do so!

SUMMARY

Risk and Risk Adjustment in Capital Projects

In this chapter we extended our analysis of capital projects to include situations involving risk. Our basic behavioral assumption throughout the chapter was that the decision maker is a *risk averter*. This means that the decision maker will be willing to accept a risky project over one that is less risky but involves the same initial outlay (project price) *only if* the risky alternative yields a sufficiently greater net present value to more than offset its added risk. To illustrate this point, the concept of risk-return indifference curves was introduced and eventually related to a probability approach to risk analysis.

We showed in this chapter that the riskiness of various investment alter-

---

8 This example has been used previously elsewhere. See Richard B. McKenzie, *Economics* (Boston: Houghton Mifflin, 1986), p. 689. Later it was argued that Disney World resulted in external costs to the citizens of Florida as the result of the increased demand for public services that resulted from its existence. See "A Sweet Deal for Disney Is Souring Its Neighbors," *Business Week* (August 8, 1988), pp. 48–49.

natives can be evaluated by examining the probability distribution of payoffs of each alternative. For each alternative, a weighted average or expected value is calculated, and this is used, along with the distribution of probable outcomes, to obtain two measures of riskiness—the *variance* and the *standard deviation* of net project returns. For projects with equal prices, lives, and expected values, we showed that a risk-averse decision maker will choose the alternative with the lowest variance. In addition the *normal distribution* was utilized to make some inferences about the probability of payoffs outside a specified range.

One result of applying the probability approach to project analysis is the attention it directs toward the question of interdependence of cash inflows. In particular we noted that the cash flow in a given time period might in some way be correlated with that in another time period. Thus a thorough analysis of a project's risk using the probability approach would have to take into account the covariance between project inflows. This increases the information requirements of the approach and complicates the calculation of variance. When combinations or portfolios of projects are evaluated, it becomes necessary to consider not only the interdependence of cash flows within each individual project but also the problem of interdependence of cash flows *between* projects.

In the last part of this chapter, some shortcuts to risk analysis were described and evaluated. Specifically, we examined the risk-*adjusted discount* rate concept and its application. Use of the risk-adjusted discount rate is viewed as a practical and acceptable approach as long as its shortcomings are understood by the project analyst. Its primary shortcoming, the fact that it treats project cash flows as becoming increasingly risky over time, can be offset by using a related method, the *certainty equivalent approach*, in which each future cash flow is separately adjusted for risk, and a risk-free discount rate is applied to the present value calculation.

The chapter closed with discussions of the views of corporation executives on the matter of risk and the treatment of risk and externalities in project evaluation. We concluded that it would be reasonable to evaluate risky alternatives using the risk-adjusted discount rate approach examined in the light of what is known about interdependence of project cash flows. In addition, we implied that it would be wise for capital project analysts to review carefully the external costs and benefits related to each project and to assess the probable consequences of internalization of such costs and benefits.

This chapter has dealt almost entirely with the more obvious quantitative aspects of project evaluation under risk. However, many capital projects have both inflows of benefits and elements of cost or price that might easily escape analysis if a strictly private or internal point of view is taken by the firm's managers or project evaluators. In the next chapter, we extend our discussion not only to such externalities—and, in some cases, nonquantitative considerations—but also to the question of project evaluation in the public sector.

QUESTIONS

1. What is the economic nature of risk? How can risk be described using a trade-off concept?
2. What is meant by the term *expected return*?
3. What is the usual assumption regarding the risk attitude of decision makers in economic theory? What other kinds of attitudes toward risk exist? Describe each attitude in terms of the behavior of the decision maker in a risk situation.
4. What is a probability distribution of returns? How can it be related to the risk associated with a given capital project?
5. Suppose two projects have the same lives and prices but that one of them (Project *A*) has an expected value that is greater than that of the other (Project *B*). Can you determine from this which project should be selected? Why or why not?
6. Explain how the concept of the standard deviation of probable returns from a capital project relates to that of risk-return indifference curves.
7. What problem in project analysis arises from the possible interdependence of cash flows in a project or a portfolio of projects?
8. What is a risk-adjusted discount rate? Explain how it is used, and discuss the problems inherent in its application to project analysis.
9. What is a certainty equivalent adjustment factor? Why do some experts argue that use of the certainty equivalent adjustment factor is a better approach than is the risk-adjusted discount rate method?
10. There is evidence that executives of medium- and large-sized corporations tend to rely on a variant of the risk-adjusted discount rate approach when evaluating capital projects. Explain how the variant described in this chapter differs from the ordinary risk-adjusted discount rate approach. Why do you think the corporation executives prefer this method?

PROBLEMS

1. Using a set of risk-return indifference curves for a single decision maker, describe a case in which the decision maker would prefer a risky investment returning an expected $1,500 to a less risky one with an expected return of $1,000. Explain how an increase in the perceived riskiness of the project with the $1,500 expected return might cause the decision maker to reject it and to choose the less risky project with the $1,000 expected return instead.

2. Suppose a one-year project has the following probable returns in relation to the percentage growth in population for a given region:

Percent Growth in Population	Net Cash Inflow of Project
1.0	$150,000
1.5	185,000
2.0	210,000
2.5	275,000

The following are the subjective probabilities of occurrence of the preceding population growth rates:

Percent Growth in Population	Subjective Probability (P_i)
1.0	0.25
1.5	0.50
2.0	0.20
2.5	0.05

What is the *expected value* of the cash inflow from the project?

3. Construct a rod graph showing a discrete probability distribution of the cash inflows from the project in Problem 2, and then determine the variance and standard deviation of the inflows. What could be said about the relation of the standard deviation to the expected value of the cash inflow if the true probability distribution of the cash inflows were normal?

4. Given the following data on two one-period capital projects, calculate (1) the expected value of each project's cash flows and (2) the standard deviation of probable cash flows from each project. Indicate which of the two projects would be chosen by a risk-averse decision maker if their prices were the same and they had similar lives.

Net Cash Flows		Subjective Probability (P_i)
Project A	Project B	
200	190	0.05
240	250	0.25
250	260	0.40
290	270	0.25
300	290	0.05

5. Belco Corporation has been evaluating two possible alternative locations for a small oil refinery. One of the locations is in the United States, whereas the other is in a nearby Latin American republic. The cost will

be $22 million if the project is built in the United States, but because of lower land and labor costs it will be only $19 million if the project is built in the Latin American country.

Recent uncertainties in the oil and gas industry have convinced Belco's managers that the lives of such projects should not be treated as longer than seven years. Management doubts that the project will have any salvage value if it is undertaken in Latin America, but it is willing to attach a $7 million after-tax salvage value to the U.S. alternative.

The estimated net annual cash inflows, which are believed to be independent, are $5 million per year if the project is located in the U.S. and $5.2 million per year if it is located in Latin America. Because of the inherent risk of changes in government regulations in the Latin American republic, Belco's managers have decided to apply a risk-adjusted discount rate of 22 percent to the inflows from the foreign alternative, while their risk-adjusted discount rate for the U.S. project will be 16 percent. Which project will they choose? (Note: PVF_a 22%, 7 = 3.4155; PVF_a 16%, 7 = 4.0386.)

6. Develop a set of certainty equivalent adjustment factors from the following information on a decision maker's preferences:

Certain Return	Equivalent Risky Return
$120,000	$160,000
170,000	210,000
250,000	300,000
325,000	400,000
500,000	625,000

7. Given the following set of risk-return indifference curves, calculate the certainty equivalent adjustment factors for an expected return of $1,400,000.

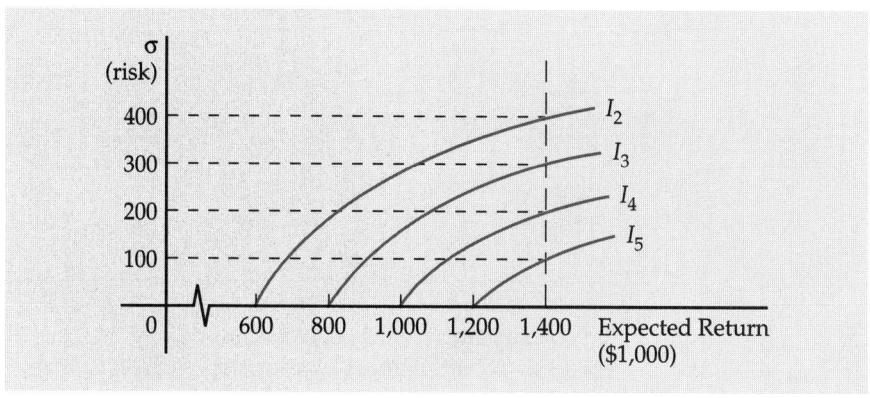

8. International Cosmographics, a small corporation in the printing industry, is considering expanding into the greeting card market. Its managers
have hired two consultants to evaluate an investment project that involves both an addition to factory space and the purchase of new printing equipment. Consultant *A* has suggested that the company adjust its
expected annual cash inflows using a risk-adjusted discount rate approach. Consultant *B* argues that such an approach is inappropriate and
that what should be used is a certainty equivalent approach that takes
into account the fact that after the first two years risk will decline because
a market share will have been established.

Consultant *B* has estimated that the following certainty equivalent
adjustment factors should be applied to the cash inflows from the project,
assuming a risk-free discount rate of 6 percent.

Year	Certainty Equivalent Adjustment Factor
1	0.9464
2	0.8957
3	0.9197
4	0.8944
5	0.8698
6	0.8458
7	0.8225
8	0.7999

Consultant *A* argues that the risk-adjusted discount rate approach is simpler and equally applicable, since a risk-adjusted discount rate of 12 percent for the first two years of project life should be applied and 9 percent
should be used for the remaining 6 years. The annual inflows (before risk
adjustment) follow. They should be treated as being independent.

Year	Net Cash Inflow
1	$100,000
2	175,000
3	200,000
4	200,000
5	200,000
6	200,000
7	200,000
8	200,000

If both risk-adjustment methodologies are applied to the preceding inflows, what difference in present value will the two approaches yield?
Explain the difference you find.

9. Using a set of risk-return indifference curves, explain how the concept of dominance makes it possible in theory to eliminate certain risk-return combinations from the "efficient set" of project portfolios.

10. American Astrotronics Corporation is evaluating two new investment projects for possible undertaking next fiscal year. One is the short-term operation of a cleaning franchise that will yield a net after-tax cash flow of $42,000 per year for the next three years. The second is short-term operation of a parking lot that will yield net after-tax cash flows of $36,000 for each of two years and $56,000 for the third and final year of operation. Neither project has a salvage value, and either can be acquired for a present outlay of $90,000.

    a. Evaluate the two projects using a risk-adjusted discount rate of 18 percent per year.

    b. If the company can undertake only one of the two projects, which should it choose? Why?

11. Garfield just won $2 million in the California lottery. Since he knows that many long-lost cat relatives will want to share in his good fortune, Garfield is trying to find the optimal place to invest his funds. At the present time, he is considering two options. The first is a real estate investment trust that is purchasing repossessed property in Texas. The second is a well-diversified mutual fund with a return closely approximating that of the market. The possible returns on the real estate investment trust, R_T, the market, R_M, and their associated probabilities, P_i, are given in the table. The risk-free rate of return, R_F, is .06.

% Growth in Real GNP	P_i	R_{T_i}	R_{M_i}
−1%	.05	−.40	−.10
1%	.3	.30	.10
2%	.5	.30	.20
3%	.15	.40	.30

    a. Calculate the expected rate of return for the real estate trust and for the market.

    b. Calculate the standard deviation of the returns for the real estate trust and for the market.

    c. With no other information regarding alternative investment opportunities, how would Garfield choose whether to invest in the real estate investment trust, the mutual fund, or a risk-free asset?

SELECTED REFERENCES

Brightman, Harvey J. *Statistics in Plain English*. Cincinnati: South-Western, 1986, Chapters 2 and 3.

Butler, J. S., and Barry Schachter. "The Investment Decision: Estimation Risk and Risk Adjusted Discount Rates," *Financial Management* 18, no. 4 (Winter 1989), pp. 13–22.

Chan, Louis K. C., and Josef Lakonishok. "Are the Reports of Beta's Death Premature?" *Financial Management* 19, no. 4 (Summer 1993), pp. 51–62.

Engler, George N. *Business Financial Management*. Dallas: Business Publications, 1975, Chapter 7 and appendices to Chapter 7.

Finnerty, John D., and Dean Leistikow. "The Behavior of Equity and Debt Risk Premiums," *Financial Management* 19, no. 4 (Summer 1993), pp. 73–84.

Fuller, Russell J., and Kent A. Hickman. "A Note on Estimating the Historical Risk Premium," *Financial Practice and Education* 1, no. 2 (Fall/Winter 1991), pp. 45–48.

Gitman, Lawrence J. *Principles of Managerial Finance*, 7th ed. New York: Harper and Row, 1994, Chapters 6 and 9.

Grundy, Kevin, and Burton G. Malkiel. "Reports of Beta's Death Have Been Greatly Exaggerated," *Journal of Portfolio Management* 22, no. 3 (Spring 1996), pp. 36–44.

Haugen, Robert A. "Finance from a New Perspective," *Financial Management*, 25, no. 1 (Spring 1996), pp. 86–97.

Mansfield, Edwin. *Statistics for Business and Economics*. New York: Norton, 1980, Chapter 3.

Mao, James C. T. *Corporate Financial Decisions*. Palo Alto, Cal.: Pavan, 1976, Chapters 7 and 8.

Moyer, R. Charles, James R. McGuigan, and William J. Kretlow. *Contemporary Financial Management*, 6th ed. St. Paul: West, 1995, Chapter 11.

Naylor, Thomas H., and John M. Vernon. *Microeconomics and Decision Models of the Firm*. New York: Harcourt, Brace and World, 1969, Chapter 16. (Chapter is written by E. T. Byrne, Jr.)

Neveu, Raymond R. *Fundamentals of Managerial Finance*, 3d ed. Cincinnati: South-Western, 1989, Chapter 12.

Sick, Gordon A. "A Certainty-Equivalent Approach to Capital Budgeting," *Financial Management* 15, no. 4 (Winter 1986), pp. 23–32.

Simon, Julian. *Applied Managerial Economics*. Englewood Cliffs, N.J.: Prentice-Hall, 1975, Chapters 3, 6, 11, and 17.

"The New Rocket Science," *Business Week* (November 2, 1992), pp. 131–135.

Weston, J. Fred, Scott Besley, and Eugene F. Brigham. *Essentials of Managerial Finance*, 11th ed. Fort Worth, Tex.: The Dryden Press, 1996, Chapters 5 and 14.

INTERNATIONAL CAPSULE III

Project Analysis in a Multinational Setting

Chapters 13 and 14 provided a brief introduction to the subject of capital projects and their evaluation. There the emphasis was on comparison of alternative investment opportunities available to the firm over the long run. As we saw, the procedures normally followed in project evaluation take into account the price tags attached to various undertakings and the stream of benefits the firm expects to receive from each of them. The methodology of determining the net present value (*NPV*) of the alternatives is fairly straightforward and involves the use of proforma income statements based on discounted future revenues and costs for some specified project life. But a number of complexities enter the analysis when capital budgeting techniques are applied to international projects.

INTERNATIONAL DIMENSIONS OF PROJECT ANALYSIS

Today, the most common setting for international capital budgeting decisions is one in which a large firm is evaluating whether or not to set up a subsidiary in a foreign country, or, perhaps, whether or not to add to the fixed assets of an existing foreign subsidiary. In multinational finance, the country where a

foreign subsidiary is located is commonly called the "host country," the firm that owns the subsidiary the "parent firm," and the country where the parent firm is located the "home country." The basic framework for analysis of foreign capital projects is the same as that used for domestic projects. However, in the case of international projects, the evaluation is complicated by a number of factors that do not enter the picture in home country capital project analysis. Some of the more important considerations follow.

1. Should the capital budgeting analysis be conducted from the viewpoint of the parent company, that of the foreign subsidiary, or both?
2. Will remittances of profits from the foreign operation be restricted by the host country of the subsidiary?
3. What will be the income tax treatment of subsidiary earnings by the host government and parent company income by its home government?
4. Will there be differential rates of inflation between the home country and the host country of the subsidiary?
5. How will net flows of income to the parent company be affected by changes in foreign exchange rates between its currency and that of the subsidiary?

6. What are the political risks associated with investment in the host country?

7. What additional factors will affect the cost of capital and therefore the discount rate applicable to the project?

From this list, it should be apparent that many of the differences between domestic and international capital projects call for quantitative adjustments that will affect either the discounted cash flows or the rate of discount for any given international investment undertaking. In addition, a firm planning a significant foreign investment project will have to ascertain whether or not there are unusual elements that may increase or decrease the initial amount of investment (project price). For example, a government may require that a firm undertake certain ancillary investments (worker housing, medical clinics, etc.) along with its investment in plant facilities, or it may provide subsidies to foreign firms that invest in certain types of activities deemed essential for economic growth.

Parent vs. Subsidiary

While a thorough analysis of a foreign capital project might include a capital budgeting analysis from the point of view of the subsidiary as an independent firm operating in the foreign country, it is widely argued by financial experts that the overriding consideration in analyzing a foreign capital project is whether or not the project is acceptable when analyzed from the viewpoint of the parent company. The two viewpoints may produce different results because of limitations on the amount of profits that can be transferred to the parent and because of the tax treatment of such flows. If the objective of the firm is to maximize shareholder wealth, then it is the cash flows to the parent that are available to pay dividends and use for reinvestment pur-

poses that will determine whether or not a foreign project is acceptable.[1]

Adjustment of Project Cash Flows

Cash flows into a projected foreign subsidiary are estimated as in any capital budgeting analysis on the basis of anticipated annual sales revenues, operating costs, and depreciation, as well as the salvage value that may occur from disposition of fixed assets at the end of the project. These calculations usually are made in the currency of the country where the subsidiary is located (local currency).

If the subsidiary is destined to sell only in the local market, an analysis of local demand will be required for the revenue estimates. This may not be an easy matter for the parent company, since the determinants of local demand may differ from those used to analyze demand in the home country. Operating costs may differ in the foreign country for a variety of reasons ranging from labor union practices to such cost items as those associated with locally purchased materials and parts and local charges for insurance, utilities, and government-provided services. Moreover, both cost and revenue estimates may have to be adjusted for anticipated inflation. Finally, the net

---

1 Contemporary research on international capital budgeting shows that many firms do use the subsidiary's point of view rather than that of the parent. This is partially explained by the historical evidence that remittances are seldom permanently blocked and that firms can use transfer pricing and other techniques to get around restrictions on remittances of earnings. See, for example, Vinod B. Bashevi, "Capital Budgeting Practices at Multinationals," *Management Accounting* (August 1981), pp. 32–35; and Marjorie Stanley and Stanley Block, "An Empirical Study of Management and Financial Variables Influencing Capital Budgeting Decisions for Multinational Corporations in the 1980s," *Management International Review* 23, no. 3 (1983), pp. 61–71.

cash flow of the subsidiary will depend also on the host country's laws regarding income taxes and allowable depreciation.

Once the net cash inflow to the subsidiary is determined, a number of additional adjustments must be made in order to arrive at the net inflow to be received by the parent company. First, the funds remitted annually by the subsidiary must be converted into the currency of the parent. This is not a simple matter, since the exchange rate applicable to one time period may differ substantially from that applicable to another. While forecasting exchange rates is difficult, any tendency for a rate to move in a predictable direction should be taken into account. With the flows to the parent now expressed in its own currency, the next adjustment would be for income taxes owed by the parent to the home country. In general the United States tax laws have provided that a parent company may credit any foreign income taxes paid against the U.S. tax liability on remittances. Thus the tax on earnings transferred annually to the parent from the subsidiary is reduced by the amount of foreign income taxes already paid. There may be a final inflow to the parent due to transfer of funds from the sale of the entire project or some of its assets at the end of the project's life. A home country tax liability may be incurred, depending on the relation between the sale price and book value of the assets sold.

Risk and the Discount Rate

It is widely recognized that risk in foreign capital projects may differ from risk in home country capital projects. Besides exchange rate risk, there are important elements of political risk that can affect anticipated project inflows. For example, if the host country has an unstable government, flows into the subsidiary may be interrupted by economic or social disorder. There is also the possibility that the host country may expropriate or confiscate foreign businesses. Clearly, the evaluation of a foreign capital project must take these additional types of risk into account.

There is a temptation to argue that the firm can allow for the additional risks associated with foreign projects by applying a higher discount rate than that used in home country analyses. In fact, many firms do take this approach.[2] However, it is argued that doing so is too simplistic and overlooks such possibilities as the fact that a fall in the value of the foreign currency, for example, may either decrease or increase the net inflows, depending on where output is sold and the sources of inputs. A high discount rate may also penalize early inflows excessively and not penalize distant inflows enough.

Because of these complications, many analysts argue that, wherever possible, adjustment for the foreign risks of a project should be handled by adjusting its forecasted cash flows. Then, when the cash flows to the parent are determined, they are discounted at a rate that reflects only overall business and financial risk. In effect this is the same rate used for home country projects. However, if the firm's presence in a country with extremely high foreign risk (such as Libya in the 1980s) increases its overall risk of bankruptcy, this would likely drive up its cost of obtaining funds and thus also the discount rate.

EXAMPLE OF A FOREIGN PROJECT

Perhaps the best way to understand how foreign capital project analysis differs from analysis done for investments at home is to consider an example of such a project. In our

---

2 See David K. Eiteman and Arthur I. Stonehill, *Multinational Business Finance*, 5th ed. (Reading, Mass.: Addison-Wesley, 1989), p. 524.

example we will follow the pattern used for the capital project study in Chapter 13 (Clickwash), indicating where specific steps are taken to adjust for foreign operations. The name of our parent firm will be MacWash, Inc., and its product line will be washing machines. MacWash is considering an investment in a plant in a developing country, Lavaria, where the sales of modern laundry detergents have been growing rapidly. The company has developed a hand-operated washing machine that takes advantage of the new detergents and can be used in areas where electricity is not widely available. It believes Lavarians will respond dramatically to the introduction of this product, especially if it is produced in their country.

MacWash will have to set up a subsidiary that is incorporated in Lavaria. The initial investment (project price) will be $4,800,000. Studies indicate that the subsidiary can be expected to have annual gross sales receipts amounting to 12,000,000 units of local currency. In Lavaria, the local currency is the Elsie, abbreviated $L\mathcal{C}$. Annual operating costs including depreciation are estimated to be $L\mathcal{C}7,200,000$. The income tax rate in Lavaria is 25 percent, and the subsidiary will have allowable straight-line depreciation of $L\mathcal{C}800,000$ per year. The Elsie is a stable currency and is expected to remain at $L\mathcal{C}1 = \$0.30$ throughout the life of the project, which MacWash knows will be six years. At the end of the six years, the Lavarian Development Bank will pay MacWash $L\mathcal{C}11,200,000$ (the book value of the project) and take over the plant. The U.S. tax rate is 34 percent. MacWash has decided to use a risk-adjusted discount rate of 14 percent for the project, even though it currently uses only a 12 percent rate on domestic investments. Finally, Lavaria does not restrict remittances or assess additional taxes against them.

Table III–1 is a worksheet for the MacWash project. The top portion of the table

shows the project's net cash inflows in local currency. This is what the subsidiary in Lavaria would receive as a firm incorporated there. The bottom half of the sheet continues the analysis to determine the net present value (*NPV*) of the project from the viewpoint of the parent. Here the annual net cash inflows to the parent are converted to U.S. dollars, and the additional U.S. tax liability is deducted. The present value of the net aftertax inflows for the six-year period is then added to that of the net aftertax inflow from the development bank payment occurring at the end of the six years to obtain the present value (*PV*) of the net cash inflows to the parent. Finally, the *NPV* of the project is obtained by subtracting its price from the *PV* of the net cash inflows. Since the *NPV* is positive, the project should be accepted.

Although our MacWash example is greatly simplified, it does call attention to three of the important foreign variables that must be considered in any analysis of this type—taxes, exchange rates, and political risk. A different tax treatment of income or remittances by Lavaria or of foreign source income by the United States might possibly yield a negative *NPV* for the project. This is one reason why it would not be prudent to evaluate the project from the standpoint of the subsidiary alone. A weakening of the Elsie would present additional problems, since the $L\mathcal{C}$ earnings of the subsidiary might not translate into a sufficient net cash inflow to the parent to make the project feasible. Finally, this project is acceptable with the end payment from the Lavarian development bank but would not be acceptable without it. If the Lavarians were to delay this payment very much, its *PV* would fall and likely make the project unacceptable.

In practice, capital budgeting analyses of projects such as this one can become extremely complex. Since a project of this type is often fraught with uncertainties, it is not uncom-

Table III–1   Worksheet for MacWash Foreign Capital Project

Annual Gross Receipts from Sales		LĆ12,000,000
Less:		
Annual Cost of Operations		LĆ7,200,000
Net Income Before Taxes		
		LĆ4,800,000
Less:		
Income Tax (Lavaria, 0.25)		LĆ1,200,000
Net Income		LĆ3,600,000
Plus:		
Depreciation		LĆ800,000
Annual Net Inflow from Project		LĆ4,400,000
Annual Net Inflow to Parent (LĆ = $0.30)		$1,320,000
Less:		
U.S. Income Tax	$489,600[a]	
Credit Local Tax	(360,000)	
		$ 129,600
Parent Net Annual Inflow After Taxes		$1,190,400
PV of 6-Year Net Inflow [PVF_a (14%, 6) = 3.8887]	$4,629,108	
PV of Development Bank Purchase		
Payment [LĆ11,200,000 × .30] = $3,360,000		
Times PVF (14%, 6) =	$1,530,816	
PV of Net Inflow to Parent		$6,159,924
Project Price		($4,800,000)
NPV of Project		$1,359,924

[a][.34 × LĆ4,800,000 × .30 = .34 × $1,440,000]

mon to simulate a number of scenarios, including a worst-case possibility, before making a final decision on it. However, despite the difficulties involved and the additional risks that confront a firm when it operates on foreign turf, the widespread success of multinational corporations suggests that the rewards are often well worth the effort.

QUESTIONS AND PROBLEMS

1. How is foreign capital project analysis similar to home country project analysis? How is it different? Identify specific considerations the firm must take into account in foreign project analysis that do not exist in home country analysis.
2. Do firms ever employ a higher risk-adjusted discount rate for foreign than for domestic capital budgeting? Why or why not? Discuss the use of such a rate as opposed to the adjustment of project flows as an approach to foreign capital project analysis.
3. Reevaluate the MacWash project of Table

III-1 on the assumption that the Lavarian Elsie will have the following values over the life of the project:

Year	Dollar Value of One Elsie
1	$0.30
2	0.34
3	0.32
4	0.28
5	0.28
6	0.28

4. Garibaldi Pizza Machine Corporation (a U.S. firm) is evaluating an investment project in Blutonia. The government of Blutonia is anxious to establish a capital goods industry and believes pizza machines would be a good place to start, since Blutonians prefer high-calorie foods. The plan calls for Garibaldi to set up a subsidiary in Blutonia at an initial outlay cost of $5.2 million (U.S.). It will be allowed to operate the subsidiary for four years and return all the profits to the United States each year. At the end of the four years, the subsidiary must be turned over to the Blutonian government, which will sell it to local private investors and retain all proceeds from the sale.

The local currency is the Bluto. At the inception of the project, the value of one Bluto is $0.50 U.S. It is projected that the before-tax earnings of the subsidiary will be as follows:

Year	Earnings Before Taxes (Blutos)
1	2,000,000
2	4,000,000
3	6,000,000
4	6,000,000

The subsidiary will have a cash inflow from allowable depreciation of 200,000 Blutos per year. The Bluto is expected to remain stable. The corporate income tax rate in Blutonia is 20 percent, while in the United States it is 38 percent. Garibaldi currently uses a risk-adjusted discount rate of 12 percent for international projects.

a. What will be the estimated after-tax net cash inflows to the parent?

b. Should Garibaldi accept the project?

SELECTED REFERENCES

Booth, Laurence D. "Capital Budgeting Frameworks for the Multinational Corporation," *Journal of International Business Studies* (Fall 1982), pp. 114–123.

Eiteman, David K., and Arthur I. Stonehill. *Multinational Business Finance*, 5th ed. Reading, Mass.: Addison-Wesley, 1989, especially Chapters 16–18.

Lessard, Donald R. "Evaluating Foreign Projects: An Adjusted Present Value Approach." In *International Financial Management*, ed. D. R. Lessard. New York: Wiley, 1985.

Madura, Jeff. *International Financial Management*, 2d ed. St. Paul: West, 1989, especially Chapters 15–16.

Weston, J. Fred, and Bart W. Sorge. *Guide to International Financial Management*. New York: McGraw-Hill, 1977.

INTEGRATING CASE 4A

A "Guaranteed" Foreign Investment

Western Consolidated Industries, a diversified manufacturing firm, has been negotiating with the government of a large Latin American country regarding a proposal to install and operate a packaging equipment plant in a new industrial park located outside the nation's capital city. The foreign government's current offer would allow Western Consolidated to operate the plant for a period of six years and to transfer its after-tax profits to the United States each year. The foreign tax rate on profits would be equal to that in the United States (46 percent), so that under U.S. tax laws no U.S. income tax would be due. Presently there are two variations of the project that would be acceptable to the foreign government.

PROPOSAL I

Western Consolidated would install a plant with facilities for manufacturing two types of packaging machines: Type A, a light-duty machine commonly used by small packaging firms, and Type B, a heavy-duty machine capable of handling larger jobs and faster rates of output. The government would guarantee the following quantities sold and prices for the six years that Western Consolidated is permitted to operate the plant:

| | Type A | | Type B | |
Year	Price	Quantity Sold	Price	Quantity Sold
1	$12,000	50	$22,000	20
2	13,000	50	24,000	20
3	14,000	60	26,000	40
4	16,000	60	28,000	40
5	18,000	60	30,000	60
6	20,000	60	32,000	60

At the end of the six years of operation, the government would buy the plant from Western Consolidated at U.S. book value, thereby returning the remainder of invested capital to the company with no gain on the sale and therefore no U.S. tax due.

Western Consolidated's management estimates that the initial outlay to install the plant will be $1,200,000 and that the book value of the plant to be returned at the end of the sixth year will be $960,000. Annual fixed costs, including depreciation, will be $200,000 for the first year of operation and will increase 10 percent each year over the remaining five years. For any one year, the average variable cost of each type of unit is expected to be constant, but AVC will have to be adjusted upward for rising input prices. The AVC estimates by year for the two types of machines are as follows:

Year	AVC_A	AVC_B
1	$ 9,600	$15,500
2	10,400	17,100
3	11,200	17,940
4	12,000	19,320
5	14,400	20,250
6	16,000	21,500

The Latin American government has agreed to make all guaranteed payments in U.S. dollars, so that Western Consolidated will run no exchange-rate risk. Management normally uses a discount rate of 12 percent for its U.S. investments, and it has been argued that the same rate should be applied to this foreign project because the government guarantees will minimize risk.

PROPOSAL II

Under this alternative, Western Consolidated would install a somewhat less flexible plant with facilities for producing only the Type B packaging machine. The initial outlay on the plant installation would be only $960,000, but the book value that would be returned at the end of six years would also be less: $768,000. Annual total fixed costs for this type of plant will be only $180,000 in the first year of operation but will increase by 10 percent each year. The prices guaranteed for the Type B machine would be the same as those stated for each year in Proposal I. In addition, the above data on AVC for the Type B machine would continue to be applicable. However, the guaranteed quantity sold of the Type B machine when it is the only kind produced would be as follows:

Year	Quantity Sold of Type B
1	50
2	60
3	60
4	80
5	100
6	100

The tax rate of 46 percent on profits will apply as in Proposal I, and the purchase of the plant at book value will ensure that no capital gains taxes will be due on the amount received when the government takes over the operation at the end of six years. Finally, the company's management will use a 12 percent discount rate in the evaluation of this alternative, again because of the low level of risk assured by government guarantees.

QUESTIONS

(*Hint:* When evaluating project inflows, be sure to reduce annual gross profits by the amount of foreign profits taxes paid.)

1. Is Proposal I an acceptable capital project? Why or why not?
2. Is Proposal II an acceptable capital project? Why or why not?
3. If the discount rate is raised to 14 percent, would either proposal be acceptable?
4. What kinds of information about the projects or the environment of the country might lead to a decision to employ an even higher discount rate to evaluate inflows?

INTEGRATING CASE 4B

Shanghai Magnificent Harmony Foundry II

Happy Mr. Fei! His manhole cover project (Case 2B, "Shanghai Magnificent Harmony Foundry I," following Chapter 8) has been deemed a smashing success, as he was able to obtain U.S. trade preference status and iron ore prices did not increase. The Central Management Committee is so impressed with Fei's handling of the matter that they now want him to search out other types of simple cast-iron products that could be exported to the United States.

On a trip to the United States, Fei discovered that the health and fitness boom has created dramatic increases in demand for all types of exercise equipment. Cast-iron weights for body-building programs at fitness centers and gyms seemed to be selling very well in the U.S. market. Fei realized that it would be a simple matter for Shanghai Magnificent Harmony Foundry (SMHF) to cast the circular weights used on lifting bars, but producing the bars themselves would present an additional problem.

To be competitive with other producers of weight-lifting equipment, Fei will have to provide lifting bars to the U.S. firms that would distribute the cast-iron weights. These bars must be of forged metal, and they are normally machined and chromium plated to improve their appearance and deter rust. While SMHF has sufficient idle capacity in forging to manufacture the bars, it has no facilities for machining and chrome plating and will have to invest in both types of equipment to realize the new project. The cost of the equipment is estimated to be 960,000 Renminbi Yuan, or 200,000 U.S. dollars at the official exchange rate applicable to both offshore sales and valuation of capital investments.

Because of a slowdown in China's shipbuilding industry, SMHF will be able to release some casting capacity to Fei for export-oriented production of the weights. This is estimated to be 500 short tons per year (2,000 lbs. = one short ton) over the next five years.

Fei has been told that the weight-lifting equipment undertaking must be evaluated with a five-year project life, since management expects it will have to reallocate the casting capacity to parts for shipbuilding as demand recovers in that sector. If casting capacity increases due to government allocation of investment funds, exports of the new product would be continued, but there is certainly no guarantee of this.

Given the success of his previous project, Fei is certain that no tariff will have to be paid on the weight-lifting equipment. For every pound of weights sold, 0.25 lb. of lifting bars (straight bars, curling bars, and dumbbell bars) will be sold. The simple cast-iron weights will have to be sold at the world market price of cast iron, which comes to $0.48 per lb. delivered to U.S. West Coast ports. His net price for both weights and bars will have to be reduced by $0.06 per lb. for freight. The landed price of the bars will be double that of the weights. Fei estimates that the forging, machining, and chrome-plating processes will increase the cost of the bars by 75 percent in comparison with ordinary cast-iron products. Further, he believes that all of the 500-ton output can be sold each year.

Fei has been instructed to evaluate the weight-lifting equipment project over the five-year time horizon using a risk-adjusted discount rate of 18 percent per year. The Central Management Committee has chosen not to require this project to carry any allocated fixed costs. Variable cost per pound of product will be the same as for manhole covers (see SMHF I), with appropriate adjustment for the production of the lifting bars. The bars and weights must sum to the available capacity allocated to the project. Fei has been told not to assume any salvage value for the equipment. Assume that because the project will not be assessed income taxes, Fei will not be able to achieve any tax savings from depreciation of the new equipment.

QUESTIONS

1. From the data given in this case, will the project be acceptable given the investment that must be made to do the plating of the bars?
2. Calculate the impact that the following would have on the project:
   a. A reduction in the risk-adjusted discount rate to 15 percent per year.
   b. A shortening of the project life to four years, given the original (18 percent per year) risk-adjusted discount rate.

PART 5

The Firm and the Public Sector

15

ECONOMICS OF PUBLIC SECTOR DECISIONS

In this chapter and the two that follow, we direct attention to the economic interrelationships between business firms and government. We begin at an operational level, adapting the optimizing decision rules discussed in previous chapters to problems of public sector decision making. We will find that many of the economic principles developed in the context of the profit-maximizing firm can be carried over to certain types of public managerial problems. However, the nature of much of the public sector's product is such that some new tools of analysis must also be developed.

This chapter deals primarily with managerial decisions concerning the supply of goods and services by the public sector. In Chapter 16 we address the matter of the effects of one of the public sector's products, laws and regulations, on private firms and their managers. Finally, Chapter 17 is devoted to an overview of recent developments in the sphere of government-business relationships and an attempt to identify trends that will define the environment of business firms and managerial decision makers in the not-too-distant future.

MICRO- VERSUS MACROECONOMICS IN PUBLIC SECTOR ANALYSIS

In the United States, public sector purchases of goods and services amount to about 20 percent of GNP. Much of our national economic policy focuses on the *macroeconomic* variables (aggregate consumption expenditures, gross private domestic investment, total government expenditures, taxes, and the money supply) that determine the level of employment and activity in the economy. In a very broad and general sense, the GNP is an indicator of the well-being of the nation's citizens, and increases in real GNP (i.e., GNP adjusted for changes in the purchasing power of the dollar) can be interpreted as improvements in the overall standard of living, as long as they are not outstripped by population increases and the picture is not distorted by shifts in the distribution of income among individuals or groups. Of course, the way in which resources are utilized by government is another important factor affecting the well-being of a society.

The federal government through its budgetary processes and its management of monetary policy, attempts to make the decisions necessary to move toward the attainment of an overall goal of full employment and relatively stable prices. However, in the process of managing the federal budget and the activities subsumed under it, literally thousands of *microeconomic* decisions must be made each day in the agencies and the bureaus that are responsible for the particular uses to which government-obtained resources are put. As some well-known public expenditure experts have stated:

> The evaluation of aggregate expenditure and taxation levels is an important ingredient in establishing national goals and priorities. However, expenditures are not made in the aggregate, but rather for specific goods and services. Whether the aggregate level is ideal in part depends on whether these specific expenditures can be justified on an individual basis.[1]

Administrators working in public bureaus and agencies (whether local, state, or federal) frequently occupy slots not unlike those held by business managers. Therefore the decision analyses developed for profit-maximizing firms can prove very useful to such administrators, even if the objective of their agency seems remote from the notion of economic profit. To apply managerial economics to the problems of public sector microeconomic decisions, we must first take a close look at the nature of public sector output and the objectives its production is meant to fulfill. We then emphasize in the balance of this chapter the techniques used in making public sector decisions relating to governmental output of specific goods and services.

THE PUBLIC SECTOR'S PRODUCT

The public sector (for our purposes, federal, state, and local government) produces an output of goods and services that consists mainly of public goods and *mixed goods* (goods that are partly public). In Chapter 14 we noted that an essential characteristic of a public good is that it provides benefits to parties who do not engage in a market transaction to obtain it. We also called these benefits *external benefits* or *third-party benefits*.

Perhaps the most obvious example of a public good is national defense. The benefits to all members of our society as a result of "consuming" national defense are generally considered to be significant. However, we do not individually engage in market transactions to purchase national defense, and the amount any given consumer would be willing to pay for defense would probably be zero if the consumer thought that the defense would be supplied whether or not he or she paid anything for it.

A **pure public good** is a product or service that is indivisible and nonexcludable.

Economists say that a good is a **pure public good** if it is *indivisible* (if one

---

1 Gary Fromm and Paul Taubman, *Public Economic Theory and Policy* (New York: Macmillan, 1973), p. 28.

person cannot consume a unit of it apart from other units) and *nonexcludable* (if it is difficult or impossible to keep it from consumers who do not pay for it). Aside from national defense, other examples of public goods are scenic views, lakes and rivers, food and drug regulation, criminal justice, and "free" radio and television. Clearly, not all public goods are produced by the public sector—God or NBC may be the supplier of some of them.

The public sector also produces a large quantity of mixed goods that provide third-party benefits, as well as private benefits, to users who pay (perhaps not the full cost) for the privilege of using them. Postal service, public housing projects, state and federal parks, and toll roads are all examples.

Finally, the public sector does produce certain goods that are almost purely private. For example, the Tennessee Valley Authority (TVA), which was set up primarily to control floods and provide rural electricity, produces fertilizer that is sold to farmers in the marketplace alongside similar products made by private industry. However, in this case it can be argued that an important reason for the production by the public sector of such a divisible and excludable good as fertilizer is that such production results in social benefits that exceed the private benefits to farmers from their use of the product. For example, excess or off-peak generating capacity can be used in fertilizer production rather than left idle, and the TVA is able to conduct research on the production and use of fertilizer in depressed agricultural areas. Thus, even when an element of the public sector's output takes on the appearance of a private good, its character can be expected to be mixed because of external benefits related to its production.

Although we have so far characterized public and mixed goods by focusing on external benefits that accompany their production, it should be noted that the production of many goods (including public, mixed, and private goods) also entails external costs. As we will see in the following section, both external costs and external benefits raise serious problems regarding the extent to which a free market system can achieve an economically efficient allocation of resources.

RESOURCE ALLOCATION AND THE SUPPLY OF PUBLIC GOODS

If government undertakes to supply a particular good or service, it must withdraw resources from the private sector, usually by purchasing them in the market. Since a reallocation of resources and a change in the economy's output follow, it is important that government decision makers ascertain whether these products result in an increase in the general well-being of the citizenry as a whole. There are really two parts to this question. First, will the government activity result in a more efficient allocation of resources? And second, will the distribution of income be altered in a way that is likely to improve the general well-being? The second question is necessary, since the provision of certain types of public sector output may involve taking income from one group of citizens and transferring it to another. At this point, however, we will concentrate on answering only the first of the two questions.

The resource allocation question applies both to privately produced goods and to public sector output. In theory the amount of any good that should be supplied at a point in time is the quantity that *equates the marginal social cost of the good with its marginal social benefit*. We need a few definitions to understand this concept.

First, the marginal *private* economic cost of a good includes all explicit and implicit costs of its production that are borne by the producer. A product's **marginal social cost** differs from its marginal private cost by the amount of external costs (third-party costs) that accompany the production of an incremental unit of output. This cost includes the value to consumers of any alternative product or products whose production is reduced or eliminated. If there are no external costs, marginal social cost and marginal private cost will be identical at each level of output.

In similar fashion we can define **marginal social benefit** as the sum of marginal private benefits and marginal external or third-party benefits. The private benefits accrue to those who directly pay a price for the good, while the external benefits are enjoyed by either the purchasers and/or nonpurchasers but are not accounted for in the product's market price. Of course, where there are no external benefits, marginal social benefit and marginal private benefit will be identical at each level of output.

If we argue that all sorts of benefits and costs can be given a dollar value, we can proceed very straightforwardly to the rationale behind the assertion that a good should be provided up to the quantity where marginal social cost equals marginal social benefit. Actually, this principle is a simple extension of the profit-maximizing decision rule for a firm: that the firm should produce up to the point where its marginal revenue equals its marginal cost. Where the decision-making unit is a governmental unit rather than a firm, we merely substitute "social benefit" for revenue and "social cost" for private cost:

> To maximize the **net social benefit** received from a good or service, it should be produced up to the point where its marginal social benefit is equal to its marginal social cost. The net social benefit of a good is equal to its total social benefit less its total social cost.

In Figure 15–1, we illustrate a total social benefit curve and a total social cost curve, both of which are increasing functions of the quantity of public good X. Net benefits are maximized at Q_X^*, where marginal social cost equals marginal social benefit. In the lower panel, the marginal social cost curve intersects the marginal social benefit curve at Q_X^*, and the slopes of the two curves ensure that for levels of output greater than Q_X^*, additions to social cost will exceed additions to social benefit. Thus, Q_X^* is the amount of output that will maximize society's net benefit from production of this good.

A theoretically optimal allocation of society's resources exists when for

The **marginal social cost** of a good is equal to the marginal private cost of producing it plus any marginal external costs imposed on third parties by its production. The marginal social cost of a good reflects the value of resources used in its production.

The **marginal social benefit** of a good is equal to the marginal private benefits the good provides plus any additional external or third-party benefits.

The **net social benefit** of a good is equal to its total social benefit less its total social cost.

Figure 15–1   Maximization of Net Social Benefits

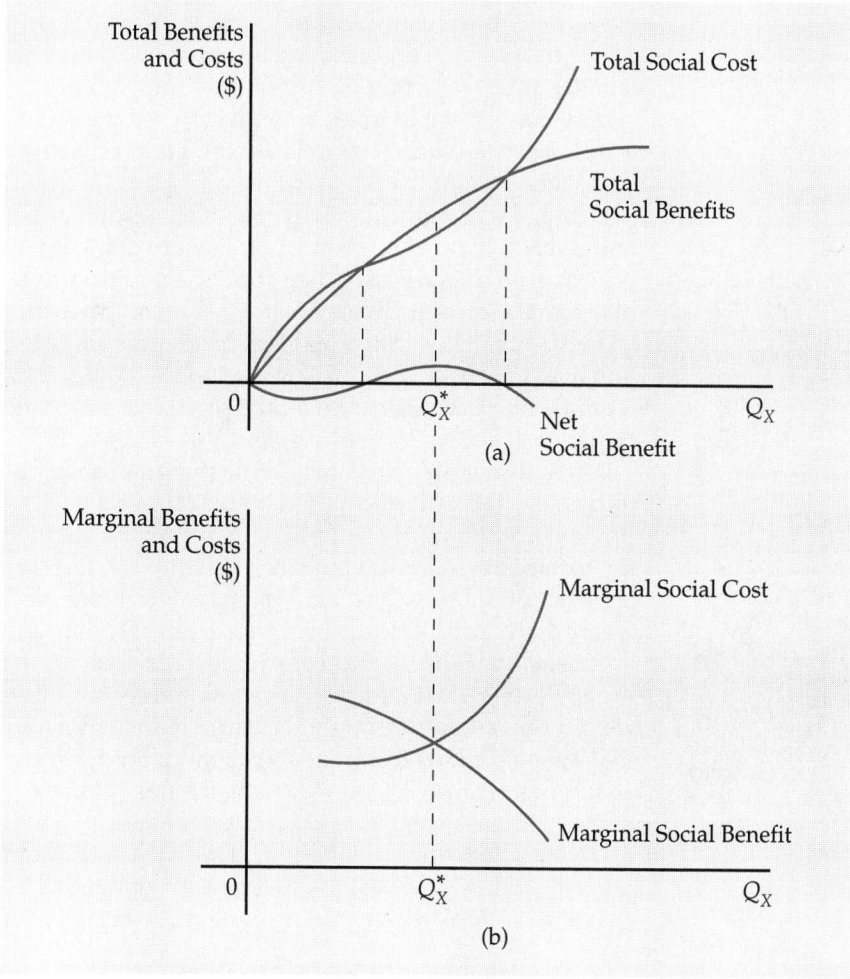

The optimal quantity of a public good is produced where the marginal social benefit of the good equals its marginal social cost. At Q_x^*, net social benefit—the difference between total social benefit and total social cost—is maximized. Production beyond Q_x^* would add more to social cost than to social benefit.

all goods the condition that $MSB = MSC$ is attained. We can further examine this principle by looking at a two-good case, where X and Y are the goods, where both costs and benefits are measured in dollars, and where initially we have

(15–1)

$$MSB_X = MSC_X = 20,$$

and

$$MSB_Y = MSC_Y = 40.$$

Thus the social cost of producing the marginal or last unit of X is \$20, while that of producing the marginal unit of Y is \$40. Obviously, it is also true that

(15–2)
$$\frac{MSB_X}{MSC_X} = \frac{MSB_Y}{MSC_Y} = 1.$$

Now assume that the following conditions exist:

1. All resources are fully employed.
2. Marginal social benefit *falls* as the quantity of each good produced is increased.
3. Marginal social cost is constant at \$20 per unit of X and \$40 per unit of Y.

What will happen to equation (15–2) if one more unit of Y is produced? First of all, a marginal social cost of \$40 will be incurred; this means *two* units of X production must be forgone. Since MSB_X will *rise* as the quantity of X is reduced, and MSB_Y will *fall* as the quantity of Y is increased, the result must be

(15–3)
$$\frac{MSB_X}{MSC_X} > 1 > \frac{MSB_Y}{MSC_Y}.$$

For example, we might have

(15–4)
$$\frac{22}{20} > 1 > \frac{38}{40}.$$

What are these ratios saying? The answer is much the same as the one we derived in the theory of production with regard to the substitution of inputs in the long run. In particular, for the new output combination, the social *benefit gained* from a *dollar's worth of expenditure* on Product X is \$22/\$20 = \$1.10, whereas the social *loss* from spending a *dollar less* on resources to produce Y is \$38/\$40 = \$0.95. Clearly, resources are *misallocated* in the new position [equation (15–4)]. The production of Y should be reduced and that of X increased until the original position is again attained and $MSB_X/MSC_X = MSB_Y/MSC_Y = 1$.

Finally, we should note that marginal social *cost* is likely to *increase* as production of a good increases and decrease as production falls. This more realistic assumption would not change the directions of the inequalities in equations (15–3) and (15–4), since MSC_X would be less than 20 and MSC_Y would be greater than 40. Our case would simply be reinforced by having both marginal social benefits *decrease* and marginal social costs *increase* as the output of a good expands.

MANAGERIAL PERSPECTIVE

The $5 Billion Mistake

Long Island Lighting Company (LILCO) had a problem on its hands—a $5.3 billion problem. Its Shoreham nuclear plant, completed at the end of 1983, had not received a license to operate and was not likely to receive one. The reason was that nearby communities were not satisfied with LILCO's emergency evacuation plan.

Finally, then New York Governor, Mario Cuomo, decided that the plant must not start up. After a great deal of negotiation, the state of New York agreed to take the plant off LILCO's hands for $1. However, the $1 price included an agreement to dismantle the plant and haul away the pieces, at least when someone came up with a safe way to dispose of the radioactive core. Moreover, the state guaranteed LILCO annual rate increases of 5% for at least three years and perhaps as long as 10 years. As a result, LILCO customers would have to pay for part of LILCO's expensive white elephant. The state guarantee made it possible for LILCO to raise its rates repeatedly, and in 1996, they were the highest in the continental United States. By raising its rates, LILCO was able to continue paying dividends to its investors and retain its ability to borrow. Needless to say, this was a much better deal for LILCO's investors than for consumers.

References: Charles M. Studness, "LILCO: The Ultimate Failure of Regulation," *Public Utilities Fortnightly* (March 1, 1996), pp. 33–36; and "The $5 Billion Nuclear Waste," *Time* (June 6, 1988), p. 55.

We can now summarize the implications of the preceding discussion. First, for a given income distribution, efficient resource allocation will take place when, for n goods,

(15–5)
$$\frac{MSB_a}{MSC_a} = \frac{MSB_b}{MSC_b} = \ldots = \frac{MSB_n}{MSC_n} = 1.$$

This condition simply means that a dollar's worth of social benefit is received for an additional dollar spent on the production of each good. Any deviation from this condition will result in a situation where too much of some good (or goods) and too little of some other good (or goods) is produced.

Furthermore, we can make the following important statement:

No incremental activity (j) should be undertaken where $MSC_j > MSB_j$.

Where the production of public goods is concerned, therefore, it is justifiable to increase output only where $MSB_j/MSC_j \geq 1$—that is, when the incremental social benefit exceeds or equals the incremental social cost of the activity.

The incremental benefit-cost ratio (MSB/MSC) of a project is equal to the marginal social benefit divided by the marginal social cost of an incremental unit of the project. The net benefit obtained from a project or activity will be maximized by increasing the size of the project or scope of the activity up to the point where the incremental benefit-cost ratio, MSB/MSC, is equal to 1.

The fraction MSB/MSC is called the **incremental benefit-cost ratio**; and in cost-benefit analysis it is employed to determine the optimal *size* of a given public sector activity or project. In the following section, we will contrast this ratio with the ratio of *total* benefits to *total* costs, B/C, a concept frequently utilized to identify worthwhile projects and rank-order them. The ratio B/C is often called the **average benefit-cost ratio**, or simply the **benefit-cost ratio**.

COST-BENEFIT ANALYSIS: A PROCEDURAL OUTLINE

The **benefit-cost ratio** (B/C) for an activity or project is equal to the present value of its benefits divided by the present value of its cost. A project is acceptable from a social welfare point of view if and only if its B/C is greater than or equal to 1.

Cost-benefit analysis is an extension of capital project analysis to public sector project decisions that attempts to take into account the economic criteria for an optimal allocation of society's resources.

Cost-benefit analysis is simply the extension of capital project analysis, described earlier in Chapters 13 and 14, to public sector microeconomic decisions. It proceeds from the notion that the aggregate output of government or any subsector thereof consists of an array of alternative projects, each having costs and benefits and each of which can be undertaken at various sizes or operated at various levels of output. To the extent that each of these is carefully screened, their aggregate is likely to have the most beneficial effect on national well-being.

The steps usually taken in the construction of a cost-benefit analysis for a government undertaking are as follows:

1. Specify objectives and identify constraints.
2. Formulate alternative means of meeting objectives.
3. Estimate costs of each alternative.
4. Estimate benefits attributable to each alternative.
5. Select the best alternative.

Every item in the preceding list poses a substantial problem or set of problems for the decision maker. First, the objectives of a public expenditure project are often easy to state in general terms but are difficult to quantify. If, for example, our objective is to improve mass transit services in a given metropolitan area, how can we state it specifically? Do we just want to move a given number of people in less time? Should *more* service be available to a broader range of potential users? What kind of service should we offer (buses, streetcars, subway)? What about passenger comfort? Will the project impose environmental costs or perhaps reduce them?

Some of the preceding questions will be unanswerable until the study is completed, since each of the possible outputs will have a social cost that might exceed its social benefit. In addition, the constraint structure will help to identify feasible characteristics of the preliminary planning objectives. For example, it might be clear at the outset that the metropolitan government can afford to consider only projects with an initial capital outlay of $24 million or less. Thus no combination of services requiring a larger outlay could be considered. There may also be technological constraints. (For example, if the city is located near sea level, a subway might be an impossibility.) Finally, there may be political or institutional constraints or barriers that limit the way in which the undertaking can be designed. For example, if a separately incorporated area that is opposed to a metropolitan transit system lies in the way of one possible alternative route, then the route may not be feasible.

Once the objectives and the constraints are well understood, alternative proposals for the undertaking can be formulated. The next step is to delineate the costs and benefits for each alternative. Then a dollar value estimate must be obtained for each item of cost and benefit. This is not a simple procedure, since a correct analysis of the alternatives must consider *all* economic costs and benefits attributable to each.

In the calculation of costs and benefits, items are usually categorized as *direct* or *indirect* costs or benefits. **Direct costs** of an undertaking include research and planning outlays, initial capital outlay, and maintenance and operating expenses over the project's life. Some items of direct cost will be difficult to estimate because they are implicit. For example, the cost of using government-owned resources (perhaps land) in the project would be estimated using an opportunity cost approach. In the case of land, the cost would be estimated by ascertaining its present value in its next best use.

Indirect costs of a project are generally those costs related to externalities that are outputs of the project not accounted for in outlays of the government for project components. For example, if streets must be dug up to construct a subway, the resulting disruption of traffic and business activity will have real costs to society. These kinds of costs are always difficult to estimate because of their partly nonmarket nature. Nonetheless, they must enter into the analysis; and, indeed, a good part of the literature on cost-benefit analysis is directed precisely toward issues of measurement. The one maxim that is universally mentioned by writers on the subject is that such costs should be estimated using the closest possible approximation to the market value of their negative effects. For example, one might use the average value of a working motorist's time to estimate the cost of disruption caused by public works construction.

On the benefits side, **direct benefits** generally accrue to *users* of the project's facilities or primary outputs. In passenger transportation, for example, the main direct benefits accrue to riders of the transportation system. Direct benefits may also accrue to persons employed in the construction and/or operation of the facilities if such persons were previously unemployed. Otherwise, employment associated with the project may simply reflect changes in the distribution of employment, which may produce little or no net social gain.

Much like indirect costs, **indirect benefits** stem mainly from externalities. Thus a system of public mass transit may eliminate congestion for nonusers of the system, and it may enhance the environment by reducing ex-

The **direct costs** of a project or activity are the costs directly associated with the project or activity.

The **direct benefits** of a project or activity are the benefits obtained by the users of the project or activity.

The **indirect benefits and costs** associated with a project or activity are external, or third-party, benefits and costs.

haust fumes. A roundabout means of estimation may be necessary to come up with a figure for the dollar value of such benefits. Indeed, the elusiveness of indirect benefits, and especially of their estimation, is one of the major dangers in cost-benefit analysis. This point will be discussed further in a following section.

Since some costs and virtually all benefits will be flows occurring over time, it will be necessary to discount the dollar value of such streams. In the final analysis, the evaluation of each alternative undertaking will rest on the trade-off between the present value of project cost and the present value of benefits. For the field of public investment, the matter of the appropriate discount rate (the *social* rate of discount) has been the subject of much controversy. At this point, it is sufficient for us to note that it is generally a lower rate than that used in the private sector, since government can usually borrow at low rates of interest (for example, the low rates usually paid on municipal bonds). In a subsequent discussion, we will provide an example of the effect of changes in the discount rate on project acceptability.

In capital project analysis in Chapter 13 we saw that a project was acceptable as long as its net present value was greater than or equal to zero. Similarly, a public project or activity is acceptable as long as its net benefit is greater than or equal to zero or, equivalently, as long as its benefit-cost ratio is greater than or equal to 1. Moreover, an increase in the size of a project or activity will increase the net benefit associated with the project as long as its incremental benefit-cost ratio (MSB/MSC) is greater than 1. The net benefit of a project will therefore be maximized by increasing the project size until MSB/MSC is equal to 1. This condition implies that $MSB = MSC$ at the optimal point for the production of a project, the social welfare maximization rule discussed earlier in this chapter.

With the preceding general notions about benefit and cost estimation in mind, we now turn to an example of the application of cost-benefit analysis.

An Application to Urban Mass Transit

Perhaps the best way to illustrate steps taken in reaching a decision through the cost-benefit approach is to look at an application to a specific problem. Let us suppose that we are preparing a cost-benefit analysis of proposed improvements in the transportation system of one of the nation's 15 largest metropolitan areas. It is widely agreed that the current public transportation system, consisting solely of buses and airport limousines, is woefully inadequate. A county-wide metropolitan transit authority has been set up to deal with the problem.

The transit authority has engaged our firm to prepare a cost-benefit analysis of the metropolitan problem. A rough dollar constraint has been established for a number of possible improvement alternatives to be financed by a 20-year bond issue. The maximum amount of funds available for the improvements, which will be completed within 18 months of the sale of the

MANAGERIAL PERSPECTIVE
Valuing a Sea Otter, Asthma Attacks, and Fishing Trips

We have stated that valuing intangibles has presented public officials and economists involved in cost-benefit studies with estimation problems. However, recently natural resource economists have been increasingly in demand to do just that with respect to the environment. In the past, for example, cost-benefit studies of air pollution controls have usually included reduced medical costs among the benefits. Now a recent study has shown that people might be willing to pay as much as $10 per day to avoid the discomfort of coughing and eye irritation caused by pollution.

When the New Bedford Harbor in Massachusetts was found to be polluted by PCBs, the calculated damages included not only the loss to commercial lobster fishers, but also $11 million in damages to beachgoers. Similar calculations were done with respect to lost recreational opportunities as a result of contamination of the Eagle River in Colorado from mining operations. Exxon Corporation and the state of Alaska have both employed economists to estimate the damages to wildlife (such as sea otters) and recreational users as a result of the oil spill in Prince William Sound. In one recent case, a court ruling held that those responsible for dumping oil or toxic chemicals must either restore the environment to its original condition or pay compensation for the total value of the damages, included the loss of nonmarket benefits.

Many of these estimates of nonmarket damages involve asking people how much they would be willing to pay in higher taxes to maintain some natural resource. Some examples of values placed on intangibles include $73 per household per year for fishing trips on the Eagle River, for an aggregate annual value of $0.5 million; $10 per household per year for preserving the bald eagle in Wisconsin, for a total annual value of $30.0 million; and $25 per household for one less asthma attack per year, for an aggregate annual value of $175 million. Although such figures are still often disputed, it is becoming clear that these nonmarket or intangible costs of pollution are quite real to those who incur them.

References: "Putting a Price Tag on Nature," *Montana Business Quarterly* (Summer 1995), pp. 8–10; and "How Much Is a Sea Otter Worth?" *Business Week* (August 21, 1989), pp. 59–62.

bonds, will be $24 million. Throughout our analysis we will be able to use this figure (or a lower one) as the present value of the project price, even though as many as two years will be required to complete improvements to the system, since the metropolitan authority can earn interest on the unexpended portion of the funds raised at about the same rate as it pays bondholders.[2]

Project Design: The Alternatives

Obviously, in an urban mass transportation project, one of the main items that will determine the possible configurations of services is the demand of the users and potential users. In the present case, we know that existing bus service is considered to be inadequate and that some specific type of service between the airport and certain other points is warranted. Undoubtedly the existing transit system will have records providing information on routes and passenger utilization of services. It may even have survey data on passenger opinions regarding new routes and types of service. If not, one of the tasks of the project analysts will be to conduct such surveys. In addition, nontransit objectives (such as pollution control, noise abatement, and general aesthetics) will be items of interest to both the community and the decision makers in the transit authority. To the extent that there are such secondary objectives of the project, they must be made as explicit as possible, and the effects of different alternative solutions on these objectives (the indirect costs and benefits of each alternative) must enter into the overall project calculations.

Let us suppose that in consultation with local authorities, a set of planning objectives is generated. Let us also suppose that based on these objectives and some preliminary estimates of passenger demand, the following alternatives are chosen for evaluation:

1. Modernize and expand the existing bus fleet and continue airport limousine service (initial capital outlay: $4,000,000).
2. Combine bus modernization with helicopter service to the airport and minibus service around the central shopping area (initial capital outlay: $6,000,000).
3. Modernize the existing bus fleet and utilize an existing railway right-of-way to provide commuter train service between the airport, nearby points, and the central business district (initial capital outlay: $11,000,000).
4. Modernize the bus fleet and construct a subway line linking the central business district with the airport and intermediate points (initial capital outlay: $17,000,000).

---

2 This is possible because the bonds would be tax exempt and might therefore bear a rate of interest no higher than that earned on large-size time deposits.

5. Modernize the bus fleet and construct a monorail train line from the airport and nearby points to the central business district (initial capital outlay: $22,000,000).

With the project alternatives thus set out, the next step is to determine the cost of each alternative. In the present case, each alternative will in theory have an optimal size. That size can be expressed in dollar terms as the level of cost that is consistent with provision of service up to the point where marginal social cost equals marginal social benefit. Thus, using alternative 1 as an example, we know there is a limit beyond which additions to the bus fleet and limousine service will likely increase social cost more than they will increase social benefits. However, this does not mean that a change to another type of service, such as the types described in alternatives 2, 3, 4, and 5, would have no potential for net additions to social benefit. We are merely establishing the level of operation of alternative 1 that will provide the maximum net benefit from its employment.

Since there is already a transit system in operation, the relevant cost of each of the improvement alternatives is the present value of the *differential* in cost between the alternative and operation of the existing system *without* modification. Such costs will consist primarily of the initial outlay (from the bond issue) on new capital equipment or modernization of old equipment, the present value of the difference in operating costs over the project life, and any indirect or external costs associated with undertaking and operating the new project—over and above those generated by continued operation of the existing system.

Measurement of the preceding cost items is relatively straightforward, except in the case of indirect or external costs. For example, if we consider alternative 4 or alternative 5, there will be external costs of disruption of traffic caused by the construction of subway or monorail facilities. Indeed, construction of such facilities may require some permanent adjustment in street routes (some may be blocked off by the rapid transit lines and become dead ends), which imposes external costs on motorists in a given area. These costs will by nature be more difficult to estimate than will direct capital costs or operating expenses.

Once the present value of the cost differential for each alternative has been estimated, the calculation of benefits begins. Again, the relevant measure is the differential between benefits generated by each new alternative and benefits that would occur if the existing system were continued over the time period identified as the project life.

Turning our attention now to the question of benefits, we expect that most of the incremental benefits will accrue to passengers who use the transit system and pay a fare for the service. However, public transportation is a mixed good that in almost all circumstances generates external benefits. For example, we can expect that nonusers of the transit system will benefit from reduced congestion if the system attracts riders who formerly drove their cars to destinations served by mass transit. In addition, businesses may benefit from reduced expenditures on employee parking facilities or company-subsidized car pool arrangements. Obviously, in this and in almost all public investment projects, we are dealing with a *flow* of benefits over time. Thus the appropriate measure of benefits will be the present value of the differential benefits generated by each alternative.

In Table 15–1 we show an enumeration of the differential costs and benefits attributable to alternative 1. As mentioned previously, the direct cost items are generally the easiest to estimate. The indirect cost items, pollution and noise, are difficult but not impossible to estimate. One well-known procedure is to ascertain the effects of pollution and noise on land values and then use this figure as a proxy for external cost. Obviously, where diesel fumes become noxiously thick, land values are likely to suffer. Fortunately, data on the effects of pollution and environmental decay on land values can frequently be obtained.

In the benefits portion of Table 15–1, we see the estimation problem in a different light. To some extent the direct benefits can be estimated by ascertaining the price that users of the service would be willing to *pay* to ride the system at the optimal level of operation. In fact, this is the theoretically correct way to estimate private benefits to users. However, it may be somewhat difficult to estimate, *ex ante*, the fare that will yield the optimal level of use

Table 15–1   Present Value of Differential Costs and Benefits of Mass Transit Improvements: Alternative 1[1]

Differential Costs	
(a) Direct:	
1. Initial capital outlay	$ 4,000,000
2. *PV* of operating cost differential	2,900,000
(b) Indirect:	
1. *PV* of additional pollution and noise	600,000
Total Differential Costs (*PV*)	$ 7,500,000
Differential Benefits	
(a) Direct:	
1. *PV* of time saved by users	$ 2,500,000
2. *PV* of motor fuel saved by users	3,000,000
3. *PV* of other automobile-operating expenses saved	
by users	2,000,000
(b) Indirect:	
1. *PV* of reduced congestion to motorists	2,000,000
2. *PV* of parking and car pool savings of businesses	1,000,000
Total Differential Benefits (*PV*)	$10,500,000

[1]The project life is assumed to be 20 years, and the discount rate is 5 percent. The $3,500,000 *PV* of future differential costs is a discounted stream of $280,847 per year. The $10,500,000 *PV* of future differential benefits is a discounted stream of $842,541 per year.

(the passenger volume consistent with *MSC* = *MSB*). Nevertheless, surveys can be used to determine approximately the number of people who would use the new service, given various prices.

As far as indirect benefits are concerned, the *PV* of reduced congestion to motorists can be estimated by calculating the amount of time that would be saved and then multiplying that figure by an appropriate dollar value per hour. The *PV* of savings to businesses from reduced expenditures on parking facilities and car pool arrangements can be estimated from data supplied by firms.

Once estimation problems have been surmounted, an enumeration such as Table 15–1 is prepared for each alternative. From these enumerations of costs and benefits, data for selecting the best alternative are calculated. Note that from Table 15–1, we have for alternative 1 a ratio of total differential benefits to total differential costs of $10,500,000/$7,500,000 = 1.40. Since the differential benefits exceed the differential costs, or the average benefit-cost ratio is greater than 1, alternative 1 is an acceptable project. In fact, any alternative that has an average benefit-cost ratio greater than 1 is acceptable, since it generates *net* social benefits.

Table 15–1 has been prepared using a discount rate of 5 percent to calculate the present values of future costs and benefits (operating costs, indirect costs, and all of the differential benefits). At this point we provide no rationale for the use of the 5 percent rate and proceed as though the rate itself were not an issue, but the effect of changing the discount rate will be examined later in this chapter.

In Table 15–2 we present summary data on the five alternative projects.

Table 15–2   Cost-Benefit Comparison of Five Alternative Metropolitan Mass Transit Projects[1]

Alternative No.	PV of Differential Costs (C)	PV of Differential Benefits (B)	B/C	$\frac{\Delta B}{\Delta C}$	Net Differential Benefits (B-C)
1	$ 7,500,000	$10,500,000	1.40		$3,000,000
				1.56	
3	12,000,000	17,500,000	1.46		5,500,000
				1.18	
2	17,500,000	24,000,000	1.37		6,500,000
				0.74	
5	27,000,000	31,000,000	1.15		4,000,000
				0.71	
4	34,000,000	36,000,000	1.06		2,000,000

[1]All future differential costs and benefits are discounted at a rate of 5 percent per annum for 20 years. See Table 15–3 for division of costs between capital outlay and discounted future flows, as well as annual benefit inflows.

Using the average benefit-cost ratio as an accept-reject criterion, we see that all five of the projects are acceptable, since $B/C > 1$ for each one of them.

In Table 15–2 the projects have been listed in order of *ascending cost*. This is a convenient format for our next step—the selection of the optimal project. What we need to know in order to select the best alternative is whether the additional costs incurred when going from a smaller project to a larger one are offset or more than offset by the additional benefits attributable to the larger project. The *incremental benefit-cost ratio*, $\Delta B/\Delta C$, answers this question. A move from a smaller undertaking to a larger one (in terms of total differential costs) is warranted as long as $\Delta B/\Delta C > 1$. Thus, according to Table 15–2, alternative 2 should be selected, since it yields net benefits above alternatives 1 and 3, whereas selecting either alternative 5 or alternative 4 over alternative 2 would add more to differential costs than to differential benefits.[3]

The preceding procedure is simply a way to approximate the condition $MSB = MSC$ where data are discrete or "lumpy" rather than continuous and smooth. From our earlier discussion of profit maximization and its relation to benefit-cost analysis, it should be evident that net benefits will be maximized when the project selected is the largest one for which $\Delta B/\Delta C > 1$. Indeed, the last column of Table 15–2 substantiates this result, since net differential benefits are largest for alternative 2.

PUBLIC INVESTMENT AND THE DISCOUNT RATE

Although the discount rate was assumed not to be an issue in the foregoing example, it has been the subject of much concern in public investment projects for two reasons. First, there has been a long debate among economists on how to determine the appropriate discount rate for public capital projects. Second, the choice of the discount rate in many cases affects the decision as to which of several alternative projects is optimal. In fact, we will see shortly that our decision in the urban transit example will be altered if a sufficiently higher discount rate is applied to the future streams of benefits and costs. Before we examine the effects of various discount rates on project selection, however, it will be useful for us to consider the question of the *theoretically correct rate.*

---

3 The student should note that if alternative 3 had yielded an incremental cost-benefit ratio less than 1, it would have been appropriate to compare alternative 2 with alternative 1, rather than with alternative 3. For example, if the *PV* of differential costs for alternative 3 had been $15,500,000 instead of $12,000,000, its $\Delta B/\Delta C$ would have been $7,000,000/ $8,000,000 = 0.88. We would then check $\Delta B/\Delta C$ between alternative 1 and alternative 2. We would find for this increment that $\Delta B/\Delta C$ = $13,500,000/$10,000,000 = 1.35. Accordingly, our rule should be that when projects are listed in ascending order of costs, each successively larger project should be compared with the last project for which $\Delta B/\Delta C > 1$ to determine whether or not it should be undertaken. To test your understanding, show that alternative 5 would be the best choice if the *PV*s of differential costs for alternatives 3 and 2 were $15,500,000 and $21,500,000, respectively.

The "Appropriate" Discount Rate

The rate of discount that in theory should be applied to public investment projects is called the **social rate of discount** by economists. Since public investment usually involves a reallocation of resources from private to public sector use, many economists argue that the opportunity cost, in terms of rate of return, for the private sectors from which the public undertaking would draw its resources constitutes the appropriate rate of discount. Returns from public sector activities are not taxed; therefore the before-tax rate of return for the forgone private output should be used as the discount rate. Finally, analysts also want to take into account the full social costs and benefits of the forgone private output when calculating the rate of return, since this is the procedure they would normally use in estimating the costs and benefits associated with the alternative public use of the resources.[4]

Where *neither externalities nor risk* are viewed as materially affecting the opportunity-cost rate of return, the social rate of discount can be viewed as the riskless market rate of return, adjusted for federal income taxes. Thus, if a business can place its funds in riskless government bonds yielding 6 percent interest tax-free, and if the tax rate on its corporate income is 46 percent, its required before-tax rate of return on a riskless project that will generate taxable income will be

$$\frac{.06}{1 - .46} = 11.11\%.$$

If a business were to place $10,000 in a 6 percent, tax-free bond, at the end of the year it would receive a return of $600 = $10,000(.06). However, at the 46 percent income tax rate, we can see that an 11.11 percent taxable return would yield the same after-tax income, since

$$
\begin{aligned}
\$10,000(.1111) &= \$1,111 \\
1,111\,(-.46) &= \underline{\quad -511} \\
\text{Net Yield} &= \ \ \$\ 600
\end{aligned}
$$

In practice, analysts of public sector capital projects have seldom attempted to estimate a social rate of discount that reflects the opportunity cost of resources withdrawn from private use. Historically, many federally funded projects have been evaluated using a very low discount rate (4.875 percent during the late 1960s) that was thought to be appropriate because it approximated the cost to the Treasury of borrowing funds.

---

4 See David F. Bradford, "The Choice of Discount Rate for Government Investments," in Robert H. Haveman and Julius Margolis (eds.), *Public Expenditure and Policy Analysis*, 3d ed. (Boston: Houghton Mifflin, 1983), Chapter 6.

In a 1967 study of federal budgeting practices, it was discovered that 13 agencies of the government used no discount analysis at all when evaluating expenditure projects. The same study showed that the discount rates used by the 10 agencies that *did* use them to evaluate their 1969 programs ranged from zero to 12 percent.[5] Typically, the rates employed by project analysts at the federal level have been prescribed before the fact and have had little or nothing to do with the opportunity cost of resources.

After more than two decades of criticism of government use of discount rates that in most cases were too low, there has emerged a fairly broad consensus both inside and outside the public sector that rates more realistically reflecting opportunity costs should be used. Accordingly, in recent years the Office of Management and Budget of the federal government has frowned on the use of discount rates lower than 10 percent per year for the evaluation of public programs.[6]

In the final analysis, the best estimate of the appropriate social rate of discount may be the discount rate that reflects the cost of funds for a project of similar length and riskiness in the private sector. Public projects do take resources from the private sector, and the fact that a government may be able to borrow money more cheaply than a private firm because of the tax laws seems irrelevant when one is attempting to value these resources. Therefore it seems reasonable to argue that the private sector cost of funds reflects the opportunity cost of funds used by the public sector for a similar project.

Effect of Changing the Discount Rate

In the preceding discussion, we asserted that changes in the discount rate can markedly affect the outcome of a capital project evaluation. Clearly, the *higher* the discount rate, the *lower* the value of a project's net inflow of benefits, since most of these occur over long periods of time. Moreover, different projects will likely have different ratios of present costs to future costs. Where a project's costs are in large part future costs, the present value of total cost may fall dramatically as the discount rate is increased. We can return to our urban transit alternatives to demonstrate how project choice may be affected by higher discount rates.

In Table 15–3 the five mass transit projects described earlier in this chapter are reviewed, and their future costs and benefits are discounted at rates of

---

5 See Elmer B. Staats, "Survey of Use by Federal Agencies of the Discounting Technique in Evaluating Future Programs," in Harley H. Hinrichs and Graeme M. Taylor (eds.), *Program Budgeting and Benefit-Cost Analysis* (Pacific Palisades, Cal.: Goodyear, 1969), pp. 212–228.
6 Steven H. Hanke and Richard A. Walker, "Benefit-Cost Analysis Reconsidered: An Evaluation of the Mid-State Project," in Robert H. Haveman and Julius Margolis (eds.), *Public Expenditure and Policy Analysis*, 3d ed. (Boston: Houghton Mifflin, 1983), Chapter 14, especially p. 332.

Table 15–3 Effect on Different Discount Rates on Cost-Benefit Comparison of Five Alternative Metropolitan Mass Transit Projects[1]

Alternative	Discount Rate (r)	Initial Capital Outlay	PV of Future Differential Costs	PV of Total Differential Costs (C)	PV of Total Differential Benefits (B)	B/C	ΔB/ΔC r = 5%	r = 7%	r = 9%	Net Differential Benefits (B-C)
1	5%	$ 4,000,000	$ 3,500,000	$ 7,500,000	$10,500,000	1.40	1.56	1.44	1.34	$3,000,000
	7%	4,000,000	2,975,000	6,975,000	8,926,000	1.28				1,951,000
	9%	4,000,000	2,564,000	6,564,000	7,691,000	1.17				1,127,000
3	5%	6,000,000	6,000,000	12,000,000	17,500,000	1.46	1.18	1.02	0.89	5,500,000
	7%	6,000,000	5,101,000	11,101,000	14,877,000	1.34				3,776,000
	9%	6,000,000	4,395,000	10,395,000	12,818,000	1.23				2,423,000
2	5%	11,000,000	6,500,000	17,500,000	24,000,000	1.37	0.74	0.66	0.60	6,500,000
	7%	11,000,000	5,526,000	16,526,000	20,402,000	1.23				3,876,000
	9%	11,000,000	4,761,000	15,761,000	17,579,000	1.12				1,818,000
5	5%	17,000,000	10,000,000	27,000,000	31,000,000	1.15	0.71	0.63	0.57	4,000,000
	7%	17,000,000	8,501,000	25,501,000	26,353,000	1.03				852,000
	9%	17,000,000	7,325,000	24,325,000	22,706,000	0.93				(1,619,000)
4	5%	22,000,000	12,000,000	34,000,000	36,000,000	1.06				2,000,000
	7%	22,000,000	10,201,000	32,201,000	30,603,000	0.95				(1,598,000)
	9%	22,000,000	8,790,000	30,790,000	26,368,000	0.86				(4,422,000)

[1]Assumes the following annual inflows and costs for a period of 20 years:

Alternative	Annual Inflow of Differential Benefits	Annual Differential Costs
1	$ 842,547	$280,849
3	1,404,245	481,456
2	1,925,822	521,577
5	2,487,520	802,426
4	2,888,733	962,911

5, 7, and 9 percent per year. The 5 percent result is identical to that in Table 15–2, from which we determined that alternative 2 would be optimal. Note the difference in the average and incremental benefit-cost ratios for the higher rates of discount. At a discount rate of 7 percent, alternative 2 is still the project to select, since the incremental benefit-cost ratio between it and the next smallest project is 1.02. Also, its net benefits of $3,876,000 are the highest that can be obtained from any of the alternatives when the discount rate is 7 percent. If the discount rate is increased to 9 percent, alternative 2 is no longer the best choice, since the incremental benefit-cost ratio between it and the next smallest project (alternative 3) falls to 0.89. Given the 9 percent discount rate, however, *alternative 3* has an incremental benefit-cost ratio of 1.34 in comparison with alternative 1, so alternative 3 is the best choice. Note that at the 9 percent discount rate, the net differential benefits of $2,423,000 for alternative 3 are the highest for any of the projects.

From the preceding illustration, we certainly can conclude that the choice of the discount rate is important in project selection. However, our mass transit example still gives no clue as to which discount rate we should choose. Obviously, proponents of alternative 2 will not want to accept the results of the analysis at 9 percent, even if we, as consultants, argue that the 9 percent discount rate is the appropriate one. The final decision is thus likely to be a political one, but it will at least be tempered by a realistic attempt to measure what the public is getting from the various alternatives.

COST-BENEFIT ANALYSIS AND DIVERGENT PUBLIC OBJECTIVES

We have focused thus far on the selection of an optimal project from an array of alternatives, each of which serves approximately the same objective. However, public funds often must be allocated among alternative programs or investments that have greatly different objectives. For example, a city commission may have to decide whether to allocate funds from a bond issue to mass transit improvements, expansion of hospital facilities, development of new parks and recreation facilities, or improvements of streets and sewers. In such a setting, cost-benefit analysis can again be useful.

Economists generally argue that more efficiency is obtained from public expenditures *the greater the benefit per dollar spent*. Benefit per dollar of expenditure is what we measure with the average benefit-cost ratio, B/C. Thus, where alternatives involve roughly the same outlay of public funds, those with the highest B/C ratios are viewed as the best choices.

In Table 15–4 we show a list of widely divergent public investment alternatives along with the B/C ratio for each. Assuming that approximately the same dollar amount is required to fund each alternative, their rank order in terms of efficiency is D, A, C, and B. That is, they are ranked such that the alternative with the highest B/C ratio is the most desirable, followed by that

Table 15–4   Average Benefit-Cost Ratios and Ranking of Widely Divergent Public Investment Alternatives

Alternatives	Description	B/C (Average Benefit-Cost Ratio)	Project Rank
A	Mass Transit Improvements	1.17	2
B	Hospital Facilities Expansion	1.02	4
C	Development of Parks and Recreation Facilities	1.05	3
D	Improvement of Streets and Sewers	1.35	1

with the second highest ratio, and so forth.[7] Naturally, this is the point at which competing public agencies and citizens' interest groups are most likely to attack the results of a cost-benefit analysis. There is likely to be no shortage of persons who will argue that improved medical facilities are more important than better streets and sewers, regardless of what the benefit-cost ratios show.

Public outcry against the results of cost-benefit analyses and related types of economic impact analyses (environmental impact studies, for example) is not to be taken lightly. Indeed, the history of cost-benefit analyses in the United States is a very checkered one, and economists themselves disagree on issues of cost and benefit measurement, as well as on the appropriate method of determining the social rate of discount. We investigate these problems further in the following section.

PITFALLS OF COST-BENEFIT ANALYSIS

The following passage from a contemporary study of cost-benefit analysis and its use in federal water resources management exemplifies typical problems of public investment analysis:

> The Bureau of Reclamation has traditionally been accused of using the tools of economic analysis to justify decisions that have been determined politically. Economists have long been critical of the apparent manipulation of cost-benefit analysis in project planning and approval processes . . .

---

7 If the required outlays for the various projects are *not* equal, the social welfare will be maximized if officials select that *group* of projects that yields the highest total net social benefit and still satisfies the budget constraint under which the governmental authority must operate.

studies conclude that the Bureau tends to overstate benefits and understate costs and that this policy enables projects to be built that would not be feasible if "proper" evaluation techniques were employed.[8]

Historically, the reputation of cost-benefit analysis as a policy tool has been severely damaged by over-eager users of the approach who have seldom failed to justify their pet projects in terms of stated economic benefits and costs. The Bureau of Reclamation, cited in the previous paragraph, is certainly not alone in its questionable application of cost-benefit analysis to project evaluation. The economics literature contains cases too numerous to cite where such branches of government as the Army Corps of Engineers, the Department of Agriculture, the Department of Labor, and many state and local authorities or their consultants have produced project studies involving unsound cost-benefit analyses that served mainly to foster bureaucratic ends. The saving grace of some of these documents is that they also ignited the flames of public opinion against both the projects and their sponsors. One example of such a case is the Cross-Florida Barge Canal, a long-term pet project of the Army Corps of Engineers.

The Corps of Engineers has one of the longest histories of use and abuse of cost-benefit analysis in U.S. public works. The Corps has employed cost-benefit analysis to evaluate its waterways projects since 1900.[9] The Cross-Florida Barge Canal was first proposed by President John Quincy Adams, and nine studies of its feasibility were made by the government during the period from 1826 to 1930. Some digging was done in 1930, but the project was abandoned.

Congress authorized construction of the canal as a war measure in 1942, but it took another 20 years to appropriate any funds for the project. The Corps resumed work on the canal in the early 1960s; by 1970 it had completed roughly 25 miles of the waterway and had spent about $50 million in the process. The canal was finally scuttled by President Nixon in 1971 after a successful campaign was waged against it by environmentalist groups.[10]

Throughout the period that the Cross-Florida Canal was under consideration, the Corps never failed to justify the project from a cost-benefit standpoint. A 1965 article surveying how cost-benefit analysis has been used compares a Corps of Engineers estimate of the canal's benefits with that of the railroad lobby to show a glaring example of self-serving benefit-cost studies.

---

8 Steven H. Hanke and Richard A. Walker, "Benefit-Cost Analysis Reconsidered: An Evaluation of the Mid-State Project," in Robert Haveman and Julius Margolis (eds.), *Public Expenditure and Policy Analysis*, 3d ed. (Boston: Houghton Mifflin, 1983), p. 324.

9 David N. Hyman, *The Economics of Governmental Activity* (New York: Holt, Rinehart, and Winston, 1973), p. 136.

10 See "Florida Sets Out to Restore Wetlands By Refilling a Canal Inadvisably Dug," *The Wall Street Journal*, July 5, 1990, p. A10; and "The Environment: Blocking Florida's Big Ditch," *Newsweek* (February 1, 1971), p. 55.

Whereas the Corps had come up with a benefit-cost ratio of 1.20 for the project, the railroad interests estimated the ratio to be 0.13. The Corps attributed a large share of total benefits to transportation savings, an item that was much disputed by the railroads. In addition the Corps included indirect benefits from flood control, recreational boating, fishing, and enhancement of land values in its estimate. In the railroads' study, each of these items was valued at zero! The authors of the survey article concluded:

> To what extent the divergence is due to the facts that the Corps likes to build canals and that the consultants were retained by the railroads, and to what extent it is due to the intrinsic impossibility of making accurate estimates is left entirely to the reader to decide![11]

In 1984, environmentalists in Florida won another victory over the Corps of Engineers when the South Florida Water Management District initiated a project to fill in a part of the Kissimmee River Channel, a 20-year-old Corps project that had dried up vast areas of marshlands and damaged the complex ecology of South Florida. It was reported that the Water Management District might spend as much as $65 million to undo the alleged damage caused by the channel.[12] However, the very next year, the Corps celebrated the completion of another southern dredging project, the Tennessee-Tombigbee Waterway. Bigger than the Panama Canal and with a price tag of $1.8 billion, this was widely recognized as the granddaddy of pork-barrel projects. Shortly after its opening, it was reported that barge traffic on the waterway was running at only about 5 percent of the optimistic projections that had been prepared by its proponents.[13]

The use and misuse of cost-benefit analysis are not likely to go away. The possible pitfalls of cost-benefit analysis are summarized in the following three points:

1. *Estimation*, particularly of *indirect benefits*, is not governed by strict standards, so an analysis can be "cooked" to show what its sponsors wish to show.
2. The opportunity-cost approach to the *social rate of discount* may bias the analysis against many worthwhile public undertakings.
3. The sheer *cost* of performing a credible cost-benefit analysis makes the approach unfeasible for many public investment decisions.

A good deal of research has been done on the estimation problems in cost-benefit studies; and, in general, it suggests that the estimation of direct

11 A. R. Prest and R. Turvey, "Cost-Benefit Analysis: A Survey," *The Economic Journal* (December 1965), p. 718.
12 "Now You See It, Now You Don't," *Time* (August 6, 1984), p. 56.
13 "Rivaling Cleopatra, A Pork-Barrel King Rides the Tenn-Tom," *The Wall Street Journal*, May 31, 1985, pp. 1, 10.

benefits can be adequately accomplished by careful application of the market value or opportunity-cost approaches. Extension of such valuation techniques to the estimation of indirect benefits is questionable and may be unnecessary in many cases. In fact the current trend seems to be toward leaving all but the most obvious indirect benefits out of cost-benefit calculations and including a discussion of their existence and probable extent in the non-quantitative part of project studies or reports. What is being recognized is that the opinions or values of public decision makers and their constituencies regarding nonmarket benefits (and costs) of a given public undertaking might best be expressed by the decision makers themselves rather than by professional economic analysts. Indeed, the nature of many indirect benefits is so elusive that the professional literature on them has taken to referring to them as "intangibles," "irreducibles," and "incommensurables." Thus, from the analyst's standpoint, the best prescription would seem to be to provide a very careful estimate of direct and clearly measurable costs and benefits in public investment studies but to call intangibles by their proper name and make their existence clear to public decision makers.

Turning to the discount rate dilemma, we wish to make two points. First, it is clear from research on the issue that many studies have been made using questionably low rates of discount for future streams of benefits. Certainly, proponents of the opportunity-cost approach would argue as much. Second, and perhaps of more importance, is the question of whether public investment undertakings should be measured using the same criterion, in terms of the rate of return, as that used in the private sector. A minority of analysts and policymakers argue that such projects should not. As one member of Congress has put it, the view that the appropriate discount rate for evaluation of public investment is one that reflects the opportunity cost rate for resources withdrawn from the private sector leads to the conclusion that society would benefit more from a new gadget than from the construction of a new school or sewerage system because the financial return was 5.5 percent on the gadget and only 5 percent on the school or sewerage system.[14] Nevertheless, one could respond that an economic problem would not occur in such cases if the social benefits from each project were estimated with a reasonable degree of accuracy.

Finally, we are left with the pitfall of the *cost* of cost-benefit studies. Much was learned about this problem during the administration of President Lyndon B. Johnson, when the Bureau of the Budget (now called the Office of Management and Budget) implemented an approach to government expenditure analysis known as the Planning, Programming, and Budgeting System (PPBS). Under PPBS, agencies were expected to conduct a yearly review of all

---

14 The statement was made by Senator William Proxmire and is cited in H. H. Liebhafsky, *American Government and Business* (New York: Wiley, 1971), p. 561.

MANAGERIAL PERSPECTIVE

Toronto's $400 Million SkyDome

The city of Toronto, Canada, has a domed stadium that opened in 1989 and reportedly cost between $360 and $419 million to build. Originally, city managers forecasted that it would turn a profit. In fact, SkyDome officials expected the stadium to generate a cash flow of $20 million its first year. This despite the fact that the Superdome in New Orleans, built for less than $180 million 14 years earlier, still typically was recording annual operating losses in the millions.

The SkyDome was designed as a multiple-use facility that includes a restaurant center, a hotel, and retail mall in the center of Toronto. Financing for the initial outlay came from a variety of sources: bank loans, corporate investors, presold boxes and seats, the Ontario government, metro-Toronto governments, a public stock sale, and the sale of advertising rights. The stadium has had its critics, however. Some of them argued early on that too much was given to the corporations in return for their investment. In 1994, the Ontario provincial government sold its share of the dome to a group of private investors (some of them the same ones originally involved in the project) for $111 million. It was reported that the sale resulted in a $202 million loss for the government. The only reason given for the discounted price was that the government did not want to be in the sports business.

References: Tim O'Brien, "Skydome Sold for $111 Million," *Amusement Business* (March 28–April 3, 1994) p. 11; and "After Skydome, Stadiums Will Never Be the Same," *Business Week* (March 20, 1989), pp. 136–138.

of their programs, using the cost-benefit technique. The idea was that the agencies would each rank their projects internally and that the Bureau of the Budget would oversee the process from above, making appropriate recommendations to the Executive Branch regarding interagency allocation of funds.

Although PPBS proved useful in the internal evaluation processes of the agencies, it failed as a *system*, since it proved to generate more information (in terms of sheer information volume) than the Budget Bureau could handle. Indeed, in 1969 it was reported to Congress that 1,145 positions were added to 21 agencies just to support PPBS activities.[15] Not only was PPBS

---

15 U.S. Congress, Joint Economics Committee, *Analysis and Evaluation of Public Expenditures: The PPB System*, Vol. 2 (Washington: U.S. Government Printing Office, 1969), p. 636.

costly, but Congress itself made little use of the output produced by the system and went about business as though PPBS scarcely existed. In any event the PPBS experience suggested that while cost-benefit analysis could prove quite useful in the evaluation of individual projects, its use would have to be tempered by consideration of the cost of the studies themselves and the ability of the decision-making apparatus to comprehend and absorb cost-benefit information.

THE FUTURE OF COST-BENEFIT ANALYSIS

As a policy tool, cost-benefit analysis has been heavily sold by economists in the past 15 years or so. There is no question that despite the demise of PPBS, cost-benefit analysis has survived and will continue to be an important policy evaluation tool. From the material presented in this chapter, the appropriate conclusion to draw is that judicious application of the approach is probably the closest economic analysis can get to a straightforward evaluation of the overall consequences of public investment decisions. In addition, cost-benefit analysis has had enough public exposure to make it a familiar tool to many public sector managers. Fortunately, such exposure has also bared its abuses and shortcomings, so the ability of unscrupulous users to misguide policymakers is somewhat limited. Certainly there are many public investment decisions that can be reviewed adequately using the cost-benefit approach if the pitfalls discussed here are avoided.

SUMMARY

Managerial Decisions in the Public Sector

In this chapter we have attempted in a selective way to discuss some of the issues surrounding the application of managerial economics to micro-level decisions in the public sector. We noted that one of the primary characteristics of many goods and services supplied by the public sector is that *external benefits* accrue to persons or groups who do not pay a direct charge for what they receive. The same was also shown to be true for some private sector production. We also found that both types of output (public and private sector) might be accompanied by *external costs*. To the extent such costs and benefits could be measured, it was shown that the optimal allocation of a society's resources at a given point in time would occur if each product or service were supplied up to the point where its *marginal social benefit equaled its marginal social cost*.

The chapter also provided a survey of *cost-benefit analysis*, an approach for evaluating public capital projects that attempts to take into account the economic criteria for an optimal allocation of society's resources. We applied cost-benefit analysis to five alternative proposals for improving a metropolitan area's mass transit system and related the concepts of the *average benefit-cost ratio* (*B/C*) and the *incremental benefit-cost ratio* (Δ*B*/Δ*C*) to the acceptability of projects and the determination of the optimal project size. Finally, our discussion turned to some of the problems associated with cost-benefit analysis, and we noted that application of the technique must be tempered in the light of *estimation difficulties, discount rate questions*, and the *expense* involved in preparing such studies.

We concluded that cost-benefit analysis is a tool that will likely be applied to public managerial questions in the future. In Chapter 17 we will offer some additional predictions about the future of managerial economics. First, however, in Chapter 16 we consider the interrelationships between the public and private sectors in matters of law and business regulation.

QUESTIONS

1. How can you distinguish between micro- and macroeconomic decisions of public sector managers? In what sense do some public sector managers occupy positions similar to those of managers of private firms?
2. What is the importance of externalities in the analysis of public goods? Do market prices of privately produced goods usually reflect externalities? Why or why not?
3. Theoretically, what principle determines the optimal amount supplied of a public good? Explain why this principle applies equally to privately produced output.
4. What are the procedural steps that are usually taken in the preparation of a cost-benefit analysis? How is the analysis similar to a private capital project evaluation? How is it different?
5. What is the importance of the *incremental* benefit-cost ratio in making a decision based on cost-benefit analysis? What is the importance of the *average* benefit-cost ratio? Are projects with high average benefit-cost ratios necessarily more desirable than those with lower ones? Explain.
6. Why is the discount rate a more complex issue in public managerial decision making than in private sector analysis? What problems have analysts found in the use of discount rates by federal agencies?
7. What are the main pitfalls of cost-benefit analyses? How can some of them be avoided?
8. Do you think cost-benefit analysis can prove useful in a setting where decision makers must choose between widely different projects? Why or why not? How might the average benefit-cost ratio be utilized in such a case?

PROBLEMS

1. Illustrate graphically how the socially optimal amount of a public good is determined in economic theory. Provide an appropriate verbal explanation for what you show, and discuss why the market is unlikely to provide an acceptable solution to the optimal amount problem.

2. City Councillor Foghorn has argued that a new sports stadium should be constructed, since it would provide the city annual lease receipts of $900,000 per year for the next 20 years. The capital outlay for the stadium is $15,000,000. Normally, the City Planning Department employs a discount rate of 6 percent per year in its evaluation of capital projects. It is expected that revenues from food and drink concessions will offset the city's annual operating and maintenance costs for the stadium. Given this information, do you agree with Councillor Foghorn? Why or why not?

3. Which of the following projects would be acceptable from a benefit-cost standpoint if the applicable discount rate is 9 percent per year?

Project	Project Life (Years)	Annual Differential Benefits	Annual Differential Costs	Capital Outlay
(A) Flood Control	20	$100,000	$30,000	$700,000
(B) Street Paving	15	40,000	5,000	250,000
(C) Playground Eqpt.	12	10,000	1,000	75,000
(D) Rat Control	5	30,000	20,000	40,000
(E) Street Lighting	20	20,000	7,000	100,000
(F) Alarm System	20	80,000	10,000	500,000

4. Although the projects in Problem 3 are not comparable in size or scope, you have been asked to rank those that are acceptable. In what order would you rank the projects based solely on the given information? Explain why.

5. The Board of County Commissioners is attempting to choose one project from among the following drainage control alternatives:

Drainage Control District	Capital Outlay	Annual Differential Costs	Annual Differential Benefits
Northeast	$180,000	$17,000	$34,000
Northwest	160,000	20,000	33,000
Central	175,000	22,000	32,000
Southeast	150,000	16,000	33,000
Southwest	165,000	20,000	35,000

If the appropriate discount rate is 6 percent per year and such projects are normally viewed as having a 20-year life, which project should the commissioners choose?

6. How would your response to the preceding problem change if the appropriate discount rate were 9 percent per year instead of 6 percent per year?

7. The City Parks and Recreation Department is considering the expansion alternatives shown in the following table for the next fiscal year. Projects *A* and *D* are located in high-crime areas. Therefore the city council has instructed the Parks and Recreation Department to add a 10 percent premium to the annual differential benefits given for each of these projects. Evaluate the five alternatives based on the table, the council's adjustment for Projects *A* and *D*, and a standard city policy of utilizing a life of 20 years and a discount rate of 6 percent for capital projects.

Project	Initial Capital Outlay	Annual Differential Operating Expense	Annual Differential Benefits
(A) Build New Swimming Facility at Royer Park	$110,000	$10,000	$20,000
(B) Improve J.F.K. Park Playground Area	70,000	4,000	8,500
(C) Build Tennis Center at G. W. Park	120,000	12,000	21,000
(D) Install Lighting at Thorp Track & Field Facility	80,000	5,000	13,000
(E) Add 2,000 Seats to Memorial Gym	105,000	6,000	17,000

This problem can be solved with Decision Assistant

D1. The City of New Urbania is considering projects for its new fiscal year. The city's residents propose new projects for the city council's consideration. The city council tries to balance the benefits of each proposed project with the associated costs. The list of projects has been consolidated and analyzed. Below is the tentative list for consideration.

Sports facility—a project to construct a large domed stadium and sports facility. The project has been one of considerable interest to many of the city's citizens who are avid sports fans. It is anticipated that should the facility be completed, the city could attract major league football and baseball teams. It is anticipated the facility will require an initial capital outlay of $60 million. The project is expected to have a life of 20 years. In addition, it is expected to have differential costs of $20 million per year and differential benefits of $28 million per year.

Convention facility—a project to expand the city's convention facility. The city has enjoyed a history of tourism and conventionism based on its mild weather, excellent facilities, and central location. The additional facilities will require an initial capital outlay of $30 million. The project will have a life of 20 years with differential benefits of $15 million per year and differential costs of $10 million.

Flood control—a multifaceted approach to one of the city's oldest problems, poor flood control. This project includes a combination of dams, reservoirs, and drainage improvements. The Army Corps of Engineers has estimated the initial capital outlay will be $1.5 million. Differential benefits total $0.5 million per year with differential costs of $0.25 million per year. The project is expected to have a life of 20 years.

Street maintenance—a project to refurbish many of the older city streets. The project will have a life of 10 years. Initial capital outlay is estimated by the city to be $12.5 million. Differential costs are estimated at $10 million while differential benefits are projected to be $14 million.

Airport maintenance—a modernization project designed to bring the city's aging airport up to standards. Initial capital outlay is estimated to be $35 million. The project is expected to have a life of 15 years. Differential benefits are expected to be $6.5 million with differential costs of $2.5 million.

Park expansion—a project to purchase additional land for conversion into parks. The city has been the beneficiary of many beautification awards, partly due to the number of parks it provides for its citizens. Initial capital outlay is estimated to be $0.7 million. The project is expected to have a life of 10 years. Differential costs are projected to be $25,000 and differential benefits are estimated to be $150,000.

Biomedical industrial park—a project to acquire acreage for an industrial park engaged in biomedical research. The city has identified biomedical research as the next technological wave, and as such it should provide many jobs for the city. Initial capital outlay is expected to be $1 million. The project is expected to have a life of 25 years. Differential benefits are expected to be $0.85 million. Differential costs are projected to be $0.8 million.

a. Use the Net Present Value, Future Value, IRR tool in the *Managerial Economics Decision Assistant* to assist the city in evaluating the cost-benefit of each of these projects independently.
b. Write a report giving your recommendation regarding each project if the applicable discount rate is 9 percent. Be sure to include a cost-benefit ratio calculation for each project in your report.

(*HINT:* Use the Present Value, Future Value, IRR tool by calculating the present value of differential costs—including the initial capital outlay at Period 0—*separately* from the present value of differential benefits. You can then use the Calculator tool to determine the cost-benefit ratio.)

SELECTED REFERENCES

Allen, Joan W., Keon S. Chi, Kevin A. Devlin, Mark Fall, Harry P. Hatry, and Wayne Masterman. *The Private Sector in State Service Delivery: Examples of Innovative Practices.* Washington, D.C.: The Urban Institute Press, 1989.

Baker, Samuel, and Catherine Elliott (eds.). *Readings in Public Sector Economics.* Lexington, Mass.: D. C. Heath, 1990.

Baumol, William J. "On the Discount Rate for Public Projects." In Robert H. Haveman and Julius Margolis (eds.). *Public Expenditure and Policy Analysis.* Chicago: Rand-McNally, 1977, pp. 161–179.

Boadway, Robin W., and David E. Wildasin. *Public Sector Economics*, 2d ed. Boston: Little, Brown, 1984.

Fisher, Ronald C. *State and Local Public Finance.* Glenview, Ill: Scott, Foresman, 1988.

Fromm, Gary, and Paul Taubman. *Public Economic Theory and Policy.* New York: Macmillan, 1973, especially Chapters 1–5.

Haveman, Robert H., and Julius Margolis (eds.). *Public Expenditure and Policy Analysis*, 3d ed. Boston: Houghton Mifflin, 1983.

Hinrichs, Harley H. "Government Decision Making and the Theory of Benefit-Cost Analysis," In Harley H. Hinrichs, and Graeme M. Taylor (eds.). *Program Budgeting and Benefit-Cost Analysis.* Pacific Palisades, Cal.: Goodyear, 1969, pp. 9–20.

Liebhafsky, H. H. *American Government and Business.* New York: Wiley, 1971, pp. 559–562.

Lynch, Thomas D. *Public Budgeting In America*, 3d ed. Englewood Cliffs, N.J.: Prentice Hall, 1990.

Palm, Thomas, and Abdul Quayum. *Private and Public Investment Analysis.* Cincinnati: South-Western, 1985.

Prest, A. R., and R. Turvey. "Cost-Benefit Analysis: A Survey." *The Economic Journal* (December 1965).

Zerbe, Richard O., Jr., and Dwight D. Dively. *Benefit-Cost Analysis In Theory and Practice.* New York: HarperCollins, 1994.

16

LEGAL AND REGULATORY ENVIRONMENT OF THE FIRM

Businesses do not operate in a legal vacuum, and infractions of laws designed to regulate their activities can prove costly both to firms and to individual managers or officers of a firm. There is no shortage of examples to make this point. For example, in 1996, 11 major drug producers, including such well-known firms as Merck, Pfizer, and Bristol Meyers-Squibb, agreed to pay $351 million to settle a civil suit charging that they fixed prices by charging drugstores higher prices than they charged managed-care groups and mail-order pharmacies.[1] In that same year, Archer-Daniels-Midland Company agreed, with two Japanese firms, to a $45 million settlement stemming from charges they had conspired to fix prices for lysine, an amino acid that promotes rapid growth in chickens and hogs.[2] In 1993, Miles, Inc., maker of S.O.S. steel wool pads agreed to plead guilty to price fixing and to pay a $4.5 million fine.[3] Between 1983 and 1985, investigations of price-fixing conspiracies in the electrical contracting industry yielded jail sentences for at least 14 executives, and 33 companies paid fines, damages, and legal expenses totaling more than $20 million.[4]

While jail sentences are not common in cases involving violations of business practices or antitrust laws, over the past two decades some judges have argued that managers simply will not obey the law if they suffer no personal consequences for their actions. A significant number of judges now believe that fines and damages payments are insufficient deterrents to corporate law-breaking, since some firms just view them as a cost of doing business.

The question of purposeful lawbreaking in business management has deep ethical dimensions. Some laws that adversely affect businesses are poorly designed and deserve to be challenged. Others are well designed to foster business competition and to protect consumers. Managers who break

---

1 "Settlement Cleared in Pharmacies' Suit Over Price Fixing, but Debate Lingers," *The Wall Street Journal*, June 24, 1996, p. B5.
2 "Judge Approves $45 Million Pact in Civil Suit on ADM Price Fixing," *The Wall Street Journal*, July 22, 1996, p. B5.
3 "S.O.S. Pad Maker Agrees to Pay Fine for Price Fixing," *The Wall Street Journal*, October 1993, p. B3.
4 "Busting a Trust: Electrical Contractors Reel Under Charges They Rigged Bids," *The Wall Street Journal*, November 29, 1985, pp. 1, 5.

any law relating to their responsibilities within a firm are courting trouble, especially if the law involves well-established maxims of business behavior. Moreover, even in the case of bad or ill-conceived laws, civil disobedience can be viewed only as a measure of last resort.

Of course, many businesses find themselves in costly legal proceedings because of *mistakes* made by managers rather than because of intentional lawbreaking. Such mistakes are frequently the result of ignorance of the law on the part of a specific decision maker or group, but the old saying that "ignorance of the law is no excuse" can make legal mistakes very costly indeed. The typical manager is not a lawyer and cannot be expected to have a very complete knowledge of all the legal ramifications of business decision making. In general, the best that can be expected is that managers have a broad conception of the purview of business law and government regulations, so that they will know when to seek legal advice and thus avoid some of the pitfalls that laws and regulations hold for the firm. In addition, a competent manager should be able to recognize the possibility that a rival firm or group of firms might be damaging his or her firm through illegal business practices.

In this chapter we attempt to provide an overview of the legal and regulatory environment in which firms operate in the United States. We emphasize those areas of regulation that bear on the economic decisions of managers whose objective is to maximize the firm's value over the long run. We look first at the nature of business law and the types of laws that apply to the firm, and then we turn to a very specific part of business regulation: the antitrust laws. The major facets of antitrust law are discussed, and this is followed by an examination of administrative agencies that both create and enforce laws affecting business. A later section deals with the specific problem of regulated industries, such as public transportation and utilities. Finally, we return to the question of the behavior of managers in the context of what we have said about the legal and regulatory environment in the United States and provide a general prescription for including legal and regulatory variables in the short- and long-run decision processes of the firm.

MANAGERS AND THE LAW

In the preceding chapter we noted that one of the most important "products" of the public sector is laws and regulations. Rules of the game are necessary to attain and secure both social and economic order. Indeed, countries and societies where rules of the game are ill defined or cast aside by an oligarchy are often plagued by civil strife. The need for a system of rules is obvious, but the extent to which economic regulations should supplant market-determined solutions to a society's problems of production and distribution of output has long been a burning issue.

From the standpoint of the manager of a business firm, government regulations are a very mixed bag. Much of the conventional wisdom of the private sector leans toward "that government is best that governs least," but it seems clear that if government did not regulate business, many firms could not survive. For example, small firms could easily be destroyed by predatory pricing strategies of large firms if government failed to make such practices illegal or failed to enforce sanctions against such activities. Thus, from the private point of view of the business firm, most managers today are sufficiently enlightened to realize that government regulations produce both costs and benefits; that is, some of the regulations have positive effects on the firm and others affect it adversely.

In the United States, private sector managers have only recently been made aware of an apparently new potential cost of decision making—that of *personal liability*. Historically, the corporate form of organization has caused penalties for breaking business rules and regulations to be exacted in the form of monetary payments (fines and/or damage settlements) from the firms that break the law. In cases where culpability could be traced to specific managers, their fines were usually paid from corporate coffers. As a result, the costs of lawbreaking in the business sector were viewed by many managers as just another business expense. The Department of Justice has taken a very dim view of this attitude and recently has begun to demand that judges mete out prison sentences to executives who knowingly break antitrust laws. The electrical contractors' case cited previously is one example.

TYPES OF LAW AFFECTING THE FIRM

Criminal law pertains to acts that are viewed as offenses against a federal, state, or local government.

Tort law deals with injuries sustained by private parties as a result of nonperformance of a duty created by law.

Contract law pertains to the establishment of contractual obligations and to wrongful acts in breach of contract.

Setting aside for the moment the special areas of antitrust laws, business practices laws, and the regulations of administrative agencies, we may divide the laws affecting the firm into basically three types: criminal law, the law of torts, and the law of contracts. All three of these have their bases partly in English common law, civil law (Roman law), and statutory law (that law produced by local, state, or federal legislative bodies). In all three types of law, procedures are set up to determine who is a wrongdoer (person or corporation) and what should be done about a wrongful act. **Criminal law** deals with wrongful acts that are viewed as offenses against the state or government. **Tort law** has to do with injuries sustained by private parties because of a wrongful act involving the breach of a duty created by law. **Contract law**, of course, deals with the establishment of contractual obligations (agreements between parties) and wrongful acts in breach of contract. A single wrongful act can simultaneously be a crime, a tort, and a breach of contract. For example, suppose that a firm enters into a conspiracy to divide markets, which causes it to break a contractual agreement with one of its distributors and to interfere with contracts made between other suppliers and their distributors. In such a case the firm will have not only violated the antitrust laws (a crime) and broken a contract, but also intentionally interfered with contracts of a third party (a tort).

Business Crime

Criminal wrongdoing in business is seldom the result of a managerial mistake. Often it involves some willful wrong act such as receiving stolen goods, embezzlement, arson, false labeling, swindling, or obtaining goods through false pretenses. Mistakes are more likely to result in violations of state and federal antitrust laws or fair business practices laws, although in some cases such violations do constitute crimes. For example, many supplier firms in the franchise food business require franchisees to enter into tying agreements whereby all types of food inputs must be bought from the franchiser. Such contracts are often unwittingly drawn in a manner that places both parties in violation of federal antitrust laws. Although criminal penalties are not likely to be assessed against managers in such a case, the fact remains that the breaking of the federal antitrust sanction against such behavior is viewed as an offense against the state. We will return to this problem in the section on antitrust violations.

Torts

In today's business environment the largest volume of tort cases occurs in the area of *negligence*. We can define negligence as failure to exercise reasonable care in performing a duty created by law. Underlying the whole negligence field is a concept known as the "duty of care," which is in its simplest terms the duty of a person or firm to act prudently or carefully so as not to harm other persons or things. The notion extends all the way from industrial accidents to product liability and rests on the idea of a "reasonable person" concept. That is, all steps that a reasonable person would take to avoid injuring other persons or things within his or her zone of influence should be adhered to. It is a variable standard that can be applied to all sorts of cases, and in any given case its precise definition rests with the jury.

In cases of negligence, there are three major determinations to be made: (1) Was the defendant negligent? (2) Was there contributory negligence on the part of the plaintiff or plaintiffs? and (3) What is the extent of injury to the plaintiff or plaintiffs? The injury phase of many legal proceedings can be both involved and costly, since expert analysis and testimony may be necessary. Frequently, parties on both sides of an injury case will hire expert witnesses (physicians, economists, engineers) to estimate damages and testify in court. The value of life itself becomes an issue when the tort involves a wrongful death.

Besides negligent acts or omissions that result in personal harm or damage to property, other common business torts are invasion of privacy; slander; trespassing on land; interference with contracts between others; and infringement of copyrights, patents, or trademarks.

Contracts

A *contract* is a binding agreement between two or more parties (persons, corporations, partnerships, government entities), wherein one of the parties is obliged to do or refrain from doing a specific act and the obligation incurred is recognized or enforced by law. Most business activities involve a contract of one kind or another.

For example, a person or a firm agrees to sell something to another party for a specified amount, or a firm agrees to purchase raw materials from a supplier at a stated price. For a contract to exist, there must be an offer made by one party (the offeror) and an acceptance by another party (the offeree). A typical written contract will include the date of the agreement, the name and address of each party to the contract, a statement of the agreement or *promise* made by each party, the *consideration* received or to be received by each party as the price of the respective promise, and the signature of the parties.

Contracts can, of course, be very intricate, and our only purpose here is to make several important points about them and about contract law. Clearly, in the case of a large corporation, legal counsel will be available for the preparation of contractual agreements normally and regularly used, as well as for special types of contracts regarding capital projects, mergers, acquisitions, and so forth. Small businesses will also obtain legal expertise when entering into complex agreements or contracts involving large undertakings. However, many everyday transactions involve contracts that are not prepared by an attorney and in some cases are not even in writing.

A good general rule regarding agreements intended to be contractual is that they should be *written*. Nonetheless, oral contracts can be valid and enforceable; thus it is important to understand that an oral agreement may be a contract. Further, in every state, there are certain kinds of contracts that cannot be enforced unless they are evidenced by a writing. The Uniform Commercial Code (UCC), which has been adopted in whole or in part by all 50 states, provides that sales contracts for goods where the price is $500 or more are not enforceable (with certain exceptions) unless there is some writing sufficient to indicate that a contract for sale has been made between the parties and signed by the party against whom enforcement is sought or by a qualified agent or broker. Other agreements that generally must be evidenced by a writing (not necessarily a contract, but perhaps just a memorandum or a note) are those involving a duty that cannot be performed within one year of the date of contract, those involving the sale or transfer of real estate, and those involving a promise to pay the debt of another party.

Remedies for *breach of contract* (failure to keep the promise as originally stated) include the following: (1) rescinding the contract, (2) suing for specific performance, and (3) bringing an action for damages. The injured party may have the option to rescind the contract; that is, to treat it as discharged, provided the entire contract is rescinded and the party in breach is restored, as far as possible, to its original position (the one that existed before the contract). The rescinding party may still recover the value of any performance rendered or money paid. *Specific performance* (wherein the party in breach of contract is compelled by the court to carry out the terms of the contract) is generally available as a remedy to the injured party only in cases involving the purchase of real estate, the purchase of personal property having a unique value (works of art, old relics), or the purchase of stock essential for control of a closely held corporation.

When there is a breach of contract, the injured party is always entitled to sue for damages. The award of economic damages to the plaintiff is the most common remedy in cases involving breach of contract and, of course, may be a very costly occurrence for the party or the firm that is at fault. Ordinarily, the injured party can be compensated only for actual loss sustained as a result of the breach of contract and cannot be awarded *punitive damages* (excess damages sought in order to punish the wrongdoer). However, actual loss can include such items as the difference between a contract price and the price a purchaser had to pay to obtain goods not delivered due to breach of contract, interest expenses incurred because of a breach, and loss of *actual* and *future* profits attributable to a breach of contract. Where the future profits of an injured party are affected, damages can sometimes be quite substantial. In addition, the costs of litigation for a case involving such a claim often mount up, since it is likely that expert witnesses may be hired to estimate the damages. Estimation of damages suffered by injured parties can be a substantial portion of the litigation of cases involving violations of the antitrust laws, a subject to which we now turn.

ANTITRUST AND BUSINESS PRACTICES LAWS

Antitrust laws are laws regulating any business practices and agreements that intensify monopoly power or otherwise restrict trade.

Price fixing is the practice of a group of firms agreeing to set the price of a final or intermediate product at a specific level.

A **tying agreement** occurs when a firm agrees that goods sold or leased will be used only with other goods of the seller or lessor.

Exclusive dealing refers to a situation where a firm buying or leasing the goods of one firm agrees not to deal with competing suppliers.

Both the federal government and the states have enacted laws to preserve competition and prevent concentration of economic power in one or a few firms (antitrust laws) and to prevent deceptive and otherwise unscrupulous business methods (business practices laws). Such laws have as their objectives both the protection of individual firms from wrongful acts of other firms and consumer protection from such evils as monopoly control of prices, price discrimination, deceptive advertising, and the sale of adulterated or otherwise unfit products.

With respect to such acts as monopolization, price fixing, tying agreements, boycotts or exclusive dealing, and price discrimination, the principal body of statutes in the United States is the federal **antitrust laws**. **Price fixing** is the practice of a group of firms agreeing to set the price of a product at a specific level. **Tying agreements** occur when a buyer of certain goods agrees to purchase certain other goods only from that same seller. **Exclusive dealing** refers to a situation where a firm buying or leasing the goods of one firm agrees not to deal with competing suppliers. As explained in Chapter 11, *price discrimination* is the practice of charging different buyers different prices for the same or similar products or services, where the price differentials cannot be justified by differences in the cost of supplying them.

The antitrust laws primarily include the Sherman Act of 1890, the Clayton and Federal Trade Commission Acts of 1914, and the Robinson-Patman Act of 1936. The original Sherman Act declared in very broad terms that contracts, combinations, and conspiracies in restraint of trade are illegal, and it provided criminal penalties for persons or firms guilty of the acts of "monopolizing, attempting to monopolize" and "combining or conspiring to monopolize." The act also provided for actions in equity (damage suits) on behalf of parties injured by such illegal acts. Under the act, as amended, injured parties are to be awarded treble damages (an amount paid by the wrongdoers to the injured parties that is three times the amount of the actual economic loss).

Because the Sherman Act lacked specificity regarding the types of business conduct to be regarded as illegal and because inadequate provision had been made for enforcement of its antitrust sanctions, Congress in 1914 passed the Clayton Act and the Federal Trade Commission Act. The primary effects of these two pieces of legislation were as follows: (1) to identify some specific wrongful acts that would be punishable as antitrust violations; (2) to embody the common law approach of trial, error, and precedent into the development of the rules of antitrust; and (3) to create a federal commission (the Federal Trade Commission) with far-reaching authority to regulate business practices.

With the growth of chain stores in the 1920s and the 1930s, the Federal Trade Commission (FTC) recommended to Congress that more precise prohibitions in the area of price discrimination were needed. The result was the Robinson-Patman Act of 1936, which forbade price discrimination between buyers of like commodities purchased under like conditions and broadly prohibited price discrimination where its effect was to injure, destroy, or prevent competition. The broad nature of the act reaffirmed that the rules of antitrust would be developed on a case-by-case basis through the judicial process.

Today, the federal antitrust laws are developed to the point that it is clear that certain acts or practices will be viewed as wrongful "in and of themselves." In technical jargon such acts are called *per se violations* of the antitrust laws. The list of *per se* violations includes the following:

1. Price fixing
2. Division of markets
3. Group boycotts
4. Tying agreements

From a managerial point of view, any agreement that appears on its face or could be construed to be one or more of the preceding violations deserves careful scrutiny.

The fact that the preceding are *per se* violations of federal law does not mean that contracts between firms are unlikely to include any of them in their provisions. To the contrary, since state laws sometimes do not forbid the same acts or practices and since not all lawyers who prepare contracts are well versed in antitrust law, many contracts are written that are in violation of federal antitrust sanctions if an effect on interstate commerce can be shown. Further, the trend in the federal courts has been that an effect on interstate commerce is easily demonstrated.

MANAGERIAL PERSPECTIVE
Some Legal Aspects of Retail Pricing

Friction has frequently occurred between manufacturers of a product, company-authorized retailers who do not discount the price of the product below the manufacturer's suggested retail price, and retailers who do offer the product at a lower price. Retailers who wish to sell at discounted prices believe that it should be their right to sell their products at any price at which they can make a profit. Those sellers who refuse to discount the price and would like to have other retailers prevented from doing so argue that the discounters are able to offer the products at a lower price because they do not provide the customer service that the nondiscounting firms do. For example, the list-price stores contend that potential customers visit their showrooms to learn about the features of the various products, using the services of their sales personnel, and then actually purchase the goods through a mail-order discount house or similar establishment that offers little or no customer service other than supplying the product ordered.

There have been a number of court decisions involving these issues during the twentieth century. For example, in 1911 the Supreme Court ruled that "agreements between manufacturers and independent retailers fixing the retail price of goods are so likely to be anticompetitive that they automatically violate antitrust law." In such a case, the existence of the agreement *in itself* would be a violation of the law, regardless of whether it could be shown to have been anticompetitive in nature or to have resulted in injury to another party. In later years, the courts have issued differing rulings in cases where there were agreements between manufacturers and retailers that could possibly affect prices but that were not direct price-fixing agreements.

In 1988, the Supreme Court reached a noteworthy decision on this issue involving Sharp Corporation and Business Electronics Corporation, a discounter in the Houston area. Sharp stopped supplying Business Electronics with its product after another firm complained about Business Electronics' low prices. The Court held that the fact that a company stops doing business with a discount retailer after receiving complaints from other full-price retailers does not in and of itself constitute a violation of the antitrust laws. Justice Antonin Scalia stated that manufacturers should be able to refuse to do business with discounters who take unfair advantage of the services offered by nondiscount stores. Thus, the impact of the Court decision seemed to be that agreements between manufacturers and retailers were illegal only if they involved explicit efforts to fix prices.

In a more recent case, the Supreme Court held that a competing firm does not *automatically* have the right to sue a distributor or manufacturer for setting *maximum* retail prices, although setting maximum retail prices may violate the antitrust laws. Predatory pricing, or setting prices so low that they preclude making a profit and are designed to drive competitors out of business, is illegal. However, the Court decision indicated that for a competing firm to bring a successful suit in a situation where a manufacturer set a maximum retail price, it would be necessary to show that the firm was in fact damaged by prices that were sufficiently low to be predatory in nature. The decision did not prevent individual retailers of the merchandise or customers from bringing suits challenging the prices. (For example, dealers could argue that the maximum prices were so low that they could not offer adequate customer service, and customers could contend that the maximum prices were in fact a price-fixing scheme designed to limit competition.)

The history of these decisions by the Supreme Court shows that relationships between manufacturers and retailers and those between different retail firms may involve complex legal issues. A responsible business firm manager must be aware of potential problems in such dealings and be willing to seek legal advice.

References: Arthur Golden, Ronan Harty, Joel Cohen, and Arthur Burke, "United States," in *International Corporate Law* (Competition Law Supplement, April 1995), pp. 1087–1089; "Justices' Antitrust Ruling to Help Firms Crack Down on Retailers That Discount," *The Wall Street Journal*, May 3, 1988, p. 4; "A Red Flag for Red Tags," *Business Week*, (May 16, 1988), p. 38; and "Supreme Court Hardens Stance on Pricing Suits," *The Wall Street Journal*, May 15, 1990, p. A3.

As we mentioned in the introductory section of this chapter, penalties for violation of the antitrust laws can be quite severe—fines ranging up to $1,000,000 per violation for firms and fines and/or prison sentences for individuals. In addition the provisions that allow recovery of treble damages by injured parties further punish offenders and also constitute a strong incentive for aggrieved parties to file antitrust actions. The money damages paid by defendants often amount to many times the fines levied by the court. In 1985, for example, it was reported that MCI Communications Corporation had agreed to accept an offer by American Telephone & Telegraph to settle two antitrust suits for damages payments and other considerations valued at well above $113 million. In fact, MCI would not disclose the exact amount of the settlement, but it was publicly known that a jury had awarded $113 million in the first of the two suits. MCI's original claim was for $5.8 billion, and at one point a jury had awarded it $1.8 billion, but that decision was overturned in a new trial. The litigation between MCI and AT&T (including the regional

Bell companies) went on for 11 years.[5] AT&T also had its problems with the Justice Department, which spent six years trying to break up the company's telephone monopoly before a federal judge finally came up with a plan that did just that. The estimated costs of defending the suit over the six years were said to have been $350 to $500 million.[6] Even for small firms involved in private antitrust suits, litigation costs can be quite substantial. Moreover, if a defendant firm loses such a suit, its costs are further escalated by the requirement that it pay the plaintiff's costs of suit, including a reasonable attorney's fee.

Many cases that involve a probable antitrust violation do not end up in the federal courts. One reason is that most states have some form of antitrust legislation under which complaints can be pursued. Another is that once a federal court agrees to hear a case, it may never reach the trial stage because the plaintiff and defendant settle the damages issue in an out-of-court negotiation. Finally, minor violations that are in restraint of trade may be settled through the actions and authority of an administrative agency, such as the FTC, which is empowered to take regulatory steps to restrain persons or firms from using unfair methods of competition or deceptive or predatory practices.

Recent Developments in Antitrust

During the period from 1980 through 1988, under the administration of President Ronald Reagan, the federal government took a permissive attitude toward many business deals that in earlier years would probably have been viewed as questionable from an antitrust viewpoint. A rash of merger and acquisition activity seemed to have the potential of substantially lessening competition in a number of important industries (airlines, food and beverages, radio and television communications). Further, Secretary of Commerce Malcolm Baldrige, himself the former head of a large conglomerate, was pushing to soften the provisions of the Clayton Act in regard to anticompetitive mergers and acquisitions.

In January 1986, the Reagan administration unveiled a legislative package that largely reflected Baldrige's views. However, this occurred at a time when many members of Congress believed the Justice Department and the Federal Trade Commission were becoming lax in enforcing the antitrust laws.[7] As a result, Congress took no action on the administration proposal, and no significant overhaul of the antitrust laws occurred before the 1988 elections, since even those lawmakers in league with the administration ap-

---

5 "MCI Says It Settled Two Antitrust Suits Against AT&T, Former Bell Companies," *The Wall Street Journal*, November 19, 1985, p. 2.

6 "Antitrust Grows Unpopular," *Business Week* (January 12, 1981), pp. 90–93.

7 "New Era for Antitrust?" *Newsweek* (January 27, 1986), p. 46; and "Antitrust: The Pendulum is Swinging Back," *Business Week* (December 9, 1985), p. 38.

parently wanted to avoid any perception that they were anticonsumer. Meanwhile, it seemed that evidence was piling up in favor of leaving the existing laws intact. For example, a Georgetown University study covering over 2,000 antitrust cases filed in federal courts during a 10-year period showed that most private suits were settled both quickly and inexpensively. Some experts were ready to argue that the existing system was working very well.[8]

Perhaps in response to a less active stance taken by the Justice Department, state attorneys general became much more aggressive in enforcing state antitrust laws and consumer protection laws during the second half of the 1980s. In some cases, the attorneys general from several states combined forces to combat what they perceived were antitrust violations.[9] Moreover, the Bush administration followed a gradual policy of increasingly vigorous enforcement of the antitrust laws.[10] When the Clinton administration took over (1993), Anne K. Bingaman was appointed Assistant Attorney General for Antitrust. Under her guidance, the Justice Department focused on sectors that were expected to be increasingly important in the U.S. economy during the twenty-first century: computers, telecommunications, financial services, and health care. The Department moved to block acquisitions, such as Microsoft's bid for Intuit, an important firm in the personal finance market, when it believed competition would be stifled.[11]

The role of the Baby Bells in the information networks and the pricing practices of the airlines were among the antitrust issues in the courts during the 1990s. The issue surrounding the Baby Bells was whether their ownership of the telephone lines gave them an unfair advantage over other suppliers of information through computer networks. These other suppliers argued that because the Baby Bells would have a monopolistic advantage, they should not be allowed to supply these sorts of information services. In 1993, however, the Supreme Court ruled that the Bells could offer such services as home shopping, stock reports, and transmission of medical records. New legislation in 1996 set the stage for open competition in telecommunications, allowing the Bells to enter long-distance markets and other providers to enter local phone markets.[12]

In the early 1990s, the Justice Department conducted a number of investigations regarding the pricing practices of the airlines. One of the issues was

---

8 "Antitrust: the Pendulum is Swinging Back," *Business Week* (December 9, 1985), p. 38.

9 "Attorneys General Flex Their Muscles," *The Wall Street Journal*, July 13, 1988, p. 21.

10 "FTC's Hard Line on Price Fixing May Foster Discounts," *The Wall Street Journal*, January 11, 1991, pp. B1, B6; "Psst! The Trustbusters Are Back in Town," *Business Week* (June 25, 1990), pp. 64–67; and "Putting the 'Anti' Back in the Antitrust Division," *Business Week* (June 19, 1989), pp. 64–70.

11 "The Cops Are Coming," *Business Week* (June 10, 1996), pp. 32–33.

12 "Winners and Losers in the New Deregulated Telecommunications Environment," *Telecommunications* (May 1, 1996), p. 26; and "Supreme Court Rules Baby Bells Can Branch Out," *San Antonio Express-News* (November 16, 1993), p. 1-C.

whether a commonly owned computer network that the airlines utilized to publish fares was anticompetitive. In late 1992, the Justice Department filed a suit charging eight airlines and the operators of the computer system of illegal pricing practices, although the airlines did not directly negotiate with one another to set the prices. Although certain airlines reached a settlement with the Justice Department, others continued to fight the lawsuit. However, it appeared that many airlines were modifying their pricing practices as the case made its way through the courts. An earlier price-fixing suit also involving the electronic fare exchange brought by the Justice Department was settled with all of the major airlines agreeing to a compensation scheme for customers.[13]

ADMINISTRATIVE AGENCIES AND THE LAW

Today, it is well recognized in the United States that government administrative agencies have both legislative and judicial powers. In general, Congress and the courts have delegated such authority to the agencies because of the difficulty inherent in making judgments and setting up rules and regulations where the problems and information involved are of a highly technical nature. We have already mentioned the FTC, an agency that takes direct action outside the courts in matters involving competition and business practices. Other federal agencies that operate similarly in various fields of administration affecting business are the Interstate Commerce Commission, the Internal Revenue Service, the International Trade Commission, the Federal Maritime Commission, the Environmental Protection Agency, and the Federal Communications Commission.[14]

Typically, an administrative agency develops standards and rules, as well as means for dealing with violations of such regulations. The latter include fines, confiscation of property, informal settlements, and **consent decrees** (agreements by wrongdoers to adjust their behavior along lines specified by the agency), as well as procedures for investigating possible wrongful acts and providing a remedy. An action is usually initiated by a *complaint*, which may be filed by an alleged injured party or initiated by the agency itself. The complaint is served on the alleged wrongdoer, who is given time to answer it. The agency may then proceed with a hearing, and the administrator (generally a panel or a commission) makes a decision either dismissing the complaint or requiring the wrongdoer to take certain actions or

A **consent decree** is a statement of certain provisions agreed to by both the government and the defendant.

---

13 "American Air's Fliers Won't Get Fare Warnings," *The Wall Street Journal*, February 25, 1993, pp. B1, B8; "Airlines Charged With Scheme to Raise Fares," *The Wall Street Journal*, December 22, 1992, pp. A3, A5; and "More Airlines To Settle Suit On Price-Fixing," *The Wall Street Journal*, June 23, 1992, pp. A3, A8.

14 We have mentioned only a few of the 120 or so federal government departments, bureaus, and agencies that implement regulatory programs.

refrain from doing certain things. The order of an administrative agency may not be self-enforcing, and the law generally provides that either the administrator may turn to the courts for enforcement or the wrongdoer may appeal the administrator's ruling through the courts. The phase involving investigation of the complaint may be quite detailed and may require that the alleged wrongdoer supply a great deal of business information to federal or state investigators. In fact, the modern tendency is for prehearing investigations to become very long and involved.

As an example of the actual procedures of a regulatory agency and the effects of its activities on individual firms, we will review briefly a case that was heard by the U.S. Tariff Commission (now called the International Trade Commission) in 1973.[15] A complaint involving the sulphur industry was brought to the Treasury Department (Bureau of Customs) by U.S. sulphur producers. The U.S. firms alleged that producers of by-product sulphur located in Western Canada were selling sulphur in the United States at less-than-fair value, a practice that violated the Federal Antidumping Act of 1921. The act provided that imported goods could not be sold in the United States at prices below their adjusted home market price (fair value) if the effect of such sales was to injure competing U.S. producers.

The immediate effect of the complaint was to set off a Treasury Department investigation of the *fact* of less-than-fair-value sales (dumping) by the Canadians. Treasury Department investigators demanded to see the relevant records of no less than five Canadian firms, some of which were affiliates of U.S.-based multinational corporations. The firms were compelled to supply the data, since the Treasury could direct its customs officials to withhold shipments of Canadian sulphur at U.S. ports of entry in the event of non-compliance. After several months of investigation, the Treasury reported to the Tariff Commission that the fact of less-than-fair-value sales had been established, and it was determined that the Commission would hear the case.

The next step in the prehearing activities was to allow the parties time to prepare their cases. The issue at the hearing would be whether or not, or to what extent, the U.S. producers were damaged by the Canadian dumping. Thus both sides launched substantial research efforts to examine this point. The Canadians were permitted by their own antitrust authorities to mount a common defense to the charge that they had injured U.S. producers. They engaged several top Washington and New York law firms to work with their in-house attorneys and an economic consultant on the preparation of their defense.

The Commission had three options available to it on the injury question. First, it could decide, based on the evidence presented by both sides, that there had been no injury. In this case the Canadian defendants would be out

---

15 This account is based on *Elemental Sulphur from Canada*, Hearings Before the United States Tariff Commission, Antidumping Investigation, No. AA1921-127, Washington, 1973.

their costs of litigation but would otherwise have to do nothing. A second possibility would be a finding that the U.S. producers had indeed suffered injury. In this instance antidumping duties would be assessed the *customers* of the Canadian firms, based on the amount of product they had imported and the margin between the U.S. price and the less-than-fair-value price on each shipment. (Obviously, from the standpoint of the Canadian sellers, this was no way to win friends, and they would probably decide to reimburse the buyers to keep them as customers.) A final possibility for the Commission was to decide that a "likelihood of injury" existed, although actual injury could not be established. In this event, and this *was* the Commission's ultimate decision, antidumping duties would not be assessed, but the Canadians would be warned not to dump in the future and would be subject to Treasury Department monitoring of their shipments for a period of three years. Thus, although antidumping duties (which in this case would have amounted to about $225,000) were not assessed, the Canadian producers, by the end of the case, had probably spent a like sum on their defense.

It is clear from the preceding discussion that the power and reach of administrative agencies is strong and pervasive. Although parties adversely affected by their decisions do have appeal rights, the courts seldom rule against the agencies *if* they are willing to admit an appeal at all. In fact, the courts tend to reverse administrative agency decisions only when they are contrary to law or when it can be proved that the administrator's exercise of authority was "arbitrary or capricious." The latter charge is rarely argued successfully.

THE REGULATED INDUSTRIES

Some administrative agencies deal exclusively with specific industries that provide public services under conditions of monopoly or near monopoly. For example, electric and gas utilities are broadly subject to regulation by the Federal Power Commission, and their retail pricing within each state is usually governed by a state public utilities commission. Other economic sectors characterized by regulation of conditions of service and price are transportation and communications.

A **natural monopoly** is present where economies of scale are sufficiently large that if two or more firms were to be involved in the production of the industry output, unit cost would be higher than for a monopoly.

Firms in these sectors are often described as **natural monopolies** for two primary reasons. First, it is a matter of public convenience that within a given market area, a large number of sellers of a public utilities type of good are not allowed to operate. (Imagine what it would mean to have, for example, four competing natural gas retailers digging up the streets of a given town to install pipelines!) Second, the fixed capital investment of public utilities suppliers is usually very large, since there are economies of scale in the production of their output and since variations in demand between peak-load periods and slack periods require that they have a capacity far in excess of *average* output. The result is that although the marginal cost of output may be very low and may even fall as output increases, average costs (particularly

AFC) will be very high when output is well below capacity. With too many firms in a given market area, each one would have a strong incentive to cut price and increase output. Only the largest and strongest would survive. In fact, the only way smaller firms could continue to exist would be through a policy of price regulation that would maintain the high prices necessary for them to cover their inordinately high fixed costs. The onerous consequences for consumers in such a setting are obvious.

Price Regulation in Theory

Government, having determined that monopoly or partial monopoly is inevitable in certain economic activities such as public utilities, has taken on the task of regulating the prices that such monopolies can charge. Economic theory has provided some guidelines on this problem, and we can summarize the theoretical case briefly with the help of Figure 16–1.

Figure 16–1   Marginal Cost vs. Average Cost Pricing for a Regulated Public Utility Firm

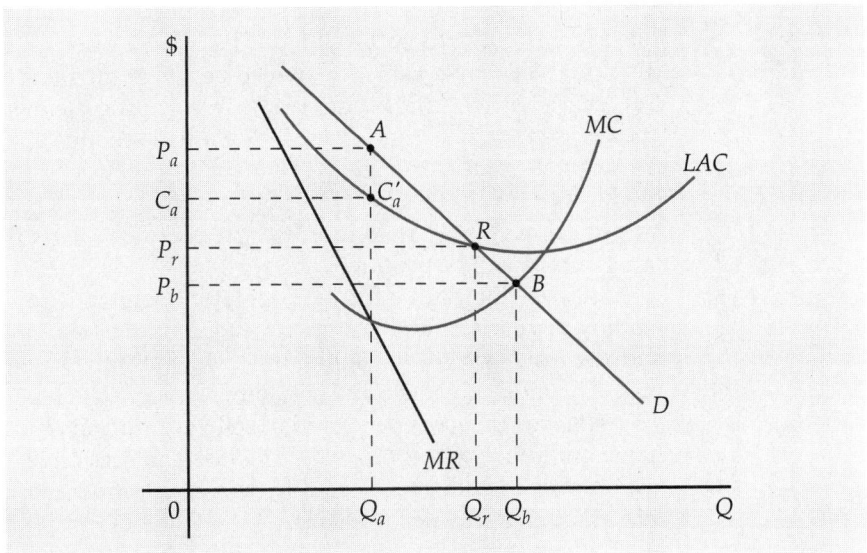

The unregulated profit-maximizing monopoly would produce where $MR = LMC$ (at Q_a) and charge a price of P_a. In this case economic profit is equal to $(P_a - C_a) \times Q_a$. If the government were to follow a marginal cost pricing policy and set a ceiling price of P_b (where LMC intersects demand curve D), the firm would produce Q_b units of output if it produced at all. However, the firm would be incurring an economic loss at Q_b, so it would leave the industry in the long run. If the government were to follow a policy of average cost pricing, it would set a ceiling price of P_r, where LAC intersects D. In this situation, the firm would produce Q_r units of output and receive a normal profit.

Figure 16–1 depicts a monopoly firm that is assumed to be a public utility. Of course, one of government's options in such a situation is simply to allow the firm to make its own pricing decisions, in which case the firm would charge price P_a for each unit of its output and supply quantity Q_a to its customers. From a social point of view, this has two undesirable consequences. First, the firm will have greater-than-normal profits (equal to the area of rectangle $C_aP_aAC_a'$), which can persist indefinitely, since no other firms can enter its market. Second, if price is regarded as a measure of the marginal social benefit of the output to consumers and the firm's marginal cost approximates marginal social cost, the socially optimal output is Q_b, which is consistent with marginal social benefit equaling marginal social cost.

From a resource allocation point of view, it has been argued that a policy of marginal cost pricing, in which the regulators establish price P_b and that price becomes the marginal revenue curve of the firm up to Q_b, would provide the socially optimal result. At Q_b, marginal social benefit would be equal to marginal social cost. Furthermore, the firm could do no better than to produce Q_b, since for smaller outputs, $P_b = MR > MC$. For larger outputs, the original marginal revenue curve once again depicts the correct marginal revenue value, and $MR < MC$.

Of course, the problem with price P_b is that it will not cover the firm's long-run average cost of production. For the firm to stay in business at Q_b, a subsidy will have to be provided. The lowest price on the given demand curve that *will* cover LAC is P_r, which occurs at the intersection of the firm's LAC curve with the market demand curve. Setting the regulated price at P_r is known as *average cost pricing*; and, as we will see, this approach is similar to the one that regulatory agencies pursue in practice. Although average cost pricing assures that profit will be only normal and increases the quantity of output (from Q_a to Q_r in Figure 16–1), it does not ensure that the socially optimal output will be produced.

Another alternative for the regulatory agency is to allow the utility to employ price discrimination in a way that increases the quantity of output and the firm's profit. In Figure 16–2, we show the same firm as in Figure 16–1. This time, however, the regulators have instructed the firm to use *price discrimination* or *block pricing* and to sell Q_r of output at price P_r and an additional amount, Q_rQ_b, at price P_b. (The firm can accomplish this by providing each customer with a reduced rate on consumption over and above a specified amount, a practice regularly followed by electric utilities.) On amount Q_r of the total quantity sold, $TR = TC = 0P_rRQ_r$ and profit is only normal. On the additional quantity sold at P_b, amount Q_rQ_b, total revenue is equal to area $Q_rP_b'BQ_b$; however, the additional cost the firm incurs is equal to the shaded area under the marginal cost curve (an amount obtained by summing all the individual MCs of the units of output between Q_r and Q_b). Since the incremental cost of the output sold for P_b is less than the incremental revenue (by an amount equal to area $ZP_b'B$), the firm will be quite happy to oblige the regulators.

Figure 16–2   Use of Price Discrimination to Increase Output and Profits
of a Regulated Utility

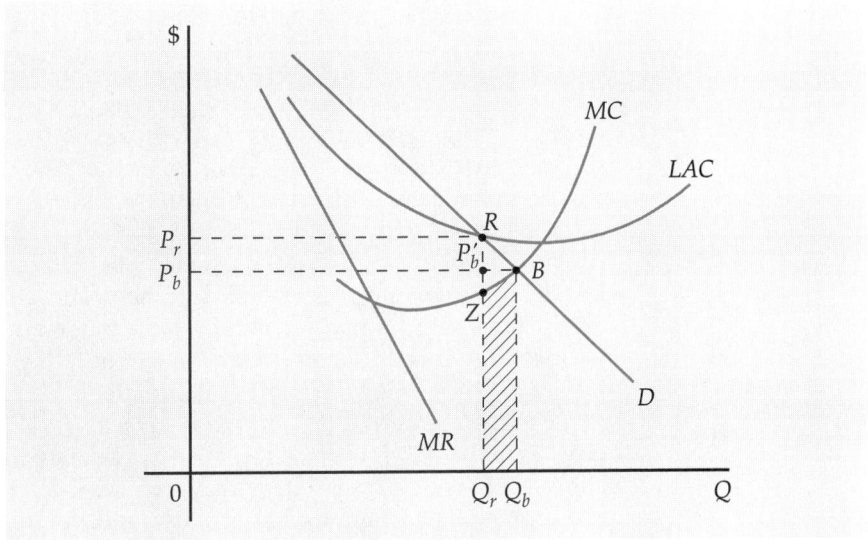

This graph illustrates government regulation with a combined average cost and marginal cost
pricing policy. Here, the government sets a ceiling price of P_r on the first Q_r units of output (average cost pricing). Then, the regulators instruct the firm that it may practice price discrimination and charge a lower price, such as P_b, for additional units. If the firm establishes a price of P_b
on incremental units beyond Q_r, it will sell an additional $Q_b - Q_r$ units. The firm would receive
incremental revenue equal to the area $Q_r P_b' B Q_b$ on these units and incur an incremental cost given
by the shaded area within $Q_r Z B Q_b$. The firm, therefore, would receive an incremental profit on
these units equal to $Z P_b' B$, and the public would benefit from the opportunity to buy the additional units at the lower price.

Price Regulation in Practice

Although economic analysis has provided some useful tools for studying
regulatory pricing, it must be conceded that, in practice, price regulation employs the method of trial, error, and precedent in much the same fashion as
is used in antitrust and other regulatory matters. Typically, the rates set by
regulatory authorities are the result of hearings in which accounting data on
costs, equity capital, and sales revenues substitute for the cost and revenue
functions necessary for the solutions familiar to economic theorists. The result
is that emphasis is placed on ensuring the regulated firm a "fair rate of return" on its investment, subject to the provision of an acceptable level of service to consumers.

   The notion of a fair rate of return is similar to the theoretical concept of
average cost pricing. That is, if we define total costs in their economic sense

MANAGERIAL PERSPECTIVE

The Cost of Regulation Can Make a Hospital Sick

Most people know that government regulation imposes costs as well as benefits on society, but sometimes the magnitude of the cost is far greater than is generally recognized. A 430-bed nonprofit hospital in the San Francisco area illustrates this point. The hospital estimates that the annual cost of dealing with various regulatory bodies and government-mandated paperwork is about $7.8 million.

The current average daily census of patients in the hospital is the same, 250 people, as it was in 1966, but the hospital staff is 75 percent larger (from 448 to 734 people). Part of this increase can be accounted for by a greater number of people treated on an outpatient basis as well as by a greater proportion of seriously ill inpatients.

Nevertheless, complying with the governmental requirements requires a staff of 140 full-time employees, plus many hours on the part of physicians as they cooperate with government-mandated audits and utilization review programs. For example, four full-time and one part-time employee spend all their time reviewing patient records. Another nine or ten people investigate the appropriateness of hospitalization.

The Federal Peer Review Act requires that all government-reimbursed hospital care be reviewed by an independent agency employed by the Health Care Finance Administration. It takes 20 employees just to supply the information needed for these audits. In addition, to obtain Medicare funds, the hospital must also be audited by the Joint Commission on Accreditation of Health Care Organizations. The hospital has added four people to the medical staff office to assist physicians with completing paperwork. An additional three data processors are also required.

The point of this story is not that all government regulation is bad, but that it all costs society in terms of resources that could be used elsewhere. Thus, the benefits and costs of each government regulation must be evaluated if the welfare of society is to be maximized.

Moreover, it is clear that a business firm cannot ignore the cost of government regulations in its long-term planning. To do so would substantially underestimate the firm's costs and could lead to unprofitable investment.

References: "One Hospital Tells the Cost of Regulation," *The Wall Street Journal*, June 26, 1990, p. A18; and Richard L. Clarke, "Tame the Healthcare Paperwork Monster," *Healthcare Financial Management* (April 1993), p. 12.

as including a return to entrepreneurship or investment that is sufficient to keep industry output at or near the socially desirable level in the long run, then when price equals long-run average cost ($P = LAC$), such a return is assured. Of course, our model of Figures 16–1 and 16–2 showed that such a rate of return is not necessarily consistent with the $P = MC$ socially optimal level of output.

Accordingly, public utilities have been permitted to employ price discrimination to push output beyond the level that would likely be supplied with a single-rate approach. Discrimination has been of both the rate-block type, or "second degree discrimination" and the segmented-market type, or "third degree discrimination" (see Chapter 11 for an example). In the latter case, separate rates have been established for commercial, industrial, and residential users. Some studies have shown that the result of these practices in public utilities pricing has been to favor commercial and industrial users at the expense of the residential consumer.[16]

WHOSE INTERESTS DO REGULATORS SERVE?

From the preceding discussion, it should be clear that in the case of public utility rate setting, one of the jobs of regulators is to make sure that privately owned utility firms are profitable. Many analysts have suggested that in public utilities (and even more so in transportation, communications, and banking), the regulators have represented producer interests much better than they have those of the public in general. A study published in 1971 summed up the situation as follows:

> The regulatory agencies have become the natural allies of the industries they are supposed to regulate. They conceive their primary task to be to protect insiders from new competition—in many cases from any competition.
>
> The Civil Aeronautics Board prevents qualified airlines from entering markets they desire to serve. The Interstate Commerce Commission keeps new motor carriers from competing with existing carriers. The Comptroller of the Currency and the Federal Reserve Board prohibit new banks from opening. In none of these fields is there any natural barrier to entry. There may be neither technical nor valid economic reasons for such decisions. Instead, the primary purpose often seems to be nothing more nor less than the protection of the "ins" from new competition by the "outs."[17]

---

16 See Paul W. MacAvoy, ed., *The Crisis of the Regulatory Commissions: An Introduction to a Current Issue of Public Policy* (New York: Norton, 1970); James Miller III and Bruce Yandle, eds., *Benefit/Cost Analysis of Social Regulation* (Washington, D.C.: American Enterprise Institute, 1979); and George C. Eads and Michael Fix, eds., *The Reagan Regulatory Strategy: An Assessment* (Washington, D.C.: Urban Institute, 1984).

17 Morton Mintz and Jerry S. Cohen, *America, Inc.: Who Owns and Operates the United States?* (New York: Dial Press, 1971), p. 103.

As many writers have indicated, the trucking industry provides an outstanding example of the protection of established interests by government regulatory agencies. Trucking in interstate commerce is regulated by the Interstate Commerce Commission (ICC). The ICC was established in the nineteenth century to regulate the railroads, which had been engaging in discriminatory rate wars that had proved detrimental to both themselves and their customers. As trucking developed in the twentieth century, the ICC first attempted to protect the railroads from the competing motor carriers. Eventually, its role changed to that of protector of large established trucking companies from the competition of smaller firms. The result was a maze of regulations that stifled competition and a licensing policy that blocked entry through elaborate and expensive procedural requirements.

For example, in his book *Economic Concentration: Structure, Behavior, and Public Policy*, John M. Blair cites the case of a small trucking firm in the mid-South that petitioned the ICC to obtain approval to extend its routes to two small Alabama towns not served by any large carrier. After more than *four years* of proceedings, the Commission granted the firm limited approval to serve only one of the two towns. Another writer reported in 1975 that ICC regulations caused a carrier to detour 800 miles out of its way and waste 160 gallons of fuel on a trip from Dallas to San Diego.[18] In 1978 *Newsweek* reported that independent trucking was about to die because of continued ICC restrictions on routes and "certificates of authority" (licenses).[19] However, a crack appeared in the facade of protection and restriction that the regulatory agencies had constructed over the years.

Alfred E. Kahn, a respected economist in the fields of regulation and antitrust who had been appointed Chairman of the Civil Aeronautics Board (CAB) by President Jimmy Carter, began to dismantle the system of fare regulation that for many decades had determined the prices charged by airlines. Kahn allowed the firms much freer rein in the area of price competition and permitted entry of firms into certain key markets where access had been restricted. The immediate result was a flurry of fare reductions and a tremendous increase in passenger traffic (an indication of highly elastic demand for the service).[20] Eventually, the CAB was eliminated from the roster of federal agencies, and its duties, which no longer included setting fares, were transferred to the Department of Transportation.

In the wake of air fare deregulation, the federal government took action to reduce legal restrictions and thus—it was hoped—increase competition in two other important economic sectors, banking and trucking. The Depository

---

18 See John M. Blair, *Economic Concentration: Structure, Behavior, and Public Policy* (New York: Harcourt, Brace, Jovanovich, 1972), p. 397; and Mark Frazier, "Highway Robbery—Via the ICC," *Readers' Digest* (January 1975), p. 72.

19 "The Joy of Truckin'," *Newsweek* (February 20, 1978), p. 68.

20 "The Double Standard of CAB Enforcement," *Business Week* (August 14, 1978), p. 26.

Institutions Deregulation and Monetary Control Act, passed by Congress in 1980, was designed to put savings banks and credit unions on a more-or-less equal footing with commercial banks, particularly by relaxing restrictions on the types of loans that could be made and allowing widespread use of interest-bearing checking accounts. Although competition increased, so did the cost of borrowing. Thus the final impact on consumers was difficult to assess.

Steps toward deregulation of the trucking industry were spelled out in the Motor Carrier Act of 1980. Specifically, the Act made entry into the industry much easier and provided for the removal of numerous geographical and commodity restrictions that had plagued independent truckers. According to one report, 2,700 restriction-removal applications filed during the first five months of 1981 were approved by the ICC.[21] The same source noted that service seemed to be qualitatively better, while both shipping rates and profits had fallen off.

Nevertheless, problems remained with *intrastate* regulation of trucking. In 1992, *Business Week* reported that Procter & Gamble saved 26 percent of the total shipping cost of restocking Tide detergent in San Antonio, Texas, by hauling it from Alexandria, Louisiana, rather than from Dallas, although the Dallas location was 30 miles closer. Shipping from Raleigh, North Carolina, to Richmond, Virginia, a distance of 146 miles, cost $204. However, a similar shipment from Danville, Virginia, to Richmond, also 146 miles, cost $539. Such discrepancies between intrastate and interstate trucking rates existed in many other states.[22] By 1995, however, intrastate trucking was virtually deregulated as an offshoot of airline deregulation, since carriers such as Federal Express and United Parcel Service that have combined air and ground service could not be regulated by state authorities.[23]

The Federal Communications Commission (FCC) is another agency that has taken numerous steps to reduce regulation in the past decade or so. The FCC is in charge of overseeing the telecommunications and broadcasting industries. In the wake of the breakup of American Telephone & Telegraph Company (1984), the FCC chose to allow smaller nonmonopoly phone companies to change prices or add services without approval and instituted lotteries as a method of distributing licenses for new services such as cellular mobile telephones. In regard to broadcasting, it relaxed regulations on television programming aimed at children, loosened guidelines requiring programming on community issues, eliminated time and frequency limits on television commercials, and relaxed rules limiting economic concentration in station ownership.

---

21 James C. Miller, III, "First Report Card on Trucking Deregulation," *The Wall Street Journal,* March 8, 1982, p. 22. (Mr. Miller was chairman of the FTC when this article was written.)
22 At that time, 42 states regulated intrastate trucking. See *Business Week* (April 6, 1992), p. 30.
23 "Courts Block Attempts to Restore Intrastate Trucking Regulation," *Traffic Management* (April 1995), p. 25; and Michael Totty, "Trucking Deregulation Shifts Into High," *The Wall Street Journal,* April 13, 1994, p. T1.

With the passage of the Telecommunications Act of 1996, the FCC entered a new era. The Act was aimed at promoting efficiency through further deregulation of the communications sector and the intermingling of telephone, broadcasting, and internet services. Regarding implementation of its provisions, *Business Week* noted that "Congress booted many of the thorny details to the FCC."[24] For example, under the Act new firms that enter local telephone service are provided access to the networks of existing firms. However, the fees that existing carriers can charge for use of their equipment are not clearly defined, and the FCC will have to develop the rules for them. In the cable TV industry, the FCC is now charged with defining "effective competition," a condition that will determine when rate regulation can be ended in a local market.

By the 1990s, some notes of caution were being sounded regarding overzealous deregulation of economic life. The telecommunications industry was still unsettled as rival firms vied for market share. While consumers had more choices, they were often confronted with a confusing array of options that was not easy to analyze. Price-gouging was occurring in certain phone markets. (See Managerial Perspective on phone deregulation.) In trucking, small independent operators feared that the deregulation they had counted on for access to routes would simply run them out of business as giant firms freely expanded. The magnitude of the debacle in the thrift industry led to changes in the regulation of banks and savings and loans.[25] In Fall 1991, Congress passed the Federal Deposit Insurance Corporation Improvement Act. Among other provisions, this law mandated prompt corrective actions by the federal regulators when they find that a bank has inadequate capital. It also required a review of any failure that resulted in substantial costs to the Federal Deposit Insurance Corporation. Earlier, in 1989, Congress had passed the Financial Institutions Reform, Recovery and Enforcement Act, a similar bill that applied to the thrift industry.[26]

Even Alfred Kahn was worried when a wave of mergers swept through the airline industry. In a television interview, he remarked that he had favored deregulation to foster competition but that he had never suggested that the antitrust laws be repealed. By the spring of 1990, a number of airlines (including People's Express and Air Florida) had gone out of business, and a number of the remaining airlines had merged so that the eight remaining

---

24 "Showtime for the Watchdog: Now, the FCC Must Set the Rules for Reform," *Business Week* (April 8, 1996), p. 86.

25 One source estimated that the problems in the thrift industry had resulted in an $80 billion cost to taxpayers by the fall of 1993. See "Catching Up With the Sick-Thrift Five," *Business Week* (December 13, 1993), p. 6; and "Bonfire of the S & Ls," *Newsweek* (May 21, 1990), pp. 20–32.

26 See "Too-Big-to-Fail After FDICIA," Federal Reserve Bank of Atlanta *Economic Review*, 78, no. 1 (January/February 1993), pp. 1–14; "Banking Conditions and Legislation," Federal Reserve Bank of Dallas *Financial Industry Issues* (3d Quarter 1992); and "The New Banking Law Toughens Regulation, Some Say Too Much," *The Wall Street Journal*, November 29, 1991, pp. A1, A8.

major domestic airlines had 95 percent of the landing slots. Pan American and Eastern were later added to the list of airlines that had ceased operations. Moreover, by the end of 1993, TWA had entered and emerged from bankruptcy reorganization, and Continental had entered and emerged from its *second* bankruptcy reorganization in eight years.[27]

Partially as a result of a scarcity of airport gates and landing slots, the barriers to entry for new carriers had become quite high. Nevertheless, a number of new airlines began operations, enticed by the availability of repossessed aircraft and laid off workers from other airlines.[28] Although greatly increased traffic improved airline profits in 1995 and 1996, a number of firms were in shaky financial condition, and even the strongest carriers were unsure what the future would bring.

REGULATION OF "UNREGULATED INDUSTRIES"

The relationship between many businesses and the regulatory agencies they must deal with is quite different from that enjoyed by firms in the so-called regulated industries (public utilities, communications, transportation). In manufacturing, for example, such agencies as the Occupational Safety and Health Administration (OSHA), the Environmental Protection Agency (EPA), and the Equal Employment Opportunity Commission (EEOC) are often viewed as unwelcome interlopers who both limit and *add costs to* the process of production.

Actually, the costs of regulation are borne by all of us in several ways. First, if the regulations implement policies that affect the production (and cost) functions of the firms they oversee, the likely result will be lower output and higher prices for the products of the regulated firms. Such a result would follow any time the marginal cost curve (*MC*) of a firm shifts upward. If the shift merely represents internalization of costs that were formerly borne

---

27 "Continental: In for the Short Haul," *Business Week* (December 6, 1993), pp. 120–122; "TWA Regroups, Emerges From Bankruptcy Shield," *The Wall Street Journal*, November 4, 1993, p. B5; "Eastern, The Wings of Greed," *Business Week* (November 11, 1991), pp. 34–36; "Pan Am Ceases Operations, Race Opens To Get Its Valuable Latin America Routes," *The Wall Street Journal*, December 5, 1991, p. A6; The Lorenzo Legacy Haunts Continental," *Business Week* (December 17, 1990), p. 28; "Pan Am Seeks Chapter 11 Shield, Gets UAL-Backed Cash Infusion," *The Wall Street Journal*, January 9, 1991, p. A3; and "Eastern Airlines Shuts Down Operations," *San Antonio Express-News*, January 19, 1991, pp. 1-B, 4-B. By 1996, TWA had also emerged from a second bankruptcy. See "St. Louis Blues: TWA Struggles to Improve Performance," *The Wall Street Journal*, September 27, 1996, p. B4.

28 See "Takeoff Is Bumpy for Start-Up Airlines As They Try to Grab a Piece of the Sky," *The Wall Street Journal*, July 11, 1993, pp. B1, B11; "The Big Time Beckons the Small Birds," *Business Week* (March 29, 1993), pp. 57–58; "Can These Upstart Airlines Handle the Heavy Weather?" *Business Week* (October 1, 1990), pp. 122–123; "Control of Major Airports by Carriers Is Focus of Justice Department Inquiry," *The Wall Street Journal*, June 18, 1990, p. A3; and "Skies Are Deregulated, But Just Try Starting a Sizable New Airline," *The Wall Street Journal*, July 19, 1989, pp. A1, A8.

(via externalities) by third parties, we know, from our earlier analysis of social costs and benefits in Chapter 15, that the resultant adjustment in output and price may be a socially acceptable result.

Of course, managers of profit-oriented firms are unlikely to take kindly to regulatory internalization of costs, even when the objective of such internalization is one with obvious social merit, such as pollution control or noise control. Installation of equipment that has no effect on the final product but involves substantial investment and adds to both fixed and variable costs of production is not the sort of change that managers can be expected to welcome. Often, regulatory standards call for strict policing of the production process. The costs of such monitoring have frequently been shifted away from the regulatory agency to the firms themselves, necessitating the hiring of "compliance officers" and cadres of specially trained personnel.

From the point of view of the consuming and taxpaying public, it is not always clear that the course of regulatory agencies leads to social gains. The great debates over such regulatory innovations as cars that will not start when seat belts are unfastened and the use of saccharin as a sugar substitute are cases in point. Further, some regulatory agencies have tended to duplicate the activities of others or to proliferate their rules and reporting requirements to an absurd degree. OSHA, which has been in existence since 1971, provides a splendid example of the latter. In 1978, it was reported that OSHA had decided to repeal 1,100 of the more than 10,000 rules it had generated since its inception.[29] Moreover, an earlier study reported that OSHA had placed in the Code of Federal Regulations about 140 standards pertaining to wooden ladders used on construction jobs.[30]

After 1980, many of the regulatory agencies became less aggressive under the leadership of Reagan appointees. This certainly occurred at OSHA, which began its retrenchment by backing off on numerous "nuisance" regulations. Between 1981 and 1985, OSHA produced only two standards on toxic substances. In 1985, it was reported that the AFL-CIO viewed the agency as nearly "irrelevant" in the effort to control workplace hazards. Business firms, which at first had criticized OSHA for excessive regulation, were reported to have become tired of waiting for OSHA to come up with standards for such dangers as chemical exposure. Some had resorted to setting strict standards on their own.[31] Their incentive, of course, was fear of litigations brought against them by workers and the general public. Both business and labor argued that OSHA needed to be revamped, but for different reasons. In 1996,

---

29 "The Regulation Mess," *Newsweek* (June 12, 1978), p. 86.
30 Richard B. McKenzie and Gordon Tullock, *Modern Political Economy* (New York: McGraw-Hill, 1978), p. 330. Also see Robert Stewardt Smith, *The Occupational Safety and Health Act: Its Goals and Its Achievements* (Washington, D.C.: American Enterprise Institute for Public Policy Research, 1976), p. 11.
31 "The Pressure on OSHA to Get Back to Work," *Business Week* (June 10, 1985), pp. 55–56.

the debate on OSHA continued, and it was suggested that the agency shift its emphasis from enforcement and penalties to helping firms design appropriate health and safety programs. Businesses, in particular, hoped for reductions in monitoring of firms with good safety records and additional relief from nuisance regulations.[32]

As this book goes to press, it seems that in general deregulation has been good for the U.S. economy. Competition in many industries is vigorous, in some cases even where the number of firms has declined because of failures, mergers, or acquisitions. Where concentration of economic power is on the increase, lawmakers, regulators, and the courts will probably have to decide whether new policies need to be developed. In addition, there are those who argue that regulation is still imposing substantial burdens on U.S. consumers. For example, a University of North Carolina researcher has reported a finding that only 13 of 33 key safety regulations succeeded in saving lives at a cost below $4 million per individual saved. He also found that regulations on wood preservatives adopted in 1990 impose costs of $6.3 trillion per life saved. Other researchers have argued that the annual costs to the economy of federal government regulations of all kinds is on the order of $500 to $650 billion.[33] This compares with total federal spending for all purposes of $1.5 trillion in 1995. Clearly, government regulation is costly, but there is virtually no chance that all of it could be eliminated, and very few people would argue that all of it should. Probably, the healthiest outcome of the deregulation trend is that we now tend to look at regulation more carefully and to ask critical questions about the impact of specific existing regulations or proposed new ones.

LAWS, REGULATIONS, AND THE FIRM'S STRATEGY

Regulatory changes can produce both costs and benefits for the firm. In the short run, when a regulatory change causes an adjustment of the firm's marginal cost or marginal revenue function, it is likely that profit maximization will require a change in either output or price or both. At a minimum the firm's managerial strategy should include evaluation of the impact of current or expected regulatory changes on its short-run price-output decision. Other short-run strategies may include efforts to influence the regulatory process itself through participation on government advisory committees, support of trade organizations, and lobbying efforts. However, it is in the firm's long-run planning that analysis of the legal and regulatory environment often is of major importance.

---

32 Kenneth Silverstein, "OSHA Reform," *Adhesives Age* (July 1996), p. 6.
33 "Tomorrow's Economic Argument," *Economist* (July 27, 1996), pp. 19–21; and Murray Weidenbaum, "Getting Our Economic House in Order," *Vital Speeches of the Day* (September 1, 1996), pp. 703–704.

From Chapters 13 and 14, we know that the present value of the firm's activities depends on what new undertakings it chooses to pursue and how these projects contribute to its future stream of profits. Obviously, when a firm's managers analyze a new investment venture, they may find that legal or regulatory variables could substantially affect the venture's outcome. A decision to accept or reject a project could easily depend on anticipated costs attributable to laws or regulations or merely uncertainty regarding the regulatory environment.

What questions should management ask regarding legal and regulatory variables in the process of capital project evaluation? The following are some of the more obviously important ones:

1. What *currently existing laws and regulations* have particular bearing on the project's outcome?
2. What are the *anticipated changes* in laws or regulations that will affect the project?
3. What *regulatory agencies* have jurisdiction over the proposed project?
4. Do rival firms enjoy *regulatory privileges*, and how will they react to a new entrant into their territory?
5. Are firms that *supply inputs* for the projected activity or that *purchase* its *output* subject to peculiar regulatory constraints?
6. Will a successful undertaking of the project require substantial expenditures on *litigation* or *representation* before regulatory agencies?
7. In general, to what extent do regulatory uncertainties add to the project's *risk*?

Once a thorough survey of the possible regulatory impacts on a given capital project is completed, the net present value (NPV) of the project can be appropriately adjusted for regulatory variables. This can be accomplished in a number of ways. For example, regulatory costs can be deducted from the project's annual flow of receipts if they recur each year, or they can be added to the price of the project if they are relevant only to getting it started. Anticipated future benefits from regulation can be added to project inflows. Finally, the matter of regulatory risks can be handled through adjustment of the discount rate. The important point is to make certain that legal and regulatory impacts are not overlooked, since they often can make or break a given business venture.

SUMMARY

The Legal Environment and Managerial Economics

In this chapter we have emphasized how the legal and regulatory environment affects the economic decisions made by managers of business firms. Our major focus has been the avoidance of mistakes that may occur because of indifference toward or ignorance of the firm's obligations under the law. We briefly surveyed the types of laws affecting the firm in its everyday relationships with other firms, with individual persons, and with the various levels of government. *Antitrust law* was reviewed, with emphasis on some of the kinds of business activities that constitute *per se violations* of the federal law (price fixing, division of markets, group boycotts, and tying agreements).

The last half of this chapter dealt with the important issue of *administrative or regulatory agencies* and their relation to the firm. We noted that such agencies both make and enforce laws and that the expertise of their administrators is seldom overturned by the courts. From the historical record of the so-called regulated industries (public utilities, transportation, communications), we found that the relationship between private business and the regulators is not always adverse and that, in fact, regulatory agencies may have actually promoted the concentration of economic power in many sectors of the economy.

A feature of our discussion of the regulated industries was the extension of the monopoly model to the question of *price-setting by regulatory commissions*, a common approach in public utilities management. In general, we found that such commissions emphasize a *fair return on investment* in public utilities capacity and allow price discrimination in the rate schedules of public utilities firms.

The final sections of this chapter dealt with the effects of miscellaneous regulatory measures on the operations of firms outside the regulated industries. The impact of such measures on production and prices was discussed, and we questioned whether *regulatory costs* might exceed the social benefits gained from some recent rules and standards. The chapter closed with a discussion of *strategies* the firm might employ to bring regulatory variables into the decision process. It was argued that in the short run the firm's managers should pay special attention to the *effects of regulation* on *marginal cost* and *marginal revenue*, being prepared to alter price and output in order to maximize profit under changing constraints. Our prescription for the firm's long-run strategy was that *regulatory variables should be explicitly included in capital project analyses* through adjustment of project prices, inflows, and discount rates.

QUESTIONS

1. What is the difference between a crime and a tort? Give some examples of business activities that may result in litigation because a tort has occurred.

2. What kinds of contracts must generally be evidenced by a writing? Are oral agreements ever recognized as contracts? What are the usual remedies for breach of contract?

3. What are the principal antitrust laws of the United States, and what kinds of activities do they prohibit?

4. For what kinds of penalties do the federal antitrust laws provide? Is it possible to find corporate executives guilty of crimes when the antitrust laws are violated?

5. Do government administrative agencies have legislative or judicial powers? What is the relationship of Congress and the courts to administrative agencies and their activities?

6. What means can administrative agencies use to enforce their regulations? How is action against violations of business regulations initiated in cases where administrative agencies have jurisdiction?

7. Explain why firms such as electric utilities are viewed as natural monopolies.

8. What is marginal cost pricing? Use a diagram to explain why a marginal cost pricing policy might make subsidization of a public utility firm a necessity.

9. What is average cost pricing? How is average cost pricing related to the regulatory concept of a fair rate of return?

10. What kinds of price discrimination are used by public utilities? Why do regulators permit the utilities to discriminate?

11. Why does the imposition of new regulations often result in reductions in output and increases in the prices charged by firms? Use a diagram to explain how the profit-maximizing output of a single firm would change because of the imposition of new costs related to regulation.

12. Discuss some of the steps that managers of firms can take to ensure that regulatory variables are taken into account when long-run decisions are being made.

SELECTED REFERENCES

Adams, Walter, and James Brock. *Antitrust Economics on Trial*. Princeton, N.J.: Princeton University Press, 1991.

Areeda, Phillip. *Antitrust Analysis: Problems, Text, Cases*, 3d ed. Boston: Little, Brown, 1981, especially Chapter 1.

Blair, John M. *Economic Concentration: Structure, Behavior, and Public Policy*. New York: Harcourt, Brace, Jovanovich, 1972, Chapters 21–24.

Blair, Roger D., and James M. Fesmire. "The Resale Price Maintenance Policy Dilemma," *The Southern Economic Journal* 60, No. 4 (April 1994), pp. 1043–1047.

Breit, William, and Kenneth G. Elzinga. *The Antitrust Casebook*. Chicago: The Dryden Press, 1982.

Carlton, Dennis W., and Jeffrey M. Perloff. *Modern Industrial Organization*, 2nd ed. New York: HarperCollins, 1994.

Conry, Edward J., Gerald R. Ferrera, and Karla H. Fox. *The Legal Environment of Business*. Boston: Allyn and Bacon, 1993.

Kleit, Andrew N., and Malcolm B. Coate. "Are Judges Leading Economic Theory? Sunk Costs, The Threat of Entry and the Competitive Process," *The Southern Economic Journal* 60, no. 1 (July 1993), pp. 103–118.

Kwoka, John E. Jr., and Lawrence J. White, eds. *The Antitrust Revolution: The Role of Economics*. New York: HarperCollins, 1994.

Moore, Gary A., Arthur M. Magaldi, and John A. Gray. *The Legal Environment of Business: A Contextual Approach*. Cincinnati: South-Western, 1987.

Salop, Steven C., and Lawrence J. White. "Antitrust Goes to College," *Journal of Economic Perspectives*, 3, no. 3 (Summer 1991), pp. 193–202.

Schiller, Bradley R. *The Economy Today*, 6th ed. New York: McGraw-Hill, 1994, Chapters 26 and 27.

17

THE FIRM AND THE FUTURE

Throughout this book we have attempted to emphasize decision making by business managers who generally operate under the traditional private sector assumption that the firm's objective is to maximize profit. Early in our discussion, we took a simplistic, short-run view of profit maximization, which disregarded the important fact that firms usually exist over a substantial time span. Later, we expanded our techniques to view the firm's profit as a net inflow of periodic receipts that can be evaluated in present value terms.

Our analysis of the profit-maximizing firm has encompassed many elements of the decision-making environment wherein managers must play their assigned roles. Production relationships, costs, demand, and pricing problems were examined in detail. Thereafter, we extended our discussion to the questions of new investment undertakings and the analysis of public sector managerial decisions. In general, factors external to the firm became increasingly important as the topics of discussion gained both complexity and realism. Rival behavior, input market conditions, global developments, and laws and regulations all make the manager's job more challenging. In addition, as our international capsules have shown, the decision to operate in a foreign environment brings with it new complications, but many familiar economic tools can be employed to analyze and deal with them.

In the future we can expect technology and market conditions to change. These adjustments will not affect the *conditions* for profit maximization, but they will alter the *data* that managers must analyze. Changes in laws and regulations, in the structure of firms, and in the international environment are perhaps the kinds of adjustments that will most tax administrative abilities in the years to come. In our concluding chapter we survey some likely changes in the environment in which both private and public sector managers will have to function as decision makers.

REGULATION, DEREGULATION, AND PRIVATIZATION

Efforts to reduce the role of the federal government in controlling the micro-economy have constituted the most striking change affecting business in the United States over the past two decades. Earlier, during the 1960s and 1970s, the productive activities of both business and government became increasingly constrained by laws and regulations intended to promote the general welfare through internalization of costs formerly associated with, but not allocated to, the production of specific goods and services. Thus businesses were confronted with the task of responding to many new regulations involving issues that ranged from control of environmental pollution, for example, to the establishment of new worker-safety codes. The 1980s and 1990s, on the other hand, brought us deregulation and privatization (sale of government-owned enterprises to the private sector), both with mixed—but still not fully understood—results. At the dawn of a new century, we are still assessing these comparatively recent developments.

Deregulation and privatization are intended to improve economic efficiency by increasing competition and fostering increases in productivity. The United States took the lead on deregulation in transportation and banking. The result was a flurry of activity in the form of expansion of old firms into new markets as well as entry by new firms. At the present time, it is clear that there have been gains from these changes, but there also have been some offsetting losses. In air transportation, there has been a major shakeout of firms, and even the most powerful of those that remain have at times found it difficult to operate profitably in an atmosphere of destructive fare wars.[1] A possible danger is that monopoly problems will result from the numerous mergers that have been allowed to take place. In trucking, expansion of large firms that have the staying power to remain in marginally profitable markets for long periods of time may lead to reduced competition as smaller firms fail.[2] In banking, the number of failures, especially of savings and loan associations, increased markedly when firms aggressively made loans on ill-conceived or excessively risky projects. In 1990, as a result of speculative lending and mismanagement that accompanied deregulation, the government's Resolution Trust Corporation (RTC), an entity set up to manage and ultimately get rid of properties that reverted to government entities after foreclosure, claimed assets valued at $186 billion were under its wing. In Texas alone, over 18,000 properties were being overseen by the RTC.[3] Remarkably, by the end of 1995, when the RTC was dissolved, all but $8 billion of these assets had been sold.[4]

While deregulation has yielded some problems that its proponents did not anticipate, results are just coming in on the movement toward privatization of government-owned firms or of activities formerly carried out by government agencies. Some cities have contracted with private firms for provision of such services as public transportation, street sweeping, and land-

---

1 "American West Airlines: Making Reorganization Work," *Air Transport World* (February 1995), pp. 26–34; and "Ready to Soar Again?" *Business Week* (April 26, 1993), pp. 26–28.
2 "Trucking Failures Hit All-Time High Again," *Traffic Management* (August 1992), pp. 16–17.
3 "S&L Property Taken Over by Government," *San Antonio Express-News* (October 21, 1990), p. 1-E.
4 "Closing Shop," *America's Community Banker* (February 1996), p. 8.

fill management. Also relatively new on the American scene is the private enterprise prison.[5] Its backers claim that it reduces the cost of operating a penal system, while its detractors fear that the search for efficiency may impose real costs on prison inmates and, eventually, on the community at large. There have already been some cases where privately run prisons have failed, leaving in their wake problems ranging from what to do with prisoners to job losses for neighboring towns.[6]

Dissatisfaction with the performance of public school students has led some school systems to contract out their management to private firms. There have been some modest successes in these ventures, but there have been many problems, too. One of the largest providers, Educational Alternatives, Inc., in 1996 had its contract with the Baltimore Board of School Commissioners canceled. *Business Week* reported that the firm had promised big savings and rapid improvement in students' test scores but "... delivered little of either." Another source reported in 1995 that the firm had hoped for a 25 percent profit on the Baltimore contract, but that based on the problems it had encountered, 9 percent was more realistic.[7]

Outside the United States, there has been a virtual tidal wave of privatizations, with many countries following the example of Great Britain. There, a major step was taken toward privatization with the denationalization of British Gas, which occurred in late 1986. While the move definitely raised some revenue for the British government, it is not clear that any efficiency gains have occurred. British Gas historically was an efficient supplier from a technical standpoint, and the change did not bring any significant competitors into the market. In 1993, the British Monopolies and Mergers Commission recommended breaking up British Gas into smaller entities in order to promote competition.[8] Britain continued along the privatization path in 1996, when its government-owned railroads were sold. In France, a wave of privatization occurred during the brief tenure (only two years) of conservative Prime Minister Jacques Chirac. However, a Socialist government less friendly to such policies was elected in 1988 and began in 1990 to restructure shareholding and reshuffle the chief officers of several privatized firms. In July of that year, the Socialists launched a proposal to nationalize a private firm in the nuclear power plant construction business. Then the tables turned again, and in 1993–1994, the French government put many of its holdings up for private purchase.[9] In 1996, France was balking at privatization of its national

5 "Making Crime Pay," *Fortune* (June 29,1992), pp. 111–112.

6 "It's a Bust: Many For-Profit Prisons Hold No Profits—Nor Even Any Inmates," *The Wall Street Journal*, June 18, 1991, pp. A1, A12.

7 "Hard Lessons at For-Profit Schools," *Business Week* (January 29, 1996) pp. 76–77; and "Privatization Picks," *Chief Executive* (January 1995), pp. 24–26.

8 "The Greatest Assets Ever Sold," *Economist* (August 21, 1993), pp. 13–14.

9 "Europe for Sale," *Business Week* (July 19, 1993), pp. 38–39.

phone company, but the European Community had scheduled telecommunications competition for 1998 under a plan that would force government to divest its telcom holdings.[10]

It is likely that the future will bring even further deregulation and privatization. Governments and businesses will have a lot of learning and re-learning to do as the fallout from this process continues. In all probability, some of the newly private endeavors will provide impressive results as obsolete organizational structures and modes of production are replaced with others that are more rational. However, rational behavior responds to incentives, and sometimes the incentives built into a government policy are not those that were intended by its formulators. Where unexpected or undesirable results are obtained, we can be sure that further modification of policy will occur.

DEVELOPING COUNTRIES AND THE EASTERN BLOC

The move toward rationalizing economic activity has swept contagiously through many developing countries and has won over many leaders in Eastern Europe as well. Countries that spent much of the past 50 years developing centrally controlled economic systems fraught with incentive-stifling bureaucracies and mismanaged government-owned enterprises have searched for ways to rescue their faltering economies. Economic gurus prescribed strong medicine in the form of "shock treatments" combining monetary austerity with privatization to move countries such as Poland and Russia to free markets and private enterprise almost overnight.[11] However, the dismantling of the Eastern Bloc's system of international trade left firms and government enterprises with no external markets, and privatization did not progress as quickly as its proponents imagined it would.

Many observers have looked hopefully toward Germany for a model of how to reform Eastern Europe. West Germany took the bull by the horns when it chose to reunify with East Germany. The costs of that reunification have been tremendous, and development in the east has proceeded much more slowly than anticipated.[12] It remains to be seen whether Germany will provide a laboratory for determining the kinds of steps that can be taken in places such as Poland, Bulgaria, Romania, and, of course, the Confederation of Independent States to both speed up development and integrate an eco-

---

10 Malcolm Taylor, "Private Party," *Communications International* (January 1996), pp. 26–28.
11 "Good Guru Guide," *Economist* (January 25, 1994), pp. 21–26; and "The High Cost of Jeffrey Sachs," *Forbes* (June 21, 1993), p. 52.
12 Ulrich Heileman and Wolfgang H. Reinicke, "Together Again: The Fiscal Costs of German Unity," *Brookings Review* (Spring 1995), pp. 42–45; and "Germany: Is Reunification Failing?" *Business Week* (November 15, 1993), pp. 48–50.

nomically depressed population into the mainstream of the world economy. What Germany has been doing for its underdeveloped east may not transfer to culturally different countries, and it is unlikely that any Eastern European state will be able to integrate itself with the West on terms anything like those the East Germans have enjoyed.

In the West, rapidly industrializing countries such as Mexico, Argentina, and Chile have moved swiftly to privatize government enterprises and deregulate economic life. (The Mexican privatization program was virtually complete by 1994 and covered the steel industry, telephones, banking, and hundreds of other activities.) Some have lifted trade barriers, and many have become more open to foreign investment and joint domestic/foreign ventures. Meanwhile, the Pacific Rim countries have turned supplying the U.S. consumer market into an economic bonanza. The flourishing economies of such ministates as Hong Kong, Taiwan, Singapore, and some of their neighbors certainly have suggested that development has as much to do with organization and incentives as it does with resources. The region's giant, China, has shown that it still has substantial political obstacles to overcome before more rapid growth can occur.[13] However, it continues to move toward greater integration with the world economy, and industrialized countries everywhere are keenly eyeing its mass market.

It appears that joint private-state ventures are very likely to become a driving force in the economic integration of industrialized countries with both the developing countries and the noncapitalist economies. The joint-venture approach does not constitute a new strategy, for there have been some joint ventures in many of these countries for a long time. However, most barriers to establishment of such ties have fallen, with the public sector in the host countries making foreign participants more and more welcome. All of this is cause for optimism as well as a veritable fountain of both challenges and opportunities for present and future managers.[14] It will be important for managers in this new environment to be not only analytical, but also flexible and innovative. It will also be important for international investors to take advantage of the existing managerial know-how of host-country executives and to help them develop new management skills.[15]

---

13 Mike Johnson, "China: The Last True Business Frontier," *Management Review* (March 1, 1996), pp. 39–43; "A Survey of Asia," *Economist* (October 30, 1993), special insert following p. 61; and *Fortune Special Issue: Asia in the 1990s*, Time Magazines Inc. (Fall 1989).

14 Joint venturing in these countries can be dangerous both financially and physically. In 1996, a U.S. hotel investor was assassinated, gangster style, in a Moscow subway station. He had been having trouble with his Russian partners (including the city government) for some time. See "Slain Businessman Battled Odds in Russia," *The Wall Street Journal*, November 5, 1996, p. A19; and "A Plague of Disjointed Ventures, " *Business Week* (May 1, 1995), p. 55.

15 Paul Lawrence and Charalambos Vlachoutsicos, "Joint Ventures in Russia: Put the Locals in Charge," *Harvard Business Review* (Jan./Feb. 1993), pp. 44–54.

SOCIAL COSTS AND "ACCOUNTABILITY"

For three decades now, there has been widespread public concern about third-party costs imposed on consumers by both business and government. Individuals and interest groups have demanded reforms aimed at internalizing economic costs that were shifted to them as goods and services were produced. High on the list of consumer complaints have been the damaging effects of pollution and other environmental and health hazards. While many reform measures have been taken, these kinds of problems are far from solved. Further, the awakening of consumers to the possibility of holding businesses liable for external costs has precipitated legal action on a broader front. The number of product liability and malpractice suits has skyrocketed, as have the settlements obtained by plaintiffs in such litigations.

The emergence of massive liability claims against businesses has made it clear that some new policies regarding the way torts are handled are likely to be developed. At issue is the question of fairness, both to injured parties and to those who damaged them. These problems were dramatically brought to light by several cases that were in their settlement phases during the latter half of the 1980s and the early 1990s. One was that of Manville Corporation (formerly Johns-Manville), a manufacturer of asbestos-based building materials. As the connection between asbestos and lung cancer (asbestosis) became firmly established, Manville was hit with thousands of lawsuits from both workers and consumers. It became clear to management that court findings in favor of the plaintiffs would bankrupt the company, so they filed for bankruptcy in advance of settlement of the claims. In 1988, Manville emerged as a reorganized company, and a trust fund of $2.5 billion was set up to compensate victims of asbestosis. This fund was much smaller than the total claims of plaintiffs ($50 billion), and legal problems continued to plague the company. Manville later became a holding company for two subsidiaries in the paperboard and non-asbestos building materials business. Finally, in 1996, one of the subsidiaries was sold, and Manville assumed the name of the other (Schuller).[16]

Two other major liability cases against private companies also made headlines during the latter half of the 1980s. The first involved A. H. Robins Company, makers of the Dalkon Shield (an intrauterine contraceptive device). Massive claims were filed against the company by women who apparently had suffered internal damage from using the device. Like Manville, A. H. Robins filed for bankruptcy, and subsequent deliberations included both the question of the firm's reorganization and provision for compensation of

---

16 "End of the Line: Manville Is No More," *Fortune* (April 29, 1996), pp. 42; and "Law: Manville Trust Claims," *The Wall Street Journal*, January 19, 1993, p. B2.

the plaintiffs. The second case, that of Union Carbide, involved a deadly gas leak at its pesticide plant in Bhopal, India. Thousands were killed, blinded, or maimed as the gas cloud wafted through heavily populated areas near the plant. Carbide did not file for bankruptcy, but instead waged a legal campaign to limit its liability. It made an offer to the Indian government, but that offer was rejected. Eventually a settlement was reached, but it was viewed as unsatisfactory to many in India.[17]

An Insurance Crisis?

As liability claims and judgments have mounted, business insurers have moved to protect themselves from losses. In certain cases, this has meant outright refusal to insure against losses from certain activities or certain types of products. In recent years, there have been many news accounts of medical practitioners leaving some fields because of the excessive costs of insurance. Businesses, and even small local governments, were from time to time denied insurance coverage. Critics of the insurance industry cited substantial profits as evidence that the industry was not in trouble. They argued that the firms' greed led them to refuse to deal in certain types of risks.

The hue and cry about liability judgments has led many politicians to call for legislation providing a cap on settlements. Most congressional experts doubt that any widespread legislation of this sort will be forthcoming soon. However, those who need insurance have begun to look for alternatives, displaying just the kind of market response that most economists would predict. For example, a significant number of corporations, industry groups, and nonprofit organizations have turned to financing their own risks by setting up "captive" insurance companies. The corporations that have taken this route include well-known names such as AT&T and Hewlett-Packard. Many such captives have been set up in Vermont, which has designed legislation friendly to them.[18] Both industry and the private sector have set up risk-pooling schemes to become self-insured. In California, beach communities banded together to form a self-insurance pool when private companies refused to extend their insurance against claims resulting from injuries and deaths at public beaches and recreational areas. Innovations have occurred in health insurance as well, where firms and public sector organizations have developed self-insurance plans. The lesson here is that there is usually a rational solution available for an economic problem, and that if existing firms in the private sector do not come up with a solution, someone else probably will. The future is likely to bring us some limitations on tort liability, but it is also likely to be

---

17 "Bhopal Legacy Still Being Felt," *Occupational Hazards* (February 1996), p. 28; and "Wounded Giant: Union Carbide Offers Some Sober Lessons in Crisis Management," *The Wall Street Journal*, January 28, 1992, pp. A1, A9.

18 "Vermont Gets 20 Closer to Captive Goal," *Business Insurance* (August 26, 1996), p. 20.

marked by significant innovations in the way firms and governments provide in advance for such contingencies.[19]

Accountability and the Manager

In Chapter 16, we noted how important it is for managers to understand the legal environment that affects the firm in regard to the questions addressed by antitrust and business practices laws. Here, we have seen that tort liability has recently become increasingly important to the business sector. Further, it is an area where changes in laws and regulations, and in the options available to both firms and their customers, may be imminent. As these changes unfold, the competent manager will have to be both knowledgeable about them and flexible enough to adjust the firm's operations in ways appropriate to the new circumstances. This may mean modifying products or processes, or even withdrawing certain lines from the market. Clearly, it also means that new capital projects can be accurately evaluated only when all of the potential changes in the legal and regulatory environment are taken into account.

As we have pointed out a number of times in preceding chapters, it is increasingly true that managerial responsibility extends beyond the firm's income statement to the consequences of virtually all of its activities. Today, "accountability" has become a major issue in both business and government, and the courts are tending to deal more harshly with corporate lawbreaking and those deemed responsible for it.[20] Thus managers, for their *own protection* as well as that of their firms and stockholders, must keep abreast of legal and regulatory matters falling within the scope of their operations and seek competent advice when treading on unfamiliar ground.

STRUCTURE AND ORGANIZATION OF FIRMS

While the increasing complexity of the environment surrounding managerial decisions has provided some real challenges to decision makers, it also has contributed to some structural and organizational adjustments in today's firms. Corporate managers have realized that the environment of modern business has made it increasingly risky to pursue a nondiversified strategy. A firm with all of its eggs in one basket, in terms of product line or markets, leaves itself open not only to swings in profits caused by changing rules and regulations, but also often to the uncertainties of the international marketplace and high-level international politics. Prior to the 1980s, many firms in the steel and petroleum industries of the United States constituted cases in point. Since they were vertically integrated and had not diversified their in-

---

19 "Congressional Issues on Hold," *Business Insurance* (July 29, 1996), pp. 1, 10.
20 "Catching Up With the Sick-Thrift Five," *Business Week* (December 13, 1993), p. 6.

vestments as much as some other large firms, they became highly dependent on government policy, both domestic and international, to ensure continued profitability. This was not entirely the doing of the firms themselves, since some of their international rivals were paragovernment firms that did not have to sell their output at profit-maximizing prices.

In the United States, two of the primary reactions of management to contemporary regulatory and international trade and investment complexities have been the conglomerate movement and the multinationalization of the corporate sector. The conglomerate movement has broadly diversified the assets of many large corporations through mergers and acquisitions that tend to insulate firms from profit fluctuations attributable to dependency on a narrow product base. On the other hand, "going multinational" for many firms has meant diversifying markets for traditional lines of products. Presumably, for a significant number of firms, both of these approaches may serve their growth, profit, and stability objectives better than other strategies.

A third approach to the contemporary business environment is the joint government/private sector investment project which was mentioned earlier. It is likely that U.S. firms have had more experience with this means of diversifying risk in their overseas operations than in their domestic activities. The reason for this is the strong presence of American private investment in such developing areas as Latin America and Africa. Nationalism in these parts of the world led governments to prohibit or at least severely constrain firm ownership by foreign interests. Although U.S. firms sometimes resisted attempts to force them into a joint-venture format, it is clear that the joint-venture approach can reduce risk and increase bargaining clout with local government agencies.

More recently, firms in all industrialized countries have more actively sought joint ventures with foreign public and private interests to produce goods for both domestic consumption and export. This trend has been a necessity in former noncapitalist countries where governments controlled the means of production. However, joint government/private sector undertakings have been occurring even in Western Europe as an offshoot of the privatization process. An example is the merger in late 1993 of Volvo and Renault, with the French government retaining a 47 percent share of the new company.[21]

Despite the recent developments in deregulation and privatization, it is evident that government and business will become increasingly entwined in the future. We can expect to see very close communication between the public and private sectors and even more joint government/private sector investment projects, especially in places such as China and the Confederation of Independent States. Government participation and worker purchases of

21 "Who's Driving Renault-Volvo?," *Economist* (September 11, 1993), pp. 61–62.

shares in some corporations may blur the notion of ownership. Nevertheless, we believe that private initiative will remain important because of the driving force of technology and the key role that individual managers and small firms play in fostering innovation.

ECONOMICS AND TOMORROW'S MANAGER

This chapter has been about change—and more specifically about the kinds of changes that we think will shape the environment of tomorrow's managers. We did not predict any great changes in economic analysis that would revolutionize the role of the manager or managerial economist. No such changes are expected. Rather, we emphasized trends and recent developments in the external environment of the firm that are likely not so much to affect managerial behavior as they are to affect the data and constraints managers must work with. Clearly, the tasks of managers will become more difficult as these factors multiply and as the organizational structure of the firm increases in complexity.

We believe that the basic principles and the approaches to problem solving that we have tried to teach in this text constitute important economic foundations for tomorrow's managers. Students who understand what we have said and can solve the kinds of problems found in the preceding chapters have attained a degree of economic know-how and literacy that will help them to analyze future problems in a managerial setting. The techniques learned here should have enduring application to future problems.

Of course, managerial economics does not end with this chapter or this book. We have only scratched the surface, particularly where techniques of quantitative analysis are concerned. We hope that students who have found this book interesting will endeavor to push their knowledge of the subject considerably further. We also hope that those who cannot devote more time to the study of managerial economics will be able to remember and use in their future careers what they have learned here.

INTEGRATING CASE 5

Bayville Convention Center

The Board of Supervisors of the city of Bayville is faced with a dilemma. For a number of years, there has been an undercurrent of community interest in building a convention center on a large downtown tract of land that has remained vacant since dilapidated public housing was torn down. (The former tenants were relocated to new facilities in a less congested area.) Several older downtown hotels recently have undergone renovation, and two new luxury hotels have been built. Presently, there is excess capacity in downtown hotel rooms. Although the central city's commercial and financial districts have undergone a renaissance, population has shifted to the suburbs, and downtown retail trade has declined. Finally, the downtown area has had a long-term drainage and flood control problem that recently has been improved by large public investment in several runoff canals.

The community is divided over the convention center proposal. Naturally, the hoteliers and downtown commercial interests favor construction of the convention center. They have enlisted the help of the Economic Development Alliance (EDA), a group of industrialists with a progrowth stance, to further public sector consideration of the project. The EDA, at its own expense, has prepared a feasibility study for the center. Initially, the Board of Supervisors welcomed this gesture, since city funds for such an effort were severely limited. However, when the study was released, certain civic groups and some members of the board began to criticize it. In general, they argued that the EDA had painted an overly optimistic picture of the convention center project.

The EDA investigated four possible sizes for the convention center. In their study they assumed a useful life of 20 years and no salvage value, since this approach is generally used by the city planning department. The sizes, estimated construction costs, and estimated operating costs of the alternative convention centers follow:

Convention Center Size (sq. ft.)	Construction Cost (dollars)	Annual Operating Cost (dollars)
130,000	$23,000,000	$ 900,000
160,000	30,000,000	1,500,000
210,000	43,000,000	2,000,000
240,000	50,000,000	2,700,000

The EDA projected *annual* operating revenues from the center to be $2,400,000 if the 130,000-square-foot structure were built. Revenue was expected to increase by 37.5 percent if the size of the center were increased to 160,000 square feet. The 210,000-square-foot center would provide 25 percent more operating revenue than would the 160,000-square-foot alternative, and an increase in size from 210,000 to 240,000 square feet would yield a further increment of 12 percent in annual operating revenue. Indirect benefits, attributable primarily to expenditures of conventioneers in the local economy, were also estimated for each size center. The indirect benefits estimates follow:

Convention Center Size (sq. ft.)	Annual Estimated Indirect Benefits (dollars)
130,000	$1,800,000
160,000	2,475,000
210,000	3,625,000
240,000	4,027,000

The EDA and downtown business interests have taken a strong position, advocating that the 240,000-square-foot center should be built, since it would yield net benefits to the community at discount rates of both 6 and 9 percent per annum. The EDA has argued that there is no use to building any of the smaller proposed centers when the largest one proves to be a viable alternative.

A. L. Tella, chairperson of a citizens group called the Bay Area Council of United People (BACUP) has led the opposition to the center and has appeared before the supervisors to criticize the EDA study. Tella has argued that the study has several shortcomings. Among them, Tella has listed the following:

1. The EDA is promoting too large a project, given the alternatives, particularly if the 9 percent discount rate is appropriate.
2. The 9 percent discount rate is too low for present conditions, since BACUP estimates the opportunity cost of resources withdrawn from the private sector to be approximately 12 percent.

3. The EDA's study is lopsided because it considers only the indirect benefits from the center and does not identify any indirect costs.

BACUP has demanded that the Board of Supervisors employ a consultant to evaluate the EDA's study and to indicate what modifications would be necessary to provide a more accurate assessment of the convention center proposal.

QUESTIONS

Suppose you were hired as a consultant to evaluate the EDA study. Using only the data given in the case, answer the following questions:

1. How would you assess the EDA's choice of the 240,000-square-foot center?
2. What would you say about the impact of using a 12 percent discount rate, rather than a 9 percent one, to evaluate the alternative projects?
3. What would be your approach to the criticisms regarding the handling of indirect costs and benefits?

APPENDIX A

Mathematical Appendix

It is very important that a student of economics understand what a functional relationship is and how it can be depicted graphically. Therefore, we begin this appendix with a brief review of functions and graphs. Moreover, it is helpful, though *not essential*, for a student of managerial economics using this text to have an understanding of the fundamental techniques of differential calculus and optimization. Accordingly, we review these procedures in this appendix so that those students who have had no previous formal training in calculus can achieve a working knowledge of the mathematical tools that are helpful in understanding basic economic theory.

FUNCTIONS AND GRAPHS

If we say that *y is a function of x*, we mean that some variable y depends upon the value of another variable x. For each value of x, there is *one and only one* value of y. We call x the *independent variable* and y the *dependent variable*. We can write this relationship in mathematical notation as

$$y = f(x).$$

One function commonly used in economics is the total cost function. An example of one that has constant average variable cost is

$$TC = 1{,}000 + 200Q,$$

where TC is total cost per week and Q is quantity produced per week. Table A–1 gives some corresponding values for TC and Q. These values are plotted in Figure A–1.

An example of a total cost function with first decreasing and then increasing unit cost is

$$TC = 50 + 20Q - 15Q^2 + 5Q^3.$$

Some values of TC and Q that satisfy this function are presented in Table A–2 and are plotted in Figure A–2.

703

Table A–1   Some Values for Total Cost and Quantity when $TC = 1{,}000 + 200Q$

Q	TC
0	$1,000
5	2,000
10	3,000
15	4,000
20	5,000

Figure A–1   A Total Cost Function, $TC = 1{,}000 + 200Q$

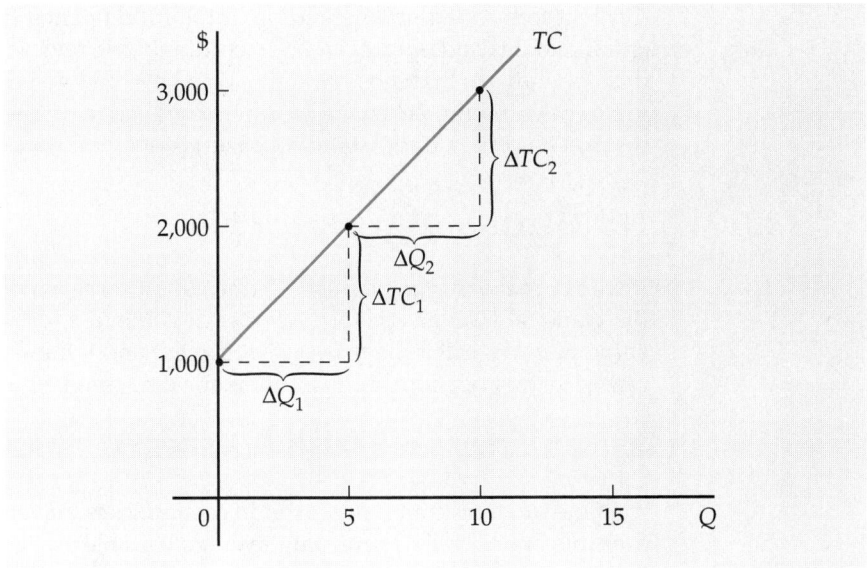

Table A–2   Some Values of Total Cost and Output when $TC = 50 + 20Q - 15Q^2 + 5Q^3$

Q	TC	Average Cost
0	$ 50	—
1	60	$60.00
2	70	35.00
3	110	36.67

Figure A–2   A Total Cost Function, $TC = 50 + 20Q - 15Q^2 + 5Q^3$

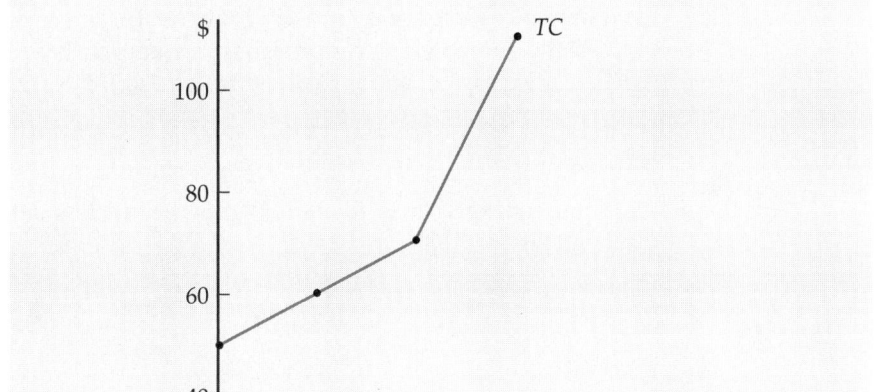

The *slope* of a function $y = f(x)$ that can be graphed as a straight line is given by the change in y divided by the change in x, $(\Delta y / \Delta x)$. Technically, as we will see later, the slope of *any* function $y = f(x)$ is given by the derivative dy/dx, which is only approximated by $\Delta y / \Delta x$ if $y = f(x)$ *cannot* be graphed as a straight line. In Figure A–1 we observe that $\Delta TC_1 / \Delta Q_1 = \Delta TC_2 / \Delta Q_2 = 1{,}000/5 = 200$. Note that for our example and for any straight line (*linear*) function, the average rate of change $\Delta y / \Delta x$ of a function $y = f(x)$ is the slope of that function and is the *coefficient* of the x variable. Thus a function of the form $y = a + bx$ can be graphed as a straight line with the slope equal to b and an intersection with the y axis at a. To discuss the slope of a function such as that sketched in Figure A–2, which cannot be graphed as a straight line (*is nonlinear*), we must first define the concepts of "limit" and "derivative."

LIMITS

The concept of the limit of a function is fairly simple. Specifically, it refers to the value, if any, that the dependent variable approaches as the independent variable approaches infinitely close to—but does not reach—a given value.

Since any particular value (except $+\infty$ or $-\infty$) can be approached from either the positive or negative direction, we can define both right-hand and left-hand limits. The left-hand limit of a function $f(x)$ as x approaches some number x_0 is the value that $f(x)$ approaches as x approaches x_0 from the negative or left-hand direction and is denoted by $\lim_{x \to x_0^-} f(x)$. The right-hand limit refers to the value that $f(x)$ approaches as x approaches x_0 from the positive or right-hand direction and is denoted by $\lim_{x \to x_0^+} f(x)$.

These concepts can be illustrated with the function defined as follows and drawn in Figure A–3:

$$f(x) = 1, \text{ when } x < 2$$

$$f(x) = 2, \text{ when } x = 2$$

$$f(x) = 3, \text{ when } x > 2.$$

Consider $\lim_{x \to 2^-} f(x)$. The value of $f(x)$ approaches 1.0 as x approaches, but does not equal, 2.0 from the left-hand side. However the value of $f(x)$ approaches 3.0 as x approaches (*but does not equal* 2) from the right-hand side,

Figure A–3   Graph of the Function $y = f(x)$,
where $f(x) = 1$, when $x < 2$,
$f(x) = 2$, when $x = 2$, and
$f(x) = 3$, when $x > 2$

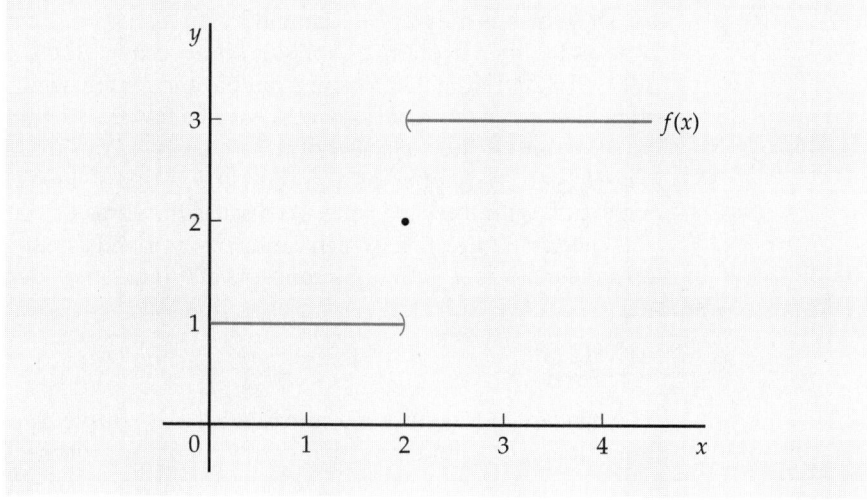

so $\lim\limits_{x\to 2^+} f(x) = 3$. Note that the right-hand and left-hand limits of this function are not equal as x approaches 2.0.

We are now in a position where we can define the overall limit of a function $f(x)$ as x approaches x_0 as $\lim\limits_{x\to x_0} f(x) = \lim\limits_{x\to x_0^-} f(x) = \lim\limits_{x\to x_0^+} f(x)$. This limit exists only when the left-hand and right-hand limits both exist and are equal to each other. To illustrate the concept of an overall limit, we will redefine the function given previously, so that

$$f(x) = 1, \text{ for } x \gtrless 2$$

$$f(x) = 2, \text{ for } x = 2,$$

and it is graphed in Figure A–4. In this case $\lim\limits_{x\to 2^-} f(x) = 1 = \lim\limits_{x\to 2^+} f(x)$; therefore, $\lim\limits_{x\to 2} f(x)$ exists and is equal to 1. Note that $\lim\limits_{x\to 2} f(x)$ does *not* equal $f(2)$ in this case. However, $\lim\limits_{x\to x_0} f(x)$ *may* equal $f(x_0)$.

DIFFERENCE QUOTIENT

Before we proceed any further, we must develop the concept of the difference quotient. The different quotient, $\Delta y/\Delta x$, of some function $y = f(x)$ is equal to

Figure A–4   Graph of the Function $y = f(x)$,
where $f(x) = 1$, for $x \gtrless 2$, and
$f(x) = 2$, for $x = 2$

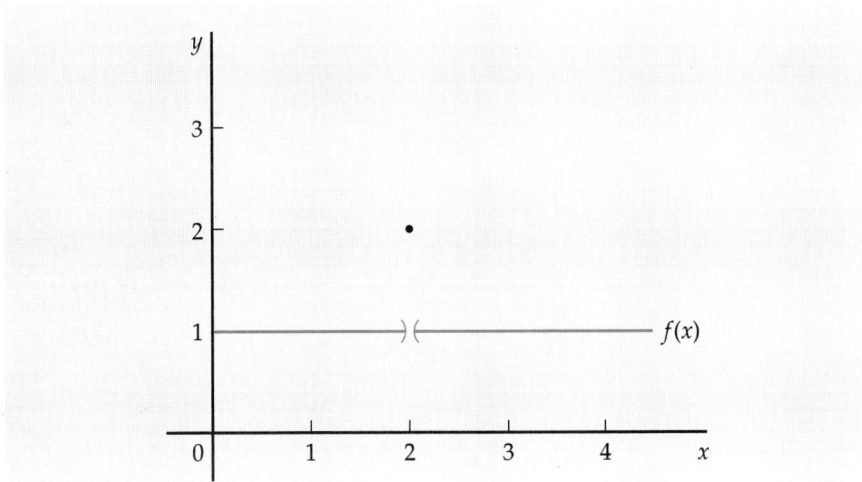

$\dfrac{f(x_0 + \Delta x) - f(x_0)}{\Delta x}$ over some x interval $(x_0, x_0 + \Delta x)$ and gives the *average rate of change* of the function over that interval. We also indicated above that $\Delta y / \Delta x$ gives the slope of a linear function. For example, let us use the function $y = f(x) = 2x + 1$ and examine the difference quotient where $x_0 = 1$ and $\Delta x = 2$. (See Figure A–5).

At $x = 1$, the value of $f(x) = 3$. At $x = 1 + \Delta x$, or 3, $f(x) = 7$. Thus, over the interval $(1,3)$ for x, $\Delta y / \Delta x = \dfrac{f(x_0 + \Delta x) - f(x_0)}{\Delta x} = \dfrac{7 - 3}{2} = 2.$

THE DERIVATIVE

We are now ready to examine the concept of the derivative of a function. The derivative dy/dx of a function $y = f(x)$ at x_0 is defined as

$$\frac{dy}{dx} = \lim_{\Delta x \to 0} \frac{\Delta y}{\Delta x} = \lim_{\Delta x \to 0} \frac{f(x_0 + \Delta x) - f(x_0)}{\Delta x}.$$

What we are saying is that the derivative dy/dx at x_0 is the limit of the difference quotient as the change in x approaches zero. Note here that it is *not* the

Figure A–5   Graph of the Function $y = 2x + 1$

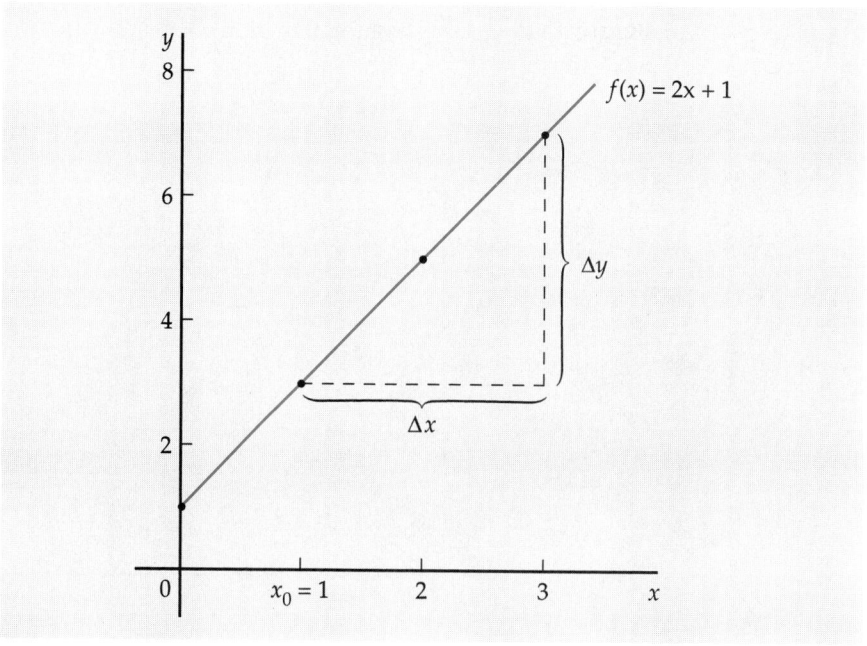

limit of the *function f(x)* at x_0 with which we are concerned, but rather the *limit of the difference quotient*, $\Delta y/\Delta x$.

Examine once more the function used in Figure A–5, which is redrawn in Figure A–6. The derivative, dy/dx, of $f(x)$ where $f(x) = 2x + 1$ at $x = 1$ is thus the $\lim\limits_{\Delta x \to 0}$ of $\dfrac{f(1 + \Delta x) - f(1)}{\Delta x}$, which is equal to $\lim\limits_{\Delta x \to 0}$ $\dfrac{2(1) + 2\Delta x + 1 - 3}{\Delta x} = 2$. In fact, we can easily demonstrate that for any x_0 we pick, the derivative of this function at that point equals 2, or $\lim\limits_{\Delta x \to 0}$

$$\frac{f(x_0 + \Delta x) - f(x_0)}{\Delta x} = \lim_{\Delta x \to 0} \frac{2x_0 + 2\Delta x + 1 - 2x_0 - 1}{\Delta x} = 2.$$ In this case dy/dx will equal $\Delta y/\Delta x$, since $f(x)$ is linear and its slope is constant. The derivative is, then, the *instantaneous* rate of change of a function at a point ($x = x_0$), whereas the difference quotient is the *average* rate of change over some interval ($x_0, x_0 + \Delta x$). Again, we emphasize that the difference quotient and the derivative are equal in the previous example because $f(x)$ was a straight line and, therefore, its slope did not change. (The instantaneous rate of change and the average rate of change of the function are, therefore, equal in this case).

Figure A–6 Graph of the Function $y = 2x + 1$, Showing a Constant Difference Quotient

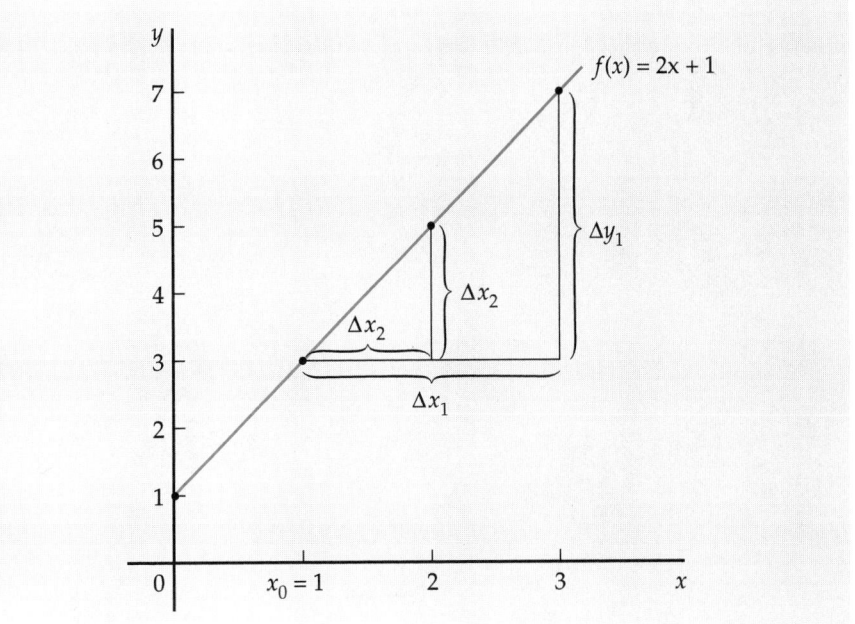

We can further illustrate the relationship between the derivative dy/dx and the difference quotient $\Delta y/\Delta x$ by contrasting the slope of a line tangent to a curve at a point with that of a line connecting two points on the curve, as done in Figure A–7 for the function $y = f(x) = 10x - x^2$.

Line segment DE is tangent to $f(x)$ at point A, and its slope is equal to the value of the derivative dy/dx at point A because the tangent to $f(x)$ at point A must have the same slope or rate of change as $f(x)$ at that point. Segments AC and AB have slopes equal to $\Delta y_1/\Delta x_1$ and $\Delta y_2/\Delta x_2$, respectively. We can see that as the length of a line segment joining point A and another point on $f(x)$ gets shorter and shorter, the slope of such a line segment approaches that of the tangent DE. For example, $\Delta y_1/\Delta x_1 = 8/2 = 4$, and $\Delta y_2/\Delta x_2 = 5/1 = 5$. The derivative dy/dx at $x = 2$ is given by the

$$\lim_{\Delta x \to 0} \frac{10(x + \Delta x) - (x + \Delta x)^2 - 10x + x^2}{\Delta x}$$

$$= \lim_{\Delta x \to 0} \frac{10x + 10\Delta x - x^2 - 2x\Delta x - \Delta x^2 - 10x + x^2}{\Delta x}$$

$$= \lim_{\Delta x \to 0} \frac{10\Delta x - 2x\Delta x - \Delta x^2}{\Delta x} = 10 - 2x = 6 \text{ at } x = 2.$$

We should pause here to note the conditions required for the derivative dy/dx of $f(x)$ at x_0 to exist, which are as follows:

Figure A–7   The Derivative dy/dx and the Difference Quotient $\Delta y/\Delta x$ for a Nonlinear Function, $y = 10x - x^2$

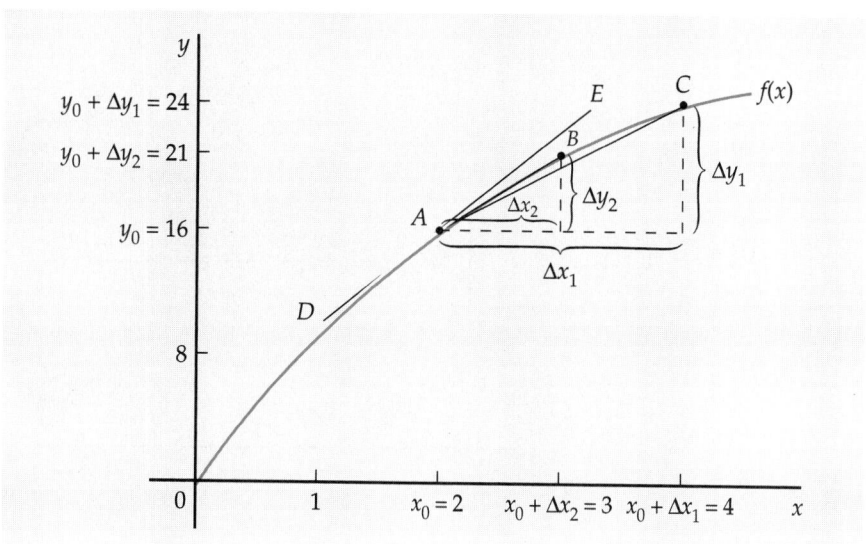

1. $\lim\limits_{x \to x_0} f(x)$ must exist.

2. $\lim\limits_{x \to x_0} f(x) = f(x_0)$. This condition requires that $f(x)$ be continuous; that is, it must not have a "hole" at $f(x_0)$. The function in Figure A–4 is *not* continuous at $x = 2$.

3. The function $f(x)$ must have no "sharp corners" at x_0, so that the slope of a line tangent to $f(x)$ at $x = x_0$ is defined. An example in which conditions 1 and 2 are met but the slope of the tangent is not defined at $x = x_0$ is shown in Figure A–8. The reason that the slope of the tangent is not defined at $x = x_0$ in Figure A–8 is that we could draw an infinite number of lines, each with a different slope, tangent to $f(x)$ at that point.

RULES FOR DIFFERENTIATION

It would be possible to derive all of the following formulas for finding the derivative dy/dx of a function $y = f(x)$ by using the definition of a derivative and finding the limit as Δx approaches zero of the difference quotient $\Delta y/\Delta x$ for each function, as we did for the functions $f(x) = 2x + 1$ and $f(x) = 10x - x^2$ earlier. However, it is sufficient that students using this text be able to understand and to apply these rules, so we will not prove them here.

1. *Constant Rule*
   If $y = f(x) = C$, a constant, then $dy/dx = 0$.
   Example: If $y = 100,000$, then $dy/dx = 0$.
   This rule is easy to comprehend if one recalls that the graph of a constant function is a horizontal line, which has a zero slope.

2. *Power Function Rule*
   If $y = f(x) = Cx^n$, then $dy/dx = nCx^{n-1}$.

Figure A–8   Graph of a Function $y = f(x)$ that is not Differentiable at x_0

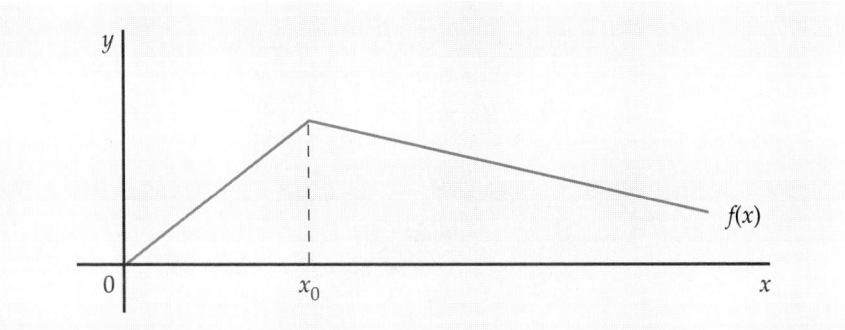

Examples: If $y = x$, then $dy/dx = 1x^0 = 1$.

If $y = 2x^{10}$, then $dy/dx = 10(2)x^9 = 20x^9$.

If $y = 15x^{-3}$, then $dy/dx = -45x^{-4}$.

If $y = ax^{50}$, then $dy/dx = 50ax^{49}$.

3. *Sum-Difference Rules*

   a. If y equals the sum of two functions, $y = f(x) + g(x)$, then

   $$dy/dx = f'(x) + g'(x), \text{ where } f'(x) = \frac{df(x)}{dx} \text{ and } g'(x) = \frac{dg(x)}{dx}.$$

   Example: If $y = 10x^2 + 5x$,
   $$dy/dx = 20x + 5.$$

   b. If y equals the difference of two functions, $y = f(x) - g(x)$, then $dy/dx = f'(x) - g'(x)$.

   Example: If $y = 4x - 10x^2$,
   $$dy/dx = 4 - 20x.$$

   Note that these rules can be extended to the sum or difference of any number of functions.

4. *Product Rule*

   If y is the product of two functions, $y = f(x) \cdot g(x)$, then $dy/dx = f'(x) \cdot g(x) + g'(x) \cdot f(x)$.

   Example: If $\quad y = (2x + 6)(3x^4 + 1)$,
   $$dy/dx = 2(3x^4 + 1) + 12x^3(2x + 6)$$
   $$= 6x^4 + 2 + 24x^4 + 72x^3$$
   $$= 30x^4 + 72x^3 + 2.$$

5. *Quotient Rule*

   If y is a quotient of two functions, $y = f(x)/g(x)$, then $dy/dx = \dfrac{f'(x) \cdot g(x) - g'(x) \cdot f(x)}{[g(x)]^2}.$

   Example: If $y = \dfrac{5x}{2x + 1}$,

   $$dy/dx = \frac{5(2x + 1) - 2(5x)}{(2x + 1)^2} = \frac{5}{(2x + 1)^2}.$$

6. *Chain Rule or Function-of-a-Function Rule*

   If $y = g(z)$, where $z = f(x)$, then $dy/dx = \dfrac{dy}{dz} \cdot \dfrac{dz}{dx} = g'(z) \cdot f'(x)$.

   Intuitively, the chain rule makes sense, for it indicates that a change in x will product a change in z, which will, in turn, produce a change in y. Thus, dy/dx, or the rate of change of y with respect to x, is given by the rate of change of z with respect to x, dz/dx, multiplied by the rate of change of y with respect to z, or dy/dz.

   Example: $y = 4z^2$, where $z = 3x^5 + 5$
   $$dy/dx = 8z \cdot 15x^4 = 8(3x^5 + 5) \, 15x^4$$
   $$= 120x^4(3x^5 + 5) = 360x^9 + 600x^4.$$

7. *Inverse Function Rule*
   If $y = f(x)$ defines a one-to-one mapping between x and y such that y is steadily increasing *or* steadily decreasing as x increases and if the derivative dy/dx exists, then the derivative dx/dy of the inverse function $x = f^{-1}(y)$ exists and $dx/dy = 1/(dy/dx)$. Note that here f^{-1} refers to the *inverse* function, *not* $1/[f(y)]$.
   Example: If $y = 5x + 2$, then

$$x = \frac{1}{5}y - \frac{2}{5},$$

and

$$\frac{dx}{dy} = \frac{1}{5} = \frac{1}{dy/dx}.$$

OPTIMIZATION

Much of economics deals with optimization, or the maximization or minimization of something. For example, one important variable that firms would usually like to *maximize* is *profit*. Firms normally wish to *minimize costs*, subject to the requirement that a specific level of production is maintained.

The First Derivative Test

The derivative is quite useful as a tool in optimization—a procedure that involves finding a maximum or minimum value of some function, as indicated previously. To understand how the derivative can be helpful in locating such points, observe the functions $y = f(x)$ in Figure A–9, panel (a), and $y = g(x)$ in Figure A–9, panel (b). Note that $f(x)$ reaches a (relative) maximum at x_1 and that $g(x)$ reaches a (relative) minimum at x_2. Also, note that the slope of $f(x)$ at $x = x_1$ equals the slope of $g(x)$ at $x = x_2$, which equals zero. Since the derivative dy/dx, also denoted by $f'(x)$ and $g'(x)$, respectively, gives the slopes of these functions (different for each function), then dy/dx also must equal zero at x_1 for $f(x)$ and at x_2 for $g(x)$. In fact, if dy/dx exists at such points, it is *necessary* that $dy/dx = 0$ for any function $y = f(x)$ to be at a maximum or a minimum. This result makes sense if we reflect that the function is not changing at minimum or maximum points (as long as the function is differentiable); thus, the function has a slope equal to zero at those points. That $dy/dx = 0$ at a possible maximum or minimum point is called the *first derivative test*. The graphs of $f'(x)$ for $f(x)$ in Figure A–9, panel (a), and $g'(x)$ for $g(x)$ in Figure A–9, panel (b), would appear similar to those drawn in Figure A–10, panels (a) and (b), respectively.

Figure A–9   Graph of a Function with a Maximum and a Function with a Minimum

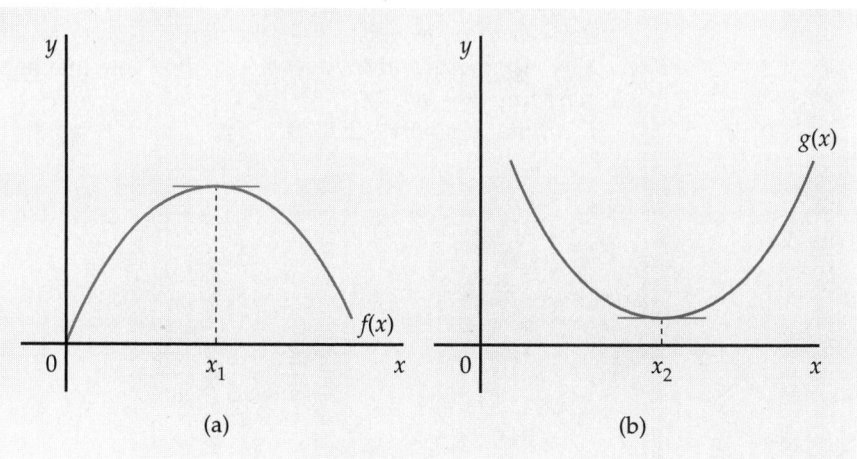

Figure A–10   The First Derivative of each of the Functions in Figure A–9

However, $dy/dx = 0$ is not a *sufficient* condition to ensure that $f(x)$ is at a maximum or minimum value at that point. To see why this is so, consider the function in Figure A–11. At $x = x_0$, the slope of the function (dy/dx) equals zero, but $f(x_0)$ is neither a relative maximum or minimum and is an example of an *inflection point*. An inflection point of a function $y = f(x)$ occurs at a point where the derivative dy/dx reaches a maximum or minimum. If we were to graph dy/dx for the function $y = f(x)$ in Figure A–11, it would look similar to the curve in Figure A–12.

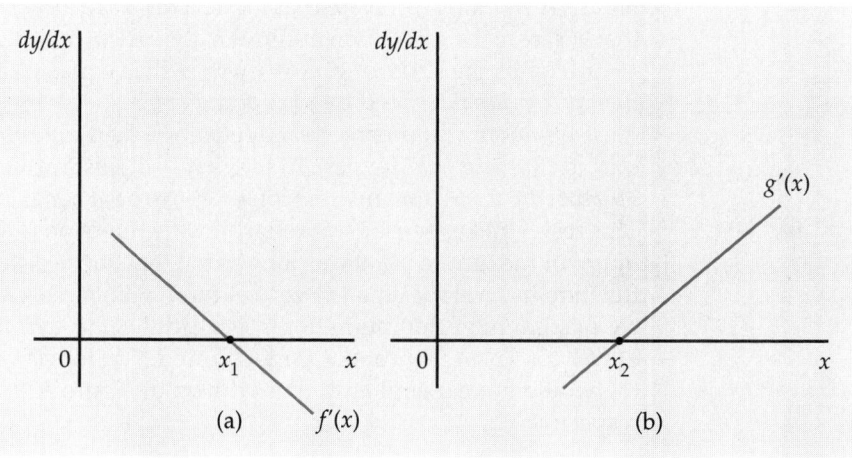

Figure A–11   Graph of a Function $y = f(x)$ with an Inflection Point at x_0

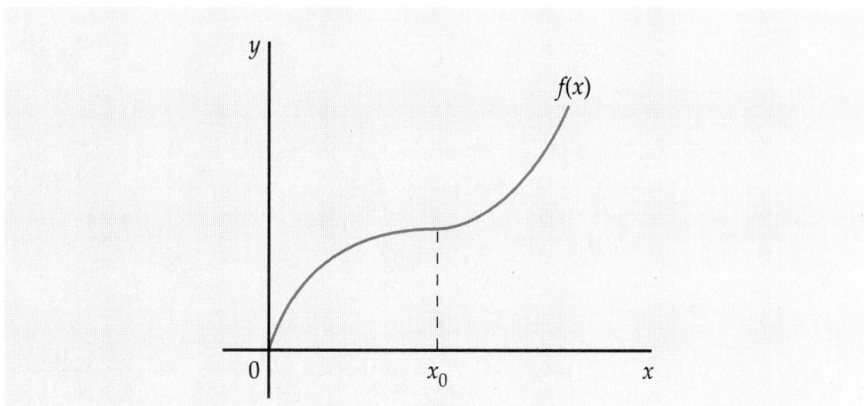

We emphasize that while $dy/dx = 0$ at x_0 is a *necessary* condition for the function $y = f(x)$ to be at a relative *maximum* or *minimum* at x_0, it is *not* a necessary condition for an *inflection point*. This fact is illustrated in Figure A–13. At x_0, dy/dx is at a maximum, and hence, $f(x_0)$ is an inflection point. However, dy/dx is not equal to zero at x_0.

If $dy/dx = 0$ for some $x = x_0$, one way of discriminating between an inflection point and an extreme point (maximum or minimum) of $f(x)$ is to examine the sign of dy/dx for points on either side of x_0. If dy/dx *changes signs* at x_0, the function $f(x)$ reaches an extremum (maximum or minimum) at $f(x_0)$. If dy/dx does not change signs, then $f(x)$ has an inflection point at x_0. This point can be grasped by examining Figures A–9, A–10, A–11, A–12, and A–13. However, a more convenient test is discussed in the next section.

Figure A–12   Graph of dy/dx for $y = f(x)$ in Figure A–11

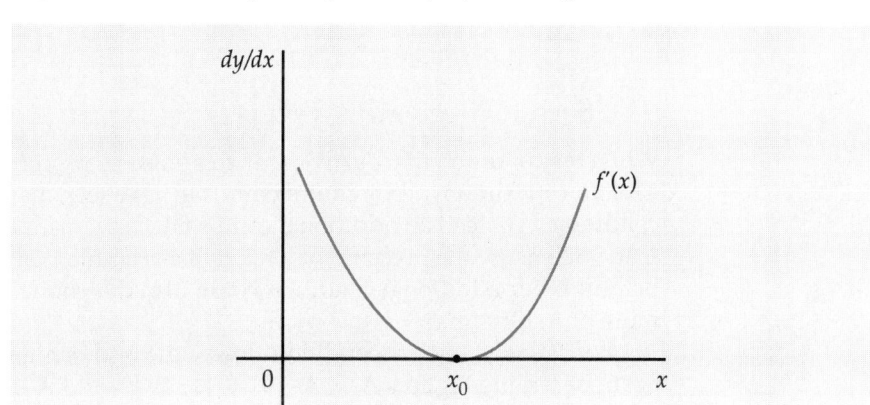

Figure A–13   Graph of a Function $y = f(x)$ and Its Derivative dy/dx Showing an Inflection Point

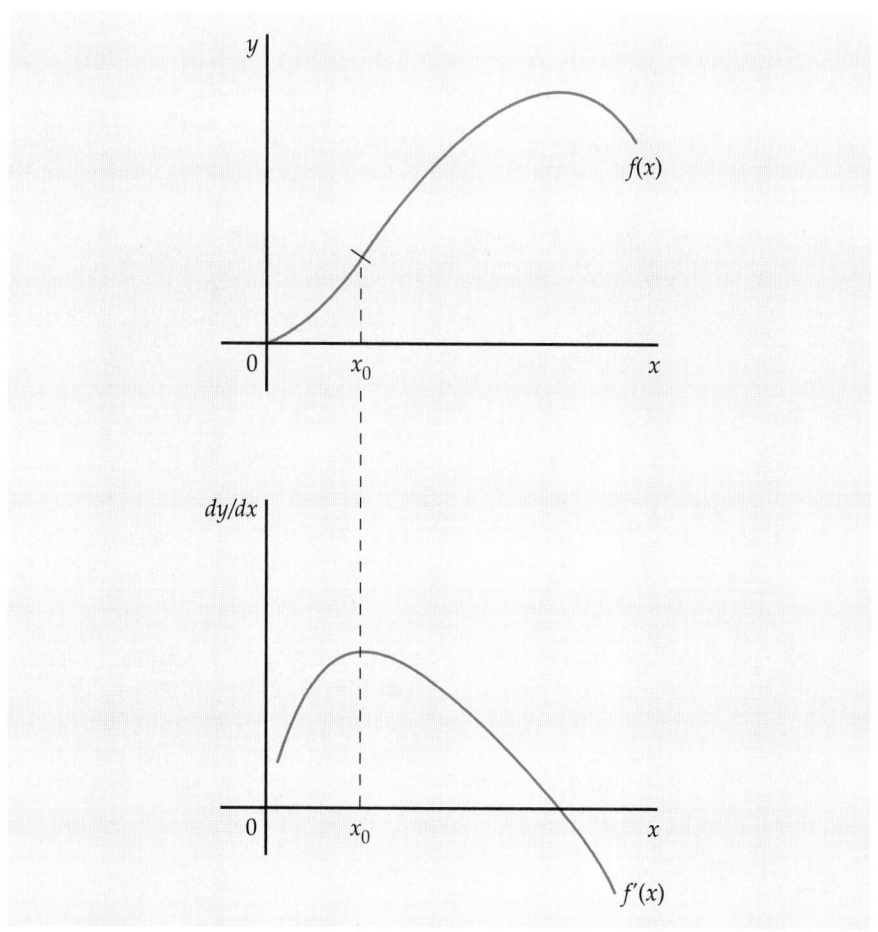

The Second Derivative Test

While the condition that $dy/dx = 0$ at x_0 is a necessary condition for $f(x_0)$ to be a relative maximum or minimum point, we have seen that it is not a sufficient condition. We need an additional condition, convenient to apply that, when met, will ensure the presence of a relative extremum of $f(x)$ at x_0. It would be helpful if our additional condition could also discriminate between a maximum or minimum.

Fortunately, such a condition does exist and can easily be grasped by again observing Figures A–9, A–10, A–11, A–12, and A–13. Notice from Figures A–9 and A–10 that dy/dx is *decreasing* when $f(x)$ reaches a *maximum* and is *increasing* when $g(x)$ is at a *minimum*. However, as noted previously, dy/dx *itself* reaches an extreme value at an inflection point. This information suggests the usefulness of a *second derivative test*.

The second derivative of a function $y = f(x)$, denoted by $f''(x)$ or d^2y/dx^2, gives the instantaneous rate of change or the slope of the *first* derivative, $f'(x)$. It is found by taking the derivative of $f'(x)$ in the same manner as one finds $f'(x)$ by taking the derivative of $f(x)$. For example, if $y = 3x^3 - 4x^2 + 5$, then $f'(x) = 9x^2 - 8x$, and $f''(x) = 18x - 8$.

The second derivative test asserts that the function $y = f(x)$ reaches a *maximum* at some point $x = x_0$ if $f'(x_0)$ is equal to zero *and* $f''(x_0)$ is negative, which indicates $f'(x)$ is decreasing at x_0. Similarly, $f(x)$ reaches a *minimum* at x_0 if $f'(x_0)$ equals zero and $f''(x)$ is positive. We have graphed $f''(x)$ and $g''(x)$ for Figure A–9, panels (a) and (b), respectively, in Figure A–14, panels (a) and (b).

Example: $f(x) = x^3 - 6x^2 + 10$
$\qquad f'(x) = 3x^2 - 12x$
$\qquad f'(x) = 0$ when $x^2 - 4x = 0$ or $x = 0, 4$
$\qquad f''(x) = 6x - 12$
$\qquad$ At $x = 0, f''(x) = -12$ and $f(0)$ is a relative maximum value.
$\qquad$ At $x = 4, f''(x) = 12$ and $f(4)$ is a relative minimum value.

The second derivative test is inconclusive, however, if both $f'(x_0)$ *and* $f''(x_0)$ equal zero. Such a result may indicate an inflection point, as would be the case for the functions in Figures A–11 and A–13. However, it may also in-

Figure A–14   The Second Derivative of each of the Functions in Figure A–9

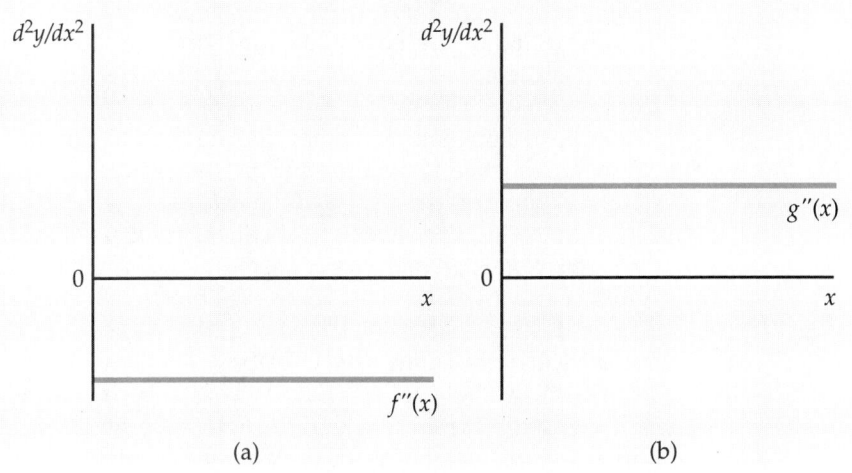

(a)   (b)

dicate a relative extremum. For example, at $x = 0$ for the function $f(x) = Cx^4$, $f'(x_0) = f''(x_0) = 0$, but $x = 0$ is a minimum point of $f(x)$.

TOTAL, AVERAGE, AND MARGINAL RELATIONSHIPS

In economics we deal with many total, average, and marginal relationships—such as total, average, and marginal cost and total, average, and marginal profit. Since the total, average, and marginal functions for all of these variables have basically the same relationships with each other, we will briefly discuss those relationships here. The total function states the relationship between an independent variable and the total amount of some other variable, such as output to total dollar cost of production, output to total dollar profit of a firm, or the amount of an input to the total output of the firm. The average function is obtained by dividing the total function by the independent variable. The marginal function is obtained by taking the derivative of the total function with respect to the independent variable. Graphically, the value of the *average* function for some value of the independent variable is given by the *slope of the line drawn from the origin of the graph of the total function to the corresponding point on the total function*. The value of a *marginal* function for some value of the independent variable is given by the *slope of the total function at that point*. When the average function reaches a maximum or minimum, the line drawn from the origin to the corresponding point on the total curve is tangent to the total curve at that point, and the value of the average function is thus equal to the value of the marginal function at that point. Examples of the relationships among total, average, and marginal product of an input and those among total, average, and marginal cost are shown in Figure A–15 and Figure A–16, respectively.

Note that when the average function is *decreasing*, the marginal function, whether decreasing or increasing, is taking on values *smaller than* those of the average function. This relationship is necessary for the average function to diminish. Similarly, if the average function is *increasing*, the marginal function, whether increasing or decreasing, must be taking on values *larger than* those of the average function. If the average function is not changing in value, it must be at a maximum, a minimum, or an inflection point; and the marginal function must be at a value equal to that of the average function.

A student can easily grasp the nature of the relationship between a marginal function and an average function if grade point averages (GPAs) are considered. Consider your current semester GPA to be a marginal function and your cumulative GPA to be an average function. It is a well-known fact among students that if the GPA achieved during the current semester (say, 2.50) is smaller than the cumulative GPA (say, 3.00 up to that semester), the cumulative GPA will have fallen at the end of the current semester. The cumulative GPA will *still fall* at the end of the next semester if the GPA for that semester rises (say, to 2.60) but is still below the cumulative GPA at the beginning of

Figure A–15   Relationships Among Total, Average, and Marginal
                    Product Functions

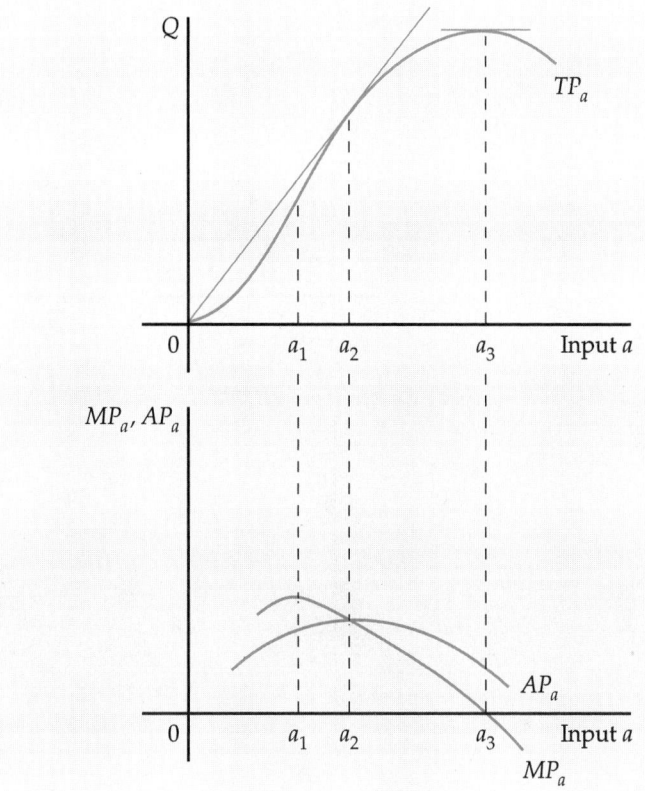

that semester. On the other hand, if the current semester GPA (say, 3.70), is greater than the cumulative GPA (say, 3.00), the cumulative GPA will rise at the end of the semester. Only when the current semester's GPA is equal to the cumulative GPA will the cumulative GPA remain the same.

PARTIAL DERIVATIVES

We will conclude this appendix with a brief discussion of partial derivatives and optimization conditions for a function with two independent variables and a few remarks about the total differential. We are interested in a partial

Figure A–16   Relationships Among Total, Average, and Marginal Cost
Functions

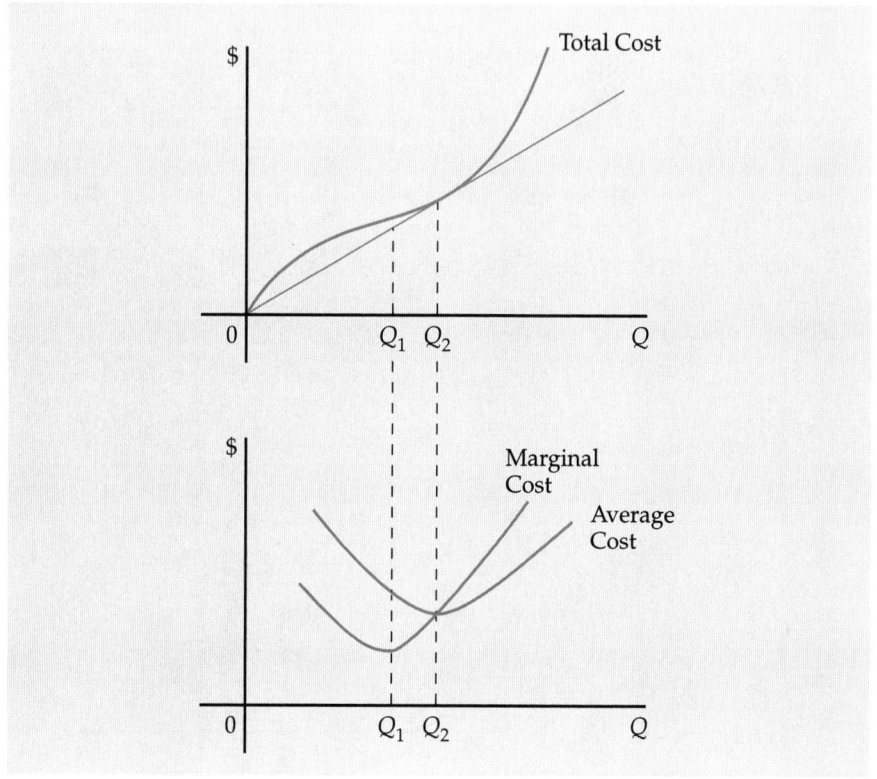

derivative when we have a dependent variable that is a function of two or
more independent variables, and we wish to know the individual effect that
a change in one independent variable (while the other is held constant) will
have on the dependent variable. To find a partial derivative, take the derivative of the function with respect to the variable in question, treating the other
independent variable or variables in the same manner as a constant. Several
examples of the procedure follow:

Example 1:

If $y = f(x,z) = x^3 + 5x^2z + 3xz^2 + 10z^3 + 10$, then

$\partial y / \partial x = 3x^2 + 10xz + 3z^2$, and

$\partial y / \partial z = 5x^2 + 6xz + 30z^2$.

Example 2:

$$\text{If } y = \frac{6x^2}{z}, \quad \text{then}$$

$$\frac{\partial y}{\partial x} = \frac{12x}{z}, \quad \text{and}$$

$$\frac{\partial y}{\partial z} = \frac{-6x^2}{z^2}. \quad \left(\text{Use the quotient rule for } \partial y/\partial z.\right)$$

Example 3:

$$\text{If } Q = f(K,L) = 15K^{2/3}\, L^{1/3}, \text{ then}$$

$$\partial Q/\partial K = 10K^{-1/3}\, L^{1/3}, \text{ and}$$

$$\partial Q/\partial L = 5K^{2/3}\, L^{-2/3}.$$

If $Q = f(K,L)$ is a production function with inputs capital (K) and labor (L), then $\partial Q/\partial K$ and $\partial Q/\partial L$ can be interpreted as the marginal products of capital and labor, respectively.

OPTIMIZATION CONDITIONS WITH TWO INDEPENDENT VARIABLES

The optimization conditions for a function with two independent variables are similar to those with one independent variable. The *first-order* condition for a maximum or a minimum of a function $y = f(x,z)$ is that

$$\partial y/\partial x = f_x = 0, \text{ and}$$
$$\partial y/\partial z = f_z = 0.$$

The *second-order* condition for a *maximum* is that

$$\frac{\partial(f_x)}{\partial x} = f_{xx} < 0,$$

$$\frac{\partial(f_z)}{\partial z} = f_{zz} < 0,$$

and

$$f_{xx} \cdot f_{zz} > \left[\frac{\partial(f_x)}{\partial z}\right]^2 = \left(f_{xz}\right)^2.$$

The *second-order* condition for a *minimum* is that

$$f_{xx} > 0,$$
$$f_{zz} > 0,$$

and

$$f_{xx} \cdot f_{zz} > (f_{xz})^2.$$

The condition that $f_{xx} \cdot f_{zz}$ be greater than $(f_{xz})^2$ ensures (assuming the other conditions are met) that the point in question is a relative maximum or minimum rather than a *saddle point*, which is roughly the three-dimensional counterpart of an inflection point. Again, satisfaction of the second-order conditions is not *necessary* for an extremum to exist at a point, but their satisfaction together with that of the first-order conditions ensures that a relative extremum *does* exist at that point.

For example, consider the function $y = f(x,z) = x^2 - 4x - 2xz - 8z + 2z^2$. Then

$$f_x = 2x - 4 - 2z, \text{ and}$$
$$f_z = -2x - 8 + 4z.$$

To find a maximum or minimum point(s), we first set f_x and f_z equal to zero and solve the two equations simultaneously, as follows:

$$2x - 2z - 4 = 0$$
$$-2x + 4z - 8 = 0$$
$$2z - 12 = 0$$
$$z = 6.$$

Solving for x from the first equation, we find

$$2x - 2(6) - 4 = 0,$$
$$2x - 12 - 4 = 0,$$
$$2x - 16 = 0, \quad \text{and}$$
$$x = 8.$$

To check the second-order conditions for the point $f(x,z) = f(8,6)$ we find

$$f_{xx} = 2,$$
$$f_{zz} = 4, \quad \text{and}$$
$$f_{xz} = -2.$$

Since f_{xx} and f_{zz} are greater than zero and $f_{xx} \cdot f_{zz} > (f_{xz})^2$ or $2(4) > 4$, $f(x,z) = f(8,6)$ is a *minimum* point.

TOTAL DIFFERENTIAL

We will close with a brief discussion of the total differential. The total differential of a function attempts to measure the change in the value of a function as a result of infinitely small changes in all independent variables. If $y = f(x,z)$, the total differential, dy, is defined as

$$dy = f_x dx + f_z d_z,$$

where dx and dz represent infinitely small changes in x and z, respectively. The total differential can be approximated at a specific point by using discrete (but small) changes in x and z as

$$\Delta y = f_x \Delta x + f_z \Delta_z.$$

Example 1:

$$\text{If } Q = 15K^{2/3} L^{1/3}, \text{ then}$$
$$dQ = 10K^{-1/3} L^{1/3} \, dK + 5K^{2/3} L^{-2/3} \, dL.$$

Example 2:

$$\text{If } Q = K^2 + 10KL, \text{ then}$$
$$dQ = (2K + 10L) \, dK + 10K \, dL.$$

We can approximate dQ at $K = 10$ and $L = 5$ by substituting in those values for K and L in the preceding equation for dQ and substituting $\Delta K = \Delta L = .01$ for dK and dL, respectively. Thus we obtain

$$\Delta Q = [2(10) + 10(5)] \, (.01) + 10(10)(.01)$$
$$70(.01) + (100)(.01) = 1.7.$$

Such a procedure can be useful, for example, in estimating the effect that changes in the quantities of factors of production will have on total output produced by the firm. In fact, in the preceding example, $\Delta Q = 1.7$ could be interpreted as the *estimated* change in total output if capital and labor were to be changed from 10 and 5 to 10.01 and 5.01 units, respectively.

SELECTED REFERENCES

Brennan, Michael J. *Preface to Econometrics*, 3d ed. Cincinnati: South-Western, 1973.

Bressler, Barry. *A Unified Introduction to Mathematical Economics*, New York: Harper and Row, 1975.

Chiang, Alpha C. *Fundamental Methods of Mathematical Economics*, 3d ed. New York: McGraw-Hill, 1984.

Dinwiddy, Caroline. *Elementary Mathematics for Economists*. Cambridge: Oxford University Press, 1967.

APPENDIX B

Interest Factor Tables

Table B–1 Compound Amount of $1 (CVF)

Period	1%	2%	3%	4%	5%	6%	7%	8%	9%	10%	12%
1	1.0100	1.0200	1.0300	1.0400	1.0500	1.0600	1.0700	1.0800	1.0900	1.1000	1.1200
2	1.0201	1.0404	1.0609	1.0816	1.1025	1.1236	1.1449	1.1664	1.1881	1.2100	1.2544
3	1.0303	1.0612	1.0927	1.1249	1.1576	1.1910	1.2250	1.2597	1.2950	1.3310	1.4049
4	1.0406	1.0824	1.1255	1.1699	1.2155	1.2625	1.3108	1.3605	1.4116	1.4641	1.5735
5	1.0510	1.1041	1.1593	1.2167	1.2763	1.3382	1.4025	1.4693	1.5386	1.6105	1.7623
6	1.0615	1.1262	1.1941	1.2653	1.3401	1.4185	1.5007	1.5869	1.6771	1.7716	1.9738
7	1.0721	1.1487	1.2299	1.3159	1.4071	1.5036	1.6058	1.7138	1.8280	1.9487	2.2107
8	1.0829	1.1717	1.2668	1.3686	1.4774	1.5938	1.7182	1.8509	1.9926	2.1436	2.4760
9	1.0937	1.1951	1.3048	1.4233	1.5513	1.6895	1.8385	1.9990	2.1719	2.3579	2.7731
10	1.1046	1.2190	1.3439	1.4802	1.6289	1.7908	1.9671	2.1589	2.3673	2.5937	3.1058
11	1.1157	1.2434	1.3842	1.5395	1.7103	1.8983	2.1048	2.3316	2.5804	2.8531	3.4785
12	1.1268	1.2682	1.4258	1.6010	1.7958	2.0122	2.2522	2.5182	2.8126	3.1384	3.8960
13	1.1381	1.2936	1.4685	1.6651	1.8856	2.1329	2.4098	2.7196	3.0658	3.4522	4.3635
14	1.1495	1.3195	1.5126	1.7317	1.9799	2.2609	2.5785	2.9372	3.3417	3.7975	4.8871
15	1.1610	1.3459	1.5580	1.8009	2.0789	2.3965	2.7590	3.1722	3.6424	4.1772	5.4736
16	1.1726	1.3728	1.6047	1.8730	2.1828	2.5403	2.9522	3.4259	3.9703	4.5949	6.1304
17	1.1843	1.4002	1.6528	1.9479	2.2920	2.6927	3.1588	3.7000	4.3276	5.0544	6.8660
18	1.1961	1.4282	1.7024	2.0258	2.4066	2.8543	3.3799	3.9960	4.7171	5.5599	7.6899
19	1.2081	1.4568	1.7535	2.1068	2.5269	3.0256	3.6165	4.3157	5.1416	6.1158	8.6127
20	1.2202	1.4859	1.8061	2.1911	2.6533	3.2071	3.8697	4.6609	5.6043	6.7274	9.6463
21	1.2324	1.5157	1.8603	2.2788	2.7859	3.3995	4.1405	5.0338	6.1087	7.4002	10.8038
22	1.2447	1.5460	1.9161	2.3699	2.9252	3.6035	4.4304	5.4365	6.6585	8.1402	12.1003
23	1.2571	1.5769	1.9736	2.4647	3.0715	3.8197	4.7405	5.8714	7.2578	8.9542	13.5523
24	1.2697	1.6084	2.0328	2.5633	3.2250	4.0489	5.0723	6.3412	7.9109	9.8496	15.1786
25	1.2824	1.6406	2.0938	2.6658	3.3863	4.2918	5.4274	6.8485	8.6229	10.8346	17.0000
26	1.2952	1.6734	2.1566	2.7725	3.5556	4.5493	5.8073	7.3963	9.3990	11.9180	19.0400
27	1.3082	1.7069	2.2213	2.8834	3.7334	4.8223	6.2138	7.9880	10.2449	13.1098	21.3248
28	1.3213	1.7410	2.2879	2.9987	3.9200	5.1116	6.6488	8.6271	11.1669	14.4208	23.8838
29	1.3345	1.7758	2.3565	3.1186	4.1160	5.4183	7.1142	9.3172	12.1719	15.8629	26.7498
30	1.3478	1.8113	2.4272	3.2434	4.3218	5.7434	7.6122	10.0626	13.2674	17.4491	29.9598
35	1.4166	1.9999	2.8138	3.9461	5.5159	7.6859	10.6765	14.7853	20.4135	28.1019	52.7994
40	1.4888	2.2080	3.2620	4.8010	7.0398	10.2855	14.9743	21.7244	31.4085	45.2583	93.0506
45	1.5648	2.4378	3.7816	5.8412	8.9847	13.7643	21.0022	31.9203	48.3257	72.8888	163.9868
50	1.6446	2.6915	4.3838	7.1067	11.4670	18.4197	29.4566	46.9013	74.3549	117.3878	289.0005
55	1.7285	2.9716	5.0821	8.6463	14.6350	24.6496	41.3143	68.9134	114.4037	189.0539	509.3174
60	1.8166	3.2809	5.8915	10.5196	18.6784	32.9867	57.9454	101.2563	176.0238	304.4724	897.5906

Period	14%	15%	16%	18%	20%	24%	28%	30%	32%	36%	40%
1	1.1400	1.1500	1.1600	1.1800	1.2000	1.2400	1.2800	1.3000	1.3200	1.3600	1.4000
2	1.2996	1.3225	1.3456	1.3924	1.4400	1.5376	1.6384	1.6900	1.7424	1.8496	1.9600
3	1.4815	1.5209	1.5609	1.6430	1.7280	1.9066	2.0972	2.1970	2.3000	2.5155	2.7440
4	1.6890	1.7490	1.8106	1.9388	2.0736	2.3642	2.6844	2.8561	3.0360	3.4210	3.8416
5	1.9254	2.0114	2.1003	2.2878	2.4883	2.9316	3.4360	3.7129	4.0075	4.6526	5.3782
6	2.1950	2.3131	2.4364	2.6995	2.9860	3.6352	4.3980	4.8268	5.2898	6.3275	7.5295
7	2.5023	2.6600	2.8262	3.1855	3.5832	4.5077	5.6295	6.2748	6.9826	8.6054	10.5413
8	2.8526	3.0590	3.2784	3.7588	4.2998	5.5895	7.2057	8.1573	9.2170	11.7034	14.7579
9	3.2519	3.5179	3.8030	4.4354	5.1598	6.9310	9.2234	10.6044	12.1665	15.9166	20.6610
10	3.7072	4.0455	4.4114	5.2338	6.1917	8.5944	11.8059	13.7858	16.0597	21.6465	28.9254
11	4.2262	4.6524	5.1173	6.1759	7.4301	10.6571	15.1115	17.9215	21.1988	29.4392	40.4955
12	4.8179	5.3502	5.9360	7.2875	8.9161	13.2148	19.3428	23.2979	27.9825	40.0373	56.6937
13	5.4924	6.1528	6.8858	8.5993	10.6993	16.3863	24.7587	30.2873	36.9368	54.4508	79.3711
14	6.2613	7.0757	7.9875	10.1472	12.8392	20.3190	31.6912	39.3734	48.7566	74.0531	111.1195
15	7.1379	8.1370	9.2655	11.9736	15.4070	25.1956	40.5647	51.1854	64.3587	100.7122	155.5673
16	8.1372	9.3576	10.7480	14.1289	18.4884	31.2425	51.9228	66.5410	84.9535	136.9685	217.7942
17	9.2764	10.7612	12.4676	16.6721	22.1861	38.7407	66.4612	86.5033	112.1385	186.2770	304.9116
18	10.5751	12.3754	14.4625	19.6730	26.6233	48.0384	85.0703	112.4541	148.0229	253.3367	426.8760
19	12.0556	14.2317	16.7765	23.2142	31.9479	59.5676	108.8900	146.1903	195.3902	344.5378	597.6267
20	13.7433	16.3664	19.4607	27.3927	38.3375	73.8638	139.3791	190.0474	257.9150	468.5715	836.6768
21	15.6674	18.8214	22.5744	32.3234	46.0050	91.5912	178.4052	247.0614	340.4475	637.2573	
22	17.8608	21.6446	26.1863	38.1416	55.2060	113.5730	228.3587	321.1794	449.3909	866.6689	
23	20.3613	24.8913	30.3761	45.0070	66.2472	140.8306	292.2991	417.5330	593.1960		
24	23.2119	28.6249	35.2363	53.1083	79.4966	174.6298	374.1428	542.7930	783.0186		
25	26.4615	32.9187	40.8741	62.6677	95.3958	216.5408	478.9026	705.6304			
26	30.1661	37.8565	47.4139	73.9478	114.4750	268.5107	612.9951	917.3188			
27	34.3894	43.5349	55.0001	87.2584	137.3700	332.9531	784.6340				
28	39.2039	50.0652	63.8002	102.9649	164.8440	412.8621					
29	44.6924	57.5749	74.0082	121.4985	197.8128	511.9485					
30	50.9493	66.2111	85.8495	143.3682	237.3754	634.8164					
35	98.0982	133.1740	180.3130	327.9907	590.6653						
40	188.8793	267.8601	378.7190	750.3613							
45	363.6697	538.7612	795.4382								
50	700.2131										
55											
60											

Table B-2 Compound Amount of an Annuity of $1 ($CVF_a$)

Period	1%	2%	3%	4%	5%	6%	7%	8%	9%	10%	12%
1	1.0000	1.0000	1.0000	1.0000	1.0000	1.0000	1.0000	1.0000	1.0000	1.0000	1.0000
2	2.0100	2.0200	2.0300	2.0400	2.0500	2.0600	2.0700	2.0800	2.0900	2.1000	2.1200
3	3.0301	3.0604	3.0909	3.1216	3.1525	3.1836	3.2149	3.2464	3.2781	3.3100	3.3744
4	4.0604	4.1216	4.1836	4.2465	4.3101	4.3746	4.4399	4.5061	4.5731	4.6410	4.7793
5	5.1010	5.2040	5.3091	5.4163	5.5256	5.6371	5.7507	5.8666	5.9847	6.1051	6.3528
6	6.1520	6.3081	6.4684	6.6330	6.8019	6.9753	7.1533	7.3359	7.5233	7.7156	8.1152
7	7.2135	7.4343	7.6625	7.8983	8.1420	8.3938	8.6540	8.9228	9.2004	9.4872	10.0890
8	8.2857	8.5830	8.8923	9.2142	9.5491	9.8974	10.2598	10.6366	11.0284	11.4359	12.2997
9	9.3685	9.7546	10.1591	10.5828	11.0265	11.4913	11.9780	12.4875	13.0210	13.5794	14.7756
10	10.4622	10.9497	11.4639	12.0061	12.5778	13.1808	13.8164	14.4866	15.1929	15.9374	17.5487
11	11.5668	12.1687	12.8078	13.4863	14.2067	14.9716	15.7836	16.6455	17.5602	18.5311	20.6546
12	12.6825	13.4121	14.1920	15.0258	15.9171	16.8699	17.8884	18.9771	20.1406	21.3842	24.1331
13	13.8093	14.6803	15.6178	16.6268	17.7129	18.8821	20.1406	21.4953	22.9532	24.5226	28.0291
14	14.9474	15.9739	17.0863	18.2919	19.5985	21.0150	22.5504	24.2149	26.0190	27.9748	32.3925
15	16.0968	17.2934	18.5989	20.0236	21.5784	23.2758	25.1290	27.1520	29.3607	31.7723	37.2796
16	17.2578	18.6392	20.1568	21.8245	23.6573	25.6724	27.8880	30.3242	33.0031	35.9495	42.7532
17	18.4303	20.0120	21.7615	23.6975	25.8402	28.2127	30.8401	33.7501	36.9734	40.5444	48.8835
18	19.6146	21.4122	23.4143	25.6454	28.1321	30.9055	33.9989	37.4501	41.3010	45.5988	55.7496
19	20.8107	22.8404	25.1168	27.6712	30.5387	33.7598	37.3788	41.4461	46.0180	51.1587	63.4395
20	22.0188	24.2972	26.8703	29.7780	33.0656	36.7853	40.9953	45.7618	51.1596	57.2746	72.0522
21	23.2390	25.7831	28.6763	31.9691	35.7189	39.9924	44.8650	50.4227	56.7639	64.0020	81.6985
22	24.4713	27.2988	30.5366	34.2479	38.5048	43.3919	49.0055	55.4566	62.8727	71.4021	92.5023
23	25.7160	28.8447	32.4527	36.6178	41.4300	46.9954	53.4359	60.8931	69.5311	79.5423	104.6026
24	26.9732	30.4216	34.4263	39.0825	44.5015	50.8151	58.1763	66.7645	76.7889	88.4965	118.1549
25	28.2429	32.0300	36.4591	41.6458	47.7265	54.8640	63.2487	73.1057	84.6998	98.3461	133.3335
26	29.5253	33.6706	38.5528	44.3116	51.1128	59.1558	68.6761	79.9541	93.3227	109.1806	150.3335
27	30.8205	35.3440	40.7094	47.0841	54.6684	63.7051	74.4834	87.3504	102.7217	121.0986	169.3735.
28	32.1287	37.0509	42.9306	49.9675	58.4017	68.5274	80.6972	95.3385	112.9666	134.2085	190.6983
29	33.4499	38.7919	45.2186	52.9661	62.3218	73.6390	87.3459	103.9655	124.1335	148.6292	214.5821
30	34.7844	40.5677	47.5751	56.0848	66.4378	79.0573	94.4601	113.2827	136.3054	164.4921	241.3319
35	41.659	49.994	60.461	73.651	90.318	111.432	138.234	172.314	215.705	271.018	431.658
40	48.886	60.402	75.401	95.026	120.797	154.758	199.630	259.052	337.872	442.580	767.080
45	56.479	71.891	92.718	121.027	159.695	212.737	285.741	386.497	525.840	718.881	1358.208
50	64.461	84.577	112.794	152.664	209.341	290.325	406.516	573.756	815.051	1163.865	2399.975
60	81.670	114.05	163.05	237.99	353.58	533.12	813.52	1253.2	1944.7	3034.8	7471.6

Period	14%	15%	16%	18%	20%	24%	28%	30%	32%	36%	40%
1	1.0000	1.0000	1.0000	1.0000	1.0000	1.0000	1.0000	1.0000	1.0000	1.0000	1.0000
2	2.1400	2.1500	2.1600	2.1800	2.2000	2.2400	2.2800	2.3000	2.3200	2.3600	2.4000
3	3.4396	3.4725	3.5056	3.5724	3.6400	3.7776	3.9184	3.9900	4.0624	4.2096	4.3600
4	4.9211	4.9934	5.0665	5.2154	5.3680	5.6842	6.0155	6.1870	6.3624	6.7251	7.1040
5	6.6101	6.7424	6.8771	7.1542	7.4416	8.0484	8.6999	9.0431	9.3983	10.1461	10.9456
6	8.5355	8.7537	8.9775	9.4420	9.9299	10.9801	12.1359	12.7560	13.4058	14.7986	16.3238
7	10.7305	11.0668	11.4139	12.1415	12.9159	14.6153	16.5339	17.5828	18.6956	21.1261	23.8533
8	13.2327	13.7268	14.2401	15.3270	16.4991	19.1229	22.1634	23.8576	25.6782	29.7315	34.3947
9	16.0853	16.7858	17.5185	19.0858	20.7989	24.7124	29.3691	32.0149	34.8952	41.4349	49.1525
10	19.3372	20.3037	21.3214	23.5212	25.9586	31.6434	38.5925	42.6193	47.0617	57.3514	69.8135
11	23.0444	24.3492	25.7328	28.7550	32.1503	40.2378	50.3984	56.4050	63.1214	78.9979	98.7388
12	27.2706	29.0016	30.8501	34.9309	39.5804	50.8948	65.5099	74.3265	84.3202	108.4372	139.2343
13	32.0885	34.3518	36.7861	42.2184	48.4965	64.1096	84.8527	97.6244	112.3027	148.4745	195.9280
14	37.5808	40.5045	43.6719	50.8177	59.1958	80.4959	109.6114	127.9117	149.2395	202.9253	275.2991
15	43.8421	47.5802	51.6594	60.9649	72.0349	100.8149	141.3026	167.2851	197.9961	276.9783	386.4185
16	50.9800	55.7172	60.9249	72.9385	87.4419	126.0104	181.8673	218.4705	262.3547	377.6904	541.9856
17	59.1172	65.0748	71.6728	87.0674	105.9303	157.2529	233.7901	285.0115	347.3081	514.6589	759.7798
18	68.3935	75.8360	84.1405	103.7395	128.1164	195.9936	300.2512	371.5146	459.4465	700.9358	
19	78.9686	88.2113	98.6029	123.4125	154.7396	244.0320	385.3213	483.9687	607.4692	954.2725	
20	91.0241	102.4430	115.3794	146.6267	186.6875	303.5996	494.2112	630.1589	802.8594		
21	104.7675	118.8094	134.8401	174.0194	225.0250	377.4634	633.5901	820.2063			
22	120.4348	137.6308	157.4145	206.3428	271.0298	469.0544	811.9951				
23	138.2957	159.2754	183.6008	244.4843	326.2356	582.6274					
24	158.6570	184.1667	213.9769	289.4912	392.4827	723.4578					
25	181.8689	212.7916	249.2132	342.5994	471.9792	898.0874					
26	208.3304	245.7103	290.0872	405.2668	567.3750						
27	238.4966	283.5667	337.5010	479.2146	681.8499						
28	272.8857	327.1016	392.5010	566.4729	819.2197						
29	312.0896	377.1665	456.3010	669.4377	984.0637						
30	356.7817	434.7412	530.3091	790.9360							
35	693.552	881.152	1120.699	1816.607							
40	1341.979	1779.048	2360.724	4163.094							
45	2590.464	3585.031	4965.191	9531.258							
50	4994.301	7217.488									
60	18535.	29219.									

Table B–3 Present Value of $1 (PVF)

Period	1%	2%	3%	4%	5%	6%	7%	8%	9%	10%	12%
1	0.9901	0.9804	0.9709	0.9615	0.9524	0.9434	0.9346	0.9259	0.9174	0.9091	0.8929
2	0.9803	0.9612	0.9426	0.9246	0.9070	0.8900	0.8734	0.8573	0.8417	0.8264	0.7972
3	0.9706	0.9423	0.9151	0.8890	0.8638	0.8396	0.8163	0.7938	0.7722	0.7513	0.7118
4	0.9610	0.9238	0.8885	0.8548	0.8227	0.7921	0.7629	0.7350	0.7084	0.6830	0.6355
5	0.9515	0.9057	0.8626	0.8219	0.7835	0.7473	0.7130	0.6806	0.6499	0.6209	0.5674
6	0.9420	0.8880	0.8375	0.7903	0.7462	0.7050	0.6663	0.6302	0.5963	0.5645	0.5066
7	0.9327	0.8706	0.8131	0.7599	0.7107	0.6651	0.6228	0.5835	0.5470	0.5132	0.4523
8	0.9235	0.8535	0.7894	0.7307	0.6768	0.6274	0.5820	0.5403	0.5019	0.4665	0.4039
9	0.9143	0.8368	0.7664	0.7026	0.6446	0.5919	0.5439	0.5002	0.4604	0.4241	0.3606
10	0.9053	0.8204	0.7441	0.6756	0.6139	0.5584	0.5084	0.4632	0.4224	0.3855	0.3220
11	0.8963	0.8043	0.7224	0.6496	0.5847	0.5268	0.4751	0.4289	0.3875	0.3505	0.2875
12	0.8875	0.7885	0.7014	0.6246	0.5568	0.4970	0.4440	0.3971	0.3555	0.3186	0.2567
13	0.8787	0.7730	0.6810	0.6006	0.5303	0.4688	0.4150	0.3677	0.3262	0.2897	0.2292
14	0.8700	0.7579	0.6611	0.5775	0.5051	0.4423	0.3878	0.3405	0.2992	0.2633	0.2046
15	0.8614	0.7430	0.6419	0.5553	0.4810	0.4173	0.3624	0.3152	0.2745	0.2394	0.1827
16	0.8528	0.7285	0.6232	0.5339	0.4581	0.3936	0.3387	0.2919	0.2519	0.2176	0.1631
17	0.8444	0.7142	0.6050	0.5134	0.4363	0.3714	0.3166	0.2703	0.2311	0.1978	0.1456
18	0.8360	0.7002	0.5874	0.4936	0.4155	0.3503	0.2959	0.2502	0.2120	0.1799	0.1300
19	0.8278	0.6864	0.5703	0.4746	0.3957	0.3305	0.2765	0.2317	0.1945	0.1635	0.1161
20	0.8196	0.6730	0.5537	0.4564	0.3769	0.3118	0.2584	0.2145	0.1784	0.1486	0.1037
21	0.8114	0.6598	0.5376	0.4388	0.3589	0.2942	0.2415	0.1987	0.1637	0.1351	0.0926
22	0.8034	0.6468	0.5219	0.4220	0.3419	0.2775	0.2257	0.1839	0.1502	0.1228	0.0826
23	0.7955	0.6342	0.5067	0.4057	0.3256	0.2618	0.2109	0.1703	0.1378	0.1117	0.0738
24	0.7876	0.6217	0.4919	0.3901	0.3101	0.2470	0.1971	0.1577	0.1264	0.1015	0.0659
25	0.7798	0.6095	0.4776	0.3751	0.2953	0.2330	0.1843	0.1460	0.1160	0.0923	0.0588
26	0.7721	0.5976	0.4637	0.3607	0.2812	0.2198	0.1722	0.1352	0.1064	0.0839	0.0525
27	0.7644	0.5859	0.4502	0.3468	0.2679	0.2074	0.1609	0.1252	0.0976	0.0763	0.0469
28	0.7569	0.5744	0.4371	0.3335	0.2551	0.1956	0.1504	0.1159	0.0896	0.0693	0.0419
29	0.7494	0.5631	0.4243	0.3207	0.2430	0.1846	0.1406	0.1073	0.0822	0.0630	0.0374
30	0.7419	0.5521	0.4120	0.3083	0.2314	0.1741	0.1314	0.0994	0.0754	0.0573	0.0334
35	0.7059	0.5000	0.3554	0.2534	0.1813	0.1301	0.0937	0.0676	0.0490	0.0356	0.0189
40	0.6717	0.4529	0.3066	0.2083	0.1420	0.0972	0.0668	0.0460	0.0318	0.0221	0.0107
45	0.6391	0.4102	0.2644	0.1712	0.1113	0.0727	0.0476	0.0313	0.0207	0.0137	0.0061
50	0.6081	0.3715	0.2281	0.1407	0.0872	0.0543	0.0339	0.0213	0.0134	0.0085	0.0035
55	0.5786	0.3365	0.1968	0.1157	0.0683	0.0406	0.0242	0.0145	0.0087	0.0053	0.0020
60	0.5505	0.3048	0.1697	0.0951	0.0535	0.0303	0.0173	0.0099	0.0057	0.0033	0.0011

Period	14%	15%	16%	18%	20%	24%	28%	30%	32%	36%	40%
1	0.8772	0.8696	0.8621	0.8475	0.8333	0.8065	0.7813	0.7692	0.7576	0.7353	0.7143
2	0.7695	0.7561	0.7432	0.7182	0.6944	0.6504	0.6104	0.5917	0.5739	0.5407	0.5102
3	0.6750	0.6575	0.6407	0.6086	0.5787	0.5245	0.4768	0.4552	0.4348	0.3975	0.3644
4	0.5921	0.5718	0.5523	0.5158	0.4823	0.4230	0.3725	0.3501	0.3294	0.2923	0.2603
5	0.5194	0.4972	0.4761	0.4371	0.4019	0.3411	0.2910	0.2693	0.2495	0.2149	0.1859
6	0.4556	0.4323	0.4104	0.3704	0.3349	0.2751	0.2274	0.2072	0.1890	0.1580	0.1328
7	0.3996	0.3759	0.3538	0.3139	0.2791	0.2218	0.1776	0.1594	0.1432	0.1162	0.0949
8	0.3506	0.3269	0.3050	0.2660	0.2326	0.1789	0.1388	0.1226	0.1085	0.0854	0.0678
9	0.3075	0.2843	0.2630	0.2255	0.1938	0.1443	0.1084	0.0943	0.0822	0.0628	0.0484
10	0.2697	0.2472	0.2267	0.1911	0.1615	0.1164	0.0847	0.0725	0.0623	0.0462	0.0346
11	0.2366	0.2149	0.1954	0.1619	0.1346	0.0938	0.0662	0.0558	0.0472	0.0340	0.0247
12	0.2076	0.1869	0.1685	0.1372	0.1122	0.0757	0.0517	0.0429	0.0357	0.0250	0.0176
13	0.1821	0.1625	0.1452	0.1163	0.0935	0.0610	0.0404	0.0330	0.0271	0.0184	0.0126
14	0.1597	0.1413	0.1252	0.0985	0.0779	0.0492	0.0316	0.0254	0.0205	0.0135	0.0090
15	0.1401	0.1229	0.1079	0.0835	0.0649	0.0397	0.0247	0.0195	0.0155	0.0099	0.0064
16	0.1229	0.1069	0.0930	0.0708	0.0541	0.0320	0.0193	0.0150	0.0118	0.0073	0.0046
17	0.1078	0.0929	0.0802	0.0600	0.0451	0.0258	0.0150	0.0116	0.0089	0.0054	0.0033
18	0.0946	0.0808	0.0691	0.0508	0.0376	0.0208	0.0118	0.0089	0.0068	0.0039	0.0023
19	0.0829	0.0703	0.0596	0.0431	0.0313	0.0168	0.0092	0.0068	0.0051	0.0029	0.0017
20	0.0728	0.0611	0.0514	0.0365	0.0261	0.0135	0.0072	0.0053	0.0039	0.0021	0.0012
21	0.0638	0.0531	0.0443	0.0309	0.0217	0.0109	0.0056	0.0040	0.0029	0.0016	0.0009
22	0.0560	0.0462	0.0382	0.0262	0.0181	0.0088	0.0044	0.0031	0.0022	0.0012	0.0006
23	0.0491	0.0402	0.0329	0.0222	0.0151	0.0071	0.0034	0.0024	0.0017	0.0008	0.0004
24	0.0431	0.0349	0.0284	0.0188	0.0126	0.0057	0.0027	0.0018	0.0013	0.0006	0.0003
25	0.0378	0.0304	0.0245	0.0160	0.0105	0.0046	0.0021	0.0014	0.0010	0.0005	0.0002
26	0.0331	0.0264	0.0211	0.0135	0.0087	0.0037	0.0016	0.0011	0.0007	0.0003	0.0002
27	0.0291	0.0230	0.0182	0.0115	0.0073	0.0030	0.0013	0.0008	0.0006	0.0002	0.0001
28	0.0255	0.0200	0.0157	0.0097	0.0061	0.0024	0.0010	0.0006	0.0004	0.0002	0.0001
29	0.0224	0.0174	0.0135	0.0082	0.0051	0.0020	0.0008	0.0005	0.0003	0.0001	0.0001
30	0.0196	0.0151	0.0116	0.0070	0.0042	0.0016	0.0006	0.0004	0.0002	0.0001	0.0000
35	0.0102	0.0075	0.0055	0.0030	0.0017	0.0005	0.0002	0.0001	0.0001	0.0000	0.0000
40	0.0053	0.0037	0.0026	0.0013	0.0007	0.0002	0.0001	0.0000	0.0000	0.0000	0.0000
45	0.0027	0.0019	0.0013	0.0006	0.0003	0.0001	0.0000	0.0000	0.0000	0.0000	0.0000
50	0.0014	0.0009	0.0006	0.0003	0.0001	0.0000	0.0000	0.0000	0.0000	0.0000	0.0000
55	0.0007	0.0005	0.0003	0.0001	0.0000	0.0000	0.0000	0.0000	0.0000	0.0000	0.0000
60	0.0004	0.0002	0.0001	0.0000	0.0000	0.0000	0.0000	0.0000	0.0000	0.0000	0.0000

Table B-4 Present Value of an Annuity of $1 ($PVF_a$)

Period	1%	2%	3%	4%	5%	6%	7%	8%	9%	10%	12%
1	0.9901	0.9804	0.9709	0.9615	0.9524	0.9434	0.9346	0.9259	0.9174	0.9091	0.8929
2	1.9704	1.9416	1.9135	1.8861	1.8594	1.8334	1.8080	1.7833	1.7591	1.7355	1.6901
3	2.9410	2.8839	2.8286	2.7751	2.7233	2.6730	2.6243	2.5771	2.5313	2.4869	2.4018
4	3.9020	3.8077	3.7171	3.6299	3.5460	3.4651	3.3872	3.3121	3.2397	3.1699	3.0373
5	4.8534	4.7135	4.5797	4.4518	4.3295	4.2124	4.1002	3.9927	3.8897	3.7908	3.6048
6	5.7955	5.6014	5.4172	5.2421	5.0757	4.9173	4.7665	4.6229	4.4859	4.3553	4.1114
7	6.7282	6.4720	6.2303	6.0021	5.7864	5.5824	5.3893	5.2064	5.0330	4.8684	4.5638
8	7.6517	7.3255	7.0197	6.7327	6.4632	6.2098	5.9713	5.7466	5.5348	5.3349	4.9676
9	8.5660	8.1623	7.7861	7.4353	7.1078	6.8017	6.5152	6.2469	5.9953	5.7590	5.3282
10	9.4713	8.9826	8.5302	8.1109	7.7218	7.3601	7.0236	6.7101	6.4177	6.1446	5.6502
11	10.3677	9.7869	9.2526	8.7605	8.3064	7.8869	7.4987	7.1390	6.8052	6.4951	5.9377
12	11.2551	10.5754	9.9540	9.3851	8.8633	8.3839	7.9427	7.5361	7.1607	6.8137	6.1944
13	12.1338	11.3484	10.6350	9.9856	9.3936	8.8527	8.3577	7.9038	7.4869	7.1034	6.4235
14	13.0038	12.1063	11.2961	10.5631	9.8987	9.2950	8.7455	8.2442	7.7862	7.3667	6.6282
15	13.8651	12.8493	11.9380	11.1184	10.3797	9.7123	9.1079	8.5595	8.0607	7.6061	6.8109
16	14.7180	13.5778	12.5611	11.6523	10.8378	10.1059	9.4467	8.8514	8.3126	7.8237	6.9740
17	15.5623	14.2929	13.1661	12.1657	11.2741	10.4773	9.7632	9.1216	8.5437	8.0216	7.1196
18	16.3984	14.9921	13.7535	12.6593	11.6896	10.8276	10.0591	9.3719	8.7557	8.2014	7.2497
19	17.2261	15.6785	14.3238	13.1339	12.0854	11.1582	10.3356	9.6036	8.9502	8.3649	7.3658
20	18.0457	16.3515	14.8775	13.5903	12.4623	11.4700	10.5940	9.8181	9.1286	8.5136	7.4694
21	18.8571	17.0113	15.4151	14.0292	12.8212	11.7641	10.8355	10.0168	9.2923	8.6487	7.5620
22	19.6605	17.6581	15.9369	14.4511	13.1631	12.0416	11.0613	10.2007	9.4425	8.7716	7.6446
23	20.4559	18.2923	16.4436	14.8568	13.4887	12.3034	11.2722	10.3711	9.5803	8.8832	7.7184
24	21.2435	18.9140	16.9356	15.2470	13.7987	12.5504	11.4694	10.5288	9.7067	8.9848	7.7843
25	22.0233	19.5235	17.4132	15.6221	14.0940	12.7834	11.6536	10.6748	9.8226	9.0771	7.8431
26	22.7953	20.1211	17.8768	15.9828	14.3753	13.0032	11.8258	10.8100	9.9290	9.1610	7.8957
27	23.5597	20.7070	18.3270	16.3296	14.6431	13.2106	11.9867	10.9352	10.0266	9.2373	7.9425
28	24.3166	21.2813	18.7641	16.6630	14.8982	13.4062	12.1371	11.0511	10.1162	9.3066	7.9844
29	25.0659	21.8444	19.1884	16.9837	15.1412	13.5908	12.2777	11.1584	10.1983	9.3696	8.0218
30	25.8078	22.3965	19.6004	17.2920	15.3726	13.7649	12.4091	11.2578	10.2737	9.4269	8.0552
35	29.4087	24.9987	21.4872	18.6646	16.3743	14.4983	12.9477	11.6546	10.5669	9.6442	8.1755
40	32.8349	27.3555	23.1147	19.7927	17.1592	15.0464	13.3317	11.9246	10.7574	9.7791	8.2438
45	36.0948	29.4902	24.5186	20.7199	17.7741	15.4559	13.6056	12.1084	10.8813	9.8628	8.2825
50	39.1964	31.4237	25.7297	21.4820	18.2560	15.7620	13.8008	12.2335	10.9617	9.9148	8.3045
55	42.1476	33.1749	26.7743	22.1084	18.6335	15.9906	13.9400	12.3186	11.0141	9.9471	8.3170
60	44.9555	34.7610	27.6754	22.6233	18.9293	16.1615	14.0392	12.3765	11.0481	9.9672	8.3240

Period	14%	15%	16%	18%	20%	24%	28%	30%	32%	36%	40%
1	0.8772	0.8696	0.8621	0.8475	0.8333	0.8065	0.7813	0.7692	0.7576	0.7353	0.7143
2	1.6467	1.6257	1.6052	1.5656	1.5278	1.4568	1.3916	1.3609	1.3315	1.2760	1.2245
3	2.3216	2.2832	2.2459	2.1743	2.1065	1.9813	1.8684	1.8161	1.7663	1.6735	1.5889
4	2.9137	2.8550	2.7982	2.6901	2.5887	2.4043	2.2410	2.1662	2.0957	1.9658	1.8492
5	3.4331	3.3522	3.2743	3.1272	2.9906	2.7454	2.5320	2.4356	2.3452	2.1807	2.0352
6	3.8887	3.7845	3.6847	3.4976	3.3255	3.0205	2.7594	2.6427	2.5342	2.3388	2.1680
7	4.2883	4.1604	4.0386	3.8115	3.6046	3.2423	2.9370	2.8021	2.6775	2.4550	2.2628
8	4.6389	4.4873	4.3436	4.0776	3.8372	3.4212	3.0758	2.9247	2.7860	2.5404	2.3306
9	4.9464	4.7716	4.6065	4.3030	4.0310	3.5655	3.1842	3.0190	2.8681	2.6033	2.3790
10	5.2161	5.0188	4.8332	4.4941	4.1925	3.6819	3.2689	3.0915	2.9304	2.6495	2.4136
11	5.4527	5.2337	5.0286	4.6560	4.3271	3.7757	3.3351	3.1473	2.9776	2.6834	2.4383
12	5.6603	5.4206	5.1971	4.7932	4.4392	3.8514	3.3868	3.1903	3.0133	2.7084	2.4559
13	5.8424	5.5832	5.3423	4.9095	4.5327	3.9124	3.4272	3.2233	3.0404	2.7268	2.4685
14	6.0021	5.7245	5.4675	5.0081	4.6106	3.9616	3.4587	3.2487	3.0609	2.7403	2.4775
15	6.1422	5.8474	5.5755	5.0916	4.6755	4.0013	3.4834	3.2682	3.0764	2.7502	2.4839
16	6.2651	5.9542	5.6685	5.1624	4.7296	4.0333	3.5026	3.2832	3.0882	2.7575	2.4885
17	6.3729	6.0472	5.7487	5.2223	4.7746	4.0591	3.5177	3.2948	3.0971	2.7629	2.4918
18	6.4674	6.1280	5.8178	5.2732	4.8122	4.0799	3.5294	3.3037	3.1039	2.7668	2.4941
19	6.5504	6.1982	5.8775	5.3162	4.8435	4.0967	3.5386	3.3105	3.1090	2.7697	2.4958
20	6.6231	6.2593	5.9288	5.3528	4.8696	4.1103	3.5458	3.3158	3.1129	2.7718	2.4970
21	6.6870	6.3125	5.9731	5.3837	4.8913	4.1212	3.5514	3.3198	3.1158	2.7734	2.4979
22	6.7430	6.3587	6.0113	5.4099	4.9094	4.1300	3.5558	3.3230	3.1180	2.7746	2.4985
23	6.7921	6.3988	6.0442	5.4321	4.9245	4.1371	3.5592	3.3253	3.1197	2.7754	2.4989
24	6.8352	6.4338	6.0726	5.4510	4.9371	4.1428	3.5619	3.3272	3.1210	2.7760	2.4992
25	6.8729	6.4642	6.0971	5.4669	4.9476	4.1474	3.5640	3.3286	3.1220	2.7765	2.4994
26	6.9061	6.4906	6.1182	5.4804	4.9563	4.1511	3.5656	3.3297	3.1227	2.7768	2.4996
27	6.9352	6.5135	6.1364	5.4919	4.9636	4.1541	3.5669	3.3305	3.1233	2.7771	2.4997
28	6.9607	6.5335	6.1520	5.5016	4.9697	4.1566	3.5679	3.3312	3.1237	2.7773	2.4998
29	6.9831	6.5509	6.1655	5.5098	4.9747	4.1585	3.5686	3.3317	3.1240	2.7774	2.4998
30	7.0027	6.5660	6.1772	5.5168	4.9789	4.1601	3.5692	3.3321	3.1242	2.7775	2.4999
35	7.0701	6.6166	6.2153	5.5386	4.9915	4.1644	3.5708	3.3330	3.1248	2.7777	2.5000
40	7.1051	6.6418	6.2335	5.5482	4.9966	4.1659	3.5712	3.3332	3.1249	2.7778	2.5000
45	7.1232	6.6543	6.2421	5.5523	4.9986	4.1664	3.5714	3.3333	3.1250	2.7778	2.5000
50	7.1327	6.6605	6.2462	5.5541	4.9994	4.1666	3.5714	3.3333	3.1250	2.7778	2.5000
55	7.1376	6.6636	6.2482	5.5549	4.9998	4.1666	3.5714	3.3333	3.1250	2.7778	2.5000
60	7.1401	6.6651	6.2491	5.5553	4.9999	4.1666	3.5714	3.3333	3.1250	2.7778	2.5000

APPENDIX C

Answers to Selected Odd-Numbered Problems

Chapter 2

1. c. $E_p = -4.33$; $E_p = -0.45$.

3. b. Marginal revenue would equal price; marginal revenue would be less than price.

5. a. $Q_2 = 23,590$.   **b.** $\Delta TR = +\$87,200$.

7. a. 56,000 stuffed animals.   **b.** Total revenue would increase by $48,000.

9. 7,600 cars.

C1. $TR = 120Q - 1.5Q^2$; $MR = 120 - 3Q$; $AR = 120 - 1.5Q$.

C3. a. $AR = P = 142 - .05Q$; $TR = Q(P) = 142Q - .05Q^2$; $MR = dTR/dQ = 142 - 0.1Q$.
b. max. $TR = \$100,820$.   **c.** Inelastic; $|E_p| = 0.78$.   **d.** $E_p = -1.70$; TR will increase if price is cut, since $|E_p| > 1$.

C5. a. 0.72.   **b.** Normal; $E_I > 0$.   **d.** -10.   **e.** Elastic; $|E_p| > 1$.

C7. a. $Q_x = 1,228 - 20P_x$.   **b.** Complements, since the coefficient of P_y is negative.
c. -4.39.   **d.** Total revenue will be maximized at $Q_x = 614$; $P_x = \$30.70$, and total revenue will be $18,849.80.

Appendix 3

1. a. The slope, b, is -237.84 and the intercept, a, is 287.57.   **b.** $R^2 = .97$.
d. $147.26 < Y < 190.04$.   **e.** The estimates should be more reliable in a large sample since both $\hat{\sigma}_a$ and $\hat{\sigma}_b$ become smaller as the sample size becomes larger.

Chapter 5

1. a. The robots are more productive per dollar spent and probably should be bought.
b. $96/P_L = 0.25$; $0.25P_L = 96$; $P_L = 96/0.25 = \underline{\$384}$.   **c.** Does she expect any change in the wage rate of artists or in the operating costs of robots? Either or both will affect her decision.

3. Use more capital, less labor, since $\dfrac{MP_K}{P_K} > \dfrac{MP_L}{P_L}$.

5. Purchase the machine.

7. **a.** Constant returns to scale; doubling the inputs results in a doubling of the level of output.   **d.** This is not a least cost combination because output per additional dollar spent is greater for capital.

9. **d.** 30 units and 20 units of input a, respectively.   **e.** Immediately after $a = 20$ units.

11. Robot, because additional output per additional \$1 is greater for the robot.

C1. **a.** $100 = 4KL + 3L^2 - (1/3)L^3$.

b. $dQ = 4L\, dK + (4K + 6L - L^2)dL = 0$,

$-4L\, dK = (4K + 6L - L^2)dL$,

$$\frac{dK}{dL} = \frac{4K + 6L - L^2}{-4L}.$$

This expression can also be derived using

$$\frac{dK}{dL} = -\frac{MP_L}{MP_K}$$

$$MP_L = \frac{\partial Q}{\partial L} = 4K + 6L - L^2,$$

$$MP_K = \frac{\partial Q}{\partial K} = 4L, \text{ so}$$

$$\frac{dK}{dL} = \frac{-\left(4K + 6L - L^2\right)}{4L}.$$

c. From (b), $MP_L = 4K + 6L - L^2$.
When $K = 5$, $MP_L = 20 + 6L - L^2$.

d. $L = 3$.

C3. **a.** $Q = 576$.   **b.** $L = 6$.   **c.** $Q = 234.67$ at $L = 4$.

C5. **a.** $Q = 2{,}258.67$.   **b.** $L = 10$.   **c.** $Q = 1{,}106.67$.   **d.** $AP_L = 119$.

Appendix 5

1. $Q = 55{,}200$ units; $K = 10$; $L = 190$; $\lambda = 96$.

Chapter 6

3. **a.** \$900.   **b.** \$3.00.   **c.** 400.   **d.** \$700.   **e.** \$3.50.

5. **b.** Between 40 and 100 units of output; between 40 and 100 units of output and 2 and 4 units of labor.

9. a. *LAC* will decrease since there are increasing returns to scale.   **b.** Combination is least cost, since $MP/P = 2.5$ for both inputs.   **c.** In the table, $TFC = Z(P_z) = 48$, and $TVC = Y(P_y) = Y(14)$.

11. b. $AFC = \$504/180 = \$2.80$.   **c.** $P_b = \$42$.

C1. a. $SMC = 240 - 8Q + Q^2$; $AVC = 240 - 4Q + (1/3)Q^2$; $SAC = (1,000/Q) + 240 - 4Q + (1/3)Q^2$.   **b.** $Q = 4$.   **c.** $Q = 6$.

C3. a. $AFC = 800/20 = 40$.   **b.** $Q = 10$.   **c.** $Q = 15$; $AVC = 26.25$.

C5. a. Home plant: \$30.50; Foreign plant: \$29.00.   **b.** Home plant: \$30.00; Foreign plant: \$25.00.

Chapter 7

1. Profit-maximizing price = \$14.67; output = 6.

3. Profit-maximizing price = \$3.50; output = 50; profit = \$50.

5. Profit-maximizing price = \$600; output = 60; profit = \$10,000.

7. b. Profit-maximizing price = \$140; output = 6,000.

9. a. 30,000 cases per month.   **b.** Yes, because the net increase in profit contribution is \$144,000.

11. a. $Q = 20$; $P = \$290$.   **b.** Profit = \$1,333.33.

C1. a. $Q = 10.5$.   **b.** $Q = 6$.   **c.** Profit = \$66.

C3. a. $P = 220 - Q$; $TR = 220Q - Q^2$.   **b.** $Q = 14$; $P = \$206$.   **c.** Profit = \$437.33.

C5. $Q = 40$; $P = \$1,240$; Profit = \$14,666.67.

C9. a. $C = 170$; $I = 245$.   **b.** Profit = \$10,670.   **c.** $\lambda = 22.7$.

Chapter 8

1. a. 500,000 raw pineapples and 2,500,000 cans of pineapple.   **b.** \$725,000.

5. b. The opportunity costs associated with the road grader, roller, and power trowel are \$100, \$0, and \$200, respectively.   **c.** 0; 0. Because at the profit-maximizing point, both asphalt and concrete paving should be done, which implies that L_A and $L_C = 0$.

7. a. $Q_A = 2$; $Q_B = 4$.   **b.** Since process C is not employed, total output = $Q_A + Q_B = 6$.

9. b. \$165,000; $S_1 = 15,000$; $S_2 = S_3 = 0$.   **c.** \$0; \$0.3125.

Chapter 9

3. Total profit = –\$6,160, so by producing, the firm will lose more than the \$4,000 fixed costs. It should shut down.

7. a. $Q = 56$ is optimal output.   **b.** Profit = –\$468, a loss minimum.

C1. $127.50.

C3. **a.** $Q = 480; P = \$60.80$.   **b.** Profit = $16,780.

C5. **a.** $Q = 100; P = \$195$.   **b.** $2,450.

C7. **a.** $Q = 30$.   **b.** $\pi = \$2,200$.   **c.** i. $LAC = 660 - 9Q + 0.05Q^2$.   ii. $Q = 90$; $P = LAC = \$255; \pi = 0$.

Chapter 10

3. **a.** $.10.   **b.** Price = $.07. Each booth will sell 1,667 kisses and earn $116.69.
  c. Yes, if firms cooperated, each could produce 1,250 kisses at a unit price of $.10.

5. **a.** $280.   **b.** 10,000 units.   **c.** 15,000 units.

7. Firms 1, 2, and 3 should be allocated 23,000, 19,250, and 7,750 barrels per year, respectively.

C1. **a.** $P = \$8.75; Q = 7,500$ homes.   **b.** $16,125.   **c.** $P = \$8.00; Q = 6,000$ homes.
  d. Profit is decreased by $5,125 when advertising expenditures are cut by $5,000.
  e. Restore advertising to its original level.

C3. **a.** $Q = 12$.   **b.** $508.

C5. **a.** Large firm will maximize profit at $Q = 3,000$ and charge a price of $44.   **b.** Small firms' quantity supplied will be 1,220.   **c.** For Aqualor, profit will be $14,000.

C7. $Q_A = 500; Q_T = 400$.

Chapter 11

5. **b.** Profit is maximized with two shifts, producing 100% B.

7. **a.** Yes.   **b.** 3,800 carryout servings; 2,400 eat-in servings.   **c.** Price for carryout is $3.10, and price for eat-in is $3.60.

C1. **a.** $Q_z = 2,000; Q_b = 1,900$.   **b.** $P_z = \$800; P_b = \$1,900$.

C3. The firm should produce 3,620 units of the joint products but sell only 3,000 units of vinegar. $P_w = \$83.80; P_v = \$15$; Profit = $154,670.40.

C5. $Q = 3,690; P_f = \$63.10; P_O = \$17.50; \pi = \$138,259.30$. There is excess codfish oil of 190.

C7. **a.** $Q_g = 1,340; Q_c = 820$.   **b.** $P_g = \$150.20; P_c = \$99.60$.   **c.** Profit = $37,884.
  d. Price will be $114.05 in both markets. $Q_g = 2,063; Q_c = 97$; Profit is $1,292.

Chapter 12

1. The firm should produce 84 sweatshirts because at that point, the $MRP_L = \$4.50 = MC_L =$ the wage rate.

3. Forty workers should be employed. Because employment of its members would likely decrease, a union would not necessarily bargain for the highest wage.

5. a. Four bartenders should be employed, and the average price of one drink should be set at $2.70.   **b.** $7.00/hour.

C1. $L = 9.25$, so use 9 workers.

Chapter 13

1. a. $67,019.   **b.** $38,276.   **c.** $15,568.

3. The greatest present value in Problem 2 = $286,825.

5. The project is not acceptable at a discount rate of 9% as the *NPV* is –$93,306. At a discount rate of 6%, the *NPV* is $18,709 so the project is acceptable.

7. a. Not acceptable.   **b.** Not acceptable.   **c.** Acceptable.

9. a. About 13%.   **b.** Since the *NPV* is $50,314, management should be advised to accept the project (assuming there is no further adjustment of the discount rate for risk).

Appendix 13

1. $61,316.

3. $13,951.

5. $407,124.

7. $11,754.

Chapter 14

3. Variance = $\sigma^2 = 835,687,500$.

Std. Deviation = $\sigma = 28,908.26$.

5. Belco will choose the U.S. refinery. The Latin American project has a negative net present value.

7.

Level of Risk (σ)	Certainty Equivalent Adjustment Factor (α)
400	0.4286
300	0.5714
200	0.7143
100	0.8571

11. a. $E(R_T) = 0.28$; $E(R_M) = 0.170$.   **b.** $\sigma_T = 0.16$; $\sigma_M = 0.09$.   **c.** He would choose in accordance with his preferences regarding risk and return.

Chapter 15

3. Projects B, E, and F are acceptable. The others are not acceptable.

5. The Southeast project has the highest B/C and net differential benefits. Also, $\Delta B/\Delta C$ is less than 1.0 for higher cost projects. Therefore the Southeast project should be chosen.

7. Project D has the highest benefit-cost ratio, so it would be ranked first. The other two acceptable projects, A and E, have approximately the same B/C ratios, so they would be ranked equally behind project D.

GLOSSARY

A

antitrust laws: Laws regulating any business practices and agreements that intensify monopoly power or otherwise restrict trade.

arc marginal product: An approximation to marginal product over some range of output; is equal to the change in total product divided by the change in the variable input.

arc marginal revenue: The average rate of change of total revenue with respect to quantity sold over some range of output.

average fixed cost: Fixed cost per unit of output in the short run. Equal to total fixed cost divided by level of output.

average/marginal relationship: The average cannot rise unless the related marginal value is above it; the average cannot fall unless the corresponding marginal value is below it; the average value must equal the marginal value when the average is at a maximum or a minimum.

average product (of a variable input): Total output divided by the number of units of the input in use. It gives output per unit of input.

average profit: Profit per unit of output. Average profit is found by dividing total profit by quantity of output. It is also equal to price minus average cost.

average revenue: Revenue per unit sold. Average revenue is equal to total revenue divided by quantity sold, and as long as only one price is charged, is equal to price.

B

barometric forecasting: Forecasting techniques that involve the use of current values of certain variables, called indicators, to predict future values of other economic variables.

barriers to entry: Conditions that make it difficult for new firms to enter an industry or market where existing firms have long-run interests.

benefit-cost ratio (B/C): The present value of the benefits divided by the present value of the cost of a project. A project is acceptable from a social welfare point of view if and only if its B/C is greater than or equal to 1.

bilateral monopoly: A market structure characterized by having only one buyer and one seller of a particular good or service.

bundling: A strategy that offers a package deal to consumers on the purchase of two or more products.

C

capital budgeting: The process by which a firm determines how to allocate investment expenditure among alternative projects.

cartel: A group of firms that have joined together to make agreements on pricing and market strategy.

change in demand: A shift in a demand curve for a good or services caused by a change in some variable other than the price of the given good or service.

change in quantity demanded: A change in the amount of a good or service that consumers are willing to purchase over some time period, which is caused by a change in the price of the good or service.

complementary goods: Products or services that are usually used with one another and have a negative cross price elasticity of demand.

compounding: The process of computing the value of a current sum of money at some future date.

consent decree: A statement of certain provisions agreed to by both the government and the defendant.

consumer's surplus: The difference between the maximum value a consumer places on a given quantity of a good he or she purchases and the money amount that is actually paid to obtain that quantity.

consumption spending: Expenditures by individuals for newly produced goods and services (excluding housing).

contestable markets: Oligopolistic markets characterized by free and costless entry and exit and by a lack of rival reaction on the part of existing firms.

contract law: Laws that pertain to the establishment of contractual obligations and to wrongful acts in breach of contract.

cost-benefit analysis: An extension of capital project analysis to public sector project decisions that attempts to take into account the economic criteria for an optimal allocation of society's resources.

cost elasticity: The percentage change in long-run total cost from a 1 percent change in output.

criminal law: Laws that pertain to acts that are viewed as offenses against a federal, state, or local government.

cross price elasticity of demand: The cross price elasticity of demand for Product X with respect to the price of Product Y is a measure of the relative responsiveness of quantity demanded of X to changes in P_Y.

cross-section data: Observations of a particular variable at a single point in time.

cyclical factors: Factors related to fluctuations in the general level of economic activity.

D

demand curve: Graphical representation of the relationship between the quantity demanded of a good and its price.

demand function: Relates the quantities of a product that consumers will purchase during some specific period to the variables that influence their decisions to buy or not to buy the good or service. Examples of such variables include the price of the good or service, prices of related goods or services, and income of potential consumers.

determinants of demand: Those variables other than a good's own price that affect the amount of the good buyers are willing and able to buy at some point in time. Some examples are income, prices of related goods, tastes, and advertising.

determinants of supply: Those variables other than a good's own price that affect the amount of the good sellers are willing and able to sell at some point in time. Some examples are input prices, technology, and various kinds of taxes.

direct benefits: The benefits obtained by the users of a project or activity.

direct costs: The costs directly associated with a project or activity.

discount rate: The rate of interest used to compute a present value.

discounting: The process of computing the present value of a sum of money to be received in the future.

diseconomies of scale: Technological and organizational disadvantages that accrue to the firm as it increases output in the long run. Diseconomies of scale increase long-run average costs.

E

economic region of production: The range in an isoquant diagram where both inputs have a positive marginal product. It lies inside the ridge lines.

economies of scale: Technological and organizational advantages that the firm encounters as it increases output in the long run. Economies of scale reduce long-run average costs.

economies of scope: Occur when the average cost of undertaking two or more activities together is less than the sum of the costs of each activity separately.

efficient portfolio: A project or a combination of investments that will involve the least risk for a given rate of return.

efficient set: The set of all efficient portfolios.

equilibrium price: The price at which the quantity demanded by consumers of a product is equal to the quantity supplied by sellers of a product.

exclusive dealing: A situation wherein a firm buying or leasing the goods of one firm agrees not to deal with competing suppliers.

expansion path: The line connecting all of the least cost combinations of input points for a particular ratio of input prices.

expected value: A weighted average of the possible outcomes, which is obtained by multiplying each outcome by the probability associated with it and then summing the resulting values.

explicit costs: Those costs of production that involve a specific payment by the firm to some person, group, or organization outside the firm. Also known as *historical costs*.

F

first-degree price discrimination: A theoretical concept that refers to charging a different amount, specifically the maximum amount a consumer is willing and able to pay, for each unit purchased.

fixed costs: Those costs that cannot be eliminated in the short run.

forecasting: The process of analyzing available information regarding economic variables and relationships and then predicting the future values of certain variables of interest to the firm or to economic policymakers.

free entry: The absence of barriers to entry into a market. In a market characterized by free entry, profit serves the function of drawing new firms into the industry when greater than normal.

future value: The amount that would be accumulated at some future date if a sum of money held today were invested now at a particular rate of interest.

G

GATT (General Agreement on Tariffs and Trade): The mechanism set up by the market economies after World War II to reduce barriers to international trade. It had over 100 member countries in 1993, and many former Eastern Bloc nations were hoping to join the group.

government expenditures: Expenditures for newly produced goods and services, including government investment expenditures, by all levels of government.

gross domestic product: The market value of all final output produced within the geographical area of a country during a given time period (generally one year).

gross national product: The market value of final goods and services produced with factors of production owned by residents of a country during some time period, usually one year.

H

historical costs: Costs of the firm for which explicit payment has been made sometime in the past or for which the firm is committed in the future. Also known as *explicit costs*.

I

implicit (opportunity) costs: Costs that do not involve actual payment by a firm to factors of production but nevertheless represent cost to the firm in the sense that in order to use certain inputs in the production process, the firm has had to abandon opportunities to use them elsewhere.

income elasticity of demand: A measure of the relative responsiveness of the quantity demanded of a product to the changes in income.

incremental benefit-cost ratio: The change in total benefits divided by the change in total costs, obtained by moving to the project with the next higher level of price or initial outlay.

incremental cost: The additional costs that will be incurred by the firm if it undertakes a new project or produces an additional batch of output.

incremental profit: Incremental revenue minus incremental cost resulting from an activity of a firm.

incremental revenue: The additional revenue that a firm will receive by undertaking a particular project.

indirect benefits: External, or third party, benefits associated with a project.

indirect costs: External, or third party, costs associated with a project.

inferior good: A product or service with a negative income elasticity of demand.

internal rate of return (*IRR*): The net annual percentage yield of a project, obtained by solving for the discount rate that will cause the net present value of the project to be equal to zero.

investment spending: (GNP definition) All purchases of capital goods—including buildings, equipment, and inventories—by private businesses and nonprofit institutions. Includes all expenditures for residential housing.

isocost line: Gives all combinations of two inputs that can be utilized for a given dollar cost to the firm, assuming given and fixed input prices.

isoprofit curve: Indicates the different combinations of two products that will result in equal profit for the firm.

isoquant: Indicates the various combinations of two inputs that would enable a firm to produce a particular level of output.

K

kinked demand curve: Occurs when rival firms will not follow the price increase of a single firm in an oligopoly but will cut prices when another firm does so. Such a demand curve is relatively elastic for prices above the going market price and much less elastic for lower prices.

L

law of diminishing returns: A technical proposition which asserts that if equal increments of one variable input are added while the amounts of all other inputs remain fixed, total product may increase, but after some point, the *additions* to total product will decrease.

least cost combination of inputs: That input combination that will enable a firm to produce a given level of output at the lowest possible cost or to produce the greatest output for a given dollar cost.

linear programming: A mathematical technique whereby a firm can make optimizing decisions in a situation where the function to be maximized or minimized is linear and subject to linear constraints that are in the form of inequalities.

long run: Time period sufficiently long that all inputs are variable.

long-run average cost: Long-run total cost divided by the level of output. Measures cost per unit of output when all inputs are variable.

long-run marginal cost: The rate of change of long-run total cost as the level of output changes.

long-run total cost: The minimum economic cost of producing each possible level of output when the time period is sufficiently long to change all inputs of the firm's production function.

M

macroeconomics: The branch of economic analysis that deals with aggregate economic variables such as the economy's total output, central government spending and tax policy, and money supply and interest rates.

marginal cost of an input: The rate of change of a firm's total cost with respect to a change in the amount of an input. *Arc* marginal cost of an input is given by the change in a firm's total cost divided by the change in the input.

marginal cost of capital (*MCC*): The discount rate that represents the marginal cost of investment funds to the firm. Calculated as a weighted average of the after-tax cost of funds from each source.

marginal or **incremental analysis:** Examines how changes in certain economic variables affect other economic variables; for example, how a change in the output of a firm affects both sales revenue and cost or how an increase in household income affects savings.

marginal product (of a variable input): The rate of change of total output with respect to changes in the variable input—other inputs kept fixed. *Arc* marginal product is an approximation to marginal product and is given by the change in the total product divided by the change in the variable input.

marginal profit: The rate of change of total profit with respect to changes in the level of the firm's output. *Arc* marginal profit is found by dividing the change in total profit by the change in quantity of output. Marginal profit is also equal to marginal revenue minus marginal cost.

marginal rate of (technical) substitution of two inputs (MRS): Indicates the rate at which two inputs can be substituted for each other while a constant level of production is maintained. The marginal rate of substitution is equal to minus one times the slope of an isoquant.

marginal revenue: The rate of change of total revenue with respect to quantity sold. Marginal revenue indicates to a firm how total revenue will change if there is a change in the quantity sold of a firm's product. An approximation to marginal revenue is the change in total revenue divided by the change in quantity sold. We call this value *arc marginal revenue*.

marginal revenue product of an input: The rate of change of total revenue with respect to change in the variable input. The marginal revenue product of an input is equal to the marginal product of the input multiplied by the net marginal revenue.

marginal social benefit: The marginal private benefit of a good or service (usually measured by its price) plus any marginal external or third-party benefits.

marginal social cost: Marginal private cost plus marginal external cost.

market segmentation: See *price discrimination*.

market share curve: Shows the amounts the firm can actually sell at various prices as all firms in the industry adjust price together.

markup pricing: A pricing technique whereby a certain percentage of cost of goods sold or of price is added to cost of goods sold, in order to obtain the market price.

microeconomics: The study of individual economic units such as consumers, business firms, or specific government agencies.

monopolistic competition: A market structure characterized by the existence of many firms in the industry (but with an element of product differentiation so that each firm has some control over price) and by free entry into and exit from the industry.

monopoly: A market structure characterized by the existence of only one firm in the industry. For a firm to retain monopoly control, there must be complete barriers to entry into and exit from the industry.

monopsonistic competition: A market with many buyers of a differentiated product.

N

natural monopoly: An industry where the existence of only one firm is a matter of public convenience and allows for the maximum benefits of economies of scale.

net cash flow: Any increase in revenues brought about by the project less any increase in operating expenses and depreciation, multiplied by $(1 - T)$, where T is the firm's marginal income tax rate. The incremental depreciation associated with the project is then added to the preceding sum.

net exports: Value of newly produced U.S. goods and services purchases by foreigners (exports) less the value of newly produced foreign goods purchased by the United States (imports).

net marginal revenue: Marginal revenue from the sale of a firm's final product *minus* a specific portion of marginal production cost. In the case of transfer pricing, the portion of marginal production cost that is deducted from MR to obtain final product net marginal revenue (NMR_F) is the marginal cost of the final division, not including the cost of the transfer product. In determining the optimal amount of a variable input, net marginal revenue is defined as marginal revenue minus marginal cost of components.

net present value (NPV): The present value of the net cash inflows minus the present value of the cost outlays of an investment. An investment project is acceptable if its *NPV* is greater than or equal to zero.

net social benefit: The total social benefit less the total social cost of an activity.

normal good: A product or service with a positive income elasticity of demand.

O

oligopoly: A market structure characterized by the existence of a few dominant firms in an industry (each of which recognize their mutual interdependence) and by substantial barriers to entry into the industry.

oligopsony: A market with a few buyers, or a few dominant buyers.

P

perfect competition: A market structure in which (a) the firm takes market price as given, since an individual firm produces only a small fraction of total industry output; (b) the products of all firms are undifferentiated; (c) there is freedom of entry into or exit from the industry; (d) there are no artificial interferences with the activities of buyers and sellers; and (e) all buyers and sellers have perfect knowledge of market conditions.

present value: The value today of a stream of receipts to be received in the future. Present value is obtained by discounting the stream of receipts using an appropriate discount rate.

price discrimination: The practice of charging different prices for the same product, either by offering buyers lower prices on marginal or incremental quantities purchased or by dividing groups of buyers into separate markets. The latter is also known as *market segmentation.*

price elasticity of demand: A measure of the relative responsiveness of quantity demanded of a product to a change in its price. The price elasticity of demand indicates how total revenue will change as a result of a change in price.

price fixing: The practice of a group of firms agreeing to set the price of a product at a specific level.

price leadership: Occurs when a firm in an oligopoly sets a price that subsequently determines what other members of the industry will charge for their products.

principal-agent problem: This occurs when one party is entrusted with making a decision on behalf of another party in a setting where the goals of the two may differ.

private costs of a firm: The sum of the explicit and implicit costs that the firm incurs.

product differentiation: A wide variety of activities, such as design changes and advertising, that rival firms employ to attract customers by distinguishing their product from competitors' products.

production function: A mathematical statement of the way that the quantity of output of a product depends on the quantities used of various inputs or resources.

profit maximization: Making the greatest economic profit possible.

profit-maximizing rule: Produce up to the point where marginal revenue is equal to marginal cost and at higher output levels marginal revenue is less than marginal cost, as long as price is greater than or equal to average variable cost in the short run or long-run average cost in the long run. Also known as *loss-minimizing rule.*

pure public good: A product or service that is indivisible and nonexcludable.

R

returns to scale: Refers to how output changes when all inputs are increased by the same multiple (e.g., doubled or tripled).

ridge lines: The lines connecting the points where the marginal product of an input is equal to zero (one line for each input) in the isoquant map and forming the boundary for the economic region of production.

risk averse investor: An investor who, given a choice between two investments with the same expected return, will always prefer the less risky one.

risk neutral investor: An investor who is indifferent between two investments with the same expected return, regardless of their risk.

risk seeker: An investor who, given a choice between two investments with the same expected return, will always prefer the riskier one.

S

seasonal factors: Factors connected with a specific season of the year.

second-degree price discrimination: The practice of charging successively lower prices for block-type increases in quantity purchased.

semivariable costs: Costs that are fixed over some ranges of output and variable over others.

short run: A time period sufficiently short that at least one input is fixed.

short-run average total cost: The cost per unit of output in the short run. Equal to short-run total cost divided by the level of output. Also equal to average fixed cost plus short-run average variable cost for each level of output.

short-run average variable cost: The variable cost per unit of output produced in the short run. Equal to short-run total variable cost divided by the level of output.

short-run marginal cost: The rate of change of *either* short-run total cost or short-run total variable cost as the level of output changes in the short run.

short-run total cost: All of the private economic costs of the firm in the short run. Equal to total fixed cost plus short-run total variable cost.

short-run total variable cost: The sum of all private economic costs of the firm that vary with its level of output in the short run.

social costs of a firm: The private costs that society in general incurs because of a firm's activities. Social costs include private costs plus any additional costs that the firm imposes on society but for which it does not pay.

social rate of discount: The rate of discount appropriate for evaluating public sector projects.

substitute goods: Products or services that can be substituted for one another and that have a positive cross price elasticity of demand.

T

third-degree price discrimination: The practice of dividing groups of consumers into separate markets and charging a different price in each market.

time series data: Observations of a specific variable over a number of time periods.

tort law: Laws that deal with injuries sustained by private parties as a result of nonperformance of a duty created by law.

total fixed cost: Total dollar amount of costs that do not vary with the level of output.

total product function (of a variable input): Indicates the maximum output that can be obtained from different amounts of one variable input, while all other inputs are kept fixed.

total profit: Total revenue minus total costs, including opportunity costs. Also known as *economic profit*.

total revenue: Total dollar sales volume of a firm, which is equal to price times quantity sold.

trend analysis: A forecasting technique that relies primarily on historical data to predict the future.

trend factors: Factors related to movements in economic variables over time.

two-part pricing: A strategy that divides the amount a consumer pays for a good or service into an access fee and a price per unit.

tying agreement: Occurs when a firm agrees that goods sold or leased will be used only with other goods of the seller or lessor.

V

variable costs: Those costs that vary with the level of a firm's output.

variance: One measure of the dispersion about the expected value or mean of a set of data or possible outcomes of a project.

INDEX

Windows® Small Business Server 2008

Administrator's Companion

Charlie Russel
Sharon Crawford

PUBLISHED BY
Microsoft Press
A Division of Microsoft Corporation
One Microsoft Way
Redmond, Washington 98052-6399

Library of Congress Control Number: 2008940535

Printed and bound in the United States of America.

1 2 3 4 5 6 7 8 9   QWT   4 3 2 1 0 9

Distributed in Canada by H.B. Fenn and Company Ltd.

A CIP catalogue record for this book is available from the British Library.

Microsoft Press books are available through booksellers and distributors worldwide. For further information about international editions, contact your local Microsoft Corporation office or contact Microsoft Press International directly at fax (425) 936-7329. Visit our Web site at www.microsoft.com/mspress. Send comments to mspinput@microsoft.com.

Microsoft, Microsoft Press, Active Directory, ActiveSync, ActiveX, Aero, ClearType, Excel, Hyper-V, Internet Explorer, MS, MSDN, MS-DOS, MSN, Outlook, PowerPoint, SharePoint, Silverlight, Visio, Visual SourceSafe, Win32, Windows, Windows NT, Windows PowerShell, Windows Server, and Windows Vista are either registered trademarks or trademarks of the Microsoft group of companies. Other product and company names mentioned herein may be the trademarks of their respective owners.

The example companies, organizations, products, domain names, e-mail addresses, logos, people, places, and events depicted herein are fictitious. No association with any real company, organization, product, domain name, e-mail address, logo, person, place, or event is intended or should be inferred.

This book expresses the author's views and opinions. The information contained in this book is provided without any express, statutory, or implied warranties. Neither the authors, Microsoft Corporation, nor its resellers, or distributors will be held liable for any damages caused or alleged to be caused either directly or indirectly by this book.

Acquisitions Editor: Martin DelRe
Developmental Editor: Karen Szall
Project Editor: Melissa von Tschudi-Sutton
Editorial Production: Custom Editorial Productions, Inc.
Technical Reviewer: Randall Galloway; Technical Review services provided by Content Master,
                 a member of CM Group, Ltd.
Cover: Tom Draper Design

Body Part No. X15-25192

For Denise and David

Loss and possession, death and life are one,
There falls no shadow where there shines no sun.

—Hɪʟᴀɪʀᴇ Bᴇʟʟᴏᴄ

Contents at a Glance

Contents

What do you think of this book? We want to hear from you!

Microsoft is interested in hearing your feedback so we can continually improve our
books and learning resources for you. To participate in a brief online survey, please visit:

www.microsoft.com/learning/booksurvey/

What do you think of this book? We want to hear from you!

Microsoft is interested in hearing your feedback so we can continually improve our books and learning resources for you. To participate in a brief online survey, please visit:

www.microsoft.com/learning/booksurvey/

Acknowledgments

I t is simply impossible to research and write a book of this breadth and length without help, and we've been particularly fortunate in the help we've received.

First, Roger Benes of Microsoft Canada played a crucial and very much appreciated role in helping to make critical connections for us. Plus he's a good and valued friend. Also from Microsoft Canada, we're indebted to Mark Dikinson who took that connection to the next step, and to Sasha Krsmanvic, Charlie's super MVP Lead, for always being there when we really needed an answer.

Building and running the kind of hardware it takes to do a book like this is a challenge, even with the ability to virtualize. Hewlett-Packard Canada generously lent us an excellent ML350G5 server to use while writing this book. It's both powerful and quiet, making it perfect for an SBS server (especially the quiet part since so often our servers share space with people). We're indebted to Gordon Pellose and Alan Rogers at HP Canada, and Sharon Fernandez and David Chin of Hill & Knowleton, HP's public relations firm in Canada.

We also had the use of another excellent Hewlett-Packard server, a rack-mount DL380G5, thanks to Greg Rankich of Xtreme Consulting Group, Inc. and Dan Cox of Hewlett-Packard USA—a great help to us and much appreciated.

All the screen captures in this book were made using HyperSnap from Hyperionics. Capturing screens in Server Core was a special challenge, but Greg Kochiniak of Hyperionics created a special build of HyperSnap for us just for Server Core. Now *that's* customer support!

The Microsoft SBS MVPs, and SBS Family MVPs, give unstintingly of their expertise and skills to the entire community. When we had questions, they had answers! A special thanks to SBS MVP Andy Goodman for a key answer at a critical time. And, of course, to the SBS Diva, Susan Bradley, who read every word of this book and provided important feedback

We also got regular and consistent support and help from the SBS Product team. They are one of the most dedicated and community-focused product teams we've ever had the pleasure to work with, and we really appreciate their help and support. Nicholas King also provided key answers around virtualization support, and Kevin Beares, the Community Lead for SBS amongst his many other roles, was instrumental as well.

Over the years, we've worked with many different publishers, but none have been as dedicated and professional and just a pleasure to work with as Microsoft Press. It starts with Martin DelRe, whom we've known and worked with for many years now. Thank you, Martin, you're a true professional. Our project editor this time was again Melissa von Tschudi-Sutton, who has been a pleasure to work with throughout this long process. We deeply appreciate her enthusiasm, feedback, editorial insights, and patience. And especially her ability to act appreciative and totally unsurprised when we manage to meet a deadline.

Randall Galloway was our technical editor, and we much valued his efforts and comments throughout the process. Our indexer at Hyde Park Publishing Services and desktop publisher at Custom Editorial Productions did an excellent and much appreciated job. The editorial team of Megan Smith-Creed and Becka McKay performed a meticulous and sensitive edit for which we're very grateful. And last but absolutely not the least, the production and support people at Microsoft Press without whom this book would not exist. It is a pleasure to work with a team of professionals of this caliber. Thank you.

As always, we thank the people from past collaborations whose contributions to everything we write can't be overstated: Rudolph S. Langer and David J. Clark.

Introduction

If you run a small business with between 5 and 75 personal computers (PCs), you don't need us to tell you that the highly competitive marketplace, economic cycles, time pressures, and technological demands are constantly exerting pressure on your bottom line.

Your business needs the same technologies that large companies need. You need the ability to share information with customers, partners, and employees. You have the same worries about spam, malware, and security. And you have the same need to manage resources and employee access to those resources. The major difference is that small businesses usually have to cope without an in-house IT staff.

Windows Small Business Server 2008 allows small businesses to operate at the same technology level as much larger organizations, but without the added costs of maintaining a network administration department.

Windows Small Business Server 2008 Administrator's Companion is a reference, assistant, and coach for the busy network administrator, whether the administrator is on the scene or accessing the network from another location.

How to Use This Book

Even though Windows Small Business Server 2008 has automated many, many of the tasks associated with configuring and securing a network, this book is required when you want to do something slightly out of the ordinary—or when you need additional understanding of what a wizard is doing. Look for the following book elements:

 Under the Hood   Because wizards are so efficient at what they do, it can be very difficult to know what's going on in the background. Sidebars titled "Under the Hood" describe the technical operations being performed by the wizard. These sidebars also include methodological information to help you understand Windows Small Business Server.

 Real World   Everyone can benefit from the experiences of others. "Real World" sidebars contain elaboration on a particular theme or background based on the adventures of other users of Windows Small Business Server.

> **NOTE**   Notes include tips as wells as alternate ways to perform a task or some information that needs to be highlighted

IMPORTANT Boxes marked Important shouldn't be skipped. (That's why they're called Important.) Here you'll find security notes, cautions, and warnings to keep you and your network out of trouble.

MORE INFO We use these boxes to point you to a recommended resource for additional information on key topics.

 ON THE COMPANION MEDIA These notes refer to scripts and other information found on the CD included as part of the book.

 SECURITY ALERT Nothing is more important than security when it comes to a computer network. Security elements should be carefully noted and acted on.

BEST PRACTICES Best practices provide advice we have gained from our own technical experience.

PLANNING As we stress throughout the book, proper planning is fundamental to the smooth operation of any network. These boxes contain specific and useful hints to make that process go smoothly.

What's In This Book

Windows Small Business Server 2008 Administrator's Companion is divided into seven parts. The first four roughly correspond to the developmental phases of a Windows Small Business Server network. Part 5 deals with Premium Edition features and Part 6 covers maintenance and troubleshooting. The last part is made up of appendices with helpful information.

Part I: Preparation and Planning

Planning and preparation are the *sine qua non* for any kind of network. It comes down to the old saying, "If you don't have the time to do it right, how will you find the time to do it over?" Chapters 1 through 4 are all about doing it right the first time.

Part II: Installation and Setup

Chapters 5 through 8 take you through the process of installing Windows Small Business Server and performing initial configurations using the Getting Started Tasks. This section includes helpful chapters on configuring Windows SBS virtualization and migrating from Windows SBS 2003.

Part III: Performing Basic Tasks

The chapters in this part cover the day-to-day tasks of running a network: configuring disks, setting up user accounts, arranging the sharing of information among users, adding and removing computers and printers, managing software updates, and backing up and restoring data.

Part IV: Performing Advanced Tasks

Chapters 17 through 22 provide insight and information about managing e-mail, connectivity technologies, and using Group Policy. In this part, you'll also find chapters about setting up and managing a Microsoft Office SharePoint site.

Part V: Premium Edition Features

Chapters 23 through 25 address features found the in Windows SBS 2008 Premium Edition. These chapters are about installing a second server, installing Microsoft SQL Server, and adding Terminal Services to your network.

Part VI: Maintenance and Troubleshooting

Chapter 26 covers the extensive library of monitoring tools in Windows Small Business Server. Chapter 27 is all about how to save your business, your network, and yourself in the face of the many varieties of disaster that can afflict networks.

Appendices

The appendices include an introduction to networking, instructions for automating installation, and a list of resources for the users of Windows SBS 2008.

System Requirements

The following are the minimum system requirements to run the companion CD provided with this book:

- Microsoft Windows XP, with at least Service Pack 2 installed and the latest updates installed from Microsoft Update Service
- CD-ROM drive
- Internet connection

- Display monitor capable of 1024 x 768 resolution
- Microsoft Mouse or compatible pointing device
- Adobe Reader for viewing the eBook (Adobe Reader is available as a download at *http://www.adobe.com.*)

DIGITAL CONTENT FOR DIGITAL BOOK READERS   If you bought a digital-only edition of this book, you can enjoy select content from the print edition's companion CD. Visit *http://go.microsoft.com/fwlink/?LinkId=133803* to get your downloadable content. This content is always up-to-date and available to all readers.

Talk to Us!

We've done our best to make this book as accurate and complete as a single-volume reference can be. However, Windows Small Business Server 2008 is large and we are but human, so we're sure that alert readers will find omissions and even errors (though we fervently hope not too many of those). If you have suggestions, corrections, or tips, please write and let us know at SBS2008@scribes.com. We really do appreciate hearing from you.

Support for This Book

Every effort has been made to ensure the accuracy of this book and companion content. Microsoft Press provides corrections for books through the Web at *http://www.microsoft.com/mspress/support/search.aspx*.

To connect directly to Microsoft Help and Support to enter a query regarding a question or issue you may have, go to *http://support.microsoft.com*.

If you have comments, questions, or ideas regarding the book or companion content or if you have questions that are not answered by querying the Knowledge Base, please send them to Microsoft Press using either of the following methods:

E-mail: *mspinput@microsoft.com*

Postal mail:
Microsoft Press
Attn: *Windows Small Business Server 2008 Administrator's Companion* editor
One Microsoft Way
Redmond, WA 98052-6399

Please note that product support is not offered through the preceding mail addresses. For support information, please visit the Microsoft Product Support Web site at *http://support.microsoft.com*.

## CHAPTER 1

Introducing Windows Small Business Server 2008

Only a few decades ago, all you needed to run your small business were the tools of whatever your business actually was, plus a couple of adding machines, a cash drawer, and some hand-written ledgers. Most of us now would view a business of the 1950s or 1960s as being so quaint as to be positively Dickensian.

Today, even the smallest business needs e-mail and a Web site. Businesses need business applications—spreadsheets, databases, and word processing—that work together. Businesses large and small need to be able to share resources—printers, fax machines, Internet access—on networks that are stable, reliable, and above all, secure.

This latest iteration of Windows Small Business Server provides all the above and a good deal more in an all-in-one package. Its combination of technologies allows a small business to have the efficiencies of a much larger operation. And as your business grows, Small Business Server allows you to easily add users, servers, and applications, or expand into other Microsoft technologies.

Windows Small Business Server Editions

Windows SBS 2008 is available in two editions: standard and premium. Both editions are based on the Windows Server code base and include Microsoft Exchange Server mail server, Internet Information Services (IIS) Web server, Routing and Remote Access Service (RRAS), Windows SharePoint Services for collaboration, Windows Server Update Services for update management across the network, and a fax server.

The premium edition adds the standard edition of Microsoft SQL Server 2008 (32-bit or 64-bit) and a license for the standard edition of Windows Server 2008 (32-bit or 64-bit) for running a second server.

> **IMPORTANT** Windows SBS Server is available only for the x86-64 (64-bit) architecture. This is to fit the requirements of Exchange Server 2007, which is 64-bit only.

Standard Edition

If you already have an earlier edition of Windows Small Business Server, you know it's an excellent solution to many of the problems faced by smaller businesses. It provides a high level of protection for your business information, improves productivity, and is affordable.

Newest Server Technology

Probably the best new "feature" in Windows SBS 2008 is that it's built on Windows Server 2008. You get all the advantages of Windows Server 2008—high levels of security and control over your network, sophisticated report and management tools, enhanced access to e-mail, the Internet, and business applications—all in a single, integrated, low-maintenance package.

64-Bit Architecture

The major shift for Windows SBS Server from 2003 to 2008 is from 32-bit architecture to 64-bit. When Exchange Server 2007 was released in a 64-bit version only, the shift was inevitable. It's also a desirable shift. 32-bit Windows was rapidly coming up against its own limitations.

A 32-bit operating system is limited to 4 gigabytes (GB) of RAM (random access memory). A 64-bit operating system can have up to 32 GB of RAM. That in and of itself is a significant difference. But the real difference is in the area of address space. Vastly increased amounts of address space help minimize the time spent swapping processes in and out of memory by storing more of those processes in RAM rather than on the hard disk. This, in turn, can increase overall program performance.

A 32-bit computer works very well for most programs, however. For example, spreadsheet programs, Web browsers, and word-processing programs will run at about the same speed on either a 32-bit or a 64-bit computer. However, when you're running a server and hosting multiple clients, a mail server, and shared applications and files, a 64-bit computer is much preferred.

For more on how 64-bit architecture works, see Chapter 2, "Understanding 64-Bit Windows."

UNDER THE HOOD   Understanding Address Space

Computer CPUs are designed so that the address (location) of any particular piece of data in virtual memory is tracked by a single integer register. Thus the total amount of data the computer can keep in its working field depends on the width of these registers.

Early in the development of personal computers, a consensus arose that 32 bits was an optimal register size. This would enable 232 addresses (4 GB) to be referenced. At a time when computers had only a few megabytes (MB) of memory, a memory address limit of 4 GB was considered large enough to assign a unique address to almost anything countable.

However, over time memory became less expensive and computers with 2 GB of RAM (for example) are far from uncommon. The need for additional address space can become pressing. Switching to a 64-bit register increases the available address space to approximately 16 terabytes (16,000 GB). Half of the address space is reserved for the operating system and half for applications.

Greater Security and Data Protection

Windows SBS 2008 comes with built-in antivirus and anti-spam with 120-day trial subscriptions to Microsoft Forefront Security for Exchange Server and Windows Live OneCare for Server.

SBS Console

When you install Windows SBS 2008, you'll immediately notice that the interface is more polished and accessible. Part of that is the new SBS Console (Figure 1-1), a central organizational point from which you can perform many administrative tasks associated with Windows SBS.

NOTE A shortcut to the console is automatically placed on the server desktop.

From Users And Groups at the top of the console window, you can add users and groups (Figure 1-2) as well as configure these objects.

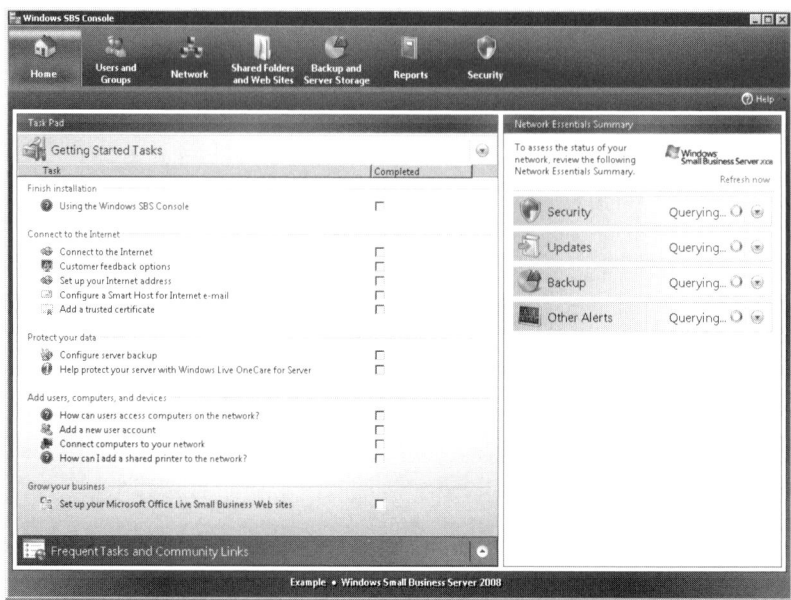

FIGURE 1-1 The Windows SBS Console

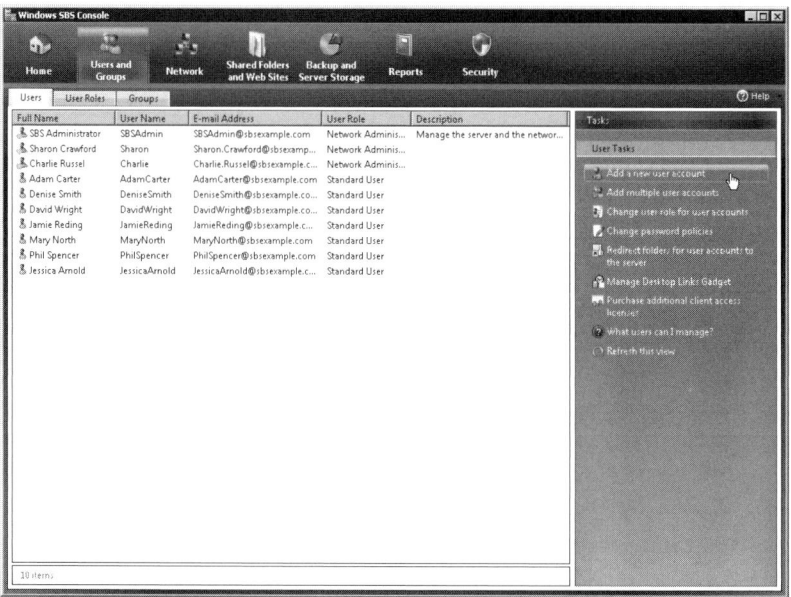

FIGURE 1-2 Users and groups in the SBS Console

Similarly, click Network to add or remove computers, manage devices such as printers, and configure your Internet connection and other networking features (Figure 1-3).

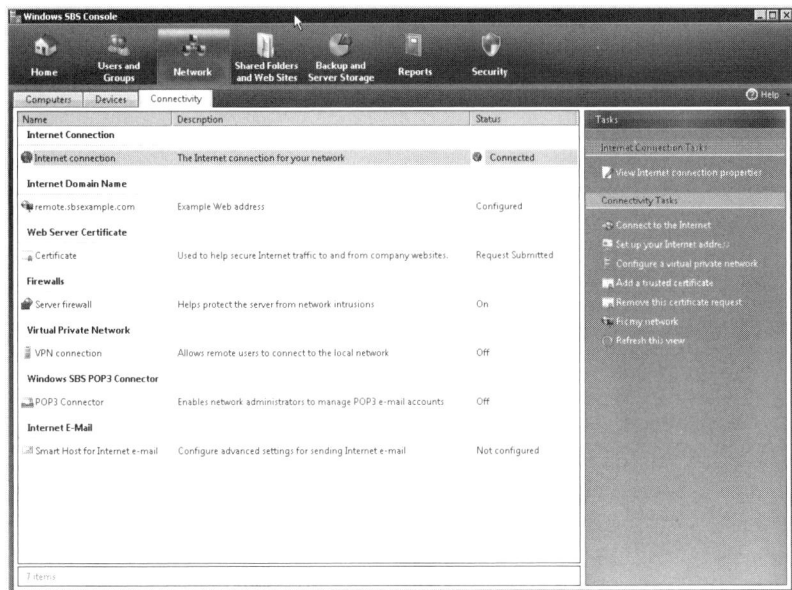

FIGURE 1-3 The SBS Console Network section

Other areas of the console connect you to the tools for shared folders, backup, report generation, and security. Chapter 17, "Windows SBS Console versus Server Manager," provides more information on the use of SBS Console.

Remote Web Workplace

Native to Windows SBS, Remote Web Workplace allows users to remotely access their e-mail, the desktop of computers they're authorized to use, and shared applications. A streamlined, customizable Remote Web Workplace is integrated with Windows SharePoint Services 3.0, including support for Windows mobile devices.

A user who logs on to Remote Web Workplace sees a home page (shown in Figure 1-4) that provides easy access to e-mail, your internal Web site, and whichever computers you've authorized.

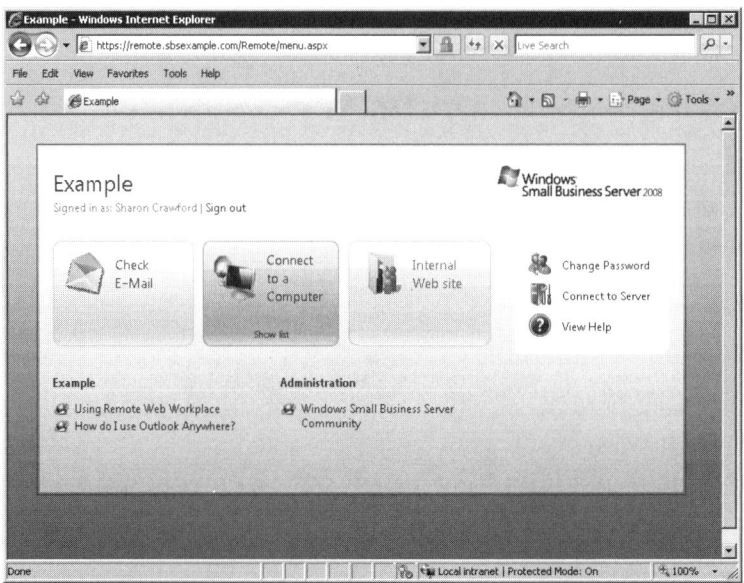

FIGURE 1-4 The home page for Remote Web Workplace

Chapter 14, "Managing Computers on the Network," includes information on how to configure and use Remote Web Workplace.

SharePoint Services

SharePoint is a browser-based collaboration and document-management platform included in Windows SBS 2008. SharePoint sites take file storage to a new level, providing meeting points for team collaboration and allowing users to collaborate on documents, tasks, and events.

SharePoint doesn't replace an entire file server (it imposes, for example, a file-size limitation of 5 GB), but it does provide a way for users to collaborate on tasks, documents, and events while sharing contacts and other information.

Deploying and using SharePoint Services is covered in Chapter 22, "Customizing a Share-Point Web Site."

Backup

The new Windows Server backup incorporates faster backup technology and simplifies data or operating system restoration. Information on configuring and running backup is found in Chapter 16, "Configuring Backup."

Premium Edition

The premium edition has all the features of the standard edition plus a license for the standard edition of Windows Server 2008 (32-bit or 64-bit) to run a second server, and the standard edition of SQL Server 2008 (32-bit or 64-bit).

Having a second server running Windows Server 2008 adds all sorts of capabilities to your SBS network, as described in the next sections.

Virtualization

Underutilization of servers is much more common than you might think. If you deploy a second server, you may be using perhaps 10 or 20 percent of the server's capabilities. The rest, though bought and paid for, remains idle. Being able to virtualize numerous servers on a single computer is an easy way to maximize a server's utility while reducing management and administrative costs.

Multiple operating systems—Windows, Linux, and others—can be deployed in parallel on a second server using Hyper-V.

You need the premium edition that includes the Windows Server 2008 license to install the Hyper-V role for virtualization on a second server. For more on how to use virtualization, see Chapter 6, "Configuring SBS in Hyper-V."

SQL Server 2008

Got a line-of-business application that needs a database server? SQL Server 2008 is part of the premium edition and has downgrade rights to SQL Server 2005, if your application requires that version.

> **NOTE** Users of SQL Server will require premium Client Access Licenses, which are more expensive than regular CALs.

SQL Server 2008 is much more than a traditional relational database management system. It includes features that make it applicable for large data warehouses as well as ad hoc departmental databases. It includes enhanced support for XML, spatial data, transparent data encryption, and policy-based management.

Chapter 24, "Installing SQL Server 2007," includes information on installing and configuring SQL Server 2008.

Terminal Services

With the addition of a second server, you can add Terminal Services (TS) RemoteApp and TS Web Access. TS RemoteApp allows users to access remote applications with just one click. The application then runs completely transparently as if it were installed on the user's local computer. TS Web Access allows the configuration of a Web page from which users can access remote desktops as well as remote applications.

All the details of using Terminal Services are found in Chapter 25, "Adding a Terminal Server."

Hardware Requirements

The hardware requirements for Windows SBS Server are detailed in Tables 1-1 and 1-2. Bear in mind that actual requirements can vary based on your system configuration and the applications and features you need to use. Processor performance is dependent not only on the clock frequency of the processor, but also on the number of cores and the size of the processor cache.

As always, disk space requirements for the system partition are approximate. Additional available hard disk space may be required if you are installing over a network.

TABLE 1-1 Hardware Requirements for Windows Small Business Server 2008 Standard Edition

HARDWARE		MINIMAL	OPTIMAL	MAXIMUM
Processor	Type	x64 (AMD64 or Intel EM64T)	x64 (AMD64 or Intel EM64T)	x64 (AMD64 or Intel EM64T)
	Number	1	2	4
	Cores	1	2–4	16 (current)
RAM		4 GB	6–8 GB	32 GB
Disk	System	60 GB	80 GB	2 terabytes
	Data		512 GB	256 terabytes (64K clusters)
NIC		10/100 Ethernet adapter	GbE	GbE or any Windows Server 2008–supported network interface
DVD		Yes	Yes	Yes
Video		1024 × 768	1024 × 768 or higher	1024 × 768 or higher
Keyboard/Mouse		Yes	Yes	Yes
External Disks (for backup)		USB or eSATA	USB or eSATA	USB or eSATA
Modem		Required for fax services	Required for fax services	Required for fax services

TABLE 1-2 Hardware Requirements for Windows Small Business Server 2008 Premium Edition Second Server

HARDWARE		MINIMAL	OPTIMAL	MAXIMUM
Processor	Type	32-bit or x64	32-bit or x64	32-bit or x64
	Number	1	2	4
	Cores	1	2–4	16 (current)
RAM		2 GB	6–8 GB (x64) or 4 GB (32-bit)	32 GB (x64) or 4 GB (32-bit)
Disk	System	10 GB	40 GB	2 terabytes
	Data		512 GB	256 terabytes (64 KB clusters)
NIC		10/100 Ethernet adapter	GbE	GbE or any Windows Server 2008–supported network interface
DVD		Yes	Yes	Yes
Video		1024 × 768	1024 × 768 or higher	1024 × 768 or higher
Keyboard/Mouse		Yes	Yes	Yes

Restrictions on Windows SBS 2008

Because Windows Small Business Server is designed for smaller organizations—and because of its bargain price—you will face specific limits when working with the package. These limits are not recommendations—they're boundaries that can't be transcended.

- Windows Small Business Server is limited to 75 users.
- Only one computer in a domain can be running Windows Small Business Server.
- Windows Small Business Server must be the root of the Active Directory forest.
- Windows Small Business Server cannot trust any other domains. It cannot have any child domains.

IMPORTANT Each edition of Windows SBS Server 2008 comes with five Client Access Licenses (CALs). If you have the premium edition, you can buy additional standard or premium CALs. If you have the standard edition, you can purchase additional standard CALs. A change with this version of Windows SBS Server is that you can purchase CALs individually or in groups, the size of which you determine.

Summary

This chapter is just a brief introduction to Windows SBS Server 2008. As you move on to specialized chapters, you'll learn the advantages of various features and how to best make use of them in your organization.

The next three chapters address planning and preparation. Of particular importance is the next chapter, "Understanding 64-Bit Windows," a subject that mystifies many but is made clear here.

Understanding 64-Bit Windows

Windows Small Business Server (SBS) 2008 is a complete architectural change from earlier versions of SBS—it is built on the 64-bit version of Windows Server 2008. This is a radical change for those who have only been using 32-bit Windows. Gone are the memory constraints inherent in 32-bit Windows, and with them some of the limitations inherent in SBS.

In this chapter, we'll cover some of the underlying reasons for the change to 64-bit, how it affects what you can (and can't) do with Windows Small Business Server 2008, and how this change will also affect the clients on your SBS network.

⊕ *REAL WORLD*   **Overcoming the Fear Factor**

We've been running 64-bit Windows—first as Windows XP Professional x64 Edition and now the 64-bit versions of Windows Vista and Windows Server 2008—since early in 2005, and we have to admit, it was a bit of a struggle early on. Drivers were the biggest issue, because all drivers had to be rewritten for 64-bit. But careful selection of hardware solved that issue, and we were up and running.

What we quickly figured out was that pretty much all of our programs worked—just as we expected them to. They were just as fast (in some cases a bit faster), and the few things that didn't work were predictable and expected. But even more important was that Windows XP Professional x64 Edition looked, felt, and behaved just like our familiar 32-bit Windows XP Professional.

Oh, there were a few differences, but they were trivial compared to the similarities. Windows XP x64 just felt "right."

On the Windows Server side, the driver issues are pretty much long gone. It would be hard today to buy any server-class computer that doesn't support 64-bit Windows. Windows Small Business Server 2008 will work on virtually any server you buy today, with the obvious exception of one based on Intel's Itanium processor. Those servers are 64-bit, but have a completely different architecture and are entirely focused on the enterprise side of the server market.

Why the Change?

The first question most users ask about the move to 64-bit for Windows Small Business Server 2008 is "Why?" A simple answer is because Microsoft Exchange 2007 is available only on 64-bit Windows Server. But the real answer is a bit more complex.

Windows Small Business Server 2003, which is 32-bit only, runs adequately on current, 64-bit-capable server hardware. Our main server here is an HP ML350G5. It is fully 64-bit-capable but can also run 32-bit Windows Server, allowing us to install Windows Small Business Server 2003 R2 on it without issue. But if we did, we'd lose access to most of the 16 gigabytes (GB) of RAM we've installed on the server, because Windows Small Business Server 2003 supports only 4 GB of RAM. With 64-bit Windows Small Business Server 2008, we can see and use all 16 GB of RAM, and SBS 2008 will actually support 32 GB of RAM.

The limitations on RAM are especially important with SBS because we run so much on a single server. Even adding a second server to offload some of the burden still leaves many SBS 2003 servers with memory constrained. The move to 64-bit removes those constraints and allows us to use more powerful servers. Tables 2-1 and 2-2 compare the memory limits of 32-bit and 64-bit Windows Server.

TABLE 2-1 General Memory Limits

GENERAL MEMORY LIMITS	SBS 2003 (32-BIT)	32-BIT WINDOWS SERVER 2008	64-BIT WINDOWS SERVER 2008
Total virtual address space	4 GB	4 GB	16 terabytes
Virtual address space per 32-bit process	2 GB (3 GB if system is booted with /3GB switch, which is not recommended)	2 GB (3 GB if system is booted with /3GB switch)	4 GB if compiled with /LARGE-ADDRESSAWARE (2 GB otherwise)

GENERAL MEMORY LIMITS	SBS 2003 (32-BIT)	32-BIT WINDOWS SERVER 2008	64-BIT WINDOWS SERVER 2008
Virtual address space per 64-bit process	Not applicable	Not applicable	8 terabytes
Paged pool	47 MB	47 MB	128 GB
Non-paged pool	256 MB	256 MB	128 GB
System PTE	660 MB to 900 MB	660 MB to 900 MB	128 GB

TABLE 2-2 32-Bit versus 64-Bit Windows Server 2008 Versions

PHYSICAL MEMORY AND CPU LIMITS	32-BIT	64-BIT
Windows Server 2008 Standard	4 GB / 1 to 4 CPU sockets	32 GB / 1 to 4 CPU sockets
Windows Small Business Server 2008	Not applicable	32 GB / 1 to 4 CPU sockets
Windows Server 2008 Enterprise	64 GB / 1 to 8 CPU sockets	2 terabytes / 1 to 8 CPU sockets
Windows Server 2008 Datacenter	64 GB / 1 to 32 CPU sockets	2 terabytes / 1 to 64 CPU sockets

NOTE Microsoft counts CPUs according to the number of physical CPU sockets that are present—not according to the number of cores. With current processors that support four cores on a single CPU, Windows Small Business Server 2008 supports 16 cores.

Another consideration is that Windows Server 2008 is the last version of Windows Server that will support 32-bit. The limitations of the 32-bit architecture and memory model make the move to 64-bit compelling, and Microsoft has already announced that the current version of Windows Server 2008 will be the last 32-bit version of Windows.

What Are the Advantages?

Why the big push to 64-bit by Microsoft for their server operating systems? Is it just the memory limitations of 32-bit, or are there other, compelling reasons? In our opinion, there are four compelling reasons to use 64-bit for servers: memory, performance, security, and virtualization.

Memory

The 32-bit versions of Windows Server use a flat memory addressing scheme, limiting these versions to a 2^{32} address space. This means a virtual memory address space of only 4 GB, which is divided into 2 GB of virtual memory address space for the operating system and 2 GB of virtual memory address space for applications.

By contrast, 64-bit versions of Windows Server support 16 terabytes of virtual memory address space, divided equally between that reserved for the operating system and that available to applications.

The actual RAM supported by various versions of Windows Server is related to, but somewhat different from, the actual memory address space. Enterprise and Datacenter editions of 32-bit Windows Server use a technique called *Physical Address Extension* (PAE) to support larger RAM configurations. PAE uses a memory address window within the 4 GB of the 32-bit address space to swap in segments of memory located at addresses beyond 4 GB. This is less efficient than a flat memory address model, obviously, but is the only solution to supporting RAM configurations of more than 4 GB with 32-bit Windows.

The 64-bit versions of Windows Server support different amounts of RAM, but the differentiation is a marketing difference, not a technology difference. The 64-bit versions of Windows Server 2008 Standard (and Windows Small Business Server 2008 that runs on Standard) support 32 GB of RAM, while the Enterprise and Datacenter versions support 2 terabytes of RAM. But all of them have the same 16 terabytes of virtual memory address space.

Performance

The performance and efficiency of 64-bit Windows also benefits from an improved overall I/O efficiency and throughput. With support for greater physical memory and memory address space, caches can be substantially larger than in 32-bit Windows, enabling Windows Small Business Server 2008 to fully utilize the improved I/O hardware available, such as PCI Express and PCI-X 266, to improve overall I/O performance. The larger address space allows more I/O to be in progress simultaneously. Even 32-bit applications can benefit from this improvement, especially those that need to use the /3GB switch. When using the /3GB switch, Windows is forced into a constrained address space, limiting the amount of non-paged pool available. This can cause non-paged pool to be exhausted when there are several I/O requests outstanding

 UNDER THE HOOD   Registers

Processors have many ways to store information that applications will need, but each storage location has a cost associated with retrieving that information. The fastest and lowest cost locations are local registers on the processor. These are fast, local slots where applications (and the operating system) can store values that will be needed shortly. Data stored in registers is available for reuse at full processor speeds and is faster than even cached data in an on-chip cache. 32-bit x86 processors have a mere eight general-purpose registers, making them significantly register-poor as compared to Reduced Instruction Set Computing (RISC) processors. Worse, because the x87 floating-point architecture is stack-oriented, floating-point arithmetic instructions require at least one of the operands to be on top of the stack. This leads to further inefficiencies and relatively poor floating-point performance.

The x64 architecture addresses this by doubling the number and size of the registers available. Although 32-bit x86 processors are limited to eight 32-bit general-purpose registers, eight floating-point registers, and eight Streaming Single Instruction-Stream, Multiple Data-Stream (SIMD) Extensions (SSE) or SSE2 registers, the 64-bit x64 architecture has sixteen 64-bit wide general-purpose registers and sixteen 128-bit wide SSE/SSE2 registers.

Another improvement in 64-bit Windows Server is a faster I/O subsystem. There are a couple of reasons for this. First, the operating system is no longer constrained by the limited address space available to it in 32-bit Windows. This limitation can become especially important for server functions that create and release many connections, such as an active Web server. In 32-bit Windows, this can lead to fragmentation of the address space used by Windows and the eventual slowing down of the server, or an inability of the server to accept additional connections. With 64-bit Windows, this address space is far larger, allowing the Web server to function at full speed.

Another way that the I/O subsystem benefits from 64-bit Windows is a wider data path, allowing faster disk reads and writes and faster memory access. Disk-intensive operations are significantly faster in 64-bit Windows.

Security

All 64-bit-capable processors include support for the hardware data execution protection (DEP) bit. DEP controls which areas of memory can be used to execute code, protecting against buffer overflows. This protection helps to prevent the kinds of attacks that led to the Code Red and the SQL Slammer worms, though good coding practices are equally important.

 UNDER THE HOOD **Buffer Overflows**

When an application buffer is stuffed with more data than it is designed to handle, the buffer spills the extra data into unexpected areas of memory, putting data where it wasn't supposed to be. This creates a buffer overflow. *Buffer overflow* is a generic term for exploits that load executable code into areas that are supposed to contain only data and then jump program execution into that code by overloading heaps, stacks, and other memory pools. For example, if your e-mail client is designed to handle attachments with a maximum of 255-character file-names, and you receive a message that has a filename with 256 characters, a buffer overflow can occur. When this happens, memory space adjacent to that filename buffer gets overwritten and malicious code can end up being executed with the privileges associated with the original program. The infamous MSBlaster worm was this type of exploit. The hardware DEP in x64 processors protects against this type of exploit.

This buffer overflow protection is combined with Microsoft's PatchGuard tech-nology, which prevents non-Microsoft-originated programs from patching the Windows kernel. This technology, available only on 64-bit Windows, prevents kernel mode drivers from extending or replacing kernel services, including system service dispatch tables, the interrupt descriptor table (IDT), and the global descriptor table (GDT). Third-party software is also prevented from allocating kernel stacks or patch-ing any part of the kernel.

In some ways, however, an even more important security feature of Windows Small Busi-ness Server 2008 (and all 64-bit versions of Windows Server 2008) is the requirement that every driver be signed to assure the authenticity of the driver provider. This won't prevent a badly written driver from causing problems, but it will ensure that when you download and install a driver, you know that it really is written by the company that claims to have written it. This helps to protect against an important and difficult-to-detect security loophole that could allow an unscrupulous virus or root kit author to provide an imitation of a commonly used driver that contained code that would let the author bypass Windows security.

 SECURITY ALERT Always know the source of any driver you install on any computer in your network. If you need a driver for an HP component, go directly to the HP site or to the Windows Update site to obtain the driver. Do not download from some third-party site. Signed drivers can help ensure that you are getting what you think you're getting, but they aren't required for the 32-bit computers on your network.

Virtualization

One of the most important features that is available only on 64-bit Windows is Hyper-V. Hyper-V is hypervisor-based native virtualization, available only on x64 versions of Windows Server 2008, which uses the hardware virtualization capabilities of the latest Intel and AMD processors to provide a robust, fast, and resource-conserving virtual environment.

Because Hyper-V is built into Windows Server 2008, it runs more efficiently and natively. A server running Hyper-V has multiple *partitions*, each running natively on the underlying hardware. The first partition is known as the *parent partition* and acts as the hardware and operating system control partition for all the other partitions where virtualized operating systems run. The other partitions are *child partitions*, each with its own operating system, running directly on the hypervisor layer. Windows Small Business Server 2008 can run as a child partition, but shouldn't be used for the parent partition. We'll cover virtualization and Windows Small Business Server 2008 in more detail in Chapter 6, "Configuring SBS in Hyper-V."

What Are the Challenges?

So is moving to 64-bit all good and wonderful? Or do special challenges need to be considered and dealt with to make the transition easier? Not surprisingly, the transition to 64-bit is not without some special concerns, including drivers, hardware, and software considerations.

Drivers

Every driver for Windows Small Business Server 2008 must be 64-bit and must be a signed driver. This means that before you buy a new 64-bit–capable server, you need to verify that the manufacturer fully supports 64-bit Windows Server 2008. If your environment includes other hardware, such as printers, that are directly controlled by SBS, you need to make sure that there are drivers available for that hardware. We'll cover how to configure SBS to support both 64-bit and 32-bit clients for your printers in Chapter 13, "Installing and Managing Printers." But if you're buying one or more printers for your SBS network, verify that they have drivers for 64-bit Windows Server 2008 available.

Hardware and Software Considerations

There are some general hardware considerations you should take into account when moving to Windows Small Business Server 2008, as well as some software considerations that are specific to 64-bit Windows in general. One consideration you don't have to worry about is whether you're running AMD or Intel processors. There is full binary compatibility between AMD's AMD64 and Intel's EM64T, allowing Windows Small Business Server 2008 to use the same binary whether the underlying processor is an AMD or an Intel processor.

Server-Grade Hardware

As we've mentioned earlier, you need to make sure that any hardware you use with your Windows Small Business Server 2008 network has the proper signed drivers available that support 64-bit Windows Server 2008. But more than that, it makes sense to go beyond the lower consumer-grade hardware, especially printers. Because you're sharing that printer across your entire network, having a better printer makes sound financial sense and also makes it easier to support. Many consumer-grade printers have no actual intelligence built into the printer, but are entirely dependent on the operating system to work. Server-grade (also referred to as business-grade) printers support a full printer control language in the printer itself, usually either PCL or PostScript. Having a server-grade printer removes many of the compatibility issues associated with printer drivers, because even if there isn't a perfect match for your printer, there will be one that is close.

> **NOTE** All-in-one printer/fax/scanner devices present a particular challenge in 64-bit Windows—very few of them have drivers that support all of their functionality. If you absolutely have to have this kind of device, you'll probably have better luck connecting it to a centrally located personal computer.

32-Bit Software Compatibility

Windows Small Business Server 2008 uses the Windows On Windows 64-bit (WOW64) subsystem to support 32-bit applications running on 64-bit Windows. The WOW64 subsystem provides a high-performance 32-bit Windows environment that supports existing 32-bit Windows applications. Because of the underlying hardware compatibility of the x64 architecture, 32-bit applications are able to run at full speed in the WOW64 subsystem. Because of the larger available memory address space and the greater efficiencies of the x64 processor architecture, many applications actually run faster in WOW64 than they do in 32-bit Windows.

WOW64 isolates 32-bit applications from 64-bit applications, but it provides for interoperability and data exchange across the boundary through COM and remote procedure call (RPC) and through transparent cut and paste. WOW64 runs 32-bit applications seamlessly while preventing file and registry collisions between 32-bit and 64-bit versions of an application.

An important WOW64 limitation is that 32-bit applications cannot load 64-bit DLLs and 64-bit applications cannot load 32-bit DLLs. This means that 32-bit ActiveX controls, for example, cannot be run in the 64-bit version of Internet Explorer, and this is why 32-bit and 64-bit versions of Internet Explorer are both included with all 64-bit versions of Windows. The 32-bit version is the default.

Another limitation is that 32-bit DLLs that provide context-sensitive menu extensions to Windows Explorer don't work. They must be rewritten to run natively in 64-bit.

Legacy Software in 64-Bit Windows

Running legacy software in 64-bit Windows has some special concerns. The vast majority of 32-bit software will work without issue in the WOW64 subsystem. The only real exceptions to this are applications that have specialized drivers, such as antivirus software, disk defragmentation utilities, and so on. These generally use special file system drivers. Check with your software vendor—many provide updated versions that work well with 64-bit Windows.

What won't work are 16-bit or MS-DOS applications. There is no support at all in any 64-bit version of Microsoft Windows for 16-bit applications. Nor is there any support for pure DOS applications. (This does not mean that all applications written to run from the command line won't work—just not older MS-DOS applications such as DOS Edit, or one of our favorites, Vern Berg's List.)

If you do need to run a legacy application that can't run in 64-bit Windows, creating a virtual machine running a 32-bit version of Windows that is used just for that application is a useful workaround. Or move the application to a workstation on your network.

What About Clients?

Windows Small Business Server 2008 provides full support for 64-bit Windows clients. That said, the need for 64-bit at the client level is still far less compelling than it is for servers. 32-bit Windows is quite adequate for the vast majority of desktop and laptop computers used in business today. The exceptions to this are development workstations, drawing and computer-aided design (CAD) workstations, or other specialized workstations used for memory-intensive applications that must be able to address greater than 4 GB of RAM.

The 64-bit business versions of Windows Vista and Windows XP both support up to 128 GB of RAM and two physical processors. If you have specialized needs for very large RAM workstations, 64-bit is definitely the way to go. But most users will find 32-bit Windows sufficient. Table 2-3 shows the support matrix for processors and RAM in Windows Vista and Windows XP.

TABLE 2-3 32-bit versus 64-bit Windows Clients

WINDOWS EDITION	MAXIMUM RAM		# OF CPU SOCKETS	
	32-bit	**64-bit**	**32-bit**	**64-bit**
XP Professional	4 GB	128 GB	2	2
XP Tablet PC Edition	4 GB	Not applicable	2	Not applicable
XP Media Center Edition (not supported in SBS network)	4 GB	Not applicable	1	Not applicable
Windows Vista Business	4 GB	128 GB	2	2
Windows Vista Enterprise (available only with Software Assurance)	4 GB	128 GB	2	2
Windows Vista Ultimate	4 GB	128 GB	2	2
Windows Vista Home Basic (not supported in SBS network)	4 GB	8 GB	1	1
Windows Vista Home Premium (not supported in SBS network)	4 GB	16 GB	1	1

Summary

In this chapter we've covered how 64-bit computing is different from the familiar 32-bit, as well as how it's really the same. We've highlighted some of the key reasons why Windows Small Business Server 2008 is available only as a 64-bit solution. The next chapter covers how to design and prepare a network prior to installing Windows Small Business Server. We also cover naming conventions, how to plan for adequate network security, and how to calculate the number and type of licenses you'll need.

CHAPTER 3

Planning Your SBS Network

Before you actually start installing Windows Small Business Server 2008, you should spend some time and thought planning what your network will look like. Time spent now, *before* you actually start installing anything, will save you time, energy, and complications later. By designing your network infrastructure, naming conventions, and network security before you actually implement them, you'll prevent having to modify or rebuild your network later.

Planning the Network Infrastructure

The first tasks in designing a network for your company are evaluating the computing needs of the organization, choosing an Internet connection method and local network type, and selecting network devices. You also need to choose server hardware as well as client hardware and software.

 UNDER THE HOOD   **Network Operating Systems**

On an ordinary PC, the role of the operating system is to manage the file system, handle the running of applications, manage the computer's memory, and control the input and output to attached devices such as cameras, printers, and scanners. A network operating system expands that role, managing the following:

- **Centralized security**

- **Remote file systems**

- **Running shared applications**

- **Input and output to shared network devices**

- **CPU scheduling of networked processes**

When multiple computers are connected in a *workgroup*, as shown in Figure 3-1, the result is called a *peer-to-peer network*: a network without a central server and with no network operating system.

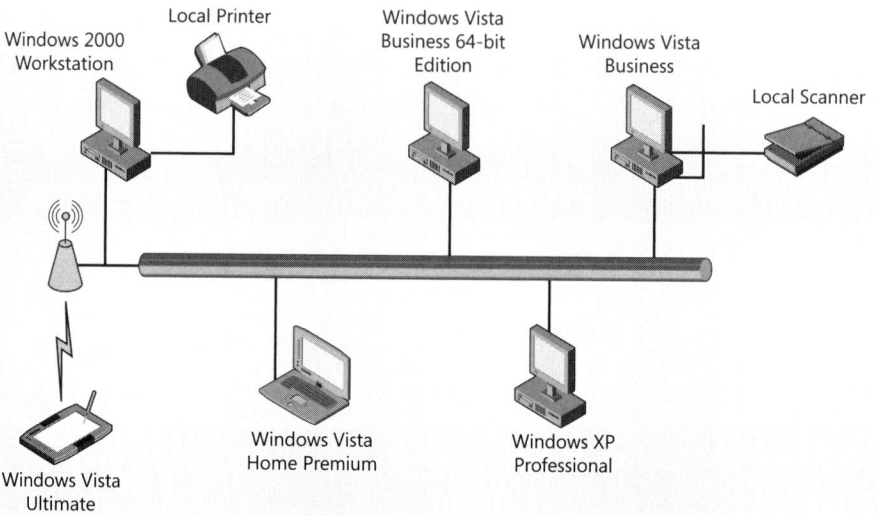

FIGURE 3-1 A peer-to-peer network, which has no central server or management

Adding one or more servers running Windows Server 2008, or Windows Small Business Server 2008, as shown in Figure 3-2, is a *client/server network*—one or more servers and multiple clients, all sharing a single security policy. The servers provide both the resources and the security policy for the network, and the clients are the computers that use the resources managed by the server.

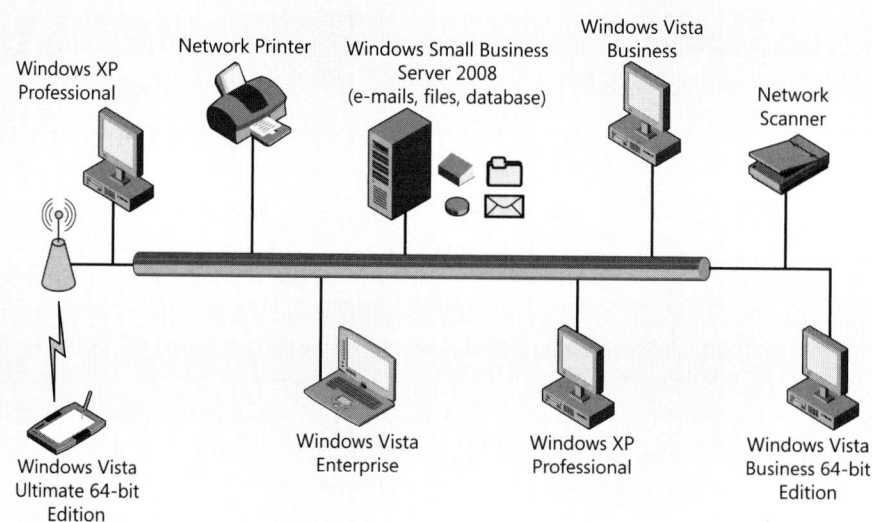

FIGURE 3-2 A client/server network, which has a central management and resource server

Servers Use Network Operating Systems

Because Windows Small Business Server has to supply services to as many as 75 users, and you're depending on it to run your business, a high-powered, robust operating system and highly reliable hardware are essential. When your users rely on a server to get their work done and keep your business running, you certainly don't want frequent failures—you don't even want to reboot!

In addition to supplying print, file, or other services, the network operating system has to provide network security. Different businesses and organizations have varying security needs, but *all* must have some level of data protection. Therefore, the system must offer a range of configurable security levels, from the relatively nonintrusive to the very stringent.

Clients Use Workstation Operating Systems

Like other computers, client computers on a network need an operating system. However, a client operating system doesn't need to manage the resources for other computers, or manage security for the network. Rebooting a workstation can be a pain for the user but doesn't usually disrupt anyone else's work.

On a Windows Small Business Server network, clients can run Microsoft Windows XP Professional (including Windows XP Tablet PC Edition and Windows XP Professional x64 Edition) and business editions of Windows Vista. However, for best performance and security, Windows XP SP3 or later, or Windows Vista SP1, should be deployed on clients.

Determining Your Needs

Before designing a network, decide which features of Windows Small Business Server 2008 your business needs; doing so helps ensure that the network design is dictated by business needs instead of by fancy technology. Key needs to consider include:

- Centralized user account management
- Centralized update management
- Web and e-mail access for employees
- File sharing and centralized file storage
- Database storage using Microsoft SQL Server
- Printer sharing
- Centralized backup
- Centralized fax server

- Remote access to the internal network via the Internet, including remote access directly to the user's desktop from the Web.
- Facilitation of group projects via a Windows SharePoint Services intranet or "team" Web site

You also must decide how important the following factors are, as well as what resources are available to support your choices:

- Performance
- Reliability
- Security

> **PLANNING**   Get a thorough idea of what kind of work will be done on the network, when and where it will be done, and by whom. For example, your organization might need to do payroll every other Friday, during which time the file server and printers are under a heavy load.

Choosing an Internet Connection

To choose an Internet connection method, you must balance an organization's bandwidth needs and budget against the available Internet connection methods. The following sections discuss how to do this, as well as how to choose an Internet service provider (ISP).

Determining Bandwidth Needs

First, determine the baseline level of bandwidth you require. You can then balance this against the organization's budget and performance goals. Allow for 100 kilobits per second (Kbps) of download bandwidth and 50 Kbps of upload bandwidth for each simultaneous user of e-mail and the Web. If remote access via Virtual Private Network (VPN) is important, allow for a minimum of 100 Kbps of upload bandwidth for each simultaneous remote access user. Table 3-1 lists a number of Internet connection speeds and the number of users supported for each speed, assuming that users will be browsing the Web and using e-mail. This table does not include requirements for VPN connections.

> **IMPORTANT**   Running an Internet-accessible Web server on your network requires at least 50 Kbps or more of upload bandwidth per simultaneous visitor, depending on the size of images or files. This can quickly swamp your Internet connection, which is why most small businesses pay for Web hosting.

TABLE 3-1 Bandwidth Requirements for Web Browsing and E-Mail

DOWNLOAD/UPLOAD SPEED	NUMBER OF USERS
256/128 Kbps	1–5
512/256 Kbps	5–10
768/384 Kbps	5–15
1024/512 Kbps	10–20
1536/768 Kbps	15–30

NOTE These bandwidth numbers are not intended to be definitive—they are a planning baseline. Each organization and its users have different usage patterns and needs, and you should evaluate your needs accordingly. Be prepared to add more bandwidth if necessary. Your users will never complain that the Internet connection is too fast, but they will definitely complain if it's too slow!

 UNDER THE HOOD **Bits and Bytes**

Network speeds are measured in either kilobits per second (Kbps) or megabits per second (Mbps), whereas download speed and hard disks are rated in kilobytes per second (KBps) or megabytes per second (MBps). For example, a 640-Kbps DSL connection might download files at 60 KBps from a fast Web site, but a 1.5-Mbps cable Internet connection might download at 180 KBps from the same site. (Some of the bandwidth is used up by transmission overhead and inefficiencies.) When you compare network speeds, make sure you're using the same units of measurement.

Types of Internet Connections

To choose an Internet connection method, you need to know which methods are available as well as their performance characteristics. Table 3-2 lists the most common connection methods and their speeds.

TABLE 3-2 Internet Connection Types

TYPE OF CONNECTION	DOWNLOAD SPEED	UPLOAD SPEED	NOTES
Dial-up	28.8–53 Kbps	28.8–40 Kbps	Analog telephone line. Sometimes referred to as Plain Old Telephone Service (POTS).
ISDN (Integrated Services Digital Network)	64–128 Kbps (one channel or two)	64–128 Kbps (one channel or two)	Must be within 50,000 feet of a telephone company central office (CO). Connection is dial-up (not persistent).
ADSL (Asynchronous Digital Subscriber Line)	256 Kbps–8 Mbps	128 Kbps–1 Mbps	Must be within 18,000 feet of a CO.
IDSL (ISDN over DSL)	128–144 Kbps	128–144 Kbps	Works at greater distances from a CO than other DSL variants.
SDSL (Synchronous DSL)	128 Kbps–2.3 Mbps	128 Kbps–2.3 Mbps	Must be within 20,000 feet of a CO.
Cable	128 Kbps–8 Mbps	128 Kbps–1 Mbps	Must have access to broadband cable service; speed can fluctuate depending on the number of users on a given cable loop.
Microwave wireless	256 Kbps–10+ Mbps	256 Kbps–10+ Mbps	Must be in line of sight to ISP's antenna; maximum distance 10 miles.
Frame relay/T1	56 Kbps–1.54 Mbps	56 Kbps–1.54 Mbps	Good availability; very reliable; consistent throughput; expensive.
802.11b (WiFi)	Up to 11 Mbps	Up to 11 Mbps	Speed decreases with increasing distance from access point.
802.11g or 802.11a	Up to 54 Mbps	Up to 54 Mbps	Speed decreases with increasing distance from access point.
802.11n	Up to 540 Mbps	Up to 540 Mbps	Speed decreases with increasing distance from access point.

TYPE OF CONNECTION	DOWNLOAD SPEED	UPLOAD SPEED	NOTES
Geosynchronous satellite	150 Kbps–3 Mbps	33.6 Kbps–128 Kbps	Requires line of sight to satellite (southern sky in North America). Unsuitable for real-time multimedia because of high latency.
Ethernet	10 to 1000 Mbps	10 to 1000 Mbps	Limited availability. Backbone connection might be DSL or T1, limiting actual bandwidth.

Choosing ISPs

After determining the preferred connection type and bandwidth, it's time to actually find ISPs. Two Web sites to check are *http://www.cnet.com/internet-access/* and *http://www.dslreports.com*. In addition to speed and cost, look for the following features:

- **Static IP address** To host any kind of Internet-accessible service such as e-mail, Microsoft Outlook Anywhere, VPNs, or Web sites, you need a static IP address or an ISP that supports the Dynamic DNS service, or you need to manage your external DNS with a DNS service that supports dynamic updates, such as *http://www.zoneedit.com*. SBS 2008 includes support for tzo.com dynamic DNS if you use the built-in wizards to register or transfer your domain name.

- **Terms of Service and Ports** Many ISPs have terms of service (TOS) on consumer-grade accounts that prohibit hosting e-mail servers, or they have a policy that blocks specific ports such as port 25. You need to ask before you buy.

- **Transfer limitations** If the ISP has a monthly data transfer limit, make sure that the limit isn't lower than your anticipated usage—charges for going beyond the limit can be significant.

- **Web hosting** If you want the ISP to host the organization's Internet Web site, look for virtual hosting (so that your organization can use its own domain name) with enough disk space on the ISP's Web servers.

- **Backup Internet connection** If your business is dependent on always being connected to the Internet, choose a secondary Internet connection with sufficient bandwidth to allow you to limp along in case the primary Internet connection fails. This second Internet connection should use a different ISP and a different connection technology. You can use a dual WAN router to use both connections simultaneously.

Choosing a Network Type

The next step in designing a network is to choose a network type. (See Table 3-3.) Start by looking at where your computers are physically located. If you can easily run cable between all computers, the choices are simple: Gigabit Ethernet (GigE) or Fast Ethernet (100BaseT).

Choose GigE if your budget can afford it and your wiring supports it; otherwise, stick to Fast Ethernet. If you're installing new cabling, hire a professional cabling expert. Spending money on good wiring now can save you a *lot* of problems in the future.

If the computers are widely scattered or mobile, consider including some wireless *access points* (APs), which are network devices that permit wireless clients access to a wired network. Fast Ethernet is more than twice as fast as the current wireless standards, more reliable, more secure, and cheaper as well. For these reasons, use wireless networks to supplement wired networks, not to replace them. For more information about wireless access points, see the section titled "Choosing a Wireless Standard: 802.11a/b/g/n" later in this chapter.

> **IMPORTANT** All wireless technologies have the potential to introduce security risks. When using wireless networking, always use appropriate security measures, such as Wireless Protected Access (WPA), 802.11i (WPA2), or 802.1x. For more information, see the section titled "Planning for Security" later in this chapter.

TABLE 3-3 Common Network Types

TECHNOLOGY	SPEED	SPEED (REAL WORLD)	CABLING	MAXIMUM DISTANCE	OTHER HARDWARE REQUIREMENTS
Fast Ethernet	100 Mbps	94 Mbps	Cat 5, Cat 5e, Cat 6	328 feet from hub or switch	Fast Ethernet hub or switch
Gigabit Ethernet	1000 Mbps	327 Mbps	Cat 5e or Cat 6	328 feet from hub or switch	Gigabit hub or switch
802.11b (WiFi)	11 Mbps	4.5 Mbps	Wireless	1800 feet (60–150 feet typical indoors)	802.11b or 802.11g access point (AP), 32 users per AP
802.11a	54 Mbps	19 Mbps	Wireless	1650 feet (50–100 feet typical indoors)	802.11a AP, 64 users per AP
802.11g	54 Mbps	13 Mbps	Wireless	1800 feet (60–150 feet typical indoors)	802.11g AP, 32 users per AP
802.11n	540 Mbps	130 Mbps	Wireless	7200 feet (100–500 feet typical indoors)	802.11n AP, 32 users per AP

NOTE Wireless speeds vary greatly depending on distance from the access point, and the number and type of walls, floors, and other interference between the access point and the client device.

BEST PRACTICES Avoid the consumer-focused HomePNA and HomePlug network types. They're more expensive, slower, less secure, and less reliable than Ethernet or a properly configured 802.11a/b/g/n wireless network.

Choosing the Right Network Cable

Choosing the right cable for a wired Fast Ethernet (100 Mbps) network is easy—Cat 5 cable. However, there are exceptions to this rule that pertain to existing installations and new construction.

Cables in an existing network might not be usable. 10-megabit Ethernet equipment might be usable for small networks until it can be replaced, but expect to replace it soon—you'll find it slow. Coaxial (thinnet) Ethernet and Cat 3 Unshielded Twisted Pair (UTP) cables are unreliable and slow and should be replaced.

New construction should run several strands of Cat 5e or, ideally, Cat 6. Although Cat 5 cable can be used with Gigabit Ethernet, it is marginal at best. Cat 5e and Cat 6 cables are more reliable and provide headroom for possible 10-Gigabit Ethernet standards. Cables should converge at a reasonably clean, centrally located wiring closet with adequate power, ventilation, and security for all servers and network devices. (Be sure to leave room for future growth.)

Shielded Cat 5, Cat 5e, and Cat 6 cables are available for situations that potentially involve high levels of electromagnetic interference (such as antennas). You should use plenum-grade cable any time wiring is placed in a drop ceiling. (Before running cable in a drop ceiling, talk to the building manager.)

Choosing a Wireless Standard: 802.11a/b/g/n

Currently you can choose from four wireless standards: 802.11b, 802.11a, 802.11g, and 802.11n. Here's what you need to know about each (also see Table 3-3):

- **802.11b** 802.11b is the most widely deployed standard, though the speed is limited (11 Mbps theoretical; 5 Mbps or even less in the real world). 802.11b supports a maximum of 32 users per AP, and a maximum of three simultaneous channels in use in the same location. Channels separate wireless networks, with each channel providing 11 Mbps of bandwidth. You should not buy new equipment that only supports 802.11b, but you can use existing equipment.

- **802.11g** 802.11g is faster than 802.11b (54 Mbps theoretical; 13 Mbps real-world), and backward-compatible with 802.11b, making it the best choice for most organizations. 802.11g supports a maximum of 32 users per AP, and a maximum of three simultaneous channels in use in the same location.

- **802.11a** 802.11a is the fastest standard (54 Mbps theoretical; 19 Mbps real-world) and is more tolerant of microwave interference and network congestion because it uses the 5 GHz frequency band. 802.11a supports a maximum of 64 users per AP, and a maximum of eight channels in use simultaneously in the same location. 802.11a is not compatible with either 802.11b or 802.11g.

  If you decide to use 802.11a network devices, stick with devices from the same vendor and consider a tri-mode 802.11a/b/g device that will allow other devices, such as laptops with built-in 802.11b/g connectivity, to work on the wireless network. (This strategy also permits the highest network density, with 11 channels available simultaneously for wireless networks.)

- **802.11n** 802.11n is faster than 802.11g (up to 540 Mbps theoretical; 100-130 Mbps real-world), and backward-compatible with 802.11g and 802.11b. Most 802.11n equipment is in the same frequency band (2.4 GHz) as 802.11b/g, but the draft standard supports dual-band equipment that can also use the 5 GHz range of 802.11a. This dual-band equipment provides the greatest flexibility and compatibility and is especially good at avoiding interference from other equipment. However, the 802.11n standard is still, after several years of talking, only a draft standard. Choosing equipment from a single OEM is the safest choice for compatibility at the highest speeds.

Choosing Network Devices

After selecting a network type and Internet connection method, create a network diagram to visually show which network devices are needed and then select the necessary devices for the network, such as switches, wireless access points, firewalls, and network adapters.

> **BEST PRACTICES** Choose a single brand of network hardware, if possible. This ensures greater hardware compatibility, simplifies administration, and makes obtaining vendor support easier.

Diagramming the Network

Creating a diagram of the network can quickly show which devices you need and where they should be located, as shown in Figure 3-3.

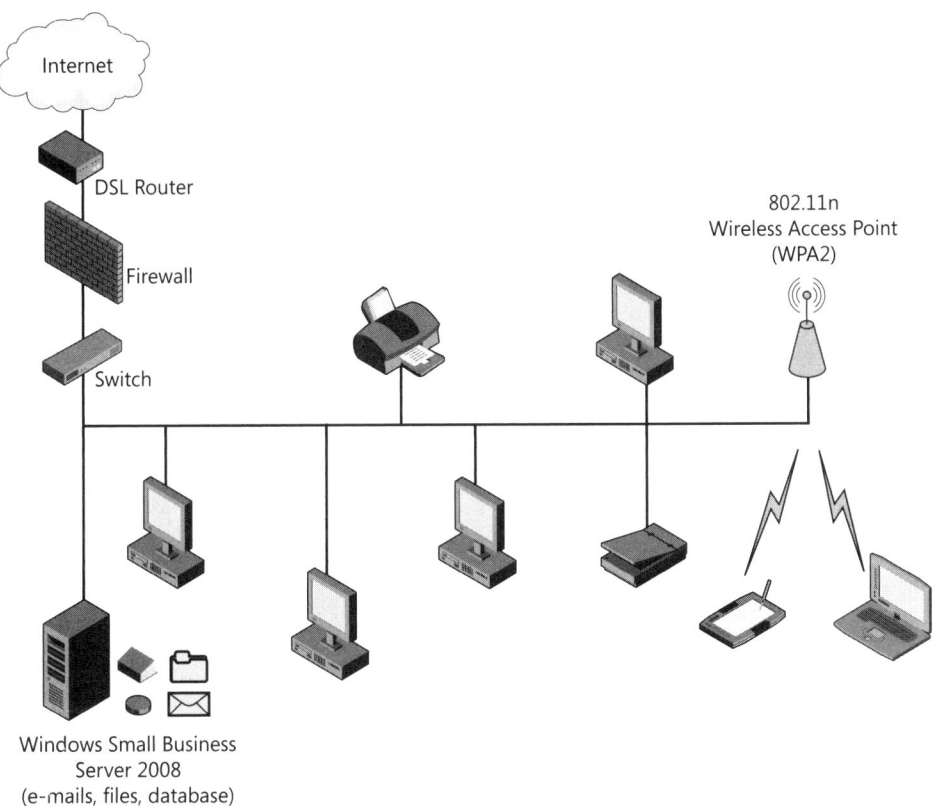

Internet

DSL Router

Firewall

Switch

802.11n
Wireless Access Point
(WPA2)

Windows Small Business
Server 2008
(e-mails, files, database)

FIGURE 3-3 A network with the Windows Small Business Server computer connected directly to the Internet

Use the following list as a guide when creating the network diagram:

- **Internet connection** The Internet connection usually comes in the form of a telephone or coaxial cable that connects to a DSL or cable router. It is traditionally represented by a cloud at the top of the drawing and a line that connects to the router or firewall.

- **DSL or cable modem** The Internet usually enters the organization in the form of a telephone or cable line that plugs into a DSL or cable modem.

- **Firewall** The DSL or cable modem is then plugged into the firewall, which should be a router or firewall. Some modems are combined with built-in routers that have basic firewall capabilities.

- **Perimeter network** This is an optional area of the network between the DSL or cable modem and the firewall, where low-security devices such as wireless access points can be placed.

- **Internal network** The internal network includes the Small Business Server computers, the client computers, and any network-connected devices, such as printers.

Choosing a Network Switch

Ethernet networks use the star network topology (also known as *hub and spoke*), which means that all network devices must be plugged into a central hub or switch. Choosing the right switch requires evaluating the following factors:

- **Switch or hub** Don't buy a hub unless you have a specialized need and understand why you're doing it. Get a switch instead. Switches are inexpensive, provide additional performance, and facilitate mixing 10-Mbps, 100-Mbps, and 1-Gbps devices on the same network segment.

- **Number of ports** Make sure that the switch provides more than enough ports for all computers, access points, network printers, and Network Attached Storage (NAS) devices on the network.

- **Speed** Fast Ethernet (100/10 Mbps) switches offer sufficient performance for most small businesses, but GigE (1000/100/10 Mbps) switches are hardly different in price and provide extra bandwidth for heavily used file servers and high-quality streaming video where the network cabling will support it.

- **Management** Managed switches provide the ability to view the status of attached devices from a remote connection, which can be useful for off-site technicians. In general, save the cash and stick with an unmanaged switch unless the cost difference is slight or the organization uses an off-site consultant who wants the ability to remotely administer switches.

Choosing Wireless Access Points

As you learned earlier in the chapter, wireless access points permit clients to wirelessly connect to a wired network. Access points are often integrated into routers, but they are also available as standalone devices that must be plugged into a switch like any other network device. Avoid wireless "gateway" or router products for connecting to your internal network—they will complicate your network management and TCP/IP configuration. They're fine for externally connected wireless access points. Some wireless routers can be reconfigured to be simple access points.

When choosing an access point, consider the following features:

- Routers with built-in access points are often no more expensive than standalone access points and are useful when creating a perimeter network. But be sure that they can be used as a pure access point—many can function only as a router, which will complicate your network setup.

- Access points should support 802.11i (WPA2) or WPA encryption. WEP is simply not acceptable for any wireless device connected to your internal network.

- Access points should support 802.1x (RADIUS) authentication if you want to provide the highest level of security and ease of use to a wireless network.

> **IMPORTANT** Two "features" that some suggest to improve wireless security are disabling of SSID broadcasts and Media Access Control (MAC) address filtering. Don't bother. They are a significant and ongoing administrative burden, and a hacker with a port scanner can easily defeat them anyway.

- Some access points have two or more antennas that can be adjusted for better coverage; others support external antennas that can be mounted on a wall for better placement.

- Standalone wireless bridges (often referred to as *wireless Ethernet bridges*) and some access points provide the ability to wirelessly bridge (connect) two wired networks that can't be connected via cables. There are a number of different types of bridging modes, including Point-to-Point and AP Client. Point-to-Point uses two wireless bridges to link two wired networks. AP Client uses an AP on the main network (to which wireless clients can connect) and a wireless bridge in AP Client mode on the remote network segment, acting as a wireless client.

    Clients on the other side of a wireless bridge will experience slower performance to the main network segment because of the shared wireless link, so use wireless bridges with discretion, and always use bridges and APs made by the same manufacturer.

- Don't include "turbo" or other high-speed modes offered by some manufacturers in your buying criteria. They provide little performance gain, if any, in the real world.

 REAL WORLD **Placing Access Points for the Best Coverage**

Wireless access points have a limited range, especially in the environment of a typical office. The indoor range of 802.11b, 802.11g, and tri-mode 802.11a access points is usually around 60–100 feet at the highest connection speed, and 25–75 feet for first-generation, single-mode 802.11a access points. That said, 2.4-GHz cordless phones, microwave ovens, and Bluetooth devices can cause serious interference with 802.11b and 802.11g networks (but not with 802.11a networks) when they are turned on. Fluorescent lights, metal walls, computer equipment, furniture, and standing too close to the access point can also reduce the range of wireless networks. Unfortunately, there is no reliable way to quantify these variables—trial and error is the best way to position access points. The promise of 802.11n is that it will at least double these effective distances, but without an agreed standard and a solid base of deployment experience, we're cautiously optimistic. Our initial tests of 802.11n do appear to provide a more stable and reliable signal at a significantly greater distance than our previous 802.11a/g equipment. There are some useful guidelines when selecting access point locations:

- Place the access point and wireless network card antennas as high as possible to get them above objects that might attenuate the signal.

- If you place access points in the plenum (the space inside a drop ceiling or raised floor), make sure you obtain access points or enclosures certified for plenum installation.

- Place the access point in the center of the desired coverage area to provide the best coverage while also reducing the publicly exposed "surface area" of the network.

- Use multiple access points as necessary to cover multiple floors or large offices, or to service a large number of clients simultaneously. Twenty clients per 802.11b or 802.11g AP is a reasonable maximum, with an average of no more than two to four simultaneously active users per AP yielding the best network performance.

- Use wireless bridges to place another Ethernet network segment (or another wireless access point) in a location unreachable by cables. Wired clients on this segment communicate with other wired devices on this segment at the speed of the wired network (1000/100/10 Mbps); however, communication with the main network segment takes place at the speed of the wireless network (10-100 Mbps real-world bandwidth).

- When selecting channels for access points, *sniff* (search by using a wireless client) for the presence of other networks and then choose an unused channel, preferably one that is four or more channels separated from other channels in use. For example, channels 1, 6, and 11 can all be used without interference.

Choosing a Firewall Device or Router

Windows Small Business Server 2008 is designed to connect directly to a firewall and does not provide any direct protection for the rest of the SBS network. This is a major change from earlier versions of SBS that acted as the gateway between the Internet and the internal network when SBS was deployed with two network cards (NICs). Windows Small Business Server 2008 includes the new Windows Firewall that is part of Windows Server 2008 to protect the server, but should be protected by an additional, separate, firewall that will also act to protect the computers on the internal network.

You should look for the following features on your network firewall device:

- **Packet filtering** Firewalls should support inbound packet filtering and Stateful Packet Inspection (SPI).

- **Protection from specific attacks** Firewalls should support protection from the denial-of-service (DoS) attacks and other common attacks such as Ping of Death, SYN Flood, LAND Attack, and IP Spoofing.

- **Network Address Translation (NAT)** NAT is the backbone of most firewall devices, providing basic security and Internet connectivity to internal clients.

- **VPN pass-through** To permit properly authenticated Internet users to establish VPN connections with a Windows Small Business Server computer behind a firewall, the firewall must support VPN pass-through of the desired VPN protocol (PPTP, L2TP, and/ or IPSec).

- **VPN tunnels** Some firewall devices provide direct support for establishing VPN connections. If you do choose to use a firewall device to establish VPN connections with clients and servers in remote offices, make sure the firewall supports the necessary number of simultaneous VPN tunnels.

- **UPnP support** Windows Small Business Server can automatically configure firewalls that support Universal Plug and Play (UPnP) to work with Windows Small Business Server services such as Exchange Server and remote access (by opening the necessary ports on the firewall). UPnP support can be found in most consumer firewall devices as well as in some business firewalls.

> **NOTE** Enabling UPnP on a dedicated firewall device makes configuring the device to work with Windows Small Business Server easy, but it does have security implications. We suggest using UPnP to do the initial setup of the firewall device, if the device supports it, but then disabling UPnP completely.

- **Dual-WAN support** Some firewalls come with support for two WAN connections to increase speed and reliability, which is a great solution for networks looking for a reliable Internet connection. Other firewalls provide a serial port so that an external dial-up modem can be used as a backup connection, but this connection is much slower.

- **Content filtering** Most firewalls make blocking certain Web sites possible, such as Web sites containing specified keywords. Many businesses use this feature to reduce the employees' ability to visit objectionable Web sites, although most content filters are largely ineffective.

- **Built-in wireless access point** Firewalls with built-in access points and switched, GigE, wired ports combine several functions and can be a cost-effective solution. However, their primary function is to protect the network, and that should be the first and most important evaluation criterion.

Choosing Server Hardware

If you have a server that can meet the capacity needs of the network or can be upgraded to do so while allowing for future growth, by all means use this server. But realistically, with the change to 64-bit in Windows Small Business Server 2008, you should plan on buying a new server as part of your migration plan. See Chapter 7, "Migrating from Windows Small Business Server 2003," for more information about migrating to Windows Small Business Server 2008 from an existing SBS domain.

When evaluating server hardware, refer to Table 3-4, which lists the minimum configurations necessary for adequate performance at different load levels. The sidebar titled "Determining Server Load" later in this chapter provides more information about configuration and performance.

TABLE 3-4 Minimum Server Configurations for Different Load Levels

COMPONENT	LIGHT LOAD	MEDIUM LOAD	HEAVY LOAD
CPU	Pentium Core 2 Duo 2.0 GHz or AMD Turion64 X2	Dual or quad core Xeon or Opteron processor supporting x64	Dual Xeon or Opteron processors, with at least two cores each
Memory	5–6 GB	6–8 GB	8–12 GB
Storage	Two or more hard drives with 100 GB available for Windows Small Business Server 2008	Three-drive, hardware-based RAID using SATA or SAS drives	Four-drive (or more), hardware-based SCSI or SAS RAID
LAN Network Adapter	100/10 Mbps PCI card	1000/100/10 Mbps PCI card	1000/100/10 Mbps PCI-x or PCIe card
Backup	Two or more external USB hard drives	Two or more external eSATA or USB hard drives	Two or more external eSATA or USB hard drives

See Chapter 11, "Disk Management," for more information on RAID. See Chapter 12, "Storage Management," for more information about choosing the appropriate storage solution. See Chapter 16, "Configuring Backup," for more information about creating a backup strategy and choosing backup devices.

 UNDER THE HOOD **Determining Server Load**

The appropriate hardware for a Windows Small Business Server 2008 server depends on the load you place it under. Think of load as equal to the number of requests per unit of time multiplied by the difficulty of fulfilling each request.

The easiest way to determine load is to sample the performance of the existing server over a range of conditions. Of course, this is tricky when you're constructing a new network or restructuring an existing network. Consider the following factors:

- **The usage pattern over time (number of requests per unit of time)** A server that handles an average load can easily become swamped at key times, such as at the beginning and end of a workday, when many users simultaneously log on or log off; during lunch, when users might browse the Internet for personal use; or around deadlines, when many users make heavy use of file, e-mail, or database services.

- **The kinds of user requests (the complexity of each request)** This determines which server subsystems are stressed most heavily. Database serving stresses storage, memory, and possibly CPU; file serving stresses mostly storage and I/O; Internet access places some load on storage and network I/O; Exchange Server stresses storage, memory, and to some extent CPU.

Choosing Client Hardware and Software

When selecting client computers for use on a network, choose systems that are fast enough to perform adequately when running Windows XP Professional or Windows Vista Business. (See Table 3-5 for recommended configurations.) Other operating systems, such as Windows 2000, Mac OS X, and Linux, can be made to work on a Windows Small Business Server 2008 network; however, they won't provide full support for many of the features of Windows Server 2008.

TABLE 3-5 Recommended Client Computer Configurations

COMPONENT	MINIMUM CONFIGURATION	BETTER CONFIGURATION
Operating System	Windows XP Professional	Windows Vista Business or Enterprise
CPU	Pentium 4 2.0 GHz or faster	Dual-core processor, 2.0 GHz or faster
RAM	256 MB	2 GB
Hard Drive	30 GB	100 GB
Network Adapter	Fast Ethernet or 802.11g	GigE, 802.11n
Display	15-inch monitor running at 800 x 600 resolution	17-inch monitor running at 1024 x 768 resolution

Computers too slow to adequately run a Windows XP operating system can be put to use as Terminal Server clients. In this configuration, users connect to a separate Windows Server 2008 computer running the Terminal Server Role. The Terminal Server can provide a full desktop display, or it can be used to supplement the display by running key applications on the Terminal Server and displaying them on the client using the TS RemoteApps feature introduced in Windows Server 2008. The Terminal Server computer *cannot* be the same physical computer as the main Windows Small Business Server computer unless virtualization is used to run multiple *virtual machines* (VMs) on a single physical computer. With a Terminal Server, all processing is done on the server, and the display is sent back to the client computer, which can run any supported Terminal Server client operating system.

This approach can make more efficient use of resources, and make central management easier. The new TS RemoteApps simplifies deploying resource-intensive applications to users without having to upgrade everyone's computer. For more information on Terminal Server, see Chapter 25, "Adding a Terminal Server."

Choosing Naming Conventions

Creating naming conventions makes choosing names for computers, shared folders, and users easier and lends consistency to the network. This consistency results in a more user-friendly network. For help with naming users, see Chapter 9, "Managing Users and Groups." For help with naming shared folders, see Chapter 10, "Shares and Permissions."

Choosing a Domain Name for the Network

The domain name is the most important and politically sensitive name on the network. Do not make this decision without consulting everyone who has a stake in the result. By getting others involved in the process, you'll have a much greater chance of acceptance. Some questions to ask when choosing a domain name include:

- Is the name easy to remember and does it make sense for the company? This could be the company name in its most common form or an abbreviation.

- Is the name 15 characters or shorter? Use only letters, numbers, the underscore, and a hyphen in the name to ensure DNS and NetBIOS compatibility.

- Is the name available? If the name is already in use as an Internet domain name for another company, you'll have to choose a different name.

- If you already have an Internet Web site, use the same name, without the extension, for your internal domain name. For example, if the company uses www.example.com for its Internet Web site, use *example* for the domain name. The Windows Small Business Server 2008 Installation Wizard will automatically add a .local extension to the name you choose.

- As soon as you choose a domain name, register it (preferably with .com, .net, or .org) on the Internet so that another company can't purchase it.

IMPORTANT   Changing a domain name is difficult and can cause numerous problems on a network, so picking a name that will last is important.

 REAL WORLD   **Internal Domain Name v. Internet Domain Name**

There are two domain names you need to worry about when setting up your network: the Internet domain name that the outside world sees for your company and e-mail, and the internal domain name that Windows Small Business Server uses. They are usually related but not identical. The public, Internet domain name needs to be globally unique, officially registered with a Domain Naming Service, and clearly identifiable as your company. The internal, Windows name can be anything at all, though it should usually be the same as the external, public one, but with a different top-level domain. So if your company is Example Widgets and your public Internet domain name is example.com, your internal Windows domain name could be something like example.local. This makes it easy to keep track of and gives you complete control over managing the internal DNS of your Windows Small Business Server network while allowing you to have a reliable third party manage your public DNS records.

Although it is technically possible to change your public name, it's neither easy nor painless, and it's virtually impossible to change your internal name without having to completely rebuild your network from scratch. So it's worth spending time up front to make sure you're choosing a name that is appropriate and has the support of all parties.

Another possibility is to choose a completely generic name for your internal domain that has nothing whatsoever to do with your company name. This works great if you change your public name, because nothing has to change on your network. But it's not an approach we like. We've always preferred naming based on the company name—it's just easier for everyone to understand and remember.

Naming Computers

It's easy for *you* to keep a map of what the different clients and servers are called and where they are on the network, but if you make life hard on users, you pay in the long run. So naming all the computers after Shakespearean characters or Norse gods might make sense to you, but it isn't going to help users figure out that Puck is the Windows Small Business Server computer and Odin is the desktop used for payroll. On the other hand, using Srv1 for the SBS server tells everyone immediately which computer it is. When naming computers, use a consistent convention and sensible names, such as the following:

- SRV1 or SBSSRV for the Windows Small Business Server 2008 computer
- FrontDesk for the receptionist's computer

In this book, we'll be using a somewhat more complicated naming convention that identifies the physical host computer, the role of the computer, and the IP address of the computer. Thus our SBS server is hp350-sbs-02, signifying that it's running on the Hewlett-Packard ML350 G5 server, it's running Windows Small Business Server 2008, and that the final octet of its IP address is .02. There are several virtual machines running on that HP server, so it gets a fair workout.

Planning for Security

It is far easier to implement effective security measures to protect your SBS network if you plan for security *before* you actually start installing software. In the following sections, we'll cover some of the most common attack vectors and the preliminary steps you can take in this planning stage to prepare your defenses.

- **Careless or disgruntled employees and former employees** Internal users and former users are the biggest risk factors to data loss and data theft on most computer networks. Whether from laziness, disregard of security policies, or outright malice, the internal user is often the most dangerous on your network. To help prevent this, refer to the section titled "Ensuring Physical Security" in this chapter as well as to Chapter 8, "Completing the Getting Started Tasks."

- **Internet hackers** All computers and devices attached directly to the Internet are subject to random attacks by hackers. According to the Cooperative Association for Internet Data Analysis (CAIDA), during a random three-week time period in 2001 more than 12,000 DoS attacks occurred: 1200 to 2400 of these attacks were against home computers, and the rest were against businesses. If your organization has a high profile, it might also be subject to targeted attack by hackers who don't like your organization or who are engaging in corporate espionage. For more information about securing a network against Internet hackers, see the section titled "Securing Internet Firewalls" in this chapter.

- **Wireless hackers and theft of service** Wireless access points are exposed to the general public looking for free Internet access and to mobile hackers. To reduce this risk, refer to the section titled "Securing Wireless Networks" in this chapter.

- **Viruses and worms** Networks are subject to virus exposure from e-mail attachments, infected documents, and worms such as CodeRed and Blaster that automatically attack vulnerable servers and clients. Refer to the section titled "Securing Client Computers" in this chapter for more information.

Ensuring Physical Security

Although security is not something that can be achieved in absolute terms, it should be a clearly defined goal. The most secure operating system and network in the world is defenseless against someone with physical access to a computer. Evaluate your physical environment to decide what additional security measures you should take, including:

- Place servers in a locked server room. And control who has keys!
- Use case locks on your servers and don't leave the keys in them.
- Place network hubs, routers, and switches in a locked cable room or wiring closet.
- Install case locks on client systems or publicly accessible systems.
- Use laptop locks when using laptops in public.
- Use BitLocker to encrypt the data on laptops that contain sensitive data.

Securing Client Computers

Even a highly secure network can be quickly compromised by a poorly secured client computer—for example, a laptop running an older version of Windows with sensitive data stored on the hard drive. To maximize the security of client computers, use the following guidelines (refer to Chapter 8 and Chapter 14, "Managing Computers on the Network," for more security procedures):

- **Use a secure operating system** Use Windows XP Professional or Windows Vista on all client computers, with a strong preference for Windows Vista on laptops.

- **Use NTFS, file permissions, BitLocker, and EFS** Use NTFS for all hard drives and apply appropriate file permissions so that only valid users can read sensitive data. Encrypt sensitive files on laptop computers using the Encrypting File System (EFS), and encrypt the system drive on laptops using BitLocker (Windows Vista Enterprise and Ultimate only).

- **Keep clients updated** Use the Automatic Updates feature of Windows XP and Windows Vista to keep systems updated automatically, or use Windows Update. Ideally, use the Windows Software Update Service (WSUS) integrated into Windows Small Business Server 2008 to centrally control which updates are installed, as described in Chapter 15, "Managing Software Updates."

- **Enable Password Policies** Password Policies is a feature of Windows Small Business Server 2008 that requires user passwords to meet certain complexity, length, and uniqueness requirements, ensuring that users choose passwords that aren't trivial to crack.

> **NOTE** Remembering passwords has become an increasingly difficult prospect, leading to the resurgence of the yellow-sticky-note method of recalling them. It's important to discourage this practice and encourage the use of distinctive but easy-to-remember passphrases.

- **Install antivirus software** Antivirus software should be installed on the Windows Small Business Server 2008 computer as well as on all clients. The best way to do this is to purchase a small-business antivirus package that supports both clients and the server. Exchange Server scanning is included in Windows Small Business Server 2008, as is the server version of Windows OneCare. There are also good third-party solutions specifically designed for the SBS market from several vendors.
- **Install antispyware software** Antispyware software should be installed on all client computers on the network and configured for real-time monitoring and daily full scans.
- **Sign and encrypt e-mail** Companies with the need to send secure e-mail should set up users to send digitally signed and possibly encrypted e-mail. If a small number of users need this capability, purchase digital IDs from an Internet Certificate Authority such as VeriSign (*http://www.verisign.com*) or Thawte (*http://www.thawte.com*). If a large number of users requires this ability, consider installing Certificate Services (included in Windows Small Business Server 2008) and creating your own digital IDs.
- **Keep Web browsers secure** Unpatched Web browsers are a significant security issue. Always keep Web browsers updated with the latest security updates.

Securing Wireless Networks

Wireless networks using the 802.11b, 802.11a, 802.11g, and 802.11n standards are very convenient but also introduce significant security vulnerabilities if not properly secured. To properly secure wireless networks, follow these recommendations:

- Change the default password of all access points.
- Change the default SSID. Pick a name that doesn't reveal the identity or location of your network.
- Enable 802.11i (WPA2) encryption on the access points.
- If the access points don't support WPA2, or at least WPA, don't use them on your internal network.

NOTE WPA and WPA2 provide two methods of authentication: an "Enterprise" method that makes use of a RADIUS server, and a "Personal" method known as WPA2-Personal that uses a Pre-Shared Key (PSK) instead of a RADIUS server.

- Companies with many wireless clients should consider using the included Active Directory Certificate Services and Network Policy Server of Windows Small Business Server 2008 server to enable 802.1x Authentication (using NPS as a RADIUS server). This procedure is discussed in Chapter 19, "Managing Connectivity."
- Disable the ability to administer access points from across the wireless network.

Securing Internet Firewalls

Most external firewall devices are secure by default, but you can take some additional steps to maximize the security of a firewall:

- Change the default password for the firewall device! We know this seems obvious, but unfortunately, it is all too often ignored.
- Disable remote administration or limit it to responding to a single IP address (that of your network consultant).
- Disable the firewall from responding to Internet pings. OK, we admit this is controversial. It's certainly a best practice, but it can also make troubleshooting a connectivity issue remotely a lot harder.
- Enable Stateful Packet Inspection (SPI) and protection from specific attacks such as the Ping of Death, Smurf, and IP Spoofing.
- Leave all ports on the firewall closed except those needed by the Windows Small Business Server 2008 server.
- Regularly check for open ports using trusted port-scanning sites. We use *http://www.dslreports.com*.
- Keep the firewall updated with the latest firmware versions, available for download from the manufacturer's Web site.

Summary

In this chapter we've covered how to design or prepare a network prior to installing Windows Small Business Server. We've also covered basic naming conventions and how to plan for adequate network security. The next chapter covers planning for fault tolerance and fault avoidance on your SBS network to help you build a reliable SBS network that can support your business.

Planning Fault Tolerance and Avoidance

Even the most optimistic system administrator knows that sooner or later she or he will be faced with a major problem. We'll cover preparing for disasters in depth in Chapter 27, "Disaster Planning," and you should refer to that chapter for information on how to prepare for major problems and how to build a disaster recovery plan to respond quickly and efficiently to major trouble. But as exhilarating as it may be to work through a major problem and successfully recover from it, it's far better to avoid major problems as much as possible.

This chapter focuses on the hardware and software tools that help you to build a highly available and fault-tolerant SBS environment. Remember, however, that hardware and software are only a small part of the equation—building and deploying for fault tolerance requires time, a clear understanding of the necessary tradeoffs, and—most important—discipline. Yes, you can avoid most computer downtime, but you'll need to be realistic about what your resources are, and what you can reasonably afford to spend. Because SBS does not support clustering, your options for high availability are somewhat limited, but you can still take some important steps to improve your availability and fault tolerance. Your primary focus needs to be on building fault tolerance into your server and network infrastructure.

Building fault-tolerant systems doesn't come without costs, in both effort and money. In this chapter we'll try to help you make informed decisions about where to most cost-effectively (and resource-effectively) build fault tolerance into your SBS environment. To use this information, you should have a clear understanding of the business needs you're trying to resolve and a realistic assessment of the resources available to meet those requirements. When planning for a highly available and fault-tolerant deployment, you should consider all points of failure and work to eliminate any single point of failure. Redundant power supplies, dual disk controllers, multiple network interface cards (multihoming), and fault-tolerant disk arrays (RAID) are all strategies that you can and should employ.

Mean Time to Failure and Mean Time to Recover

The two most common metrics used to measure fault tolerance and avoidance are the following:

- **Mean time to failure (MTTF)** The mean time until the device will fail
- **Mean time to recover (MTTR)** The mean time it takes to recover after a failure has occurred

Although a great deal of time and energy is often spent trying to lower the MTTF, it's important to understand that even if you have a finite failure rate, an MTTR that is zero or near zero may be indistinguishable from a system that hasn't failed. Downtime is generally measured as MTTR/MTTF, so increasing the MTTF will reduce the downtime—but at a significant cost. Trying to increase the MTTF beyond a certain point can be prohibitively expensive. A more cost-effective and realistic strategy, especially in the small business space where resources are finite and customers are very cost-conscious, is to spend both time and resources on managing and reducing the MTTR for your most likely and costly points of failure.

Most modern electronic components have a distinctive "bathtub" curve that represents their failure characteristics, as shown in Figure 4-1. During the early life of the component (referred to as the burn-in phase), it's more likely to fail; when this initial phase is over, a component's overall failure rate remains quite low until it reaches the end of its useful life, when the failure rate increases again.

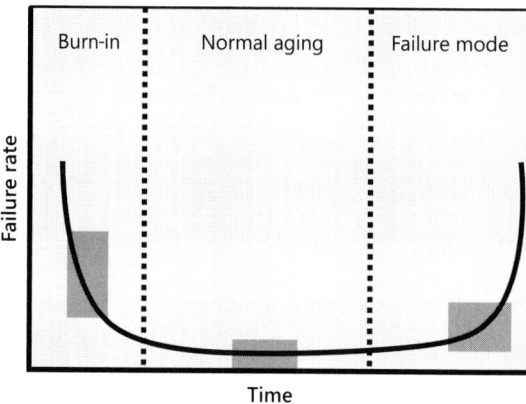

FIGURE 4-1 The normal statistical failure rates for mechanical and electronic components: a characteristic "bathtub" curve

The typical commodity hard disk of 10 years ago had an MTTF on the order of three years. Today, the manufacturer's published MTTF for a typical commodity hard disk is more likely to be 35 to 50 years, with MTTF ratings of server-oriented hard drives hitting 134 years! At least part of that difference is a direct result of counting only the portion of the curve in the normal aging section while taking externally caused failure out of the equation. Therefore, a hard disk that fails because of an improperly filtered power spike doesn't count against the MTTF of the disk, nor does a disk that fails in its first week or two. This might be nice for the disk manufacturer's statistics, but it doesn't do much for the system administrator whose system has crashed because of a disk failure.

As you can see, it's important to look at the total picture and carefully evaluate all the factors and failure points on your system. Only by looking at the whole system, including the recovery procedures and methodology, can you build a truly fault-tolerant environment.

Protecting the Power Supply

The single biggest failure point for any network is its power supply. If you don't have power, you can't run your computers. It seems pretty obvious, and most of us slap an uninterruptible power supply (UPS) on the order when we're buying a new server. However, this barely scratches the surface of what you can and should do to protect your network from power problems. You need to protect your network from four basic types of power problems:

- **Local power supply failure**   Failure of the internal power supply on a server, router, or other network component
- **Voltage variations**   Spikes, surges, sags, and longer-term brownouts
- **Short-term power outages**   External power failures lasting from fractions of a second to several minutes
- **Long-term power outages**   External power failures lasting from several minutes to several hours or even days

Each type of power problem poses different risks to your network and requires somewhat different protection mechanisms. The level of threat that each one poses to your environment varies depending on the area where you are located, the quality of power available to you, and the potential loss to your business if your computers are down.

Local Power Supply Failure

Computer power supplies have made substantial gains in the last 10 years, but they are still one of the greatest risk points. All the power conditioning, uninterruptible power supplies, and external generators in the world won't help much if your server's power supply fails. Most servers these days either come with a redundant power supply or have the option of including one. Take the option! The extra cost associated with adding a redundant power supply to a server or critical piece of network hardware is far less than the cost of downtime if the power supply fails. We found this out the hard way recently—our main server turned out to have a run of bad power supplies. The manufacturer knew about the problem, and replaced them without question. But if it hadn't been for the second power supply in it, we'd have been down and out until the replacement got to us. As it was, the manufacturer also replaced the second power supply in the server without waiting for it to fail because it was part of the same batch of bad power supplies.

If your server, router, or other piece of network hardware doesn't have the option of a redundant power supply, order a spare power supply for it when you order the original hardware. Don't count on the hardware manufacturer's "four-hour response time," especially when you consider the cost to your business even if they actually repair the equipment in four hours. If you have a spare power supply in a well-marked cabinet where you can easily find it, you can quickly and with minimal disruption replace the failed power supply and return the equipment to full functionality. Then you can afford to wait patiently for the manufacturer's service response.

> **NOTE** Most major manufacturers use proprietary components in their servers. This usually means that you can't count on using an off-the-shelf component, such as a power supply, but must use one specifically designed to fit the particular brand and model of server you have.

 REAL WORLD It's Only Useful if You Can Find It!

Having a good supply of critical spares is a great idea, but sometimes reality intrudes. Storage can be the weak link here. Most server rooms are not nearly as spacious as we would like them to be, and in the SBS world a server room may be little more than a lockable closet. If that's the case, make sure the closet has adequate, filtered ventilation and cooling—servers produce a significant amount of heat and a poorly ventilated environment will greatly shorten the life of your server.

Dust is the enemy of your server—it will impede cooling and can actually short out electrical components. Server rooms should not have carpeting. And remove any printers from the area—printers are dust generators.

All too often the spare parts end up jammed into a bin or shoved onto an upper shelf with inadequate or nonexistent identification. If your network is down and you need a power supply to get it back up, you don't want to be pawing through a jumble of spare parts looking for the right power supply.

Make every effort to develop a single, central, secure location for all spare parts. At least then you have only a single place to search. Then make sure the manufacturer's part number is visible, and clearly label the computer or computers each part is for. Protect the part from dust and spilled coffee by keeping it in a sealed plastic storage bag.

We like to tape a list of the manufacturer's part numbers, details of the installed hardware, and the list of spare parts we have right inside the case cover of the server itself. It's easy to find and doesn't end up getting lost. It does you no good to have a spare power supply if you can't find it or don't know you have it. And don't forget to include the location of any special tools required. It never ceases to amaze us how many different and apparently unique screwdriver bits we need to get into our various computers! We started our toolkit with an inexpensive computer toolkit and add tools to it as needed.

Finally, practice! If you've never replaced a power supply before, and you don't have clear and detailed instructions, it will take you orders of magnitude longer to replace it when the server is down and everyone is yelling and the phone keeps ringing. By practicing the replacement of the power supplies in your critical hardware, you'll save time and reduce the stress involved.

Ideally, document the steps you need to perform and include well-illustrated and detailed instructions on how to replace the power supplies of your critical hardware as part of your disaster recovery standard operating procedures. If you can swap out a failed power supply in 10 minutes, rather than waiting hours until an outside technician arrives, you've saved more than enough money to pay for the spare part several times over.

 REAL WORLD SNMP

Simple Network Management Protocol (SNMP) has been around for a long time, and provides a standardized way for devices, including computers, to provide feedback about their health. Many OEM servers come installed with third-party management suites that can be configured to notify you of significant events such as power variations, CPU temperatures, and disk events that can be a precursor to hard disk failure. If your server comes with such a tool, by all means use it.

Voltage Variations

Even in areas with exceptionally clean power that is always available, the power that is supplied to your network inevitably fluctuates. Minor, short-term variations merely stress your electronic components, but major variations can literally fry them. You should never, ever simply plug a computer into an ordinary wall socket without providing some sort of protection against voltage variations. The following sections describe the types of variations and the best way to protect your equipment against them.

Spikes

Spikes are large but short-lived increases in voltage. They can occur because of external factors, such as lightning striking a power line, or because of internal factors, such as a large motor starting. The most common causes of severe voltage spikes are external and outside your control. The effects can be devastating. A nearby lightning strike can easily cause a spike of 1,000 volts or more to be sent into equipment designed to run on 110 to 120 volts. Few, if any, electronic components are designed to withstand large voltage spikes of several thousand volts, and almost all will suffer damage if they're not protected from them.

Protection from spikes comes in many forms, from the $19.95 power strip with built-in surge protection that you can buy at your local hardware store to complicated arrays of transformers and specialized sacrificial transistors that are designed to die so that others may live. Unfortunately, those $19.95 power strips just aren't good enough. They are better than nothing, but barely. They have a limited ability to withstand really large spikes.

More specialized (and more expensive, of course) surge protectors that are specifically designed to protect computer networks are available from various companies. They differ in their ability to protect against really large spikes and in their cost. There's a fairly direct correlation between the cost of these products and their rated capacity and speed of action within any company's range of products, but the cost for a given level of protection can differ significantly from company to company. As always, if the price sounds too good to be true, it is.

In general, these surge protectors are designed to work by sensing a large increase in voltage and creating an alternate electrical path for that excessive voltage that doesn't allow it to get through to your server. In the most severe spikes, the surge protectors should destroy themselves before allowing the voltage to get through to your server. The effectiveness of these standalone surge protectors depends on the speed of their response to a large voltage increase and the mechanism of failure when their capacity is exceeded. If the surge protector doesn't respond quickly enough to a spike, bad things will happen.

Most UPSs also provide some protection from spikes. They have built-in surge protectors, plus isolation circuitry that tends to buffer the effects of spikes. The effectiveness of the spike protection in a UPS is not directly related to its cost, however—the overall cost of the UPS is more a factor of its effectiveness as an alternative power source. Your responsibility is to read the fine print and understand the limitations of the surge protection a given UPS offers. Also remember that just as with simple surge protectors, large voltage spikes can cause the surge protection to self-destruct rather than allow the voltage through to your server. That's the good news; the bad news is that instead of having to replace just a surge protector, you're likely to have to repair or replace the UPS.

NOTE Online or continuous UPSs are far more effective at protecting downstream electronic equipment than standard reactive UPSs. Even though an online UPS typically costs 1.5 to 2 times the price of a standard reactive UPS of the same capacity, it's money well spent.

Finally, one other spike protection mechanism can be helpful—the constant voltage transformer (CVT). You're not likely to see one unless you're in a large industrial setting, but they are often considered to be a sufficient replacement for other forms of surge protection. Unfortunately, they're not really optimal for spike protection. They do filter some excess voltage, but a large spike is likely to find its way through. However, in combination with either a fully protected UPS or a good standalone surge protector, a CVT can be quite effective. They also provide additional protection against other forms of voltage variation that surge protectors alone can't begin to manage.

Surges

Voltage surges and spikes are often discussed interchangeably, but we'd like to make a distinction here. For our purposes, a surge lasts longer than most spikes and isn't nearly as large. Most surges last a few hundred milliseconds and are rarely over 1,000 volts. They can be caused by many of the same factors that cause voltage spikes.

Providing protection against surges is somewhat easier than protecting against large spikes. Most of the protection mechanisms just discussed also adequately handle surges. In addition, most CVTs are sufficient to handle surges and might even handle them better if the surge is so prolonged that it threatens to overheat and burn out a simple surge protector.

Sags

Voltage sags are short-term reductions in the voltage delivered. They aren't complete voltage failures or power outages and are shorter than a full-scale brownout. Voltage sags can drop the voltage well below 100 volts on a 110- to 120-volt normal line and cause most servers to reboot if protection isn't provided.

Standalone surge protectors provide no defense against sags. You need a UPS or a very good CVT to prevent damage from a voltage sag. Severe sags can overcome the rating of all but the best constant voltage transformers, so you generally shouldn't use a CVT as the sole protection against sags. A UPS, with its battery power supply, is an essential part of your protection from problems caused by voltage sag.

Brownouts

A brownout is a planned, deliberate reduction in voltage from your electric utility company. Brownouts most often occur in the heat of the summer and are designed to protect the utility company from overloading. They are not designed to protect the consumer, however.

In general, a brownout reduces the available voltage by 5 to 20 percent from the normal value. A CVT or a UPS provides excellent protection against brownouts, within limits. Prolonged brownouts might exceed your UPS's ability to maintain a charge at the same time that it is providing power at the correct voltage to your equipment. Monitor the health of your UPS carefully during a brownout, especially because the risk of a complete power outage increases if the power company's voltage reduction strategy proves insufficient.

The best protection against extended brownouts is a CVT of sufficient rating to fully support your critical network devices and servers. If you live in an area that is subject to brownouts, and your budget can afford it, a good CVT is an excellent investment. This transformer takes the reduced voltage provided by your power company and increases it to the rated output voltage. A good constant voltage transformer can handle most brownouts for an extended time without problems, but you should still supplement the CVT with a quality UPS and surge protection between the transformer and the server or network device. This extra protection is especially important while the power company is attempting to restore power to full voltage, because during this period you run a higher risk of experiencing power and voltage fluctuations.

Short-Term Power Outages

Short-term power outages last from a few milliseconds to a few minutes. They can be caused by either internal or external events, but you can rarely plan for them even if they are internal. A server that is unprotected from a short-term power outage will, at the very least, reboot or, at the worst, fail catastrophically.

The best protection against a short-term power outage is a UPS in combination with high-quality spike protection. Be aware that many momentary interruptions of power are accompanied by large spikes when the power is restored. Further, a series of short-term power outages often occur consecutively, causing additional stress to electronic components.

Long-Term Power Outages

Long-term power outages, lasting from an hour or so to several days, are often accompanied by other, more serious problems unless your server room is in a very remote location. Long-term power outages can be caused by storms, earthquakes, fires, and the incompetence of electric power utilities, among other things. As such, plans for dealing with long-term power outages should be part of an overall disaster recovery plan. (See Chapter 27 for more on disaster planning.)

Protection against long-term power outages really becomes a decision about how long you want or need to function if all power is out. If you need to function long enough to be able to gracefully shut down your network, a simple UPS or a collection of them will be sufficient, assuming that you've sized the UPS correctly. However, if you need to be sure that you can maintain the full functionality of your SBS network during an extended power outage, you're going to need a combination of one or more UPSs and an auxiliary generator. But before you start spending money on generators and failover switches, evaluate the overall infrastructure supplying your power. If you're dependent on Internet connectivity to do business, it does you no good to be up and running in the middle of a two-day power outage if your Internet is also down.

 REAL WORLD **Generators Require Serious Expertise and Maintenance**

We've been involved with more than one operation that depended on—and implemented—auxiliary generators to support their operations during extended power outages, including our office, thanks to the regular extended outages that the weather here causes. The results of having an auxiliary generator have been rather mixed, however. The one lesson we've learned the hard way is that simply buying and installing an auxiliary generator will do little, if anything, to keep you up and running when the power goes out. Generators are complex mechanical and electrical machines that require specialized expertise and consistent, conscientious processes and maintenance.

If your situation requires an auxiliary generator to supplement your UPSs, you should carefully plan your power strategy to ensure that your generator has sufficient clean load capacity to provide the power your network will require in the event of a long-term power outage. Make sure you have a sufficient fuel source to power the generator for as long as you reasonably expect to have power out.

> **IMPORTANT** For all but the smallest businesses, a generator powered by piped-in natural gas is a far safer and more appropriate solution than a gasoline-powered generator with all the potential issues that storage of gasoline can entail.

To install and set up the generator, you'll need the expertise of a licensed electrician who has experience installing and configuring generator failover switches. Test your solution to make sure you didn't miss anything! Further, you should regularly test the effectiveness of your disaster recovery plans and make sure that all key personnel know how to start the auxiliary generator manually in the event it doesn't start automatically. Finally, you should have a regular preventive maintenance (PM) program in place that services and tests the generator and ensures that it is ready and functioning when you need it. This PM program should include both static tests and full load tests on a regular basis, and should also call for periodically replacing the fuel to the generator if it's gasoline powered. One of the best ways to do all of this is to plan and execute a "disaster day" for testing your entire disaster recovery plan in as close to real-world conditions as possible, including running your entire operation from the backup generator.

Disk Arrays

The most common computer hardware malfunction is probably a hard disk failure. Even though hard disks have become more reliable over time, they are still subject to failure, especially during their first month or so of use. They are also vulnerable to both catastrophic and degenerative failures caused by power problems. Fortunately, disk arrays have become the norm for servers, and good fault-tolerant RAID systems are available in Windows Small Business Server 2008 and RAID-specific hardware supported by SBS. The choice of software or hardware RAID, and the particulars of how you configure your RAID system, can significantly affect the cost of your servers. To make an informed choice for your environment and needs, you must understand the tradeoffs and the differences in fault tolerance, speed, configurability, and so on.

Hardware v. Software

RAID can be implemented at the hardware level, using RAID controllers, or at the software level, either by the operating system or by a third-party add-on. SBS supports both hardware RAID and its own software RAID.

Hardware RAID implementations require dedicated controllers and cost somewhat more than an equivalent level of software RAID. However, for that extra price, you get a faster, more flexible, and more fault-tolerant RAID. When compared to the software RAID provided in SBS 2008, a good hardware RAID controller supports more levels of RAID, on-the-fly reconfiguration of the arrays, hot-swap and hot-spare drives (discussed later in this chapter), and dedicated caching of both reads and writes.

Software RAID requires that you convert your disks to dynamic disks. Converting your boot disk (C drive) is probably not a good idea. Dynamic disks can be more difficult to access if a problem occurs, and the SBS setup and installation program provides only limited support. For maximum fault tolerance, we recommend using hardware mirroring (RAID 1) on your system drive; if you do use software mirroring, make sure your disaster recovery scenarios fully encompass booting from the second disk of a failed mirror. Or just say no to having your boot disk as part of a software RAID array.

RAID Levels for Fault Tolerance

Except for level 0, RAID is a mechanism for storing sufficient information on a group of hard disks so that even if one hard disk in the group fails, no information is lost. Some RAID arrangements go even further, providing protection in the event of multiple hard disk failures. The more common levels of RAID and their appropriateness in a fault-tolerant environment are shown in Table 4-1.

TABLE 4-1 RAID Levels and Their Fault Tolerance

LEVEL	NUMBER OF DISKS*	SPEED	FAULT TOLERANCE	DESCRIPTION
0	N	+++	- - -	Striping alone. Not fault-tolerant—it actually increases your risk of failure—but does provide for the fastest read and write performance.
1	2N	+	++	Mirror or duplex. Slightly faster read than single disk, but no gain during write operations. Failure of any single disk causes no loss in data and minimal performance hit.
3	N+1	++	+	Byte-level parity. Data is striped across multiple drives at the byte level with the parity information written to a single dedicated drive. Reads are much faster than with a single disk, but writes operate slightly slower than a single disk because parity information must be generated and written to a single disk. Failure of any single disk causes no loss of data but can cause a significant loss of performance.
4	N+1	++	+	Block-level parity with a dedicated parity disk. Similar to RAID 3 except that data is striped at the block level.
5	N+1	+	++	Interleaved block-level parity. Parity information is distributed across all drives. Reads are much faster than a single disk but writes are significantly slower. Failure of any single disk provides no loss of data but results in a major reduction in performance.

LEVEL	NUMBER OF DISKS*	SPEED	FAULT TOLERANCE	DESCRIPTION
6	N+2	+	+ +	Replicated interleaved block-level parity. Parity information is distributed across all drives with two parity blocks on separate drives for every stripe. Reads are much faster than a single disk but writes are significantly slower. Failure of any two disks provides no loss of data but results in a major reduction in performance.
0+1 and 10	2N	+ + +	+ +	Striped mirrored disks or mirrored striped disks. Data is striped across multiple mirrored disks or multiple striped disks are mirrored. Failure of any one disk causes no data loss and no speed loss. Failure of a second disk could result in data loss. Faster than a single disk for both reads and writes.
Other	Varies	+ + +	+ + +	Array of RAID arrays. Different hardware vendors have different proprietary names for this RAID concept. Excellent read and write performance. Failure of any one disk results in no loss of performance and continued redundancy.

*In the Number of Disks column, N refers to the number of hard disks required to hold the original copy of the data. The plus and minus symbols show relative improvement or deterioration compared to a system using no version of RAID. The scale peaks at three symbols.

NOTE RAID is an excellent solution for fault tolerance, but it can't protect you against corruption caused by hardware or software failures. Only a good backup of data from before the corruption can protect against that.

When choosing the RAID level to use for a given application or server, consider the following factors:

- **Intended use** Will this application be primarily read-intensive, such as file serving, or will it be predominantly write-intensive, such as a transactional database? SBS servers are heavily write-intensive, at least on the disks that Microsoft Exchange uses. Virtualization is also highly disk-intensive.
- **Fault tolerance** How critical is this data, and how much can you afford to lose?

- **Availability** Does this server or application need to be available at all times, or can you afford to be able to reboot it or otherwise take it offline for brief periods?

- **Performance** Is this application or server heavily used, with large amounts of data being transferred to and from it, or is this server or application less I/O-intensive? If this is your main SBS server, it's heavily used.

- **Cost** Are you on a tight budget for this server or application, or is the cost of data loss or unavailability the primary driving factor?

You need to evaluate each of these factors when you decide which type of RAID to use for a server or portion of a server. No single answer fits all cases, but the final answer requires you to carefully weigh each of these factors and balance them against your situation and your needs. The following sections take a closer look at each factor and how it weighs in the overall decision-making process.

Intended Use

The intended use, and the kind of disk access associated with that use, plays an important role in determining the best RAID level for your application. Think about how write-intensive the application is and whether the manner in which the application uses the data is more sequential or random. Is your application a three-square-meals-a-day kind of application, with relatively large chunks of data being read or written at a time, or is it more of a grazer or nibbler, reading and writing little bits of data from all sorts of different places?

If your application is relatively write-intensive, you'll want to avoid software RAID or RAID 5 and RAID 6 if other considerations don't require them. With RAID 5 and RAID 6, any application that requires more than 50 percent writes to reads is likely to be at least somewhat slower, if not much slower, than it would be on a single disk or a RAID 1 mirror. You can mitigate this to some extent by using more but smaller drives in your array and by using a hardware controller with a large cache to offload the parity processing as much as possible. RAID 1, in either a mirror or duplex configuration, provides a high degree of fault tolerance with no significant penalty during write operations—a good choice for the system disk.

If your application is primarily read-intensive, and the data is stored and referenced sequentially, RAID 3 or RAID 4 might be a good choice. Because the data is striped across many drives, you have parallel access to it, improving your throughput. And because the parity information is stored on a single drive rather than dispersed across the array, sequential read operations don't have to skip over the parity information and are therefore faster. However, write operations are substantially slower, and the single parity drive can become an I/O bottleneck during write operations.

NOTE RAID 3 and RAID 4 have been largely supplanted by other RAID technologies, primarily RAID 5 and RAID 10. In an SBS environment, RAID 3 and RAID 4 are unlikely to be an appropriate choice, and you should only consider them for specialized applications.

If your application is primarily read-intensive and not necessarily sequential, RAID 5 and RAID 6 are obvious choices. They provide a good balance of speed and fault tolerance, and the cost is substantially lower than the cost of RAID 1 or RAID 10. Disk accesses are evenly distributed across multiple drives, and no single drive has the potential to be an I/O bottleneck. However, writes require calculation of the parity information and the extra write of that parity, slowing write operations down significantly. Windows Small Business Server file shares are a good fit for RAID 5 and RAID 6, but avoid them for the volume that holds write intensive database files.

If your application provides other mechanisms for data recovery or uses large amounts of temporary storage that doesn't require fault tolerance, a simple RAID 0, with no fault tolerance but fast reads and writes, is a possibility—but we strongly advise against RAID 0 on an SBS server.

Fault Tolerance

Carefully examine the fault tolerance of each of the possible RAID choices for your intended use. All RAID levels except RAID 0 provide some degree of fault tolerance, but the effect of a failure and the ability to recover from subsequent failures are different.

If a drive in a RAID 1 mirror or duplex array fails, a full, complete, exact copy of the data remains. Access to your data or application is unimpeded, and performance degradation is minimal, although you do lose the benefit gained on read operations of being able to read from either disk. Until the failed disk is replaced, however, you have no fault tolerance on the remaining disk. After you replace the failed disk, overall performance is significantly reduced while the new disk is initialized and the mirror is rebuilt. Modern RAID controllers can vary the speed of data reconstruction when replacing a failed disk, allowing you to balance the speed of regeneration against the performance degradation.

In a RAID 3 or RAID 4 array, if one of the data disks fails, a significant performance degradation occurs because the missing data needs to be reconstructed from the parity information. Also, you'll have no fault tolerance until the failed disk is replaced. If the parity disk fails, you'll have no fault tolerance until it is replaced, but also no performance degradation. After you replace the failed disk, overall performance is significantly reduced while the new disk is initialized and the parity information or data is rebuilt.

In a RAID 5 array, the loss of any disk results in a significant performance degradation, and your fault tolerance will be gone until you replace the failed disk. After you replace the disk, you won't return to fault tolerance until the entire array has a chance to rebuild itself, and performance is seriously degraded during the rebuild process.

In a RAID 6 array, the loss of any disk results in a significant performance degradation, but you will still be fault tolerant. The failure of a second disk will not cause data loss, but will leave you with no fault tolerance. After you replace a failed disk, you won't return to full fault tolerance until the entire array has a chance to rebuild itself, and performance is seriously degraded during the rebuild process.

RAID systems that are arrays of arrays can provide for multiple failure tolerance. These arrays provide for multiple levels of redundancy and are appropriate for mission-critical applications that must be able to withstand the failure of more than one drive in an array.

Availability

All levels of RAID, except RAID 0, provide higher availability than a single drive. However, if availability is expanded to also include the overall performance level during failure mode, some RAID levels provide definite advantages over others. Specifically, RAID 1 and its derivatives, RAID 10 and RAID 0+1, provide enhanced availability when compared to RAID levels 3, 4, 5, and 6 during failure mode. The performance degradation is minimal when compared to a single disk if one half of a mirror fails, whereas a RAID 5 or RAID 6 array has substantially compromised performance until the failed disk is replaced and the array is rebuilt.

In addition, RAID systems that are based on an array of arrays can provide higher availability than RAID levels 1 through 6. Running on multiple controllers, these arrays are able to tolerate the failure of more than one disk and the failure of one of the controllers, providing protection against the single point of failure inherent in any single-controller arrangement. RAID 1 that uses duplexed disks running on different controllers—as opposed to RAID 1 that uses mirroring on the same controller—also provides this additional protection and improved availability.

Hot-swap drives and hot-spare drives (discussed later in this chapter) can further improve availability in critical environments, especially hot-spare drives. By providing for automatic failover and rebuilding, they can reduce your exposure to catastrophic failure and provide for maximum availability.

Performance

The relative performance of each RAID level depends on the intended use. The best compromise for many situations is arguably RAID 5 or RAID 6, but you should be suspicious of that compromise if your application is fairly write-intensive. Especially for relational database data and index files where the database is moderately or highly write-intensive, the performance hit of using RAID 5 or RAID 6 can be substantial. A better alternative is to use RAID 0+1 or RAID 10.

Whatever level of RAID you choose for your particular application, it will benefit from using more small disks rather than a few large disks. The more drives contributing to the stripe of the array, the greater the benefit of parallel reading and writing you'll be able to realize—and your array's overall speed will improve.

Cost

The delta in cost between RAID configurations is primarily the cost of drives, potentially including the cost of additional array enclosures because more drives are required for a particular level of RAID. RAID 1—either duplexing or mirroring—is the most expensive of the conventional RAID levels because it requires at least 33 percent more raw disk space for a given amount of net storage space than other RAID levels.

Another consideration is that RAID levels that include mirroring or duplexing must use drives in pairs. Therefore, it's more difficult (and more expensive) to add on to an array if you need additional space on the array. A net 144-gigabyte (GB) RAID 0+1 array, comprising four 72-GB drives, requires four more 72-GB drives to double in size, a somewhat daunting prospect if your array cabinet has bays for only six drives, for example. A net 144-GB RAID 5 array of three 72-GB drives, however, can be doubled in size simply by adding two more 72-GB drives for a total of five drives.

RAID arrays based on 2.5-inch drives are rapidly replacing traditional 3.5-inch drives. The smaller 2.5-inch drives take up less physical space for the same amount of total storage, while consuming substantially less power and generating less heat. The initial cost of the array is essentially similar to that of an equivalent array using 3.5-inch drives, but the ongoing costs are less. Our current preferred array system uses eight 2.5-inch SAS drives configured as RAID 0+1. The entire array fits in the space of a pair of standard CD/DVD drives in our HP ML350 tower.

Hot-Swap and Hot-Spare Disk Systems

Hardware RAID systems can provide for both hot-swap and hot-spare capabilities. A hot-swap disk system allows failed hard disks to be removed and a replacement disk inserted into the array without powering down the system or rebooting the server. When the new disk is inserted, it is automatically recognized and either will be automatically configured into the array or can be manually configured into it. Additionally, many hot-swap RAID systems allow you to add hard disks into empty slots dynamically and automatically or manually increase the size of the RAID volume on the fly without a reboot.

A hot-spare RAID configuration uses an additional, preconfigured disk or disks to automatically replace a failed disk. These systems can be configured to automatically regenerate the array in the event of a failure, thus maintaining maximal redundancy. When combined with a RAID configuration that can withstand multiple drive failures, such as RAID 6, a hot-spare system provides a very high degree of redundancy and availability.

Even where you don't have hot-spare drive already configured into your array, it makes sense to always keep a matching spare drive available in your replacement-parts cabinet. Hard drives aren't all that expensive, and having a spare will save you time if you have a drive failure in your array. Plus, with drive sizes and technology changing rapidly, it can be annoying to try to find a matching drive two or three years after you buy the original array.

Redundant Networking

Having a server up and running does you little good if the server can't communicate with the rest of your network or the outside world. Building redundancy into your power and disk systems is important, but does you little good if you can't communicate with your network.

Protecting against a network-card failure can be as simple as having a spare network card, ideally of the same type as is in your server. In the event of a failure, replacing the card takes only a few minutes longer than it takes to reboot the server, if you can find the spare. A better option is to leave the spare card plugged in to a spare slot, but disabled in Windows. Finally, if your server supports it, using network card teaming provides redundancy in the event of failure with higher throughput under normal operation. But be sure your application supports teamed networking before implementing.

When your network interface is on the motherboard, as is common these days, it's generally not as easy to provide identical redundant network interfaces, unless they are built into the server. Nonetheless, having a server-quality network card available and ready to drop into the server in the event of a failure can make recovery much quicker.

If your business depends on Internet connectivity (and whose business doesn't at least require e-mail these days?), one point of failure that can easily be missed is your Internet connection. Solving this, however, is not at all difficult—simply replace your standard router with a dual-WAN router and bring in a second Internet service. We have both cable and DSL available to our office, so we added a Xincom dual-WAN router that does basic load balancing when both connections are working, but still provides acceptable bandwidth when either connection is down.

Finally, under networking, we strongly suggest your server have a low-level network port that can be used to connect to the server directly even if the operating system is unresponsive. If you have an HP, this is called an iLO port (short for integrated lights out). For Dell, it's a DRAC (Dell Remote Access Card). Other server manufacturers have similar technologies. This is a network card that is powered up and reachable well before any operating system gets loaded, and it is managed entirely in firmware.

Other Spare Parts

So you've got a spare power supply, a spare hard drive for your array, and your NICs are teamed. Is that enough? Well, it puts you way ahead of many businesses, but are there any other parts that you should keep available? Any other peripheral or card that you couldn't run your business without is a good candidate for a spare. Another candidate is a spare video card, though this is less critical. You can, after all, always Remote Desktop into the server if you need to, and replacement video cards are easy and quick to come by.

Any other cards or peripherals that you would have problems doing without for the time it takes to get a new one to replace a failure is a good candidate for your spare-parts cabinet. We like to keep a spare network switch with a few spare network cables available. Another smart choice is to keep a spare of your DSL modem or boundary router.

Summary

Building a highly available and fault-tolerant system requires you to carefully evaluate both your requirements and your resources to eliminate single points of failure within the system. You should evaluate each of the hardware subsystems within the overall system for fault tolerance and ensure that recovery procedures are clearly understood and practiced to reduce recovery time in the event of a failure. UPSs, redundant power supplies, redundant networking, and RAID systems are all methods for improving overall fault tolerance.

Now that we've covered the planning and preparation of your SBS network, it's time to move on to the actual installation and setup of SBS. In the next part we'll cover new installations, migrating from an existing SBS or Windows Server network, and some special considerations for using virtualization to build your SBS network. The first chapter in this next part covers a typical first-time installation of Windows Small Business Server 2008.

Installing SBS 2008

This chapter covers performing a clean installation of Windows Small Business Server 2008. All installations of SBS 2008 are clean installs, because there is no direct upgrade path from an existing SBS installation—only a migration. We'll cover migrations in detail in Chapter 7, "Migrating from Windows Small Business Server 2003," so if you're installing in an existing Windows domain environment—either SBS or Windows Server—you'll want to jump ahead to Chapter 7.

If you're installing in a virtual environment, and it's a fresh install, then go ahead and read this chapter, but hold off on actually performing any of the steps until you've had a chance to read Chapter 6, "Configuring SBS in Hyper-V."

Planning

Chapters 2 through 4 have already covered most of the planning issues associated with installing SBS, but there are a few last things to take care of. You should have the hardware all assembled, but now it's time to verify the physical configuration of the network, decide on what IP address range you'll be using, and choose network names. You'll also want to decide how the storage on your SBS server should be apportioned. The installation wizard for Windows Small Business Server 2008 is quite good and asks only a few basic questions about your business and the network names and passwords you want to use. Everything else is saved for the Getting Started task list after the installation completes.

Planning Partitions

One of the things that doesn't get explicitly asked is how to partition your hard disk space. The default installation will put everything on a single partition that takes up all the space on your first hard disk. SBS 2008 makes it fairly easy to move data such as user shares and Microsoft Exchange data to new locations whenever you want, so careful planning up front isn't critical, especially if some of your hard disk space won't be visible until the operating system is fully installed and you can install drivers for the space.

Our recommendation is to at least create a partition for the initial installation, and to size it appropriately for the system drive of SBS. We recommend that you create a partition during the initial installation screens for Small Business Server 2008 that is *at least* 60 gigabytes (GB) in size. (80 to 120 GB is a more realistic minimum.)

REAL WORLD   Dividing Storage

Although you can have a single large partition and put everything on it, there are compelling reasons to divide hard-drive space into at least three different partitions, even if you are using hardware RAID. The three partitions are:

- The primary operating system partition.

- A partition for static storage. Use this for primarily read-intensive storage such as company-wide shared folders, application installations, and installation sources.

- A partition for data, logs, and other volatile information. This will be the most active partition and should have a storage technology optimized accordingly.

Dividing your storage space into logical partitions in this way makes backups and disaster recovery easier and allows you to focus your efforts on the critical data partition.

Planning Location and Networking

The other planning step you should take prior to installing SBS 2008 is to decide your physical layout and networking layout. The main areas of concern for the physical layout are:

- **Server security**   Is the server secure from physical access?

- **Network device security**   Are the main network devices secure from physical access?

- **Ease of access**   Is it easy to get to the server, and the connections to it, for maintenance?

- **Expandability**   Is there room to add servers as your business grows?

Your SBS server should be physically protected and have limited access that is controlled and monitored. Although not every small business has the luxury of an air-conditioned server room with high-security access control, there are still basic steps you can and should take. The server (and main networking equipment) should be in a separate room that can be locked. In a pinch, using a lockable cage in a multipurpose room can work, but then choose your servers for their noise level. A keycode lock is a good choice because it can be easily changed if an employee leaves, and most keycode locks allow for separate keys for individuals and for determining who has been in the room. See Chapter 3, "Planning Your SBS Network" for more on planning for security.

Planning the logical networking is another important step to make sure you've done before starting the actual install. We like to use a simple spreadsheet that shows the necessary information we'll need for the installation. Details on the spreadsheet include:

- Internet service provider (ISP) information, including account names, IP addresses, support phone number, and so on.
- Internal network details, including IP address range, router IP address, number and names of clients, and number and names of servers.
- DNS and NetBIOS names that will be used for the new network.
- Router configuration, including any updates that are required to the router, what its default settings are if you have to reset it, what settings you've changed on the router to configure it for SBS, and so on. If your router is UPnP-enabled, SBS can make at least some of the changes for you automatically.

NOTE Many routers default to 192.168.0.1, 192.168.1.1, or 10.0.0.1 for their IP address. If you have to reset the router, make sure you have a well-documented way to upload a configuration file to return it to the configuration you've chosen for your network. Leaving the router at one of these common defaults can create issues setting up virtual private networks, so it's not recommended.

Preparing the Server

Finally, there are a few last steps to take before launching the installation:

- Make sure the server is sized appropriately for the load under which you plan to place it. For more information on server sizing, see Chapter 3.
- If you're installing on an existing server, back up all data and record any important settings.
- Remove the Uninterruptible Power Supply (UPS) management cable from the server (even if it's USB).
- Upgrade the system BIOS to the latest version available.
- Set the boot order in the BIOS to boot from the DVD before the hard disk.
- Locate any mass storage drivers necessary for the system.
- Configure the firewall or router as required.

Installation

The actual installation of Windows Small Business Server 2008 has been significantly simplified compared to earlier versions of SBS. The initial installation of the operating system asks fewer questions, and the installation of the SBS portion also asks far fewer questions. Plus both can be automated or semi-automated using answer files. We'll walk through a basic installation first and then address customizations, advanced settings, and automation.

Installation Process

The installation process for Windows Small Business Server 2008 is a two-stage process. The first stage installs 64-bit Windows Server 2008 Standard, and the second stage installs SBS itself. The important thing here is that the underlying operating system is Windows Server 2008 Standard. There are only three limitations placed on Windows Server 2008 by SBS:

- SBS can only be in a single domain environment—no trust relationships are possible.
- The initial SBS server must hold all of the Flexible Single Master Operation (FSMO) roles. Additional domain controllers can be installed in the SBS network, but none of the FSMO roles can be moved.
- A maximum of 75 users or device Client Access Licenses (CALs) are allowed.

Installing the Base Operating System

Installing the underlying Windows Server 2008 Standard operating system can be done using any of the deployment methods supported by Windows Server 2008, but you will usually do it by booting from the Windows Small Business Server 2008 Disk1 and following these steps:

1. At the initial screen of the Install Windows Wizard, shown in Figure 5-1, set the localization information for this installation of SBS.

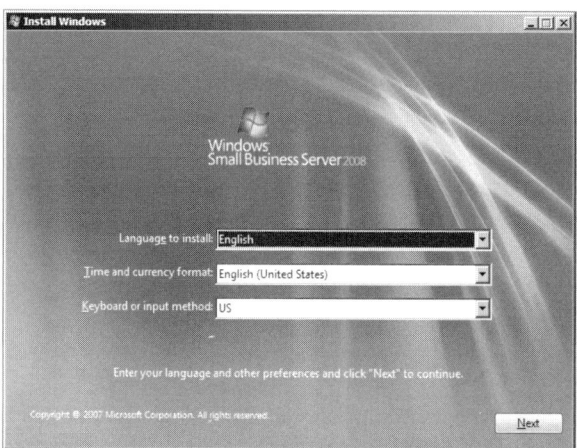

FIGURE 5-1 The localization page of the Install Windows Wizard

2. Click Next to open the Install Now page of the Install Windows Wizard, as shown in Figure 5-2.

FIGURE 5-2 The Install Now page of the Install Windows Wizard

3. Click Install Now to open the Type Your Product Key For Activation page of the Install Windows Wizard. Enter your SBS 2008 product key. To simplify product activation, select the Automatically Activate Windows When I'm Online check box. If this is a test setup, clear the check box—you'll have 30 days to use and test SBS before you'll need to activate.

4. Click Next to open the Please Read The License Terms page. Read the license and select the I Accept The License Terms check box. You don't have a choice, after all, but it's good to know what you're actually agreeing to.

5. Click Next to open the Which Type Of Installation Do You Want page shown in Figure 5-3. Upgrade will be disabled—your only choice is Custom (Advanced).

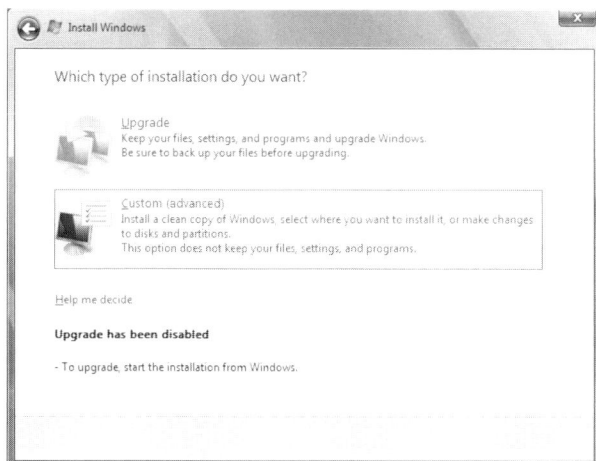

FIGURE 5-3 The Which Type Of Installation Do You Want page of the Install Windows Wizard

6. Click Custom (Advanced) to open the Where Do You Want To Install Windows page. You'll see a list of available drives and partitions you can install SBS on.

7. If the drive you want to use isn't listed, click Load Driver to open the Load Driver dialog box shown in Figure 5-4. Drivers can be loaded from floppy disk, CD, DVD, or a USB flash drive.

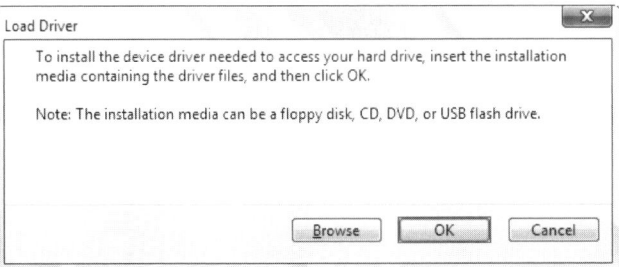

FIGURE 5-4 The Load Driver dialog box during Windows Installation

8. Click OK to have Windows search attached removable media and display the results on the Select The Driver To Be Installed page, shown in Figure 5-5. If the driver isn't displayed, click Browse and navigate to the device and folder where the driver is located.

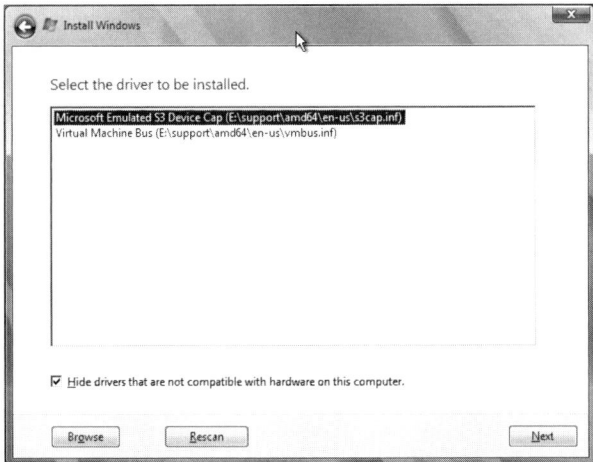

FIGURE 5-5 The Select The Driver To Be Installed page of the Install Windows Wizard

9. Click Next to load the selected driver and return to the Where Do You Want To Install Windows page. Select the partition where you want to install Windows.

10. Click Next to begin the actual installation of Windows Server 2008 Standard. No further questions will be asked until the SBS portion of the installation begins.

Installing the SBS Portion

After the underlying operating system is installed, Windows will log on and the SBS installation will automatically start. This installation will configure your time zone, your networking, and your server and Windows domain names; configure your business information; and set your administrator account and password for the SBS domain. Also during this process, you'll have a chance to install any required networking drivers if Windows doesn't have a built-in driver for your network card and to download the latest updates to protect your server.

> **NOTE** Windows Small Business Server 2008 installation requires that a functioning network card be detected prior to installation. If your network card is not automatically detected by Windows Server 2008, you'll need to download the driver and have it available before the installation of SBS can proceed.

To install the SBS portion of the Windows Small Business Server 2008, continue the installation from step 10 of the preceding section. When the operating system finishes installing and restarts your server, the SBS installation will begin automatically, as shown in Figure 5-6.

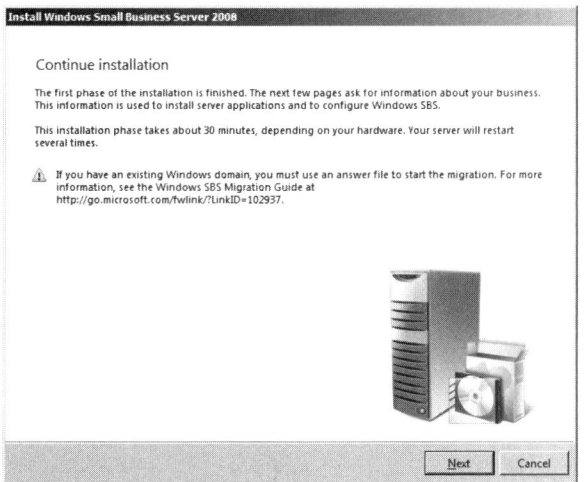

FIGURE 5-6 The Continue Installation page of the Install Windows Small Business Server 2008 Wizard

Continue the installation by following these steps:

1. Click Next on the Continue Installation page of the Install Windows Small Business Server 2008 Wizard to open the Verify The Clock And Time Zone Settings page shown in Figure 5-7.

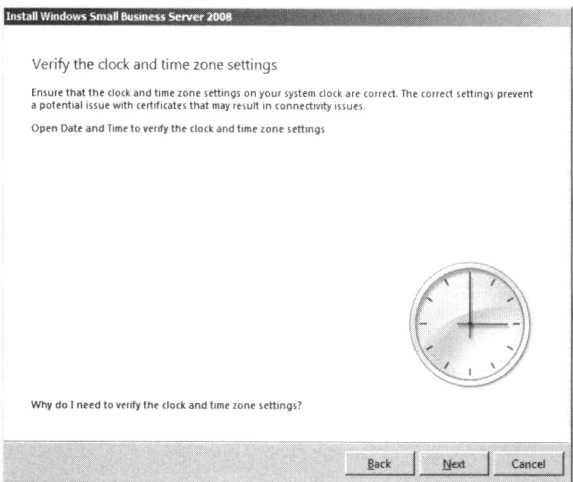

FIGURE 5-7 The Verify The Clock And Time Zone Settings page of the Install Windows Small Business Server 2008 Wizard

2. Click the Open Date And Time To Verify The Clock And Time Zone Settings link to the standard Windows Date And Time dialog box. Set the time zone and current date and time if they aren't correct and then click OK to return to the Verify The Clock And Time Zone Settings page.

3. Click Next to open the Get Important Updates page. (If your network adapter hasn't been detected, you will not see this page—instead, you'll have an opportunity to load drivers for the network adapter.)

4. Click Go Online And Get The Most Recent Installation Updates (Recommended). This will download only critical updates that are directly related to installation issues.

5. When the update check is complete, click Next to open the Company Information page shown in Figure 5-8.

6. Fill in the fields on the Company Information page. This information will be used to customize various other areas of SBS. Nothing is required here, but there's no good reason not to enter the information either—none of it is sent to Microsoft.

7. Click Next to open the Personalize Your Server And Your Network page shown in Figure 5-9. Here you need to enter a name for your server and an internal domain name that will be used for the SBS network.

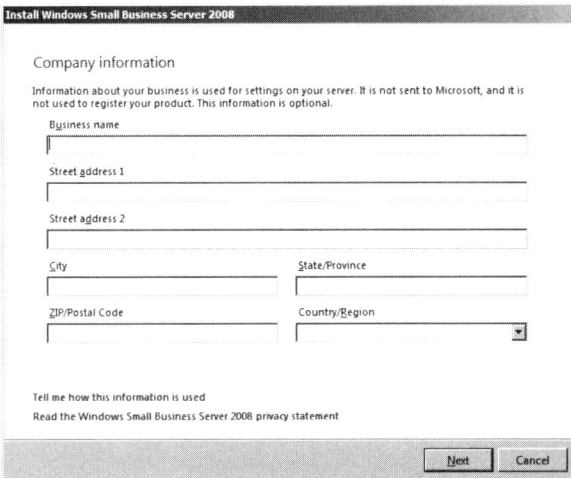

FIGURE 5-8 The Company Information page of the Install Windows Small Business Server 2008 Wizard

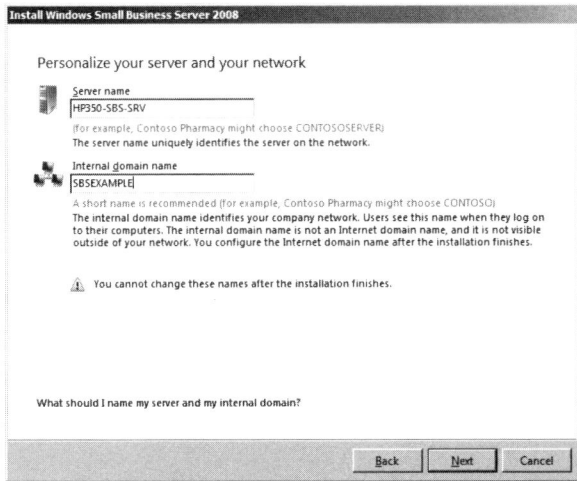

FIGURE 5-9 The Personalize Your Server And Your Network page of the Install Windows Small Business Server 2008 Wizard

REAL WORLD   Choose a Generic Domain Name

The temptation is to choose a simple domain name that somehow reflects the name of the company you're building the SBS server for. This makes perfect sense and no one will question it. In fact, this is what we used to do when we set up networks for our customers. And it seemed to work fine. Until the first time one of them merged with another small company and changed their name to reflect the new company. And we had to tell them that there wasn't any way to change the domain name.

The only solution was to rebuild the network from scratch, with all the pain and risk that involved. We learned an important lesson, however. Although it's important to choose a name that makes sense to users—because they'll see it every time they log on to their workstations—make it a generic name that reflects the functionality, not the specific company name.

We now use a generic internal domain name, SBSNETWORK. Everyone understands what it is, but it doesn't cause issues if the company later has a name change.

8. Click Next to open the Add A Network Administrator Account page shown in Figure 5-10. Enter a name for the administrator and an account name (user name) for the account. SBS 2008 requires that the main administrator account *not* be Administrator. See the Under the Hood sidebar for more details on the Administrator account.

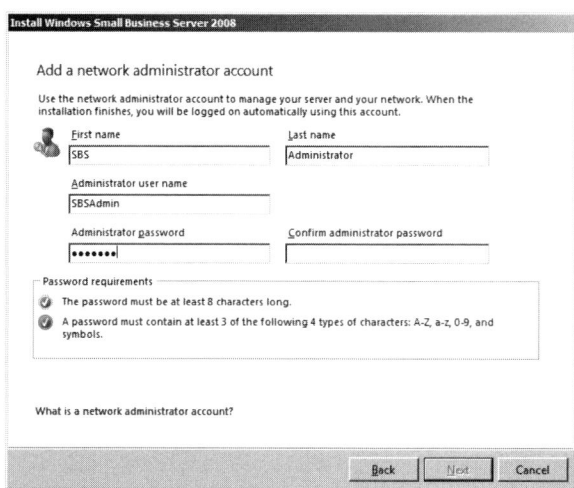

FIGURE 5-10 The Add A Network Administrator Account page of the Install Windows Small Business Server 2008 Wizard

NOTE   SBS lets you know if your password meets the current complexity and length requirements as you enter it.

9. Enter a password for the new administrator account and click Next to open the confir-
    mation page shown in Figure 5-11. If everything looks correct, click Next to install SBS.

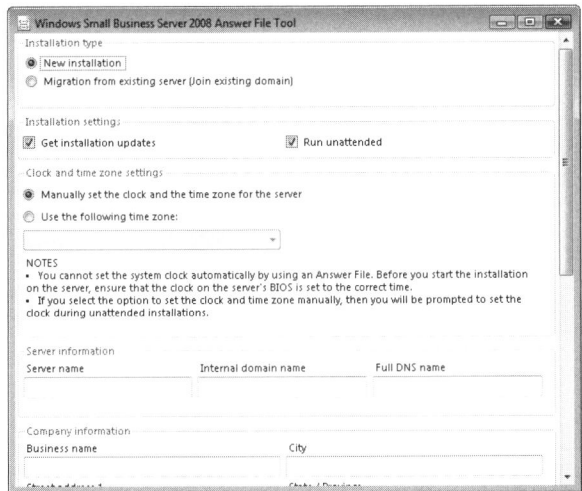

FIGURE 5-11 The That Is All The Information Needed confirmation page of the Install Windows
Small Business Server 2008 Wizard

UNDER THE HOOD   Administrator 500 Account

SBS requires you to create a new administrator account during a new installation.
(We called this account "SBSAdmin" in the previous examples.) This administrator account is used for all future administration of SBS, and the original *Administrator* account—often referred to as the 500 account from an easily recognizable
portion of the account's globally unique identifier (GUID)—is disabled.

The new administrator account password is synchronized with the Directory Service
Restore Mode (DSRM) Administrator account password, used to recover Active
Directory if there's a problem. So far, so good. But when the password changes for
the new administrator account, the underlying DSRM Administrator account is *not*
updated. This means that the DSRM Administrator password is tied to that original
password, and you'll need to keep a permanent record of it in case you need to
recover from a problem with Active Directory.

We understand the reasons why the developers disable the *Administrator* account,
but we think it's unfortunate that there isn't a solution in place that would allow the
passwords to remain synchronized. However, because SBS 2008 is built on Windows
Server 2008, you can use the restartable AD DS feature, combined with appropriate
registry changes, to enable other recovery scenarios. For more information on using
Restartable AD DS, see *http://technet.microsoft.com/en-us/library/cc732714.aspx*.

Using the SBS Answer File Generator

New in Windows Small Business Server 2008 is the ability to simplify the SBS portion of the installation using an answer file. The answer file is required for doing a migration from an existing domain environment, but it's optional for a clean new installation. It does, however, have some advantages because it allows you to customize some portions of the install that aren't available in the normal install. Disk1 of Windows Small Business Server 2008 includes a tool called the SBS Answer File Generator (SBSAfg.exe) to create an answer file. SBSAfg.exe is located in the \Tools directory. To use SBSAfg.exe, follow these steps:

1. Copy the file SBSAfg.exe from the SBS 2008 Disk1 to your local hard disk. Where you copy it isn't important as long as you can find it.

2. From Windows Explorer, double-click SBSAfg to start the SBS Answer File Tool, shown in Figure 5-12.

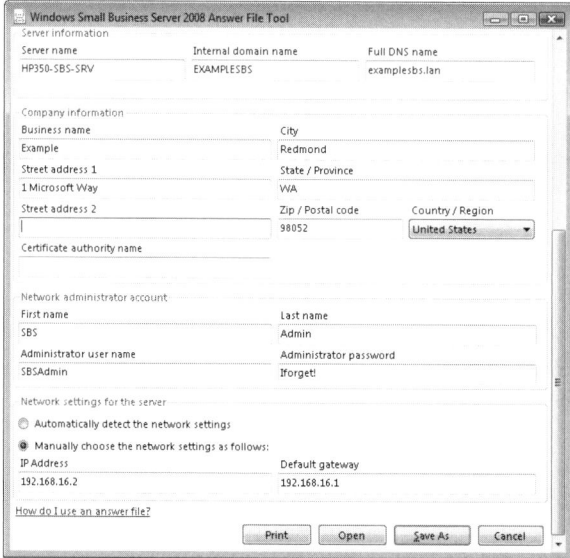

FIGURE 5-12 The Windows Small Business Server 2008 Answer File Tool

3. Fill in the fields of the Answer File Tool to configure your installation of SBS. If you leave a required field blank, you'll be prompted for that value during the installation.

4. When you've filled in the fields of the Answer File Tool, click Save As to save the answer file. The filename should be SBSAnswerFile.xml.

5. To use the answer file, copy it to removable media such as a USB flash drive or USB hard drive and connect the USB drive to the SBS server prior to the initial SBS installation screen (shown earlier in Figure 5-6) and SBS will automatically load the answer file and proceed to use it during the installation. You can also copy it to the root of any hard disk attached to the SBS server.

NOTE If you create an empty XML file with the name SBSAnswerFile.xml and make it available to the SBS installation process, as described in step 5, you will have additional options available during the installation process.

NOTE If you're installing on a Hyper-V child partition, where there is no USB available, you can use a virtual floppy drive (VFD) with the SBSAnswerFile.xml on it. Floppy disks work just as well for automating the installation.

Using the answer file is the only way you can specify a different internal root DNS domain name other than ".local". If you use the standard SBS installation, it will automatically add a .local to the internal domain name. But when using an answer file, you can specify any root DNS domain to add. You'll see in Figure 5-12 that we used .lan as the internal DNS root domain.

Summary

This chapter has covered the steps required to prepare for and perform a clean installation of Windows Small Business Server 2008. After installation, additional configuration specific to your environment is done using the Getting Started task list, as discussed in Chapter 8, "Completing the Getting Started Tasks."

Chapter 6, which follows, discusses Hyper-V in general and describes the special considerations for installing SBS in a Hyper-V environment. These considerations, while specific to Hyper-V, are also relevant in a general way for any virtualization environment. Chapter 7 covers migrating an existing Windows Server or Windows Small Business Server environment to Windows Small Business Server 2008.

Configuring SBS in Hyper-V

Hyper-V is Microsoft's new hypervisor-based, native Windows Server 2008 virtualization solution. While not for everyone, we think that using virtualization (and specifically Hyper-V) to build your SBS network is a very cost-effective solution that can provide an excellent end-user experience while also enabling improved disaster recovery and ease of management.

When we wrote the *Microsoft Windows Small Business Server 2003 Administrator's Companion*, virtualization was a tiny fraction of the market and almost exclusively the province of very large organizations. Microsoft had no virtualization products and provided little or no support for companies and individuals using virtualization. By the time we wrote *Microsoft Windows Small Business Server 2003 R2 Administrator's Companion*, there was already a huge shift in place. Microsoft had bought out a virtualization company and had two products on the market: Virtual PC and Virtual Server. More and more companies were looking to virtualization as a way to consolidate servers, reduce server room footprints, and provide flexible test environments. Virtualization had gone from the "Hey, that's kinda neat" phase to the "Hmmm, you know, that might just make sense" phase. Companies large and small were actively investigating virtualization, planning how to use it, or already deploying it.

Now, fast forward a couple of years, and virtualization is a way of life for many of us. We couldn't begin to do what we need to do without being able to virtualize, and we're actively deploying virtual solutions in production. Microsoft has gone from having a couple of virtualization products to having a suite of solutions around virtualization, including building it right into the operating system with the inclusion of Hyper-V in Windows Server 2008.

Why has virtualization suddenly become such a compelling scenario? What has changed? We think that two very important changes are driving the move to virtualize: official support from Microsoft and the wide availability of x64 hardware.

Official support means that if you have an issue with Windows or just about any of the Microsoft server applications, and you're running in a virtualized environment, you're still supported, and Microsoft support won't say, "Sorry, we don't support you on Virtual Server." This is an important concern for anyone using virtualization in a production environment.

The wide availability of x64 hardware is also driving the move to virtualization. The biggest limiting factor for running virtualization on 32-bit Windows is the RAM limitation. By moving to x64 Windows Server, especially Windows Server 2008 with native Hyper-V, running many server workloads on a single physical server is easy. For example, while writing this book, we've been using an HP ML350G5 server with 16 gigabytes (GB) of RAM and two dual-core processors. That lets us easily run two copies of Windows Small Business Server 2008 in virtual machines and several Windows Vista and Windows XP virtual machines as well.

In this chapter, we'll cover the specifics of installing and configuring SBS in a Hyper-V environment while we also provide a general overview of Hyper-V and cover basic installation and configuration.

Hyper-V Overview

Windows Server 2008 (and thus Windows Small Business Server 2008) includes built-in virtualization with the Hyper-V Server Role. Hyper-V is hypervisor-based, native virtualization that uses the hardware virtualization capabilities of the latest Intel and AMD processors to provide a robust, fast, and resource-conserving virtual environment.

Emulation versus Hypervisor

There are two basic methods of virtualizing operating systems: emulation and hypervisor. *Emulation* builds an execution environment on top of the underlying operating system of the host computer and uses software to simulate the hardware that is made available to the guest operating systems.

A *hypervisor* is software that runs directly on the hardware of the physical server and provides a narrow hardware abstraction layer between the hardware and the base operating system. The hypervisor can use the native hardware support in current Intel and AMD processors to improve the overall performance and security of the hypervisor.

Because Hyper-V is a hypervisor and is built in to Windows Server 2008, it runs more efficiently and natively. A server running Hyper-V has multiple partitions, each running natively on the underlying hardware. The first partition is known as the parent partition and acts as the hardware and operating system control partition for all the other partitions where virtualized operating systems run. The other partitions are child partitions, each with their own operating systems, running directly on the hypervisor layer, as shown in Figure 6-1.

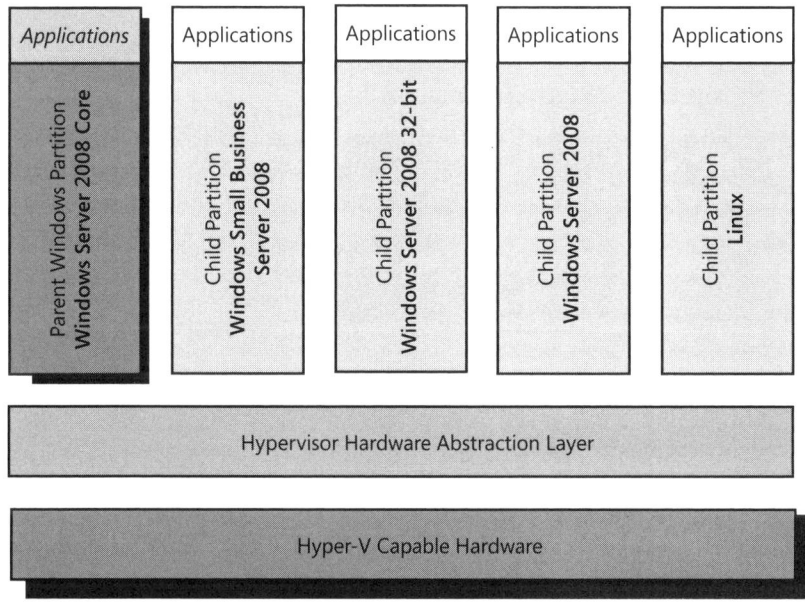

FIGURE 6-1 Windows Server 2008 Hyper-V architecture

Windows Server 2003 supported using Microsoft Virtual Server 2005 R2 as a virtualization solution. Virtual Server is not a hypervisor-based virtualization: It is designed to run on top of an existing operating system—the host operating system—and provide an emulated hardware environment for guest operating systems, as shown in Figure 6-2.

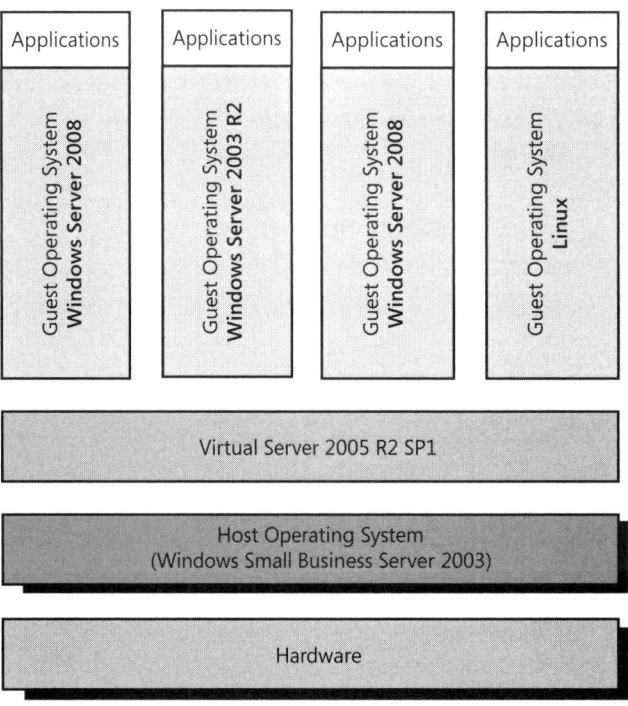

FIGURE 6-2 Microsoft Virtual Server architecture

Hyper-V runs on x64 versions of full Windows Server 2008 and Server Core, as well as the new Hyper-V Server. In most cases, Server Core, or the standalone Hyper-V Server, which is based on Server Core, should be the preferred parent partition for a server that will be used for virtualization. This limits the resource footprint of the parent partition and also makes it easier to protect, because the number of services and attack vectors is fewer on Server Core.

Requirements

The requirements for enabling the Hyper-V Role on Windows Server 2008 are as follows:

- x64 version of Windows Server 2008
- Hardware virtualization support (Intel-VT or AMD-V–enabled CPUs)
- Hardware Data Execution Protection (DEP)–enabled (Intel XD bit or AMD NX bit)

In addition to the requirements for the parent partition of Windows Server 2008, each child partition requires approximately 75 megabytes (MB) of RAM and the hard disk space used by the operating system in the child partition.

Finally, it is important that your server have a minimum of two NICs installed, exclusive of any special management NICs such as an HP iLO. One of these NICs will be reserved for remote management of the parent server and ensures that you can always connect to the parent partition to manage the child partitions.

Any virtualization solution puts a lot of stress on the hardware of the I/O subsystem, especially the disk subsystem. Each virtual hard disk is a file, and with multiple operating systems each writing to files independently and concurrently, a lot of I/O traffic is writing to the parent partition's file system. As a result, a weak or slow I/O subsystem will quickly become the bottleneck limiting the overall performance of the virtual machines.

Also, unlike many applications, virtualization tends to be write-intensive, making it essential that you plan your RAID subsystem accordingly. RAID 5 is a much less appealing alternative as a base RAID choice for the parent operating system. You also do not want to run software RAID on the parent Windows Server 2008.

Any RAID subsystem works better the more disks it has. A RAID 0+1 array that has four 400-GB disks has 800 GB of disk space available, but it is not as fast as a RAID 0+1 array of eight 200-GB disks, which provides the same 800 GB of disk space. By adding extra disks, the writing and reading from the array is distributed across more disks, putting less load on each individual disk.

The same stresses apply to the networking portion of the I/O subsystem that apply to the disk portion. Because many virtual machines can connect through a single physical NIC, you'll want to specify fast and resource-sparing network cards for your Hyper-V server. Here's a clue: a $20 GigE network card is not going to provide the same satisfactory experience as a quality, server-class network card connected to either the PCI-X or PCIe busses.

If you're building or specifying a server for Hyper-V (or any virtualization product), don't skimp on the I/O subsystem. A fast RAID controller with a large cache and a wide array with as many disks as you can manage is an important performance choice. And be especially aware of redundancy. If your Hyper-V server fails because you've had two disks in a RAID 5 array fail, not only is the one physical server down, but your SBS server and every other virtual machine running on that server are also down.

Installation

Installing Hyper-V on Windows Server 2008 uses the native Windows Server 2008 tools—either the graphical Server Manager, or the command-line version, ServerManagerCmd.exe. When installing on Windows Server 2008 Core, use the OCSetup.exe utility.

Installing On Windows Server Core

To install the Hyper-V Role on Server Core, first complete the normal installation of Windows Server 2008 by selecting the appropriate version (Enterprise or Standard) of Server Core as the operating system being installed. Then perform basic initial configuration of the operating system, including setting the IP addresses, setting the server name, and configuring the Windows Firewall, as detailed in the following section. You will not be joining the Server Core to the domain, because the domain will be a child of the Core parent partition. Scripts to simplify the installation and initial configuration are provided on the companion media that accompanies this book. You will need to enable remote administration as part of the base Server Core installation because there is no way to directly manage or create virtual machines on Server Core—the Hyper-V Management Console won't run on Server Core.

 COMPANION MEDIA   The previously mentioned scripts—initsetup1.cmd and initsetup2.cmd—are in the Scripts folder on this book's companion media.

When you've completed the base operating system configuration, use the following commands to add the Hyper-V Role:

```
bcdedit /set hypervisorlaunchtype auto
start /w ocsetup Microsoft-Hyper-V
```

You'll need to reboot the server after these commands have been run.

NOTE   The preceding bcdedit command is not strictly required, but if you don't run it, you need to do two reboots before Hyper-V is fully operational.

Initial Configuration

The initial steps you'll need to perform on a Server Core installation can vary depending on what Roles you're installing, but in a basic Hyper-V-only installation, these are the essential basic steps:

- Set a fixed IP address.
- Change the server name to something reasonable.
- Enable remote management through Windows Firewall.
- Enable remote desktop.
- Activate the server.

Table 6-1 contains the settings we'll be using during this install scenario.

TABLE 6-1 Settings for Initial Server Core Configuration (Example)

SETTING	VALUE
IP Address (Management NIC)	192.168.51.4
Gateway	192.168.51.1
DNS Server	192.168.51.2
IP Address (Child Partition NIC)	192.168.16.2
Gateway	192.168.16.1
DNS Server	192.168.16.2
Server Name	hp350-core-04
Default Desktop Resolution	1024x768
Remote Management	Enable for All Profiles
Windows Activation	Activate

IMPORTANT Normally, servers used for SBS 2008 are equipped with only a single network card because SBS 2008 only supports a single NIC configuration. However, if you are using Hyper-V virtualization, you'll want a second NIC to ensure that you maintain management access to the physical computer even if there are problems with the virtualized SBS. That second NIC can be connected to the same subnet (range of IP addresses) as the primary NIC, or it can be on a completely separate network, as in our test network here.

To configure the initial settings of a Server Core installation, follow these steps:

1. Log on to the newly installed Windows Server 2008 computer. You'll be prompted to change your initial password.

2. At the initial command window, start a second command window by typing the following command:

   ```
   Start cmd
   ```

   Although not an absolute requirement, it's often handy to have a second window open when you've only got the command line to work from.

3. If you're running on two different subnets, determine which network adapter is connected to which subnet. If both have DHCP servers, a simple **ipconfig** will give you the information you need.

4. Set up your management network first by running the following commands, modified to match your environment. Our settings are taken from Table 6-1.

   ```
   netsh interface ipv4 show interfaces
   netsh interface ipv4 set address name="2" source=static
   ```

```
address=192.168.51.4        mask=255.255.255.0
gateway=192.168.51.1
netsh interface ipv4 add dnsserver name="2" address=192.168.51.2 index=1
netdom renamecomputer %COMPUTERNAME% /newname: hp350-core-04
```

5. If there were no problems encountered, run `shutdown /t 0 /r` to reboot your server. Figure 6-3 shows a typical session.

FIGURE 6-3 Initial configuration of the management interface for Server Core

6. When the server restarts, log back on. If you use two CMD windows, you'll need to start the second one. Server Core isn't smart enough to do it automatically.

7. Run the following commands, as shown in Figure 6-4.

```
Netsh advfirewall set allprofiles settings remotemanagement enable
Netsh advfirewall firewall set rule group="Remote Administration" new enable=yes
Netsh advfirewall firewall set rule group="Remote Desktop" new enable=yes
Cscript %windir%\system32\scregedit.wsf /AR 0
Cscript %windir%\system32\scregedit.wsf /CS 0
```

8. Restart the server and log back on. Run the following command (and answer "Y" when prompted) to set up Windows Remote Management (WinRM):

```
Winrm quickconfig
```

9. If your copy of Windows Server 2008 does not have the RTM version of Hyper-V, please download and copy the RTM version to the server, and run the install. The file can be downloaded from the link in Microsoft Knowledge Base article 950050 at *http://support.microsoft.com/kb/950050/*.

10. Run the following command and then restart the server as requested:

```
<path>\Windows6.0-KB950050-x64.msu
```

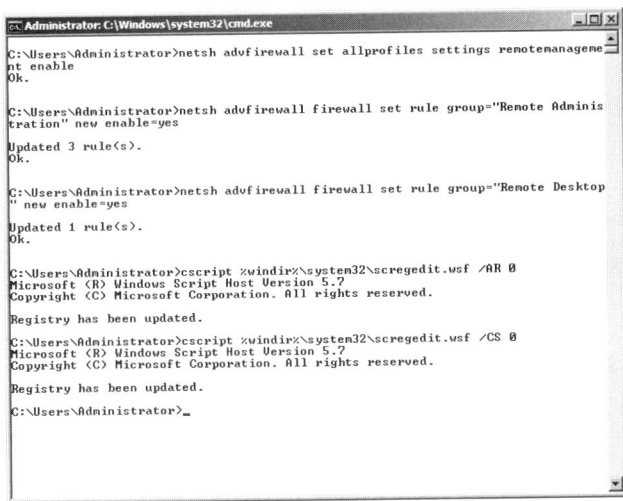

FIGURE 6-4 Configuring Server Core firewall and registry settings

Installing the Hyper-V Role

When you've completed the initial configuration of the Windows Server 2008 Server Core, you can then add the Hyper-V Role to your server. To enable the Hyper-V Role to the server, use the following commands, as shown in Figure 6-5.

```
Bcdedit /set hypervisorlaunchtype auto
Start /w ocsetup Microsoft-Hyper-V
```

IMPORTANT Syntax for **ocsetup** commands are very fussy and case sensitive.

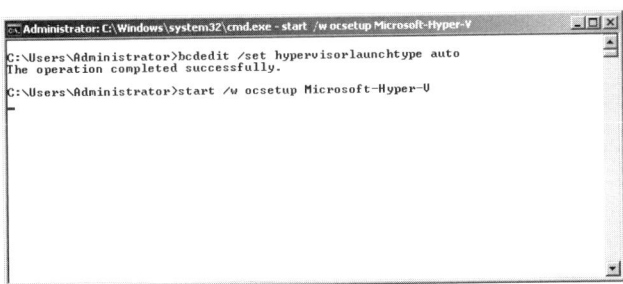

FIGURE 6-5 Enabling the Hyper-V Role on Windows Server 2008 Server Core

You'll need to restart your server at least once following these commands, and then Hyper-V will be installed and ready to configure.

Installing on Full Windows Server 2008

To install the Hyper-V Role on full Windows Server 2008, first complete the normal installation and configuration of Windows Server 2008, as described in Chapter 23, "Installing the Second Server." When initial configuration has completed, you can install the Hyper-V Role using the following steps:

1. Open the Server Manager console if it isn't open already.

2. Select Add Roles from the Action menu to open the Before You Begin page of the Add Roles Wizard.

3. Read the advice on the Before You Begin page. It's actually good advice and a useful reminder. If you've read the page, understand all its implications, and don't ever want to see the page again, select the Skip This Page By Default check box. We leave it unchecked, personally.

> **NOTE** If you've already run the Add Roles Wizard and have selected Skip This Page By Default, you won't see the Before You Begin page of the Add Roles Wizard.

4. Click Next to open the Select Server Roles page of the Add Roles Wizard.

5. Select Hyper-V from the list of Roles.

6. Click Next to open the Hyper-V page, as shown in Figure 6-6. This page describes the Hyper-V Role and includes a Things To Note section that has cautions and advisories specific to the Hyper-V Role. The page also has a link to several Additional Information pages with up-to-date information on Hyper-V.

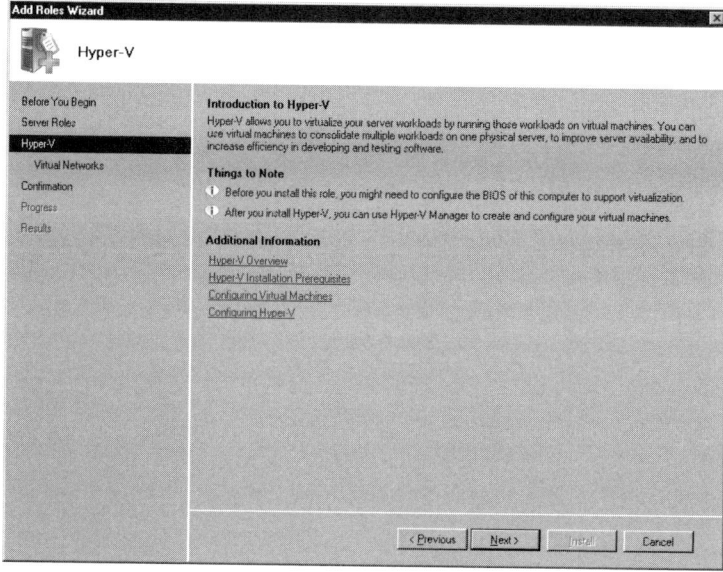

FIGURE 6-6 The Hyper-V page of the Add Roles Wizard

7. When you've read the Things To Note, click Next to open the Create Virtual Networks page shown in Figure 6-7.

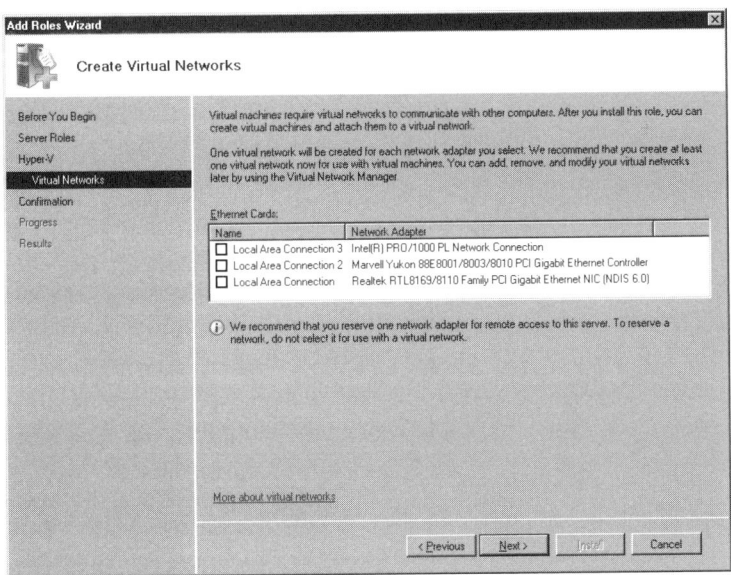

FIGURE 6-7 The Create Virtual Networks page of the Add Roles Wizard

8. Select the Ethernet Cards you want to create Virtual Networks for. The general rule is to leave at least one network card not used for virtual networks to ensure that you maintain full remote connectivity to the server.

9. When the Add Roles Wizard has all the information necessary to proceed, it will open the Confirm Installation Selections page. If everything looks correct, click Install to begin the installation.

10. When the installation completes, you'll see the Installation Results page. The Hyper-V installation will require a reboot. Click Close to complete the wizard. Click Yes to reboot now.

11. After the server reboots, log back on with the same account that you used to add the Hyper-V Role. The Resume Configuration Wizard will open, and when the configuration is complete, you'll see the final Installation Results page, as shown in Figure 6-8.

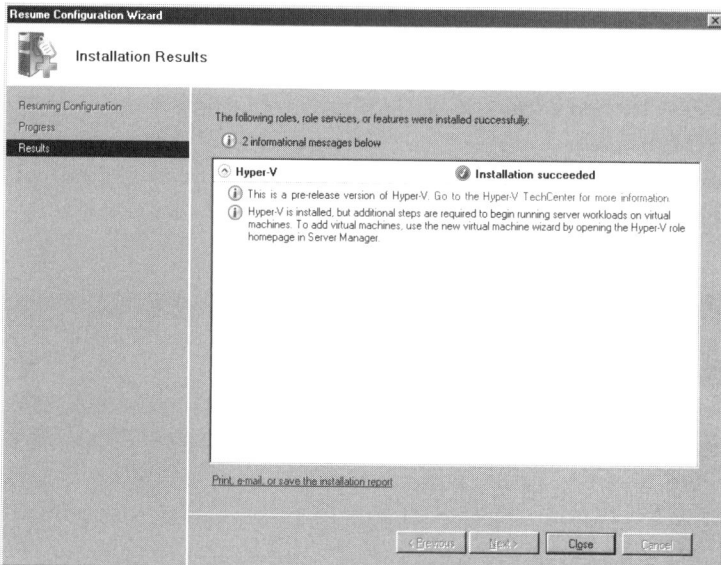

FIGURE 6-8 The Installation Results page of the Resume Configuration Wizard

12. Click Close to exit the wizard.

Initial Configuration

After you've installed the Hyper-V Role, you need to actually configure Hyper-V and then start adding virtual machines. The management tool for Hyper-V is the Hyper-V Manager console. Like other management consoles in Windows Server 2008, it integrates into the Server Manager console. You can use it there or run it standalone. We prefer standalone, frankly. Open Administrative Tools and select Hyper-V Manager from the list to run the Hyper-V Manager console standalone.

> **NOTE** You could run the Hyper-V Manager console by starting it from the command line, but unlike other Windows Server 2008 management consoles, it's not put in %windir%\system32. It is actually in %ProgramFiles%\Hyper-V, which isn't on your path. The command line for this is:
>
> ```
> "%ProgramFiles%\Hyper-V\virtmgmt.msc" (quotes required)
> ```

> **NOTE** If you're running Hyper-V on Server Core, you'll need to install the Hyper-V management tools onto a Windows Vista or Windows Server 2008 computer and run them remotely. See Microsoft Knowledge Base article 952627 at *http://support.microsoft.com /kb/952627/*. You'll use the same steps as if you were running the console locally, but you'll have to connect to the server first.

Configuring Networks

The first step after installing Hyper-V is to configure your networks. This step in the Add Roles Wizard creates the network and attaches it to the network cards you selected, but it makes the new networks available only as a private network connection, which isn't terribly useful if you need to connect your virtual machines to the outside world or another network. And, of course, if you installed on Server Core, no network configuration has been done at all.

Hyper-V supports three kinds of virtual networks:

- **External** An external network is a virtual network switch that binds to the physical network adapter, providing access to resources outside the virtual network. An external network can be assigned to a VLAN.

- **Internal** An internal network is a virtual network switch that allows virtual machines on the server to connect to each other and to the parent partition. An internal network can be assigned to a VLAN.

- **Private** A private network is a virtual network switch that allows virtual machines to connect to each other but provides no connection between the virtual machines and the physical computer.

To set your networks to be external networks, allowing them to connect through the physical network adapter to outside the physical computer, use the following steps:

1. Open the Hyper-V Manager console if it isn't already open.

2. Select the Hyper-V computer in the left pane and then click Virtual Network Manager in the Actions pane to open the Virtual Network Manager as shown in Figure 6-9.

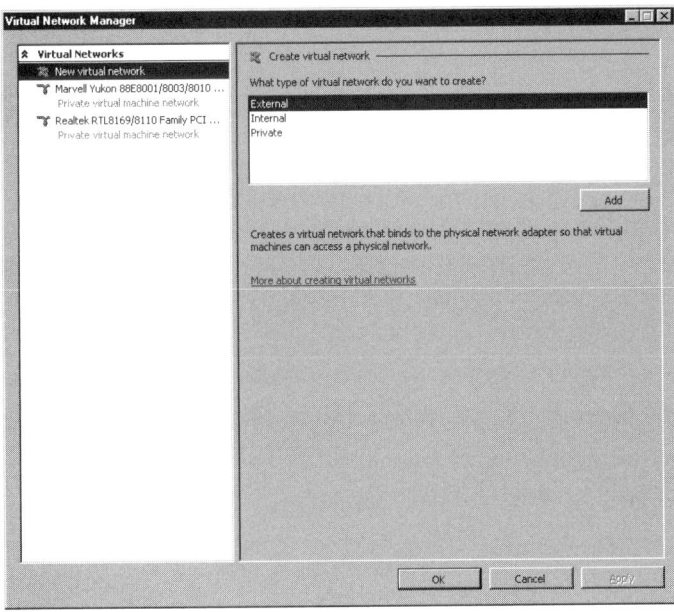

FIGURE 6-9 The Virtual Network Manager

3. Select the Virtual Network you want to make an external network. Edit the name to provide a more meaningful description and add any notes you want to add.

4. Select External and then select the physical network adapter you want to connect this virtual network to from the drop-down list, as shown in Figure 6-10.

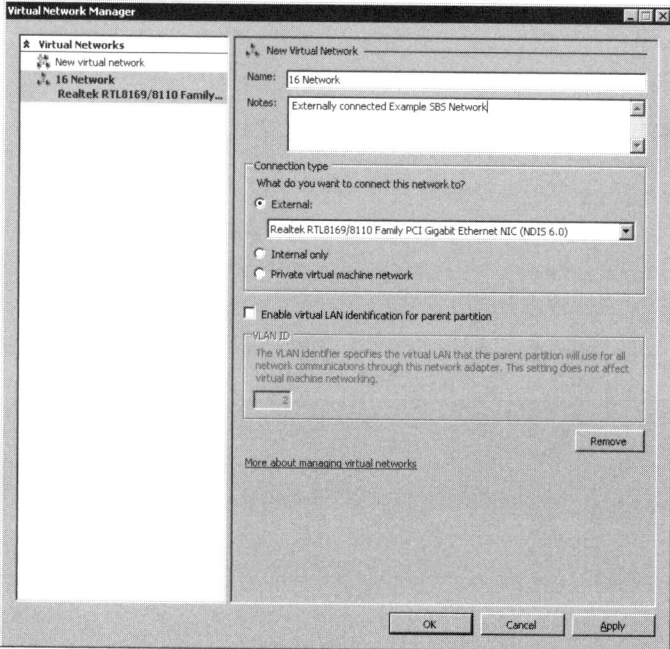

FIGURE 6-10 Attaching a virtual network to a physical adapter to create an external network

5. Click OK to close the Virtual Network Manager and apply your changes.

Server Settings

The next step in configuring your Hyper-V server is to set the overall server settings and the user-specific settings. General server settings include the default location for hard disks and the default location for virtual machines. User-specific settings include keyboard settings and saved credentials.

To set the server settings for a Hyper-V server, use the following steps:

1. Open the Hyper-V Manager console if it isn't already open.

2. Select the Hyper-V computer in the left pane and then click Hyper-V Settings in the Actions pane to open the Hyper-V Settings dialog box, shown in Figure 6-11.

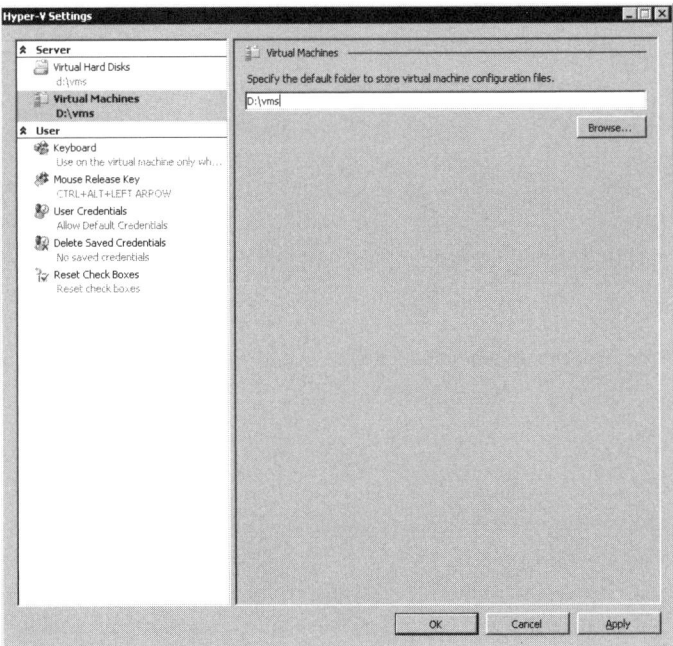

FIGURE 6-11 The Hyper-V Settings dialog box

3. Select Virtual Hard Disks in the left pane and enter the top of the path to use as a default for storing the VHD files used by virtual machines. You can change the actual path of any specific VHD later. This just sets the default location.

4. Select Virtual Machines in the left pane and set the default path for storing virtual machine snapshot files.

5. Select Keyboard in the left pane and specify how special Windows key combinations (such as Alt+Tab and Ctrl+Esc) are used.

6. Select Mouse Release Key and set the default key combination to release a captured mouse when connecting to a virtual machine that doesn't have Integration Components installed.

7. Select Delete Saved Credentials or Reset Check Boxes to remove any saved credentials on the server or to reset all the Don't Ask Me Again check boxes on the server.

8. Click OK to change the settings and return to the main Hyper-V Manager.

The default locations that Microsoft has chosen for VHD files and snapshot files frankly just don't make any sense at all. The default location is on the system drive of the parent partition. That's just a really bad idea. Your VHD files could take up hundreds of gigabytes of space, possibly terabytes of space. Do they really think that your system drive is the right place for all that? Well, we certainly don't. Frankly, we think they should either ask the question during the install, or actually go out and inspect your system and choose an appropriate default based on your system configuration. But they didn't make that choice, so you need to take steps to fix it.

The default location for snapshots is also on the system drive of the parent partition, and again these are files that are going to take up a lot of space. Plus, putting these files on the system drive is a bad decision for performance.

We suggest creating one or more disk volumes specifically for storing VHDs and snapshots. This makes backups easier, allows you to store your VHDs on your fastest array, and just makes good sense. Even if you had to completely rebuild the server, by having your VHDs and snapshot files on separate volumes, you greatly simplify the recovery process.

Creating a Virtual Machine

Okay—enough of that getting-ready stuff and basic configuration. The real reason we're running Hyper-V is to actually create and use virtual machines (VMs), so let's get down to it. There are several different ways you can make a VM, but they all start with the Hyper-V Manager console.

> **NOTE**   System Center Virtual Machine Manager (SCVMM) 2008 will support Hyper-V, including for creation of VMs. We can't wait! If you use more than one or two VMs and support more than one host server, SCVMM is a great product. And we're pretty cautious about saying things like that.

The basic steps for creating a VM are as follows:

- Create a new VM, giving it a name and location.
- Assign RAM to the VM.
- Connect to a network.
- Assign or create a Virtual Disk.
- Specify where the operating system will be loaded from.

The New Virtual Machine Wizard handles all these basic steps but is pretty limited, and insufficient for creating a VM for SBS. You'll want to actually configure the VM further before installing SBS or the SBS second server on your VM. We'll start by walking through the steps for creating a VM and then show you how to change that basic VM to be a bit more useful and flexible.

Creating a Basic VM

To create a new VM, follow these steps:

1. Open the Hyper-V Manager console if it isn't already open.

2. Select the Hyper-V computer in the left-hand pane, click New, and then click Virtual Machine on the Actions menu to start the New Virtual Machine Wizard.

3. If you haven't disabled the Before You Begin page, you can read the description of what's going to happen or click the More About Creating Virtual Machines link to open the Help pages for creating a VM. Select the Do Not Show This Page Again check box so that you don't have to see this page again.

4. Click Next to open the Specify Name And Location page, shown in Figure 6-12.

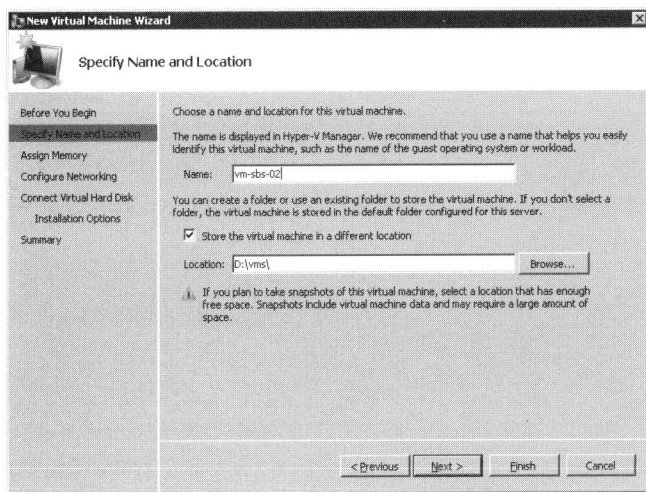

FIGURE 6-12 The Specify Name And Location page of the New Virtual Machine Wizard

5. Enter a name for the VM and select the Store The Virtual Machine In A Different Location check box. When you select this check box, all the files for this VM will be stored in a directory with the same name as the VM, shown below in the Location field.

> **NOTE** For this first VM, with a name of vm-sbs-02 and a default location of D:\vms\, the result will be a new directory of D:\vms\vm-sbs-02, with the files and subdirectories of the VM stored in it.

6. Click Next to open the Assign Memory page, shown in Figure 6-13. Specify the amount of memory that will be assigned to the new VM. You should specify the same amount of memory that you would specify for the RAM of a physical SBS computer, but *do not exceed the memory of the host physical computer.*

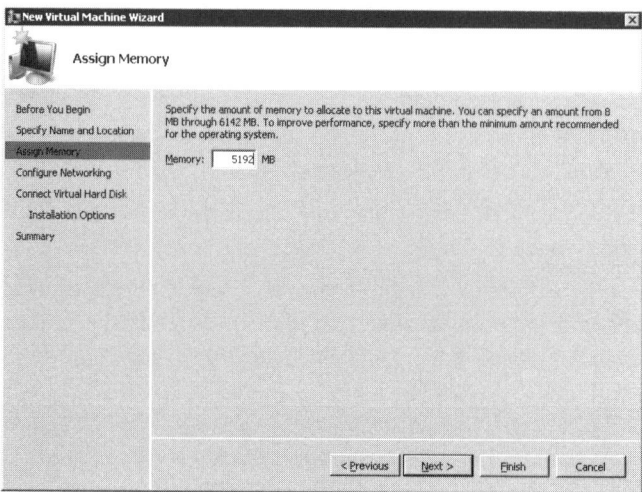

FIGURE 6-13 The Assign Memory page of the New Virtual Machine Wizard

7. Click Next to open the Configure Networking page. Select the network that the VM will be connected to, as shown in Figure 6-14.

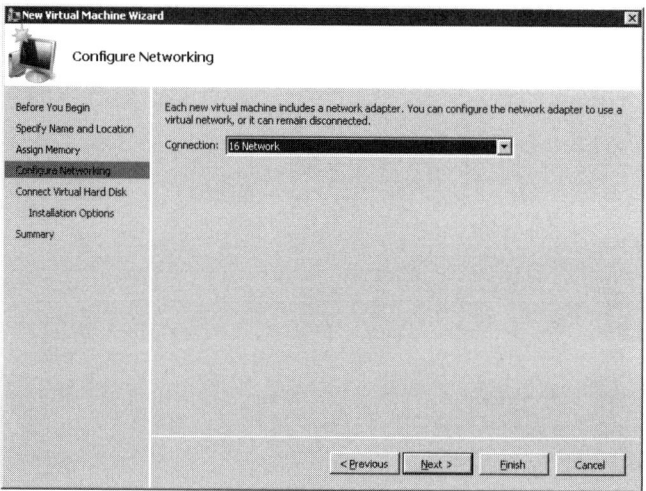

FIGURE 6-14 The Configure Networking page of the New Virtual Machine Wizard

8. Click Next to open the Connect Virtual Hard Disk page, shown in Figure 6-15.

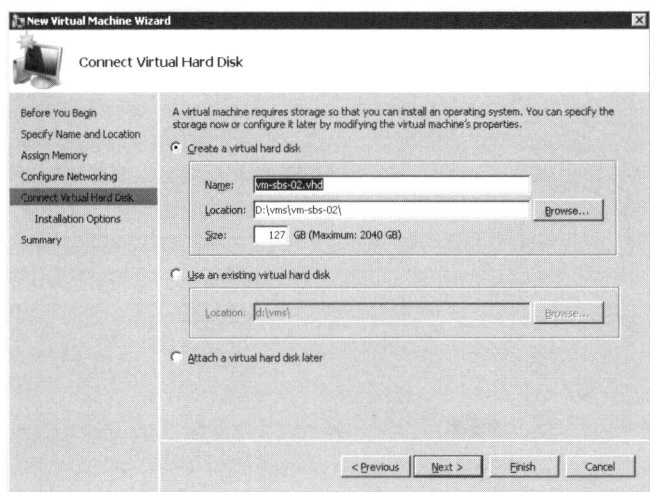

FIGURE 6-15 The Connect Virtual Hard Disk page of the New Virtual Machine Wizard

9. Select Create A Virtual Disk to create a new, automatically expanding, virtual disk with a nominal size of 127 GB. Accept the default location and name or modify as appropriate for your environment. If you think you'll need a system disk larger than 127 GB, change the Size field.

> **IMPORTANT** The maximum size of an IDE VHD in Hyper-V is 2 terabytes (2040 GB, actually). But a dynamically expanding virtual hard disk doesn't actually take up any more room on your physical hard disk or array than it needs to. As you expand your use of the VM, the size of the disk will continue to grow, up to the size you set when you create the disk.

10. Click Next to open the Installation Options page, as shown in Figure 6-16.

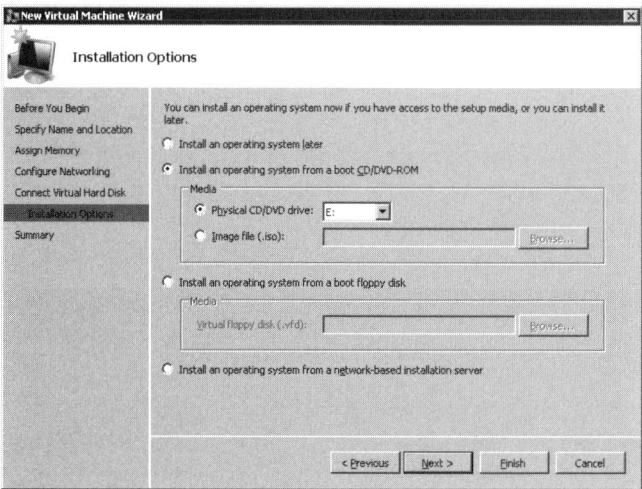

FIGURE 6-16 The Installation Options page of the New Virtual Machine Wizard

The choices are as follow:

- **Install An Operating System Later** This option requires you to configure how your operating system will be installed manually before starting the VM.

- **Install An Operating System From A Boot CD/DVD-ROM** This option allows you to connect to the physical computer's CD or DVD drive, or to mount an ISO file stored on the physical computer's hard disk as if it were a physical CD/DVD drive.

- **Install An Operating System From A Boot Floppy Disk** This option allows you to connect to a virtual floppy disk (.vfd) file as if it were a physical floppy drive.

- **Install An Operating System From A Network-Based Installation Server** This option changes the BIOS setting for the VM to enable a network boot from a PXE server and also changes the network card for the VM to be an emulated Legacy Network Adapter instead of the default synthetic network adapter. If you're deploying using a WDS server, choose this option.

11. Click Next to open the Completing The New Virtual Machine Wizard summary page or click Finish to skip the last step. On the last page you can choose to automatically start the new VM as soon as you close the wizard, but we think that's a bad option. Just skip it—you should probably adjust the settings for the new VM before you start it anyway.

Machine Settings

After you've created the VM for your SBS server, you should make some changes to the machine settings that the New Virtual Machine Wizard has configured. To adjust the settings of a VM, select the VM in the center Virtual Machines pane of Hyper-V Manager and click Settings on the Action menu to open the Settings dialog box for the VM, as shown in Figure 6-17.

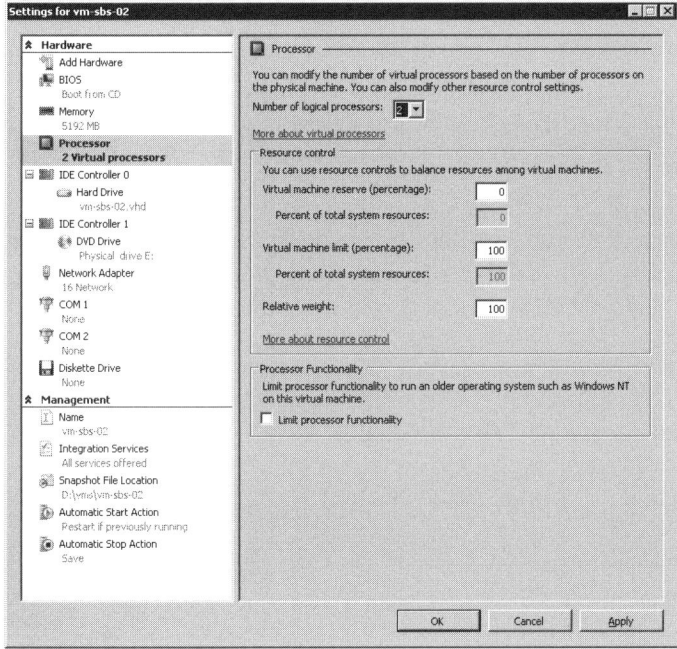

FIGURE 6-17 The Settings dialog box for the vm-sbs-02 virtual machine

The settings page of a VM allows you to control the virtual hardware available to that VM. The settings that can be changed on a VM include the following:

- **Add Hardware** Add a SCSI Controller, Network Adapter, or Legacy Network Adapter.

- **BIOS** Change the boot order and Numlock state.

- **Memory** Set the amount of memory assigned to the VM. Each VM is limited to 64 GB of memory.

- **Processor** Set the number of logical processors assigned to the VM. This is limited to the number of logical processors available on the host computer, or four logical processors, whichever is fewer. Hyper-V is limited to a maximum of 16 logical processors per host computer in the initial release. For SBS 2008, assign at least two logical processors.

- **IDE Controllers 0, 1** Set the drives connected to each IDE controller. Both Hard Disk and DVD Drive types are supported on IDE controllers.

- **SCSI Controller(s)** Set the drives connected to the synthetic SCSI controller. Each SCSI controller is assigned to SCSI ID7 and can support up to six virtual SCSI drives. SCSI drives cannot be used as boot drives and are not available until integration components are installed. Even if your physical drives are SCSI or SAS, do not choose SCSI here for your boot disk. That must always be IDE.

- **Network Adapters** Set the network, Mac type, and VLAN connections of the synthetic network adapters. Each VM is limited to a maximum of eight network adapters. SBS 2008 only supports a single network.

- **Legacy Network Adapters** Set the network, Mac type, and VLAN connections of the legacy network adapters. Each VM is limited to a maximum of four legacy network adapters.

- **COM 1, COM 2** Set the named pipe used to communicate with the physical host computer.

- **Diskette Drive** Set the virtual floppy drive (.vfd) that is connected to the virtual floppy drive. No pass-through to the physical floppy drive on the host (parent) computer is supported. Use VFDs for SBS Answer Files to automate deployment.

Memory and CPU

Hyper-V supports a maximum of four processors and 64 GB of RAM per VM. On host computers with fewer than four processors, you'll be limited to the number of logical processors on the host itself. And you need to be careful not to over-specify the RAM for VMs on a physical computer. You need to leave at least 500 MB of RAM for the host partition, plus a bit (less than 100 MB) per running VM.

Disks and Controllers

Hyper-V uses a pair of synthetic IDE controllers for hard disks and DVD drives by default. You must use an IDE for the boot hard disk—the synthetic SCSI controller won't have drivers available in the operating system until after the Integration Services are installed.

If you're familiar with the IDE controller in Virtual Server 2005, you'll know that it was slow and only supported hard disks up to 127 GB. We quickly learned to use Virtual Server's SCSI controller and floppy disk to load the drivers during installation, greatly speeding up the process. But that workaround is no longer necessary. The new IDE controller in Hyper-V has full LBA-48 support, and it's much faster than the old Virtual Server one.

Before you can add additional disks and connect them to a SCSI controller, you need to add the SCSI controller. By default, a new VM doesn't include a SCSI controller. When you add the controller, you can also add one or more disks to the controller.

 REAL WORLD Choosing Disk Types

Hyper-V supports three virtual disk types—dynamically expanding disks, fixed-sized disks, and differencing disks.

Dynamically expanding disks are created with a maximum size, and this is the size that the operating system of the VM sees. But the actual .vhd file of the disk takes up only as much space on your physical hard disk or array as absolutely required for the current contents of the VM drive. As the VM requires more storage space, Hyper-V automatically grows the .vhd file. This is very efficient of hard disk space, allowing you to add space only as absolutely required. But it does mean a slight performance hit every time the disk needs to grow, and more important, the .vhd file tends to become somewhat fragmented over time, also impacting performance. Nonetheless, we almost always use this type of disk for our VMs except where absolute performance is an issue.

A fixed-size disk is also a .vhd file, but instead of growing only as big as it needs to, when it needs to, it is created at the full size on disk that it needs to be. It takes a significant time to create the .vhd file, but it will be created as a contiguous file (or as contiguous as the underlying fragmentation of your physical disk or array allows).

A differencing disk is an interesting disk type. It is like a dynamic disk in that it gets only as large as it needs to. But a differencing disk is a great way to combine the disk space requirements of multiple VMs. You create the original "base" VM and then mark the disks as read-only. You can actually delete the VM that created the base disks. Now you create one or more VMs that have the same operating system and you create them with differencing disk(s). The differencing disk points to the original base .vhd file, and the only thing that gets saved to the differencing disk is any change from the base VM. This allows multiple VMs to share the same base, simplifying deployment of different versions of the same base system—very useful for quickly building test networks.

The biggest disadvantage of differencing disks is speed. As more VMs point back to the original VHD files, the access to that VHD can be slowed. And if anything causes a change to the original VHD, all the VMs that point to it can be lost. Over time, the size advantage of differencing disks is also reduced as updates and service packs are applied to the differenced VMs. But for a test environment? Differencing disks can be a great speed and resource saver.

The final option is to point directly to the physical partition. This is the fastest option but provides the least flexibility. You might choose this option if you are running Microsoft SQL Server on a VM and you have a performance-sensitive application. But even there, we tend to avoid it if at all possible, choosing a fixed-size disk instead. The difference in speed is negligible, but the flexibility difference is significant.

Network Adapters

When you create a new VM, it will automatically include a single network adapter. Unless you choose to install the operating system from the network, it will add one of the synthetic network adapters that are new to Hyper-V. These work great and are definitely the preferred choice—unless you are running an operating system that doesn't have Integration Services available for it. If that's the case, you'll need to change this adapter to a legacy network adapter. You can't directly change the adapter type—you'll need to delete the existing one and add a legacy adapter.

Because SBS 2008 includes the necessary Integration Components built into the base operating system, you should always choose a synthetic network adapter unless you are using PXE to boot from the network.

COM and Floppy

Hyper-V automatically configures a pair of virtual COM ports (COM1 and COM2) and a virtual floppy disk drive for each VM. But it doesn't actually connect them to anything. To connect a COM port to the host computer, you need to use named pipes. For floppy disks, you need to create a virtual floppy disk file (.vfd). A VFD file is an image of a floppy disk. There is no way in Hyper-V to connect directly to any existing floppy drive on the server.

Working with a Virtual Machine

Working with a Hyper-V VM is almost identical to working with a physical computer. You should do virtually everything you need to do from the client operating system, just as you would on a physical computer. You can connect to the client operating system using Remote Desktop when that is a supported option, and you can always connect using the Virtual Machine Connection. You can open the Virtual Machine Connection to a particular VM by either double-clicking the VM in the Hyper-V Manager console or by selecting it and then clicking Connect on the Action menu. You can connect either locally from the parent partition or remotely if you're running the Hyper-V Remote Management Tools. This connection is to the VM the same as the physical keyboard, mouse, and monitor of a physical computer. However, there are some actions that need to be performed from the parent partition, either from the Hyper-V console or from the menu bar of the Virtual Machine Connection.

Starting, Stopping, Saving, Snapshotting

To start a VM, you need to either set the VM to automatically start or use the Hyper-V Manager console to start the VM. Right-click the VM in the console and select Start from the menu. If you have the Virtual Machine Connection for that VM open, you can select Start from the Action menu.

To stop a VM, you should shut down the operating system in the VM. You can initiate this from the Hyper-V Manager console or on the Virtual Machine Connection Action menu, if Integration Services are installed in the VM. You can also stop a VM by right-clicking the VM in the console and selecting Turn Off , but this can cause corruption issues for the VM's operating system and is not recommended when other alternatives are available.

You can save a VM from the Hyper-V Manager console or the Virtual Machine Connection for that VM by selecting Save from the Action menu. This will save the current state of the VM to disk and is similar to hibernating a physical computer. It does release memory and resources back to the parent partition.

Pausing a VM is similar to putting a physical computer into sleep mode. It's not actively doing anything, but it also doesn't release any of the VM's resources back to the parent partition, except that it isn't using a CPU or doing any disk I/O. But the RAM it has allocated to the VM stays unavailable to other VMs.

Snapshots are one of the ways that VMs are more useful and flexible than any physical computer. Snapshots allow you to take a "picture" of a running virtual machine at an exact moment in time and save it. You can revert back to that snapshot later, starting up the VM at that exact configuration. This is *extremely* useful for building test computers, because it lets you try a new configuration or software application without the risk of having to rebuild the computer if something really bad happens or just wasting the time trying to get back to where you were before the change if it didn't work.

Snapshots can be a powerful tool, giving you the ability to try something with the calm assurance that you can recover completely if it doesn't work. And snapshots happen in seconds. Just select the VM in the Hyper-V Manager console, right-click, and select Snapshot. The VM can be running or not—it doesn't matter.

After you create a snapshot, the VM returns to its previous state. You can rename the snapshot, check the settings that applied at the time of the snapshot, delete it, or even delete an entire snapshot subtree. All these actions are available from the Actions pane of the Hyper-V Manager console or from the Action menu of the Virtual Machine Connection. You can also revert a VM to its previous snapshot or select another snapshot in the tree and apply it.

As you can see, powerful stuff, and the possibilities are something you'll just have to work with a bit to begin to understand.

Clipboard

The Hyper-V Virtual Machine Connection supports a limited ability to pass the contents of your clipboard between the parent partition and the running VM. Only text can be passed, but this allows you to replay the text as keystrokes into the VM. To use this capability, you need to copy text to your clipboard on the parent partition using Ctrl+C or any other method. Then, in the child partition, prepare the location you want to type the text into and select Type Clipboard Text on the Clipboard menu of the Virtual Machine Connection. The text is typed into the child partition at the cursor, one character at a time.

The other feature of the Hyper-V Virtual Machine Connection Clipboard menu is a screen capture utility. A pretty limited one, frankly, but it works if what you need to do is capture the entire screen of the child computer. To capture the screen, just select Capture Screen from the Virtual Machine Connection Clipboard menu. This puts the screen into your clipboard, and from there you can paste it into Microsoft Paint or any other graphics program.

The ability to capture screens is an essential for any documentation task, and often important for troubleshooting as well. Having an exact picture of the situation at a specific point in time just makes everything clearer, in our experience. The screen capture utility in Hyper-V only does the full screen—you can't get screen shots of individual windows or buttons—because the keystrokes are usually captured from the parent partition, not the child. Our solution is to use a small utility that is much smarter at screen shots than anything we could do with the built-in facilities of Windows—HyperSnap (*http://www.hyperionics.com*). There are other good screen capture utilities out there, but we've been using HyperSnap for more than 13 years now, and it does an excellent job. We can capture exactly what we want and save it in any format we can imagine. Plus, if we do need to manipulate an image for some reason, HyperSnap has the ability to do that, too. We load a copy of HyperSnap into every test computer we run, using Group Policy to deploy it. And when we needed screen shots for Server Core? Hyperionics did a custom version for us that worked where nothing else had.

SBS in Hyper-V

Microsoft has announced that running SBS Standard and Premium in a Hyper-V child partition is supported, and that using the Second Server as a parent partition, with only the Hyper-V Role enabled, is fully supported and still allows installation of the Second Server as a child partition. Further, if no additional Roles are installed in the parent partition, and the parent partition is used as part of an SBS network, the partition does not need to be domain joined, simplifying deployment. See the "Microsoft server software and supported virtualization environments" Knowledge Base article (*http://support.microsoft.com/?kbid=957006*) for up-to-date virtualization support statements. So, that sounds like we think everything is good with running Hyper-V, right? Well, no.

We think that one scenario is a really, really bad idea, even if it is technically possible. You should *not* run the Hyper-V Role inside your primary SBS server. Way too many other things are going on with any SBS server to also add in the Hyper-V Role, and it is not a supported scenario.

Hyper-V should always run in a partition where little or nothing else is going on. The parent partition should be just that—strictly a parent. This keeps the attack surface of the entire set of virtual machines smaller, reduces the number of reboots required, and keeps the resources for the VM, which should be the ones doing the heavy lifting.

We can imagine scenarios in which the parent partition is also running a couple of key infrastructure Roles as well—DNS and DHCP come to mind. We generally prefer not to do this, but it can make life a bit easier in some scenarios. However, when you start running any other Roles beyond Hyper-V on your parent partition, you've changed the licensing equation.

Licensing

With Windows Server 2008 Standard, including SBS Second Server, you are entitled to what are called 1+1 licensing rights. This means that you can use the same physical license to install Windows Server 2008 on the parent partition and the first child partition, *as long as the only Role you install into the parent is Hyper-V.* That's an important limitation. As soon as you start adding in other Roles, you lose the right to run a child partition without buying a full license for it.

Windows Server 2008 Enterprise gives you the right to install a parent partition and four child partitions, as long as that parent partition is used only for the Hyper-V Role. As soon as you add in any other Roles to the parent, you lose one of your secondary rights.

Windows Server 2008 Datacenter gives you the right to install a parent partition and as many child partitions as you want. Of course, the actual cost of a Datacenter license is just a bit out of the reach of most small businesses.

Configuration

When you configure a child partition for SBS Standard, you should allocate the same level of hardware resources to the child as you would to a physical server running SBS Standard. This means a *minimum* of 4 GB of RAM, but we think 6 GB is a more appropriate minimum for any production environment. And at least two processor cores. Use the synthetic network adapters, which are much faster than the legacy emulation ones. And create the same number of virtual hard disks for your server as you would have arrays with a physical computer. We like to have a minimum of three disks—one for the system, one for user space, and one for Microsoft Exchange data. Even if your circumstances require you to have them sitting on the same RAID array, having three separate virtual disks puts you in a position to add additional arrays if you need to, and you can easily move the VHDs over to the new array to balance the load.

The one configuration that we see happening increasingly as consultants and others begin to understand the power and capabilities of 64-bit servers is the "SBS Premium in a Box" deployment. This starts with a small Hyper-V parent partition, possibly running Server Core, and then two child partitions—the first running the main SBS server and the second running the SBS second server with SQL Server on it. Or, in many deployments, a Windows Server 2008 Standard server running Terminal Services.

This all-in-one solution could easily be supported on a single, well-thought-out, mid-range server, with two quad-core CPUs and 12-16 GB of RAM—and a good SAS disk array.

Summary

Virtualization is a hot topic these days, and with good reason. The new capabilities of 64-bit servers and Microsoft's new Hyper-V technology make it a compelling option in many scenarios. In this chapter we've covered the basics of using Hyper-V to virtualize Windows Small Business Server 2008. In the next chapter, we cover migrating from an existing Windows Small Business Server 2003 network to SBS 2008.

## CHAPTER 7

Migrating from Windows Small Business Server 2003

With Windows Small Business Server 2008, there is no "upgrade" from the previous version, or any other version. The only way to preserve an existing deployment of SBS, including e-mail and Active Directory, is to migrate to SBS 2008. This change is a direct result of the change in underlying architecture to from 32-bit to 64-bit.

Migration is far more complex than a clean install or in-place upgrade, although the SBS team has made a significant effort to simplify the most common cases. However, SBS 2008 requires some significant changes to your network that you need to plan out ahead of time:

- SBS 2008 supports only a single NIC. The preferred SBS 2003 configuration is two NICs.

- SBS 2008 Premium does not include ISA. If you're an SBS 2003 Premium customer running ISA as your firewall, you'll need to replace it with an alternative.

- Your new SBS 2008 server will have a different name than your existing SBS 2003 server, and a different IP address. The migration process will configure DNS to correct for this.

- The new Companyweb SharePoint site will replace your existing Companyweb site. You can maintain existing content in an Oldcompanyweb SharePoint site.

- When you start the migration, there really is no "undo" button. And you'll have 21 days to complete the process and remove the old server from the network.

These are all significant issues, in our opinion. But if you prepare your existing SBS server properly and plan your migration thoroughly before beginning the process, the migration will succeed.

The Migration Process

Before you start your SBS 2008 migration, you should read and understand this chapter and Microsoft's migration guide titled "Migrate to Windows Small Business Server 2008 from Windows Small Business Server 2003" at *http://technet.microsoft.com/library/cc546034.aspx*. This migration guide will be updated as issues arise and are resolved, so you should always check the Web site for the most current information.

The steps in a successful migration are as follows:

1. Prepare your existing SBS server for migration.

2. Create the SBSAnswerFile.xml using the SBS AnswerFile Generator tool.

3. Install SBS 2008, using the Answer File to run in migration mode.

4. Use the Migration Wizard to migrate data and settings from your existing SBS 2003 server to your new SBS 2008 server.

5. When migration is complete, demote your existing SBS 2003 server to domain member and then remove it from the domain. You must reformat the server before you can reuse it.

6. If you're using Folder Redirection in SBS 2003, you'll need to delete the old GPO for folder redirection.

7. Perform optional post-migration tasks—including mapping users to computers and enabling folder redirection—and Microsoft Exchange tasks such as POP3 connectors and mailbox quotas.

 REAL WORLD **A Migration Alternative**

With SBS 2003, the Microsoft solution for migration caused significant user disruption and was only a viable solution if you needed to change your SBS domain name for some reason. In our *Microsoft Windows Small Business Server 2003 R2 Administrator's Companion* book, we recommended an alternative solution— Swing Migration (see *http://www.sbsmigration.com*). Swing Migration uses a temporary domain controller to capture the Active Directory, DNS, and other information from the existing domain controller (the source SBS server) and transfer that to the new SBS 2003 server, allowing the new SBS server to retain the exact same name and IP address as the original source SBS server. Microsoft Exchange data is generally moved with a simple forklift technique, and SharePoint sites are handled in a similar fashion—overall, an excellent and time-effective way to manage a migration that has several virtues over other methods, including:

- No disruption or change to SBS client computers.

- No disruption in e-mail or other network functions except for the final switchover, which can easily be done during normal downtimes. Most work is done offline and can be done on a flexible schedule.

- Full data and configuration protection.

- The ability to restart the process at any point in time with no risk of data loss if there is a problem.

Unfortunately, Swing Migration as it exists for SBS 2003 will not completely work for SBS 2008, although we can see some definite benefits to using a similar process. It certainly covers the server name and IP address change issue, and we can envision how to work around most of the possible e-mail issues.

We expect that Jeff Middleton, Microsoft MVP for SBS and principal of *www.sbsmigration.com*, will have a full version of Swing Migration for SBS 2008 soon, and we expect it to be a very good offering, especially if your migration project is not a perfect fit for the Microsoft assumptions. We've known Jeff for several years now, and even though his final version of Swing isn't yet available, we have enough confidence in him to recommend it fully. Because, ultimately, what you really need for any migration is just that—confidence.

Preparing Your Server

The most important part of any migration to SBS 2008 involves properly preparing your existing SBS server. The time and thought you spend on a full and careful preparation of your existing SBS server has a direct impact on the success of your migration. Don't just start a migration without first preparing. Read this entire chapter carefully, and read Microsoft's migration guide as well. Be sure you understand what will happen and what the requirements are before you start.

The steps for preparing your server are as follows:

1. Do a full and complete backup of the existing SBS server.

2. Install all current service packs and other updates on the server.

3. Configure your network for the migration.

4. Configure Active Directory.

5. Run the Best Practices Analyzer to verify the health of the existing SBS network.

6. Clean up and optimize the current Microsoft Exchange mailboxes.

7. Use the Migration Preparation Tool to extend the Active Directory schema, modify the Microsoft Exchange Server mode, and extend the time that both versions of SBS can be running to 21 days.

8. Identify line-of-business applications running on the existing SBS server and plan for their migration.

Back Up Existing SBS Server

The first and most important step in any migration is making sure you have a full and verified backup. We all do backups, and we hope that we never need to use them. But if you aren't taking steps to actually verify that your backup can be restored, you haven't really got a backup you can count on. Before beginning any SBS migration, it's essential that you establish a sound fallback position that will allow you to recover in case something goes wrong. Of course, nothing should go wrong, but we're firm believers in Murphy's Laws.

For details on how to back up your existing SBS server, see *http://go.microsoft.com /fwlink/?LinkId=27140*, or see Chapter 13, "Backing Up and Restoring Data," in our *Microsoft Windows Small Business Server 2003 R2 Administrator's Companion* book.

In *addition* to doing a conventional backup using SBS Backup, we strongly suggest making an image backup of at least the system volume of your existing SBS server and any other volumes that are used to store core SBS data files such as Microsoft Exchange data files. This will allow for a faster full recovery in the event that you have to cancel the migration for some reason. Products we've used for this image backup include StorageCraft, Acronis, and Windows Home Server. Currently we're using and really liking Windows Home Server for this.

Whatever backup methods you use, you should *verify the integrity* of the backup by doing a test restore. For image backups, this means restoring the entire partition image to a disk of equal or greater size and, at a minimum, verifying that files can be read and opened. For an SBS Backup test, you should restore multiple files from different locations to an alternate location and verify that the files can be opened and read.

Install Current Updates

It seems obvious to us, but bears repeating nonetheless—bring your current SBS server up to date, installing all current service packs and security updates. If you're running SBS 2003 R2, with built-in Windows Server Update Service (WSUS), this should be happening automatically. But even if you're sure you are up to date, connect to Microsoft Update to verify.

The migration process expects minimum levels of service packs, and not being fully "patched up" can create issues in the migration. Given that the migration is a one-way process, you really don't want to get well into it and find you have a blocker. Hopefully, the tools in this preparation stage will catch any blockers before you start, but it's still just a really good idea to get all your updates installed before you start.

Network Configuration

Before you can migrate to SBS 2008, you need to configure your existing SBS server for a single NIC. This means a significant change for most SBS networks, because the preferred configuration for SBS 2003 calls for two NICs—one connected to the external Internet and one connected to the internal SBS network. All traffic on the internal network actually passes through the SBS server to get to the Internet, as shown in Figure 7-1.

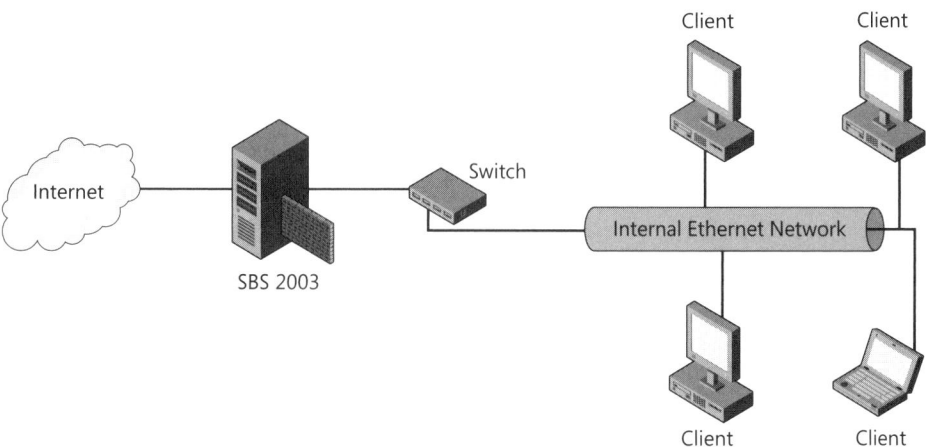

FIGURE 7-1 Default two-NIC configuration for SBS 2003

This configuration also uses SBS as the firewall for the SBS network—something it does quite well when running SBS 2003 Premium Edition with Internet Security and Acceleration Server (ISA) 2004. Because SBS 2008 requires a single NIC configuration, you need to change your SBS 2003 configuration before the migration. In a single NIC configuration, as shown in Figure 7-2, you'll need to add a router and firewall to your existing SBS network, along with reconfiguring the default gateway and other settings for your client computer and devices.

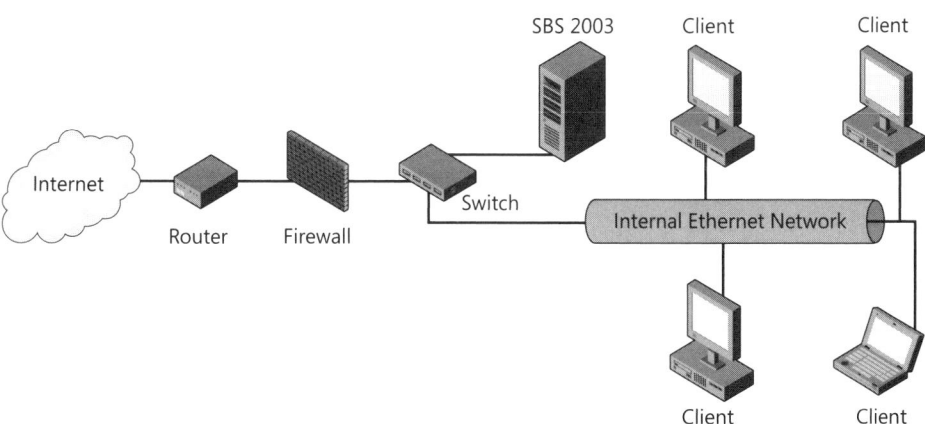

FIGURE 7-2 Single-NIC configuration for SBS 2003

Most consumer-grade routers include minimal firewall capabilities, but they really aren't sufficient to properly protect an SBS network. You should either add a firewall appliance in addition, or buy a true firewall router such as one of the TZ series firewalls from Sonicwall (*http://www.sonicwall.com/us/products/TZ_Series.html*). Other possibilities include Watch-Guard firewalls (*http://www.watchguard.com*) and Netgear ProSafe firewalls (*http://www.netgear.com/Products/VPNandSSL/WiredVPNFirewallRouters.aspx*).

The basic process of network reconfiguration uses the following steps:

1. Reconfigure DHCP for shorter license times (optional).
2. Disable or remove the Internet-facing NIC in your existing SBS server.
3. Run the Configure E-Mail And Internet Connectivity Wizard (CEICW) to reconfigure networking.
4. Install a router/firewall and connect to the Internet.
5. Connect the router/firewall to a switch on the internal Ethernet.
6. Run the Remote Access Wizard to disable VPNs and reconfigure Routing And Remote Access (RRAS).
7. Reconfigure client computers and devices with fixed IP addresses and verify DHCP configuration.

DHCP Reconfiguration

Although it's not absolutely required, you can simplify DHCP address reconfiguration on your SBS network if you shorten the lease time in advance of beginning the migration. This will allow client computers and devices on your network to get updated network information without a reboot in a reasonable time frame. The default DHCP lease duration is eight days. To change the duration, follow these steps:

1. Log on to your existing SBS server with an account that has administrative privileges.
2. Open the DHCP console (dhcpmgmt.msc).
3. In the left pane, drill down and select the scope you want to change.
4. Select Properties from the Action menu to open the Scope Properties dialog box shown in Figure 7-3.
5. Change the Lease Duration For DHCP Clients to a shorter time. We like to set an 8-hour lease here.
6. Click OK to close the Scope Properties dialog box and return to the DHCP console. Close the DHCP console.

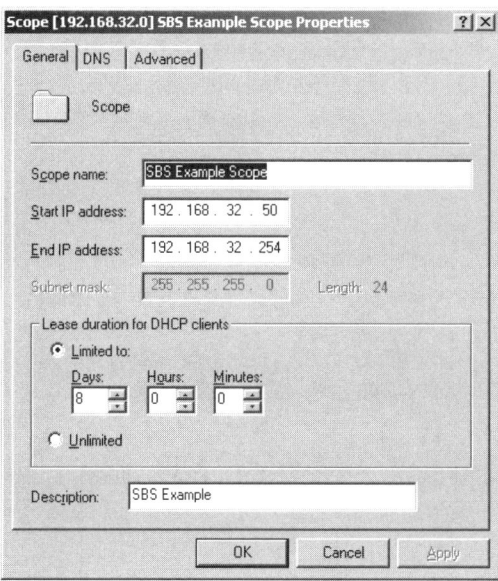

FIGURE 7-3 The Scope Properties dialog box for a DHCP scope

Disable or Remove Second NIC

The first essential step in reconfiguring your network from a two-NIC SBS network to a single-NIC network is to disconnect the externally facing NIC from your existing Internet connection and disable or remove the network card. You can get away with disabling it, but then you'll have more complaints from the SBS wizards, so we prefer removing it physically from the server. After you've removed the network card, you need to reconfigure your SBS network to the IP address range you'll use for your Internet connection.

 REAL WORLD **Address Ranges**

Because you're reconfiguring your network anyway, now is a good time to make a decision about the IP address range you want to use. The default range of many routers is 192.168.0.xxx or 192.168.1.xxx. The easy answer is to use whatever the default range of your new router/firewall is. We actually don't much like that solution because it can cause complications down the road if you're ever in a situation where you need to set up a static VPN to another network that has chosen that range. We prefer choosing pretty much any of the other possibilities in the private "C-class" range—anywhere from 192.168.2.xxx to 192.168.254.xxx. The default range for SBS 2003 is actually 192.168.16.xxx, and that's a good choice that doesn't seem to interfere with any other common ones we've seen. On our networks here we have used 192.168.16.xxx and 192.168.51.xx for our test networks.

When you've decided the range for your new SBS network, you can complete the reconfiguration by following these steps:

1. Shut down the SBS server.

2. Disconnect the Internet-facing network cable from the server, open the server enclosure, and remove the network card.

3. Turn on the server. It will likely take longer than usual to restart—be patient.

4. Log on to the server with the main Administrator account.

5. In the left pane of the Server Management console, click Internet And E-Mail to show the Manage Internet And E-Mail page as shown in Figure 7-4.

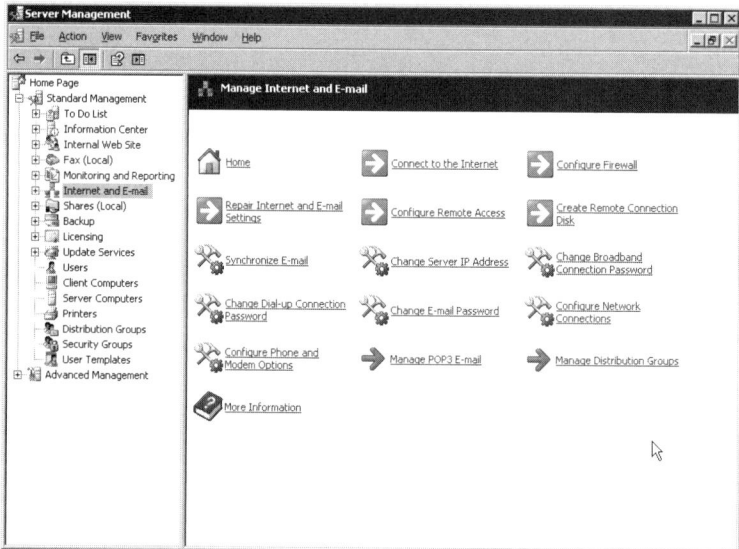

FIGURE 7-4 The Manage Internet And E-Mail page of the SBS Server Management console

6. Click Connect To The Internet to open the CEICW.

7. Click Next to open the Connection page of the CEICW, as shown in Figure 7-5.

8. Select Broadband and click Next to open the Broadband Connection page, as shown in Figure 7-6. Select A Local Router Device With An IP Address from the My Server Uses drop-down list.

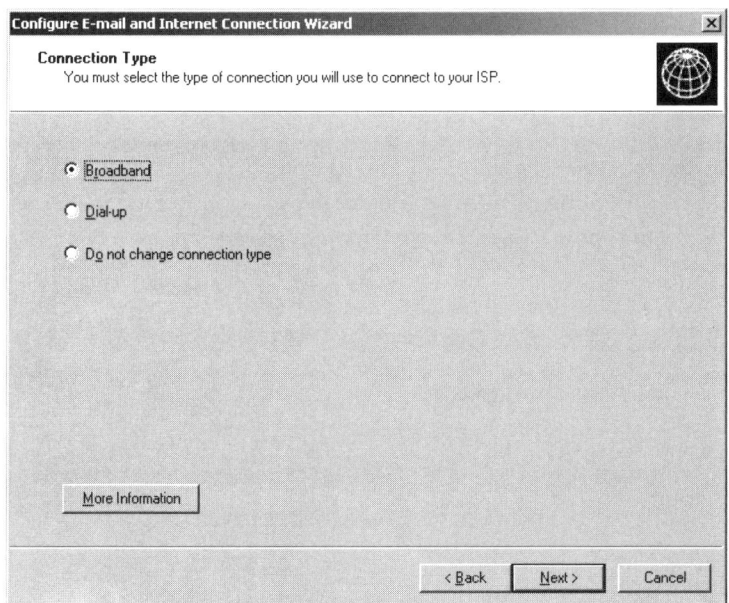

FIGURE 7-5 The Connection page of the CEICW

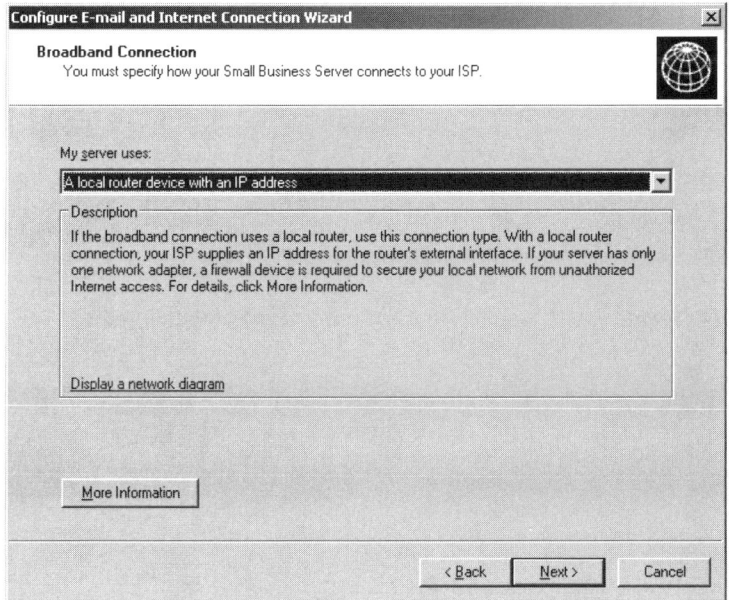

FIGURE 7-6 The Broadband Connection page of the CEICW

9. Click Next to open the Router Connection page shown in Figure 7-7. Type in the IP address you will be using with your new router/firewall and the IP addresses for your ISP's DNS servers.

NOTE If your router/firewall does DNS forwarding, you can use the IP address of the router/firewall for the Primary DNS Server address and leave the Secondary DNS Server address blank. If you want to always use root hints for DNS, you can leave these blank.

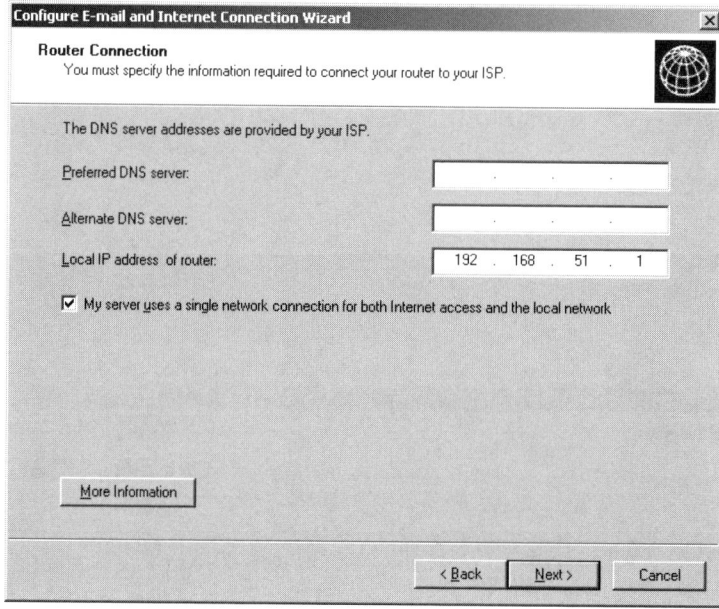

FIGURE 7-7 The Router Connection page of the CEICW

10. Select the My Server Uses A Single Network Connection For Both Internet Access And The Local Network check box.

11. Click Next. If the IP address of the router/firewall is in a different address range from your previous internal address, you'll see the message shown in Figure 7-8.

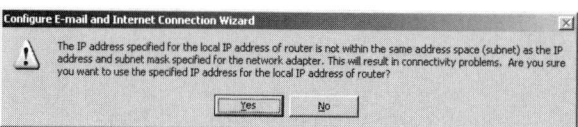

FIGURE 7-8 The warning message generated during network reconfiguration

12. Click Yes to open the information message shown in Figure 7-9. Because we're not connected to anything at this point, click No.

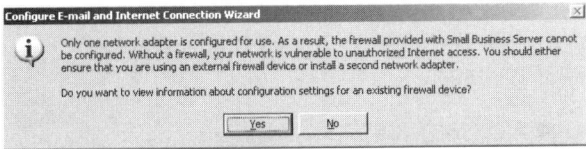

FIGURE 7-9 The firewall informational message of the CEICW

13. On the Web Services Configuration page, select the services that you want to be available when your existing SBS server is back online.

14. Click Next twice more and then click Finish to complete the wizard.

15. Click Close when the CEICW finishes.

If you've chosen to use a different IP address range for your SBS network than the one you're currently configured to use, now is a good time to change it by following these steps:

1. On the Manage Internet And E-Mail page of the Server Management console, click Change Server IP Address to open the Change IP Address Tool dialog box shown in Figure 7-10.

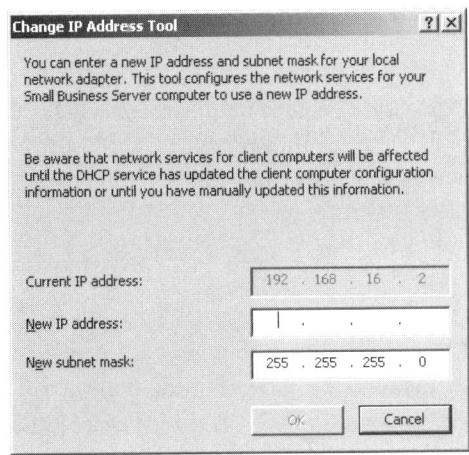

FIGURE 7-10 The Change IP Address Tool

2. Type in the new IP address for the server and click OK. When the tool completes, you'll see the message shown in Figure 7-11.

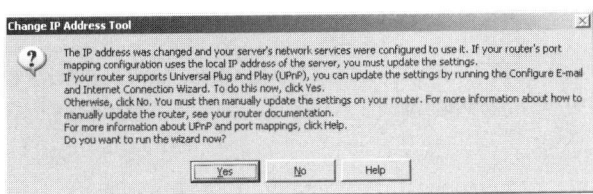

FIGURE 7-11 When you change the server's IP address, it offers to run the CEICW again.

3. Select No to complete process and close the Change IP Address Tool dialog box. As shown in Figure 7-12, the IP address has been reconfigured to point to the new router/firewall that we will install at 192.168.51.1.

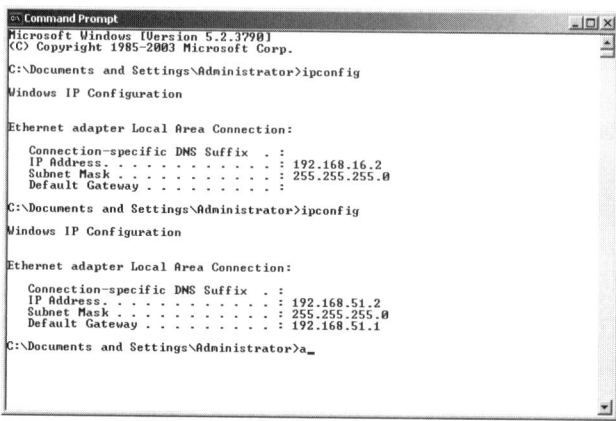

FIGURE 7-12 The IP address has changed on the server.

> **NOTE** If you have fixed IP devices on your network, you'll need to manually reconfigure their default gateway. This won't matter for devices that don't need to connect to the Internet, such as printers, but if you have additional servers or workstations that use fixed IP addresses, you should reconfigure them now to point to the new router.

Install Router and Firewall

After you've reconfigured your existing SBS to use a single network card, you need to reconnect it to the Internet. You need to insert a router into the network, if you don't already have one, and configure it for the network address range that you've chosen for your SBS network.

In many cases, you'll already have a router in place—we did. But that router is likely not a full-fledged firewall. Now is the time to replace it or add an additional firewall appliance. When you do, you'll need to configure the firewall for your SBS network. The ports SBS 2003 uses include:

- **25** Simple Mail Transport Protocol (SMTP), used by Microsoft Exchange for incoming and outgoing e-mail.
- **80** Hypertext Transfer Protocol (HTTP) Outbound, this port is used to surf the Web. Inbound, it can be used to initially connect to the Remote Web Workplace site.
- **443** Hypertext Transfer Protocol Secure (HTTPS), used outbound for connecting to secure Web sites and inbound for connecting to Remote Web Workplace.
- **444** Companyweb, used to connect to the SharePoint Companyweb intranet site. Only open this port if your users connect to Companyweb when working remotely.

- **3389** Remote Desktop Protocol (RDP), only used if you allow direct RDP connections from remote locations to your SBS server. If you do enable this for remote management, you should limit the IP addresses that are allowed to connect to specific, known IP addresses.
- **4125** Remote Web Workplace (RWW), used by RWW for connecting remote users to their desktops.

Additional ports might be in use for specific applications on your network, but these are the basic incoming ports that are used by SBS.

After you've installed and configured your router, connect it to your SBS network as shown earlier in Figure 7-2. Verify that you have connectivity from the server and from your workstations to a known site. If a workstation doesn't have connectivity, reboot and try again. Verify that the DHCP assigned IP address is in the correct range.

 UNDER THE HOOD   **ISA Server**

The requirements for migrating SBS 2003 Premium Edition networks that are using ISA Server are somewhat different. The basic premise is the same—you need to reconfigure your network to use a single NIC. But you'll also need to remove the ISA Firewall Client from computers on your network. Microsoft's migration guide says that you can leave ISA in place during the migration as long as you are running at least ISA 2004 SP3, but we think this just confuses the issue and leaves additional places where there could be problems during the migration.

We started to write up a full set of steps for uninstalling ISA and reconfiguring the workstations on your network, but then we found an excellent resource from Kevin Weilbacher, an SBS MVP. He has posted a step-by-step guide to removing ISA 2004 from SBS 2003, and he is actively maintaining it, updating it to cover issues as they're reported, with input from many of the other SBS MVPs. For full details on how to remove ISA 2004, see *http://msmvps.com/blogs/kwsupport/archive /2008/09/07/uninstalling-isa-2004.aspx*.

Disable VPNs

Before you begin the migration, you need to disable virtual private networking to the SBS server. If you need VPN access, you should choose a router/firewall that can act as a VPN endpoint. Ultimately, however, we think a better overall solution is to use RWW and avoid VPNs whenever possible.

To disable VPNs on the existing SBS server, follow these steps:

1. Log on to the server with the main Administrator account.
2. Open Server Management console if it doesn't open automatically.

3. In the left pane of the Server Management console, click Internet And E-Mail. The Manage Internet And E-Mail page opens.

4. Click Configure Remote Access to open the Remote Access Wizard.

5. Click Next on the Welcome page to open the Remote Access Method page as shown in Figure 7-13.

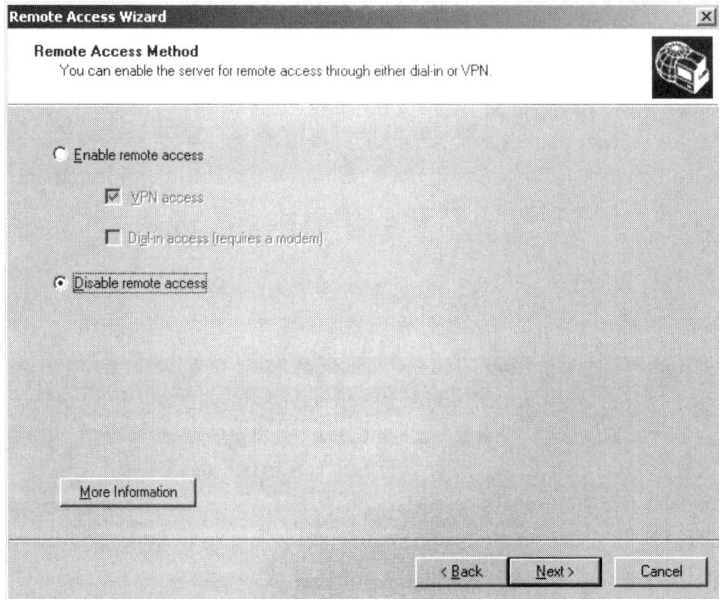

FIGURE 7-13 The Remote Access Method page of the Remote Access Wizard

6. Select Disable Remote Access, click Next, and then click Finish.

7. When the wizard completes, click Close to return to Server Management console.

This completes the network reconfiguration for your SBS migration. Now is a good time to verify that all the computers and devices on your network are working as you'd expect and can connect properly. Pay particular attention to devices such as printers, wireless access points, and Web cams that have a fixed or DHCP reservation address to make sure that they are communicating correctly with the rest of the network.

Configuring Active Directory

Before you can complete the migration to SBS 2008, you need to raise the domain and forest functional levels of your current SBS 2003 Active Directory. The migration requires that the Active Directory forest and domain functional level be Windows Server 2003. The default for SBS 2003 is Microsoft Windows 2000 functional level.

You can't move to a Windows Server 2003 functional level if there are any Windows 2000 or earlier domain controllers in your SBS domain. If there are, you must first demote them from being domain controllers. For Windows 2000, run Dcpromo.exe as a domain administrator to demote the legacy Windows 2000 domain controller. If you still have Windows NT 4 domain controllers in your network, you'll need to rebuild these servers as non-domain controllers or remove them from the network entirely.

To raise the domain and forest functional level of your SBS 2003 Active Directory, follow these steps:

1. Log on to the SBS 2003 server with an account that has both Domain Admins and Enterprise Admins privileges. The Administrator account is a good choice for this.

2. Click Start, then click Administrative Tools, and then click Active Directory Domains And Trusts to open the Active Directory Domains And Trusts console shown in Figure 7-14, or you can type **domain.msc** at the Run menu.

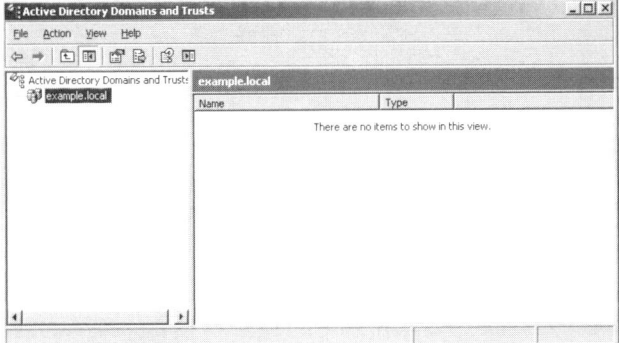

FIGURE 7-14 The Active Directory Domains And Trusts console

NOTE Raising the domain functional level is an irreversible change. You can't later lower the functional level.

3. Click the domain (example.local in Figure 7-14) and select Raise Domain Functional Level from the Action menu to open the dialog box shown in Figure 7-15.

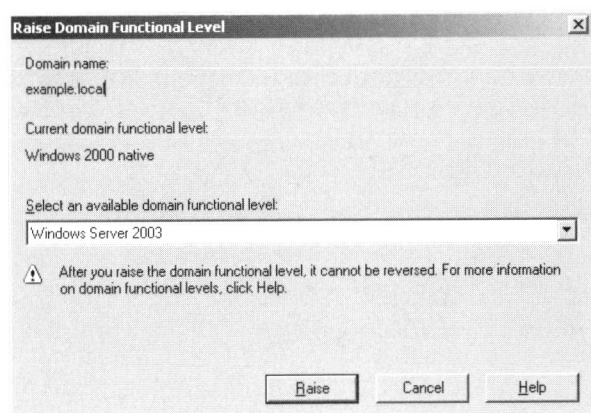

FIGURE 7-15 The Raise Domain Functional Level dialog box

4. Select Windows Server 2003 from the drop-down list (this should be the only choice in most SBS networks) and then click Raise to raise the domain functional level.

NOTE If the Current Domain Functional Level is shown as Windows Server 2003, you won't be able to change the functional level.

5. Click OK at the warning that this change can't be reversed, and click OK again at the success message.

6. Click Active Directory Domains And Trusts in the left pane at the top of the tree.

7. Click Raise Forest Functional Level on the Action menu to open the Raise Forest Functional Level dialog box shown in Figure 7-16.

NOTE Raising the forest functional level is an irreversible change. You can't later lower the functional level.

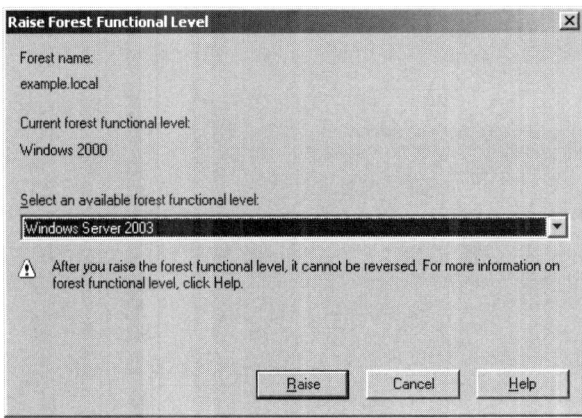

FIGURE 7-16 The Raise Forest Functional Level dialog box

8. Click Raise to see the warning message that this change is irreversible as shown in Figure 7-17.

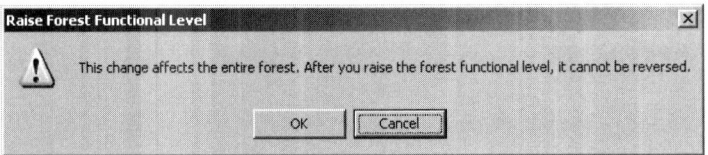

FIGURE 7-17 Raising the forest functional level is irreversible.

9. Click OK. If the raise was successful, you'll see the informational message in Figure 7-18.

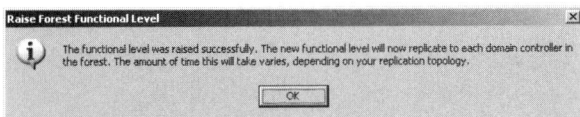

FIGURE 7-18 The Raise Forest Functional Level success informational message

10. Click OK to close the message and then close the Active Directory Domains And Trusts dialog box.

Best Practices Analyzer (BPA)

The BPA is a useful tool to run against your SBS server regardless of whether you're planning on migrating to SBS 2008 immediately or later on. The BPA can identify all kinds of problems in an SBS environment with more than 200 errors, warnings, and informational messages about the health of your SBS network.

You can download the BPA from *http://go.microsoft.com/fwlink/?LinkId=113752* and then install it on your SBS 2003 server. The Knowledge Base article for the BPA is 940439. When you've downloaded the BPA, execute the SBS2003SP1-KB940439-x86-enu.exe file to install it. (The actual filename varies depending on the language.)

You can then run the BPA using the following steps:

1. Click Start, click All Programs, and select SBS Best Practices Analyzer Tool.

2. The first time you run the BPA, you'll be asked if you want to check for new versions every time you start it, and you'll be offered an opportunity to check now. Say yes to automatic updates, and do check now—even with a fresh download, we still got a newer version after the check.

3. From the Welcome screen shown in Figure 7-19, you can select the options to use for a scan or view a previous scan.

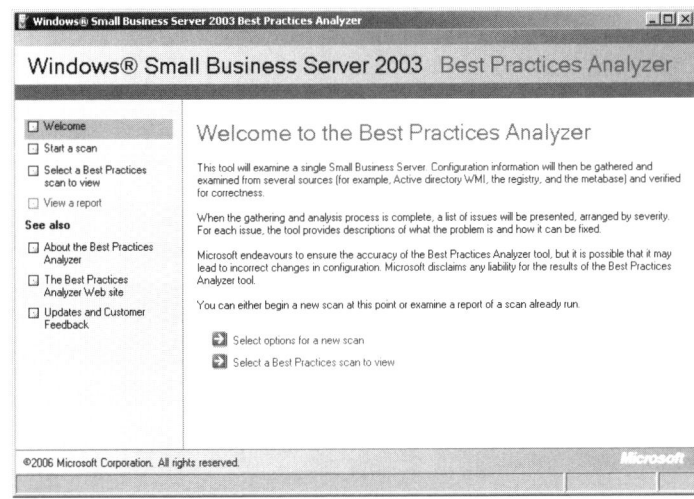

FIGURE 7-19 The Welcome screen of the SBS Best Practices Analyzer

4. Click Select Options For A New Scan to open the Start A Scan page shown in Figure 7-20.

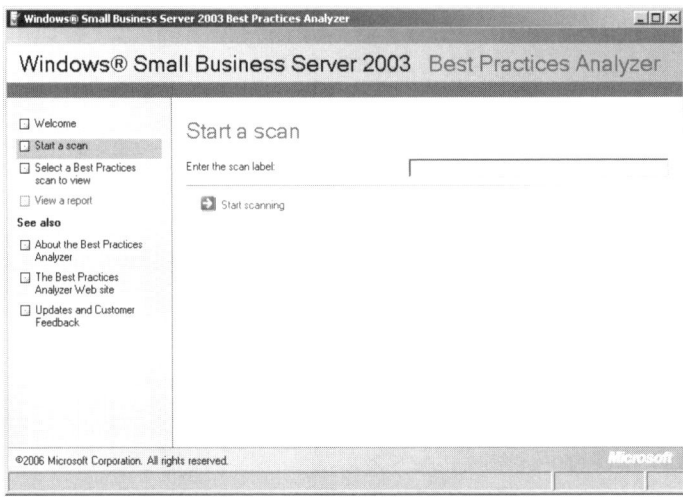

FIGURE 7-20 The Start A Scan page of the SBS BPA

5. Type in a label for the scan and click Start Scanning. When the scan completes, you'll see a summary of the results as shown in Figure 7-21.

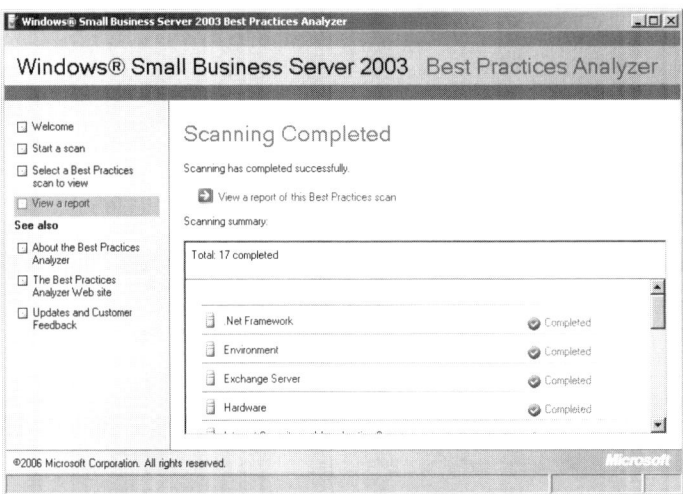

FIGURE 7-21 The Scanning Completed summary page of the SBS BPA

6. To view the results of the scan, click View A Report Of This Best Practices Scan. A typical report is shown in Figure 7-22.

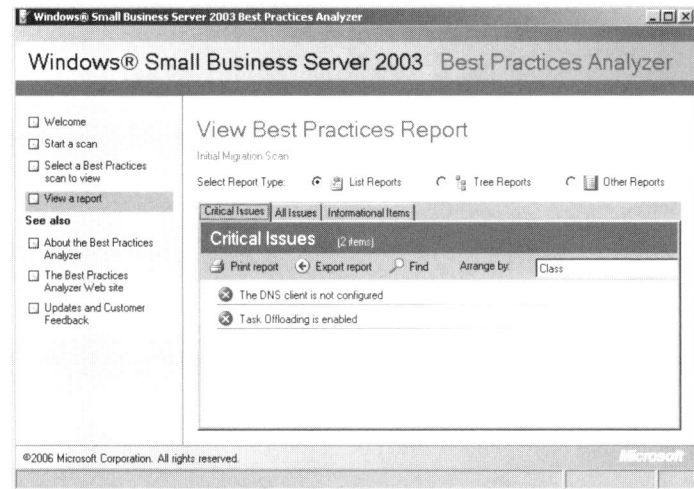

FIGURE 7-22 A typical report from an SBS BPA scan

7. Click any listed issue to see more details on the issue, including links to Knowledge Base articles on how to correct the issue. Figure 7-23 shows the detail screen for the DNS issue shown in Figure 7-22.

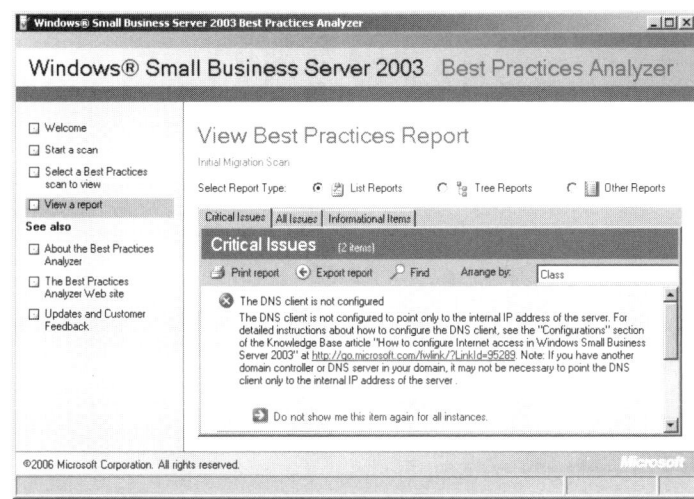

FIGURE 7-23 The DNS Client Is Not Configured details from the SBS BPA

8. After you've corrected the issues that could prevent a successful migration, run the BPA again by repeating steps 4 through 7 to verify that all the problems are corrected. At a minimum, you should correct all critical issues, and you should carefully evaluate the issues listed in the All Issues section and correct any that are possible problems for your migration.

Optimize Exchange Mailboxes

You should have your users optimize their Microsoft Exchange mailboxes to reduce the time it takes to migrate them to Exchange 2007. If you've been enforcing strict mailbox limits, this likely isn't a major issue, but if you've got a couple of users who are special and have seriously large mailboxes, now is a good time to try to get this under control. Anything that removes excess mail from the mailboxes is a good thing, but the most obvious steps are:

- Ask all users to empty their Deleted Items folders.
- Ask all users to empty their Junk E-Mail folders.
- Ask all users to archive all mail items older than some reasonable date.

After users have had a reasonable amount of time to clean up their mailboxes, it's usually useful to examine the mailbox store in Exchange to see whether any outstandingly large mailboxes remain. This allows you to have a more direct discussion with the owner of the mailbox to help reduce its size. You can check the size of mailboxes by opening the Exchange System Manager and navigating to Servers, then *servername*, then First Storage Group, then Mailbox Store, then Mailboxes, as shown in Figure 7-24.

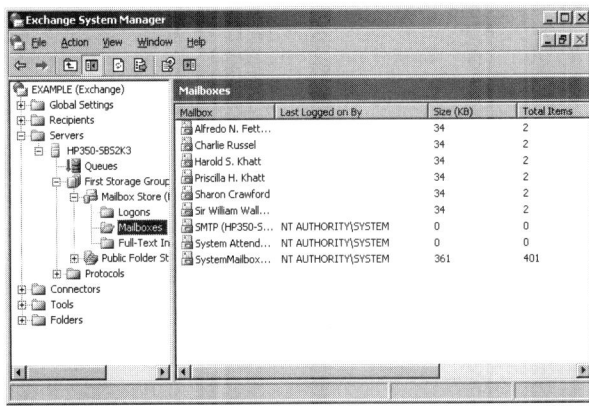

FIGURE 7-24 A very empty Microsoft Exchange Mailbox store

NOTE The mailboxes listed in Figure 7-24 are not typical of a working system but reflect what you would see on a brand-new system.

Running the Migration Preparation Tool

There are several tasks that need to be done on all SBS 2003 networks to prepare for the actual migration, including the following:

- Upgrade the Active Directory schema.
- Set the Microsoft Exchange Server mode.

■ Extend the time that two SBS servers can coexist in the same network.

To make life easier for the migration, these tasks are automated with the Migration Preparation Tool.

There's one other task we'll cover in this section—synchronizing the time source. On most SBS networks this should already be OK, but it's critical for the proper migration to the new SBS 2008 server, so we'll make sure it's correct and synched to an external source.

IMPORTANT The changes made by the Migration Preparation Tool are irreversible. You should ensure that you have a fully tested backup of your existing SBS 2003 server before running the Migration Preparation Tool. The *only* way to return to your original configuration is to restore your backup.

Before you start the migration, you need to upgrade the Active Directory schema to align with the schema used by SBS 2008. To upgrade the schema, you *must* be logged on to the existing SBS server with an account that is a member of the Domain Admins, Enterprise Admins, and Schema Admins groups. The default Administrator account is in all three groups. To verify that the account you are using is in the necessary groups, open Active Directory Users And Computers and double-click the account you are using. Click the Member Of tab to see a list of groups the account belongs to, as shown in Figure 7-25.

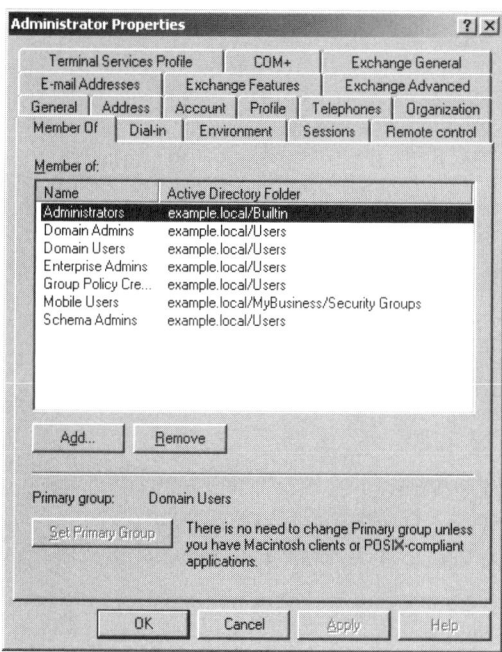

FIGURE 7-25 The Member Of tab of the Administrator account properties

To run the Migration Preparation Tool, use the following steps:

1. Log on to your SBS 2003 server with an account that has Domain Admins, Enterprise Admins, and Schema Admins privileges.

2. Insert the first SBS 2008 DVD into the DVD drive of the server.

   NOTE If you don't have a DVD drive on your existing SBS server, insert the DVD in a client workstation and copy the entire tools directory to a location on the server and run SourceTool from there.

3. Open Windows Explorer and navigate to the Tools directory of the DVD drive.

4. Double-click SourceTool.exe to open the Migration Preparation Tool shown in Figure 7-26.

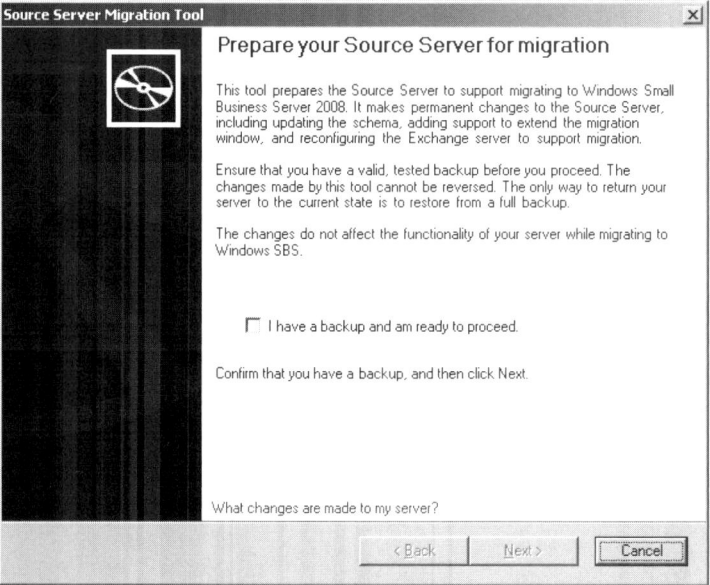

FIGURE 7-26 The opening page of the Source Server Migration Tool Wizard

5. Select the I Have A Backup And Am Ready To Proceed check box and then click Next. The tool will start updating your schema, extending your coexistence time, and configuring Exchange Server. The process takes several minutes and provides very little feedback, so just be patient. The largest chunk of time is for the schema upgrade.

6. When the tool completes its tasks, you'll get a confirmation message that it completed. You can click Finish to close the tool or click Create An Answer File to open the Answer File Generator now.

7. When you exit the Migration Preparation Tool, you'll be prompted to reboot. You should reboot your server before going any further.

After you reboot, you need to make sure your existing SBS 2003 server is correctly synchronized with an external time source. To set the time synchronization on your SBS server, use the following steps:

1. Log on to your existing SBS server with an account that has Domain Admins privileges.

2. Open a command window (Cmd.exe). Type the following commands in the window, as shown in Figure 7-27.

```
w32tm /config /syncfromflags:domhier /reliable:no /update
net stop w32time
net start w32time
```

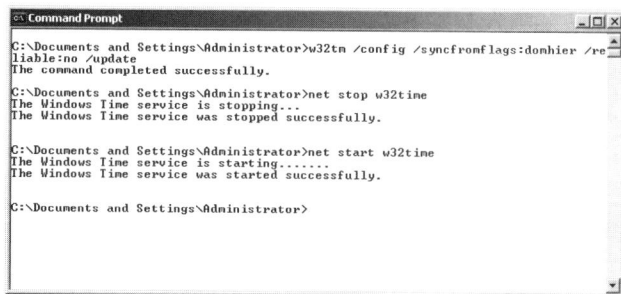

FIGURE 7-27 Configuring Windows Time synchronization

3. Close the command window.

> **IMPORTANT** If you are running SBS 2003 and SBS 2008 in virtual machines on a Hyper-V server, the parent partition *must* have the same time zone, date, and time as the child partitions.

Finally, before you can migrate your existing SBS 2003 server, you need to ensure that any line-of-business applications are moved off the main SBS server or that you have a clear migration path to move them to another server on your SBS network after the migration completes. Remember that after you migrate to SBS 2008, your old SBS server must be completely decommissioned and removed from the network. Before you can return it to the SBS network, you need to format the system disk and reinstall an operating system. The old and new SBS servers can only coexist on the network for a maximum of 21 days.

Creating a Migration Answer File

When you have your existing SBS server prepared for migration, you need to create an answer file that can be used to install SBS 2008. You *must use an answer file* for the installation of SBS 2008 if you are migrating. Fortunately, there's an excellent Answer File Generator tool on the SBS 2008 installation DVD. But there is one step we need to take first—creating a new SBS administrator account.

Administrator Account

SBS 2003 creates a default Administrator account during initial installation and setup. This account, often referred to as the *500 account* because of a distinctive portion of the GUID for the account, is the master account from which all things spring. This is a legacy from when we were less security-aware and less concerned about having everything installed by and dependent on a well-known account.

Today, that is far from a best practice, and in SBS 2008, the Administrator account is disabled by default. So to ensure that we have an account for both servers that has the necessary privileges to complete the migration, we're going to first create a new administrator account and make that account part of all the groups that the current Administrator account is part of. This new account must have Domain Admins, Enterprise Admins, and Schema Admins privileges, at a minimum. In fact, we're simply going to make a copy of the Administrator account.

To create the new administrator account, follow these steps:

1. Log on to the existing SBS 2003 server with an account with at least Domain Admins privileges.

2. Click Start and open Active Directory Users And Computers from the Administrative Tools folder.

3. Open the Users folder in the left pane and select the Administrator account in the right pane.

4. Select Copy from the Action menu to open the Copy Object – User dialog box shown in Figure 7-28.

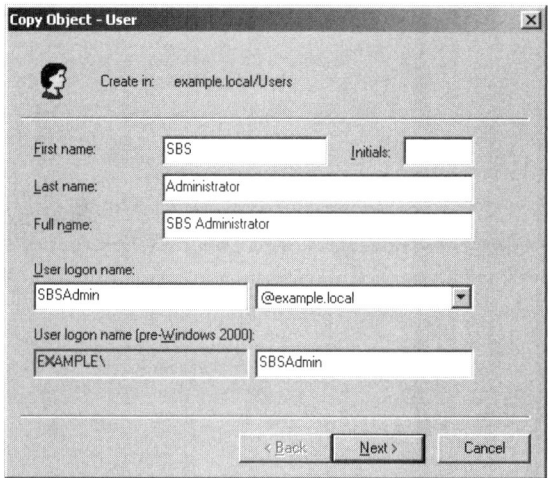

FIGURE 7-28 Creating a new administrator account for SBS 2003

5. After supplying the new administrator account, click Next to fill in password information for the new account, as shown in Figure 7-29. Use a password of at least eight characters that is a mixture of uppercase and lowercase, special characters, and numerals to ensure that it meets complexity requirements for SBS 2008.

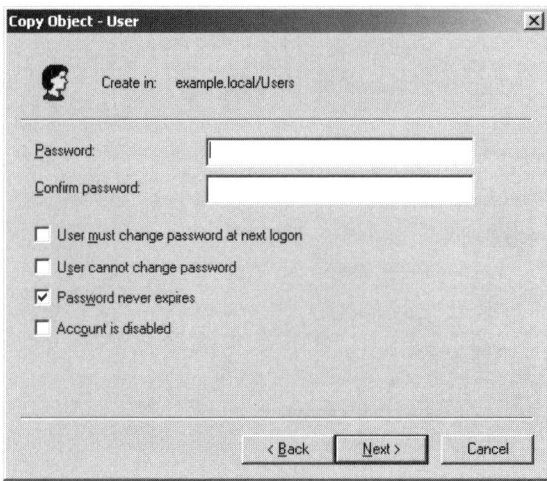

FIGURE 7-29 Setting the password for the new administrator account

6. Click Next to open the Exchange mailbox creation of the Copy Object – User dialog box, as shown in Figure 7-30.

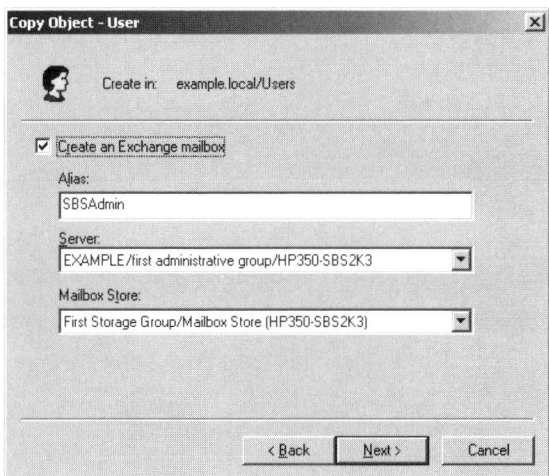

FIGURE 7-30 Creating the Exchange mailbox for the new administrator account

7. Click Next and then click Finish to create the account. The account will be created in the Users container, which isn't where we want it.

8. Expand the MyBusiness OU container and then expand the Users OU under it so that you can see the SBSUsers OU as shown in Figure 7-31.

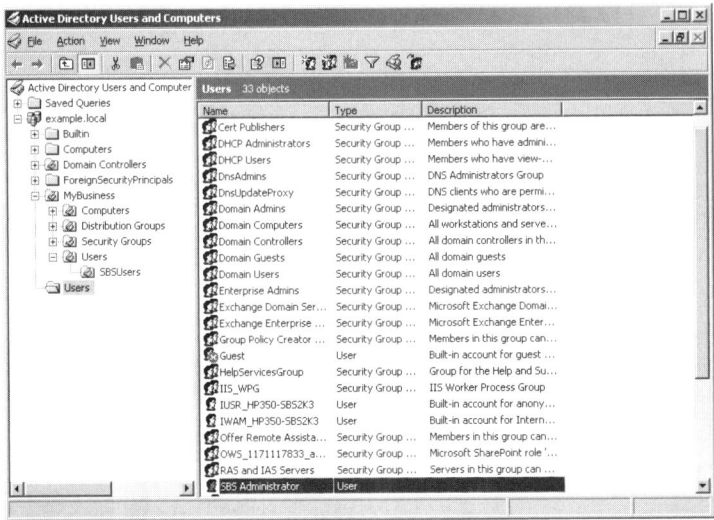

FIGURE 7-31 The MyBusiness OU is expanded so that you can see the SBSUsers OU.

9. Select the new user you just created and drag it into the SBSUsers OU. You'll see the warning shown in Figure 7-32.

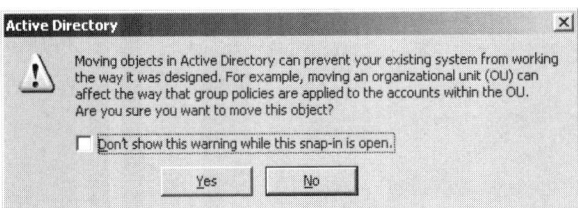

FIGURE 7-32 The warning about moving objects in Active Directory

10. Click Yes to move the user. Figure 7-33 shows the SBSUsers OU with the new administrator account in it.

11. Close Active Directory Users And Computers.

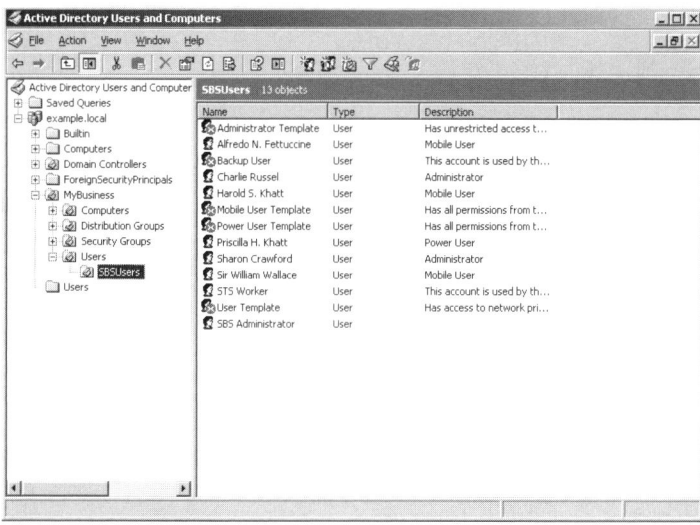

FIGURE 7-33 The SBSUsers OU with the new SBS Administrator account in it

Using the SBS Answer File Generator

The SBS Answer File Generator (SBSAfg.exe in the Tools folder of the Installation DVD) can be used to automate a fresh, new install of SBS, and we've covered it in some detail in Chapter 5, "Installing SBS 2008." But it has a second and more important function—it is used to generate an answer file for enabling a migration installation. You *must* use an answer file when doing a migration. You do not have the option of doing it purely interactively.

Before you start the answer file generator, you should make sure you have all the information required. Put together a table with all the answers you'll need. This will help ensure you're not missing a vital piece of information before you start. Table 7-1 shows our working table for the migration of our Example.local SBS 2003 network to SBS 2008.

TABLE 7-1 Answer File Checklist for SBS 2003 Migration

FIELD	ANSWER	REQUIRED
Get Installation Updates	Yes	No, but recommended.
Run Unattended	Yes	No.
Use Time Zone	GMT-8	No, but will stop to wait if not set.
Windows Live OneCare For Server	No	No.

FIELD	ANSWER	REQUIRED
Microsoft Forefront Security For Exchange Server	Yes	No.
Business Name	SBS Example	Optional. Not sent to Microsoft.
Street Address 1	1 Microsoft Way	Optional. Not sent to Microsoft.
Street Address 2		Optional. Not sent to Microsoft.
City	Redmond	Optional. Not sent to Microsoft.
State	WA	Optional. Not sent to Microsoft.
Zip/Postal Code	98052	Optional. Not sent to Microsoft.
Country/Region	United States	
Certificate Authority Name		Leave blank for self-issued cert.*
Domain Administrator Account Name	SBSAdmin	Yes.
Password	Iforget!	Yes.
Source Server Name	HP350-SBS2k3	Yes.
Source Domain Name	Example.local	Yes.
Default Gateway	192.168.51.1	Yes.
Source Server IP Address	192.168.51.2	Yes.
Destination Server Name	HP350-SBSMIG	Yes.
Destination Server IP Address	192.168.51.3	Yes.
DHCP Server Running On Source Server	Yes	Highly recommended. Will allow the migration process to move DHCP to the destination server.

When using a self-signed certificate, you should leave the Certificate Authority Name field blank. SBS will create the certificate and use the correct authority name. It's very easy to choose a name that will cause problems, and by the time the installation fails, you'll have wasted a significant amount of time.

When you have all the settings for your migration written down, it's time to run the SBS Answer File Generator using the following steps:

1. Double-click the SBSAfg.exe file in the \Tools directory of the first DVD (the Installation DVD) of the SBS 2008 distribution media.

2. In the Installation Type section of the Windows Small Business Server 2008 Answer File Tool (Figure 7-34), select Migration From Existing Server (Join Existing Domain).

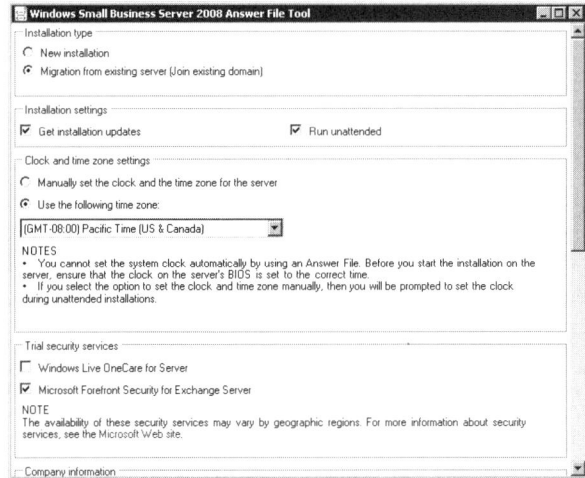

FIGURE 7-34 The Windows Small Business Server 2008 Answer File Tool

3. Fill in the fields according to the table you created, making sure to scroll to the end of the file so you don't miss any.

4. Click Print to print a copy of the settings to the default printer if you want a hard copy of the settings.

> **IMPORTANT** The printout has the administrative password clearly visible. This will also be the domain recover password. Protect the printout accordingly and destroy it when it's no longer required.

5. Click Save As to save a copy as SBSAnswerFile.xml. You can save the copy to a local hard disk, to a network share, or to removable media.

> **IMPORTANT** The SBSAnswerFile.xml file that is generated has the administrative password in plain text. This will also be the domain recover password. Protect the file until you use it and delete it when you're done.

6. Click Cancel to close the Answer File Generator.

7. Copy SBSAnswerFile.xml to the root directory of the removable media you will use during installation of SBS 2008. This can be a USB key disk, a floppy disk, or other removable media that your server can read during the installation.

Installing SBS 2008

Okay—we've prepared our server, created our answer file, and we're ready to go. Time to install SBS 2008. We're going to follow the normal steps covered in Chapter 5, except that we're using the answer file we created earlier in this chapter. Insert the removable media with the SBSAnswerFile.xml, insert your Installation DVD, and turn on the server.

> **NOTE** You won't actually need the answer file to be available until the Windows Server 2008 portion of the installation completes.

You need to set your BIOS to boot from the DVD drive as the first option to ensure that the server boots from the DVD. Then walk through the normal Windows Server 2008 installation steps as covered in Chapter 5. During the initial Server 2008 phase, you'll enter your SBS Standard or SBS Premium Installation key. Do not use the key for the second server if you have SBS 2008 Premium—that's a separate key that you need to save for your second server installation. You'll also choose your installation disk, and you can set the size of your system volume for SBS at this time. Do not set it at fewer than 60 gigabytes (GB), and we really prefer 80 GB or more. It's a real pain to increase the size later, and there are just too many things that end up going onto your primary system volume.

After you've answered the initial installation questions, the installation of Windows Server 2008 proceeds automatically. When it completes and the system reboots, the installation of SBS will automatically begin if the SBSAnswerFile.xml file is available and you've set the answer file for unattended installation. Even if you've selected the Run Unattended check box in the SBS Answer File Generator, the installation will stop if it is missing a critical piece of information. If you've left the Run Unattended check box cleared, the SBS installation process will use the answers you've provided in the file, but will expect manual input from you to move from step to step.

The server will reboot several times during the installation, but if you've filled out the answer file fully and you've selected the Run Unattended check box, you should be able to start it, answer the initial questions, and go away for a while. Have lunch. Play a game of racquetball. The whole process may be automated, but it's still slow. When the installation is complete, you'll see the Installation Finished screen shown in Figure 7-35.

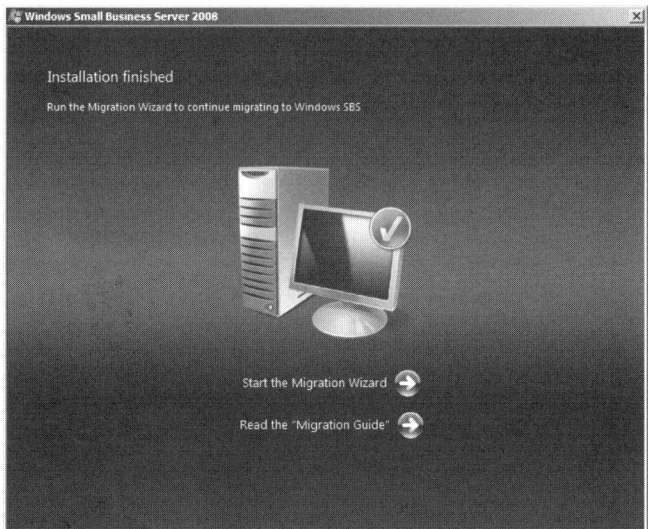

FIGURE 7-35 The Installation Finished screen, ready to start the migration from SBS 2003 to SBS 2008

Migrating Settings and Data

When you've completed the installation of SBS 2008 into your SBS 2003 network, you have 21 days to complete the migration and decommission the original server. There are several steps in the process, some automated, some not.

Reconfigure Folder Redirection

The first step if you're using Folder Redirection in your existing SBS 2003 network is to reconfigure that to point to a folder on your new SBS 2008 server. If the SBS 2008 installation program put all your initial shares on the C drive, you'll want to fix that first. We had that happen on our initial test migration because the second hard disk wasn't recognized until we were fully installed and could load drivers. You can wait to do all this until the rest of your migration is complete, but we like to only have to touch things as little as possible, so we used the following batch file to switch things around.

MoveShares.cmd

```
@Echo Off
REM Batch file to move the initial shares on an SBS 2008 installation

setlocal
REM This assumes D: will be the drive where users data goes. Change as needed.
set _Users=D:\Users

mkdir %_Users%
mkdir %_Users%\FolderRedirections
mkdir %_Users%\Public
mkdir %_Users%\Shares

dir %_Users%
echo if the above looks correct, then...
pause

xcopy \\%ComputerName%\Public\* %_Users%\Public /i /e
net use RedirectedFolders /delete
net use Public /delete
net use UsersShares /delete

net share RedirectedFolders=%_Users%\FolderRedirections /grant:everyone,full
net share Public=%_Users%\Public /grant:everyone,full
net share UsersShares=%_Users%\Shares /grant:everyone,full
```

Now that we've moved those over, let's change our folder redirection to point to the new server. (You can skip this step entirely if you haven't enabled Folder Redirection on your existing SBS 2003 network.)

To change the folder redirection, use the following steps:

1. Log on to the new SBS 2008 server with an administrative account.

2. Open Group Policy Management in the Administrative Tools folder to open the Group Policy Management console (gpmc.msc). In the left pane, navigate to Group Policy Objects as shown in Figure 7-36.

3. Right-click Small Business Server Folder Redirection and select Edit to open the Group Policy Management Editor as shown in Figure 7-37.

4. In the left pane of the Group Policy Management Editor, navigate to User Configuration, then Policies, then Windows Settings, then Folder Redirection.

5. In the right pane, right-click Documents and select properties to open the Documents Properties dialog box.

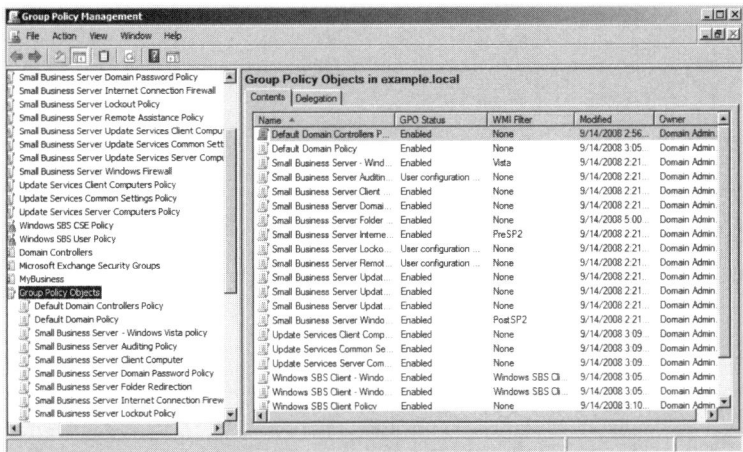

FIGURE 7-36 The Group Policy Management console

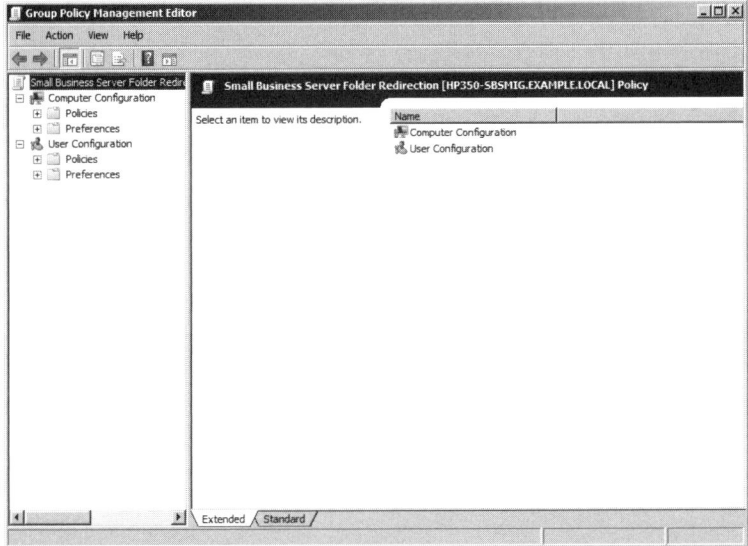

FIGURE 7-37 The Group Policy Management Editor

6. From the Setting drop-down list, select Basic – Redirect Everyone's Folder To The Same Location. From the Target Folder Location drop-down list, select Create A Folder For Each User Under The Root Path, as shown in Figure 7-38.

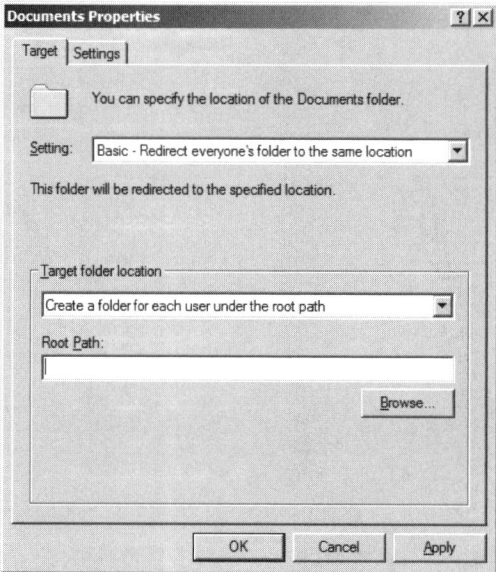

FIGURE 7-38 Setting the folder redirection path

7. In the Root Path field, type **\\\<*SBS2008servername*>\RedirectedFolders**, replacing *<SBS2008servername>* with the name of your new SBS 2008 server. Figure 7-39 shows the result for our hp350-sbsmig server used for the test migration.

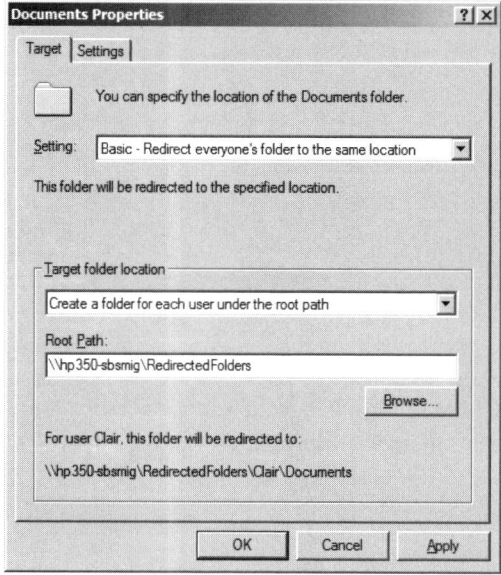

FIGURE 7-39 Folder Redirection on our SBS 2008 test migration server

8. Click OK and then click Yes in the warning dialog box.

9. Close the Group Policy Management Editor to return to the Group Policy Management console and then close the console.

Using the Migration Wizard

From the time that Windows Small Business Server 2008 is first installed and running on your existing SBS network, you have a maximum of 21 days to complete the migration. Required tasks listed in the Migration Wizard must be completed in the order listed. Optional tasks can be completed later because the other tasks in the task list are not dependent on them. The tasks in the Migration Wizard are listed in Table 7-2.

TABLE 7-2 Tasks in the Migration Wizard

TASK	REQUIRED OR OPTIONAL
Change data storage locations on the new SBS 2008 server	Optional
Configure networking	Required
Configure Internet address	Required
Migrate network settings from old SBS server	Optional
Migrate Exchange Server mailboxes	Required if Exchange used
Clean up legacy Group Policy settings	Optional
Migrate users' shared data	Optional (but not if you're the user!)
Migrate Companyweb	Optional
Migrate fax data	Optional
Migrate user accounts and groups	Required
Migrate SQL Server data	Optional and not in the wizard
Migrate line-of-business applications	Optional and not in the wizard
Decommission the old SBS 2003 server	Required

You can start and stop the Migration Wizard as often as necessary. Each time you open it after the initial time, it opens to the Migration Wizard Home page.

> **NOTE** For the steps of this wizard, we've chosen to break the process up in sections that correspond to the individual tasks in the wizard. Each section begins with a heading and includes a series of steps. You can complete each section independently of the other sections, except that each required task in the wizard must be performed in order.

Starting the Migration Wizard

To run the Migration Wizard, follow these steps:

1. Log on to the new SBS 2008 server with an account that has administrative privileges.

2. Open the Windows SBS Console if it doesn't open automatically.

3. Click Migrate To Windows SBS to open the Migrate To Windows Small Business Server 2008 Wizard. The first time you run the wizard, you'll see a Welcome page.

4. Click Next to open the Migration Wizard Home page, shown in Figure 7-40.

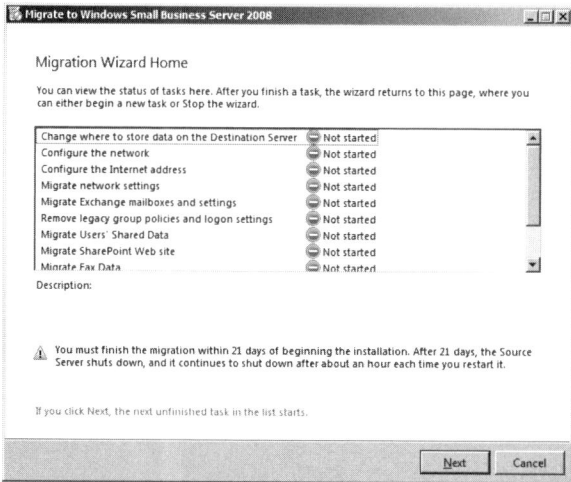

FIGURE 7-40 The Migration Wizard Home page before starting the migration

5. Select Change Where To Store Data On The Destination Server and click Next to open the page shown in Figure 7-41.

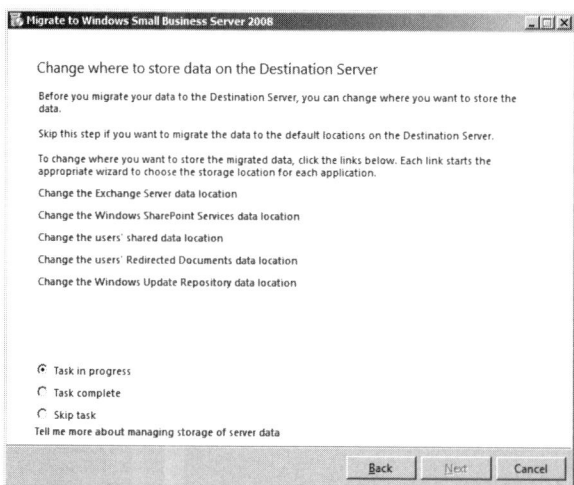

FIGURE 7-41 The Change Where To Store Data On The Destination Server page

6. This is an optional task, so you can choose to skip the task. Because the default location for Exchange Server data is on the C drive, we definitely want to change that, so click Change The Exchange Server Data Location to open the Move Exchange Server Data Wizard.

7. Click Next and your server hard drives are examined. When the wizard finishes the examination, it prompts you with the warning Server Backup Is Not Configured, as shown in Figure 7-42. We know that, so click OK.

FIGURE 7-42 Warning that Server Backup isn't configured

8. On the Choose A New Location For The Data page, shown in Figure 7-43, select the location you want to use for the data and click Move.

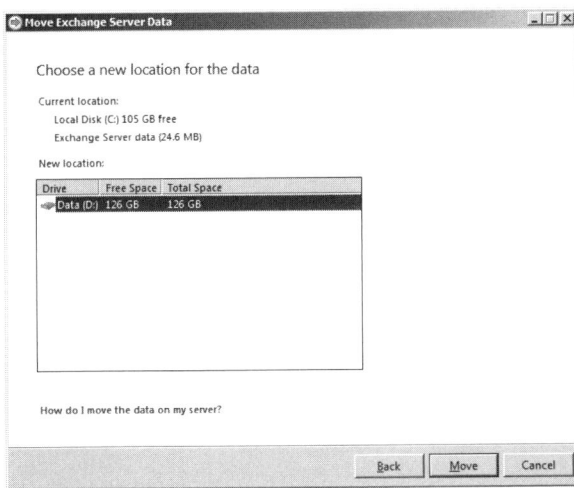

FIGURE 7-43 The Choose A New Location For The Data page of the Move Exchange Server Data Wizard

9. Click Finish when the task completes.

10. Complete the rest of the relocations on this page now or complete them later. SBS includes wizards that simplify these tasks even after the migration is complete.

11. Click Skip Task when you've completed all the steps you want to do at this time and then click Next to return to the Migration Wizard Home page.

Configure the Network

To configure the network, follow these steps:

1. Click Next to move to the Set Up The Network page.

2. Click the Start The Connect To The Internet Wizard link to open the Before You Begin page of the Connect To The Internet Wizard, shown in Figure 7-44.

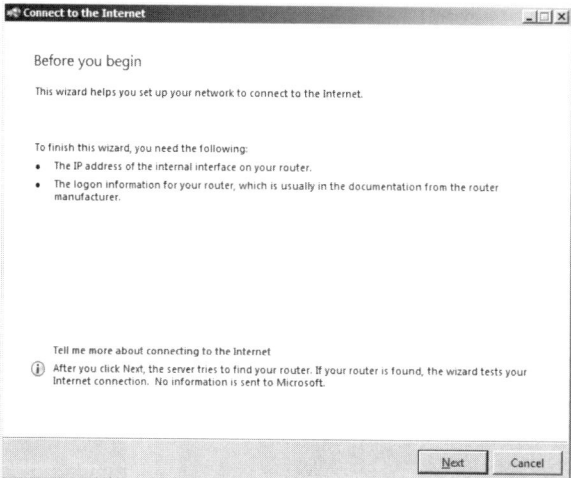

FIGURE 7-44 The Before You Begin page of the Connect To The Internet Wizard

3. Click Next and the wizard will start detecting your current network and locating your router. When it completes, you'll see the page shown in Figure 7-45.

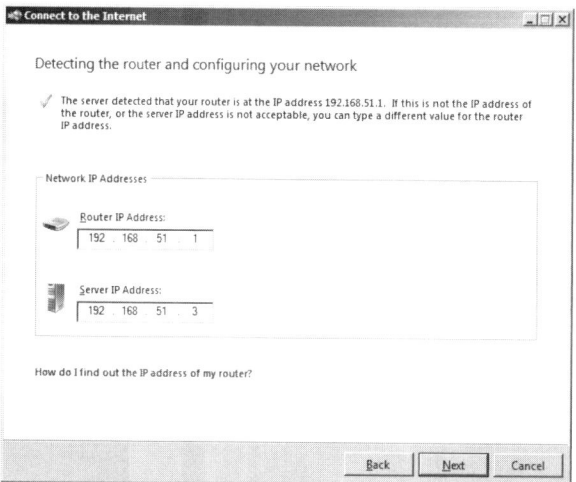

FIGURE 7-45 The Connect To The Internet Wizard has correctly detected the router and server IP addresses.

4. Click Next. If you have a UPnP router, the wizard will automatically configure it. If you don't, you'll see a page describing how to manually configure the settings required.

5. Click Finish to return to the Migration Wizard Home page. The Configure The Network task now shows as Completed.

Configure the Internet Address

To configure the Internet address, follow these steps:

1. Click Next to open the Configure The Internet Address page. Read the warning about certificate distribution to remote users. If you are using self-signed certificates, and you don't do this now, your users will be locked out of RWW and Outlook Web Access until you distribute new certificates to them.

2. Click Start The Internet Address Management Wizard when you're ready to move your RWW and OWA sites to the new SBS 2008 server.

3. Click Next on the Before You Begin page (after reading it) to open the Do You Want To Register A New Domain Name page, shown in Figure 7-46.

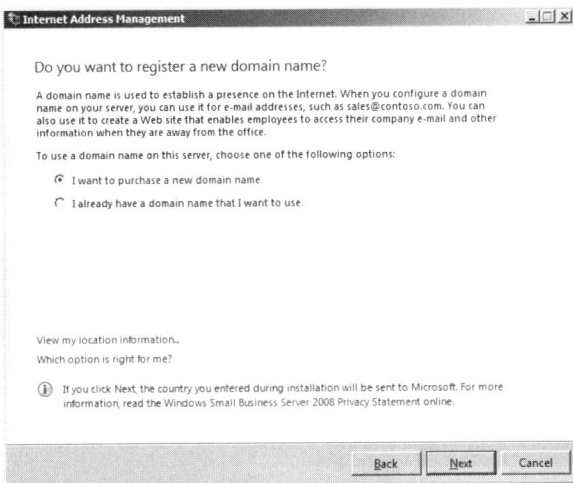

FIGURE 7-46 The Do You Want To Register A New Domain Name page of the Internet Address Management Wizard

4. Select the appropriate choice for your network. If you're not changing your Internet domain name, choose I Already Have A Domain Name That I Want To Use.

5. Click Next to open the How Do You Want To Manage Your Domain Name page, shown in Figure 7-47. If you're already managing your domain name, there's no reason to change.

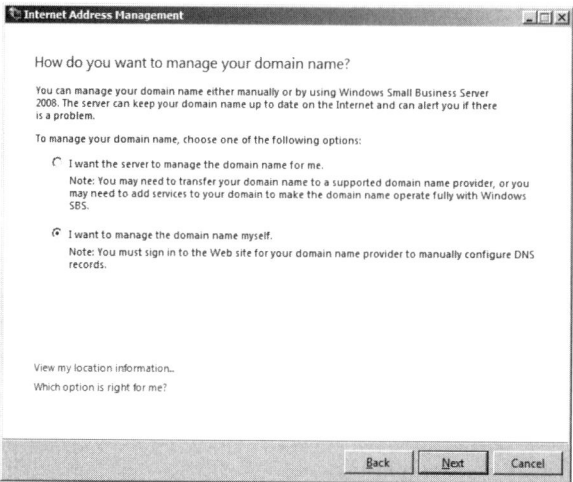

FIGURE 7-47 SBS 2008 can automatically manage DNS records and your domain name.

6. Click Next to open the Store Your Domain Name Information page of the wizard, as shown in Figure 7-48.

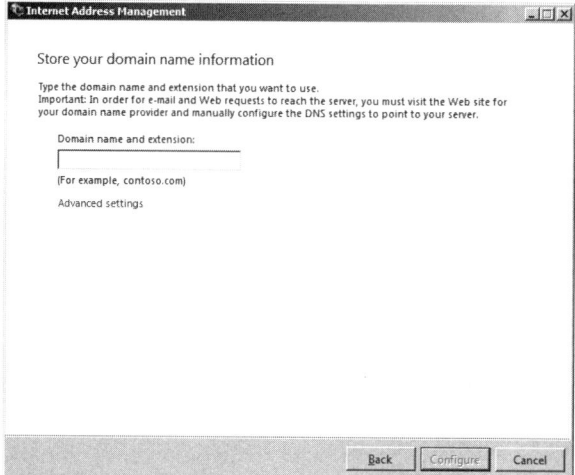

FIGURE 7-48 The Store Your Domain Name Information page of the Internet Address Management Wizard

7. Type your Internet domain name in the Domain Name And Extension field and then click Configure. This will configure your RWW site, your Exchange e-mail address, and your Internet router if it supports UPnP. If it doesn't, you need to manually configure the settings on the router.

8. Click Finish when the wizard completes to return to the Configure The Internet Address page of the Migration Wizard.

9. Click Task Complete and then click Next to return to the Migration Wizard Home page.

Migrate Network Settings

To migrate network settings, follow these steps:

1. Click Next to open the Migrate Network Settings page of the Migration Wizard, shown in Figure 7-49.

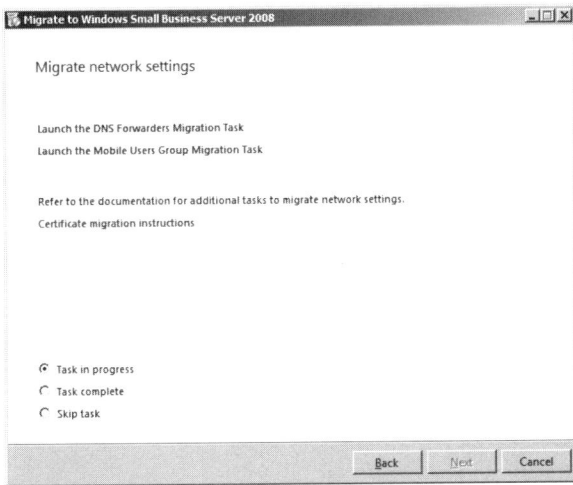

FIGURE 7-49 The Migrate Network Settings page of the Migration Wizard

2. Click Launch The DNS Forwarders Migration Task. When the task completes, you'll see the informational message shown in Figure 7-50.

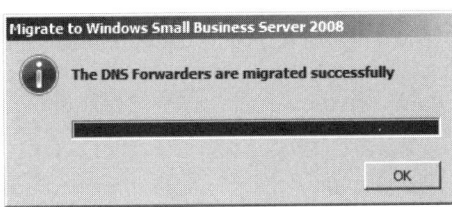

FIGURE 7-50 The DNS Forwarders have been migrated successfully.

3. Click OK to return to the Migrate Network Settings page.

4. Click Launch The Mobile Users Group Migration Task to migrate the Mobile Users group. The Mobile Users group is not a default SBS 2008 Security Group.

5. Click OK when the wizard completes to return to the Migrate Network Settings page.

6. Click Task Complete and then click Next to return to the Migration Wizard Home page.

Migrate Exchange Mailboxes and Settings

To migrate Exchange mailboxes and settings, follow these steps:

1. Click Next to open the Migrate Exchange Mailboxes And Settings page of the Migration Wizard, as shown in Figure 7-51.

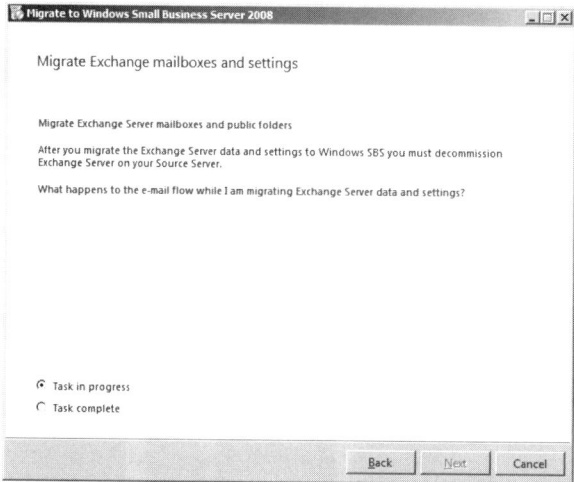

FIGURE 7-51 The Migrate Exchange Mailboxes And Settings page

2. Click the Migrate Exchange Server Mailboxes And Public Folders link to open the Windows Help file on migrating Microsoft Exchange.

3. Carefully read the information in the help file, paying particular attention to the behavior of Microsoft Forefront for Exchange Server. If you installed Forefront as part of the SBS 2008 install, it will already be scanning mailboxes and will *remove attachments that it considers dangerous*. Warn your users before you start migrating their mailboxes to save any attachments they want to keep.

> **IMPORTANT** Microsoft Forefront for Exchange will automatically delete any attachments it decides are dangerous. The default "dangerous" extensions can include normal business documents and compressed archives that your users don't want to lose.

4. Click the Remove Internet Connectors link below the list of file extensions that get deleted to open the Help file page shown in Figure 7-52.

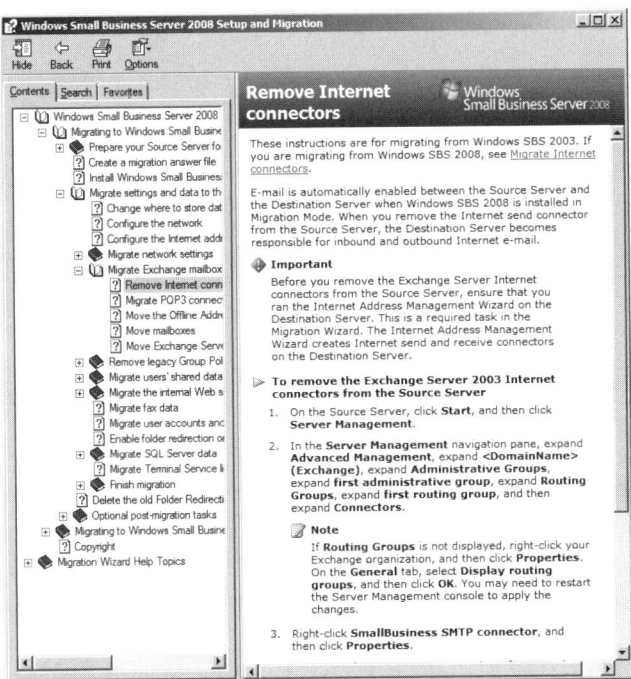

FIGURE 7-52 The Remove Internet Connectors help page

5. Follow the instructions to remove the Internet Connectors from your SBS 2003 server. On the SBS 2003 server, make sure you document any special settings on the connectors.

6. On the SBS 2008 server, if your organization uses POP3 connectors, click Migrate POP3 Connectors to see the instructions for migrating the POP3 connectors to the new server. If you don't use POP3 connectors, you can skip these steps.

7. Click Move The Offline Address Book to open the instructions for moving your offline address book.

8. When the Offline Address Book(s) have been moved, click Move Mailboxes in the help file to see instructions for moving mailboxes. Moving mailboxes takes a significant amount of time—and if you haven't done a thorough cleanup, it will take even longer. The results of our little test network are shown in Figure 7-53.

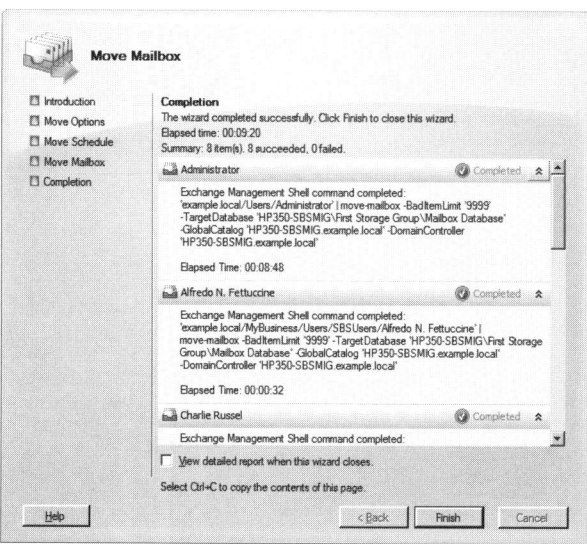

FIGURE 7-53 The results of the Move Mailbox Wizard

9. Click Finish to close the Move Mailbox Wizard.

10. Click Move Exchange Server Public Folders in the help file and follow the instructions for moving Public Folders to your new SBS 2008 server. This set of instructions appears to be about removing public folders, but if you read carefully, you'll see it actually moves them. This process can take several hours to several days.

11. After the task completes, decommission the Exchange Server on the SBS 2003 server.

12. Click Task Complete and then click Next to return to the Migration Wizard Home page.

Remove Legacy Group Policies and Logon Settings

To remove legacy Group Policies and logon settings, follow these steps:

1. Click Next to open the Remove Legacy Group Policies And Logon Settings page. These scripts and Group Policies have already been migrated but now need to be removed, because they're not compatible with SBS 2008. If you have customizations in these scripts or Group Policies, you'll need to save them and reapply the customizations after the migration is complete using the new methods in SBS 2008.

2. Log on to the SBS 2003 server with an administrative account.

3. Click Start and then click Run.

4. Type **\\localhost\sysvol\<*domainname.local*>\scripts** and then press Enter to open Windows Explorer in the replication folder for logon scripts. (Replace <*domainname.local*> with your domain name. In our test network, it's example.local.)

5. Delete or rename the SBS_LOGIN_SCRIPT.bat file, as shown in Figure 7-54.

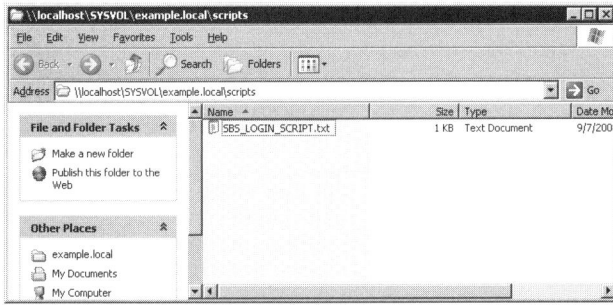

FIGURE 7-54 Renaming the login script file will prevent it from running.

6. If any of your users have custom logon scripts, disable them in Active Directory Users And Computers.

7. Return to the Migration Wizard and click Remove Old Group Policy Objects. Follow the instructions in the help file to remove the old GPOs.

> **NOTE** If you have customizations in your legacy SBS GPOs, you'll want to save them to a different location and then rebuild them after the migration completes.

8. Be careful to not remove the new SBS GPOs. Most of these start with Windows SBS. The old GPOs mostly start with Small Business Server in the GPO name.

9. Follow the instructions to remove the SBS 2003 WMI Filters, and then close the Group Policy Management console and return to the Migration Wizard.

10. Click Task Complete and then click Next to return to the Migration Wizard Home page.

Migrate Users' Shared Data

To migrate users' shared data, follow these steps:

1. Click Next to open the Migrate Users' Shared Data page of the Migration Wizard.

2. Click How Do I Migrate Users' Shared Data to open the help topic on moving the users' shares.

3. Follow the steps to re-create the shared folders on the new SBS 2008 server and copy the data from the old server.

4. When you've finished, click Task Complete and then click Next to return to the Migration Wizard Home page.

Migrating Companyweb

Migrating the Companyweb site is an imperfect solution at best. Because of the change in versions between the SharePoint in SBS 2003 and the SharePoint in SBS 2008, the migration of the SharePoint site moves the existing Companyweb to a new OldCompanyweb site.

Unless you have made significant customizations and your users have data stored in the SBS 2003 Companyweb site, you can skip this step. But if you do decide to migrate your SBS 2003 Companyweb, follow these steps:

1. Click Next to open the Migrate Your Internal Web Site page of the Migration Wizard.

2. Click the Migrate The Internal Web Site link to open the help topic on migrating Companyweb.

3. Follow the steps carefully. When you're finished, click Task Complete and then click Next to return to the Migration Wizard Home page.

4. If you opt to not migrate the site, or to migrate the site later, click Skip Task and then click Next to return to the Migration Wizard Home page.

Migrating Fax Data

To migrate fax data, follow these steps:

1. Click Next to open the Migrating Fax Data page of the Migration Wizard.

2. Select where you want to store your fax data on the new SBS 2008 server. You can choose either the default location for the fax service or Companyweb. The option to store in Companyweb is a new option in SBS 2008.

3. Click the Click To Start Migrating Your Fax Data link to begin the migration.

4. When the migration completes, click OK to return to the Migrate Fax Data page.

5. Click Task Complete and then click Next to return to the Migration Wizard Home page.

6. If you opt to not migrate the fax data, or if you don't use the fax service, click Skip Task and then click Next to return to the Migration Wizard Home page.

Migrating Users and Group

As a normal part of Active Directory replication when the SBS 2008 server was installed, the users and groups have already been migrated. But they aren't yet visible in the Windows SBS Console. To make them visible in the Windows SBS Console, follow these steps:

1. Click Next to open the Migrate Groups page of the Migration Wizard.

2. Click Display The Security Group Migration Instructions to open the help topic.

3. Follow the instructions to open ADSIEdit and modify each security and distribution group to add the Created value to the msSBSCreationState attribute for each group, as shown in Figure 7-55.

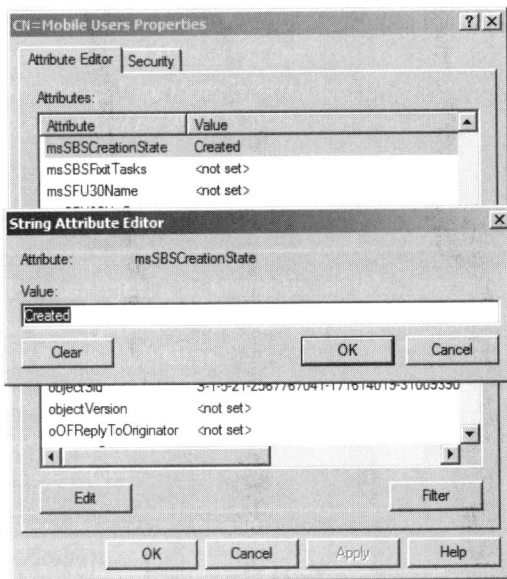

FIGURE 7-55 Using ADSI Edit to set the attributes of a migrated group

4. Set the groupType attribute as described and then close the Properties dialog box for the group.

5. When you have modified the groups that you want to have visible in the Windows SBS Console, close ADSIEdit and then close the help file to return to the Migration Wizard.

6. Click Next to open the Migrate User Accounts page of the Migration Wizard.

7. Click the Run The Change A User Role Wizard link to open the Select New User Role page of the Change A User Role Wizard, as shown in Figure 7-56.

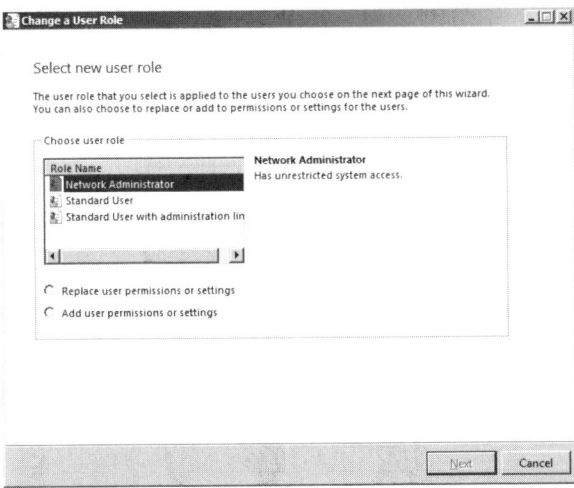

FIGURE 7-56 The Select New User Role page of the Change A User Role Wizard

8. Select Replace User Permissions Or Settings and select the role you want to assign to these users.

9. Click Next to open the Select User Account page. This page will probably be blank when you start.

10. Click Display All User Accounts In The Active Directory to show all the accounts as shown in Figure 7-57.

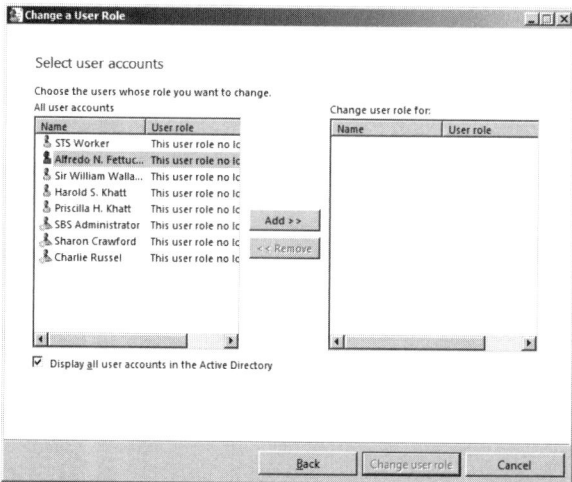

FIGURE 7-57 The Select User Accounts page of the Change A User Role Wizard

11. Select the users you want to change and click Add to move them to the right pane.

12. Click Change User Role to update the users. Click Finish when the wizard completes to return to the Migrate User Accounts page.

13. Repeat steps 7 through 12 until all the accounts you want to manage in the Windows SBS Console have been migrated. (Don't bother with special accounts such as the STS Worker account shown in Figure 7-57.)

14. Click Task Complete and then click Next to return to the Migration Wizard Home page.

Finish the Migration

When you finish migrating users and groups, the next step is to finish the migration and de-commission the source server. When you click Next on the Migration Wizard Home page, you get one last chance to complete any steps you marked as skipped, as shown in Figure 7-58.

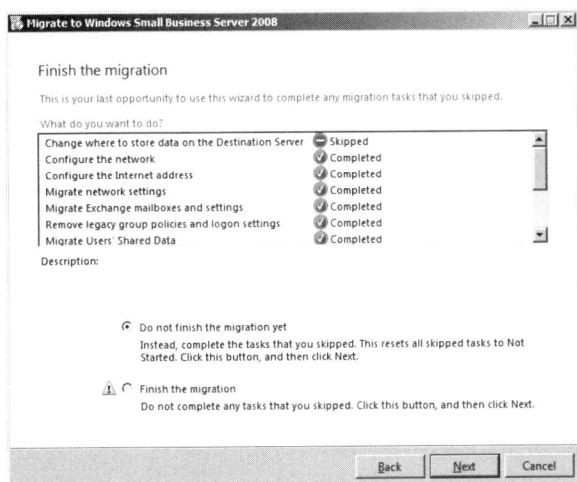

FIGURE 7-58 One last chance to complete skipped tasks before the wizard is done

If there are any optional tasks that you delayed because you weren't ready to complete them, now is the time to complete them. Select Do Not Finish The Migration Yet and then click Next to reset the Skipped flag and mark them Not Started, as shown in Figure 7-59.

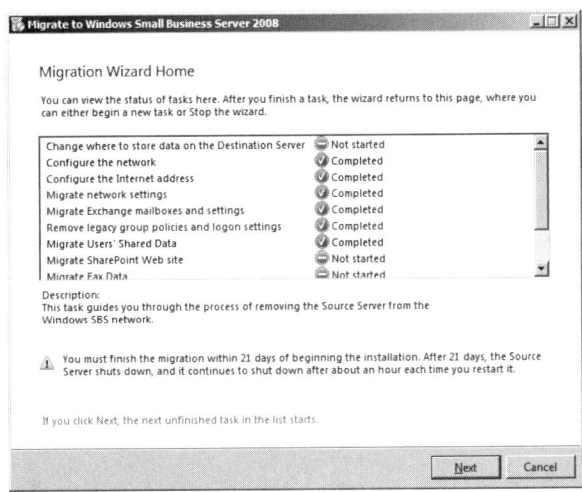

FIGURE 7-59 Restarting the Migration Wizard to do tasks skipped the first time

Click Next to begin doing the optional tasks you skipped previously. When you're all finished, and you get to the end of the tasks list again, click Next and then select Finish The Migration if you have any skipped tasks that you don't want to do.

Finally, click Next open the Finish The Migration page. On this page, you are told to demote the old SBS 2003 server to no longer be a domain controller. To demote the SBS 2003 server, follow these steps:

1. Log on to the SBS 2003 server with an administrative account.

2. Open a command window. At the prompt, type **dcpromo** and press Enter to open the Active Directory Installation Wizard, as shown in Figure 7-60.

FIGURE 7-60 The Welcome page of the Active Directory Installation Wizard

3. Click Next and the Global Catalog server warning shown in Figure 7-61 will be displayed.

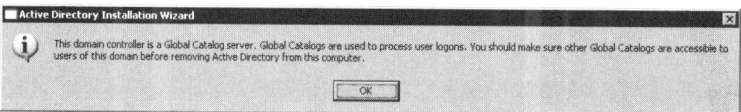

FIGURE 7-61 The Global Catalog server warning when demoting your source SBS 2003 server

4. Click OK to open the Remove Active Directory page shown in Figure 7-62.

5. Leave the check box cleared and click Next to open the Administrator Password page.

6. Type in a password, type it in again to confirm it, then click Next to open the Summary page.

7. Click Next and the wizard will remove Active Directory and demote the original SBS 2003 server to a domain member.

8. When the wizard completes successfully, click Finish and then click Restart Now.

9. On the Finish The Migration page of the Migration Wizard, select The Source Server Is No Longer A Domain Controller and click Next.

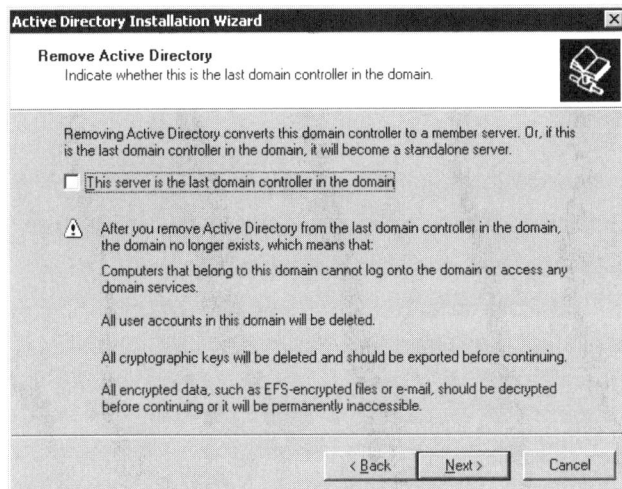

FIGURE 7-62 The Remove Active Directory page of the Active Directory Installation Wizard

10. Disconnect the original SBS 2003 server from the network and do not reconnect it until you have completely reformatted it and installed a new operating system.

11. On the SBS 2008 server, open the Windows SBS Console if it isn't open.

12. Click Network in the navigation bar and then click Computers, as shown in Figure 7-63.

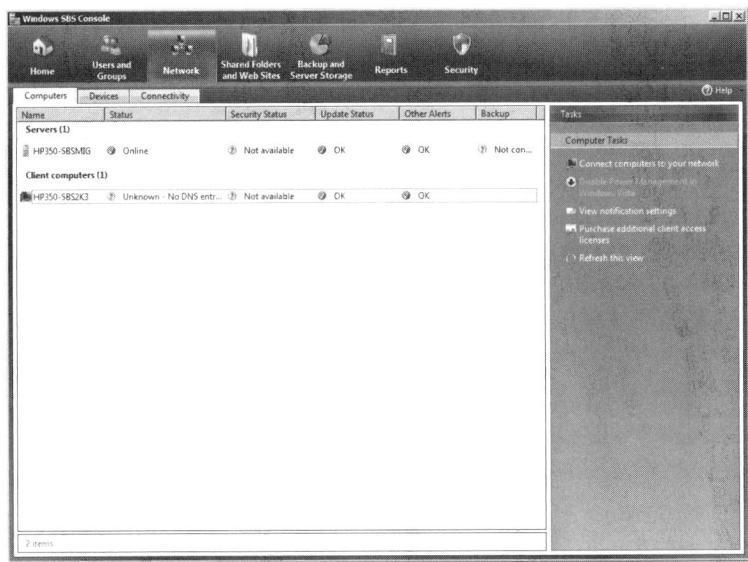

FIGURE 7-63 The Computers tab of the Windows SBS Console

13. Select the former SBS 2003 computer in the Client Computers section and click Remove in the Tasks pane.

14. Click Yes at the prompt and the SBS 2003 computer is removed from the domain.

Re-Enabling Folder Redirection

After the migration tasks are complete, you can re-enable Folder Redirection for user accounts. SBS 2008 allows you to do folder redirection by individual user account instead of requiring you to do it as an all-or-none proposition.

To enable folder redirection, follow these steps:

1. Open the Windows SBS Console if it isn't open.

2. Select Users And Groups in the navigation bar and then click Users.

3. Click Redirect Folders For User Accounts To The Server in the Tasks pane to open the Folder Redirection Properties dialog box shown in Figure 7-64.

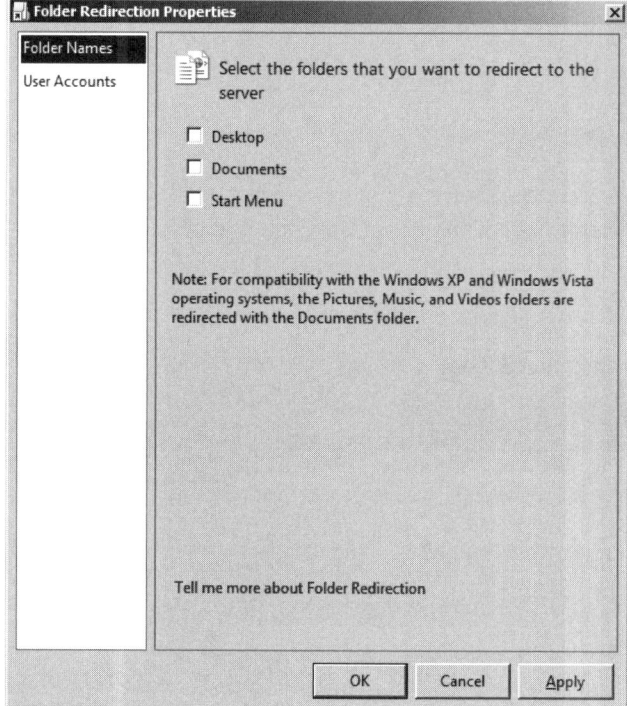

FIGURE 7-64 The Folder Names page of the Folder Redirection Properties dialog box

4. Select the folders that you want to redirect and then click User Accounts in the left pane to open the User Accounts page shown in Figure 7-65.

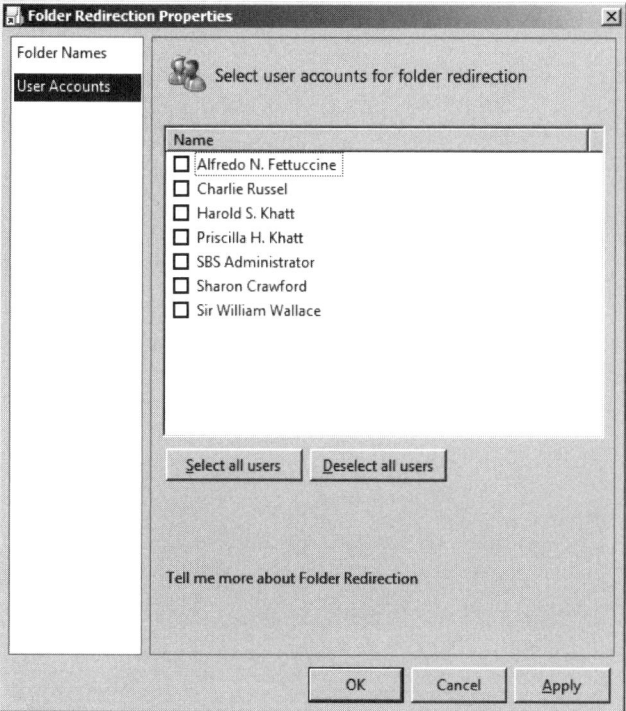

FIGURE 7-65 The User Accounts page of the Folder Redirection Properties dialog box

5. Select the accounts you want to use folder redirection on and then click OK to redirect the accounts.

6. Click Close at the success message to return to the Windows SBS Console.

Summary

In this chapter, we've covered the migration from an SBS 2003 network to an SBS 2008 network. Each migration will be slightly different and will present its own set of challenges. By being fully prepared and understanding all the steps that are involved in a migration, you'll be in the best position to have a successful migration with a minimum of disruption to your end users. In the next chapter, we cover the Getting Started Tasks that all installations need to complete. Some of these tasks will have been completed as part of the migration, but others remain.

Completing the Getting Started Tasks

Once Windows Small Business Server 2008 is installed, there's the usual array of chores to be completed, configured, and set up before your network is complete. Not all of these chores have to be done at once and some don't need to be done at all, but you do need to review the list.

Start by opening the Windows SBS Console. When you select Home, you'll see the list displayed in Figure 8-1. In this chapter, we'll cover the Getting Started Tasks in order and then the items under the Network Essentials Summary.

FIGURE 8-1 You'll see the Getting Started Tasks when you select Home on the Windows SBS Console.

Using the Windows SBS Console

The Windows SBS Console is a handy tool that you can use from any location—the Windows SBS server computer, a client computer, or remotely—to manage users, groups, network settings, shared resources, backup, and security.

Select Home from the navigation bar and then click the Using The Windows SBS Console link to open a help file describing Windows SBS Console functions.

> **IMPORTANT** Advanced administrative tasks are performed using Windows Server 2008 tools available from the Administrative Tools menu. For example, to manage non-Windows SBS users and computers, use Active Directory Users And Computers Management Console.

Connect to the Internet

Normally, if the connection is already set up and the router is properly configured, the Internet connection is made during the installation of Windows SBS 2008. You will only need to run the Connect To The Internet Wizard if the connection was not made for some reason during installation. If you change your router or Internet provider, you might need to run the wizard again in the future.

To manually connect, click the Connect To The Internet link to get started. The initial page of the Connect To The Internet Wizard advises you on what you need to proceed, namely:

- The IP address for the router you'll be connecting from
- The logon information necessary to connect to the router

When you've collected that information, click Next and follow these steps:

1. The Connect To The Internet Wizard attempts to detect your router (see Figure 8-2).

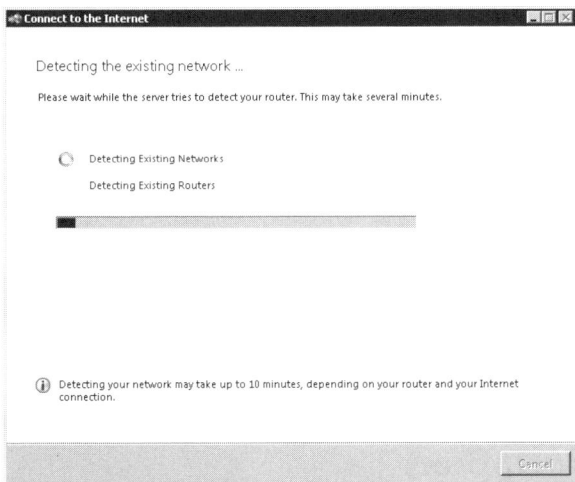

FIGURE 8-2 Detecting your network router

2. The next page of the Connect To The Internet Wizard displays the IP address of the router and of the server (Figure 8-3). If either or both of the addresses are incorrect, type in the corrections. Click Next.

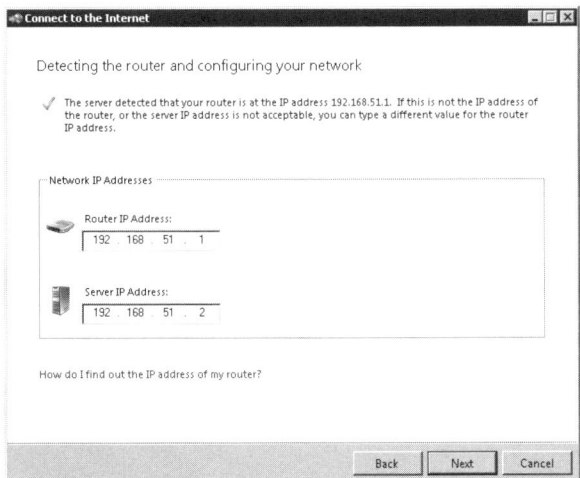

FIGURE 8-3 The wizard displays the IP addresses detected.

3. As shown in Figure 8-4, the wizard proceeds to locate and configure the router and the server. When the process is finished, a notification appears announcing that the Internet connection is completed. Click Finish.

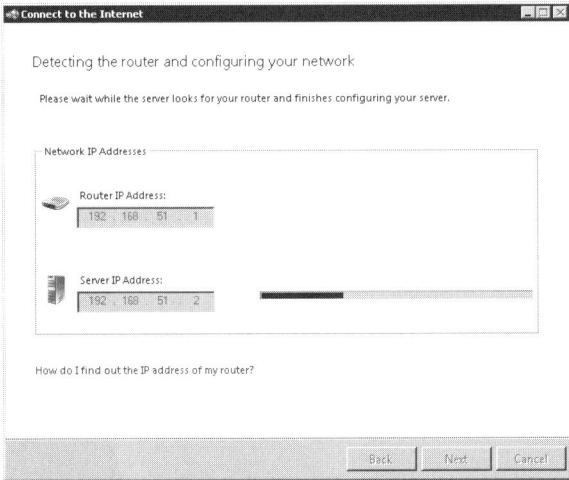

FIGURE 8-4 Detecting the router and completing the Internet connection

Customer Feedback Options

The Customer Feedback Options is an area of considerable importance to Microsoft and even to us end users—in the long run. In the short term, you may well wonder why you should participate in a program unlikely to be of direct benefit to you.

Well, it's something like paying taxes for schools when you have no children or your children are all adults. We pay those taxes because an educated populace is a greater social good. On a less lofty level, the Customer Experience Improvement Plan should result in better software in the future. And because this is software used by hundreds of millions of people, some considerable social good should therefore emerge.

Click Customer Feedback Options and then click Read More About The Program Online and decide for yourself.

Set Up Your Internet Address

Before you can set up your Internet presence, you must gather a variety of information:

- You must have an Internet domain name. If you don't have one, you must register one with a domain registration service. You will need a prospective name and several alternatives and a credit card to pay the registration fee.

- If you already have an Internet domain name, you'll need the name of your Internet provider as well as the logon information for the provider.

Choosing an Internet Domain Name

When choosing an Internet domain name, you want a name that clearly identifies your organization without being too long or too abbreviated—both are difficult to remember.

For example, if your business name is a long one, such as Alfie's Aquatic Adventure and Scuba Diving School, good choices for domain names might be AlfiesAquatics.com or AlfiesAdventure.com. A name that's too long tries the patience of people looking for your site.

Names that are too short have their own hazards. AAASDS may be the company's initials, but they don't provide much in the way of information.

NOTE Don't get hung up on having to have a .com extension. You're much more likely to be able to get a name you like with a .net, .biz, or .info extension.

Registering a New Domain Name

Click the Set Up Your Internet Address link to view the list of what you'll need to start the process, click Next, and follow these steps:

1. As shown in Figure 8-5, the Internet Address Management Wizard asks you to choose between purchasing a new domain name or using one you already have. Select I Want To Purchase A New Domain Name and then click Next.

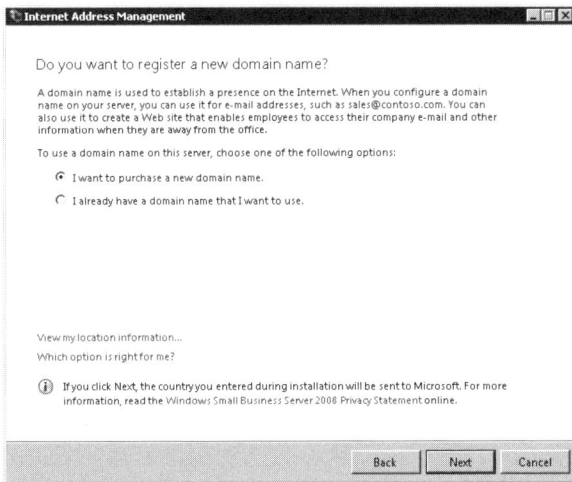

FIGURE 8-5 Getting a new domain name

2. Type the domain name you want to register and select the extension from the drop-down list. Click Next.

3. Select a domain name provider from the list provided (Figure 8-6) and then click Next.

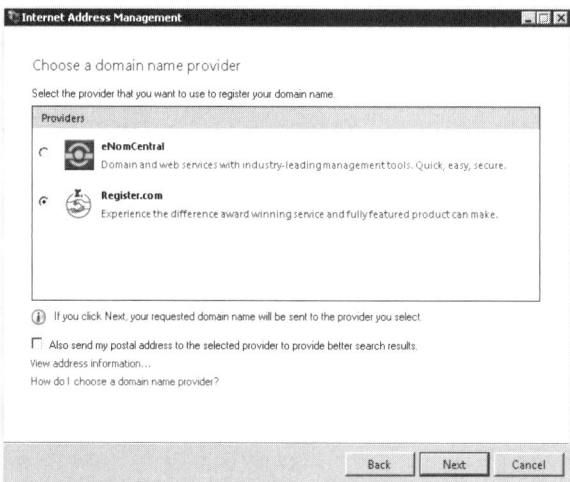

FIGURE 8-6 Choosing a domain name provider

NOTE Including your postal address improves the search, because some national extensions are available only to residents. For example, you must be in Canada to register a domain name with the .ca extension.

4. If the domain name you chose is not available, possible variations appear in the Available Domain Names list. Accept one of those or search again. If the name is available, you can register it, as shown in Figure 8-7. Click Register Now to be connected to the domain name registry company.

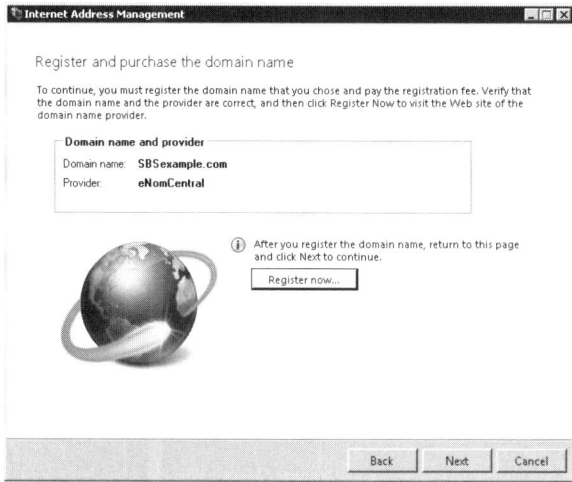

FIGURE 8-7 If the domain name is available, you're given an opportunity to register it.

5. After completing the registration, return to the page in Figure 8-7 and then click Next.

6. On the Store Your Domain Name Information page (Figure 8-8), enter the domain name and the user name you registered (if they're not already entered) and the password you used when registering. Click Configure to complete the process.

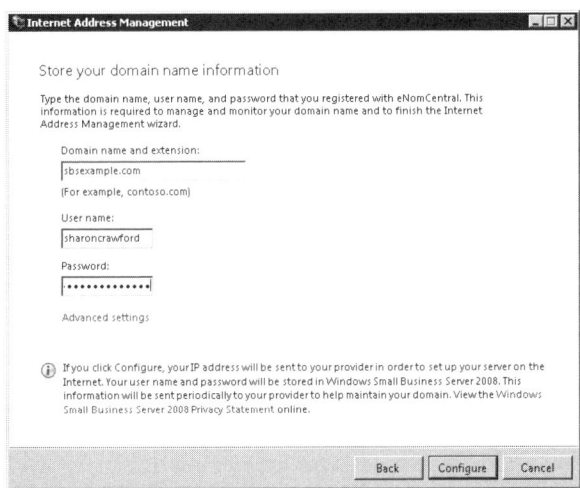

FIGURE 8-8 Storing the domain registration information

Using an Existing Domain Name

If you already have a registered domain name, you can easily set up your presence on the Internet. Before you start, you'll need the domain name and the name and logon information for your domain provider. When you're ready, click the Set Up Your Internet Address link and follow these steps:

1. Read the introductory material and then click Next.

2. On the Do You Want To Register A New Domain Name page, select I Already Have A Domain Name and then click Next.

3. You next have to choose whether you want the server to manage the domain name or manage it yourself. See the sidebar titled "Who Manages the Domain Name?" for more information. Make your selection and click Next. (If you choose self-management, skip to the section titled "Managing Your Domain Name" later in this chapter.)

4. On the Type The Domain Name That You Want To Use page, type the domain name you own and select the extension from the drop-down list (Figure 8-9). Click Next.

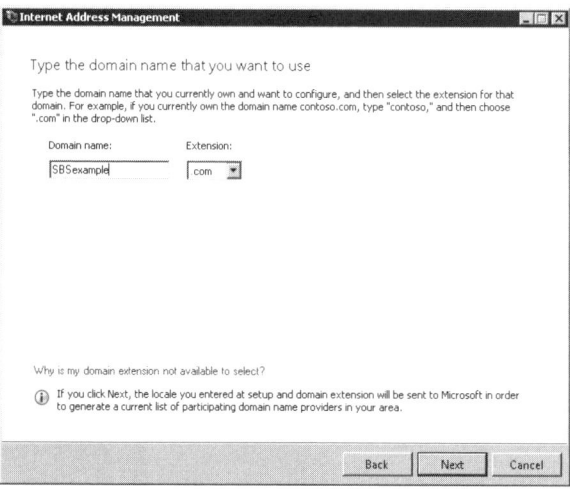

FIGURE 8-9 Entering the existing domain name you want to use

5. Choose a domain name provider from the partner list and click Next.

6. Click Visit Web Site and follow the instructions provided. Then return to the Update Domain Name Registration With Your Provider page and click Next.

7. On the Store Your Domain Name Information page, type the domain name and the user name you registered (if they're not already entered) and the password you used when registering. Click Configure to complete the process.

The Internet Address Management Wizard will proceed to configure your server as shown in Figure 8-10.

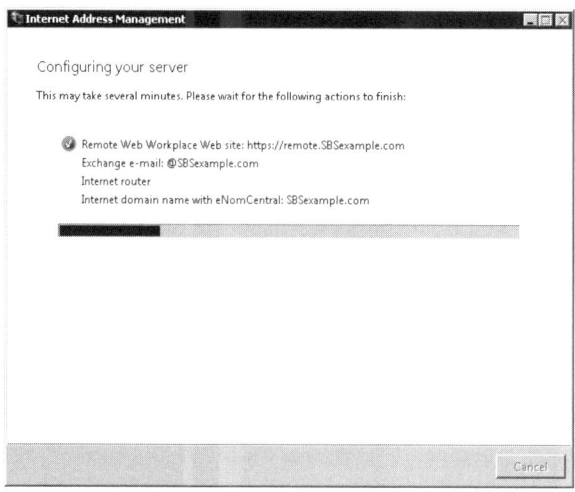

FIGURE 8-10 The wizard configures Windows SBS 2008 to use your domain name.

Who Manages the Domain Name?

When you have an existing domain name, you can do the management of the name yourself or let the server do it for you. It's considerably easier to let the server manage the domain name, but the key issues are:

- Is your name registered with one of the domain name providers partnered with Microsoft? If yes, let the server manage the domain name.
- If your name is registered with another domain name provider, are you willing to have the registration transferred to one of the Microsoft partners? If yes, let the server manage the domain name.

However, you may have no choice but to manage the domain yourself if one of the following applies:

- The wizard doesn't list the domain name extension for your existing domain name.
- No partner domain name providers are listed for your country or region.

If the server manages the domain name, the wizard configures the following:

- Domain Name System (DNS)
- Certification Authority
- Internet Information Services (IIS)
- Simple Mail Transfer Protocol (SMTP) mail policies for Exchange Server
- The UPnP architecture, if supported by your router

If you manage the domain name yourself, you must add DNS records to your server as shown in the following table.

DNS RESOURCE RECORDS TO ADD FOR SERVER SELF-MANAGEMENT

RESOURCE RECORD NAME	RECORD TYPE	SETTING	DESCRIPTION
Remote	A	Static IP address of the WAN side of your router or firewall (provided by your Internet Service Provider)	Maps your domain name to the WAN IP address
MX	Alias	Remote yourdomainname.ext	Provides message routing for e-mail to mailrecipient@ yourdomainname.ext

RESOURCE RECORD NAME	RECORD TYPE	SETTING	DESCRIPTION
SPF	TXT	v=spf1 a mx ~all	Helps to prevent your e-mail from being labelled as spam by recipient mail servers
_autodiscover_tcp	SRV	Service: _autodiscover Protocol: _tcp Priority: 0 Weight: 0 Port: 443 Target host: remote. yourdomainname.ext	Allows Office Outlook 2007 with Service Pack 1 and Windows Mobile 6.1 e-mail clients to automatically identify and set up Outlook Anywhere (RPC over HTTP)

For more information on adding DNS records, see Chapter 18, "Configuring and Managing E-Mail." Or you can simplify things even further by using a DNS management service independent of your domain name registrar or Internet Service Provider. (Type **DNS management** into an Internet search engine for options.)

Managing Your Domain Name

If you already have a registered domain name and want to manage it yourself, you'll need the domain name and the name and logon information for your domain provider. When you're ready, click the Set Up Your Internet Address link and follow these steps:

1. Read the introductory material and then click Next.

2. On the Do You Want To Register A New Domain Name page, select I Already Have A Domain Name and then click Next.

3. Type in the domain name and extension (Figure 8-11) and then click Configure.

The Internet Address Management Wizard configures the server to use your domain name (Figure 8-12). To ensure that your Remote Web Workplace, e-mail, and other features work correctly, make sure the DNS settings are correctly configured.

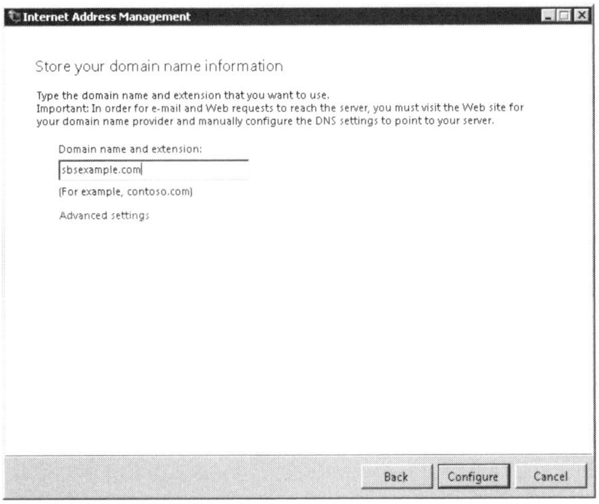

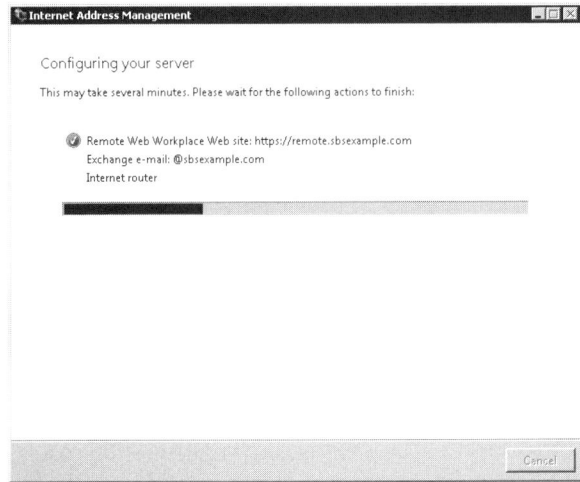

FIGURE 8-11 Domain information for self-management

FIGURE 8-12 The wizard configures your server to use your domain name.

Configure E-Mail

As soon as you've made your Internet connection, you should configure e-mail. Refer to Chapter 18 for information on setting up all forms of e-mail.

Add a Trusted Certificate

Certificates are used to verify the identity of servers on the Internet. Certificates also encrypt data to make a Remote Web Workplace connection secure.

The default installation of Windows SBS 2008 configures what is called a *self-issued* certificate. This certificate lets users securely access your Web sites if they install it on their remote computer or device. However, if users try to access your Web sites without installing the certificate on their remote computer, they receive a certificate warning. The warning tells users that the certificate being used to secure the Web site is not trusted, and as a result the site is not trusted. The user must click through the warning to gain access to the Web site. And in these times when users are rightfully warned about malicious and deceptive Web sites, many will be reluctant to take what appears to be a risk.

A trusted certificate verifies the authenticity of your server and the identity of the person or organization applying for a certificate. When you have a trusted certificate, remote users no longer have to install your certificate on their computers. So it is to your advantage to acquire a trusted certificate.

Purchasing a Certificate

Certificates can be purchased from a variety of providers on the Internet—just type **trusted certificate** in a search engine. Or you can click the Add A Trusted Certificate link in the Getting Started Tasks list and follow these steps. (If you have an existing certificate you want to use, skip to the section titled "Using an Existing Certificate" later in this chapter.)

1. Read the introductory material on the Before You Begin page and then click Next.

2. Select I Want To Buy A Certificate From A Certificate Provider and then click Next.

3. Verify the information for the trusted certificate, as shown in Figure 8-13. Click Next.

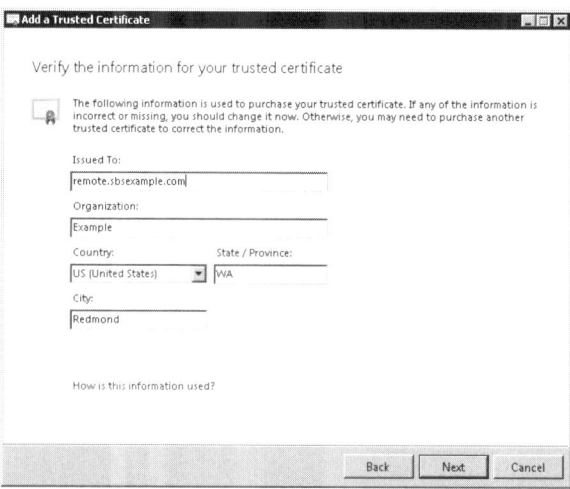

FIGURE 8-13 Verifying information for your certificate

4. The Generate A Certificate Request page displays encoded data from your server that is needed by the certificate provider (Figure 8-14). Click Save To File to save a copy to a location you specify and then click Copy to copy the data to your clipboard. Click Next.

5. Follow the instructions to purchase and then install a certificate.

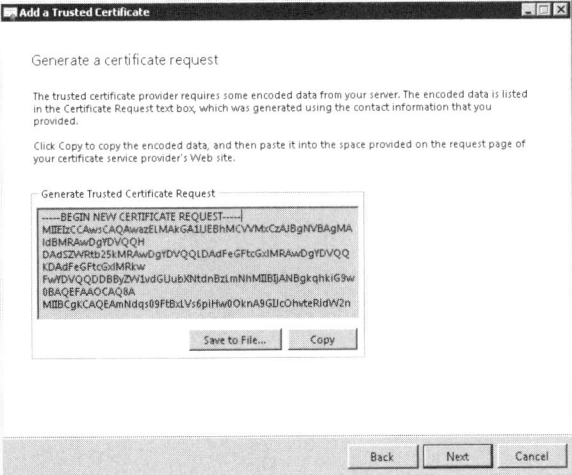

FIGURE 8-14 Generating a request for a trusted certificate

Using an Existing Certificate

If you have a certificate and it's available for export, you can move it to Windows SBS 2008.

Exporting a Trusted Certificate

To export a trusted certificate, follow these steps:

1. Log on to the server where the certificate currently exists. Click Start and then click Run. Type **mmc** in the Open box and click OK.

2. Select Add/Remove Snap-ins from the File menu.

3. In the Add Or Remove Snap-ins dialog box, select Certificates from the Available Snap-ins list (Figure 8-15) and then click Add.

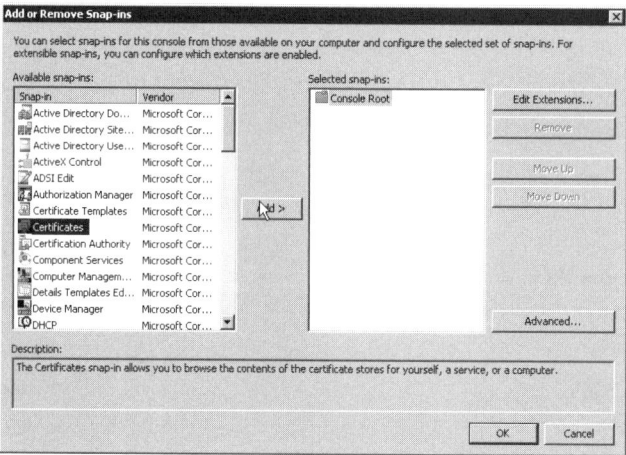

FIGURE 8-15 Constructing a Certificates management console

4. In the pop-up window, click Computer Account. Click Next.

5. In the Select Computer dialog box, select Local Computer. Click Finish and then click OK.

6. Expand Certificates, expand Personal, and then click Certificates.

7. Right-click the certificate to be exported, click All Tasks, and then click Export, as shown in Figure 8-16.

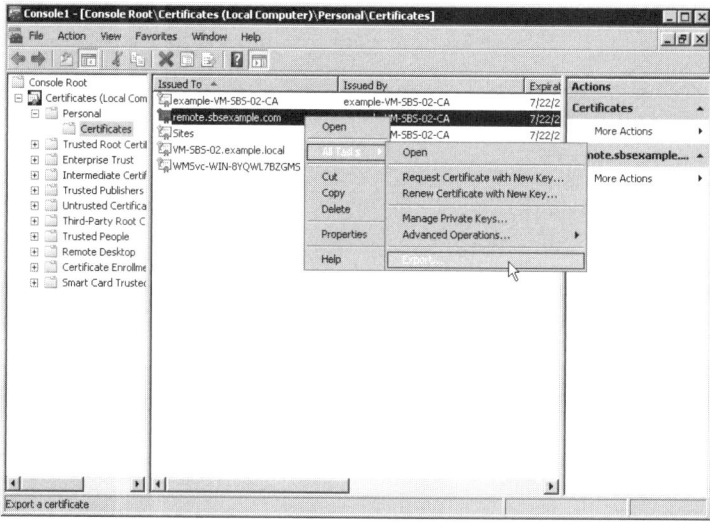

FIGURE 8-16 Exporting a certificate

8. On the Welcome To The Certificate Export Wizard page of the Certificate Export Wizard, click Next.

9. Verify that Yes, Export The Private Key is selected and then click Next.

10. Select Include All Certificates In The Certificate Path If Possible and Export All Extended Properties and then click Next. Do not select Delete The Private Key If The Export Is Successful. Enter a strong password to protect the certificate file and then click Next.

11. Save the .pfx file (giving it an easily identifiable name, such as *trustcertificate.pfx*) to a secure location and then click Next. Click Finish to complete.

IMPORTANT There may be several certificates with the same name. Be sure to choose a certificate that has a valid expiration date and that was issued by the expected trusted authority. If you're not sure which certificate to choose, open Internet Information Services (IIS), establish which certificate IIS is using, and choose that one.

Importing a Trusted Certificate

When the trusted certificate has been exported, you will need to import it to the Windows SBS server and then run the wizard to add a trusted certificate. This process involves quite a few steps, but each one is fairly simple:

1. Move the previously created .pfx file to the Windows SBS server.

2. Log on to the server running Windows SBS 2008. Click Start and then click Run. Type **mmc** in the Open box and click OK.

3. Select Add/Remove Snap-ins from the File menu.

4. In the Add Or Remove Snap-ins dialog box, select Certificates from the Available Snap-ins list and then click Add.

5. In the pop-up window, click Computer Account. Click Next.

6. In the Select Computer window, select Local Computer. Click Finish and then click OK.

7. Expand Certificates, expand Personal, and then click Certificates.

8. Right-click Certificates, select All Tasks, and then select Import, as shown in Figure 8-17.

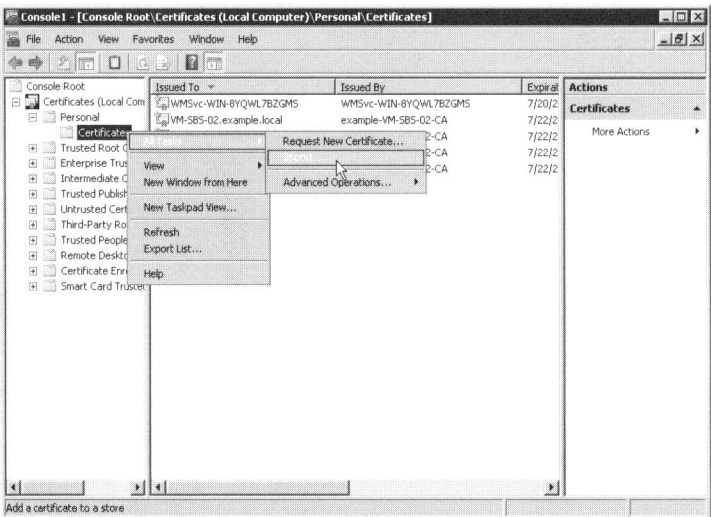

FIGURE 8-17 Importing a certificate

9. The Certificate Import Wizard starts. Click Next on the Welcome To The Certificate Import Wizard page.

10. Type or browse to the location of the saved .pfx file and then use the drop-down list to change the extension to Personal Information Exchange (.pfx). Click Open and then click Next.

11. Type the password that you used in the Export procedure, verify that Mark This Key As Exportable and Include All Extended Properties are selected, and then click Next.

12. Be sure that the certificate will be imported to the Personal folder and then click Next. Click Finish to complete the import.

For applications to be able to use the certificate, after the trusted certificate has been imported, you must run the Add A Trusted Certificate Wizard.

1. Click the Add A Trusted Certificate link on the Getting Started Tasks page.

2. Read the introductory material on the Before You Begin page and then click Next.

3. On the Get The Certificate page, click I Want To Use A Certificate That Is Already Installed On The Server and then click Next.

4. On the Choose An Installed Certificate page, click the certificate that you just imported and then click Next.

Protect Your Server with Live OneCare

Windows SBS 2008 comes with a trial version of Windows Live OneCare, an automatic, self-updating service to protect your server against viruses, spyware, and other threats to your system. The service is free for four months, so you can use it and decide if you want to buy it after the free trial period expires.

To begin using Windows Live OneCare, click the Help Protect Your Server With Windows Live OneCare For Server link to open the Getting Started dialog box shown in Figure 8-18.

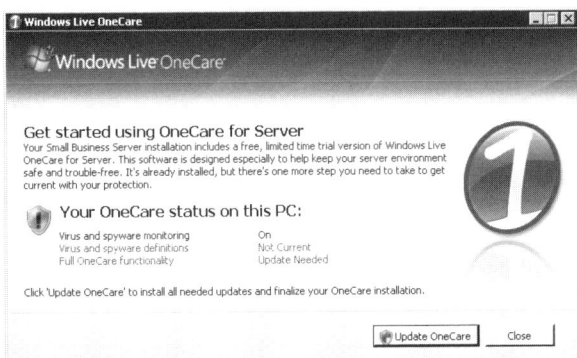

FIGURE 8-18 Starting Live OneCare

Click Update OneCare and follow these steps:

1. Confirm the language choice and click Next.

2. Read the Terms Of Use and select I Accept The Terms Of Use. Click Next.

3. OneCare downloads and installs updates. This may take a while, though not as long as the dialog box estimates.

When OneCare finishes updating, a reboot may be required.

Using Live OneCare

The protective functions of Live OneCare can be automated (advisable) or performed manually. It's best to set up a schedule to automatically tune up your server and check for viruses and spyware. You can run these programs manually as well. To open Live OneCare, select All Programs from the Start menu and then select Windows Live OneCare.

On the Home page (Figure 8-19), you can click a link to perform a scan or select Change Settings to automate scans.

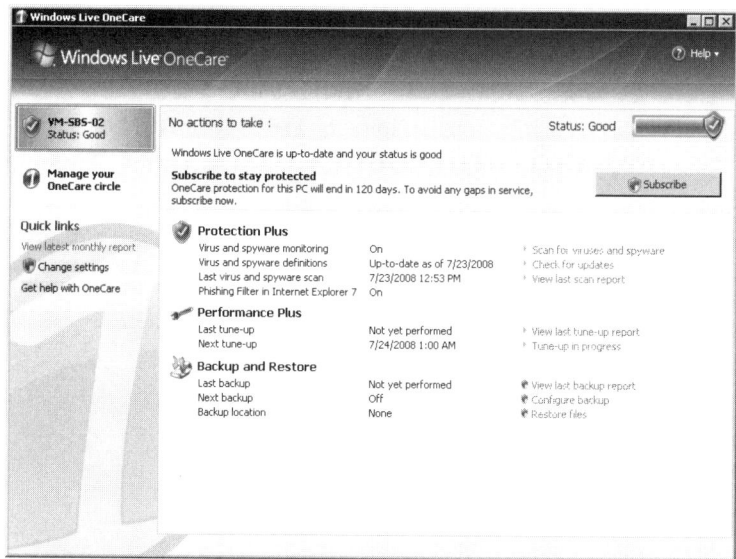

FIGURE 8-19 The Live OneCare home page

Different scans, not surprisingly, perform different functions.

- **Scan For Viruses And Spyware** Click this link to manually perform scans to find viruses, spyware, Trojans, and worms. You can choose from three options:
  - Quick Scan checks the locations on your computer where viruses and spyware are most likely to be found. It's not a comprehensive scan, and it won't evaluate other clean-up or tune-up issues on your computer.
  - Complete Scan searches everywhere, including external drives.
  - Custom Scan searches areas you specify.
- **Start Tune-up Scan** The tune-up scan, shown in Figure 8-20, performs the following:
  - Removes unnecessary files if Tune-up is set to remove files. Click Change Settings and then click Tune-up to add this option.
  - Scans for viruses and other undesirable software.
  - Checks for files that need backing up.
  - Checks for high-priority security updates from Microsoft.

The Tune-up scan takes quite some time to perform, so be sure to schedule it during off hours.

Click the Change Settings link to customize settings for these scans as well as settings for a log of Live OneCare activity.

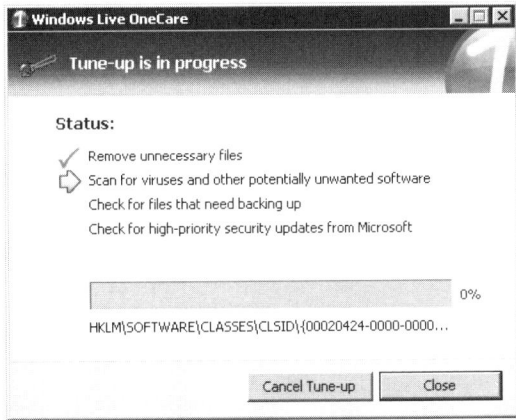

FIGURE 8-20 The Tune-up scan starts.

NOTE For all the details on setting up backup operations, see Chapter 16, "Configuring Backup."

Add Users, Computers, and Devices

For details on these links, see the following chapters:

- **How Can Users Access Computers On The Network?** Chapter 9, "Managing Users and Groups"
- **Add A New User Account** Chapter 9
- **Connect Computers To Your Network** Chapter 14, "Managing Computers on the Network"
- **How Can I Add A Shared Printer To The Network?** Chapter 13, "Installing and Managing Printers"

Network Essentials Summary

The Home page of the Windows SBS Console shows a real-time summary of fundamental network health. Click any of the links to review the nature of any alerts or warnings.

- **Security** The Security Center reports the details of warnings or alerts and directs you to the tools to solve them.
- **Updates** Warns if necessary updates aren't installed. Follow the link to the Update Center to correct the problem.

- **Backup** Alerts you if backups have not been performed. See Chapter 25, "Adding a Terminal Server," for details on configuring your backup plan.

- **Other Alerts** Warns of other potential problems, such as clients without virus protection or security updates.

Summary

This chapter has addressed the processes necessary to complete the Getting Started Tasks, including making a connection to the Internet, acquiring an Internet domain name, and handling trusted certificates.

You can always return to the Home page of the Windows SBS Console to perform tasks that you've postponed and rerun the wizards you've already used.

In the next chapter, we move on to the details of creating and configuring individual user accounts as well as the use of groups to refine and simplify the administration of your Windows SBS 2008 network.

Managing Users and Groups

When it comes to a network, the users and administrators all have different sets of needs, and some of those needs can come into conflict. For the most part, users need reliable access to the files, folders, applications, printers, and other devices required to do their jobs. What they don't need are error messages, delays, or any other obstructions. The person in charge of the network has his or her own needs, such as shielding need-to-know material from those who don't need to know and protecting the users from themselves. The key to bringing these needs into balance is the configuration of groups and users—the topic of this chapter.

Understanding Groups

Because Windows Server 2008 is the underlying operating system for SBS 2008, all the built-in security groups integral to Windows Server 2008 still exist. However, many of these groups are intended for much larger, multidomain networks, so the designers of Windows Small Business Server created a subset of organizational units to simplify administration.

In practice, a group is usually a collection of user accounts. The point of groups is to allow the network administrator to assign rights and permissions to groups rather than to individual users. Groups can be customized and users added or removed in a single step.

SBS allows two group types: security and distribution. Most groups are *security groups* because they're the only groups through which permissions can be assigned. Each security group is also assigned a *group scope*, which defines how permissions are assigned to the group's members.

User rights are assigned to security groups to establish what members of the group can or cannot do. Some rights are automatically assigned to some groups—for example, a user who is a member of the Remote Web Workplace Users group has the ability to connect using Remote Web Workplace.

E-mail distribution groups, on the other hand, are not security-enabled and can be used *only* with e-mail applications to send e-mail to sets of users.

 REAL WORLD   **Why Use Groups at All?**

Groups are an effective way of simplifying administration. If you have just a few users, it's possible to manage permissions for each user manually, though it's additional busywork most administrators won't welcome. And with SBS, it could prove to be positively onerous, because SBS controls access to many features based on group membership. You can easily use SBS without changing any of the default groups or adding to them at all. Just use the built-in templates to add users, and you'll end up with the correct permissions and rights.

The real strength of groups is that when you change the rights of the group, you change them for everyone in the group, without having to do anything else. This makes it easy to update the rights of users on your network without having to go in and change every single account.

For example, when you have a number of people who travel or telecommute, you don't need to keep track of which users have the right to log on remotely if you add them all to the Virtual Private Network Users group. Changes to that group—granting access to a special share, for example—require only that you assign the right to the group, in just one step.

NOTE   Permissions and user rights are different creatures, though easily mistaken for one another. Permissions determine what resources members of a group can access. User rights determine what members of a group can or cannot do.

Creating Groups

Creating new groups is exceedingly easy in Windows SBS 2008—so easy that you should think carefully before you over-complicate your network with too many groups. Too many distribution groups is merely a nuisance, but too many security groups can have unforeseen consequences, such as conflicting permissions that can keep people from getting access to the resources they need.

Setting Up a Distribution Group

To create a new distribution group, follow these steps:

1. Open the Windows SBS Console and select Users And Groups.

2. Click the Groups tab and then select Add A New Group in the Tasks pane. The Add A New Group Wizard launches. Read the Getting Started text and then click Next.

3. In the Add A New Group dialog box, as shown in Figure 9-1, type in a Group Name and Description. Select Distribution Group in the Group Type box and then click Next.

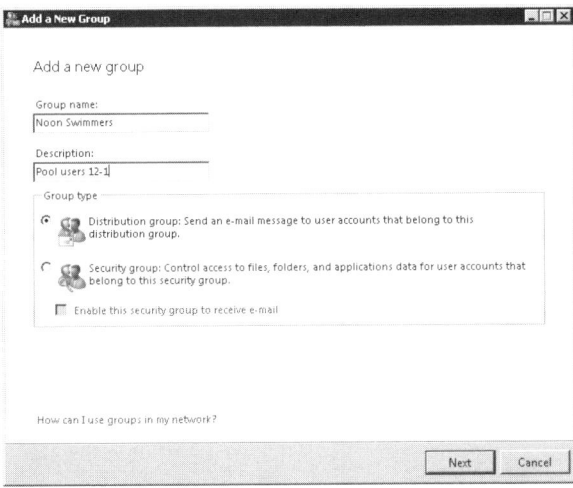

FIGURE 9-1 A new group needs a name and a description.

4. On the Create A Group E-Mail Address page, the group name will be automatically entered. You can change the e-mail address for this group, although the default name—linked as it is to the group name—is probably the easiest to remember and use. In the E-Mail Delivery Options box, you can select the check box to allow people external to your organization to send mail to the address. Leave the check box cleared if you want the address to be completely internal. Click Next.

5. Select the groups or individuals you want to include in this distribution group. When all members have been added to the Group Members list, click Add Group.

NOTE To add members later, simply click Add Group. Even without members, the group will be created and added to the list of groups.

Creating a Security Group

The process of adding a security group is slightly more complicated than creating a distribution group, but following these steps will make it simple:

1. Open the Windows SBS Console and select Users And Groups.

2. Click the Groups tab and then select Add A New Group in the Tasks pane. The Add A New Group Wizard launches. Read the Getting Started text and then click Next.

3. Enter a Group Name and a Description. In the Group Type area, select Security Group. If you want to be able to send e-mail to this group, select the Enable This Security Group To Receive E-mail check box, as shown in Figure 9-2. Click Next.

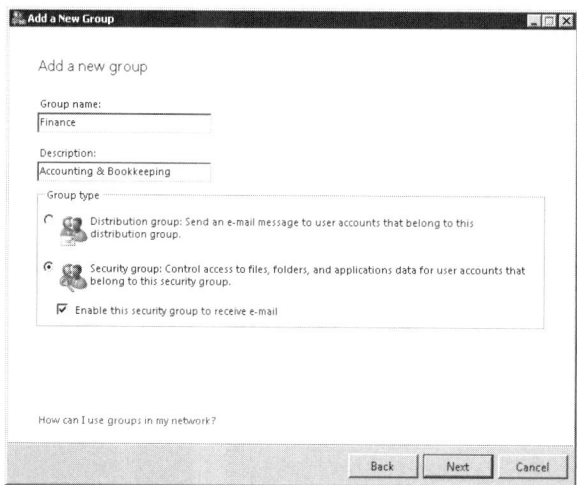

FIGURE 9-2 Name and select the group type for a new security group.

NOTE If your security group will not be receiving e-mail as a group, the wizard will skip to the page described in step 5.

4. On the Create A Group E-Mail Address page, the group name will be automatically entered. You can change the e-mail address for this group, although the default name is probably the easiest to remember and use. In the E-Mail Delivery Options box, you can select the check box to allow people external to your organization to send mail to the address. Leave the check box cleared if you want the address to be completely internal.

As shown in Figure 9-3, e-mail–enabled security groups have the additional option of allowing messages to be archived on your SharePoint Web site. Click Next.

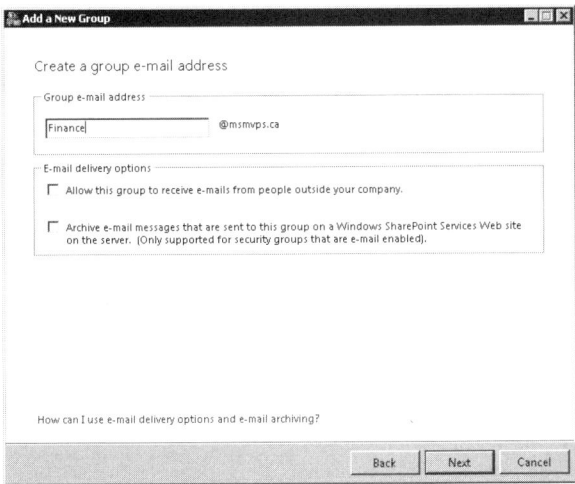

FIGURE 9-3 Security groups that are e-mail–enabled have the option of receiving e-mail from people external to the organization and the option of archiving messages on a SharePoint Services Web site.

5. On the Select Group Members For page, select the groups or individuals you want to include in this distribution group. When all members have been added to the Group Members list, click Add Group.

NOTE If you're not ready to add members to the group, just click **Add Group**. The group will be created and you can return to it and add members at some future time.

The wizard will report that the group has been created. You can view the group in the SBS Console under Users And Groups by clicking the Groups tab.

Working with Groups

If your organization is small or uncomplicated, you may be able to use the built-in groups, add a few of your own, and assign all rights and permissions through shared folders. You can even begin with that expectation. However, your organizational needs will perhaps not align exactly with the groups and tools provided in the Windows SBS Console. In that case, using other built-in groups and customizing them to your needs might be required.

A ll groups have a group scope that defines how permissions are assigned. There are three possible group scopes: global, domain local, and universal.

Global Scope

A group with a global scope is actually a bit of an anomaly in an SBS domain, because it is designed to provide global scope across multiple domains, something that SBS doesn't support. Global groups can be members of universal and domain local groups, and they can have the following members:

- Other global groups
- Individual accounts

Domain Local Scope

A domain local group controls access to specific local resources and can have one or more of the following members:

- Other domain local groups
- Global groups
- Universal groups
- Individual accounts

Universal Scope

A universal security group is another concept that is a bit awkward in the single-domain environment of SBS. Universal groups can have the following members:

- Other universal groups
- Global groups
- Individual accounts

All the built-in groups have been created with universal scope because it's the most versatile group scope.

Built-in Universal Groups

The built-in groups with universal scope are, with few exceptions, the groups that all users belong to. Table 9-1 lists the security universal groups that are specific to Windows SBS 2008. These are the groups you see when you open the Windows SBS console, select Users And Groups, and then click the Groups tab.

TABLE 9-1 SBS-Specific Universal Security Groups

GROUP NAME	DESCRIPTION
User Roles	Descriptions of user roles.
Windows SBS Admin Tools Group	Members can access and use the Administration tools in Remote Web Workplace.
Windows SBS Fax Administrators	Members can administer the Windows SBS fax service.
Windows SBS Fax Users	Members can make use of the Windows SBS fax service.
Windows SBS Folder Redirection Accounts	Members have folders redirected to the SBS Users folder on the server.
Windows SBS Link Users	Members can access the Link List in Remote Web Workplace.
Windows SBS Remote Web Workplace Users	Members can access Remote Web Workplace.
Windows SBS SharePoint_MembersGroup	Members can perform usual functions on the internal Website such as adding, deleting, customizing, and updating material.
Windows SBS SharePoint_OwnersGroup	Members can administer the internal Website.
Windows SBS SharePoint_VisitorsGroup	Members have read-only access to the internal Website.
Windows SBS Virtual Private Network Users	Members have remote access to the network.

Built-in Domain Local Groups

Built-in domain local groups are created when Windows Small Business Server is installed. These groups can't be members of other groups and their group scope can't be changed. Table 9-2 shows the built-in local groups.

TABLE 9-2 Built-in Domain Local Groups

GROUP NAME	DESCRIPTION
Account Operators	Members can add, change, or delete user and group accounts.
Administrators	Members can perform all administrative tasks on the computer. The built-in Administrator account that is created when the operating system is installed is a member of the group. When a member server or a client running Windows Vista, Windows XP Professional, or Windows 2000 Professional joins a domain, the Domain Admins group is made part of this group.

GROUP NAME	DESCRIPTION
Allowed RODC Password Replication Group	Members can have their passwords replicated to all Read-only Domain Controllers.
Backup Operators	Members can log on to the computer, back up and restore the computer's data, and shut down the computer. Members cannot change security settings but can override them for purposes of backup and restore.
Cert Publishers	Members are allowed to publish certificates to the directory.
Certificate Service DCOM Access	Members can connect to Certificate Authorities.
Cryptographic Operators	Members can perform cryptographic procedures.
Denied RODC Password Replication Group	Members of this group cannot have their passwords replicated to an RODC. Default members are Cert Publishers, Domain Admins, Domain Controllers, Enterprise Admins, Group Policy Creator Owners, Read-only Domain Controllers, and Schema Admins. This group appears in the Builtin list when an RODC is created in the domain.
DHCP Administrators	Members can administer the DHCP service. No default members.
DHCP Users	Members have read-only access to DHCP services. No default members.
Distributed COM Users	Members can activate, launch, and use Distributed COM objects on this computer.
DnsAdmins	Members are DNS administrators. No default members.
Event Log Readers	Members can read event logs from local computers.
Guests	Members have the same access as members of the Users group. The Guest account has fewer rights and is a default member of this group.
IIS_IUSRS	Used by Internet Information Services.
Incoming Forest Trust Builders	Members can create incoming one-way trusts.
Network Configuration Operators	Users can have access to managing some network configurations.
Performance Log Users	Members can schedule some performance counters.
Performance Monitor Users	Provides backward compatibility to allow members access to performance counters locally and remotely.
Pre–Windows 2000 Compatible Access	A backward-compatibility group to allow read access on all users and groups in the domain.

GROUP NAME	DESCRIPTION
Print Operators	Members can manage printers and print queues on domain printers.
RAS And IAS Servers	Servers in this group can access remote access properties of users.
Remote Desktop Users	Members are allowed to connect remotely.
Replicator	Supports file replication in a domain. Do not add user accounts of actual users to this group. If necessary, you can add a "dummy" user account to this group to permit you to log on to Replicator services on a domain controller and manage replication of files and directories.
Server Operators	Members can administer servers.
Terminal Server License Servers	Members can update user accounts in Active Directory to track and report Terminal Server per user Client Access Licenses usage.
Users	Members can log on to the computer, access the network, save documents, and shut down the computer. Members cannot install programs or make system changes. Authenticated Users and Domain Users are members by default.
Windows Authorization Access Group	Members have access to the computed *tokenGroupsGlobal-AndUniversal* attribute on *User* objects.

It takes only a glance at this list of groups to see that many are unlikely to be used in a Small Business Server network. However, look a bit further under the domain name in Active Directory Users And Computers and click the Users node (shown in Figure 9-4) to see more groups.

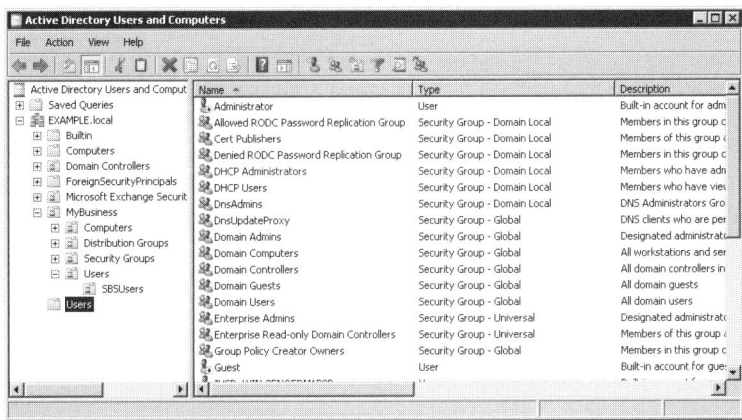

FIGURE 9-4 Additional groups you can use in Windows SBS

The following sections describe some more commonly used groups.

Built-in Global Groups

Default global groups are created to encompass common types of accounts. By default, these groups do not have inherent rights; an administrator must assign all rights to the group. However, some members are added to these groups automatically, and you can add more members based on the rights and permissions you assign to the groups. Rights can be assigned directly to the groups or by adding the default global groups to domain local groups. Table 9-3 lists the commonly used default global groups.

TABLE 9-3 Built-in Global Groups

GROUP NAME	DESCRIPTION
DnsUpdateProxy (installed with DNS)	Members are DNS clients that can provide dynamic updates to DNS on behalf of other clients. No default members.
Domain Admins	This group is automatically a member of the domain local Administrators group, so members of Domain Admins can perform administrative tasks on any computer in the domain. This group is automatically a member of the Administrators group and the Denied RODC Password Replication group. The Administrator account is a member of this group by default.
Domain Computers	All computers in the domain are members.
Domain Controllers	All domain controllers in the domain are members. This group is automatically a member of the Denied RODC Password Replication group.
Domain Guests	The Guest account is a member by default. This group is automatically a member of the domain local Guests group.
Domain Users	The Administrator account and all user accounts are members. The Domain Users group is automatically a member of the domain local Users group.
Group Policy Creator Owners	Members can create and modify Group Policy for the domain. The Administrator account is a member of this group by default. This group is also a member of the Denied RODC Password Replication group.
Read-Only Domain Controllers	Members are the Read-only Domain Controllers in the domain.

NOTE Setting rights and permissions for groups and assigning groups to use shared folders are subjects covered in Chapter 10, "Shares and Permissions."

Managing User Roles

Gaining access to the network requires a domain user account, which authenticates the identity of the person making the connection and controls what resources a user has a right to access.

In Windows SBS 2008, by default all user accounts fall into one of three roles, or categories:

- Standard User
- Standard User with Administrative Links
- Network Administrator

Each user account you add will be based on one of these user roles (or on another user role that you create). In the interests of sanity (your own), keep the number of user roles to a minimum. It is far easier to control access through group membership rather than creating multiple user roles.

The Standard User Role

A Standard User has access to shared folders, e-mail, the Internet, printers, fax services, Remote Web Workplace, and SharePoint Services. All of these access points can be configured within the Standard User role. To make changes to the Standard User role, start the Windows SBS Console and follow these steps:

1. Click Users And Groups and then click the User Roles tab.

2. Right-click Standard User and select Edit User Role Properties. The Standard User Properties dialog box will open, as shown in Figure 9-5. In the left pane, click a category to see the settings for this role.

   - General displays a description of the role.

   - Remote Access shows how the user role can access the network from a remote location. By default, anyone with this user role can access Remote Web Workplace and is automatically a member of the Windows SBS Remote Web Workplace Users. An optional setting is to allow the user role to access the Virtual Private Network. Selecting this check box adds all users assigned to this role to the Windows SBS Virtual Private Network Users group.

   - E-Mail allows you to set a maximum mailbox size. Clear the check box if you don't want to impose a limit on the amount of disk space a user can use for storing mail.

   - Folders is a page for managing and redirecting folders for the user role. As on the E-Mail page, you can enforce a limit on the size of shared folders. In addition, folder redirection can be set and a folder redirection quota imposed.

   - Groups shows the group membership for users assigned this role. You can add a group membership by clicking Add; you can remove a group membership by highlighting a group and clicking Remove.

- Web Sites allows the choice of sites to be available to this user role.

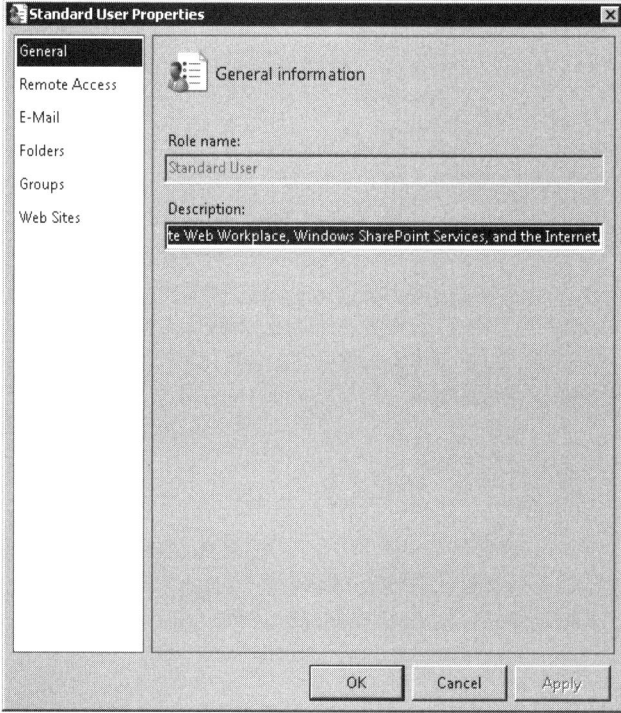

FIGURE 9-5 Settings for a standard user role

IMPORTANT All the users assigned the same role will have the same settings. Changes you make to a user role won't just change future user accounts, they will change all accounts assigned to that role.

3. Click OK when finished. You are asked if you want to apply the customization to all accounts based on the role. Click Yes and the user role changes are applied.

The Standard User with Administrative Links Role

The Standard User with Administrative Links role has, as you'd suspect, the Standard User role access plus membership in groups that gives users assigned this role the ability to perform administrative tasks. Click the Groups link to view the groups that this role includes.

Network Administrator Role

The Network Administrator role provides unrestricted system access to any account it is assigned to. The E-mail and Folders settings are the same as for the other default roles. Remote Access and Web Sites are different, however. On the Remote Access page, you can add or remove access to the virtual private network, but not the Remote Web Workplace (on by default). Similarly, the Web Sites page allows Outlook Web Access to be granted or withheld, but all accounts based on the Network Administrator role will have access to Remote Web Workplace and the internal Web site.

If your network is administered by a third-party provider, access to Outlook Web Access and your virtual private network (if you even have one) isn't necessary, but an administrator must be able to log on to the server.

Creating a New User Role

Perhaps you have some users for whom none of the standard user roles is appropriate. In that case, it's simple to create a new user role by following these steps:

1. Open the Windows SBS console, select Users And Groups, and then select User Roles.

2. In the Tasks pane, select Add A New User Role to start the wizard.

3. In the Add A New User Role page (Figure 9-6), enter a User Role Name and a Description.

4. By default, the new user role is set to be based on the existing Standard User role. Clear the check box if you want to start from scratch, or choose another user role to base the new role on.

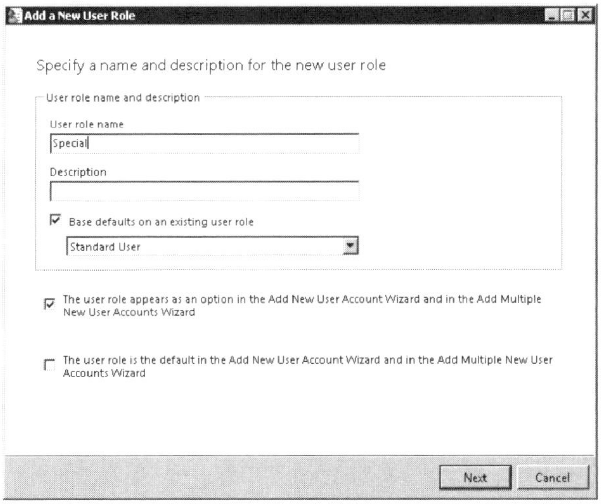

FIGURE 9-6 Creating a new user role

5. Also by default, the new user role will appear as an optional choice when creating new user accounts. Clear the check box if you don't want the role to display in the Add New User Account Wizard or the Add Multiple New User Accounts Wizard.

6. To make the new user role the default choice when adding new user accounts, select the check box labeled The User Role Is The Default In The Add New User Account Wizard And The Add Multiple New User Accounts Wizard. Click Next.

7. On the Choose User Role Permissions (Group Membership) page, add or remove group memberships. Remember that all user accounts you base on this role will inherit these same memberships. When you've adjusted group memberships, click Next.

8. On the Choose E-Mail Settings page, enforce or remove a mailbox size quota for this user role. Outlook Web Access is on by default, but you can remove that as well if you want. Click Next.

9. Choose the remote access settings for this user role, as shown in Figure 9-7. Click Next when you have made the appropriate selections.

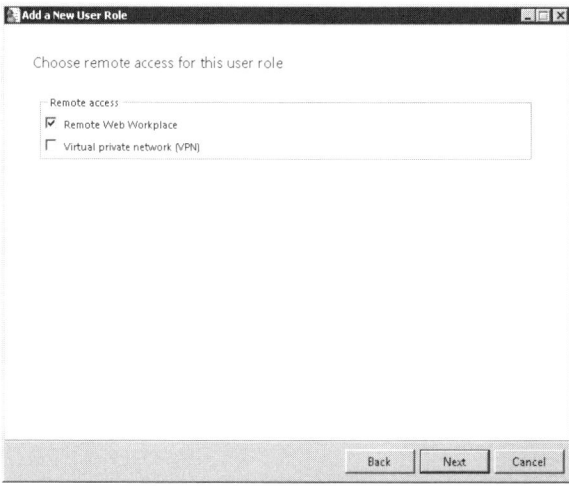

FIGURE 9-7 Choosing remote access settings for a new user role

10. On the Choose Share Folder Access For This User Role page, choose the Shared Folder settings for the user role. Select Back to return to previous pages to change any of your selections. When finished, click Add User Role.

11. The New User Role Was Added Successfully To The Network page (Figure 9-8) announces that the new user role has been added and provides an option to add a user account or multiple user accounts. Click Finish or one of the selection areas to proceed to adding accounts.

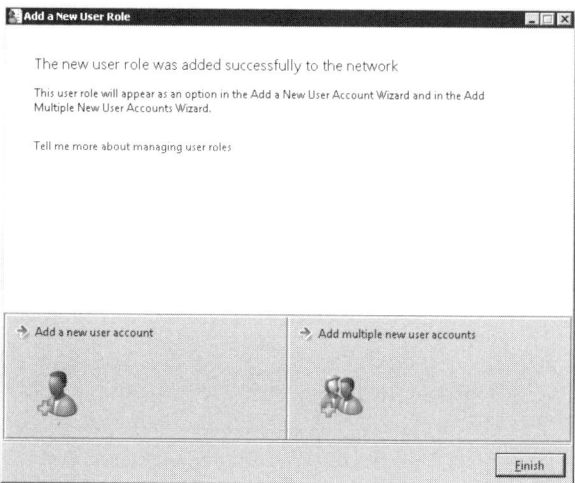

FIGURE 9-8 After a new user role has been added, you can proceed to adding user accounts.

Adding a New User Account

User roles are essentially templates that make the adding of user accounts remarkably simple. To add a new user account, open the Windows SBS Console, select Users And Groups, select Users, and then follow these steps:

1. In the Tasks pane, select Add A New User Account to start the wizard. On the Add A New User Account And Assign A User Role page (Figure 9-9), enter the full name, user name, e-mail address, and other relevant information. Choose the user role to base the new account on. Click Next.

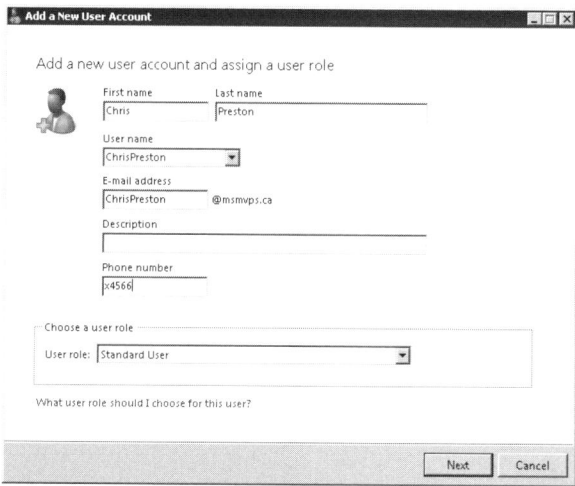

FIGURE 9-9 Adding a new user account

2. Enter and confirm a password for this account. (See the next section, "Making Secure Passwords," for more information on creating a strong password.)

3. Click Add User Account.

Making Secure Passwords

By default, Windows SBS requires a password at least eight characters in length. In addition, a password must contain at least three of the following four elements:

- Uppercase letters
- Lowercase letters
- Numbers
- Non-alphanumeric characters

For example, a password such as JuxCLNU1 satisfies the requirement. It has eight characters, and among them are uppercase letters, lowercase letters, and a number. Similarly, tuidqx!7*5 is also a valid password, consisting of ten characters including lowercase letters, numbers, and non-alphanumeric characters.

The problem with these passwords is their complete lack of memorability. They're the sort of passwords that get written on sticky notes and left around for anyone to find. A solution is to encourage users to be imaginative when creating a password.

Among the best passwords are alphanumeric acronyms of phrases that have a meaning to the user but are not likely to be known to others. This makes the password easy for the user to remember, while at the same time making it hard for an outsider to guess. For example, a password that meets all requirements is ThinkOT[] (for "Think outside the box"). Or [Thinkit] ("Think inside the box").

Another good password isn't a word at all, but a passphrase—an entire phrase or sentence, complete with spaces (which count as non-alphanumeric characters) and punctuation. "A picture is worth 1000 words" is an example of a passphrase that meets all requirements: length, uppercase and lowercase letters, numbers, and non-alphanumeric characters.

Users should also be advised to avoid catchphrases that they themselves use a lot and certain patterns that would be easy for another person to guess, such as:

- A rotation or reuse of the characters in a logon name.
- The user's name or initials, the initials of his or her children or significant other, or any of these items combined with other commonly available personal data such as a birth date, telephone number, or license plate number.

It pays to educate your users about passwords and password privacy, but most of all, it pays to heed your own advice: Make sure the password you select for administration is a good password, and change it frequently. Doing so will help you avoid the consequences of having somebody break into your system and wreak havoc in your very own kingdom. If users remote in to the network from home or other remote sites, include more security than domain-level password authorization.

Adding Multiple User Accounts

Rather than add users one at a time, you can group similar users together and add their accounts simultaneously. To add multiple user accounts, open the Windows SBS Console, select Users And Groups, select Users, and then follow these steps:

1. In the Tasks pane, click Add Multiple User Accounts to launch the wizard.

2. On the first page (Figure 9-10), choose the user role these accounts will be based on and then click Add.

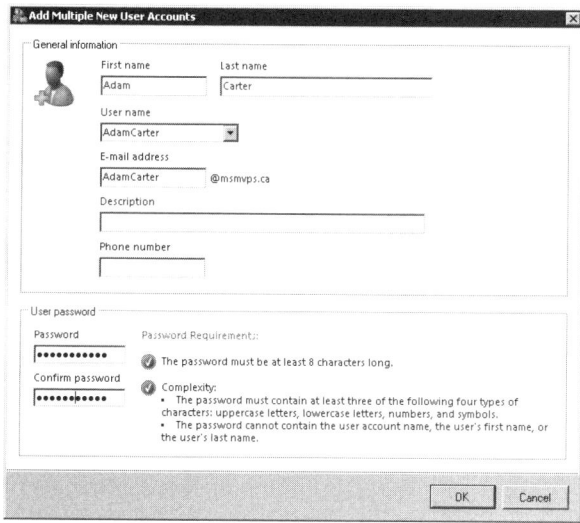

FIGURE 9-10 Adding multiple user accounts

3. Enter the general information about the user and a password, just as you would when adding a single user. Click OK when finished.

4. Click Add again to add another user. When you've completed adding the multiple user accounts, you can highlight a user account to edit or remove it.

5. Click Add User Accounts. A dialog box opens and adds the multiple users, as shown in Figure 9-11.

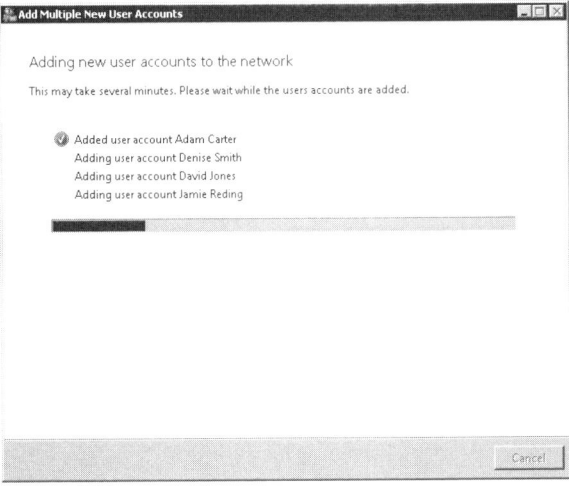

FIGURE 9-11 New accounts are added to the network.

Giving Users Access to Computers

To log on to a computer on the network, users need a user account and permission to access the computer. So after you create a user account, the next step is to allow access. From the server, open the Windows SBS console, click Users And Groups, and then follow these steps:

1. Click the Users tab and then double-click the user account.

2. On the Properties page, click Computers.

3. Select the computers that you want to allow this user account to access and grant the user account the appropriate level of access.

4. If appropriate, select the Can Remotely Access This Computer check box. Click OK when finished.

You can always return to this page to change or update computer access for a user.

Summary

In this chapter we've covered the uses for groups and the simple creation of user accounts. Next we move on to configuring these users and groups to accomplish the work of your network without getting in each other's way.

Shares and Permissions

Anyone who has used a computer for any length of time is familiar with the concept of *sharing*. One shares photos and videos and writings with others. This isn't necessarily done on a network—sharing is often done via e-mail or on a Web site.

On a business network, sharing is the key to getting work done. However, not everything needs to be shared with everyone, which is why the use of shares is always linked with the use of permissions.

Share Permissions v. File Permissions

There are two kinds of permissions involved in any shared folder—those on the actual share and those imposed by the underlying file system. These permissions are *subtractive*. This means that only the most restrictive permission will win. Managing permissions on both the share and the file system at the same time can often be quite confusing, and it's difficult to keep track of the details of both. We generally recommend using the underlying NTFS file permissions to control access and setting the share permissions to Full Control for everyone for most normal shares. The NTFS file permissions give much greater granularity and control over exactly what level of access is granted. However, in some cases using a more restrictive share permission is useful. When you do use a more restrictive share permission, indicate in the share name that the share is restricted.

Whatever your choice, avoid configuring both share permissions *and* NTFS permissions, because the result can be unpredictable and hard to troubleshoot.

Share Permissions

Windows SBS provides easy ways to share folders. After a folder is shared, restrictions can be added or removed in the form of *share permissions*. These permissions apply only at the folder level—not at the file level—and are limited to allowing or denying Full Control, Read, and Change. Table 10-1 summarizes the three types of access, from most restrictive to least restrictive.

TABLE 10-1 Types of Share Permissions

SHARE PERMISSION	TYPE OF ACCESS
Read	Allows viewing of file and subfolder names, viewing data in files, running programs
Change	Allows the access under Read, plus allows adding files and subdirectories to the shared folder, changing data in files, and deleting files and subdirectories
Full Control	Allows all the access under Change, plus allows changing permissions and taking ownership

Share permissions determine the maximum access allowed over the network. They don't affect a user who logs on locally or a terminal server user of the computer where the shared folders are stored.

File Permissions

File permissions are also called NTFS permissions and the terms are used interchangeably. File permissions, unlike share permissions, control user access regardless of where it originates. Local users, Terminal Services users, and network users are all treated equally.

File permissions can be set on folders and even down to individual files. This means that for any file, you can give individual users different types of access. Although you can set such detailed permissions, avoid doing so. Always try to operate with the simplest possible permissions. Set as few restrictions as possible. Assign permissions to groups, not individuals. Simplify, simplify, simplify. Your life will be easier in both the short and long term.

REAL WORLD User Account Control

For many years, various smart alecks (including ourselves) have been warning administrators not to do everything using the Administrator account. Save that account for when you need it, we said. Use a standard user account most of the time, we implored. Of course, no one paid the slightest bit of attention, and here's the inevitable result: User Account Control.

User Account Control (UAC) is a security feature introduced in Windows Vista that is now a component of the Windows Server 2008 operating system. It's based on the security theory of least privilege. The idea is that users should have the absolute minimum privilege necessary to perform assigned tasks. This may sound as though it contradicts our advice to operate with the simplest possible permissions, but in fact it does not. Shares and permissions remain the best way to allow or restrict access to files and folders.

The goal of UAC is to reduce the exposure of the operating system by requiring users to run in standard user mode, minimizing the ability of users to make changes that could destabilize their computers or expose the network to undetected virus infections on their computers.

Prior to Windows Vista, the Windows usage model has been one of assumed administrative rights. Software developers assumed their programs could access and modify any file, registry key, or operating system setting. Even when Windows NT introduced security and differentiated between granting access to administrative and standard user accounts, users were guided through a setup process that encouraged them to use the built-in Administrator account or one that was a member of the Administrators group. A second problem is that even standard users sometimes need to perform tasks that require administrative rights, such as installing software and opening ports in the firewall.

The UAC solution is to require administrative rights less frequently, enable legacy applications to run with standard user rights, make it easier for standard users to access administrative rights when they need them, and enable administrative users to run as if they were standard users.

NTFS Permissions

The ability to assign enforceable permissions to files and folders is part of the NTFS file system. If you assign NTFS permissions, you need to understand how they work and how they are different for a file and for the folder that contains the file.

What Permissions Mean

NTFS permissions affect access both locally and remotely. Share permissions, on the other hand, apply only to network shares and don't restrict access on the part of any local user (or terminal server user) of the computer on which you've set the share permissions. Windows 2008 Server has a set of standard folder permissions that are combinations of specific kinds of access. The individual permissions are Full Control, Modify, Read & Execute, List Folder Contents, Read, and Write. Each of these permissions consists of a group of special permissions. Table 10-2 shows the special permissions and the standard permissions to which they apply.

TABLE 10-2 Special Permissions for Folders

SPECIAL PERMISSION	FULL CONTROL	MODIFY	READ & EXECUTE	LIST FOLDER CONTENTS	READ	WRITE
Traverse Folder/ Execute File	Yes	Yes	Yes	Yes	No	No
List Folder/Read Data	Yes	Yes	Yes	Yes	Yes	No
Read Attributes	Yes	Yes	Yes	Yes	Yes	No
Read Extended Attributes	Yes	Yes	Yes	Yes	Yes	No
Create Files/ Write Data	Yes	Yes	No	No	No	Yes
Create Folders/ Append Data	Yes	Yes	No	No	No	Yes
Write Attributes	Yes	Yes	No	No	No	Yes
Write Extended Attributes	Yes	Yes	No	No	No	Yes
Delete Subfolders and Files	Yes	No	No	No	No	No
Delete	Yes	No	No	No	No	No
Read Permissions	Yes	Yes	Yes	Yes	Yes	Yes
Change Permissions	Yes	No	No	No	No	No
Take Ownership	Yes	No	No	No	No	No

File permissions include Full Control, Modify, Read & Execute, Read, and Write. As with folders, each of these permissions controls a group of special permissions. Table 10-3 shows the special permissions associated with each standard permission.

TABLE 10-3 Special Permissions for Files

SPECIAL PERMISSION	FULL CONTROL	MODIFY	READ & EXECUTE	READ	WRITE
Traverse Folder/ Execute File	Yes	Yes	Yes	No	No
List Folder/Read Data	Yes	Yes	Yes	Yes	No
Read Attributes	Yes	Yes	Yes	Yes	No
Read Extended Attributes	Yes	Yes	Yes	Yes	No
Create Files/Write Data	Yes	Yes	No	No	Yes
Create Folders/ Append Data	Yes	Yes	No	No	Yes
Write Attributes	Yes	Yes	No	No	Yes
Write Extended Attributes	Yes	Yes	No	No	Yes
Delete Subfolders and Files	Yes	No	No	No	No
Delete	Yes	Yes	No	No	No
Read Permissions	Yes	Yes	Yes	Yes	Yes
Change Permissions	Yes	No	No	No	No
Take Ownership	Yes	No	No	No	No

IMPORTANT Groups or users granted Full Control on a folder can delete any files and subfolders, no matter what the permissions are on the individual files or subfolders. Any user or group assigned Take Ownership can become the owner of the file or folder and then change permissions and delete files or even entire subfolder trees, no matter what the permissions were before that user or group became the owner.

How Permissions Work

If you take no action at all, the files and folders inside a shared folder have the same permissions as the share. Permissions for both directories and files can be assigned to the following:

- Groups and individual users on this domain

- Global groups, universal groups, and individual users from domains that this domain trusts
- Special identities such as Everyone and Authenticated Users

The important rules for permissions can be summarized as follows:

- By default, a folder inherits permissions from its parent folder. Files inherit their permissions from the folder in which they reside.
- Users can access a folder or file only when they are granted permission to do so or they belong to a group that has been granted permission.
- Permissions are cumulative, but the Deny permission trumps all others. For example, if the Sales group has Read access to a folder and the Finance group has Modify permission for the same folder, and Wally is a member of both groups, Wally has the higher level of permission, which is Modify. However, if the Sales group permission is changed to explicitly Deny, Wally is unable to use the folder, despite his membership—and ostensibly higher level of access—in the Finance group.
- Explicit permissions take precedence over inherited permissions. Inherited Deny will not prevent access if an object has an explicit Allow permission.
- The user who creates a file or folder owns the object and can set permissions to control access.
- An administrator can take ownership of any file or folder.

Considering Inheritance

Just to complicate matters a bit more, there are two types of permissions: explicit and inherited. *Explicit permissions* are the ones you set on files or folders you create. *Inherited permissions* are those that flow from a parent object to a child object. By default, when you create a file or a subfolder, it inherits the permissions of the parent folder. If the Allow and Deny boxes are shaded when you view the permissions for an object, the permissions are inherited.

If you don't want the child objects to inherit the permissions of the parent, you can block inheritance at the parent level or child level. *Where* you block inheritance is important. If you block at the parent level, no subfolders will inherit permissions. If you block selectively at the child level, some folders will inherit permissions and others will not.

To make changes to inherited permissions, follow these steps:

1. Right-click the folder and select Properties.
2. Click the Security tab and then click Advanced.
3. On the Permissions tab of the Advanced Security Settings For dialog box, highlight the permission you want to change and click Edit.
4. Clear the check box for Include Inheritable Permissions From This Object's Parent. (See Figure 10-1.)

You'll be given the option to copy existing permissions to the object or to remove all inherited permissions. The object will no longer inherit permissions from the parent object and you can change permissions or remove users and groups from the Permissions list.

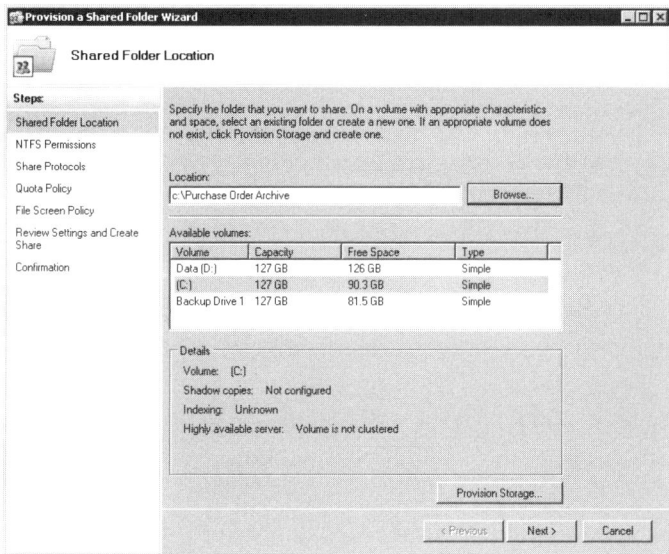

FIGURE 10-1 Changing inheritance

You can also change inherited permissions by changing the permissions of the parent folder or by explicitly selecting the opposite permission—Allow or Deny—to override the inherited permission.

Adding a Shared Folder

Sharing a folder is an easy process in Windows SBS because, as usual, there's a wizard to guide you. Start by opening the Windows SBS Console and then clicking Shared Folders And Web Sites. In the Tasks pane, click Add A New Shared Folder and follow these steps:

1. Enter the location for the shared folder as shown in Figure 10-2. If you don't know the exact address, click the Browse button. When the location is specified, click Next.

> **NOTE** In the lower potion of the dialog box is a button labeled Provision Storage, and though this sounds like a place to store your grain for the coming winter, it is in fact a link to set up storage for the shared folder. Unless you have a Storage Area Network (SAN), you can safely disregard it. If you do have a SAN, click the button to specify a storage subsystem.

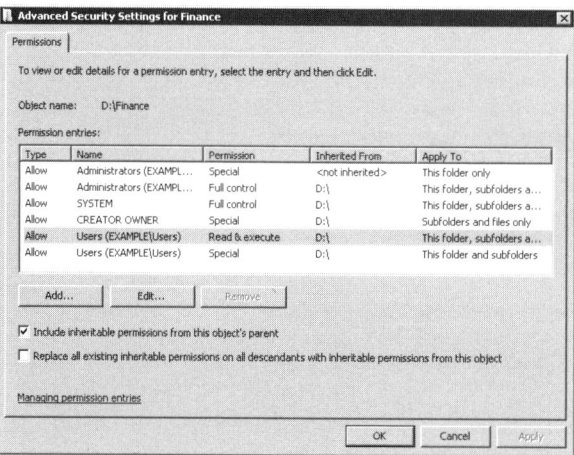

FIGURE 10-2 Specifying the location for a new shared folder

2. On the NTFS Permissions page, you can accept the NTFS permissions or change them. If you decide to change the permissions, first read the section titled "NTFS Permissions." Click Next.

3. On the Share Protocols page (Figure 10-3), choose the protocol that users will use to access the share. Unless you have NFS installed on the computer, the default is SMB (Server Message Block), a native-to-Windows protocol used for shares since Windows NT. Click Next.

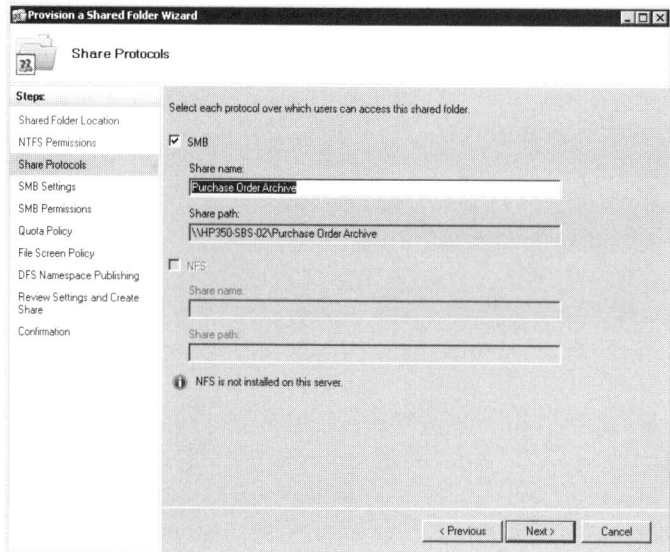

FIGURE 10-3 Specifying a protocol for the share

4. On the SMB Settings page, you can view the User Limit, Access-Based Enumeration, and Offline Settings for the folder. Click Advanced to change any of these. Click Next.

5. On the SMB Permissions page (Figure 10-4), select the share permissions you want and then click Next.

> **NOTE** For details on share permissions, see the section titled "Share Permissions" earlier in this chapter.

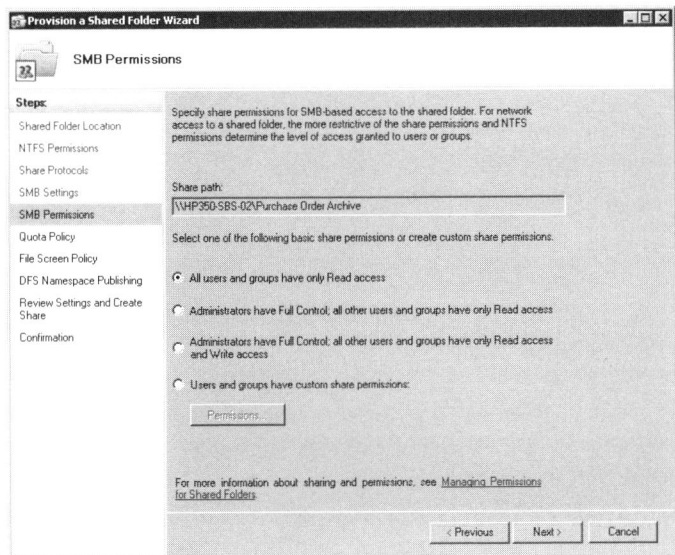

FIGURE 10-4 Setting share (SMB) permissions

6. On the Quota Policy page, you can set a quota to limit the size of the shared folder. Click Next.

> **NOTE** For more on quotas, see Chapter 12, "Storage Management."

7. On the File Screen Policy page, you can apply a file screen to limit the types of files the shared folder can contain. Choose a template from the drop-down list (as shown in Figure 10-5) and a summary of the file screen properties appears. Click Next.

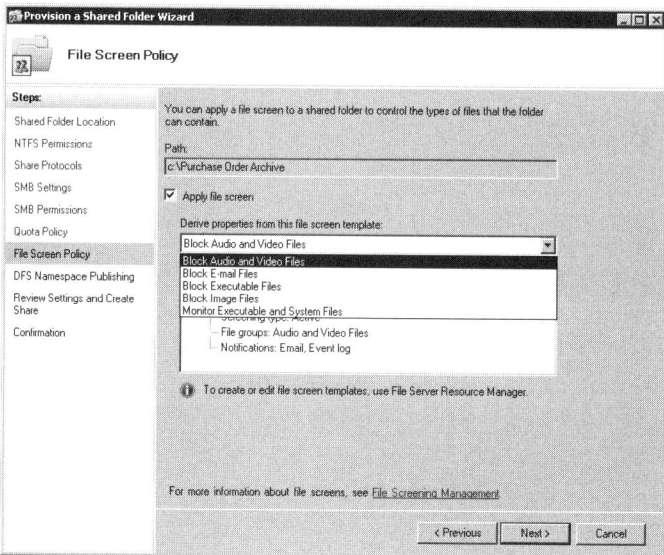

FIGURE 10-5 Configuring file screening for a shared folder

8. On the DFS Namespace Publishing page, you can choose to publish the share to a DFS namespace. (Using and creating a DFS namespace is described in Chapter 12.) Click Next.

9. On the Review Settings And Create Share page, review the settings. Click Previous to change settings. If the settings are correct, click Create.

10. A Confirmation page opens verifying the creation of the share.

Removing a Shared Folder

To stop sharing a folder, open the Windows SBS Console and follow these steps:

1. Click Shared Folders And Web Sites.

2. Select the folder you want to stop sharing.

3. In the Tasks pane, click Stop Sharing This Folder.

4. A warning appears pointing out that if you stop sharing the folder, users will no longer be able to access it over the network. Click Yes to confirm.

> **IMPORTANT** If you remove a share when someone is connected to the folder, it will cause a forced disconnect, which could produce a loss of data. Even if data is not lost, an unexpected and forced disconnect will surely produce user annoyance.

Changing Share Permissions

Changing the permissions on a shared folder is easily done. Open Windows SBS Console, select Shared Folders And Web Sites, and then follow these steps:

1. Select the share. In the Tasks pane, click Change Folder Permissions.

2. To change the permissions for a user or group listed, highlight the name as shown in Figure 10-6 and make the changes in the Permissions area.

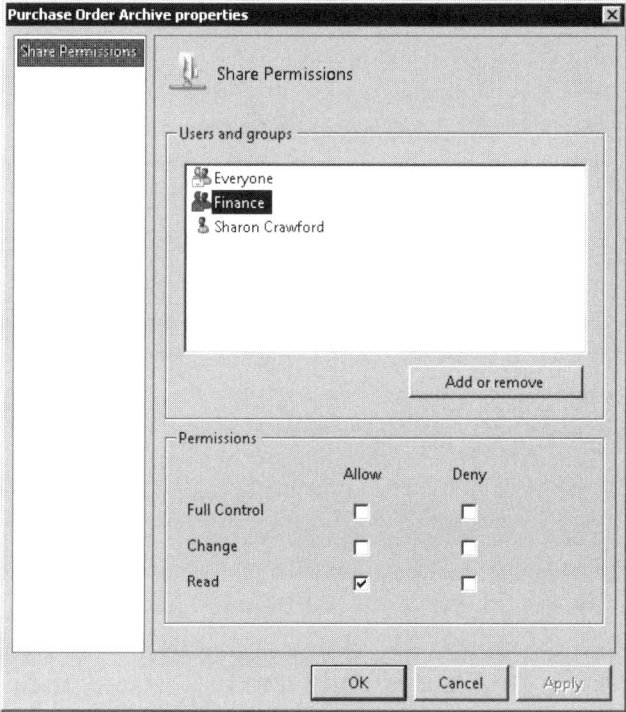

FIGURE 10-6 Changing permissions for users and groups

3. To add or remove users from this share, click Add Or Remove to open the Shared Folders dialog box shown in Figure 10-7. To add users or groups, highlight the name in the All Users And Groups list and then click Add.

4. To remove users and groups, highlight the name in the Selected Users And Groups list and click Remove.

5. Click OK when finished.

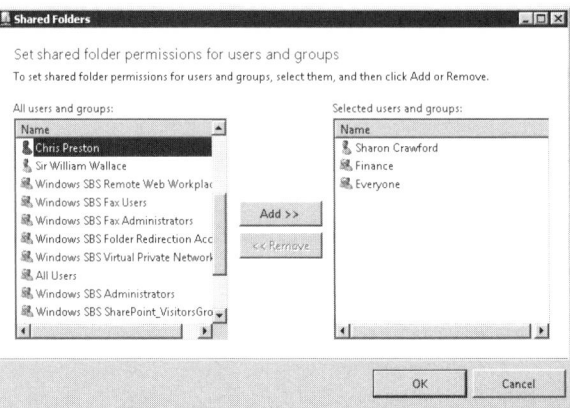

FIGURE 10-7 Changing users and groups for shared folders

Special Shares

In addition to shares created by a user or administrator, the system creates a number of special shares that shouldn't be modified or deleted. These include the administrative shares: the ADMIN$ share and the hidden shares for each hard drive volume (C$, D$, E$, and so on). These shares allow administrators to connect to drives that are otherwise not shared. These shares are not visible by default and can be connected only by administrators.

Special shares exist as part of the operating system's installation. Depending on the computer's configuration, some or all of the following special shares might be present (and none should be modified or deleted):

- **ADMIN$** Used during the remote administration of a computer. The path is always the location of the folder in which Windows was installed (that is, the system root). Only administrators can connect to this share.

- **driveletter$** The root folder of the named drive. Only administrators can connect to these shares on Windows SBS servers or clients.

- **IPC$** Used during remote administration and when viewing shared resources. This share is essential to communication and can't be deleted.

- **NETLOGON** Used while processing domain logon requests. Do not remove.

- **SYSVOL** Required on domain controllers. Do not remove.

- **PRINT$** A resource that supports shared printers.

To connect to an unshared drive on another computer, you need to be logged on using an account with the necessary rights. Use the address bar in any window and type the address using the following syntax:

\\computer_name\[driveletter]$

To connect to the system root folder (the folder in which Windows SBS is installed) on another computer, use the following syntax:

\\computer_name\admin$

Ownership and How It Works

Every object on an NTFS volume has an owner. By default, the owner is the person who created the file or folder. The owner controls how permissions are set on the object and to whom permissions are granted. Even if the owner is denied access, the owner can always change permissions on an object. The only way to prevent this is for the ownership to change.

Ownership of an object can change in any of the following ways:

- An administrator can take ownership.
- Any user or group with Administrative Rights on the computer where the object resides can take ownership.
- The owner can transfer ownership to another user if the owner has Administrative rights or User Account Control is turned off.

Taking Ownership of an Object

To take ownership of an object, you must be logged on as an administrator or as a remote user with Administrative Rights, and then follow these steps:

1. Right-click the object and select Properties. Click the Security tab.
2. Click Advanced and then click the Owner tab. Click Edit.
   - To change the owner to a user or group that is not listed, click Other Users And Groups. In the Select User, Computer Or Group dialog box, type the name of the user or group, click Check Names, and then click OK.
   - To change the owner to a user or group that is listed, in the Change Owner To box, click the new owner.
3. To change the owner of all subcontainers, select the Replace Owner On Subcontainers And Objects check box.

Transferring Ownership

Users with administrative credentials can transfer ownership of an object by following these steps:

1. Right-click the object and select Properties. Click the Security tab.
2. Click Advanced and then click the Owner tab. Click Edit.
3. If the proposed new owner is in the Change Owner To list, select the name as shown in Figure 10-8 and click OK.

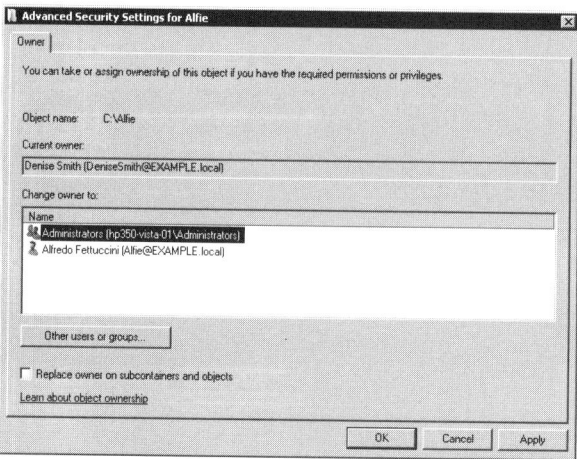

FIGURE 10-8 Transferring ownership

4. If the proposed new owner isn't listed, click Other Users Or Groups to open the Select User, Computer Or Group dialog box.

5. Locate the new owner and click OK.

6. Select the new owner in the Change Owner To list and click OK.

 REAL WORLD Uses for Share Permissions

As stated earlier in this chapter, it's generally best to use NTFS file permissions instead of share-level permissions to control access to shared resources over the network. Using share-level permissions alone gives you significantly less control over the specific permissions being granted, and they're less secure than file system permissions because they apply only to users connecting over the network.

However, there are some exceptions to this rule. For example, you might want to permit all authenticated users to access a volume in a certain subfolder but allow only a certain group to access the root directory. In this instance, you can create two file shares: one at the subfolder level with no share-level security (Full Control For Everyone), and one at the root folder level with share-level security to allow only the specified group access.

Somewhat more useful is the ability to hide file shares by adding the dollar sign character ($) to the end of the share name. This notation allows any user to connect to the share—provided that she knows the share name. After users connect, they're still bound by NTFS security permissions, but this approach can be handy for storing advanced tools so that an administrator can access them from a user's system or user account. File security isn't really an issue—you just don't want users messing around with the files.

Effective Permissions

Admittedly, the subject of permissions can be fraught with anxiety—one reason simplicity should be your watchword. However, there will be times when a resource will have acquired a kudzu-like accretion of permissions and it will be your job to wield the machete.

To determine what the effective permissions are on an object—that is, what permissions apply to a given user or group—follow these steps:

1. Right-click the file or folder for which you want to view permissions. Select Properties.

2. Click the Security tab and then click Advanced. Click the Effective Permissions tab.

3. Click the Select button to open the Select User, Computer Or Group dialog box.

4. Locate the user or group you want and then click OK. The selected check boxes (as shown in Figure 10-9) indicate the effective permissions of the user or group for that file or folder.

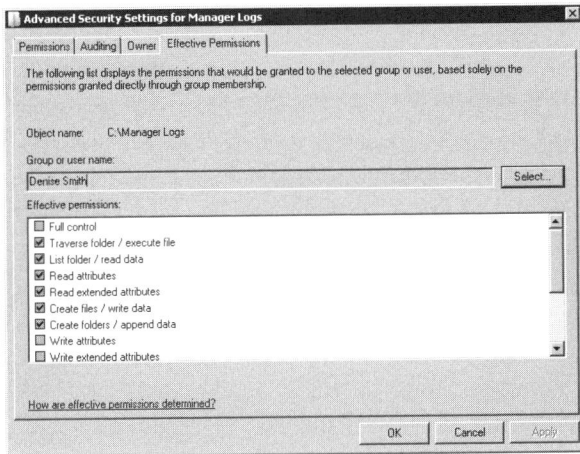

FIGURE 10-9 Viewing effective permissions

> **NOTE** Share permissions are not part of the effective permissions calculation. Access to shared folders can be denied through share permissions even when access is allowed through NTFS file permissions.

Factors That Are Considered in Determining Effective Permissions

The factors that are considered when determining effective permissions are as follows:

- Global group membership
- Local group membership (except when accessing objects remotely)

- Local permissions
- Local privileges (except when accessing objects remotely)
- Universal group membership

Defining User Rights

As if various kinds of permissions weren't enough, we must also address the concept of user rights. What users can and cannot do depends on the rights and permissions that have been granted to them. Rights generally apply to the system as a whole. The ability to back up files or to log on to a server, for example, is a right that the administrator can grant or withhold. Rights can be assigned individually, but most often they are characteristics of groups, and a user is assigned to a particular group on the basis of the rights that the user needs.

Permissions, as discussed earlier in this chapter, indicate the access that a user (or group) has to specific objects, such as files, directories, and printers. For example, the question of whether a user can read a particular directory or access a network printer is a permission.

Rights, on the other hand, are divided into two types: privileges and logon rights. *Privileges* include such functions as the ability to run security audits or force shutdown from a remote system—obviously not tasks that are done by most users. *Logon rights* are almost self-explanatory: They involve the ability to connect to a computer in specific ways. Rights are automatically assigned to the groups in Windows SBS 2008, although they can be assigned to individual users as well. Assignment by group is usually preferred, so whenever possible, assign rights by group membership to keep administration simple.

When membership in groups defines rights, rights can be removed from a user by simply removing the user from the group. Table 10-4 lists the logon rights and the groups to which they are assigned by default.

TABLE 10-4 Logon Rights Assigned to Groups by Default

NAME	DESCRIPTION	GROUPS ASSIGNED THE RIGHT ON THE SBS DOMAIN CONTROLLER	GROUPS ASSIGNED THE RIGHT ON WORK-STATIONS AND SERVERS
Access This Computer From The Network	Permits connection to the computer through the network	Administrators, Authenticated Users, Everyone	Administrators, Backup Operators, Users, Everyone
Allow Logon Locally	Permits logging on to the computer interactively	Administrators, Account Operators, Backup Operators, Print Operators, Server Operators	Administrators, Backup Operators, Users
Allow Logon Through Terminal Services	Allows logging on as a Terminal Services client	Administrators	Administrators, Remote Desktop Users

In Windows SBS, it is much simpler to control logon access through individual user ac-counts (see the section titled "Giving Users Access to Computers" in Chapter 9, "Managing Users and Groups," for more information) unless your network is relatively large and you are using Windows Server 2008 built-in groups in addition to Windows SBS groups.

Managing Default User Rights Assignments

To see the user rights assignment on the Windows SBS server, select Administrative Tools from the Start menu and then select Local Security Policy. Expand Local Policies and then click User Rights Assignment.

To change one of the policies, right-click the name and select Properties. If the Add User Or Group button is available (Figure 10-10), you can click it to add additional users who will have the user right.

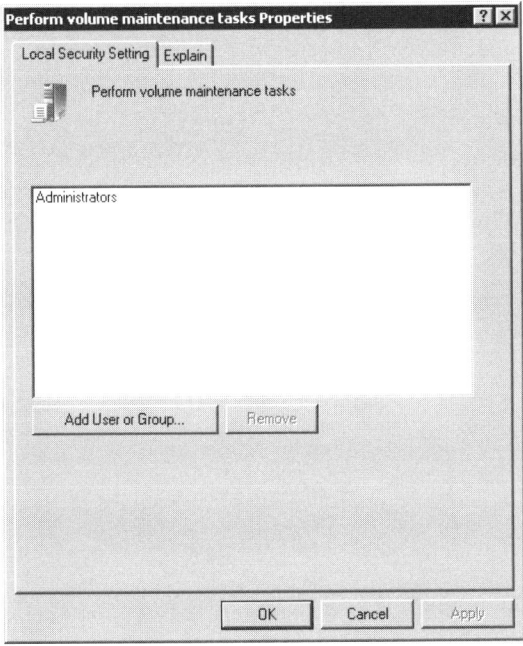

FIGURE 10-10 Additional users or groups can be granted this user right.

If the Add User Or Group button is unavailable, this user right can be granted only by add-ing the user or group to the groups already listed.

Summary

This chapter and the previous one have concerned themselves with users, groups, and their abilities and restrictions. In the next chapter, we move to hardware and the management of hard drives, volumes, and storage.

Disk Management

Arguably the single most important function that a server provides to the rest of the network is to be a central, secure, managed file storage area. By centralizing file storage on a server, it becomes an order of magnitude easier to ensure the safety, integrity, recoverability, and availability of the core files of your business. Instead of having files spread all across the network on individual users' computers, you have them in a single place—easier to share among collaborators, easier to back up, easier to recover in the event of a disaster, and easier to secure so that only those people who *should* have access to a file, do. The downside to having all your important files in a single location is the potential for a single point of failure. You need to make sure that your files are seriously protected and always available—your business depends on them. This makes it imperative that you carefully manage the underlying disks that support your file storage and that those disks be both redundant and thoroughly backed up.

Storing, securing, backing up, and making available the core files of your business is a bigger topic than we could fit in a single chapter, so we've spread it out and organized it according to the various functions involved. But we can't stress this enough: *All* of the pieces are essential to a safe, secure, and available network. Don't shortchange any of them. In this chapter, we'll cover the underlying disk management that makes it possible to store your files and protect against loss, corruption, or disaster. In Chapter 12, "Storage Management," we'll cover the features of Microsoft Windows Small Business Server 2008 that enable you to manage storage, protect critical files, and provide versioning of shared files to protect against corruption or misadventure. Additional backup and recovery details are covered in Chapter 16, "Configuring Backup." Finally, in Chapter 4, "Planning Fault Tolerance and Avoidance," and Chapter 27, "Disaster Planning," we go over the steps to ensure that your data systems and network are both highly available and can be recovered in the event of a serious disaster.

The Search for Disaster Protection

Traditionally, large businesses have used a variety of techniques to ensure that files stored on a server were both secure and safe. These solutions tend to be expensive, but when spread across all the supported workstations and buried in a large MIS budget, they are feasible. The same solutions would *not* be feasible or acceptable in most small businesses, but that doesn't change our very real need to protect ourselves from disaster. Fortunately, both hardware and software solutions can provide a very high level of security and safety at a budget more in keeping with the realities of a small business. However, before we can talk about those solutions, let's make sure we all understand the terminology of disk management. Let's review some definitions.

- **Physical drive** The actual hard disk itself, including the case, electronics, platters, and all that stuff. Not terribly important to the disk administrator.

- **Partition** A portion of the hard disk. In many cases, this is the entire hard disk space, but it needn't be.

- **Master Boot Record (MBR)** A technique for partitioning a hard disk. This is the default method for Windows Small Business Server 2008. MBR-partitioned disks are limited to a maximum of four partitions per disk, and a maximum size of 2 terabytes.

- **GUID Partition Table (GPT)** A technique for partitioning a hard disk, GPT is replacing MBR for larger hard disks and large storage arrays. Windows Small Business Server 2008 supports GPT-partitioned disks for all disks except the boot disk. GPT disks support 128 partitions and are required for disks (or arrays) larger than 2 terabytes.

- **Allocation unit** The smallest unit of managed disk space on a hard disk or logical volume. Also called a *cluster*.

- **Primary partition** A portion of the hard disk that's been marked as a potentially bootable logical drive by an operating system. MS-DOS could support only a single primary partition, but Windows Server 2008 can support four primary partitions on an MBR hard disk and 128 primary partitions on a GPT hard disk.

- **Extended partition** A non-bootable portion of the hard disk that can be subdivided into logical drives. There can be only a single extended partition per hard disk, but this partition can be divided into multiple logical drives. Extended partitions are *deprecated* in Windows Small Business Server 2008 and can't be directly created from the GUI.

- **Volume** A unit of disk space composed of one or more sections of one or more dynamic disks.

- **Simple volume** The dynamic equivalent of a partition. A portion of a single dynamic disk, a simple volume can be assigned either a single drive letter or no drive letter and can be attached (mounted) on zero or more mount points.

- **Extended volume** Similar to, and sometimes synonymous with, a spanned volume, an extended volume is any dynamic volume that has been extended to make it larger than its original size. When an extended volume uses portions of more than one physical disk, it is more properly referred to as a *spanned volume*.

- **Logical drive** A section or partition of a hard disk that acts as a single unit. An extended partition can be divided, for example, into multiple logical drives.

- **Logical volume** Another name for a logical drive.

- **Basic disk** A traditional disk drive that is divided into one or more partitions, with a logical drive in each primary partition. Basic disks do not support the more advanced functions of disk management, but they can be converted to dynamic disks in many cases.

- **Dynamic disk** A managed hard disk that can be used to create various volumes.

- **RAID (redundant array of independent [formerly "inexpensive"] disks)** The use of multiple hard disks in an array to provide for larger volume size, fault tolerance, and increased performance. RAID comes in different levels, such as RAID 0, RAID 1, and RAID 5. Higher numbers don't necessarily indicate greater performance or fault tolerance, just different methods of doing the job.

- **Spanned volume** A collection of portions of hard disks combined into a single addressable unit. A spanned volume is formatted like a single drive and can have a drive letter assigned to it, but it will span multiple physical drives. A spanned volume—occasionally referred to as an *extended volume*—provides no fault tolerance and increases your exposure to failure but does permit you to make more efficient use of the available hard disk space.

- **Striped volume** Like a spanned volume, a striped volume combines multiple hard disk portions into a single entity. A striped volume uses special formatting to write to each of the portions equally in a stripe to increase performance. A striped volume provides no fault tolerance and actually increases your exposure to failure, but it is faster than either a spanned volume or a single drive. A stripe set is often referred to as *RAID 0*, although this is a misnomer, because plain striping includes no redundancy.

- **Mirror volume** A pair of dynamic volumes that contain identical data and appear to the world as a single entity. Disk mirroring can use two drives on the same hard disk controller or can use separate controllers, in which case it is sometimes referred to as duplexing. In case of failure on the part of either drive, the other hard disk can be split off so that it continues to provide complete access to the data stored on the drive, providing a high degree of fault tolerance. This technique is called *RAID 1*.

- **RAID 5 volume** Like a striped volume, this combines portions of multiple hard disks into a single entity with data written across all portions equally. However, it also writes parity information for each stripe onto a different portion, providing the ability to recover in the case of a single drive failure. A RAID 5 volume provides excellent throughput for read operations but is substantially slower than all other available options for write operations.

- **SLED (single large expensive disk)** Now rarely used, this strategy is the opposite of the RAID strategy. Rather than using several inexpensive hard disks and providing fault tolerance through redundancy, you buy the best hard disk you can and bet your entire network on it. If this doesn't sound like a good idea to you, you're right. It's not.

- **JBOD** Just a bunch of disks. The hardware equivalent of a spanned volume, this has all the failings of any spanning scheme. The failure of any one disk will result in catastrophic data failure.

> **NOTE** Additional RAID levels are supported by many hardware manufacturers of RAID controllers. These include RAID 0+1, RAID 10, RAID 6, and RAID 50. For more details on various RAID levels, see the manufacturer of your RAID controller or *http://en.wikipedia.org /wiki/RAID#Standard_levels*.

 UNDER THE HOOD **Disk Technologies for the Server**

The first time we wrote a chapter about disk management, there were basically three possible technologies available: Modified Field Modification (MFM), Pulse Frequency Modulation (PFM), and Small Computer System (or Serial) Interface (SCSI). Unless you were a total geek (and had oodles of money), your systems used either MFM or PFM, and RAID wasn't even an option. Over time, SCSI became the only real choice for the vast majority of servers and even became mainstream on high-end workstations. Servers at the high end might use fiber, but SCSI had the vast majority of the server disk market.

Integrated Device Electronics (IDE), later called *Advanced Technology Attachment* (ATA), became the standard on the personal computer. However, IDE never made serious inroads into the server market, because although it was fast for single tasks, it lacked the inherent multitasking support and bus mastering that a server disk interface technology required, and there were no real hardware RAID solutions that supported it. Avoid it on your server except as secondary storage.

Recently, the introduction of Serial ATA (SATA) technology has made serious inroads into the lower end of the server marketplace. With SATA RAID controllers built into many motherboards, and standalone SATA RAID boards that support eight or more SATA drives and have substantial battery-backed RAM cache onboard, many low- to mid-range servers are finding SATA RAID solutions to provide a cost-effective alternative to SCSI. Although most SATA RAID controllers lack the ability to hot-swap a failed drive and generally don't have the ultimate performance potential of SCSI or Serially Attached SCSI (SAS), they are still quite attractive alternatives where cost is a primary factor. SATA also makes sense as secondary or "near-line" storage for a server.

The new kid on the block, however, is SAS. This is the most interesting addition to the server storage equation in quite a while. Using the same thin cables and connectors as SATA, with none of the configuration nuisance of traditional SCSI, SAS is definitely the way to go. When combined with new 2.5-inch drives, the ability to put a really large amount of very fast storage in a small space has taken a significant step forward. Many SAS controllers fully support SATA drives also, allowing you to combine the two technologies on the same controller. With the main bottleneck for servers continuing to be I/O in general, and especially disk I/O, there will continue to be pressure to find new and faster methods to access disk-based storage. SAS, combined with 2.5-inch drives, enables fast and flexible storage arrays in remark-ably smaller spaces, and with lower energy and cooling requirements.

Choosing the Storage Solution for Your Network

The first decision you need to make when planning your storage solution for SBS is really made when you specify your server. If your budget can afford it, you should definitely con-sider choosing a hardware RAID solution that lets you add disks on the fly and reconfigure the array without turning off the server or rebooting. This is absolutely the best and most flexible storage solution for protecting your data and could take the form of hot-swappable SAS hard drives, or even a Storage Area Network (SAN). The best choices aren't cheap, and in most cases you need to make at least some portion of the decision as part of the original server purchase.

 REAL WORLD **Network Attached Storage**

Although most hardware storage solutions require you to make decisions very early in the buying process, a growing number of Network Attached Storage (NAS) solutions can provide a cost-effective way to increase the storage flexibility of your SBS network. Many of the available solutions, especially at the lower end of the price range, are designed more for home networks and digital media sharing than for business networks. However, there are also excellent NAS servers available that are based on Microsoft Windows Storage Server. These provide the greatest flexibility and support for an SBS network, and we prefer them when adding a NAS to an SBS network. For more on Windows Storage Server–powered NAS servers, see *http://www.microsoft.com/windowsserversystem/wss2003*.

Another interesting option (and one we'll discuss in much greater detail later in Chapter 16) is Windows Home Server. Although it is not designed primarily as a NAS, it supports much of the same functionality, while adding in the ability to do client backups very efficiently. If your need for a NAS is primarily to add some near-line storage for occasional use files or to store local backups, we think Windows Home Server is a very interesting alternative, and one we're using on our personal SBS network.

When the server is actually in place and is being used, you can't really make a change to the underlying hardware that would allow you to use a hardware RAID solution—at least not easily. But you *can* use the built-in facilities of SBS to make your existing disk subsystem more fault-tolerant by using dynamic disks and the software RAID of SBS, as described in the section titled "RAID 5 Volumes" later in this chapter.

Storage Connection Technologies

If you're reading this chapter before you buy your server, congratulations on being a thorough person. If not, some of these decisions have already been made, but you may well find that you will have to add storage. If you do, you'll want to focus on storage solutions designed and optimized for servers—a very different set of needs from the typical workstation. Your choices are:

- **Integrated Device Electronics (IDE)** Strictly a client solution. Inexpensive, but not really appropriate on a server. Now being replaced even at the client end by SATA.

- **Serial Advanced Technology Attachment (SATA)** A newer and faster version of IDE. Still primarily a workstation solution, but acceptable when combined with hardware RAID for smaller servers.

- **External Serial Advanced Technology Attachment (eSATA)** A way to use SATA for external, secondary, or backup storage.

- **Small Computer System Interface (SCSI)** Perfect for servers and high-end workstations, but significantly more expensive than SATA. Has the ability to have up to 13 drives per SCSI channel.

- **Serially Attached SCSI (SAS)** Perfect for large servers. This is a relatively new technology that is rapidly becoming the mainstream server storage interface. Prices are still higher than SATA or IDE.

- **Internet SCSI (iSCSI)** Important for Storage Area Networks (SANs) and can even be used as a boot device for SBS servers, but the complexities and costs put this outside the range of most small businesses.

- **FireWire** Hot-pluggable. A good choice as a backup storage device.

- **Universal Serial Bus (USB)** Only appropriate if you use USB 2.0. Good for CD and DVD drives. Hot-pluggable. A good choice as a backup storage device.

- **Fiber Channel** Great if you have large amounts of money to spend.

- **Network Attached Storage (NAS)** A good way to provide large amounts of storage that can be flexible to meet your needs. Specify Windows Storage Server–based NAS for the greatest flexibility and compatibility.

- **Storage Area Networks (SAN)** Faster and more flexible than the typical NAS, but also much more expensive and difficult to configure. Generally not for small business networks.

- **Solid State Disks (SSD)** Initially used primarily for notebook computers, these are starting to find their way into servers, especially high-density servers in data centers, where their power savings are a plus. Still too pricy for most small business networks.

Managing Disks

There are two different kinds of disks in Windows Small Business Server 2008: basic disks and dynamic disks. *Basic disks* are the conventional disks we're used to. *Dynamic disks* were introduced in Windows 2000 Server and support additional management and agglomeration options.

Basic disks support two different kinds of partitions: primary and extended. Extended partitions are deprecated in Windows Server 2008, although they can still be created from the command line using DiskPart.exe. And any existing disks you have with extended partitions will be recognized without a problem. If you need to create a disk with many different volumes on it (more than four), create the disk as a GPT disk rather than an MBR type.

Dynamic disks use volumes instead of partitions and support the additional management, redundancy, and agglomeration features of SBS, including Spanned Volumes, Striped Volumes (RAID 0), Mirrored Volumes (RAID 1), and RAID 5.

The primary method for managing disks on an SBS server is the Disk Management console. This can be used as a standalone console by running diskmgmt.msc from the command line, or from Server Manager as shown in Figure 11-1.

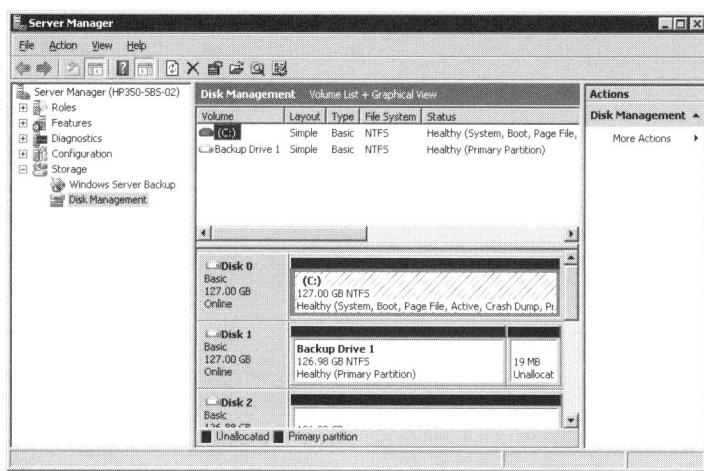

FIGURE 11-1 The Disk Management console from inside Server Manager

The Disk Management console is divided into two panes. The top pane shows the drive letters (volumes) associated with the local disks and gives their properties and status; the bottom pane has a graphical representation organized by physical drive.

NOTE In this chapter, for simplicity, the rest of our screen shots run Disk Management as a standalone console, but the exact same functions are available from inside Server Manager as well.

 REAL WORLD Hardware RAID

Although Disk Management provides an excellent software RAID solution, hardware RAID is also now widely available, from either the original server vendor or from third parties, and it provides substantial advantages over software RAID. Hardware RAID solutions range from a simple RAID controller to fully integrated, standalone subsystems. Their features vary, as does their cost, but all claim to provide superior performance and reliability over a simple software RAID solution such as that included in Windows Small Business Server 2008. In general, they do. Some of the advantages they can offer include:

- Hot-swap and hot-spare drives, allowing for virtually instantaneous replacement of failed drives.

- Integrated, battery-protected disk caching for improved disk performance.

- A separate, dedicated system that handles all processing, for improved overall performance.

- Increased flexibility and additional RAID levels, such as RAID 10 and RAID 0+1, which are a combination of striping (RAID 0) and mirroring (RAID 1) that provide for fast read and write disk access with full redundancy.

Single Server

Although not all hardware RAID systems provide all the possible features, they all have the potential to improve the overall reliability and performance of your hard disk subsystem. With SBS being predominantly a single-server environment, you have your entire business running on that single server. This makes hardware RAID a particularly sound investment for your SBS server.

NAS and SAN

Many NAS systems are built on hardware RAID, providing an easy and cost-effective way to expand your original server storage in a highly fault-tolerant way. However, it pays to look closely at exactly what you are buying—some are built on RAID 0, which is not fault-tolerant at all and actually increases your risk.

We only briefly mentioned Storage Area Networks (SANs) earlier, and we won't mention them again. Although they are excellent, fast, flexible, and highly fault-tolerant, they are only for those with really large IT budgets at this point. Plus, they can be rather tricky to implement and configure. Given the strong advances in NAS, we think NAS provides a better solution for those running on realistic budgets.

Windows Home Server

A new player in the standalone storage market is Microsoft's Windows Home Server (WHS). Designed primarily to provide a single storage location for the home market, WHS is based on Windows Server 2003 and provides many of the functions of a NAS server. WHS uses a new Drive Extender technology to allow you to add hard drives to the server without having to do any reconfiguration at all—WHS extends the file system across the new drive automatically, increasing the available disk space. WHS also does Client Backup really well (see Chapter 16) and automatically duplicates files across multiple disks, providing redundancy.

Although it is not what we would choose for storage on an SBS network of 50 to 75 users, WHS can certainly be a viable choice on smaller SBS networks, and it definitely has a role as a client backup solution for key workstations in an SBS network of any size.

Partitions and Volumes

In Windows Server 2008, the distinction between volumes and partitions is somewhat murky. When using Disk Management, a regular partition on a basic disk is called a *simple volume*, even though technically a simple volume requires that the disk be a dynamic disk.

As long as you use only simple volumes or partitions, you can easily convert between a basic disk (and partition) and a dynamic disk (and a volume). Once you use a feature that is only supported on dynamic disks, however, changing back to a basic disk will mean data loss.

BEST PRACTICES Recovering or rebuilding a server that has a dynamic disk for the boot disk can be tricky. We suggest keeping your boot disk (C) a basic disk and use hardware mirroring (RAID 1) to safeguard its contents, and only use dynamic disks for other disks on your server.

 REAL WORLD **Dynamic v. Basic Disks**

We used to be big fans of dynamic disks. They provided increased flexibility and functionality in a way that was pretty transparent. And they were a huge step forward when they were introduced in Windows 2000. At the time, RAID controllers were both more expensive and less functional, and many servers didn't have hardware RAID on them. That's simply not the case anymore.

If using dynamic disks increases your options, isn't that a good thing? Well, yes. But—and it's a big but—a dynamic disk complicates the disaster recovery process, and we dislike anything that creates potential issues in a disaster recovery scenario. We definitely don't think dynamic disks are appropriate for a system disk. And we just have a hard time seeing the upside, given the functionality that a good RAID controller provides.

If you do find a need that can't be solved any other way, by all means use dynamic disks. There's no apparent performance cost, and you use the same tools to manage both dynamic disks in SBS and basic disks. But avoid converting your system disk to dynamic. And make sure your disaster recovery procedures are updated appropriately.

Adding a Partition or Volume

Adding a new drive or partition to an SBS server is straightforward. First, obviously, you need to physically install and connect the drive. If you have a hot-swappable backplane and array, you don't even have to shut the system down to accomplish this task. If you're using conventional drives, however, you need to shut down and turn off the system.

After the drive is installed and the system is turned on again, SBS automatically recognizes the new hardware and makes it available. If the disk is a basic disk that is already partitioned and formatted, you can use it immediately. If it's a brand new disk that has never been partitioned or formatted, you need to prepare it first. If it's a dynamic disk or disks, but from another computer, you can use it as soon as you import it. If the disk is a basic disk that has already been formatted, you aren't prompted to upgrade it to a dynamic disk. If the disk has never been used before, the Initialize And Convert Disk Wizard prompts you.

Adding a New Disk Using the Initialize Disk Wizard

When you install a new hard drive, the drive is automatically recognized, and the Initialize And Convert Disk Wizard starts when you open Disk Management. To add a new disk, complete the following steps:

1. Open Disk Management.
2. If Disk Management recognizes a new disk, you see the first page of the Initialize Disk Wizard, shown in Figure 11-2. This wizard initializes a disk so that it can be recognized by Windows Small Business Server 2008 and lets you select whether the disk should be an MBR or GPT disk.

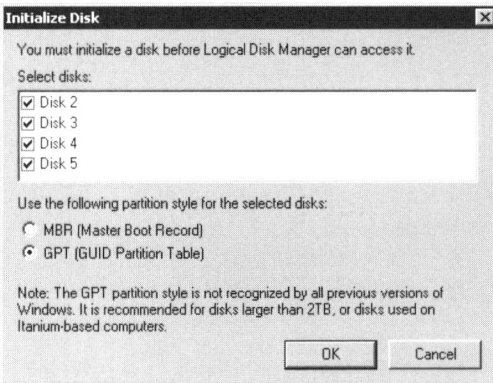

FIGURE 11-2 The Initialize Disk Wizard

3. Clear any disks you don't want to initialize and select the partition style for the disks.

When the wizard finishes, you're at the main Disk Management console, shown in Figure 11-3. Notice that the disk is still not formatted or allocated and is highlighted in black (if you haven't changed the default color settings for the Disk Management console).

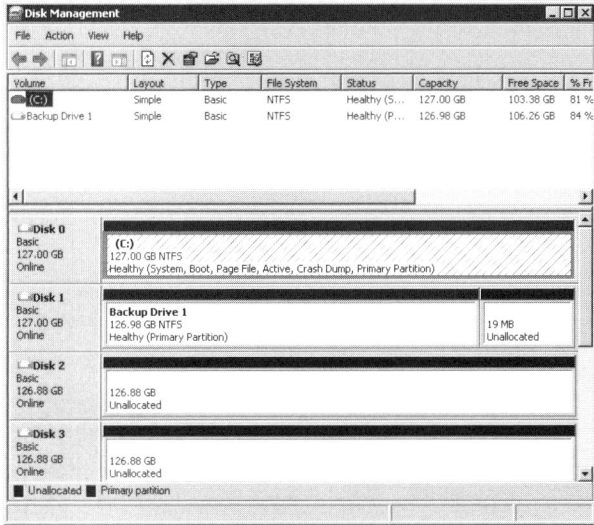

FIGURE 11-3 The main Disk Management console, showing the new disks

Creating a Simple Volume or Partition

To create a new simple volume or partition, complete the following steps:

1. In the Disk Management console, right-click the unallocated disk and choose the type of new volume you want to create. To create a partition, select New Simple Volume, as shown in Figure 11-4.

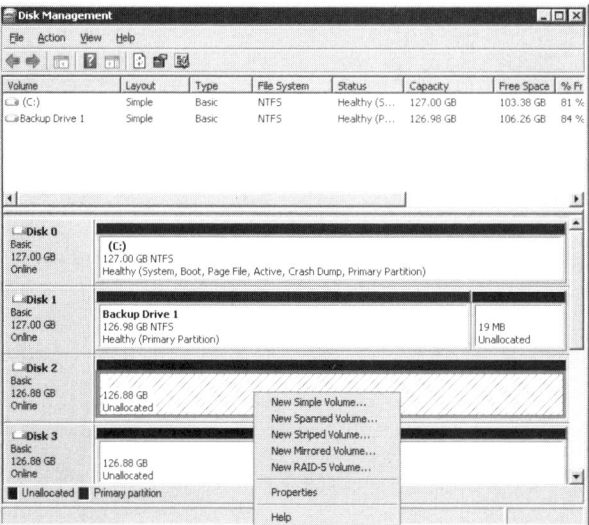

FIGURE 11-4 Creating a new volume on an unallocated disk

2. The New Simple Volume Wizard opens to guide you through the process of creating the new volume on the dynamic disk.

3. Click Next to open the Specify Volume Size page. Specify the size of volume you'll be creating, as shown in Figure 11-5.

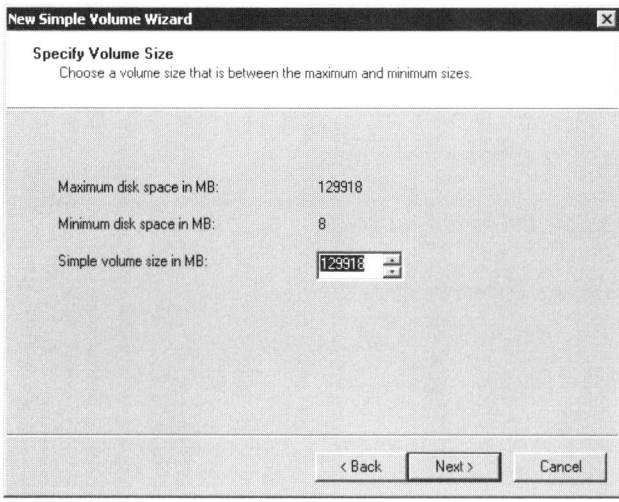

FIGURE 11-5 The Specify Volume Size page of the New Simple Volume Wizard

4. Click Next to open the Assign Drive Letter Or Path page. The next available drive letter will be selected by default. For details on mounted volumes, see the section titled "Mounting a Volume" later in this chapter.

5. Click Next to open the Format Partition page shown in Figure 11-6. Specify the format options for the volume, including:

   - **File System** The only supported file system for Windows Small Business Server 2008 is NTFS, except for removable devices such as USB key drives.

   - **Allocation Unit Size** The default value is 4 kilobyte (KB) sectors. This is a reasonable balance, but choose a larger size, such as 16 KB or even 64 KB, if you know that this volume will only be used to hold very large files (such as a volume dedicated to virtual hard disks, for example, or large database files).

   - **Volume Label** Specify a meaningful label that identifies the volume.

   - **Perform A Quick Format** Saves waiting for full formatting but is not recommended on new disks, since no verification pass is performed.

   - **Enable File And Folder Compression** Only an option if the allocation unit size is less than 16 KB. And never recommended.

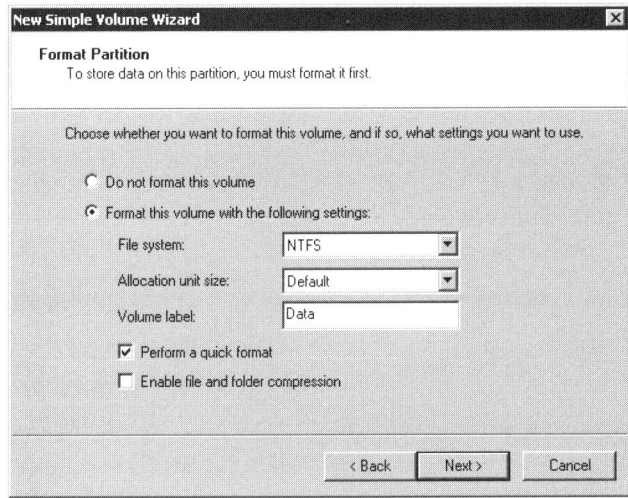

FIGURE 11-6 The Format Partition page of the New Simple Volume Wizard

6. Click Finish to close the wizard and begin provisioning the volume. You return to the Disk Management console, where you see the new volume, as shown in Figure 11-7.

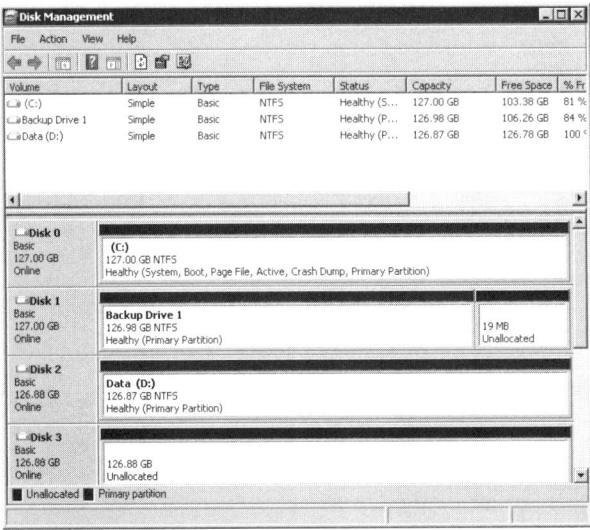

FIGURE 11-7 The new Primary Partition (Simple Volume) has been created.

 UNDER THE HOOD **Command Line**

SBS adds to the system administrator's toolkit a complete command-line interface for managing disks—DiskPart.exe. This command-line utility is scriptable or can be used interactively. The following simple script creates a volume on an existing dynamic disk and assigns it to the next available drive letter:

```
REM Filename: MakeVol.txt
REM
REM This is a DiskPart.exe Script. Run from the command line
REM or from another script, using the syntax:
REM
REM    diskpart /s MakeVol.txt > logfile.log
REM
REM to run this script and dump the results out to a log file.
REM
REM This script creates a simple volume of 28 Gb on disk #3, and then
REM assigns a drive letter to it. Note that this does NOT format
REM the volume -- that requires using the format command, not part
REM of diskpart.exe

REM First, list out our disks. Not required for scripting, but useful
REM to show the overall environment if we need to troubleshoot problems
list disk

REM Next, select which disk will have the simple volume created on it.
```

```
select disk 3

REM Now, create the volume...
create volume simple size=28672

REM Assign without parameters will choose the next available HD letter.
Assign
```

Creating a RAID 1 (Mirror) or RAID 5 Volume

The process of creating a mirrored (RAID 1) or RAID 5 volume is similar to creating a simple volume, except that the disks will be converted to dynamic disks first, and you'll need to select the disks to add to the volume.

To create a new simple volume or partition, complete the following steps:

1. In the Disk Management console, right-click an unallocated disk and choose New RAID 5 Volume or New Mirrored Volume to open the New RAID 5 Volume Wizard (or New Mirrored Volume Wizard).

2. Click Next to open the Select Disks page, as shown in Figure 11-8.

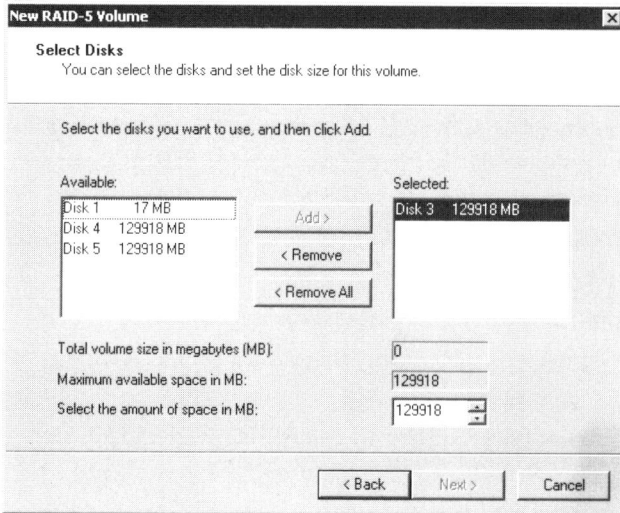

FIGURE 11-8 The Select Disks page of the New RAID 5 Volume Wizard

3. Select the disks to add to the volume and then specify the amount of space on each disk to use for the volume. The maximum for all disks is the amount of unallocated space on the disk with the least available space.

4. Click Next to open the Assign Drive Letter Or Path page shown in Figure 11-9. See the section titled "Mounting a Volume" later in this chapter for more on mounted volumes.

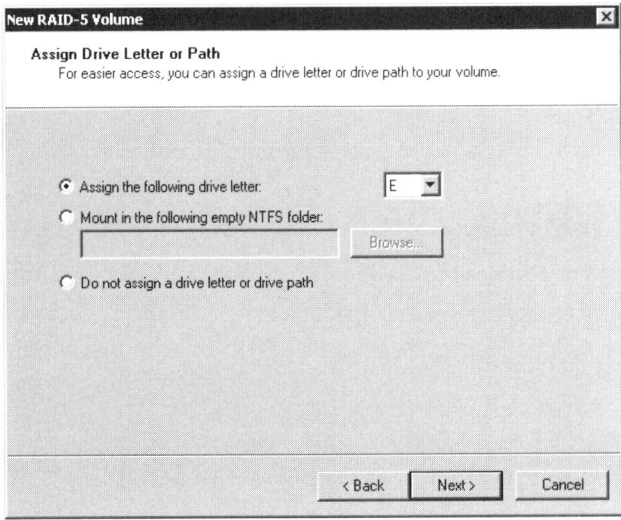

FIGURE 11-9 The Assign Drive Letter Or Path page of the New RAID 5 Volume Wizard

5. Click Next to open the Format Volume page. The formatting options are the same as for a simple volume or partition:

- **File System**   The only supported file system for Windows Small Business Server 2008 is NTFS, except for removable devices such as USB key drives.

- **Allocation Unit Size**   The default value is 4 KB sectors. This is a reasonable balance, but choose a larger size, such as 16 KB or even 64 KB, if you know that this volume will only be used to hold very large files (such as a volume dedicated to virtual hard disks, for example, or large database files.)

- **Volume Label**   Specify a meaningful label that identifies the volume.

- **Perform A Quick Format**   Saves waiting for full formatting but is not recommended on new disks because no verification pass is performed.

- **Enable File And Folder Compression**   Only an option if the allocation unit size is less than 16 KB. And never recommended.

6. Click Finish to accept your settings and provision the RAID volume. If the disks are currently basic disks, you'll see the warning message shown in Figure 11-10.

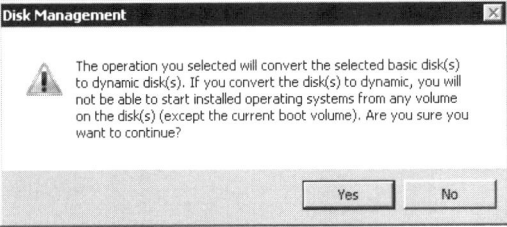

FIGURE 11-10 The Disk Management warning for converting to dynamic disks

7. Click Yes, and the disks will be converted and the provisioning will begin.

 UNDER THE HOOD **Formatting Options**

Even though SBS can recognize hard drives that are formatted in any of the three file system formats (FAT, FAT32, and NTFS), only NTFS is supported by Windows Small Business Server 2008. Although it is technically possible to format any drive except the system drive as FAT or FAT32, it is neither recommended nor supported.

You can choose to quick-format a drive to make it available more quickly, but this option simply removes the file entries from the disk and does no checking for bad sectors. Choose quick formatting only when recycling a disk that has already been formatted and you are confident it hasn't been damaged.

On an NTFS volume or partition, you can specify the allocation unit size. This option lets you tune the disk for a particular purpose, depending on the disk's size and intended function. A database storage volume that will contain large database files managed by the database program might lend itself to large allocation units (also called *clusters*), whereas a disk that must hold many small files is a candidate for smaller clusters. However, the default sizes are an excellent compromise for most situations—modify them only with caution and with a clear understanding of the consequences for your environment.

You can also choose to enable disk and folder compression on NTFS volumes and partitions. This causes all files and folders on the volume (as opposed to individual files or folders you select) to be compressed. Compression can minimize the amount of hard disk space used by files but has a negative impact on performance while making disaster recovery more problematic. Given the cost of hard drive space today, we think this is just a bad idea.

Deleting a Partition or Volume

Deleting a partition and deleting a volume are essentially the same task. When you delete a partition or volume, the entire volume or partition is deleted. However, if you've got an older disk with an extended partition on it that you use with SBS, you won't be able to delete the extended partition until you delete all of the logical drives in the partition. You can directly delete a primary partition or a volume.

In all cases, when you delete a volume, logical drive, or partition, you end up with free or unallocated space and no data on the volume, drive, or partition when you're done, so make sure you have a good backup if there's a chance you might later need any of the data. To delete a partition or volume, follow these steps:

1. Right-click the partition or volume and select Delete Volume.

2. At the Delete RAID 5 Volume warning, shown in Figure 11-11, click Yes to delete the volume.

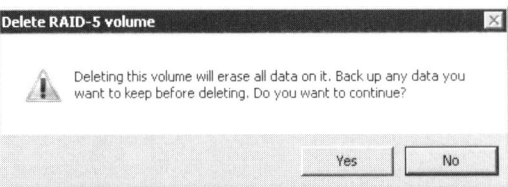

FIGURE 11-11 The Delete RAID 5 Volume warning

When the volume or partition is completely deleted, the space it occupied will be unallocated. Space that is unallocated on dynamic disks can be used to create mirrors, extend an existing volume, create a RAID array, or otherwise manage the storage on your server. Space that is unallocated on basic disks can be partitioned or used to extend a partition.

 REAL WORLD **Extended Partitions**

Extended partitions were a mechanism used by earlier versions of Windows to get around the limitation of MBR disks that only allowed a maximum of four partitions. If you have extended partitions on your disks for some reason, you can create logical drives on the partition using DiskPart.exe. However, you no longer have a graphical way to create an extended partition or a logical drive, nor any real need to do so. With Windows Small Business Server 2008 providing full support for GPT disks, the old limit of a maximum of four partitions on a disk is gone—GPT disks in Windows Server 2008 support 128 partitions. If you have any existing MBR disks that include an extended partition because you moved a disk from another computer to your SBS computer, we suggest you remove the existing extended partition and convert the disk to GPT.

Extending or Shrinking a Volume

Windows Small Business Server 2008 has the ability to extend or shrink a volume, on the fly, without shutting down the server or rebooting. When you shrink a volume, you create unallocated space on the volume. That unallocated space can then be used to extend another volume.

Shrinking a Volume

The ability to shrink a volume is a new feature added to Windows Server 2008, giving you greater flexibility in managing your disks. Before Windows Server 2008, you had to use a third-party application to shrink a volume. And even now, third-party applications such as Acronis Disk Director give you greater flexibility and control over resizing partitions and volumes than Disk Management. With Disk Management, you can shrink down the unused space on a volume, recovering some of that empty space to use on other volumes, but the most you can expect to recover is about 50 percent of the free space on the volume. If the file system on the volume is fragmented, you might not get even that much.

To shrink a volume, follow these steps:

1. Open the Disk Management console if it isn't already open.

2. Select the volume you want to shrink and right-click to open the menu shown in Figure 11-12.

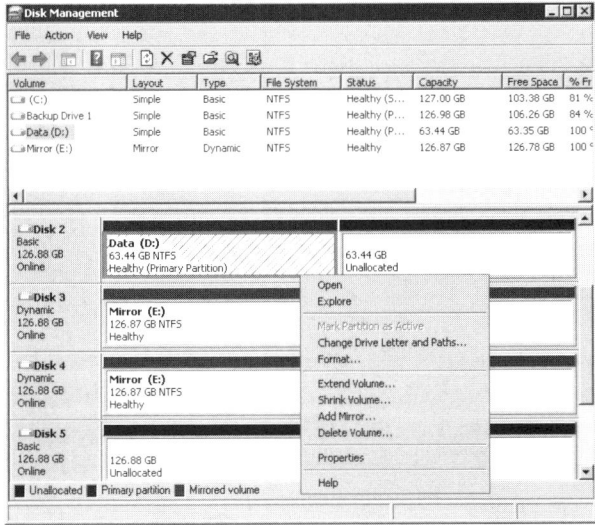

FIGURE 11-12 The Action menu for simple volume

3. Select Shrink Volume from the menu to open the Shrink dialog box shown in Figure 11-13.

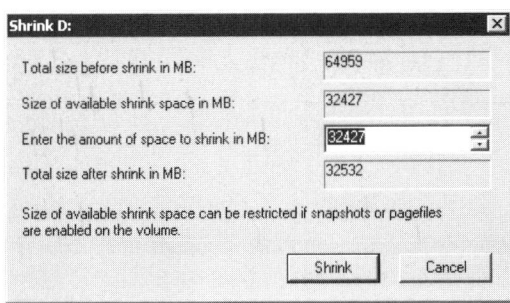

FIGURE 11-13 The Shrink dialog box for the simple volume D

4. Select the amount to shrink the volume and then click Shrink to change the size of the volume.

Extending a Volume

You can add space to a volume without having to back up, reboot, and restore your files if it is a simple volume or a spanned volume. You do this by converting the volume to a spanned or extended volume that incorporates unallocated space on any disk. Unfortunately, you can't increase the size of a RAID 5 or RAID 0 (striped) volume simply by adding disks to the array, unless you're using a version of hardware RAID that supports this functionality. To extend a volume, complete the following steps:

1. In the Disk Management console, right-click the volume you want to extend. Choose Extend Volume to open the Extend Volume Wizard.

2. Click Next to open the Select Disks page and select one or more disks from the list of disks that are available and have unallocated space. Click Add to add the selected disk or disks and indicate the amount of space you want to add, as shown in Figure 11-14.

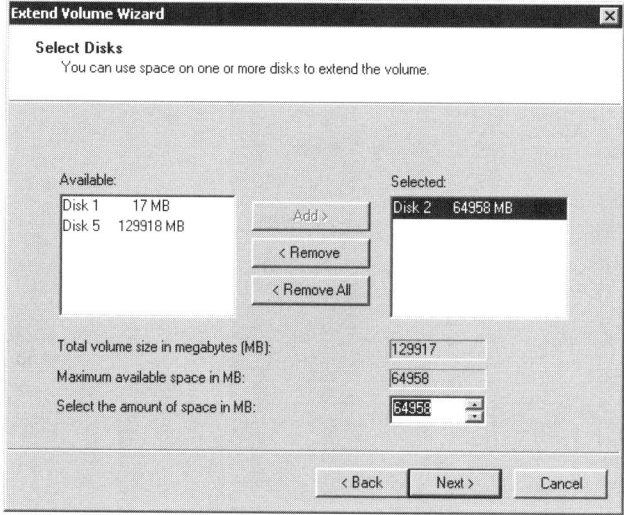

FIGURE 11-14 The Select Disks page of the Extend Volume Wizard

3. Click Next and the Extend Volume Wizard displays a final confirmation page before extending the volume. Click Finish to extend the volume. The extended volume is shown in Figure 11-15.

> **IMPORTANT** A spanned (extended) volume is actually less reliable than a simple disk. Unlike a mirror or RAID 5 volume, which has built-in redundancy, a spanned or striped volume will be broken and all its data lost if any disk in the volume fails.

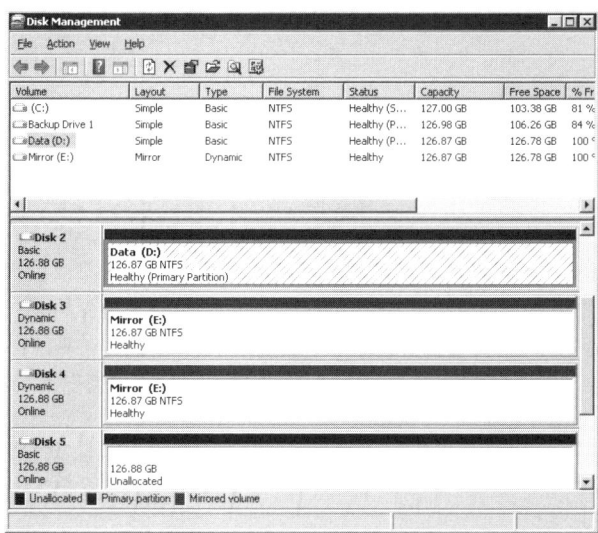

FIGURE 11-15 The Disk Management console, showing the new extended volume D

 REAL WORLD **Extending—Friend or Foe?**

Most people responsible for supporting a busy server have wished at some point that they could simply increase the space of a particular volume or drive on the fly when it got low on space—preferably without having to bring the system offline for several hours while the entire volume is backed up and reformatted to add the additional hard disks, the backup is restored, and the share points are re-created. Fun? Hardly. Risky? Certainly. And definitely a job that means coming in on the weekend or staying late at night—in other words, something to be avoided if at all possible.

All this makes SBS's ability to create additional space on a volume without the need to back up the volume, reformat the disks, and recreate the volume a seductive feature. However, unless you're running hardware RAID, you should think twice before jumping in. Only simple or spanned volumes allow you to add additional storage on the fly, and because neither is redundant, using them exposes your users to the risks of a failed drive. Yes, you have a backup, but even under the best of circumstances, you'll lose some data if you need to restore a backup. Further, using spanned volumes actually increases your risk of a hard disk failure. If any disk used as part of thespanned volume fails, the entire volume is toast and will need to be restored from backup.

Why, then, would anyone use spanning? Because they have hardware RAID to provide the redundancy. This combination offers the best of both worlds—redundancy provided by the hardware RAID controller and flexibility to expand volumes as needed, using Disk Management. Yet another compelling argument for hardware RAID, as if you needed any more.

NOTE Windows Small Business Server 2008 uses the terms *extended* and *spanned* nearly interchangeably when describing volumes. Technically, however, a spanned volume must include more than one physical disk, whereas an extended volume can also refer to a volume that has had additional space added to the original simple volume on the same disk.

Adding a Mirror

When your data is mission-critical and you want to make sure that the data is protected and always available no matter what happens to one of your hard disks, consider mirroring the data onto a second drive. SBS can mirror a dynamic disk onto a second dynamic disk that is at least the same size as the original so that the failure of either disk does not result in loss of data. To mirror a volume, you can either select a mirrored volume when you create the volume, or you can add a mirror to an existing volume. To add a mirror to an existing volume, complete the following steps:

1. In the Disk Management console, right-click the volume you want to mirror. If a potential mirror is available, the shortcut menu lists the Add Mirror command.

2. Choose Add Mirror to display the Add Mirror dialog box, shown in Figure 11-16.

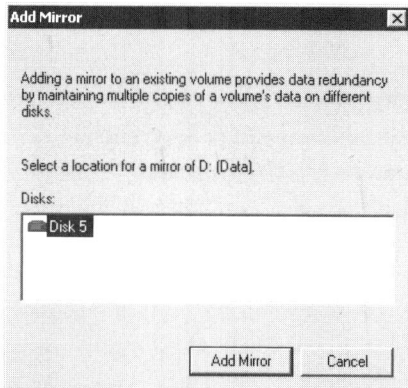

FIGURE 11-16 The Add Mirror dialog box

3. Select the disk to use for the mirror and click Add Mirror. If either or both of the disks are basic disks, you'll get a warning that the change will convert the disks to dynamic disks. Click Yes to proceed.

4. The mirror is created immediately and starts duplicating the data from the original disk to the second half of the mirror. This process is called *regeneration*, or sometimes *resynching*. (The process of regeneration is also used to distribute data across the disks when a RAID 5 volume is created.)

NOTE Regeneration is both CPU-intensive and disk-intensive. When possible, create mirrors during slack times or during normally scheduled downtime. Balance this goal, however, with the equally important goal of providing redundancy and failure protection as expeditiously as possible.

BEST PRACTICES To improve your overall data security and reliability, mirror your volumes onto disks that use separate controllers whenever possible. This process is known as *duplexing* and eliminates the disk controller as a single point of failure. It can also speed up both reading and writing to the mirror, because the controller and bus are no longer potential bottlenecks.

Drive Failure in a Mirrored Volume

If one of the disks in a mirrored volume fails, you can continue to have full access to all your data without loss. SBS marks the failed disk as missing and takes it offline. It also, however, takes the other half of the mirror and marks it as failed, as shown in Figure 11-17. This doesn't mean your data is lost. But it does mean you can't access it until you break the mirror. The missing disk will then need to be replaced and the mirror re-created to restore redundancy.

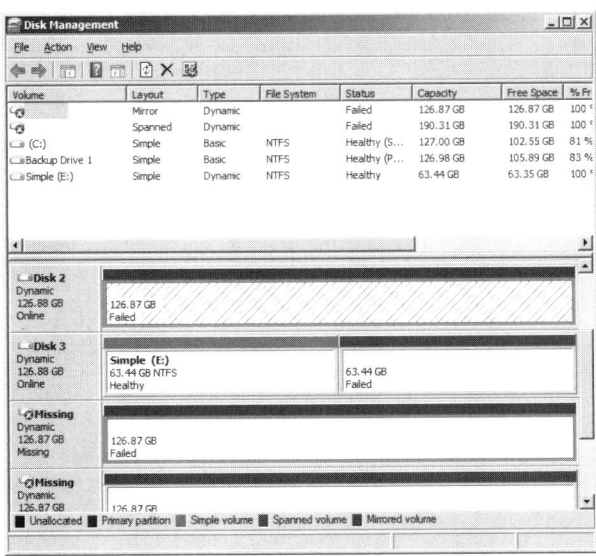

FIGURE 11-17 A missing disk causes a failure on both halves of a mirror.

To recover access to the data that was on the failed mirror, you need to remove the mirror and reactivate the good disk by following these steps:

1. Open Disk Management if it isn't already open.

2. Right-click the mirrored disk that shows as online (Disk 2 in Figure 11-17.)

3. Select Remove Mirror from the shortcut menu to open the Remove Mirror dialog box shown in Figure 11-18.

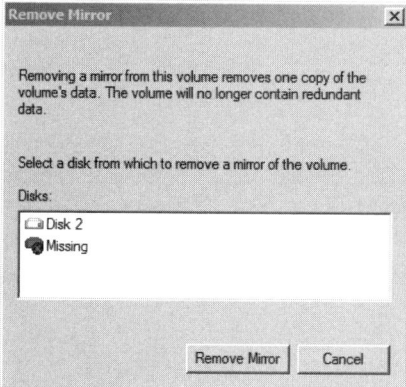

FIGURE 11-18 The Remove Mirror dialog box

4. Select the missing or offline disk and click Remove Mirror. You'll be prompted to confirm the removal. Click Yes, and the mirror is removed, but the disk is still not available because the drive letter mapping has to be reestablished.

5. Right-click the now healthy volume and select Change Drive Letter And Paths For Data to open the dialog box shown in Figure 11-19.

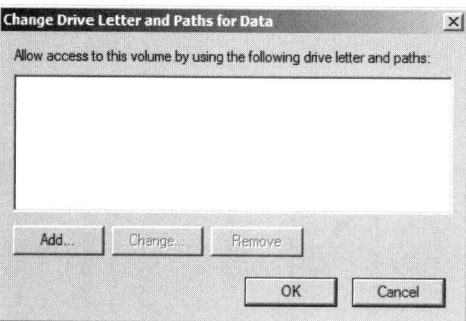

FIGURE 11-19 The Change Drive Letter And Paths For Data dialog box

6. Click Add to open the Add Drive Letter Or Path dialog box, select a drive letter from the drop-down list, and click OK. If you attempt to use the same drive letter as the drive had in the past, you'll see the warning message shown in Figure 11-20.

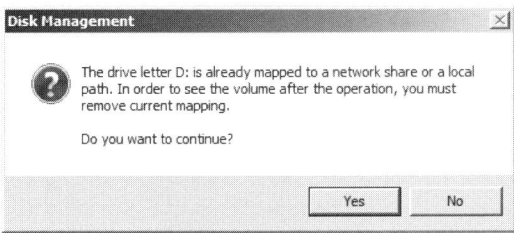

FIGURE 11-20 Disk Management warns when you try to map a drive letter that it has a remembered connection to.

7. Click Yes and the drive letter is assigned and the disk is available.

If you need to make additional disk space available on your system and you have no additional disks available, you can remove the mirror from a mirrored volume. When you remove a mirror, the data on one of the disks is untouched, but the other disk becomes unallocated space. Of course, you will have lost all redundancy and protection for the data, so you need to take steps to restore the mirror as soon as possible. Until then, you might want to modify your backup schedule for the remaining disk. To remove a mirror, complete the following steps:

1. In the Disk Management console, right-click either half of the mirror. Choose Remove Mirror from the shortcut menu. The Remove Mirror dialog box opens.

2. Select the disk you want to remove from the mirror. Click Remove Mirror. You get one last chance to change your mind. Click OK, and the disk you highlighted becomes unallocated space.

Breaking a Mirror

If a disk fails and you can't replace it with an identical one, break the mirror until a replacement becomes available. Breaking a mirror severs the connection between the two disks, allowing the remaining disk to continue to function normally until a replacement disk becomes available. When the replacement disk is available, the mirror can be re-created.

You might also find it useful to break a mirror even when both disks are still functioning, because you then end up with two identical copies of the same data. One half of the broken mirror continues to have the same drive letter or mount point, while the second half of the broken mirror is assigned the next available drive letter. To break a mirror, complete the following steps:

1. In the Disk Management console, right-click either disk of the mirrored volume.

2. Choose Break Mirrored Volume from the shortcut menu. You're asked to confirm that you really want to break it.

3. Click Yes, and the mirror is broken. You'll have two volumes. One retains the drive letter or mount point of the original mirror, and the other is assigned the next available drive letter. They will both contain exact duplicates of the data at the instant of the break but will immediately start to diverge as they are modified.

RAID 5 Volumes

Windows Small Business Server 2008 supports a software implementation of RAID 5 that allows you to have a redundant file system without the 50-percent capacity overhead of using mirrored volumes. The overhead on a RAID 5 volume decreases for each additional disk you add to the volume, making this the most space-efficient method of providing redundancy in SBS.

Unfortunately, this efficiency doesn't come without some costs. RAID 5 arrays are inherently slower at write operations than even a plain old standalone drive. You also don't have the flexibility that you have with mirrored volumes in SBS. You can't simply remove a drive from a RAID 5 volume, nor can you break a failed drive out of the volume, allowing the remaining drives to regenerate. Further, when a disk fails on a RAID 5 volume, not only is the volume no longer redundant, but it also gets a lot slower because both read and write operations must calculate the correct value for every byte read or written.

Some of the tasks you do with a mirror also apply to a RAID 5 volume. You can:

- Create the RAID 5 volume.
- Assign a mount point or drive letter to the RAID 5 volume.
- Format the RAID 5 volume.
- Continue to use the RAID 5 volume after the failure of one of the disks in the volume.

What you can't do with the software RAID in SBS is add or remove disks from the RAID 5 volume after you have created it, except for replacing a failed disk. To be able to dynamically add and remove disks from a RAID 5 array, you must choose a hardware RAID array that supports dynamic reconfiguration.

 REAL WORLD **Assigning Volume Names**

The name you assign to a volume, partition, or drive should tell you something about it rather than simply mimicking the drive letter. A volume name like "Big140SAS" tells you pretty conclusively that it's that big new SAS drive you just bought—unless, of course, you already have a half-dozen of them on your server, in which case you're going to need to come up with a more effective name. On the other hand, a volume name of "C_DRIVE" is just about useless, because the drive letter is available from anywhere that the volume name is. A common scheme is to assign volume names based on the primary use of the volume, so "UserHome" or "DB_STORE" make it pretty clear which volume it is from a logical (but not necessarily physical) view. We've moved to preferring this logical view of volume names— in an era of widely available hardware RAID solutions, combined with virtualized servers and virtual hard drives, the particular physical characteristics of a drive are less important than the logical ones. On our server, it's all part of a large SAS array underneath anyway.

Mounting a Volume

SBS borrows a concept from the UNIX world by adding the ability to mount a volume or partition on a subfolder of an existing drive letter. A mounted volume can also have a drive letter associated with it, although it does not need to, and it can be mounted at more than one point, giving multiple entry points into the same storage.

A volume must be mounted on an empty subfolder of an existing NTFS volume or drive. FAT and FAT32 drives do not support mounted volumes. You can mount only a single volume at a given mount point, but you can then mount further volumes on top of an existing mounted volume, with the same rules and restrictions as any other mount. An important caution, however: The properties of a drive do not show all the available disk space for that drive, because they do not reflect any volumes mounted on the drive. Further, mounted volumes are not supported with Windows Services for UNIX on shared Network File System (NFS) exports.

Mounted volumes can be used to provide a mix of redundant and non-redundant storage in a logical structure that meets the business needs of the business while hiding the complexities of the physical structure from the users, but it does pose potential issues during disaster recovery and for some kinds of file access.

The volume being mounted appears to users as a simple directory. This feature makes it possible to create larger file systems that use multiple hard disks without the inherent risks of using spanned volumes, because the failure of any one of the mounted volumes affects only the directories that were part of that volume. To mount a volume, complete the following steps:

1. From the Disk Management console, right-click a volume or partition. Choose Change Drive Letter And Paths from the shortcut menu. The Change Drive Letter And Paths dialog box opens.

2. Click Add to open the Add Drive Letter Or Path dialog box shown in Figure 11-21.

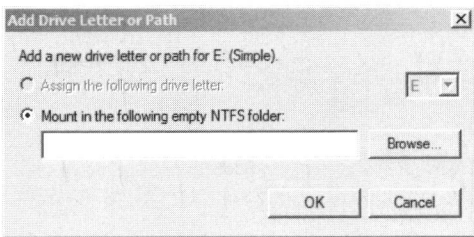

FIGURE 11-21 The Add Drive Letter Or Path dialog box used to mount a volume

3. You can type the mount point or click Browse to select or create a mount point. Any empty directory that resides on a nonremovable NTFS volume can be the mount point.

4. After you select or type the mount point, click OK, and the volume or partition is mounted.

IMPORTANT It's actually easy to get yourself into trouble with this new feature. Disk Management lets you make multiple levels of mounted volumes, including ones that are recursive. You're well advised to mount volumes only at the root level of a drive. Trying to mount below that point can lead to confusion and make management and documentation difficult. Also, verify with your backup vendor that mount points are fully supported by their application.

Summary

In this chapter, we covered the details of how to manage the hard disks on your Windows Small Business Server 2008 computer, and how to configure them for data integrity and redundancy. In the next chapter, we'll cover the configuration and management of file storage on your SBS server.

Storage Management

Even relatively small networks need a lot of storage, and as time passes and the network grows, the need for storage grows exponentially, not merely arithmetically. Fortunately, hard drives have become cheaper even as their storage capacity increases. Unfortunately, that circumstance often leads to attempts to manage storage requirements by simply buying more disks. Like many quick fixes, this can work for a while but leads to backup and archival complications and can end up making it even more difficult to manage the storage of your network.

With a bit of planning and a bit more implementation, you can keep your storage *manageable*.

Distributed File System (DFS)

Distributed File System (DFS) allows you to group shared folders located on different servers and present them to users as a virtual tree of folders known as a *namespace*. A namespace has many benefits, including increased availability of data, load sharing, and simplified data migration. DFS Replication allows administrators to replicate folders in a bandwidth-efficient manner using the remote differential compression (RDC) algorithm that replicates only the changed blocks within a file.

DFS Namespaces and DFS Replication are useful for the following purposes:

■ Organizing a large number of file shares scattered across multiple servers into a contiguous namespace so that users can find the files they need

■ Improving the availability and performance of file shares, especially in network environments with multiple sites, where DFS Namespaces can redirect users to the closest available server

■ "Caching" data at a branch office so that users can access files at a local file server, which then efficiently replicates with a central file server across a WAN connection

- Centralizing backup from branch offices by replicating all data from the branch office to a central server that is backed up regularly
- Keeping two or more file shares in sync over LAN or WAN links

NOTE You can use DFS to create a loosely coupled collaboration environment where DFS Replication replicates data between multiple servers. However, DFS Replication does not include the ability to check out files (as you'd check out books from a library) or replicate files that are in use, such as multi-user databases. Therefore, use Windows SharePoint Services in environments where users regularly attempt to edit the same file at the same time from different locations.

DFS Terminology

Much of the terminology in DFS is very specific to the DFS environment. Acquainting yourself with these terms will save a lot of confusion later.

- **Namespace** A namespace is a virtual view of shared folders. The folders can be in a variety of locations but appear to the user as a single tree.
- **Namespace server** A namespace server hosts a namespace. The namespace server can be a member server or a domain controller.
- **Namespace root** The namespace root is the shared folder that serves as the root for a particular namespace. Because DFS is a virtual file system, the namespace root can be any shared folder on an NTFS partition.
- **Folders** Folders in a DFS Namespace can provide structural depth to a hierarchy or can contain folder targets that map to shares.
- **Folder target** A folder target is the UNC path of a shared folder or another namespace that is associated with a folder in a namespace. The folder target is where data and content are stored.

NOTE Folders can contain folder targets or other folders, but not both at the same level in the hierarchy.

DFS clients automatically choose a folder target in their site, if available, reducing intersite network utilization. If more than one target is available on the client's site, each client randomly selects a target, spreading the load evenly across all available servers. If a target goes down, the client automatically picks a different target. (This process is called *client failover*.) When the original target comes back online, the client automatically switches back to the preferred target if the namespace server and the client support client failback. In this way, targets provide fault tolerance, load balancing, and site awareness. You can use DFS Replication to keep folder targets synchronized.

Namespace Type

There are two types of DFS Namespaces: standalone and domain-based. A standalone namespace (for example, \\srv1\public) stores all namespace information on the registry of the namespace server instead of in Active Directory. Any server running Windows 2000 Server or later can host a standalone namespace, regardless of whether the server belongs to a domain (though servers running Windows Server 2003 and Windows 2000 Server do not support all features of DFS Namespaces).

Standalone namespaces can host more folders (up to 50,000 folders with targets) than domain-based namespaces (which can hold up to 5,000 folders with targets), but the only way to provide redundancy for a standalone namespace root is to use a server cluster. You cannot use multiple namespace servers to host a standalone namespace as you can with a domain-based namespace.

However, you can replicate folders in a standalone namespace as long as all replication members belong to the same Active Directory forest as in a Windows SBS domain. Domain-based namespace roots (for example, \\example.local\public) differ from standalone namespace roots in a couple of ways. First, you must host domain-based namespace roots on a member server or domain controller of an Active Directory domain. Second, domain-based namespace roots automatically publish the DFS topology in Active Directory. This arrangement provides fault tolerance and network performance optimization by directing clients to the nearest target.

Choose a standalone namespace if the network does not use Active Directory or if the namespace contains more than 5,000 folders with targets. Otherwise, choose a domain-based namespace to use multiple namespace servers for redundancy and to take advantage of Active Directory for site-aware client referrals.

You can also combine the two. For example, you can create a domain-based namespace that includes a standalone root as a folder. Before creating namespaces, design the namespace hierarchy in a similar manner to the way you designed the domain structure for the organization.

Create a namespace structure that is logical, easy to use (for end users!), and matches the organization design, and then get the key stakeholders in the project to sign off on the design. Enlist some representative users from the organization to review the namespace design and provide feedback.

Namespace Server Requirements

The following servers can host multiple namespaces:

- Windows Server 2008 Enterprise
- Windows Server 2008 Datacenter
- Windows Server 2003 R2, Enterprise Edition
- Windows Server 2003 R2, Datacenter Edition

- Windows Server 2003, Enterprise Edition
- Windows Server 2003, Datacenter Edition

Servers running the following operating systems can host only a single namespace:

- Windows Server 2008 Standard
- Windows Server 2003 R2, Standard Edition
- Windows Server 2003, Web Edition
- Windows Server 2003, Standard Edition
- All versions of Windows 2000 Server

Namespace Client Requirements

To access the DFS folder structure, you need a DFS client. Users can access file shares that are part of a DFS Namespace without a DFS client; however, the user does not benefit from any of the DFS features, such as hierarchical namespaces, multiple folder targets, and site-aware client referrals.

The following operating systems include full support for DFS Namespaces, including support for client failback to the preferred folder target:

- Windows Server 2008
- Windows Vista Business, Windows Vista Enterprise, Windows Vista Ultimate
- Windows Server 2003 R2
- Windows Storage Server 2003 R2
- Windows Server 2003 with SP2, or SP1 and the Windows Server 2003 client failback hotfix
- Windows XP Professional with SP3, or SP2 and the Windows XP client failback hotfix

The client failback hotfixes are described in Microsoft Knowledge Base article 898900 at *http://support.microsoft.com/kb/898900*.

Users who are running the following operating systems can access namespaces, but if a folder target becomes unavailable and then later comes back online, the computer will not fail back (return) to the preferred folder target:

- Windows Storage Server 2003
- Windows XP Professional
- Windows Preinstallation Environment (Windows PE) (Windows PE can access stand-alone namespaces, but it cannot access domain-based namespaces.)
- Windows 2000 Server
- Windows 2000 Professional
- Windows NT Server 4.0 with Service Pack 6a
- Windows NT Workstation 4.0 with Service Pack 6a

To use DFS to best advantage, clients with the ability to fail back are preferred.

DFS Replication

Before deploying DFS Replication, verify that all the following tasks have been done:

- Extend (or update) the Active Directory Domain Services (AD DS) schema to include Windows Server 2003 R2 or Windows Server 2008 schema additions.

> **NOTE** For information about extending the AD DS schema, see *http://technet.microsoft.com/en-us/magazine/cc462798.aspx?pr=blog.*

- Install the File Services role with the DFS Replication role service on all servers that will act as members of a replication group.
- Ensure that all members of the replication group are running Windows Server 2008 or Windows Server 2003 R2.
- Install DFS Management on a server to manage replication.
- Store replicated folders on NTFS volumes.
- Verify that your antivirus software is compatible with DFS Replication.

File Replication Service

File Replication Service (FRS), introduced in Windows Server 2000, replicates files and folders that are stored in DFS folders or in the SYSVOL folder on domain controllers. FRS in Windows Server 2008 is an optional role service of the File Services server role that allows replication of content with other servers that use FRS instead of DFS Replication.

DFS Replication replaces FRS for replication of DFS folders on servers running Windows Server 2003 R2 or Windows Server 2008. In domains that use the Windows Server 2008 domain functional level, DFS Replication replaces FRS for the SYSVOL folder as well.

Neither DFS Replication nor FRS support file support checkout or merging. If two or more users modify the same file simultaneously on different servers, DFS Replication uses a conflict-resolution method of last writer wins for files that are in conflict (that is, a file that is updated at multiple servers simultaneously) and earliest creator wins for name conflicts. DFS Replication moves the other copies to a conflict folder on the losing server but does not replicate this folder by default, unlike FRS, so the folder remains on the local server. To avoid conflicts, use Windows SharePoint Services when users in multiple locations need to collaborate on the same files at the same time. (Windows SharePoint Services allows users to check out files.)

DFS Replication, like FRS, is a multimaster replication engine that detects changes in a file by monitoring the update sequence number (USN) journal and replicating the changed file when the file is closed. Unlike FRS, DFS Replication uses a version vector exchange protocol to determine what parts of the file are different and then uses the RDC protocol to replicate only changed blocks of files larger than 64 kilobytes (KB). This makes DFS Replication much more efficient at replication than FRS, which is particularly important when replicating with servers across a WAN link. DFS Replication does not replicate files that make use of EFS encryption.

Replication Topologies

DFS Replication can make use of several of topologies: hub and spoke, full mesh, and custom. These topologies are familiar to most network administrators, but here is a quick review:

- **Hub and spoke** This topology is also known as a *star topology*. Each server replicates with a central server, minimizing the use of WAN links. This topology is similar to an Ethernet network, which uses a hub or switch as the center of the network. Choose this topology to reduce network usage when the replication group has more than 10 members, or when members of the replication group are in a site connected via a WAN connection.

- **Full mesh** All servers replicate with all other servers. Choose this topology when the replication group has fewer than 10 servers and all links have low enough costs (performance or monetary) to allow each server to replicate with every other server. The full mesh topology minimizes the time it takes to propagate changes to all members of the replication group and increases reliability by replicating with all members of the replication group, but it also increases network traffic from replication.

- **Custom** This topology allows you to manually specify replication connections.

Installing DFS Management

To manage a DFS Namespace and DFS Replication, you must first install DFS Management.

Select Server Manager from the Administrative Tools menu and install the File Services role on the server. Then follow these steps:

1. In Server Manager, expand the Roles node, right-click File Services, and then select Add Role Services (Figure 12-1).

2. Select Distributed File System, as shown in Figure 12-2, and then click Next.

3. On the Create A DFS Namespace page, select Create A Namespace Now and provide a name. Alternatively, you can choose to create the namespace later. Click Next.

4. On the Select Namespace Type page, select Domain-based Namespace and click Next.

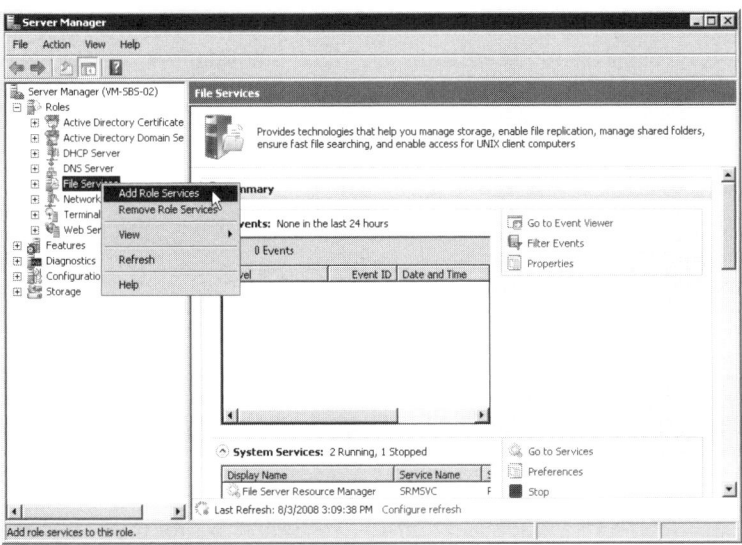

FIGURE 12-1 Adding role services

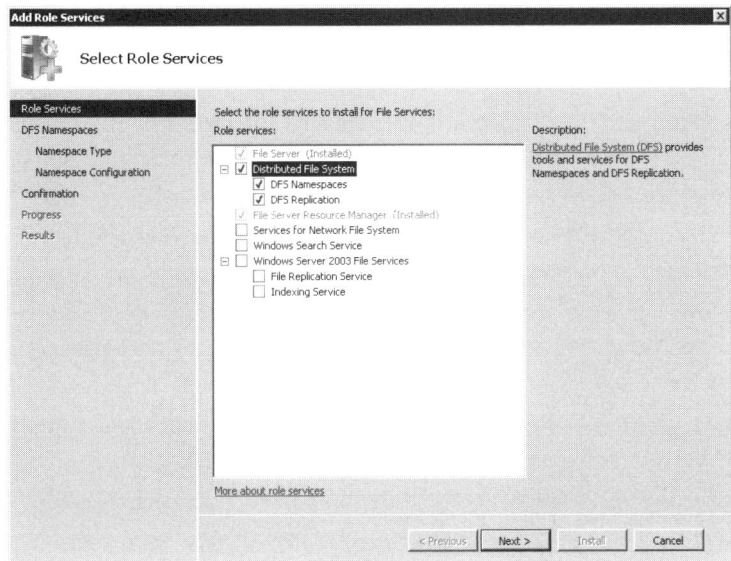

FIGURE 12-2 Selecting the file services to install

5. On the Configure Namespace page, click Add to add folders to the namespace. In this process, shown in Figure 12-3, you can browse for folder targets and place the targets in the folders you choose. Click OK.

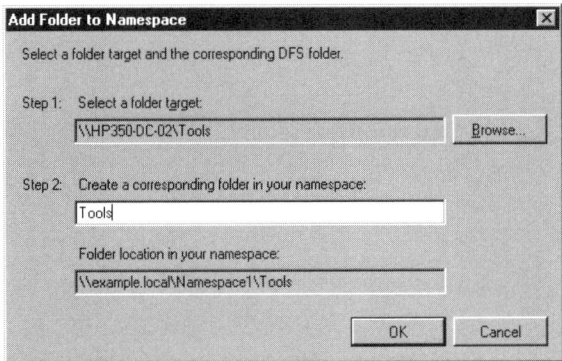

FIGURE 12-3 Adding a folder to the namespace

6. When you have finished adding shares to the namespace, click Next.

7. Review the selections and click Install.

Creating or Opening a Namespace Root

The first step in working with DFS Namespaces is to create a namespace or open an existing namespace root. If you created a namespace root when installing DFS Management, you can use this procedure to open it; otherwise, follow these steps to create one:

1. Launch DFS Management from the Administrative Tools folder. Navigate to DFS Management and then to Namespaces node.

2. To open an existing namespace root, right-click Namespaces and choose Add Namespace To Display. To create a new namespace root, right-click Namespaces and choose New Namespace. The New Namespace Wizard appears.

3. On the Namespace Server page, type the name of the server that you want to host the namespace root and then click Next. If the DFS service is disabled, click Yes in the Warning dialog box to start the DFS service and set its start-up setting to Automatic.

4. On the Namespace Name And Settings page, type the name to use for the namespace root. This name appears as the share name to users—for example, \\example.local\ public. The New Namespace Wizard creates the namespace root in the %SYSTEM-DRIVE%:\DFSRoots\name folder and gives all users read-only permissions. To change these settings, click Edit Settings. Click Next.

5. On the Namespace Type page (shown in Figure 12-4), choose whether to create a domain-based namespace or a standalone namespace and then click Next.

   ■ Select Domain-Based Namespace to store the namespace on multiple servers in Active Directory. An example of a domain-based namespace is \\example.local\public.

- Select Stand-Alone Namespace to create the namespace on a single server or server cluster. An example of a standalone namespace is \\srv1\public.

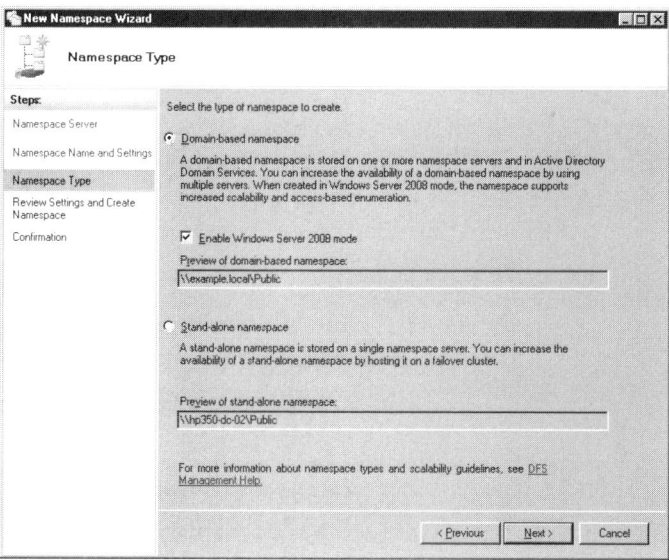

FIGURE 12-4 Choosing the namespace type

6. On the Review Settings And Create Namespace page, click Create. The New Namespace Wizard creates the namespace root. Correct any errors using the Previous button and then click Close.

Creating a Namespace from a Command Prompt

To create a namespace from a command prompt, use the `Dfsutil /Addftroot` or `Dfsutil /Addstdroot` commands. For example, to create the same namespace shown in Figure 12-4, follow these steps:

1. Open the command window. Start the DFS service and set the start-up type to Automatic if it is not already by typing the following commands:

```
Sc Start Dfs
Sc Config Dfs Start= Auto
```

2. Create a folder and file share for the namespace root by typing the following commands:

```
Md E:\Public
Net Share Public=E:\Public
```

3. Create the domain-based namespace root by typing the following command:

```
Dfsutil /Addftroot /Server:Srv1 /Share:Public
```

Adding Namespace Servers

The namespace root is the most important part of the namespace. Without it, clients cannot access any DFS folders. Because of this, the first step in creating a more fault-tolerant namespace is to add namespace servers to the namespace root. If possible, add at least one namespace server on each site where users need access to the DFS Namespace by following these steps:

1. In the DFS Management console, navigate to Namespaces, right-click the domain-based namespace root you want to replicate, and then choose Add Namespace Server.

2. In the Add Namespace Server dialog box, type the path to the namespace server and then click OK. Windows creates the namespace root on the target server in the %SYSTEMDRIVE%:\DFSRoots*name* folder and gives all users read-only permissions. To change these settings, click Edit Settings.

3. If the DFS service is disabled, click Yes in the Warning dialog box to start the DFS service and set its start-up setting to Automatic.

4. To add a namespace server to a namespace from a command prompt, create the appropriate shared folder, verify that the DFS service is started and the start-up type is set to Automatic, and then use the Dfsutil /Addftroot command. For example, open a command window and then type **Dfsutil /Addftroot /Server:Srv2/Share:Public**.

Adding DFS Folders

DFS folders allow users to navigate from the namespace root to other file shares on the network without leaving the DFS Namespace structure. To create a DFS folder, follow these steps:

1. Right-click the namespace root to which you want to add a folder and then choose New Folder. This displays the New Folder dialog box, shown in Figure 12-5.

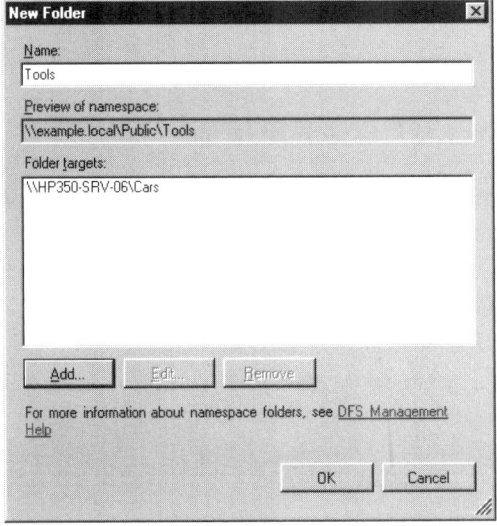

FIGURE 12-5 Creating a new folder

2. Type a name for the folder in the Name box. To create a folder that contains other DFS folders, click OK without adding any target folders. This creates a layer of structure to the namespace.

3. To add target folders, click Add and then type the shared folder's UNC or DNS path, or click Browse to browse to the shared folder.

4. Add any additional folder targets and then click OK.

If you added multiple folder targets, click Yes in the Replication dialog box to create a replication group for the folder targets, or click No to set up a replication group later (or not at all). If you click Yes, the Replicate Folder Wizard appears with some settings already entered. For more information, see the section titled "Creating a Replication Group" later in this chapter.

To create a DFS folder from a command prompt, create the appropriate file shares and then use the Dfscmd /Map command. (You cannot add DFS folders without folder targets from a command prompt.) For example, open the command window and then type the following commands:

```
Dfscmd /Map \\Example.local\Public\Software \\Dc1\Software
Dfscmd /Add \\Example.local\Public\Software \\Srv2\Software
```

> **NOTE** To publish a DFS folder or namespace root in Active Directory so that users can find the folder or namespace when searching Active Directory for shared folders, right-click the appropriate container in the Active Directory Users And Computers console, choose New, choose Shared Folder, and then type the path of the namespace or DFS folder in the Network Path box.

Changing Advanced Settings

The default settings for DFS Management are appropriate for most installations, but if you need to change advanced namespace settings such as the referral order, change how namespace servers poll domain controllers for DFS metadata, or delegate DFS management permissions, use the information in the following sections.

Changing Namespace Referral Settings

To change the cache duration, the order in which domain controllers or namespace servers refer clients to namespace servers and folder targets, or the failback settings for an entire namespace, right-click a namespace root or folder, choose Properties, and click the Referrals tab (Figure 12-6).

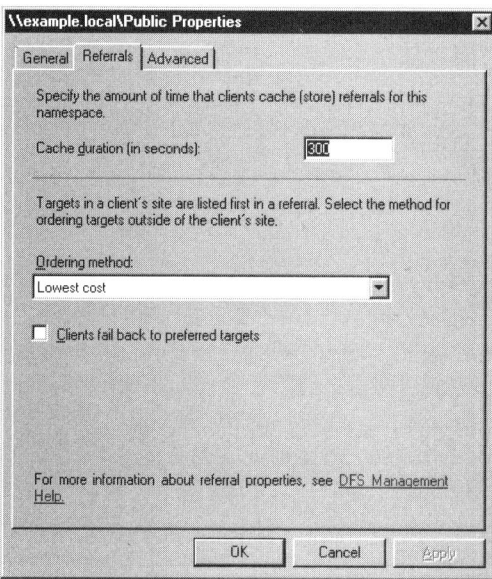

FIGURE 12-6 The Referrals tab of a namespace Properties dialog box

Use the following list to complete the process:

- In the Cache Duration box, specify how long clients should cache referrals before poll-ing the domain controller or namespace server for a new referral.

- In the Ordering Method drop-down box, choose how domain controllers and namespace servers should refer clients to folder targets and namespace servers.

- Select the Clients Fail Back To Preferred Targets option to force a client to switch back to using its preferred server when it comes back online.

The preferred server is based on site and any custom referral ordering settings you specify on folder targets. This setting is supported by clients running Windows XP with Service Pack 2 and the post-SP2 Windows XP client failback hotfix, Windows Server 2003 with Service Pack 1 and the Windows Server 2003 client failback hotfix, and Windows Server 2003 R2. See Knowl-edge Base article 898900 at *http://support.microsoft.com/kb/898900/* for information on how to obtain this hotfix.

Overriding Referral Settings on Individual Folders

DFS folders inherit referral settings from the namespace root unless you specifically override them. To override the referral settings for a folder, right-click the appropriate folder, choose Properties, click the Referrals tab, and then specify the settings you want to override.

To explicitly set a single folder target as the preferred target or set the folder target as a target of last resort, right-click the folder target, choose Properties, click the Advanced tab, select the Override Referral Ordering check box, and then specify the priority for the target folder.

Delegating Management Permissions

DFS Management sets the permissions on the namespace object in Active Directory or in the registry of the namespace server (when using a standalone namespace). To change the ability of users to perform common management tasks, use the following list:

- **Create and manage namespaces** To view, add, or remove groups who can manage namespaces, right-click the Namespaces node, choose Delegate Management Permissions, and then use the Delegate Management Permissions dialog box.

- **Manage individual namespaces and replication groups** To view groups that can manage a namespace or replication group, select the namespace or replication group and then click the Delegation tab. To remove management permissions for a group, right-click the group and choose Remove. To give management permissions for the namespace to a group, right-click the namespace, choose Delegate Management Permission, type the name of the group in the Select Users Or Groups dialog box, and then click OK.

- **Create and manage replication groups** To view, add, or remove groups that can manage replication, right-click the Replication node, choose Delegate Management Permissions, and then use the Delegate Management Permissions dialog box.

Changing Namespace Polling Settings

To change how namespace servers poll domain controllers for the latest namespace metadata in a domain-based namespace, right-click the appropriate namespace, choose Properties, click the Advanced tab, and then choose one of the following polling methods:

- **Optimize For Consistency** Polls the primary domain controller (PDC) emulator for new namespace polls data every hour and after each change to the namespace. Use this setting when the network contains 16 or fewer namespace servers to minimize the time it takes to propagate namespace changes to all namespace servers. This is the default setting.

- **Optimize For Scalability** Polls the nearest domain controller every hour for changes to the namespace. Use this setting when the network contains more than 16 namespace servers to reduce the load on the PDC emulator. However, choosing this setting increases the amount of time it takes to propagate namespace changes to all namespace servers. Servers running Windows 2000 Server do not support this setting and continue to use the Optimize For Consistency polling method.

To enable the Optimize For Scalability polling method from a command prompt, use the Dfsutil /Rootscalability command. For example, open the command window, change to the directory in which you placed the Dfsutil.exe file, and then type:

Dfsutil/Root:Example.local\Public/Rootscalability/Enable.

Backing Up and Restoring the DFS Folder Targets

The DFS Namespaces database for domain-based DFS is stored in Active Directory, and you can back it up and restore it using Active Directory–aware backup methods. To back up the listing of folder targets for a standalone namespace root, type the following text at a command prompt (replacing *ServerName* and *Namespace* with the name of the appropriate server name and namespace root):

DFScmd /View *ServerName**Namespace*/Batch >DFS_backup.bat

To restore this DFS structure, re-create the DFS Namespace and then run the batch file you created.

> **NOTE** In addition to backing up the DFS topology, back up the contents of the actual file shares routinely. Always test the backup before relying on it. You can use the `Dfsradmin Replicationgroup` command to export DFS Replication settings such as replication group members and connections.

Using DFS Replication

An easy-to-use, fault-tolerant, and high-performance file system is not worth much if the data you want to access is unavailable or out of date. To ensure that files are available to users even if a server goes down, create additional folder targets (as described earlier in this chapter) and use DFS Replication to keep the folder targets in sync. You can also use DFS Replication to synchronize folders that are not part of a DFS Namespace—for example, to replicate data from a branch office to a server in the main office that you back up regularly and reliably.

Creating a Replication Group

A *replication group* is defined as two or more servers that participate in replication. Replication groups define the replication topology used by members for replication. To create a replication group, follow these steps:

1. Click Start, point to Administrative Tools, and then click DFS Management.

2. In the console tree, right-click the Replication node and then click New Replication Group.

3. Follow the instructions in the New Replication Group Wizard.

 UNDER THE HOOD **Conflict Resolution During the Initial Replication**

f other members of the replication group have data in the replicated folders, Windows takes the following actions during the initial replication:

■ If an identical file already exists on the target server (any server other than the primary member), the primary member does not replicate the file.

- If a file already exists on a target server but the file is not identical to the version on the primary member, Windows moves the file on the target server to the local conflict folder and then replicates the primary member's version of the file, even if this file is older than the version on the target server.

- If a file exists on a target server that is not present on the primary member, Windows does not replicate it during the initial replication but does replicate it during subsequent replications to other members, including the primary member.

After the initial replication, the primary member role goes away and replication is multiple-master-based. Do not delete, rename, or move files on the primary member or any member that has already replicated until the first replication is complete. (Look for Event 4104 in the DFS Replication log.) Deleting, renaming, or moving files before the first replication is complete can cause the files to reappear if they existed on a target that had not yet replicated.

Replicating a DFS Folder

To create a replicated folder in a new replication group that replicates a DFS folder, use the following steps:

1. Right-click the appropriate folder under the Namespaces node of DFS Management, and choose Replicate Folder. The Replicate Folder Wizard appears.

2. On the Replication Group And Replicated Folder Name page, confirm the name for the replication group and for the replicated folder. (The name for the replication group must be unique on the domain. To add to an existing replication group, use the instructions in the following sections.)

3. On the Replication Eligibility page, review the target folders that will be replicated. Click Next.

4. On the Primary Member page, select the server that holds the data that you want to use as the seed for the initial replication.

5. On the Topology Selection page, select one of the following replication topologies:

   - **Hub And Spoke**   Spoke servers replicate with one or two central hub servers. Hub servers replicate with all other hub servers by using the full mesh topology, as well as with designated spoke servers. Choose this topology in large network environments and environments with multiple branch offices. This topology requires a minimum of three members.

   - **Full Mesh**   All servers replicate with all other servers. Choose this topology when there are fewer than 10 servers in the replication group and all links have low enough costs (performance or monetary) to allow each server to replicate with every other server instead of a central hub server.

- **No Topology**   This option does not specify a topology and postpones replication until you specify a replication topology manually. To specify a replication topology after creating the replication group, right-click the replication group in the DFS Management snap-in and then choose New Topology.

6. On the Hub Members page that appears if you chose the Hub And Spoke topology, specify the hub servers.

7. On the Hub And Spoke Connections page that appears if you chose the Hub And Spoke topology, verify that the wizard lists the proper spoke servers. To change the required hub server with which a spoke member replicates preferentially, or the optional hub member with which a spoke member replicates if the required hub member is unavailable, select the spoke server, click Edit and then specify the required hub and the optional hub.

8. On the Replication Group Schedule And Bandwidth page, choose when to replicate and the maximum amount of bandwidth you want DFS Replication to use.

9. To create a custom schedule, choose Replicate During The Specified Days And Times and then click Edit Schedule. You can create a custom schedule that uses Coordinated Universal Time (UTC) or the local time of the receiving server.

10. On the Review Settings And Create Replication Group page, review the settings and then click Create. Review for errors and then click Close. Windows then replicates topology and replication settings to all domain controllers. A replication group member polls its nearest domain controller regularly. (By default, replication group members perform a lightweight poll every five minutes for Subscription objects under the local computer container and a full poll every hour.) It receives the settings after Windows updates the domain controller. To change the replication polling interval, use the Dfsrdiag command.

Creating a Branch Office Replication Group

To create a replication group that replicates a single branch server with a single hub server, use the following steps:

1. In the DFS Management snap-in, right-click Replication and choose New Replication Group. The New Replication Group Wizard appears.

> **NOTE**   Creating replicated folders within an existing replication group is faster than creating a new replication group for each replicated folder, because the replication group automatically applies its schedule, topology, and bandwidth-throttling settings to the new replicated folder.

2. On the Replication Group Type page, choose Replication Group For Data Collection.

3. On the Name And Domain page, type a name for the replication group that is unique on the domain, specify in which domain to host the replication group, and optionally type a description of the replication group.

4. On the Branch Server page, type the name of the branch server that holds the data that you want to replicate with the hub server.

5. On the Replicated Folders page, click Add and then use the Add Folder To Replicate dialog box to specify the local folder on the branch server to replicate with the hub server. Click OK when you are finished.

6. On the Hub Server page that appears if you chose Replication Group For Data Collection on the Replication Group Type page, type the name of the hub server that serves as a replication target for the replicated folders.

7. On the Target Folder On Hub Server page, specify the local folder on the hub server in which you want to place replicated data from the branch server. This folder is usually located in a folder or volume that you back up regularly.

8. On the Replication Group Schedule And Bandwidth page, choose when to replicate and the maximum amount of bandwidth you want to allow DFS Replication to use. To create a custom schedule, choose Replicate During The Specified Days And Times and then click Edit Schedule. You can create a custom schedule that uses Coordinated Universal Time (UTC) or the local time of the receiving server.

9. On the Review Settings And Create Replication Group page, review the settings, and then click Create. Review for errors and then click Close.

Windows then replicates topology and replication settings to all domain controllers. A replication group member polls its nearest domain controller regularly. (By default, replication group members perform a lightweight poll every five minutes for Subscription objects under the local computer container and a full poll every hour.) It receives the settings after Windows updates the domain controller. To change the replication polling interval, use the Dfsrdiag command.

Creating a Multipurpose Replication Group

To create a replication group that replicates any number of servers with any number of other servers, use the following steps:

1. In the DFS Management snap-in, right-click Replication and choose New Replication Group. The New Replication Group Wizard starts.

2. On the Replication Group Type page, choose Multipurpose Replication Group.

3. On the Name And Domain page, type a name for the replication group that is unique on the domain, specify in which domain to host the replication group, and optionally type a description of the replication group.

4. On the Replication Group Members page, add the servers on which you want to replicate content.

5. On the Topology Selection page, choose a replication technology.

6. On the Hub Members page that appears if you chose the Hub And Spoke topology, specify the hub servers.

7. On the Hub And Spoke Connections page that appears if you chose the Hub And Spoke topology, verify that the wizard lists the proper spoke servers. To change the required hub server with which a spoke member replicates preferentially, or the optional hub member with which a spoke member replicates if the required hub member is unavailable, select the spoke server, click Edit, and then specify the required hub and the optional hub.

8. On the Replication Group Schedule And Bandwidth page, choose when to replicate and the maximum amount of bandwidth you want to allow DFS Replication to use. To create a custom schedule, choose Replicate During The Specified Days And Times and then click Edit Schedule. You can create a custom schedule that uses Coordinated Universal Time (UTC) or the local time of the receiving server.

9. On the Primary Member page, select the server that holds the data that you want to use as the seed for the initial replication.

10. On the Folders To Replicate page, click Add and then use the Add Folder To Replicate dialog box to specify the folder to replicate. Click OK when you are finished.

11. On the Local Path Of *Folder* On Other Members page, select a replication member that you want to participate in replication of the specified folder, click Edit, and then use the Edit Local Path dialog box to enable replication and specify the local folder on the target server in which to place replicated data from the hub server. Repeat this step for every replicated folder you specify in the Replicated Folders page.

12. On the Review Settings And Create Replication Group page, review the settings and then click Create. Review for errors and then click Close.

Windows then replicates topology and replication settings to all domain controllers. A replication group member polls its nearest domain controller regularly. (By default, replication group members perform a lightweight poll every five minutes for Subscription objects under the local computer container and a full poll every hour.) It receives the settings after Windows updates the domain controller. To change the replication polling interval, use the Dfsrdiag command.

Managing Replication Groups

Select a replication group and then use the Memberships, Connections, Replicated Folders, and Delegation tabs of the DFS Management console to manage the replication group, as discussed in the following list.

NOTE Click a column heading to change how Windows groups items in the view. To add or remove columns, right-click the column heading and choose Add/Remove Columns.

Use the following options on the Memberships tab to view and manage the member servers for each replicated folder:

- To disable a member of the replication group, right-click the member and then choose Disable. Disable members that do not need to replicate a specific replicated folder. Do not disable members temporarily and then enable them—doing so causes roughly one kilobyte of replication traffic per file in the replicated folder, and overwrites all changes on the disabled member. (See the Under the Hood sidebar titled "Conflict Resolution During the Initial Replication" earlier in this chapter for more information.)

- To delete a member of the replication group, right-click it and then choose Delete.

- To add a member server that participates in replication, right-click the replication group in the DFS Management console, choose New Member, and then use the New Member Wizard to specify the local path of the replicated folders, connections, and schedule.

- To change the size of the conflict or staging folders or to disable the retention of deleted files, right-click the member, choose Properties, click the Advanced tab, and then use the Quota boxes. The conflict folder stores the "losing" files that Windows deletes when it encounters two versions of the same file during replication as well as the most recently deleted files in the replicated folder, and the staging folder queues replication data.

> **NOTE** The default size of the staging folder is 4,096 megabytes (MB), but by increasing the size of the staging folder, you can increase the performance of replication group members that replicate with a large number of replication partners or that contain large files that change often. Look for event ID 4208 in the DFS Replication event log; if this event appears multiple times in an hour, increase the staging folder size 20 percent until the event no longer appears frequently.

- To create a report showing the replication health as well as RDC efficiency, right-click the replication group, choose Create Diagnostic Report, and then use the Diagnostic Report Wizard to create the report.

- To verify the replication topology, right-click the replication group and then choose Verify Topology.

On the Connections tab, view and manage all replication connections. To add a new replication connection between two members of a replication group, right-click the replication group and choose New Connection. Then use the New Connection dialog box to specify the sending member, the receiving member, the schedule, and whether to create a one-way replication connection or a two-way connection.

Use the following options on the Replicated Folders tab to view and manage all replicated folders:

- To add a new replicated folder to the replication group, right-click the replication group in the DFS Management console, choose New Replicated Folder, and then use the New Replicated Folder Wizard to specify the primary member and the local folders to replicate.

- To omit certain file types or subfolders from replication, click the Replicated Folders tab, right-click the replicated folder, choose Properties, and then use the File Filter and Subfolder Filter boxes on the General tab.

- To share a replicated folder on the network and optionally add the folder to a DFS Namespace, right-click the replicated folder, choose Share And Publish In Namespace, and then use the Share Or Publish Replicated Folder Wizard.

> **NOTE** RDC increases processor utilization on the server, so you might want to disable it on servers with slow processors or high-speed links, and in environments that replicate only new content or files smaller than 64 KB. To disable RDC on a connection, click the Connections tab, right-click the member, choose Properties, and then clear the Use Remote Differential Compression (RDC) check box. You can also change the minimum file size that RDC engages from the 64-KB default size by using the Dfsradmin ConnectionSet command. Monitor RDC statistics and CPU utilization before and after disabling RDC to verify that you reduce processor utilization enough to warrant the increased network traffic.

On the Delegation tab, view and manage administrative permissions. See the section titled "Delegating Management Permissions" earlier in this chapter for information about the Delegation tab.

> **NOTE** To change the replication polling interval, which controls how often a server checks for updated files, use the Dfsrdiag command.

Using File Server Resource Manager

The File Server Resource Manager (FSRM) is installed as a role service of the File Services Role and is made up of three tools:

- Storage Reports Management
- Quota Management
- File Screening Management

These tools allow administrators of Windows Server 2008 file servers to keep track of storage growth and usage, as well as create hard or soft policies limiting the amount and type of files that users can save in specific folders.

> **NOTE** In the SBS Console you can set the size of individual users' shared folders. Other quotas you might want to set would be on public folders or central company resource folders.

Scheduling Storage Reports

FSRM supports reporting in Dynamic Hypertext Markup Language (DHTML), HTML, Extended Markup Language (XML), Comma-Separated Values (CSV) text, or plain text, making it easy to view reports or process them using scripts, Microsoft Office Excel, or other applications.

FSRM can search and report on the following files and events. Additional reports can be defined and included in the list.

- Duplicate files
- File screening audit
- Files by file group
- Files by owner
- Large files
- Least-recently accessed files
- Most-recently accessed files
- Quota usage

File Server Resource Manager is automatically installed when you install Windows SBS Server 2008. To use it, you need only open Server Manager from the Administrative Tools menu and then follow these steps:

1. In the left pane, expand Roles, then File Services, then Share And Storage Management, and then File Server Resource Manager.

2. Right-click Storage Reports Management and select Schedule A New Report Task (Figure 12-7).

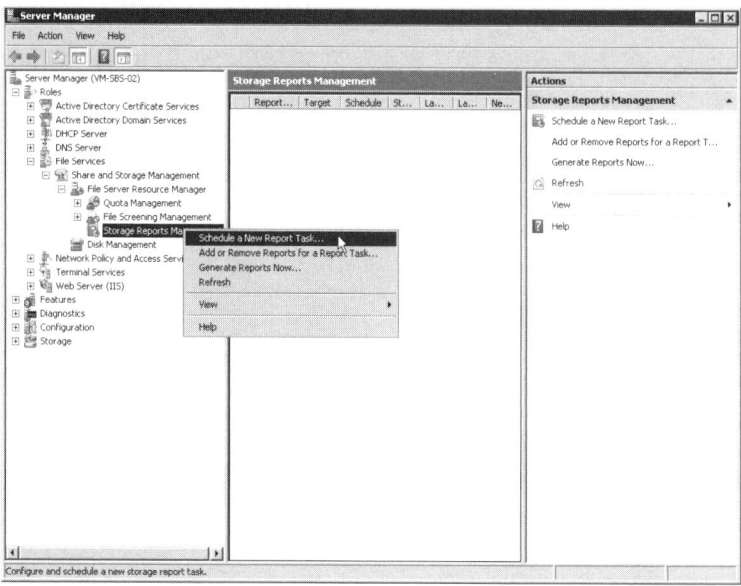

FIGURE 12-7 Starting a new report

3. The Storage Reports Task Properties dialog box opens (Figure 12-8).

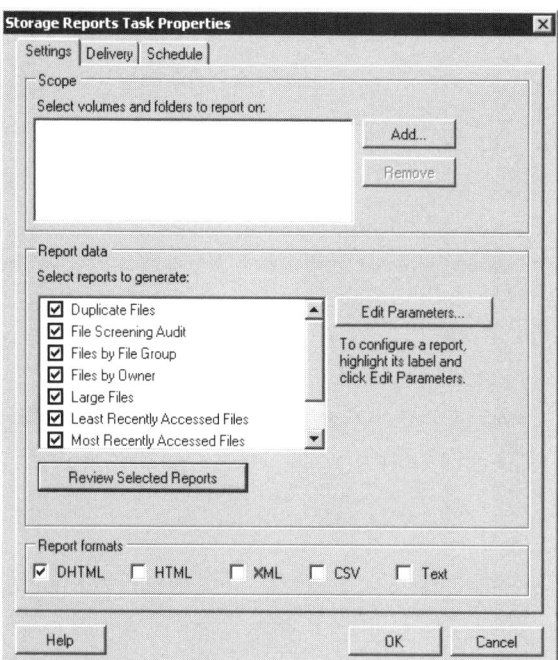

FIGURE 12-8 Configuring a storage report

4. In the Scope section of the dialog box, click Add to select the local folders that you want to monitor.

5. In the Report Data section of the dialog box, select the reports that you want to generate. To view the settings for all selected reports, click Review Selected Reports. To adjust the settings for a report, select the report and then click Edit Parameters.

6. In the Report Formats section of the dialog box, select the formats in which you want to generate the reports.

7. Click the Delivery tab, select the Send Reports To The Following Administrators check box, and type the e-mail addresses of the administrators who should receive the storage reports, using a semicolon to separate addresses.

8. Click the Schedule tab and then click Create Schedule. In the Schedule dialog box (Figure 12-9), set the date and time for the report to be generated.

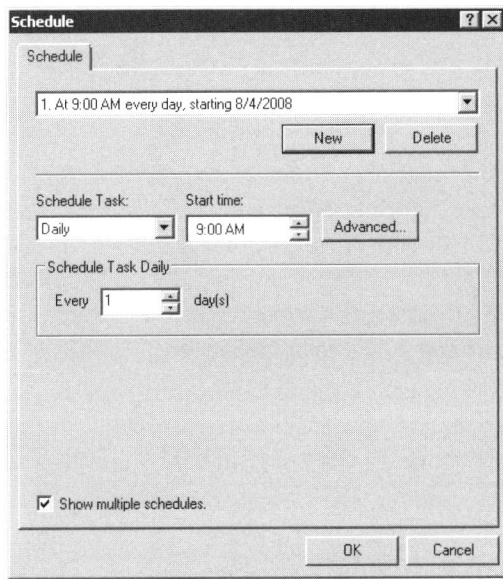

FIGURE 12-9 Setting a report schedule

9. When all three tab selections are made, click OK. The new scheduled report task appears in the File Server Resource Manager console.

To run the scheduled report immediately, right-click it and choose Run Report Task Now. The Generate Storage Reports dialog box appears, asking whether you want to view the reports immediately, or whether File Server Resource Manager should generate the reports in the background for viewing later from the report storage folder.

UNDER THE HOOD   Storage Reports and Performance

To create a storage report, Windows creates a Scheduled Task in the Task Scheduler library that uses the Volume Shadow Copy Service to take a snapshot of the specified storage volumes and then creates the storage report from this snapshot using XML style sheets stored in the %WINDIR%\system32\srm\xslt folder. This process minimizes the performance impact on the server, but it does degrade file server performance temporarily.

Schedule your storage reports during off-peak times to minimize the impact on users and combine reports whenever possible. Because all storage reports in a storage report task use the same snapshot, you can minimize the performance impact on a server by consolidating your reports to minimize the number of snapshots required.

Using Directory Quotas

One way to slow the growth of storage on a network is to limit the amount of disk space each user can utilize on a server. Windows Server 2008 provides two ways of doing this—disk quotas and directory quotas. Directory quotas allow you to manage storage at a folder level. You can create quota templates and auto quotas that Windows automatically applies to subfolders and newly created folders. Directory quotas, unlike disk quotas, look at the actual amount of disk space used by a file and provide powerful notification capabilities.

Directory quotas apply to all users as a group; disk quotas apply to individual users. Both directory quotas and disk quotas apply to a single server. Quotas can use either hard limits, which prevent users from exceeding their quotas, or soft limits, which only provide a warning and notification.

> **NOTE**   Directory quotas are preferred in Windows SBS 2008. If you choose to use disk quotas, you can set them by opening a disk's Properties dialog box and clicking the Quota tab.

Directory Quota Types

Directory quotas come in three varieties:

- **Quotas**   Sets the total amount of disk space that a folder and all subfolders can consume. For example, if you create a quota that limits the \Users folder to 10 gigabytes (GB), the total contents of this folder and all subfolders cannot exceed 10 GB in size. If one user uses 9 GB of file space, all the other users combined are limited to 1 GB.

- **Auto Quotas** Sets the amount of disk space that the first level subfolders (child folders) of a folder can consume. For example, if you create an auto quota for the \Users folder and set the limit at 2 GB, each first level of subfolder (for example, \Users\Charlie; \Users\Wally) is limited to 2 GB in size. An auto quota does not set a limit on the contents of the parent folder, only the subfolders (child folders).
- **Quota Templates** Standardizes and centralizes quota and auto quota settings. When you change the settings of a quota template, you can automatically apply the changes to all quotas that use the quota template you change.

NOTE Directory quotas work only on fixed NTFS volumes; you cannot use directory quotas on removable drives or FAT volumes.

Creating Quotas and Auto Quotas

To create a quota or auto quotas, follow these steps. To create a quota template, see the section titled "Creating and Editing Quota Templates" later in this chapter.

1. In the File Server Resource Manager, expand Quota Management.
2. Right-click Quotas in the console tree and choose Create Quota.
3. The Create Quota dialog box opens, as shown in Figure 12-10.

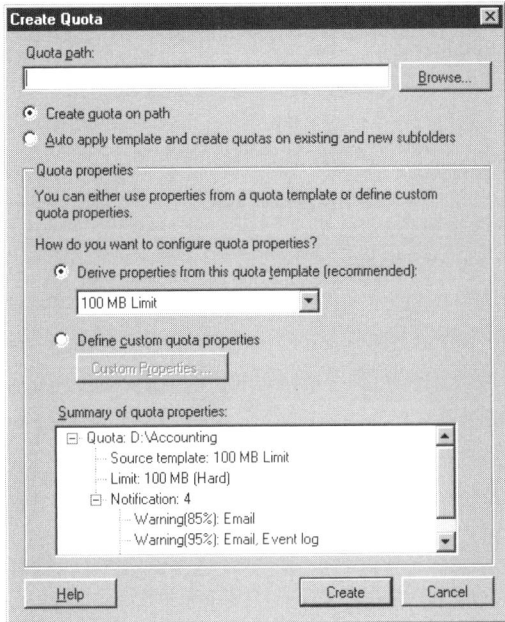

FIGURE 12-10 Creating a quota

4. Click Browse, select the folder to which you want to apply a quota, and then click OK.

5. To create a quota that limits the size of a folder, including all subfolders, select the Create Quota On Path option. To create an auto quota, which limits the size of subfolders individually (useful for setting quotas on the \Users folder), select the Auto Apply Template And Create Quotas On Existing And New Subfolders option.

6. Select the quota template you want to apply or choose Define Custom Quota Properties and click Custom Properties to create a custom quota. (You cannot create custom quotas for auto quotas.) Click Create when you are finished.

7. If you chose to create a custom quota, the Save Custom Properties As A Template dialog box appears. Use this dialog box to save the custom quota as a quota template or choose Save The Custom Quota Without Creating A Template.

8. To create a directory auto quota from a command prompt, use the Dirquota Quota Add command. For example, open a command window and then type the following command:

```
Dirquota AutoQuota Add /Path:E:\Users /SourceTemplate:"200 MB Limit Reports
To User" /Remote:Srv1
```

NOTE Use quota templates instead of custom quotas whenever possible. A quota template allows you to make changes to the template that apply to all quotas derived from the template. For example, to change the administrator e-mail address for all quotas on a server, edit the appropriate quota templates and then apply these changes to all quotas. This eliminates the need to manually update each quota.

Viewing and Managing Quotas

To view the particulars of a quota, highlight that quota in the File Server Resource Manager and view the details in the lower pane as shown in Figure 12-11.

Use the guidelines described in the following sections for additional quota management.

- To filter the display by quota type or path, click the Filter hyperlink and then use the Quota Filter dialog box.

- To disable a quota, right-click the quota and select Disable Quotas. To enable a quota, right-click and select Enable Quotas.

- To reset the peak usage data, select the quota, right-click, and select Reset Peak Usage.

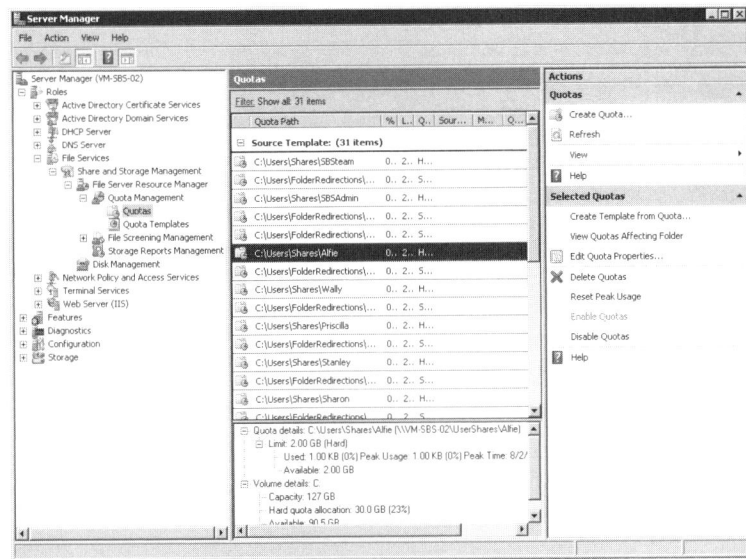

FIGURE 12-11 Viewing the details of an individual quota

Creating and Editing Quota Templates

Quota templates enable you to quickly apply standardized quota settings, as well as simultaneously update all quotas that make use of a template—when you edit a quota template, Windows gives you the option to update all quotas based on the template. To create or edit a quota template, follow these steps:

1. In the File Server Resource Manager console, right-click Quota Templates and choose Create Quota Template, or right-click an existing quota template and choose Edit Template Properties. To create a quota template based on an existing quota, right-click the quota and choose Create Quota From Template.

2. To base the template on an existing template, in the Create Quota Template dialog box choose a template from the Copy Properties From Quota Template box and then click Copy, as shown in Figure 12-12.

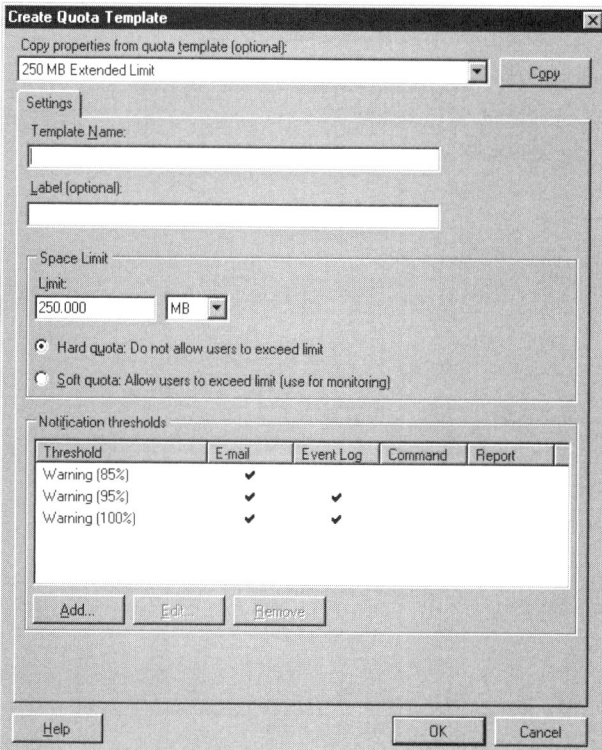

FIGURE 12-12 Creating a quota template

3. Type a name and label for the template in the Template Name and Label boxes.

4. In the Limit box, type the maximum amount of disk space each user can utilize in the specified folder.

5. Choose Hard Quota to prevent users from exceeding the limit you specify, or Soft Quota to use the quota only for monitoring.

6. In the Notification Thresholds section of the dialog box, click Add to create a new notification or select an existing notification and then click Edit to open the properties for the threshold, as shown in Figure 12-13.

7. In the Generate Notifications When Usage Reaches box, specify when to notify users. A typical configuration is to use three notification thresholds, which are often set at 85 percent, 95 percent, and 100 percent.

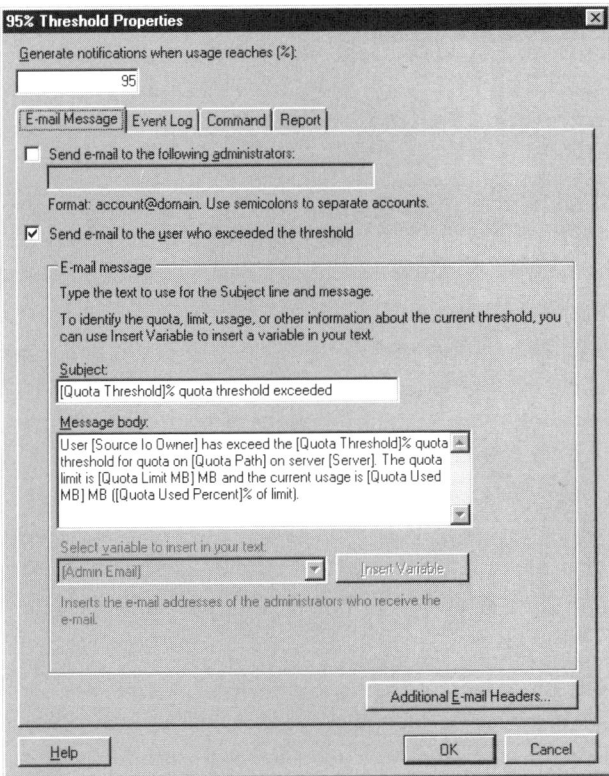

FIGURE 12-13 Notification options for a quota template

8. Specify what actions to take when a user exceeds the threshold you specify and click OK when you are finished:

- Use the E-Mail Message tab to send an e-mail notification to users who exceed the threshold. (You can also choose to send the notification to an administrator.) Use the E-Mail Message section of the tab to customize the message that Windows generates.

- Use the Event Log tab to record a log entry on the server when a user exceeds the threshold.

- Use the Command tab to run a command or script when a user exceeds the threshold.

- Use the Report tab to generate a storage report when a user exceeds the threshold.

See the section titled "Scheduling Storage Reports" earlier in this chapter for more information about storage reports.

9. Click OK when you're finished. If you're editing an existing template, the Update Quotas Derived From Template dialog box opens. Choose one of the following options and then click OK:

- **Apply Template Only To Derived Quotas That Match The Original Template** Updates quotas based on the quota template only if you have not customized them.

- **Apply Template To All Derived Quotas** Updates all quotas based on the quota template.

- **Do Not Apply Template To Derived Quotas** Does not update any quotas based on the template.

Screening Files

Administrators who use storage reports for the first time are often surprised, and occasionally dismayed, at how many audio and video files they find on file servers. In addition to the massive amounts of disk space that audio and video files consume, organizations can be exposed to legal liability if these files are obtained or shared illegally.

To help administrators control what type of files users can save on a file share, File Screening Management is part of the File Server Resource Manager console. With File Screening Management, administrators can block users from saving files with certain file types to a specific file share, as discussed in the following sections.

 REAL WORLD Controlling Audio and Video Files on Servers

f you are serious about blocking personal audio and video files on public file shares, you need two things:

- **An acceptable use policy that clearly states what users may and may not place on file shares** This policy should state that users may not save illegally obtained files of any type on company file servers, including audio and video files for which the users have not purchased a license. You might also want to state that users may only save legally obtained audio and video files to their home directory (on which you create a directory quota, limiting users to a reasonable amount of disk space).

- **A file screen that implements this policy** The best way to get people to follow a company policy is to make it hard for them to violate the policy. A file screen makes it difficult for an average user to violate an acceptable-use policy concerning audio and video files and reduces legal liability by demonstrating that the organization is taking active steps to prevent its employees from violating its written policy.

Because file screens use a filename mask and not a content mask to block files, users can still save MP3 files by changing the file extension of the file to something that isn't blocked. However, if you have a clear and unambiguous acceptable-use policy, and a file screen for that policy in place, this requires a wilful violation and a conscious attempt to cover up the violation—something that most employees are unlikely to risk.

Creating File Screens

To create a file screen, open the File Server Resource Manager console and follow these steps:

1. Click the File Screening Management node.

2. Click the File Screens container, right-click File Screens in the console tree, and choose Create File Screen. The Create File Screen dialog box opens, as shown in Figure 12-14.

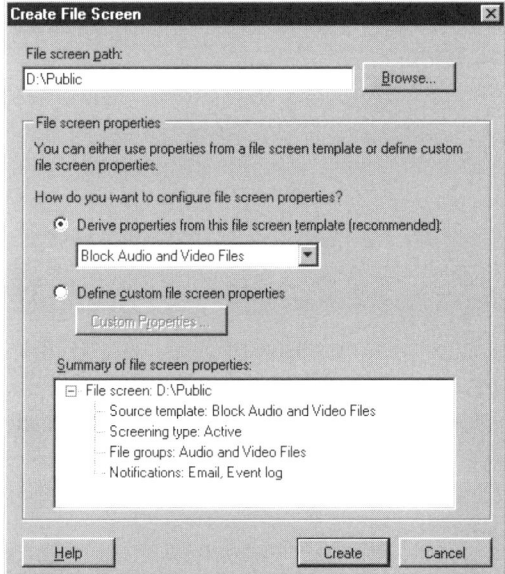

FIGURE 12-14 Creating a file screen

3. Click Browse, select the folder to which you want to apply the file screen, and then click OK.

4. Select the file screen template you want to apply or choose Define Custom File Screen Properties and then click Custom Properties to create a custom file screen. Click OK when you are finished.

5. If you chose to create a custom file screen, the Save Custom Properties As A Template dialog box appears. Use this dialog box to save the custom file screen as a file screen template or choose Save The Custom File Screen Without Creating A Template.

Creating Exceptions

To create an exception to a file screen, follow these steps:

1. Click the File Screens container, right-click File Screens in the console tree, and choose Create File Screen Exception. The Create File Screen Exception dialog box appears, as shown in Figure 12-15.

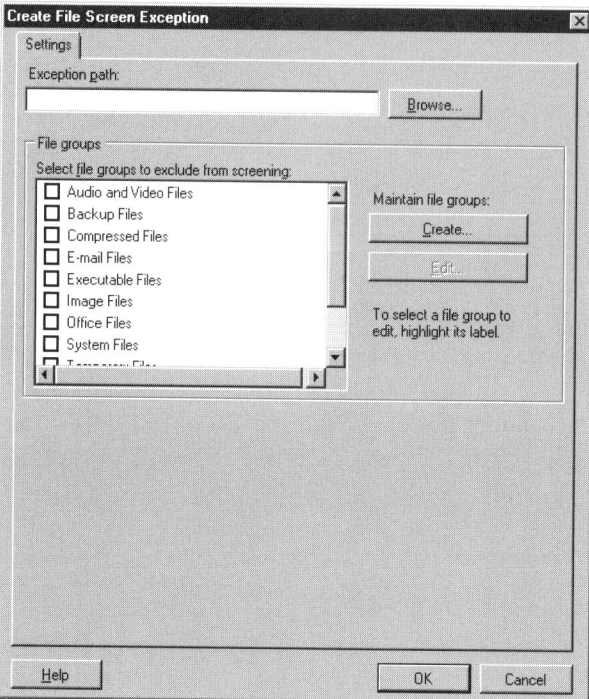

FIGURE 12-15 Creating file exceptions

2. Click Browse, select the folder to which you want to apply the file screen exception, and then click OK. The folder you select cannot already contain a file screen, but it can be a subfolder of a folder that contains a file screen.

3. Select the groups that you want to allow, excluding them from any file screens applied to parent folders. Click OK when you are finished to return to the File Server Resource Manager console.

Creating and Editing File Screen Templates

To create or edit a file screen template, follow these steps:

1. In the File Server Resource Manager console, right-click File Screen Templates and choose Create File Screen Template, or right-click an existing template and choose Edit Template Properties. To create a file screen template based on an existing file screen, right-click the file screen and choose Create A Template From File Screen.

2. To base the template on an existing template, in the Create File Screen Template dialog box, choose a template from the Copy Properties From Template box, as shown in Figure 12-16. Click Copy.

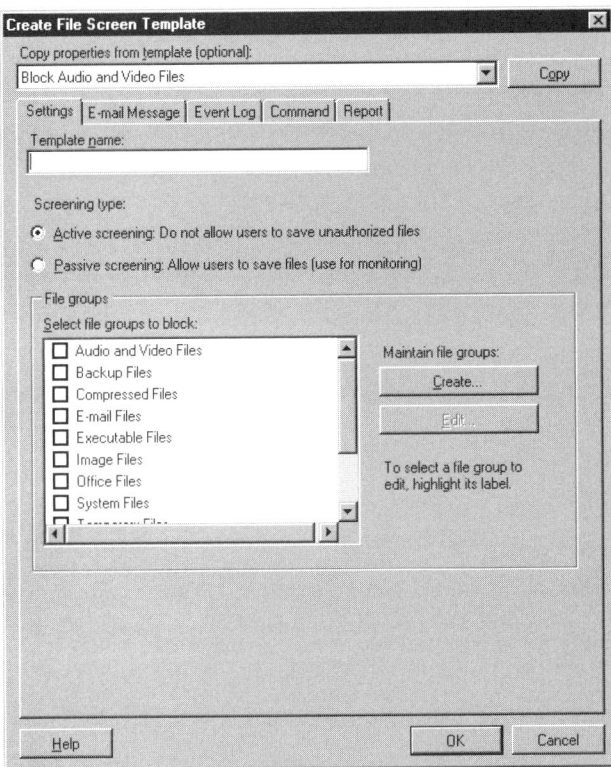

FIGURE 12-16 Working with a file screen template

3. Type a name and label for the template in the Template Name box.

4. Choose Active Screening to prevent users from saving files of the type you specify or choose Passive Screening to use the file screen only for monitoring.

5. Select the file group or groups that you want to block. To create a new file group, click Create; to edit an existing file group, select the group and then click Edit.

6. Specify what actions to take when a user saves a screened file type and then click OK:

- Use the E-Mail Message tab to send an e-mail notification to the user who saved a screened file type. (You can also choose to send the notification to an administrator.) Use the E-Mail Message section of the tab to customize the message that Windows generates.

- Use the Event Log tab to record a log entry on the server when a user saves a screened file type.

- Use the Command tab to run a command or script when a user saves a screened file type.

- Use the Report tab to generate a storage report when a user saves a screened file type. See the section titled "Scheduling Storage Reports" earlier in this chapter for more information about storage reports.

7. If you are editing an existing template, the Update File Screens Derived From Template dialog box appears. Choose one of the following options and then click OK:

- **Apply Template Only To Derived File Screens That Match The Original Template** Updates file screens based on the quota template only if you have not customized them.

- **Apply Template To All Derived File Screens** Updates all file screens based on the quota template.

- **Do Not Apply Template to Derived File Screens** Does not update any file screens based on the template.

Working with File Groups

A file group is a group of files with a common set of characteristics in their filenames. For example, the Audio and Video file group includes audio files (with .mp3, .wma, and .aac file extensions), and video files (with .wmv, .mpeg, and .mov file extensions). Storage reports use file groups when reporting on the types of files present on a file share, while file screening uses file groups to control which files to block. To create or edit a file group, follow these steps:

1. In the File Server Resource Manager console, select File Screening Management.

2. Right-click the File Groups container and choose Create File Group. The Create File Group Properties dialog box opens, as shown in Figure 12-17.

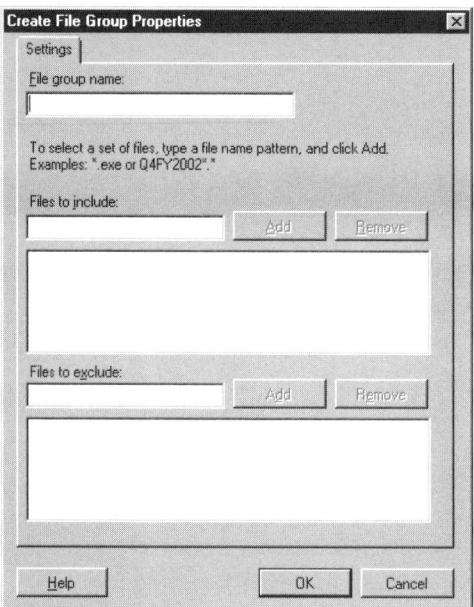

FIGURE 12-17 Creating a file group

3. Type a name for the file group in the File Group Name box.

4. In the Files To Include box, type the filename criteria to include in the group. Use asterisks (*) as wildcard characters and then click Add.

5. To exclude files from the file group, type the filename criteria to exclude from the file group in the Files To Exclude box. Click OK.

 REAL WORLD   **Creative Use of File Groups**

File screening isn't just for file extensions. It's actually based on pattern matching against the entire filename to define the file group. This means you can have a file group that matches all MP3 files by creating a file group that matches "*.mp3". But you could also have a file group that matched all Company Policy files by matching "pol*.pdf" if all your company policies are stored in files that start with "pol" and are Adobe PDF files. Or, if monthly financial reports are consistently stored as MMYYYY.XLS, you could create a file group that matched all 2008 financials by using ??2008.XLS as your pattern.

The usual tendency with file groups is to think of selecting files solely by extension. But by using the entire filename in the pattern match, you can use file groups more creatively, and also do enhanced reporting based on the file groups.

Summary

In this chapter, you've seen the details of some very sophisticated ways to manage file storage, including Distributed File System incorporating DFS Namespaces and DFS Replication, as well as the storage reports, quotas, and file screens of File Server Resource Manager.

In the next chapter, we move on to installing, sharing, and configuring printers on the network.

Installing and Managing Printers

As much as everyone would like to have a paperless office, it appears we'll all be much grayer (or balder, or both) before that completely comes to pass. Office paper consumption peaked in 1999, and since then the quantities of waste in the office paper-recycling bin have levelled off and in some places have actually begun to shrink. However, even if fewer people are printing out their e-mails before reading them, paper remains at the center of many business operations.

The cost of basic printers has declined dramatically, but companies are investing in sophisticated high-speed printers that allow users to handle jobs that once required an outside print shop. These printers are expensive both to buy and to use. Therefore, printer sharing remains an important function of enterprise networks. Setting up multiple users to share printers reduces cost and can increase printing output. You can direct routine work to low-cost-per-page printers, schedule long print jobs for off hours, and limit access to high-end printers.

In other words, there's not much you can do to keep employees from printing out the occasional grocery list or soccer schedule, but you can prevent them from doing it on the full-color laser printer with toner cartridges that cost as much as a new printer.

Understanding Print Servers

Print servers are computers (or sometimes network appliances) that manage the communications between printers and the client computers generating the print jobs.

Generally, there are two approaches to print servers. The Microsoft approach is to use a Windows computer as an "intelligent" print server that handles communication between the printers and the client computers (reducing strain on the clients) and maintains a common print queue for all clients. Microsoft print servers also make it easy to find printers on the network by name (NetBIOS, DNS, or Active Directory) and install the appropriate printer drivers.

In contrast, other operating systems, such as Linux, and printers with built-in network interfaces use a relatively "dumb" print server called the Line Printer Daemon (LPD), which acts strictly as an interface between the network and the printer. Each client maintains its own printer queue and performs all preprint processing, increasing the amount of time the computer is partially or completely unavailable for other tasks.

These two approaches aren't in opposition to each other and, in fact, the best way to connect a printer to a Windows print server is via a network connection to a printer, which usually runs the LPD service. The Windows print server connects to the printer using the traditional Line Printer Remote (LPR) service (the client-side equivalent of LPD) or via the higher-performance standard TCP/IP printer port and shares the printer on the network. The Windows print server holds the printer queue and sends each print job to LPD, which passes the job to the printer.

 UNDER THE HOOD **Printer Terminology**

Although the term *printer* is usually used to refer to both the physical device and its software interface, strictly speaking, a printer is a device that does the actual printing, and a *logical printer* is the software interface (printer driver) for the printer. You can have one logical printer associated with a single printer, or you can have several logical printers associated with a single printer. In the latter arrangement, the logical printers can be configured at different priority levels so that one logical printer handles normal printing and another handles print jobs that should be printed during off-peak hours. For a printer that supports both PostScript (PS) and Printer Control Language (PCL), two logical printers allow users to choose which type of printing to do.

A single logical printer can also be associated with multiple physical printers in a printer pool, as long as all the printers work with the same driver. Printer pools distribute the printing load more evenly, increasing performance. Because the physical printers in the pools are interchangeable, printer pools also make it possible for an administrator to add or remove physical printers without affecting the users' configurations.

Selecting Printers

Choosing the right printers for an organization is a lot like choosing the right car. There are certain practical matters to look at such as up-front cost, cost of consumables (gas, ink, or toner), and suitability to the task at hand (for example, hauling lumber or printing brochures).

Color laser printers have become affordable for most businesses, but the cost of color toner remains extremely high. However, if you have a property-sales office and need to print hundreds of high-quality color photos daily, a color laser printer is not an extravagance. A printer that will produce beautiful color at a rate of 20 or more pages per minute can be had for well under $1,000.

On the other hand, if you need lots of black-and-white pages and only occasional color, a black-and-white laser printer plus a color inkjet printer might be the most economical option. Color ink cartridges for inkjet printers are expensive, but they last a long time if used infrequently. And inkjet printers themselves are so low in cost they're practically disposable (as reprehensible as that is from an environmental point of view).

Look for printers with built-in network interfaces because they print faster, require less processing power on the print server, and can be flexibly located anywhere there's a network cable. Printers with a USB connection can be used if print volumes are low (or for backup printers), but steer clear of printers using parallel port connections—they can drastically slow a print server.

 REAL WORLD **Another Way Printers Are Like Cars**

n our office, we have three printers:

- A standard, small business–size, black-and-white laser printer (the sensible sedan)
- A multifunction color inkjet copier/scanner/printer/fax (the efficient hybrid)
- A very fast color laser printer the size of a small file cabinet (the totally impractical but cool sports car)

Printers are undoubtedly essential to your business, but there's no reason you can't have some fun at the same time.

Planning Printer Placement

In a very small office, there's no need to spend time planning printer deployment. The printers go wherever there's room for them. However, in a larger organization, you'll need to establish printer- and location-naming conventions, evaluate whether to upgrade or migrate existing print servers, and prepare for print server failures.

Naming Printers

An effective printer-naming convention is important to ensure that users can easily identify printers on the network. When creating a printer-naming convention, consider the following:

- The *printer name* can be any length up to 220 characters, which is plenty of room for any scheme you devise. Of course, the name should also be as short as possible without sacrificing clarity.

- The *share name* is the name that all clients see when they browse for a printer, use the Add Printer Wizard, or use the Net Use command. The share name can be up to 80 characters long, but again should be shorter for readability. Some older applications cannot print to printers with fully qualified printer share names (the computer name and printer share name combined) that exceed 31 characters, or to print servers where the default printer's share name exceeds 31 characters. Clients using other operating systems might also have trouble with names longer than 31 characters or names containing spaces or other special characters. But whether you have to deal with such applications or not, shorter is generally better.

Naming Printer Locations

In small organizations, finding printers is easy—just stand up and look around or ask the person sitting next to you. This doesn't work as well in larger organizations where printers have varying capabilities and might be widely scattered. Under these circumstances, users need to be able to browse or search for printers based on the criteria they want, including printer features and printer location.

Location names are similar in form to domain names and use the *name/name/name...* syntax. They start with the most general location name and become progressively more specific. Each part name can have a maximum of 32 characters and can contain any characters except the forward slash (/), which Windows reserves as a delimiter.

Keep the naming convention simple and easy to understand. End users are usually interested in the answer to only one question: "Where's my printout?"

Design/ArtStudio/HPDesignJet5500 is one example of a clear location name, as is Marketing/DirectMail/RicohTabSize.

Installing Printers

Before a Windows print server can share a printer on the network, it must first connect to the printer and install the necessary drivers. The following sections walk you through adding printers that are attached directly to the print server via USB or parallel port interface, as well as connecting to printers with built-in network adapters.

I n the consumer world, most printers are directly connected to a computer with a parallel port, USB port, or IEEE 1394 port. This solution—simple to use and to understand—is perfectly adequate and appropriate for individual users, or even most very small offices. But it has some significant disadvantages over a network-attached printer. It limits where the printer can be physically located, since it must be within a few feet of the computer that supports it. And it can seriously slow the work of the individual whose computer acts as the print server. Printer input/output is not very efficient, especially when using the traditional parallel printer port.

A network-attached printer, on the other hand, can be located virtually anywhere. If you're using standard Ethernet to connect to the printer, you'll need a network port nearby, but if you use a wireless print server, even that requirement is eliminated. As a bonus, network printing doesn't have an adverse effect on the server that supports it—you can manage all your print queues directly from the SBS server, thereby simplifying management.

If your printers don't have a network interface, you can use one of the widely available standalone print server appliances, either wireless or Ethernet. SBS treats these as if they were standard network printers, but you don't have to buy a printer with a network card included—the print server appliance has a port or ports to connect to the printer as well as a network interface.

An exception to the "all printers are network printers" rule is for the user who has a privacy (or other) need for a locally attached printer. Human resources and hiring managers are two classes of users that this might apply to.

Adding and Sharing a Network Printer

To add a network printer to your Windows SBS 2008 network, follow the instructions provided by the manufacturer of the printer. If the specific instructions are long gone, make sure you have the drivers you need (you can download them from the manufacturer's Web site, if necessary) and follow these steps:

1. Make the physical connection between the printer and a network jack using a network cable.

2. Turn the printer on. (If the printer is already on, turn it off and then on again.)

3. From the computer running Windows SBS 2008, select DHCP from the Administrative Tools menu.

4. In the DHCP task pane, expand IPv4, expand Scope, and then expand Address Leases under your domain name. Locate the DHCP address assigned to the new printer (Figure 13-1) and make a note of it.

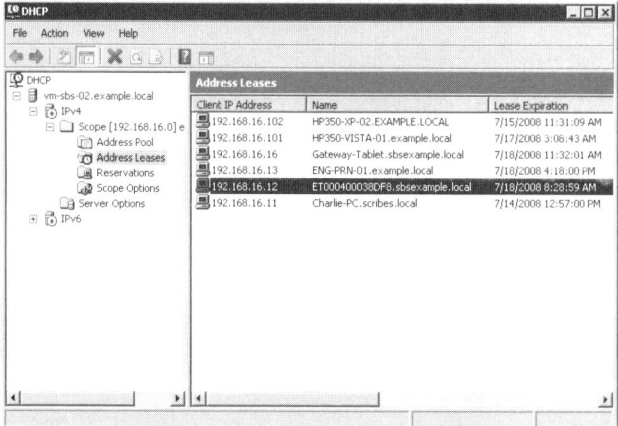

FIGURE 13-1 Locating the TCP/IP address for a network printer

5. Next, select Control Panel from the Start menu and click Printers.

6. From the File menu, select Run As Administrator and then select Add Printer (Figure 13-2).

NOTE If the menu bar isn't visible in the Printers window, press Alt to display it.

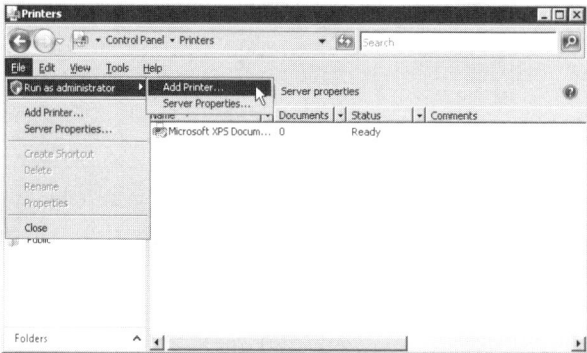

FIGURE 13-2 You must have administrative credentials and choose Run As Administrator to install a printer.

7. On the Choose A Local Or Network Printer page, select Add A Local Printer. (Stay with us—it's a network printer, but from the point of view of your installation, it's a local printer.)

8. On the Choose A Printer Port page, click Create A New Port and select Standard TCP/IP Port from the drop-down list. Click Next.

9. On the Type A Printer Hostname Or IP Address page, select Autodetect as the Device Type and then type in the IP address you noted in step 4. The Port Name is automatically filled in (see Figure 13-3). Click Next.

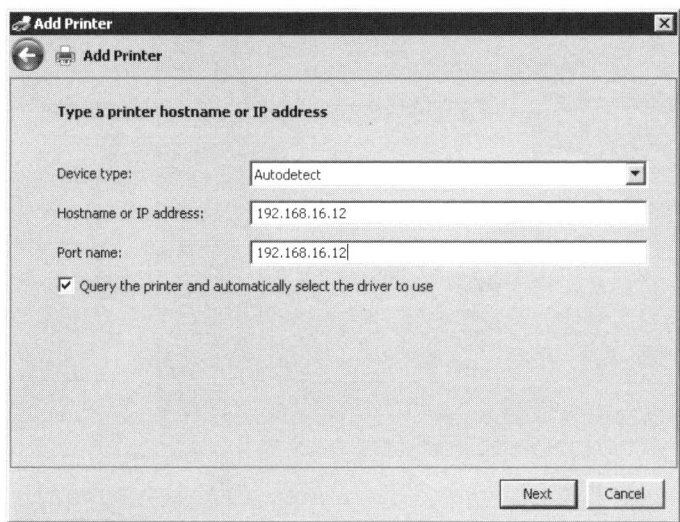

FIGURE 13-3 Entering the printer IP address

> **NOTE** Leave the check box selected to Query The Printer And Automatically Select The Driver To Use. If Windows SBS 2008 already has built-in drivers for the printer, you won't need to provide additional ones.

10. Windows SBS 2008 contacts the printer and displays the Install The Printer Driver dialog box. Choose the manufacturer name from the list on the left and the printer model from the list on the right. Click Next.

> **NOTE** The designation (MS) next to the printer name indicates that the driver is part of Windows SBS 2008. If your printer needs multiple drivers (such as Postscript in addition to PCL), click Have Disk and point to the location of the drivers.

11. On the Type A Printer Name page, accept or revise the printer name. The printer will be set as the default printer unless you clear the check box. Click Next.

12. On the Printer Sharing page, accept or revise the share name. Add a location and comments if wanted. Click Next.

13. The successful installation is announced (Figure 13-4). Print a test page to confirm that all is well. Click Finish.

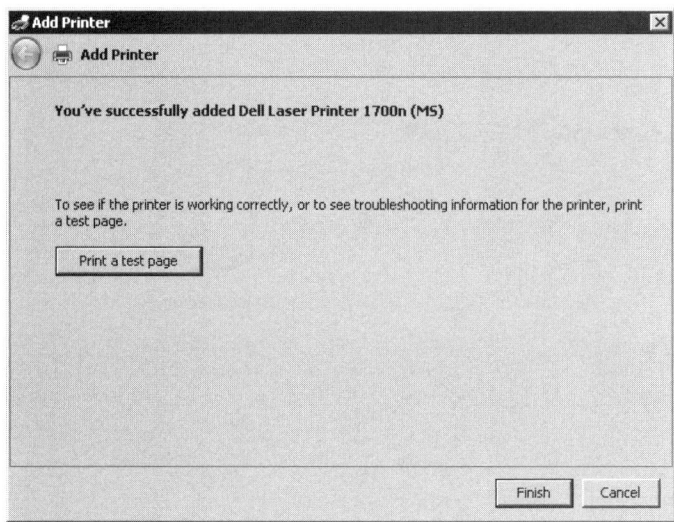

FIGURE 13-4 The successful installation is declared.

Showing a Shared Printer in Windows SBS Console

Even after a network printer is successfully installed and shared, it may still not display in the Devices list under the Network tab of Windows SBS Console. If that's the case, follow these steps:

1. Open Windows SBS Console, click Network, and then click Devices.

2. In the Tasks Pane, click Refresh This View. If the printer is still not listed, click List A Shared Printer In This Console.

3. In the Show Shared Printer In The Console dialog box, provide the network path for the shared printer or click Browse to locate the printer.

4. When the *Computer**Share* path is displayed as shown in Figure 13-5, click OK.

5. In the Windows SBS Console, click Refresh This View in the Tasks list. The printer appears in the list of printers.

Now you can manage this printer from the Windows SBS Console. Right-click the printer name to view printer jobs. Or select Printer Properties to view and modify printer settings.

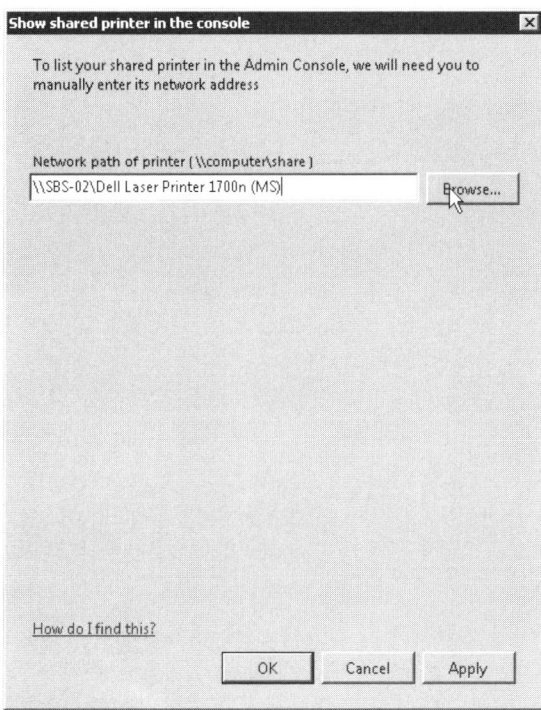

FIGURE 13-5 Entering a shared printer's network address

Sharing Locally Connected Printers

If you're using a USB or IEEE 1394 (FireWire) connection to the printer, as soon as you plug the printer into the server, Windows automatically detects, installs, and shares the printer on the network, and also publishes it in Active Directory (although you might be prompted for drivers).

Sharing a Printer Connected to a Vista Computer

From the computer running Windows Vista, click Start and then follow these steps:

1. Select Control Panel and then click Printers or Hardware And Sound\Printers.

2. Right-click the printer you want to share and select Properties.

3. On the Sharing tab, click Change Sharing Options.

4. Select the Share This Printer option, as shown in Figure 13-6, and select the check boxes for Render Print Jobs On Client Computers and List In The Directory.

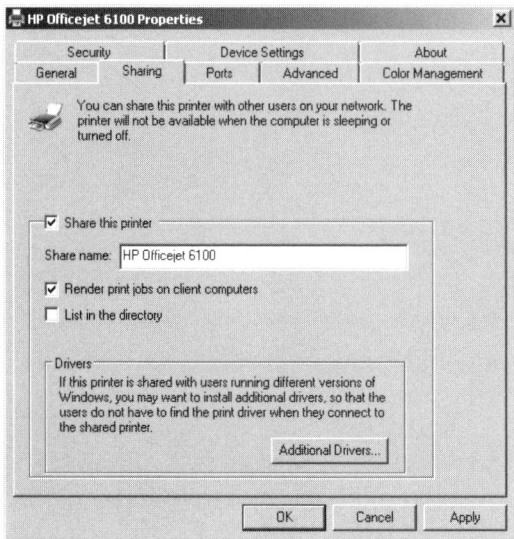

FIGURE 13-6 Sharing a local printer with other users

5. Click the General tab. In the Location text box, enter a description of the printer's location. Add additional notes in the Comment section. Click Apply.

6. Click Print Test Page to verify that the printer is correctly attached.

On the Windows SBS Console, click Network and then Devices. The printer appears in the Printers list.

Sharing a Printer Connected to a Windows XP Computer

From the computer running Windows XP, click Start and then follow these steps:

1. Select Control Panel and then click Printers And Faxes.

2. In the task pane, click Add A Printer to start the Add A Printer Wizard. Follow the instructions to complete the wizard.

3. In the details pane, right-click the printer and select Properties.

4. On the Sharing tab, select Share This Printer and then select List In The Directory. Verify that Render Print Jobs On Client Computers is selected.

5. Click the General tab. In the Location area, type the physical location of the printer.

6. Click Apply.

On the server, open the Windows SBS Console. Click Network and then click Devices. Confirm that the printer is included in the Printers list.

Sharing a Printer Connected to a Windows SBS 2008 Computer

From the computer running Windows SBS, click Start and then follow these steps:

1. Click Control Panel and then click Printers.

2. Right-click the printer you want to share and select Properties.

3. On the Sharing tab, click Change Sharing Options.

4. Select Share This Printer and select the check boxes for Render Print Jobs On Client Computers and List In The Directory.

5. Click the General tab. In the Location text box, enter a description of the printer's location. Add additional notes in the Comment section. Click Apply.

6. On the Windows SBS Console navigation bar, click Network and then click Devices. The printer will appear in the Printers list.

Adding Client Drivers for Shared Printers

Before a shared printer can be used by clients of a different architecture, such as x64 editions of Windows, you need to add the drivers for the printer to SBS. This isn't automatic when initially sharing a printer, so you'll need to add the necessary client drivers after the shared printer is created.

To install drivers for clients of different architectures, follow these steps:

1. Open the Windows SBS Console, click Network, and then click Devices. Right-click the printer and select Printer Properties.

2. Click the Sharing tab and then click the Additional Drivers button.

3. In the Additional Drivers dialog box, shown in Figure 13-7, select the check box next to any client drivers to be installed and then click OK. To install additional client drivers, you need access to the installation files for the appropriate driver version either locally or across the network.

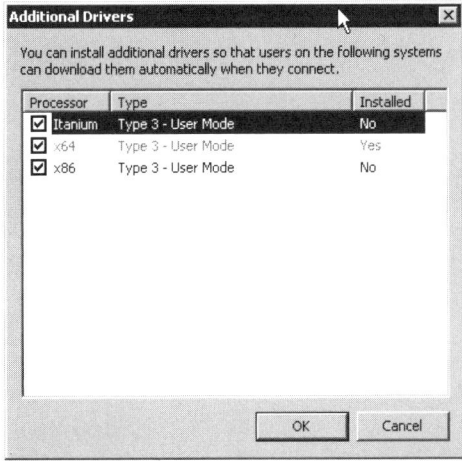

FIGURE 13-7 Selecting additional printer drivers to install

4. SBS will prompt you for the location of the appropriate drivers for the printer.

5. Click OK through the next dialog boxes to install the drivers.

Managing Printers from Windows SBS

To manage print jobs, open Windows SBS Console. Click Network and then click Devices. Right-click the printer you want to manage and select Printer Jobs from the Action menu.

- To temporarily stop a *single* document from printing, right-click the selected document and choose Pause from the Action menu. To resume printing, right-click the document and choose Resume.

- To temporarily stop *all* documents from printing, choose Pause Printing from the Printer menu. To resume printing all documents, select Pause Printing a second time from the Printer menu.

- To cancel one or more print jobs, select the documents, right-click, and choose Cancel from the Action menu. (You can also cancel print jobs by selecting them and pressing the Delete key.)

- To cancel *all* print jobs in the print queue, choose Cancel All Documents from the Printer menu.

- To restart a print job (force the document to print from the beginning again), right-click the document and choose Restart from the Action menu.

- To change the priority of a print job, right-click the print job, choose Properties from the Action menu, and then use the Priority slider to adjust the priority of the document, with 1 being the lowest priority and 99 being the highest priority.

- To specify that a print job should be printed only during a certain period, right-click the print job, choose Properties from the Action menu, select the Only From option, and choose the time range to allow the document to print. This feature is useful when you want to set a large document to print only during a time when you anticipate the printer will be free.

Managing Printers from the Command Line

Windows SBS 2008 makes command-line administration almost practical for those who are so inclined. You can perform almost all administration tasks from a command line—printers included. Use the following list of commands and scripts to get started.

- **Print** Prints the specified text file to the specified printer.

- **Lpr** Prints the specified text file to the specified LPD print queue.

- **Net print** Displays information about the specified print queue or print job. Can also hold, release, or delete print jobs.

- **Lpq** Displays information about the specified LPD print queue.

- **Net start** Starts the specified service. You can use the Net start spooler and Net stop spooler commands to start or stop the spooler service.

- **Cscript %Windir%\System32\Printing_Admin_Scripts\en-US\Prrnmngr.vbs** Adds, deletes, or lists printers on a Windows print server.

- **Cscript %Windir%\System32\ Printing_Admin_Scripts\en-US\Prrnjobs.vbs**
  Lets you view and manage the print jobs of printer shares on a Windows print server.

- **Cscript %Windir%\System32\ Printing_Admin_Scripts\en-US\Prrncfg.vbs**
  Allows you to view and change the settings of printers on a Windows print server.

- **Cscript %Windir%\System32\ Printing_Admin_Scripts\en-US\Prrnqctl.vbs**
  Pauses or resumes printing, clears the print queue, or prints test pages.

- **Cscript %Windir%\System32\ Printing_Admin_Scripts\en-US\Prrnport.vbs**
  Administers all things related to printer ports.

- **Cscript %Windir%\System32\ Printing_Admin_Scripts\en-US\Prrndrvr.vbs**
  Adds, deletes, or lists printer drivers on a Windows print server.

NOTE To view a list of parameters, type the command followed by /? at a command prompt.

Setting Security Options

Security options come into play when you have a range of printers that are separate but not at all equal. For example, you might not want everyone to print to the five-dollar-per-page dye-sublimation printer purchased for the art staff. At a more down-to-earth level, security settings can preserve printer properties or printing priorities from unauthorized changes.

To set permissions on a printer, right-click the printer, choose Printer Properties, and then use the Security tab to assign permissions to groups of users. Click Advanced to exert finer control over permissions or to enable auditing. You can view the results of the audit settings in the security log.

A printer has three levels of permissions: Print, Manage Documents, and Manage Printers. These are defined as follows:

- **Print** Users or groups with Print permission can connect to the printer; print documents; and pause, restart, or delete their own documents from the print queue. Windows by default grants members of the Everyone group the Print permission.

- **Manage Documents** Users or groups with Manage Documents permission have the Print permission along with the ability to change the settings for all documents in the print queue and to pause, restart, and delete any user's documents from the print queue. Windows grants the Creator/Owner group the Manage Documents permission level by default.

- **Manage Printers** Users or groups with Manage Printers permission have the Manage Documents and Print permissions along with the ability to modify printer properties, delete printers, change printer permissions, and take ownership of printers.

Determining Printer Availability

To set up a printer to be available only during certain times—perhaps to discourage after-hours printing—complete the following steps:

1. In the SBS Console, right-click the printer you want to modify and select Printer Properties from the Action menu.

2. Click the Advanced tab and then click Available From.

3. Select the earliest and latest times the printer is to be available to users and then click OK.

Group Priorities and Printer Availability

Changing printer availability as just described changes the printer use times for everyone and makes no further restrictions. With a few additional steps, you can set up a printer so that print jobs submitted by some users print before jobs submitted by other users; for example, you can give priority to managers or groups with tight deadlines. You can also reserve a printer for exclusive use by certain groups during certain times; for example, you can reserve a printer outside of normal business hours so that the groups you specify can print large, high-priority print jobs.

To control availability or group priority, create two or more logical printers for a single physical printer, give each logical printer a different priority and/or make it available at different times, and give different sets of users or groups permission to print to each logical printer.

Creating a Logical Printer

To create a logical printer, follow these steps:

1. Select Control Panel from the Start menu and click Printers.

2. From the File menu, select Run As Administrator and then select Add Printer.

> **NOTE** If the menu bar isn't visible in the Printers window, press Alt to display it.

3. On the Choose A Local Or Network Printer page, select Add A Local Printer.

4. On the Choose A Printer Port page, click Use An Existing Port, select the port that the physical printer is on, and then click Next.

5. On the Install The Printer Driver page, choose the manufacturer name from the list on the left and the printer model from the list on the right. Click Next.

6. Choose the version of the driver you want to use and click Next.

7. Give the printer a descriptive name that describes its function or who uses it. Click Next.

8. On the Printer Sharing page, provide the location and additional comments if wanted. Click Next.

Configuring Usage of the Logical Printer

When the logical printer exists, you next configure how it is used and by whom. Open Printers in Control Panel and follow these steps:

1. Highlight the logical printer in the list. Click the File menu and select Run As Administrator and then Properties.

   NOTE If the menu bar isn't visible in the Printers window, press Alt to display it.

2. Click the Security tab and assign permissions to the users or groups that will have special access to this printer.

3. Click the Advanced tab (shown in Figure 13-8). If the logical printer is to be available only at certain times, select Available From and set the times.

4. To change the priority of the users and groups who use this logical printer, type a number in the Priority list box. The priority range goes from 1, which is the lowest priority, to 99, which is the highest priority.

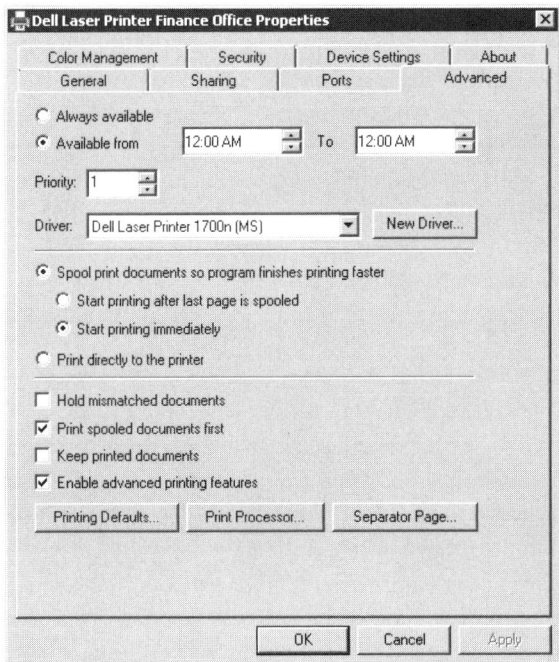

FIGURE 13-8 Advanced printer settings

5. Click OK and repeat the process for all other logical printers you created for the printer.

Viewing the Logical Printer in the SBS Console

As when installing a new printer, the logical printer will not automatically display in the list of network devices in the Windows SBS Console. If this is the case when you view the Printers list, first click Refresh This View in the Tasks pane. If the printer still doesn't appear, follow these steps:

1. Click List A Shared Printer In This Console and browse to the printer, as shown in Figure 13-9.

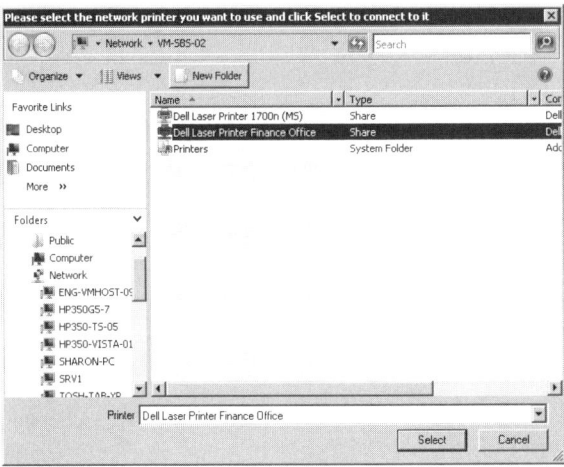

FIGURE 13-9 Selecting a printer to show in the console

2. Click Select and then click OK.
3. In the Windows SBS Console, click Refresh This View in the Tasks list. The printer appears in the list of printers.

Setting Up a Printer Pool

A printer pool consists of multiple printers sharing a single driver and appears as a single printer to users. The advantage of using a printer pool is that clients don't need to look for an available printer; they simply print to the single logical printer on the print server, which then sends the print job to the first available printer. Administration of the printers is also simplified, because all printers in the printer pool are consolidated under one driver. If you modify the properties for the single logical printer, all physical printers in the printer pool use the same settings.

To set up a printer pool, complete the following steps:

1. Select Control Panel from the Start menu and click Printers.
2. Highlight the first printer to be part of the pool. From the File menu, select Run As Administrator and then select Properties.

NOTE If the menu bar isn't visible in the Printers window, press Alt to display it.

3. Click the Ports tab.

4. Select the Enable Printer Pooling check box.

5. To add additional printers to the printer pool, select the ports to which the additional printers are connected.

IMPORTANT All printers in a printer pool must be able to use the same printer driver. If they are not identical printer models, you can sometimes achieve this by careful selection of a printer driver that will support an acceptable level of functionality for several different but related printers.

Configuring Print Spooling

Print spooling, or storing a print job on disk before printing, affects the actual printing speed as well as how clients perceive printing performance. You can change the way print spooling works to correct printing problems or to hold printed documents in the printer queue for repeated printing. To change the spool settings for a printer, highlight the printer you want to modify, click the File menu, and select Run As Administrator and then Properties.

Click the Advanced tab to modify the spool settings. The following list describes the print spool settings on the Advanced tab:

- **Spool Print Documents So Program Finishes Printing Faster** Spools the print documents to the print server, freeing the client to perform other tasks more quickly.

    To ensure that the entire document is available to the printer when printing begins, select Start Printing After Last Page Is Spooled. This step might correct some printing problems and also helps make sure that high-priority documents print before low-priority documents.

    To reduce the time it takes to print a document, select Start Printing Immediately.

- **Print Directly To The Printer** Turns off spooling, causing a performance hit on the server (though it might fix some printing problems).

- **Hold Mismatched Documents** Holds documents in the queue that don't match the current printer settings (for example, documents that require legal-size paper when letter paper is currently in the printer). Other documents in the print queue are unaffected by held documents.

- **Print Spooled Documents First** Prints the highest-priority document that is already spooled first, ahead of higher-priority documents that are still spooling. This step speeds overall printer throughput by keeping the printer from waiting for documents.

- **Keep Printed Documents** Keeps a copy of print jobs in the printer queue in case users need to print the document again. In this circumstance, the user can resubmit the document directly from the queue rather than printing from his or her application a second time.

- **Enable Advanced Printing Features** Enables metafile spooling and printer options such as page order, booklet printing, and pages per sheet (if available on the printer). Disable this when you're experiencing printer problems.

Using the Fax Service

As long as you have an e-mail address and a scanner, you have no need for a fax machine or a fax modem. Ninety percent of faxes are documents generated by your computer and can therefore be sent by e-mail. Other types of documents can be easily scanned, saved as a file, and...sent by e-mail.

If you must send faxes to recipients with fax numbers but no e-mail, you can use an Internet-based fax service for a few dollars per month.

However, there are clearly still those who need to send and receive faxes—otherwise why would Windows SBS 2008 offer a way to send, receive, and manage them? This section describes how to use the fax tools.

Adding a Fax Device

It may seem obvious, but to start and configure the fax service, you must first install a fax device. To do so, follow these steps:

1. Click Start, Control Panel, and then Phone And Modem Options.

2. In the Phone And Modem Options dialog box, click the Modems tab and then click Add to start the Add Hardware Wizard.

3. Follow the instructions on the Install New Modem page. Windows will automatically detect the modem you have attached, unless you select the Don't Detect My Modem check box. Click Next.

4. If Windows does not detect your modem, select the type of modem from the Install New Modem dialog box (Figure 13-10). Click Next.

5. Select the port(s) for the modem. Click Next.

6. Windows installs the modem and notifies you of the successful installation. Click Finish.

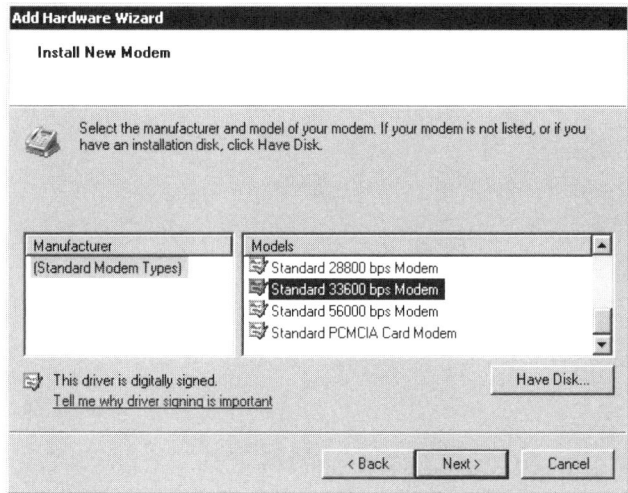

FIGURE 13-10 Designating the type of modem to install

Starting and Configuring the Fax Service

When a fax modem has been installed, you can start and configure the fax service. Open the Windows SBS Console, click Network, click Devices, and then follow these steps:

1. In the Tasks pane, click Start The Fax Service.

2. In the next dialog box (Figure 13-11), you're advised that the fax service is started but not configured. Click Yes to start the configuration process.

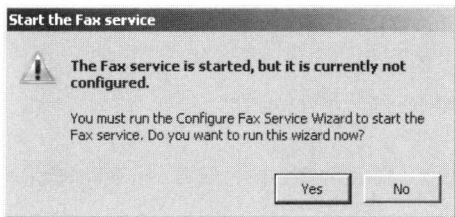

FIGURE 13-11 Click Yes to run the Configure Fax Service Wizard.

3. Enter your Organization's Name, Phone Number, Fax Number, and Address for the fax cover page. Click Next.

4. Enter the Fax Header Text that will print on faxes you send (Figure 13-12). Click Next.

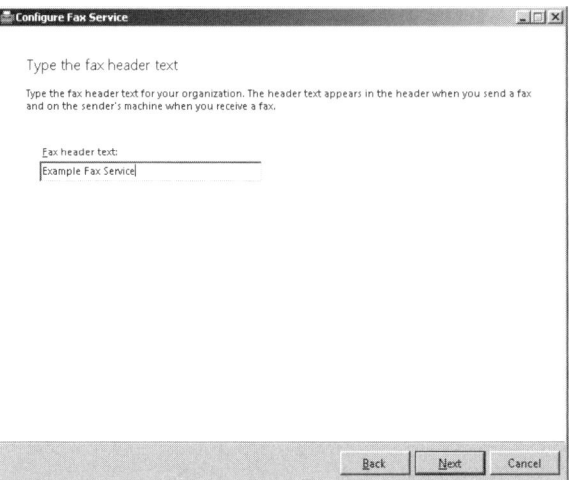

FIGURE 13-12 Entering a fax header

5. Select the modem to use for sending faxes. (If you install multiple modems, you can dedicate some to sending and others to receiving, if needed.) Click Next.

6. Select the modem to use for receiving faxes. In the case of multiple modems, you can configure different delivery options for different modems. Click Next.

7. The following four options are available for routing incoming faxes (see Figure 13-13). You can use any or all of them.

   ■ **Route Through E-mail** Deliver faxes to the e-mail address or addresses specified.

   ■ **Store In A Document Library** Deliver faxes to a document storage area of your internal Web site.

   ■ **Print** Route all faxes to a specified printer.

   ■ **Store In A Folder** Deliver all faxes to a specified folder.

8. Click Configure Fax when you've made your selections.

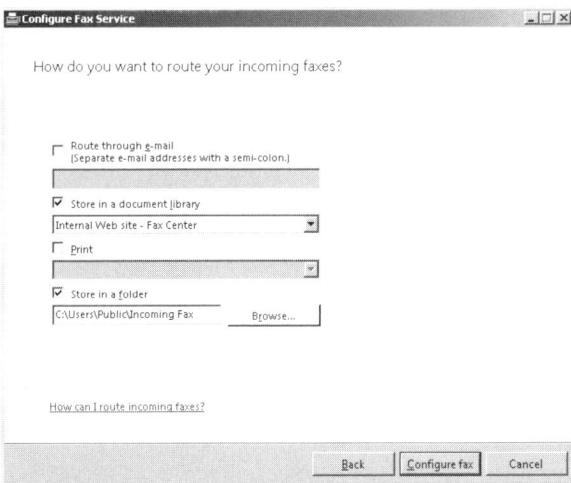

FIGURE 13-13 Choosing the destinations for incoming faxes

Managing Fax Users and Administrators

By default, all users are added to the Windows SBS Fax users group. To change membership in this group, open the Windows SBS Console., select Network, and then select Devices. In the Tasks pane, select Configure The Windows SBS Fax Users Group.

Select Add Or Remove to change the membership. Click E-mail to add an e-mail address specifically for this group.

Similarly, you can select Configure The Windows SBS Fax Administrator Group. By default, all administrators are members of this group. Click Add or Remove to change the membership of this group. Click E-mail to add an e-mail address specifically for this group.

Summary

Printing is an essential service on any network. Aside from actual network failure, few things will generate as much unrest as the inability to print documents. In this chapter, we've covered the fundamentals of printer and fax administration, along with sufficient information on planning to keep your printing operations viable into the future. Next we move on to the equally critical subject of managing computers—and their users—on the network.

Managing Computers on the Network

Windows Small Business Server 2008 streamlines the client management process, making it easy to connect computers to the network and manage them from a single console.

When you connect a client computer to the SBS network, SBS automatically configures the computer for optimal operation in an SBS environment. Existing accounts on the computer are migrated to the users assigned to that computer, the Windows Firewall configuration is set to work properly on an SBS network, and the Internet Explorer home page is set to the internal Web site.

Connecting Computers to the Network

SBS supports the 32-bit and 64-bit versions of Windows XP Professional and the Business, Enterprise, and Ultimate editions of Windows Vista. Windows Server 2003 and Windows Server 2008 are also supported, either as member servers or secondary domain controllers.

 REAL WORLD   **Domain Controllers**

There has been a longstanding misunderstanding about additional domain controllers on an SBS network: Many people believe that the main SBS server is the *only* domain controller allowed on an SBS network. This simply isn't true. You can have additional domain controllers on an SBS network. The only requirement is that these secondary domain controllers must not hold any of the Flexible Single Master Operations (FSMO, pronounced *fizmo*) roles. Those must all remain on the original SBS server.

With SBS 2008, this requirement becomes even clearer, because the Premium Edition of SBS 2008 includes a second copy of Windows Server 2008 and the right to install it on the SBS network. You can use this second server to support SQL Server (the default behavior) or to support Terminal Services, including TS RemoteApps—or you can use it as a secondary domain controller.

If you're supporting a remote site, such as a branch office, using a secondary domain controller is a very good idea. We like to take advantage of the new Read Only Domain Controller (RODC), introduced in Windows Server 2008, for that branch office.

Creating Computer Accounts

Unlike previous versions of SBS, with SBS 2008 you don't need to create a computer account ahead of time. Instead, you (or the user of the computer) plug the computer into the SBS network, you're assigned an IP address from the DHCP server, and you're then joined to the SBS domain when you use the *http://connect* page to connect the client. Or you can manually run the Launcher.exe application from a USB key.

Before you try to connect a new computer to the network, first create the user account(s) that will have access to the computer. This simplifies the setup process for the computer account and ensures that the correct user accounts are given permission to log on to the new computer.

Establishing Basic Network Connectivity

The first step in connecting a computer to an SBS network is to connect to the network and obtain a valid IP address. This process is pretty simple: plug the computer into an Ethernet switch on the network and configure the system for Dynamic Host Control Protocol (DHCP). Wireless clients must first associate with an access point and provide a WPA key.

Configuring Windows Vista and Windows Server 2008 to Use DHCP

By default, Windows Vista and Windows Server 2008 will use DHCP to configure TCP/IP, and you shouldn't have to change anything. However, if the client has been set to use a fixed IP address, you can change it back to using DHCP by completing the following steps:

1. Open the Network Connections folder shown in Figure 14-1. The easiest way to get to this in Windows Vista is to type **ncpa.cpl** in a command window or in the Search field on the Start menu.

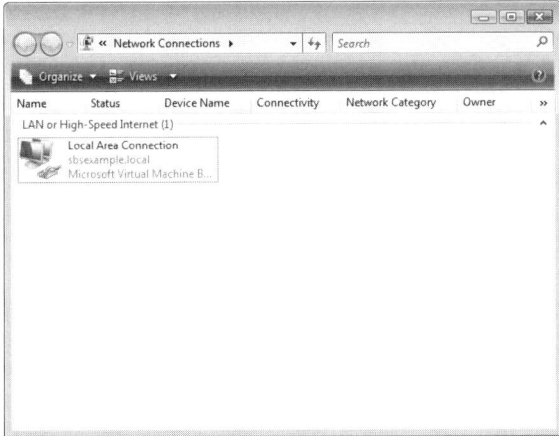

FIGURE 14-1 The Network Connections folder in Windows Vista

2. Select the network card and right-click to open the Action menu shown in Figure 14-2.

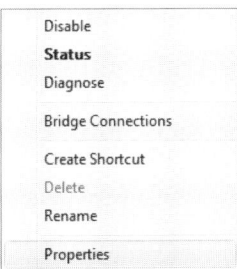

FIGURE 14-2 The Action menu for a network card

3. Select Properties to configure the properties of the Local Area Connection, as shown in Figure 14-3.

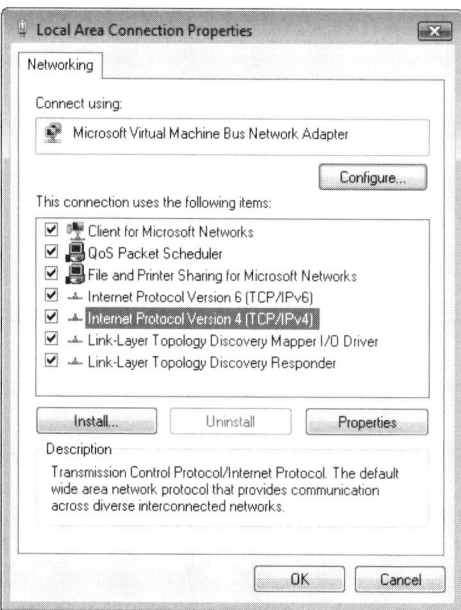

FIGURE 14-3 The Properties dialog box of the Local Area Connection

4. Select Internet Protocol Version 4 (TCP/IPv4) and click Properties to open the Internet Protocol Version 4 (TCP/IPv4) Properties page. Select Obtain An IP Address Automatically and Obtain DNS Server Address Automatically, as shown in Figure 14-4.

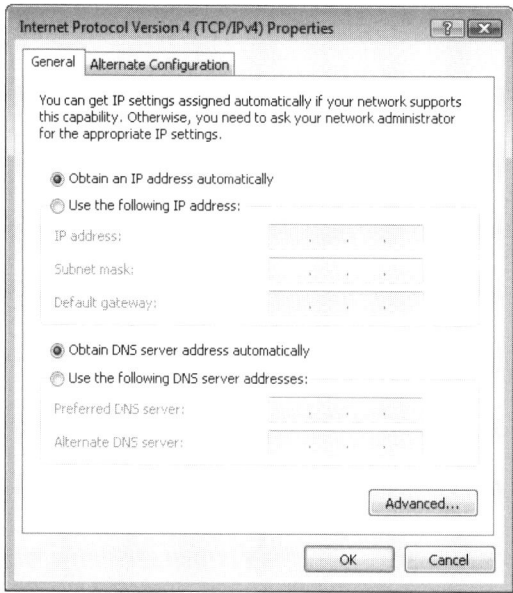

FIGURE 14-4 Internet Protocol Version 4 (TCP/IPv4) Properties page

5. Click OK and then click Close to configure the network connection to use DHCP.

For Windows Server 2008, the steps are much the same. If your server needs to have a fixed IP address, either provide a reservation in DHCP (preferred) or assign a static IP address that is within the same subnet range as your SBS server and that is excluded from the DHCP address range offered by SBS.

Configuring Windows XP and Windows Server 2003 to Use DHCP

By default, Windows XP (including x64 Edition) and Windows Server 2003 use DHCP to configure TCP/IP, and you shouldn't have to change anything. However, if the computer has been set to use a fixed IP address, you can change it back to using DHCP by completing the following steps:

1. In the Network Connections folder (available in Control Panel), right-click the appropriate network adapter (usually Local Area Connection) and choose Properties.

2. In the Local Area Connection Properties dialog box, select the Internet Protocol (TCP/IP) component and click Properties to open the Internet Protocol (TCP/IP) Properties dialog box, shown in Figure 14-5.

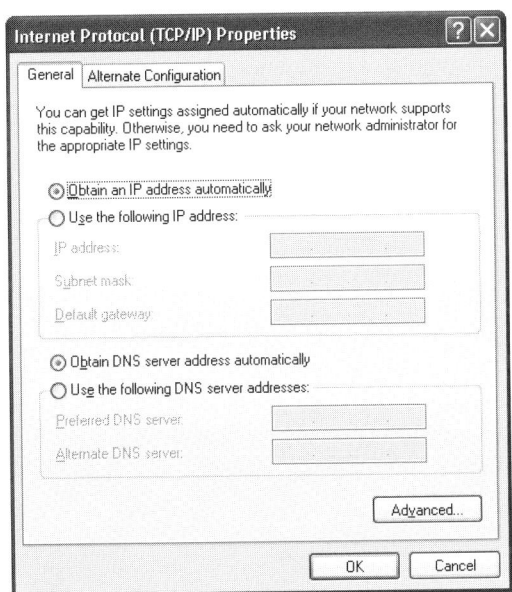

FIGURE 14-5 The Internet Protocol (TCP/IP) Properties dialog box in Windows XP

3. Verify that the Obtain An IP Address Automatically and Obtain DNS Server Address Automatically options are selected and then click OK.

NOTE If your SBS environment includes more than one server, the secondary servers are good candidates for a static IP address. If you use a static IP address, configure the server with an IP address in the excluded IP address range of 192.168.*yyy*.3 through 192.168.*yyy*.9 (where *yyy* is the subnet used by your SBS network), or add an appropriate exclusion in DHCP.

Using the Small Business Server Connect Computer Wizard

After you establish network connectivity and you've created the appropriate user accounts, the next steps in connecting a computer to an SBS network are to log on to the computer, open Internet Explorer or Firefox, and launch the Small Business Server Connect Computer Wizard by connecting to *http://connect*. This wizard configures the computer to run on the network by performing the following actions:

- Verifies that the computer meets minimum requirements to run on an SBS 2008 network
- Changes the computer's workgroup or domain membership to be a member of the SBS domain
- Configures the computer to automatically get updates from the SBS server
- Assigns users to the computer
- Optionally migrates existing local user profiles stored on the computer to new domain user profiles, preserving the data and settings of local user accounts
- Sets the browser home page to *http://companyweb*
- Enables Remote Web Workplace connections
- Configures the Windows Firewall
- Installs the SBS Vista Gadget if it's a Windows Vista client
- Configures Group Policies on the client computer to align with SBS 2008

To use the Connect Computer Wizard from Internet Explorer or Firefox, follow these steps:

1. Log on to the computer you want to connect to the SBS network and open your browser. Internet Explorer and Firefox are supported.
2. Browse to *http://connect* to open the Welcome To Windows Small Business Server 2008 home page, as shown in Figure 14-6.

FIGURE 14-6 The Welcome To Windows Small Business Server 2008 home page

3. Click Start Connect Computer Program to open the Launcher.exe application. You'll see a security warning as shown in Figure 14-7.

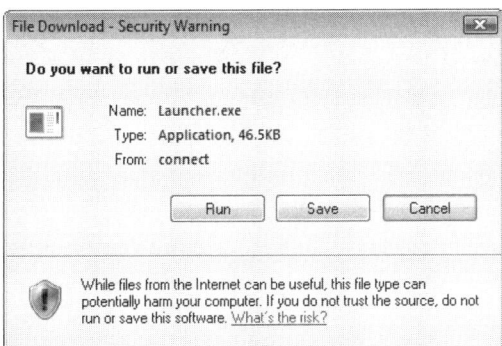

FIGURE 14-7 The File Download Security Warning for Launcher.exe

4. Click Run (and click Continue if you get a User Account Control prompt) to start the Connect Computer Wizard at the Choose How To Set Up This Computer page shown in Figure 14-8.

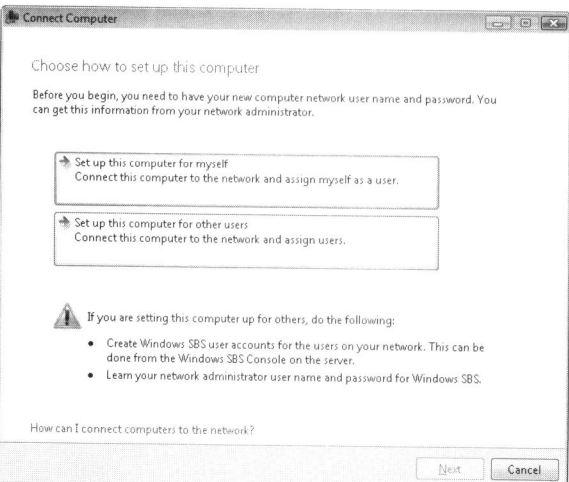

FIGURE 14-8 The Choose How To Set Up This Computer page of the Connect Computer Wizard

5. Select Set Up This Computer For Myself if you'll be the only user using this computer. Select Set Up This Computer For Other Users if this will be a shared computer, or if you're setting up another user's computer.

6. The Connect Computer Wizard verifies that the computer being connected meets minimum requirements and reports the success, as shown in Figure 14-9.

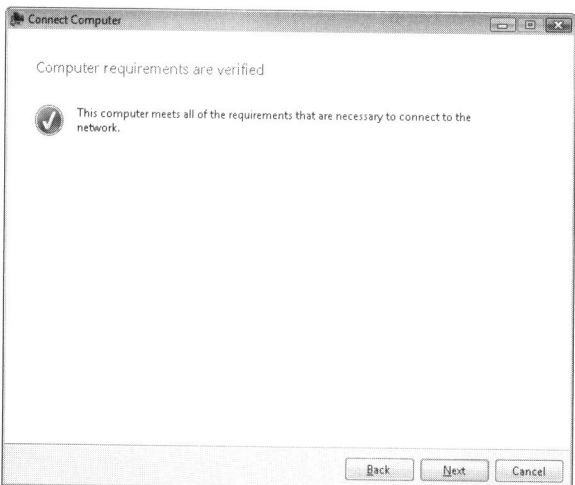

FIGURE 14-9 The Computer Requirements Are Verified page of the Connect Computer Wizard

7. Click Next to open the Type Your Network Administrator User Name And Password page of the Connect Computer Wizard. Enter the credentials for a Network Administrator account.

8. Click Next to open the Verify The Name And Description Of This Computer page of the Connect Computer Wizard. Modify the name if required, and enter an optional description for the computer, as shown in Figure 14-10.

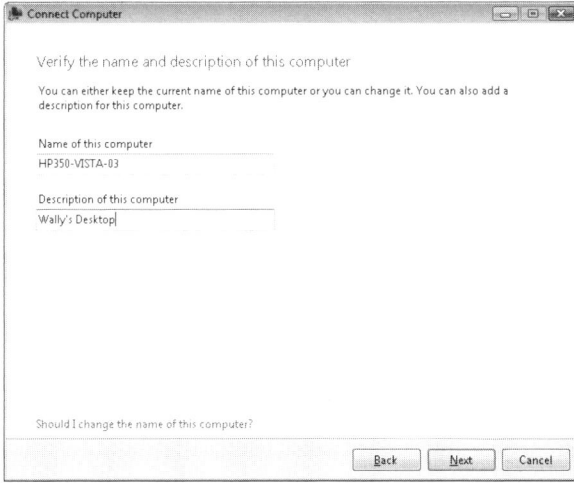

FIGURE 14-10 The Verify The Name And Description Of This Computer page of the Connect Computer Wizard

9. Click Next to open the Assign Users To This Computer page, as shown in Figure 14-11. Any Network Administrator accounts will already be assigned to the computer automatically. Select additional users in the left pane and click Add to assign them to the computer.

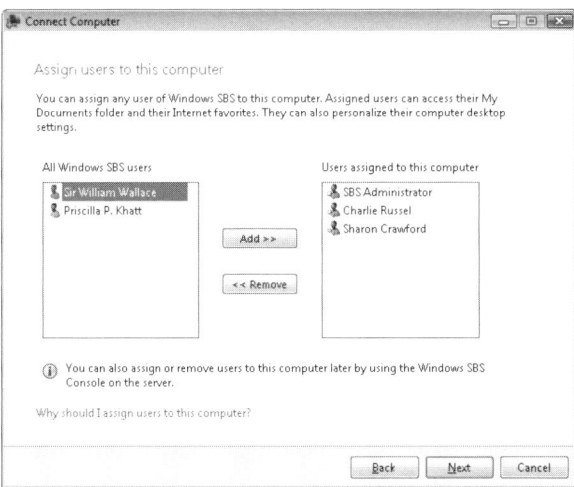

FIGURE 14-11 The Assign Users To This Computer page of the Connect Computer Wizard

10. Click Next to open the Move Existing User Data And Settings page, shown in Figure 14-12. Here you'll see a list of SBS user accounts that are assigned to the computer, with matching drop-down lists of accounts that can have their user data migrated to the new SBS account.

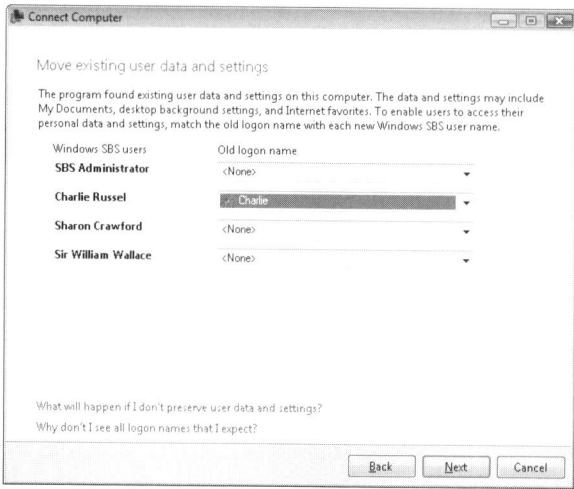

FIGURE 14-12 The Move Existing User Data And Settings page of the Connect Computer Wizard

11. Select the accounts to migrate, as shown in Figure 14-12, and click Next to open the Assign Level Of Computer Access For Users Of Windows SBS page shown in Figure 14-13. Here you assign the permission level *on the local computer* for the SBS domain account. By default, SBS Standard Users are assigned Standard User on their local computers as well, though in some scenarios you may choose to assign them Local Administrator privilege.

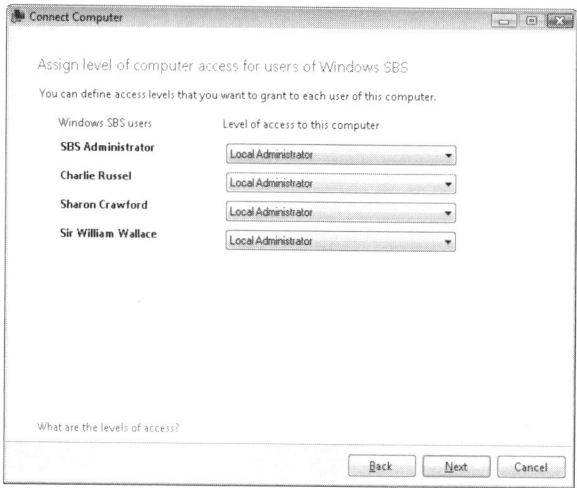

FIGURE 14-13 The Assign Level Of Computer Access For Users Of Windows SBS page of the Connect Computer Wizard

12. Click Next to open the Confirm User Data And Settings Selections page, and if every-thing is as you expected, click Next and then click Restart to begin the account migra-tion and domain join. This process might require more than one reboot, but should proceed automatically.

13. When the Connect Computer Wizard is finished, log on and click Finished.

 REAL WORLD **Local Administrator Accounts**

The SBS default is to create SBS standard users as only standard users on their local computers, and we think this is a very good idea. Most local users have no need to run with elevated privileges, and the security of your network is significant-ly improved if they don't. However, this can be a nuisance for some users who have a legitimate but only occasional need to do something that requires elevation. You could create those users as local administrators, but then that privilege is always available to them.

Another solution has been to create all PCs with a generic local administrative account that the user can use. But this becomes either unwieldy to keep track of and administer, or too generic, giving users the ability to log on to computers that aren't their own with that same password.

We think a better solution is to create one or more (depending on departmental needs and concerns) Standard User SBS domain accounts that can be assigned to individual PCs as local administrator.

These SBS Standard User accounts should only be assigned to PCs that have an actual need to occasionally elevate, and they should also only be allowed to log on during normal business hours, and only locally—no Remote Web Workplace (RWW) access for these accounts. Passwords should be changed regularly.

Now when a user needs to elevate privilege to do something, you don't need to give the user access to an account that has domain administrator privileges. The user can elevate to this special account that is a local administrator, but only a domain user.

Connecting Alternate Clients

Windows XP Professional and Windows Vista business-class clients provide the best experi-ence when running on a Windows Small Business Server 2008 network, especially Windows Vista. There's even a custom SBS gadget for the Windows Vista Sidebar. But computers run-ning older versions of Windows, such as Windows 2000 Professional or Mac OS/X, can also connect to your SBS network. They won't have all the functionality of Windows XP or Win-dows Vista, but they can be managed and used.

Connecting computers that don't meet the minimum requirements for using the Connect Computer Wizard is possible, but it requires you to manually configure and add the computers to the SBS domain and then manually assign users to the computer.

Connecting Earlier Windows Clients

To connect a Windows 2000 Professional client to SBS, you need to manually join the domain and then configure accounts on the computer by following these steps:

1. Log on to the Windows 2000 client with a local administrative account.

2. Open System Properties by right-clicking My Computer and selecting Properties.

3. Click the Network Identification tab and then click Properties to open the Identification Changes page shown in Figure 14-14.

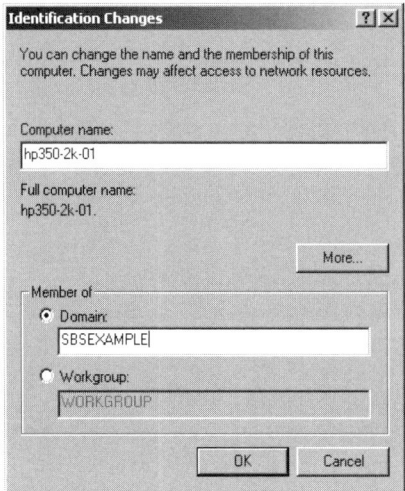

FIGURE 14-14 The Identification Changes page of the System Properties dialog box

4. Type the SBS domain name into the Domain field and click OK.

5. In the Domain Username And Password dialog box, provide the user name and password of an SBS Network Administrator account and click OK.

6. Click OK three more times to acknowledge the welcome message, the reboot warning, and to close the System Properties dialog box. Click Yes to reboot the Windows 2000 computer.

7. When the computer restarts, log on to the computer with an SBS account to ensure that everything went as expected.

Older clients, with the exception of Windows 2000 Server, are not accessible from Remote Web Workplace because they don't support Remote Desktop.

Connecting Mac OS X Clients

Mac OS/X clients can function reasonably well on an SBS network. Mac OS/X 10.4 and later versions can connect correctly to an SBS 2008 network, and versions 10.2 and 10.3 can be made to connect, though you should upgrade your version of OS/X to 10.4 or later if at all possible.

Microsoft Office 2004 and Microsoft Office:mac 2008 both work well with Microsoft Office documents from Windows clients, and Entourage works well with Microsoft Exchange.

To connect to a Windows file share, follow these steps:

1. Configure the computer to obtain its IP address using DHCP, if it doesn't already do so.

2. Select Connect To Server from the Go menu of Finder.

3. In the Connect To Server window, browse to the computer or type the address of the Windows file share, using one of the following formats:

   smb://*fullyqualifieddomainname*/sharename

   smb://*domain.name;servername*/sharename

   For example, to connect to the Data share on the hp350-sbs-srv computer, type in:

   smb://hp350-sbs-srv.example.local/Data

4. In the SMB/CIFS FilesystemAuthentication dialog box, verify the domain name, type in a Windows user name and password, and click OK.

Using Remote Desktop

Microsoft recently released an all new Remote Desktop client for the Mac, Remote Desktop Connection Client for Mac 2, which is available as a free download from the Microsoft Web site at *http://www.microsoft.com/mac/products/remote-desktop/.* This new version supports multiple connections to Windows computers, including Windows Vista and Windows Server 2008 Terminal Services, Network Level Authentication, and printing from Windows applications to Mac-connected printers. Unfortunately, Remote Desktop Connection Client for Mac 2 does not support TS RemoteApps.

Using Remote Web Workplace

Windows Small Business Server 2008 includes an updated version of the Remote Web Workplace (RWW). This Web site gives the remote user access to e-mail, her desktop at work, the internal Web site, and any TS RemoteApps–enabled remote applications that have been configured for RWW.

Connecting to RWW

Connecting to Remote Web Workplace doesn't require any special settings except that you need to be running Internet Explorer 6 (or Internet Explorer 7 from a Windows Vista computer) for full functionality. The default location for RWW is *https://remote.domainname.com*, where domainname.com is replaced by your public Internet domain name.

When you connect to RWW, you see a logon page like that shown in Figure 14-15.

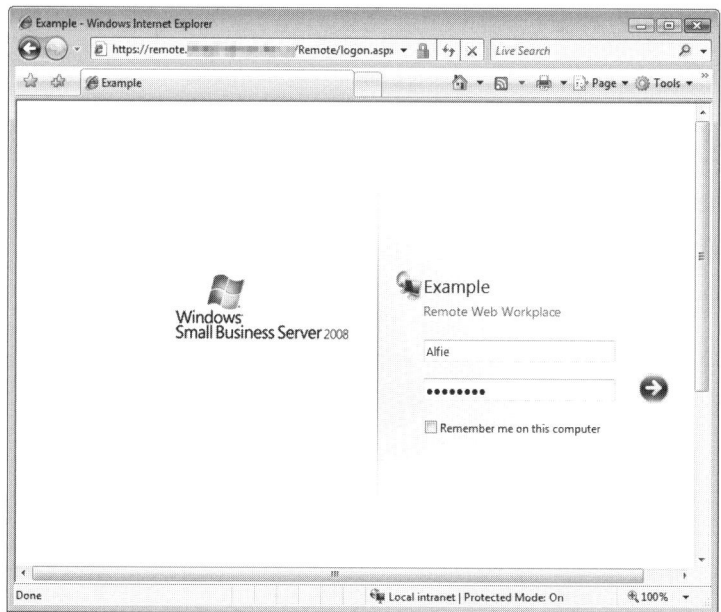

FIGURE 14-15 The Remote Web Workplace logon page

 UNDER THE HOOD   **Two-Factor Authentication**

I f your network contains sensitive information—and whose doesn't these days—
you should consider providing an additional layer of security beyond simple passwords. Windows Small Business Server 2008 sets reasonable password policies, but even the best of password policies is a balancing act between making the password difficult to crack and making it easy for users to remember and use so that they aren't tempted to write it down on the back of their keyboards. The four kinds of authentication methods or factors are:

- Something you know (password)
- Something you have (token, or physical key)

- Something you are (biometric)
- Somewhere you are (location)

Of these, only the first three are realistic and usable in a small business environment, though the fourth—location—is starting to be used by banks as one factor to be sure that the person trying to access your bank account is actually you.

Passwords alone are a single-factor authentication method, in this case something you know. Two-factor authentication requires two of the main three factors and provides a definite improvement in the surety that the person authenticating to your network is really who he claims to be.

For a second authentication factor, we like the simplicity, moderate cost, and effectiveness of a one-time password (OTP). Generated automatically by a token you carry around with you, the combination of the token, a personal identification number (PIN), and your SBS password provides an additional level of security. Requiring at least users with administrative privilege (and we think all remote users) to use two-factor authentication is a good way to improve the overall security of the sensitive data on your network.

Third-party providers of OTP tokens include AuthAnvil (*http://www.authanvil.com*), CryptoCard (*http://www.cryptocard.com*), and RSA SecureID (*http://www.rsa.com*). Of these, only AuthAnvil is focused on the small business market, with a suite of products that are fully integrated into SBS, including RWWGuard, which replaces the logon page shown in Figure 14-15 with a new page that includes an additional field to directly enter your OTP. We use RWWGuard and AuthAnvil on our SBS network.

After you've logged on RWW, you'll see the main RWW page shown in Figure 14-16. From here, you can connect to a computer on your SBS network, log on to Outlook Web Access, go to your internal home page, change your password, or if you're logged on as an administrator, connect to a server to perform system maintenance.

You can customize this RWW landing page, even adding links to applications on your network using TS RemoteApps. We'll cover customization of this site in Chapter 19, "Managing Connectivity," and TS RemoteApps is covered in Chapter 25, "Adding a Terminal Server."

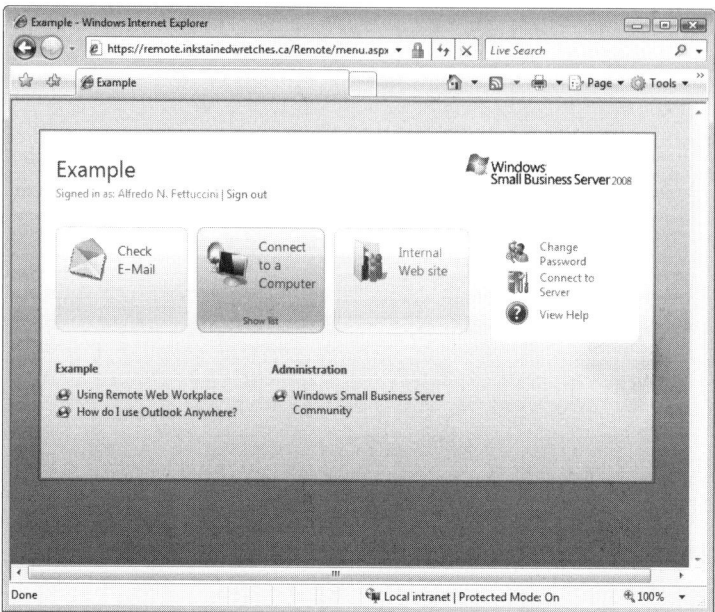

FIGURE 14-16 The main RWW landing page

Managing Computers

You can manage the clients that are available on your network, along with many of the settings that control their availability and behavior, from the Windows SBS Console. To see a list of computers joined to your SBS domain, open the Windows SBS Console and click the Network button to open the Computers page, as shown in Figure 14-17.

From the Computers page, you can see a quick status for the computers on your network: which ones are online, which ones need updates, and which ones have other problems or warnings. When you click a computer in the list, a new section of the Tasks pane opens showing you tasks you can perform that are specific to the computer selected, as shown in Figure 14-18, where we've selected computer HP350-VISTA-03.

From here we can offer remote assistance, connect directly to the computer using Remote Desktop (if the computer supports Remote Desktop), view the properties of the computer, check on update and other security-related status, and even remove the computer from the domain.

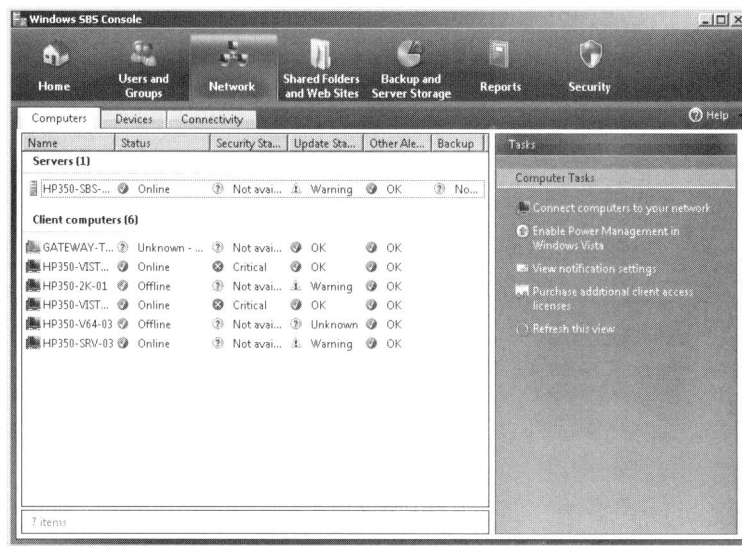

FIGURE 14-17 The Windows SBS Console Computers page

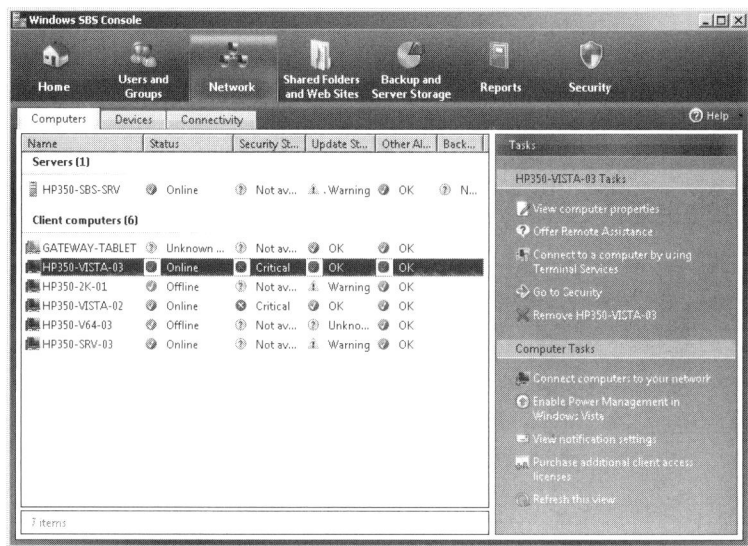

FIGURE 14-18 The Windows SBS Console Computers page with computer HP350-VISTA-03 selected

Viewing and Modifying Client Computer Settings

To view or modify the properties and settings of a client computer in SBS, select the computer in the Windows SBS Console Computers page, as shown in Figure 14-18, and click View Computer Properties in the Tasks pane to open the Properties dialog box for the computer. From here you can view the name of the computer, set the description of it, view the status of updates assigned to the computer, and control who has remote access to the computer.

To set the remote access to the computer, follow these steps:

1. Open the Windows SBS Console Computers page and click the computer you want to change the remote access for in the left pane.

2. Click View Computer Properties in the Tasks pane.

3. Click User Access in the left pane of the Properties page, as shown in Figure 14-19.

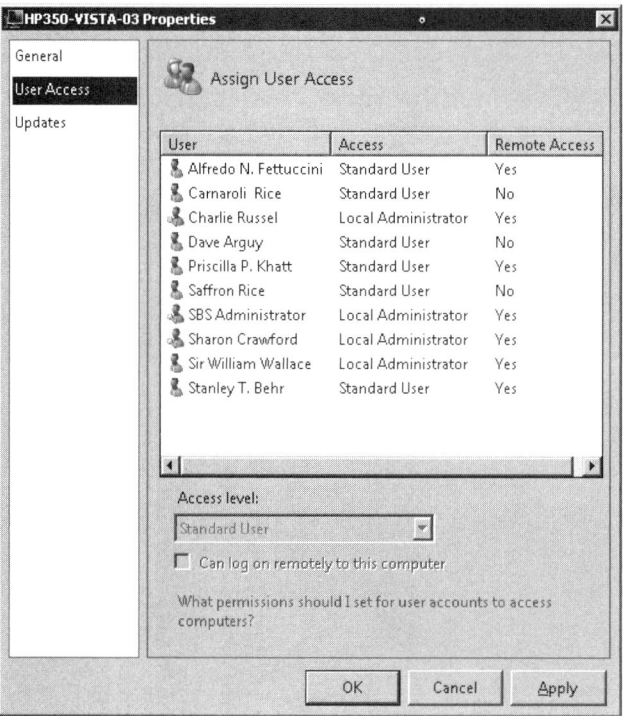

FIGURE 14-19 The Assign User Access page of the Computer Properties dialog box

4. Select the user you want to assign, modify, or remove access from, and then choose the level of access the user will have on the computer from the Access Level drop-down list.

5. Select the Can Log On Remotely To This Computer check box if the user should be allowed to log on over RWW or from a local Remote Desktop session.

6. Click OK to close the wizard.

UNDER THE HOOD   Controlling Local Access to a Computer

The SBS wizards only allow you to control remote access to a computer. Any SBS user with physical access to the computer can log on locally with at least Standard User privilege. This is not restricted by SBS in any way, despite what the help files appear to indicate. We think this is a mistake, and one that we frankly don't understand—especially since the fix to directly control who has access to a computer is fairly easy. So we wrote a little script to do it. This script uses PowerShell to directly edit the ADSI properties for a user account, enabling access to specific computers. If a computer isn't explicitly granted access, it is denied once this script is run.

```
# Script Name: set-comprestrict.ps1
# ModHist: 12/07/08 - Initial
#       :
#
#  Script to restrict a user to one or more computers on an SBS 2008
network
#     Expects: two parameters--
#         logon name (sAMAccountName)
#         client computer names (in a quoted, comma separated list)
#
#  With Thanks to Richard Siddaway (Microsoft MVP) for his help.


# Copyright 2008 by Charlie Russel and Sharon Crawford. All rights
  reserved.
#   You may freely use this script in your own environment, modifying it
    to meet
#   your needs. But you may not re-publish it without permission.
#


param($UserName, $comp)
$_OU="ou=SBSUsers,ou=Users,ou=MyBusiness,dc=SBSExample,dc=local"
$searchOU=[ADSI]"LDAP://$_OU"
$searcher= New-Object
    System.DirectoryServices.DirectorySearcher $searchOU
$searcher.filter = "(&(objectClass=User)(sAMAccountName=$UserName))"

$userResult = $searcher.FindOne()
$user = $userResult.GetDirectoryEntry()

$user.userWorkstations = $comp
"Restricting user account: $UserName to clients: $comp"

$user.SetInfo()
"Done"
```

You'll need to run this script from an elevated PowerShell console.

Another solution is to use the native Active Directory Users And Computer console. For more on using the native tools, including when you should and should not use them, see Chapter 17, "Windows SBS Console versus Server Manager." But the short answer is always use the Windows SBS Console if at all possible. Only use the native Server Manager consoles when you're really sure there's no other way to achieve the desired end result.

Remotely Managing Computers

Network Administrators can remotely manage a computer from the Windows SBS Console, either offering remote assistance to the currently logged-on user or directly connecting to the computer over Remote Desktop.

Offering Remote Assistance

One way of managing computers remotely is by directly helping users to perform their tasks. Remote Assistance gives the Network Administrator a way to share the session of a user on a Windows XP or Windows Vista computer. It is not available on computers with older Windows operating systems, such as Windows 2000 Professional, or on non-Windows computers.

When you share a session using Remote Assistance, both the user and the Network Administrator see the same thing and both can interact with the session using both keyboard and mouse.

To offer Remote Assistance, follow these steps:

1. Open the Windows SBS Console if it isn't already open.

2. Click the Network button and then select the computer you want to offer Remote Assistance to.

3. Click Offer Remote Assistance from the Tasks pane. If you haven't disabled the warning, you'll see a reminder that you need to make sure the user you want to help is logged on, as shown in Figure 14-20.

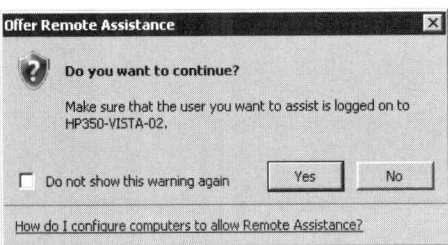

FIGURE 14-20 Warning before remote assistance is offered

4. Click Yes. The user logged on to the computer you're offering assistance to is prompted to let you share her session, as shown in Figure 14-21.

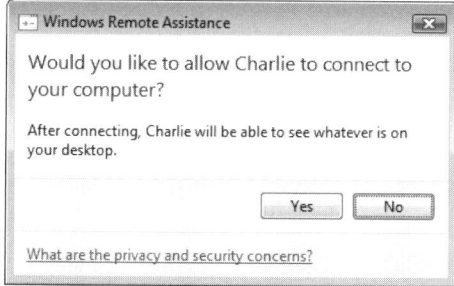

FIGURE 14-21 Windows Remote Assistance offer

5. If the user accepts the offer by clicking Yes, his desktop will be shared back to the SBS server console, and both screens will have the Remote Assistance toolbar displayed, as shown in Figure 14-22.

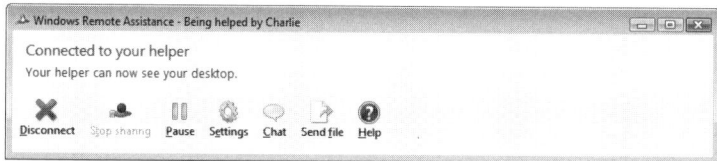

FIGURE 14-22 The Remote Assistance toolbar is displayed on both screens on top of the user's desktop.

6. When the Remote Assistance session has accomplished its task, either user can click the Disconnect button in the Remote Assistance toolbar to end the session.

Connect Remotely

Remote management tasks that can't be easily accomplished in a Remote Assistance session, or that need to be performed when no user is logged on to the remote computer, often needed to be performed by physically going to the computer and logging on with the administrator's account. A major nuisance, certainly. With the inclusion of Remote Desktop in Windows XP Professional and Windows Vista Business, Enterprise, and Ultimate Editions, administrators have an alternative—a Remote Desktop session. When you join a computer to the SBS domain using *http://connect*, one of the settings that is propagated to the new client is to enable Remote Desktop on the computer.

Although it's easy enough to directly connect to a remote computer using either the Remote Desktop link in the All Programs/Accessories folder of the Start Menu or from the command line using Mstsc.exe, the Windows SBS Console gives you direct access from the console. Just highlight the computer in the Computers page of the Windows SBS Console and click Connect To A Computer Using Terminal Services in the Tasks pane. You'll see a prompt for the connection credentials to use, as shown in Figure 14-23, and then a full-screen Remote Desktop session opens.

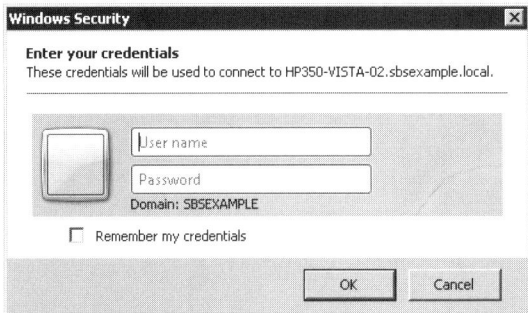

FIGURE 14-23 Remote Desktop credentials prompt

If there is an active session on the remote computer, you'll get a warning that the other user will be disconnected from the session. Unlike with Remote Assistance, you can't share a Remote Desktop session to a client computer. (The exception to this is that Remote Desktop connections to Terminal Server sessions can be shared, if necessary.)

The only real problem with using the Windows SBS Console to initiate a Remote Desktop session is that it will always be a full-screen session. That's fine for some things, but can be a nuisance if you're trying to do the same task on multiple client computers. In that event, we like to use the command line:

```
mstsc  /v:<computername> /h:<height> /w:<width>
```

So, to open three Remote Desktop sessions, each with a resolution of 1024 x 768, to the computers HP350-SRV-03, HP350-VISTA-02, and HP350-VISTA-03, a simple PowerShell command line will get the job done:

```
PSH> $RDP_Array = "hp350-srv-03","hp350-vista-02","hp350-vista-03"
PSH>foreach($computer in $RDP_Array){mstsc /v:$computer /h:768 /w:1024}
```

Removing Computers from the Network

You should remove computers from the network only if the computers are being decommissioned. When you remove a computer from the network, you make any SBS user accounts on the computer unavailable, and even if you later rejoin the computer to your SBS domain, new user profiles will be created and the old ones will be unavailable. If you do have to have a user use a computer temporarily without being part of the domain, you can usually just create a local user account on the computer and have the user log on to that account.

If circumstances require you to remove a computer from the domain, and you want to save some of the settings for an existing account, use the Windows Vista Windows Easy Transfer (WET) Wizard, or with Windows XP, the Files And Settings Transfer Wizard. This won't save everything, but it will save many of the current user's settings.

To remove a computer from the SBS domain, follow these steps:

1. Open the Windows SBS Console if it isn't already open.

2. Click the Network button and then select the computer you want to remove from the SBS domain.

3. Click Remove *Computername* in the Tasks pane.

4. When prompted, as shown in Figure 14-24, click Yes to remove the computer.

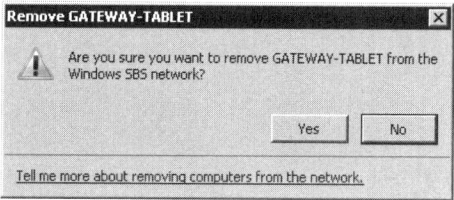

FIGURE 14-24 The Remove Computer warning message

Summary

In this chapter we've covered the basic management tasks available for individual computers on the network. Windows Small Business Server 2008 simplifies many of them by automating tasks and ensuring that computers meet the necessary requirements before they join the SBS network. In addition, by making both Remote Assistance and Remote Desktop directly available from the Windows SBS Console, the Network Administrator has direct access to computers for management and assistance.

In the next chapter we'll cover the details of setting up and managing software updates to your Windows computers on your SBS network.

Managing Software Updates

Software updates, or patches in the common parlance, are something that everyone hates, but they have become a basic part of life in the modern computing world. We hated them and complained about them when we were UNIX system administrators some 20 years ago, and we still hate them, even though the overall process of obtaining, testing, and applying them has improved greatly. We doubt that anything we can say will make you like patches any better than we do, but in this chapter we'll try to cover the basics to make the patch management process as straightforward and manageable as possible. We'll cover how SBS uses Windows Server Update Services (WSUS) to enable a fully integrated software update management solution for our SBS networks.

 REAL WORLD   **Terminology**

The first rule of patches is that Microsoft doesn't like that word. Microsoft uses several different terms, each with a slightly different meaning, but the reality is that to the rest of the world, they're still called patches. We call them patches, the magazines and newspapers call them patches, even most Microsoft employees call them patches, unless they're giving a formal presentation. So throughout this chapter, that's what we'll call them. But Microsoft does have official terminology, and we should all be clear on what it is.

- **Critical update**   A generally available fix for a critical but non-security-related bug. A critical update has an accompanying Knowledge Base article.

- **Security update**   A generally available fix for a security vulnerability. Security updates have an accompanying Knowledge Base article and a Security Bulletin.

- **Software update** A broad term that covers service packs, hotfixes, update rollups, security updates, feature packs, and so on. A software update has an accompanying Knowledge Base article.

- **Service pack** A generally available collection of fixes and feature enhancements. Service packs are cumulative and contain all currently available updates, update rollups, security updates, critical updates, and hotfixes, and they might contain fixes for problems that were found internally and have not been otherwise released. Service packs also sometimes add new features (Microsoft Windows XP SP2, for example).

- **Hotfix** A narrowly available fix for a specific issue. Hotfixes are generally available only through Microsoft Product Support Services and cannot be redistributed. Hotfixes are not tested as thoroughly as updates, update rollups, or service packs.

- **Update** A generally available fix for a specific, non-security-related, noncritical problem. An update has an accompanying Knowledge Base article.

- **Update rollup** A generally available and tested collection of hotfixes, security updates, critical updates, and updates that are packaged together. An update rollup has an accompanying Knowledge Base article.

See? All sorts of terms and terminology, and not one of them is a patch. For complete, up-to-date details on Microsoft update terminology, see *http://support.microsoft.com/kb/824684/*.

Why Patching Is Important

In the old days, when your network wasn't connected to the Internet, system administrators were the only people who installed software, and users had only a green screen terminal, deciding when to apply a patch was a fairly straightforward decision. If you were having a specific problem and you wanted a bit of overtime on the weekend, you came in and applied a patch. If no one was complaining and you didn't want to work on the weekend, you threw the tape (patches always came on tapes in those days) in the drawer and waited until you had to come in on the weekend for some other maintenance, or users started complaining about a problem that seemed related. Or you simply never got around to it at all.

Even in the more recent past it was possible to have a more considered and gradual approach to applying patches. When a vulnerability was identified, it often took months before there was any real risk to your network.

Today that approach simply won't work, as Code Red, Nimda, Slammer, and others have all too clearly demonstrated. Within hours or (at most) days of the release of a critical security update, there will almost certainly be sample exploit code posted on the Internet, telling anyone and everyone how to exploit the vulnerability. If you ignore critical security updates, you place your entire SBS network—and the data stored on it—at risk.

Applying software updates is only one part of a defense-in-depth strategy to protect your network, but it's a critical part. Don't neglect it.

 REAL WORLD **Patch Tuesday**

In the old days, patches, especially security updates, were released whenever a new vulnerability was identified and corrected. When that happened a few times a year, it wasn't a big problem, and the system administrator dealt with each patch as it came out. In most cases, you could just wait until the Service Pack came out and deal with a whole bunch of them at once. But as more and more security updates and critical updates were released on an almost daily basis, it became increasingly difficult to properly test and identify all the patches that were necessary for your system. The whole process became a serious impediment to productivity and security.

In direct response to many, many complaints, Microsoft moved to a monthly update release process. Unless there is a compelling and immediate need for a critical security update to be released off-cycle, all security updates are released once a month, on the second Tuesday of the month. This change has greatly simplified the planning and deployment of patches.

The Patching Cycle

There are (or there should be) four basic phases in the ongoing cycle of maintaining a well-patched, up-to-date network:

- Assess
- Identify
- Evaluate and plan
- Deploy

Each of these phases is essential to the successful management of patches on your network. And in a large, well-run network, each of these phases is quite formal and carefully delineated.

Given the relative simplicity of SBS networks, and the more realistic IT budgets and resources we have, you're going to have to combine and simplify the overall process a bit, and you'll probably even bypass phases on occasion. However, it's good to have an understanding of the phases and to think through the steps involved in each one, even if you're combining them. In the following sections, we'll cover each of the phases of the full patching cycle, and then provide an "SBS Version" subsection that provides a realistic description of the phase for an SBS network. Obviously, there is no single SBS version—the resources and requirements of an SBS network of 50 users are a good deal different from those of 5 users.

Assess

The *assess phase* of patch management is all about understanding what your environment is, where and how it is vulnerable and can be attacked, and what resources and procedures are in place to reduce those vulnerabilities.

When a patch is released, you can't make an informed decision about whether you need to install that patch unless you first know what software is present in your environment and what your critical business assets are that absolutely, positively must be protected. So the first step to an overall patch management process is to figure out what software you're running in your environment. All of it, we hope. Whether you build a spreadsheet, have a Microsoft Office Access database, or just keep it all in a chart in Microsoft Office Word, you need to get your software environment audited and documented.

Identify your critical business assets. Is there confidential data that you couldn't function without? Are there critical systems that must be available at all times? Are there individuals whose productivity is mission-critical? All of these are business assets that you should factor into your overall patch management strategy.

The next part of the assessment phase is to understand what security threats and vulnerabilities you currently have. Do you have legacy Windows systems that are no longer supported? Are there non-Windows systems that aren't being fully monitored and updated automatically?

Are you running old versions of software programs that can't be easily updated or replaced? Do you have public-facing Web servers that are not behind your firewall? What are your security policies and how are they enforced? These and many, many more questions need to be asked—and answered.

Finally, you need to assess your patching infrastructure and resources. How do you deploy software and patches now? Who is responsible for identifying, testing, and deploying patches? What resources are available to help with that? How rapidly can you respond to a critical vulnerability that affects your systems? What steps can you take to improve your response time?

SBS Version

If all that seems a bit much, it's really just a lot of somewhat formal words to say that what you really need to do is know what is on your network that you need to keep patched. It's also good to have a record of what kinds of patches have caused trouble for you in the past—when you see new patches that affect these areas, you'll probably want to do some additional testing before you send the patch out.

Identify

The *identify phase* is about finding out what software updates or patches are available, and how critical it is that they be deployed in your environment. You need to take the following actions:

- Discover the patch.
- Decide whether it's relevant to your environment.
- Download the patch.
- Identify the patch's criticality.

There are many ways to discover patches, but for Microsoft products, one of the best ways is to sign up for e-mail alerts. If you do this, Microsoft will send you notifications of security updates before they are actually released. The signup page is at *http://www.microsoft.com /technet/security/bulletin/notify.mspx*. You can tailor the notification method and detail level to suit your environment.

> **NOTE** This link provides alerts only for security-related patches.

Whatever method you use to discover patches, it's important that you have a way to trust the source of the patch information. All Microsoft security update alerts are signed with a publicly available PGP key, for example. And it shouldn't be necessary to say this, but just in case: Microsoft will never send a security update as an attachment to an e-mail! Never.

> **IMPORTANT** Wait, maybe you missed that. Again, for emphasis: Microsoft will *never* send a security update as an attachment to an e-mail! Never.

After you find out about a new patch, you need to decide whether it's relevant to your environment. If all your client computers are running Windows Vista SP1 (and they should be!), a patch that applies only to Windows XP isn't really relevant to your environment. However, if the patch is a critical security update for the 2007 Microsoft Office system and you run that in your environment, you'll need to apply it.

When you determine that a patch is relevant to your environment, you need to obtain the patch from a known and trusted source. For a Microsoft patch, this generally means downloading it directly from Microsoft. With SBS, this means letting WSUS download the patch by synchronizing, but we'll get to the gory details of WSUS later. Find the relevant Knowledge Base article for the patch and then cut and paste the link to the download page directly into your browser. Do not click the link in an e-mail to get your patch. Even when you have verified that the e-mail is really from Microsoft and is a legitimate e-mail, you shouldn't click the links. Get into the habit of always using cut and paste. When you use cut and paste to put a link into your browser, you greatly reduce the likelihood of a phishing attack—being unknowingly redirected to a site that looks exactly like the site you expected to go to, but is actually a site designed to steal information from you or download unwanted spyware onto your computer.

> **NOTE** Most e-mail clients today have the ability to force all e-mail to display as plain text. This is a good thing, because it prevents unscrupulous people from hiding the real destination of a link. The giveaway for detecting a bogus link will usually be that it's a link to an IP address, not the actual DNS domain name, or if it is a DNS name, it's not exactly the one you think it is. If you make the change and only read your e-mail in plain text, your e-mail won't be as pretty, but you'll be a lot safer.
>
> To enable plain-text e-mail handling in Outlook 2003, select Options from the Tools menu. Click the Preferences tab, and then click E-Mail Options. Select the Read All Standard Mail In Plain Text and Read All Digitally Signed Mail In Plain Text check boxes. Click OK and restart Outlook.

After you've downloaded the patch and read the associated Knowledge Base article, you are in a position to determine just how critical the patch is in your environment. Is this a patch that needs to be deployed immediately, with limited testing—or even with no testing? Or are there ameliorating factors that allow the patch to be deployed as part of a regular patching schedule after full testing?

SBS Version

Again, if that seemed a bit much, you're probably right. But it's actually what we had to go through before the R2 version of SBS 2003 if we didn't have some method—usually third-party—to automatically download and identify patches for our environment. With the R2 release of SBS 2003, we were able to let WSUS take care of the downloads and the initial analysis. SBS 2008 extends that to fully support WSUS version 3, but you'll still want to do some thinking before you let it fire off an automatic update to every client in the network.

Evaluate and Plan

The *evaluate and plan phase* of patch management flows naturally out of the identify phase, and in many ways is an extension of it. In this phase, you determine how to respond to the software update you've downloaded. Is it critical, or even necessary? How should it be deployed? And to whom? Should interim countermeasures be employed that will minimize your exposure to the vulnerability? What priority does the patch have?

The initial determination of need, suitability, and priority is made during the identify phase, but in the evaluate and plan phase, you should take a closer look at the patch. What priority is the patch? If it affects a critical business asset, and there's no easy or appropriate countermeasure except the patch, it will have a higher priority for testing and deployment than if there's a simple countermeasure that you can implement until the patch can be deployed. If it targets critical business assets, it's going to have a higher priority than if the only computers that are affected are several old Windows 2000 computers that aren't running any critical business applications. (But you got rid of those old Windows 2000 computers, right?)

When you've identified the priority of the patch, you need to plan the actual deployment. Which computers need to have the patch deployed to them? Are there any constraints or issues that interfere with the deployment? Who needs to be notified, and what steps need to be taken so that the deployment minimizes the disruption to the environment? If this is an emergency release, will it go through a staged deployment, or is every affected computer going to have the patch deployed as soon as possible?

SBS Version

In any SBS network larger than a few clients, you should have a couple of clients that are designated canaries. In all but emergency patch situations, these computers will have the new patches deployed to them first. If they survive the patch without major issues, you can OK the deployment onto the rest of your clients.

Unfortunately, WSUS—as included with SBS 2008—doesn't support having a special group of client computers that are treated differently from other clients. The workaround we've found is to have one (or two) users who go directly to Microsoft Update every Patch Tuesday and update their computers. This gets the update onto their computers quicker than any other method, and allows some testing time before any automatic deployment can happen. If you go this route, choose a user who has a fairly typical computer and, most important, who is willing to take on this role. Also, make sure that you carefully review the "Caveats" section of the Security Bulletin. This section details known issues and interactions that you should be aware of.

Deploy

The *deployment phase* of patch management is in many ways the easiest phase. You've done all your preparatory work; now all you need to do is the actual deployment.

First and foremost, communicate. Let everyone who will be affected know that you will be deploying a patch, and what application or area of the operating system it affects. If you know that the deployment will cause changes in behavior, tell your users before the deployment. You will have far fewer support calls if you've warned people that a certain behavior is expected than if you surprise them.

SBS Version

With SBS, we have WSUS to do the deployment and track its progress. If your canary user has survived, you should proceed with the deployment. But the same rule applies as for a really large enterprise—communicate. If users have open files, and SBS automatically deploys an update that requires a reboot, they could potentially lose work. A reminder e-mail to your users on Patch Tuesday is a good idea.

Repeat

After you've deployed a patch, the process starts over again. It really is a continuous process—or it should be. At a minimum, verify that the patch has been successfully deployed to the affected computers. Update your software map and database so that you know which computers have had the patch applied. Because our assumption is that every patch is on every computer, we only keep track of the exceptions. When a patch cycle is complete, we make a note of any issues, confirm that deployment has been successful, and get ready for the next round.

Using SBS Software Updates

SBS includes a customized and configured version of Windows Software Update Services (WSUS). The SBS team has already done the heavy lifting to get WSUS configured and working optimally for our SBS networks. When the SBS install is finished, updates are already being managed and deployed, but you can do additional customization from the Updates page of the Windows SBS Console.

Configuring Software Update Settings

The default software update settings for SBS 2008 are adequate for most small businesses, but there are additional settings you can use to customize how updates are handled on your network. You can

- Change the update level for servers and clients.
- Change the update schedule.
- Change which computers are managed by WSUS.

> **NOTE** For those familiar with SBS 2003 R2, these settings are very similar, though the interface is different.

Changing Update Level

SBS uses the following four *update levels* to control which updates for SBS and your SBS client and server computers are automatically deployed:

- **High** Automatically approves all security, critical, and definition updates, and also approves all service packs. This is the default for client computers.
- **Medium** Automatically approves all security, critical, and definition updates. This is the default for server computers.

- **Low** Automatically approves all security and definition updates. Critical updates that are not security-related will not be automatically approved.

- **None** No updates are automatically approved. Each update must be manually approved or rejected. Not a good idea.

To change the level for a class of computers, follow these steps:

1. Open the Windows SBS Console if it isn't already open.

2. Select Security on the navigation bar.

3. Click Updates, if it isn't on top, to display the Updates page, as shown in Figure 15-1.

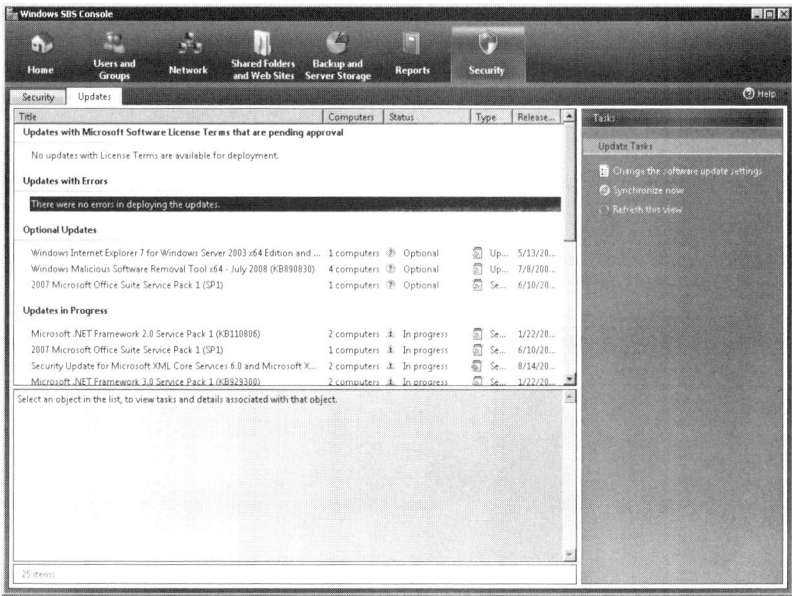

FIGURE 15-1 The Updates page of the Windows SBS Console

4. Click Change The Software Update Settings in the Tasks pane to open the Software Update Settings dialog box shown Figure 15-2.

5. Select Server Updates to change the settings for servers; select Client Updates to change settings for client PCs.

6. Select the level to use for this class of computers and then click OK to close the dialog box and change the level.

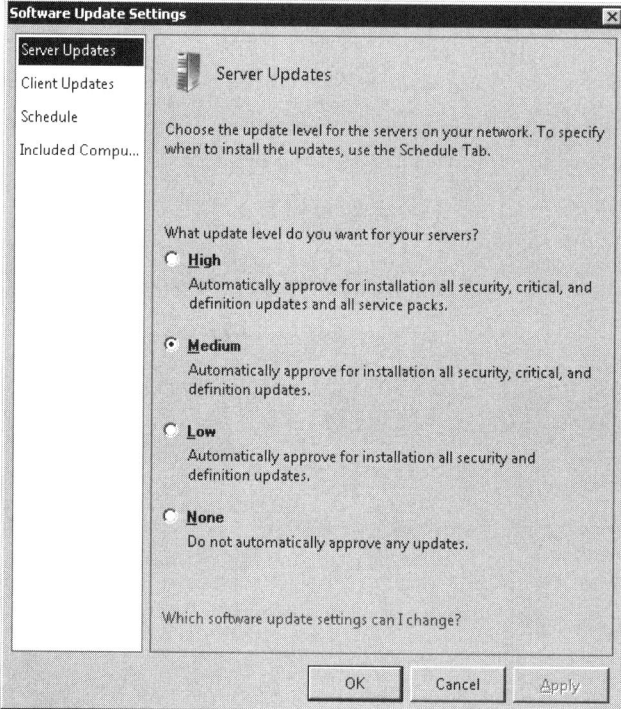

FIGURE 15-2 The Software Update Settings dialog box

Changing Update Schedule

You can change the day of the week and the time of day that automatic updates happen and also configure updates to download automatically to computers but wait for the user to initiate the installation by changing the update schedule. To change the update schedule, use the following steps:

1. Open the Windows SBS Console if it isn't already open.
2. Select Security on the navigation bar.
3. Click Updates, if it isn't on top, to display the Updates page.
4. Click Change The Software Update Settings in the Tasks pane to open the Software Update Settings dialog box.
5. Click Schedule in the left pane to open the Schedule page of the Software Update Settings dialog box, as shown in Figure 15-3.

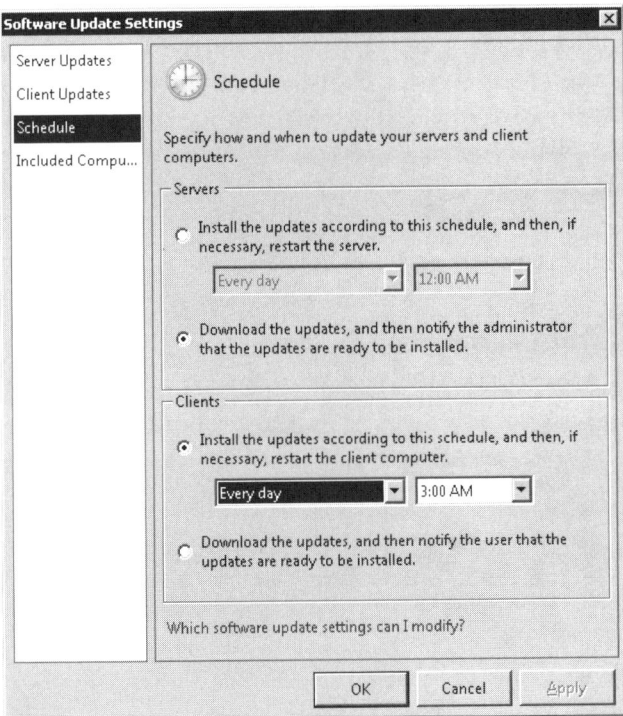

FIGURE 15-3 The Schedule page of the Software Update Settings dialog box

6. To configure automatic downloads to Client computers, select that option in the Clients section.

NOTE Configuring client computers for automatic downloads requires that an administrator initiate the install on the client.

7. To configure servers to update automatically, including automatically rebooting, change that option in the Servers section.

NOTE Configuring servers to automatically install updates is a really bad idea. This will cause the server to automatically reboot if the update requires an update, and you run a significant risk of lost work or unexpected downtime. This option should only be chosen if you've carefully considered all the alternatives and have a clear understanding of the need for automatic update installation. And even then we think that server updates should be a manual process.

8. To change the day of the week or the time of day that an automatic update is installed, select the day of the week from the drop-down list. You can choose to have updates always installed on a specific day, or on any day that they're available. The default is Every Day. The default time of day for updates is 3:00 A.M. If you have automatic backups of client computers, you should adjust this time to not interfere with the backup window.

9. When you've completed any changes to the update schedule, click OK to close the dialog box and implement the changes.

Excluding Computers from Automatic Updates

By default, software updates in SBS include all computers on your SBS network and automatically assign them to either server or client computers. You can use the exclusion to prevent any updates from being offered to a particular computer, while also excluding it from error reporting on update status.

 REAL WORLD   **Permanently Excluding Remote Users**

A reasonable question to ask is why you might want to exclude a computer from the automatic updates of SBS. One type of computer that it makes sense to exclude is the computer that never, or only rarely, connects to the network. This includes the laptops used by external employees, for example, or by salespeople who spend most of their time on the road. If you include them in the normal SBS software updates list, you'll never get a nice green check that all is well, since they are rarely available to verify their status. Nor should they primarily be using the SBS network for updates. Instead, these computers should be configured to go directly to the Microsoft Update site for updates. And we think they should be configured to automatically update from there, just as client computers on your SBS network are configured to automatically update. If anything, these computers are at greater risk because they routinely connect to unsecured networks, and thus should be maintained at a fully patched level.

To exclude a computer from automatic updates, follow these steps:

1. Open the Windows SBS Console if it isn't already open.

2. Select Security on the navigation bar.

3. Click Updates, if it isn't on top, to display the Updates page.

4. Click Change The Software Update Settings in the Tasks pane to open the Software Update Settings dialog box.

5. Click Included Computers in the left pane to open the Included Computers page of the Software Update Settings dialog box, as shown in Figure 15-4.

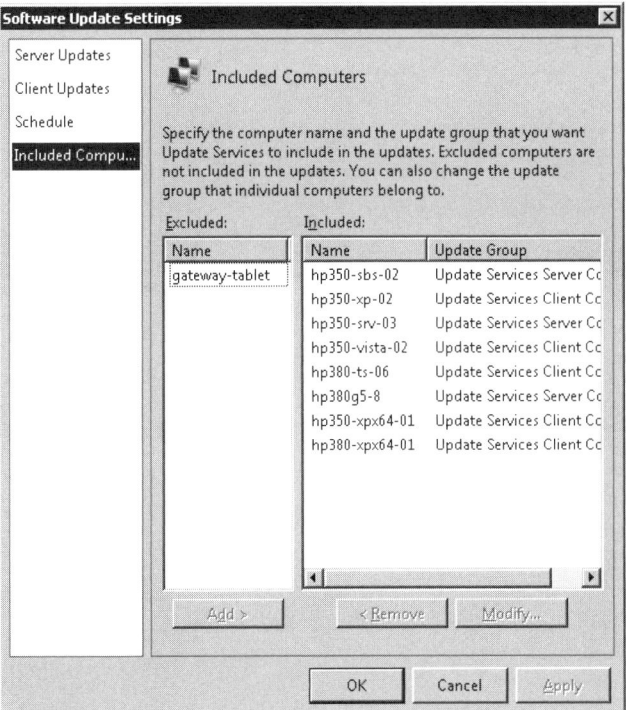

FIGURE 15-4 The Included Computers page of the Software Update Settings dialog box

6. Select the computer you want to exclude from the list of Included computers and click Remove to move it to the Excluded list.

7. When you've completed your changes to the Included Computers page, click OK to close the dialog box and apply the changes.

Modifying the Update Group

Generally, SBS correctly identifies whether a computer is a server or a client and includes it in the appropriate group for update purposes. You wouldn't normally change that setting. But if you want to force a particular computer that is a server to automatically be updated, for example, or to ensure that a particularly critical workstation isn't automatically rebooted at 3:00 A.M. the Wednesday morning after Patch Tuesday, you can modify the group the computer is in to match the behavior you need.

To modify the update group of a computer, follow these steps:

1. Open the Windows SBS Console if it isn't already open.

2. Select Security on the navigation bar.

3. Click Updates, if it isn't on top, to display the Updates page.

4. Click Change The Software Update Settings in the Tasks pane to open the Software Update Settings dialog box.

5. Click Included Computers in the left pane to open the Included Computers page of the Software Update Settings dialog box.

6. Select the computer you want to change and click Modify to open the Change The Members Of An Update Group dialog box, as shown in Figure 15-5.

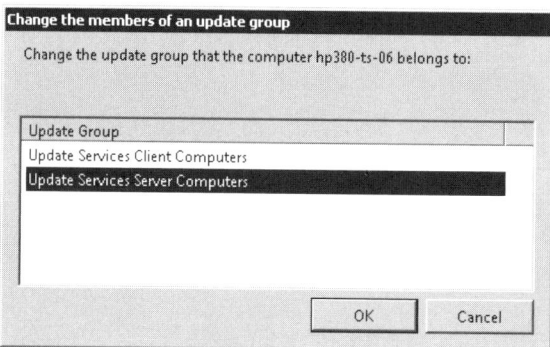

FIGURE 15-5 The Change The Members Of An Update Group dialog box

7. Select the group to move the computer to and click OK.

8. When you've completed your changes to the Included Computers page, click OK to close the dialog box and apply the changes.

Deploying Updates

Most updates are automatically accepted and deployed by the built-in rules of SBS Software Updates, but some updates are considered optional or require explicit acceptance of a separate End User License Agreement (EULA), and these will require intervention by an SBS administrator to either deploy or decline the update.

The main Updates page, shown in Figure 15-6, includes the overall status of updates on your SBS network, and also the specific details of any selected update. In the details pane of the Updates page, you can find more information on the specifics of the update, what applications or versions of Windows it applies to, and whether it will require a reboot. The details also include a link to the appropriate Knowledge Base article or download page for the update.

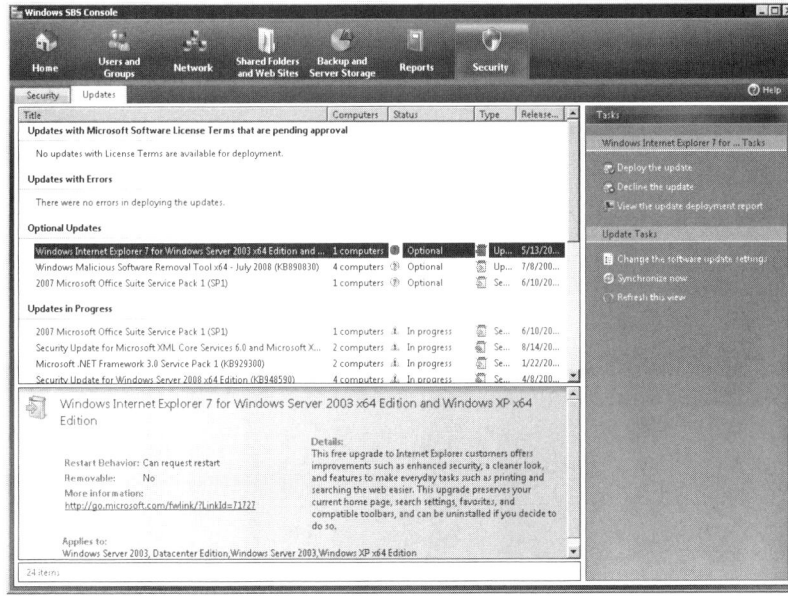

FIGURE 15-6 The Updates page, showing details for an optional update

To deploy or decline an update, follow these steps:

1. Open the Windows SBS Console if it isn't already open.

2. Select Security on the navigation bar.

3. Click Updates, if it isn't on top, to display the Updates page.

4. Select the update you want to deploy or decline in the main pane of the Updates page and read the description of the update in the details pane.

5. Click Deploy (or Decline) in the Tasks pane to open the Software Updates dialog box shown in Figure 15-7. (The Decline dialog box is essentially the same, except that it says Decline instead of Deploy.)

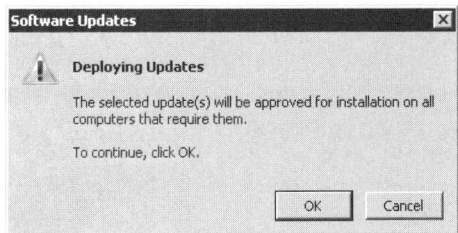

FIGURE 15-7 The Software Updates Deploying Updates dialog box

6. Click OK to deploy (or decline) the update. If the update requires a separate EULA ac-knowledgement, such as the Windows Internet Explorer 7 update highlighted in Figure 15-6, you'll be prompted to accept the Software License Terms, as shown in Figure 15-8.

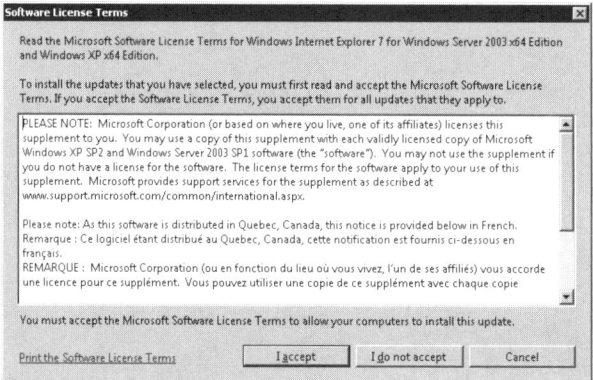

FIGURE 15-8 The Software License Terms dialog box allows the administrator to accept for all computers affected by the update.

7. Click I Accept and the update is deployed. You'll see a final acknowledgement message that the update is scheduled for deployment in the next 4 to 24 hours.

8. Click OK and the update will be added to the Updates In Progress section.

 UNDER THE HOOD **Changing Your Mind**

When you decline an update, it disappears from the SBS Updates page com-pletely. There's really no way to change your mind and decide to deploy it from within the Windows SBS Console. To approve an update that has been previ-ously declined, you'll need to use the native WSUS console. Use the following steps to approve an update that has either been automatically declined by SBS Software Updates, or that you've manually declined:

1. Open the Update Services console by selecting Microsoft Windows Server Up-date Services 3.0 SP1 in the Administrative Tools folder of the Start menu.

2. In the left pane of the Update Services console, navigate to Updates, then to All Updates, and then select Declined from the Approval drop-down list in the All Updates center pane. Click Refresh to update the view.

3. Select the update you want to approve from the list of declined updates and click Approve on the Actions pane.

4. In the Approve Updates dialog box, select the groups of computers to approve the update for and select Approved from the drop-down list of options.

5. Click OK to approve the update and click Close to close the progress dialog box.

6. Close the Update Services console.

Using the native Update Services console is not something you should ordinarily do, since it can interfere with the normal operation of the SBS Software Updates. But sometimes it's just the only way to do something, as in this case.

Viewing Update Deployment Reports

When updates are showing in the Updates In Progress section of the Updates page, it often means that some computers have had the update deployed, but others are still pending for one reason or another (usually because the affected computer has been offline). To see what the status is for all the computers affected, follow these steps:

1. Open the Windows SBS Console if it isn't already open.

2. Select Security on the navigation bar.

3. Click Updates, if it isn't on top, to display the Updates page.

4. Select the update you want to see the deployment report for and click View The Update Deployment Report on the Tasks menu to open the Deployment Report for the update, as shown in Figure 15-9.

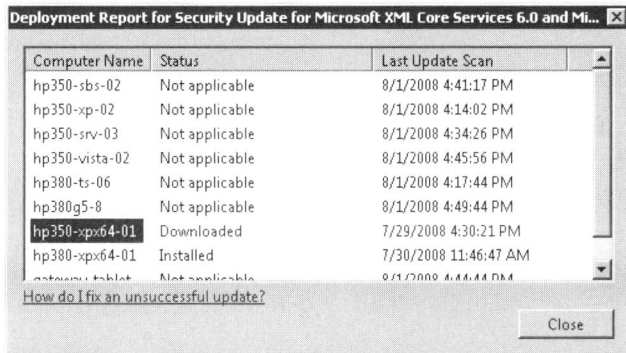

Computer Name	Status	Last Update Scan
hp350-sbs-02	Not applicable	8/1/2008 4:41:17 PM
hp350-xp-02	Not applicable	8/1/2008 4:14:02 PM
hp350-srv-03	Not applicable	8/1/2008 4:34:26 PM
hp350-vista-02	Not applicable	8/1/2008 4:45:56 PM
hp380-ts-06	Not applicable	8/1/2008 4:17:44 PM
hp380g5-8	Not applicable	8/1/2008 4:49:44 PM
hp350-xpx64-01	Downloaded	7/29/2008 4:30:21 PM
hp380-xpx64-01	Installed	7/30/2008 11:46:47 AM
gateway-tablet	Not applicable	8/1/2008 4:44:44 PM

How do I fix an unsuccessful update?

FIGURE 15-9 The Deployment Report for a security update

5. When you've identified which computers are causing the update to not complete, you can take the appropriate steps to correct the situation.

Synchronization

SBS synchronizes with the Microsoft servers once a day, at 10:00 P.M. local time. Normally, this is a sufficiently frequent and timely synchronization that you shouldn't need to do anything special to synchronize. In the event of an active outbreak of a critical exploit that affects your network, however, or for any other reason you need to manually synchronize the SBS Software Updates, you can trigger an update manually at any point in time. To initiate an update, follow these steps:

1. Open the Windows SBS Console if it isn't already open.

2. Select Security on the navigation bar.

3. Click Updates, if it isn't on top, to display the Updates page.

4. Click Synchronize Now on the Tasks pane to open the Software Updates Synchronize Now confirmation dialog box, shown in Figure 15-10.

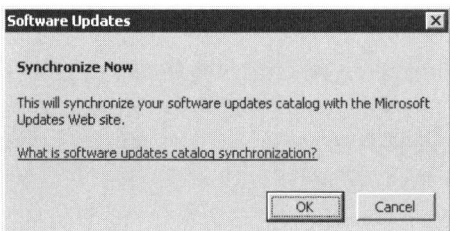

FIGURE 15-10 The Synchronize Now confirmation dialog box

5. Click OK and the synchronization will begin, and the Software Updates dialog box will change to a progress dialog box. When the synchronization completes, you'll see the dialog box shown in Figure 15-11.

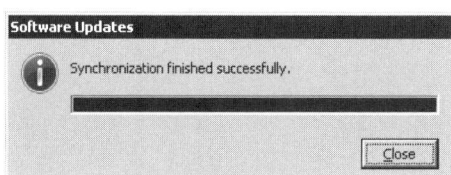

FIGURE 15-11 The Software Updates synchronization has completed.

6. Click Close to return to the Windows SBS Console.

Third-Party Solutions

SBS Software Updates does a good job of managing the various patches for Microsoft products on your SBS network. It has a single, integrated, and consistent method for patch management that will meet the basic needs of the majority of SBS environments. And it's certainly easier to get set up and working correctly than using the regular Windows Software Update Services download from Microsoft.com. But having said all that, there are limitations. WSUS will only manage updates of Microsoft products, and it doesn't give you the fine-grained control that some SBS networks might need. If your needs go beyond the basics of SBS Software Updates, you need to go either to a product such as Microsoft's Systems Center

Essentials (SCE), or to a third-party product. SCE is a good product, and well-suited to larger SBS networks, but it should be installed on its own server, not on the main SBS 2008 server.

An alternative to the Microsoft patch management solutions that we've used and like a lot is Shavlik's NetChk Protect (*http://www.shavlik.com/netchk-protect.aspx*). This is a full-featured, powerful product that gives you the ability to create multiple patch groups, control the download and deployment actions and schedules for each group differently, and even patch computers that aren't part of your SBS domain but are connected to your network. It supports patching of popular non-Microsoft products that you're likely to have on your SBS network, such as WinZip, Firefox, Apple QuickTime, and Adobe Acrobat.

Other alternatives that we've not used but that have come recommended by fellow SBS administrators include PatchLink Update (*http://www.lumension.com*) and BigFix (*http://www.bigfix.com*).

Summary

In this chapter, we've covered both the process of patch management and the mechanics of using Windows Small Business Server 2008 Software Updates. In the next chapter, we'll cover another critical security process—backing up and restoring your SBS network.

Configuring Backup

Backup is one of those chores that everyone knows is necessary but everyone hates to deal with. In Windows Small Business Server 2008, the solution can be simple if you only need to do disaster recovery backups of the server. A bit more work is required to set up more sophisticated backup solutions (using Windows Home Server), but all solutions can become completely automatic and transparent after the initial configuration is done.

The backup function in Windows SBS Console provides a friendly interface for scheduling and configuring your backups. It's still Windows Server Backup underneath, and some functions are available only through Windows Server Backup on the Administrative Tools menu.

Configuring the Backup Service

Windows Server Backup is installed automatically, but it must be configured for your purposes. To start the configuration, open Windows SBS Console, click Backup And Server Storage, and then follow these steps:

1.   In the Tasks pane, click Configure Server Backup to start the Configure Server Backup Wizard, as shown in Figure 16-1, and then click Next.

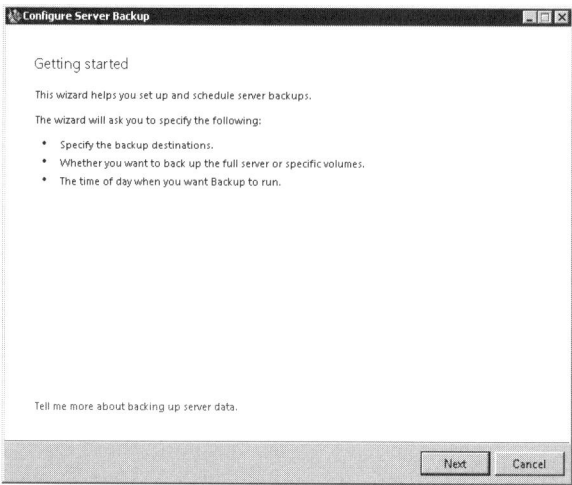

FIGURE 16-1 Starting the Configure Server Backup Wizard

2. On the Specify The Backup Destination page, select one or more external drives as destinations for your backup. As detailed in Table 16-1, the location you choose for storing the backups also has consequences in terms of what can be restored. Click Next.

> **IMPORTANT** The drives you select will be reformatted when backup is configured. Make sure the drives are empty or have nothing on them that needs to be saved.

TABLE 16-1 Backup Locations

STORAGE LOCATION	WHAT CAN BE RECOVERED	WHAT CANNOT BE RECOVERED	DETAILS
Local hard disk	Files, folders, applications, and volumes. System state and operating system if the backup contains all the critical volumes.	Operating system if the backup is on the same physical disk as one or more critical volumes.	The local disk you choose will be dedicated for storing your scheduled backups and will not be visible in Windows Explorer.
External hard disk	Files, folders, applications, and volumes. System state and operating system recoveries if the backup used contains all the critical volumes.		Backups can be easily moved offsite for disaster protection.

STORAGE LOCATION	WHAT CAN BE RECOVERED	WHAT CANNOT BE RECOVERED	DETAILS
DVD, other optical media, removable media	Entire volumes.	Applications, individual files.	Media must have at least 1 gigabyte (GB) free space.

3. Type in label information for each backup disk. Click Next.

4. On the Select Drives To Back Up page, select the individual drives or click Back Up All to include all drives. Generally, you should back up the following:

   ■ Exchange Server data

   ■ Windows SharePoint Services data

   ■ Microsoft SQL Server databases that support your line-of-business applications

   ■ Redirected users' document folders

   ■ Users' shared data folders

5. Click Next to specify the backup schedule, as shown in Figure 16-2. Select the frequency and the times of day. By default, Configure Server Backup schedules a backup to run daily at 5:00 P.M. and 11:00 P.M. However, you can adjust the backup schedule according to the needs of your organization. Click Custom and you can schedule multiple backups at times you choose. Click Next.

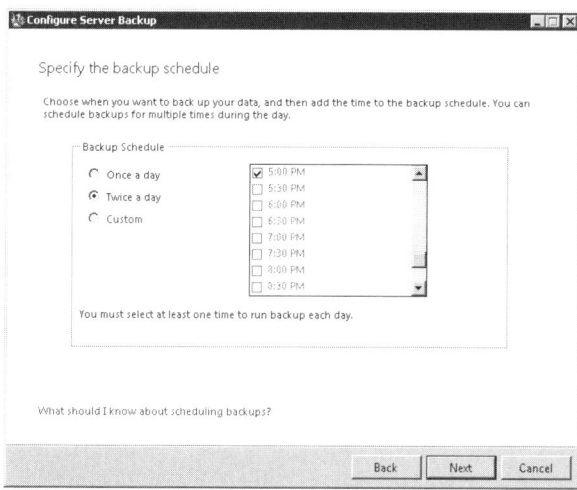

FIGURE 16-2 Setting backup times

6. Confirm the selection you've made and click Configure. The backup configuration will complete.

UNDER THE HOOD Ntbackup Users

Current users of Ntbackup.exe who switch to the Windows SBS 2008 Backup should consider the following:

- Settings for creating backups aren't upgraded when you upgrade to Windows SBS 2008, so you'll need to reconfigure your settings.

- You need a separate, dedicated disk for running scheduled backups.

- Only NTFS-formatted volumes on a locally attached disk can be backed up.

- Windows Server Backup supports backing up to external and internal disks. You can no longer back up to tape.

You can't recover backups created with Ntbackup.exe by using Windows SBS Backup. However, a version of Ntbackup.exe is available as a download for users who want to recover data from backups created using Ntbackup.exe. The downloadable version of Ntbackup.exe is only for recovering backups for older versions of Windows and can't be used to create new backups. To download Ntbackup.exe, see *http://go.microsoft.com/fwlink/?LinkId=82917*.

Changing the Backup Configuration

Your backup settings can be modified through the Windows SBS Console. Select Backup And Server Storage. The Tasks pane lists changes you can make.

Modifying Backup Destinations

In the SBS Console, click Backup And Server Storage, highlight the server to change, and choose Add Or Remove Backup Destinations to open the Server Backup Properties dialog box (Figure 16-3).

In the Server Backup Properties dialog box, follow these steps:

1. Click Backup Destination in the left pane.

2. Click Add Or Remove Drives.

3. Select the drives you want to add and clear the drives you want removed. Click Next.

4. If you've added a drive, you are asked to provide a label for it (Figure 16-4).

5. On the confirmation page, review your selections and click Configure.

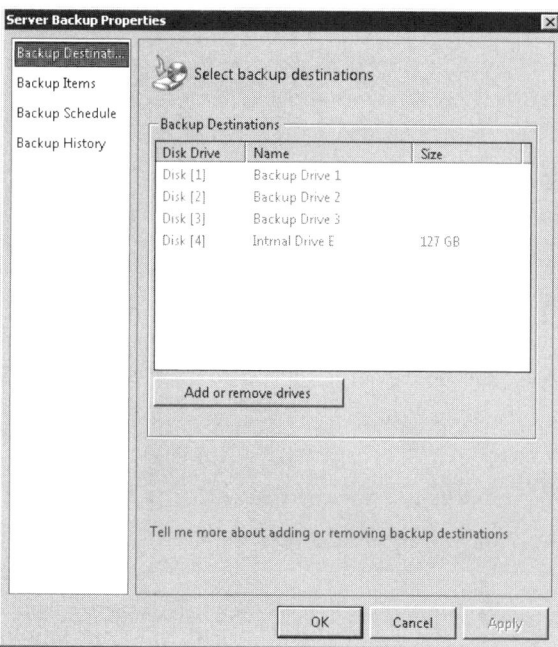

FIGURE 16-3 The Server Backup Properties dialog box

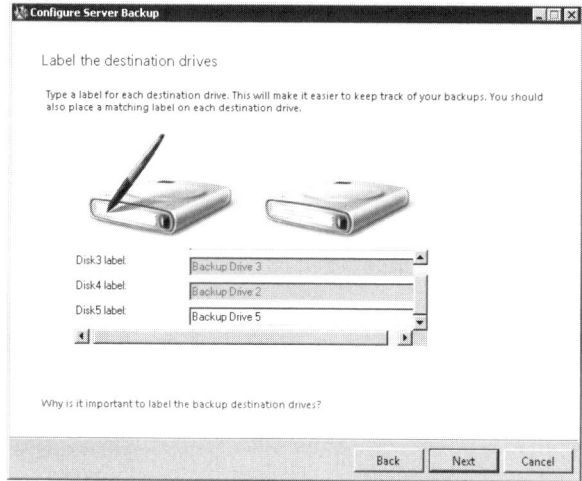

FIGURE 16-4 Labelling a new backup destination drive

Changing Items to Be Backed Up

In the SBS Console, click Backup And Server Storage, highlight the server to change, choose Add Or Remove Backup Items to open the Server Backup Properties dialog box, and then follow these steps:

1. Select Backup Items in the left pane.

2. Select the drives you want to add and clear the drives you want removed. Click OK.

Modifying the Backup Schedule

In the SBS Console, click Backup And Server Storage, highlight the server to change, choose Change Backup Schedule to open the Server Backup Properties dialog box, and then follow these steps:

1. Select Backup Schedule in the left pane.

2. Select one of the options for the backup schedule and then click OK.

   - Choose Once A Day and a backup will be performed every day at 11:00 P.M. local time.

   - Choose Twice A Day and backups will be performed daily at 5:00 P.M. and 11:00 P.M. local time.

   - Choose Custom and you can select a backup schedule of your own devising.

> **IMPORTANT** Store your external storage drives offsite and regularly rotate them to protect your data against disaster.

View Backup History

To check your backup history, open the SBS Console and click Backup And Server Storage. Highlight the server to view and choose View Backup History to open the Server Backup Properties dialog box.

Select Backup History in the left pane and a list of previous backups displays.

REAL WORLD   Data Protection Manager

In a larger Windows SBS environment, you probably depend on Microsoft Server–based platforms—including SQL Server, Microsoft SharePoint Server, or Microsoft Exchange—to manage and deliver information within your organization. In that case, Data Protection Manager is a better choice than the default Windows SBS backup.

True, you'll have to purchase it, and it requires a dedicated standalone server. That's two licenses plus the cost of the hardware just to get started. So it's not as cheap as using the Windows Server Backup.

However, Data Protection Manager (DPM) offers many benefits:

- Zero data-loss recovery for Microsoft applications.

- Shorter backup windows and smaller full backups thanks to patented Express Full technology. Scheduling a "backup window" is no longer necessary, which is a great advantage in environments where 24/7 uptime is required.

- Typical file recovery from tape can take hours; DPM performs the same function in minutes.

- DPM enables self-service user recovery, letting users access and retrieve files directly within Windows Vista, Windows XP, the 2007 Microsoft Office system, Microsoft Office 2003, and Microsoft Office XP applications without administrator intervention.

- Automates the scheduling of backups with Service Level Agreement–based policies.

- Advanced monitoring alerts administrators only when an actionable error occurs.

- Efficiently uses standard hardware through innovative de-duplication technology, reducing the volume of disk needed, and providing disk-based backup at a fraction of the cost of proprietary hardware solutions.

- Customers can consolidate both disk- and tape-based backup infrastructure onto Data Protection Manager 2007, reducing the number of backup and recovery applications and managing both disk and tape from a single interface.

DPM 2007 includes integrated support for both disk and tape media in a number of common configurations:

- **Disk-to-Disk**   Data can be moved from the source disk to the DPM-attached secondary disk using a very efficient block-level replication solution.

- **Disk-to-Disk-to-Tape**   After data is on a DPM-attached secondary disk, it can be moved to DPM-attached tape media, where it is written using the industry-standard MTF format. Data transfer rates capable of saturating an LTO3 drive are supported.

- **Disk-to-Tape**   If you don't require secondary disk backup, data can be moved directly to DPM-attached tape drives.

Using the Backup Once Wizard

The Backup Once Wizard is intended as a supplement to regularly scheduled backups, not as a substitution for them. For example, you can use the Backup Once Wizard for the following situations:

- Volumes that are not included in regular backups
- Volumes that contain important items before making changes such as installing updates or new features
- Backups of regularly scheduled items to a location other than where scheduled backups are stored

If you are using a local disk, be sure the disk supports either USB 2.0 or IEEE 1394 and is internal or attached to the server. If using DVDs, make sure that a DVD writer is connected to the server and online, and that you have enough blank DVDs to store the contents of all the volumes that you want to back up. Backups to DVDs can span multiple DVDs if the backup is too large for a single DVD.

> **NOTE** Using Backup Once is not the same as the Backup Now link in Windows SBS Console. Backup Now performs a full backup using the settings you've already configured. Backup Once allows configuring as you go.

To create a manual backup on a local disk, DVD, or removable media, follow these steps:

1. Open Administrative Tools and click Windows Server Backup.
2. In the Actions pane, under Windows Server Backup, click Backup Once to start the Backup Once Wizard. On the Backup Options page, select one of the following options and then click Next:
   - The Same Options That You Used In The Backup Schedule Wizard For Scheduled Backups
   - Different Options
3. If you select the Same Options, the next page will be a Confirmation page. Select Backup and the backup will proceed. If you select Different Options, on the Select Backup Configuration page, select one of the following options and then click Next:
   - Select Full Server to back up all volumes on the server.
   - Click Custom to back up only certain volumes and then click Next. On the Select Backup Items page, select the check boxes for the volumes that you want to back up. Volumes that contain operating system components or applications are included in the backup by default to enable operating system recovery and system state recovery options. These recovery options can be excluded by clearing the Enable System Recovery check box (Figure 16-5).

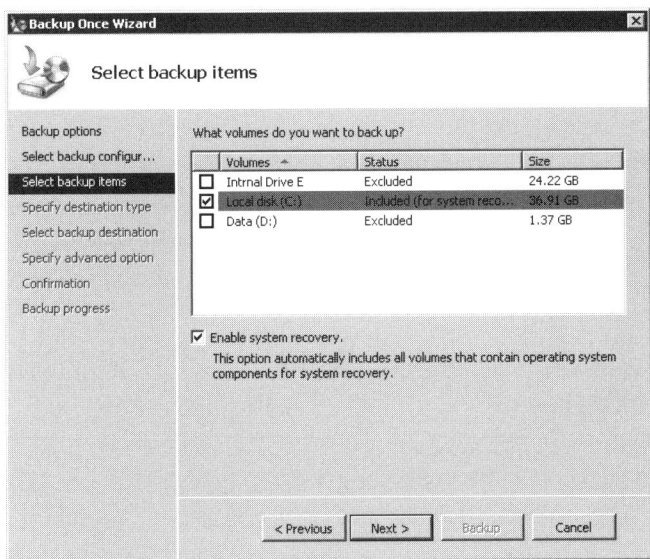

FIGURE 16-5 Selecting backup items

4. On the Specify Destination Type page, select Local Drives and then click Next.

5. On the Select Backup Destination page, select the destination for the backup from the drop-down list. If you choose a hard disk, be sure that the disk has enough free space. If you choose a DVD drive or other optical media, indicate whether you want the contents to be verified after they are written to (Figure 16-6).

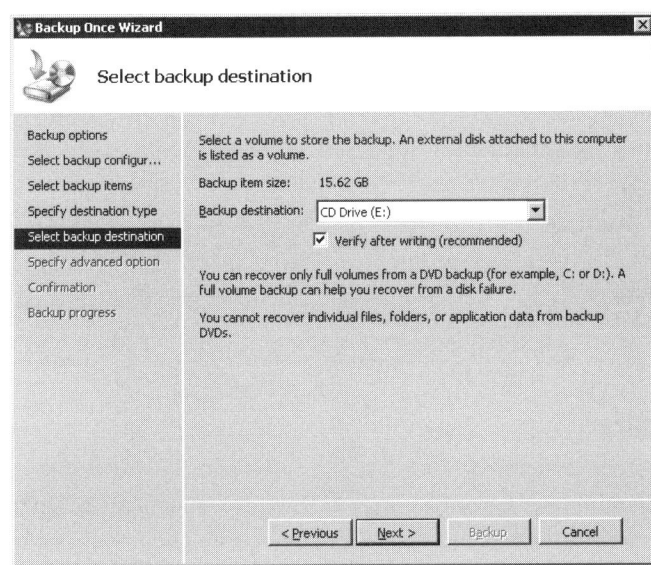

FIGURE 16-6 Selecting the backup destination

6. On the Specify Advanced Options page, choose whether you want to make a copy or full Volume Shadow Copy Service (VSS) backup. You should select VSS Full Backup if you are sure you are not using another product to create backups. Otherwise, choose VSS Copy Backup. Click Next.

7. On the Confirmation page, review the details and then click Backup.

8. On the Backup Progress page, you can view the status of the backup. If you are backing up to a DVD, you are notified to insert the first DVD in the drive, and then if the backup is too large for a single DVD, you will be prompted for subsequent DVDs as the backup progresses.

Recovering Backups

There's not much point to doing regular backups unless you can recover what you need when you need it. After your first full backup and periodically thereafter, you should test that your backups can be restored.

Recovering Your Server

The backups you've created with Windows Server Backup can be used to recover your operating system, system state, volumes, application data, backup catalog, and local files and folders. Different tools are used to recover different objects. For example:

- The Recovery Wizard in Windows Server Backup can recover files, folders, applications, and volumes.

- Windows Setup disk or a separate installation of the Windows Recovery Environment can recover the operating system and the full server (all volumes).

- Wbadmin start systemstaterecovery can recover the system state.

- The Catalog Recovery Wizard can recover the backup catalog. This wizard is available only when the backup catalog is corrupted.

> **NOTE** You can perform all of these recovery procedures using the Wbadmin command described later in the chapter.

Recovering Volumes

When you restore a full volume using the Recovery Wizard, all contents of the volume are restored—you can't select individual files or folders to recover. To recover just certain files or folders and not a full volume, see the sections titled "Recovering Files and Folders from the Local Server" and "Recovering Files and Folders from Another Server" later in this chapter.

To recover selected volumes, follow these steps:

1. Open the Administrative Tools menu and select Windows Server Backup.

2. In the Actions pane, under Windows Server Backup, click Recover to start the Recovery Wizard.

3. On the Getting Started page, specify whether the volumes will be recovered from backups stored on this computer or another computer and then click Next.

4. If you are recovering volumes from backups stored on another computer, do the following steps and then click Next:

   a. On the Specify Location Type page, indicate whether the backup that you want to restore from is on Local Drives or a Remote Shared Folder.

   b. If you are recovering from a local drive, on the Select Backup Location page, select the location of the backup from the drop-down list. If recovering from a remote shared folder, type the path to the folder on the Specify Remote Folder page and then click Next. The path to the backup will be \\<Remote Server> <Remote-SharedFolder>\WindowsImageBackup\<ComputerName>\<YourBackup>.

5. If you are recovering from this computer, on the Select Backup Location page, select the location of the backup from the drop-down list. If you are recovering from DVD or removable media, you are prompted to insert the device or first DVD in the series. Click Next.

6. For a recovery either from the local computer or another computer, on the Select Backup Date page, select the date from the calendar and the time from the drop-down list of backups you want to restore from. Click Next.

7. On the Select Recovery Type page, select Volumes and then click Next.

8. On the Select Volumes page, select the check boxes associated with the volumes in the Source Volume column that you want to recover. Then, from the associated drop-down list in the Destination Volume column, select the location that you want to recover the volume to. Click Next.

> **IMPORTANT** A message informs you that any data on the destination volume will be lost when you perform the recovery. Be sure the destination volume is either empty or doesn't contain information that could be needed later.

9. On the Confirmation page, review the details and then click Recover to restore the specified volumes.

10. On the Recovery Progress page, you can view the status of the recovery operation and determine whether it was completed successfully.

Recovering Files and Folders from the Local Server

Occasionally files will be corrupted or overwritten, and it's necessary to recover them from the most recent backup. To recover individual files and folders, follow these steps:

1. Open the Administrative Tools menu and select Windows Server Backup.

2. In the Actions pane, under Windows Server Backup, click Recover to start the Recovery Wizard.

3. On the Getting Started page (Figure 16-7), select This Server. Click Next.

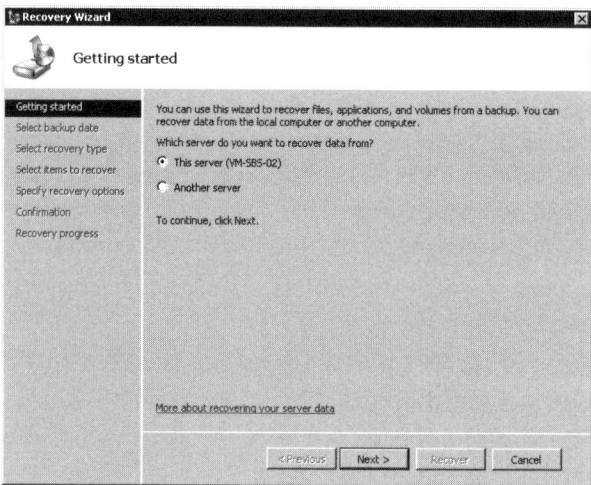

FIGURE 16-7 Starting the recovery process

4. On the Select Backup Date page, select the date and time of the backup you want to recover from. Click Next.

5. On the Select Recovery Type page, select Files And Folders as the type of recovery. Click Next.

6. On the Select Items To Recover page, under Available Items, expand the list until the folder you want is visible (Figure 16-8). Click a folder to display the contents in the adjacent pane, click each item that you want to restore, and then click Next.

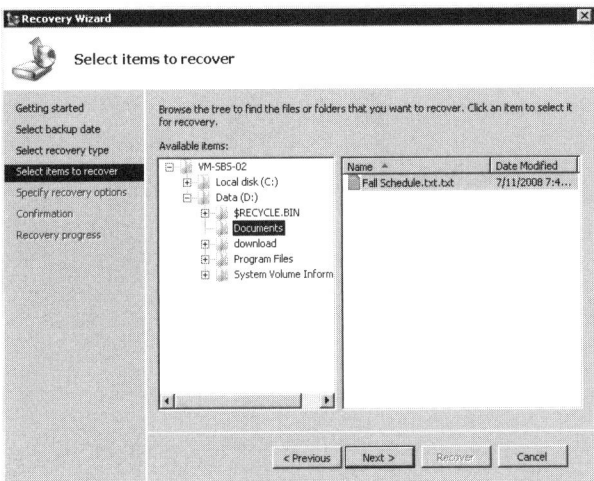

FIGURE 16-8 Selecting the items to be recovered

7. On the Specify Recovery Options page, under Recovery Destination, select one of the following:

   ■ Original Location

   ■ Another Location (type the path to the location or click Browse to select it)

8. Under When the Wizard Finds Files And Folders In The Recovery Destination, choose one of the following options and then click Next:

   ■ Create Copies So I Have Both Versions Of The File Or Folder

   ■ Overwrite Existing Files With Recovered Files

   ■ Don't Recover Those Files And Folders

9. On the Confirmation page, review the details and then click Recover to restore the specified items.

10. The Recovery Progress page displays the status of the recovery operation (Figure 16-9). Click Close when the process is finished.

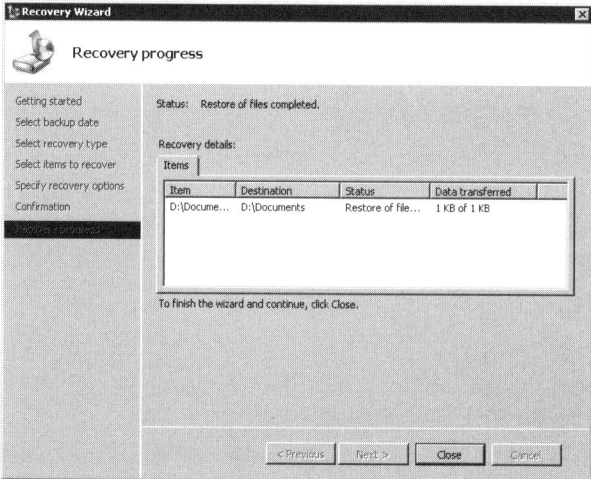

FIGURE 16-9 The recovery is complete.

Recovering Files and Folders from Another Server

To recover files and folders from a backup on another server, follow these steps:

1. Open the Administrative Tools menu and select Windows Server Backup.

2. In the Actions pane, under Windows Server Backup, click Recover to start the Recovery Wizard.

3. On the Getting Started page, select Another Server and click Next.

4. On the Specify Location Type page, select one of the following options and then click Next:

   - Local Drives
   - Remote Shared Folder

5. If you are recovering from a local drive, on the Select Backup Location page, select the location of the backup from the drop-down list. If you are recovering from a remote shared folder, type the path to the folder on the Specify Remote Folder page and then click Next. The path to the backup will be \\<Remote Server><RemoteSharedFolder>\WindowsImageBackup\<ComputerName>\<YourBackup>.

6. On the Select Backup Date page, select the date from the calendar and the time from the drop-down list of backups you want to restore from. Click Next.

7. On the Select Recovery Type page, select Files And Folders and then click Next.

8. On the Select Items To Recover page, expand the list under Available Items until the folder you want is visible. Click a folder to display the contents in the adjacent pane, click each item that you want to restore, and then click Next.

9. On the Specify Recovery Options page, under Recovery Destination, select one of the following options and then click Next:

   - Original Location
   - Another Location (type the path to the location or click Browse to select it)

10. Under When the Wizard Finds Files And Folders In The Recovery Destination, select one of the following options and then click Next:

   - Create Copies So I Have Both Versions Of The File Or Folder
   - Overwrite Existing Files With Recovered Files
   - Don't Recover Those Files And Folders

11. On the Confirmation page, review the details and then click Recover to restore the files and folders.

12. On the Recovery Progress page, view the status of the recovery operation to determine whether it was completed successfully.

Recovering Applications and Data

The Recovery Wizard in Windows Server Backup can be used to recover applications and data from a backup, provided that the application in question uses Volume Shadow Copy Service (VSS) technology so that it is compatible with Windows Server Backup. Also, the VSS writer for the application must have been enabled before you created the backup being used for recovery. Most applications do not enable the VSS writer by default. You will have to explicitly enable it. If the VSS writer was not enabled for the backup, you will not be able to recover applications from it.

To recover an application, follow these steps:

1. Open the Administrative Tools menu and click Windows Server Backup.

2. In the Actions pane, under Windows Server Backup, click Recover to start the Recovery Wizard.

3. On the Getting Started page, specify whether the application will be recovered from backups run on this computer or another computer and then click Next.

4. If you are recovering applications from backups stored on another computer, do the following steps and then click Next:

   a. On the Specify Location Type page, indicate whether the backup that you want to restore from is on Local Drives or a Remote Shared Folder.

   b. If you are recovering from a local drive, on the Select Backup Location page, select the location of the backup from the drop-down list. If recovering from a remote shared folder, type the path to the folder on the Specify Remote Folder page (Figure 16-10) and then click Next. The path to the backup will be \\<Remote Server><RemoteSharedFolder>\WindowsImageBackup \<ComputerName>\<YourBackup>.

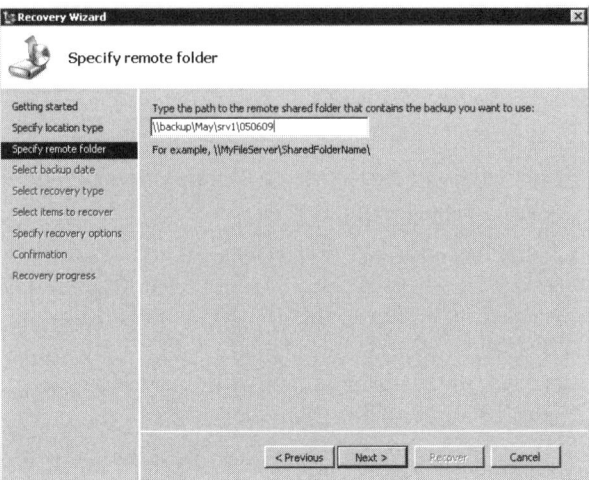

FIGURE 16-10 Specifying the path to the remote shared folder

    c. If you are recovering from this computer, on the Select Backup Location page, select the location of the backup from the drop-down list and then click Next.

5. On the Select Backup Date page, select the date from the calendar and the time from the drop-down list of the backup that you want to restore from and then click Next.

6. On the Select Recovery Type page, click Applications and then click Next.

7. On the Select Application page, under Applications, select the application to recover. If the backup that you are using is the most recent and the application you are recovering supports a roll-forward of the application database, you will see a check box labelled Do Not Perform A Roll-Forward Recovery Of The Application Databases. Select this check box if you want to prevent Windows Server Backup from rolling forward the application database that is currently on your server. Click Next.

> **IMPORTANT** Roll-forward recovery uses information stored in transaction log files to return a database to the state it was in at an exact point in time. To perform a roll-forward recovery, archival logging must be enabled and a full backup image of the database must be available, as well as access to all archived log files created since the last successful backup image.
>
> If a roll-forward recovery isn't possible, a version recovery will be performed. Version recovery is the process used to return a database to the state it was in at the time a particular backup image was made.

8. On the Specify Recovery Options page, under Select How Do You Want To Recover The Application Data, select one of the following options and then click Next:

    ■ Recover To Original Location

- Recover To Another Location (Type the path to the location or click Browse to select it)

9. On the Confirmation page, review the details and then click Recover to restore the listed items.

10. On the Recovery progress page, view the status of the recovery operation to determine whether it was completed successfully.

Recovering the Operating System

You can recover your server operating system or full server by using a Windows SBS Installation DVD and a backup created with Windows Server Backup. The Windows Installation disk allows access to the System Recovery Options page in the Windows Recovery Environment.

Before you start, you need to determine the following:

- Where you will recover to
- What backup you will use
- Whether you will perform an operating system–only or full server recovery
- Whether you will reformat and repartition your disks

NOTE When recovering to a new hard disk, the new disk must be at least as large as the disk that contained the volumes that were backed up—no matter what size those volumes were. For example, if you backed up only one 50-GB volume on a 1-terabyte disk, you have to use a 1-terabyte or larger disk when restoring.

To recover the operating system or the full server using a Windows SBS Setup disk, follow these steps:

1. Insert the Windows SBS Setup disk into the DVD drive and turn on the computer. The Install Windows Wizard appears.

2. Specify language settings and then click Next.

3. Click Repair Your Computer.

4. Setup searches the hard disk drives for an existing Windows installation and then displays the results in System Recovery Options. If you are recovering the operating system onto a separate computer, the list should be empty. (No operating system should be on the computer.) Click Next.

5. In the System Recovery Options dialog box, click Windows Complete PC Restore to start the Windows Complete PC Restore Wizard.

6. Select Use The Latest Available Backup (Recommended) or Restore A Different Backup and then click Next.

7. If restoring a different backup, on the Select The Location Of The Backup page, choose one of the following options:

- Select the computer that contains the backup that you want to use and then click Next.
- On the Select The Backup To Restore page, click the backup you want to use and then click Next.
- Click Advanced to browse for a backup on the network and then click Next.

NOTE If the storage location contains backups from multiple computers, be sure to click the correct row for the backups for the computer that you want to use.

8. On the Choose How To Restore The Backup page, do the following steps:

   a. Select Format And Repartition Disks to delete existing partitions and reformat the destination disks to be the same as the backup. This enables the Exclude Disks button. Click this button and then select the check boxes associated with any disks that you want to exclude from being formatted and partitioned. The disk that contains the backup that you are using is automatically excluded.

   b. Select the Only Restore System Disks check box to perform an operating system–only recovery.

   c. Click Install Drivers to install any needed device drivers for the hardware that you are recovering to.

   d. Click Advanced to stipulate whether the computer is restarted and the disks are checked for errors immediately after the recovery.

   e. Click Next.

9. Confirm the details for the restoration and then click Finish.

Restoring a Backup Catalog

The details of your backups are stored in a file called a *backup catalog*. This file contains information about which volumes are backed up and where they're located. Windows Server Backup stores the catalog in the same place that you store your backups. If the catalog file is corrupted, Windows Server Backup sends you an alert and an event is added to the event log (Event 514). Before you can perform additional backups, the catalog must be restored or deleted.

If you have no backups that you can use to recover the catalog, the corrupted file must be deleted. This means information about previous backups is lost and the backups can't be accessed using Windows Server Backup. Therefore, it's important to create a new backup immediately after deleting the catalog file.

NOTE The Catalog Recovery Wizard is available only when Windows Backup Server detects that the catalog file is corrupted.

To recover a backup catalog, follow these steps:

1. Open the Administrative Tools menu and click Windows Server Backup.

2. In the Actions pane, under Windows Server Backup, click Recover to start the Catalog Recovery Wizard.

3. On the Specify Storage Type page, select one of the following options:

   ■ If you don't have a backup to use to recover the catalog and you just want to delete the catalog, select I Don't Have Any Usable Backups, click Next, and then click Finish.

   ■ If you do have a backup that you can use, specify whether the backup is on a local drive or remote shared folder and then click Next.

4. Do one of the following:

   ■ On the Select Backup Location page, if the backup is on a local drive (including DVDs), select the drive that contains the backup that you want to use from the drop-down list. If you are using DVDs, make sure the *last* DVD of the series is in the drive. Click Next.

   ■ If the backup is on a remote shared folder, on the Specify Remote Folder page, type the path to the folder that contains the backup that you want to use and then click Next.

   A message informs you that backups taken after the backup that you are using for the recovery will not be accessible. Click Yes.

5. On the Confirmation page, review the details and then click Finish to recover the catalog.

6. On the Summary page, click Close.

After the catalog recovery is completed or you have deleted the catalog, you must close and then reopen Windows Server Backup to refresh the view.

Using the Wbadmin Command

The Wbadmin command allows you to back up and restore volumes and files from the command line. Wbadmin replaces the Ntbackup command released with previous versions of Windows. You can't use Wbadmin to recover backups created with Ntbackup. However, if you need to recover backups made with Ntbackup, you can download a version of Ntbackup usable with Windows Server 2008. This downloadable version of Ntbackup allows you to perform recoveries of legacy backups, but you cannot use it on Windows Server 2008 to create new backups. To download this version of Ntbackup, see *http://go.microsoft.com/fwlink/?LinkId=82917*.

The next sections list Wbadmin commands and syntax. Table 16-2 lists and describes the parameters used with Wbadmin. For additional assistance, type **Wbadmin /?** at a command prompt.

Wbadmin enable backup

The following subcommand enables or configures scheduled daily backup:

```
Wbadmin enable backup
[-addtarget:{backuptargetdisk | backuptargetnetworkshare}]
[-removetarget:{backuptargetdisk | backuptargetnetworkshare}]
[-schedule:timetorunbackup]
[-include:volumestoinclude]
[-allcritical]
[-user:username]
[-password:password]
[-inheritacl:inheritacl]
[-quiet]
```

Wbadmin disable backup

The following subcommand disables running scheduled daily backups:

```
wbadmin disable backup
[-quiet]
```

Wbadmin start backup

The following subcommand runs a backup job:

```
wbadmin start backup
[-backupTarget:{TargetVolume | TargetNetworkShare}]
[-include:VolumesToInclude]
[-allCritical]
[-vssFull]
[-noVerify]
[-user:UserName]
[-password:Password]
[-noInheritAcl]
[-quiet]
```

Wbadmin stop job

The following subcommand stops a running backup or recovery job:

```
Wbadmin stop job
[-quiet]
```

Wbadmin start recovery

The following subcommand runs a recovery based on the specified parameters:

```
wbadmin start recovery
-version:VersionIdentifier
-items:VolumesToRecover | AppsToRecover | FilesOrFoldersToRecover}
-itemtype:{Volume | App | File}
[-backupTarget:{VolumeHostingBackup | NetworkShareHostingBackup}]
[-machine:BackupMachineName]
[-recoveryTarget:{TargetVolumeForRecovery | TargetPathForRecovery}]
[-recursive]
[-overwrite:{Overwrite | CreateCopy | Skip}]
[-notRestoreAcl]
[-skipBadClusterCheck]
[-noRollForward]
[-quiet]
```

Wbadmin start systemstatebackup

The following subcommand creates a backup of the system state of a computer. A backup of the system state can only be saved to a locally attached disk (either internal or external). It cannot be saved to a DVD or to a remote shared folder. In addition, only the system state and system applications can be recovered from this backup—volumes and files cannot be recovered from this backup.

```
wbadmin start systemstatebackup
-backupTarget:<VolumeName>
[-quiet]
```

Wbadmin start systemstaterecovery

The following subcommand runs a system state recovery based on the supplied parameters:

```
wbadmin start systemstaterecovery
-version:VersionIdentifier
-showsummary
[-backupTarget:{VolumeName | NetworkSharePath}]
[-machine:BackupMachineName]
[-recoveryTarget:TargetPathForRecovery]
[-excludeSystemFiles]
[-authsysvol]
[-quiet]
```

Wbadmin start sysrecovery

The following subcommand runs a system recovery based on specified parameters. This command can be run only from the Windows Recovery Environment, and it is not listed by default in the usage text of Wbadmin. (You can access the Windows Recovery Environment from a Windows Server 2008 installation DVD by inserting the DVD and following the steps in the wizard until you see the option Repair Your Computer. Click this link to open the System Recovery Options dialog box.)

```
wbadmin start sysrecovery
-version:VersionIdentifier
-backupTarget:{VolumeHostingBackup | NetworkShareHostingBackup}
[-machine:BackupMachineName]
[-restoreAllVolumes]
[-recreateDisks]
[-excludeDisks]
[-dfsAuth]
[-skipBadClusterCheck]
[-quiet]
```

Windows Recovery Environment

Windows Recovery Environment (Windows RE) is a recovery platform designed to automatically repair common causes of unbootable operating system installations. When the computer fails to start, Windows automatically fails over into this environment, and the Startup Repair tool in Windows RE automates diagnosis and repair. In addition, Windows RE is a starting point for various tools for manual system recovery.

Windows RE is a partial version of the operating system plus a set of tools you can use to carry out operating system or full server recoveries, using a backup that you created earlier using Windows Server Backup.

Wbadmin get versions

The following subcommand reports on the available backups:

```
wbadmin get versions
[-backupTarget:{VolumeName | NetworkSharePath}]
[-machine:BackupMachineName]
```

Wbadmin get status

The following subcommand reports the status of the current backup or recovery:

```
wbadmin get status
```

TABLE 16-2 Wbadmin Parameters

PARAMETER	DESCRIPTION
-addtarget	Storage location for backup. Disk is formatted before use and any existing data on it is permanently erased.
-allCritical	Automatically includes all critical volumes (volumes that contain system state data). Can be used along with the *-include* option.
-backupTarget	Storage location for this backup. Requires a hard disk drive letter (f:) or a Universal Naming Convention (UNC) path to a shared network folder (*servername**sharename*). If a shared network folder is specified, this backup will overwrite any existing backup in that location.
-dfsAuth	Marks the restore as authoritative. Can be used only when the server being recovered is hosting folders that are being replicated by Distributed File System Replication (DFSR). This parameter makes the recovered version of the replicated folders the authoritative copy, thereby overwriting the version stored on other members of the replication group. If this parameter is not used, the data is restored as a nonauthoritative copy.
-excludeDisks	Can be used only with the *-recreateDisks* parameter. Must be input as a comma-delimited list of disk identifiers (as listed in the output of Wbadmin get disks). Excluded disks are not partitioned or formatted. This parameter helps preserve data on disks that you do not want modified during the recovery.
-include	Comma-delimited list of volume drive letters, volume mount points, or GUID-based volume names to include in the backup.
-noInheritAcl	If specified, the computer-name folder applies ACLs for the user whose credentials were given when running the backup and access to the Administrators group and Backup Operators group on the computer with the shared network folder. If *-noInheritAcl* is not used, the ACL permissions from the remote shared folder are applied to the <ComputerBackedUp> folder by default so that anyone with access to the remote shared folder can access the backup.
-items	Comma-delimited list of volumes, applications, and files to recover.
	If *-itemtype* is Volume, it can be only a single volume that is specified by providing the volume drive letter, volume mount point, or GUID-based volume name.
	If *-itemtype* is App, it can be only a single application. Applications that can be recovered include SQL Server and Windows SharePoint Services. You can also use the value *ADExtended* to recover an installation of Active Directory.
	If *-itemtype* is File, it can be files or directories, but it should be part of the same volume, and it should be under the same parent.

PARAMETER	DESCRIPTION
-itemtype	Type of items to recover. Must be Volume, App, or File.
-machine	Specifies the name of the computer for which you want to recover the backup. Should be used when *-backupTarget* is specified.
-notrestoreacl	Can be used only when recovering files. Specifies to not restore the security ACLs of the files being recovered from backup. By default, the security ACLs are restored (the default value is true). If this parameter is used, the default ACLs for the location that the files are being restored to are applied.
-noVerify	If specified, backups written to removable media (such as a DVD) are not verified for errors. If not specified, backups written to such media are verified for errors.
-overwrite	Valid only when recovering files. Specifies the action to take when a file that is being recovered already exists in the same location. *Overwrite* causes the recovery to overwrite the existing file with the file from the backup. *CreateCopy* causes the recovery to create a copy of the existing file so that the existing file is not modified. *Skip* causes the recovery to skip the existing file and continue with recovery of the next file.
-password	Password for the user name that is specified by the parameter *-user*.
-quiet	Runs the command with no prompts to the user.
-recoveryTarget	Specifies the drive to restore to. Use if this drive is different than the one that was previously backed up. Can also be used for restorations of volumes, files, or applications. If you are restoring a volume, you can specify the volume drive letter of the alternate volume. If you are restoring a file or application, you can specify an alternate backup path.
-recreateDisks	Restores a disk configuration to the state that existed when the backup was created.
-recursive	Can be used only when recovering files. Recovers the files in the folders and all files subordinate to the specified folders. By default, only files that reside directly under the specified folders are recovered.
-removetarget	Storage location specified in the existing backup schedule.
-restoreAllVolumes	Restores all volumes from the selected backup. If this parameter is not specified, only critical volumes (volumes that contain system state data) are restored from the selected backup. Useful when you need to restore noncritical volumes during system recovery.

PARAMETER	DESCRIPTION
-schedule	Comma-delimited times of day specified as HH:MM.
-showsummary	Can be used only with `Wbadmin start sysstaterecovery`. Reports the summary of the last run of this command. This parameter cannot be accompanied by any other parameters.
-skipBadClusterCheck	Can be used only when recovering volumes. This skips checking your recovery destination disks for bad cluster information. If you are restoring to an alternate server or hardware, this switch should not be used. You can manually run the command chkdsk /b on your recovery disks at any time to check them for bad clusters and then update the file system information accordingly.
-user	Specifies the user name with write access to the backup destination (if it is a shared network folder). The user needs to be a member of the Administrators or Backup Operators group on this computer.
-version	Specifies the version of the backup in MM/DD/YYYY-HH:MM format, as listed by `Wbadmin get versions`.
-vssFull	If specified, performs a full backup using Volume Shadow Copy Service (VSS). Each file's history is updated to reflect that it was backed up.
	If this parameter is not specified, `Start Backup` makes a copy backup, but the history of files being backed up is not updated.
	Caution: Do not use this parameter when using a non-Microsoft program to back up applications.

Windows Home Server

If Windows Server Backup works perfectly fine, why invest in another backup product? Well might you ask. If you need more than disaster recovery for servers, Windows Home Server (WHS) is the ideal solution. It does everything Server Backup does plus client computer backup in a simple solution that is easy to configure and use.

> **NOTE** Although WHS isn't just for home use, the inclusion of that term explains why WHS is limited to backing up no more than 10 computers. However, if you're just backing up server data and critical client computers, you'll be able to easily stay under that limit.

When you buy a Windows Home Server, you buy the hardware and software combined. You merely plug it in to your network, turn it on, and configure it through the WHS home page (see Figure 16-11).

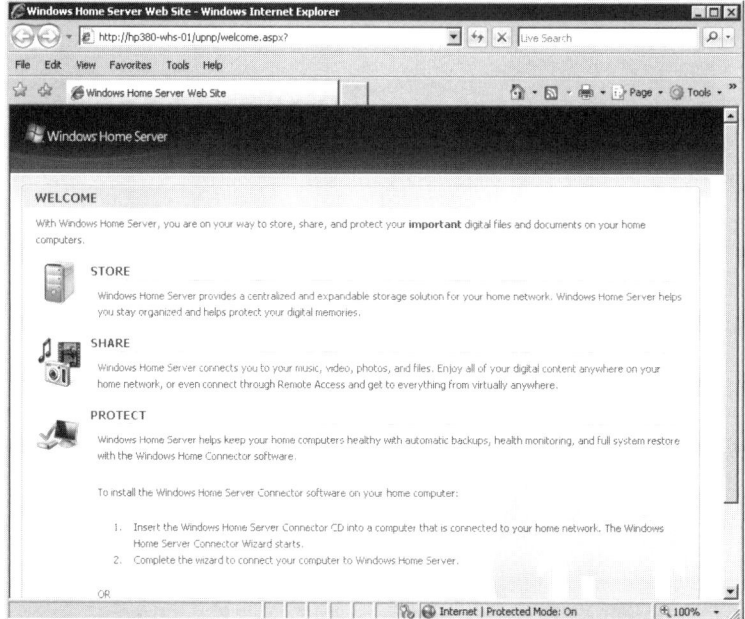

FIGURE 16-11 The Windows Home Server home page

Or you can buy the system builder version and install it on a computer yourself. Although you can install Windows Home Server on an old desktop you have around, you're much better off with robust and fairly recent hardware.

Table 16-3 lists the minimum and recommended hardware for WHS.

TABLE 16-3 Hardware Requirements for Windows Home Server

HARDWARE	MINIMUM	RECOMMENDED
CPU	1GHz Pentium 3 (or equivalent)	Pentium 4, AMD x64, or newer processor. Windows Home Server includes a 32-bit operating system, which runs on 32-bit and 64-bit (Intel EM64T and AMD x64) architectures. It's likely that future versions of Windows Home Server will support only 64-bit processors, so it's prudent to use a 64-bit compatible processor to take the hassle out of upgrading.
RAM	512 MB	512 MB

HARDWARE	MINIMUM	RECOMMENDED
Hard drives	70 GB internal hard drive as the primary and any number of additional hard drives of any capacity	At least two internal hard drives with 300 GB as the primary drive.
Network interface card	100 Mbps Ethernet network interface card	100 Mbps (or faster) Ethernet network interface card from the Windows Server Catalog Web site (*http://go.microsoft.com /fwlink/?LinkId=86748*).

You'll also need the following in order to install WHS:

- **DVD Drive (internal or external DVD drive)** Your WHS computer must be capable of booting from this internal or external DVD drive in order to install Windows Home Server.

- **Display** A compatible monitor

- **Keyboard and mouse**

After WHS is installed, you won't need a monitor, mouse, and keyboard. All configurations can be done from a WHS client.

The following operating systems supported by Windows SBS are also supported to work with Windows Home Server:

- Windows Vista Business

- Windows Vista Business N (European Union only)

- Windows Vista Enterprise

- Windows Vista Ultimate

- Windows XP Professional with SP2

- Windows XP Tablet Edition with SP2

NOTE Windows XP Professional X64 edition is not supported by WHS even though it is supported by Windows SBS.

IMPORTANT You must use a wired connection to connect your home server to your broadband router or to a switch that is connected to your broadband router. After WHS is set up, computers that use wireless connections will be able to connect wirelessly to WHS.

Connecting to Windows Home Server

You must run Windows Home Server Connector on each computer that will use WHS for backup.

To install the Windows Home Server Connector software, insert the Windows Home Server Connector CD into a computer connected to your network. The Windows Home Server Connector Wizard starts. Complete the wizard to connect your computer to Windows Home Server.

Or, if you purchased a server with WHS installed, browse to the WHS computer using the format *http://WHS_Server_Name* and follow the instructions.

> **NOTE** You should also download the WHS Toolkit (Figure 16-12). The Toolkit is a collection of tools that help with troubleshooting any problems you may have.

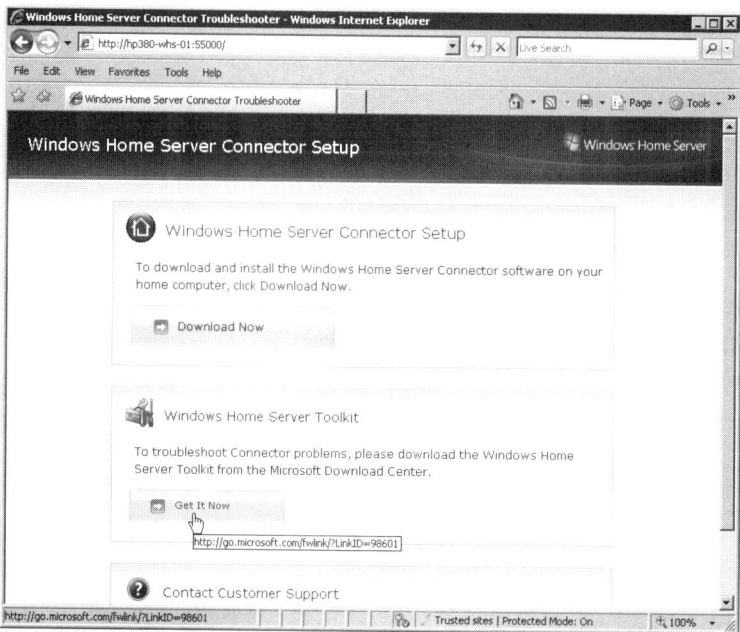

FIGURE 16-12 Click to download the WHS Toolkit.

After the connector is installed, an icon is placed in the notification area. Right-click it to open the connection to the WHS Console (Figure 16-13).

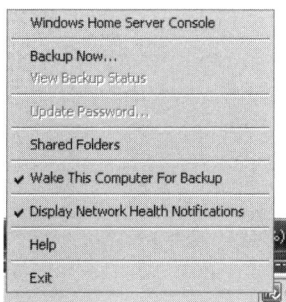

FIGURE 16-13 WHS menu

From the console, you can initiate backups, confirm the health of your network and shared folders, and check the status of your available storage (Figure 16-14).

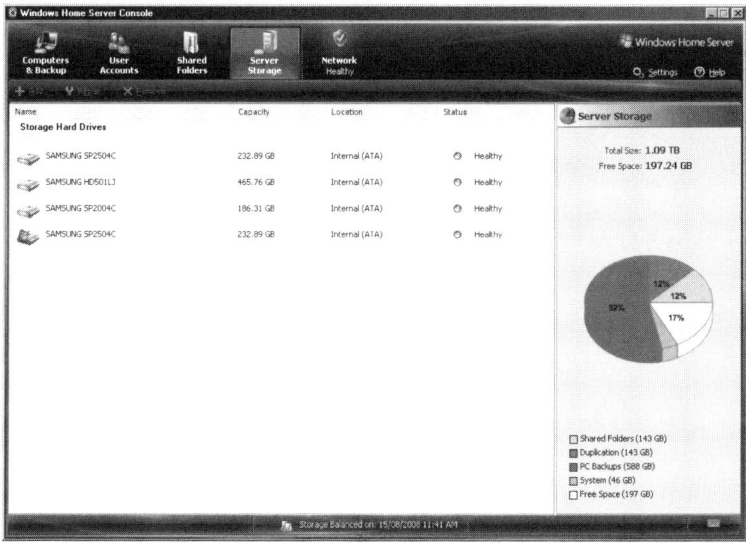

FIGURE 16-14 Checking the storage capacity on WHS

NOTE The initial backup of a computer to WHS is no faster than a conventional backup. Subsequent backups, however, are very quick indeed, because WHS rapidly calculates which blocks of data have changed and only backs up the changed blocks.

Summary

Windows Server Backup provides a basic but configurable backup and recovery tool that makes scheduling backups and restoring backed-up information easier and faster. However, if you need to back up critical client computers, an even easier solution is Windows Home Server with its slick interface and easy-to-use tools.

In the next chapter, we move on to an analysis of the Windows SBS Console and Server Manager.

PART IV

Performing Advanced Tasks

Windows SBS Console v. Server Manager

The Windows SBS Console is the heart of the Windows Small Business Server 2008 experience and is *the* preferred tool for managing SBS. Whenever possible, use the Windows SBS Console. The wizards and features built into the console are designed to work correctly with SBS and to simplify the tasks you need to perform.

That being said, Windows Server 2008 includes a completely new Server Manager console that is a huge improvement on earlier management consoles. There will be some tasks that you'll likely need to use Server Manager for, so it's useful to familiarize yourself with it and to understand when to use it or the native standalone management consoles for Windows Server 2008. In this chapter, we describe:

- Adding Roles and Features
- Managing Roles
- Using the native consoles

The native Windows Server 2008 Server Manager is the tool you'll use to add a Role, Role Service, or Feature to SBS, and it is also a good gateway into native Windows Server 2008 management tasks. There are some tasks, however, that without a doubt are best left to the Windows SBS Console, and we cover those as well, pointing out where using the native tools of Windows Server 2008 is not an optimal choice.

Adding (and Removing) Roles and Features

Adding and removing Roles from Windows Server 2008 (and thus Windows Small Business Server 2008) can be done from either the Server Manager console or the command line. Both methods perform the same tasks and follow the same logic for which services get installed. But this is definitely a place where it's a whole lot easier to use the GUI, so unless you're deploying dozens of identical servers, just use Server Manager. (I can't believe we said that—we're the quintessential command-line types for almost everything. But this is one time where graphical just makes sense.)

 UNDER THE HOOD   **Server Manager—A New Way to Do Old Tasks**

Previous versions of Windows Server used a freeform method for adding and removing the various features and abilities of Windows Server. This method could easily allow unnecessary services to be enabled, exposing the server to risk. Equally, it was possible to disable a critical feature or ability of Windows Server, causing other services or features not to work correctly. Troubleshooting these issues was time-consuming and frustrating, and the overall security of the server could be compromised. The Configure Your Server Wizard and the Manage Your Server Wizard of Windows Server 2003 were an attempt to resolve some of these issues by providing a simple interface that allowed for a single place to add or remove roles and manage those that were already on the server.

Windows Server 2008 takes these old wizards and completely replaces them with the new Server Manager. The goal of Server Manager is to be the one place where you can add, manage, or remove Roles, Role Services, and Features on the server—your "one-stop shop" for all management tasks on Windows Server 2008. For SBS, we've already got our primary interface—the Windows SBS Console. Most management tasks can be handled directly there. But you can't add Roles from there, you can't add Features, and some management tasks just don't lend themselves to highly standardized wizards, frankly. For all those things, you need Server Manager or the standalone consoles. Plus, if you're running SBS Premium, you'll need Server Manager to manage the included copy of Windows Server 2008 Standard.

What's different about Server Manager (and its command-line version) is that it's a requirement for adding Roles, Role Services, or Features. When we first ran across this requirement to always use Server Manager for these tasks, we weren't very happy about it. In fact, we complained loudly and with a good deal of enthusiasm to more than one set of ears inside Microsoft. We saw it as an unnecessary and unproductive dumbing-down of Windows Server.

Everyone we said this to kept telling us to be patient and work with it. Well, we hate to admit it, but they were right. This is just a whole lot better and smarter way to install Roles. Not only do you get the right minimum level of dependent services, but you also have the right configuration and exceptions for Windows Firewall—automatically.

Roles, Role Services, and Features

Windows Server 2008 makes a distinction between a server *Role*, a *Role Service*, and a *Feature*. Server Roles are broad groupings of common functionality that help define what a server is used for. Thus a file server would have the File Services Role installed, and a terminal server would have the Terminal Services Role installed.

Each of these broadly defined Roles has available one or more Role Services. A Role Service is a particular functionality that is available only for the Role for which it is a Role Service. Thus for a file server with the File Services Role installed, the following Role Services are available: File Server, Distributed File System (and its subsidiary services, DFS Namespaces and DFS Replication), File Server Resource Manager, Services for Network File System, Windows Search Service, and Windows Server 2003 File Services (including its two subsidiary services, the File Replication Service and the Indexing Service). For the Terminal Services Role, the following Role Services are available: Terminal Server, TS Licensing, TS Session Broker, TS Gateway, and TS Web Access.

Features are Windows Server 2008 functionality that doesn't require a specific Role to be installed. Features are useful across a wide variety of server configurations. Features include broad, general-purpose functionality, such as Windows PowerShell, as well as narrow but non-role-specific functionality, such as Internet Storage Name Server (iSNS) and Message Queuing.

Adding and Removing Roles

Roles reflect the tasks and services we expect of our servers. The File Services Role includes various aspects of using SBS as a file server, one of the most basic tasks of our SBS servers. Most Roles that should be installed on the main SBS server are installed automatically as part of the installation of Windows Small Business Server 2008. And you should be very cautious about installing any additional Roles on the main SBS server. SBS is a complicated and busy server already, and adding additional Roles or functionality is not usually recommended. Instead, add a second server to your SBS network to add additional Roles whenever possible, or use the second server that is part of the Premium Edition of SBS.

Add a Role

Using the Server Manager console, you can add a Role using the following steps:

> **NOTE** In these steps, we'll add the Terminal Server Role to our SBS 2008 Premium Edition second server. The steps are essentially similar for any Role, though the exact screens and choices will be slightly different.

1. Open the Server Manager console if it isn't open already.
2. Select Add Roles from the Action menu to open the Before You Begin page of the Add Roles Wizard, as shown in Figure 17-1.

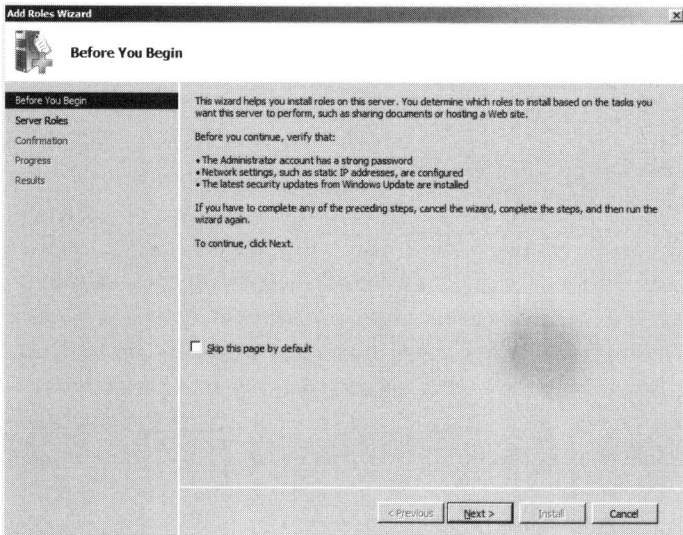

FIGURE 17-1 The Before You Begin page of the Add Roles Wizard

3. Read the advice on the Before You Begin page. It's actually good advice and a useful reminder. If you've read the page, understand all its implications, and don't ever want to see the page again, select the Skip This Page By Default check box. (Personally, we like to leave it cleared.)

4. Click Next to open the Select Server Roles page, as shown in Figure 17-2.

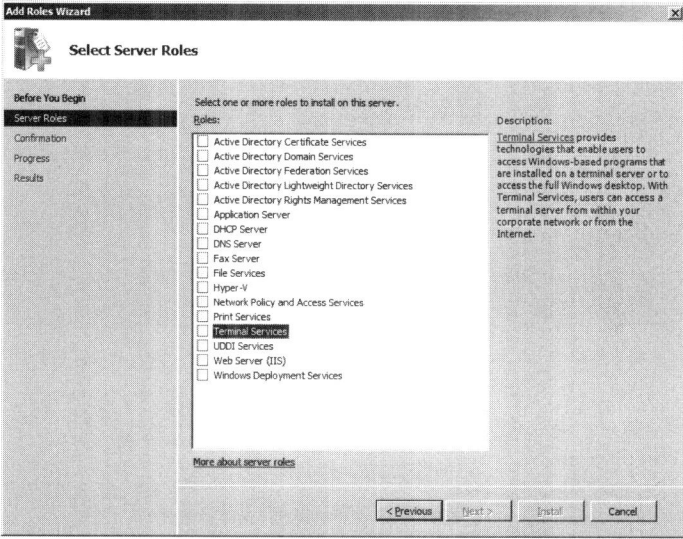

FIGURE 17-2 The Select Server Roles page of the Add Roles Wizard

5. Select the Server Role(s) you want to add. You can select more than one, but doing so makes it much more likely that you'll have to reboot before the installation completes.

6. Click Next to open the page for the first Role that will be installed, as shown in Figure 17-3 (if you selected Terminal Services in the previous step). This page describes the Role that is being installed and includes a Things To Note section that contains cautions or advisories specific to the Role being installed. There is also a link to an Additional Information page with up-to-date information on the Role being installed.

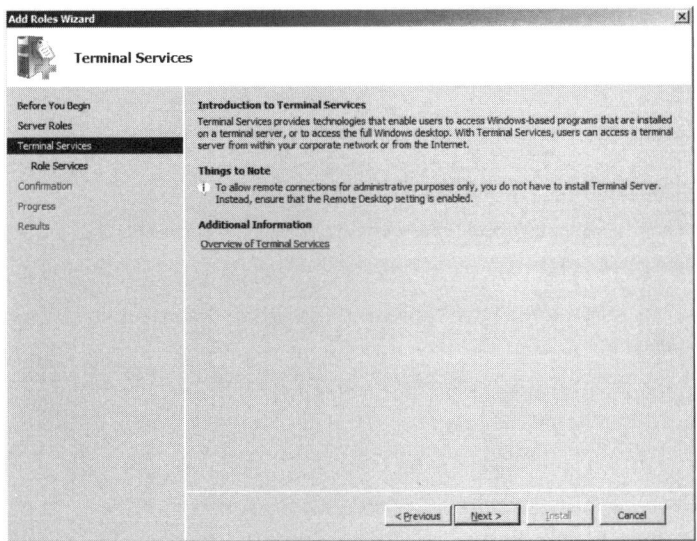

FIGURE 17-3 The Terminal Services page of the Add Roles Wizard

7. After you've read any Things To Note, click Next to open the Select Role Services page shown in Figure 17-4.

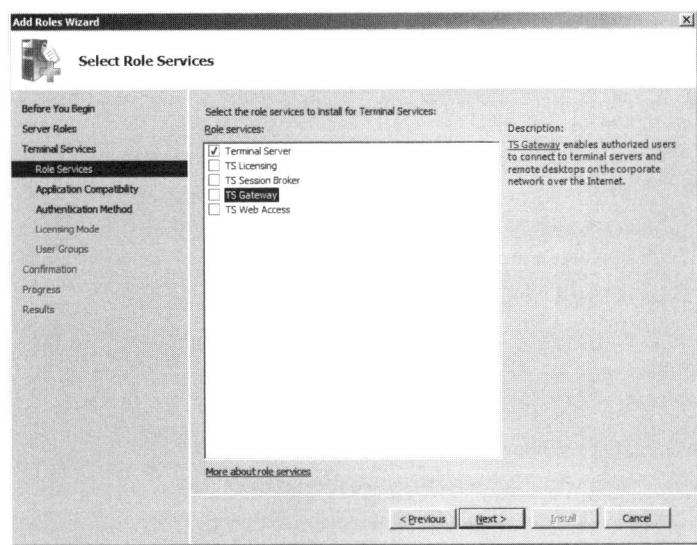

FIGURE 17-4 The Select Role Services page of the Add Roles Wizard

8. Select the Role Services you want to add at this time. If you select a Role Service that has a dependency on another Role, Role Service, or Feature, you'll see a pop-up dialog box describing the additional functionality that will be installed, as shown in Figure 17-5.

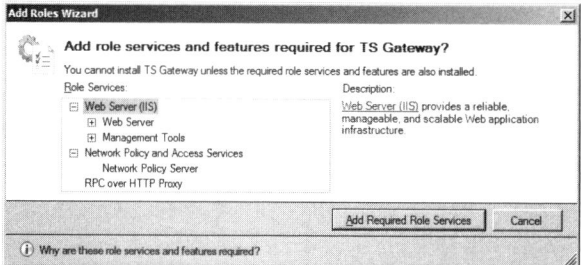

FIGURE 17-5 The Add Role Services And Features Required For TS Gateway page of the Add Roles Wizard

9. Click Add Required Role Services to continue and return to the Select Role Services page or click Cancel if you want to change your Role Services selection.

10. Click Next to open the next page in the Add Roles Wizard. From here to the end of the wizard, the specific pages will vary depending on what Roles and Role Services you've selected.

NOTE For Terminal Services in an SBS environment, when you get to the Select User Groups Allowed Access To This Terminal Server page, it's useful to add the Windows SBS Remote Web Workplace Users group, as shown in Figure 17-6.

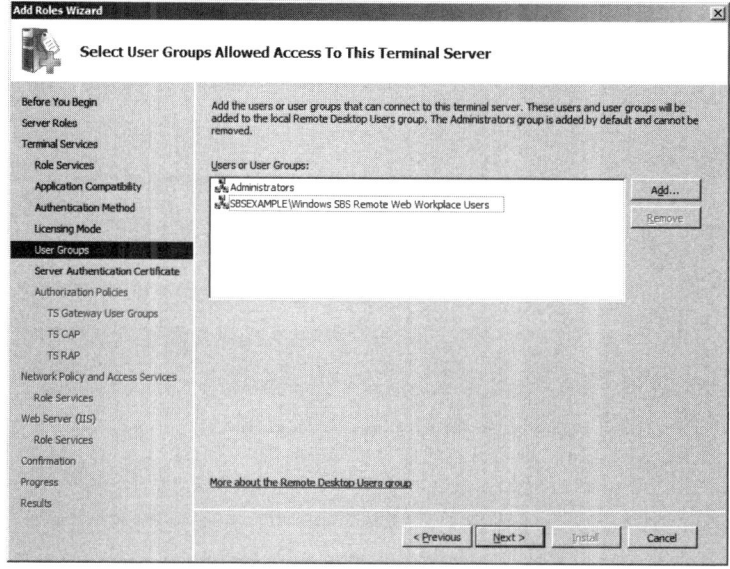

FIGURE 17-6 The Select User Groups Allowed Access To This Terminal Server page of the Add Roles Wizard

11. After the Add Roles Wizard has all the information necessary to proceed, it will open the Confirm Installation Selections page. This is your last chance to make sure you've selected the Roles and Role Services you expected and configured any necessary settings appropriate for your environment. If everything looks correct, click Install to begin the installation.

12. After the installation completes, you'll see the Installation Results page, shown in Figure 17-7. This page indicates whether the installation requires a restart or any other warnings or errors. Click Close to complete the wizard.

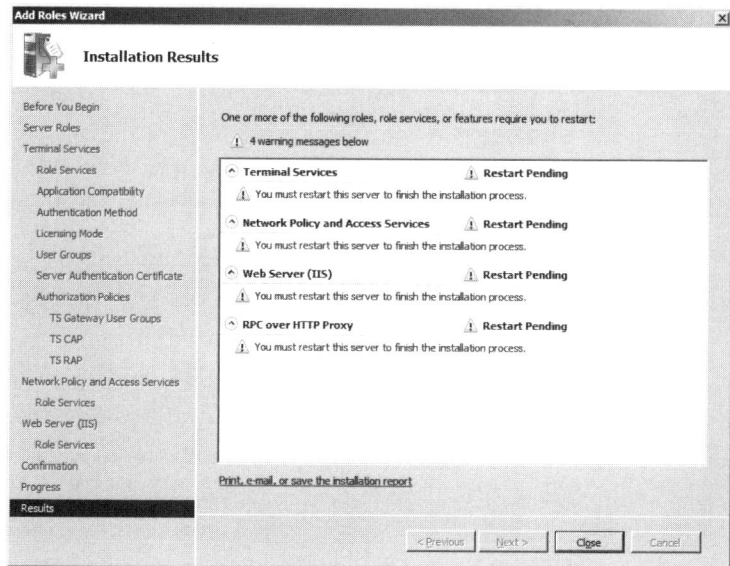

FIGURE 17-7 The Installation Results page of the Add Roles Wizard

13. If your installation required a restart, you'll be prompted to restart the server. You might as well do it now, because you can't install anything else while a restart is pending.

14. If your installation requires a restart, be sure to log back on with the same account you used to add the Role. The installation can't complete until you log back on with that account. The Resume Configuration Wizard will open and complete the installation of the Roles and Role Services you selected. Click Close when the installation is complete.

Removing a Role

You can use either the graphical Server Manager console to remove a Role, or you can use the command-line utility ServerManagerCmd.exe. Both have the same functionality: They remove only the explicit Role selected. They will not usually remove any Roles or Role Services that were added during the initial Role installation to support the Role being removed—unless the Role, Role Service, or Feature requires the Role that is being removed. That's a bit confusing, isn't it? Okay, how about a specific example that makes it a bit clearer: Let's say you installed the Terminal Services Role with all its Role Services. You'll also have Network Policy And Access Services installed, along with Web Server (IIS). You can uninstall the entire Terminal Services Role and neither the Network Policy And Access Services nor Web Server (IIS) Roles will be removed. But if you remove the Web Server (IIS) Role, it will also remove the RPC Over HTTP Proxy Feature, as shown in Figure 17-8.

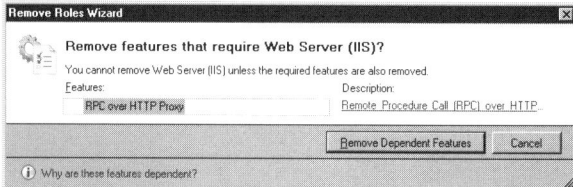

FIGURE 17-8 Removing the Web Server (IIS) Role forces removal of the RPC Over HTTP Proxy Feature.

To remove a Role using the Server Manager console, follow these steps:

1. Open the Server Manager console if it isn't already open.

2. Select Remove Roles from the Action menu to open the Before You Begin page of the Remove Roles Wizard.

3. Read the advice on the Before You Begin page. It's actually good advice and a useful reminder. If you've read the page, understand all its implications, and don't ever want to see the page again, select the Skip This Page By Default check box. Personally, we leave it cleared.

4. Click Next to open the Remove Server Roles page, as shown in Figure 17-9. Clear the Roles you want to remove.

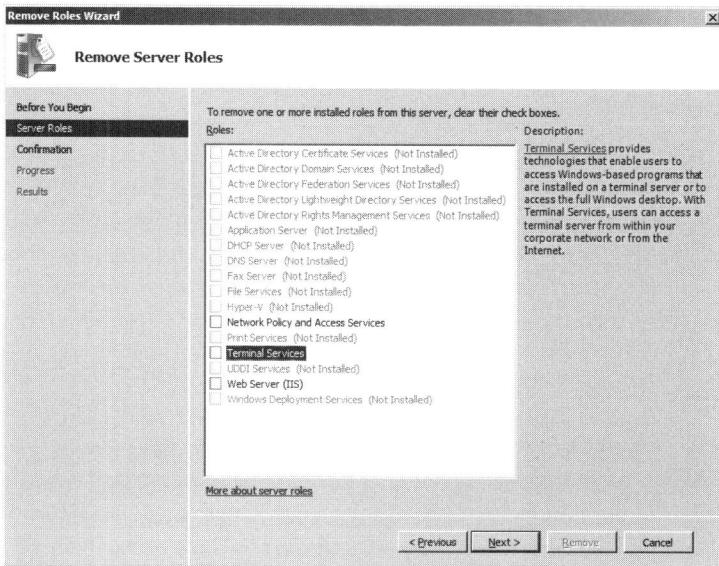

FIGURE 17-9 The Remove Server Roles page of the Remove Roles Wizard

5. If there are any dependent features, you'll be prompted to remove them also, as shown earlier in Figure 17-8.

6. When you've cleared the check boxes for any Roles you want to remove, click Next to open the Confirm Removal Selections page, as shown in Figure 17-10. This page will often include one or more informational messages. Be sure you understand all implications of removing the Role or Roles.

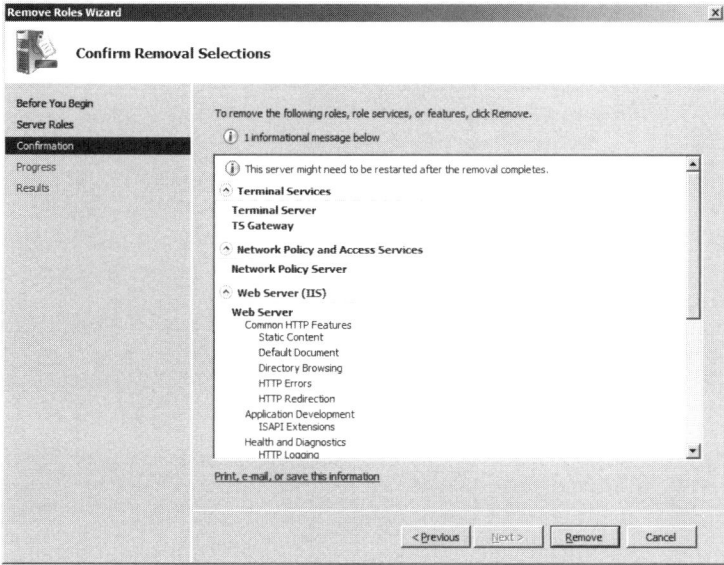

FIGURE 17-10 The Confirm Removal Selections page of the Remove Roles Wizard

> **NOTE** You can print, e-mail, or save the information in the Confirm Removal Selections page by clicking below the informational window.

7. Click Remove to actually begin the removal.

8. When the removal has completed, you'll see the Removal Results page, as shown in Figure 17-11. If any of the Roles or Features require a restart, you'll see a message warning you that a restart is pending. In our experience, removing just about anything requires a restart.

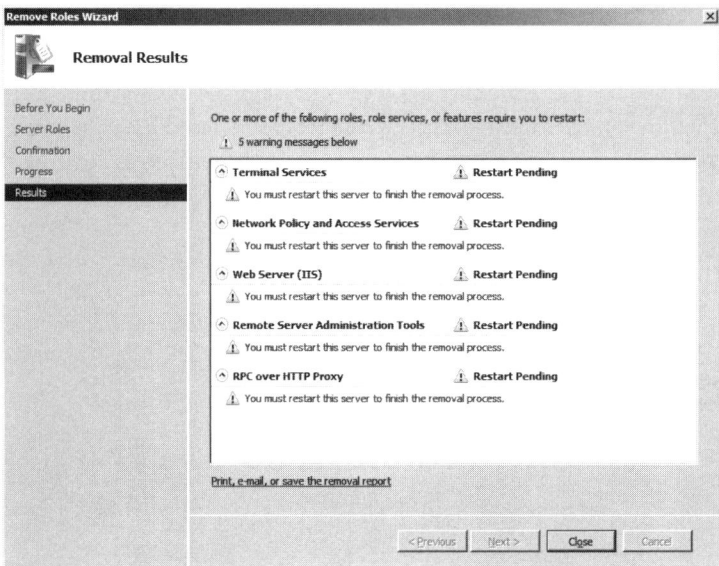

FIGURE 17-11 The Removal Results page of the Remove a Role Wizard

9. Click Close and then click Yes if prompted for a restart.

10. If your removal requires a restart, be sure to log back on with the same account you used to remove the Role. The removal can't complete until you log back on with that account. The Resume Configuration Wizard will open and complete the removal of the Roles you selected. Click Close when the removal is complete.

Adding and Removing Role Services

In most situations, you'll add or remove Role Services as a part of adding and removing the Roles they are services for. But often enough you'll start out with one set of Role Services for a particular Role, and at some point discover the need to add a Role Service or even remove a Role Service for something that's no longer needed.

The process of adding and removing Role Services is much the same as adding and removing Roles and follows many of the same steps. Adding a Role Service requires that the Role for that service be installed. You can't add the TS Licensing Role Service without having the Terminal Services Role installed.

Adding a Role Service

You can use either the command line or the graphical Server Manager console to add a Role Service. To add the TS Licensing Role Service to the main SBS server, which already has the TS Gateway Role Service installed, follow these steps:

1. Open the Server Manager console if it isn't already open.

2. Click Terminal Services in the left pane and select Add Role Services from the Action menu to open the Add Role Services Wizard, as shown in Figure 17-12.

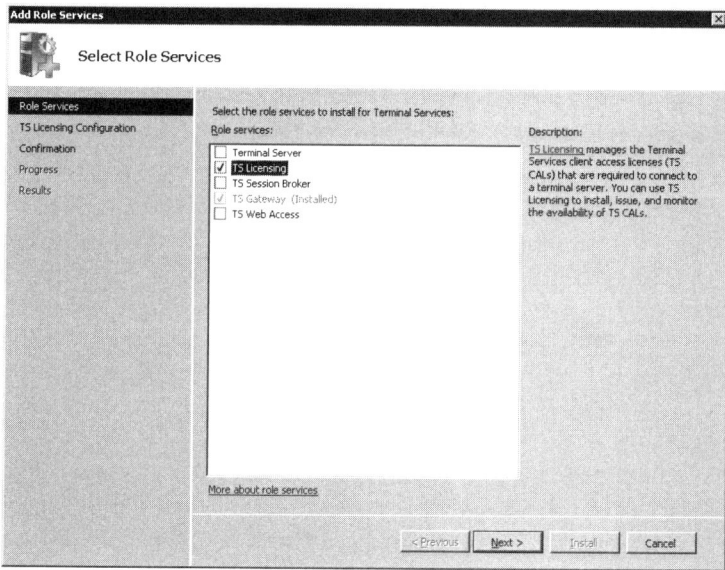

FIGURE 17-12 The Select Role Services page of the Add Role Services Wizard

3. Select the Role Service you want to add and click Next. If this Role Service has configuration choices, you'll have one or more pages of wizard to address. With the TS Licensing Role Service, you'll have the Configure Discovery Scope For TS Licensing page shown in Figure 17-13.

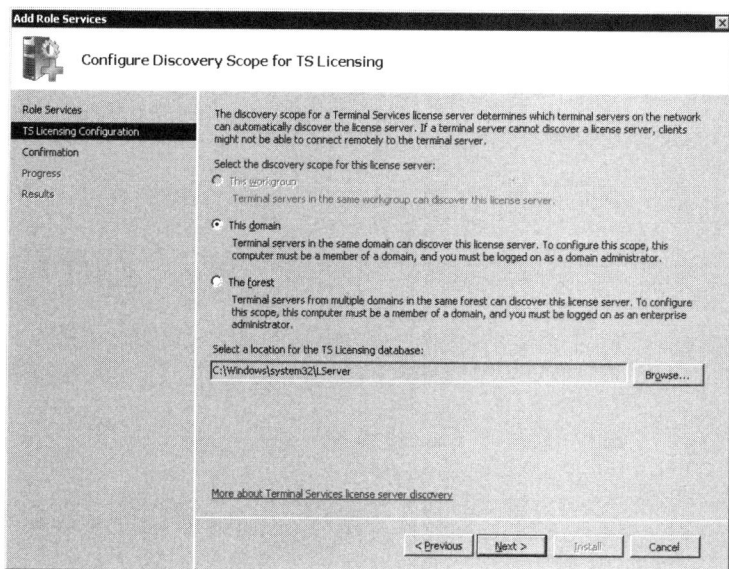

FIGURE 17-13 The Configure Discovery Scope For TS Licensing page of the Add Role Services Wizard

4. Select This Domain or The Forest. With SBS it doesn't really matter, because we have only a single domain in our forest.

5. Click Next to open the Confirm Installation Selections page.

6. Click Install to begin the installation.

7. After the installation is complete, the Installation Results page will open, as shown in Figure 17-14. If no restart is required, click Close to complete the installation.

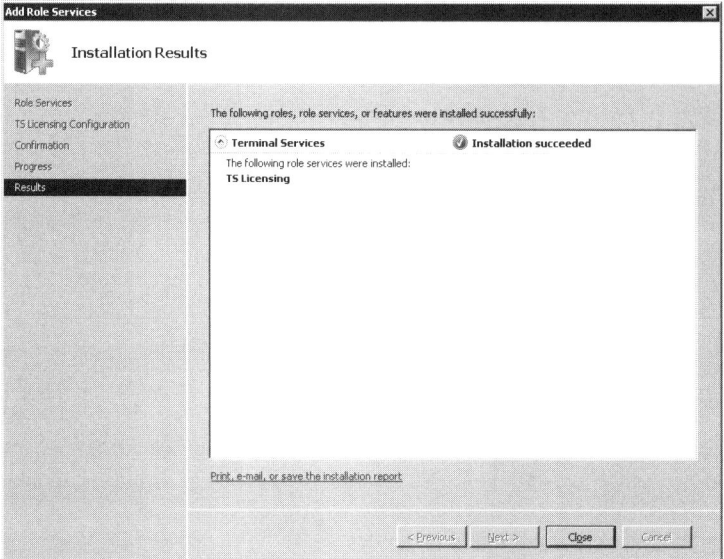

FIGURE 17-14 The Installation Results page of the Add Role Services Wizard

Removing a Role Service

Removing a Role Service doesn't necessarily remove the Role. For example, you can remove the TS Licensing Role Service without affecting other Role Services of the Terminal Services Role.

As always, you can use either the command line or the graphical Server Manager console to remove Role Services. As with removing Roles, we have a hard time understanding why anyone would use the command line to remove a Role Service, but there's no particular reason not to. To remove the TS Licensing Role Service of the Terminal Services Role, follow these steps:

1. Open the Server Manager console if it isn't already open.

2. Select the Terminal Services role in the left pane of the Server Manager console.

3. Select Remove Role Services from the Action menu to open the Select Role Services page of the Remove Role Services Wizard, as shown in Figure 17-15.

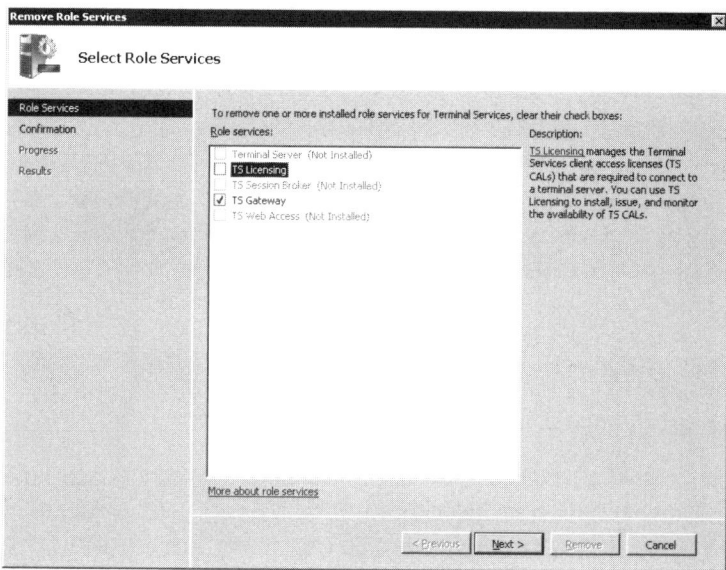

FIGURE 17-15 The Select Role Services page of the Remove Role Services Wizard

4. Clear TS Licensing and click Next to open the Confirm Removal Selections page.

5. Click Remove to begin the removal process. When the process completes, you'll see the Removal Results page, as shown in Figure 17-16.

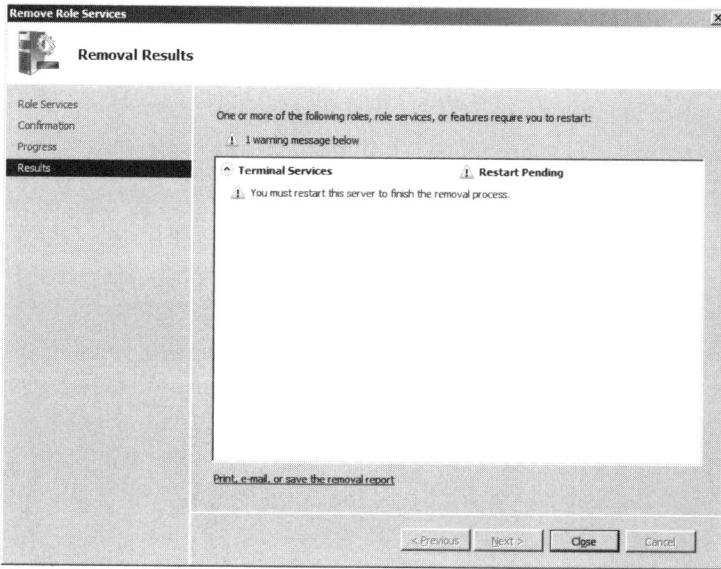

FIGURE 17-16 The Removal Results page of the Remove Role Services Wizard

6. Click Close to exit the wizard. Click Yes to restart the server if prompted.

7. If removing the Role Services requires a restart, be sure to log back on with the same account you used to remove the Role Service. The removal can't complete until you log back on with that account. The Resume Configuration Wizard will open and complete the removal of the Role Service you selected. Click Close when the removal is complete.

> **NOTE** Many Roles and Role Services that can be added without a restart are not so well-behaved when being removed. Expect to have to reboot when removing a Role or Role Service.

Adding and Removing Features

Adding or removing a Feature in SBS 2008 is a very similar process to adding or removing a Role. The difference is that Features are independent of the Roles on a server—a Feature can be added regardless of the Roles that are already on the computer. Again, as with adding a Role, if there's a dependency, the Add Features Wizard will automatically prompt you to add the required additional Roles or Features.

Adding Features

Adding a Feature to Windows Server 2008 usually doesn't require other Features or Roles, though there are exceptions. The exceptions include Message Queuing, which has several subsidiary Features dependent on the main Message Queuing Feature, and the .NET Framework 3.0 Features, which also has several subsidiary Features.

To install the three basic Features we have on every server, follow these steps:

1. Open the Server Manager console if it isn't already open.

2. Select Features in the left pane of the Server Manager console.

3. Select Add Features from the Action menu to open the Select Features page of the Add Features Wizard, as shown in Figure 17-17.

4. Select the Features you want to install and click Next to begin the installation process.

5. When the process completes, you'll see the Installation Results page. If this page shows that one or more of your Features has a pending restart, you'll need to restart the server before continuing.

6. Click Close to exit the wizard. Click Yes to restart the server if prompted.

7. If your installation requires a restart, be sure to log back on with the same account you used to add the Features. The installation isn't complete until you log back on with that account. The Resume Configuration Wizard will open and complete the installation of the Features you selected. Click Close when the installation is complete.

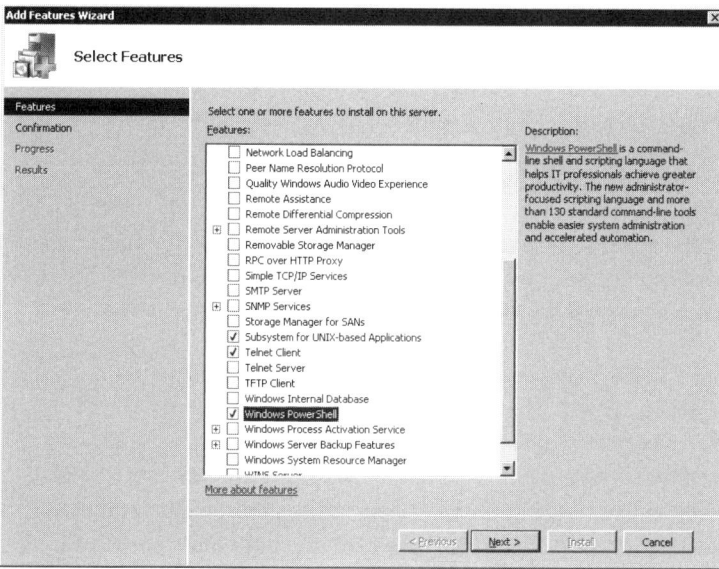

FIGURE 17-17 The Select Features page of the Add Features Wizard

To install the same three Features using the command line, use the following command:

```
servermanagercmd -install Telnet-Client PowerShell Subsystem-UNIX-Apps
```

In our experience, these three Features can be installed together without requiring a server restart. We've added the preceding command line to our standard build configuration, ensuring that the tools we need and expect are available on all servers.

> **NOTE** Windows PowerShell is installed by default on the SBS first server but is not installed by default on the Premium Edition second server or on a standard Windows Server 2008 installation. And it is not available if you're installing Windows Server 2008 Server Core.

Removing Features

Removing a Feature from Windows Server 2008 usually doesn't affect other Features or Roles, though there are exceptions, including the .NET Framework 3.0 Feature, which has several subsidiary Features.

To remove a Feature, follow these steps:

1. Open the Server Manager console if it isn't already open.
2. Select Features in the left pane of the Server Manager console and then highlight the Feature you want to remove.
3. Select Remove Features from the Action menu to open the Select Features page of the Remove Features Wizard.

4. Clear the check box of the Feature you want to remove, click Next, and then click Remove to begin the removal process.

5. When the process completes, you'll see the Removal Results page. If this page shows a pending restart, you'll need to restart the server before continuing.

6. Click Close to exit the wizard. Click Yes to restart the server if prompted.

7. If your removal requires a restart, be sure to log back on with the same account you used to add the Features. The removal isn't complete until you log back on with that account. The Resume Configuration Wizard will open and complete the removal of the Features you selected. Click Close when the wizard is finished.

Using the Native Consoles

For many tasks, even most tasks, you should use the Windows SBS Console. There's even an Advanced Mode version that has links to the native consoles for the most commonly required tasks that don't have special SBS wizards. But whether you get to those consoles from the Advanced Mode Windows SBS Console, start them directly, or use Server Manager, the behavior is the same.

Using the Advanced Mode of the Windows SBS Console

The simplest way to work with the most commonly used native consoles is to open them from the Advanced Mode of the Windows SBS Console, shown in Figure 17-18.

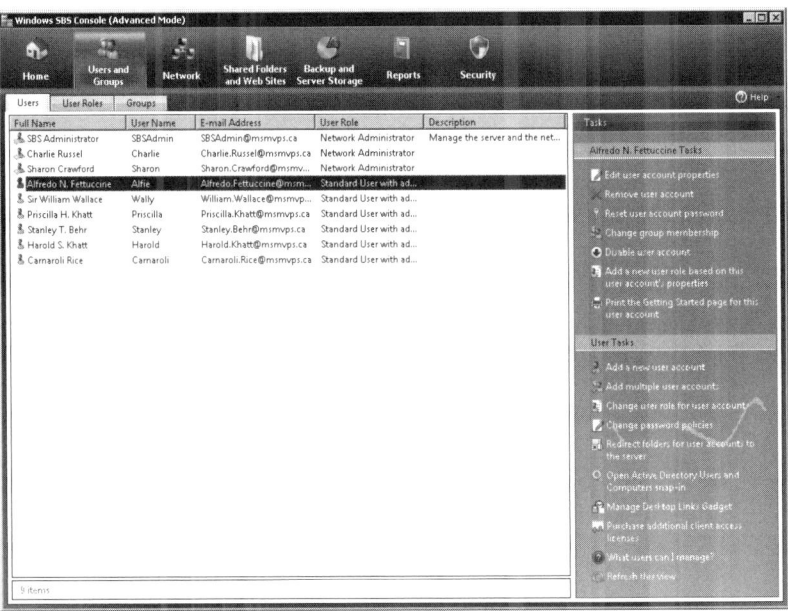

FIGURE 17-18 The Users page of the Windows SBS Console (Advanced Mode)

As we can see in the figure, there is an additional option in the Tasks pane of the Users page—a link to Open Active Directory Users And Computers Snap-in. The Active Directory Users And Computers (ADUC) console is the native mechanism for managing users and computers in Windows Server 2008. And there are definitely tasks that can only be performed easily from the ADUC console, not from the Windows SBS Console. For example, you can't add a contact from the Windows SBS Console—you need to use ADUC for that.

 REAL WORLD **Improving Communications with Contacts and Distribution Groups**

The local affiliate of an international charitable organization where Charlie lives uses Windows Small Business Server as their infrastructure server, supporting both employees and board members with e-mail, database, and other services. One of the ways they use SBS is to maintain Distribution Groups for the working committees of the affiliate. Instead of everyone maintaining separate (and all too often out-of-date) e-mail lists, by hosting them on the SBS server, there's a single place to maintain the groups. Most of the members of the Distribution Groups are not users on the SBS network, but contacts.

To set up the Distribution Groups, Charlie created a Contacts folder in the MyBusiness organizational unit of their SBS domain. Volunteers are added to this folder by importing a list of names and e-mail addresses generated from their central volunteer database into a comma-separated variable length (CSV) file and then imported into Active Directory using a Windows PowerShell script to update existing contacts or create new ones, as required. As the various working committees change over time, the Distribution Group membership is updated, but the single address for the committee doesn't change.

As Charlie and the other board members and volunteers have found, this central management of committee lists, made possible by Windows Small Business Server, has greatly simplified communications in the affiliate. To send a message to all the members of the construction committee, for example, a single e-mail address is used. Board members, who have User accounts on the system, can easily centralize their e-mail to their preferred e-mail address by also having a contact e-mail address and forwarding to that.

To use the Advanced Mode of Windows SBS Console to create a contact, follow these steps:

1. Click Start, All Programs, Windows Small Business Server, and then click Windows SBS Console (Advanced Mode) to open the console. (Be smart—put a link to this on your desktop or pin it to the Start menu.)

2. Click Users And Groups and then click Users if it isn't in front.

3. In the Tasks pane, on the right, click Open Active Directory Users And Computers Snap-in to open ADUC, as shown in Figure 17-19.

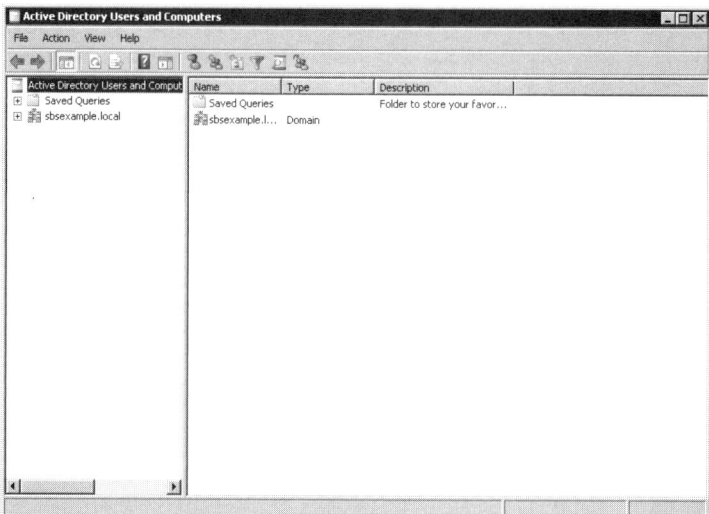

FIGURE 17-19 Active Directory Users And Computers console

4. Expand the domain name in the left pane and navigate to the MyBusiness OU.

5. Click MyBusiness, select New, and then select Organizational Unit from the shortcut menu to open the New Object – Organizational Unit dialog box shown in Figure 17-20.

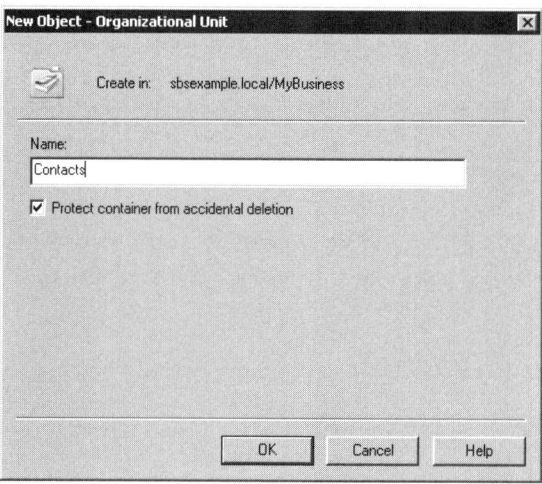

FIGURE 17-20 The New Object – Organizational Unit dialog box

6. Type in a name for the container and click OK to create the OU.

7. Right-click the OU you just created, select New, and then select Contact, as shown in Figure 17-21.

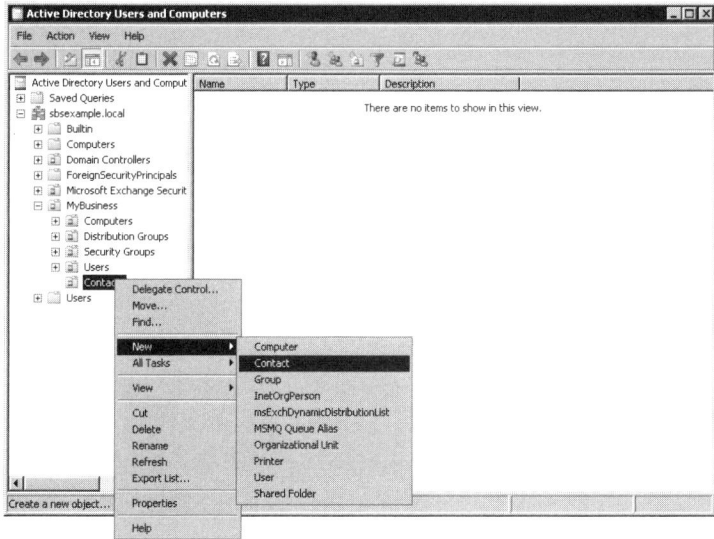

FIGURE 17-21 Creating a new contact

8. In the New Object – Contact dialog box, shown in Figure 17-22, fill in the fields for the new contact. We find it useful to add **(external)** to the name field when adding secondary e-mail addresses for users who will have an account on the SBS server.

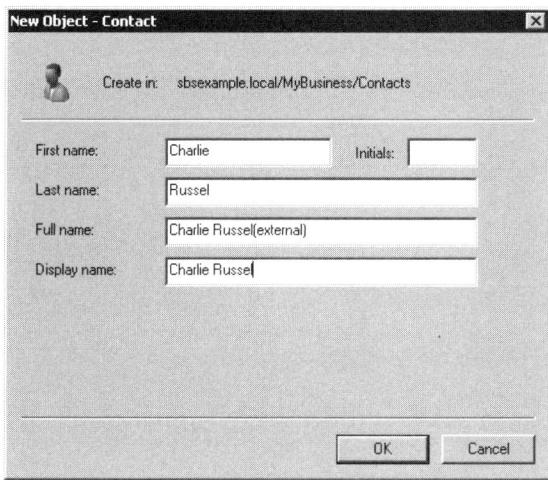

FIGURE 17-22 The New Object – Contact dialog box

9. Click OK to create the contact.

10. Select Properties from the Action menu to open the Properties dialog box for the new contact and enter an e-mail address, as shown in Figure 17-23.

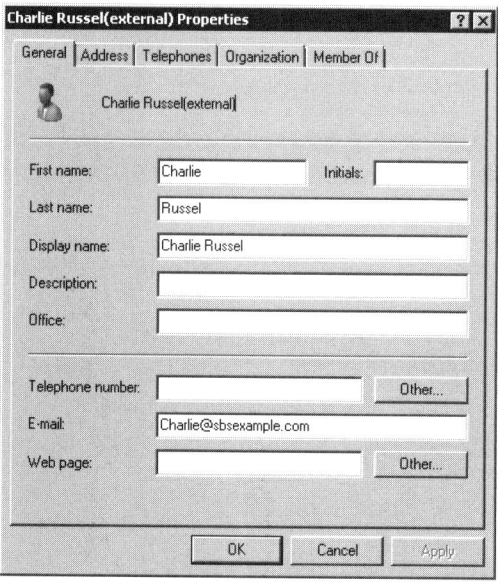

FIGURE 17-23 The Properties dialog box for a contact

11. Click OK to save the changes.

Using Server Manager

A good way to see all the management interface for any server, regardless of the number of Roles installed, is to use the Windows Server 2008 Server Manager. This combines administrative, management, and monitoring functionality into a single console, giving you a single place to manage and monitor all the functionality of your SBS server that isn't managed and monitored from the SBS Console.

The most important part of the Server Manager console, shown in Figure 17-24, is the Roles section. Here you have not only a summary of events, messages, and general health of the Roles that are installed on your server, but also direct access to the individual management consoles for each role.

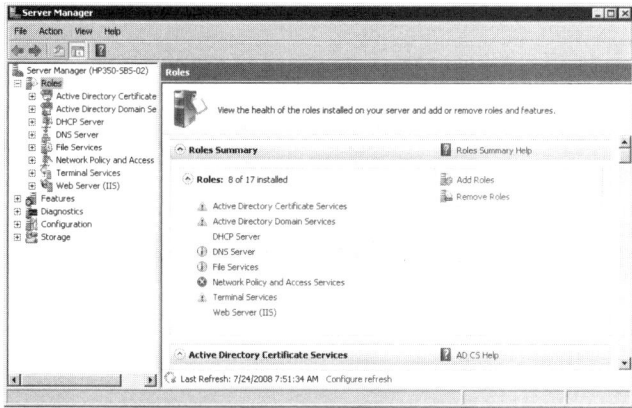

FIGURE 17-24 The Roles page of the Server Manager console

We'll use the Server Manager console to take care of a bit of configuration we need to do on our hp350-sbs-02.sbsexample.local server—configuring the printer and a couple of key workstations for DHCP reservations. This is something that simply can't be done directly from the SBS Console. And we *could* manually configure each of them with static IP addresses, but we prefer to use DHCP whenever possible, so the best solution is a DHCP reservation. It ensures that key workstations are always at the address we expect, but if we need to make a major change to the network addressing, it's all handled at one location, saving us from having to go around and manually configure individual devices or workstations.

To open the DHCP console in Server Manager and add a DHCP reservation, follow these steps:

1. Open the Server Manager if it isn't already open, and click Roles in the left pane.

2. Expand the Roles section and then expand the DHCP Server section by clicking the little plus sign (⊞) to the left of the section you want to expand.

3. Drill down to the IPv4 Address Leases for your SBS server, as shown in Figure 17-25.

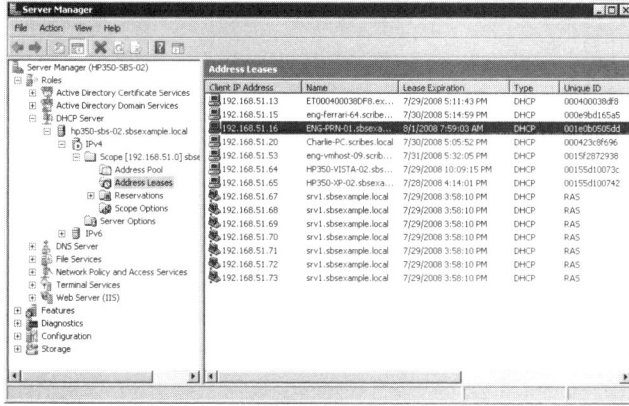

FIGURE 17-25 The IPv4 Address Leases for our SBSEXAMPLE network

4. Highlight the device that you want to give a DHCP reservation to—in our case, the HP 3505 Color LaserPrinter that is in the Engineering office—ENG-PRN-01.

5. We always put our printers in the .40-.49 IP address range, for no particular reason, so we'll assign this printer a DHCP reservation at 192.168.51.40.

6. Right-click Reservations in the left pane and select New Reservation, as shown in Figure 17-26.

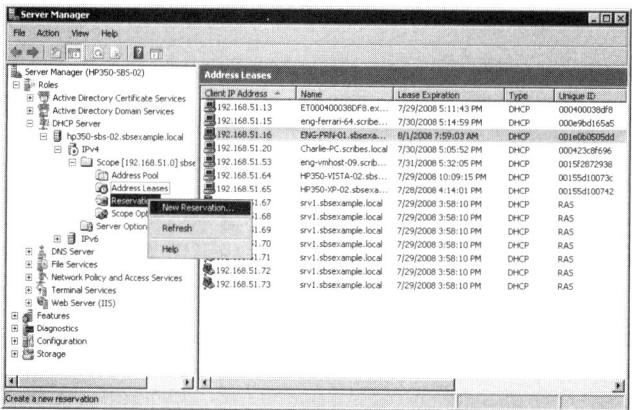

FIGURE 17-26 The right-click menu for DHCP Reservations

NOTE If the New Reservation option isn't available, try clicking Reservations in the left pane once and then clicking Address Leases again. Now right-click Reservations and the choice should be available.

7. In the New Reservation dialog box, type in the name of the device or computer in the Reservation Name field, the IP address where it will reside in the IP Address field, and the Unique ID shown in the current Address Leases display for the MAC Address, shown in Figure 17-27.

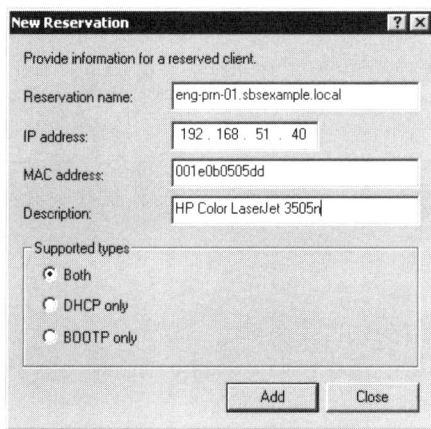

FIGURE 17-27 The New Reservation dialog box for a DHCP Reservation

8. Click Add and the new DHCP reservation is created. The IP address of the device will not, however, immediately start using the reservation. The change will occur either the next time the computer or device requests a new DHCP lease or when it restarts. To simplify things, we suggest forcing a restart after you have made the change.

Directly Opening Native Consoles

Although using the Server Manager console to access the management consoles for the roles and features on your server is a simple way to get at all of them from one location, we often find that it is awkward to navigate when a lot of roles are installed, and we also hate giving up any of our screen real estate for that left pane. So, our solution is to simply open the native management consoles directly. The GUI way is to open the Start menu and click Administrative Tools. This gives you a list of the available Administrative consoles, as shown in Figure 17-28.

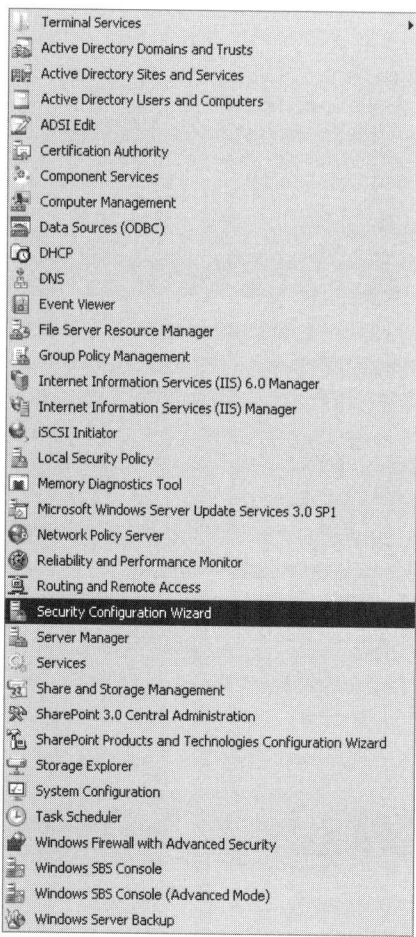

FIGURE 17-28 The available Administrative consoles on a Windows Small Business Server 2008 server

The other way is to open them directly, either from the Run menu or by using a Cmd or Windows PowerShell window. Our preference is to keep a Windows PowerShell window open on the desktop and use that. Table 17-1 has a list of the management consoles, along with a couple of keyboard shortcuts for control panel applications that are easier to get at from the command line.

TABLE 17-1 Command-Line Shortcuts

COMMAND LINE	CONSOLE OR APPLICATION
Adsiedit.msc	Active Directory Service Interface (ADSI) Editor*
Azman.msc	Authorization Manager
Certmgr.msc	Certificates Manager
Certsrv.msc	Certificate Authority Manager

COMMAND LINE	CONSOLE OR APPLICATION
Certtmpl.msc	Certification Templates Console
Comexp.msc	Component Services Console
Compmgmt.msc	Computer Management Console*
Devmgmt.msc	Device Manager*
Dhcpmgmt.msc	DHCP Console*
Diskmgmt.msc	Disk Management Console*
Dnsmgmt.msc	DNS Manager Console*
Domain.msc	Active Directory Domains and Trusts
Dsa.msc	Active Directory Users And Computers*
Dssite.msc	Active Directory Sites And Services
Eventvwr.msc	Event Viewer*
Fsmgmt.msc	Shared Folders (File Services Manager)
Fsrm.msc	File Server Resource Manager
Gpedit.msc	Group Policy Editor
Gpmc.msc	Group Policy Management Console*
Gpme.msc	Group Policy Management Editor*
Gptedit.msc	Group Policy Starter GPO Editor
Lusrmgr.msc	Local Users And Groups Manager (not for use on a domain controller)
Napclcfg.msc	Network Access Protection (NAP) Client Configuration Console
Nps.msc	Network Policy Server Console
Perfmon.msc	Performance Monitor*
Pkiview.msc	Private Key Infrastructure (PKI) Viewer
Rrasmgmt.msc	Routing And Remote Access Manager
Remoteprograms.msc	TS RemoteApp Manager*
Rsop.msc	Resulting Set Of Policies Console
Secpol.msc	Local Security Policy Console
Servermanager.msc	Server Manager Console*
Services.msc	Services*
Storagemgmt.msc	Share And Storage Management Console*
Storexpl.msc	Storage Explorer Console
Tapimgmt.msc	Telephony Console

COMMAND LINE	CONSOLE OR APPLICATION
Taskschd.msc	Task Scheduler*
Tpm.msc	Trusted Platform Module (TPM) Management
Tsadmin.msc	Terminal Services Manager*
Tsconfig.msc	Terminal Services Configuration*
Tsgateway.msc	Terminal Services Gateway Manager
Tsmmc.msc	Remote Desktops Console
Virtmgmt.msc	Hyper-V Manager* (Note: This manager is not on your default path but is installed in C:\Program Files\Hyper-V if present.)
Wbadmin.msc	Windows Server Backup Console*
WF.msc	Windows Firewall with Advanced Security Console*
Wmimgmt.msc	Windows Management Instrumentation (WMI) Manager
Appwiz.cpl	Control Panel: Programs And Features*
Desk.cpl	Control Panel: Display Settings*
Firewall.cpl	Control Panel: Windows Firewall
Hdwwiz.cpl	Control Panel: Add Hardware Wizard
Inetcpl.cpl	Control Panel: Internet Properties (Internet Explorer)
Intl.cpl	Control Panel: Regional And Language Options
Main.cpl	Control Panel: Mouse Properties*
Mmsys.cpl	Control Panel: Sound
Ncpa.cpl	Control Panel: Network Connections*
Powercfg.cpl	Control Panel: Power Options
Sysdm.cpl	Control Panel: System Properties*
Telephon.cpl	Control Panel: Phone And Modem Options
Timedate.cpl	Control Panel: Date And Time

*These are the items we use regularly and that we think are worth learning. Also, .MSC is part of the environment variable PATHEXT, allowing you to skip typing the .msc part of the program name when you want to open one of the management consoles.

Summary

The majority of all your daily management tasks in Windows Small Business Server 2008 can be, and should be, performed using the Windows SBS Console, or the Windows SBS Console Advanced Mode. But there will inevitably be some tasks that either can't be performed from there or that are more easily performed using the native Windows Server 2008 management interface. Before you use the native tools, always verify that you're not doing something that has a built-in SBS wizard. Whenever an SBS wizard is available, you should use it. The wizards almost always do several tasks in an integrated way that would be difficult to do directly using the native management tools, and you'll have a better-behaved and easier-to-manage SBS environment if you stick to the wizards whenever you can.

In the next chapter, we'll cover configuring and managing e-mail, including the initial setup and configuration of Microsoft Exchange Server 2007.

Configuring and Managing E-Mail

One of the central pillars of Windows Small Business Server 2008 is Microsoft Exchange Server 2007. Exchange Server is installed as part of both SBS 2008 Standard and SBS 2008 Premium and provides a robust, full-featured, and flexible e-mail and collaboration infrastructure.

Managing the Exchange infrastructure in a large organization is the task of one or more full-time Exchange administrators, but with Windows Small Business Server, most of the heavy lifting has been done by the SBS team. The initial installation and configuration of Exchange are handled automatically as part of the SBS install and the Getting Started Tasks list.

Basic E-Mail Configuration

The default Exchange Server configuration is set up when you run the initial pass of the Set Up Your Internet Address Wizard and the Configure A Smart Host For Internet E-Mail Wizard. If you haven't completed these tasks, as described in Chapter 8, "Completing the Getting Started Tasks," you need to do that first.

Before you can run the Set Up Your Internet Address Wizard, shown in Figure 18-1, you need to either have your Internet domain name registered or have a good idea of the one you want to register, along with a couple of alternatives in case the one you want isn't available. If you already have a domain, you'll need to know whether you want to manage the DNS settings for it yourself or have SBS manage it for you. Personally, we prefer managing it ourselves, using a service such as ZoneEdit.com as our DNS provider, but for many small businesses, it's just as easy to have SBS manage the domain for you.

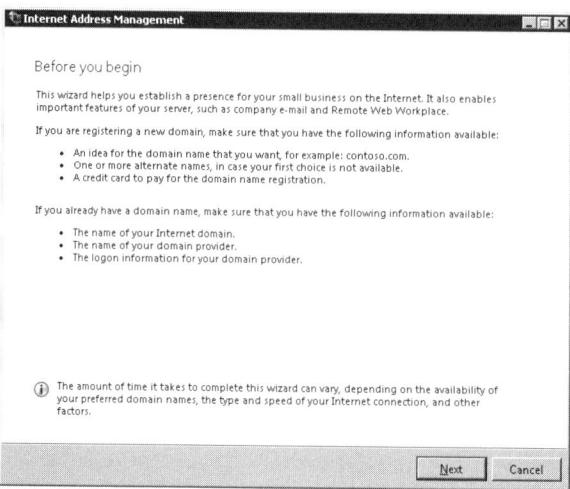

FIGURE 18-1 You need some basic information about your Internet domain name before you can configure e-mail and your Internet address.

Configuring Internet Mail

There are two basic methods for sending e-mail from SBS: direct delivery and forwarding. Direct delivery uses DNS to route e-mail directly to the server that the DNS records point to for the recipient's e-mail domain. E-mail doesn't "pass through" any other Simple Mail Transport Protocol (SMTP) servers along the way and is shown as being directly sent from your SBS Internet domain.

The second method forwards all your mail to another SMTP server that is configured to both accept incoming e-mail for forwarding and to understand how to find the correct destination for the e-mail. Most Internet service providers (ISPs) provide this kind of forwarding server, known as a *Smart Host*.

 REAL WORLD **DNS E-Mail Routing?**

Choosing forwarding (Smart Host) as your e-mail delivery mechanism has some drawbacks, not the least of which is that all e-mail from your Windows Small Business Server will show that it has been forwarded from your ISP. This used to be a significant problem, but as the attempts to control unsolicited commercial e-mail (UCE, or more commonly, spam) have matured, many ISPs don't give you a choice. If you're on their network, you have to use their SMTP server or they simply block your outgoing e-mail. This is especially true if you have a dynamic IP address, because home computers that have malware installed on them are a common source of spam. In an attempt to prevent propagation of that spam, many ISPs are deliberately blocking TCP port 25 (the default port used by SMTP).

Unfortunately, some very fussy e-mail domains refuse to accept mail that has passed through a mail forwarder, and even those who are not that absolute can end up blocking your e-mail when your ISP gets on their blocklist—something you have no control over.

The solution is to have a fixed IP address on a business-class account with your ISP. This ensures that your IP address is a block of addresses that your ISP won't block, and that other servers on the Internet will recognize as fixed addresses. This kind of account is usually a good deal more expensive than a basic floating IP address account designed for a home user. But you're *not* a home user, and you'll have far fewer problems if you use a business-class account.

The default configuration for Exchange Server is to deliver e-mail to recipients directly, not through a Smart Host. Use that configuration by preference—only use a Smart Host if you experience problems sending e-mail or if you're using a service such as Exchange Defender (*www.exchangedefender.com*) that acts as both an inbound filter and an outbound verifier.

Enabling a Smart Host

If you need to use a Smart Host, SBS has a wizard to help configure it for you. Hardly a surprise—SBS has a lot of wizards. Usually you will have configured this by running the Configure A Smart Host For Internet E-Mail Wizard when you did the initial set up of SBS, but circumstances can change, so you can always run this later as well.

To configure SBS to use a Smart Host for Internet e-mail, follow these steps:

1. Open the Windows SBS Console if it isn't already open.

2. Select Network on the top navigation bar and then click Connectivity to open the Connectivity page, shown in Figure 18-2.

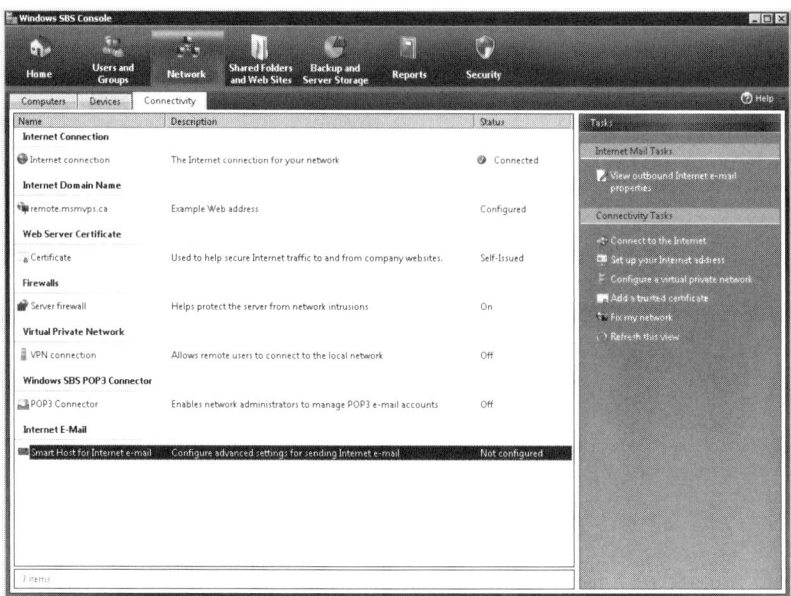

FIGURE 18-2 The Connectivity page of the Windows SBS Console

3. Select Smart Host For Internet E-mail and then click View Outbound Internet E-mail Properties in the Tasks pane to open the Configure Internet Mail Wizard shown in Figure 18-3.

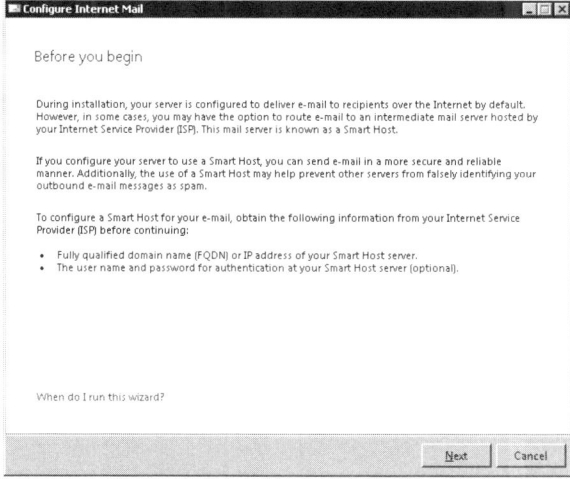

FIGURE 18-3 The Before You Begin page of the Configure Internet Mail Wizard

4. Click Next to open the Specify Settings For Outbound Internet Mail page shown in Figure 18-4.

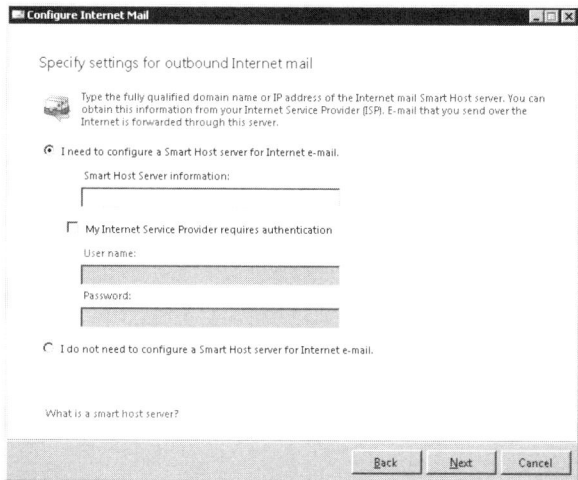

FIGURE 18-4 The Specify Settings For Outbound Internet Mail page of the Configure Internet Mail Wizard

5. Enter the information provided by your ISP for connecting to their Smart Host. Some ISPs require you to provide authentication to connect. This information is usually available on the support pages of your ISP.

6. Click Next to begin the configuration and then click Finish to close the wizard.

Enabling DNS E-Mail Sending

Using DNS for e-mail delivery is the behavior for Exchange Server in SBS. If you haven't configured a Smart Host, you don't need to do anything at all to use DNS e-mail sending. But if you've configured for Smart Host and need to change back to using DNS, you run the same wizard as when you configured for Smart Host. Follow these steps:

1. Open the Windows SBS Console if it isn't already open.

2. Select Network on the top navigation bar and then click Connectivity to open the Connectivity page shown earlier in Figure 18-2.

3. Select Smart Host For Internet E-mail and then click View Outbound Internet E-mail Properties in the Tasks pane to open the Configure Internet Mail Wizard.

4. Click Next to open the Specify Settings For Outbound Internet Mail page shown in Figure 18-5.

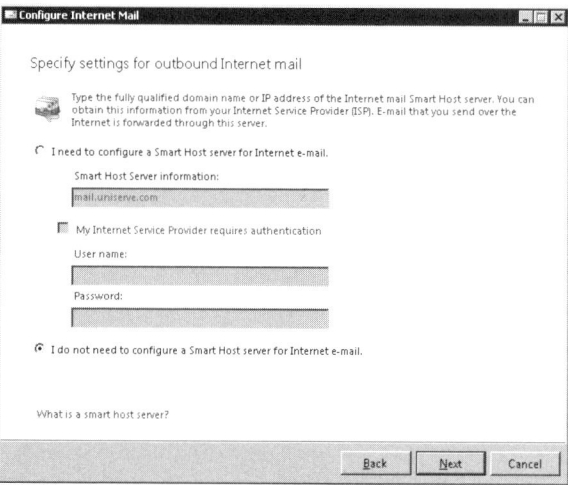

FIGURE 18-5 Removing the Smart Host to return to DNS e-mail delivery

5. Select I Do Not Need To Configure A Smart Host Server For Internet E-mail.

6. Click Next to begin the configuration and then click Finish to close the wizard.

POP3 E-Mail

Some small businesses still rely on external e-mail accounts, and they can be useful during the transition to a new SBS installation. We think using Microsoft Exchange is a far better solution overall, but SBS does support using external, Post Office Protocol v3 (POP3) e-mail accounts. The Window SBS POP3 Connector has changed in SBS 2008 from the version in SBS 2003 in three important ways:

- POP3 e-mail is brought to the SBS server using SMTP, allowing for full scanning and filtering and direct integration into Exchange.

- POP3 e-mail can be scheduled for retrieval every five minutes.

- The POP3 connector no longer supports generic e-mail boxes. Each e-mail box must be explicitly configured and assigned.

Configuring POP3 e-mail requires you to know the e-mail account properties—including the mail server, account name, and password—for each POP3 e-mail account you want to add.

S etting up a POP3 e-mail account requires some details about the account and about the settings used by the account provider. These settings can be usually be found on the support pages of the ISP or mail account provider. The settings you'll need to know before you can set up an account are:

- **POP3 Server** The DNS name or IP address of the POP3 server. Often *pop.ispname.com* or similar.

- **Port** The TCP port to connect to the server. The default for regular POP3 is 110, and for SSL encrypted POP3 it is 995.

- **Secure Socket Layer** Used to encrypt traffic to and from the POP3 server. Select only if your ISP or POP3 mail provider supports SSL encryption.

- **Logon Type** A drop-down list of supported types—Basic, Secure Password Authentication (SPA), or Authenticated POP (APOP). If your ISP doesn't support SSL, and supports only Basic authentication, your account name and password are being transmitted in plaintext. If you must use a provider that only supports plaintext, do *not* connect from a public wireless hotspot and do *not* use the same password you use for anything important.

You'll also need to know the full account name and password for the account. You should warn users not to change their passwords for the account without notifying whoever is responsible for maintaining the POP3 Connector.

Adding a POP3 Account

The process for adding POP3 accounts is simple, but tedious if you have more than a few to add. There's no way we know of to add them with a script.

To add a POP3 e-mail account, follow these steps:

1. Open the Windows SBS Console if it isn't already open.

2. Select Network on the top navigation bar and then click Connectivity to open the Connectivity page shown earlier in Figure 18-2.

3. Select POP3 Connector in the main pane and then click View POP3 Connector Properties in the Tasks pane to open the Windows SBS POP3 Connector dialog box, shown in Figure 18-6.

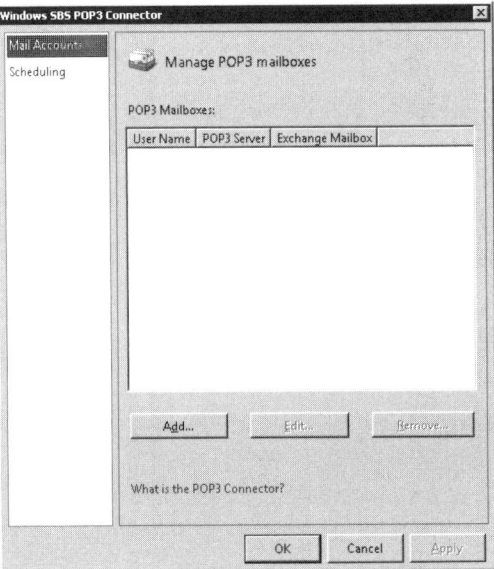

FIGURE 18-6 The Windows SBS POP3 Connector dialog box

4. Click Add to open the POP3 Mailbox Accounts page of the Windows SBS POP3 Connector dialog box, as shown in Figure 18-7. Enter the information to connect to the account. For details on the various settings, see the Under the Hood sidebar titled "POP3 Account Settings" earlier in this chapter.

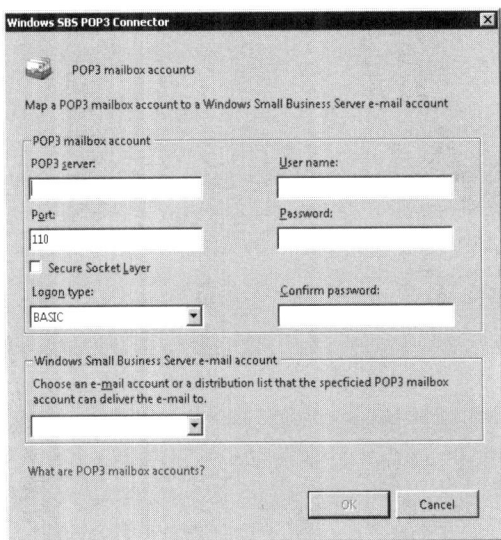

FIGURE 18-7 The POP3 Mailbox Accounts page of the Windows SBS POP3 Connector dialog box

5. Click OK to return to the Manage POP3 Mailboxes page. From here you can add additional mailboxes, edit an existing mailbox, or remove a mailbox.

6. When you've finished adding mailboxes, click OK to close the dialog box and implement the change.

Setting POP3 Retrieval Frequency

SBS allows you to control how often the POP3 connector retrieves messages from POP3 accounts. This control is limited to a single setting for any and all POP3 accounts—you can't set a different frequency on a per-account basis, unfortunately. The default retrieval frequency is every 15 minutes, but you can configure the POP3 connector to retrieve POP3 mail as often as every five minutes if you need to or scale back to only once every few hours, if that's more appropriate.

 REAL WORLD **POP3 Frequency**

One of the common complaints raised by users of SBS 2003 was the inability to set the POP3 frequency to more often than every 15 minutes. Microsoft has addressed this by allowing retrieval of POP3 mail every five minutes in SBS 2008. But just because you *can* do something doesn't necessarily mean you should.

Setting the POP3 retrieval interval too short can create a situation in which the connector never actually completes. When large documents are attached to e-mail, and the network is busy, a five-minute interval can be too short a time to retrieve all the e-mail for a site. This leads to churning and a generally unsatisfactory experience for users. If your e-mail is so time-sensitive that you need to retrieve it more often than every 15 minutes, we'd strongly suggest moving your primary e-mail to Microsoft Exchange. Well, actually, we'd recommend that anyway, but it's especially true for organizations that expect instant e-mail.

To set the POP3 retrieval frequency, use the following steps:

1. Open the Windows SBS Console if it isn't already open.
2. Select Network on the top navigation bar and then click Connectivity to open the Connectivity page shown earlier in Figure 18-2.
3. Select POP3 Connector in the main pane and then click View POP3 Connector Properties in the Tasks pane to open the Windows SBS POP3 Connector dialog box.
4. Click Scheduling in the left pane to open the Set POP3 Connector Schedule page, shown in Figure 18-8.
5. Change the Schedule section to automatically retrieve e-mail at the interval desired. If you need to manually initiate a POP3 e-mail retrieval, click Retrieve Now.
6. Click OK to initiate the schedule and return to the Connectivity page.

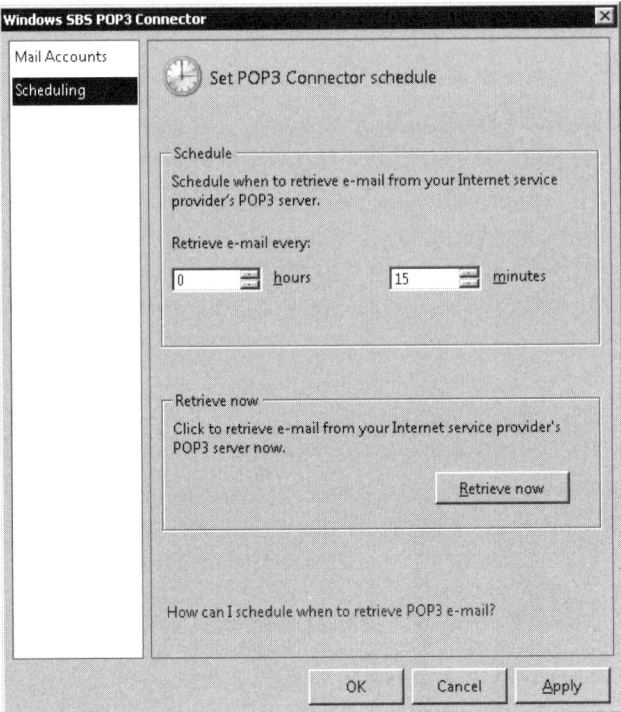

FIGURE 18-8 The Set POP3 Connector Schedule page

Advanced E-Mail Configuration

Although most things that you'll need to do for e-mail configuration are easily handled from the Windows SBS Console, there are a few things that require running the Exchange Management Console, shown in Figure 18-9, or using Windows PowerShell scripts. Anything that can be done in the Exchange Management Console can also be done using Windows PowerShell in the Exchange Management Shell.

Trying to cover everything that can be done to configure Microsoft Exchange Server 2007 is an entire book, and not something we'll even try to do in this chapter. What we'll do is use a couple of examples to give you an idea of what kinds of things can be configured, and how to find them and use the Exchange Management Console to accomplish them. For additional details, we strongly suggest a bit of exploration through the graphical console, or when you need more help, we suggest the *Microsoft Exchange Server 2007 Administrator's Companion, Second Edition* (Microsoft Press, 2008).

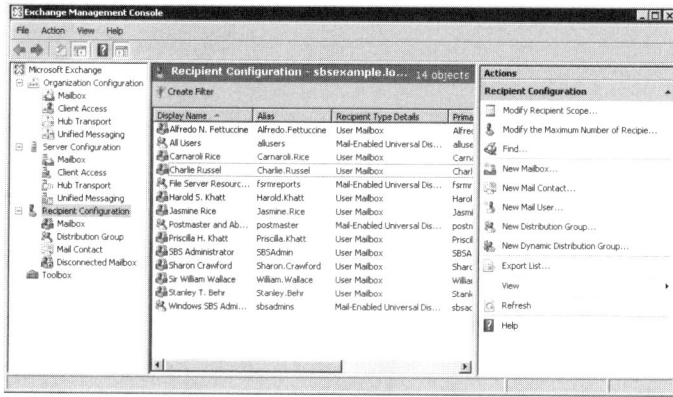

FIGURE 18-9 The Exchange Management Console

Using Contacts

In Microsoft Exchange terms, a contact is someone who doesn't need an Active Directory user account and doesn't have mail stored in Exchange. But a contact does need to be both a contact in Active Directory and be mail-enabled in Microsoft Exchange. If you've created someone as a contact in Active Directory, he or she still needs to be mail-enabled in Exchange. If you're creating the contact directly in Exchange, you will also be adding him or her to Active Directory at the same time, so it's usually more efficient to add contacts directly from within the Exchange Management Console or using the New-MailContact PowerShell cmdlet.

Mail-Enabling Existing Contacts

You can mail-enable existing contacts from your Active Directory if they've already been created there. To mail-enable a contact, follow these steps:

1. Open the Exchange Management Console if it isn't open.

2. Navigate to Recipient Configuration and then click Mail Contact in the left pane of the console.

3. Click New Mail Contact in the Actions pane to open the New Mail Contact Wizard shown in Figure 18-10.

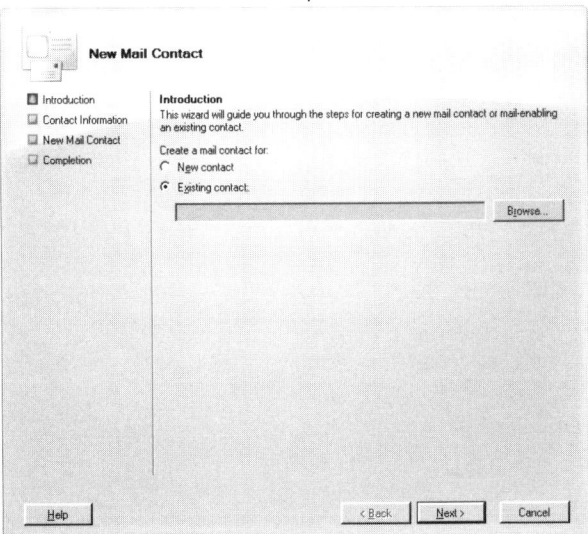

FIGURE 18-10 The Introduction page of the New Mail Contact Wizard

4. Click Existing Contact and then click Browse to open the Select Contact dialog box shown in Figure 18-11. You'll see a list of all Active Directory contacts that are not currently mail-enabled.

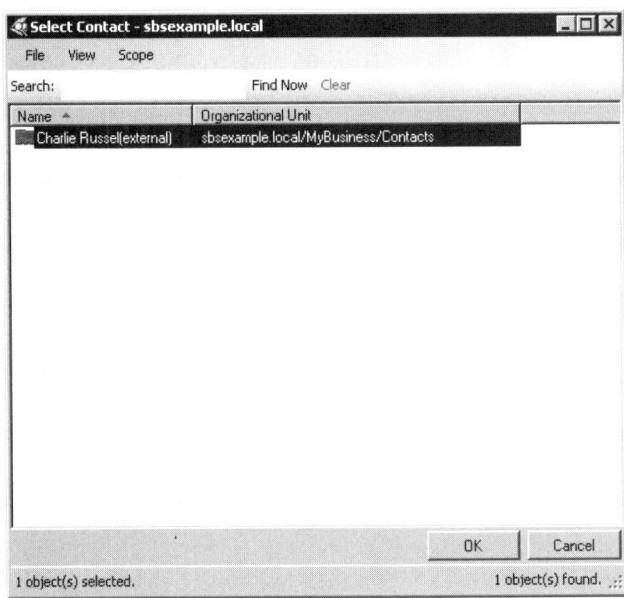

FIGURE 18-11 Browsing to find an Active Directory contact that needs to be mail-enabled

5. Select the contact you want to mail-enable and click OK to return to the Introduction page of the New Mail Contact Wizard.

6. Click Next to open the Contact Information page of the New Mail Contact Wizard, as shown in Figure 18-12. Most of the fields will already be filled in because this is an existing contact.

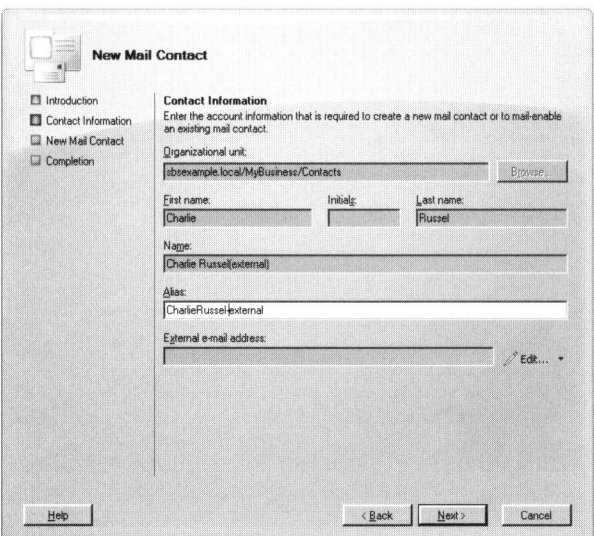

FIGURE 18-12 The Contact Information for an existing Active Directory contact that is being mail-enabled

7. Click Edit to open the SMTP Address dialog box shown in Figure 18-13.

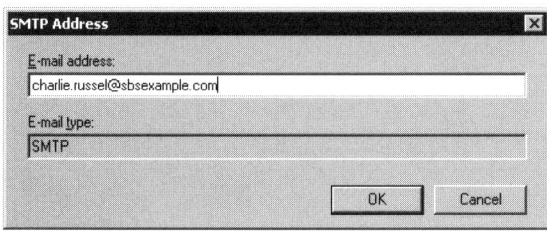

FIGURE 18-13 Adding an SMTP address to mail-enable a contact

8. Type in the e-mail address for the contact and click OK to return to the Contact Information page of the New Mail Contact Wizard.

9. Click Next to open the New Mail Contact page shown in Figure 18-14. This summarizes the actions that are about to taken and is your last chance to cancel or correct the information.

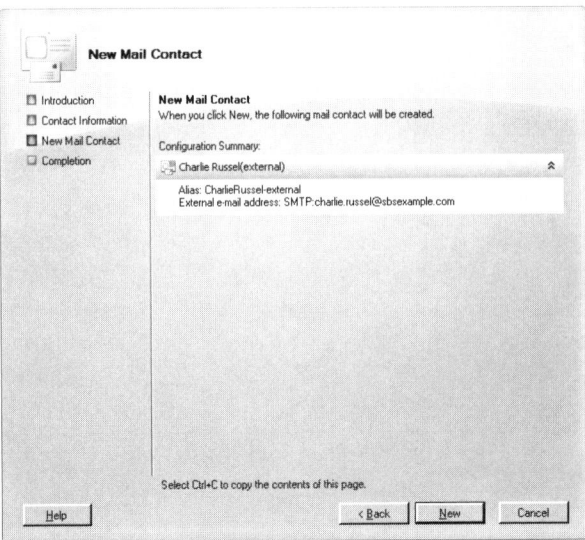

FIGURE 18-14 The New Mail Contact page shows the new mail-enabled contact that will be created.

10. Click New to create the contact and open the Completion page shown in Figure 18-15.

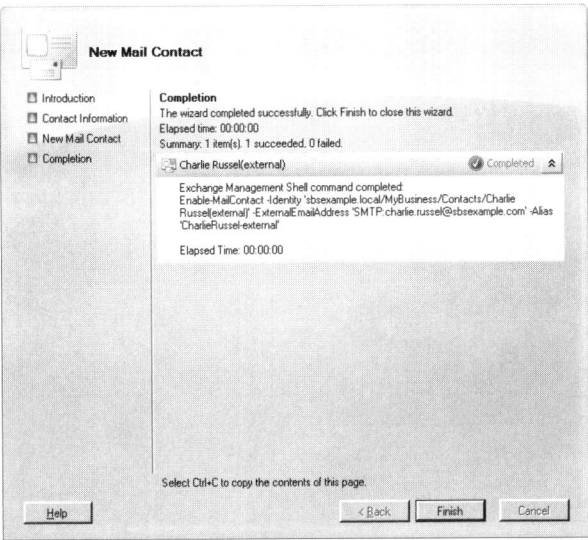

FIGURE 18-15 The Completion page shows the actual Windows PowerShell script that was executed.

11. Click Finish to close the New Mail Contact Wizard and return to the Exchange Management Console.

NOTE Press Ctrl+C on the Completion page of the New Mail Contact Wizard (or any other Wizard in Microsoft Exchange 2007) to copy the contents of the page to the clipboard. This will include the Windows PowerShell script that was executed to complete the task. You can then paste this into your favorite editor (we use Gvim, but even Notepad will work) and use it as the basis to build future scripts.

Adding a New Mail-Enabled Contact

The steps for creating a new mail-enabled contact are similar to those for updating an existing Active Directory contact to be mail-enabled. However, when you're creating a new contact, you'll need to have additional information about the contact and know which Organizational Unit you want the contact to reside in.

Use the following steps to create a new mail-enable contact:

1. Open the Exchange Management Console if it isn't already open.

2. Navigate to Recipient Configuration and then click Mail Contact in the left pane of the console.

3. Click New Mail Contact in the Actions pane to open the New Mail Contact Wizard.

4. Select New Contact and click Next to open the Contact Information page shown in Figure 18-16.

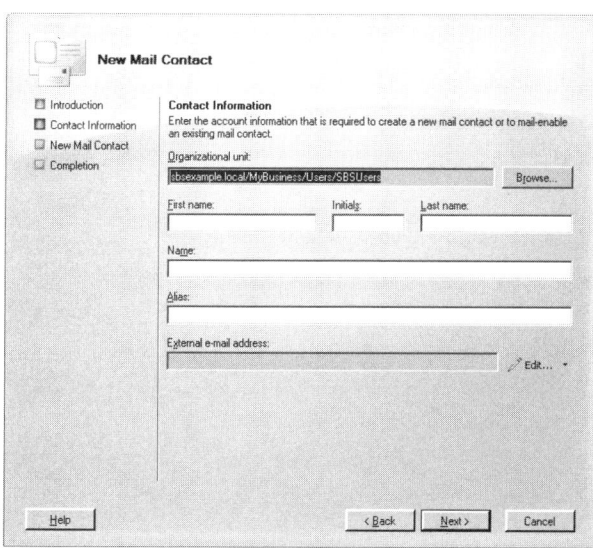

FIGURE 18-16 The Contact Information page for creating a new mail-enabled contact

5. Click Browse to open the Select Organizational Unit dialog box shown in Figure 18-17.

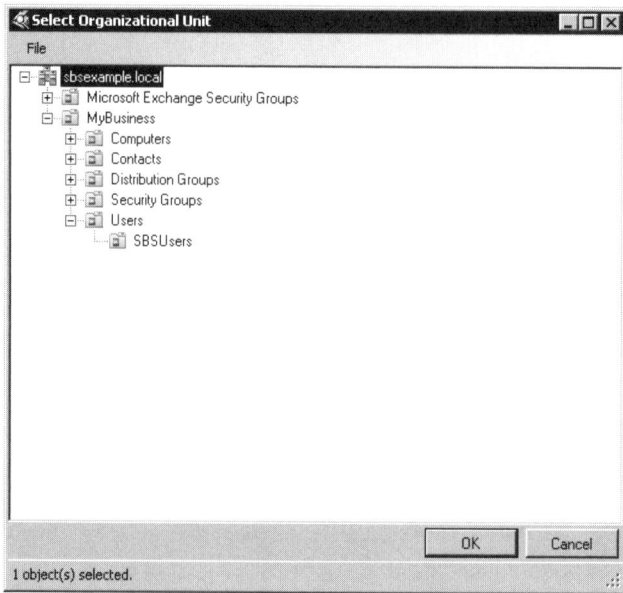

FIGURE 18-17 The Select Organizational Unit dialog box

6. Select the OU to use for this contact and click OK to return to the Contact Information page.

7. Fill in the rest of the information for the Contact, including an alias. The alias field will be filled in as you add a first and last name. We think it's a good idea to have a way to make it clear that this is an external contact in the alias, because you'll be sending e-mail to this contact outside your organization.

8. Click Edit to open the SMTP Address dialog box and enter the SMTP address for the contact.

9. Click OK to return to the Contact Information page and then Click Next to open the New Mail Contact. This summarizes the actions that are about to taken and is your last chance to cancel or correct the information.

10. Click New to create the contact and open the Completion page.

11. Click Finish to close the New Mail Contact Wizard and return to the Exchange Management Console.

UNDER THE HOOD   **Where to Put Contacts**

The default location used by the Exchange Management Console for new contacts is the SBSUsers OU. This is probably not ideal, since by the naming alone, plus the hierarchy, it should have Users, not Contacts, as its members. We think it's a good idea to create an OU just to hold your contacts, making it clear what they are and helping to keep things organized.

Where to put the Contacts OU? And what to call it? Well, as for what to call it, Contacts seems like a perfectly good name, and it has the virtues of being both descriptive and simple. For where, we like to put it under the MyBusiness OU, because that's where everything for SBS tends to go, and then leaving it at the first level below that, as shown in Figure 18-17. But, ultimately it doesn't really matter—just choose a place that works for you and then stick to it.

Adding an Additional E-Mail Domain Name

One request we see regularly in the SBS newsgroups is how to add an additional e-mail domain that SBS can receive e-mail for. Often a small-business owner combines several businesses under a single office and a single SBS network but still needs to be able to receive e-mail to each of those business names. Exchange Server makes that easy to implement. You can add additional domains that Exchange accepts mail for and automatically update the e-mail addresses of your users to include the additional domains.

Before you can accept e-mail for another domain, however, you need to make sure that the outside world knows about that domain and how to reach it. You need to register your second domain name with one of the Internet registrars, and you need to set up DNS records for the domain. Those records need to include an MX record that sends mail to your SBS server. This record should point to the public IP address of your router.

Accepting e-mail for an additional domain, however, is only part of the equation. You also need to change the recipient policies so that the new domain will propagate to your users.

When you're ready to have Exchange Server receive e-mail for an additional domain, use the following steps to add the domain:

1. Open the Exchange Management Console if it isn't already open.

2. Navigate to Hub Transport in the Organizational Configuration container in the left pane and then click the Accepted Domains tab in the center pane, as shown in Figure 18-18.

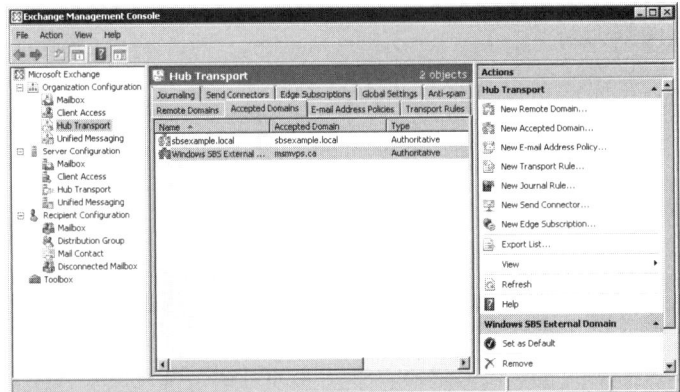

FIGURE 18-18 The Accepted Domains for our test SBS network

3. Click New Accepted Domain in the Actions pane to open the New Accepted Domain Wizard shown in Figure 18-19.

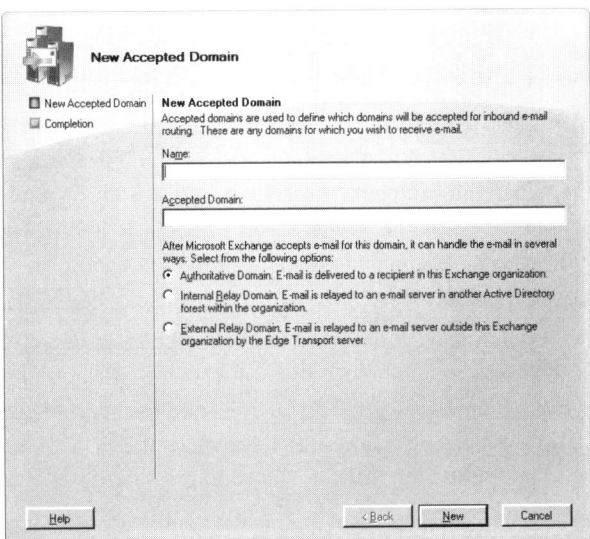

FIGURE 18-19 The New Accepted Domain Wizard

4. Enter a name for the domain you want to receive e-mail for and then enter the DNS domain name in the Accepted Domain field.

5. Click New and then click Finish when the task has completed. As with all other commands in the Exchange Management Console, you can save the Windows PowerShell script that was executed to complete the command on the Completion page before you close the wizard.

6. Click New E-mail Address Policy in the Actions pane to open the New E-mail Address Policy Wizard shown in Figure 18-20.

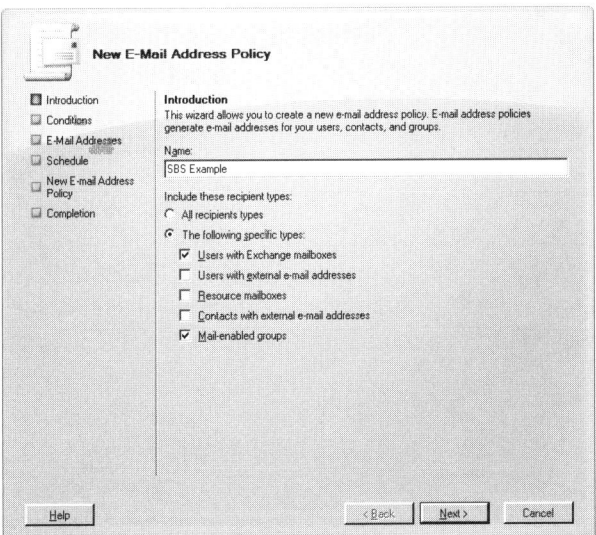

FIGURE 18-20 The Introduction page of the New E-mail Address Policy Wizard

7. Type in a name for the new policy and select the following types of mailboxes that will be included in the policy: Users With Exchange Mailboxes and Mail-Enabled Groups, as shown in Figure 18-20. This should be a good starting point for most SBS networks, though if you're heavy users of Resource mailboxes (such as for scheduling conference rooms), you may want to add them as well.

8. Click Next to open the Conditions page of the New E-mail Address Policy Wizard. You can use these conditions to filter which recipients the policy applies to. Click Preview to see a list of the accounts that will be affected by the current set of conditions. In most cases, you should leave the conditions blank on this page.

9. Click Next to open the E-mail Addresses page.

10. Click Add to open the SMTP E-mail Address dialog box shown in Figure 18-21.

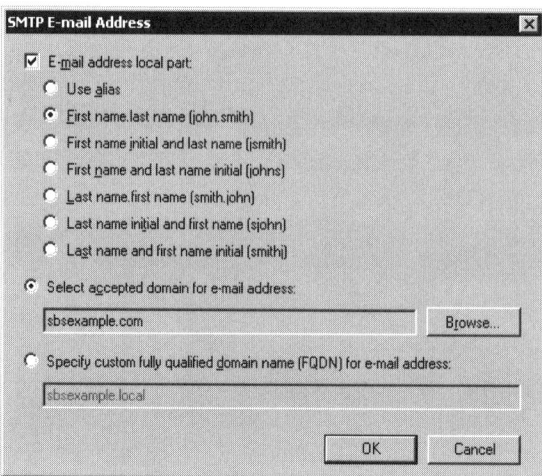

FIGURE 18-21 The SMTP E-mail Address dialog box of the New E-mail Address Policy Wizard

11. Select the format of the e-mail address to use and then click Select Accepted Domain For E-mail Address.

12. Click Browse to select the new accepted domain you added earlier.

13. Click OK to return to the E-mail Addresses page, which will now show the address policy that will be applied and click OK.

14. Click Next twice to open the Configuration Summary, as shown in Figure 18-22.

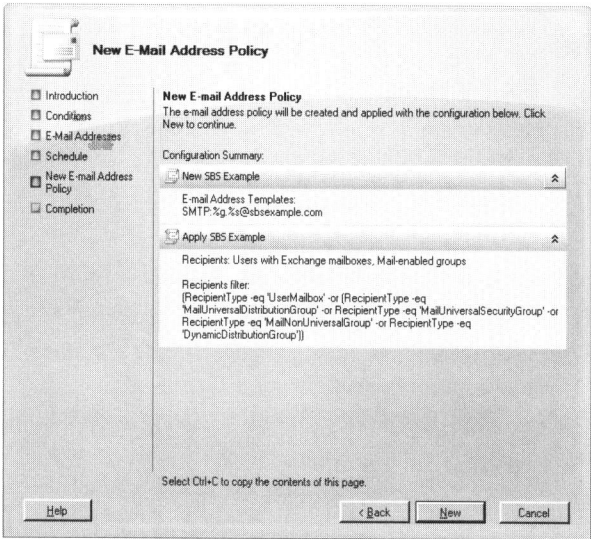

FIGURE 18-22 The new e-mail address policy that will be applied

15. Click New to apply the policy and then click Finish on the Completion page to close the wizard.

16. Select the original Windows SBS E-mail Address Policy and click Change Priority in the Actions pane to open the Change E-mail Address Policy Priority dialog box shown in Figure 18-23.

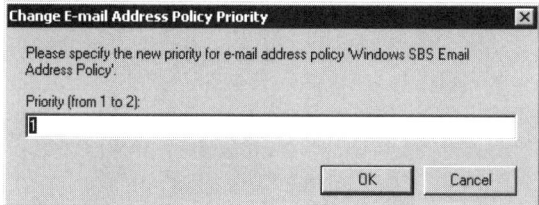

Change E-mail Address Policy Priority

Please specify the new priority for e-mail address policy 'Windows SBS Email Address Policy'.

Priority (from 1 to 2):

1

OK   Cancel

FIGURE 18-23 Set the address policy you want to control the Reply address to a priority of 1.

17. Click OK and then click Apply in the Actions pane to open the Apply E-mail Address Policy Wizard shown in Figure 18-24. Select Immediate, click Next, and then click Apply to apply the change.

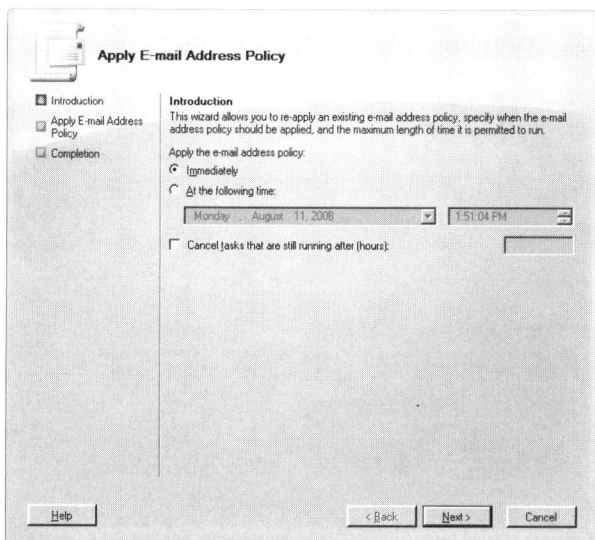

FIGURE 18-24 Set when you want the address policy change to be implemented.

18. Click Finish to close the wizard and return to the Exchange Management Console. You're now receiving e-mails for the new domain.

UNDER THE HOOD Using Windows PowerShell for Exchange Management

The Microsoft Exchange Server 2007 Management Console is built entirely on Windows PowerShell. All the commands and functionality that can be performed in the console can also be done from the Exchange Management Shell. Although most things are easily done from the Exchange Management Console, doing repetitive tasks from a graphical console can be a pain and is also far more prone to errors. Using the Windows PowerShell command line that the Exchange Management Shell provides gives you the ability to automate routine tasks.

For those not very familiar with Windows PowerShell, using the Exchange Management Console and then saving the Windows PowerShell script that was actually performed on the Completion page of the wizard gives you a great starting point for building your own scripts to perform similar tasks. A useful resource is the Exchange Team Blog at *http://msexchangeteam.com/*.

Another good resource is Windows PowerShell itself, which is an extremely self-discoverable language. You can start by getting a list of all the Exchange-specific Windows PowerShell commands:

```
Get-Excommand > ExchangeCommands.txt
```

This creates a file that has a list of all the Exchange-specific Windows PowerShell commands. If you see a command that looks like it might do what you want, such as creating a new distribution list, get some help with that command:

```
Help New-DistributionGroup
```

You can get additional help, including examples of using the command, by adding the –detailed switch to the help command:

```
Help New-DistributionGroup –detailed
```

To get some more general help with Windows PowerShell, try the following:

```
Help about*
```

This will give you a list of available general help topics and is a great way to start your Windows PowerShell Discovery Tour.

Forefront Server Security for Exchange Server

Windows Small Business Server 2008 includes a 120-day, full-featured, evaluation copy of Microsoft Forefront Server Security for Exchange Server as the anti-malware front end to Microsoft Exchange Server. Forefront uses multiple antivirus engines to provide an enhanced level of security as it scans each e-mail message entering your organization (including POP3 e-mail), and it also scans each time a message is accessed, continuing the protection.

The base configuration of Forefront Server Security is automatically handled by the SBS installation routine, if you choose to install Forefront as part of your initial installation. Where additional configuration is required, you'll need to use the Forefront Server Security Administrator console, shown in Figure 18-25, to make any changes.

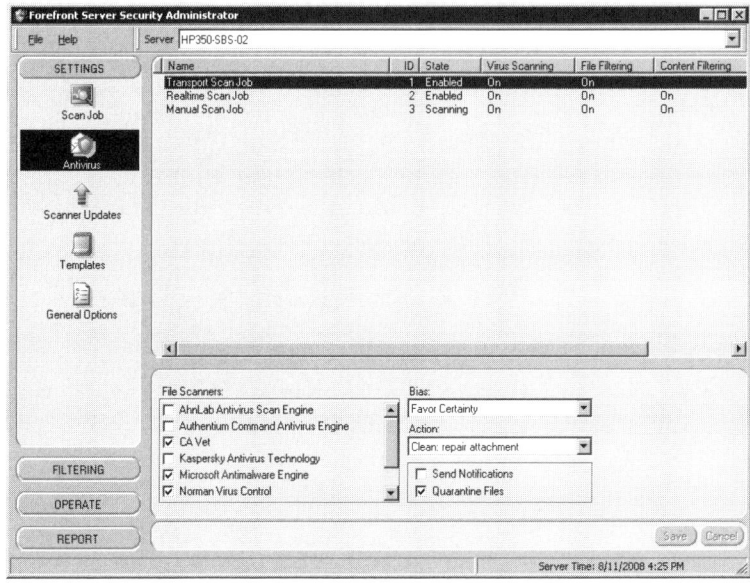

FIGURE 18-25 The Forefront Server Security Administrator console

We think it's great that Microsoft has enabled and configured Forefront, but we don't expect adoption to be all that high with only a 120-day evaluation edition included. If you don't currently have antivirus software that scans your incoming e-mail, by all means install Forefront and try it out. It's a good product. But if you and your customers already have a working solution that supports SBS 2008, we can't see installing Forefront and disabling or not installing your current solution. What you don't want to do is try to run Forefront and any other e-mail scanning antivirus software at the same time.

Summary

In this chapter, we've covered the basics of setting up and configuring Microsoft Exchange Server 2007, which is a core component of Windows Small Business Server 2008. We included how to configure the new POP3 E-mail Connector for SBS. We covered two more advanced topics, mail-enabling contacts and adding an additional e-mail domain name, as a window into the rich additional feature set that is possible with the Exchange Management Console or by using the Exchange Management Shell and Windows PowerShell. All the commands that are performed from the Exchange Management Console can be saved as Windows PowerShell scripts and executed directly from Windows PowerShell as scripts or interactive commands.

In the next chapter, we'll cover connectivity, including TCP/IP, Remote Web Workplace, Virtual Private Networks, and Wireless connectivity.

CHAPTER 19

Managing Connectivity

Connectivity is a huge topic that can often span many chapters, so we're going to be a bit constrained to cover it all here in a single chapter. One of the reasons we can, of course, is that Windows Small Business Server includes well-designed wizards for many of the connectivity tasks we face in configuring and managing an SBS network. Some of these wizards have already been covered in other chapters:

- The Internet Connection Wizard, to configure your Internet connection (covered in Chapter 8, "Completing the Getting Started Tasks")

- The Internet Address Management Wizard, to set up and manage your Internet domain name (covered in Chapter 8)

- The Add A Trusted Certificate Wizard, to obtain and deploy a trusted certificate for your Internet Domain (covered in Chapter 8)

- The Configure Internet Mail Wizard, to configure Microsoft Exchange to use a smart host for mail delivery (covered in Chapter 18, "Configuring and Managing E-Mail")

That's an important list of wizards and covers some of the biggest areas of network connectivity, but it does still leave quite a bit for this chapter, including:

- DHCP and DNS

- Wireless connectivity

- Firewall configuration

- Remote Web Workplace (RWW)
- Virtual Private Networks (VPNs)
- Fixing network problems

This last topic focuses on the Fix My Network Wizard, which replaces the Configure E-Mail And Internet Connectivity Wizard (CEICW) of SBS 2003.

DHCP and DNS

SBS manages DHCP and DNS with no user intervention required in most cases. SBS configures itself to be the only DHCP server on the network, and the primary DNS server as well. You should normally not have to change any of the DNS or DHCP settings on your network for basic operation, but there can be specialized needs that require additional configuration. For example, on our network, we prefer to have a larger excluded range of IP addresses that the DHCP server can't use because of how we configure key workstations and printers.

> **NOTE** The tools you need for DHCP and DNS are the DHCP console (dhcpmgmt.msc) and the DNS Manager console (dnsmgmt.msc), respectively. You can open these consoles from the Administrative Tools menu, from the Advanced Windows SBS Console, or directly from the command line. We use the command line.

Managing DHCP

DHCP automatically provides computers on the local network segment with valid IPv4 addresses and important additional configuration settings, including the addresses of DNS servers and the default gateway, along with other configuration settings if needed. SBS manages the core DHCP settings automatically, but you can add additional settings as appropriate for your environment, as well as view and manage the current address leases and exclusions. If your network includes printers or other devices that require unchanging IP addresses, you can either exclude the address from use by DHCP and manually set the device, or configure DHCP for an address reservation to ensure that the device always gets the same address. On our network, we also assign DHCP reservations to key workstations so that they're at predictable IP addresses to simplify troubleshooting.

> **NOTE** Although it isn't required to exclude a DHCP address that you assign a reservation to, we prefer to exclude an entire range of addresses and then use DHCP reservations within that range for computers and devices we want predictable addresses for. Not the normal way, but it works for us and our admittedly specialized needs.

DHCP Options Scope

I n SBS, you can set DHCP options at three different levels—Server, Scope, and Reservation. Options set at the Server level apply to all DHCP address leases on the server and therefore on your SBS network. Normally, SBS has only a single DHCP scope, so options you set at the Scope level are also applied to all DHCP address leases. Options set at the DHCP Scope level override any options set at the Server level.

When you create a DHCP reservation, you commit a specific network card to a specific IP address on your SBS network. You can also, as part of the DHCP reservation, configure additional options for that DHCP client. Any options set at the DHCP Reservation level will override those set at the Scope or Server level.

SBS expects to be the only DHCP server on your network, and if it senses another DHCP server, it will stop the DHCP Server service to prevent handing out duplicate IP addresses. During initial installation of SBS, if there are other DHCP servers on your network (such as your router), the setup process either disables the other DHCP server if it responds to a UPnP request, or prompts you to disable the server manually. Although it's technically possible to use some other DHCP server rather than the SBS server, the SBS wizards are designed to function best if SBS controls the DHCP server functionality.

Viewing Current DHCP Address Leases

To view the addresses currently leased to clients, complete the following steps:

1. Open the DHCP console if it isn't already open.

2. In the left pane, expand the containers until you can select Address Leases (as shown in Figure 19-1) to view a list of currently assigned IP addresses and their corresponding host names.

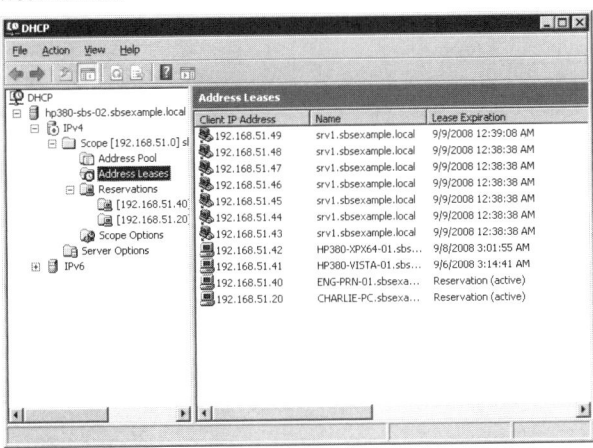

FIGURE 19-1 Viewing assigned IP addresses

Creating Exclusions in DHCP

The pool of addresses that a DHCP server can lease to clients is called a *scope*. For any device on the network that has a static IP address within the scope, you need to create an exclusion to prevent the DHCP server from handing out that address to a client.

 REAL WORLD DHCP Exclusions

The default configuration of DHCP in SBS creates an exclusion for IP addresses from .1 to .10 in your SBS network subnet (192.168.51 in the screenshots in this chapter). This leaves more than 240 addresses in the subnet that can be handed out by the DHCP server. We prefer to have a larger exclusion on our network to allow for additional fixed IP addresses for key workstations and devices on the network. These are usually configured as DHCP reservations but can also be configured as fixed IP addresses. We add an additional exclusion from .11 to .40 to allow plenty of room for those fixed IP addresses, which still leaves more than 200 DHCP addresses for computers and devices on the network.

To create an exclusion, complete the following steps:

1. Open the DHCP console if it isn't already open.

2. In the left pane, expand the containers until you can select Address Pool.

3. Select New Exclusion Range from the Action menu.

4. In the Add Exclusion dialog box, shown in Figure 19-2, use the Start IP Address and End IP Address boxes to specify the range of IP addresses you want to exclude. To exclude a single IP address, type it in the Start IP Address box and leave the End IP Address box blank.

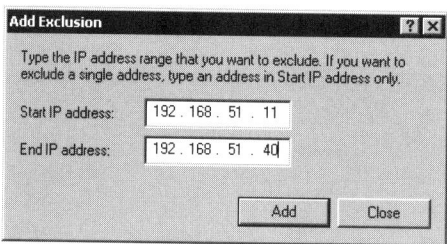

FIGURE 19-2 The Add Exclusion dialog box

5. Click Add to create the exclusion. Create any additional exclusions and then click Close when you're finished.

Adding a DHCP Reservation

As an alternative to manually setting and managing IP addresses for fixed IP devices, such as printers, you can use DHCP to assign an address and configuration settings to the device and then use a DHCP reservation to ensure that the device always gets that address and that no other device or client is assigned that address. Because reservations inherit the Scope options and can be easily modified from a single point, it's much better to use a reservation instead of manually setting or managing IP addresses for devices that support DHCP.

 UNDER THE HOOD **Finding the MAC Address**

Before you can add a reservation to DHCP, you need to know the Media Access Control (MAC) address of the DHCP client you want to make a reservation for. Although you could read the MAC address off the network device (there's a sticker somewhere on the device with the address), that's hardly easy in most cases. So, how to easily get the MAC address? The two ways we know are using the getmac command (available only on Windows Server 2003 and Windows Server 2008) and the ipconfig command.

To obtain the MAC address using the ipconfig command, go to the client computer (or make a remote desktop connection) and type **ipconfig /all** at the command prompt. The MAC address is listed as the physical address. Using ipconfig / all doesn't require elevation.

To obtain the MAC address using the getmac command, type the following from a command prompt:

getmac /s *computer* **/v**

Where *computer* is the IP address, host name, or DNS name of the remote computer you want the MAC address for.

Finally, you can obtain the MAC address of any current DHCP client by looking at the current DHCP lease for the client—the MAC address is shown in the Unique ID column.

To create a DHCP reservation, complete the following steps:

1. Open the DHCP console if it isn't already open.

2. In the left pane, expand the containers until you can select Reservations.

3. Select New Reservation from the Action menu to open the New Reservation dialog box shown in Figure 19-3. The fields are as follows:

- **Reservation Name**   Usually the DNS name for the device or client. Choose a name that conforms to DNS naming requirements for best compatibility.
- **IP Address**   The IP address that you are reserving for this device or client.
- **MAC Address**   The Media Access Control or hardware address of the network card for the device or client. This is a hexadecimal number that is globally unique and is generally printed directly on the device.
- **Description**   A descriptive phrase that will make it easier to identify the specific device the reservation is assigned to.
- **Supported Types**   The choices are Both, DHCP Only, or BOOTP Only. BOOTP is an older protocol for automatically assigning IP addresses and configuration details that is no longer commonly used, but selecting the Both option is the best choice unless you have a specific reason not to.

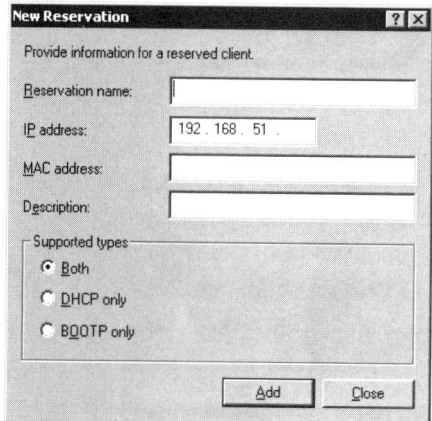

FIGURE 19-3 The New Reservation dialog box

4. Click Add and the reservation is added. The reservation inherits the configuration options that have been set for the DHCP scope, and you can add specific options for each reservation.

Setting DHCP Options

The process for setting DHCP options is essentially the same regardless of the level you set the option at. As described in the Under the Hood sidebar titled "DHCP Options Scope" earlier in this chapter, each level of DHCP inherits options from the higher level, but can override them. As an example of setting DHCP options, we'll set the Host Name option for the DHCP reservation for our printer. (The printer is assigned a DHCP reservation at 192.168.51.40.)

To set the host name for the printer using a DHCP option, use the following steps:

1. Open the DHCP console if it isn't already open.

2. In the left pane, expand the containers until you can select Reservations.

3. Select the DHCP reservation for the printer in the left pane and select Configure Options from the Action menu to open the Reservation Options dialog box.

4. Scroll down in the Available Options to 012 Host Name and select the check box next to it, as shown in Figure 19-4.

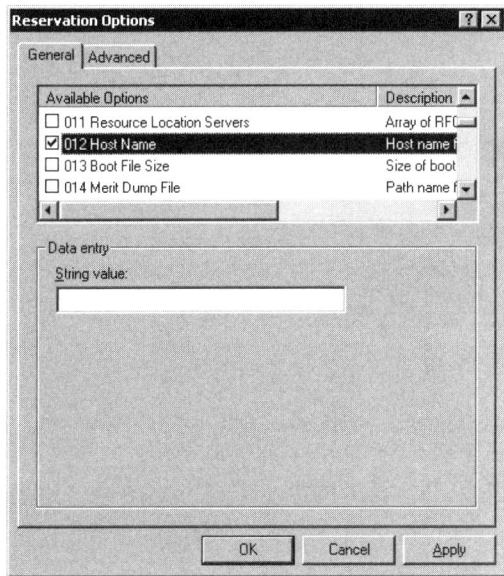

FIGURE 19-4 Setting the host name for a DHCP reservation

5. Type the host name for the printer in the String Value field and click OK to return to the DHCP console.

Enabling DNS Updates

On an SBS server, the DHCP server is by default not configured to automatically update the DNS server when it assigns an IP address to a client. This is not a problem for Windows clients because they update their own records. But if you have other types of DHCP clients, you can configure DHCP to handle the DNS update automatically.

To enable DHCP to automatically update the DNS records, follow these steps:

1. Open the DHCP console if it isn't already open.

2. Right-click IPv4, select Properties, and then click the DNS tab to open the IPv4 Properties dialog box, shown in Figure 19-5.

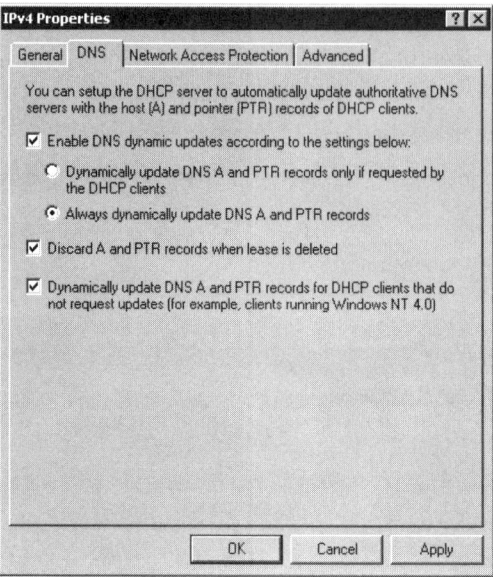

FIGURE 19-5 The DNS tab of the IPv4 Properties dialog box

3. Select the Enable DNS Dynamic Updates According To The Settings Below check box. If you have dumb devices, such as printers, also select the Dynamically Update DNS A And PTR Records For DHCP Clients That Do Not Request Updates check box.

4. When you've made your changes, click OK to return to the DHCP console.

Managing DNS

SBS uses the DNS server service for local name resolution only. SBS automatically creates three DNS zones—two forward lookup zones and a reverse lookup zone. It creates a forward lookup zone for the internal domain (sbsexample.local), which allows you to use a DNS name to resolve an IP address with computers and devices on the internal network. It also creates a "split DNS" for resolution of your public DNS name by creating a local version for use by internal clients so they can reach the public resources such as RWW and Outlook Anywhere without actually leaving the internal network. External clients can't reach that internal server, so their DNS queries for these resources point to the public IP address of your SBS network. SBS also creates a reverse lookup zone (51.168.192.in-addr.arpa in the screenshots in this chapter), which enables you to resolve the DNS name associated with a particular IP address (a useful trick for troubleshooting). All three zones use secure dynamic updates so that Windows clients can automatically and securely update their own DNS records.

SBS manages DNS automatically for Windows clients. Non-Windows clients and devices, however, will not have DNS records automatically created and maintained. In most situations, this is perfectly OK, but if you need to ensure that client IP addresses are fully resolvable on the SBS network, you'll need to either manually create and maintain the records or configure DHCP to automatically update them as described earlier.

Adding a DNS Record

You can manually configure DNS records for fixed IP address clients or for clients that use a DHCP reservation. By adding the records, you ensure that these clients' IP addresses can be resolved from their names, simplifying management and troubleshooting. However, this does require that you maintain the records and ensure their accuracy, and manual editing and maintenance of DNS records is something to avoid if at all possible. However, for special devices that you need to assign a fixed IP address to, and that don't handle DHCP well, manually adding the records to the DNS server is the only solution. To add A and PTR (Address and Pointer) records to the SBS DNS server, follow these steps:

1. Open the DNS Manager console if it isn't already open.

2. Select the internal DNS domain in the left pane as shown in Figure 19-6 (sbsexample. local in the screenshot).

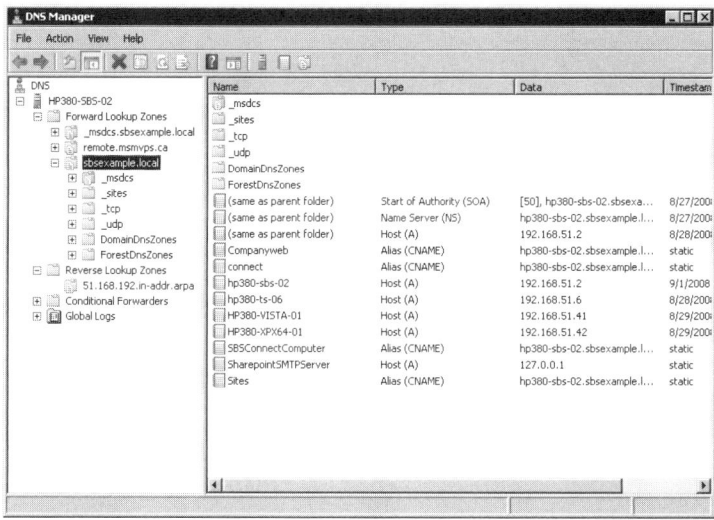

FIGURE 19-6 The DNS forward lookup zone for the internal network

3. Select New Host (A Or AAAA) from the Action menu to open the New Host dialog box shown in Figure 19-7.

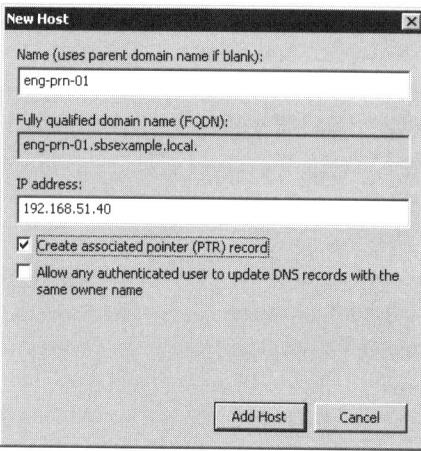

FIGURE 19-7 Adding a new host record for the printer

4. Fill in the host name and IP address for the new DNS record and select the Create Associated Pointer (PTR) Record check box to also create a reverse lookup record for the device.

5. Click Add Host and then click OK in the DNS message dialog box to create the record.

6. Click Done to return to the DNS Manager console.

NOTE If you later delete the A record, the associated PTR record is not automatically deleted. You must manually delete it from the reverse lookup zone.

DNS Forwarding

When a client makes a DNS query of a DNS server, and the server doesn't have the information either in its own records or in its cache of known IP addresses from previous queries, there are three possible options for the server:

- Return record not found
- Forward the query to a nearby server that might have the information
- Forward the query to one of the Internet's root DNS servers

Obviously the first option isn't terribly useful, unless you're creating a very private test network and you don't want any queries going outside it.

The second option, DNS forwarding, was the default behavior for SBS 2003 and is still the default if you migrate from SBS 2003 to SBS 2008. In SBS 2003, the DNS server was configured to automatically forward DNS requests that it didn't have the answer for to the DNS server of your Internet service provider (ISP). This was efficient because the ISP's DNS servers were usually no more than a hop or two away, and the answer was quickly returned. This is a good idea if you trust your ISP to have accurate and safe DNS servers.

The third option is for the server to forward any DNS query for which it doesn't have the answer to the Internet's DNS root servers. This option, which uses root hints, is somewhat slower than querying the ISP's servers that are a lot closer, but it does ensure an accurate answer.

 REAL WORLD **DNS Poisoning Attacks**

The standard setup for most internal DNS servers, including SBS 2003, was to set up your DNS server as a primary zone and then configure it to forward all other requests to your ISP's designated DNS servers. This resulted in fast and private support for internal name resolution while providing the fastest resolution of names outside your private network and reducing overall traffic for your ISP and the Internet as a whole. Unfortunately, this exposes your network to DNS poisoning attacks such as the widespread cache corruption attack that affects all versions of BIND before version 9. If some malicious program manages to subvert the DNS servers maintained by your ISP because your ISP hasn't gotten around to updating them, your DNS server will pass that problem on to your internal clients.

The problem is especially a concern if your ISP is somewhat slow to apply patches to its DNS servers, as seems to be the case for many ISPs, both large and small. BIND is the most common DNS server software used by ISPs, and several vulnerabilities have been identified against BIND, especially versions before BIND 9. Patches to correct these vulnerabilities are available, but if your ISP is slow to apply the patch, you could be exposed.

If you don't specify a server to forward to, your DNS server will use root hints to directly resolve the address. This might be somewhat slower, and it certainly increases the overall traffic on the Internet, but if the root servers are poisoned, we're all in trouble. If you trust your ISP to maintain its servers adequately, go ahead and forward to their servers. Personally, we've stopped doing so, and we're really glad that SBS 2008 doesn't do this either.

If you do trust your ISP, and you want to configure SBS 2008 for DNS forwarding, use the following steps:

1. Open the DNS Manager console if it isn't already open.
2. Right-click the SBS server in the left pane and select Properties.
3. Click the Forwarders tab, as shown in Figure 19-8.

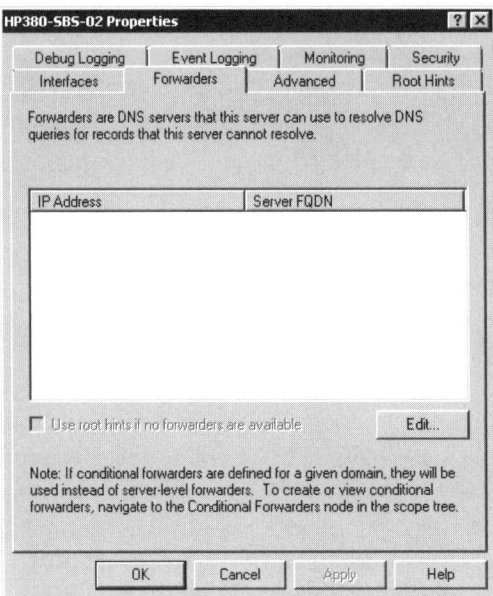

FIGURE 19-8 The Forwarders tab of the DNS Server Properties dialog box

4. Click Edit to open the Edit Forwarders dialog box shown in Figure 19-9.

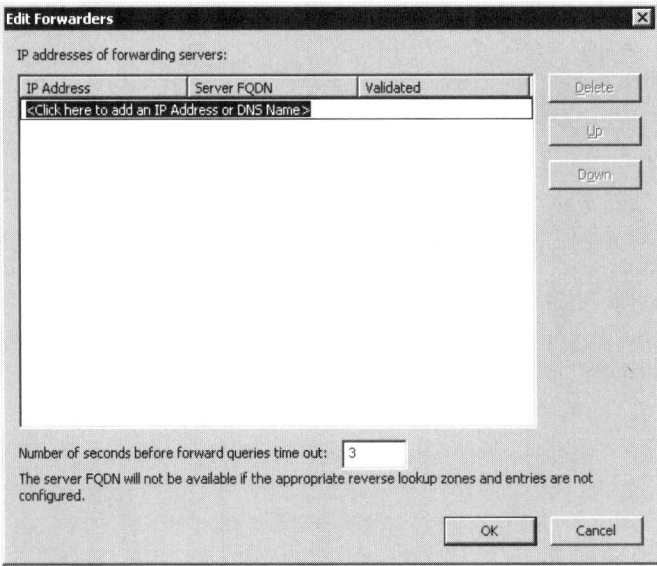

FIGURE 19-9 The Edit Forwarders dialog box of DNS Server properties

5. Click the Click Here To Add An IP Address Or DNS Name field and type either the IP
    address or DNS name of the DNS server you want to forward queries to.

6. Click OK to close the Edit Forwarders dialog box, or add additional entries as desired.

7. Leave the Use Root Hints If No Forwarders Are Available box selected unless you want the failure or nonavailability of your ISP's DNS server to cause DNS queries to fail on your network.

8. Click OK to close the DNS Server Properties dialog box and return to the DNS Manager console.

Wireless Connectivity

Wireless connectivity has become an essential business tool. We expect to be able to connect wirelessly wherever we go, and increasingly our expectations are met. But providing wireless access inside your SBS network is a bit different. You still generally need to do it, but you need to take serious precautions to ensure that you don't compromise security.

We've heard arguments on all sides of the wireless security question, from those who appear to think that simply hiding your wireless network is all that's required, to those who claim there is no such thing as a secure wireless and we shouldn't ever use or allow it. As with most such arguments, the answer is somewhere in the middle. Exactly where in the middle is really about your own comfort level and perception of risk.

There are ways to implement full Two Factor Authentication (TFA) for wireless connectivity, and they can be done even on a small network if you want and need to spend the resources to do it. (For more on TFA, see the Real World sidebar titled "Two Factor Authentication and RWW" later in the chapter.)

Wireless security has come a long way from the early days of wireless networking. Initially, there was Wired Equivalent Privacy (WEP) that came in two levels—64-bit and 128-bit. Unfortunately, the algorithm for WEP was seriously flawed, and by 2001 there were widely available decryption programs that let virtually anyone who wanted to compromise WEP security. We now believe that WEP is actually worse than no security: It is so easy to compromise that it should be considered no security at all, but it gives users a false sense of safety.

WEP was replaced with Wi-Fi Protected Access (WPA), and finally by WPA2. WPA2 (also known by its Institute of Electrical and Electronics Engineers, or IEEE, standard designation of 802.11i) has two levels of security: WPA2-Enterprise and WPA2-Personal.

WPA2-Enterprise uses an 802.1X, or RADIUS, server to distribute different initial keys to every user. This 802.1X server can use TFA to further increase security. Realistically, implementing WPA2-Enterprise is more than most SBS networks can do, but if you want to try it, a good starting place is this document on TechNet: *http://www.microsoft.com/technet/network/wifi/ed80211.mspx*.

WPA2-Personal uses a pre-shared key (PSK) of 8 to 63 characters in length and can use either Advanced Encryption Standard (AES) or Temporal Key Integrity Protocol (TKIP) encryption. TKIP is simpler to do, but it has been compromised and we don't recommend it. When WPA2-Personal is used with AES and has a minimum 16 character PSK, it provides an acceptable security for most small businesses and can be easily implemented. Another important requirement is to choose a wireless network name (SSID) that is not the default on your wireless access point (WAP).

The basic requirements for secure Wireless access to your SBS network are:

- Use one or more wireless access points (*not* routers).
- Use a static IP address or DHCP reservation for the WAP.
- Disable the DHCP server on the WAP.
- Change the SSID of the WAP to one that is appropriate for the network but is neither the default nor something that too clearly identifies your company.
- Change the password of the WAP to a password of at least 12 characters.
- Enable AES as the only encryption method.
- Choose a pre-shared key of at least 16 characters. Alternately, use a USB key and Windows Connect Now (WCN) if your WAP supports it. WCN will generate a random 64-character key.

 REAL WORLD Wireless Security Strategies

A variety of security strategies for wireless networking have been suggested and used over the years—some useful and some not. The following list details our evaluation of several of these strategies.

- **MAC Address Filtering** This strategy allows only a statically managed list of MAC addresses to access the wireless network. It's a nice idea, but this strategy is easy to defeat with a sniffer, because MAC addresses can be easily spoofed. Plus, a static list of "allowed" MAC addresses is a hopeless mess to manually maintain. All in all, it's a complete waste of time.

- **SSID Hiding** This strategy requires that the client know the name of the wireless network to be able to connect to it. And even if the network is known and configured into the Windows client, that client must continually probe to make sure that the network is present. This requirement causes all sorts of problems and limits the ability of Windows to manage connections. The strategy is totally useless because anyone with access to the packets in the air can read the SSID from the commonly sent 802.11 management frames in a matter of seconds. On the other hand, broadcasting the SSID, when combined with appropriate security, makes the network easier to manage and easier for users as well. Hiding the SSID is another complete waste of time.

- **WEP Encryption**   The original encryption standard for wireless, this standard uses either a 40-bit or 104-bit key (along with a fixed 24-bit initialization vector). It is easily hacked by anyone with bad intentions and will keep only the most casually curious out of your network. WEP keys are static keys and must be manually maintained. Every time a user who has wireless access leaves the organization, the WEP keys need to be changed. A network protected with WEP alone should be considered completely unsecured.

- **WPA**   The original WPA encryption standard is based on RC4, which can be compromised. However, because it changes keys with sufficient frequency and derives the new keys in an improved way as compared to WEP, it was a significant improvement over WEP and could generally be implemented without buying new hardware. With 802.1X authentication and the appropriate authentication method, the initial encryption keys are automatically generated.

- **WPA2**   The WPA2 encryption is based on AES and is much more secure than RC4, while the WPA2 standard incorporates additional security measures beyond just encryption. Both pre-shared key (WPA-Personal) and RADIUS/802.1X authentication (WPA2-Enterprise) scenarios are supported. This is the minimum wireless security standard you should allow on your SBS network.

- **IEEE 802.11i**   This is the underlying standard for WPA2, which is described in the preceding bullet point.

- **VPNs**   One solution to setting up secure wireless networks is to place the wireless network outside your main network and use a VPN connection to the main network. This approach has the advantage of getting around the insecurities of older equipment but has inherent problems. If the external access point is open and unsecured, it leaves the client exposed to any other computer in range. It also imposes a performance hit and requires a VPN connection for every client. Machine group policies are not applied, and the overall reliability of the connection and the administrative overhead are significant issues as well. Finally, as we describe later in the chapter, VPNs have inherent risks that we prefer to avoid.

- **IEEE 802.1X**   Using 802.1X as the authentication mechanism for WPA or WPA2 encryption is an excellent solution, but implementing it on most SBS networks isn't realistic.

We know some of these points are a bit controversial, but we also think that it's possible to allow wireless clients on your internal SBS network—but only if you set realistic minimum standards and don't use ineffective "security" measures that provide a false sense of security while actually doing little, if anything, to protect you from an attack.

Windows Firewall

The Windows Firewall in Windows Server 2008 is the same basic firewall included in Windows Vista and adds many new features and capabilities compared to the Windows Firewall included in SBS 2003 R2. These new features include outbound filtering; filtering based on SIDs; a better management UI; configuration for local, remote, local port, remote port, and protocol; and tight integration with IPSec. The other big change is location-specific policies—there are three separate firewall profiles: a domain profile, a private profile for computers that aren't domain members but are on secured networks, and a public profile for computers that reside on publicly accessible networks. And, finally, per-user rules are now supported. Although these profiles aren't terribly useful for the SBS server itself, which only uses the domain profile, the same profiles are used by Windows Vista computers and can be enforced with Group Policy.

In SBS, the Windows Firewall is on by default. All of the wizards in SBS and Windows Server 2008 that are used to add Roles and Features will automatically set the necessary Windows Firewall rule(s) to ensure proper functionality while still securing the server.

SBS 2003 R2 had a built-in firewall, but most of the wizards used to configure the server were not designed to configure the firewall, and most environments had Windows Firewall disabled on servers, relying on an external firewall, or ISA 2004 on SBS Premium servers, to protect the network. In SBS 2008, the expectation is that Windows Firewall remains enabled.

The Windows Server 2008 Windows Firewall allows more granular control over the configuration and settings than previous versions. To open the Windows Firewall With Advanced Security console, shown in Figure 19-10, type **wf.msc** at the command prompt, click the Windows Firewall With Advanced Security in the Administrative Tools folder, or open Firewall Settings under Security in the Windows SBS Console.

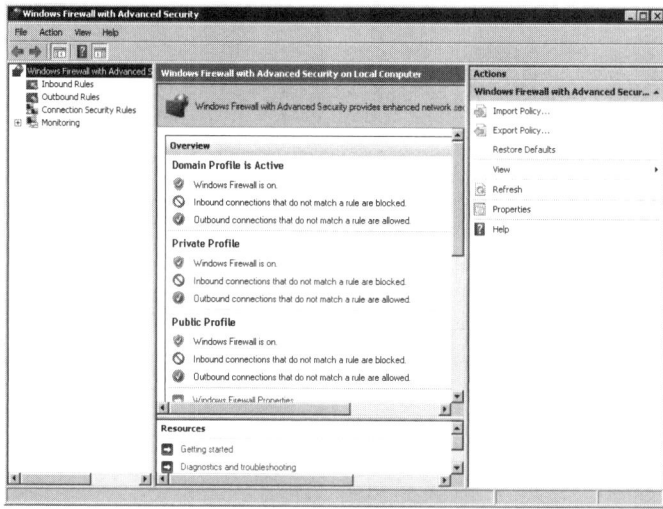

FIGURE 19-10 The Windows Firewall With Advanced Security console

Windows Firewall has three profiles: a domain profile, a private profile, and a public profile. Each profile can have different inbound and outbound rules as needed. To build a specific rule, click Inbound Rules or Outbound Rules and then click New Rule. Custom rules can be set for programs or for ports.

Setting Firewall Policies Using Group Policy

Use Group Policy to ensure a consistent application of Windows Firewall policies across the domain. Using normal Group Policy rules, as discussed in Chapter 20, "Using Group Policy," you can set up a Group Policy to manage a group of systems. Use the built-in WMI filters of SBS Group Policy to set specific policies for different types of clients and servers.

Firewall Rule Basics

When building Windows Firewall rules, there are three possible actions for a connection that matches the rule:

- Allow the connection.
- Only allow a connection that is secured through the use of IPSec (authenticated bypass).
- Explicitly block the connection.

The order of precedence for Windows Firewall rules is:

- Authenticated bypass
- Block connection
- Allow connection
- Default profile behavior

This means that if you have a Block rule and an Allow rule, and your connection meets both criteria, *the block rule will always win*. By being as specific as possible with your rules, you have less likelihood of conflict and more direct control. Port rules are much more general than application rules and should be avoided whenever possible.

Rule Definitions

Building rule definitions is the process of building up a combination of conditions and specific access types into a rule that either allows or disallows a connection.

Rules can be defined for the following:

- **Programs** These are specific applications that are either allowed or disallowed by the rule.
- **Ports** These allow or disallow a protocol through a specific port or set of ports.
- **Predefined** These include several preconfigured and well-known services and programs.
- **Custom** These can combine programs, ports, and specific interfaces into a custom rule.

Rules can allow or disallow traffic to or from programs, system services, computers, or users.

Rules can use the following protocol values:

- Any
- IANA IP protocol numbers
- TCP
- UDP
- ICMPv4
- ICMPv6
- Others, including IGMP, HOPOPT, GRE, IPv6-NoNxt, IPV6-Opts, VRRP, PGM, L2TP, IPv6-Route, and IPv6-Frag

Rules for local ports (UDP or TCP) can include:

- All ports
- Specific ports (comma-separated list)
- Dynamic RPC
- RPC Endpoint Mapper
- Edge Traversal

Rules for remote ports (TCP and UDP) can include:

- All ports
- Specific ports (comma-separated list)

Rules for ICMP traffic (ICMPv4 and ICMPv6) can be:

- All ICMP types
- Specific types of ICMP traffic

Rules can be for a local IP address scope of:

- Specific IPv4 or v6 address or list of addresses
- Range of IPv4 or v6 addresses or list of ranges
- Entire IPv4 or v6 subnet or list of subnets

Rules can be for a remote IP address scope of:

- Specific IPv4 or v6 address or list of addresses
- Range of IPv4 or v6 addresses or list of ranges
- Entire IPv4 or v6 subnet or list of subnets
- Predefined set of computers (local subnet, default gateway, DNS servers, WINS servers, DNS servers, or a list of such items)

Rules can specify an interface type of:

- All interface types
- Local area network
- Remote access
- Wireless

Rules can include program types of:

- All programs
- System (a special keyword that restricts traffic to the system process)
- Specific path and .exe name to an executable

Rules for services can:

- Apply to all programs and services
- Apply to services only
- Apply to a specified service

There are three predefined special local ports:

- **Dynamic RPC** Used by applications and services that receive dynamic RPC traffic over TCP. (Does not include traffic over Named Pipes.)
- **RPC Endpoint Mapper** Used only with the RPCSS service and allows traffic to the endpoint mapper.
- **Edge Traversal** Only used with the iphlpsvc (Teredo) service and allows the traffic to be decapsulated by the Teredo service on a dynamic port.

Additional rules can be set to allow only secure connections. For secure connections, you can specify that the connection:

- Requires encryption
- Allows connections only from specified computers in Active Directory
- Allows connections only from specified users or security groups in Active Directory

IMPORTANT Whenever possible, resist the temptation to create specific Windows Firewall rules for specific computers or users. Although this is technically possible, it can quickly become a management and documentation nightmare. Use the SBS security groups and OUs to control firewalls. This is flexible, easy to maintain, and easily documented.

Creating a Firewall Policy

You create firewall policies by combining rules and assigning them to groups of users or computers either through a WMI filter or an OU. As an example, use the following steps to create a rule that blocks Live Messenger from a server computer.

1. Open the Group Policy Management Console.

2. Navigate to the SBSServers OU, as shown in Figure 19-11.

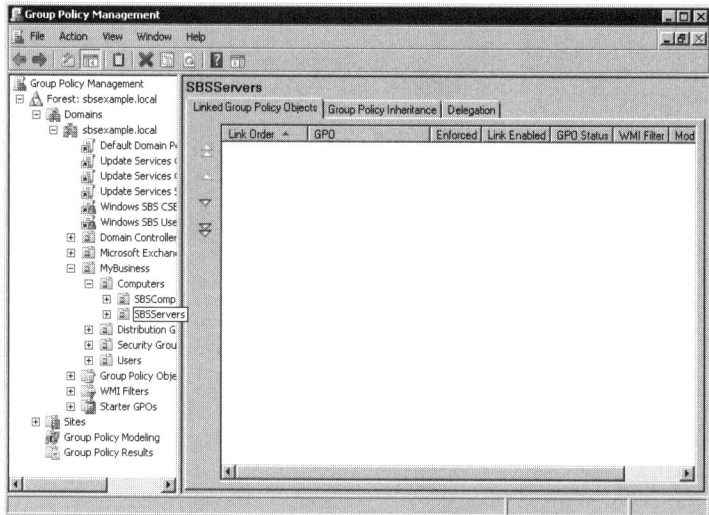

FIGURE 19-11 The SBSServers OU in the Group Policy Management Console

3. Right-click SBSServers and select Create A GPO In This Domain And Link It Here to open the New GPO dialog box shown in Figure 19-12.

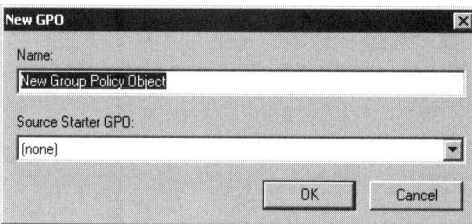

FIGURE 19-12 The New GPO dialog box

4. Give the GPO a name and click OK.

5. Highlight the new policy in the Linked Group Policy Objects pane, right-click, and select Edit to open the Group Policy Management Editor, shown in Figure 19-13.

6. Navigate to the Outbound Rules container of Windows Firewall With Advanced Security, as shown in Figure 19-13.

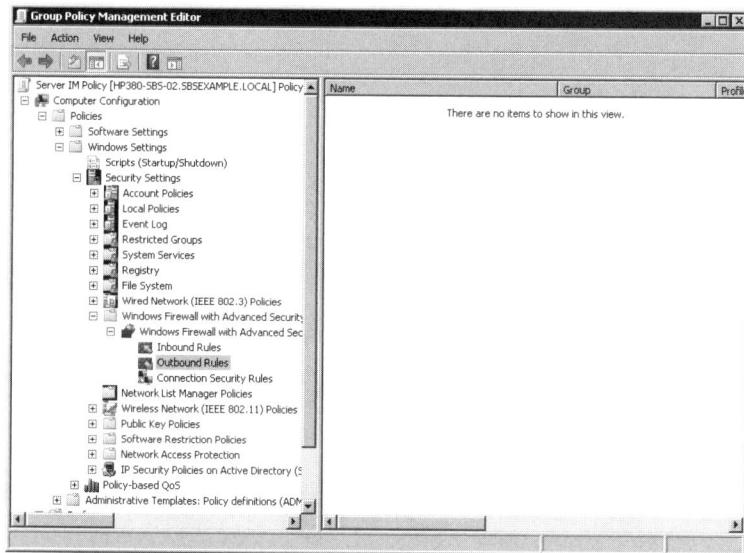

FIGURE 19-13 The Group Policy Management Editor

7. Right-click Outbound Rules and select New Rule to open the New Outbound Rule Wizard shown in Figure 19-14.

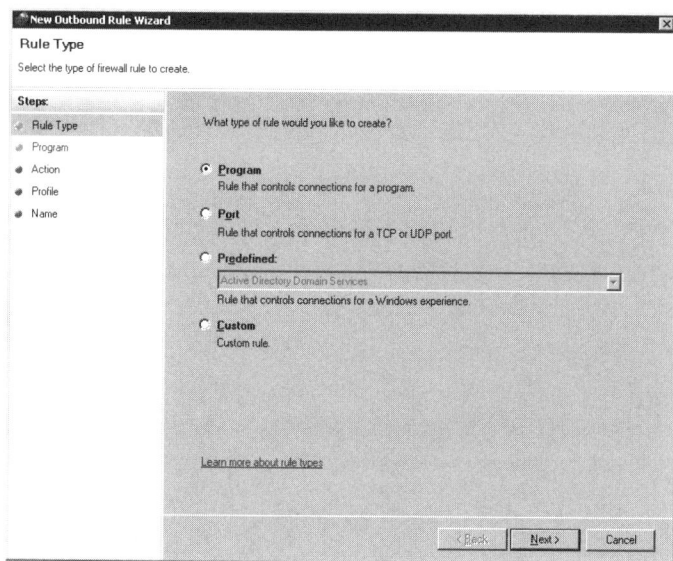

FIGURE 19-14 The Rule Type page of the New Outbound Rule Wizard

8. Select Program and click Next to open the Program page, as shown in Figure 19-15.

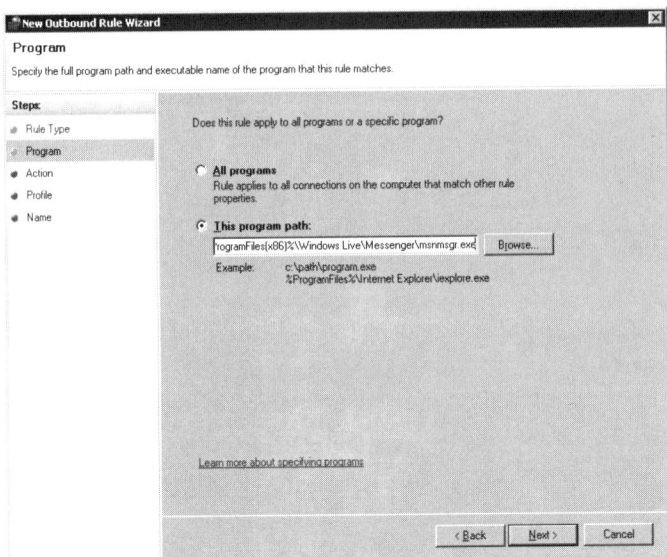

FIGURE 19-15 The Program page of the New Outbound Rule Wizard

9. Select This Program Path and type the full path to Windows Live Messenger (**%ProgramFiles(x86)%\Windows Live\Messenger\msnmsgr.exe**).

10. Click Next to open the Action page. Select Block The Connection.

11. Click Next to open the Profile page shown in Figure 19-16. Select all three profiles.

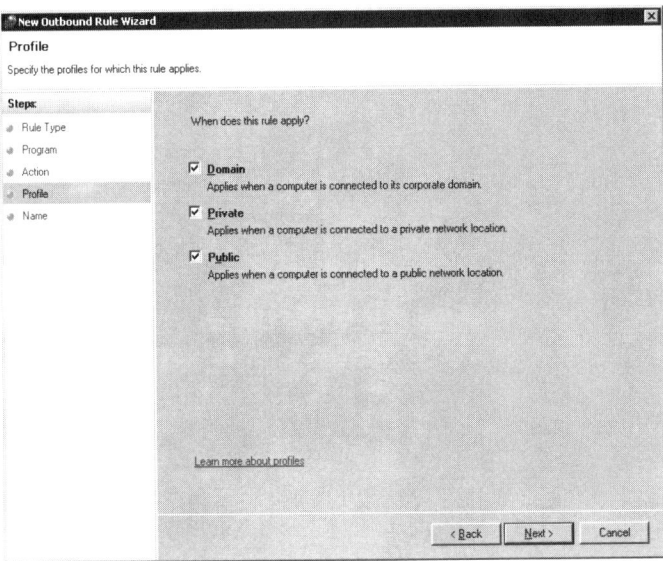

FIGURE 19-16 The Profile page of the New Outbound Rule Wizard

12. Click Next to open the Name page. In the Name field, type **Windows Live Messenger** and add a description.

13. Click Finish to create the rule. The result is shown in Figure 19-17.

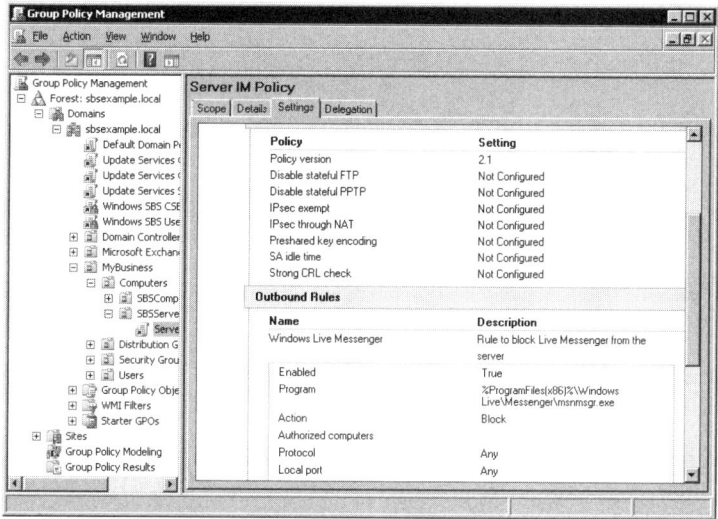

FIGURE 19-17 The Group Policy Management Console, showing the new Outbound Rule

NOTE This block rule is hardly sufficient to block all instances or types of instant messaging from the servers on an SBS network, but we present it to show how the Firewall Policy rules work and are configured.

Remote Web Workplace (RWW)

Remote Web Workplace (RWW) was introduced in SBS 2003 and has been the source of not a little envy from enterprise networks that had nothing equivalent. In SBS 2008, RWW has been improved and updated to use the new features of Windows Server 2008, while getting an overall facelift and several small, but we think highly useful, improvements.

The basic premise of RWW is to provide a secure way for remote users to access the resources of the SBS network. Users connect to the RWW landing page, and from there they can do the following:

- Connect to their desktops in the office
- Connect to the company's internal Web site (Companyweb)
- Read e-mail using Outlook Anywhere
- Change their passwords
- Connect to additional help or features as available

Administrative users have additional options, including the ability to connect to the SBS server or other servers on the network.

Configuring RWW Computer List

A major change in SBS 2008 RWW is the ability to limit the list of computers that a user sees when logging on to RWW. In SBS 2003, the list of computers showed all the available workstations in the domain—not a big deal in an SBS domain of 5 users, but a bit of a pain in an SBS network of 50 users.

In SBS 2008, each user sees only the list of computers that he or she is allowed to connect to. The list is created initially when you join the computer to the SBS network, as shown in Figure 19-18.

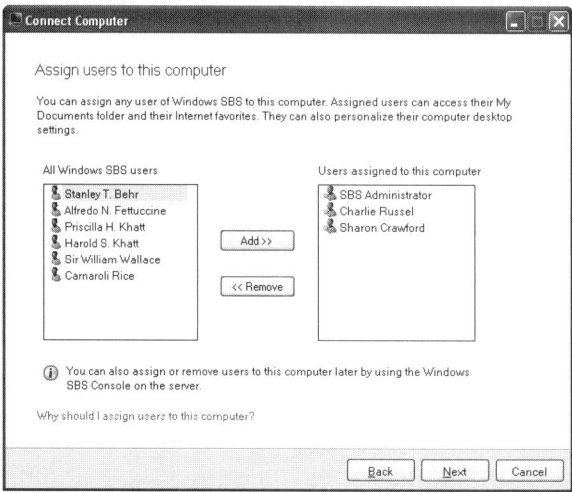

FIGURE 19-18 Assigning users to a computer during initial deployment of the computer

After computers are set up, however, you can easily change this list. We tend to think from a user perspective, rather than a computer perspective, so we change it by configuring the computers that a user account is assigned to. To change the list of computers that a user can connect to from RWW, use the following steps:

1. Open the Windows SBS Console if it isn't already open.

2. Click Users And Groups in the navigation bar and then click the Users tab.

3. Select the user you want to modify and then click Edit User Account Properties in the Tasks pane to open the Properties dialog box for the user, as shown in Figure 19-19.

4. Click Computers in the left pane to open the Set Network Computer Access dialog box, shown in Figure 19-20.

5. Select the computer you want to grant access to and select the Can Remotely Access This Computer check box.

6. Click OK to close the Properties dialog box for the user and return to the Windows SBS Console.

Removing access for a user follows essentially the same steps.

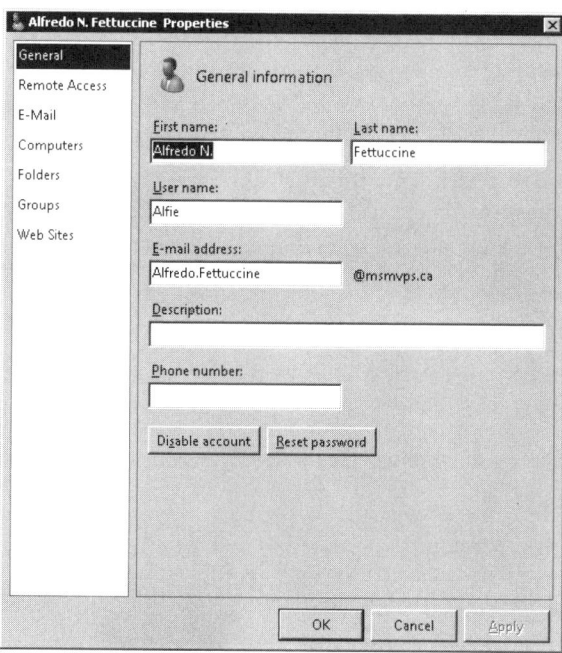

FIGURE 19-19 The Properties dialog box for user Alfredo N. Fettuccine

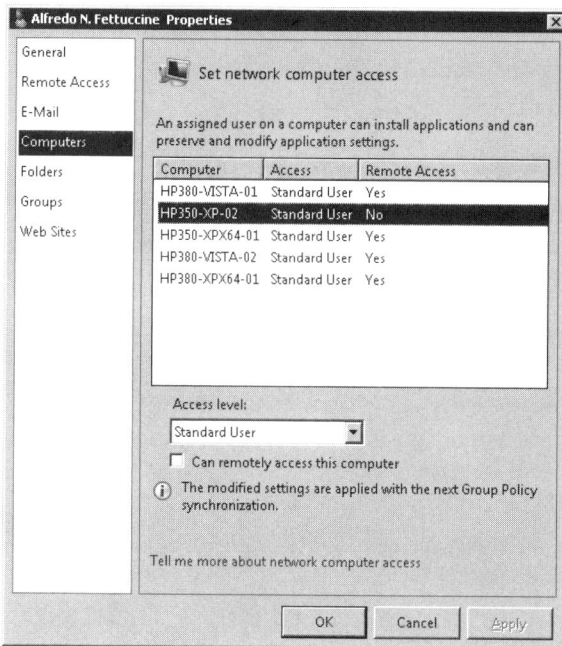

FIGURE 19-20 The Set Network Computer Access dialog box

Enabling RWW Access to a Terminal Server

One of the things that we expected to just work, but that doesn't, is having a terminal server show up in Remote Web Workplace as a computer that users can log onto. When we added a Windows Server 2008 computer to our SBS network and enabled the Terminal Server role on the server, we expected it to automatically be added to the RWW list, but it didn't happen. We did some poking around and asked some of our SBS MVP friends and came up with the solution. (Thanks, Handy Andy!) First, there are some minimum requirements:

- The terminal server must be joined to the SBS domain.
- TS Licensing must be installed and activated on the SBS Network.
- Users must be added to the Remote Desktop Users local group on the terminal server.
- The TS Licensing mode (per user or per device) for the server must be assigned.

When you've met these minimum requirements, use the following steps to enable the terminal server for RWW:

IMPORTANT The following steps include editing the registry. Editing the registry is deceptively simple but can have disastrous results—up to and including making your computer unable to boot. Be careful and don't make any changes without knowing exactly why you're making them and what the consequences are. There—you've been warned.

1. Log on to the SBS server with an account that has Network Administrator privileges.
2. Open Active Directory Users And Computers from the Administrative Tools menu.
3. Navigate to the SBSComputers OU, as shown in Figure 19-21.

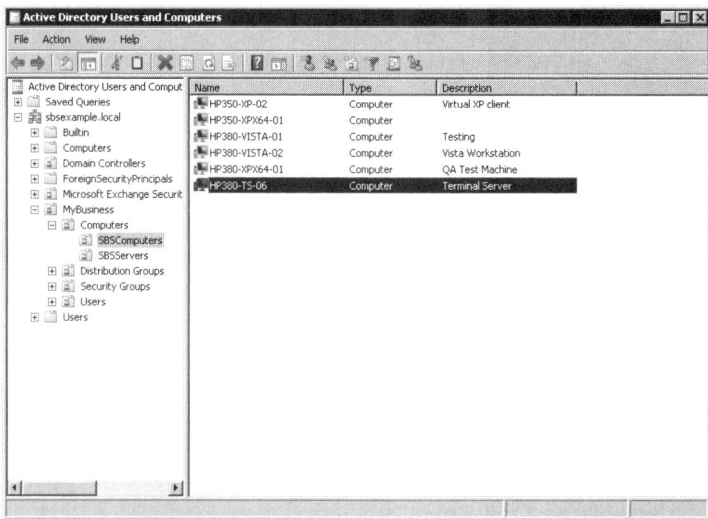

FIGURE 19-21 The SBSComputers OU, showing the terminal server in the wrong OU

4. Select the terminal server and drag it into the SBSServers OU.

5. Click Yes when you see the warning message shown in Figure 19-22.

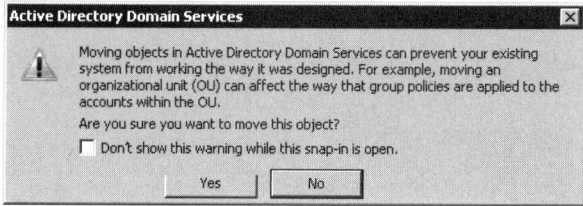

FIGURE 19-22 The Active Directory Domain Services warning message about moving objects

6. Close the Active Directory Users And Computers console.

7. Open the registry editor (Regedit.exe).

8. Navigate to HKEY_LOCAL_MACHINE\SOFTWARE\Microsoft\SmallBusinessServer.

9. If there is a RemoteUserPortal key, open it. If it doesn't exist, create it.

10. Create a new multi-string value (REG_MULTI_SZ) called TsServerNames, as shown in Figure 19-23.

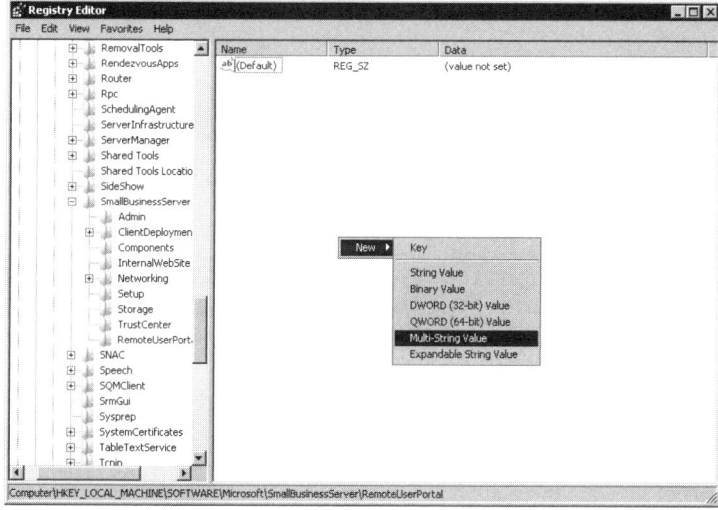

FIGURE 19-23 Creating a new multi-string value

11. Edit the multi-string value, adding the exact server names of your terminal servers, each on its own line, as shown in Figure 19-24.

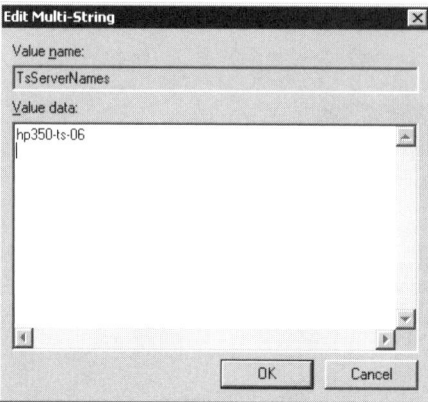

FIGURE 19-24 Modifying a new multi-string value

12. Click OK to close the Edit Multi-String editor and then close the registry editor.

13. Open the Windows SBS Console if it isn't already open.

14. Click Shared Folders And Web Sites in the navigation bar and then click the Web Sites tab.

15. Select the Remote Web Workplace Web site in the main pane and click Disable This Site in the Tasks pane.

16. Click Enable This Site in the Tasks pane.

Whew. That was a bit more work than we really expected. The SBS team has done a really good job of making SBS work as we'd hope and expect. But this one they missed.

Enabling or Disabling a User for RWW

You can enable or disable the access of individual users to RWW. Normally, all users are enabled for RWW, but if you want only a subset of your users to have the privilege to log in to RWW, you can disable the access of those you want to exclude.

Follow these steps to enable or disable a user from Remote Web Workplace:

1. Open the Windows SBS Console if it isn't already open.

2. Click Users And Groups in the navigation bar and then click the Groups tab.

3. Select the Windows SBS Remote Web Workplace Users security group in the main pane and then click Edit Group Properties in the Tasks pane to open the Properties dialog box for the group, as shown in Figure 19-25.

4. Select a user account in the Group Members pane and click Remove to remove the user.

5. To add a user account, click Add to open the Change Group Membership dialog box shown in Figure 19-26.

6. Select one or more users or groups in the left pane and click Add to add them to the group.

7. Click OK and then click OK again to exit the dialog box and return to the Windows SBS Console.

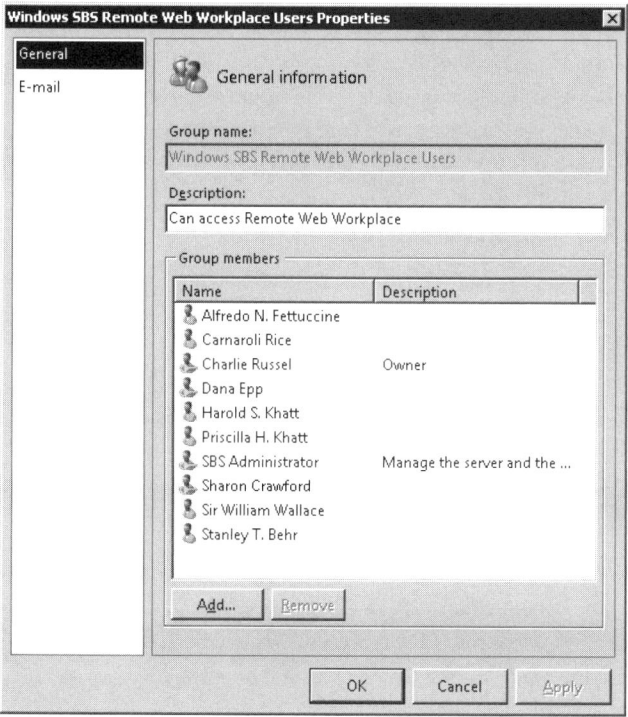

FIGURE 19-25 The Properties dialog box for the Windows SBS Remote Web Workplace Users security group

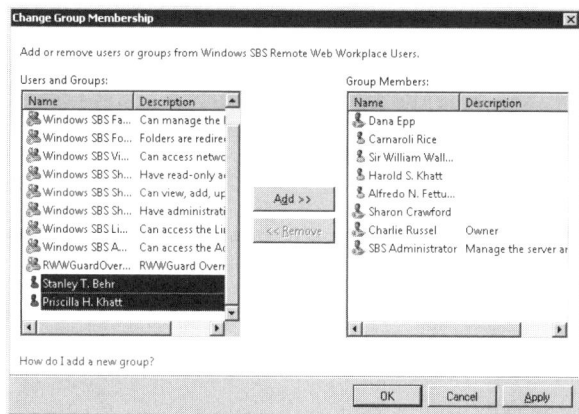

FIGURE 19-26 The Change Group Membership dialog box

REAL WORLD Two Factor Authentication and RWW

Remote Web Workplace is a secure way to connect to your SBS network. It uses IPSec tunneling and uses the authentication of Microsoft's Active Directory (your user name and password) to grant access to the resources of your SBS network. That said, if your SBS network contains sensitive information and you're subject to regulatory requirements for data protection, you should consider Two Factor Authentication (TFA) on RWW, especially for any accounts that are either Network Administrators or have special access to sensitive data.

Authentication is the process of ensuring that the individual who requests access to a resource is, in fact, the individual he claims to be. There are four basic kinds of authentication—"what-you-know," "who-you-are," "what-you-have," and "where-you-are." TFA requires that any user requesting remote access to the resources of your SBS network use two methods to uniquely identify himself. The first method is the user name and password of the user, and the second is some other factor. The real beauty of TFA is that even if one of your factors is compromised, it's useless without the second factor.

The basic user name and password is a what-you-know factor, and it's the most commonly used form of authentication. When combined with a sort of loose where-you-are factor—that is, at the console of your own PC—and when passwords or passphrases are sufficiently complex, it's a good method of authentication.

Who-you-are authentication is usually some form of biometric analysis—fingerprint readers, retina scanners, and even visual recognition software—all are forms of who-you-are authentication. We're not big fans of the most common of these, fingerprint readers. They're rather easily defeated from what we've seen to date.

What-you-have authentication is usually something like a smart card or a one-time password generator. Microsoft uses smart cards for their TFA, but we think one-time passwords are a lot easier to deal with and deploy in a small business. You don't require deploying smart card readers for everyone, and the overall costs are significantly less as a result.

Finally, where-you-are authentication uses your physical location as a proof of who you are. An example is the variable authentication process that some banks are implementing. It starts with the IP address and computer name you're connecting to your bank from. The bank knows that the IP address is typical for you and only asks a standard set of verification questions. But if you were to connect from a public wireless access point while on vacation, the bank would immediately be more cautious about whom you claim to be, and the secondary verification process would be more detailed. This kind of variable authentication process is expensive to implement and outside the scope of most small businesses.

We use TFA for remote access to our SBS network. We've implemented Scorpion Software's RWWGuard and AuthAnvil (*http://www.scorpionsoft.com*) to require a one-time password in addition to the normal RWW logon, as shown in Figure 19-27.

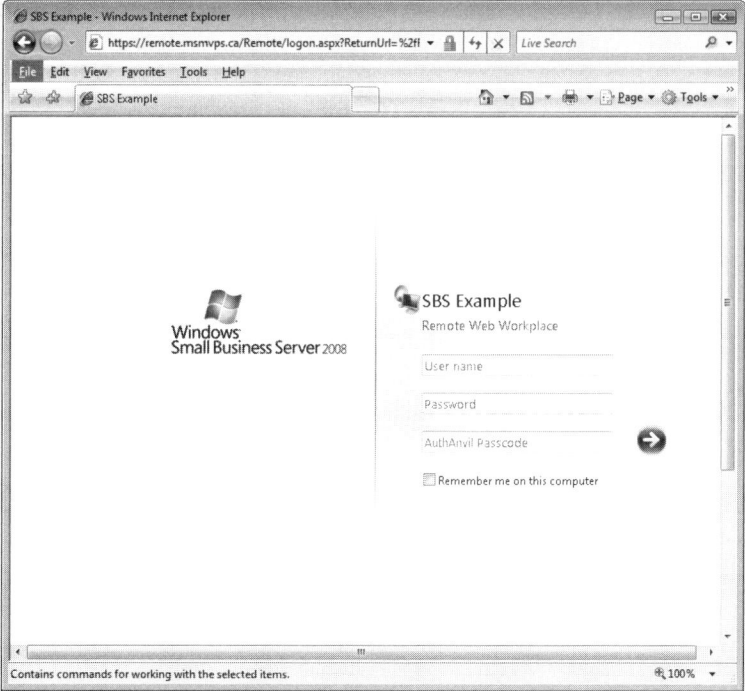

FIGURE 19-27 The RWWGuard logon page

What we really like about RWWGuard is that it's almost completely transparent. It looks and feels just like SBS, except for the one additional field for our one-time password. And the AuthAnvil key fob with those one-time passwords is on our keychain.

RWW Links List

There are two separate lists of links that are visible below the main buttons of the RWW home page: Organization Links and Administration Links. By default, all users are able to see the Organization links, but only users with the Network Administrator role, or the Standard User With Administration Links role, are able to see the Administration links.

You can customize these links, adding or removing them as appropriate for your network, and you can also configure which users have the links visible. To change which links are visible in RWW, follow these steps:

1. Open the Windows SBS Console if it isn't already open.

2. Click Shared Folders And Web Sites in the navigation bar and then click the Web Sites tab.

3. Click the Remote Web Workplace link in the left pane and then click View Site Properties in the Tasks pane to open the Properties dialog box for RWW.

4. Click Home Page Links in the left pane of the Properties dialog box to open the Home Page Links For Remote Web Workplace dialog box shown in Figure 19-28.

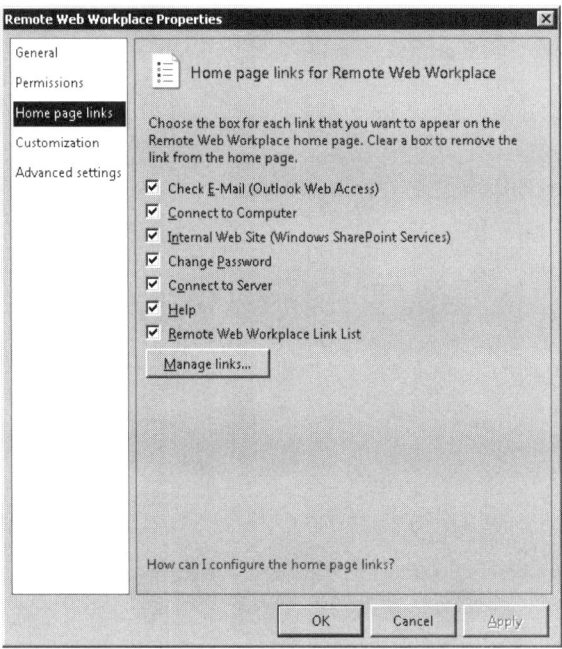

FIGURE 19-28 The Home Page Links For Remote Web Workplace dialog box

5. Clear the check boxes for any links you don't want to have visible on RWW. This will affect all users.

6. Click Manage Links to open the Remote Web Workplace Link List Properties dialog box, shown in Figure 19-29.

7. To disable either Organization Links or Administration Links, clear them on the General Settings page of the Remote Web Workplace Link List Properties dialog box.

8. Click Permissions in the left pane to open the Manage Gadget Permissions page, shown in Figure 19-30.

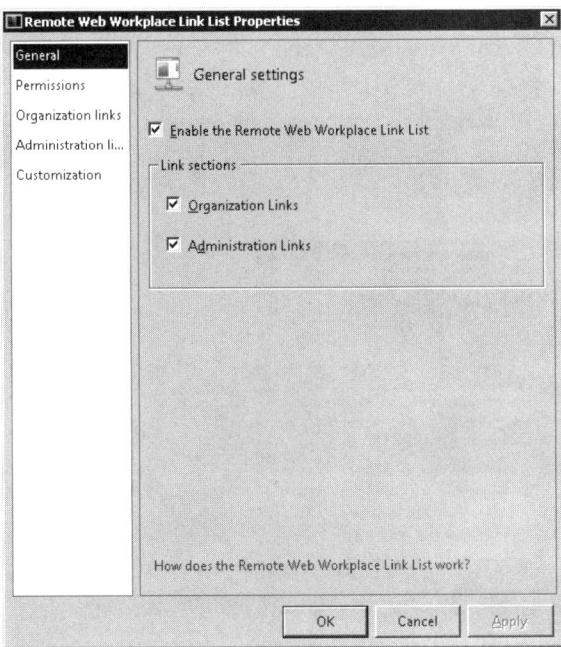

FIGURE 19-29 The General page of the Remote Web Workplace Link List Properties dialog box

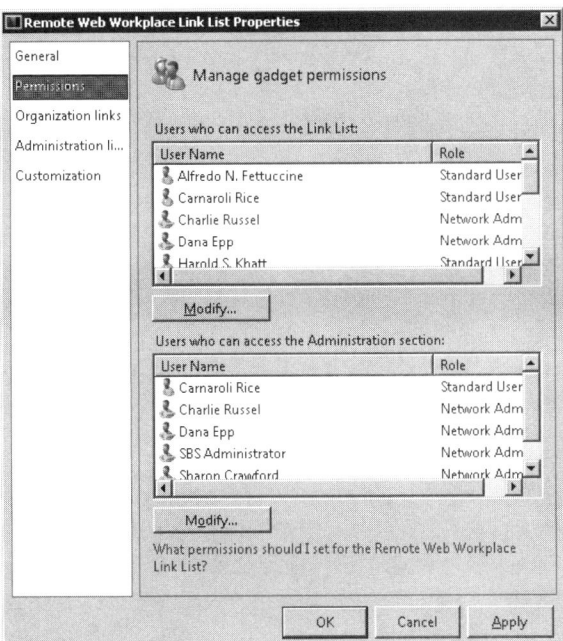

FIGURE 19-30 The Manage Gadget Permissions page of the Remote Web Workplace Link List Properties dialog box

9. Click Modify beneath the list you want to change permissions for to open the Change Group Membership dialog box for the security group.

10. Click Organization Links to open the Manage Organization Links page shown in Figure 19-31. Links added here will be visible to all SBS users who have permission to log on to RWW. (See Chapter 25, "Adding a Terminal Server," for details on adding links here for TS RemoteApps.)

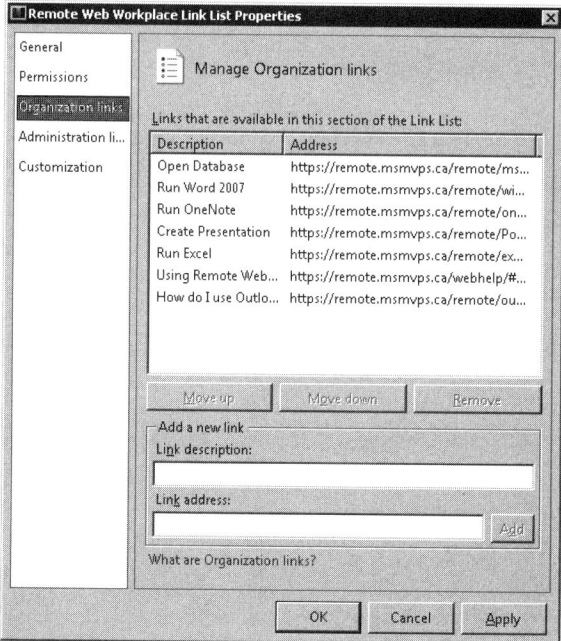

FIGURE 19-31 The Manage Organization Links page of the Remote Web Workplace Link List Properties dialog box showing several added TS RemoteApps links

11. Click Administration Links to open the Manage Administration Links page. Links added here are only visible to users with either Network Administration or Standard User With Administration Links roles.

12. Click Customization in the left pane to open the Customize Link List Section Names page, shown in Figure 19-32. The only change you can make here is to change the names of the two sets of links.

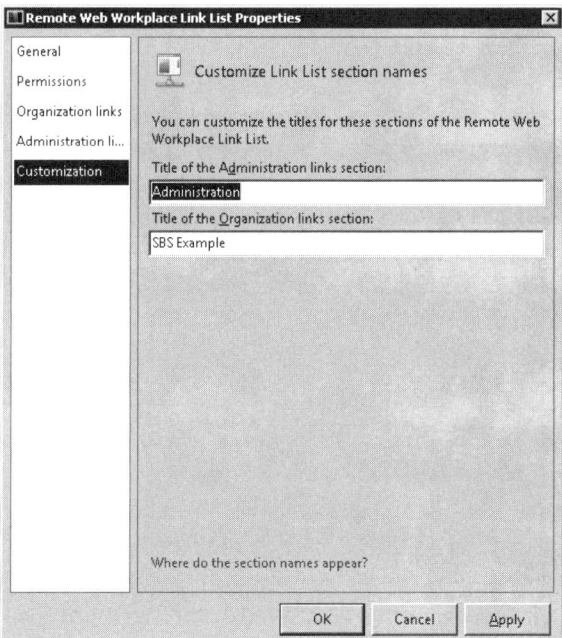

FIGURE 19-32 The Customize Link List Section Names page of the Remote Web Workplace Link List Properties dialog box

13. When you've completed your changes to the RWW Web site properties, click OK to exit and apply the changes.

Virtual Private Networks (VPNs)

Most operations that users and administrators need to do from remote locations can, and should, be performed using Remote Web Workplace. RWW gives your users a secure portal to connect to the resources of the SBS network and is the preferred way to access the network from a remote location.

If you do have a compelling need to implement VPN onto your SBS network, we strongly suggest that you carefully limit the users that have VPN privileges and that you ensure that their computers are fully patched and protected at all times. VPNs significantly increase your security risk from an unpatched and compromised computer causing problems on your SBS network. Because VPNs allow a remote computer to directly connect to the network, any malware on the remote computer has full access to your SBS network.

E ven though we generally try to avoid VPNs whenever possible and use RWW for all our remote access needs, one operation that we regularly perform still works better over a VPN: applying the monthly round of updates to the server. Applying patches remotely is always something that has the potential to cause disruption, but it's also something that's a part of just about every SBS administrator's life. With VPNs, there is less likelihood of the connection being disrupted and not reinstated than with RWW, in our experience.

The problem, of course, is that to enable VPNs for patching, you have to enable a whole additional role on the server and start up more services. And we're firm be-lievers in keeping the running services to as small a number as possible. So what are the alternatives if RWW is out for patching? One is to use a firewall or router that is a VPN endpoint, offloading this from the SBS server entirely. This didn't work well in a two-NIC SBS 2003 environment, but it works quite well in a single-NIC SBS 2008 environment. The second alternative is to enable RDP directly to the SBS server. This works but has some significant security implications. If you do this, we'd strongly suggest that you configure your firewall or router to accept the RDP request only from a specific IP address or set of addresses, and we'd also strongly suggest imple-menting AuthAnvil or another form of TFA on the SBS server (which isn't a bad idea in any case).

Enabling VPNs

Enabling VPNs to your SBS network is a simple process. You run the Set Up Virtual Private Networking Wizard from the Windows SBS Console, and you configure your router or firewall for VPN passthrough. If you have UPnP enabled, SBS will make the change on the router for you. But we don't enable UPnP on our network, so we get to do that step manually.

To enable VPN access to your SBS network, use the following steps:

1. Open the Windows SBS Console if it isn't already open.

2. Click Network in the navigation bar and then click the Connectivity tab.

3. Select VPN Connection in the main pane and then click Configure A Virtual Private Network in the Tasks pane to start the Set Up Virtual Private Networking Wizard shown in Figure 19-33.

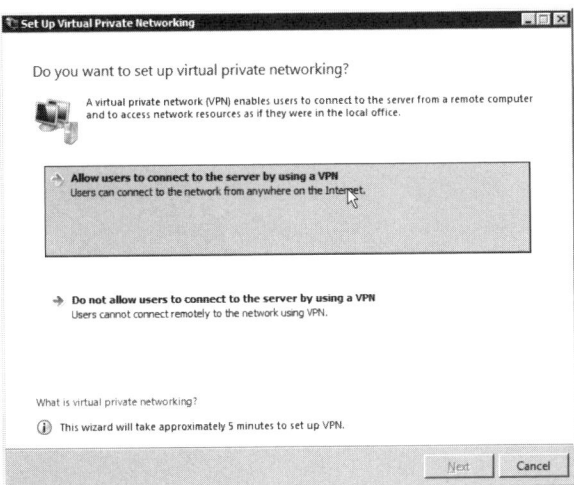

FIGURE 19-33 The Set Up Virtual Private Networking Wizard

4. Click Allow Users To Connect To The Server By Using A VPN. When the wizard completes, you'll see a status page that tells you the wizard completed successfully and includes any warnings, as shown in Figure 19-34.

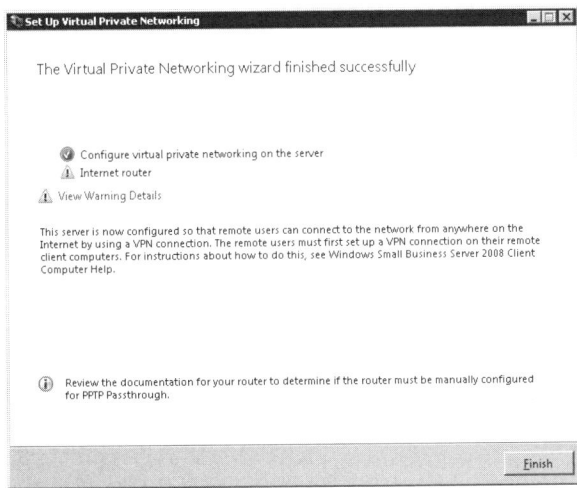

FIGURE 19-34 With UPnP turned off, you'll get a warning that the router wasn't configured.

5. If you get a warning, click View Warning Details to see what the warning is about. If you have UPnP turned off on your router, you'll see the warning details shown in Figure 19-35.

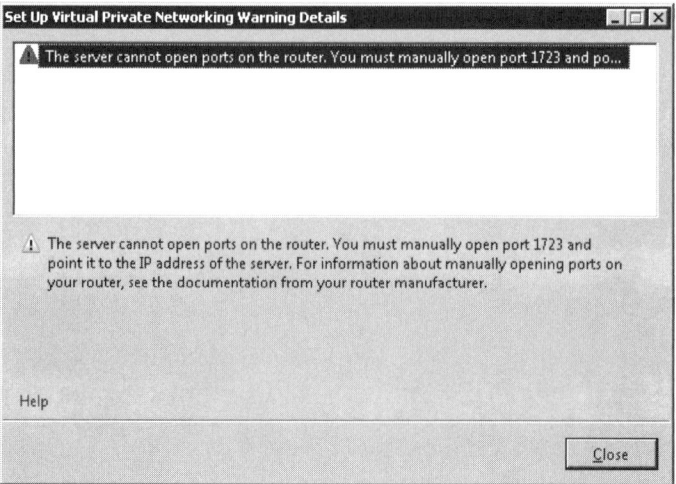

FIGURE 19-35 With UPnP off, you must manually configure ports on your router.

6. Click Close to close the Set Up Virtual Private Networking Warning Details page and then click Finish to close the wizard.

7. If you don't have UPnP enabled on your router, open Internet Explorer and log on to the router.

8. The details for each router are different, but you need to configure the router to forward port 1723 to the IP address of the SBS server. You may also need to configure PPTP Passthrough. Most routers have an automatic method (often called Virtual Servers) for configuring port forwarding. Consult your router documentation.

9. After the router is configured, you'll probably need to restart the router. When you do, VPNs will be enabled on your SBS network.

Configure VPN Permissions

By default, only users with the Network Administrator role are enabled for VPN access. To add additional users, you need to add them to the Windows SBS Virtual Private Network Users security group. As with most things in SBS, there's more than one way to get there, but we use the following steps:

1. Open the Windows SBS Console if it isn't already open.

2. Click Network on the navigation bar and then click the Connectivity tab.

3. Select VPN Connection in the left pane and then click View Virtual Private Network Properties in the Tasks pane to open the Virtual Private Networking Properties dialog box, shown in Figure 19-36.

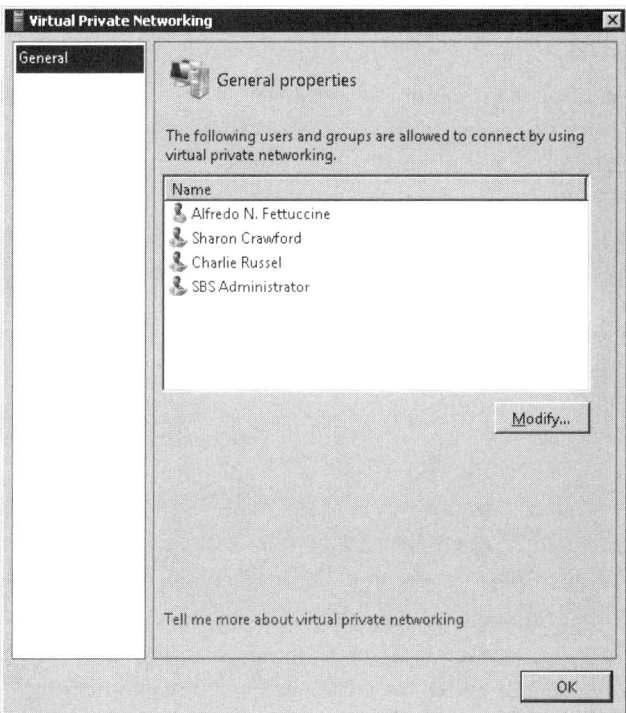

FIGURE 19-36 The Virtual Private Networking Properties dialog box

4. Click Modify to open the Change Group Membership dialog box for the Windows SBS Virtual Private Network Users security group, shown in Figure 19-37.

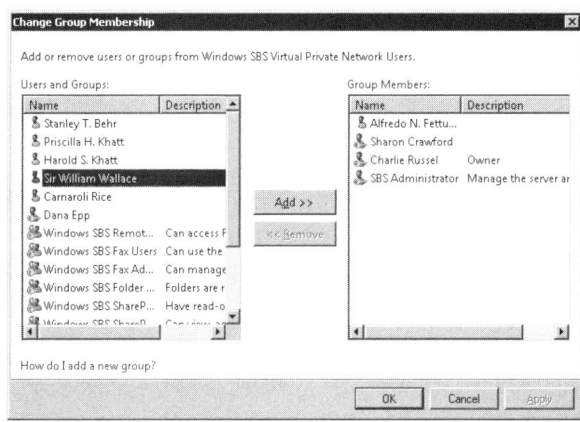

FIGURE 19-37 The Change Group Membership dialog box for the Windows SBS Virtual Private Network Users security group

5. Select users or groups of users in the left Users And Groups pane and click Add to add them to the Windows SBS Virtual Private Network Users security group.

6. Select users or groups of users in the right Group Members pane and click Remove to remove them from the Windows SBS Virtual Private Network Users security group. Only members of the Windows SBS Virtual Private Network Users security group have permission to use a VPN to connect to the SBS network.

7. When you've finished making your changes, click OK twice to save the changes and return to the Windows SBS Console.

Fixing Network Problems

In a perfect world, networks would never fail, no one would ever have to change a network card, IP addresses would be automatically assigned and never change, and no one would ever have to try to troubleshoot a network connectivity problem. Well, IPv6 helps with some of this, but we're afraid that there's still a long way to go until we reach network nirvana. Until we do, however, there's the Fix My Network Wizard in SBS.

We have to say right up front that when we heard the name for this new wizard, we were more than a little concerned. It sounded a lot like something that you might run on a home PC—usually with less than optimal results. But then we remembered that for SBS 2003, the SBS team had already created one of the best network configuration wizards we've ever used—the Configure E-mail And Internet Connectivity Wizard. Affectionately known as the CEICW (say that fast three times), the CEICW was a sort of one-stop shop for resetting all your network settings back to where they belonged. The CEICW was really good at what it did, but it did have some limits. It couldn't tell that your IP address had changed, and it didn't recognize that your router wasn't responding, along with a few other things that we sort of wished it did. There were also times when you needed to run a different wizard or actually resort to using the native Windows Server tools.

With the Fix My Network Wizard in SBS 2008, the SBS team has taken the concept of the CEICW and extended and improved it significantly. The actual initial configuration of Internet domain name and e-mail, along with public DNS names, have been separated out as discrete tasks with their own wizards, which makes a lot of sense. When you've done those, they really aren't likely to change much. But it's all the other things that seem to go wrong with networking.

The Fix My Network Wizard, shown in Figure 19-38, is located on the Connectivity page of the Network section of the Windows SBS Console. This wizard can identify and in most cases fix problems with DHCP, DNS, logons, network access (both local and remote), Internet connectivity, RWW, e-mail, and VPNs. In some cases, you might need to run the wizard multiple times, and if you have UPnP disabled on your router, you'll need to manually make any router changes that it identifies.

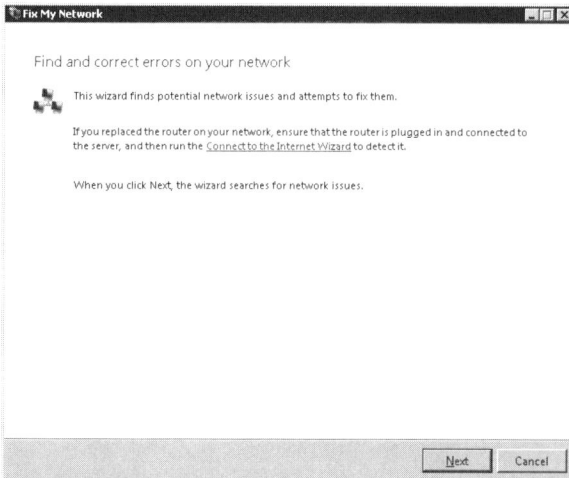

FIGURE 19-38 The initial page of the Fix My Network Wizard

When we ran the Fix My Network Wizard on our network, which appeared to be working as expected, we got the Potential Network Issues page shown in Figure 19-39.

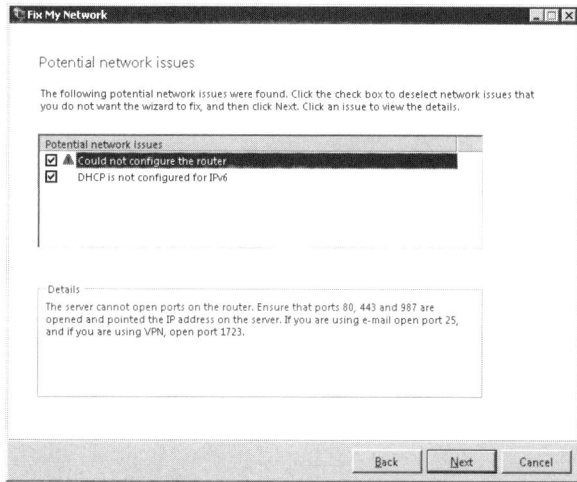

FIGURE 19-39 A typical Potential Network Issues page of the Fix My Network Wizard

We weren't too concerned about the first item on the list, because we already knew we had disabled UPnP on our router. But the second one was news to us, so we cleared the check box on the router issue and clicked Next to see what would happen. The wizard worked away for about 10 or 15 seconds, and then gave us the results page shown in Figure 19-40.

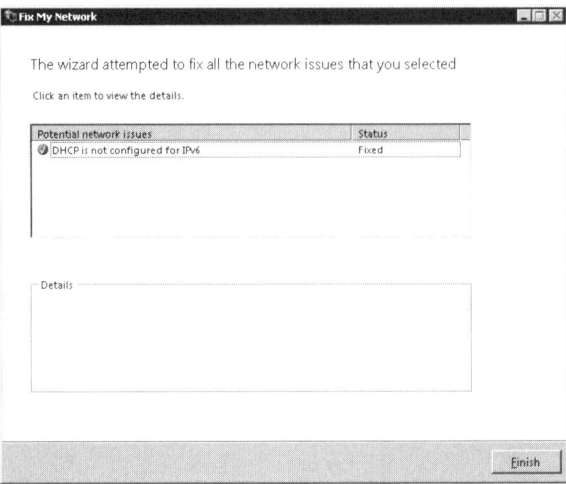

FIGURE 19-40 The Fix My Network Wizard has fixed our DHCP.

The one limitation of the Fix My Network Wizard is that it won't run successfully if you have more than a single network card enabled on your SBS server. Because that's not a supported configuration, the wizard reports the issue and offers to disable the extra NIC. Our solution is to simply disable the NIC prior to running the Fix My Network Wizard on our production network, which does have more than one network card in the server because of the unusual networking requirements here with all of our test networks.

Summary

Connectivity is a huge topic, and this chapter has tried to cover the most important areas for SBS networks. We've covered DHCP and DNS, wireless connectivity, firewall configuration, Remote Web Workplace (RWW), Virtual Private Networks (VPNs), and the Fix My Network Wizard. In the next chapter, we'll cover Group Policy and how you can use it to help manage your SBS network.

Using Group Policy

In one form or another, Group Policy is all about security. The policies in place after installation include rules about logons, software installation, passwords, and other settings that have an effect on how safe your network will be. You may not need to change most of these settings. However, you do need to know how the policies work, how to make changes, and how to configure new policies for your particular circumstances.

The configuration of intelligent security policies has the serendipitous effect of potentially increasing productivity by providing a barrier against those great time-wasters: the accidental loss of vital folders, deletion of files, and the inadvertent introduction of viruses and other malicious software to the network. Group Policy also helps the cause of productivity by making it easier for users to find what they need to work efficiently.

Although it's true that Windows SBS does most of the Group Policy work for you, and the underlying Windows 2008 Group Policy is aimed mainly at very large networks, there are still some Group Policy settings that can be very useful in a Windows SBS setting. For example, you can configure the mapped drives for all the client computers (see the section titled "Drive Maps" later in this chapter) or create a Group Policy object that will control software distribution (see the section titled "Deploying Applications with Group Policy" later in this chapter).

So even if you don't want to get into all the complexities that Group Policy can present, you can make use of some aspects and actually simplify your life.

Components of Group Policy

Group Policy consists of the following configurable components:

- **Security Settings** Configures security for users, computers, and domains
- **Scripts** Specifies scripts for computer startup and shutdown, as well as for user logon and logoff events
- **Preference Items** Configures unenforced settings for users and computers
- **Folder Redirection** Places special folders such as Documents or specified application folders on the network
- **Software Settings** Assigns applications to users

Group Policy Objects

A collection of policy settings is called a Group Policy object (GPO). A GPO contains policies that affect computers and policies that affect users. Computer-related policies include computer security settings, application settings, and computer startup and shutdown scripts. User-related policies define application settings, folder redirection, assigned and published applications, user logon and logoff scripts, and user security settings. In cases of conflicting policies, the convention is that computer-related settings override user-related settings.

In a GPO, most settings have three possible states: enabled, disabled, and not configured. Group policies are inherited and cumulative. When you associate a GPO with an Active Directory container, the Group Policy is applied to all computer and user accounts in the container.

Group Policy is an abstraction consisting of two parts: a Group Policy container (GPC) and a Group Policy template. Both parts are contained in a Group Policy object (GPO). The GPO is what we work with directly. The GPO contains all the settings that can apply to users and computers. When those settings are changed, the changes are made to the GPO. The two components of the GPO exist in different places.

The GPC is the Active Directory component of the GPO and includes subcontainers with version information, status information, and a list of which Group Policy extensions are employed in the GPO. It also contains some information used by clients, such as the software installation policy.

The GPT is a set of files in the SYSVOL folder on the server. When you create a GPO, the corresponding GPT folder structure is created automatically. The actual name of the folder for the GPT is the *globally unique identifier* (GUID) for the GPO—a number that is useful to the computer but is otherwise incomprehensible. To see the policy folder, look in %SystemRoot%\SYSVOL\sysvol\domain_name\policies. But *do not* change this folder in any way. Work on Group Policy through the Group Policy Management console (GPMC).

Managing Group Policies

The Group Policy Management console (GPMC) provides a comprehensive overview of Group Policy in a single console. All Group Policy management tasks can be performed in the GPMC except configuring individual policies in GPOs.

When you want to configure individual policies, the GPMC will launch the Group Policy Object Editor with the policy loaded.

To see the group policies specifically defined for Windows SBS, select Administrative Tools from the Start menu and then select Group Policy Management. Expand Forest and then Domains until you get to MyBusiness as shown in Figure 20-1.

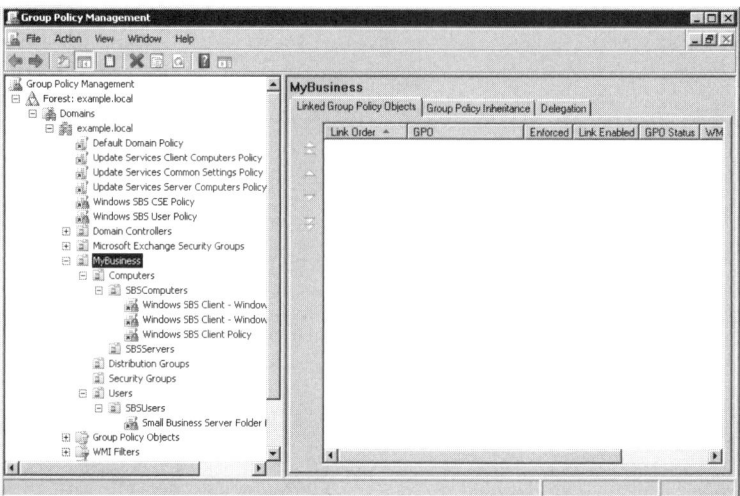

FIGURE 20-1 Viewing SBS Group Policy

To view or modify an existing GPO, right-click the GPO and select Edit as shown in Figure 20-2.

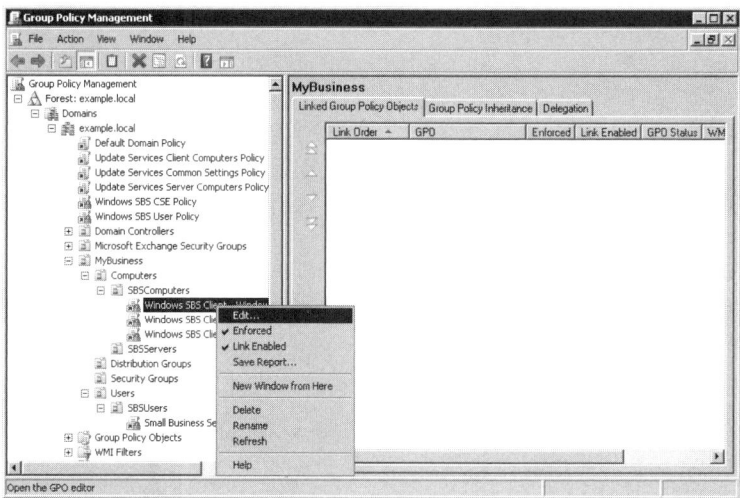

FIGURE 20-2 Choosing to edit a GPO

This action opens the Group Policy Management Editor (Figure 20-3), wherein you can expand various items in the console to view existing settings.

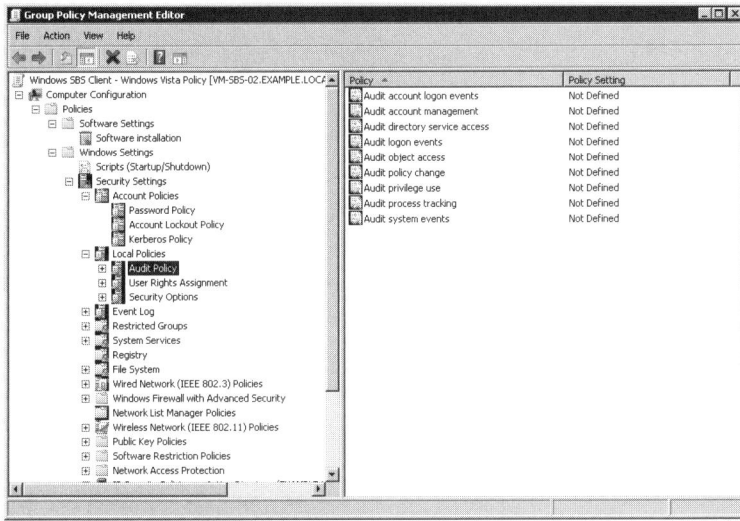

FIGURE 20-3 Viewing group policies

Order of Inheritance

As a rule, Group Policy settings are passed from parent containers down to child containers. This practice means that a policy that is applied to a parent container applies to all the
containers—including users and computers—that are below the parent container in the
Active Directory tree hierarchy. However, if you specifically assign a Group Policy for a child
container that contradicts the parent container policy, the child container's policy overrides
the parent Group Policy.

If policies are not contradictory, both can be implemented. For example, if a parent
container policy calls for an application shortcut to be on a user's desktop, and the child
container policy calls for another application shortcut, both appear. Policy settings that are
disabled are inherited as disabled. Policy settings that are not configured in the parent container remain unconfigured.

Overriding Inheritance

Several options are available for changing how inheritance is processed. One option, called
enforcing the GPO link, prevents child containers from overriding any policy setting set in a
higher level GPO. This option is not set by default on all GPOs.

Enforcing a GPO Link in the GPMC

To enforce a link, open the Group Policy Management console, right-click the Group Policy
object link in the console tree, and select Enforced, as shown in Figure 20-4.

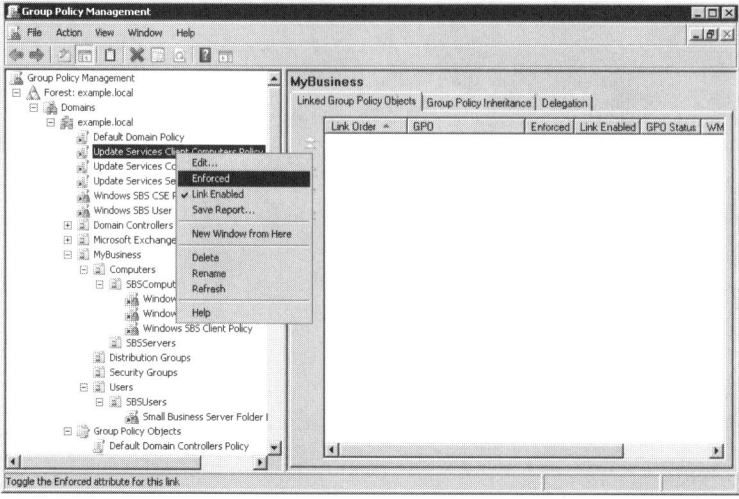

FIGURE 20-4 Enforcing a GPO link

A second option is Block Inheritance. When you select this option, the child container does not inherit any policies from parent containers. In the event of a conflict between these two options, the Enforced option always takes precedence. Simply stated, Enforced is a link property, Block Inheritance is a container property, and Enforced takes precedence over Block Inheritance.

Setting Block Inheritance

To enable Block Inheritance, open the Group Policy Management console and right-click the domain or organizational unit (OU) for which you want to block inheritance. Select Block Inheritance, as shown in Figure 20-5.

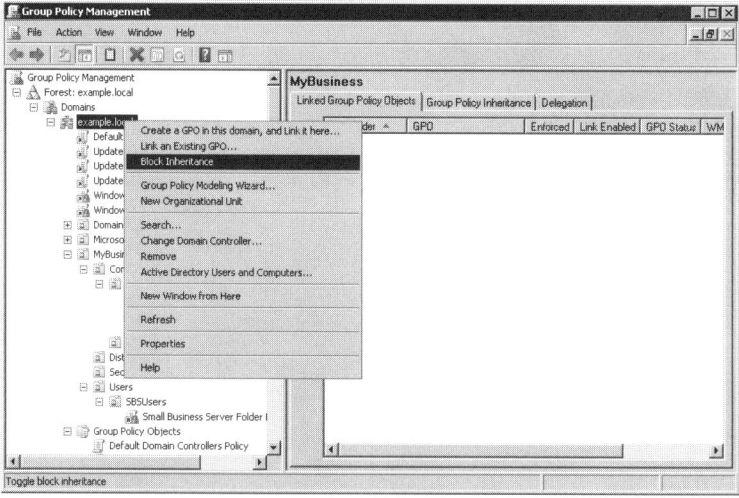

FIGURE 20-5 Setting block inheritance for a domain

Order of Implementation

Group policies are processed in the following order:

1. Local GPO
2. GPOs linked to the site in the order specified by the administrator
3. Domain GPOs, as specified by the administrator
4. OU GPOs, from largest to smallest OU (parent to child OU)

The GPO with the lowest link order is processed last, and therefore has the highest precedence. If multiple GPOs attempt contradictory settings, the GPO with highest precedence wins.

Exceptions to this order are GPOs with enforced or disabled links, GPOs with disabled user or computer settings, and OUs (or the whole domain) set to block inheritance. To see the order of precedence for GPOs for a domain or OU, open the Group Policy Management console, and in the console tree, select the domain name or the OU. In the details pane, click the Group Policy Inheritance tab, as shown in Figure 20-6.

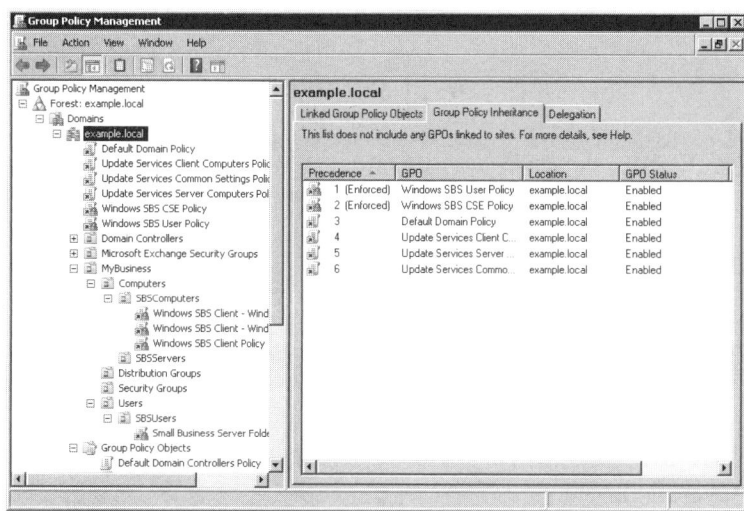

FIGURE 20-6 Viewing a domain's Group Policy order of inheritance

Creating a Group Policy Object

The installation of Windows SBS creates an Active Directory domain that includes a Default Domain Policy, a Default Domain Controllers Policy, and several policies specifically for Small Business Server. When you need to set up a GPO of your own, follow these steps:

1. Select Group Policy Management from the Administrative Tools menu and navigate to the container to which you want the new GPO to apply.

2. Right-click the domain, site, or OU and select Create A GPO In This Domain, And Link It Here.

3. In the New GPO dialog box, type in a name for the Group Policy object and click OK.

4. Right-click the new GPO and select Edit to launch the Group Policy Object Editor.

5. Specify settings for the GPO. When you're finished, close the Group Policy Object Editor.

6. In the Group Policy Management console, right-click the domain name or the OU this GPO is to be associated with and select Link An Existing GPO.

7. In the Select GPO dialog box, select the GPO to link and click OK.

To shorten the process by one step, you can also right-click the domain or OU and select Create A GPO In This Domain, And Link It Here.

NOTE Try to keep the total number of GPOs as low as possible. The processing of each GPO takes time, and too many objects can slow logons and logoffs. The number of settings within a GPO doesn't matter—it's the total number of GPOs.

 UNDER THE HOOD Inside the Group Policy Object Editor

When you create a new GPO or edit an existing one, the Group Policy Object Editor is automatically launched. In the console tree, two nodes—Computer Configuration and User Configuration—display. Under each node are extensions for Software Settings, Windows Settings, and Administrative Templates.

Use the Computer Configuration folders to customize policies for computers on the network. These policies go into effect when the computer is turned on and the operating system starts. Settings in these folders apply to any user who logs on to the computer. For example, if you have computers in a training room for which you want to enforce a strict environment, the Computer Configuration node is where you configure those settings.

The User Configuration node contains settings for customizing environments or setting policies for users on the network. User Configuration policies come into play when a specific user logs on to the network.

Deleting a Group Policy Object

To delete a GPO, right-click it in the Group Policy Management console and select Delete. When you delete a GPO, all links to the GPO will also be deleted. Be sure that you are logged on with an account that has sufficient permissions.

Neither the Default Domain Policy nor the Default Domain Controllers Policy can be deleted.

Managing Group Policy Links

With numerous GPOs on a network, it's important to keep track of GPO links within the domain. To find out what links exist for a particular GPO, follow these steps:

1. Select Group Policy Management from the Administrative Tools menu.

2. Right-click the domain name in the console tree and select Search.

3. In the Search Item drop-down list, select GPO-links.

4. Click Add and then click Search.

5. In the Search Results box shown in Figure 20-7, double-click a GPO to view its links and other settings.

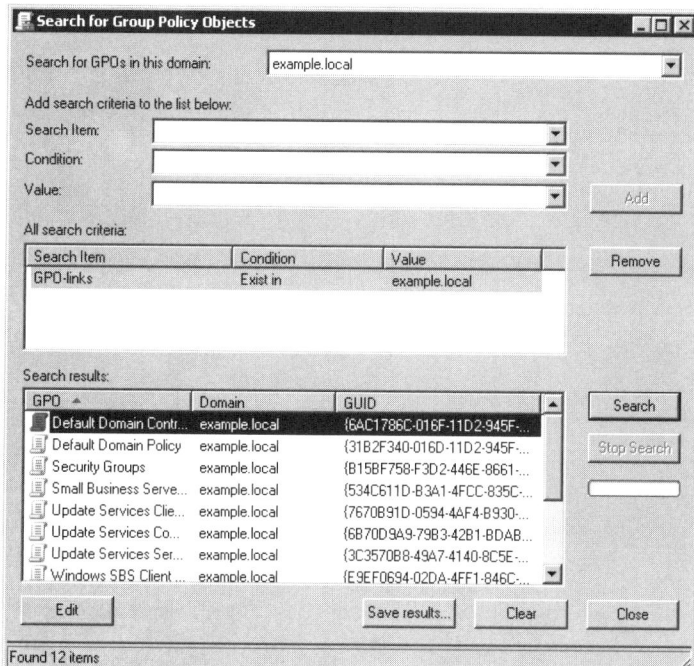

FIGURE 20-7 Finding GPO links

Setting the Scope of the GPO

A GPO applies to all the users and computers in the container with which the GPO is associated. Most GPOs default to applying to Authenticated Users—namely, everyone who can log on to the network. Inevitably, there are GPOs that should apply only to some. To filter the application of a GPO, follow these steps:

1. Select Group Policy Management from the Administrative Tools menu.

2. Select the Group Policy object you want to filter and click the Scope tab.

3. On the Scope tab in the Security Filtering section, click Add and locate the groups or users who should have the policy applied to them, as shown in Figure 20-8. Make your selection and click OK.

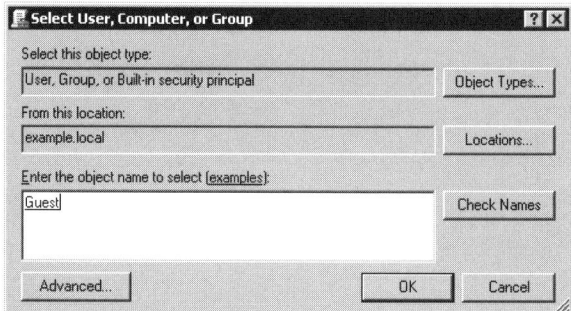

FIGURE 20-8 Selecting groups or users to which the GPO applies

If Authenticated Users appears in the Security Filtering list on the Scope page, select it and click Remove. This ensures that the GPO is applied only to the groups or users you added.

Enabling and Disabling GPO Links

To check or change the status of a GPO link, follow these steps:

1. Select Group Policy Management from the Administrative Tools menu.

2. In the console tree, navigate to Group Policy Objects under your domain name and select the GPO.

3. On the Scope tab, links are listed and the status of the link is shown under Link Enabled. To change the status, right-click the link and select Link Enabled from the shortcut menu, as shown in Figure 20-9.

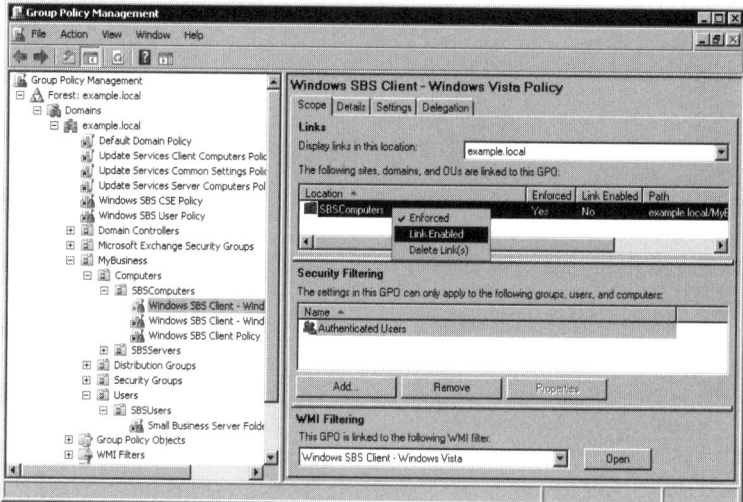

FIGURE 20-9 Enabling a GPO link

Disabling a Branch of a GPO

If a GPO has an entire node under User Configuration or Computer Configuration that's not configured, disable the node to avoid processing those settings. This speeds startup and logon for all users subject to that GPO. To disable a node, open the Group Policy Management console and follow these steps:

1. In the console tree, expand Group Policy Objects.

2. Right-click the GPO that contains the User or Computer settings you want to disable, point to GPO Status, and then choose one of the following options shown in Figure 20-10:

   - Click User Configuration Settings Disabled to disable user settings for the GPO.
   - Click Computer Configuration Settings Disabled to disable computer settings for the GPO.

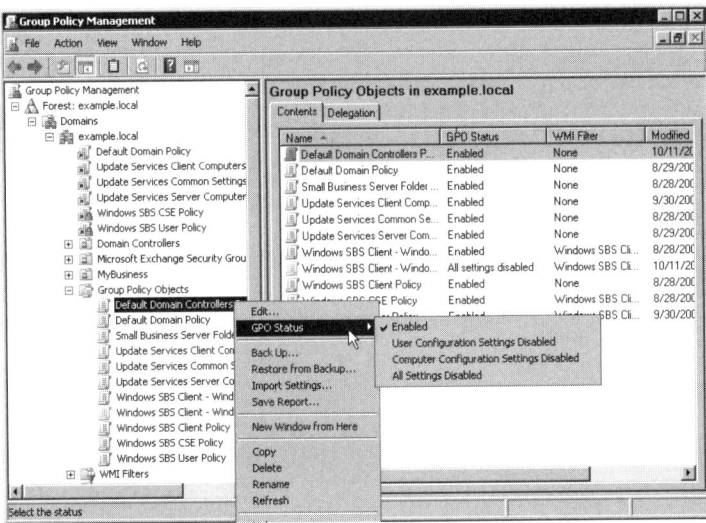

FIGURE 20-10 Disabling a branch of a GPO

A check mark next to User Configuration Settings Disabled or Computer Configuration Settings Disabled indicates that the option is currently selected.

Refreshing Group Policy

Policy changes are immediate, but they are not instantly propagated to clients. Client computers request policy only when one of the following occurs:

- The computer starts.
- A user logs on.
- An application requests a refresh.
- A user requests a refresh.
- A Group Policy refresh interval is enabled and the interval has elapsed.

By default, Group Policy refreshes in the background every 90 minutes with a random offset of 0 through 30 minutes added so that not all computers request a refresh at the same time.

If you find the default refresh too long or too short, you can change the refresh interval by following these steps:

1. Select Group Policy Management from the Administrative Tools menu.

2. To add the setting to an existing GPO, right-click the GPO and select Edit. To create a new GPO, right-click the domain name or OU and select Create A GPO In This Domain, And Link It Here. Supply a name for the new GPO, right-click it in Group Policy Management console, and select Edit.

3. In the console tree, expand Computer Configuration, expand Policies, expand Administrative Templates, expand System, and then select Group Policy, as shown in Figure 20-11.

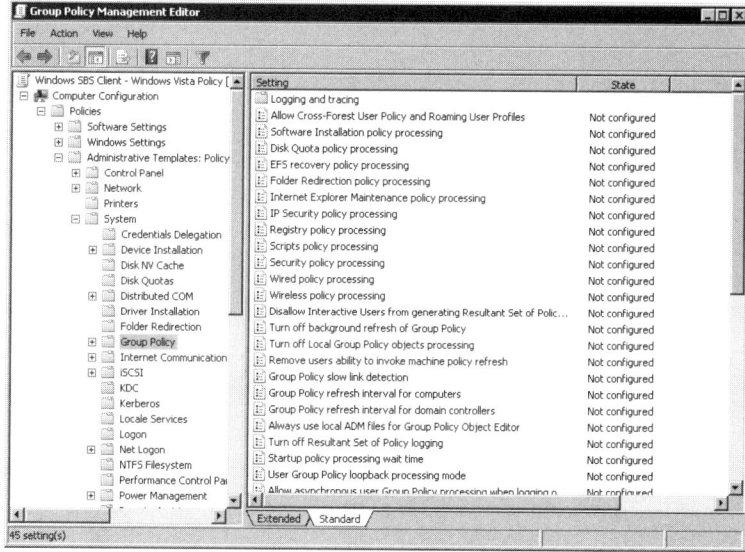

FIGURE 20-11 Group Policy settings for Group Policy node

4. In the details pane, double-click Group Policy Refresh Interval For Computers.

5. On the Settings tab, select Enabled and then supply the new settings. Click OK when finished.

> **NOTE** Don't make the interval very short, because a large amount of network traffic is generated by each refresh.

Because policy can be set at several levels, when you look at a policy object, what you see is both local policy and the policy in effect on the system. Local policy and actual policy in effect may not be synonymous if the computer is inheriting settings from domain-level policies. If you make a policy setting and it isn't reflected in effective policy, a policy from the domain is overriding your setting.

It's also possible that the policy change hasn't been refreshed since the change was made. To force a policy refresh for the local computer, open a Command Prompt window and type the following:

```
gpupdate [/target:{computer | user}] /force
```

Backing Up a Group Policy Object

A valuable feature, new in the Group Policy Management console, is the ability to back up and restore GPOs. Include regular backup of all GPOs as part of your overall planning-for-disaster strategy. To back up a GPO, follow these steps:

1. Open the Group Policy Management console. In the console tree, navigate to Group Policy Objects in the domain that contains the GPO to be backed up.

   - To back up a single GPO, right-click the GPO and select Back Up.
   - To back up all GPOs in the domain, right-click Group Policy Objects and select Back Up All (Figure 20-12).

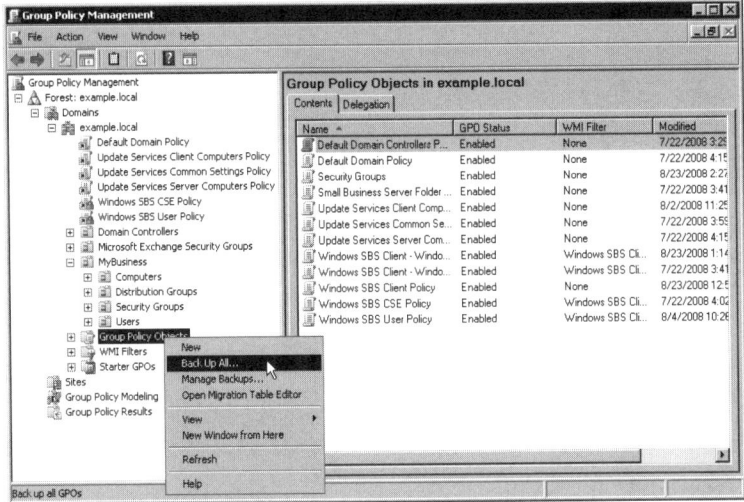

FIGURE 20-12 Backing up all GPOs

2. In the Back Up Group Policy Object dialog box, type the path to the backup location and then click Back Up.

3. After the operation completes, click OK.

> **NOTE** Because the only reason to back up GPOs—or anything else, for that matter—is to protect data that might have to be restored one day, be sure that the backup folder is secure and can be accessed only by authorized administrators.

Restoring a Group Policy Object

You can easily restore GPOs that have been backed up. If you back up all the GPOs in a container, you can restore all of them, some of them, or one at a time.

To restore backed-up GPOs, complete these steps:

1. Select Group Policy from the Administrative Tools menu.

2. In the console tree, navigate to Group Policy Objects.

3. To restore a previous version of an existing GPO or to restore a deleted GPO, right-click Group Policy Objects and select Manage Backups.

4. In the Manage Backups dialog box, select the GPO to restore and click Restore.

When you have a lot of GPOs to sort through, select the check box that allows you to display only the latest versions of the backed-up GPOs. If you're unsure of which GPO to restore, highlight them one at a time and click View Settings.

Deploying Applications with Group Policy

Managing software on client computers can be a tedious task, but you can use Group Policy to deploy applications automatically. The Group Policy Software Installation extension enables you to deploy applications to computers in the domain or forest using Group Policy and includes the capability to do the following:

- Publish applications so that users can view and install programs from the network

- Assign applications to users or computers so that the applications are installed automatically when users need them or on the next restart or logon

- Target applications to different groups using Group Policy

- View installation status using Group Policy Results

Publish or Assign Applications

To deploy an application, create or edit the appropriate Group Policy object (GPO) and add the application's Windows Installer package to either the user or computer policy, depending on whether you want it to apply to users or computers. The next time the user logs on or the computer restarts, Active Directory applies the relevant policy to the user or computer, depending on the package settings you specify in the GPO. Table 20-1 lists the GPO settings for installation actions.

TABLE 20-1 GPO Settings Needed for Specific Actions

ACTION	SETTING REQUIRED
Automatically install the application	Install This Application At Logon
Add the application to a list of installable programs in Programs And Features	Publish
Add a shortcut to the application in the Start menu and install it on first use	Assign the Application (Don't use the Install This Application At Logon setting.)

An application published in Active Directory becomes available from Programs And Features for the users to whom the GPO applies. An assigned application, on the other hand, can be assigned to either users or computers and is installed without any action on the user's part. Assigned applications appear on the Start menu and are installed on first use, unless you specify that they should be fully installed at the next logon.

Assign essential applications to users or computers so that these applications are always available, and publish optional programs to make it easy for users to find applications when they need them. Do not assign or publish an application to both computers and users. Table 20-2 summarizes the differences between publishing and assigning applications.

TABLE 20-2 Outcomes When Publishing v. Assigning Applications

	PUBLISHED APPLICATIONS	APPLICATIONS ASSIGNED TO USERS	APPLICATIONS ASSIGNED TO COMPUTERS
After deployment, when is the software available for installation?	Immediately	After the next logon*	After the next reboot*
How is the software installed?	Through Programs And Features in Control Panel	Automatically on first use or after the next logon event (Icons are on the Start menu or desktop.)	Automatically installed on reboot*
Is the software installed when an associated file is opened?	Yes	Yes	Already installed
Can a user remove the software?	Yes, using Programs And Features	Yes, but the software is available again after the next logon	No, but software repairs are allowed. Local administrators can uninstall.
Package types supported	Windows Installer and .zap files	Windows Installer	Windows installer

Windows XP and Windows Vista clients process Group Policy asynchronously as a background refresh during startup and logon, which shortens startup times but requires two restarts to install assigned software to computers and users at logon.

Creating a Software Distribution Point

To deploy applications using Group Policy, first create a software distribution point on the network that contains the setup files for the applications. (Make sure you have appropriate licenses for the applications.)

To create a software distribution point, use the following steps:

1. Design and create a DFS or shared folder structure for software.

2. Set the following NTFS permissions on the software distribution folder. (Set the share permissions to Everyone = Full Control to prevent conflicting file and share permissions.)

   - Authenticated Users = Read and Execute
   - Domain Computers = Read and Execute
   - Administrators = Full Control

IMPORTANT Permissions that are incorrectly set are a common cause of problems when deploying software with Group Policy, so verify that file and share permissions are set properly on the software distribution folder.

3. Copy the application setup files to the folder created in step 1, or use an administrative setup command to install the setup files to the folder.

Consult the software manufacturer for specific instructions and recommendations.

NOTE To publish the software distribution folder in Active Directory so that users can find the folder when searching Active Directory for shared folders, right-click the appropriate container in the Active Directory Users And Computers console, choose New, select Shared Folder, and then type the path of the DFS folder or shared folder in the Network Path box.

Creating a GPO for Software Deployment

Create a new GPO for deployed applications by following these steps:

1. Open Group Policy Management from the Administrative Tools folder on the Start menu.

2. Right-click the domain or OU where you want to create the GPO and select Create A GPO In This Domain, And Link It Here, as shown in Figure 20-13.

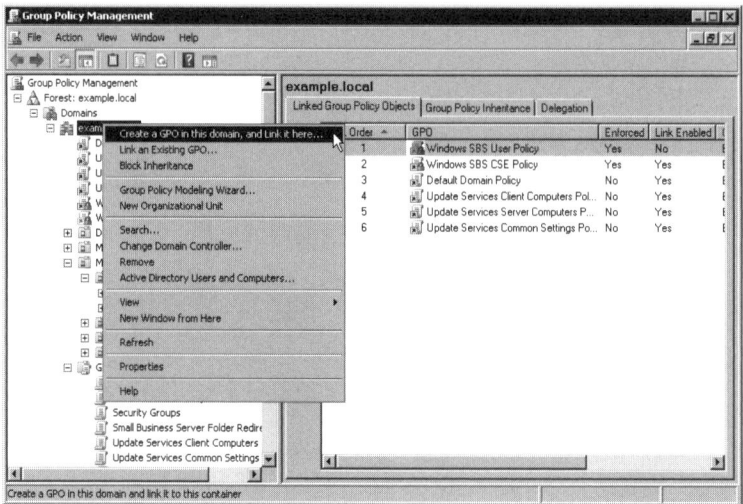

FIGURE 20-13 Creating a new GPO

3. In the New GPO dialog box, type in a name for the GPO as shown in Figure 20-14 and click OK.

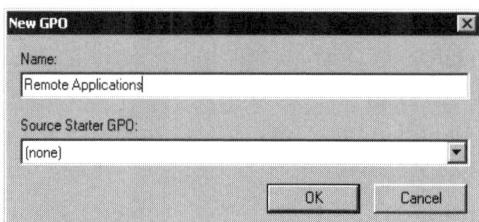

FIGURE 20-14 Providing a name for the new GPO

4. Navigate to the new GPO in the left pane and under Security Filtering click Add to assign this GPO to specific users or computers.

Configuring the Group Policy Software Installation Extension

There are a number of options that control how Group Policy deploys and manages software packages. These options determine how packages are added to the GPO, the amount of control users have over an installation, and the default application for a given file extension, as well as which categories you can use for grouping applications. The following sections cover these options.

NOTE Software installation settings for applications deployed to users are not shared with applications that are deployed to computers. Each type of deployment maintains its own set of applications and settings.

Setting Software Installation Options

To change the default settings for the Group Policy Software Installation extension, first open the Software Installation Properties dialog box by performing the following steps:

1. Open the Group Policy Management console from the Administrative Tools menu.

2. Right-click the GPO you created for application deployment and select Edit.

3. Under Computer Configuration or User Configuration, expand Policies and then expand Software Settings.

4. Right-click Software Installation and select Properties, as shown in Figure 20-15, to open the Software Installation Properties dialog box.

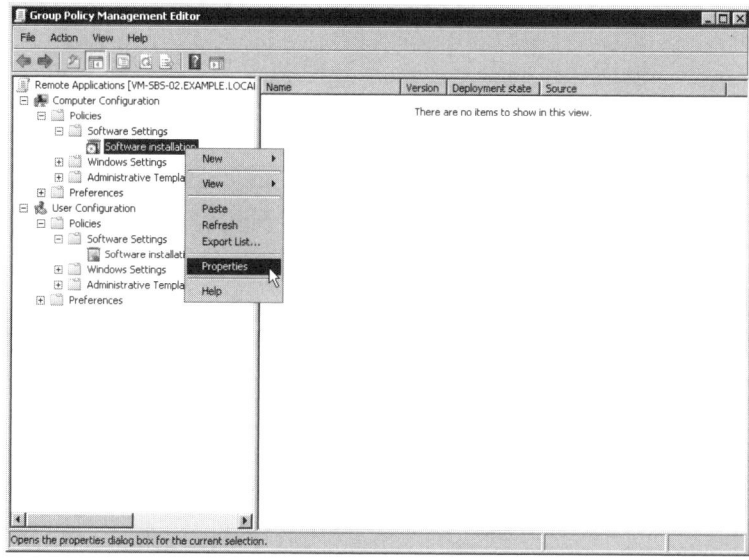

FIGURE 20-15 Selecting Software Installation properties

NOTE Software Installation settings for applications deployed to users are not shared with applications that are deployed to computers. Each type of deployment maintains its own set of applications and settings.

5. On the General tab (Figure 20-16), specify the location of the software distribution point.

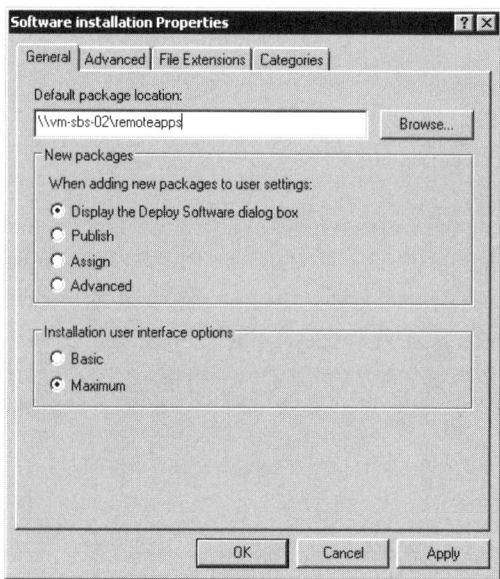

FIGURE 20-16 The Software Installation Properties dialog box

6. In the New Packages area, specify the default behavior for new software packages. Table 20-3 shows the choices.

TABLE 20-3 Default Behavior Options When Adding New Packages

OPTION	WHAT IT DOES
Display The Deploy Software Dialog Box	Displays a dialog box asking whether to publish (User Configuration only) or assign the application, or whether to customize the configuration
Publish (User Configuration Only)	Automatically publishes the application using default settings
Assign	Automatically assigns the application using default settings
Advanced	Displays the applications advanced properties allowing a customized installation

7. In the Installation User Interface Options area, choose Basic for limited visibility to the user of the installation process; choose Maximum for full visibility during installation.

8. Click the Advanced tab to set additional options for the software packages under this GPO:

- To uninstall applications automatically when the GPO no longer applies to the user or computer, select Uninstall The Applications When They Fall Out Of The Scope Of Management.

- To add OLE information as part of the application deployment, select Include OLE Information When Deploying Applications.

- To allow standard .MSI applications to be deployed to 64-bit computers, select Make 32-Bit X86 Windows Installer Applications Available To Win64 Machines. (This is the default behavior.)

- To allow legacy 32-bit applications (.zap files) to be deployed to 64-bit computers, select Make 32-Bit X86 Down-level (.zap) Applications Available To Win64 Machines.

9. To set up a list of software categories, thereby making it easier for users to find the applications they want, click the Categories tab, click Add, and type the category name. Categories apply to the entire domain, not just the current GPO. Click OK when finished.

> **NOTE** The File Extensions tab will be empty when you first create a new GPO, because Windows lists only file extensions associated with packages already present in the GPO. Later you can return to this tab to select the order in which file extensions should be recognized.

Adding a Software Package to a Group Policy

Before Group Policy can assign or publish applications that you copy to the software distribution point discussed earlier in this chapter, you must add the installation packages to the GPO. To add a package to a GPO, follow these steps:

1. Install the application to the software distribution point using an administrative setup command or by manually copying the setup files, as discussed in the section titled "Creating a Software Distribution Point" earlier in this chapter.

2. Open the Group Policy Management console from the Administrative Tools menu.

3. Right-click the GPO you created for application deployment and select Edit to open the Group Policy Management Editor.

4. Select either User Configuration or Computer Configuration, expand Policies, and then expand Software Settings.

5. Right-click Software Installation, choose New, and then choose Package, as shown in Figure 20-17.

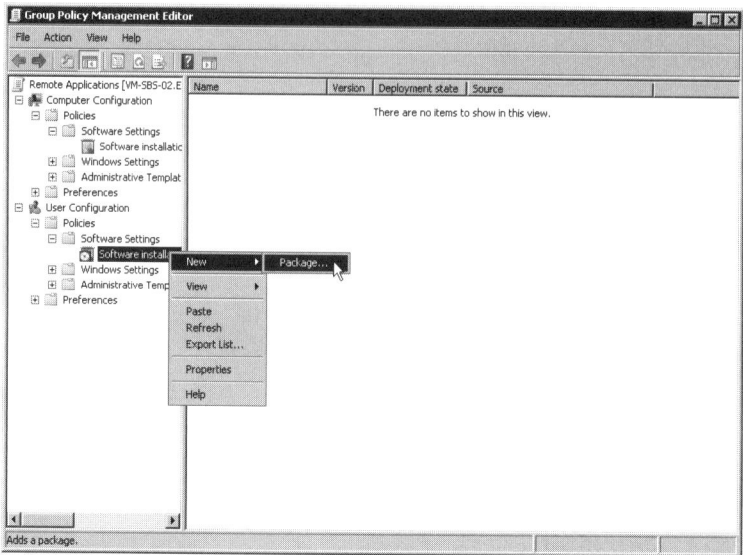

FIGURE 20-17 Installing a new software package

6. Select either the Windows Installer Package (*.msi) or select a file type from the drop-down list of file types. (Note that you can deploy .zap files only to users, not computers.)

7. Navigate to the software distribution point you created and select the package, as shown in Figure 20-18. Do not use a local file path.

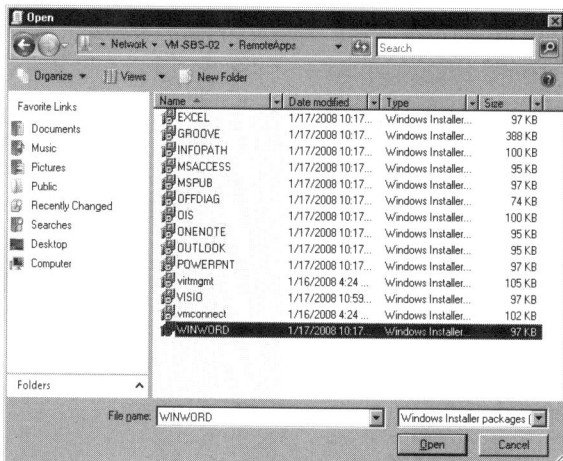

FIGURE 20-18 Selecting a software distribution package

8. Click Open to open the Deploy Software dialog box and choose from the following options for how to deploy the package. When you have made your selections, click OK.

- Select Published to publish the application in Active Directory with the default settings (available only with User Configuration).

- Select Assigned to assign the application with the default properties.
- Select Advanced to modify how Windows deploys the application.

NOTE Windows deploys packages after the second logon or restart for Windows XP clients, after the first logon or restart for Windows 2000 clients, and after the first logon or restart if you enable the Always Wait For The Network At Computer Startup And Logon policy.

Group Policy Preferences

Group Policy Preferences help you configure, deploy, and manage operating system and application settings that you cannot manage by using Group Policy. Examples include mapped drives, scheduled tasks, and Start menu settings. Using Group Policy Preferences is often a better alternative than logon scripts for configuring these settings. Group Policy Preferences are built into the Group Policy Management console.

Networks customarily have two types of settings: enforced settings (Group Policy) and optional settings (preferences). Enforced settings can't be changed by users. Preferences, on the other hand, can be changed by users. By specifically deploying preferences, you can create configurations that are more suitable for your organization than the operating system's default settings. Deploying preferences is usually done through logon scripts or default user profiles.

So what are the differences between Group Policy Preferences and Group Policy? The primary difference is that Group Policy is enforced and Group Policy Preferences are not. Table 20-4 shows the other key differences.

TABLE 20-4 Group Policy v. Group Policy Preferences

GROUP POLICY SETTINGS	GROUP POLICY PREFERENCES
Settings are enforced.	Preferences are not enforced.
User interface is disabled.	User interface is not disabled.
Adding policy settings requires application support and constructing Administrative templates.	Preference items for files and registry settings are easily created.
Requires Group Policy–aware applications	Supports non-Group Policy–aware applications
Filtering is based on Windows Management Instrumentation (WMI) and requires writing WMI queries.	Supports item-level targeting.
Alternative user interface is provided for most policy settings.	Uses a familiar, easy-to-use interface for configuring most settings.

Figure 20-19 shows a decision tree for choosing between Group Policy settings and Group Policy Preferences.

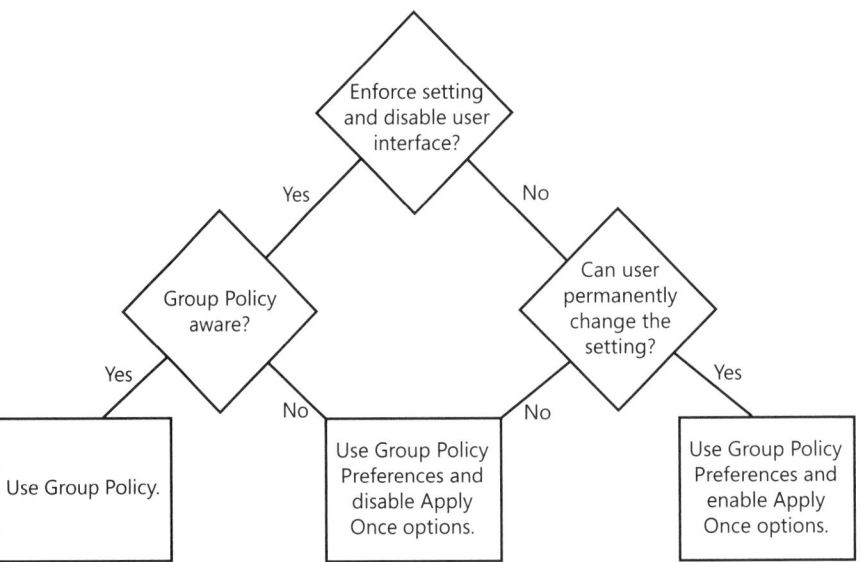

FIGURE 20-19 Deciding between Group Policy and Group Policy Preferences

To view Group Policy Preferences, start Group Policy Management from the Administrative Tools menu and follow these steps:

1. Navigate to Group Policy Objects. Right-click Default Domain Controllers Policy and select Edit.

2. Under Computer Configuration, expand Preferences, expand Windows Settings, and then expand Control Panel Settings.

3. Under User Configuration, expand Preferences, expand Windows Settings, and then expand Control Panel Settings.

As you can see in Figure 20-20, the Computer Configuration and User Configuration lists are very similar. However, even when the names are identical, the properties may differ. The following preferences do not overlap: Applications, Drive Maps, Internet Settings, Regional Options, and Start Menu under User Configuration; and Network Shares and Network Options under Computer Configuration.

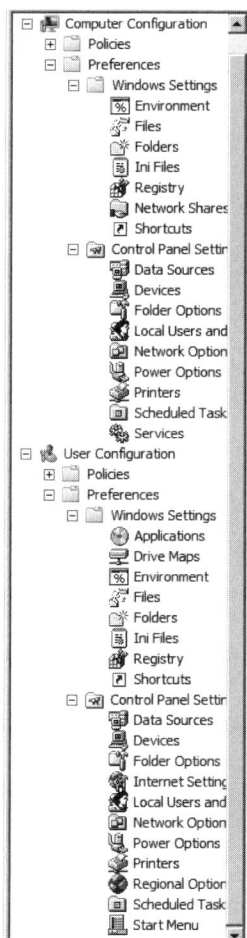

FIGURE 20-20 Group Policy Preferences extensions

Using Group Policy Preferences for Windows

Like Group Policy settings, preferences are almost infinitely configurable. In the next sections, we'll discuss a sample of these extensions, beginning with the Windows settings.

Drive Maps

The Drive Maps setting allows you to create, update, and delete mapped drives and their properties. To create a mapped drive preference item, follow these steps:

1. Start Group Policy Management.

2. Right-click the GPO that will contain the new preference item and then click Edit.

3. In the console tree, navigate to User Configuration, expand the Preferences folder, and then expand the Windows Settings folder. Right-click the Drive Maps node, point to New, and select Mapped Drive.

4. In the New Drive Properties dialog box, select one of the following actions for Group Policy to perform:

- **Create** Creates a new mapped drive
- **Replace** Deletes an existing mapped drive and creates a new one
- **Update** Changes specific settings of an existing mapped drive
- **Delete** Removes a mapped drive

5. Enter drive map settings, which are described in Table 20-5.

TABLE 20-5 Drive Map Settings

SETTING NAME	ACTION	DESCRIPTION
Location	Create, Replace, or Update	To create or replace an existing mapped drive, type in a fully qualified UNC path. To modify an existing drive mapping, leave this field empty. Note: This field also accepts processing variables. Press F3 for a list of acceptable variables.
Reconnect	Create, Replace, or Update	Select this box to save the mapped drive in the user's settings and reconnect to it at subsequent logons.
Label As	Create, Replace, or Update	Provide a descriptive label. This field also accepts preference processing variables. Press F5 for a list.
Drive Letter	Create, Replace, or Update	To assign the first available drive letter, select Use First Available Starting At and choose a drive letter. To assign a specific drive letter, select Use and then select a drive letter.
Drive Letter	Update	To change an existing drive mapping, select Existing and then select the drive letter.
Drive Letter	Delete	To delete all drive mappings, select Delete All, Starting At and then select the beginning drive letter. To delete a specific mapping, select Delete and then select the drive letter.

SETTING NAME	ACTION	DESCRIPTION
Connect As	Create, Replace, or Update	To map a drive using credentials other than those of the currently logged-on user, type the name and password to be used.
Hide/Show This Drive	Create, Replace, or Update	To prevent the drive from being displayed in Windows Explorer, select Hide This Drive. To allow it to display, select Show This Drive. These settings take priority over the Hide/Show All Drives setting.

6. Click the Common tab and select the options you want. For more information, see the section titled "Configuring Common Options" later in this chapter.

7. Click OK. The new preference items displays in the details pane.

The new mapped drive will display when a user logs on (Figure 20-21).

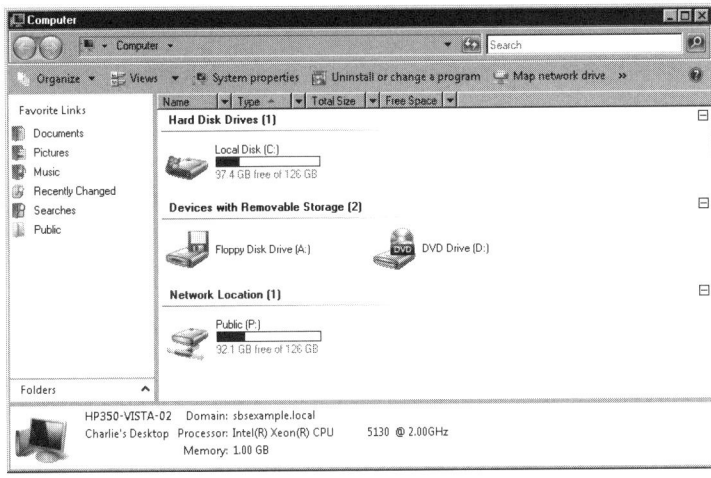

FIGURE 20-21 A drive mapped by Group Policy Preferences

Files

With the Files preference extension, you can copy, modify the attributes of, replace, or delete files. The extension supports wildcard characters in file paths and environment variables.

Before configuring a file preference item, review the behavior of each type of action and setting shown in Table 20-6.

TABLE 20-6 File Settings

SETTING	ACTION	DESCRIPTION
Source File(s)	Create, Replace, or Update	Enter the location from which to copy the source file. The field can include variables. You can use a local or mapped drive or a fully qualified UNC path.
Destination File	Create, Replace, or Update and the Source File(s) field includes wildcards	Enter the location to which to copy files or the location of the files to be changed. You can use a local or mapped drive (from the perspective of the client) or a fully qualified UNC path.
Delete File(s)	Delete	Type the path to the file(s) from the perspective of the client. The field can include wildcard characters.
Suppress Errors On Individual File Actions	Replace, Update, or Delete	Select this check box to allow multiple files to transfer during the replace, delete, or update operation even if one or more files fail to transfer.
Attributes	Create, Replace, or Update	Select attributes for the file(s) being transferred. If necessary to complete an operation, the Read Only attribute will be reset.

To create a new file preference item, follow these steps:

1. Start Group Policy Management from the Administrative Tools menu.
2. Right-click the Group Policy object (GPO) that will contain the new preference item and then click Edit.
3. In the console tree under Computer Configuration or User Configuration, expand the Preferences folder and then expand the Windows Settings folder.
4. Right-click Files, point to New, and select File.
5. In the New Files Properties dialog box, select one of the following actions from the drop-down list:

   - **Create** Copies a file or multiple files from a source to a destination and then configures the file attributes for computers or users.
   - **Delete** Removes a file or multiple files.
   - **Replace** Overwrites files at the destination location with replacement files. If the file does not exist at the destination, the Replace action copies the file from the source location to the destination.
   - **Update** Modifies attributes of an existing file.

6. Enter the file settings, which are described in Table 20-6.

7. Click the Common tab and select the options you want. (For more information, see the next section, titled "Configuring Common Options.")

8. Click OK. The new preference item appears in the details pane.

Configuring Common Options

All Group Policy preference items have a Common tab and many items share common options, including the following:

- **Stop Processing Items In This Extension If An Error Occurs** More than one item can be configured in each extension. If this option is selected, a failed preference item will stop the remaining preference items from processing.

> **NOTE** Preference items are processed from the bottom of the list, moving toward the top. If you select this option, items processed before the failing item will still be processed successfully. This option only stops preference items that follow the failed item.

- **Run In Logged-On User's Security Context (User Policy Option)** By default, user preferences are processed using the security context of the SYSTEM account. Select this option and the preference items are processed in the security context of the logged-on user. This lets the preference extension access resources as the user and not as the computer. This can make a difference when using mapped drives and other network resources.

- **Remove This Item When It Is No Longer Applied** By default, Group Policy doesn't remove preferences when the GPO is removed from the user or computer. Select this option and the preference item is removed when the GPO is removed.

- **Apply Once And Do Not Reapply** The results of preference items are rewritten each time Group Policy refreshes, which is every 90 minutes by default. Select this option and preferences will apply once for the computer, no matter how many users share the computer. Select this option in user configuration and the item will be applied once on each computer the user logs in to.

- **Item-Level Targeting** You can use item-level targeting to apply preference items to individual users and computers. You can include multiple preference items, each tailored for selected users or computers and each targeted to apply settings only to the relevant users or computers.

Using Group Policy Preferences for Control Panel

In addition to the Windows category, you can make preference settings under Control Panel.

Devices

Use the Devices preference item to centralize the enabling or disabling of specific types of hardware for users or computers. You may configure an entire class of devices such as Ports (COM & LPT) or narrow the selection to a particular type of device such as Communications Port (COM2). To configure a Device preference item, follow these steps:

1. Start the Group Policy Management console.
2. Right-click the GPO that will contain the new preference item and then click Edit.
3. In the console tree under Computer Configuration or User Configuration, expand the Preferences folder and then expand the Control Panel Settings folder.
4. Right-click Devices, point to New, and select Device.
5. In the New Device Properties dialog box, select Use This Device (Enable) or Do Not Use This Device (Disable) from the Action drop-down list.
6. Enter the Device settings. (See Table 20-7 for descriptions.)
7. Click the Common tab and select the desired options. (For more information, see the section titled "Configuring Common Options" earlier in this chapter.)
8. Click OK. The new preference item appears in the details pane.

TABLE 20-7 Device Settings

SETTING	ACTION	DESCRIPTION
Device Class	Enable or Disable	Click the Browse button to select the enabled or disabled device class plus the device type, if required.
Device Type	Enable or Disable	If a device type is selected, it will appear in this field.

Using Group Policy Results

The Group Policy Results tool gathers information on all existing policies to determine the policies in effect and the order in which they are applied. To use Group Policy Results, follow these steps:

1. Open Group Policy Management from the Administrative Tools menu.
2. Right-click Group Policy Results and select Group Policy Results Wizard. Click Next.
3. On the Computer Selection page, accept the default setting of This Computer or select Another Computer. Click Next.
4. On the User Selection page (Figure 20-22), select the user for whom you want to view policy settings. Click Next.

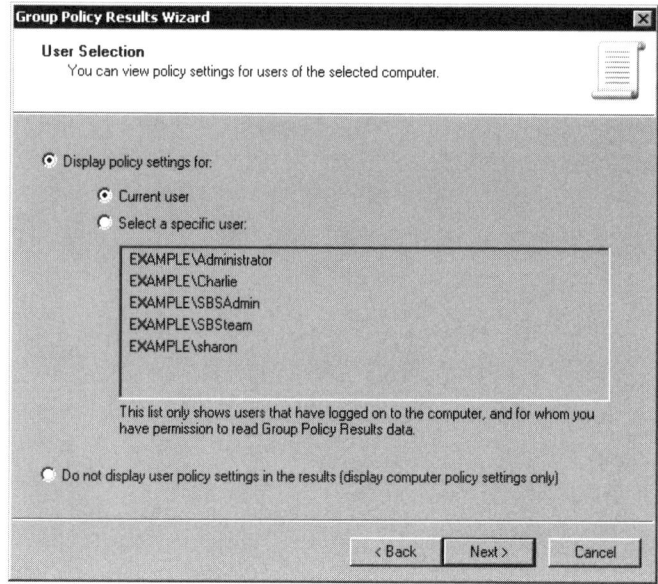

FIGURE 20-22 The User Selection page in the Group Policy Results Wizard

5. Review your selection on the Summary Of Selections page. Click Back to change the selections. Click Next to accept them. Click Finish.

Review the Group Policy Results. You can also right-click the report name and select Advanced View (Figure 20-23). This will open a Resultant Set Of Policy (Figure 20-24) that details every aspect of policy for the selected user or computer.

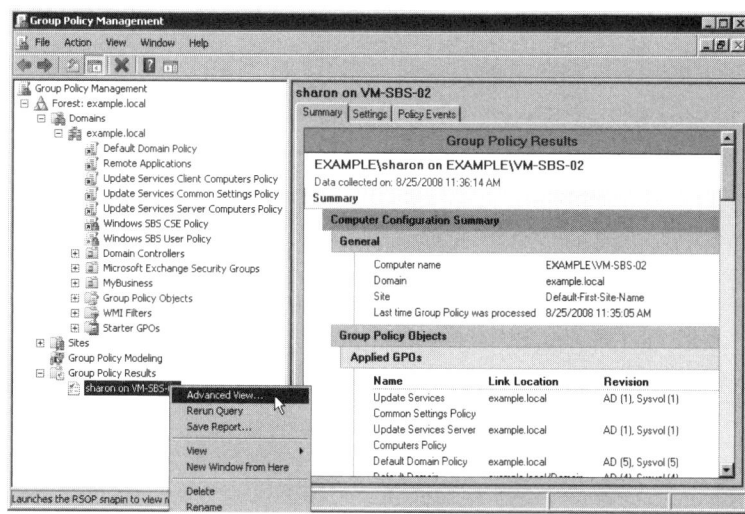

FIGURE 20-23 Group Policy Results

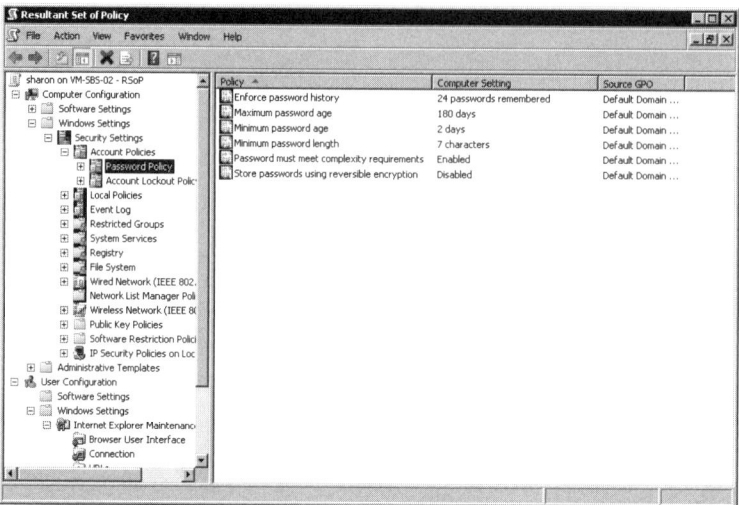

FIGURE 20-24 Advanced view of Group Policy Results

Summary

In this chapter, we've described some common uses of Group Policy and Group Policy Preferences, all in pursuit of organizing and centralizing security and other settings. In the next chapter, we move on to configuring and gathering reports on your Windows SBS network's operations.

Managing Reports

Monitoring and analyzing network reports is frequently far down on an administrator's to-do list. Reports get attention only when something goes wrong or there's a strong suspicion that something is about to go horribly wrong. The purpose of this chapter is to encourage even a modest amount of attention to reports *before* that oh-no moment arrives.

Windows SBS comes with detailed reports built in. These reports are already configured and scheduled, though you can modify all settings. In addition, you can create your own reports for specific circumstances. First, we'll review the two built-in reports—the Summary Network Report and the Detailed Network Report.

Network Reports

To view the default Summary Network Report, open the SBS Console, click Reports, and then highlight Summary Network Report, as shown in Figure 21-1.

This report is run once a day by default. The Detailed Network Report (Figure 21-2) runs once a week by default. Both these times and frequencies can be reconfigured.

The summary and detailed reports have exactly the same options, just configured differently. Both have the same content and schedule options and you can configure e-mail options in the same way.

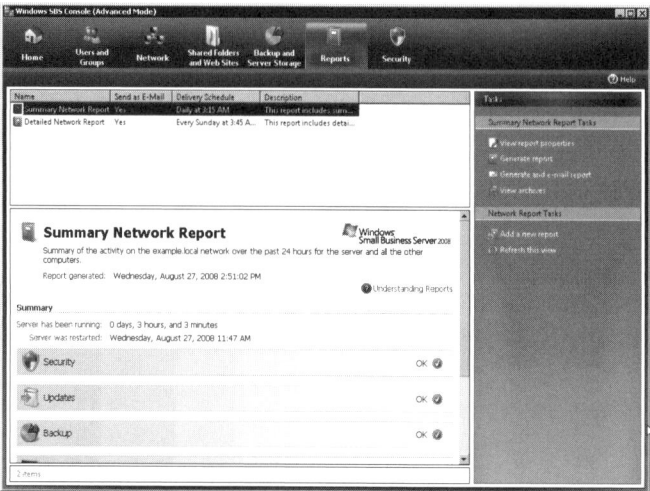

FIGURE 21-1 Viewing the Summary Network Report

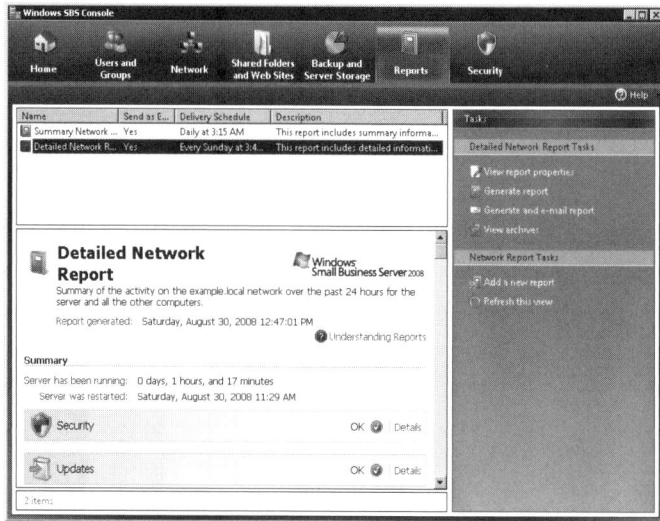

FIGURE 21-2 The weekly Detailed Network Report

Customizing the Summary Report

The default Summary Network Report really doesn't tell you much more than you can see on the Home page of the Windows SBS Console. However, you can easily customize it to display selected reports on network health. To customize the Summary Network Report, follow these steps:

1. Click Reports in the Windows SBS Console.

2. Right-click the Summary Network Report and select View Report Properties.

3. The Summary Network Report Properties dialog box opens on the General page. You can change both the report name and description by typing in new ones. Click Content.

4. On the Content page, shown in Figure 21-3, select the areas you want to include on the report.

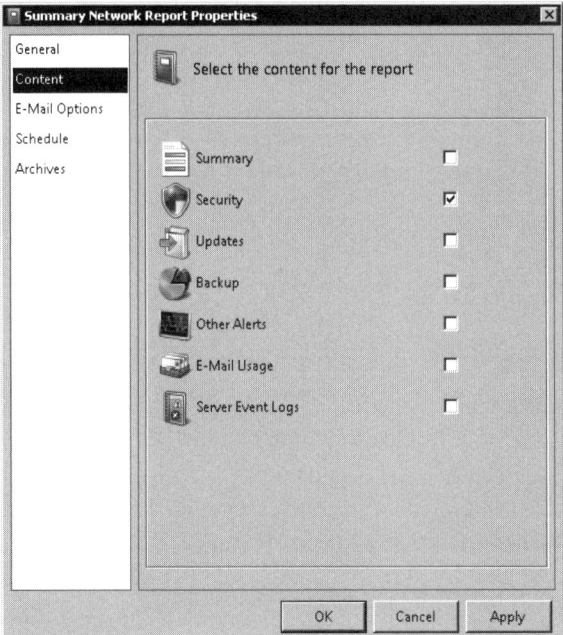

FIGURE 21-3 Selecting the content to include in the Summary Report

5. Click E-Mail Options. Select the user accounts that should receive the report when it's generated. Enter the e-mail addresses for additional recipients in the Other E-mail Addresses box. When you enter multiple e-mail addresses, separate each address with a semicolon.

6. Select Schedule to specify the frequency and time when the report will be generated.

7. Click Archives to view a list of past reports. To see a report, select a report and click View Report. The report will display in an Internet Explorer window (Figure 21-4). Click OK when finished.

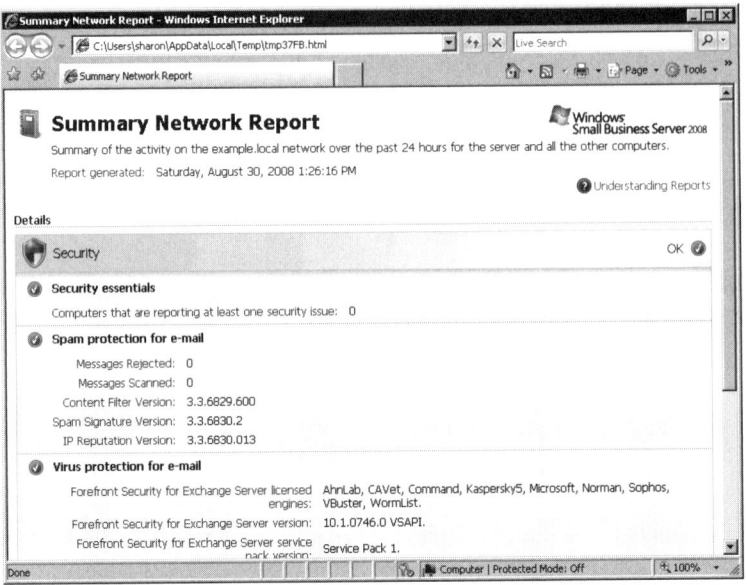

FIGURE 21-4 Viewing an archived Summary Report

NOTE When editing report properties, you don't need to go through the pages in order. Select only the ones you need to modify and click OK when finished.

Customizing the Detailed Report

To customize the Detailed Network Report, follow these steps:

1. Click Reports in the Windows SBS Console.

2. Right-click Detailed Network Report and select View Report Properties.

3. The Detailed Network Report Properties dialog box opens on the General page. You can change both the report name and description by typing in new ones. Click Content.

4. On the Content page, select the areas you want to include on the report.

5. Click E-Mail Options. Select the user accounts that should receive the report when it's generated, as shown in Figure 21-5. Enter the e-mail addresses for additional recipients in the Other E-Mail Addresses box. When you enter multiple e-mail addresses, separate each address with a semicolon.

6. Click Schedule to specify the frequency and time the report will be generated. The day of the week and time can be changed for weekly reports, or you can choose a daily report and specify the time of day to generate the report (Figure 21-6).

7. Click Archives to view a list of past reports. To see a report, select it and click View Report. The report will display in an Internet Explorer window. Click OK when finished.

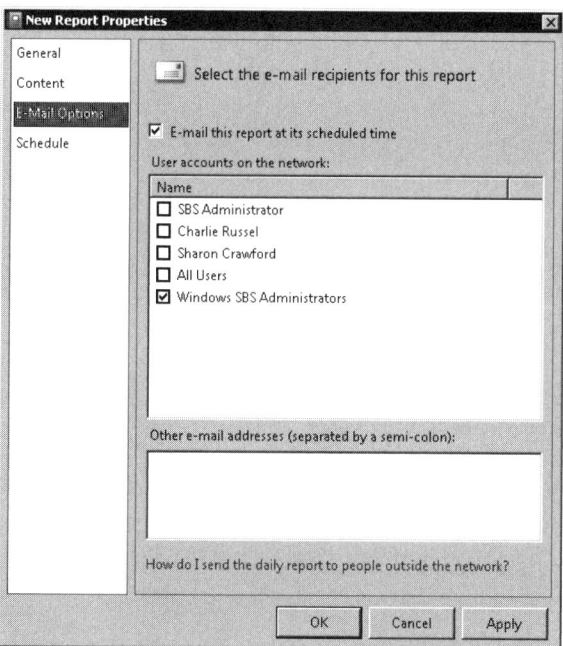

FIGURE 21-5 Selecting e-mail accounts that will receive the report

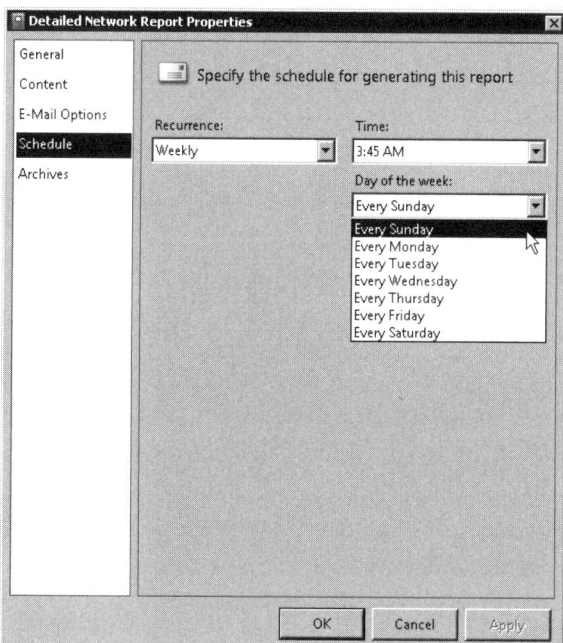

FIGURE 21-6 Changing the report schedule

Creating a New Report

Using the same format as the Summary and Detailed Reports, you can build a new report to suit your specific needs. For example, let's say you outsource certain administrative tasks, and you want to send a regular security report to the person who handles the outsourced tasks. You'd follow these steps to create that report:

1. Click Reports in the Windows SBS Console.

2. In the Tasks pane, click Add A New Report.

3. On the General page, type in a name and description for the report, as shown in Figure 21-7.

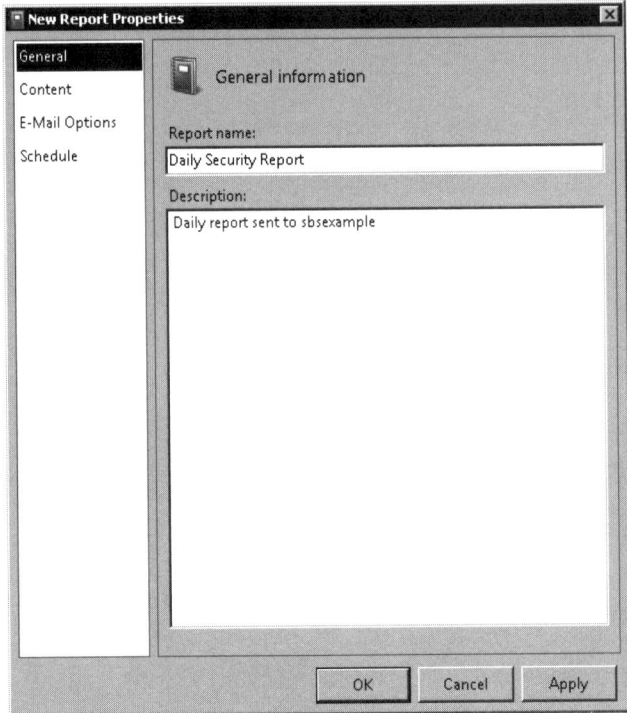

FIGURE 21-7 Creating a new custom report

4. Click Content. Select the subject(s) you want included in the report.

5. Click E-Mail Options. Select the addresses to e-mail the report to and add the addresses of any others not already listed (Figure 21-8). When you enter multiple e-mail addresses, separate each address with a semicolon.

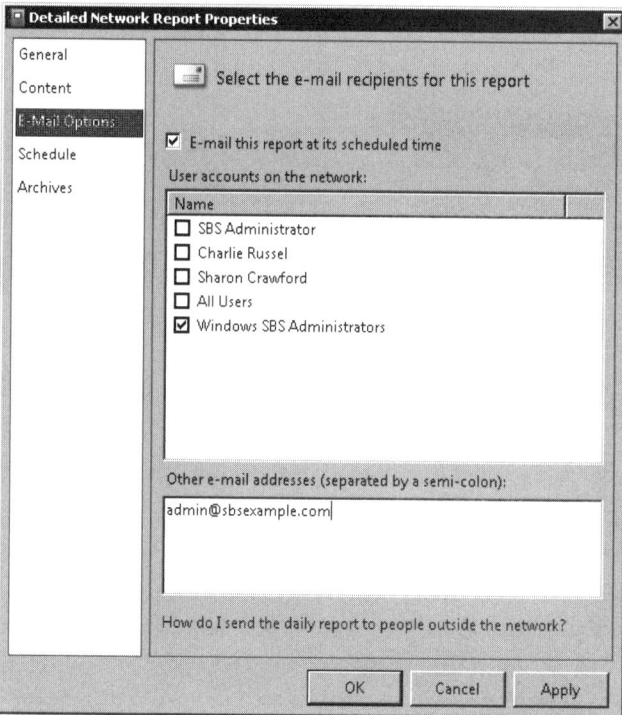

FIGURE 21-8 Selecting e-mail addresses that will receive the report

6. Click Schedule to specify the frequency and time when the report will be generated. The day of the week and time can be changed for weekly reports. Or you can choose a daily report and specify the time of day to generate the report.

7. Click OK when you're finished to save the new report and add it to the list in the Windows SBS console.

NOTE The Archives page isn't available until the report has been saved.

Configuring Alerts

Windows SBS has a large set of included alerts. To view the alerts, select Network in the Windows SBS Console and then select Computers. In the Tasks pane, click View Notification Settings.

In the Notification Settings dialog box, there are three pages of notifications to choose from.

Alerts for Services

On the Services page (Figure 21-9), you'll find a list of services with their startup type.

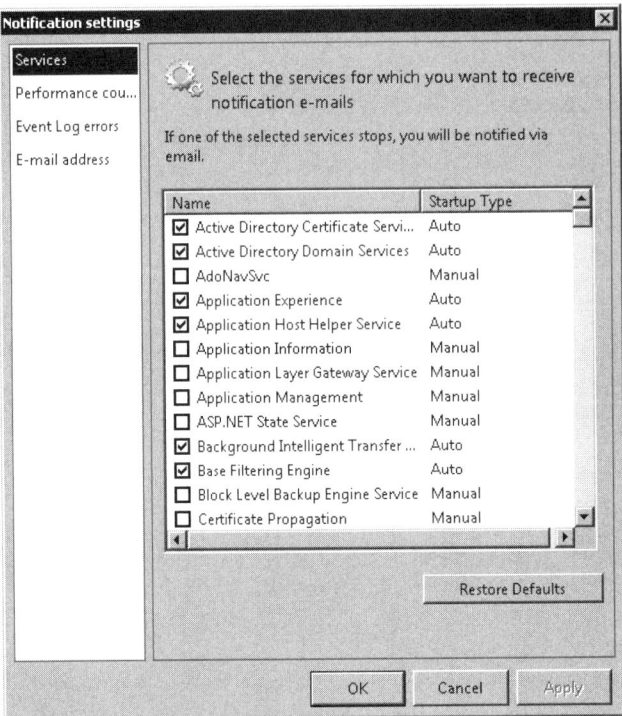

FIGURE 21-9 Setting notifications for services

As you can see, many of the services are already marked for notification. Select additional services to receive notification if the service stops. When a service stops, an alert is sent to the Home page of Windows SBS Console and will also appear on any subsequently generated Summary or Detailed Report that includes other alerts, as shown in Figure 21-10.

> **NOTE** Click E-Mail Address and specify an e-mail address to receive notifications. To send to multiple e-mail addresses, separate them using a semicolon.

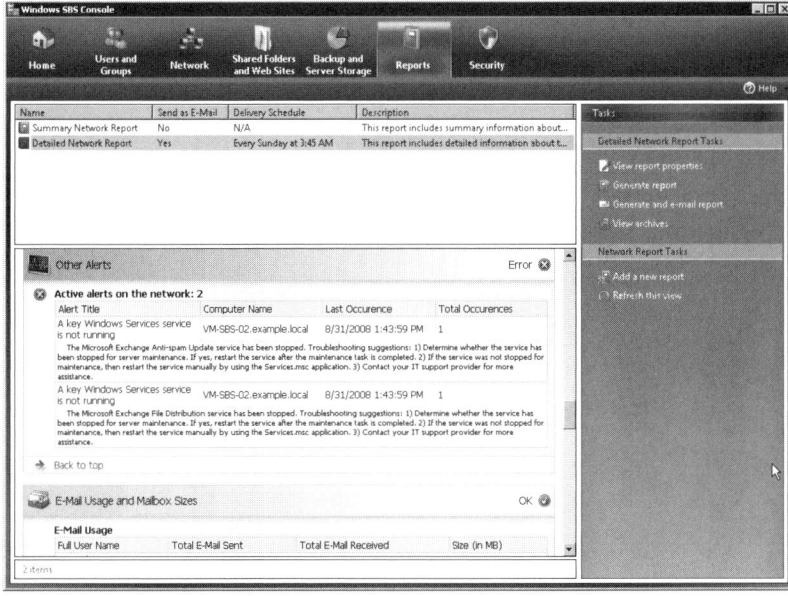

FIGURE 21-10 An alert that services have stopped

Performance Counter Alert

On the Performance Counter page of the Notification Settings dialog box, Percent Free Disk Space is selected by default. You can clear the check box to remove the notification, though we'd be hard-pressed to understand why anyone would do so.

To change the threshold for the notification, highlight Percent Free Disk Space and then click Edit. In the Edit box (Figure 21-11), enter a threshold for notification. Click OK when finished.

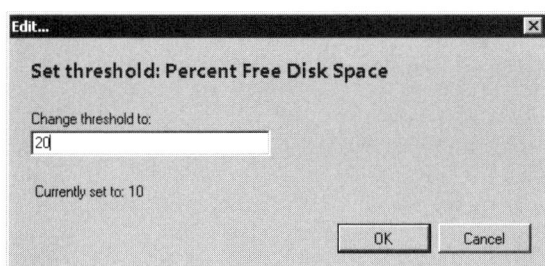

FIGURE 21-11 Changing the notification threshold

Event Log Error Alerts

On the Event Log Errors page shown in Figure 21-12, a large number of potential Event Log errors are listed.

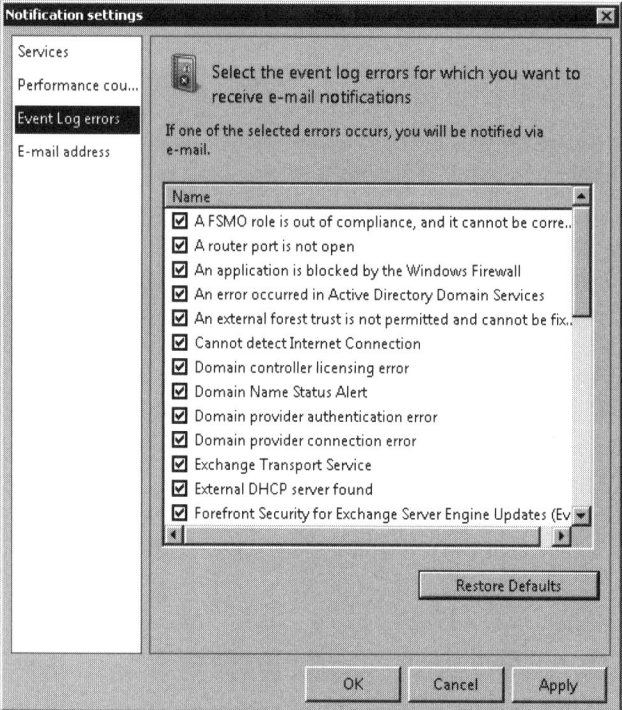

FIGURE 21-12 Selecting Event Log error notifications

Select or clear errors according to your needs. Click OK when finished.

> **NOTE** Click E-Mail Address and specify an e-mail address to receive notifications. To send to multiple e-mail addresses, use a semicolon to separate addresses.

Creating Custom Alerts

You can create a custom alert that adds alert information to reports and enables users to receive e-mail notifications when the specified event occurs. The custom alert provides information about a specific event that has occurred, which will enable a system administrator to quickly correct a problem.

Creating an Alert for a Stopped Service

Creating an alert is a multistep process but not at all difficult. In this example, we'll configure an alert to appear when the Exchange Transport Service fails to start.

Acquire a GUID

To create a custom alert, you need to first acquire a GUID (globally unique identifier) that will be assigned to the alert. To acquire a GUID, complete these steps:

1. Select All Programs from the Start menu and then click Windows PowerShell.

2. At the command prompt, type the following command:

   ```
   [System.Guid]::NewGuid().ToString()
   ```

3. Record the GUID that's returned (see Figure 20-13).

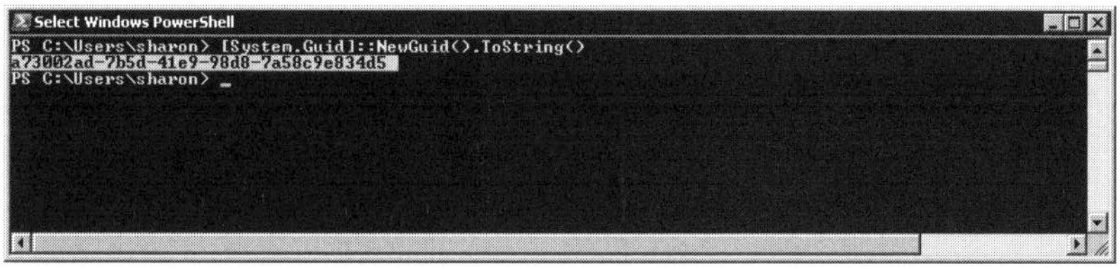

FIGURE 21-13 Acquiring a GUID

> **NOTE** An even easier way to get a GUID is to go to *www.guidgen.com* and a GUID is generated the moment you connect. Copy it and save it for use later.

Find Event Information

Next, you must obtain information about the event that will be associated with the custom alert. To acquire the information you need, follow these steps:

1. Select Event Viewer from the Administrative Tools menu.

2. Locate the event log where the event is recorded. In this example, we're creating an alert that will appear when a particular service fails to start.

3. In the events pane (Figure 21-14), select the event to associate with the custom alert. (For this example, we're using an event with the ID of 7000.) The event ID will be used later in this document, so make note of the number.

4. Click the Details tab and select Friendly View. Click the plus sign to expand System as shown in Figure 21-14.

5. Make note of the Provider Name and Channel.

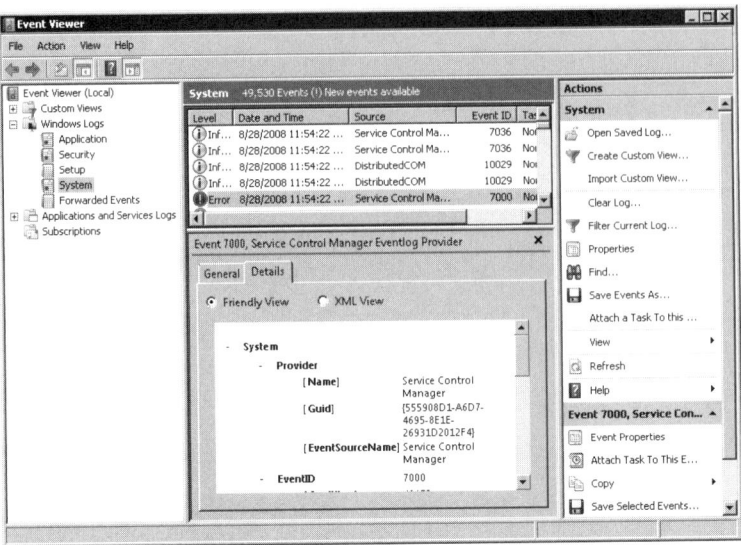

FIGURE 21-14 Viewing event information

Create and Save an .xml File

Next, to create an .xml file that contains the elements and attributes to generate the custom alert, follow these steps:

1. Open NotePad.

2. Add the following data to the NotePad file:

```xml
<?xml version="1.0" encoding="utf-8" ?>
<AlertDefinitions>
  <AlertDefinition ID=" a73002ad-7b5d-41e9-98d8-7a58c9e834d5"
                   Default="1"
                   Title="Exchange Transport Service"
                   Source="Service Control Manager">
  </AlertDefinition>
</AlertDefinitions>
<Parameters>
  <Path>System</Path>
  <Provider>Service Control Manager</Provider>
  <SetEventID>7000</SetEventID>
  <ClearEventID>7036</ClearEventID>
</Parameters>
```

Table 21-1 lists the attributes and parameters for the alert definition.

TABLE 21-1 Attributes and Parameters for a Custom Alert

PARAMETER	DESCRIPTION
ID	The GUID that uniquely identifies the custom alert. Use the GUID that you obtained earlier.
Default	Defines that the alert is enabled and will be preserved when defaults are restored.
Title	The name for the alert when displayed in Windows SBS Console.
Source	The application that the alert is monitoring. In this case, it's the Service Control Manager.
Path	Name of the event log where the alert is recorded. Use the Channel value you recorded.
Provider	Use the Provider name you acquired.
SetEventID	ID number of the event that triggers the alert.
ClearEventID	This is an optional element that specifies the ID number of the event that clears the alert. If this element is not defined, the alert will be cleared after 30 minutes. If this element is defined, the alert will only be cleared if the specified event occurs.

3. Save the file as *filename*.xml.

4. Copy the .xml file to the %programfiles%\Windows Small Business Server\Data\Monitoring\ExternalAlerts directory on the computer that is running the Windows SBS 2008 operating system.

5. Select Services from the Administrative Tools menu.

6. Right-click Windows SBS Manager service and select Restart (as shown in Figure 21-15).

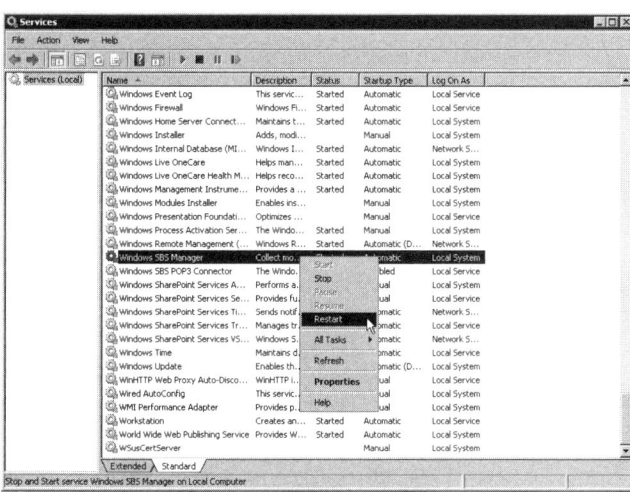

FIGURE 21-15 Restarting the SBS Manager service

Depending on the source for the alert, you may not see the notification for some time. Windows SBS Console polls for changes every 30 minutes, so if you want to check sooner than that, go to the Reports tab, right-click a report that includes Other Alerts (such as the Detailed Network Report), and select Generate Report.

The resultant report will show whether the custom alert has been activated (Figure 20-16).

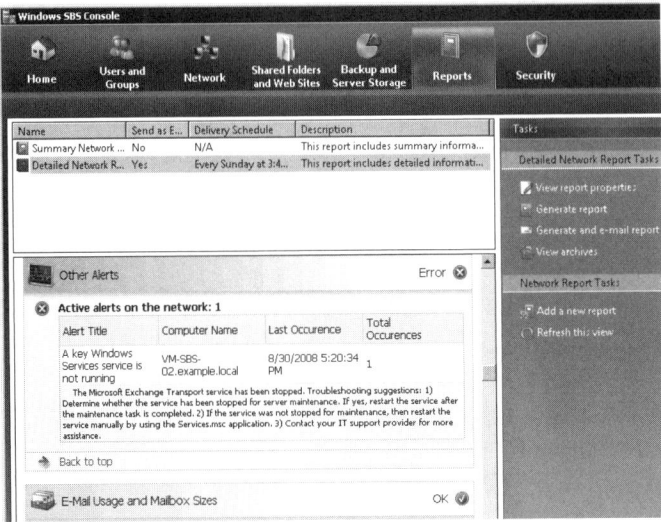

FIGURE 21-16 Report showing an activated custom alert

Custom Alert for Backup Failure

Backups are so crucial to the security of your network that when one fails, you want to know about it sooner rather than later. This section explains what you need to create an .xml file that will generate an alert.

Acquire a GUID

To acquire a GUID, complete these steps:

1. Select All Programs from the Start menu and then click Windows PowerShell.

2. At the command prompt, type the following command:

   ```
   [System.Guid]::NewGuid().ToString()
   ```

3. Make note of the GUID that's returned.

4. Open NotePad and add the following data to the NotePad file, substituting the GUID you acquired in the GUID field:

   ```
   <?xml version="1.0" encoding="utf-8" ?>
   <AlertDefinitions>
   <AlertDefinition ID="GUID" Default="1"
   ```

```
Title="Backup Failure" Source="Server">
    <Parameters>
    <Path>Application</Path>
    <Provider>Microsoft-Windows-Backup</Provider>
    <SetEventID>546</SetEventID>
    </Parameters>
</AlertDefinition>
</AlertDefinitions>
```

5. Save the file with the .xml extension and copy it into the %programfiles%\Windows Small Business Server\Data\Monitoring\ExternalAlerts directory on the computer that is running the Windows SBS 2008 operating system.

6. Select Services from the Administrative Tools menu. Right-click the Windows SBS Manager service and then click Restart.

NOTE For more on building your own alerts as well as security add-ins, visit *http://msdn.microsoft.com/en-us/library/cc721702.aspx.* Additional custom alerts can be downloaded free at *www.codeplex.com/sbs.*

Summary

In this chapter, we've covered the somewhat limited Reports component of the Windows SBS Console. Fortunately, more detailed notifications can be had through View Notification Settings and particularly through devising custom alerts.

Next, we move on to creating and customizing a useful Windows SharePoint site on the network.

Customizing a SharePoint Site

W indows Small Business Server 2008 includes Windows SharePoint Services 3.0 Service Pack 1, and the SBS installation automatically creates an internal Web site called Companyweb, which is a custom SharePoint site designed for small businesses. This default site meets the needs of most small businesses with little customization required, but you can easily add features to Companyweb to make it even more useful for your environment and needs without being a developer or Web designer.

SharePoint keeps getting better with each version, and whole books have been written about how to create, manage, and develop for SharePoint sites. We won't pretend to try to cover everything, but in this chapter we'll cover some of the features and configuration of Companyweb and SharePoint in general, and show you how to add a useful set of links to TS RemoteApps.

Introducing SharePoint Services

Windows SharePoint Services is a Web-based collaboration and document management system that is easily and quickly deployed to provide an effective intranet solution for businesses of all sizes. In SBS, SharePoint is installed automatically, and an internal Web site (*http://companyweb*), shown in Figure 22-1, is created and configured with a range of features that make sense for small businesses.

> **NOTE** In this chapter, we shorten Windows SharePoint Services to simply SharePoint. Windows SharePoint Server 2007, which is designed for hosting multiple, independent, SharePoint portals, is a separate product.

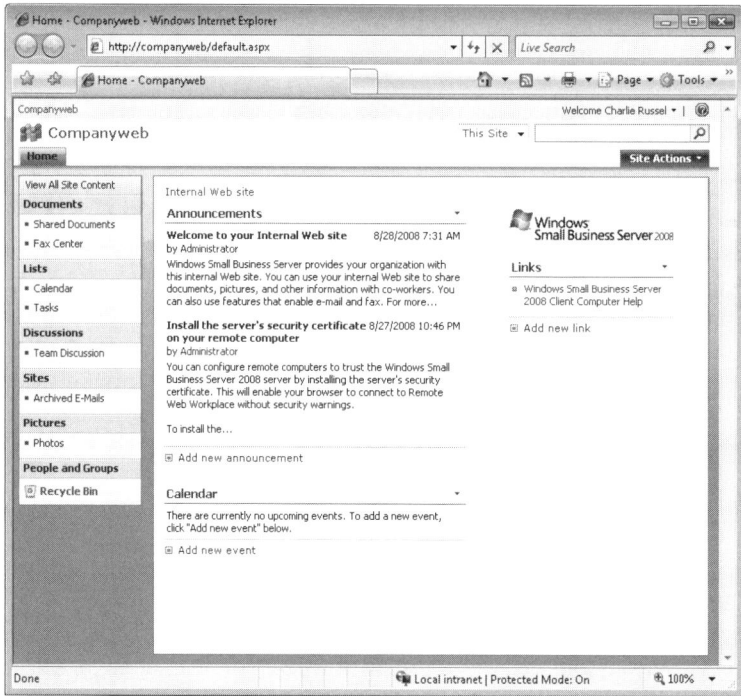

FIGURE 22-1 The default internal Web site for SBS 2008

The main center pane of Companyweb has a section for announcements and a calendar section. On the left pane are links into other main areas of the Web site, including document libraries, a fax library, calendar and tasks lists, a team discussion area, and a photo library. These items are generally available from other pages of the Web site, giving you quick access without having to navigate back to the home page. On the righthand side of the page is the Links pane, a place to put links to important external resources or applications that users can run.

The default Companyweb site is a good starting point, but there are plenty of ways you can extend it and add additional features and sections without having to be a Web developer. Of course, if you *are* a Web developer, you can use myriad options to create additional features and functionality. SharePoint is easily extensible, and there are good books for both professional developers and interested users.

Understanding SharePoint Items

Let's start by looking at the pieces that can make up a SharePoint site. Some have been around since the earliest days, but others are new to version 3 of SharePoint.

- **Libraries** Libraries come in various formats, including:
  - Document libraries for storing and collaborating on documents, including basic versioning features

- Picture libraries for storing photos and graphics

- Form libraries for storing InfoPath form templates

- Wiki page libraries that let you build interactive basic wiki sites

- **Lists** Lists come in various formats for presenting and storing list-based information, including:

    - Communications lists such as announcements and contacts

    - Tracking lists such as links, calendar, and tasks

    - Custom lists including a datasheet view

- **Web pages** Web pages include a basic Web page, sites, and workplaces or a Web Parts page.

- **Discussions** Discussions are a type of list used to build a basic forum for ongoing collaborative discussions.

- **Tasks** Tasks come in both basic tasks lists and project tasks that include Gantt chart functionality to graphically track project status.

Understanding SharePoint Roles

SharePoint has three basic user roles for a site: visitor, member, and owner. In SBS 2008, three security groups correspond to these roles: Windows SBS SharePoint_VisitorsGroup, Windows SBS SharePoint_MembersGroup, and Windows SBS SharePoint_OwnersGroup.

For the default Companyweb site, the CompanyWeb Visitor group has only the Windows SBS SharePoint_VisitorsGroup as a member. This group can read but can't edit the site or its contents, nor can they add discussion items. By default, no SBS Users are in Windows SBS SharePoint_VisitorsGroup, though you can move users into it.

For the default Companyweb site, the CompanyWeb Member group has only the Windows SBS SharePoint_MembersGroup as a member. This group can read, write, and contribute to the Companyweb site, including posting to discussions and customizing the site. By default, all user accounts with Standard User role and Standard User with Administrative Links role are part of this group.

For the default Companyweb site, the CompanyWeb Owner group has only the Windows SBS SharePoint_OwnersGroup as a member. This group has full administrative rights on the Companyweb site and can create new workspaces, change user and site permissions, and create new user roles and permissions. By default, all Network Administrators are part of this group.

The CompanyWeb Member group is a powerful group that has the ability to change the look and feel of your Companyweb site; can add or delete sections, documents, or articles; and generally has very nearly the full power of the Owner, with the sole exception of not being able to control the permissions of other users. As shown in Figure 22-2, there is a lesser level of permissions called Contribute, which still allows users to view, add, and update content, but doesn't give them full design capabilities. We think this is a more appropriate role for most users and you should consider changing the default permissions for CompanyWeb Members to Contribute instead of Design.

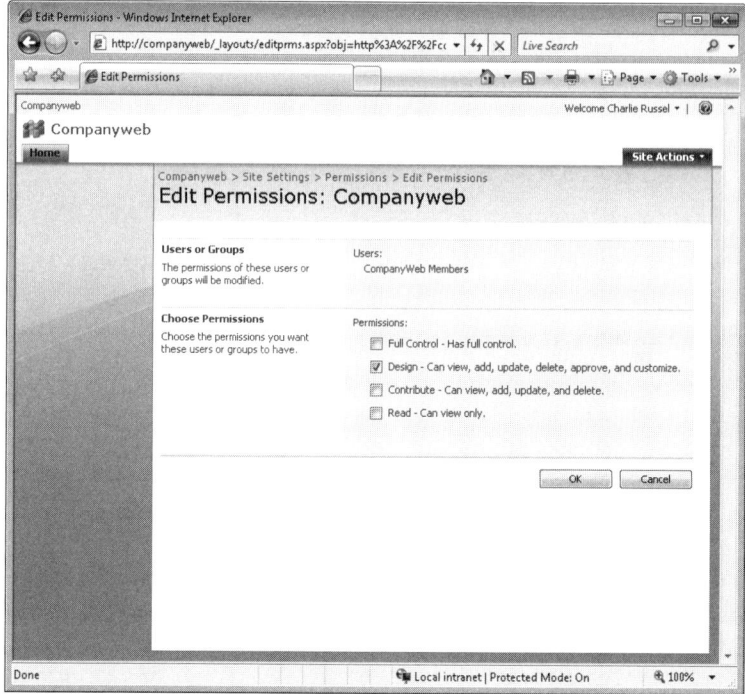

FIGURE 22-2 The default permissions for CompanyWeb Members are Design permissions

To change the permissions for all CompanyWeb Members, follow these steps:

1. Log on to the Companyweb site with an account that has Owner permissions.

2. On the main Companyweb page, select Site Settings from the Site Actions drop-down list to open the Site Settings page shown in Figure 22-3.

3. Click Advanced Permissions under Users And Permissions to open the Permissions: Companyweb page shown in Figure 22-4.

4. Click CompanyWeb Members to open the Edit Permissions: Companyweb page shown in Figure 22-2.

5. Clear the Design – Can View, Add, Update, Delete, Approve, And Customize check box and check the Contribute – Can View, Add, Update, And Delete check box.

6. Click OK to return to the Permissions: Companyweb page.

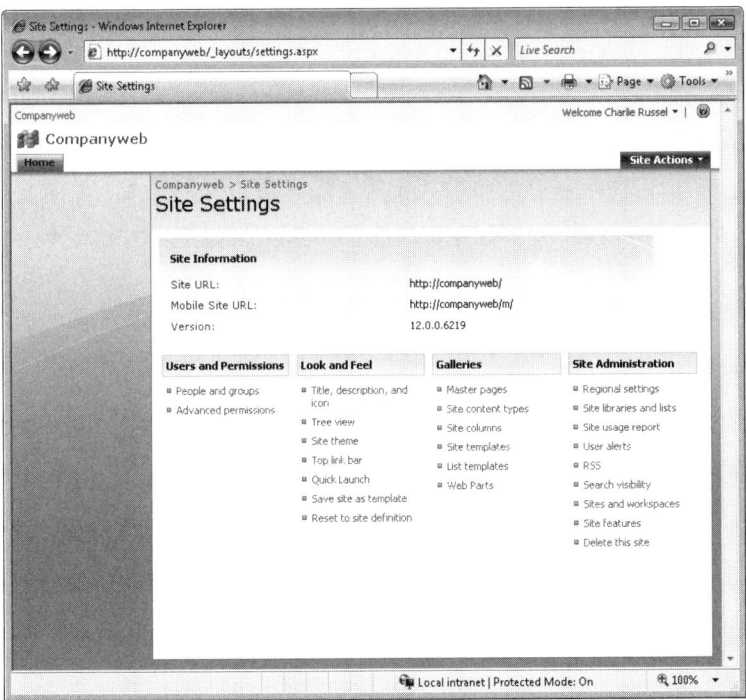

FIGURE 22-3 The Site Settings page of the Companyweb site

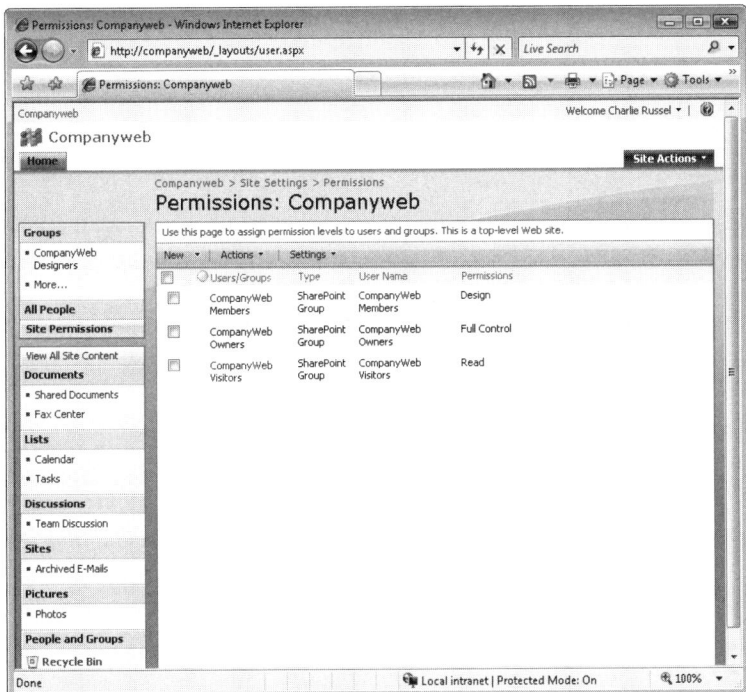

FIGURE 22-4 The Permissions: Companyweb page

From the Permissions: Companyweb page you can also create a new group and assign permissions and users to it, or directly add users and assign them permissions. These permissions are carried throughout the site.

To edit the permissions for a particular section of the Companyweb site, open that section of the site and then select Settings from the Settings drop-down list. Here you can customize the particular section and edit the permissions for the section. As an example, let's modify the permissions of the default Shared Documents Library to allow our user "Alfie" to have full control of the library, using these steps:

1. Open *http://Companyweb* if it isn't already open.

2. Click Shared Documents in the left pane to open the Shared Documents page, shown in Figure 22-5.

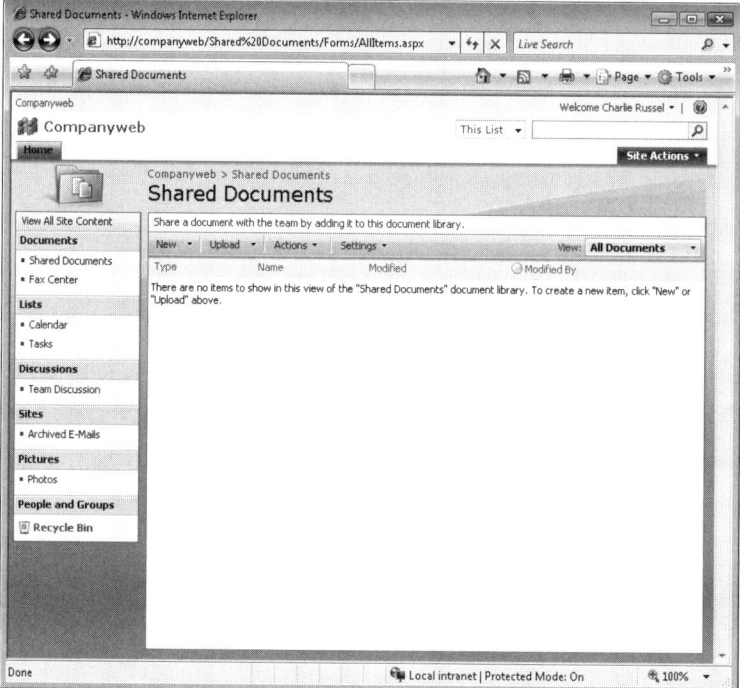

FIGURE 22-5 The Shared Documents library of the default Companyweb site

3. Click Settings in the menu bar above the main library list and select Document Library Settings from the drop-down list, as shown in Figure 22-6.

4. Select Permissions For This Document Library from the Permissions And Management section to open the Permissions: Shared Documents page shown in Figure 22-7.

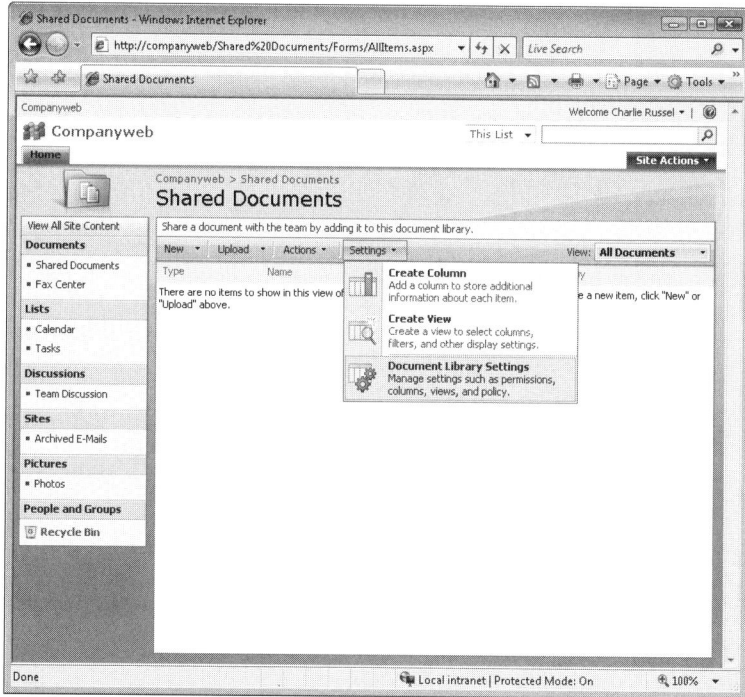

FIGURE 22-6 Changing the settings for the Shared Documents library

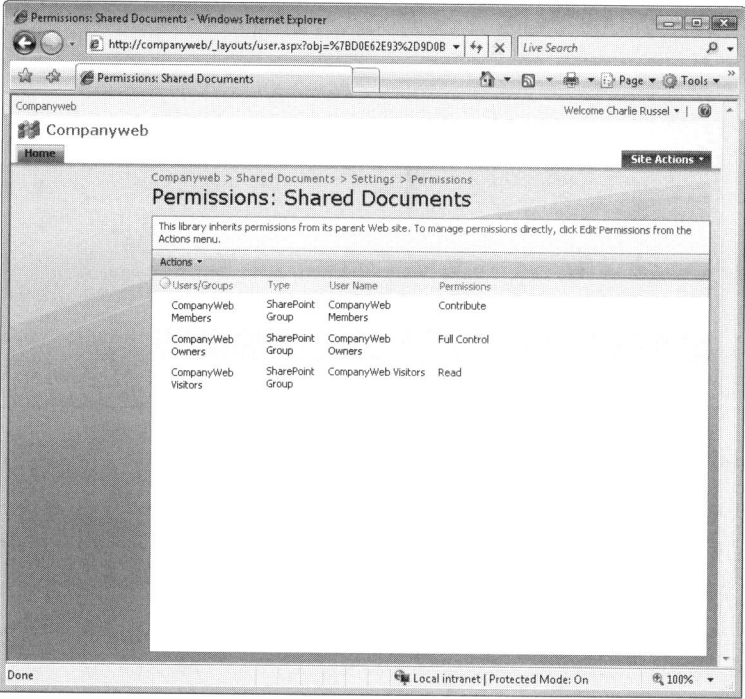

FIGURE 22-7 Changing the Permissions for the Shared Documents library

5. Click Edit Permissions from the action menu. You'll see the warning message shown in Figure 22-8.

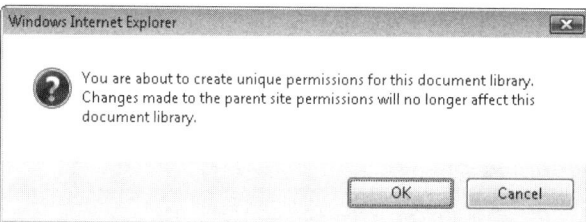

FIGURE 22-8 Warning message when you change permissions on a document library

IMPORTANT This is a good time to emphasize that after you change permissions on a portion of a site, you lose the inheritance that makes it easy to keep track of what permissions are granted. If you do need to change permissions as we are in this example, be sure to clearly document the changes. Or resist the temptation and find another way to manage things. It is possible, however to revert to inherited permissions, using the Actions drop-down list of a section that is no longer inheriting.

6. Click OK and the page changes as shown in Figure 22-9 to show that it is no longer inheriting permissions.

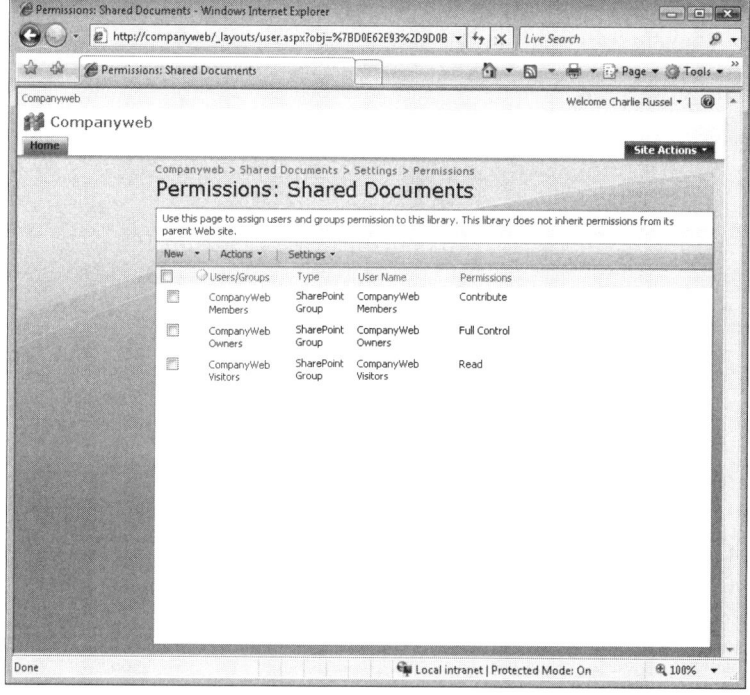

FIGURE 22-9 The Shared Documents library is no longer inheriting permissions from the site.

7. Select Add Users from the New menu to open the Add Users: Shared Documents page shown in Figure 22-10.

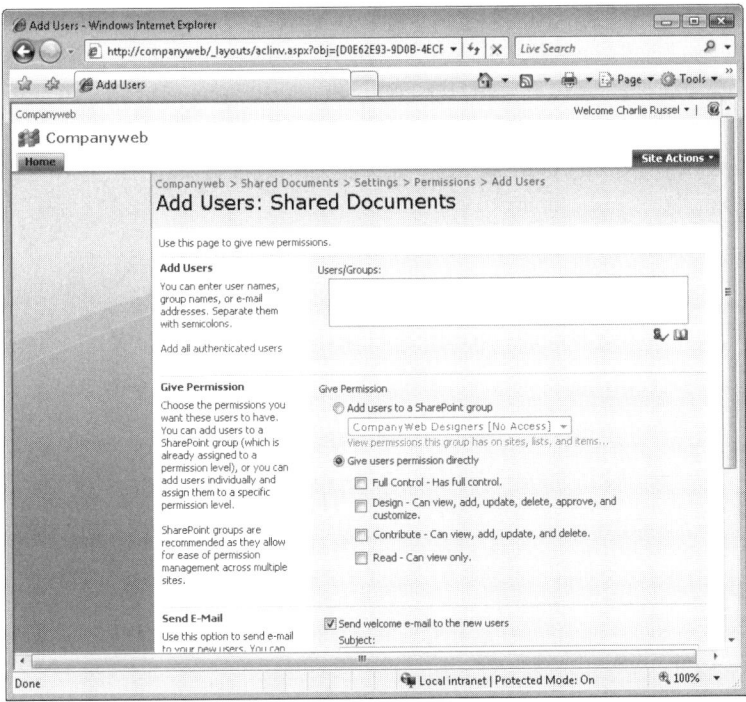

FIGURE 22-10 The Add Users: Shared Documents page

8. Type **Alfie** in the Users/Groups box and click the Check Names button in the lower right of the box. SharePoint verifies the user and substitutes his full name, Alfredo N. Fettuccine.

9. Select Full Control – Has Full Control from the Give Users Permission Directly section.

10. If you want to send Alfie an e-mail message telling him that he's in charge now, select the Send Welcome E-mail To The New Users check box and edit the message as appropriate.

11. Click OK to make the change and return to the Permissions: Shared Documents folder.

Customizing Companyweb

You can customize Companyweb to add additional lists, links, and libraries. Working with a SharePoint site to customize it is pretty straightforward and follows a similar logic wherever you are. We'll start by adding a regular IT Team meeting and creating a Workspace for it that allows IT team members to file their reports ahead of time and add comments to other's reports.

Adding a Workspace

Adding a Workspace creates an area where a group of users can directly interact and share documents and discussions, separate from the overall document libraries. For our example, let's first create a recurring meeting and assign users to the meeting, following these steps:

1. From the main Companyweb page, click Add New Event in the Calendar section of the center pane to open the Calendar: New Item page.

2. Type in a title and location for this meeting, set the time and date to next Monday at 9 AM, finishing at 10 AM, and add a description as shown in Figure 22-11.

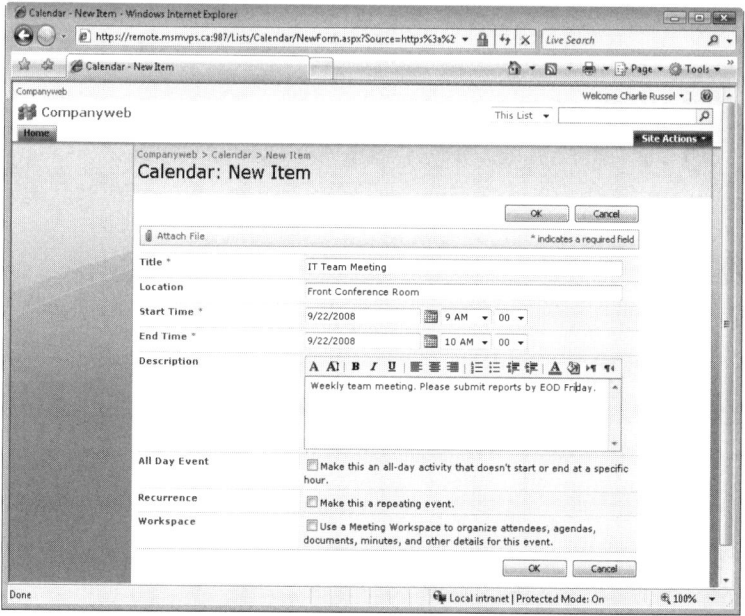

FIGURE 22-11 Adding a new Calendar item

3. Select the Make This A Repeating Event check box. The Recurrence section will expand as shown in Figure 22-12.

4. Set the meeting for Weekly and set it to end after 10 occurrences.

5. Select the Use A Meeting Workspace... check box and click OK to open the New Meeting Workspace page shown in Figure 22-13.

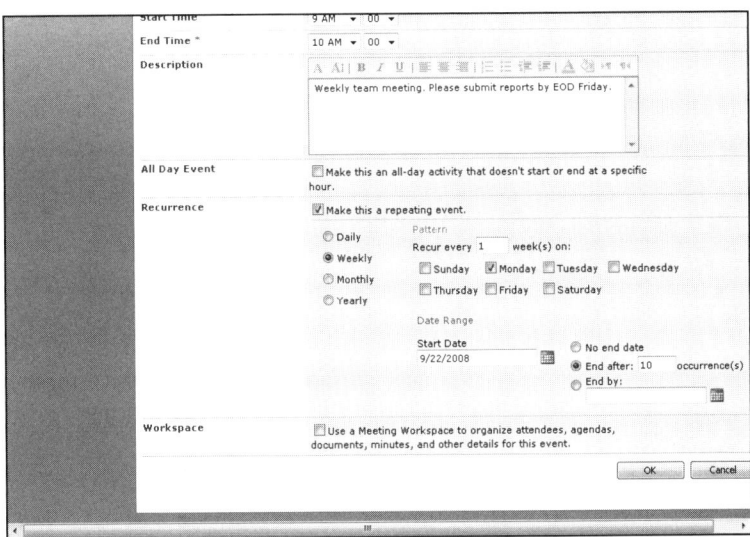

FIGURE 22-12 The Make This A Repeating Event section of a new calendar item

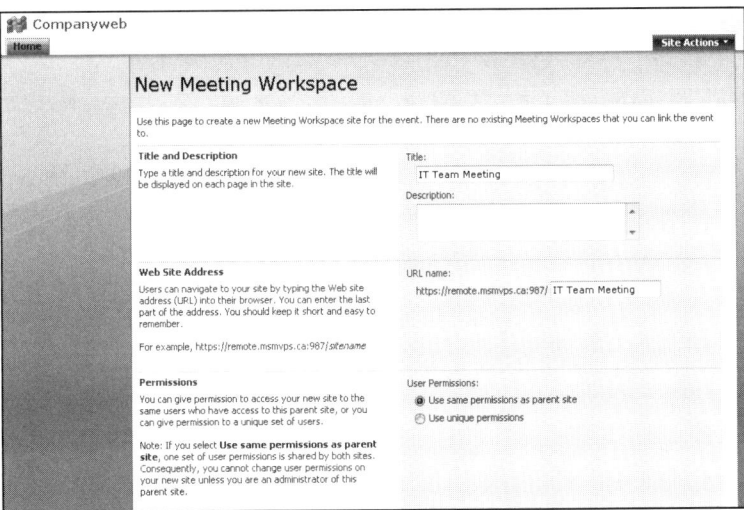

FIGURE 22-13 Creating a new workspace for the IT team meeting

6. Select Use Unique Permissions in the User Permissions section and click OK to open the Template Selection page.

7. Select Basic Meeting Workspace for this meeting and click OK to open the Set Up Groups For This Site page shown in Figure 22-14.

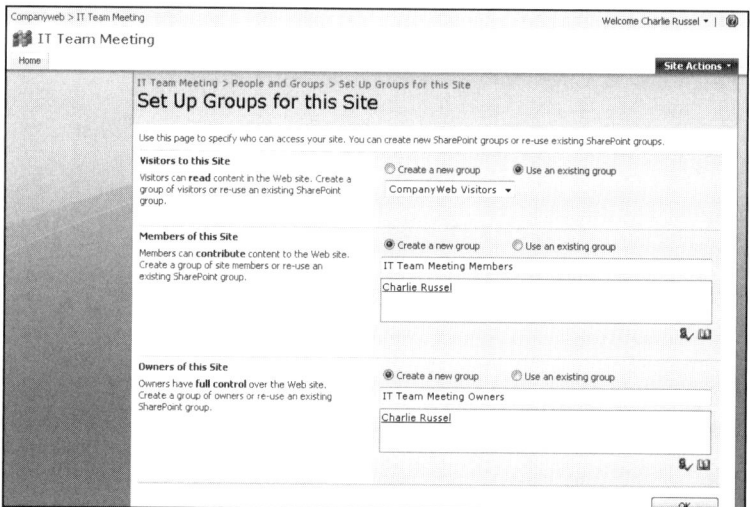

FIGURE 22-14 The Set Up Groups For This Site page

8. Add users as members of this site by selecting the Create A New Group option and typing in their account names, separated by semicolons. Click the Check Names icon to verify the names.

9. To add additional owners, repeat the previous step with names for the owners of this site.

10. When you've set the permissions as you want, click OK to open the Workspace you've created, as shown in Figure 22-15.

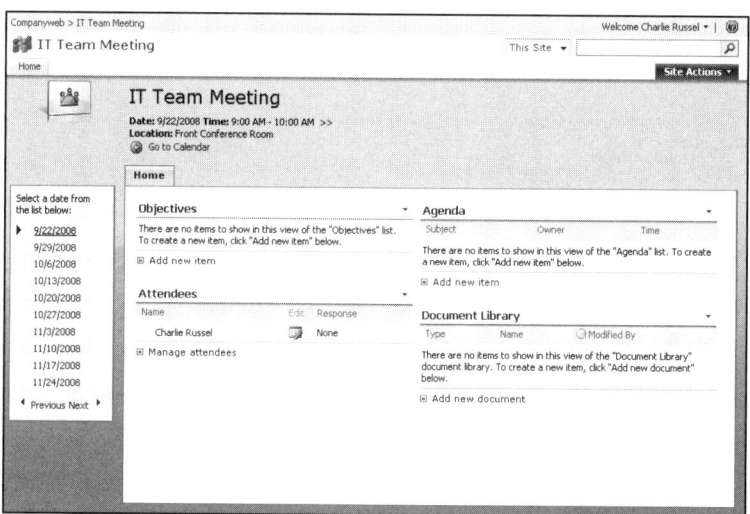

FIGURE 22-15 The new IT Team Meeting site

11. Click Manage Attendees to open the Attendees page and click New to open the Attendees: New Item page shown in Figure 22-16. Type in the name for the attendee and click OK.

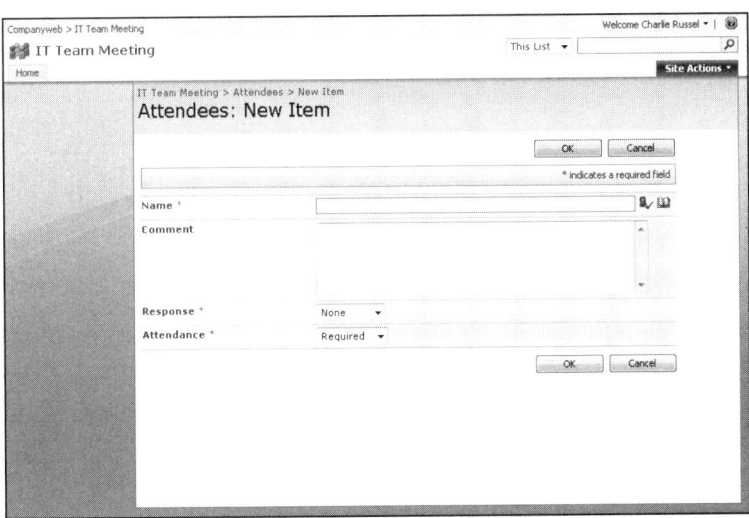

FIGURE 22-16 The Attendees: New Item page

12. Repeat the previous step until you've added all the attendees to the list, as shown in Figure 22-17.

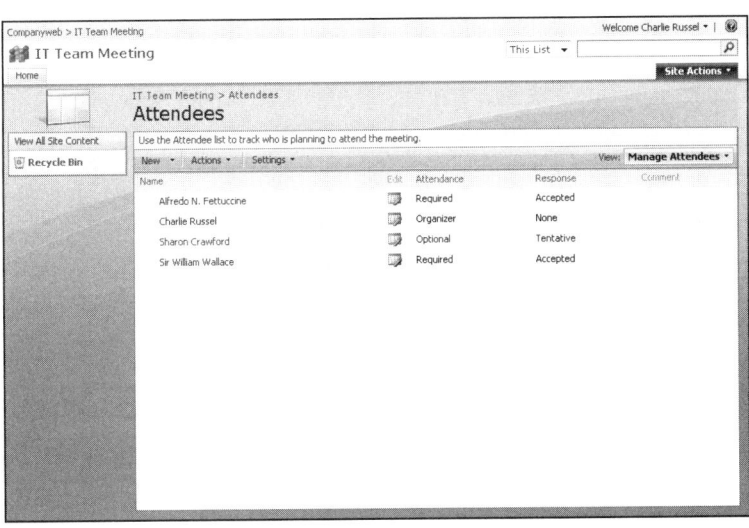

FIGURE 22-17 Attendees have been added to our team meeting.

13. Click IT Team Meeting in the upper left to return to the main page for this workspace.

14. Click Add New Item in the Agenda section to create an agenda for the current meeting, as shown in Figure 22-18.

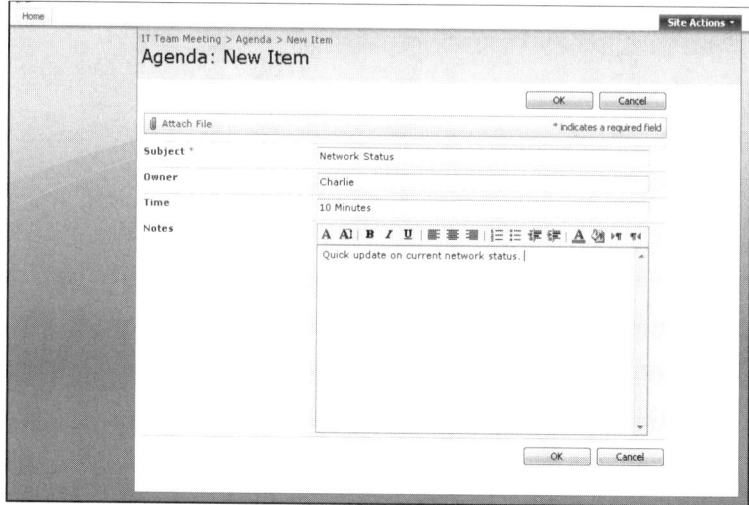

FIGURE 22-18 Adding an agenda item to the meeting

15. Repeat the previous step as required to add items to the agenda, as shown in Figure 22-19.

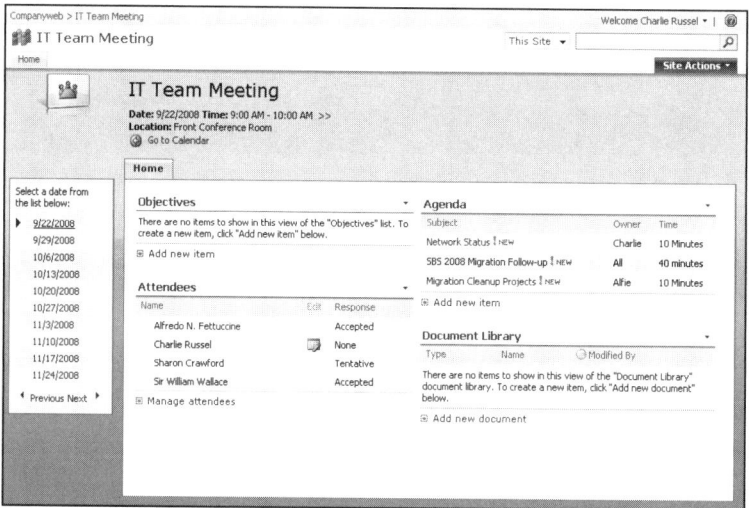

FIGURE 22-19 The agenda for the next IT Team Meeting is filled out.

16. Click Companyweb in the top bar to return to the main Companyweb site.

Adding TS RemoteApps Links

You can add links to TS RemoteApps programs to your Companyweb SharePoint site. This gives your users direct access to applications from their main Companyweb page. The process has five basic steps:

- Add the TS WebAccess role service on the SBS 2008 server.
- Add the missing .NET Framework 3.0 features.
- Register the Web Part as a safe control.
- Create a folder to store the Web Part.
- Add the Web Part to Companyweb.

The first two steps involve the native Windows 2008 Server Manager. If you need a refresher on Server Manager, see Chapter 17, "Windows SBS Console v. Server Manager."

Add TS WebAccess Role Service

The default installation of SBS includes the TS Gateway role service of Terminal Services, but doesn't include the TS WebAccess role service, so the first thing we need to do is add that role service, using the following steps:

1. Open Server Manager from the Start menu.
2. Expand Roles and then click Terminal Services.
3. Select Add Role Services from the action menu to open the Select Role Services page shown in Figure 22-20.

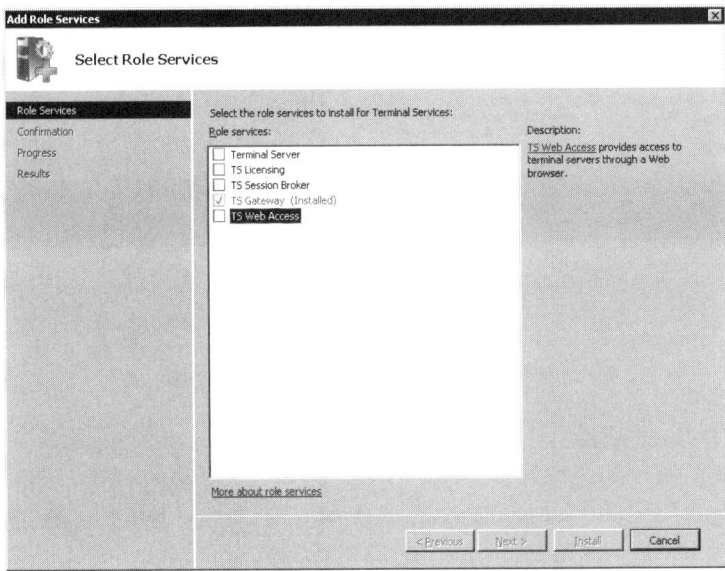

FIGURE 22-20 The Select Role Services page of the Add Role Services Wizard for Terminal Services

4. Select TS WebAccess and click Next to open the Confirm Installation Selections page.

5. Click Install and then click Close to return to Server Manager. Leave it open. We have one more task while we're in Server Manager.

> **NOTE** In most cases you won't need to restart the SBS server when you add this role service, but you might need to add additional updates the next time the server checks for updates.

Adding the .NET Framework 3.0 Feature

The default install of SBS includes a portion of the .NET Framework 3.0, but not all the pieces we need, so we need to add that to the server, using the following steps:

1. Open Server Manager if it isn't already open.

2. Click Features in the left pane and select Add Features from the action menu to open the Add Features Wizard, shown in Figure 22-21.

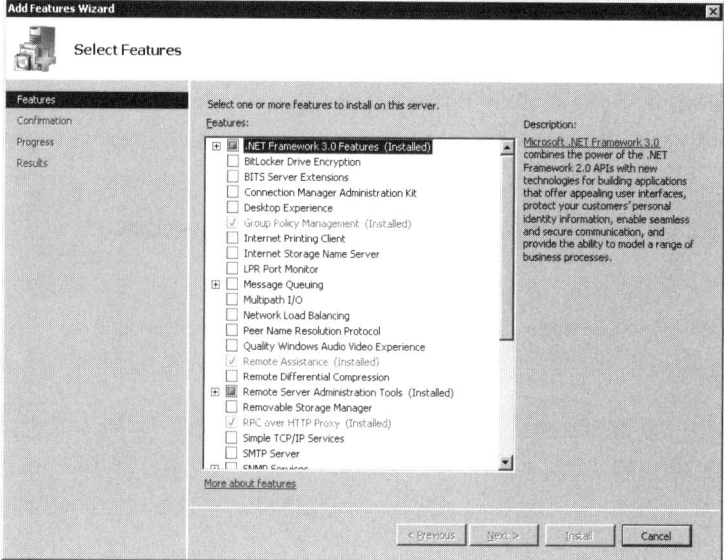

FIGURE 22-21 The Add Features Wizard

3. Expand .NET Framework 3.0 Features (Installed) and select the WCF Activation check box.

4. Click Next to open the Confirm Installation Selections page and then click Install to begin the installation.

5. Click Close to close the Add Features Wizard and return to Server Manager.

6. You can close Server Manager. We're done with it for now.

Register the Web Part as Safe

Next we need to register the Web Part we're going to use as a *safe control*. This allows it to run without needing an elevated prompt. To register the Web Part, follow these steps:

1. Open an elevated Cmd or PowerShell command prompt using Run As Administrator.

2. Change to the directory where the configuration file for Companyweb is and open web.config in Notepad or your favorite plain text editor, as shown in Figure 22-22.

```
cd "C:\Program Files\Windows Small Business Server\Bin\webapp\InternalWebSite"
notepad web.config
```

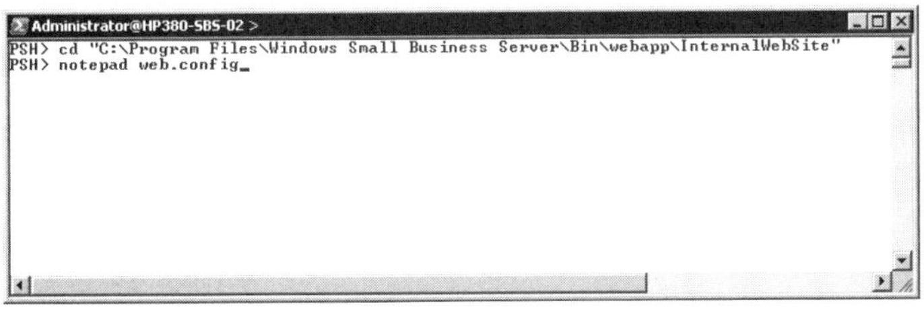

FIGURE 22-22 Editing the web.config file for Companyweb

3. In the web.config file, locate the <SafeControls> section of the file. At the end of the section of SafeControl Assembly entries, add the following line:

```
<SafeControl Assembly="TSPortalWebPart, Version=6.0.0.0, Culture=neutral,
PublicKeyToken=31bf3856ad364e35"
Namespace="Microsoft.TerminalServices.Publishing.Portal" TypeName="*" Safe="True"
AllowRemoteDesigner="True" />
```

> **NOTE** Add this as a single line, with no line breaks.

4. Save the change and exit Notepad. Keep the elevated command prompt open. You'll need it in the next section.

> **IMPORTANT** Always make a copy of important files before editing them—just in case.

Create a Folder to Store the Web Part

Next you need to create a folder to hold the Web Part and its images, and to give the Network Services account full control on the folder. Use the following steps:

1. In the elevated command prompt from the previous section, type the following command:

```
mkdir "C:\Program Files\Common Files\Microsoft Shared\Web Server
Extensions\wpresources\TSPortalWebPart\6.0.0.0__31bf3856ad364e35\images"
```

> **NOTE** Notice the two underscores after 6.0.0.0 in the preceding single command line.

2. Change directories to the parent folder of the images folder you just created:

   ```
   cd "C:\Program Files\Common Files\Microsoft Shared\Web Server
   Extensions\wpresources\TSPortalWebPart\6.0.0.0__31bf3856ad364e35"
   ```

3. Give the Network Service account full control over the images folder you created in Step 1:

   ```
   icacls images /grant NetworkService:F
   ```

4. Close the Command Prompt window if you see a success message, as shown in Figure 22-23.

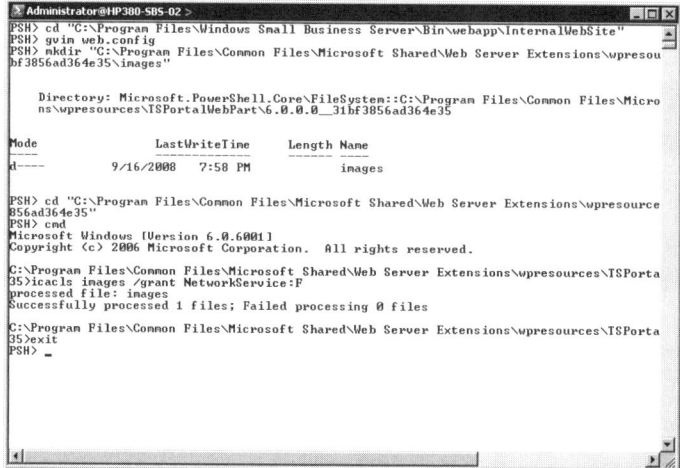

FIGURE 22-23 The Windows PowerShell session for marking the Web Part safe and creating an images folder for it

Add the Web Part to Companyweb

Finally, the reason we're doing all this—to add the Web Part to Companyweb, follow these steps:

1. Open Companyweb with an account that has SharePoint Owner privileges.

2. Select Site Settings from the Site Actions menu to open the Site Settings page.

3. Click Web Parts under the Galleries section to open the Web Part Gallery page, as shown in Figure 22-24.

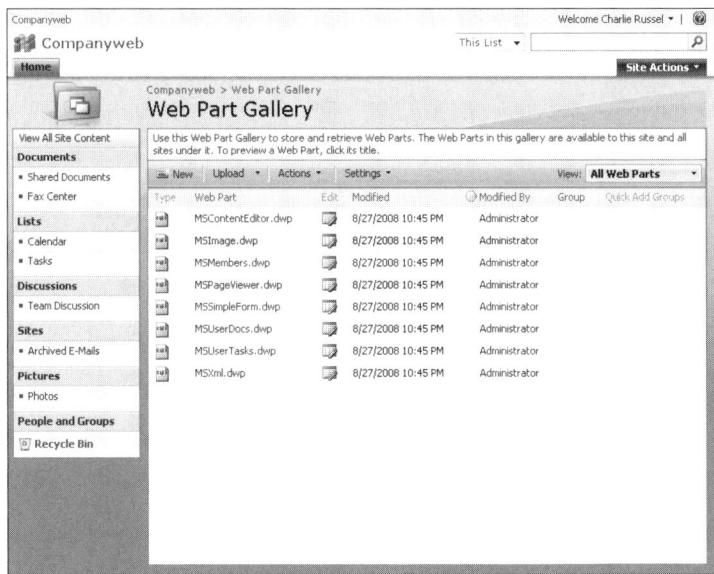

FIGURE 22-24 The Web Part Gallery page

4. Click New to open the Web Parts Gallery: New Web Parts page, scroll down to the bottom, and select the Microsoft.TerminalServices.Publishing.Portal.TSPortalWebPart check box, as shown in Figure 22-25.

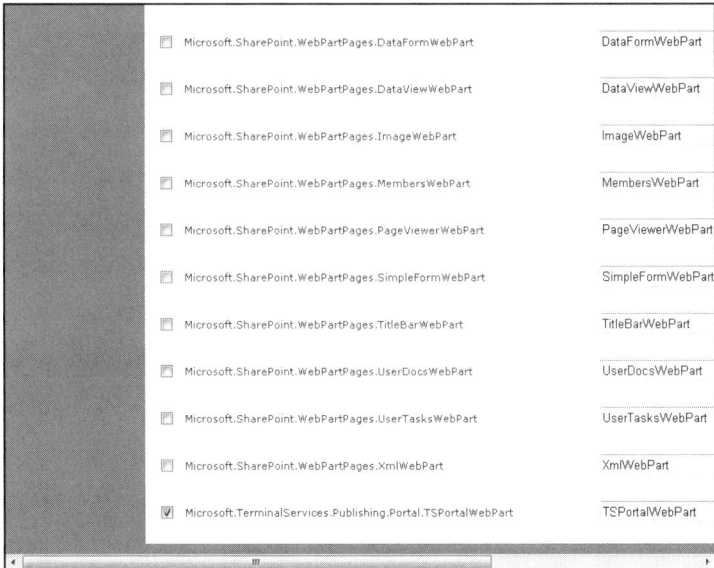

FIGURE 22-25 Adding the TS RemoteApps Web Part

5. Click Populate Gallery to add the Web Part and return to the Web Part Gallery.

6. Click Home to return to the main Companyweb page.

7. Select Edit Page from the Site Actions menu to open Companyweb in edit mode, as shown in Figure 22-26.

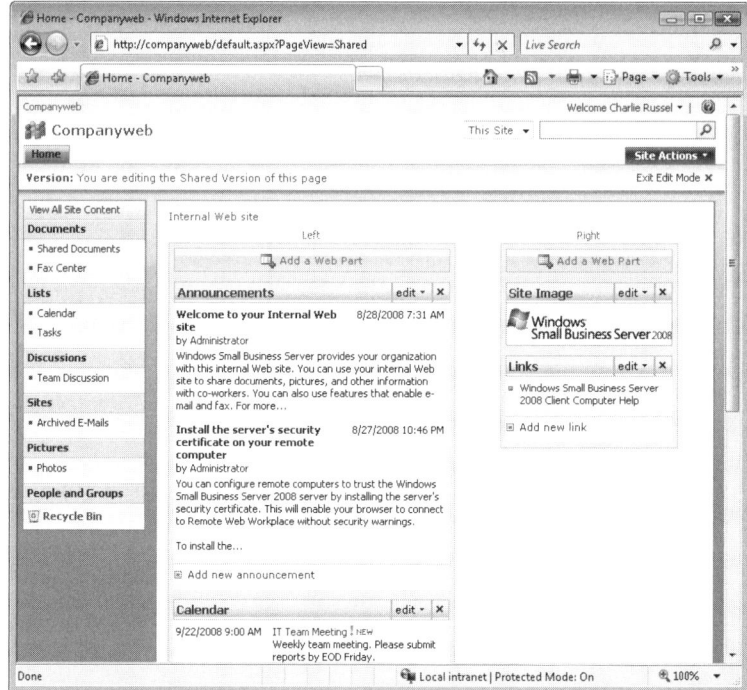

FIGURE 22-26 The Companyweb site in edit mode

8. In the Right section, click Add A Web Part to open the Add Web Parts To Right page, shown in Figure 22-27.

9. Scroll down to the Miscellaneous section and select the TSPortalWebPart check box.

10. Click Add to return to the Companyweb page in edit mode, with the Web Part added.

11. Drag the Web Part below the Site Image.

12. Click Edit in the upper-right corner of the Web Part and then select Modify Shared Web Part to open the TS Web Access properties.

13. Type in the name of the Terminal Server to connect to in the Terminal Server Name field and click OK to close the properties of the Web Part.

14. If you see the error shown in Figure 22-28, you need to add the SBS server to the TS Web Access Computers local security group on your Terminal Server.

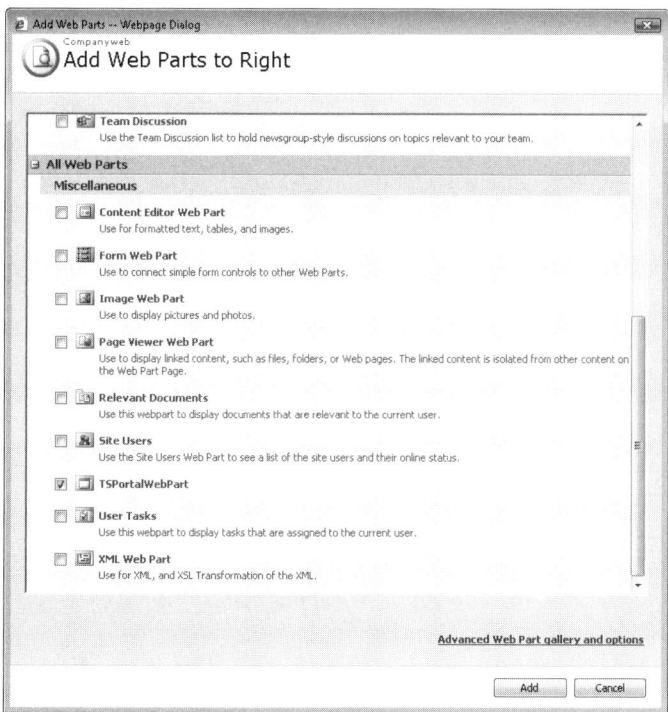

FIGURE 22-27 The Add Web Parts To Right page

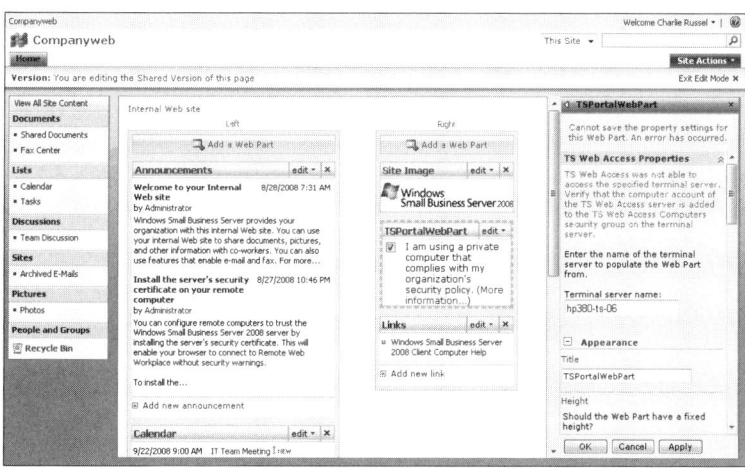

FIGURE 22-28 By default, the SBS server doesn't have permission to access the list of TS RemoteApps.

Follow these steps to add the SBS server to the TS Web Access Computers security group on your Terminal Server:

a. Log on to the Terminal Server with an administrative account.

b. Open Computer Management in the Administrative Tools folder.

c. Expand Local Users And Groups and then click Groups.

d. Double-click TS Web Access Computers Properties to open the dialog box in Figure 22-29.

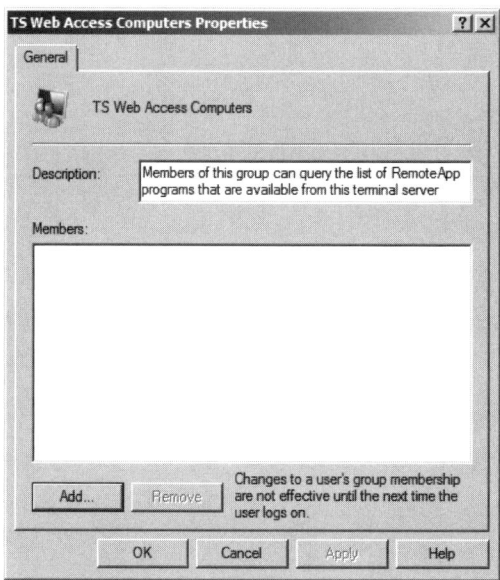

FIGURE 22-29 The TS Web Access Computers Properties dialog box

e. Click Add to open the Select Users, Computers, Or Groups dialog box shown in Figure 22-30.

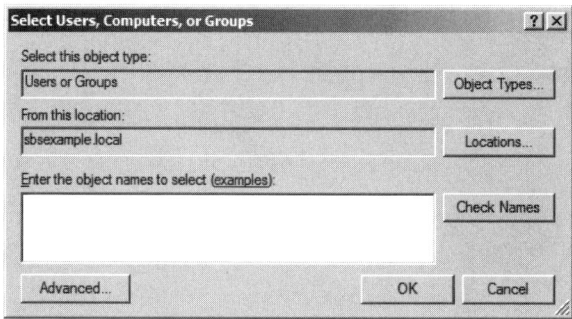

FIGURE 22-30 The Select Users, Computers, Or Groups dialog box. Note that Object Types doesn't include Computers by default.

f. Click Object Types and select Computers. Click OK to return to the Select Users, Computers, Or Groups dialog box.

g. In the Enter The Object Names To Select (Examples) field, type the name of your SBS server and click Check Names.

h. Click OK to return to the TS Web Access Computers Properties dialog box.

i. Click OK and then close the Computer Management console.

15. Return to the Companyweb site in edit mode and click OK again. The TS RemoteApps are populated on the SharePoint site automatically.

16. Click Exit Edit Mode to return to the Companyweb site, with the application icons in the right pane, as shown in Figure 22-31.

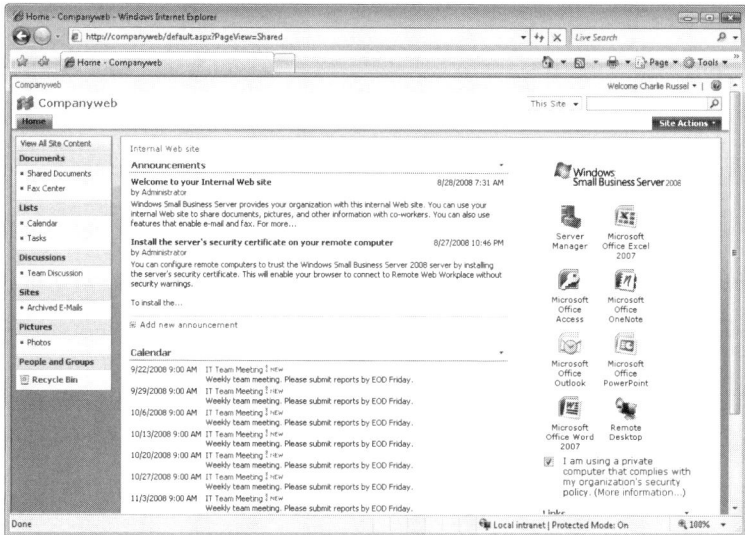

FIGURE 22-31 When permissions are correct, the available TS RemoteApps automatically populate the Companyweb home page.

17. Click any of the applications to open a TS RemoteApp. Figure 22-32 shows Microsoft OneNote 2007 running on a Windows Vista computer that doesn't have any applications installed on it at all.

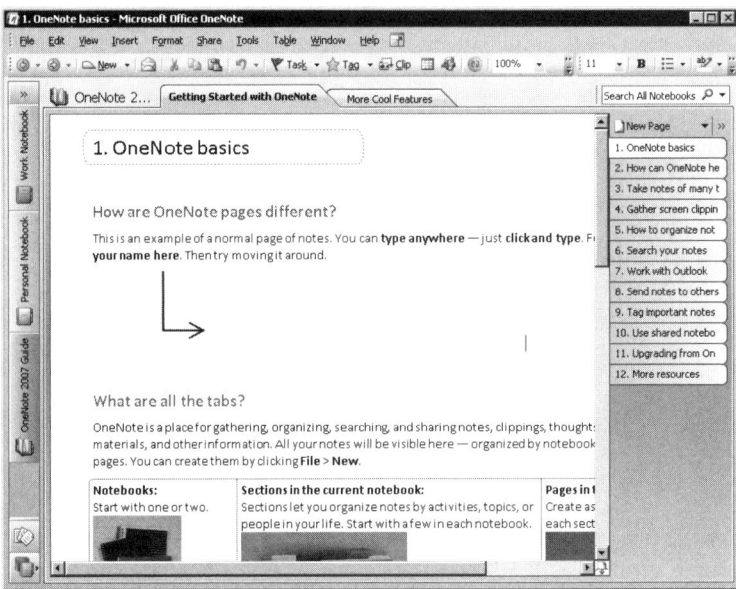

FIGURE 22-32 Running OneNote as a TS RemoteApp

This just begins to scratch the surface of what you can do with SharePoint and the Companyweb site, but we think the new features that are enabled with SharePoint Services 3.0 are exciting. And having our TS RemoteApps on the Companyweb page is a great addition.

Summary

In this chapter, we've covered customizing the default SharePoint site, Companyweb. We shown how to modify permissions, add a workspace, and modify the site to use Companyweb as a TS Web Access portal for running remote applications directly from Companyweb.

In the next part, we move on to installing and using the Premium Edition features, including installing the second server, installing Microsoft SQL Server 2008, and configuring Terminal Services on the second server.

Installing the Second Server

Windows Small Business Server 2008 Premium includes a full copy of Windows Server 2008 Standard that can be used for any purpose desired, as long as it's installed on the SBS network. SBS Premium includes both 32-bit and 64-bit versions of Windows Server 2008, so you can choose the option that makes the most sense in your network environment. We, of course, are going with 64-bit for our own SBS network.

Because the second server is full Windows Server 2008 Standard, you can install any of the normal roles and features on the server as you would any other copy of Windows Server 2008 Standard, including Hyper-V and Terminal Services. Windows Server 2008 Standard includes "1+1" virtualization licensing, allowing for virtualization of a single instance of Windows Server as a child partition—but only if the parent partition is used solely for the Hyper-V role. We think a very interesting scenario will be to install the second server as a Hyper-V parent and then install the second server again virtualized to support any additional roles and features, including Microsoft SQL Server (covered in Chapter 24, "Introducing SQL Server 2008 Standard Edition for Small Business") and the Terminal Server Role (covered in Chapter 25, "Adding a Terminal Server").

Another choice for some environments will be to install the second server as an additional domain controller. This can make a lot of sense if the second server will be used to support a remote site; for example, where a local infrastructure server, with Active Directory Domain Services, DNS, DHCP, File Server, and Print Server roles would likely be installed.

Minimum System Requirements

There are no special requirements for installing the second server that make it different from installing any other version of Windows Server 2008. Your minimum requirements and steps remain the same. The official minimum requirements are shown in Table 23-1, along with our commentary on those requirements and suggested real-world minimums.

TABLE 23-1 Minimum System Requirements for Second Server

HARDWARE	REQUIREMENTS	COMMENTS
Processor	32-bit: 1 GHz 64-bit, x64: 1.4 GHz 64-bit, Itanium: Itanium 2	2 GHz or greater is more realistic. And Itanium is not shipped as part of SBS 2008, nor does it realistically make any sense for an SBS network.
RAM	512 MB	1 gigabyte (GB) of RAM is a more realistic minimum; 2 GB is recommended. For Server Core, 1 GB of RAM is normally sufficient for typical infrastructure workloads.
Disk	10 GB	No less than 40 GB of hard disk space on the system drive, please. And if your server has more than 16 GB of RAM, increase the minimum to at least 50 GB.
Optical Drive	DVD-ROM	A CD-ROM drive is no longer sufficient, though it's still technically possible to get special CD-ROM–based installation media. For network installations, no optical drive is required.
Video	800 × 600	1024 × 768 is a more realistic minimum. Some screens will be difficult to use at a resolution below 1024 × 768.
Other	Keyboard and mouse	
Network	Not required	Who are they kidding? A supported network card is required for joining a domain or almost anything you'll want to do with Windows Server 2008.

Notice what is not on the list of required hardware—a floppy drive! Finally, in Windows Server 2008, we can get rid of the floppy requirement, even if we need to load drivers for our hard disk controller. Drivers can now be loaded from CD or DVD, from a USB flash drive, or from floppy disk.

 REAL WORLD **64-Bit and Signed Drivers**

As we've seen for installing the main SBS server, signed 64-bit drivers are required for 64-bit versions of Windows Server 2008. This requirement means that you must do your homework and make sure that your vendors provide full support for their hardware in 64-bit Windows Server 2008. We continue to be surprised by the slow response from even major vendors to provide signed 64-bit drivers, so if you need to use hardware cards or peripherals that aren't part of the server you ordered from your server vendor, be sure to verify the availability of a supported, signed driver for that hardware card or peripheral before installing a 64-bit version of Windows Server 2008. Remember, you have the option of choosing the 32-bit version if it is more appropriate for your environment.

Of course, if a driver isn't available, choose a vendor that does have a driver to retain all the advantages that 64-bit provides. Personally, we're choosing to change hardware vendors where we find deficiencies in 64-bit driver support. And we're telling our old hardware vendors exactly why we're dropping them, too.

Installation and Initial Configuration

Installation and configuration of Windows Server 2008 has changed significantly from the process we're all more or less familiar with from Windows Server 2003. There are far fewer steps required to actually begin the installation, with hardly any input required from the user. You don't even need to enter a Product ID (PID)—see the Under the Hood sidebar "PID-less Installs." Eventually you'll have to enter the PID before you can activate the server, but a lot of steps that used to be required before the installation process would begin have now been moved to the initial configuration stage.

 UNDER THE HOOD **PID-less Installs**

Windows Server 2008 normally requires you to enter a PID for installation. But you can simply skip entering the PID and then you'll have to select exactly which version of Windows Server 2008 you're installing. You'll get a couple of extra prompts and warnings, but if you only want to run a demonstration or evaluation environment for 30 days or fewer, just skip entering the PID. You'll have a fully functional Windows Server 2008 installation for those 30 days.

If you decide to convert a server installed without a PID to a fully activated Windows Server 2008 server, you need to enter a PID for the exact same version of Windows Server 2008 that you said you were installing when you initially installed. That means if you used retail media to install the server, you must provide a retail key. If you used the SBS 2008 media, you use the key provided with SBS 2008. You can't change which version is installed without completely reinstalling Windows Server 2008.

To enter a product key for a server installed without a PID, use the slmgr.vbs -ipk command.

Installation

Installing Windows Server 2008 from standard distribution media onto a clean server with no operating system on it requires just seven screens at the very beginning and the entire rest of the installation will complete without further interruption. You don't need to enter any network information, computer name, domain name, or any other information except the actual PID associated with the installation and the language to install.

Use the following steps to install Windows Server 2008 onto a bare server using standard DVD media:

1. Turn on the server and immediately insert the Windows Server 2008 DVD for the architecture Windows Server 2008 you want to install. If the primary hard disk hasn't got a bootable operating system on it, you'll go directly into the Windows Server 2008 installation process. If the disk has a bootable operating system on it, you might be prompted with Press Any Key To Boot From CD Or DVD. If you are, press a key.

2. When the initial Install Windows page appears, shown in Figure 23-1, select the language and other regional settings to use for this installation.

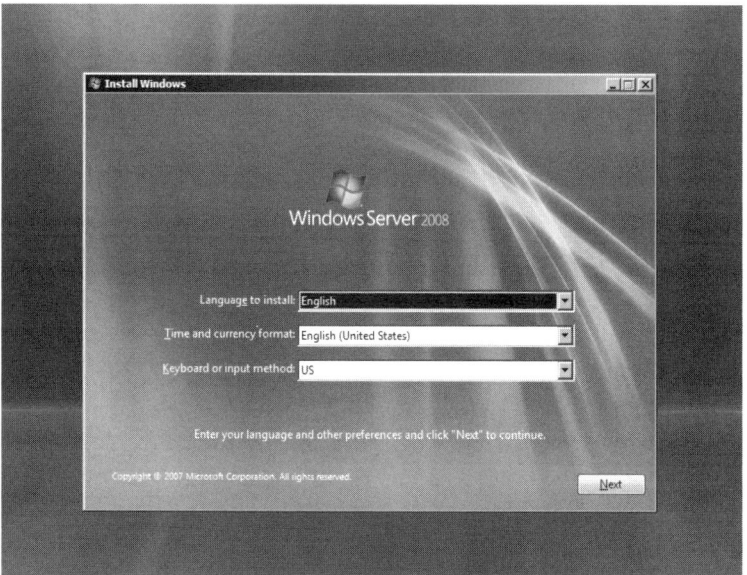

FIGURE 23-1 The initial page of the Install Windows Wizard

3. Click Next to open the page shown in Figure 23-2. From here you can choose to repair a corrupted Windows Server 2008 installation or get additional information before installing.

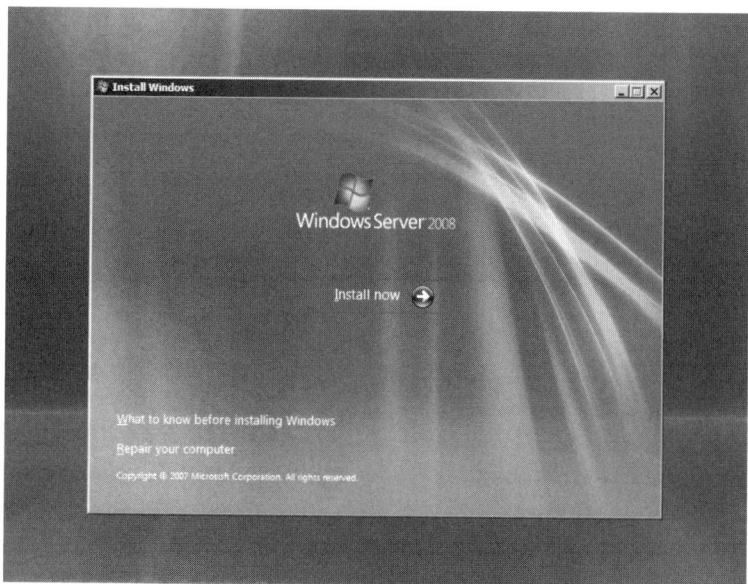

FIGURE 23-2 The Install Now page of the Install Windows Wizard

4. Click Install Now to open the Type Your Product Key For Activation page of the Install Windows Wizard, as shown in Figure 23-3.

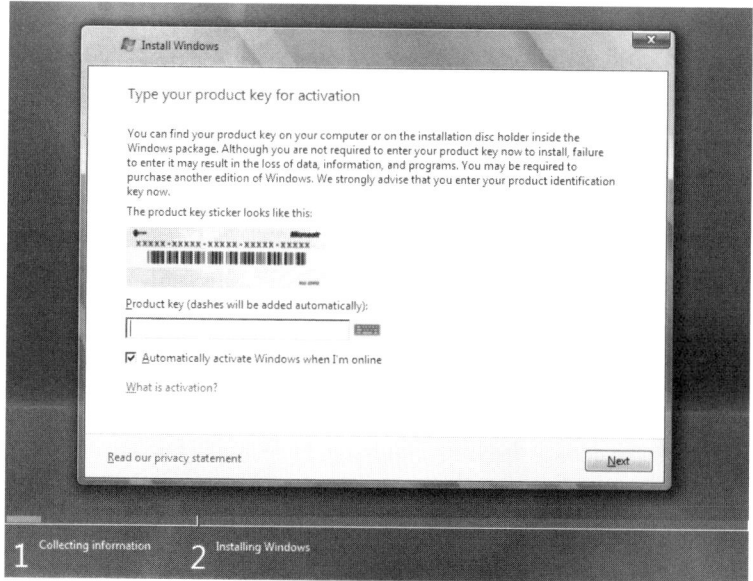

FIGURE 23-3 The Type Your Product Key For Activation page of the Install Windows Wizard

5. Type in a product key for this installation of Windows Server 2008. (See the Under the Hood sidebar titled "PID-less Installs" earlier in this chapter for information on installing without entering a product key.)

6. Leave the Automatically Activate Windows When I'm Online check box selected unless you need to control when activation occurs.

7. Click Next to open the Select The Operation System You Want To Install page of the Install Windows Wizard as shown in Figure 23-4. If you're installing without entering a product key, you'll see a much longer list of possible versions.

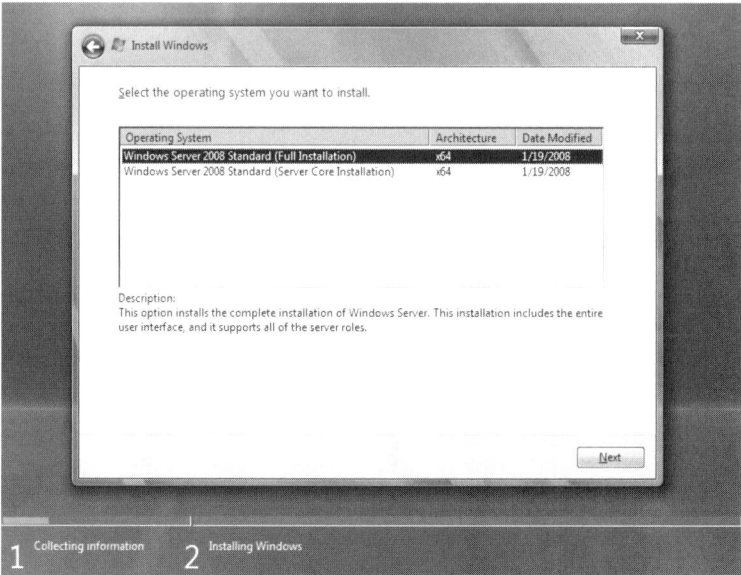

FIGURE 23-4 The Select The Operation System You Want To Install page of the Install Windows Wizard

8. Select either a Full Installation or a Server Core Installation. This selection is irrevocable—you can't change an installation at a later time from Full to Server Core, or from Server Core to Full. (For details on installing and configuring Windows Server 2008 Server Core, see Chapter 6, "Configuring SBS in Hyper-V," where we provide some scripts to simplify the process.)

9. Click Next to open the Please Read The License Terms page. Select I Accept The License Terms. You don't have a choice—either accept them or the installation terminates.

10. Click Next to open the Which Type Of Installation Do You Want page. The only choice when you boot from a DVD is Custom (Advanced), so click that to open the Where Do You Want To Install Windows page shown in Figure 23-5.

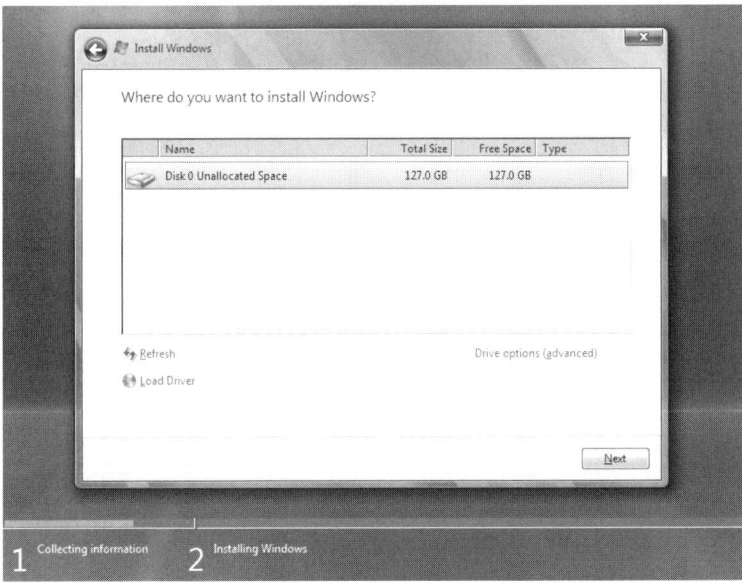

FIGURE 23-5 The Where Do You Want To Install Windows page of the Install Windows Wizard

11. The first disk on your computer will be highlighted. You can select any disk shown, or if the disk you want to install on isn't displayed, you can load any required driver at this point by clicking Load Driver. Clicking Drive Options (Advanced) will give you additional options to repartition or format the selected drive.

12. When you've selected the drive to install on, click Next and the installation will begin. You won't be prompted again until the installation completes and you're prompted for a password for the Administrator account.

 UNDER THE HOOD **Drive Options**

The default selected drive when you're installing SBS second server is the first drive as enumerated by the BIOS. You can change the selection if the drive you want isn't selected, or you can add drivers for additional controllers if the drive you want isn't visible. For those familiar with earlier versions of Windows, you'll be glad to know that Windows Server 2008 finally adds support for something besides a floppy drive for loading storage drivers during installation! As shown in Figure 23-6, you can load drivers from floppy, from CD or DVD, or from a USB flash drive.

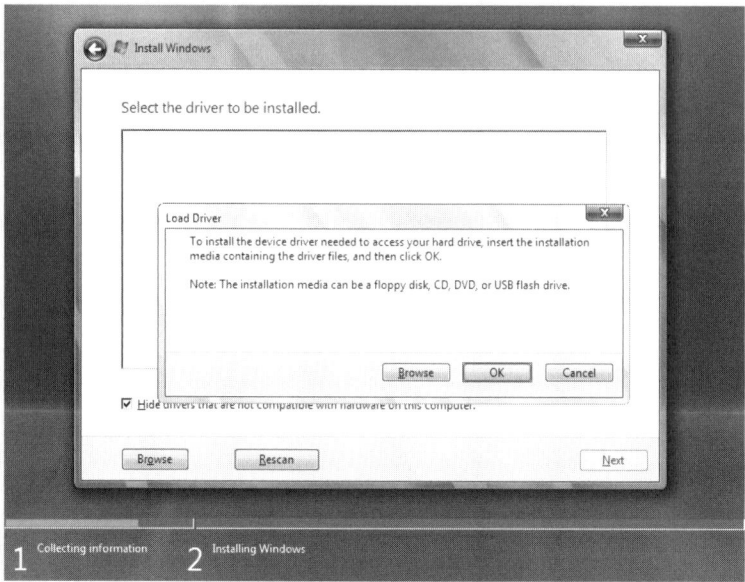

FIGURE 23-6 Windows Server 2008 supports loading storage drivers from floppy, optical drive, or USB drive.

If you need to change partitions on a drive, or format it, or even extend it to add additional space, just click Drive Options (Advanced) to display additional options for managing and configuring your disks during installation, as shown in Figure 23-7.

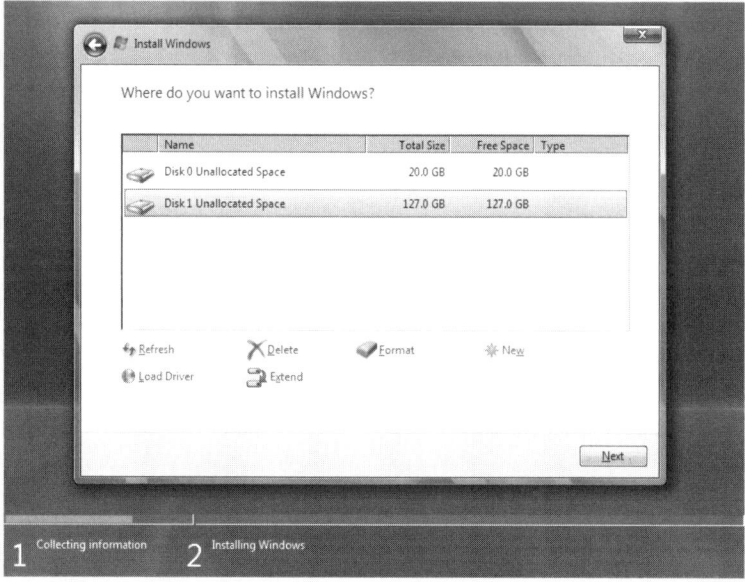

FIGURE 23-7 Advanced drive options are available during installation of Windows Server 2008.

New in SBS 2008 and Windows Server 2008 is the ability to extend existing partitions, even during the installation process. Although this isn't a feature that matters in completely new installations, it can be a useful feature when you're recycling a computer. You can extend a partition onto available unallocated space on the same disk.

NOTE If you need to open a command window during the installation process, just press Shift+F10. Now you can manually run Diskpart.exe or any other tool available at this point in the process to manually load a driver or fine-tune partitioning.

After the installation completes, Windows Server 2008 will restart and proceed to the logon screen. You'll need to enter a new password for the Administrator account, as shown in Figure 23-8, and then log on to the new server.

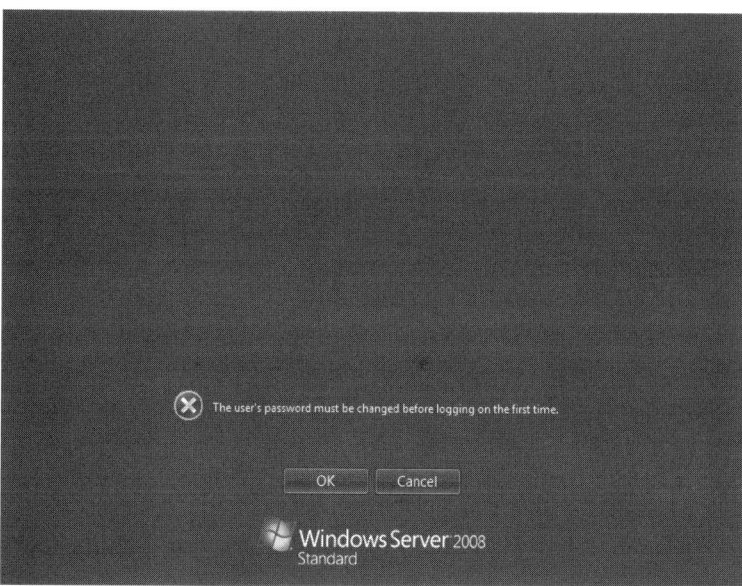

FIGURE 23-8 Setting the initial password for the Administrator account

When you log on, you'll see the Initial Configuration Tasks (ICT) Wizard, shown in Figure 23-9, which makes the initial setup of your new server easy.

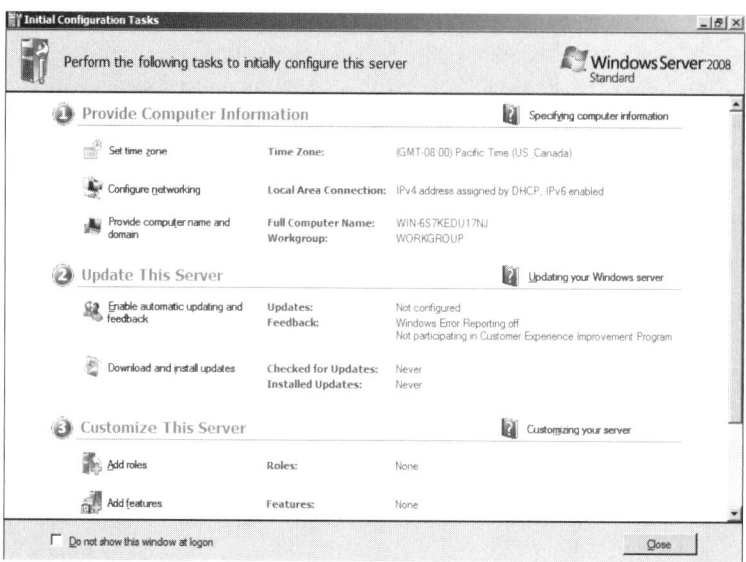

FIGURE 23-9 The Initial Configuration Tasks Wizard for Windows Server 2008

Initial Configuration

When the SBS Premium second server installation completes, there are still quite a few tasks to perform. The basic requirements haven't changed—they've just been shifted to after, in-stead of during, the install. At minimum, you'll need to perform the following tasks on a fresh server installation:

- Assign the initial Administrator account password.

- Install any hardware drivers required.

- Set the time zone.

- Configure the networking.

- Assign a name to the server.

- Join the server to the SBS domain.

- Configure automatic updates and automatic feedback settings.

- Check for updates and install them.

The first of those tasks, assigning the Administrator account password, is required before you can log on for the first time, so we've already covered that.

There are additional tasks on the Initial Configuration Tasks (ICT) Wizard that you probably want to perform as part of your initial setup:

- Add server roles.

- Add server features.

- Enable Remote Desktop.

- Configure Windows Firewall.

Exactly which roles and features you'll need to install varies depending on what the server will be used for. We'll cover the basics of adding a feature here, by adding the Windows PowerShell feature. And in Chapter 25, we'll cover adding roles in more detail. Enabling Remote Desktop is handled automatically by Group Policy in an SBS network, and Windows Firewall should also be configured automatically by the role and feature wizards and Group Policy.

Install Hardware Drivers

There's a missing piece in the ICT Wizard—no direct way to add hardware drivers for any hardware on the server that isn't recognized. Microsoft makes every effort to get as many drivers as possible on the installation DVD, but the reality is that new hardware will continue to be released, and the drivers are limited to what was available when Windows Server 2008 shipped. So some hardware might require drivers that aren't on the DVD. If these are drivers for hard disk controllers, you always have the option of adding them during the installation, but for other hardware you need to wait until Windows Server 2008 is installed.

After the installation completes, and you've logged on, you can install additional drivers as required. We think it's a good idea to do this as the first step before configuring any settings in the ICT. This is especially important if your network card isn't recognized, because you'll need connectivity to the SBS network to complete the rest of the ICT.

Setting the Time Zone

During the initial installation, Windows will pick a time zone (probably not the one you're in unless you live on the west coast of North America) and will also set the current date and time based on your computer's BIOS. To set the date and time, as well as the current time zone, click the link on the ICT Wizard to open the Date And Time dialog box shown in Figure 23-10. After you've set your server's clock and time zone, click Apply and then click OK to return to the ICT Wizard.

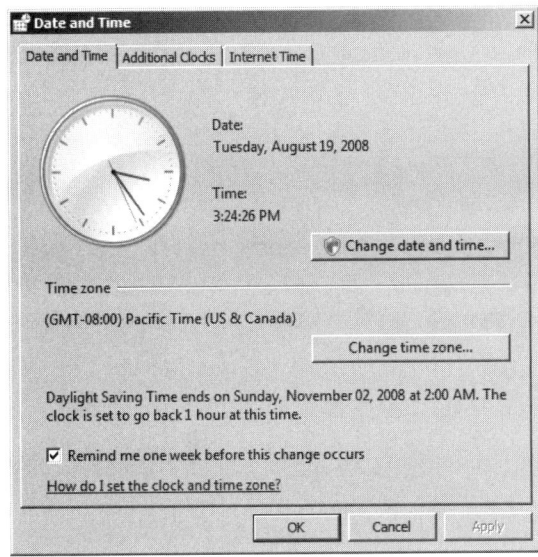

FIGURE 23-10 The Date And Time dialog box

Windows Server 2008 lets you configure two additional clocks as part of the Date And Time dialog box. If you configure additional clocks, the times in those time zones will be visible when you hover the mouse cursor over the clock.

If you regularly work with folks in another time zone, you eventually get used to the time difference and don't need additional clocks on your server. And, after all, you shouldn't be sitting at the server console in most cases anyway. But we still find it handy, and because we work with folks in Europe and Australia fairly often, we turn on two additional clocks: one set to Greenwich Mean Time (GMT), and the other set to GMT+10 hours, for Sidney, Australia. This ensures that when we call at a totally unreasonable hour, we have absolutely no excuse.

Configuring Networking

Next on the list is configuring your networking. By default, your new server has enabled both IPv4 and IPv6, and with the DHCP server running on the main SBS server, you should have automatically assigned IP addresses. For servers, we highly recommend that at least the IPv4 address be a fixed address. In most scenarios, the IPv6 address can be a stateless autoconfiguration address.

NOTE If no DHCP server is available, the server will have a link-local address—an auto-configuration IP address that is unique on the network but won't be forwarded by routers to another network. These IP addresses begin with 169.254. If your second server has an IP address in this range, check for problems with the physical network connecting the second server to the SBS server.

To configure the networking and set a fixed IP address for the server, follow these steps:

1. Click Configure Networking in the Initial Configuration Tasks window to open the Network Connections Control Panel application shown in Figure 23-11.

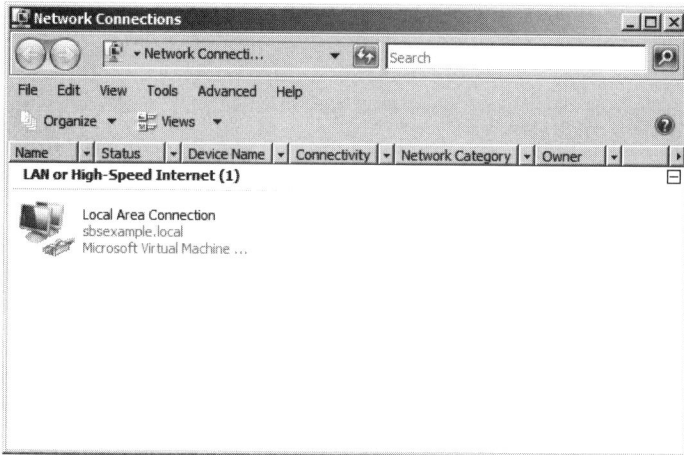

FIGURE 23-11 The Network Connections Control Panel application

2. Right-click the connection you want to configure and select Properties from the Action menu to open the Local Area Connection Properties dialog box, shown in Figure 23-12.

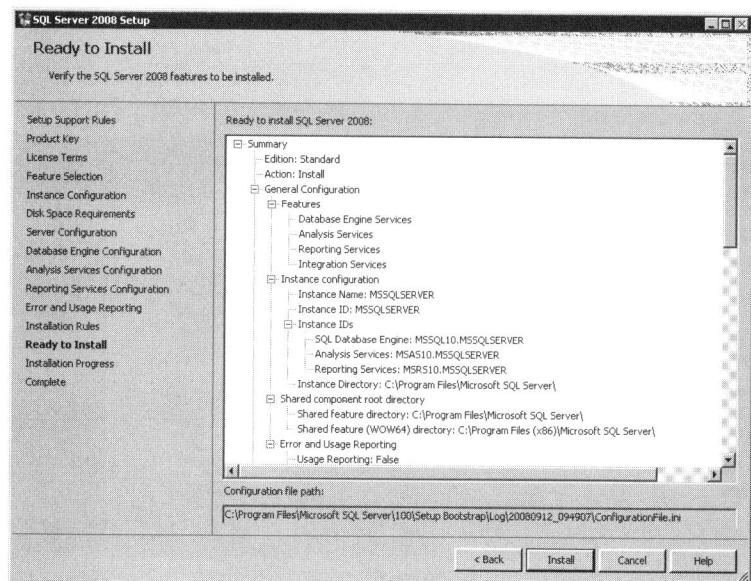

FIGURE 23-12 The Local Area Connection Properties dialog box

3. Select Internet Protocol Version 4 (TCP/IPv4) and click Properties.

4. Select Use The Following IP Address, as shown in Figure 23-13.

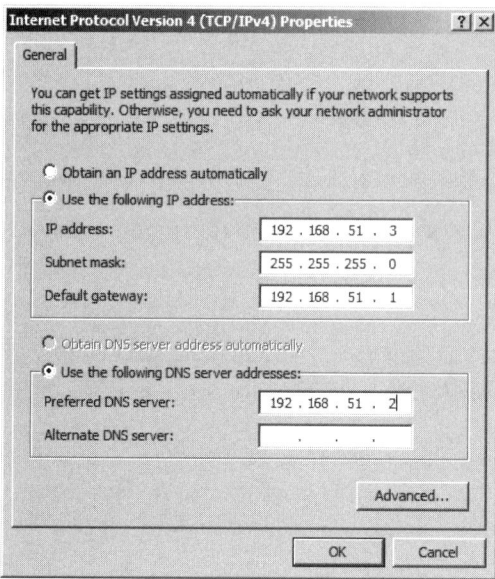

FIGURE 23-13 The Internet Protocol Version 4 (TCP/IP) Properties dialog box

5. Enter an IP address, a subnet mask, and a default gateway appropriate to your network. This should be in the range excluded from the SBS DHCP server range.

NOTE By default, the SBS server will be at 192.168.*nnn*.2, where *nnn* is the subnet used by your Internet router. On our network this is 51, so we've assigned 192.168.51.3 as the IP address for our second server. Your subnet will likely be different.

6. Specify the Preferred DNS Server for your network. This will be the IP address of the primary SBS server.

7. Click OK to close the Internet Protocol Version 4 (TCP/IP) Properties dialog box, and then click Close to complete the configuration of the connection.

8. Close the Network Connections window by clicking in the upper-right corner of the window to return to the ICT Wizard page.

Setting the Computer Name and Domain

When you have your networking configured, you're ready to give the computer a name and join it to the SBS domain. The Windows Server 2008 setup process automatically assigns a random and meaningless name to a new server. Although this name is certainly unique on the network, it's not a useful final name, so you'll want to change it.

 REAL WORLD **Naming Computers**

t's a good idea to use a computer name that is both DNS-compatible and Net-BIOS-compatible so that all types of clients see the same name for your computer. (And yes, we're going to have to live with NetBIOS for a while still—too many applications, including Microsoft applications, simply don't work properly without it.) To do this, keep the name to 15 characters or fewer and don't use asterisks or periods. To obtain the best application compatibility, use dashes instead of spaces and underscores.

Beyond that, you should use a naming convention that has some internal consistency. We've seen all sorts of naming conventions, from the literary obscurities of naming them after romantic poets or science-fiction characters, to Norse or Greek gods, to colors (with the server fronts all painted to match the color name of the server). But honestly, we like names that actually help identify functionality, location, address, hardware, domain, or some combination of these. So our SBSEXAMPLE network here includes computers with the following names:

- hp350-sbs-02 (The computer is running on a Hewlett-Packard ML350G5, it's the main SBS server, and its IP address is 192.168.51.2.)

- hp350-srv-03 (It's running on a Hewlett-Packard ML350G5, it's a server, and its IP address is 192.168.51.3.)

- hp350-vista-02 (It's running on that same Hewlett-Packard ML350G5, it's a Windows Vista VM, and it's the second one we created.)

We know it's a boring way to name things, but we think it's a lot easier to understand than trying to remember that Zeus is the main SBS server, and Athena is the second server running SQL Server.

You can save a reboot if you change the computer name and domain at the same time. Both require a reboot that will prevent other tasks from being completed, but fortunately they can be paired. To set the name and domain, follow these steps:

1. Click Provide Computer Name And Domain in the ICT Wizard to open the System Properties dialog box shown in Figure 23-14.

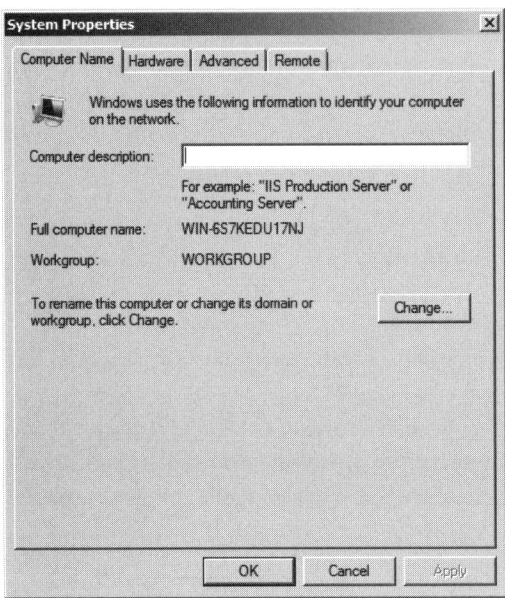

FIGURE 23-14 The System Properties dialog box

2. You can enter a description for this computer if you want, but it's hardly ever visible and thus not terribly useful.

3. Click Change to open the Computer Name/Domain Changes dialog box shown in Figure 23-15.

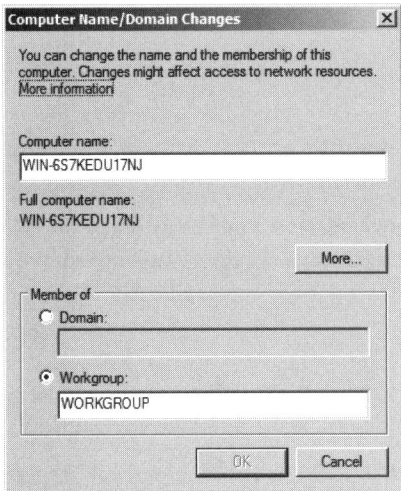

FIGURE 23-15 The Computer Name/Domain Changes dialog box

4. Type in a computer name consistent with your naming convention and then select Domain to type in the SBS domain name.

NOTE You can use either the NetBIOS version of the domain name (SBSEXAMPLE here) or the DNS version (sbsexample.local).

5. Click OK. You are prompted for credentials to perform the change, as shown in Figure 23-16. This should be the administrator account you chose for the SBS domain.

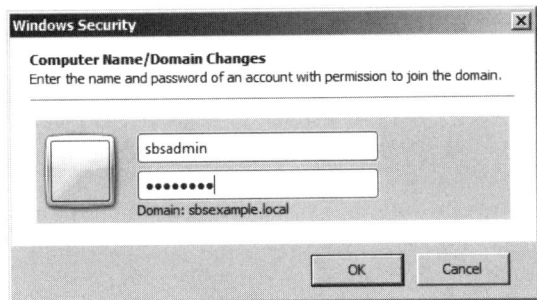

FIGURE 23-16 You must provide administrative credentials for the SBS domain.

6. Click OK. If there aren't any problems, you'll get a Welcome message like that shown in Figure 23-17.

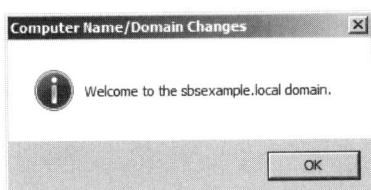

FIGURE 23-17 The Welcome message lets you know you're now joined to the domain.

7. Click OK to acknowledge the Welcome message. You'll be warned that you need to restart the server before the changes take full effect. Click Close and then click OK a couple more times and the server will reboot.

> **IMPORTANT** It's tempting at this point to try to delay the reboot to see if you can squeeze a few more things in before having to wait for the server to shut down and restart. And we understand the temptation—we're big fans of minimizing the number of reboots required and doing as many things as we can when we know we're going to have to reboot. But this is the one time when we think you shouldn't do it. You need to get that new name and security in place before anything else happens.

8. After the server has rebooted, log on with an SBS account—not the local administrator account—to complete the configuration of the server.

Enable Updates and Feedback

The next group of settings on the ICT Wizard is used to set how updates are handled and what feedback is sent to Microsoft. The first setting in this section of the ICT Wizard is to actually configure what settings are used for updates and feedback. You can make three basic choices when you click Enable Automatic Updating And Feedback on the ICT Wizard:

- Windows and Microsoft Update settings
- Windows Error Reporting settings
- Customer Experience Improvement Program settings

To configure these settings, follow these steps:

1. On the Initial Configuration Tasks Wizard, click Enable Automatic Updating And Feedback to open the dialog box shown in Figure 23-18.

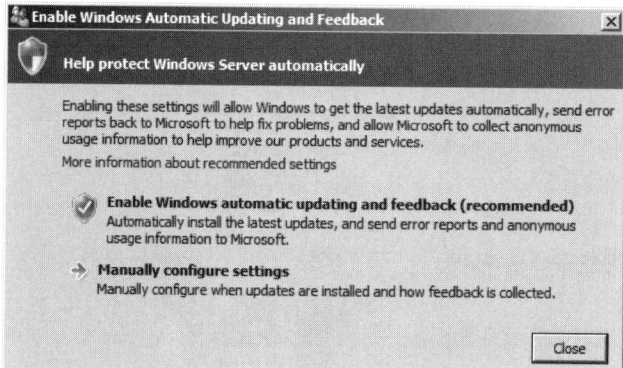

FIGURE 23-18 The Enable Windows Automatic Updating And Feedback dialog box

2. Unless you really want your server to be automatically downloading and installing updates with no warning, and with automatic reboots (again without warning), do not select Enable Windows Automatic Updating And Feedback.

3. Click Manually Configure Settings to open the dialog box shown in Figure 23-19.

4. To configure how the Windows and Microsoft updates are handled on this server, use the Windows SBS Console, as described in Chapter 15, "Managing Software Updates."

5. Click Change Settings in the Windows Error Reporting section to open the Windows Error Reporting Configuration dialog box shown in Figure 23-20.

6. Select how you want error reports handled. We think that automatically sending at least summary reports, and preferably detailed reports, is good for all of us. See the Under the Hood sidebar titled "Windows Error Reporting" for more information on what is sent and why we care. When you've made your selection, click OK to return to the Manually Configure Settings dialog box, shown in Figure 23-19.

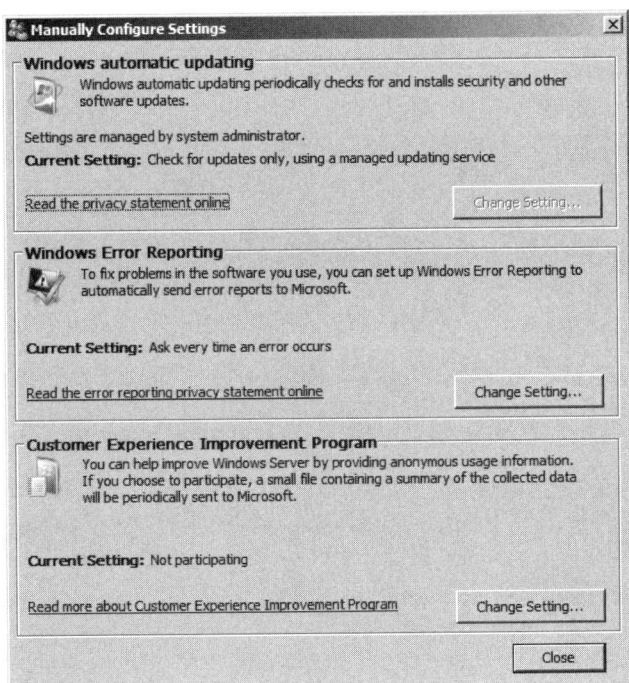

FIGURE 23-19 The Manually Configure Settings dialog box

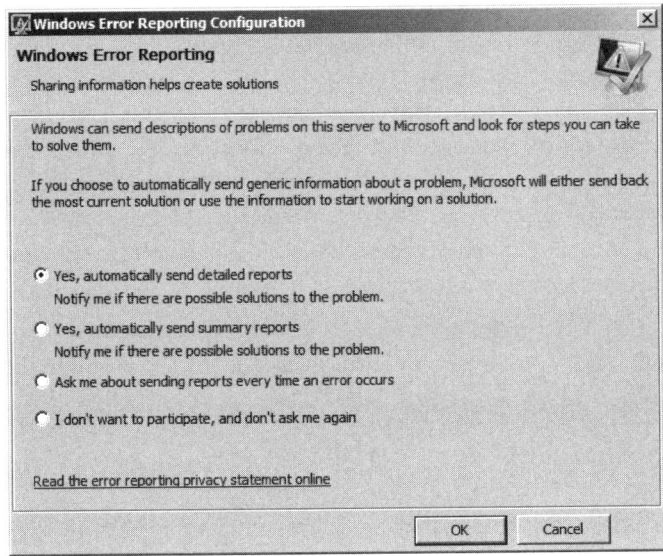

FIGURE 23-20 The Windows Error Reporting Configuration dialog box

7. Click Change Settings in the Customer Experience Improvement Program (CEIP) section to open the Customer Experience Improvement Program Configuration dialog box shown in Figure 23-21.

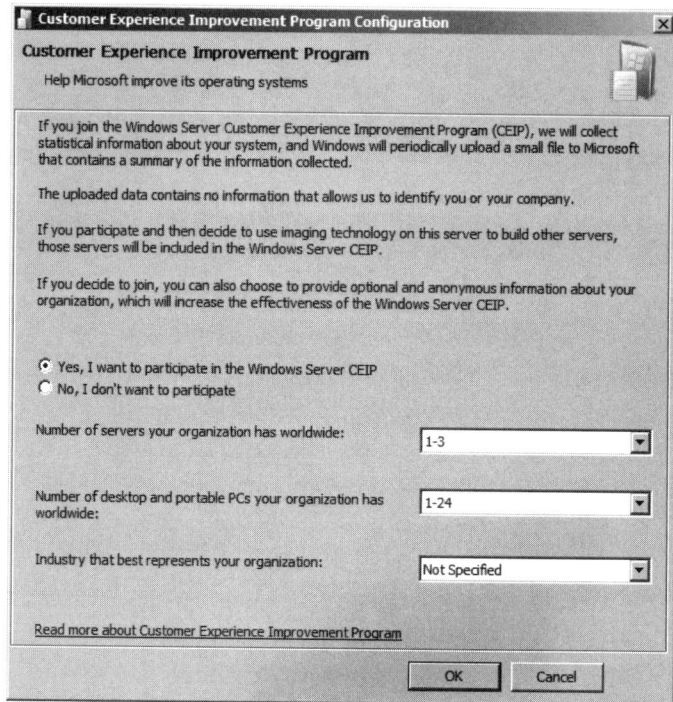

FIGURE 23-21 The Customer Experience Improvement Program Configuration dialog box

8. The default is to not automatically participate in the CEIP. When you choose to participate, no personal or organizationally identifiable information is sent to Microsoft. None. But they do gather information about your hardware and the Server Roles installed on the server, and if you include details about your organization's servers, workstations, and industry, that information is linked to the collected data. Personally, we choose to send it.

9. Make your selections, click OK, and then click Close to return to the ICT Wizard.

 UNDER THE HOOD **Windows Error Reporting**

Windows Error Reporting dates back to the old Dr. Watson errors that we all learned to hate in the earlier days of Windows. But it's come a long way since then. One of the major changes, introduced in Windows XP, was the sending of the crash dumps back to Microsoft when a program crashed or stopped responding. (This is called Online Crash Analysis, or OCA, and it found a lot of bugs!) You were asked each time if you wanted to send the crash dump, and fortunately a lot of people did, because the result has been a far more stable and solid Windows, along with much better drivers. Microsoft CEO Steve Ballmer is reliably reported to have observed that "about 20 percent of the bugs cause 80 percent of all errors, and—this is stunning to me—one percent of bugs cause half of all errors." By identifying those 20 percent of the bugs, and focusing efforts on them, we all benefit from more stable, crash-free software.

It is important to note, however, that crash dumps can contain personally identifiable information. If you're in the middle of entering your credit card number when the program you're working in crashes, chances are that the credit card number, or some portion of it, is likely to be inside that crash dump. Microsoft has made repeated—and we think credible—assurances that they will not use any personal information in those crash dumps in any way. You can read their Privacy Statement at *http://oca.microsoft.com/en/dcp20.asp*. In fact, we urge you to read it. It's clear and we think as unambiguous as possible when lawyers are involved. And we found it reassuring. We've all benefited from the errors that have been reported in the past to help make the software we use better and more reliable.

Getting Updates

The final option in the middle section of the ICT Wizard is to go online and download updates right now. Just click Download And Install Updates. The Windows Update dialog box shown in Figure 23-22 opens.

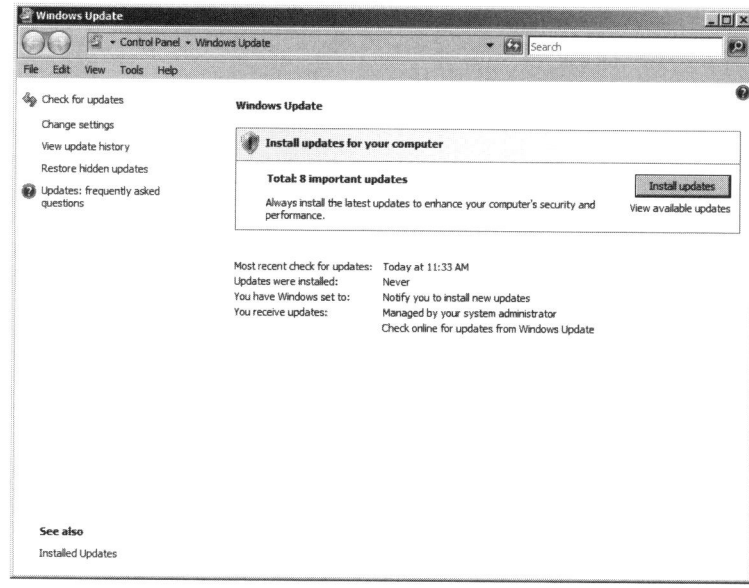

FIGURE 23-22 The Windows Update dialog box

If updates are available, they'll be displayed and you can choose to install them immediately. The default is to connect to WSUS running on the main SBS server. Install the updates and get the reboot out of the way.

Customizing the Server

The final section of the ICT Wizard is used to add Roles and Features to the server, enable remote access, and configure Windows Firewall. We can finally get down to actually setting the server up to do some real work. All the rest has just been getting ready.

We'll cover adding Roles to the server when we talk about Terminal Server in Chapter 25. Roles are a new way that Windows Server 2008 groups similar functionality together for installation and configuration. A Role is a specific set of functionality that the server needs for a particular set of uses. Roles can also have Role Services, which are subsets of the functionality in the Role and can only be installed as part of the Role.

Features can be installed on any server, without being specific to a particular function of how the server will be used. We think that at least one Feature, Windows PowerShell, should be installed on every server, so we'll cover that installation here.

The other two settings in this last section of the ICT Wizard are enabling Remote Desktop and configuring Windows Firewall.

Adding the Windows PowerShell Feature

Windows PowerShell is the new command-line shell and scripting language released by Microsoft in 2006. It is available as a download at *http://www.microsoft.com/technet/scriptcenter /topics/msh/download.mspx* for earlier versions of Windows, but is included as a feature in Windows Server 2008 and is installed automatically on the main SBS server—but not, unfortunately, on the SBS Premium second server.

Windows PowerShell has completely replaced Cmd.exe as our everyday command shell. Even if you don't write a bunch of Windows PowerShell scripts right away, just using Windows PowerShell as your command-line shell will get you started.

You need to enable the Windows PowerShell feature in Windows Server 2008 before you can use it. The ICT Wizard has an Add Features link, so let's use it to add Windows PowerShell right now, by following these steps:

1. Click Add Features in the Initial Configuration Tasks Wizard to open the Add Features Wizard, shown in Figure 23-23.

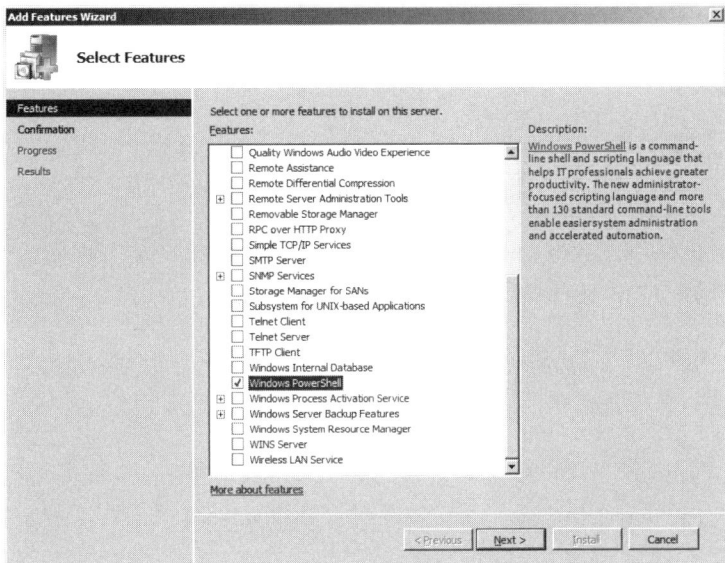

FIGURE 23-23 The Select Features page of the Add Features Wizard

2. Scroll down to near the bottom of the Features list and select Windows PowerShell, as shown.

3. Click Next to open the confirmation page. You'll see a list of features that are going to be installed, and a warning that this might require a reboot. Don't worry, the server will not reboot as long as this is the only feature you're installing.

4. Click Install to begin the actual installation. When the installation completes, you'll see the Installation Results page. Any problems will be highlighted here, or it will simply report that the installation was successful. Click Close to exit the Add Features Wizard.

Now, you're almost done. A couple of little configuration steps will simplify your use of Windows PowerShell, so let's take care of that right now.

First, let's pin Windows PowerShell to the Start menu to make it easier to use. After all, Command Prompt is there, so why shouldn't Windows PowerShell be there, too? To pin Windows PowerShell to the Start menu, follow these steps:

1. Click Start, click All Programs, and then click Windows PowerShell 1.0.

2. Right-click Windows PowerShell and select Pin To Start Menu, as shown in Figure 23-24.

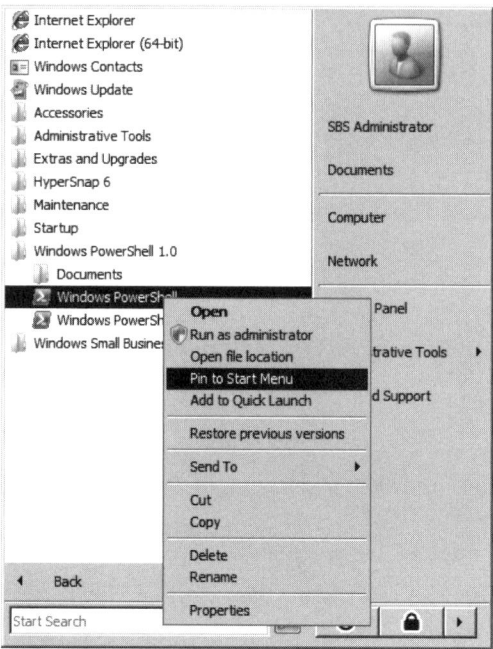

FIGURE 23-24 Pinning Windows PowerShell to the Start Menu

3. While you're there, add Windows PowerShell to your Quick Launch toolbar. Now you have easy access to Windows PowerShell without having to dig into the menus to get to it.

> **NOTE** On 64-bit Windows Server 2008, you have both a 64-bit version of Windows PowerShell and a 32-bit version called Windows PowerShell (x86). For virtually everything, you'll want to use the 64-bit shell.

By default, Windows PowerShell installs in the safest way possible, prohibiting you from running any scripts or configuration files. This lets you use the command line but severely limits your ability to customize or do much of anything with Windows PowerShell beyond simple shell commands.

This restriction is called the *execution policy* of the shell. Four levels of execution policy are available:

- **Restricted** Does not allow any scripts to be run and won't load configuration files. This is the default value.
- **AllSigned** Allows the running of scripts or configuration files signed by a trusted publisher. Even scripts that you write yourself must be signed.

- **RemoteSigned** Allows the running of scripts or configuration files that were created on the local network to run without being signed, but any script that was downloaded from the Internet must be signed by a trusted publisher.

- **Unrestricted** Allows the running of any script or configuration file, regardless of where it came from. Scripts or configuration files that originated on the Internet will prompt you before you can run them, however.

We think the default value of Restricted is a bit much, and frankly we're just not willing to get a code-signing certificate just to run our own scripts, so even AllSigned is a bit much. In an environment that fully supports code-signing certificates, and where you want to restrict the scripts that can be run to only those that are approved and signed, AllSigned makes sense. But for most SBS networks, we think RemoteSigned is a good compromise. To change the execution policy to RemoteSigned, follow these steps:

1. Click Start, right-click the Windows PowerShell, and then select Run As Administrator.

2. Select Continue at the User Account Control prompt to open Windows PowerShell with administrative privileges.

3. At the Windows PowerShell prompt, run the following command:

   ```
   Set-ExecutionPolicy RemoteSigned
   ```

4. To confirm that the change has taken effect, you can use the Get-ExecutionPolicy command, shown in Figure 23-25.

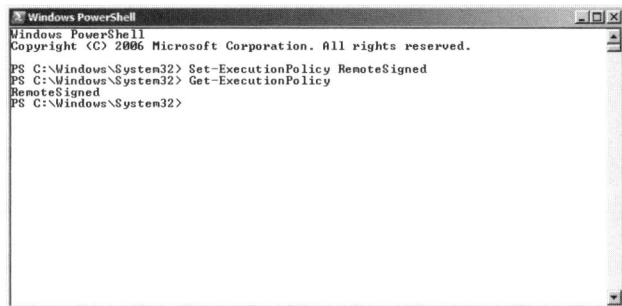

FIGURE 23-25 Configuring the Windows PowerShell Execution Policy

Remote Desktop

Next on the ICT Wizard list is a link to enable Remote Desktop. Remote Desktop allows administrators to connect directly to the server without having to sit down at the console in the server room. Windows Server 2008 introduces version 6.1 of the Remote Desktop Protocol (RDP). The Remote Desktop Client version 6.1 is included in Windows Vista Service Pack 1 (SP1) and Windows XP SP3, and version 6 clients are downloadable from Microsoft Knowledge Base Article 925876 at *http://support.microsoft.com/kb/925876*.

Version 6 and later of RDP includes many improvements over earlier versions, including 32-bit color, server authentication, resource redirection, font smoothing, and Terminal Services Remote Programs. For remote administration of a server, the most important improvement is server authentication, which ensures that you are actually connecting to the computer you think you are.

To enable Remote Desktop on the new server, you don't have to do anything at all. When the server is joined to the SBS domain, the SBS configured Group Policy will automatically enable Remote Desktop on the server. Nice.

Configure Windows Firewall

By default, Windows Firewall is enabled on all new servers. This is a very different version of Windows Firewall than the one that came with the first release of Windows Server 2003. The new Windows Firewall is location-aware, with different rules for Domain traffic, Private Network traffic, and Public Network traffic. And it's bidirectional, controlling both incoming and outgoing traffic.

As you change the roles and features enabled on the server, Windows Firewall will be automatically configured to work optimally within your SBS network. Some settings are directly controlled by SBS Group Policy, and others are configured automatically by the Windows Server 2008 role and feature wizards.

Closing the Initial Configuration Tasks Wizard

When you've finished all the steps in the ICT Wizard, you can select the Do Not Show This Window At Logon check box and click Close. This will close the ICT Wizard, and you'll never see it again. When the wizard closes, the Server Manager console will open, allowing you to continue to configure your server for additional Roles and Features, along with providing easy access to all your daily management tasks on the server.

If you're not quite sure you're completely done with the ICT Wizard, we suggest you leave the box cleared and close the ICT Wizard. This will still automatically open the Server Manager, but the next time you log on to the server, you'll see the ICT Wizard.

All the functions on the ICT Wizard are available elsewhere, but we think it's a useful and well-designed feature that pulls together all the initial steps you're likely to need to do on a new server into a single, logical place. If you've closed the ICT Wizard and turned it off, and then realize that you need to configure something that was on the ICT Wizard but can't easily locate it on the Server Manager, you can open the ICT Wizard again by running oobe from the command line.

Summary

In this chapter, we've covered the basic installation and initial configuration tasks you need to do to get your SBS Premium second server up and running. SBS does preconfigure some settings for you, but quite a few still need to be done manually. In the next chapter, we'll cover installing and configuring Microsoft SQL Server 2008 as we continue covering the features of Windows Small Business Server 2008 Premium Edition.

## CHAPTER 24

Introducing SQL Server 2008 Standard Edition for Small Business

The Premium Edition of Windows Small Business Server 2008 includes Microsoft SQL Server 2008 Standard Edition for Small Business (henceforth referred to in this chapter as SQL Server 2008). SQL Server 2008 is a set of components based around a relational database that work together to meet the data storage and analysis needs of some of the largest Web sites and enterprise data-processing systems. SQL Server 2008 works equally well for meeting the day-to-day business needs of the small business.

This chapter can't come close to telling you everything you might need to know about SQL Server—that is the subject of dozens of books. However, we can give you an overview of the features and a brief introduction to installing SQL Server.

Installation Options

You have choices when it comes to installing SQL Server 2008, although if you use it to support a particular line-of-business application, the decision might already be made for you. Windows SBS 2008 Premium Edition includes both 32-bit and 64-bit versions of SQL Server and Windows 2008 Server. The permutations are as follows:

- SQL Server 64-bit can be installed on your Windows SBS 2008 Server or, preferably, on a second server running Windows Server 2008 64-bit.

- SQL Server 32-bit can be installed on a second server running Windows Server 2008 32-bit.

Installation Restrictions

Before you begin the process of installing and deploying SQL Server, you should be aware of the following restrictions:

- The versions of SQL Server that are included in Windows SBS 2008 Premium are licensed for installation only in your Windows SBS 2008 network. You cannot install SQL Server on a server that is not in the Windows SBS 2008 domain.

- The Windows SBS 2008 CAL Suite for Premium Users or Devices is required for users or devices that access SQL Server.

- You can install SQL Server on the server running Windows SBS 2008 or on the second server that you set up for your Windows SBS 2008 domain. However, for security reasons, it's a bad idea to install the SQL Server on a domain controller. Use the second server in the Windows SBS 2008 domain.

- Do not upgrade the instance of SQL Server 2005 Express that is installed on the server running Windows SBS 2008 for monitoring (SBSMONITORING) and do not move the database to the SQL Server Standard Edition that is included in Windows SBS 2008 Premium. These types of migration are not supported.

- Don't attempt to upgrade the instance of the Windows internal database (SQL Server 2005 Embedded Edition) installed for Windows Server Update Services and for Windows SharePoint Services (MICROSOFT##SSEE) and don't move the database to the SQL Server Standard Edition that is included in Windows SBS 2008 Premium. These types of migrations are not supported.

- You can move the Windows SharePoint Services content database to SQL Server Standard Edition, but it's not a sensible idea, because then you'll need a SQL Server CAL for everyone who accesses SharePoint.

Installing SQL Server (Part One)

To install SQL Server, insert the DVD in the drive on the server and follow these steps:

1. If the startup sequence doesn't start automatically, select Computer from the Start menu and double-click the DVD drive.

2. The first dialog box that appears (Figure 24-1) advises that Microsoft .NET Framework and an updated Windows Installer will be installed as part of the SQL Server installation. Click OK.

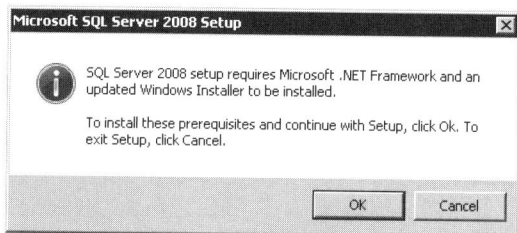

FIGURE 24-1 The SQL Server 2008 Setup dialog box

3. Next you must agree to the license terms to download the .NET Framework (Figure 24-2). Click Install after you have read and accepted.

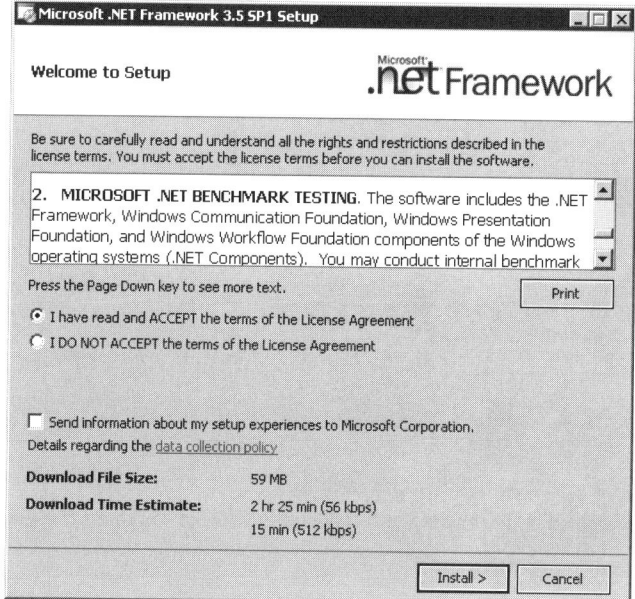

FIGURE 24-2 Accepting the licensing agreement

4. After the .NET Framework download is complete, the installation begins automatically. The installation can take several minutes. When the installation is finished, click Exit.

5. In the Windows Update Standalone Installer dialog box (Figure 24-3), click OK.

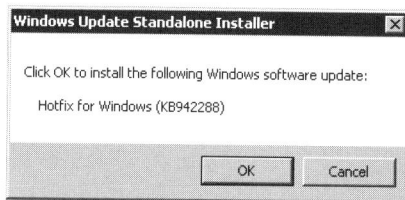

FIGURE 24-3 Click OK to install the update.

6. When the update is installed, click Restart Now.

When the computer is restarted, double-click the DVD drive again. The SQL Server Installation Center (Figure 24-4) opens. The following sections describe the links on each page.

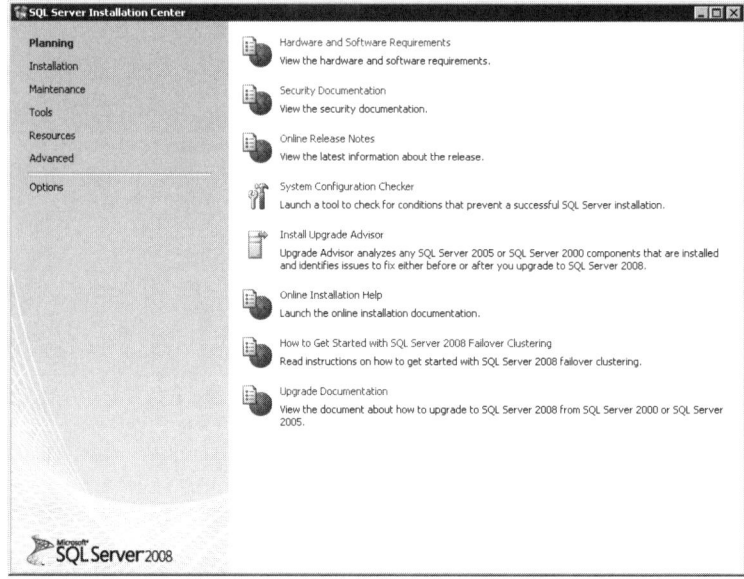

FIGURE 24-4 The SQL Server Installation Center

Planning

The SQL Server Installation Center provides a wealth of information. All that reading might be daunting at first, but 90 percent of a successful installation is in the planning. So the planning page is where we'll start.

Hardware And Software Requirements

Click the Hardware And Software Requirements link to see the minimum hardware and software requirements to install and run SQL Server 2008. The link is to the SQL Server 2008 Books Online.

Security Documentation

Click the Security Documentation link for advice on security measures. Click the links under the heading Before Installing SQL Server (Figure 24-5) for best practices.

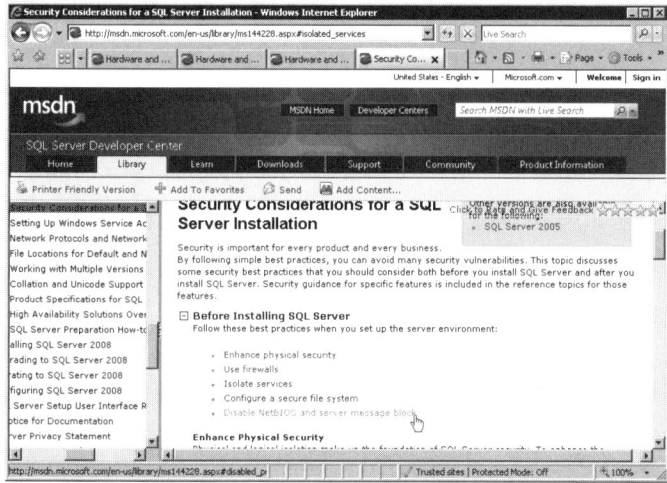

FIGURE 24-5 Online SQL Server security documentation

Online Release Notes

The Online Release Notes link takes you to the latest updates on SQL Server installation. The Release Notes document is available only online and is not on the installation media.

System Configuration Checker

The System Configuration Checker examines the computer for possible installation problems. After it runs, select Show Details to see the rules and results as shown in Figure 24-6.

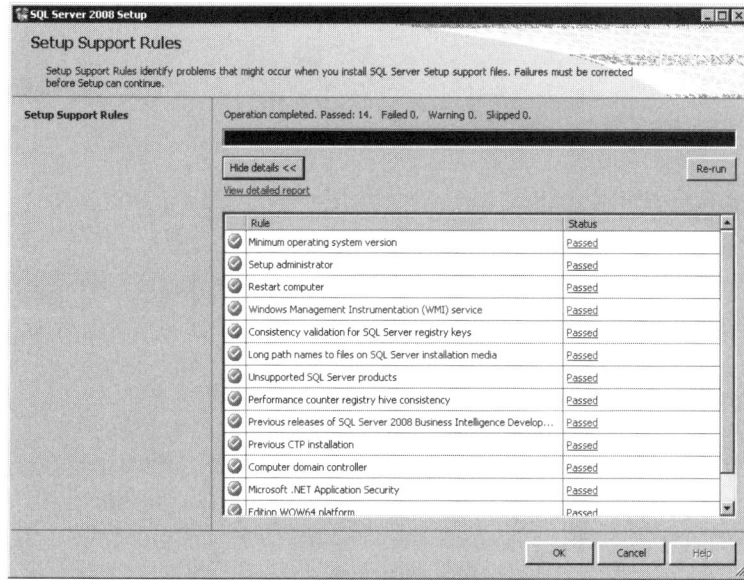

FIGURE 24-6 Results of the System Configuration Checker

Problems detected by the System Configuration Checker must be corrected before installation can continue. For even more details, click the View Detailed Report link.

Install Upgrade Advisor

Click Install Upgrade Advisor if you already have either SQL Server 2000 or SQL Server 2005 installed. Upgrade Advisor will check for any issues that need to be addressed before installing SQL Server 2008.

Online Installation Help

The Online Installation Help link connects to the MSDN SQL Server Developer Center, specifically to the Initial Installation section of SQL Server 2008 Books Online. On this page, there are links to all aspects of SQL Server, including Considerations For Installing The SQL Server Database Engine and Considerations For Installing SQL Server Management Tools.

How To Get Started With SQL Server 2008 Failover Clustering

Click the SQL Server 2008 Failover Clustering link to view information on building a SQL Server cluster. A two-node cluster can be built but will require additional licensed copies of SQL Server and Windows Server 2008.

Upgrade Documentation

Click the Upgrade Documentation link to connect to online topics including Version And Edition Upgrades, which lists the supported paths.

Installation

The Installation page of the SQL Server Installation Center includes links to wizards that will start different types of installations.

New SQL Server Stand-Alone Installation Or Add Features To An Existing Installation

Click the New SQL Server Stand-Alone Installation link to start the first-time installation of SQL Server. Return to this link to add features to an existing installation.

New SQL Server Failover Cluster Installation

Click this link to install a single-node SQL Server 2008 failover cluster.

Add Node To A SQL Server Failover Cluster

Click this link to add a second node to a single-node SQL Server failover cluster. This requires a second licensed copy of SQL Server and a second licensed copy of Windows Server 2008.

Upgrade From SQL Server 2000 Or SQL Server 2008

Click this link to upgrade your existing version of SQL Server. Be sure to first check Upgrade Documentation on the Planning page and verify that your version of SQL Server is directly upgradable to SQL Server 2008.

Search For Product Updates

Before installing SQL Server 2008, click Search For Product Updates to be sure that your Windows installation is up to date (Figure 24-7).

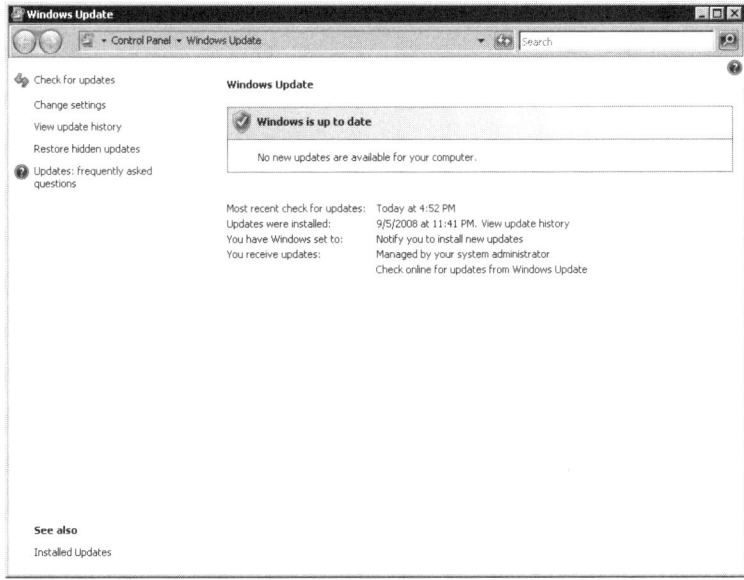

FIGURE 24-7 Check Windows updates before installing SQL Server.

Maintenance

The Maintenance page links to wizards to update or repair your SQL Server installation.

Edition Upgrade

Click the Edition Upgrade link to start the process of changing your edition of SQL Server.

Repair

This link starts a repair wizard to fix a corrupt SQL Server 2008 installation.

Remove Node From A SQL Server Failover Cluster

Click this link to remove an existing node from a failover cluster.

Tools

The Tools page of the SQL Server Installation Center includes the following three links.

System Configuration Checker

The System Configuration Checker examines the computer for possible installation problems. After it runs, select Show Details to see the rules and results. This links to the same tool as the System Configuration Checker link on the Planning page.

Installed SQL Server Features Discovery Report

When you're not sure just what SQL Server products are installed on the server, click this link to see a report. The report details any SQL Server 2000, SQL Server 2005, and SQL Server 2008 products and features that are present.

Upgrade Integration Services Packages

To upgrade SQL Server 2005 Integration Services Packages to SQL Server 2008 format, you can click this link, which is not activated until after SQL Server 2008 is installed.

Resources

The Resources page of the SQL Server Installation Center (Figure 24-8) includes multiple links to technical resources and other helpful Web sites.

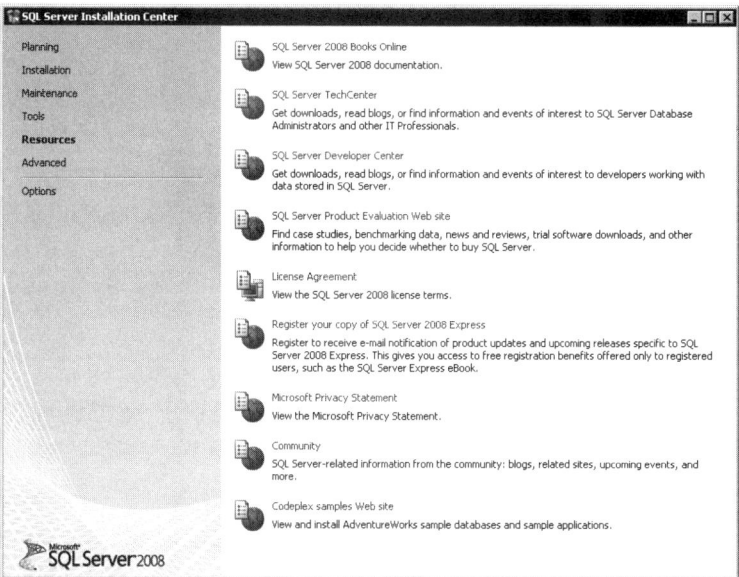

FIGURE 24-8 Resources page of the SQL Server Installation Center

Advanced

The Advanced page of the SQL Server Installation Center includes the following three advanced installation options.

Install Based On Configuration File

Click this link to launch an installation using an existing configuration file.

Advanced Cluster Preparation

Click this link to launch a wizard preparing a failover cluster installation.

Advanced Cluster Completion

This link starts a wizard that will complete a SQL Server 2008 failover cluster from a list of cluster-prepared instances.

Options

The Options page of the SQL Server Installation Center shows processor type options, but the option has already been determined by the operating system on the server where SQL Server will be installed. If the operating system is 32-bit, you can only install 32-bit SQL Server. If the operating system is 64-bit, you can only install 64-bit SQL Server.

Installing SQL Server (Part Two)

After you've reviewed all the relevant information in the previous sections and are at last ready to perform an initial installation of SQL Server, follow these steps:

1. On the Installation page of the SQL Server Installation Center, click the link for New SQL Server Stand-Alone Installation Or Add Features To An Existing Installation. SQL Server 2008 Setup launches.

2. The Setup Support Rules are run. Click Show Details to see the list of rules, as shown in Figure 24-9. Click OK if all rules show as Passed. Review any Warnings to determine their relevance to your network. Correct relevant Warnings and all Failed rules before proceeding.

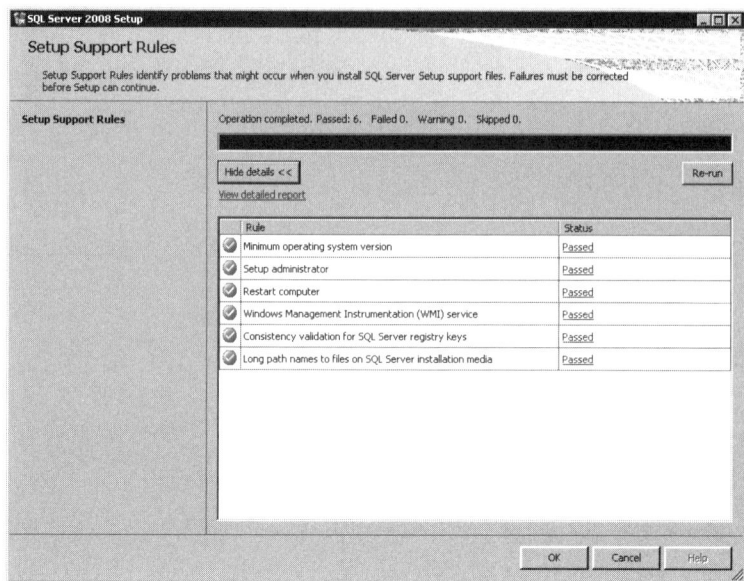

FIGURE 24-9 SQL Server checks for problems that could hinder installation.

3. Click Install on the Setup Support Files page and the support files are installed (Figure 24-10).

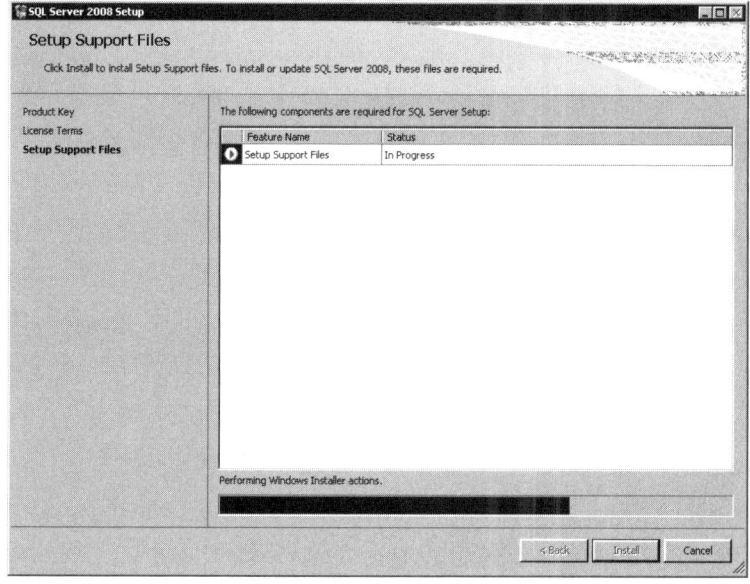

FIGURE 24-10 Installing support files

4. Another set of Setup Support Rules run. Click Show Details to see the list of rules. Click Next if all rules show as Passed. Review any Warnings to determine their relevance to your network. Correct relevant Warnings and all Failed rules before proceeding.

5. On the Product Key page, enter the product key for SQL Server 2008 Standard Edition for Small Business. Click Next.

6. Read the license terms and select the I Accept The License Terms check box. Click Next.

7. On the Feature Selection page, select the features to install. A description for each component group appears in the Description pane when you select it. See Table 24-1 for additional descriptions of the available features. Verify the location for shared features. Click Next.

TABLE 24-1 SQL Server Available Features

FEATURE	DESCRIPTION
Database Engine Services	The core service for storing and processing data.
SQL Server Replication	Replicates between and synchronizes two databases. Unnecessary for a single database.
Full-Text Search	Allows full-text queries against plain character-based data in SQL Server tables.
Analysis Services	Tools to create and administer online analytical processing (OLAP) and data-mining applications.
Reporting Services	Server and client tools to produce and manage reports.
Business Intelligence Development Studio	A development environment for Analysis Services, Reporting Services, and Integration Services solutions
Client Tools Connectivity	Tools for client/server communication.
Integration Services	Graphical tools and programmable objects for moving, copying, and converting data.
Client Tools Backwards Compatibility	Tools for clients to access earlier versions of SQL Server.
Client Tools SDK	Software development tools for programming clients.
SQL Server Books Online	Core documentation for SQL Server.
Management Tools – Basic	Includes SQL Server Management Studio.
Management Tools – Complete	Adds SQL Server Management Studio support for Reporting Services, Analysis Services, and Integration Services.
SQL Client Connectivity SDK	Software development kit for client connectivity.
Microsoft Sync Framework	Platform to enable collaboration and offline synchronization for applications, services, and devices.

8. On the Instance Configuration page, specify whether to create a Default Instance or a Named Instance. If you plan to install a single instance of SQL Server on a database server, you should create a default instance. Verify the root directory for the instance and click Next.

9. On the Disk Space Requirements page, review the available space and the amount of space required for the installation. Click Next.

> **NOTE** If the available space isn't sufficient, you can change the SQL Server features you want to install, change the installation directory to a drive with more space, or create more free space on the drive by moving other files.

10. On the Server Configuration page, assign logon accounts to the various SQL Services. Click Help for the recommended procedures. Click Next.

 UNDER THE HOOD **Service Accounts**

SQL Server 2008 requires several service accounts to run its various services. Choosing which account to use for a service account is always a tradeoff between simplicity and security. The simplest solution is to select the Local System account. You never need to worry about the password changing, and this account always has sufficient privileges. Unfortunately, running your SQL Server services under that account is not the best solution from a security standpoint. The Local System account is a powerful account, especially when it's running on your SBS server: If your security in SQL Server is breached, the entire network is compromised.

Using a regular user domain account is a possibility for the SQL Server service—it does not require any administrative privileges. But the SQL Server Agent process does require administrative privileges if your SQL Server environment uses CmdExec or ActiveScript jobs, or if you use the AutoRestart feature. If this is the case in your SQL Server environment, you should use separate service accounts for the SQL Server service and the SQL Server Agent.

Whatever domain accounts you use for SQL Server, you should use strong (long and complex) passwords. Also, when entering the domain name for a domain user account, you must use the NetBIOS name, not the DNS name. (In our environment, this means that the domain must be entered as "EXAMPLE" or "example" but not "example.local.")

11. The rest of the installation will configure the features selected in step 7. After you configure all these features and the Installation Rules are run (as seen in Figure 24-11),

the Ready To Install page (Figure 24-12) displays. Confirm that the installation tree is correct and click Install.

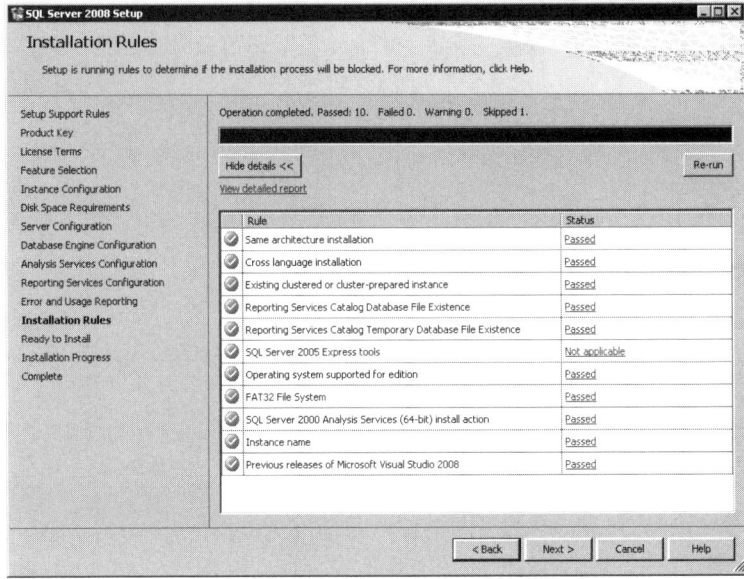

FIGURE 24-11 The final set of installation rules

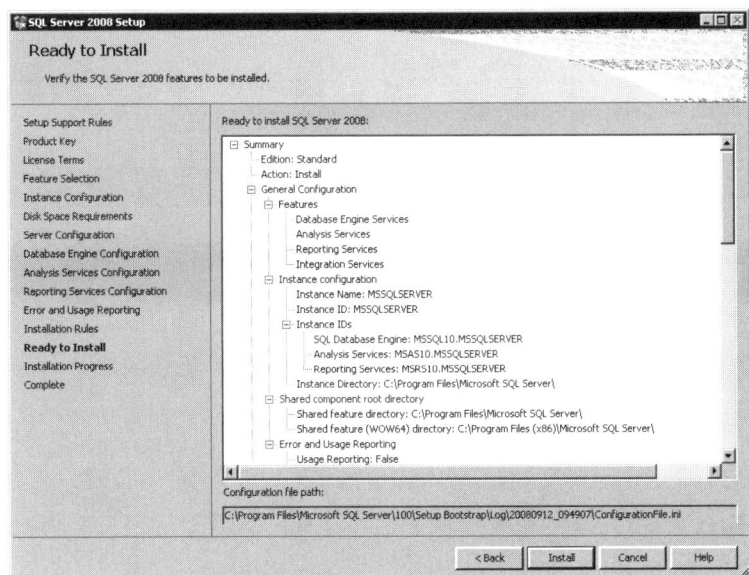

FIGURE 24-12 The list of components ready to install

12. The Installation Progress page follows the installation performance (Figure 24-13).

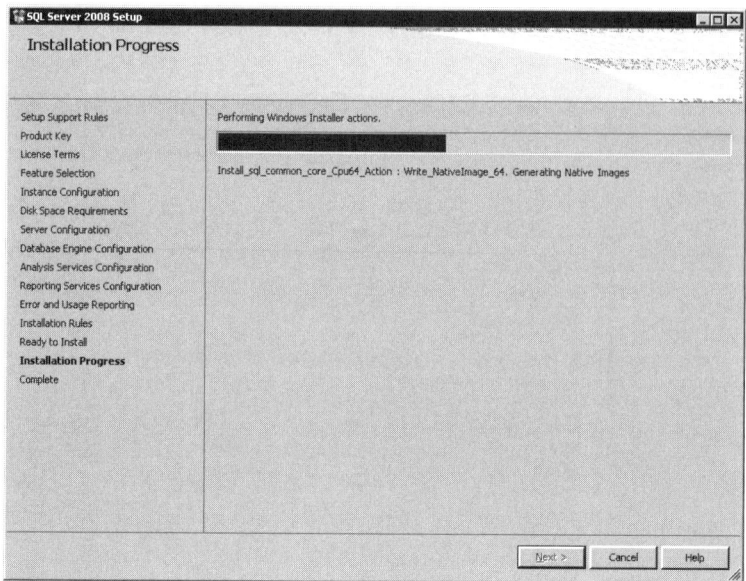

FIGURE 24-13 The Installation Progress page

13. At the completion of installation, the Installation Progress page displays the features and their status (Success or Failure). Click Next.

14. On the Complete page, as shown in Figure 24-14, review the information about your setup and notes that apply to your installation.

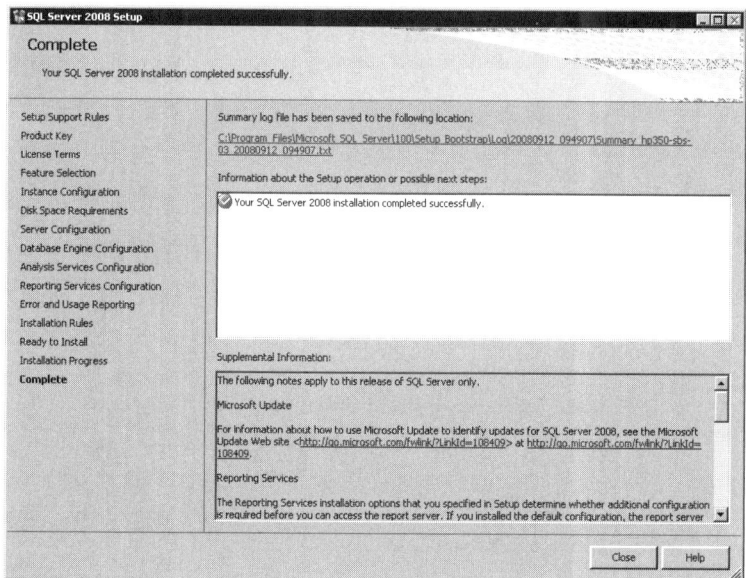

FIGURE 24-14 The Complete page for the SQL Server installation

15. Click the link at the top of the page to review an exceedingly detailed log file for the installation. This information can be very useful for any feature that failed installation. Click Close to finish.

When the installation is complete, select All Programs on the Start menu and then expand the Microsoft SQL Server 2008 entry (Figure 24-15). You can import an existing database and access the configuration tools you've installed.

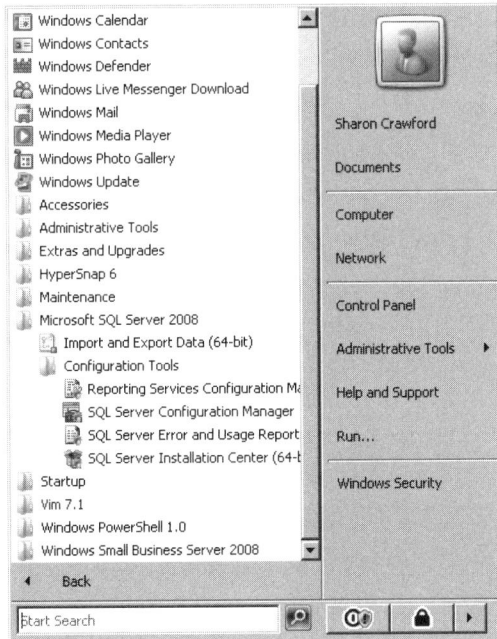

FIGURE 24-15 Your SQL Server installation on the Start menu

 REAL WORLD **Putting SQL Server to Work**

For the most up-to-date SQL Server 2008 documentation, click the links on the Resources page of the SQL Server Installation Center.

For help with setting up your database and maintaining it, two helpful books are *Microsoft SQL Server 2008 Step-by-Step* (2008) and *Microsoft SQL Server 2008 Administrator's Pocket Consultant* (2008), both from Microsoft Press.

Summary

In this chapter, we've provided a brief look at the planning and installation of SQL Server 2008 on your Windows SBS network. In the next chapter, we move on to adding and managing the very useful Terminal Services.

Adding a Terminal Server

One of the potential uses for the second server that the Premium Edition of Windows Small Business Server 2008 enables is as a Terminal Server. With the new features of Terminal Services in Windows Server 2008, we think this is a very compelling option, and one that we are implementing in our office already.

Adding a terminal server to SBS 2008 doesn't require purchasing the Premium Edition of SBS—any copy of Windows Server 2003 or Windows Server 2008 will do, though we strongly recommend Windows Server 2008. The additional features and security in Windows Server 2008 are compelling, especially those for a terminal server.

We also strongly recommend using the 64-bit version of Windows Server 2008 for a terminal server. Because of the better memory management and larger virtual memory address space, x64 versions of Windows are able to support more Terminal Server users.

New Terminal Services Features

Windows Server 2008 Terminal Services is a major update from the Terminal Services in Windows Server 2003. The three major new features are TS Gateway, TS RemoteApps, and TS Web Access. For most SBS environments, the first two of these are the most important. TS Gateway is used by the new Remote Web Workplace (RWW), and TS RemoteApps gives us the ability to use specific applications running on a terminal server as if they were local. TS Web Access is also useful, but rather than setting up a traditional Web server to provide access to applications, we'll use Microsoft Office SharePoint Server to put them directly onto Companyweb, the SBS intranet. For more on that, see Chapter 22, "Customizing a SharePoint Site."

TS Gateway

TS Gateway is automatically installed on the main SBS server and preconfigured to support RWW. In SBS 2003, RWW acted as a proxy for the Remote Desktop Protocol, using port 4125 as the incoming port to connect remote users to clients in the SBS domain. This worked well and was *the* big application in SBS 2003. In fact, it was so successful that a lot of enterprise networks were envious of the technology.

In Windows Server 2008, Microsoft added TS Gateway to allow a similar functionality, but instead of using an RDP proxy across port 4125, TS Gateway tunnels traffic over HTTPS to help form a secure, encrypted connection between remote users on the Internet and the remote computers on which their productivity applications run, even if their use is located behind a network address translation (NAT) Traversal–based router.

The SBS team chose to use the new TS Gateway functionality of Windows Server 2008 for the Remote Web Workplace, which is a good idea because it allows us to do some really cool things with RWW, including adding links to applications that can be run directly from RWW across the Internet.

TS RemoteApps

TS RemoteApps is the single best feature added to Windows Server 2008, except for Hyper-V. But Hyper-V isn't exciting—it just makes our jobs easier. TS RemoteApps is actually exciting, and it gives us a way to give our users a better experience.

Terminal Services has always enabled us to allow users to run as if they were local, but actually using the power of the server. But TS RemoteApps makes the entire process transparent to the user. The application runs on the server, using the server's memory, CPU, and resources, but it displays on the user's computer just as if it were running locally. It's uncanny how natural it feels. We use it here in our office all the time. For example, Charlie doesn't like the 2007 Microsoft Office system, especially Microsoft Office Word 2007, preferring the interface and customizations he's created for Word 2003. But he rather likes the newer Microsoft Office Outlook 2007, so he runs Word 2003 locally but uses the Outlook 2007 that is installed on our terminal server.

Because TS RemoteApps lets you create .msi files for deployment, you can use Group Policy to deploy the remote applications. The applications can even be configured to take over the file association for a file type, just as if they were local applications, again making the user experience completely natural.

TS Web Access

TS Web Access provides a Web-based front end that allows you to publish applications to a Web page for easier user access. In SBS 2008, you can extend TS Web Access to publish the links directly in the SharePoint Companyweb site. We covered how to do this in Chapter 22.

Concepts

Windows Terminal Services is a new concept for many system administrators who expect systems to be essentially single-user. It brings true multiuser capability to Windows. Each user who connects to a Windows Server 2008 server using Remote Desktop or a TS RemoteApp is actually using the resources of the server itself, not the particular workstation at which he or she is seated. The user's experience doesn't depend on the speed of the workstation—the user's workstation is actually sharing the processor, RAM, and hard disks of the server itself.

Each user gets his or her Windows Terminal Services session, and each session is completely isolated from other sessions on the same server. An errant program in one session can cause that session's user to have a problem, but other users are unaffected.

Each user who connects to a Windows Server 2008 server using Remote Desktop is actually functioning as a terminal on that server. Windows Terminal Services supports a wide variety of computers as terminals—from diskless display stations running Microsoft Windows CE entirely in memory to legacy Windows desktop computers that are otherwise too underpowered for satisfactory use. Because the terminal is responsible solely for the console functions—that is, the keyboard, mouse, and actual display—the processing and RAM requirements for the terminal are minimal. All other functioning resides on and is part of the server, although the disks, printers, and serial ports of your local workstation can be connected to the remote session.

> **IMPORTANT** Versions of Windows prior to Windows XP SP2 can't install the latest version of the Remote Desktop Client software. All client workstations should be updated to at least Windows XP SP2 or later to take full advantage of the features of Windows Server 2008 Terminal Services and to protect the security of the network.

Remote Access

Terminal Services provides an ideal solution for the mobile user who needs to be able to run network-intensive or processor-intensive applications even over a dial-up connection. Because the local computer is responsible only for the actual console, the responsiveness and bandwidth requirements are substantially better compared to trying to run applications across a slow connection. The actual bandwidth used for Windows Terminal Services can be tuned by enabling or disabling certain graphics features to improve responsiveness over a slow connection.

Central Management

Because all applications in a Windows Terminal Services session are running on the server, management of sessions and applications is greatly simplified. Any changes to applications or settings need only be made once, on the server, and these changes are seen by all future Windows Terminal Services sessions.

In addition, Windows Terminal Services allows an administrator to view what is happening in a user's session, or even to directly control it. Help desk personnel can actually see exactly what the user is seeing without leaving their desks. If the user is configured accordingly, the Help desk person can share control of the session, walking the user through a difficult problem.

REAL WORLD Requirements

The requirements for a terminal server depend on the number of users and the type of applications they run. Because each user will be executing his or her programs on the server itself, you need to determine exactly how your users work and what their real requirements are. Each installation will be different, but what follows are some guidelines to help you size your server appropriately.

RAM

Each session on the Terminal Server uses a minimum of approximately 20 megabytes (MB) of RAM just to log on. Add to this any RAM required to run the programs that each session launches. A typical user running Outlook, Word, and Microsoft Office Excel while connecting to the Internet uses approximately 40 MB of RAM, or approximately 20 MB beyond what the session itself requires. However, a power user can easily use twice that amount, and developers or other extreme users can go even farther.

CPU

Predicting exactly how much CPU power will be required per user is difficult, because each user has a different mix of applications and expectations. A dual-core, dual-processor server running an x64 version Windows Server 2008 with sufficient RAM present to avoid swapping can realistically host somewhere between 200 and 300 users—in other words, a lot more than an SBS network has to worry about. That same server running 32-bit Windows Server 2008 can probably support no more than 50 to 75 users, realistically. The limiting factor in 32-bit Windows Server is usually not the CPU, or even the RAM, but the actual virtual memory address space available to the operating system. Most 32-bit Windows Terminal Services servers run out of system page table entries (PTEs) before they become processor-bound.

Network

A typical SBS network with 100 Mbps or 1 Gps networking has more than sufficient network bandwidth to support as many Terminal Server clients as necessary. Remote users can tailor their RDP settings to limit bandwidth use over slow connections.

Licensing

Terminal Server use requires special licensing considerations. In addition to normal Client Access Licenses (CALs), which are covered by your SBS licensing, you also need to have a TS CAL for each user or device that connects to the terminal server to run an application. Unfortunately, TS CALs are not included as part of either SBS Standard or SBS Premium.

Installing Terminal Services Role

Installing the Terminal Services Role and its supporting Role Service should be one of the very first things you do on any server you plan to use as a terminal server. Important changes to how applications are installed happen automatically when you're in Application Mode on a Windows Server computer, and there can be problems if applications are installed before the server is converted to an application server. Our general preference is to run through the tasks on the Initial Configuration Tasks Wizard (ICTW), skipping only the Add Roles tasks, but joining the server to the domain, giving it a name, setting a fixed IP address, and installing the basic features we want on all servers. When that is done, and all the required restarts have been completed, it's time to install the Terminal Services Role.

> **IMPORTANT**   Before you can add the Terminal Services Role, you must move the server to the SBSServers organizational unit (OU). This is not automatically done when you join the domain—the server is actually put in the SBSComputers OU. If you don't move the server to the SBSServers OU, the Terminal Services Role cannot be added without error.

To install the Terminal Services Role, follow these steps:

1. Open the Active Directory Users And Computers snap-in, shown in Figure 25-1, from the Administrative Tools menu of the main SBS server or by typing **dsa.msc** at a command prompt.

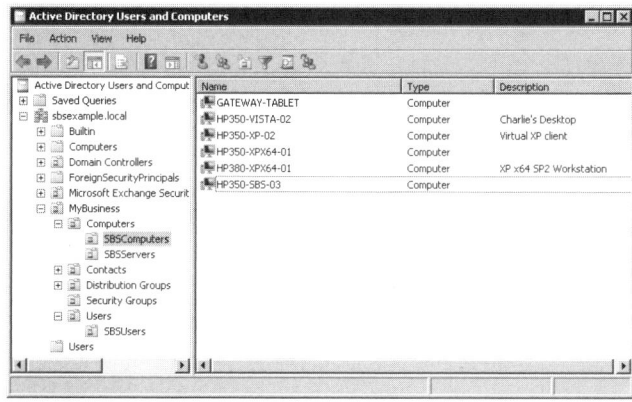

FIGURE 25-1 The Active Directory Users And Computers console

2. Navigate to the SBSComputers OU, as shown in Figure 25-1. Select the server that will be the terminal server and drag it to the SBSServers OU.

3. You'll be warned about moving objects in Active Directory, as shown in Figure 25-2. Click Yes to confirm you want to move the object.

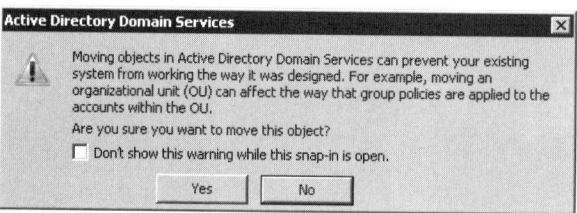

FIGURE 25-2 Moving the Terminal Server computer object to the SBSServers OU

4. Log on to the server that you want to make a terminal server.

5. Open a Windows PowerShell or command window as administrator.

6. Force a Group Policy update, as shown in Figure 25-3. This will likely require a logoff, so you shouldn't do this from a Remote Desktop session if you can avoid it. Alternately, you can simply reboot the server.

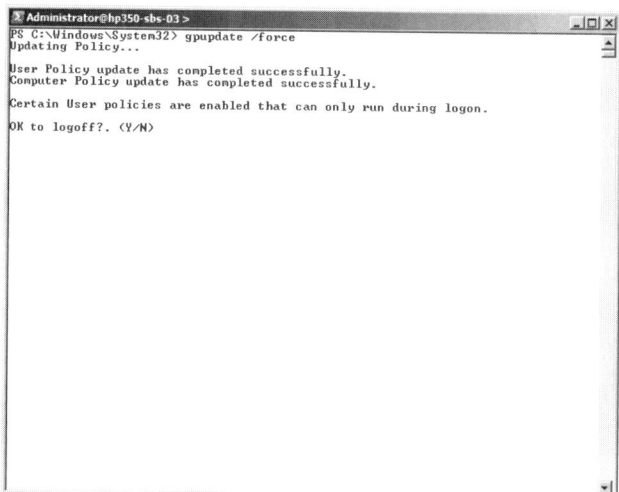

FIGURE 25-3 Forcing a Group Policy update before installing Terminal Services

7. Open the Server Manager console if it isn't already open. (If you still have the ICTW open, you can close it and the Server Manager console will open automatically.)

8. In the left pane of the Server Manager console, select Roles, as shown in Figure 25-4.

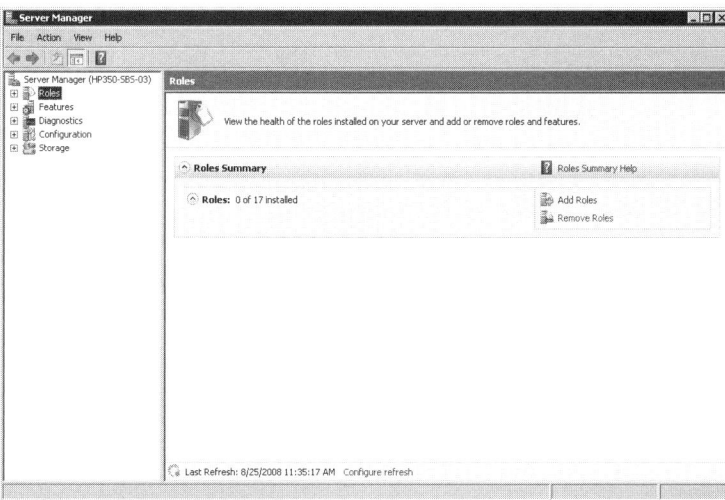

FIGURE 25-4 The main Server Manager console, with Roles selected in the left (tree view) pane

9. Select Add Roles from the action menu to open the Add Roles Wizard shown in Figure 25-5.

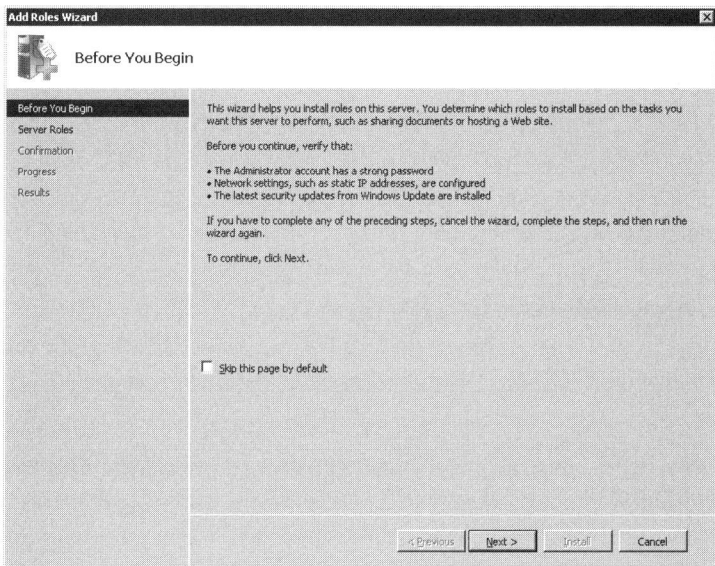

FIGURE 25-5 The Before You Begin page of the Add Roles Wizard

10. The Before You Begin page of the Add Roles Wizard contains some general informa-tion and recommended configuration settings. After you've seen this once and read it, you can select the Skip This Page By Default check box. Once is quite enough.

11. Click Next to open the Select Server Roles page. Select Terminal Services, as shown in Figure 25-6.

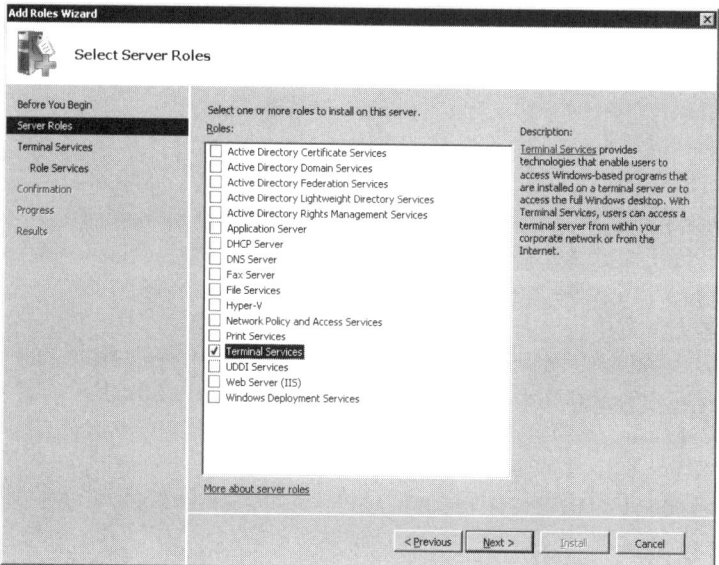

FIGURE 25-6 The Select Server Roles page of the Add Roles Wizard

12. Click Next to open the Terminal Services page. Read the brief Introduction To Terminal Services, and if you want more information on Terminal Services Roles and Role Services, click the Overview Of Terminal Services link.

13. Click Next to open the Select Role Services page, as shown in Figure 25-7. Select at least the Terminal Server Role Service.

> **NOTE** You will need to install a TS Licensing server in your SBS domain within 120 days of enabling Terminal Services. This can be installed on any Windows Server 2008 computer in the domain and can be installed at any point in that 120-day period.

14. Click Next to open the Uninstall And Reinstall Applications For Compatibility page of the Add Roles Wizard, shown in Figure 25-8. This is a good reminder that applications that have already been installed should be uninstalled and reinstalled so that they are properly multiuser aware.

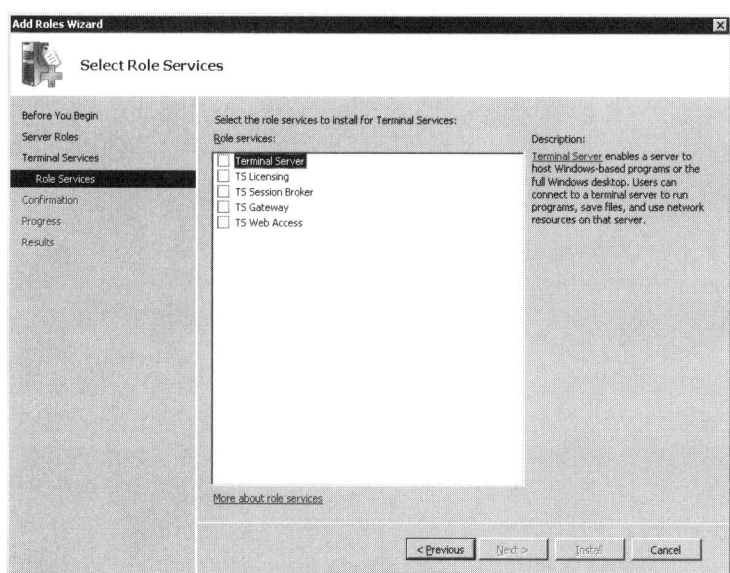

FIGURE 25-7 The Select Role Services page of the Add Roles Wizard for adding the Terminal Services Role

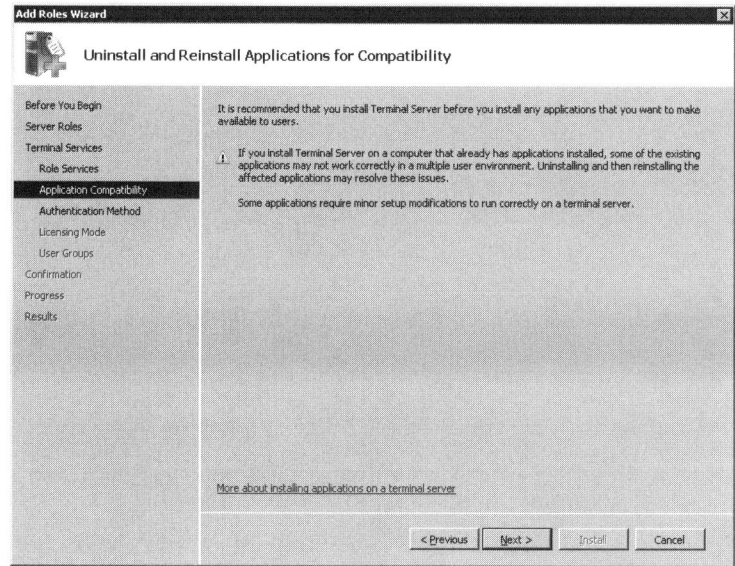

FIGURE 25-8 The Uninstall And Reinstall Applications For Compatibility page of the Add Roles Wizard

15. Click Next to open the Specify Authentication Method For Terminal Server page, shown in Figure 25-9. There are two choices for authentication:

- **Require Network Level Authentication** Choose this if all your clients will be running at least Windows XP SP3 or Windows Vista. This option is more secure and should be used when possible.

- **Do Not Require Network Level Authentication** Choose this option if you have clients that can't be upgraded to at least Windows XP SP3. Clients will still require RDP 6 or later to use TS RemoteApps.

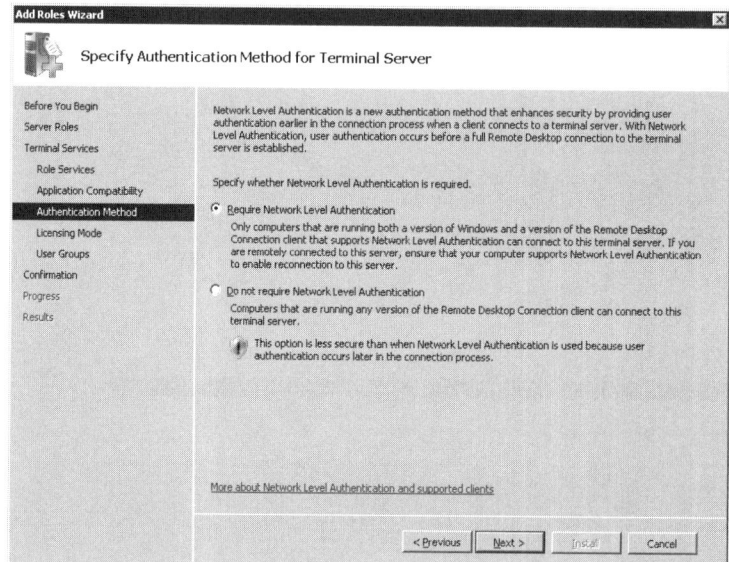

FIGURE 25-9 Setting the Authentication Level for the terminal server

16. Click Next to open the Specify Licensing Mode page, shown in Figure 25-10. Here you can choose between per-device or per-user licensing, or you can delay the decision. In most cases, unless you've already bought your CALs, postpone this for now, until you've had a chance to decide how your users will actually use the terminal server. This will allow you to make the most cost-efficient choice for licensing.

17. Click Next to open the Select User Groups Allowed Access To This Terminal Server page, shown in Figure 25-11. The default is only Administrators, so you'll want to change that. We suggest creating a Security Group specifically to control TS RemoteApps access, but you can also just give all users access, or specify each individual user.

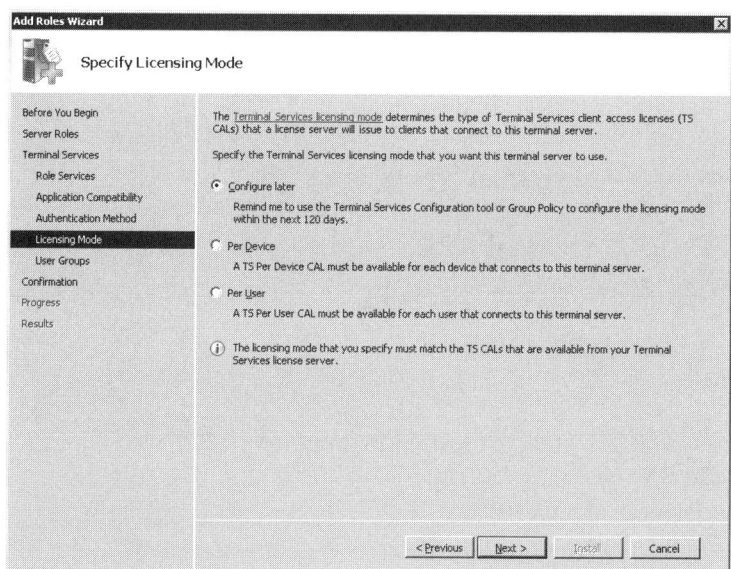

FIGURE 25-10 You can postpone the decision about which Terminal Services Licensing mode to use.

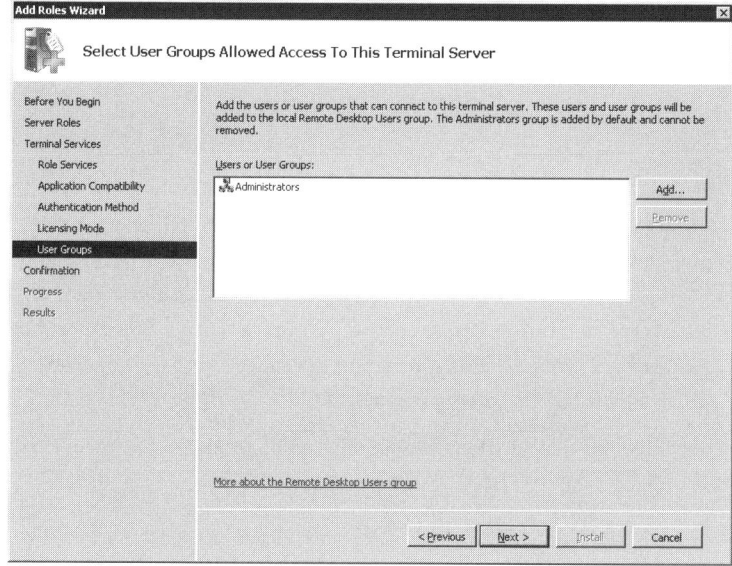

FIGURE 25-11 The Select User Groups Allowed Access To This Terminal Server page of the Add Roles Wizard

18. Click Add to specify additional users and groups that will be able to use the terminal server. To add all users, enter Domain Users in the Select Users, Computers, Or Groups dialog box, as shown in Figure 25-12. Click Check Names to make sure you've typed the group name correctly and then click OK to return to the Add Roles Wizard.

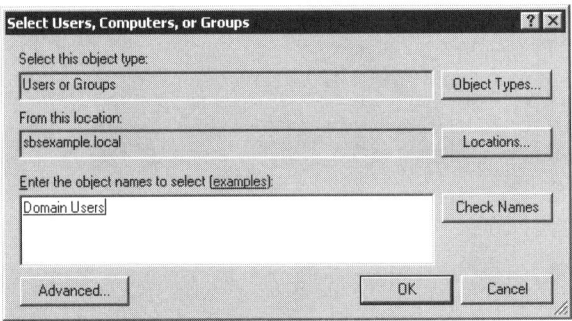

FIGURE 25-12 Selecting users and groups

19. Click Next to open the confirmation page and then click Install to begin the installation.

20. Before the installation is complete, you'll need to reboot the server. Click Close on the Installation Results page and click Yes to begin the reboot.

21. When the server has restarted, log on with the same account as you used to add the Terminal Services Role. The Installation Results page will open and the installation will complete.

 REAL WORLD Desktop Experience

By default, there is no audio on a Windows Server 2008 computer, and the default graphics level is set to a 16-bit maximum. You can improve this by adding the Windows Server 2008 Desktop Experience feature. This feature gives your client sessions the visual look and feel of Windows Vista, as well as adding other programs that are normally part of Windows Vista, including Windows Photo Gallery, Windows Mail, and Windows Media Player, among others.

You can also improve the visual look by enabling 32-bit color and audio by following these steps:

1. Open the Server Manager console if it isn't already open.

2. Navigate to Roles and then Terminal Services and then select Terminal Services Configuration in the left pane of Server Manager.

3. Select RDP-Tcp in the center Connections pane, as shown in Figure 25-13.

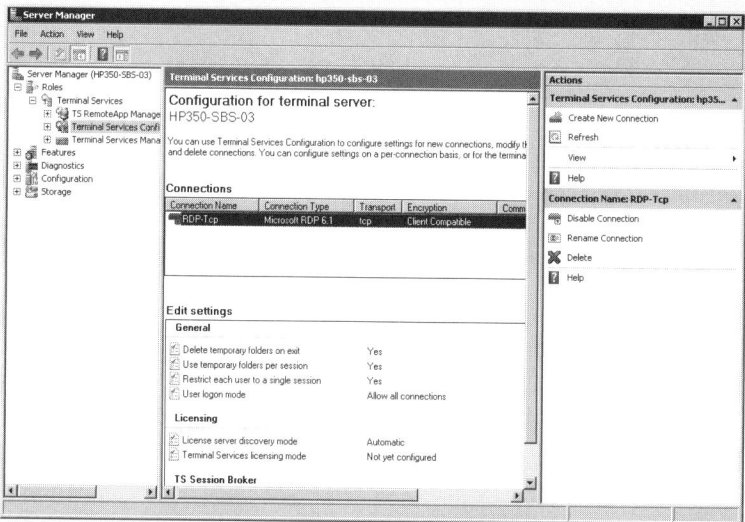

FIGURE 25-13 The RDP Configuration in Server Manager

4. Right-click the RDP-Tcp connection and select Properties to open the RDP-Tcp Properties dialog box.

5. Click the Client Settings tab, as shown in Figure 25-14.

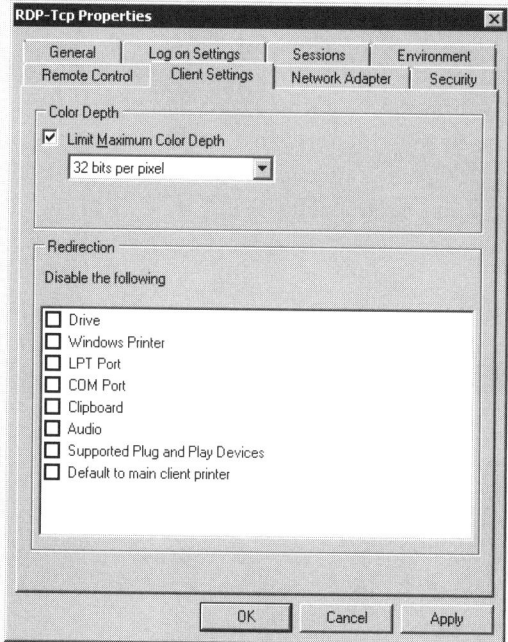

FIGURE 25-14 Setting RDP properties

6. Select a maximum color depth of 32 Bits Per Pixel from the Limit Maximum Color Depth drop-down list to enable 32-bit color.

7. Clear the check box for Audio in the Disable The Following section.

8. Click OK to close the Properties dialog box. If there are current user sessions, you'll see the warning shown in Figure 25-15.

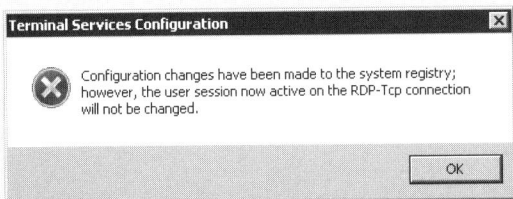

FIGURE 25-15 Warning when changing configuration with open sessions

9. By default, the Audio service is manually started on Windows Server 2008. You need to enable it before RDP clients will get audio.

10. Click Services on the Administrative Tools menu and then scroll down to Windows Audio.

11. Right-click Windows Audio and select Properties, change the Startup Type to Automatic, and then click Start to start the service.

12. Click OK and then close the Services console.

Making these changes improves the overall user experience for end users but also increases the amount of resources used per connection. That's probably not a big issue in most SBS environments, and we think it's worthwhile. Adding the Desktop Experience doesn't, however, install the games that are normally included with Windows Vista. This probably improves productivity, but we think there should at least be an option for them.

Configuring Terminal Services Licensing

Windows Server 2008 requires that at least one Windows Terminal Services license server be installed and running on any network that uses Application Server mode. If a license server is not installed within 120 days, all Windows Terminal Services connections will be disabled. Windows Terminal Services requires a separate Terminal Server CAL for each user or device in addition to any Windows Server CALs you might need. The Terminal Server Licensing server does not track per-user license usage, but it does enable you to install per-user licenses.

Installing Terminal Server Licensing

In SBS, installing the Terminal Server Licensing service on the same server that is running Terminal Services is a reasonable choice, but you can also install it on the main SBS server if you prefer. If you're going to have more than a single terminal server, it makes sense to install the TS Licensing Role Service on the main SBS server or another domain controller to enable automatic discovery by all of the terminal servers. To install TS Licensing on the computer running Terminal Services, follow these steps:

1. Open Server Manager on the server running Terminal Services if it isn't already open.

2. Select Roles, then select Terminal Services in the left pane, and then select Add Role Services from the action menu.

3. On the Select Role Services page, select TS Licensing.

4. Click Next to open the Configure Discovery Scope For TS Licensing page, shown in Figure 25-16. Select whether this license server will service only the current domain or the entire forest. Actually, select whichever you want here; the choice doesn't make any sense in an SBS environment, where we have a single domain forest.

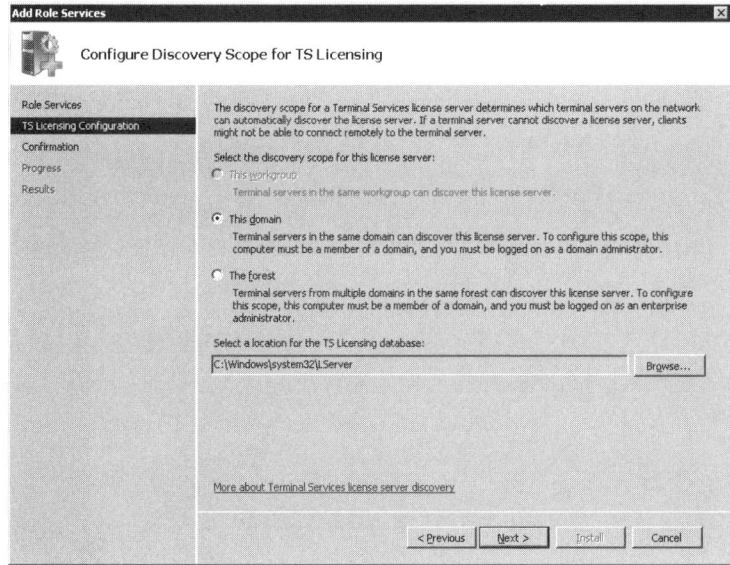

FIGURE 25-16 The TS Licensing Configuration page of the Add Role Services Wizard

5. Click Next to open the Confirm Installation Selections page. If everything looks correct, click Install to begin the installation.

6. Click Close when the installation completes.

After the TS Licensing Role Service is added, you need to activate the server before it will actually do anything. To activate the license server, follow these steps:

1. Open the Terminal Services Licensing Manager (licmgr.exe).

2. Select the TS Licensing server in the left pane and then select Activate Server from the Action menu.

3. The Terminal Server License Server Activation Wizard opens. Click Next to open the Connection Method page.

4. Select a connection method from the drop-down list. The choices are Automatic Connection, Web Browser, or Telephone. Automatic Connection requires an Internet connection from the server you are activating. Web Browser also requires an Internet connection, but it can be run from any workstation. Click Next.

5. If you've chosen Automatic, the connection will be made and then the first Company Information page is displayed, as shown in Figure 25-17. Fill in all the fields on this page—they are required. Click Next.

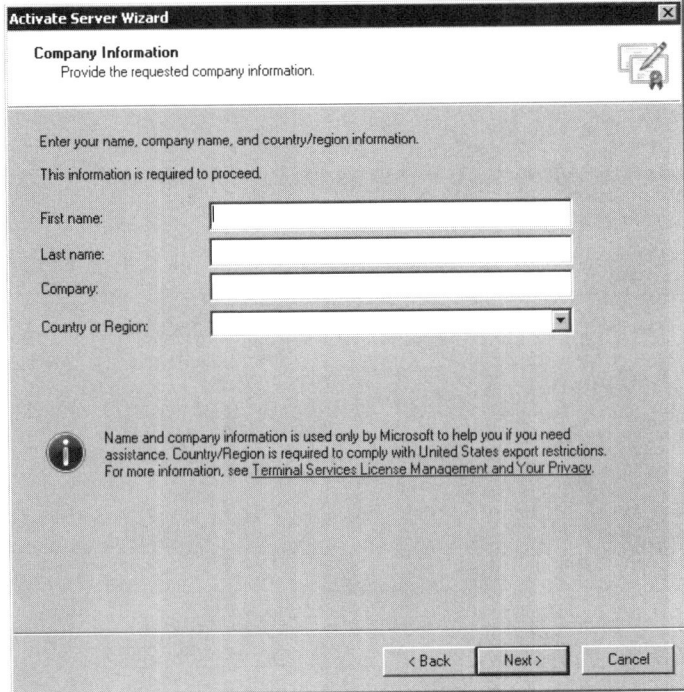

FIGURE 25-17 The required fields on the Company Information page of TS Licensing

6. The second page of company information is displayed. All information on this page is optional—fill it in only if you want to. Click Next, and if your connection is good, your server will activate and you'll be presented with the completion page. You can continue to add CALs by selecting the Start Terminal Server Licensing Wizard Now box.

7. Click Next until you get to the License Program page of the Install Licenses Wizard, as shown in Figure 25-18.

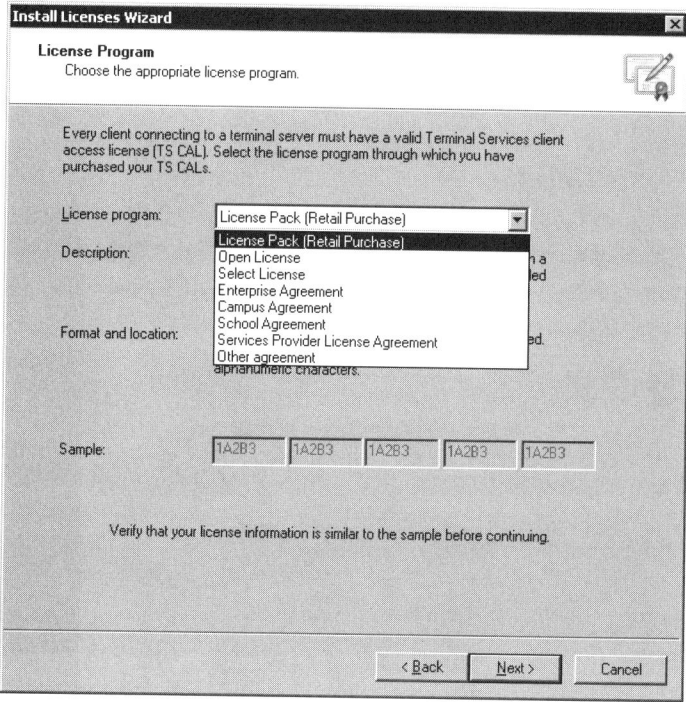

FIGURE 25-18 Choose the type of TS CALs you've purchased

8. Select the type of license you're entering from the License Program drop-down list.

9. Click Next and fill in the license code. Click Next again, and the activation will complete.

> **NOTE** Additional steps are required for either Web browser or telephone methods. If you need to reactivate your server and reinstall licenses, you will be required to use the telephone method.

Configuring TS RemoteApps

When you've installed the Terminal Services Role, along with the Terminal Server Role Service, you're ready to configure TS RemoteApps. If there is one thing in Windows Server 2008 that we think is "cool," it has to be TS RemoteApps. Instead of having users connect to a remote terminal server, open a full desktop, and then run the applications they need, TS RemoteApps allows users to run remote applications just as if they were running them locally, without opening up a desktop. The actual behavior is just like a regular application—when it needs to open an additional window, such as when you go to save a file, it automatically opens up a new window on your local workstation that has just the File Save dialog box in it. To the user, the application behaves just as it would if the application were running locally.

Applications can be published as .rdp files, or as .msi files, allowing deployment through Group Policy. When installed with an .msi file, they can even be set to take over the default extension of the application on the user's workstation, enabling automatic launch.

TS RemoteApp Manager

The TS RemoteApp Manager console (remoteprograms.msc), shown in Figure 25-19, is used to manage remote applications. From here, you can define the various settings that control which applications are available, who can connect to them, and how they're distributed and published.

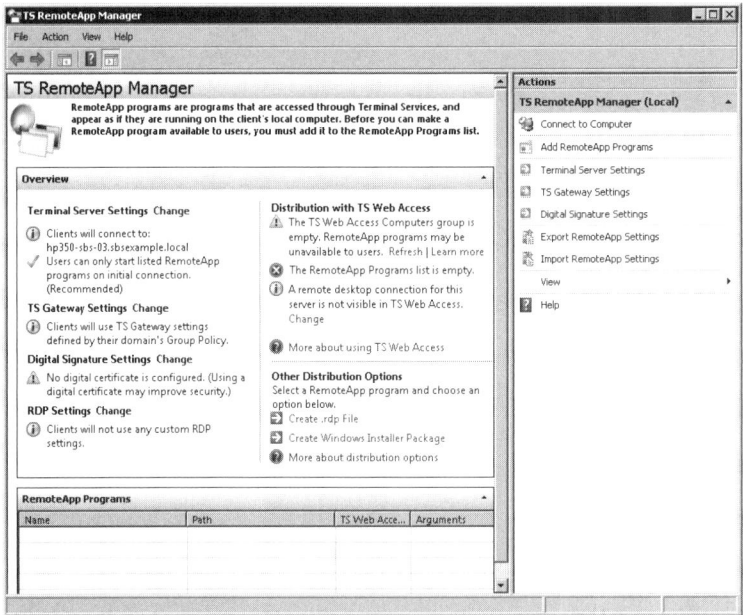

FIGURE 25-19 The TS RemoteApp Manager console

When you create a RemoteApp, you can set how it is distributed and available. You can create an .rdp file for it or a Windows Installer Package (.msi) file. Windows installer packages can be distributed using Group Policy, and have additional options as compared to .rdp files.

To add create a RemoteApp program, follow these steps:

1. Open the TS RemoteApp Manager if it isn't already open.

2. Click Add RemoteApp Programs in the Actions pane to open the RemoteApp Wizard.

3. Click Next to open the Choose Programs To Add To The RemoteApps Programs List page of the RemoteApp Wizard, as shown in Figure 25-20.

4. Select one or more programs to add to the RemoteApps programs list. You can add any programs you see in the list or use the Browse button to locate the program's executable.

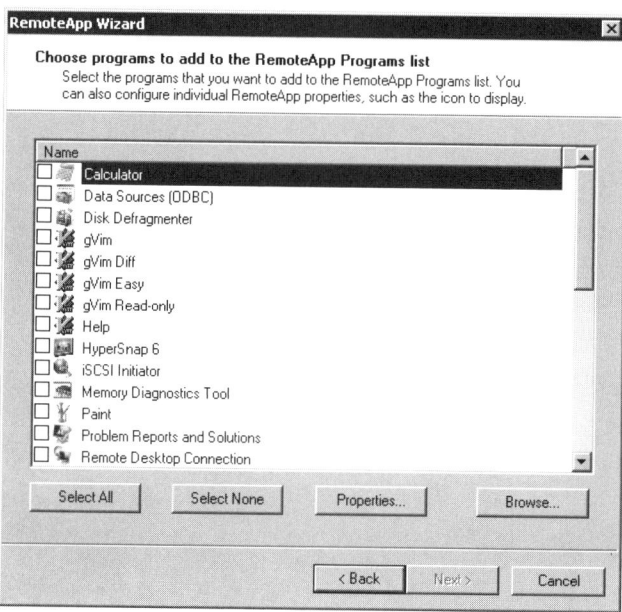

FIGURE 25-20 Choosing programs to make available through TS RemoteApps

5. To change the run properties of the application you are adding, select it from the list of programs and click Properties to open the Properties dialog box for the program, as shown in Figure 25-21 for our editor of choice, gVim.

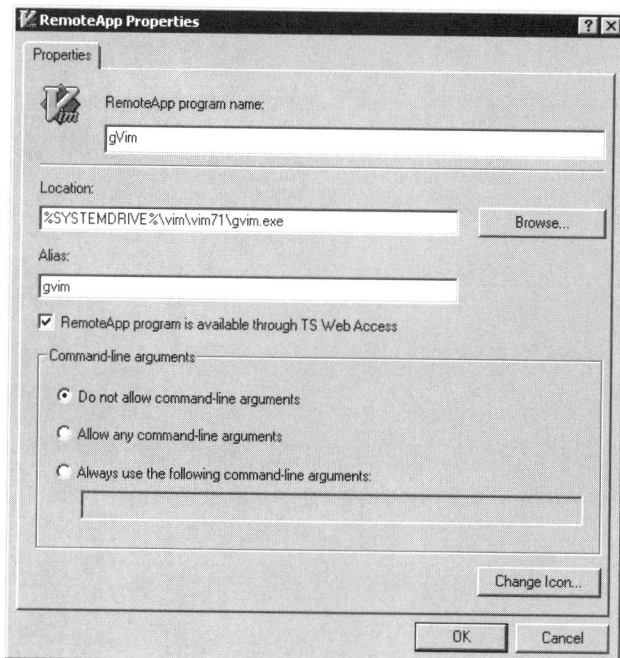

FIGURE 25-21 Setting the properties for a RemoteApp program

6. Change any application-specific properties that you want to change and then click OK to close the Properties dialog box for the application.

7. Click Next and then click Finish to add the program to the list of available RemoteApps.

Deploying with .Rdp and .Msi Files

You can easily deploy remote applications to specific computers on your network by creating .rdp or .msi files. Personally, we prefer using .msi files because they can be pushed out using Group Policy, and you can control additional settings with them. Or you can create a file share to save the files to, and users can install the files to their computers.

To create a Windows Installer Package (.msi) file, follow these steps:

1. Open the TS RemoteApp Manager if it isn't already open.

2. Select the application you want to create a package for in the RemoteApp Programs pane.

3. Click Create Windows Installer Package in the Actions pane to open the RemoteApp Wizard.

4. Click Next to open the Specify Package Settings page, shown in Figure 25-22.

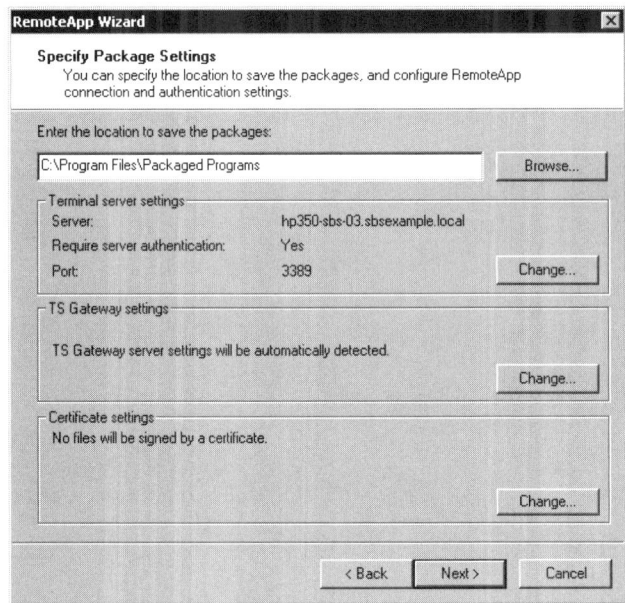

FIGURE 25-22 The Specify Package Settings page of the RemoteApp Wizard

5. Enter a location to save the package to. The default is C:\Program Files\Packaged Programs, but we think a shared folder makes more sense.

6. Change any TS Gateway, Terminal Server, or Certificate settings that need to be different for this application. There's really no need to change anything in an SBS environment.

7. Click Next to open the Configure Distribution Package page shown in Figure 25-23.

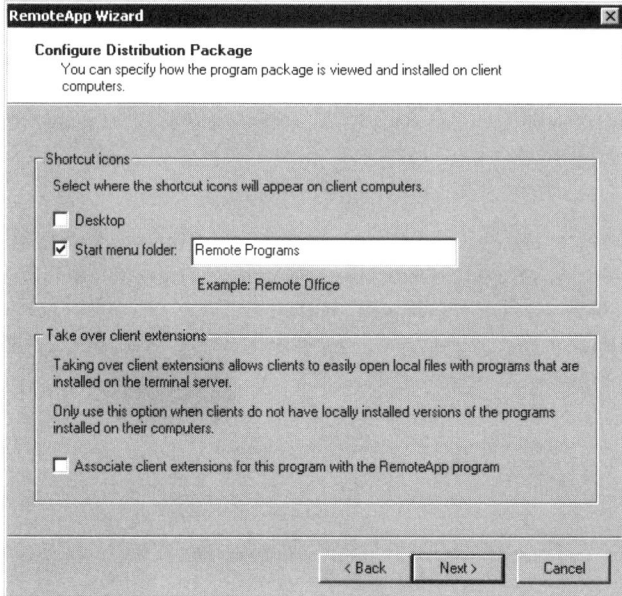

FIGURE 25-23 The Configure Distribution Package page of the RemoteApp Wizard

8. The default is to add the program to the Start Menu Folder Remote Programs. If this folder doesn't already exist, it will be created as part of the installation. You can also choose to have the RemoteApp program automatically added to the user's desktop. And you can have the remote application take over all the client extensions it would normally take over for the user's computer.

9. Click Next and then click Finish to create the Windows Installer Package.

> **NOTE** Creating an .rdp file for deployment follows similar steps but has fewer options. You can't have an RDP-deployed RemoteApp program take over the extensions on your local computer, for example.

O K, you've probably figured out by now that we think the new RemoteApps capability is one of the best new things in Windows Server 2008. We think the TS Web Access is a nice touch when used through our Companyweb, and the new TS Gateway is used by Remote Web Workplace to enable SSL tunneling instead of using port 4125.

The best of the improvements in Terminal Services, however, is RemoteApps. Now you can centralize all of your critical applications onto terminal servers and deploy them directly to users with Group Policy. Because the applications can actually capture the extensions associated with application and connect them to the remote program, the end user experience is almost completely transparent.

When Windows 2000 Server released and made Terminal Server Remote Administration mode available on every single server, we said that it was the reason to migrate to Windows 2000, and time has proven that feature to be absolutely indispensable. Well, we think two features in Windows Server 2008 are just as important: Hyper-V and TS RemoteApps.

Adding a RemoteApp to Remote Web Workplace

One of the cool things you can do with the new TS RemoteApps capability is add an application directly to the RWW landing page. This allows a user working remotely to directly and securely access an application on the SBS network without having to log on to take a full Remote Desktop session.

The basic process is:

- Create an .rdp file for the application.
- Save the .rdp file to the path where Remote Web Workplace resides on your SBS server.
- Create a new MIME type in IIS for RDP.
- Add a link to the .rdp file to the RWW page using the SBS Console.

Let's go through the process to add a link to Windows Mail to the RWW page. You need to have the Desktop Experience feature already installed on your terminal server.

First, follow these steps on the terminal server to create an .rdp file for Windows Mail:

1. Open TS RemoteApp Manager if it isn't already open (remoteprograms.msc).

2. Select Add RemoteApp Programs from the Actions menu to open the RemoteApp Wizard.

3. Click Next to open the Choose Programs To Add To The RemoteApp Programs List page.

4. Scroll down near the bottom and select Windows Mail from the list, as shown in Figure 25-24.

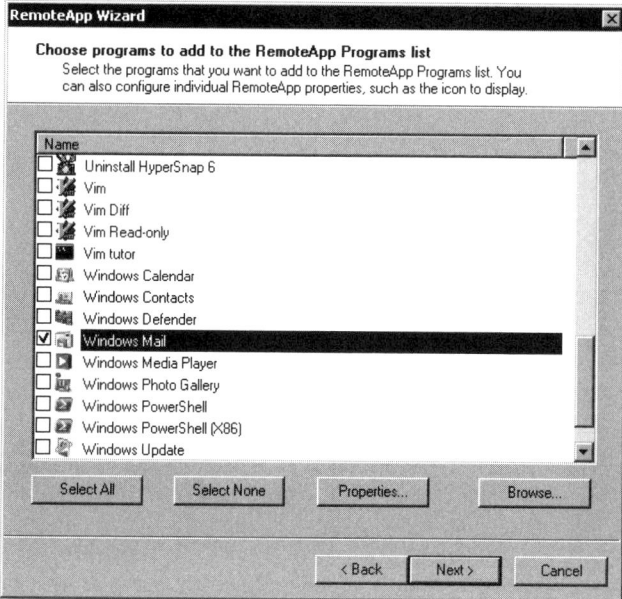

FIGURE 25-24 Selecting Windows Mail to add to the list of RemoteApps

5. Click Next and then click Finish to add Windows Mail to the list of RemoteApp programs.

6. Select Windows Mail in the list of RemoteApp Programs and then click Create .RDP File in the Actions pane to open the RemoteApp Wizard.

7. Click Next to open the Specify Package Settings page of the RemoteApp Wizard.

8. Type in the UNC path to the Public share on your SBS server for the location to save, as shown in Figure 25-25.

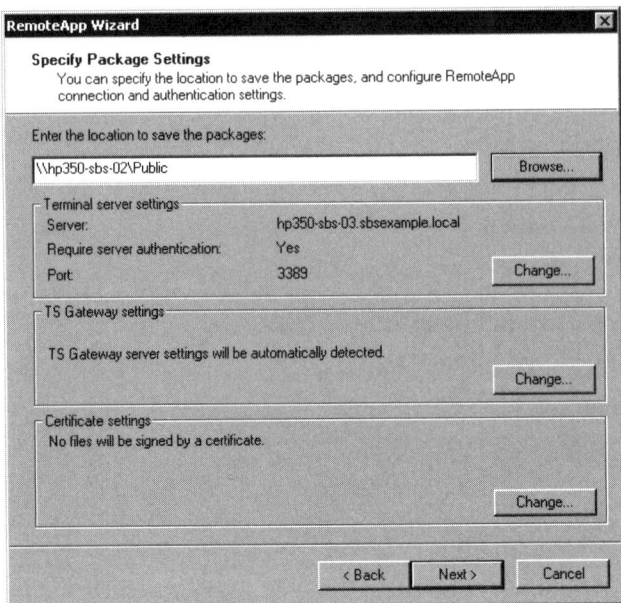

FIGURE 25-25 Save the .rdp file to the Public share of your SBS server.

9. Click Next and then click Finish to create the file.

Next, let's log on to the SBS server and move that .rdp file over to where we need it by following these steps:

1. Log on to the main SBS server with a Network Administrator account.

2. Open Windows Explorer and navigate to \\localhost\public, as shown in Figure 25-26.

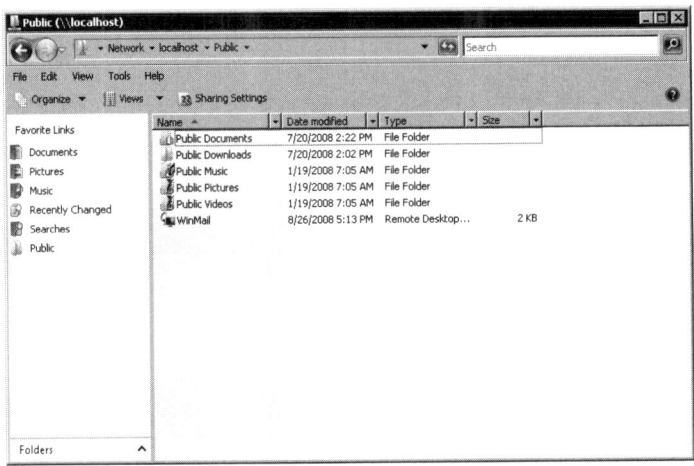

FIGURE 25-26 Locating the WinMail RDP

3. Highlight the WinMail .rdp file and copy it to the clipboard.

4. Navigate to the BIN directory for Remote Web Workplace. The default location is C:\Program Files\Windows Small Business Server\Bin\webapp\Remote\. Paste the WinMail .rdp file. You'll be prompted for permission because this is a protected folder.

Next, we need to create a new MIME type for the .rdp extension by following these steps:

1. Open the Internet Information Services (IIS) Manager from the Administrative Tools menu.

2. Highlight the server name in the left pane, navigate to Sites, then to SBS Web Applications, and finally to Remote. Click MIME Types in the center pane, as shown in Figure 25-27.

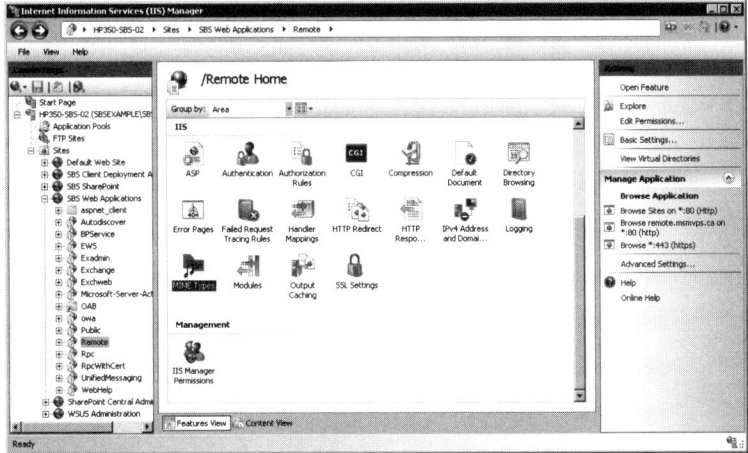

FIGURE 25-27 The IIS Manager console

3. Click Open Feature on the Actions menu to open the MIME Types in the center pane, as shown in Figure 25-28.

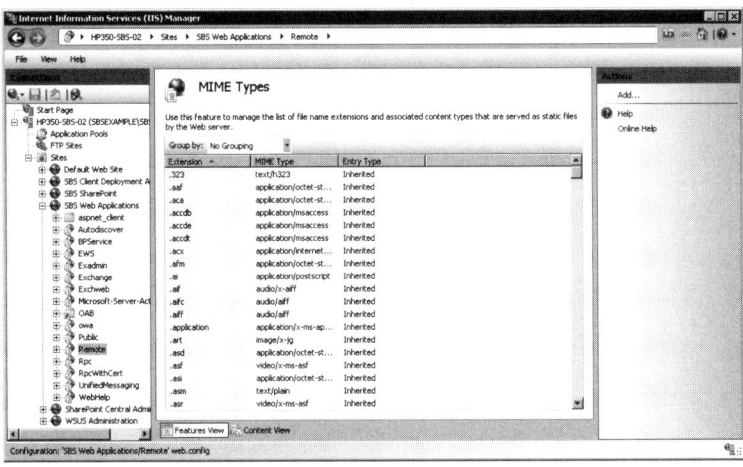

FIGURE 25-28 The MIME Types feature in IIS Manager console

4. Click Add on the Actions pane to open the Add MIME Type dialog box. Type **.rdp** in the File Name Extension field and type **application/x-remotedesktop** in the MIME Type field, as shown in Figure 25-29. Click OK.

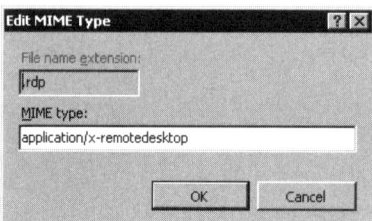

FIGURE 25-29 The Edit MIME Type dialog box

5. Right-click the server name in the left pane and select Stop from the Actions menu.

6. Right-click the server name again and select Start.

7. Close the Internet Information Services (IIS) Manager console.

Finally, we need to add the WinMail link to the RWW page by following these steps:

1. Open the Windows SBS Console if it isn't already open.

2. Click Shared Folders And Web Sites in the navigation pane and then click the Web Sites tab, as shown in Figure 25-30.

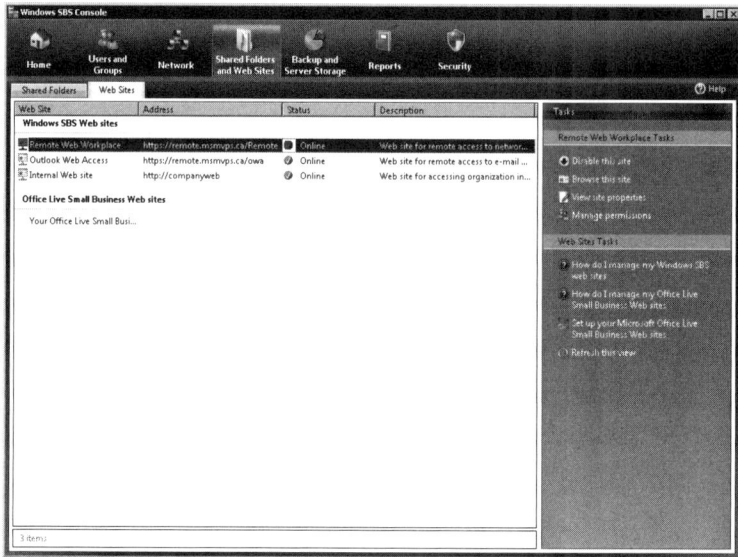

FIGURE 25-30 The Web Sites page of the Windows SBS Console

3. Select Remote Web Workplace and click View Site Properties on the Tasks pane to open the Remote Web Workplace Properties dialog box, as shown in Figure 25-31.

4. Click Home Page Links in the left pane and then click Manage Links to open the Remote Web Workplace Link List Properties dialog box, shown in Figure 25-32.

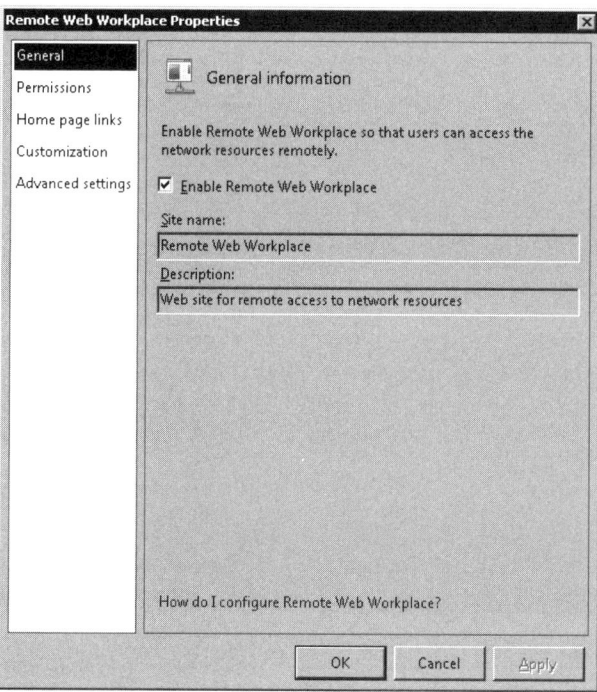

FIGURE 25-31 The Remote Web Workplace Properties dialog box

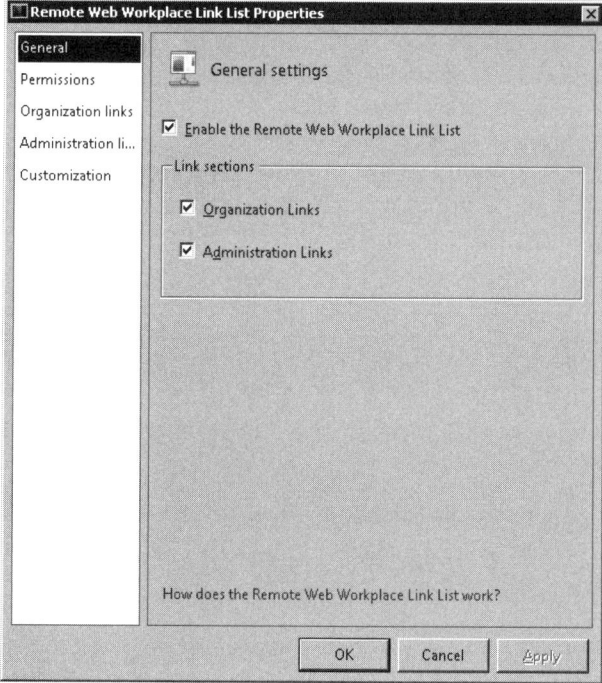

FIGURE 25-32 The Remote Web Workplace Link List Properties dialog box

5. Click Organizational Links in the left pane to open the Manage Organizational Links page in the right pane, as shown in Figure 25-33.

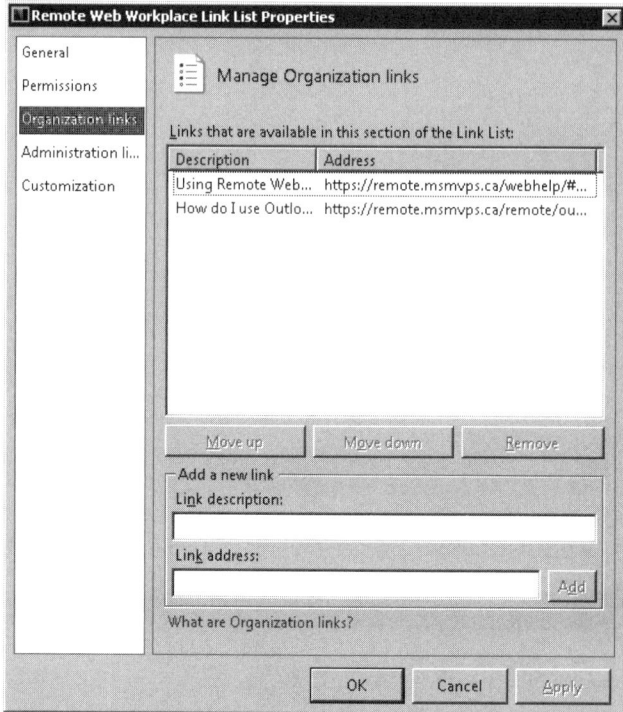

FIGURE 25-33 The Manage Organizational Links page of the Remote Web Workplace Link List Properties dialog box

6. Type **Run WinMail** in the Link Description field and then type the link to the .rdp file you added in the Link Address field. (This should be **https://remote.*example.com*/remote/winmail.rdp**, where *example.com* is replaced by your DNS name.)

7. Click Add and then click OK twice to close the Remote Web Workplace Link List Properties dialog box and return to the Windows SBS Console.

8. Highlight Remote Web Workplace, click Disable This Site in the Tasks pane, and then click Enable This Site in the Tasks pane.

9. Log on to Remote Web Workplace, and you'll see the new link, as shown in Figure 25-34.

10. The first time you run this or any other RemoteApp, you'll have to provide credentials and confirm you really want to do this. You can save your selections so you're not prompted again, if you choose.

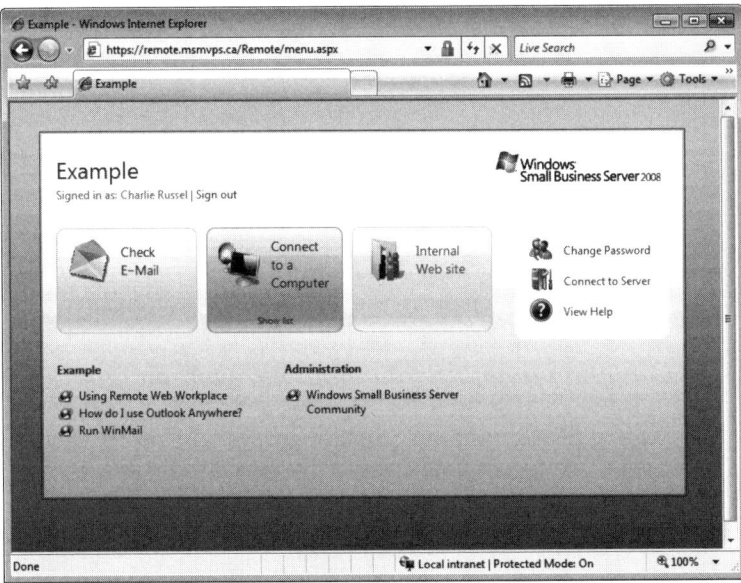

FIGURE 25-34 Remote Web Workplace showing the new link to Windows Mail

Running Windows Mail remotely probably isn't the most important application that you'll want to be able to use, but it provides a simple example for our purposes. Each business has a different application set that it needs to make available remotely, but any application that currently requires logging on to a remote desktop or using a VPN connection is an obvious choice.

Summary

Windows Server 2008 adds important new capabilities to Terminal Services. When combined with the new second server that is part of SBS Premium, adding a terminal server to an SBS network is a natural fit, enabling additional application deployment options and giving the SBS administrator or consultant the tools to rationalize resources in the SBS domain. In this chapter, we've covered the new features of Terminal Services in Windows Server 2008, the installation and configuration of the Terminal Server Role, and implementation and deployment of TS RemoteApps.

In the next section of the book, we move on to maintenance and troubleshooting of your SBS network, beginning with basic monitoring and fine-tuning of performance.

PART VI

Maintenance and Troubleshooting

CHAPTER 26

Windows SBS Reliability and Performance Monitoring

For a network to operate at its best, you must be able to recognize bottlenecks and take action to eliminate them. This chapter covers the system and network monitoring tools in Microsoft Windows Small Business Server 2008 that enable you to detect problems and tune your system to its optimum performance level.

The Windows Reliability And Performance Monitor is a simple tool that can help you track server loads, locate persistent errors, customize the data you want to collect in logs, define limits for alerts and automatic actions, generate reports, and view past performance data.

Three tools make up the Windows Reliability And Performance Monitor: Resource View, Performance Monitor, and Reliability Monitor.

To open the Windows Reliability And Performance Monitor, click Start, type **perfmon** in the Start Search box, and press Enter. Or you can select Windows Reliability And Performance Monitor from the Administrative Tools menu.

> **NOTE** For virtually every procedure in this chapter, you need to be logged on with administrative credentials.

Using Resource View

The Resource Overview page, shown in Figure 26-1, is the home page for the Reliability And Performance Monitor. On this screen, four scrolling graphs allow real-time monitoring of CPU, disk, network, and memory usage.

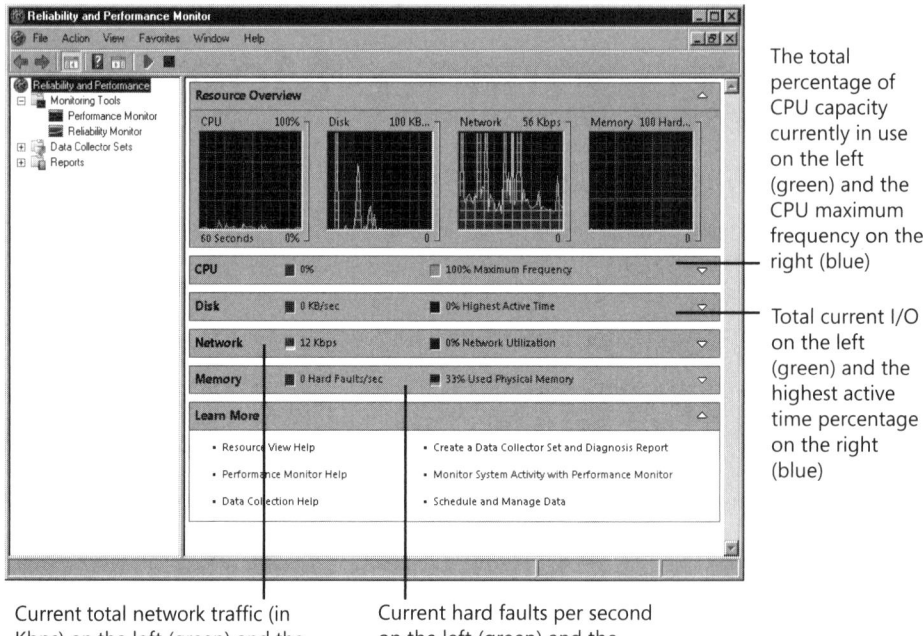

The total percentage of CPU capacity currently in use on the left (green) and the CPU maximum frequency on the right (blue)

Total current I/O on the left (green) and the highest active time percentage on the right (blue)

Current total network traffic (in Kbps) on the left (green) and the percentage of network capacity in use on the right (blue)

Current hard faults per second on the left (green) and the percentage of physical memory currently in use on the right (blue)

FIGURE 26-1 Resource Overview page

If Resource View doesn't show real time, click the green Start button in the toolbar.

The four sections below the graphs contain details about each resource. Click the graph or click the section to display the detail, as shown in Figure 26-2.

> **NOTE** Click a row and the highlight will remain on that row even when the application's position changes in the display.

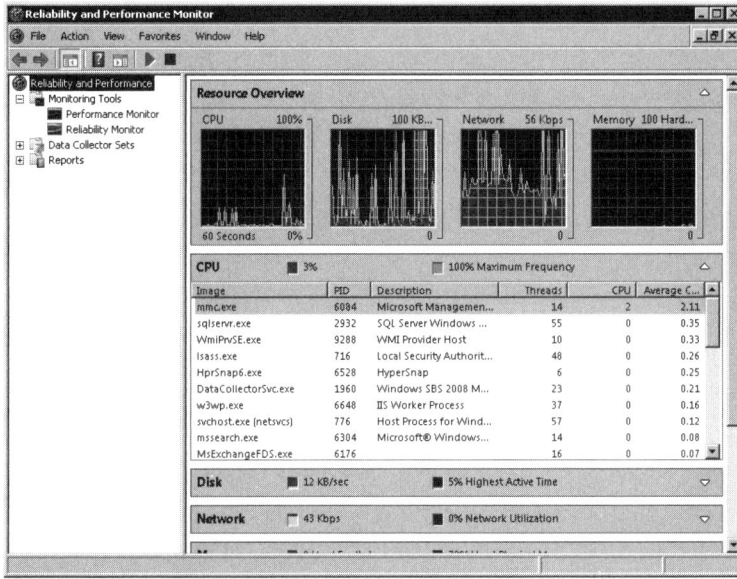

FIGURE 26-2 Displaying CPU usage in Resource Overview

> **NOTE** If the following message displays, choose Take Control: "The Windows Kernel Trace provider is already in use by another trace session. Taking control of it may cause the current owner to stop functioning properly."

Click the column header in the detail view to sort by ascending order. Click a second time to sort in descending order.

The following sections define the headers in each detail view.

CPU Details

- **Image** The application using the CPU
- **PID** The process identification for the application instance
- **Description** Name of the application
- **Threads** Number of active threads in this instance
- **CPU** Number of currently active cycles for this instance
- **Average CPU** Average CPU load over the past 60 seconds, expressed as a percentage of the total capacity of the CPU.

Disk Details

- **Image** The application using the disk

- **PID** The process identification for the application instance
- **File** The file being read or written
- **Read** The current speed (in bytes per minute) at which the file is being read
- **Write** The current speed (in bytes per minute) at which the file is being written
- **I/O Priority** The priority of the IO task
- **Response Time** Disk activity response time in milliseconds

Network Details

- **Image** The application using the network resource.
- **PID** Process identification of the application instance.
- **Address** The network address with which the local computer is exchanging information. This can be an IP address, a computer name, or a fully qualified domain name.
- **Send** Amount of data (in bytes per minute) that is being sent from the local computer to the network address.
- **Receive** The amount of data (in bytes per minute) that the application is receiving from the network address.
- **Total** The total bandwidth (in bytes per minute) of the data being sent and received.

Memory Details

- **Image** Application using memory resource
- **PID** Process identification of the application instance
- **Hard faults/min** Number of hard faults per minute being caused by the application instance

> **NOTE** A hard fault (also called a *page fault*) is not an error. It happens when a page at the address referenced is no longer in physical memory and has been swapped out or placed on a hard drive. However, an application that causes a high number of hard faults will be slow to respond, because it constantly has to read from a hard drive rather than from memory.

- **Working Set (KB)** Amount of memory (in kilobytes) currently used by the application instance
- **Shareable (KB)** Amount of the working set memory (in kilobytes) that may be available for other use
- **Private (KB)** Amount of the working set memory (in kilobytes) dedicated to the process

Using Performance Monitor

Performance Monitor is a simple tool to help you visualize what is happening on your network and on individual computers. Like Resource Overview, it can display events in real time, but it can also preserve data in logs for later viewing.

Insufficient memory or processing power can cause bottlenecks that severely limit performance. Unbalanced network loads and slow disk-access times can also prevent the network from operating optimally. Bottlenecks occur when one resource interferes with another resource's functioning. For example, if one application monopolizes the system processor to the exclusion of all other operations, there is a bottleneck at the processor.

Bottlenecks can occur in Windows subsystems or at any element of the network, for many reasons, including:

- Insufficient resources available
- A program or client monopolizes a resource
- Failure of a program, service, or device
- Software incorrectly installed or configured
- Incorrect configuration of the system for the workload

Performance Monitor helps you to identify where the bottlenecks are so that you can eliminate them.

To start Performance Monitor, click Start and type **perfmon** in the Start Search box. In the navigation tree, expand Monitoring Tools and then click Performance Monitor. The initial screen (shown in Figure 26-3) shows one counter: the percentage of processor time in use. Point at a spot in the graph and an informational window will open, giving the details of that point.

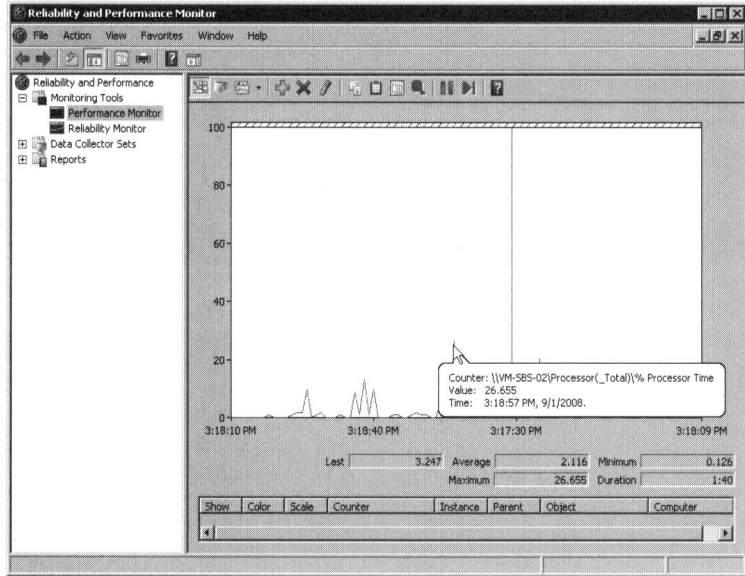

FIGURE 26-3 Performance Monitor showing the percentage of processor time in use

Adding Performance Counters

You can display any number of counters on the Performance Monitor. Simply right-click inside the Performance Monitor display and select Add Counters. This opens the Add Counters dialog box, as shown in Figure 26-4.

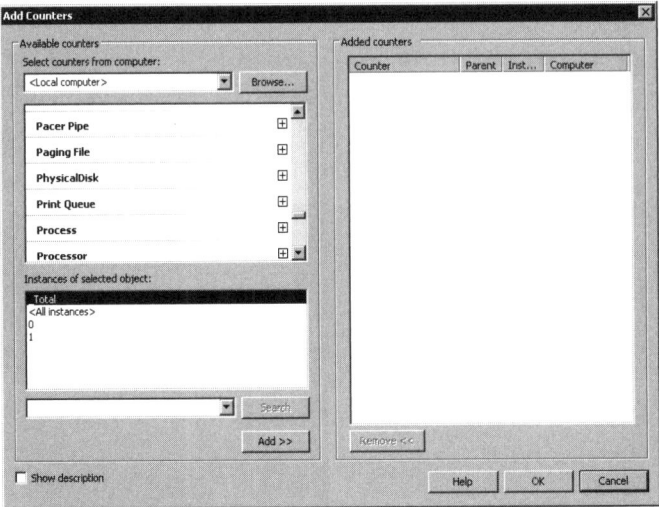

FIGURE 26-4 Viewing available counters

To add a counter to the Performance Monitor, follow these steps:

1. Select a computer from the drop-down list or click Browse to find other computers.

2. Available counters are listed below the computer selection box. You can add all the counters in a group or click the plus sign to select individual counters.

> **NOTE** Select the Show Description check box in the lower left of the window for information on what the selected counters are actually counting.

3. When you click a group or an individual counter, the current instances display in the Instances Of Selected Object window. Select a particular instance or select All Instances. To search for a particular instance, type the process name in the drop-down box below the Instances Of Selected Object pane and click Search. If your search produces no returns, highlight another group to clear the search. The search function is offered only if multiple instances are available.

4. Click Add to put the counter in the Added Counters list. Click OK when you're finished.

Changing the Performance Monitor Display

When you add multiple counters, the Performance Monitor screen can be difficult to decipher. To make the display more readable, follow these steps:

1. Right-click the Performance Monitor display and select Properties to open the Performance Monitor Properties dialog box as shown in Figure 26-5.

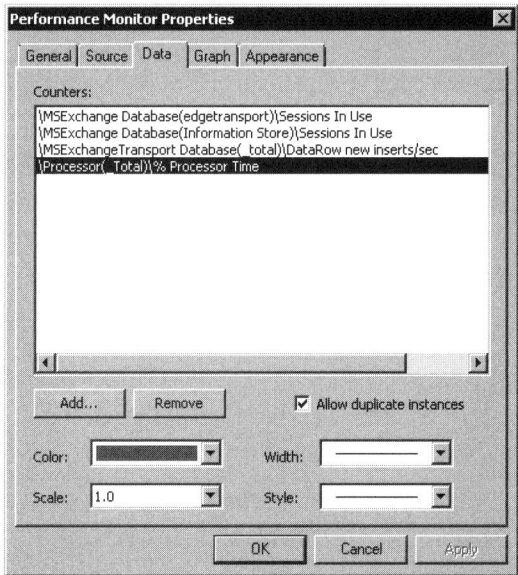

FIGURE 26-5 Changing how the Performance Monitor displays

2. Click the Data tab to select how you want the counters to display. Change the color, width, or style of the counter lines.

3. Change other display elements on the General, Graph, and Appearance tabs.

4. Click the Source tab to change the data source from Current Activity to a specified log file. For more on using performance logs, see the section titled "Managing Collected Data" later in this chapter.

Saving the Performance Monitor Display

The current display of Performance Monitor can be saved as an image or as a Web page.

To save the display as an image, follow these steps:

1. Right-click the Performance Monitor display and select Save Image As.

2. Select a location and type in a name for the saved image. The image will be saved as a .gif file.

3. Click Save.

To save the Performance Monitor display as a Web page, follow these steps:

1. Right-click the Performance Monitor display and select Save Settings As.

2. Select a location and type in a name for the saved display. The display will be saved as an .html file.

3. Click Save.

Using Reliability Monitor

Reliability Monitor provides a System Stability Index that reflects whether unexpected problems are reducing system reliability. A graph of the Stability Index over time quickly identifies dates when problems began to occur. The accompanying System Stability Report presents details to help you locate and fix the root cause of reduced reliability. Looking at changes to the system (operating system updates or adding and removing software) along with failures (application, operating system, or hardware failures), you can develop a method for dealing with the problems.

To open Reliability Monitor, select Reliability And Performance Monitor from the Administrative Tools menu. Alternatively, click Start, click the Start Search box, type **perfmon**, and press Enter. In the navigation tree, expand Monitoring Tools and click Reliability Monitor.

 UNDER THE HOOD **How Reliability Monitor Collects Data**

Reliability Monitor uses data collected by the RACAgent scheduled task, which runs by default after the operating system is installed. If this task is disabled, you must enable it manually. To enable the RACAgent scheduled task or to check on its status, follow these steps:

1. Click Start, type **taskschd.msc** in the Start Search box, and then press Enter.

2. In the navigation pane, expand Task Scheduler Library, expand Microsoft, expand Windows, and click RAC.

3. Right-click RAC, click View, and click Show Hidden Tasks.

4. Right-click RACAgent in the Console pane and select Enable.

Viewing Reliability Monitor on a Remote Computer

Information about the location of Reliability Monitor files is stored in the registry. Therefore, remote registry access is required to open data on a remote computer. To enable the Remote Registry Service, complete the following steps.

1. On the computer where you want to access Reliability Monitor data, click Start, type **services.msc** in the Start Search box, and press Enter.

2. In the Services list, right-click Remote Registry and select Start, as shown in Figure 26-6.

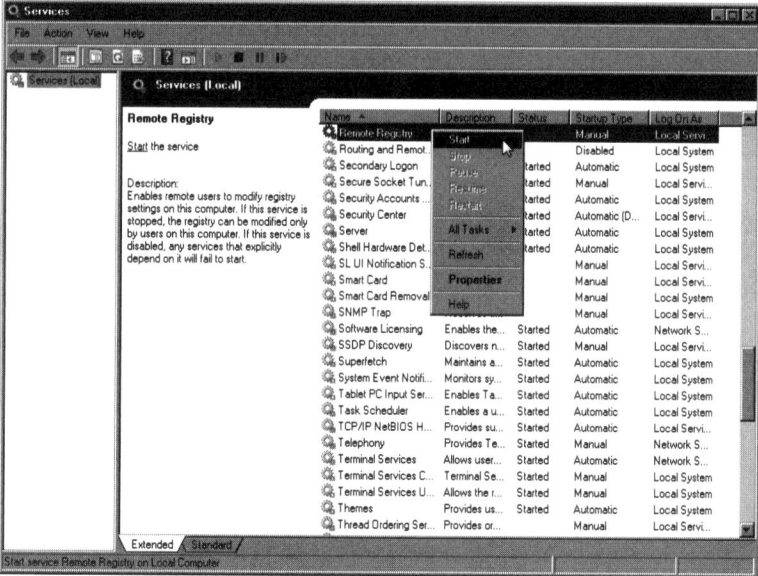

FIGURE 26-6 Starting the Remote Registry Service

How to Interpret the System Stability Index

Reliability Monitor maintains up to a year of history for system stability and reliability events. The System Stability Chart (Figure 26-7) displays a rolling graph organized by date.

The System Stability Index (SSI) generates a daily number from 1 (very unstable) to 10 (very stable). This is a weighted measurement derived over time. Recent failures are more heavily weighted than past failures. So after a problem has been resolved, the SSI number rises. On days when there is not enough data to calculate a reliable System Stability Index, the graph line is dotted. Days that the computer is turned off are not calculated in the SSI.

In the lower half of the window, the System Stability Report uses the five categories described in the following sections to track events that either affect the stability score or record software installation and removal. Click a date column in the chart and the events from that date will display in the report.

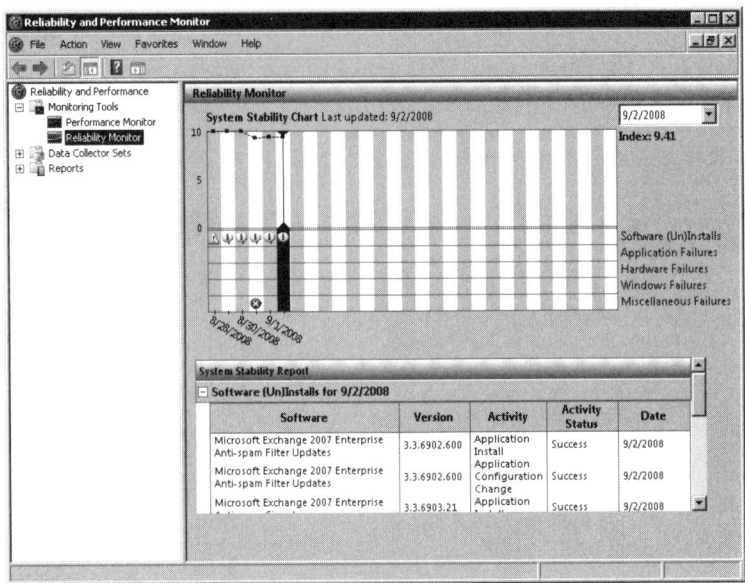

FIGURE 26-7 A sample System Stability report

Software (Un)Installs

Installations and removals are tracked in this category, which includes applications drivers, Windows updates, and parts of the operating system. The data display shows the following information:

- **Software** The name of the application, update, driver, or operating system
- **Version** The version number of the software
- **Activity** Install or uninstall
- **Activity Status** Success or failure of the activity
- **Date** Date of the activity

Software that repeatedly fails to install or uninstall might need to be updated. If it's a Microsoft application, use Windows Update to find solutions. If the application is not a Microsoft product, search the manufacturer's Web site for updates.

Application Failures

This category lists applications that have failed or stopped working. Nonresponding applications that are terminated are also included. The data display shows the following information:

- **Application** The executable program name of the application
- **Version** The version number of the application
- **Failure Type** Whether the application stopped working or stopped responding
- **Date** Date of the failure

Applications that fail or stop responding might need updates.

Hardware Failures

Memory and disk failures are in this category. The data display shows the following information:

- **Component type** Where the failure occurred
- **Device** Device that failed
- **Failure type** The type of failure that occurred
- **Date** Date of the failure

Repeated hardware failures can sometimes be resolved with software or firmware updates. Before replacing a piece of hardware, contact the manufacturer for troubleshooting instructions and advice.

Windows Failures

Operating system and boot failures are in this category. The data display shows the following information:

- **Failure type** Boot failure or operating system crash
- **Version** Version of operating system and service pack
- **Failure Detail** Shows the stop code in the event of an operating system crash; shows the reason code in the event of boot failure
- **Date** Date of the failure

Repeated operating system and boot failures can sometimes be resolved by reinstalling the operating system. Sometimes a boot failure can be caused by a hardware incompatibility. Search the Windows Knowledge Base (*http://support.microsoft.com*) for more information.

Miscellaneous Failures

This category includes failures that are not included in the previous categories but nevertheless affect system stability. Usually these will be unexpected operating system shutdowns. The data display shows the following information:

- **Failure type** Indicates what happened
- **Version** Version of the operating system and service pack
- **Failure detail** Describes the nature of the failure
- **Date** Date of the failure

Creating a Data Collector Set

Data Collector Sets are a method of monitoring and reporting in Reliability And Performance Monitor. You can collect only information that's useful to you, and you can create individual Data Collector Sets that can be viewed alone or combined with other Data Collector Sets in Performance Monitor. Data Collector Sets can be configured to generate alerts when thresholds are reached, or you can associate them with scheduling rules to data collection at specific times.

Building a Data Collector Set from a Template

Reliability And Performance Monitor includes several templates that concentrate on general system diagnosis information or collect performance data specific to server roles or applications. You can import templates created on other computers and export Data Collector Sets that you create to use on other computers.

To create a Data Collector Set from a template, follow these steps:

1. Click Start, type **perfmon** in the Start Search box, and then press Enter.

2. In the navigation pane, expand Data Collector Sets, right-click User Defined, point to New, and click Data Collector Set. The Create New Data Collector Set Wizard starts.

3. Enter a name for your Data Collector Set. Select Create From A Template and click Next.

4. From the Template Data Collector Set menu, select the template you want to use to create your Data Collector Set. A description of the data collected appears as you highlight each template (Figure 26-8).

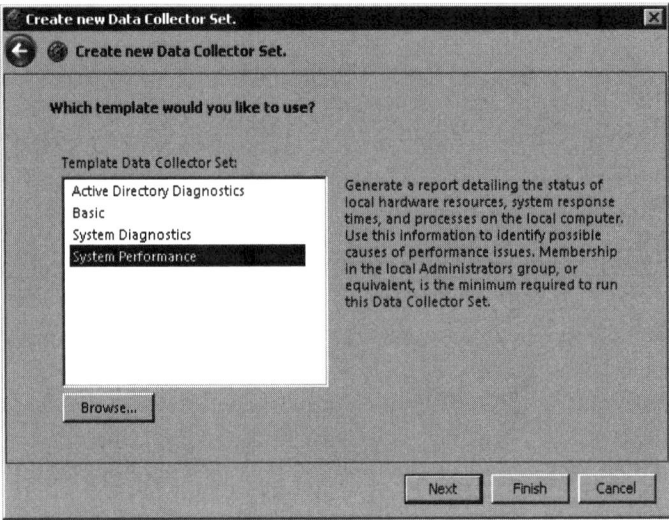

FIGURE 26-8 Highlight a template to read the description.

5. The Root Directory contains data collected by the Data Collector Set. If you want to store your Data Collector Set data in a location other than the default, click Browse or type in the directory name.

6. Click Next to choose a custom location for the Data Collector Set or to define more options. Click Finish to save the current settings and exit.

NOTE If you type in a directory name, do not enter a backslash (\) at the end of the directory name.

7. Click Next to define a user for the Data Collector Set to Run As or click Finish to save the current settings and exit.

8. When you click Next, you can configure the Data Collector Set to run as a specific user. Click Change to enter the user name and password for a user other than the default listed or click Finish to save the current settings and exit.

To start collecting data and storing it in the location specified in step 5, right-click the Data Collector Set in the navigation pane and select Start.

To view the properties of the Data Collector Set or make changes, right-click the Data Collector Set you created in steps 1 through 8 and select Properties. For more information about the properties of the Data Collector Set, see "Managing Collected Data" later in this chapter.

Importing Templates

Data Collector Set templates are stored as XML files, and you can import them directly from a local hard drive or from a network drive. To import a Data Collector Set template, run the Create New Data Collector Set Wizard and click Browse when asked which template you'd like to use. Browse to the location of the XML file you want to use, select it, and click Open.

Exporting Templates

To export a Data Collector Set for use on other computers, open Reliability And Performance Monitor, expand Data Collector Sets, right-click the Data Collector Set you want to export, and click Save Template. Select a directory in which to store the XML file and click Save.

Creating a Data Collector Set from Performance Monitor

To use the counters in a Performance Monitor display to create a Data Collector Set, follow these steps:

1. Start Performance Monitor and add counters to create a custom view you want to save as a Data Collector Set.

2. Right-click Performance Monitor in the navigation pane, point to New, and click Data Collector Set. The Create New Data Collector Set Wizard starts. The Data Collector Set you create will contain all of the data collectors selected in the current Performance Monitor view.

3. Type in a name for the Data Collector Set and click Next.

4. The Root Directory will contain data collected by the Data Collector Set. If you want to store your Data Collector Set data in a location other than the default, click Browse to navigate to the location or type in the directory name.

> **NOTE** If you type in a directory name, do not enter a backslash (\) at the end of the directory name.

5. After clicking Next, you can configure the Data Collector Set to run as a specific user. Click Change to enter a user name and password.

6. Click Finish.

To start collecting data and storing it in the location specified in step 4, right-click the Data Collector Set in the navigation pane and select Start.

Constructing a Data Collector Set Manually

You can create a customized Data Collector Set made up of performance counters, configuration data, or data from trace providers. To make such a Data Collector Set, follow these steps:

1. Open Windows Reliability And Performance Monitor.

2. In the navigation pane, expand Data Collector Sets, right-click User Defined, point to New, and click Data Collector Set.

3. Type in a name for your Data Collector Set. Select Create Manually and click Next.

4. Select Create Data Logs. Select the check boxes next to the Data Collector types you want to use and click Next.

   - **Performance Counter** Generates metric data about the system's performance
   - **Event Trace Data** Provides information about activities and system events
   - **System Configuration Information** Records the state of—and changes to—Registry keys

5. Depending on the Data Collector types you selected, you will be presented with dialog boxes to add Data Collectors to your Data Collector Set.

   - Click Add to open the Add Counters dialog box. When you are finished adding performance counters, click OK and then click Next to continue configuration or click Finish to exit and save the current configuration.

   - You can install event trace providers with the operating system or as part of a non-Microsoft application. Click Add to select from a list of available Event Trace Providers, as shown in Figure 26-9. You can select multiple providers by holding down the Ctrl key and highlighting the providers you want. When you are finished adding event trace providers, click OK and then click Next to continue configuration or click Finish to exit and save the current configuration.

6. To record system configuration data, type in the Registry keys you want to track. You must know the exact key.

7. When you've finished adding Registry keys, click Next to continue configuration or click Finish to exit and save the current configuration.

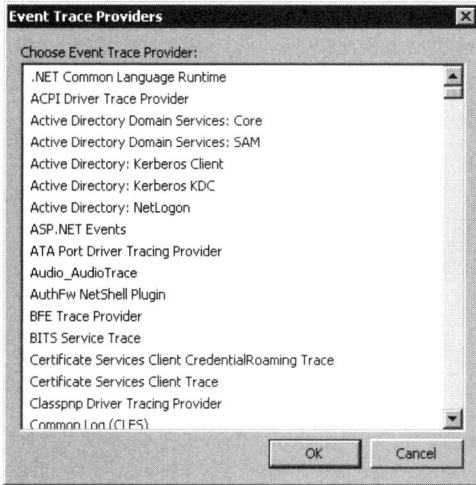

FIGURE 26-9 Selecting trace providers for a Data Collector Set

8. The Root Directory will contain data collected by the Data Collector Set. If you want to store your Data Collector Set data in a location other than the default, click Browse to navigate to the location or type in the directory name.

> **NOTE** If you type in a directory name, do not enter a backslash (\) at the end of the directory name.

9. After clicking Next, you can configure the Data Collector Set to run as a specific user. Click Change to type in the user name and password for a user other than the default listed.

10. Click Finish.

Creating a Data Collector Set to Monitor Performance Counters

Another type of Data Collector Set that you can create monitors performance counters and sends out alerts when the counters exceed or fall below thresholds you set.

First create the data set and then configure the alerts by following these steps:

1. Open Reliability And Performance Monitor. In the navigation pane, expand Data Collector Sets, right-click User Defined, point to New, and click Data Collector Set.

2. Type in a name for your Data Collector Set. Select Create Manually and click Next.

3. Select the Performance Counter Alert option and click Next.

4. Click Add to open the Add Counters dialog box. When you are finished adding counters, click OK.

5. Highlight the counter you'd like to monitor. From the Alert When drop-down list, choose whether to alert when the performance counter value is above or below the limit. In the Limit box, enter the threshold value.

6. When you've finished defining alerts, click Next to continue configuration or click Finish to exit and save the current configuration.

7. After clicking Next, you can configure the Data Collector Set to run as a specific user. Click Change to type in a user name and password.

Scheduling Data Collection

Data collection can be scheduled and log data managed using Data Collector Sets. You can store the reports after log data has been deleted so that you can still have performance statistics without storing masses of individual counter values.

To schedule when a Data Collector Set starts, follow these steps:

1. After you create a Data Collector Set, right-click the name of the Data Collector Set in the navigation pane and select Properties.

2. Click the Schedule tab.

3. Click Add to create a start date, time, or day for data collection, as shown in Figure 26-10. If you are configuring a new Data Collector Set, be sure that the start date is after the current date and time.

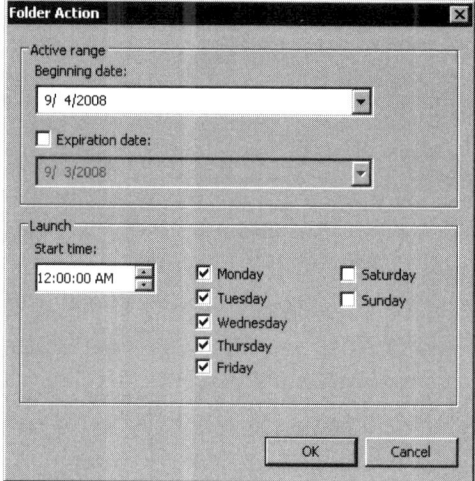

FIGURE 26-10 Scheduling a start date and time for a Data Collector Set

4. If you don't want to collect new data after a specific date, select the Expiration Date check box and supply the date.

5. Click OK when finished.

NOTE Specifying an expiration date will prevent new instances of data collection from starting after the expiration date.

To schedule when a Data Collector Set stops, follow these steps:

1. After you create a Data Collector Set, right-click the name of the Data Collector Set in the navigation pane and select Properties.

2. Click the Stop Condition tab.

3. To stop collecting data after a specified time, select Overall Duration and choose the number and units of time.

NOTE If your aim is to collect data indefinitely, don't select Overall Duration.

4. In the Limits section, you can select When A Limit Is Reached, Restart The Data Collector Set to break the data collection into separate, more manageable logs.

   ■ Select Duration to configure a time period for data collection to write to a single log file.

   ■ Select Maximum Size to restart the Data Collector Set or to stop collecting data when the log file reaches the limit.

NOTE If both limit types are selected, the collection of data will stop or restart when the first limit is reached. If you configure Overall Duration, those settings will override limits.

5. If you have set an Overall Duration, you can select Stop When All Data Collectors Have Finished so that all the counters can finish recording the most recent values before the entire Data Collector Set is stopped.

6. Click OK.

Managing Collected Data

Data Collector Sets create log files and optional report files. Data Manager allows you to configure how log data, reports, and compressed data are stored for each Data Collector Set.

To configure Data Manager for a Data Collector Set, follow these steps:

1. Open Windows Reliability And Performance Monitor, expand Data Collector Sets, and expand User Defined.

2. Right-click the name of the Data Collector Set that you want to configure and select Data Manager.

3. On the Data Manager tab, you can accept the default values or make changes according to your data retention policy. Table 26-1 describes each option.

   - Select Minimum Free Disk or Maximum Folders and previous data will be deleted when the limit is reached according to the Resource Policy you choose (Delete Largest or Delete Oldest).

   - Select Apply Policy Before The Data Collector Set Starts and previous data will be deleted before the Data Collector Set creates its next log file.

   - Select Maximum Root Path Size and previous data will be deleted when the root log folder size limit is reached.

4. Click the Actions tab. You can accept the default values or make changes. To make changes, use the Add, Edit, or Remove buttons. Table 26-2 describes each option.

5. Click OK to finish.

TABLE 26-1 Data Manager Options

OPTION	DEFINITION
Minimum Free Disk	Amount of free disk space that must be available on the drive where log data is stored. When the limit is reached, previous data will be deleted based on your Resource Policy.
Maximum Folders	Number of subfolders allowed in the data directory. When the limit is reached, previous data will be deleted according to your Resource Policy.
Resource Policy	Specifies whether the largest or the oldest log file or directory will be deleted when limits are reached.
Maximum Root Path Size	Maximum size of the Data Collector Set data directory, including all subfolders. When selected, this maximum path size overrides the Minimum Free Disk and Maximum Folders limits. When the limit of the Maximum Root Path Size is reached, previous data will be deleted according to your Resource Policy.

TABLE 26-2 Actions Properties

OPTION	DEFINITION
Age	The age of the data file in days or weeks. If the value is set to zero, the age is not considered.
Size	The size, in megabytes, of the log data folder. If the value is set to zero, the size is not considered.
Cab	A cabinet file. Cab files are archives that are created from raw log data that can be extracted later.
Data	Raw data log created by the Data Collector Set. To save disk space, the data log can be deleted after a cab file is created.
Report	Report file generated from the log data. Report files can be retained even after the log data has been deleted.

Working with Data Log Files

When log files grow large, reports are generated more slowly. If you review your logs frequently, setting limits will automatically break up logs to make them easier to view. The relog command can divide long log files into more manageable segments, or you can use it to combine multiple log files.

The relog command has the following syntax. The parameters are detailed in the following sections.

```
Relog [filename [filename ...]] [-a] [-c Path [Path ...]] [-cf filename] [-f {bin
| csv | tsv | SQL}] [-t Value] [-o {outputfile | DSN!Counterlog}] [-b M/D/YYYY
[[HH:]MM:]SS] [-e M/D/YYYY [[HH:]MM:]SS] [-config {filename | i}] [-q]
```

The *<filename [filename ...]>* parameter specifies the path name of an existing performance counter log. You can specify multiple input files.

The *–a* parameter appends output file instead of overwriting. This option does not apply to SQL format where the default is always to append.

The *–c <Path [Path ...]>* parameter specifies the performance counter path to log. To specify multiple counter paths, separate them with a space and enclose the counter paths in quotation marks (for example, "CounterPath1 CounterPath2").

The *–cf <filename>* parameter specifies the path name of the text file that lists the performance counters to be included in a relog file. Use this option to list counter paths in an input file, one per line. Default setting is all counters in the original log file are relogged.

The –f {bin | csv | tsv | SQL} parameter specifies the path name of the output file format. The default format is bin. For a SQL database, the output file specifies the DSN!CounterLog. You can specify the database location by using the ODBC manager to configure the DSN (Database System Name).

The –t <Value> parameter specifies sample intervals in "N" records. Includes every nth data point in the relog file. Default is every data point.

The –o {outputfile | DSN!CounterLog} parameter specifies the path name of the output file or SQL database where the counters will be written.

The –b <M/D/YYYY HH:MM:SS> parameter specifies begin time for copying first record from the input file. Date and time must be in this exact format: M/D/YYYY HH:MM:SS.

The –e <M/D/YYYY HH:MM:SS[AM | PM]> parameter specifies end time for copying last record from the input file. Date and time must be in this exact format: M/D/YYYY HH:MM:SS.

The –config {filename | i} parameter specifies the path name of the settings file that contains command-line parameters. Use –i in the configuration file as a placeholder for a list of input files that can be placed on the command line. On the command line, however, you do not need to use i. You can also use wildcards such as *.blg to specify many input filenames.

The –q parameter displays the performance counters and time ranges of log files specified in the input file.

The –y parameter bypasses prompting by answering "yes" to all questions.

The /? parameter displays help at the command prompt.

Viewing Reports

To help analyze collected data and identify trends, Reliability And Performance Monitor generates reports from Data Collector Sets.

To view a Data Collector Set report, follow these steps:

1. Open Windows Reliability And Performance Monitor.

2. Expand Reports and click User Defined or System.

3. Select the Data Collector Set that you want to view as a report. The report opens in the console pane, as shown in Figure 26-11.

To create a new report for a Data Collector Set, type **perfmon / report "Data_Collector_Set_name"** at a command prompt. Type **perfmon /report** without any other parameters to generate the System Diagnostics report.

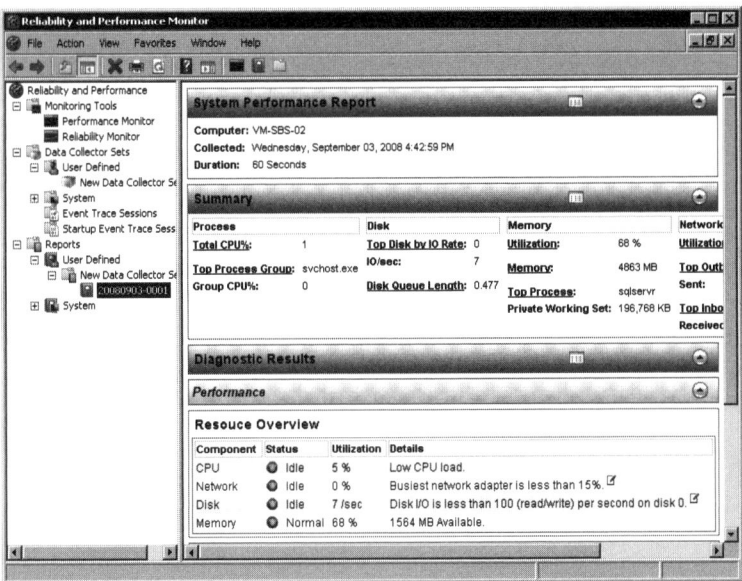

FIGURE 26-11 Viewing a Data Collector report

Summary

In this chapter, we covered the available tools for keeping track of your network's health and performance. The next chapter offers strategies for protecting your network from potential disasters.

Disaster Planning

Smart SCUBA divers dive with a buddy and carry an alternate air source, even though they've trained extensively and checked their equipment thoroughly. Schools and businesses have fire drills even though the vast majority of buildings never burn down. System administrators are no different—we do verified backups and write up disaster recovery plans we hope never to use. But we do them because there are only two types of networks: those that have experienced disaster and those that haven't—yet.

Disaster can take many forms, from the self-inflicted pain of a user or administrator doing something really, really unwise, to the uncontrollable, unpreventable results of a natural disaster such as a flood or an earthquake. In any case, your business will depend on how well you were prepared for the disaster, and how well you and your team respond to it and recover from it.

This chapter covers emergency preparedness. It discusses creating a disaster recovery plan, with standardized procedures to follow in the event of a catastrophe. It also describes how to prepare for a disaster so that if (or when) one happens, you have the tools to recover. We'll also cover some of the specialized, and in some ways easier, recovery scenarios that virtualization uses.

Planning for Disaster

Some people seem to operate on the assumption that if they don't think about a disaster, one won't happen. This is similar to the idea that if you don't write a will, you'll never die—and just about as realistic. No business owner or system administrator should feel comfortable about their degree of preparedness without a clear disaster recovery plan that has been thoroughly tested. Even then, you should continually look for ways to improve the plan—it should only be your starting point. A good disaster recovery plan is one that you are constantly examining, improving, updating, and testing. But understand your disaster plan's limitations: It isn't perfect, and even the best disaster recovery plan needs to be constantly examined and adjusted or it quickly gets out of date.

Planning for disaster or emergencies is not a single step, but an iterative, ongoing process. Systems are not mountains, but rivers, constantly moving and changing, and your disaster recovery plan needs to change as your environment changes. To put together a good disaster recovery plan—one you can bet your business on—you need to follow these steps:

1. Identify the risks.
2. Identify the resources.
3. Develop the responses.
4. Test the responses.
5. Iterate.

 REAL WORLD **Size Does Matter**

Disasters happen to businesses of all sizes and types. Small businesses are no more insulated from them than large businesses are, but generally they don't have the same levels of resources to respond to them and recover from them. A large, multinational corporation with an IT staff of several hundred worldwide certainly has more resources than a small accounting firm with an IT staff of one. As you work through the steps to build your disaster recovery plan, how you plan and implement it will vary depending the size of your company and the resources available.

Some of the steps we suggest here may be substantially more informal in a small business, but don't ignore them. No matter how small your business, if it uses and depends on Windows Small Business Server 2008, you have valuable and business-critical assets on your server, so take the steps to protect them and your business before you have a disaster. You'll save money, time, and, most important, business reputation by being able to withstand and even grow in the face of disaster.

We've been through fires, earthquakes, crashed servers, and just plain egregious error, and we've learned the hard way that disaster recovery is something that you can do a lot better if you've planned for it ahead of time. It's not sexy, and it's sometimes hard to sell to upper management, but it is worth the effort. If you're lucky, you'll never need to use all of your worst-case scenarios, but if you do need them, you'll really, really be glad you have them.

Identifying the Risks

The first step in creating a disaster recovery plan is to identify the risks to your business and the costs associated with those risks. The risks vary from the simple deletion of a critical file to the total destruction of your place of business and its computers. To properly prepare for a disaster, you need to perform a realistic assessment of the risks, the potential costs and consequences of each disaster scenario, the likelihood of any given disaster scenario, and the resources available to address the risks. Risks that seemed vanishingly remote a few years ago are now part of our everyday lives.

Identifying risks is not a job for a single person. As with all the tasks associated with a disaster recovery plan, all concerned parties must participate. There are two important reasons for this: You want to make sure that you have commitment and buy-in from the parties concerned, and you also want to make sure you don't miss anything important.

No matter how carefully and thoroughly you try to identify the risks, you'll miss at least one. You should always account for that missing risk by including an "unknown risk" item in your list. Treat it just like any other risk: Identify the resources available to address it and develop countermeasures to take should it occur. The difference with this risk, of course, is that your resources and countermeasures are somewhat more generic, and you can't really test your response to the risk, because you don't yet know what it is.

Start by trying to list all the possible ways that your system could fail. Solicit help from everyone with a stake in the process. The more people involved in the brainstorming, the more ideas you'll get and the more prevention and recovery procedures you can develop and practice. Be careful at this stage in the process to not dismiss any idea or concern as trivial, unimportant, or unlikely.

Next, look at all the ways that some external event could affect your system. (The current buzzword for this is *threat modeling*, if you care.) The team of people responsible for identifying possible external problems is probably similar to a team looking at internal failures, but with some important differences. For example, if your business is housed in a large commercial office building, you'll want to involve that building's security and facilities groups even though they aren't employees of your business. They will not only have important input into the possible threats to the business, but also they'll also have information on the resources and preventative measures already in place.

The risk identification phase is really made up of two parts—identification and assessment. They are different tasks. During the identification portion of the phase, you need to identify every possible risk, no matter how remote or unlikely. No risk suggested should be regarded as silly—don't limit the suggestions in any way. You want to identify every possible risk that anyone can think of. Then, when you have as complete a list as you can create, move on to the assessment task. In the risk-assessment task, you will try to understand and quantify just how likely a particular risk is. If you're located in a floodplain, for example, you're much more likely to think flood insurance is a good investment.

NOTE Even in a very small business, where there may be only one person involved in disaster planning, it's a really good idea to get others involved somehow in at least the identification task of risk identification. Different people think up different scenarios and risk factors, and getting more and different viewpoints involved will improve the overall result of the process.

Identifying the Resources

When you've identified the risks to your network, you need to identify what the resources are to address those risks. These resources can be internal or external, people or systems, hardware or software.

When you're identifying the resources available to deal with a specific risk, be as complete as you can, but also be specific. Identifying everyone in the company as a resource to solve a crashed server might look good, but realistically only one or two people are likely to actually be able to rebuild the server. Make sure you identify those key people for each risk, as well as the more general secondary resources they have to call on, such as Microsoft Customer Support Services (CSS) and local Microsoft partners. So, for example, the primary resource available to recover a crashed server might consist of your hardware vendor to recover the failed hardware and your own IT person or primary system consultant to restore the software and database. General secondary resources could include Microsoft Support (*http://support.microsoft.com/oas/default.aspx?gprid=3208*), Microsoft Partners in your area, and even newsgroups such as the microsoft.public.windows.server.sbs newsgroup.

An important step in identifying resources in your disaster recovery plan is to specify both the first-line responsibility and the back-end or supervisory responsibility. Make sure everyone knows who to go to when the problem is more than they can handle or when they need additional resources. Also, clearly define when they should escalate. The best disaster recovery plans include clear, unambiguous escalation policies. This takes the burden off individuals to decide when and whom to notify and makes escalation simply part of the procedure.

Developing the Responses

An old but relevant adage comes to mind when discussing disaster recovery scenarios: When you're up to your elbows in alligators, it's difficult to remember that your original objective was to drain the swamp. This is another way of saying that people lose track of what's important when they are overloaded by too many problems that require immediate attention. To ensure that your swamp is drained and your network gets back online, you need to take those carefully researched risks and resources and develop a disaster recovery plan. There are two important parts of any good disaster recovery plan:

- Standard operating procedures (SOPs)
- Standard escalation procedures (SEPs)

Making sure these procedures are in place and clearly understood by everyone involved before a disaster strikes puts you in a far better position to recover gracefully and with a minimum of lost productivity and data.

Standard Operating Procedures

Emergencies bring out both the best and worst in people. If you're prepared for the emergency, you can be one of those who come out smelling like a rose, but if you're not prepared and let yourself get flustered or lose track of what you're trying to accomplish, you can make the whole situation worse than it needs to be.

Although no one is ever as prepared for a system emergency as they'd like to be, careful planning and preparation can give you an edge in recovering expeditiously and with a minimal loss of data. It is much easier to deal with the situation calmly when you know you've prepared for this problem and you have a well-organized, tested SOP to follow.

Because the very nature of emergencies is that you can't predict exactly which one is going to strike, you need to plan and prepare for as many possibilities as you can. The time to decide how to recover from a disaster is before the disaster happens, not in the middle of it when users are screaming and bosses are standing around looking serious and concerned. If you're lucky. (We seem to have been blessed more by those who follow the more common adage: "When in trouble or in doubt, run in circles, scream and shout.")

It's just plain *hard* to stay calm and focused when you're in the middle of an emergency and there's a lot of extra stress being applied by everyone around you. But if you're properly prepared and have a clear plan, with well-written and accurate SOPs, it's a lot easier.

Your risk assessment phase involved identifying as many possible disaster scenarios and risks as you could; the resource assessment phase identified the resources for those risks. Now you need to create SOPs for recovering the system from each of the scenarios. Even the most levelheaded system administrator can get flustered when the system has crashed, users are calling every 10 seconds to see what the problem is, the boss is asking every 5 minutes when you'll have it fixed, and your server won't boot. And that's the easy case compared to the mess that can be caused by an external disaster.

Reduce your stress and prevent mistakes by planning for disasters before they occur. Practice recovering from each of your disaster scenarios. Write down each of the steps, and work through questionable or unclear areas until you can identify exactly what it takes to recover from the problem. This is like a fire drill, and you should do it for the same reasons—not because a fire is inevitable, but because fires do happen, and the statistics demonstrate irrefutably that those who prepare for a fire and practice what to do in a fire are far more likely to survive it.

Even where you know you're the only resource the company has to recover from a disaster scenario, write down the basic steps to do it. You don't need to go into minute detail, but at the very least, outline the key steps. This may be something you do for real only once in your life, so don't count on being able to remember everything. Disasters, by their very nature, raise the overall stress level and cause people to forget important steps.

Your job as a system administrator is to prepare for disasters and practice what to do in those disasters—not because you expect the disaster, but because if you do have one, you want to be the hero, not the goat. After all, it isn't often that the system administrator or IT consultant gets to be a hero, so be ready when your time comes.

The first step in developing any SOP is to outline the overall steps you want to accomplish. Keep it general at this point—you're looking for the big picture here. Again, you want everyone to be involved in the process. What you're really trying to do is make sure you don't forget any critical steps, and that's much easier when you get the overall plan down first. There will be plenty of opportunity later to cover the specific details.

After you have a broad, high-level outline for a given procedure, the people you identified as the actual resources during the resource assessment phase should start to fill in the blanks of the outline. You don't need every detail at this point, but you should get down to at least a level below the original outline. This will help you identify missing resources that are important to a timely resolution of the problem. Again, don't get too bogged down in the details at this point. You're not actually writing the SOP, just trying to make sure that you've identified all of its pieces.

When you feel confident that the outline is ready, get the larger group back together again. Go over the procedure and smooth out the rough edges, refining the outline and listening to make sure you haven't missed anything critical. When everyone agrees that the outline is complete, you're ready to add the final details to it.

The people who are responsible for each procedure should now work through all the details of the disaster recovery plan and document the steps thoroughly. They should keep in mind that the people who actually perform the recovery might not be who they expect. It's great to have an SOP for recovering from a failed router, but if the only person who understands the procedure is the IT person, and she's on vacation in Bora Bora that week, your disaster recovery plan has a big hole in it.

When you create the documentation, write down everything. What seems obvious to you now, while you're devising the procedure, will not seem at all obvious in six months or a year when you suddenly have to follow it under stress.

 REAL WORLD **Multiple Copies, Multiple Locations**

I t's tempting to centralize your SOPs into a single, easily accessible database. And you should do that, making sure everyone understands how to use it. But you'll also need to have alternative locations and formats for your procedures. Not only do you not want to keep the only copy in a single database, you also don't want to have only an electronic version—how accessible is the SOP for recovering a failed server going to be when the server has failed? Always maintain hard-copy versions as well. The one thing you don't want to do is create a single point of failure in your disaster recovery plan!

Every good server room should have a large binder, prominently visible and clearly identified, that contains all the SOPs. Each responsible person should also have one or more copies of at least the procedures he or she is either a resource for or likely to become a resource for. We like to keep copies of all our procedures in several places so that we can get at them no matter what the source of the emergency or where we happen to be when one of our pagers goes off.

Even if you're the only resource, keep multiple copies of your procedures and key phone numbers of external resources. Don't rely entirely on electronic storage, because even external electronic storage may be difficult to access if the disaster is major. But don't ignore electronic storage, either. Most of the time, it's the fastest and easiest to get to, and the most likely to be completely up to date.

After you have created the SOPs, your job has only begun. You need to keep them up to date and make sure that they don't become stale. It's no good having an SOP to recover your ISDN connection to the Internet when you ripped the ISDN line out three years ago and put in a DSL line with five times the bandwidth at half the cost.

You also need to make sure that all your copies of an SOP are updated. Electronic ones should probably be stored in a database or in a folder on SBS that is available offline. However, hard-copy documents are notoriously tricky to maintain. A good method is to make yet another SOP that details who updates what SOPs, how often, and who gets fresh copies whenever a change is made. Then put a version control system into place and make sure everyone understands his or her role in the process. Build rewards into the system for timely and consistent updating of SOPs—if 10 or 20 percent of someone's bonus is dependent on keeping those SOPs up to date and distributed, you can be sure they'll be current at least as often as the review process.

Standard Escalation Procedures

No matter how carefully you've identified potential risks, and how detailed your procedures to recover from them are, you're still likely to have situations you didn't anticipate. An important part of any disaster recovery plan is a standardized escalation procedure. Not only should each individual SOP have its own procedure-specific SEP, but you should also have an overall escalation procedure that covers everything you haven't thought of—because it's certain you haven't thought of everything.

An escalation procedure has two functions—resource escalation and notification escalation. Both have the same purpose: to make sure that everyone who needs to know about the problem is up to date and involved as appropriate, and to keep the overall noise level down so that the work of resolving the problem can go forward as quickly as possible. The resource escalation procedure details the resources that are available to the people who are trying to recover from the current disaster so that these people don't have to try to guess who (or what) the appropriate resource might be when they run into something they can't handle or something doesn't go as planned. This procedure helps them stay calm and focused. They know that if they run into a problem, they aren't on their own, and they know exactly who to call when they do need help.

The notification escalation procedure details who is to be notified of serious problems. Even more important, it should provide specifics regarding when notification is to be made. If a particular print queue crashes but comes right back up, you might want to send a general message only to the users of that particular printer letting them know what happened. However, if your e-mail has been down for more than half an hour, a lot of folks are going to be concerned. The SEP for e-mail should detail who needs to be notified when the server is unavailable for longer than some specified amount of time, and it should probably detail what happens and who gets notified when it's still down some significant amount of time after that.

This notification has two purposes: to make sure that the necessary resources are made available as required, and to keep everyone informed and aware of the situation. If you let people know that you've had a server hardware failure and that the vendor has been called and will be onsite within an hour, you'll cut down the number of phone calls exponentially, freeing you to do whatever you need to do to ensure that you're ready when the vendor arrives.

Testing the Responses

A disaster recovery plan is nice to have, but it really isn't worth a whole lot until it has actually been tested. Needless to say, the time to test the plan is at your convenience and under controlled conditions, rather than in the midst of an actual disaster. It's a nuisance to discover that your detailed disaster recovery plan has a fatal flaw in it when you're testing it under controlled conditions. It's a bit more than a nuisance to discover it when every second counts.

You won't be able to test everything in your disaster recovery plans. Even most large organizations don't have the resources to create fully realistic simulated natural disasters and test their response to each of them under controlled conditions, and even fewer small businesses have those kinds of resources. Nevertheless, there are things you can do to test your response plans. The details of how you test them depend on your environment, but they should include as realistic a test as feasible and should, as much as possible, cover all aspects of the response plan. The other reason to test the disaster recovery plan is that it provides a valuable training ground. If you've identified primary and backup resources, as you should, chances are that the people you've identified as backup resources are not as skilled or knowledgeable in a particular area as the primary resource. Testing the procedures gives you a chance to train the backup resources at the same time.

You should also consider using the testing to cross-train people who are not necessarily in the primary response group. Not only will they get valuable training, but you'll also create a knowledgeable pool of people who might not be directly needed when the procedure has to be used for real, but who can act as key communicators with the rest of the community.

Iterating

When you finish a particular disaster recovery plan, you might think your job is done, but in fact it has just begun. Standardizing a process is actually just the first step. You need to continually look for ways to improve it.

You should make a regular, scheduled practice of pulling out your disaster recovery plan with those responsible and making sure it's up to date. Use the occasion to actually look at it and see how you can improve on it. Take the opportunity to examine your environment. What's changed since you last looked at the plan? What equipment has been retired, and what has been added? What software is different? Are all the people on your notification and escalation lists still working at the company in the same roles? Are the phone numbers, including home phone numbers, up to date?

 REAL WORLD **Understand and Practice Kaizen**

Kaizen is a Japanese word and concept that means "small, continuous, improvement." Its literal translation is, "Change (kai) to become good (zen)."

So, why bring a Japanese word and concept into a discussion about disaster recovery? Because a good disaster recovery plan is one that you are constantly Kaizening. When you really understand Kaizen, it becomes a way of life that you can use in many ways.

The first thing to understand about Kaizen is that you are not striving for major change or improvement. Small improvements are the goal. Don't try to fix or change everything all at once. Instead, focus on one area, and try to make it just a little bit better.

The second part of Kaizen is that it is continuous. You must constantly look for ways to improve and implement those improvements. Because each improvement is small and incremental, you can easily implement it and move on to the next one.

Kaizen is very much about teamwork. Good Kaizen balances the load on a team and finds ways to build the strengths of the team as a whole. If you practice Kaizen and continually look for small, incremental ways to improve your work, you will soon have a better and more enjoyable workplace. As a manager, if you find ways to encourage and reward those who practice Kaizen, your team and you will grow and prosper.

Another way to iterate your disaster recovery plan is to use every disaster as a learning experience. When the disaster or emergency is over, get everyone together as soon as possible to talk about what happened. Find out what they think worked and what didn't in the plan. What tools did you not have that would have made the job go quicker or better?

Actively solicit suggestions for how the process could be improved. Then make the changes and test them. You'll not only improve your responsiveness to this particular type of disaster, but you'll also improve your overall responsiveness by getting people involved in the process and enabling them to be part of the solution.

Preparing for a Disaster

As Ben Franklin was known to say, "Failure to prepare is preparing to fail." This is truer than ever with modern operating systems, and although SBS includes a number of exceptionally useful recovery modes and tools, you still need to prepare for potential problems. Some of these techniques are covered in detail in other chapters and are discussed here only briefly, whereas others are covered here at length.

Setting Up a Fault-Tolerant System

A fault-tolerant system is one that is prepared to continue operating in the event of key component failures. This technique is very useful for servers running critical applications. Here are a few of the many ways to ensure fault tolerance in a system:

- Use one or more RAID arrays for system and data storage, protecting you from hard-disk failure. If a hard disk in the array fails, only that disk needs to be replaced—and no data is lost. See Chapter 11, "Disk Management," for information about using RAID, both software and hardware, to provide fault tolerance for your disk subsystem.

- Use multiple disk array controllers to provide redundancy if a controller fails.

- Use an uninterruptible power supply (UPS) to allow the server to shut down gracefully in the event of a power failure.

- Use multiples of everything that is likely to fail, including power supplies and network cards.

- Keep key spares available to quickly recover by replacing a failed part. If you have only a single power supply and it fails, you'll be back online a *lot* faster if you swap out a failed power supply yourself and then call your hardware vendor for a replacement for the failed one.

Backups

We've got a whole chapter on backups—Chapter 16, "Configuring Backup"—but it's important to talk briefly about them here under disaster recovery, because they're the backbone of any disaster recovery scenario. Having a backup of your critical system files is nice. Having backups of your data is nice. But having a tested backup of both of them is critical to a successful restore experience. By tested, we mean that you've actually restored the files in the backup and that you were able to read and use them.

Not every single backup will get tested for your ability to restore. That's not realistic and there's no point even pretending it's going to happen. But you should have a regular schedule of testing backups to know you can restore from them. We like to do ours at least once a week. We pick a couple of key subdirectories and restore them to a temporary location on the server.

Image backups, such as those done by Windows Server Backup, pose additional testing issues. It's a really good idea to test full system restores to ensure that your recovery scenario for a full hardware failure is viable—especially if you intend to do restores to dissimilar hardware, which is something not directly contemplated by Windows Server 2008 Backup. If you want to be able to do a restore to dissimilar hardware, you're probably going to need to use a third-party backup utility, such as Acronis True Image for Microsoft Windows Small Business Server (*http://www.acronis.com*) or StorageCraft ShadowProtect Server (*http://www.storagecraft.com*). Both of these products are designed to allow you to do backup and restore to dissimilar hardware, including physical to virtual (P2V).

Restoring from Backup

The process of restoring your SBS server from backup is something you should test and do *before* you find yourself in the middle of a disaster. And yes, we know, we're repeating ourselves. But it's really important. One last time and then we'll let it go: The only good backup is a fully tested backup. And the only reliable way to test a backup is to restore it.

When disaster strikes your SBS network, and you have to restore an entire server, you'll need the following:

- Your backup.
- Hardware to restore the backup to. If you're using the native Windows Server 2008 Backup that is part of SBS, it needs to be quite similar hardware to the server you're replacing.
- The original disk 1 from your SBS 2008 installation media, or another Windows Server 2008 Standard DVD.
- Any drivers required to for Windows Server 2008 to "see" your hard disks or your backup media. These should be on a USB key or other media that the target server can read.

When you have all the requirements together, you're ready to restore your server by following these steps:

1. Insert the first disk of the SBS 2008 installation media and turn on the server.
2. If the BIOS needs to be changed to allow the DVD drive to be the first boot device, go into the server's BIOS and make the change and then restart the server.
3. If prompted, press any key to boot from the DVD drive to bring up the initial localization page of the Windows Small Business Server 2008 installation, as shown in Figure 27-1.

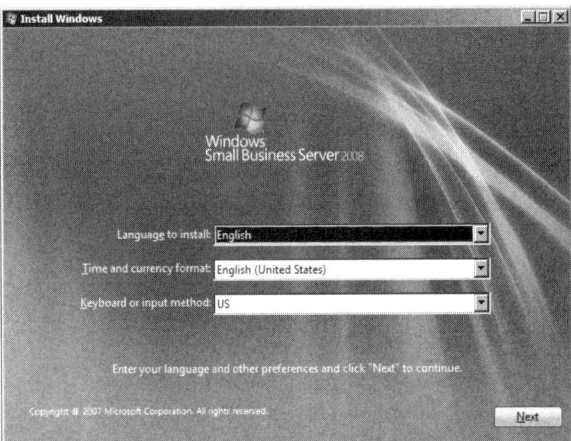

FIGURE 27-1 The localization page of the Windows Small Business Server 2008 installation

4. Set the localization options and then click Next to open the Install Now page.

5. Click Repair Your Computer to open the System Recovery Options dialog box shown in Figure 27-2. If you're restoring to a bare system, no operating system is shown, as in the figure.

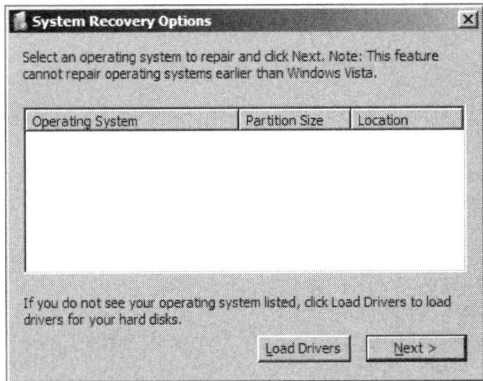

FIGURE 27-2 When restoring to a new server, no existing operating systems are present.

6. Click Load Drivers if you need to load drivers for your hard disks and follow the prompts to provide the necessary drivers.

7. Click Next to open the System Recovery Options dialog box shown in Figure 27-3.

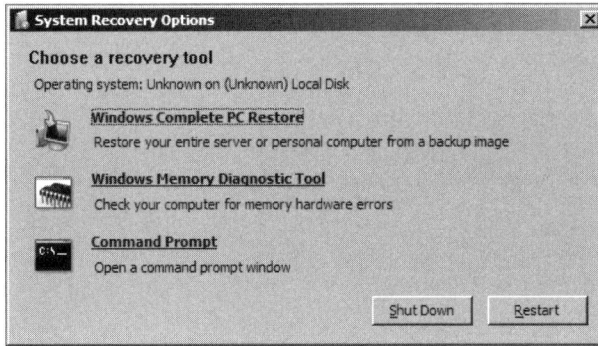

FIGURE 27-3 The System Recovery Options dialog box

8. Click Windows Complete PC Restore. Windows will search for attached backups and present the Restore Your Entire Computer From A Backup page of the Windows Complete PC Restore Wizard, as shown in Figure 27-4. The most recent backup identified on the backup disk will be highlighted.

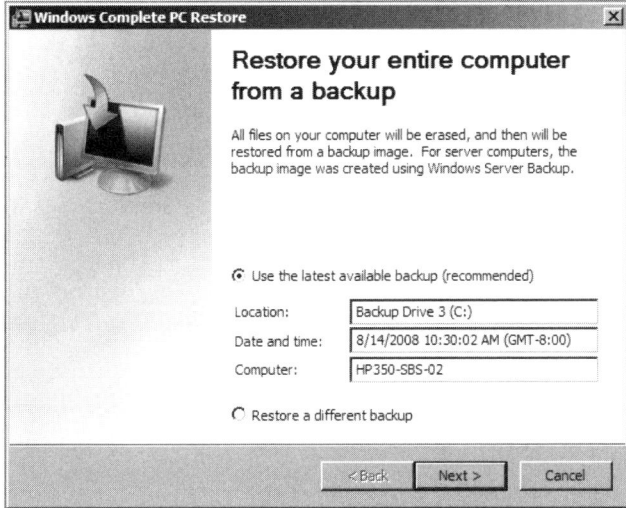

FIGURE 27-4 The most recent backup found is selected for restoration.

9. Click Next to open the Choose How To Restore The Backup page, shown in Figure 27-5. If your disks are identically sized and not yet partitioned, you won't have an option to format them and repartition.

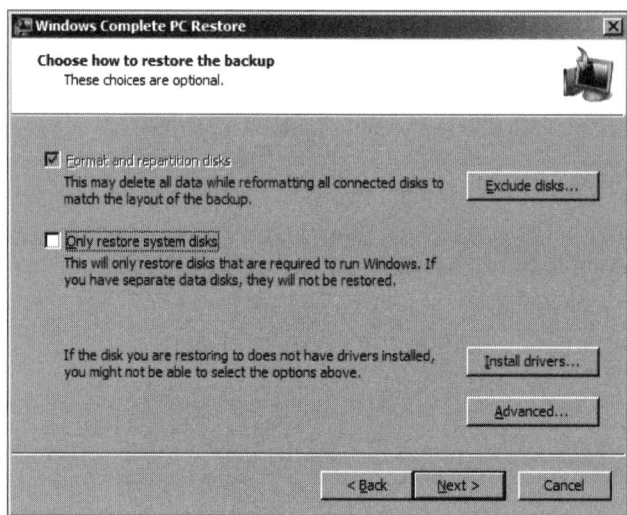

FIGURE 27-5 The Choose How To Restore The Backup page of the Windows Complete PC Restore Wizard

10. Select the Only Restore System Disks check box if you don't need to restore data partitions and disks. Even if you do, we prefer to focus on first getting a clean system restore, then restoring any additional files that need to be restored.

11. Click Next to move to the confirmation page and then click Finish.

12. Windows Complete PC Restore requires a final confirmation before restoring, as shown in Figure 27-6. Select the confirmation check box and click OK.

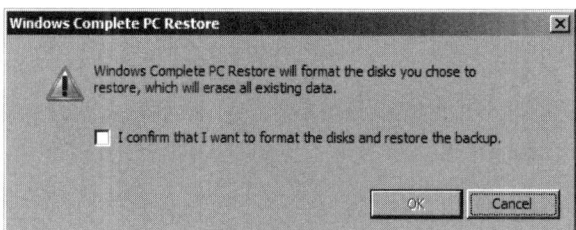

FIGURE 27-6 Final confirmation before formatting disks and restoring your computer

13. When the restore is complete, you'll be prompted to restart the server, as shown in Figure 27-7. This will include a list of disks not restored if you've chosen to only restore system disks.

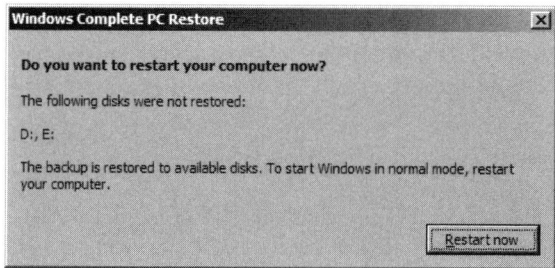

FIGURE 27-7 When the computer is restored, you need to restart.

Virtualization and Disaster Planning

The core of disaster planning is the same whether you're running SBS virtualized or on physical hardware. The five steps described in the beginning of this chapter are almost exactly the same. But there are differences when dealing with virtualized SBS. The two biggest differences to address are:

- No USB drive support inside the child partition
- Hardware independence

What do these differences mean for disaster planning? A few differences in the mechanics of backups and restores, primarily, with a possible change in the products used.

No USB Support

The lack of USB support inside the child partition is a limitation that can be addressed in several ways. The first way is to only worry about running backups from the parent partition, using Volume Shadow Services (VSS) snapshots with a VSS-aware backup product. This is a great solution in many ways, but it does have one limitation—it won't fully handle Microsoft Exchange Server log files. The simplest answer is to enable circular logging for Exchange Server, and not worry about it. A more complex answer probably requires some Windows PowerShell scripting and maybe running periodic backups to either a virtual hard disk that is assigned to the child partition, or taking advantage of something like FabulaTech's USB over Network, to connect external USB drives inside the virtualized SBS.

Having a connection to a USB drive inside the virtualized SBS will solve the backup problem, as long as other steps are being taken to ensure that a backup is being done of the system VHD as well from the parent partition. That's because the USB over Network client isn't available in the Windows PE environment used by the Windows Server 2008 restore.

An excellent choice for backing up virtual hard disks is Microsoft's Data Protection Manager 2007. It is, however, probably a bit of overkill on most small to midsized SBS networks. It requires a second server, for one thing, though you could install it on the SBS Premium Edition second server. But then you wouldn't be able to back up the second server to it.

Hardware Independence

The second difference with running SBS virtualized is all positive—hardware independence. Virtualization allows you to move virtual machines (VMs) to different physical hardware almost completely transparently. Even when you haven't fully exported a VM, the rest is easy as long as you have copies of the VHD files. A bit of configuration of the virtualization settings, and creating the virtual networks, and then when SBS is up and running, you will likely have to rerun the Connect To The Internet Wizard, and you should be fully restored.

This hardware independence gives you a lot of options as you plan for how you'll handle a disaster. Even if you don't immediately have an identical or even equivalent server available, most SBS networks could run in a somewhat reduced mode on a workstation class computer with 6 or 8 gigabytes (GB) of RAM and a dual or quad-core processor. You wouldn't have the level of redundancy available as you would in a good server, and it's not a configuration we'd recommend for any length of time, but it is more than adequate to get out of a disaster situation and get the business up and running.

Summary

Assume that disaster will eventually occur and plan accordingly. Create standardized recovery procedures and keep them up to date. When there's a lot of turmoil, as always happens in the case of a major failure, people forget important steps and can make poor decisions. Standardized procedures provide a course of action without the need for on-the-spot decisions. If you've planned for a disaster, and practiced what to do in the event of one, you'll be able to recover much more quickly than if you haven't. And recovering quickly in the event of a major disaster can be a significant competitive advantage.

Introduction to Networks

IF YOU'VE EVER MADE a phone call or used a bank ATM, you've already experienced using a network. After all, a network is simply a collection of computers and peripheral devices that can share files and other resources. The connection can be a cable, a telephone line, or even a wireless channel. The Internet itself is a network—a global network made up of all the computers, hardware, and peripherals connected to it.

Your bank's ATM consists of hardware and software connected to central computers that know, among other things, how much money you have in your account. When you call cross-country or just across town, telephone company software makes the connection from your phone to the phone you're calling through multiple switching devices. It's something we do every day, without thinking about the complicated processes behind the scenes.

Both the telephone networks and the ATM networks are maintained by technicians and engineers who plan, set up, and maintain all the software and hardware; however, the assumption underlying Windows Small Business Server is that there isn't anyone dedicated full time to maintaining the network and its operating system. Instead, Windows Small Business Server provides the Windows SBS Console —a unified administrative interface designed to meet the needs of small businesses and simplify your choices.

Servers

A server is a computer that provides services. It's really just that simple. The difficulty comes when people confuse the physical box that provides the service with the actual service. Any computer or device on a network can be a server for a particular service. A server doesn't even need to be a computer in the traditional sense. For example, you might have a print server that is nothing more complicated than a device connected to the network on one side and connected to a printer on the other. The device has a tiny little brain with just enough intelligence to understand when a particular network packet is intended for it and translate those packets into something that the printer can understand.

In Windows Small Business Server 2008, usually a single computer acts as the physical server box (though you can have secondary servers), but that box provides a variety of services to the network beyond the usual file and print services. These services meet your core business needs, including authentication and security, e-mail and collaboration, an Internet connection, sharing, faxing, and even database services and a full-featured firewall in Premium Edition.

Clients

A client is anything on the network that avails itself of a server's services. Clients are usually the other computers on the network. The client computers typically print to network printers, read e-mail, work on shared documents, connect to the Internet, and generally use services that aren't available on their local computers. Clients aren't usually as powerful as servers, but they're perfectly capable computers on their own.

Media Connecting Servers and Clients

Another portion of a network is the actual network media that connects the various servers and clients to each other. This media includes both the network cards that are part of the server or client and the physical wire (or wireless connection) between them and the various other components involved, such as hubs, routers, and switches. When all these media components work as they should, we pretty much forget about this portion of the network and take it for granted. But when a failure of one component of the network media occurs, we face troubleshooting and repairs that can be both frustrating and expensive—a good reason to buy only high-quality network components from vendors and dealers who support their products.

Features of the Windows Operating System

The Windows Server 2008 operating system that underlies Windows Small Business Server is a proven, reliable, and secure operating system with the features to run a business of virtually any size. With Windows Small Business Server, the operating system and server components have been specifically tuned to support from 5 to 75 users in a small business environment, with all the server functions residing on a single computer.

Some of the features that make Windows Server 2008 ideal for a small business server include:

- Easy installation that is almost fully automated in Windows Small Business Server
- A robust yet easy-to-administer security model using Active Directory
- The NTFS file system that fully supports long filenames, dynamic error recovery, shadow copies, user space limitations, and security
- Support for a broad range of hardware and software

Domains and Workgroups

Microsoft provides for two different networking models in their operating systems: workgroups and domains. Windows Small Business Server supports only the domain model of Microsoft networking, but it's worthwhile to go over why this decision makes sense, even in a very small business.

Do Workgroups Work?

Microsoft introduced the concept of the workgroup in 1992 with Windows for Workgroups. The workgroup is a logical grouping of several computers whose work or users are connected and who want to share their resources with each other. Usually, all the computers in a workgroup are equal, which is why such setups are referred to as *peer-to-peer networks*.

Workgroup networks are appealing because they're easy to set up and maintain. Individual users manage the sharing of their resources by determining what will be shared and who will have access. A user can allow other users to use a printer, a CD-ROM drive, an entire hard drive, or only certain files. The difficulty arises when it's necessary to give different levels of access to different users. Passwords can be used for this purpose in a limited way, but as the network gets larger, passwords proliferate and the situation becomes increasingly complicated. Users who are required to have numerous passwords start using the same one over and over or choose passwords that are easy to remember and therefore easy to guess, and there is no way to enforce a minimum password quality level. If someone leaves the company to work for your biggest competitor, passwords have to be changed and everyone in the workgroup has to be notified of the new passwords. Security, such as it is, falls apart.

Another problem that occurs when a workgroup becomes too large is that users have difficulty locating the resources they need. The informal nature of workgroups also means that centralized administration or control is nonexistent. Everything has to be configured computer by computer. This lack of central administration and control, along with the limited security, makes the workgroup model a bad choice for all but the home network.

Defining Domains

To provide a secure and easy-to-manage environment that takes full advantage of Active Directory and the collaborative features of Microsoft Exchange 2007 and the other components of Windows Small Business Server, Microsoft made the decision to use a domain-based networking environment. Management is simplified and centralized on the server, reducing the complexity and security problems caused by having to manage users, resources, and passwords across multiple clients.

A domain is really just a type of workgroup that includes a server—but a server that manages and administers all of the users and computers in the network. It is a logical grouping of users who are connected by more than the cables between their computers. The goal of a domain is to let users share resources within the group and to make it easier for the group to work. However, the key difference is that Active Directory—and the server it runs on—manages, catalogs, and secures the users, groups, computers, and resources for the entire network, providing a single point of administration and control.

Additional Users

When adding a new user to the domain, you won't need to go around to each computer and enter all the information. As the administrator, you can simply connect to the server and add the new user, using the Windows SBS Console. You can create the user's mailbox, set up a home folder, add the user to security and distribution groups, configure his or her Share Point access, set up disk quotas, and even configure a client computer—all with only a few clicks and the entering of the user name and password. The change will be immediately seen across the entire domain.

All users, including the newest, can get at their resources, no matter which computer is being used. Permission to access resources is granted to individual users (or a group of users), not to individual computers. And when you need to restrict access to a sensitive document or directory, you need to log on to only a single workstation to make the change across the entire domain. You can easily and quickly grant or restrict access by individual user or by groups of users.

Access Control

In a workgroup, there are limitations on sharing your computer's resources with the rest of the workgroup. At the simplest level, you can either share the resource or not share it. Beyond that, you can require a password for a particular level of access to the resource. This enables only a very limited ability to control access to the resource, and virtually none if your computer is physically accessible to anyone but yourself.

Windows Small Business Server provides discretionary access control, which allows, for example, some users to create a document or make changes to an existing one while other users can only read the document and still other users can't even see it. You can set access for:

- An individual file or files within a directory
- The entire directory

Windows Small Business Server lets you make selections as fine or as coarse as needed and makes the administration of security easy to manage.

Domain Components

An SBS domain has at least two main components and an optional third component:

- Domain controller
- Member server (optional)
- Workstations or clients

Let's take a look at these components.

Domain Controller

The main computer in the SBS domain is the domain controller. In many if not most SBS domains, the domain controller is the only server. It hosts Active Directory and all the components of SBS, and it also acts as the file and print server for the domain. All computers in the domain must authenticate to the domain controller, and all domain security is controlled by it.

Member Servers

In some larger SBS domains, additional Windows Server 2008 computers might be in the domain. SBS 2008 includes a second server as part of the Premium edition. These computers can be used to spread some of the network's resource load around so that the domain controller doesn't carry the whole load: SBS Premium includes SQL Server 2008 Standard, which can be loaded on either the second server, or on the main SBS server.

Another reason you might have an additional member server in your SBS domain is to host Windows Terminal Services. Terminal Services allows you to use inexpensive, easily managed desktop computers and terminals whose only function is to run applications directly on the Terminal Server computer. The Terminal Server provides the disk space and all the applications that the user has, while the terminal or computer of the user is merely a display and console (keyboard and mouse). Centralizing applications onto a Terminal Server can dramatically reduce costs and simplify administration in some scenarios. However, for security reasons, Terminal Services cannot be run from the main SBS server, so if you'll be using Terminal Services, you'll need at least one additional server on your network.

Workstations or Clients

All the Windows clients of an SBS network must be running Windows XP SP2 or later, but in most networks they will be running Windows Vista. If you have any workstations running earlier versions of Windows, they are no longer supported and should be upgraded. You can also have Mac and even UNIX or Linux clients, but their ability to integrate fully with the SBS network will be limited.

Windows clients must be running a business-class version of Windows—specifically, Windows XP Professional, Windows XP Tablet PC Edition, Windows Vista Business, Windows Vista Enterprise, or Windows Vista Ultimate.

APPENDIX B

Automating Installation

YOU CAN ALMOST COMPLETELY automate the installation of Windows Small Business Server 2008. This is a definite change from Small Business Server 2003, where the level of automation was limited to the base operating system only. But with SBS 2008, you can use the SBS Answer File Generator (discussed in Chapter 5, "Installing SBS 2008," and Chapter 7, "Migrating from Windows Small Business Server 2003") to completely automate the SBS portion of the installation.

For automating the base Windows Server 2008 installation, you need to use the Windows Server 2008 Automated Installation Kit (AIK), which you can download from *http://www.microsoft.com/downloads/details.aspx?FamilyID=c7d4bc6d-15f3-4284-9123-679830d629f2&DisplayLang=en*.

For completely automating the install, you'll need a server running Windows Deployment Services (WDS), and your network card in the target server will need to support Preboot Execution Environment (PXE) boot. (This means that you'll need to use a Legacy Network Adapter if building SBS 2008 in a virtual environment because the high speed synthetic NIC in Hyper-V doesn't support PXE.)

You'll use an unattend.xml file to define what is actually installed. The creation of this file and the details in it are covered at length in the Windows Automated Installation Kit Reference on TechNet at: *http://technet.microsoft.com/en-us/library/cc722187.aspx*. But unless you're doing a lot of identical SBS installations, we really think this is overkill. The critical installation features and steps—the ones that take up your time—are already handled as part of the normal SBS installation in SBS 2008, and you can completely automate that process using the SBS Answer File Generator. The actual operating system installation is a matter of a few clicks and typing in the Product Identification Number (PID).

Once you've done that, and selected the hard disk to install on, you're done. The installation will proceed automatically. If you've put your sbsanswerfile.xml file where it can be found, the SBS portion of the installation will take over automatically and continue as soon as Windows Server 2008 is installed.

Our overall opinion is that automating the installation beyond what the SBS Answer File Generator does is probably going to cost more time than it saves unless you're in a lab environment or a hosting environment where you are deploying at least dozens of SBS servers to make it worth the effort.

APPENDIX C

Resources

BOOKS ARE GREAT. THEY'RE easy to use and very portable. We love books. They are, however, completely static and when you need information on the latest security threat or help with new applications, there's nothing like the Internet.

This appendix lists Web sites and blogs of use to SBS users and consultants. First are links to Microsoft resources, followed by Web sites and blogs maintained by companies and knowledgeable individuals.

Microsoft Resources

http://blogs.technet.com/msrc	Microsoft Security Response Center
http://blogs.technet.com/sbs	Official SBS blog
http://blogs.technet.com/wsus	Latest information on Windows Server Update Service (WSUS)
http://blogs.technet.com/mu	Microsoft Update Product Team information
http://blogs.technet.com/sus/	The WSUS Support Team blog
http://blogs.msdn.com/ie/rss.xml	IEBlog: The Windows Internet Explorer Weblog
http://www.microsoft.com/technet/security /advisory/RssFeed.aspx?securityadvisory	Microsoft TechNet Security TechCenter
http://feeds.feedburner.com /MicrosoftDownloadCenter	Microsoft Download Center
http://www.microsoft.com/mscorp /execmail/rss.xml	Microsoft Executive E-Mail: Insights about technology and public-policy issues important to computer users from Microsoft executives
http://blogs.msdn.com/MainFeed.aspx	Microsoft MSDN blogs
http://windowsvistablog.com/blogs /MainFeed.aspx	Windows Vista Team blog
http://msexchangeteam.com/rss.aspx	The Microsoft Exchange Team blog
http://blogs.msdn.com/sqlblog/default.aspx	Microsoft SQL Server Support blog

Other Resources for SBS Users and Consultants

All the sites listed here have been found to be informative and useful. However, as with all Internet resources, you must use your judgment and think critically about what advice to follow.

http://www.eventid.net	Event details and general technical help
http://feeds.feedburner.com/smbitprosposts	SMBITPro: Small and Medium Business (SMB) IT professionals
http://blogs.msdn.com/aaron_margosis/rss.xml	Aaron Margosis' Web Log: The Non-Admin blog running with least privilege on the desktop
http://msmvps.com/blogs/donna/rss.aspx	Donna's Security Flash: PC and Internet security blog
http://blogs.iss.net/rss.php	Frequency X: Straight Dope on the Vulnerability du Jour from IBM Internet Security Systems
http://computer.forensikblog.de/en/atom.xml	Int for(ensic) blog: Notes on computer forensics, international edition
http://msinfluentials.com/blogs/jesper/rss.aspx	Jesper's Blog by Jesper Johansson, the author of Windows Server 2008 Security Resource Kit
www.smallbizserver.net	Frequently asked questions about SBS Server
http://blog.loglogic.com/atom.xml	Everything about keeping and using security logs
http://www.viruslist.com/en/rss/latestanalysis	Viruslist.com: All about Internet security
http://msmvps.com/blogs/mainfeed.aspx	Blogs by current and former Microsoft Most Valuable Professionals
http://sbs.seandaniel.com/rss.xml	SBS and related technology
http://www.symantec.com/content/en/us/enterprise/rss/securityresponse/srblogs.xml	Symantec Security Response blogs
http://smallbizthoughts.blogspot.com/feeds/posts/default?alt=rss	Small Biz Thoughts: Intended primarily for Small Business Consultants
http://feeds.trendmicro.com/MalwareAdvisories	TrendMicro's Malware Advisories
http://www.smallbiztrends.com	Small Business Trends: An online publication for small business owners, entrepreneurs, and the people who interact with them

Index

About the Authors

CHARLIE RUSSEL and **SHARON CRAWFORD** are co-authors of numerous books on operating systems. Their titles include *Windows Server 2008 Administrator's Companion*; *Microsoft Windows Small Business Server 2003 R2 Administrator's Companion*; *Microsoft Windows Server 2003 Administrator's Companion*, 2nd Edition; *Microsoft Windows XP Professional Resource Kit*, 3rd Edition; and *Upgrading to Windows 98*.

Charlie Russel is a chemist by education; an electrician by trade; a UNIX sysadmin and Oracle DBA because he raised his hand when he should have known better; an IT Director and consultant by default; and a writer by choice. Charlie is a Microsoft MVP for Windows Server, and is the author of more than two dozen computer books on operating systems and enterprise environments, including *Microsoft Windows Small Business Server 2003 Administrator's Companion*, *Microsoft Windows XP Professional Resource Kit*, 3rd Edition, and (with Robert Cordingley), the Oracle DBA Quick Reference Series. He has also written numerous white papers on Microsoft.com.

Sharon Crawford began writing computer books in 1991 and prefers it to all her previous *real* jobs, which included driving a cab and repairing subway cars in New York. She has given up looking for legitimate employment.

Sharon and Charlie live in beautiful British Columbia with one dog, varying numbers of cats, and a delightful, if somewhat distracting, view of Pender Harbour.

What do you think of this book?

We want to hear from you!

Your feedback will help us continually improve our books and learning resources for you.
To participate in a brief online survey, please visit:

microsoft.com/learning/booksurvey

...and enter this book's ISBN-10 or ISBN-13 number (appears above barcode on back cover).
As a thank-you to survey participants in the U.S. and Canada, each month we'll randomly
select five respondents to win one of five $100 gift certificates from a leading online merchant.
At the conclusion of the survey, you can enter the drawing by providing your e-mail address,
which will be used for prize notification only.*

Thank you in advance for your input!

Where to find the ISBN on back cover

Example only. Each book has unique ISBN.

* No purchase necessary. Void where prohibited. Open only to residents of the 50 United States (includes District of Columbia)
and Canada (void in Quebec). For official rules and entry dates see: **microsoft.com/learning/booksurvey**

Stay in touch!

To subscribe to the *Microsoft Press® Book Connection Newsletter*—for news on upcoming
books, events, and special offers—please visit:

microsoft.com/learning/books/newsletter